CROSSWORD
LISTS AND SOLVER

CROSSWORD
LISTS AND SOLVER

BLITZ EDITIONS

This edition produced for
Bookmart 1990.

Reprinted August 1991

Crossword Lists first published 1989
Crossword Solver first published 1988

Copyright © Bloomsbury Publishing Limited 1988, 1989

ISBN 1 85605 075 0

Printed in Great Britain by Mackays of Chatham

CROSSWORD LISTS

Edited by

Anne Stibbs

ACKNOWLEDGMENTS

Beth Bonham
Eve Daintith
John Daintith
Joan Gallagher
Robert Kerr
David Pickering
Kathy Rooney
Jessica Scholes
Gwen Shaw
Kate Smith
Brenda Tomkins
Edmund Wright

CONTENTS

GEOGRAPHY

COUNTRIES OF THE WORLD

AFGHANISTAN
Capital: Kabul
Currency: afghani (pul)
Legislature: Central Committee
Admin. Div.: Province

ALBANIA
Capital: Tirana
Currency: lek (qindar)
Legislature: People's Assembly (Kuvënd Popullor)
Admin. Div.: People's Council

ALGERIA
Capital: Algiers
Currency: dinar (centime)
Legislature: National Assembly

ARGENTINA
Capital: Buenos Aires
Currency: austral (centavo)
Legislature: National Congress: Senate; H of Deputies
Admin. Div.: Province

AUSTRALIA
Capital: Canberra
Currency: dollar (cent)
Legislature: Federal Parliament: Senate; H of Representatives
Admin. Div.: State

AUSTRIA
Capital: Vienna
Currency: schilling (groschen)
Legislature: National Assembly: Nationalrat (National Council); Bundesrat (Federal Council)
Admin. Div.: Federal State

BANGLADESH
Capital: Dhaka
Currency: taka (poisha)
Legislature: Parliament

BELGIUM
Capital: Brussels
Currency: franc (centime)
Legislature: Senate; Chamber of Representatives
Admin. Div.: Province

BOLIVIA
Capital: La Paz
Currency: boliviano (centavo)
Legislature: Congress: Senate; Chamber of Deputies
Admin. Div.: Department

BOTSWANA
Capital: Gaborone
Currency: pula (thebe)
Legislature: National Assembly

BRAZIL
Capital: Brasilia
Currency: cruzado (centavo)
Legislature: National Congress: Senate; Chamber of Deputies
Admin. Div.: State

BULGARIA
Capital: Sofia
Currency: lev (stotinka)
Legislature: National Assembly
Admin. Div.: People's Council

BURMA
Capital: Rangoon
Currency: kyat (pya)
Legislature: People's Assembly

CAMBODIA
Capital: Phnom Penh
Currency: riel (sen)
Legislature: National Assembly

CANADA
Capital: Ottawa
Currency: dollar (cent)
Legislature: Parliament: Upper House; H of Commons
Admin. Div.: Province

CHILE
Capital: Santiago
Currency: peso (centavo)
Admin. Div.: Region

CHINA
Capital: Peking
Currency: yuan (fen)
Legislature: National People's Congress
Admin. Div.: Province

COLOMBIA
Capital: Bogotá
Currency: peso (centavo)
Legislature: Congress: Senate; H of Representatives
Admin. Div.: Départmento

COSTA RICA
Capital: San José
Currency: colón (céntimo)
Legislature: Legislative Assembly

CUBA
Capital: Havana
Currency: peso (centavo)

Legislature: National Assembly of People's
  Power
Admin. Div.: Province
CYPRUS
  Capital: Nicosia
  Currency: pound (cent)
  Legislature: H of Representatives
CZECHOSLOVAKIA
  Capital: Prague
  Currency: koruna (heller)
  Legislature: Federal Assembly: H of the
  People; H of the Nations
DENMARK
  Capital: Copenhagen
  Currency: krone (öre)
  Legislature: Folketing (Diet)
  Admin. Div.: Municipality
DOMINICAN REPUBLIC
  Capital: Santo Domingo
  Currency: peso (centavo)
  Legislature: Congress
  Admin. Div.: Province
ECUADOR
  Capital: Quito
  Currency: sucre (centavo)
  Legislature: National Congress
  Admin. Div.: Province
EGYPT
  Capital: Cairo
  Currency: pound (piastre)
  Legislature: People's Assembly
  Admin. Div.: Governorate
EL SALVADOR
  Capital: San Salvador
  Currency: colón (centavo)
  Legislature: Assembly
ETHIOPIA
  Capital: Addis Ababa
  Currency: birr (cent)
  Legislature: Shengo (National Assembly)
FINLAND
  Capital: Helsinki
  Currency: markka (penni)
  Legislature: Parliament: Eduskunta-
  Riksdagen (Chamber)
  Admin. Div.: Province
FRANCE
  Capital: Paris
  Currency: franc (centime)
  Legislature: Parliament: National Assembly;
  Senate
  Admin. Div.: Département
THE GAMBIA
  Capital: Banjul
  Currency: dalasi (butut)
  Legislature: House of Representatives
  Admin. Div.: District
GERMANY, DEMOCRATIC REPUBLIC OF
  (East Germany)
  Capital: East Berlin
  Currency: Mark (Pfennig)

Legislature: People's Chamber
  (Volkskammer)
Admin. Div.: County
GERMANY, FEDERAL REPUBLIC OF (West
  Germany)
  Capital: Bonn
  Currency: Deutsche Mark (Pfennig)
  Legislature: Bundestag (Federal Diet);
  . Bundersrat (Federal Council)
  Admin. Div.: County
GHANA
  Capital: Accra
  Currency: cedi (pesewa)
  Legislature: Provisional National Defence
  Council
  Admin. Div.: Region
GREECE
  Capital: Athens
  Currency: drachma (lepton)
  Legislature: Parliament
  Admin. Div.: Nomoi (Prefecture)
GUATEMALA
  Capital: Guatemala City
  Currency: quetzal (centavo)
  Legislature: Legislative Assembly
HAITI
  Capital: Port-au-Prince
  Currency: gourde (centime)
  Legislature: National Assembly
  Admin. Div.: Département
HONDURAS
  Capital: Tegucigalpa
  Currency: lempira (centavo)
  Legislature: Congress of Deputies
  Admin. Div.: Department
HONG KONG
  Capital: Victoria
  Currency: dollar (cent)
  Legislature: Executive Council; Legislative
  Council
  Admin. Div.: District
HUNGARY
  Capital: Budapest
  Currency: forint (filler)
  Legislature: Parliament (Országgyülés)
  Admin. Div.: County
ICELAND
  Capital: Reykjavik
  Currency: króna (eyrir)
  Legislature: Parliament (Althingi): Upper
  House; Lower House
  Admin. Div.: Commune
INDIA
  Capital: New Delhi
  Currency: rupee (paisa)
  Legislature: Parliament: Council of States
  (Rajya Sabha); H of the People (Lok
  Sabha)
  Admin. Div.: State
INDONESIA
  Capital: Jakarta

Currency: rupiah (sen)
Legislature: People's Consultative Assembly
Admin. Div.: Province

IRAN
Capital: Tehran
Currency: rial (dinar)
Legislature: Islamic Consultative Assembly (Majlis)
Admin. Div.: Province (Ostán)

IRAQ
Capital: Baghdad
Currency: dinar (fils)
Legislature: National Assembly
Admin. Div.: Governorate

IRELAND, REPUBLIC OF
Capital: Dublin
Currency: pound (pence)
Legislature: Parliament (Oireachtas): H of Representatives (Dáil); Senate (Seanad)
Admin. Div.: County

ISRAEL
Capital: Jerusalem
Currency: shekel (agora)
Legislature: Knesset
Admin. Div.: Municipality

ITALY
Capital: Rome
Currency: lira (centesimo)
Legislature: Parliament: Chamber of Deputies; Senate
Admin. Div.: Region

JAMAICA
Capital: Kingston
Currency: dollar (cent)
Legislature: H of Representatives; Senate
Admin. Div.: Parish

JAPAN
Capital: Tokyo
Currency: yen
Legislature: Diet: H of Representatives (Shugi-in); H of Councillors (Sangi-in)
Admin. Div.: Prefecture

JORDAN
Capital: Amman
Currency: dinar (fils)
Legislature: Parliament
Admin. Div.: District (Muhafaza)

KENYA
Capital: Nairobi
Currency: shilling (cent)
Legislature: National Assembly
Admin. Div.: Province

KOREA, DEMOCRATIC PEOPLE'S REPUBLIC OF (North Korea)
Capital: P'yŏngyang
Currency: won (chon)
Legislature: Supreme People's Assembly
Admin. Div.: Province

KOREA, REPUBLIC OF (South Korea)
Capital: Seoul
Currency: won (jeon)

Legislature: National Assembly
Admin. Div.: Province

KUWAIT
Capital: Kuwait
Currency: dinar (fils)
Legislature: National Assembly
Admin. Div.: Governorate

LAOS
Capital: Vientiane
Currency: kip (at)
Legislature: People's Supreme Council
Admin. Div.: Province

LEBANON
Capital: Beirut
Currency: pound (piastre)
Legislature: Parliament
Admin. Div.: Governorate

LIBERIA
Capital: Monrovia
Currency: dollar (cent)
Legislature: National Assembly: Senate; H of Representatives
Admin. Div.: County

LIBYA
Capital: Tripoli
Currency: dinar (dirham)
Legislature: General People's Congress

LUXEMBOURG
Capital: Luxembourg
Currency: franc
Legislature: Council of State

MADAGASCAR
Capital: Antananaivo
Currency: franc malgache
Legislature: National People's Assembly
Admin. Div.: Province

MALAWI
Capital: Lilongwe
Currency: kwacha (tambala)
Legislature: Parliament

MALAYSIA
Capital: Kuala Lumpur
Currency: dollar (cent)
Legislature: Parliament: H of Representatives (Dewan Ra'ayat); Senate (Dewan Negara)
Admin. Div.: State

MALTA
Capital: Valletta
Currency: lira (cent)
Legislature: Parliament: H of Representatives

MAURITIUS
Capital: Port Louis
Currency: rupee (cent)
Legislature: Legislative Assembly

MEXICO
Capital: Mexico City
Currency: peso (centavo)
Legislature: General Congress: Chamber of Deputies; Senate

Admin. Div.: State
MONGOLIA
  Capital: Ulan Bator
  Currency: tugrik (mongo)
  Legislature: Great People's Khural
  Admin. Div.: Province
MOROCCO
  Capital: Rabat
  Currency: dirham (centime)
  Legislature: Parliament
  Admin. Div.: Province
NEPAL
  Capital: Kathmandu
  Currency: rupee (paisa)
  Legislature: Panchayat
  Admin. Div.: Zone
NETHERLANDS
  Capital: Amsterdam
  Currency: florin (cent)
  Legislature: Parliament (Staten-Generaal):
    First Chamber; Second Chamber
  Admin. Div.: Province
NEW ZEALAND
  Capital: Wellington
  Currency: dollar (cent)
  Legislature: Parliament: H of
    Representatives
  Admin. Div.: Region
NICARAGUA
  Capital: Managua
  Currency: córdoba (centavo)
  Legislature: National Assembly
  Admin. Div.: Region
NIGERIA
  Capital: Abuja
  Currency: naira (kobo)
  Admin. Div.: State
NORWAY
  Capital: Oslo
  Currency: krone (öre)
  Legislature: Storting: Lagting; Odelsting
  Admin. Div.: Fylker
PAKISTAN
  Capital: Islamabad
  Currency: rupee (paisa)
  Legislature: Parliament: National Assembly;
    Senate
  Admin. Div.: Province
PANAMA
  Capital: Panama City
  Currency: balboa (cent)
  Legislature: Legislative Assembly
  Admin. Div.: Province
PARAGUAY
  Capital: Asunción
  Currency: guarani (céntimo)
  Legislature: Parliament: Senate; Chamber of
    Deputies
  Admin. Div.: Department
PERU
  Capital: Lima

Currency: inti (centimo)
  Legislature: Congress: Senate; Chamber of
    Deputies
  Admin. Div.: Department
PHILIPPINES
  Capital: Manila
  Currency: peso (centavo)
  Legislature: Congress: Upper House; H of
    Representatives
  Admin. Div.: Region
POLAND
  Capital: Warsaw
  Currency: zloty (grosz)
  Legislature: Sejm
  Admin. Div.: Voivodship
PORTUGAL
  Capital: Lisbon
  Currency: escudo (centavo)
  Legislature: Assembly of the Republic
  Admin. Div.: District
ROMANIA
  Capital: Bucharest
  Currency: leu (ban)
  Legislature: Grand National Assembly
  Admin. Div.: County
SAUDI ARABIA
  Capital: Riyadh
  Currency: riyal (halalas)
  Legislature: Assembly
  Admin. Div.: Region
SEYCHELLES
  Capital: Victoria
  Currency: rupee (cent)
  Legislature: People's Assembly
SIERRA LEONE
  Capital: Freetown
  Currency: leone (cent)
  Legislature: Parliament
  Admin. Div.: Province
SINGAPORE
  Capital: Singapore City
  Currency: dollar (cent)
  Legislature: Parliament
SOUTH AFRICA
  Capital: Pretoria
  Currency: rand (cent)
  Legislature: Parliament: H of
    Representatives, H of Delegates, H of
    Assembly
  Admin. Div.: Province
SPAIN
  Capital: Madrid
  Currency: peseta (céntimo)
  Legislature: Cortes: Congress of Deputies;
    Senate
  Admin. Div.: Autonomous Community
SRI LANKA
  Capital: Colombo
  Currency: rupee (cent)
  Legislature: Parliament
  Admin. Div.: District

SUDAN
  Capital: Khartoum
  Currency: pound (piastre)
  Legislature: National Assembly
  Admin. Div.: Region
SWEDEN
  Capital: Stockholm
  Currency: krona (öre)
  Legislature: Riksdag
  Admin. Div.: Län
SWITZERLAND
  Capital: Bern
  Currency: franc (centime)
  Legislature: Parliament: Standerat;
    Nationalrat
  Admin. Div.: Canton
SYRIA
  Capital: Damascus
  Currency: pound (piastre)
  Legislature: People's Council
  Admin. Div.: Mohafaza
TAIWAN
  Capital: Taipei
  Currency: dollar (cent)
  Legislature: National Assembly
  Admin. Div.: County
TANZANIA
  Capital: Dodoma
  Currency: shilling (cent)
  Legislature: National Assembly
  Admin. Div.: Region
THAILAND
  Capital: Bangkok
  Currency: baht (stangs)
  Legislature: National Assembly: Senate; H of
    Representatives
  Admin. Div.: Province (Changwad)
TUNISIA
  Capital: Tunis
  Currency: dinar (millieme)
  Legislature: National Assembly
  Admin. Div.: Gouvernorat
TURKEY
  Capital: Ankara
  Currency: lira (kurus)
  Legislature: Grand National Assembly
  Admin. Div.: Il
UGANDA
  Capital: Kampala
  Currency: shilling (cent)
  Legislature: National Resistance Council
  Admin. Div.: Province
UNITED KINGDOM
  Capital: London

  Currency: pound (pence)
  Legislature: Parliament: H of Lords; H of
    Commons
  Admin. Div.: County
UNITED STATES OF AMERICA
  Capital: Washington, DC
  Currency: dollar (cent)
  Legislature: Congress: Senate; H of
    Representatives
  Admin. Div.: State
URUGUAY
  Capital: Montevideo
  Currency: peso (centésimo)
  Legislature: Chamber; Senate
  Admin. Div.: Department
USSR (SOVIET UNION)
  Capital: Moscow
  Currency: rouble (copeck)
  Legislature: Supreme Soviet of the USSR:
    Council of the Union; Council of
    Nationalities
VENEZUELA
  Capital: Caracas
  Currency: bolivar
  Legislature: Congress: Senate; Chamber of
    Deputies
  Admin. Div.: State
VIETNAM
  Capital: Hanoi
  Currency: dong (xu)
  Legislature: National Assembly
  Admin. Div.: Province
YUGOSLAVIA
  Capital: Belgrade
  Currency: dinar (para)
  Legislature: Federal Assembly: Federal
    Chamber; Chamber of Republics and
    Autonomous Provinces
ZAÏRE
  Capital: Kinshasa
  Currency: zaïre (likuta)
  Legislature: National Legislative Council
  Admin. Div.: Region
ZAMBIA
  Capital: Lusaka
  Currency: kwacha (ngwee)
  Legislature: National Assembly
  Admin. Div.: Province
ZIMBABWE
  Capital: Harare
  Currency: dollar (cent)
  Legislature: Parliament: Senate; H of
    Assembly
  Admin. Div.: Province

ENGLISH COUNTIES

COUNTY (Administrative Centre)

4
AVON (Bristol)
KENT (Maidstone)
5
DEVON (Exeter)
ESSEX (Chelmsford)
SALOP (name for
   Shropshire between
   1974 and 1980)
WIGHT, ISLE OF
   (Newport, IOW)
6
DORSET (Dorchester)
DURHAM (Durham)
SURREY (Kingston
   Upon Thames)
SUSSEX, EAST
   (Lewes)
SUSSEX, WEST
   (Chichester)
7
CUMBRIA (Carlisle)
NORFOLK (Norwich)
*RUTLAND (Oakham)
SUFFOLK (Ipswich)
8
CHESHIRE (Chester)
CORNWALL (Truro)
SOMERSET (Taunton)

9
BERKSHIRE
   (Reading)
CLEVELAND
   (Middlesborough)
HAMPSHIRE
   (Winchester)
WILTSHIRE
   (Trowbridge)
†W. MIDLANDS
   (Birmingham)
10
*CUMBERLAND
   (Carlisle)
DERBYSHIRE
   (Matlock)
HUMBERSIDE
   (Beverley)
LANCASHIRE
   (Preston)
†MERSEYSIDE
   (Liverpool)
N. YORKSHIRE
   (Northallerton)
SHROPSHIRE
   (Shrewsbury)
†S. YORKSHIRE
   (Barnsley)
†W. YORKSHIRE
   (Wakefield)

11
OXFORDSHIRE
   (Oxford)
†TYNE AND WEAR
   (Newcastle-Upon-
   Tyne)
*WESTMORLAND
   (Kendal)
12
BEDFORDSHIRE
   (Bedford)
LINCOLNSHIRE
   (Lincoln)
WARWICKSHIRE
   (Warwick)
13
*HEREFORDSHIRE
   (Hereford)
HERTFORDSHIRE
   (Hertford)
STAFFORDSHIRE
   (Stafford)
14
CAMBRIDGESHIRE
   (Cambridge)
LEICESTERSHIRE
   (Leicester)
NORTHUMBERLAND
   (Morpeth)

15
BUCKINGHAMSHIRE
   (Aylesbury)
GLOUCESTERSHIRE
   (Gloucester)
*HUNTINGDONSHIRE
   (Huntingdon)
NOTTINGHAMSHIRE
   (Nottingham)
16
NORTHAMPTON-
   SHIRE
   (Northampton)
17
†GREATER
   MANCHESTER
   (Manchester)
20
HEREFORD AND
   WORCESTER
   (Worcester)

*indicates a former
   county
† metropolitan county

WELSH COUNTIES

COUNTY (Administrative Centre)

5
CLWYD (Mold)
DYFED (Carmarthen)
GWENT (Cwmbran)
POWYS (Llandrindod
   Wells)
7
GWYNEDD
   (Caernarfon)
8
*ANGLESEY
   (Llangefni)
9
*GLAMORGAN
   (Cardiff)

9 —continued
*MERIONETH
   (Dolgellan)
10
*FLINTSHIRE (Mold)
S. GLAMORGAN
   (Cardiff)
W. GLAMORGAN
   (Swansea)
11
*BRECONSHIRE
   (Brecon)
*RADNORSHIRE
   (Llandrindod Wells)

12
*DENBIGHSHIRE
   (Ruthin)
MID GLAMORGAN
   (Cardiff)
13
*CARDIGANSHIRE
   (Aberystwyth)
*MONMOUTHSHIRE
   (Newport)
*PEMBROKESHIRE
   (Haverfordwest)

15
*CAERNARFON-
   SHIRE (Caernarfon)
*CARMARTHEN-
   SHIRE
   (Carmarthen)
*MONTGOMERY-
   SHIRE (Welshpool)

*indicates a former
   county

SCOTTISH REGIONS AND COUNTIES

REGION OR COUNTY (Administrative Centre)

3
*AYR (Ayr)
4
*BUTE (Rothesay)
FIFE (Fife)
*FIFE (Cupar)
5
*ANGUS (Forfar)
*BANFF (Banff)
*MORAY (Elgin)
*NAIRN (Nairn)
*PERTH (Perth)
6
*ARGYLL
  (Lochgilphead)
*LANARK (Hamilton)
ORKNEY (Kirkwall)
*ORKNEY (Kirkwall)
7
*BERWICK (Duns)
BORDERS (Newton
  St. Boswells)
CENTRAL (Stirling)

7 —continued
*KINROSS (Kinross)
LOTHIAN (Edinburgh)
*PEEBLES (Peebles)
*RENFREW (Paisley)
*SELKIRK (Selkirk)
TAYSIDE (Dundee)
*WIGTOWN
  (Stranraer)
*ZETLAND (Lerwick)
8
*ABERDEEN
  (Aberdeen)
*DUMFRIES
  (Dumfries)
GRAMPIAN
  (Aberdeen)
HIGHLAND
  (Inverness)
*ROXBURGH
  (Newtown St.
  Boswells)
SHETLAND (Lerwick)

8 —continued
*STIRLING (Stirling)
9
*CAITHNESS (Wick)
*DUMBARTON
  (Dumbarton)
*INVERNESS
  (Inverness)
10
*KINCARDINE
  (Stonehaven)
*MIDLOTHIAN
  (Edinburgh)
*SUTHERLAND
  (Golspie)
11
*CLACKMANNAN
  (Alloa)
*EAST LOTHIAN
  (Haddington)
STRATHCLYDE
  (Glasgow)

11 —continued
*WEST LOTHIAN
  (Linlithgow)
12
WESTERN ISLES
  (Lewis)
13
*KIRKCUDBRIGHT
  (Kirkcudbright)
15
*ROSS AND
  CROMARTY
  (Dingwall)
19
DUMFRIES AND
  GALLOWAY
  (Dumfries)

  *indicates former
  Scottish county

COUNTIES OF NORTHERN IRELAND

COUNTY (County Town)

4
DOWN (Downpatrick)
6
ANTRIM (Belfast)

6 —continued
ARMAGH (Armagh)
TYRONE (Omagh)

9
FERMANAGH
  (Enniskillen)

11
LONDONDERRY
  (Londonderry)

REPUBLIC OF IRELAND PROVINCES

CONNACHT   LEINSTER   MUNSTER   ULSTER

REPUBLIC OF IRELAND COUNTIES

4	6	7 —continued	8 —continued
CORK	CARLOW	LEITRIM	LONGFORD
MAYO	DUBLIN	WEXFORD	MONAGHAN
5	GALWAY	WICKLOW	9
CAVAN	OFFALY	8	ROSCOMMON
CLARE	7	KILKENNY	TIPPERARY
KERRY	DONEGAL	LAOIGHIS	WATERFORD
LOUTH	KILDARE	LIMERICK	WESTMEATH
MEATH			
SLIGO			

AMERICAN STATES

STATE	ABBREVIA-TION	NICKNAME	CAPITAL
ALABAMA	ALA	CAMELLIA	MONTGOMERY
ALASKA	ALAS		JUNEAU
ARIZONA	ARIZ	OCOTILLO	PHOENIX
ARKANSAS	ARK		LITTLE ROCK
CALIFORNIA	CAL	GOLDEN	SACRAMENTO
COLORADO	COLO	CENTENNIAL	DENVER
CONNECTICUT	CONN	NUTMEG	HARTFORD
DELAWARE	DEL	DIAMOND	DOVER
FLORIDA	FLA	SUNSHINE	TALLAHASSEE
GEORGIA	GA	PEACH	ATLANTA
HAWAII	HA	ALOHA	HONOLULU
IDAHO	IDA	GEM	BOISE
ILLINOIS	ILL	PRAIRIE	SPRINGFIELD
INDIANA	IND	HOOSIER	INDIANAPOLIS
IOWA	IA	HAWKEYE	DES MOINES
KANSAS	KAN	SUNFLOWER	TOPEKA
KENTUCKY	KY	BLUEGRASS	FRANKFORT
LOUISIANA	LA	PELICAN	BATON ROUGE
MAINE	ME	PINETREE	AUGUSTA
MARYLAND	MD	OLDLINE	ANNAPOLIS
MASSACHUSETTS	MASS	BAY	BOSTON
MICHIGAN	MICH	WOLVERINE	LANSING
MINNESOTA	MINN	NORTHSTAR	ST. PAUL
MISSISSIPPI	MISS	MAGNOLIA	JACKSON
MISSOURI	MO	SHOWME	JEFFERSON CITY
MONTANA	MONT	TREASURE	HELENA
NEBRASKA	NEBR	CORNHUSKER	LINCOLN
NEVADA	NEV	SILVER	CARSON CITY
NEW HAMPSHIRE	NH	GRANITE	CONCORD
NEW JERSEY	NJ	GARDEN	TRENTON
NEW MEXICO	N MEX	LAND OF ENCHANTMENT	SANTA FÉ
NEW YORK	NY	EMPIRE	ALBANY
NORTH CAROLINA	NC	TARHEEL	RALEIGH
NORTH DAKOTA	N DAK	SIOUX	BISMARCK
OHIO	OH	BUCKEYE	COLUMBUS

OKLAHOMA	OKLA	SOONER	OKLAHOMA CITY
OREGON	OREG	BEAVER	SALEM
PENNSYLVANIA	PA	KEYSTONE	HARRISBURG
RHODE ISLAND	RI	OCEAN	PROVIDENCE
SOUTH CAROLINA	SC	PALMETTO	COLUMBIA
SOUTH DAKOTA	S DAK	COYOTE	PIERRE
TENNESSEE	TENN	VOLUNTEER	NASHVILLE
TEXAS	TEX	LONESTAR	AUSTIN
UTAH	UT	MORMAN	SALT LAKE CITY
VERMONT	VT	GREEN MOUNTAIN	MONTPELIER
VIRGINIA	VA	OLD DOMINION	RICHMOND
WASHINGTON	WASH	EVERGREEN	OLYMPIA
WEST VIRGINIA	W VA	MOUNTAIN	CHARLESTON
WISCONSIN	WIS	BADGER	MADISON
WYOMING	WYO	EQUALITY	CHEYENNE

AUSTRALIAN STATES AND TERRITORIES

| AUSTRALIAN CAPITAL TERRITORY | NEW SOUTH WALES NORTHERN TERRITORY | QUEENSLAND SOUTH AUSTRALIA TASMANIA | VICTORIA WESTERN AUSTRALIA |

TOWNS AND CITIES

AFGHANISTAN

5
HERAT
KABUL

8
KANDAHAR

ALGERIA

4
ORAN

7
ALGIERS

ANGOLA

6
LOBITO
LUANDA

ARGENTINA

7
CORDOBA
LA PLATA
ROSARIO

11
BAHIA BLANCA
BUENOS AIRES

AUSTRALIA

5
PERTH

6
DARWIN
HOBART
SYDNEY

8
ADELAIDE
BRISBANE
CANBERRA

9
MELBOURNE
NEWCASTLE

12
ALICE SPRINGS

AUSTRIA

6
VIENNA

8
SALZBURG

9
INNSBRUCK

BANGLADESH

5
DHAKA

10
CHITTAGONG

BELGIUM

5
GHENT
LIÈGE
NAMUR
YPRES

6
BRUGES
DINANT
OSTEND

7
ANTWERP
MALINES

8
BRUSSELS

BRAZIL

5
BELEM

6
RECIFE

8
BRASILIA
SAO PAULO

11
PORTO ALEGRE

12
RIO DE JANEIRO

13
BELO HORIZONTE

BULGARIA

5
SOFIA
VARNA

BURMA

3
AVA

7
RANGOON

8
MANDALAY

CANADA

6
OTTAWA
QUEBEC
REGINA

7
CALGARY
HALIFAX
ST JOHN'S
TORONTO
8
EDMONTON
HAMILTON
KINGSTON
MONTREAL
VICTORIA
WINNIPEG
9
VANCOUVER
SASKATOON
10
THUNDER BAY
11
FREDERICTON
12
NIAGARA FALLS
13
CHARLOTTETOWN

CHILE

8
SANTIAGO
10
VALPARAISO

CHINA

4
LUTA
SIAN
5
WUHAN
6
ANSHAN
CANTON
DAIREN
FUSHUN
HARBIN
MUKDEN
PEKING
TSINAN
7
BEIJING
KUNMING
LANCHOW
NANKING
TAIYUAN
8
SHANGHAI
SHENYANG
TIENTSIN
9
CHANGCHUN
CHUNGKING

10
PORT ARTHUR

COLOMBIA

4
CALI
6
BOGOTÁ
9
CARTAGENA
12
BARRANQUILLA

CZECHOSLOVAKIA

4
BRNO
6
PRAGUE
10
BRATISLAVA

EGYPT

4
GIZA
SUEZ
5
ASWAN
CAIRO
LUXOR
TANTA
6
THEBES
7
MANSURA
MEMPHIS
ZAGAZIG
8
ISMAILIA
PORT SAID
10
ALEXANDRIA

ENGLAND

3
ELY
EYE
RYE
WEM
4
BATH
BRAY
BUDE
BURY
CLUN
DEAL
DISS
ETON
HOLT

4 —continued
HOVE
HULL
HYDE
INCE
LEEK
LOOE
LYDD
ROSS
RYDE
SHAP
WARE
WARK
YARM
YORK
5
ACTON
ALTON
BACUP
BLYTH
BOURN
CALNE
CHARD
CHEAM
COLNE
COWES
CREWE
DERBY
DOVER
EGHAM
EPSOM
FILEY
FOWEY
FROME
GOOLE
HAWES
HEDON
HURST
HYTHE
LEEDS
LEIGH
LEWES
LOUTH
LUTON
MARCH
OLNEY
OTLEY
POOLE
REETH
RIPON
RISCA
RUGBY
SARUM
SELBY
STOKE
STONE
TEBAY
THAME
TRING
TRURO
WELLS

5 —continued
WIGAN
6
ALFORD
ALSTON
ASHTON
BARNET
BARROW
BARTON
BATLEY
BATTLE
BAWTRY
BEDALE
BELPER
BODMIN
BOGNOR
BOLTON
BOOTLE
BOSTON
BRUTON
BUNGAY
BURTON
BUXTON
CASTOR
COBHAM
CROMER
DARWEN
DUDLEY
DURHAM
EALING
ECCLES
EPPING
EXETER
GORING
HANLEY
HARLOW
HARROW
HAVANT
HENLEY
HEXHAM
HOWDEN
ILFORD
ILKLEY
ILSLEY
JARROW
KENDAL
LEYTON
LONDON
LUDLOW
LYNTON
LYTHAM
MALDON
MALTON
MARLOW
MASHAM
MORLEY
NASEBY
NELSON
NESTON
NEWARK
NEWENT

6 —continued	7 —continued	7 —continued	7 —continued
NEWLYN	BILSTON	LEYBURN	WAREHAM
NEWTON	BOURTON	LINCOLN	WARWICK
NORHAM	BOWFELL	MALVERN	WATCHET
OAKHAM	BRANDON	MARGATE	WATFORD
OLDHAM	BRISTOL	MATLOCK	WEOBLEY
ORMSBY	BRIXHAM	MOLESEY	WICKWAR
OSSETT	BROMLEY	MORETON	WINDSOR
OUNDLE	BURNHAM	MORPETH	WINSLOW
OXFORD	BURNLEY	MOSSLEY	WINSTER
PENRYN	BURSLEM	NEWBURY	WISBECK
PEWSEY	CAISTOR	NEWPORT	WORKSOP
PINNER	CATFORD	NORWICH	**8**
PUDSEY	CAWSTON	OLDBURY	ABINGDON
PUTNEY	CHARING	OVERTON	ALFRETON
RAMSEY	CHATHAM	PADSTOW	ALNMOUTH
REDCAR	CHEADLE	PENRITH	AMESBURY
RIPLEY	CHEDDAR	POULTON	AMPTHILL
ROMNEY	CHESHAM	PRESCOT	AXBRIDGE
ROMSEY	CHESTER	PRESTON	AYCLIFFE
RUGELY	CHORLEY	RAINHAM	BAKEWELL
SEAHAM	CLACTON	READING	BARNSLEY
SEATON	CLIFTON	REDHILL	BERKELEY
SELSEY	CRAWLEY	REDRUTH	BEVERLEY
SETTLE	CROYDON	REIGATE	BICESTER
SNAITH	DARSLEY	RETFORD	BIDEFORD
ST IVES	DATCHET	ROMFORD	BOLSOVER
STROOD	DAWLISH	ROSSALL	BRACKLEY
STROUD	DEVIZES	ROYSTON	BRADFORD
SUTTON	DORKING	RUNCORN	BRAMPTON
THIRSK	DOUGLAS	SALFORD	BRIDPORT
THORNE	DUNSTER	SALTASH	BRIGHTON
TOTNES	ELSTREE	SANDOWN	BROMYARD
WALTON	ENFIELD	SAXELBY	BROSELEY
WATTON	EVERTON	SEAFORD	CAMBORNE
WESTON	EVESHAM	SHIFNAL	CARLISLE
WHITBY	EXMOUTH	SHIPLEY	CATERHAM
WIDNES	FAREHAM	SHIPTON	CHERTSEY
WIGTON	FARNHAM	SILLOTH	CLEVEDON
WILTON	FELTHAM	SKIPTON	CLOVELLY
WITHAM	GLOSSOP	SPILSBY	COVENTRY
WITNEY	GOSPORT	STAINES	CREDITON
WOOLER	GRIMSBY	STILTON	DAVENTRY
YEOVIL	HALIFAX	ST NEOTS	DEBENHAM
7	HAMPTON	SUDBURY	DEDWORTH
ALNWICK	HARWICH	SUNBURY	DEPTFORD
ANDOVER	HAWORTH	SWANAGE	DEWSBURY
APPLEBY	HELSTON	SWINDON	EGREMONT
ARUNDEL	HEYWOOD	SWINTON	EVERSLEY
ASHFORD	HITCHIN	TAUNTON	FAKENHAM
AYLSHAM	HONITON	TELFORD	FALMOUTH
BAMPTON	HORNSEA	TENBURY	FOULNESS
BANBURY	HORNSEY	TETBURY	GRANTHAM
BARKING	HORSHAM	THAXTED	GRANTOWN
BECCLES	IPSWICH	TILBURY	HADLEIGH
BEDFORD	IXWORTH	TORQUAY	HAILSHAM
BELFORD	KESWICK	TWYFORD	HALSTEAD
BERWICK	KINGTON	VENTNOR	HASTINGS
BEWDLEY	LANCING	WALSALL	HATFIELD
BEXHILL	LANGTON	WALTHAM	HELMSLEY
BICKLEY	LEDBURY	WANTAGE	HEREFORD

8 —continued

HERNE BAY
HERTFORD
HINCKLEY
HOLBEACH
HUNMANBY
ILKESTON
KEIGHLEY
KINGSTON
LAVENHAM
LECHLADE
LISKEARD
LONGTOWN
LYNMOUTH
MARYPORT
MIDHURST
MINEHEAD
NANTWICH
NEWHAVEN
NUNEATON
ORMSKIRK
OSWESTRY
PENZANCE
PERSHORE
PETERLEE
PETWORTH
PEVENSEY
PLAISTOW
PLYMOUTH
RAMSGATE
REDDITCH
RICHMOND
RINGWOOD
ROCHDALE
ROTHBURY
SALTBURN
SANDGATE
SANDWICH
SEDBERGH
SHANKLIN
SHELFORD
SHIPSTON
SIDMOUTH
SKEGNESS
SLEAFORD
SOUTHEND
SPALDING
STAFFORD
ST ALBANS
STAMFORD
STANHOPE
STANWELL
ST HELENS
STOCKTON
STRATTON
SURBITON
SWAFFHAM
TAMWORTH
THETFORD
THORNABY
TIVERTON

8 —continued

TUNSTALL
UCKFIELD
UXBRIDGE
WALLASEY
WALLSEND
WANSTEAD
WESTBURY
WETHERAL
WETHERBY
WEYMOUTH
WOODFORD
WOOLWICH
WORTHING
YARMOUTH

9

ALDEBURGH
ALDERSHOT
ALLENDALE
ALRESFORD
AMBLESIDE
ASHBOURNE
ASHBURTON
AVONMOUTH
AYLESBURY
BLACKBURN
BLACKPOOL
BLANDFORD
BLISWORTH
BRACKNELL
BRAINTREE
BRENTFORD
BRENTWOOD
BRIGHOUSE
BROUGHTON
CAMBRIDGE
CARNFORTH
CASTLETON
CHESILTON
CHINGFORD
CLITHEROE
CONGLETON
CRANBORNE
CRANBROOK
CREWKERNE
CRICKLADE
CUCKFIELD
DARTMOUTH
DEVONPORT
DONCASTER
DONINGTON
DROITWICH
DRONFIELD
DUNGENESS
DUNSTABLE
ELLESMERE
FAVERSHAM
FLEETWOOD
GATESHEAD
GODALMING
GRAVESEND

9 —continued

GREENWICH
GRINSTEAD
GUILDFORD
HARROGATE
HASLEMERE
HAVERHILL
HAWKHURST
HOLMFIRTH
ILCHESTER
IMMINGHAM
KETTERING
KING'S LYNN
KINGSWEAR
LAMBOURNE
LANCASTER
LEICESTER
LICHFIELD
LIVERPOOL
LONGRIDGE
LOWESTOFT
LYME REGIS
LYMINGTON
MAIDSTONE
MANSFIELD
MIDDLETON
NEWCASTLE
NEWMARKET
NEW ROMNEY
NORTHWICH
OTTERBURN
PEMBRIDGE
PENISTONE
PENKRIDGE
PENYGHENT
PICKERING
ROCHESTER
ROTHERHAM
SALISBURY
SALTFLEET
SEVENOAKS
SHEERNESS
SHEFFIELD
SHERBORNE
SMETHWICK
SOUTHGATE
SOUTHPORT
SOUTHWELL
SOUTHWOLD
STARCROSS
ST AUSTELL
STEVENAGE
STOCKPORT
STOKESLEY
STOURPORT
STRATFORD
TARPORLEY
TAVISTOCK
TENTERDEN
TODMORDEN
TONBRIDGE

9 —continued

TOWCESTER
TYNEMOUTH
ULVERSTON
UPMINSTER
UPPINGHAM
UTTOXETER
WAINFLEET
WAKEFIELD
WARKWORTH
WEYBRIDGE
WHERNSIDE
WHITHAVEN
WIMBLEDON
WINCANTON
WOKINGHAM
WOODSTOCK
WORCESTER
WYMONDHAM

10

ACCRINGTON
ALDBOROUGH
ALTRINCHAM
BARNSTAPLE
BEDLINGTON
BELLINGHAM
BILLERICAY
BIRKENHEAD
BIRMINGHAM
BRIDGNORTH
BRIDGWATER
BROMSGROVE
BROXBOURNE
BUCKINGHAM
CANTERBURY
CARSHALTON
CHELMSFORD
CHELTENHAM
CHICHESTER
CHIPPENHAM
CHULMLEIGH
COGGESHALL
COLCHESTER
CULLOMPTON
DARLINGTON
DORCHESTER
DUKINFIELD
EASTBOURNE
ECCLESHALL
FARNINGHAM
FOLKESTONE
FRESHWATER
GILLINGHAM
GLOUCESTER
HALESWORTH
HARTLEPOOL
HASLINGDON
HEATHFIELD
HORNCASTLE
HORNCHURCH
HUNGERFORD

10 —continued
HUNSTANTON
HUNTINGDON
ILFRACOMBE
KENILWORTH
KINGSCLERE
KIRKOSWALD
LAUNCESTON
LEAMINGTON
LEOMINSTER
LITTLEPORT
MAIDENHEAD
MALMESBURY
MANCHESTER
MEXBOROUGH
MICHELDEAN
MIDDLEWICH
MILDENHALL
NAILSWORTH
NOTTINGHAM
OKEHAMPTON
ORFORDNESS
PANGBOURNE
PATRINGTON
PEACEHAVEN
PONTEFRACT
PORTISHEAD
PORTSMOUTH
POTTER'S BAR
RAVENGLASS
ROCKINGHAM
SAXMUNDHAM
SHEPPERTON
SHERINGHAM
SHREWSBURY
STALBRIDGE
ST LEONARDS
STOWMARKET
SUNDERLAND
TEDDINGTON
TEIGNMOUTH
TEWKESBURY
THAMESMEAD
TORRINGTON
TROWBRIDGE
TWICKENHAM
WALSINGHAM
WARMINSTER
WARRINGTON
WASHINGTON
WEDNESBURY
WELLINGTON
WESTWARD HO
WHITCHURCH
WHITSTABLE
WHITTLESEY
WILLENHALL
WINCHELSEA
WINCHESTER
WINDERMERE
WINDLESHAM

10 —continued
WIRKSWORTH
WITHERNSEA
WOODBRIDGE
WORKINGTON

11
BASINGSTOKE
BEARMINSTER
BOGNOR REGIS
BOURNEMOUTH
BRIDLINGTON
BUNTINGFORD
CLEETHORPES
COCKERMOUTH
EAST RETFORD
GLASTONBURY
GREAT MARLOW
GUISBOROUGH
HALTWHISTLE
HAMPTON WICK
HATHERLEIGH
HIGH WYCOMBE
INGATESTONE
LEYTONSTONE
LITTLESTONE
LUDGERSHALL
LUTTERWORTH
MABLETHORPE
MANNINGTREE
MARKET RASEN
MARLBOROUGH
MUCH WENLOCK
NEW BRIGHTON
NEWTON ABBOT
NORTHAMPTON
PETERSFIELD
POCKLINGTON
RAWTENSTALL
SCARBOROUGH
SHAFTESBURY
SOUTHAMPTON
SOUTH MOLTON
STALYBRIDGE
ST MARGARET'S
STOURBRIDGE
TATTERSHALL
WALLINGFORD
WALTHAMSTOW
WESTMINSTER
WHITECHURCH
WOODHALL SPA

12
ATTLEBOROUGH
BEXHILL-ON-SEA
CASTLE RISING
CHESTERFIELD
CHRISTCHURCH
GAINSBOROUGH
GREAT GRIMSBY
GREAT MALVERN

12 —continued
HUDDERSFIELD
INGLEBOROUGH
LONG STRATTON
LOUGHBOROUGH
MACCLESFIELD
MILTON KEYNES
MORECAMBE BAY
NORTH BERWICK
NORTH SHIELDS
NORTH WALSHAM
PETERBOROUGH
SHOEBURYNESS
SHOTTESBROOK
SOUTH SHIELDS
STOKE-ON-TRENT

13
BARNARD CASTLE
BERKHAMPSTEAD
BISHOP'S CASTLE
BOROUGHBRIDGE
BRIGHTLINGSEA
BURTON-ON-TRENT
BURY ST EDMUNDS
CHIPPING ONGAR
FINCHAMPSTEAD
GODMANCHESTER
GREAT YARMOUTH
HIGHAM FERRERS
KIDDERMINSTER
KIRKBY STEPHEN
KNARESBOROUGH
LITTLEHAMPTON
LYTHAM ST ANNES
MARKET DEEPING
MARKET DRAYTON
MELCOMBE REGIS
MELTON MOWBRAY
MIDDLESBROUGH
NORTHALLERTON
SAFFRON WALDEN
SHEPTON MALLET
WOLVERHAMPTON
WOOTTON BASSET

14
BERWICK-ON-TWEED
BISHOP AUCKLAND
BISHOPS WALTHAM
CHIPPING BARNET
CHIPPING NORTON
HEMEL HEMPSTEAD
KIRKBY LONSDALE
MARKET BOSWORTH
MORTIMER'S CROSS
STOCKTON-ON-TEES
STONY STRATFORD
SUTTON COURTNEY
TUNBRIDGE WELLS
WELLINGBOROUGH
WEST HARTLEPOOL

15+
ASHTON-UNDER-
   LYNE
BARROW-IN-
   FURNESS
BISHOP'S
   STORTFORD
BURNHAM-ON-
   CROUCH
CASTLE DONINGTON
LEIGHTON BUZZARD
NEWCASTLE-ON-
   TYNE
ST LEONARDS-ON-
   SEA
STRATFORD-ON-
   AVON
SUTTON COLDFIELD
WELWYN GARDEN
   CITY
WESTON-SUPER-
   MARE

FRANCE

3
AIX
PAU

4
ALBI
CAEN
LYON
METZ
NICE

5
ARLES
ARRAS
BREST
DIJON
EVIAN
LILLE
LYONS
MACON
NANCY
NIMES
PARIS
REIMS
ROUEN
TOURS
TULLE

6
AMIENS
BAYEUX
CALAIS
CANNES
DIEPPE
LE MANS
NANTES
RHEIMS
ST MALO

6 —continued
TOULON
VERDUN

7
AJACCIO
ALENÇON
AVIGNON
BAYONNE
DUNKIRK
LE HAVRE
LIMOGES
LOURDES
ORLÉANS

8
BESANÇON
BIARRITZ
BORDEAUX
BOULOGNE
CHARTRES
GRENOBLE
SOISSONS
ST TROPEZ
TOULOUSE

9
ABBEVILLE
CHERBOURG
DUNKERQUE
MARSEILLE
MONTAUBAN
PERPIGNAN
ST ETIENNE

10
MARSEILLES
MONTELIMAR
STRASBOURG
VERSAILLES

11
ARMENTIÈRES
MONTPELLIER

15
CLERMONT-
  FERRAND

**GERMAN
DEMOCRATIC
REPUBLIC**

4
GERA
SUHL

5
HALLE

6
BERLIN
ERFURT

7
COTTBUS
DRESDEN
LEIPZIG
POTSDAM

7 —continued
ROSTOCK
SPANDAU

8
SCHWERIN

9
FRANKFURT
MAGDEBURG

11
BRANDENBURG

13
KARL-MARX-STADT

GREECE

6
ATHENS
SPARTA
THEBES

7
CORINTH
MYCENAE
PIRAEUS

8
SALONIKA

HUNGARY

4
PÉCS

8
BUDAPEST

INDIA

4
AGRA

5
AJMER
ALWAR
DELHI
KOTAH
PATNA
POONA
SIMLA

6
BARODA
BHOPAL
BOMBAY
HOWRAH
IMPHAL
INDORE
JAIPUR
JHANSI
KANPUR
KOHIMA
MADRAS
MEERUT
MYSORE
NAGPUR
RAMPUR

7
BENARES
GWALIOR
JODHPUR
LUCKNOW

8
AGARTALA
AMRITSAR
CALCUTTA
CAWNPORE
JAMALPUR
SHILLONG
SRINAGAR
VARANASI

9
AHMEDABAD
ALLAHABAD
BANGALORE
HYDERABAD

10
CHANDIGARH
DARJEELING
JAMSHEDPUR
TRIVANDRUM

11
BHUBANESWAR

INDONESIA

7
BANDUNG
JAKARTA

8
SURABAJA

9
PALEMBANG

IRAN

6
ABADAN
SHIRAZ
TABRIZ
TEHRAN

7
ISFAHAN
MASHHAD

IRAQ

5
BASRA
MOSUL

7
BAGHDAD
KARBALA

IRELAND

4
BRAY
COBH
CORK

5
BALLA
BOYLE
CLARE
KELLS
SLIGO

6
ARKLOW
BANTRY
CARLOW
CASHEL
DUBLIN
GALWAY
TRALEE

7
ATHLONE
BLARNEY
CLONMEL
DUNDALK
KILDARE
SHANNON
WEXFORD
WICKLOW
YOUGHAL

8
CLONTARF
DROGHEDA
KILKENNY
LIMERICK
LISTOWEL
MAYNOUTH
RATHDRUM

9
CONNEMARA
KILLARNEY
ROSCOMMON
TIPPERARY
WATERFORD

10
SHILLELAGH

11
BALLYMURPHY

ISRAEL

4
GAZA

5
HAIFA
JAFFA

7
TEL AVIV

9
BEERSHEBA
JERUSALEM

ITALY

4
BARI
PISA

4 —continued
ROME

5
GENOA
MILAN
OSTIA
PADUA
PARMA
SIENA
TRENT
TURIN

6
NAPLES
REGGIO
VENICE
VERONA

7
BOLOGNA
MESSINA
PALERMO
POMPEII
RAVENNA
SALERNO
SAN REMO
TRIESTE
VATICAN

8
FLORENCE
SYRACUSE

9
AGRIGENTO

JAPAN

4
KOBE

5
KYOTO
OSAKA
TOKYO

6
NAGOYA

7
FUKUOKA
SAPPORO

8
NAGASAKI
YOKOHAMA

9
HIROSHIMA

10
KITAKYUSHU

KENYA

4
LAMU

7
MOMBASA
NAIROBI

KOREA

5
SEOUL

9
PANMUNJON

LEBANON

4
TYRE

5
SIDON

6
BEIRUT

7
TRIPOLI

LIBYA

4
HOMS

6
TOBRUK

MALI

6
BAMAKO

8
TIMBUKTU

MEXICO

6
JUAREZ
PUEBLA

8
ACAPULCO
VERACRUZ

9
MONTERREY

11
GUADALAJARA

MOROCCO

3
FEZ

5
RÀBAT

6
AGADIR
MEKNES

7
TANGIER

8
TANGIERS

9
MARRAKECH
MARRAKESH

10
CASABLANCA

NETHERLANDS

5
HAGUE

6
ARNHEM
LEIDEN
LEYDEN

7
UTRECHT

8
THE HAGUE

9
AMSTERDAM
DORDRECHT
EINDHOVEN
ROTTERDAM

NEW ZEALAND

6
NAPIER
NELSON

7
DUNEDIN

8
AUCKLAND

10
WELLINGTON

12
CHRISTCHURCH

NIGERIA

4
KANO

5
ABUJA
ENUGU
LAGOS

6
IBADAN

NORTHERN IRELAND

4
MUFF

5
DOAGH
GLYNN
KEADY
LARNE
LOUTH
NEWRY
OMAGH
TOOME

6
ANTRIM
AUGHER

6 —continued
BELCOO
BERAGH
CALLAN
CARNEY
COMBER
LURGAN
RAPHOE
SHRULE

7
BELFAST
BELLEEK
CALEDON
CARRICK
CLOGHER
DERVOCK
DUNDRUM
DUNMORE
FINTONA
GILFORD
GLENARM
LIFFORD
LISBURN

8
AHOGHILL
BALLYBAY
DUNGIVEN
HILLTOWN
PORTRUSH
STRABANE
TRILLICK

9
BALLINTRA
BALLYMENA
BALLYMORE
BANBRIDGE
BELTURBET
BUSHMILLS
COLERAINE
COOKSTOWN
DUNGANNON
GLASLOUGH
KILLYBEGS
KIRCUBBIN
MONEYMORE
NEWCASTLE
PORTADOWN
RASHARKIN
ROSTREVOR
TOVERMORE

10
BALLYBOFIR
BALLYCLARE
BALLYHAISE
BALLYMONEY
BALLYRONEY
CASTLEDERG
CASTLEFINN
CUSHENHALL
DONAGHADEL

10 —continued
GLENGARIFF
KILCONNELL
MARKETHILL
PORTAFERRY
SAINTFIELD
STRANGFORD
STRANORLAR
TANDERAGEE

11
BALLYCASTLE
BALLYGAWLEY
CARRICKMORE
CROSSMAGLEN
DOWNPATRICK
DRAPERSTOWN
ENNISKILLEN
LETTERKENNY
LONDONDERRY
MAGHERAFELT
PORTGLENONE
RANDALSTOWN
RATHFRYLAND

12
CASTLEBLANEY
CASTLE DAWSON
CASTLEWELLAN
FIVE MILE TOWN
HILLSBOROUGH
INISHTRAHULL
SLIEVE DONARD
STEWARTSTOWN

13
BROOKEBOROUGH
CARRICKFERGUS
DERRYGONNELLY

14
NEWTOWN
  STEWART

NORWAY

4
OSLO

6
BERGEN

9
TRONDHEIM

PAKISTAN

6
LAHORE
QUETTA

7
KARACHI

8
PESHAWAR

9
HYDERABAD

10
RAWALPINDI

PERU

4
LIMA

5
CUZCO

POLAND

4
LODZ

5
POSEN

6
DANZIG
GDANSK
KRAKOW
LUBLIN
WARSAW

7
BRESLAU

8
PRZEMYSL

PORTUGAL

6
LISBON
OPORTO

SAUDI ARABIA

5
MECCA

6
JEDDAH
MEDINA
RIYADH

SCOTLAND

3
AYR
UIG

4
ALVA
BARR
DUNS
ELIE
KIRN
LUSS
NIGG
OBAN
REAY
RONA
STOW
WICK

5
ALLOA
ANNAN

5 —continued
APPIN
AVOCH
AYTON
BANFF
BEITH
BRORA
BUNAW
BUSBY
CERES
CLOVA
CLUNE
CRAIL
CUPAR
DENNY
DOWNE
ELGIN
ELLON
ERROL
FYVIE
GOVAN
INSCH
ISLAY
KEISS
KEITH
KELSO
LAIRG
LARGO
LEITH
NAIRN
PERTH
SALEN
TROON

6
ABOYNE
ALFORD
BARVAS
BEAULY
BERVIE
BIGGAR
BO'NESS
BUCKIE
CARRON
CAWDOR
COMRIE
CRIEFF
CULLEN
CULTER
DOLLAR
DRYMEN
DUNBAR
DUNDEE
DUNLOP
DUNNET
DUNOON
DYSART
EDZELL
FINDON
FORFAR
FORRES
GIRVAN

6 —continued
GLAMIS
HAWICK
HUNTLY
IRVINE
KILLIN
KILMUN
LANARK
LAUDER
LESLIE
LINTON
LOCHEE
MEIGLE
MOFFAT
PLADDA
RESTON
RHYNIE
ROSYTH
ROTHES
SHOTTS
THURSO
TONGUE
WISHAW
YARROW

7
AIRDRIE
BALFRON
BALLOCH
BANAVIE
BOWMORE
BRAEMAR
BRECHIN
BRODICK
CANOBIE
CANTYRE
CARBOST
CARGILL
CARLUKE
CRATHIE
CULROSS
CUMNOCK
DENHOLM
DOUGLAS
DUNKELD
DUNNING
EVANTON
FAIRLIE
FALKIRK
GALSTON
GIFFORD
GLASGOW
GLENCOE
GOLSPIE
GOUROCK
GRANTON
GUTHRIE
HALKIRK
KENMORE
KESSOCK
KILMORY
KILSYTH

7 —continued

KINROSS
KINTORE
LAMLASH
LARBERT
LYBSTER
MACDUFF
MAYBOLE
MELDRUM
MELROSE
MELVICH
METHVEN
MILMUIR
MONIKIE
MUTHILL
NEWPORT
PAISLEY
PEEBLES
POLMONT
POOLEWE
PORTREE
PORTSOY
RENFREW
SADDELL
SARCLET
SCOURIE
SELKIRK
STANLEY
STRATHY
TARBERT
TARLAND
TAYPORT
TRANENT
TUNDRUM
TURRIFF
ULLSTER
YETHOLM

8

ABERDEEN
ABERLADY
ABINGTON
ARBROATH
ARMADALE
ARROCHAR
AULDEARN
BALLATER
BANCHORY
BARRHILL
BEATTOCK
BLANTYRE
BURGHEAD
CANISBAY
CARNWATH
CREETOWN
CROMARTY
DALKEITH
DALMALLY
DINGWALL
DIRLETON
DUFFTOWN
DUMFRIES

8 —continued

DUNBEATH
DUNBLANE
DUNSCORE
EARLSTON
EYEMOUTH
FINDHORN
FORTROSE
GLENLUCE
GREENLAW
GREENOCK
HAMILTON
INVERARY
INVERURY
JEANTOWN
JEDBURGH
KILBRIDE
KILNIVER
KILRENNY
KINGHORN
KIRKWALL
LANGHOLM
LATHERON
LEUCHARS
LOANHEAD
MARKINCH
MARYKIRK
MONIAIVE
MONTROSE
MONYMUSK
MUIRKIRK
NEILSTON
NEWBURGH
NEWMILNS
PENICUIK
PITSLIGO
POOLTIEL
QUIRAING
ROTHESAY
ST FERGUS
STIRLING
STRICHEN
TALISKER
TARANSAY
TRAQUAIR
ULLAPOOL
WHITHORN
WOODSIDE

9

ABERFELDY
ABERFOYLE
ARDROSSAN
BERRIDALE
BETTYHILL
BLACKLARG
BRACADALE
BRAERIACH
BROADFORD
BROUGHTON
BUCKHAVEN
CAIRNTOUL

9 —continued

CALLANDER
CARSTAIRS
DUMBARTON
EDINBURGH
FERINTOSH
FOCHABERS
INCHKEITH
INVERARAY
INVERNESS
JOHNSTONE
KILDRUMMY
KINGUSSIE
KIRKCALDY
LEADHILLS
LOCHGELLY
LOCHINVAR
LOCHNAGAR
LOCKERBIE
LOGIERAIT
MAUCHLINE
MILNGAVIE
PETERHEAD
PITLOCHRY
PORT ELLEN
PRESTWICK
RICCARTON
RONALDSAY
ROTHIEMAY
SALTCOATS
SHIELDAIG
SLAMANNAN
ST ANDREWS
STEWARTON
ST FILLANS
STRANRAER
STRATHDON
STRONTIAN
THORNHILL
TOBERMORY
TOMINTOUL

10

ABBOTSFORD
ACHNASHEEN
ANSTRUTHER
APPLECROSS
ARDRISHAIG
AUCHINLECK
BALLANTRAE
BLACKADDER
CARNOUSTIE
CARSPHAIRN
CASTLETOWN
COATBRIDGE
COLDINGHAM
COLDSTREAM
DALBEATTIE
DRUMLITHIE
EAST LINTON
GALASHIELS
GLENROTHES

10 —continued

JOHNSHAVEN
KILCREGGAN
KILLENAULE
KILMAINHAM
KILMALCOLM
KILMARNOCK
KILWINNING
KINCARDINE
KINGSBARNS
KIRKMAIDEN
KIRKOSWALD
KIRRIEMUIR
LENNOXTOWN
LESMAHAGOW
LINLITHGOW
LIVINGSTON
MILNATHORT
MOTHERWELL
PITTENWEEM
PORTOBELLO
RUTHERGLEN
STONEHAVEN
STONEHOUSE
STONEYKIRK
STRATHAVEN
STRATHEARN
STRATHMORE
TWEEDMOUTH
WEST CALDER
WILSONTOWN

11

ABERCHIRDER
BALQUHIDDER
BANNOCKBURN
BLAIRGOWRIE
CAMPBELTOWN
CHARLESTOWN
CUMBERNAULD
DRUMMELZIER
DUNFERMLINE
ECCLEFECHAN
FETTERCAIRN
FORT WILLIAM
FRASERBURGH
HELENSBURGH
INVERGORDON
KIRKMICHAEL
LOSSIEMOUTH
LOSTWITHIEL
MAXWELLTOWN
MUSSELBURGH
PORT GLASGOW
PORT PATRICK
PRESTONPANS
PULTNEYTOWN
STRATHBLANE

12

AUCHTERARDER
BALLACHULISH

12 —continued
EAST KILBRIDE
FORT AUGUSTUS
GARELOCHHEAD
INNERLEITHEN
LAWRENCEKIRK
PORTMAHOMACK
STRATHPEFFER
TILLICOULTRY

13
AUCHTERMUCHTY
CASTLE DOUGLAS
COCKBURNSPATH
DALMELLINGTON
INVERKEITHING
INVERKEITHNIE
KIRKCUDBRIGHT
KIRKINTILLOCH
NEWTON STEWART
ROTHIEMURCHUS

SOUTH AFRICA

6
DURBAN
SOWETO

8
CAPE TOWN
MAFEKING
PRETORIA

9
KIMBERLEY
LADYSMITH

10
SIMONSTOWN

11
GRAHAMSTOWN
SHARPEVILLE

12
BLOEMFONTEIN
JOHANNESBURG

13
PORT ELIZABETH

SPAIN

4
VIGO

5
CADIZ

6
BILBAO
MADRID
MALAGA

7
BADAJOZ
CORDOBA
GRANADA
SEVILLE

8
ALICANTE
PAMPLONA
VALENCIA
ZARAGOZA

9
BARCELONA
CARTAGENA
LAS PALMAS
SANTANDER
SARAGOSSA

12
SAN SEBASTIAN

SRI LANKA

5
GALLE
KANDY

7
COLOMBO

11
TRINCOMALEE

SUDAN

6
BERBER

7
DONGOLA

8
KHARTOUM
OMDURMAN

SWEDEN

5
MALMÖ

7
UPPSALA

8
GÖTEBORG

9
STOCKHOLM

10
GOTHENBURG

11
HELSINGBORG

SWITZERLAND

4
BÂLE
BERN

5
BASEL
BASLE

6
GENEVA
ZURICH

7
LUCERNE

8
LAUSANNE

SYRIA

4
HOMS

6
ALEPPO

7
PALMYRA

8
DAMASCUS

TANZANIA

6
DODOMA

8
ZANZIBAR

TURKEY

5
IZMIR

6
ANKARA
SMYRNA

7
ERZERUM

8
ISTANBUL

9
BYZANTIUM

14
CONSTANTINOPLE

USA

4
GARY
LIMA
RENO
TROY
WACO
YORK

5
AKRON
BOISE
BRONX
BUTTE
FLINT
MIAMI
OMAHA
OZARK
SALEM
SELMA
TULSA
UTICA

6
ALBANY
AUSTIN
BANGOR
BILOXI
BOSTON
CAMDEN
CANTON
DALLAS
DAYTON
DENVER
DULUTH
EL PASO
EUGENE
FRESNO
LOWELL
MOBILE
NASSAU
NEWARK
OXNARD
PEORIA
ST PAUL
TACOMA
TOLEDO
TOPEKA
TUCSON
URBANA

7
ABILENE
ANAHEIM
ATLANTA
BOULDER
BUFFALO
CHICAGO
CONCORD
DETROIT
HAMPTON
HOBOKEN
HOUSTON
JACKSON
KEY WEST
LINCOLN
MADISON
MEMPHIS
MODESTO
NEW YORK
NORFOLK
OAKLAND
ORLANDO
PHOENIX
RALEIGH
READING
ROANOKE
SAGINAW
SAN JOSÉ
SEATTLE
SPOKANE
ST LOUIS
WICHITA
YONKERS

8
BERKELEY
BROOKLYN
COLUMBUS
DEARBORN
GREEN BAY
HANNIBAL
HARTFORD
HONOLULU
LAKELAND
LAS VEGAS
NEW HAVEN
OAK RIDGE
PALO ALTO
PASADENA
PORTLAND
RICHMOND
SAN DIEGO
SANTA ANA
SAVANNAH
STAMFORD
STOCKTON
SYRACUSE
WHEELING

9
ANCHORAGE
ANNAPOLIS
ARLINGTON
BALTIMORE
BETHLEHEM
CAMBRIDGE
CHAMPAIGN
CHARLOTTE
CLEVELAND
DES MOINES
FAIRBANKS
FORT WAYNE
FORT WORTH
GALVESTON
HOLLYWOOD
JOHNSTOWN
KALAMAZOO
LANCASTER
LEXINGTON
LONG BEACH
MANHATTAN
MILWAUKEE
NASHVILLE
NEW LONDON
NORTHEAST
PRINCETON
RIVERSIDE
ROCHESTER
WATERBURY
WORCESTER
YPSILANTI

10
ATOMIC CITY
BATON ROUGE
BIRMINGHAM

10 —continued
CHARLESTON
CINCINATTI
EVANSVILLE
GREENSBORO
GREENVILLE
HARRISBURG
HUNTSVILLE
JERSEY CITY
KANSAS CITY
LITTLE ROCK
LONG BRANCH
LOS ANGELES
LOUISVILLE
MIAMI BEACH
MONTGOMERY
NEW BEDFORD
NEW ORLEANS
PITTSBURGH
PROVIDENCE
SACRAMENTO
SAINT LOUIS
SAN ANTONIO
WASHINGTON
YOUNGSTOWN

11
ALBUQUERQUE
CEDAR RAPIDS
CHATTANOOGA
GRAND RAPIDS
MINNEAPOLIS
NEWPORT NEWS
PALM SPRINGS
SCHENECTADY
SPRINGFIELD

12
ATLANTIC CITY
BEVERLY HILLS
FAYETTEVILLE
INDEPENDENCE
INDIANAPOLIS
JACKSONVILLE
NEW BRUNSWICK
NIAGARA FALLS
OKLAHOMA CITY
PHILADELPHIA
POUGHKEEPSIE
SALT LAKE CITY
SAN FRANCISCO
SANTA BARBARA

13
CORPUS CHRISTI
ST PETERSBURGH

14
FORT LAUDERDALE

15
COLORADO
   SPRINGS

USSR

3
UFA

4
BAKU
KIEV
LVOV
OMSK
RIGA

5
BREST
GORKY
KAZAN
MEMEL
MINSK
PINSK
PSKOV
VILNA
YALTA

6
KAUNAS
MOSCOW
ODESSA
TIFLIS

7
ALMA-ATA
DONETSK
IRKUTSK
ISFAHAN
KALININ
KHARKOV
LEMBERG
TALLINN
TBILISI
VILNIUS
YAKUTSK
YEREVAN

8
NOVGOROD
SMOLENSK
TASHKENT

9
ASTRAKHAN
CHERKESSK
KARAGANDA
KRIVOI ROG
KUIBYSHEV
LENINGRAD
SAMARKAND
VOLGOGRAD

10
KÖNIGSBERG
SEVASTOPOL
STALINGRAD
SVERDLOVSK

11
KALININGRAD

11 —continued
NOVOSIBIRSK
VLADIVOSTOK

14
DNEPROPETROVSK

VENEZUELA

7
CARACAS

9
MARACAIBO

WALES

3
USK

4
BALA
HOLT
MOLD
PYLE
RHYL

5
CHIRK
FLINT
NEATH
NEVIN
TENBY
TOWYN

6
AMLWCH
BANGOR
BRECON
BUILTH
CONWAY
MARGAM
RUABON
RUTHIN

7
CARBURY
CARDIFF
CWMBRAN
DENBIGH
MAESTEG
NEWPORT
NEWTOWN
ST ASAPH
SWANSEA
WREXHAM

8
ABERAVON
ABERDARE
ABERGELE
BARMOUTH
BRIDGEND
CAERLEON
CARDIGAN
CHEPSTOW
DOLGELLY

PORTS (continued)

8 —continued
EBBW VALE
HAWARDEN
HOLYHEAD
HOLYWELL
KIDWELLY
KNIGHTON
LAMPETER
LLANELLY
LLANRWST
MONMOUTH
PEMBROKE
RHAYADER
SKERRIES
SKIFNESS
TALGARTH
TREDEGAR
TREGARON

9
ABERAERON
ABERDOVEY
ABERFFRAW
BEAUMARIS
CARNARVON
CRICCIETH
FESTINIOG
FISHGUARD
LLANBERIS
LLANDUDNO
NEW RADNOR
PONTYPOOL
PORTHCAWL
PORTMADOC
PWHLLHELI
WELSHPOOL

10
CADER IDRIS
CAERNARFON
CAERNARVON
CARMARTHEN
CRICKHOWEL
FFESTINIOG
LLANDOVERY
LLANFYLLIN
LLANGADOCK
LLANGOLLEN
LLANIDLOES
MONTGOMERY
PLINLIMMON
PONTYPRIDD
PORTH NIGEL
PORT TALBOT
PRESTEIGNE

11
ABERGAVENNY
ABERYSTWYTH
MACHYNLLETH
OYSTERMOUTH

12
LLANDILOFAWR
LLANTRISSANT

13
HAVERFORDWEST
MERTHYR TYDFIL

WEST GERMANY

4
BONN
KIEL
KÖLN

5
ESSEN
MAINZ
TRIER
WORMS

6
AACHEN
BERLIN
BOCHUM
BREMEN
CASSEL
KASSEL
LÜBECK
MUNICH
TRÈVES

7
COBLENZ
COLOGNE
HAMBURG
HANOVER
HOMBURG
KOBLENZ
MÜNCHEN

8
AUGSBURG
DORTMUND
HANNOVER
MANNHEIM
NÜRNBERG

9
BRUNSWICK
DARMSTADT
FRANKFURT
NUREMBERG
STUTTGART

9 —continued
WIESBADEN
WUPPERTAL

10
BADEN BADEN
BAD HOMBURG
DÜSSELDORF
HEIDELBERG

11
SAARBRÜCKEN

13
AIX-LA-CHAPELLE

YUGOSLAVIA

5
SPLIT

6
SKOPJE
ZAGREB

8
BELGRADE
SARAJEVO

9
LJUBLJANA

ZAÏRE

8
KINSHASA

10
LUBUMBASHI

PORTS

ALGERIA

4
ORAN

6
SKIKDA

7
ALGIERS

9
PORT ARZEW

ANGOLA

6
LOBITO
LUANDA

ARGENTINA

7
LA PLATA

11
BUENOS AIRES

AUSTRALIA

6
SYDNEY

7
DAMPIER
GEELONG

8
ADELAIDE
BRISBANE

9
MELBOURNE
NEWCASTLE

10
FREEMANTLE

11
PORT JACKSON

12
PORT ADELAIDE

BELGIUM

6
OSTEND

7
ANTWERP

9
ZEEBRUGGE

BENIN

7
COTONOU

9
PORTO NOVO

BRAZIL

4
PARA

5
BELEM

6
RECIFE
SANTOS

7
TOBARAO

10
PERNAMBUCO
12
RIO DE JANEIRO

BULGARIA

5
VARNA

BURMA

5
AKYAB
6
SITTWE
7
RANGOON
8
MOULMEIN

CAMEROON

6
DOUALA

CANADA

7
HALIFAX
KITIMAT
8
MONTREAL
9
CHURCHILL
ESQUIMALT
OWEN SOUND
VANCOUVER
11
THREE RIVERS

CHANNEL ISLANDS

8
ST HELIER
11
SAINT HELIER
ST PETER PORT

CHILE

5
ARICA
8
COQUIMBO
10
VALPARAISO

CHINA

4
AMOY
6
CHEFOO

6 —continued
HANKOW
SWATOW
WEIHAI
7
FOOCHOW
YINGKOW
8
SHANGHAI
TIENTSIN
10
PORT ARTHUR

COLUMBIA

9
CARTAGENA
12
BARRANQUILLA
BUENAVENTURA

CORSICA

6
BASTIA
7
AJACCIO

CUBA

6
HAVANA
14
SANTIAGO DE CUBA

CYPRUS

7
LARNACA
8
LIMASSOL

DENMARK

6
ODENSE
7
AALBORG
HORSENS
8
ELSINORE
9
HELSINGÖR
10
COPENHAGEN
13
FREDERIKSHAVN

ECUADOR

9
GUAYAQUIL

EGYPT

4
SUEZ
8
DAMIETTA
PORT SAID
10
ALEXANDRIA

ENGLAND

4
HULL
5
DOVER
6
LONDON
7
CHATHAM
GRIMSBY
HARWICH
TILBURY
8
FALMOUTH
NEWHAVEN
PENZANCE
PLYMOUTH
PORTLAND
SANDWICH
WEYMOUTH
9
AVONMOUTH
DEVONPORT
GRAVESEND
KING'S LYNN
LIVERPOOL
NEWCASTLE
SHEERNESS
10
BARNSTAPLE
COLCHESTER
FELIXSTOWE
FOLKESTONE
HARTLEPOOL
PORTSMOUTH
SUNDERLAND
TEIGNMOUTH
WHITSTABLE
11
CINQUE PORTS
SOUTHAMPTON
12
NORTH SHIELDS
PORT SUNLIGHT
13
MIDDLESBROUGH

FINLAND

8
HELSINKI

FRANCE

5
BREST
6
CALAIS
CANNES
DIEPPE
TOULON
7
DUNKIRK
LE HAVRE
8
BORDEAUX
BOULOGNE
HONFLEUR
9
CHERBOURG
FOS-SUR-MER
MARSEILLE
10
LA ROCHELLE
MARSEILLES

FRENCH GUIANA

7
CAYENNE

**GERMAN
DEMOCRATIC
REPUBLIC**

6
WISMAR
7
ROSTOCK

GHANA

4
TEMA
8
TAKORADI

GREECE

5
CANEA
CORFU
6
PATRAS
RHODES
7
PIRAEUS

8
NAVARINO

10
HERMOPOLIS

11
HERMOUPOLIS

HAWAII

8
HONOLULU

11
PEARL HARBOR

HUNGARY

8
BUDAPEST

INDIA

6
BOMBAY
COCHIN
HALDIA
KANDLA
MADRAS

8
CALCUTTA
COCANADA
KAKINADA

11
MASULIPATAM
PONDICHERRY

12
MASULIPATNAM

INDONESIA

6
PADANG

7
JAKARTA

8
MACASSAR
MAKASSAR
PARADEEP

IRAN

6
ABADAN

7
BUSHIRE

IRAQ

5
BASRA

IRELAND

4
COBH

4 —continued
CORK

7
DONEGAL
DUNDALK
YOUGHAL

8
DUNLEARY

12
DUN LAOGHAIRE

ISRAEL

4
ACRE
AKKO
ELAT

5
EILAT
HAIFA

6
ASHDOD

ITALY

4
BARI

5
GAETA
GENOA
OSTIA
TRANI

6
ANCONA
NAPLES
VENICE

7
LEGHORN
MARSALA
MESSINA
PALERMO
SALERNO
TRAPANI
TRIESTE

8
BRINDISI

IVORY COAST

7
ABIDJAN

JAMAICA

8
KINGSTON

9
PORT ROYAL

10
MONTEGO BAY

JAPAN

4
KOBE

5
KOCHI
OSAKA

8
HAKODATE
NAGASAKI
YOKOHAMA

9
HIROSHIMA
KAGOSHIMA

11
SHIMONOSEKI

KENYA

7
MOMBASA

KUWAIT

12
MINA AL-AHMADI

LEBANON

6
BEIRUT

LIBYA

7
TRIPOLI

8
BENGHAZI

MADAGASCAR

8
TAMATAVE

MALAYSIA

6
PENANG

9
PORT KLANG

10
GEORGE TOWN

12
KOTAKINABALU

MAURITANIA

10
NOUAKCHOTT

MAURITIUS

9
PORT LOUIS

MEXICO

7
GUAYMAS

8
VERA CRUZ

MOROCCO

4
SAFI

5
CEUTA
RABAT

6
AGADIR
TETUÁN

7
MELILLA
MOGADOR
TANGIER

9
ESSAOUIRA

10
CASABLANCA

14
MINA HASSAN TANI

MOZAMBIQUE

5
BEIRA

6
MAPUTO

NETHERLANDS

5
DELFT

8
FLUSHING

9
AMSTERDAM
EUROPOORT
ROTTERDAM

10
VLISSINGEN

NEW ZEALAND

6
NELSON

8
AUCKLAND
GISBORNE

9
LYTTELTON

NIGERIA

5
LAGOS

12
PORT HARCOURT

NORTHERN IRELAND

7
BELFAST

NORWAY

4
OSLO

6
BERGEN
LARVIK
NARVIK
TROMSO

9
STAVANGER
TRONDHEIM

10
CHRISTIANA
HAMMERFEST

13
CHRISTIANSUND

PAKISTAN

6
CHALNA

7
KARACHI

PANAMA

5
COLON

6
BALBOA

9
CRISTOBAL

PAPUA NEW GUINEA

11
PORT MORESBY

**PEOPLE'S
DEMOCRATIC
REPUBLIC OF
YEMEN**

4
ADEN

PERU

3
ILO

6
CALLAO

8
MATARINI

10
SAN JUAN BAY

PHILIPPINES

4
CEBU

6
MANILA

POLAND

6
DANZIG
GDANSK
GDYNIA

7
STETTIN

8
SZCZECIN

9
KOLOBRZEG

PORTUGAL

6
LISBON
OPORTO

PUERTO RICO

7
SAN JUAN

ROMANIA

10
CONSTANTSA

SAUDI ARABIA

6
JEDDAH

SCOTLAND

4
TAIN
WICK

5
LEITH
SCAPA

6
DUNBAR
DUNDEE

8
GREENOCK

9
ARDROSSAN
SCAPA FLOW
STORNAWAY

11
GRANGEMOUTH
PORT GLASGOW

SENEGAL

5
DAKAR

SIERRA LEONE

8
FREETOWN

SOUTH AFRICA

6
DURBAN

8
CAPE TOWN

9
MOSSEL BAY
PORT NATAL

10
EAST LONDON
SIMONSTOWN

11
RICHARD'S BAY

13
PORT ELIZABETH

SOUTH KOREA

5
PUSAN

SPAIN

5
PALMA
PALOS

6
BILBAO
FERROL
MALAGA

7
CORUNNA
FUNCHAL

8
ALICANTE
ARRECIFE
LA CORUÑA

9
ALGECIRAS
BARCELONA
CARTAGENA
LAS PALMAS
PORT MAHON

SRI LANKA

5
GALLE

7
COLOMBO

SUDAN

6
SUAKIN

9
PORT SUDAN

SWEDEN

5
LULEA
MALMÖ
WISBY
YSTAD

6
KÄLMAR

8
GÖTEBORG
HALMSTAD
NYKÖPING

9
STOCKHOLM

10
GOTHENBURG

11
HELSINGBORG

TAIWAN

6
TAINAN

7
KEELUNG

9
KAOHSIUNG

TANZANIA

6
MTWARA

11
DAR ES SALAAM

**TRINIDAD AND
TOBAGO**

11
PORT-OF-SPAIN

TURKEY

5
IZMIR

6
SMYRNA

8
ISTANBUL

14
CONSTANTINOPLE

URURGUAY

URUGUAY

10
MONTEVIDEO

USA

4
ERIE
7
DETROIT
HOUSTON
NEW YORK
NORFOLK
SEATTLE
8
NEW HAVEN
9
BALTIMORE
GALVESTON
NANTUCKET
PENSACOLA
10
BRIDGEPORT
CHARLESTON
JERSEY CITY
LOS ANGELES
NEW BEDFORD
NEW ORLEANS
PERTH AMBOY
PORTSMOUTH
11
ROCK HARBOUR
12
SAN FRANCISCO

USSR

4
BAKU
OKHA
RIGA
5
KERCH
REVAL
YALTA
6
IZMAIL
ODESSA
7
OKHOTSK
TALLINN
8
NAKHODKA
PECHENGA
TAGANROG
TIKSI BAY
9
ARCHANGEL
LENINGRAD
11
VLADIVOSTOK
13
PETROPAVLOVSK

VENEZUELA

8
LA GUIARA
12
PUERTO HIERRO

13
PUERTO CABELLO

WALES

7
CARDIFF
SWANSEA
8
HOLYHEAD
LLANELLI
PEMBROKE
9
PORTMADOC
12
MILFORD HAVEN

WEST GERMANY

4
KIEL
5
EMDEN
6
BREMEN
7
HAMBURG
8
CUXHAVEN
9
FLENSBURG
10
TRAVEMÜNDE
11
BREMERHAVEN

13
WILHELMSHAVEN

YEMEN ARAB REPUBLIC

5
MOCHA
6
AHMEDI
7
HODEIDA

YUGOSLAVIA

3
BAR
4
PULA
5
KOTOR
6
RIJEKA
7
CATTARO
9
DUBROVNIK

ZAÏRE

6
MATADI
9
MBUJI-MAYI

ISLANDS

4
BALI
CEBU
CUBA
EDGE
GUAM
JAVA
OAHU
SARK
5
BANKS
CERAM
CORFU
CRETE
DEVON
HAITI
LEYTE
LUZON

5 —continued
MALTA
PANAY
SAMAR
TIMOR
6
BAFFIN
BORNEO
CYPRUS
FLORES
HAINAN
HAWAII
HONSHU
JERSEY
KODIAK
KYUSHU
MADURA
NEGROS

6 —continued
PENANG
RHODES
SICILY
TAHITI
TAIWAN
7
BAHRAIN
BARENTS
BERMUDA
CELEBES
CORSICA
CURACAO
GOTLAND
GRENADA
ICELAND
IRELAND
JAMAICA

7 —continued
MADEIRA
MAJORCA
MINDORO
OKINAWA
PALAWAN
SHIKOKU
ST LUCIA
SUMATRA
WRANGEL
8
ALDERNEY
BARBADOS
DOMINICA
GUERNSEY
HOKKAIDO
HONG KONG
MALAGASY

8 —continued
MELVILLE
MINDANAO
SAKHALIN
SARDINIA
SOMERSET
SRI LANKA
SULAWESI
TASMANIA
TENERIFE
TRINIDAD
UNALASKA
VICTORIA
VITI LEVU
ZANZIBAR

9
ANTICOSTI
AUSTRALIA

9 —continued
ELLESMERE
GREENLAND
HALMAHERA
ISLE OF MAN
MANHATTAN
MAURITIUS
NANTUCKET
NEW GUINEA
SINGAPORE
ST VINCENT
VANCOUVER

10
CAPE BRETON
GUADELOUPE
HISPANIOLA
LONG ISLAND
MADAGASCAR

10 —continued
MARTINIQUE
NEW BRITAIN
NEW IRELAND
NEW ZEALAND
PUERTO RICO

11
AXEL HEIBERG
GUADALCANAL
ISLE OF PINES
ISLE OF WIGHT
SOUTHAMPTON

12
BOUGAINVILLE
GREAT BRITAIN
NEW CALEDONIA
NEWFOUNDLAND
NOVAYA ZEMLYA

13
NORTH EAST LAND
PRINCE OF WALES
PRINCE PATRICK
SANTA CATALINA

14
TIERRA DEL FUEGO

15
MARTHA'S
  VINEYARD
WEST SPITSBERGEN

18
PRINCE EDWARD
  ISLAND

OCEANS AND SEAS

3 & 4
ARAL (SEA)
AZOV (SEA OF)
DEAD (SEA)
JAVA (SEA)
KARA (SEA)
RED (SEA)
ROSS (SEA)
SAVA (SEA)

5
BANDA (SEA)
BLACK (SEA)
CHINA (SEA)
CORAL (SEA)
IRISH (SEA)
JAPAN (SEA OF)
NORTH (SEA)
TIMOR (SEA)
WHITE (SEA)

6
AEGEAN (SEA)
ARCTIC (OCEAN)
BALTIC (SEA)
BERING (SEA)
CELTIC (SEA)
INDIAN (OCEAN)
INLAND (SEA)
IONIAN (SEA)
LAPTEV (SEA)
NANHAI (SEA)
TASMAN (SEA)
YELLOW (SEA)

7
ANDAMAN (SEA)
ARABIAN (SEA)
ARAFURA (SEA)

7 —continued
BARENTS (SEA)
BEHRING (SEA)
CASPIAN (SEA)
DONG HAI (SEA)
GALILEE (SEA OF)
MARMARA (SEA OF)
OKHOTSK (SEA OF)
PACIFIC (OCEAN)
WEDDELL (SEA)

8
ADRIATIC (SEA)
AMUNDSEN (SEA)
ATLANTIC (OCEAN)
BEAUFORT (SEA)
HUANG HAI (SEA)
LIGURIAN (SEA)

8 —continued
SARGASSO (SEA)
TIBERIAS (SEA OF)

9
ANTARCTIC (OCEAN)
CARIBBEAN (SEA)
EAST CHINA (SEA)
GREENLAND (SEA)

10+
BELLINGSHAUSEN
  (SEA)
MEDITERRANEAN
  (SEA)
PHILIPPINE (SEA)
SETO-NAIKAI (SEA)
SOUTH CHINA (SEA)

LAKES AND LOCHS

LAKE (Country)

3
AWE (Scotland)
VAN (Turkey)

4
BALA (Wales)
CHAD (West Africa)
COMO (Italy)
ERIE (Canada, USA)
EYRE (Australia)

4 —continued
KIVU (Zaire, Rwanda)
NEMI (Italy)
NESS (Scotland)
TANA (Ethiopia)

5
FOYLE (Ireland)
GARDA (Italy)
GREAT (Australia)

5 —continued
GREAT (USA,
  Canada)
HURON (USA,
  Canada)
KIOGA (Uganda)
KYOGA (Uganda)
LÉMAN (Switzerland,
  France)

5 —continued
LEVEN (Scotland)
LOCHY (Scotland)
MAREE (Scotland)
NEAGH (Northern
  Ireland)
NYASA (Malawi,
  Tanzania,
  Mozambique)

RIVERS

5 —continued
ONEGA (Soviet Union)
TAUPO (New Zealand)
URMIA (Iran)

6
ALBERT (Uganda, Zaïre)
BAIKAL (Soviet Union)
EDWARD (Uganda, Zaïre)
GENEVA (Switzerland, France)
KARIBA (Zambia, Zimbabwe)
LADOGA (Soviet Union)
LOMOND (Scotland)
LOP NOR (China)
MALAWI (Malawi, Tanzania, Mozambique)
MOBUTU (Uganda, Zaïre)
NASSER (Egypt)
NATRON (Tanzania)
PEIPUS (Soviet Union)
POYANG (China)

6 —continued
RUDOLF (Kenya, Ethiopia)
SAIMAA (Finland)
VÄNERN (Sweden)

7
BALATON (Hungary)
DERWENT (England)
KATRINE (Scotland)
KOKO NOR (China)
LUCERNE (Switzerland)
NU JIANG (China, Burma)
ONTARIO (Canada, USA)
QINGHAI (China)
ST CLAIR (USA, Canada)
TORRENS (Australia)
TURKANA (Kenya, Ethiopia)

8
BALKHASH (Soviet Union)
CHIEMSEE (West Germany)
CONISTON (England)
DONGTING (China)
GRASMERE (England)

8 —continued
ISSYK KUL (Soviet Union)
MAGGIORE (Italy, Switzerland)
MAZURIAN (Poland)
MENINDEE (Australia)
MICHIGAN (USA)
NEUSIEDL (Austria, Hungary)
SUPERIOR (USA, Canada)
TITICACA (Peru, Bolivia)
TONLE SAP (Kampuchea)
TUNG-T'ING (China)
VICTORIA (Uganda, Tanzania, Kenya)
WINNIPEG (Canada)

9
ATHABASCA (Canada)
BANGWEULU (Zambia)
CHAMPLAIN (USA)
CONSTANCE (West Germany)
ENNERDALE (England)

9 —continued
GREAT BEAR (Canada)
GREAT SALT (USA)
MARACAIBO (Venezuela)
THIRLMERE (England)
TRASIMENO (Italy)
ULLSWATER (England)
WAST WATER (England)

10 +
BUTTERMERE (England)
GREAT SLAVE (Canada)
IJSSELMEER (Netherlands)
KARA-BOGAZ-GOL (Soviet Union)
OKEECHOBEE (USA)
TANGANYIKA (Zaïre, Burundi, Tanzania, Zambia)
VIERWALDSTÄTTER-SEE (Switzerland)
WINDERMERE (England)

RIVERS

RIVER (Country)

2 & 3
AIN (France)
ALN (England)
BUG (USSR, Poland, E. Germany)
CAM (England)
DEE (Scotland, Wales, England)
DON (USSR, Scotland, England, France, Australia)
EMS (W. Germany, Netherlands)
ESK (Australia)
EXE (England)
FAL (England)
FLY (New Guinea)
HAN (China)
KWA (Zaïre)
LEA (England)
LEE (Ireland)

2 & 3 —continued
LOT (France)
OB (USSR)
PO (Italy)
RED (USA)
RUR (W. Germany)
RYE (England)
TAY (Scotland)
URE (England)
USA (USSR)
USK (Wales, England)
WEY (England)
WYE (Wales, England)
YEO (England)

4
ADDA (Italy)
ADUR (England)
AIRE (England, France)
ALMA (USSR)

4 —continued
AMUR (Mongolia, USSR, China)
ARNO (Italy)
ARUN (Nepal)
AUBE (France)
AVON (England)
BEAS (India)
BURE (England)
CHER (France)
COLN (England)
DART (England)
DOON (Scotland)
DOVE (England)
EBRO (Spain)
EDEN (England, Scotland)
ELBE (W. Germany, E. Germany, Czechoslovakia)
EMBA (USSR)

4 —continued
ISIS (England)
JUBA (E. Africa)
KAMA (USSR)
KURA (Turkey, USSR)
LAHN (W. Germany)
LECH (W. Germany, Austria)
LENA (USSR)
LUNE (England)
LÜNE (W. Germany)
MAAS (Netherlands)
MAIN (W. Germany, Northern Ireland)
MIÑO (Spain)
MOLE (England)
NILE (Sudan, Egypt)
ODER (W. Germany, E. Germany, Czechoslovakia, Poland)

27

RIVERS

4 —continued
OHIO (USA)
OISE (France)
OUSE (England)
OXUS (USSR)
PEEL (Australia, USA)
RAVI (India, Pakistan)
REDE (England)
RUHR (W. Germany)
SAAR (W. Germany, France)
SIDA (USSR)
SPEY (Scotland)
TAFF (Wales)
TAJO (Spain)
TARN (France)
TAWE (Wales)
TAWI (India)
TEES (England)
TEJO (Brazil)
TEST (England)
TYNE (Scotland, England)
URAL (USSR)
VAAL (South Africa)
WEAR (England)
YARE (England)

5
ADIGE (Italy)
AISNE (France)
ALLAN (Scotland, Syria)
ALLER (Spain, W. Germany)
ANNAN (Scotland)
BENUE (Nigeria)
BRENT (England)
CAMEL (England)
CHARI (Cameroon, Chad)
CLYDE (Scotland, Canada)
COLNE (England)
CONGO (Zaire)
DNEPR (USSR)
DOUBS (France, Switzerland)
DOURO (Spain, Portugal)
DOVEY (Wales)
DRAVA (Italy, Austria, Yugoslavia, Hungary)
DUERO (Spain)
DVINA (USSR)
FORTH (Scotland)
FROME (Australia)
INDUS (India, Pakistan, China)
JAMES (USA, Australia)

5 —continued
JUMNA (India)
JURUÁ (Brazil)
KAFUE (Zambia)
KASAI (Angola, Zaire)
KUBAN (USSR)
LIPPE (W. Germany)
LOIRE (France)
MARNE (France)
MAROS (Indonesia)
MEUSE (France, Belgium)
MINHO (Spain, Portugal)
MURES (Romania, Hungary)
NEGRO (Spain, Brazil, Argentina, Bolivia, Paraguay, Uruguay, Venezuela)
NEMAN (USSR)
NIGER (Nigeria, Mali, Guinea)
OTTER (England)
PEACE (Canada, USA)
PEARL (USA, China)
PECOS (USA)
PIAVE (Italy)
PURUS (Brazil)
RANCE (France)
RHINE (Switzerland, W. Germany, Netherlands)
SAALE (E. Germany, W. Germany)
SAÔNE (France)
SEINE (France)
SLAVE (Canada)
SNAKE (USA)
SOMME (France)
STOUR (England)
SWALE (England)
TAGUS (Portugal, Spain)
TAMAR (England)
TIBER (Italy)
TRENT (England)
TWEED (England, Scotland)
VOLGA (USSR, USA)
VOLTA (Ghana)
WESER (W. Germany)
XINGU (Brazil)
ZAIRE (Zaire)

6
ALLIER (France)
AMAZON (Peru, Brazil)
ANGARA (USSR)
BÍO-BÍO (Chile)

6 —continued
CHENAB (Pakistan)
CLUTHA (New Zealand)
COOPER (Australia)
COQUET (England)
CROUCH (England)
DANUBE (W. Germany, Austria, Romania, Hungary, Czechoslovakia, Bulgaria)
DNESTR (USSR)
ESCAUT (Belgium, France)
FRASER (Canada)
GAMBIA (The Gambia, Senegal)
GANGES (India)
GLOMMA (Norway)
HUDSON (USA)
HUNTER (Australia)
IRTYSH (USSR)
ITCHEN (England)
JAPURÁ (Brazil)
JORDAN (Israel, Jordan)
KOLYMA (USSR)
LIFFEY (Eire)
LODDON (Australia, England)
MAMORÉ (Brazil, Bolivia)
MEDINA (USA)
MEDWAY (England)
MEKONG (Laos, China)
MERSEY (England)
MONNOW (England, Wales)
MURRAY (Australia, Canada)
NECKAR (W. Germany)
NEISSE (Poland, Germany)
OGOOUÉ (Gabon)
ORANGE (South Africa)
ORWELL (England)
PARANÁ (Brazil)
PLATTE (USA)
RIBBLE (England)
ST JOHN (Liberia, USA)
SALADO (Argentina, Cuba, Mexico)
SEVERN (England)
SUTLEJ (Pakistan, India, China)
THAMES (England)

6 —continued
TICINO (Italy, Switzerland)
TIGRIS (Iraq, Turkey)
TUGELA (South Africa)
USSURI (China, USSR)
VIENNE (France)
VLTAVA (Czechoslovakia)
WABASH (USA)
WEAVER (England)
YELLOW (China, USA, Papua New Guinea)

7
BERMEJO (Argentina)
CAUVERY (India)
DAMODAR (India)
DARLING (Australia)
DERWENT (England)
DURANCE (France)
GARONNE (France)
GIRONDE (France)
HELMAND (Afghanistan)
HOOGHLY (India)
HUANG HO (China)
LACHLAN (Australia)
LIMPOPO (South Africa, Zimbabwe, Mozambique)
LUALABA (Zaire)
MADEIRA (Brazil)
MARAÑÓN (Brazil, Peru)
MARITSA (Bulgaria)
MOSELLE (W. Germany)
ORONTES (Syria)
PECHORA (USSR)
POTOMAC (USA)
SALWEEN (Burma, China)
SCHELDT (Belgium)
SENEGAL (Senegal)
SHANNON (Eire)
SONGHUA (Vietnam, China)
SUNGARI (China)
SUWANNEE (USA)
URUGUAY (Uruguay, Brazil)
VISTULA (Poland)
WAIKATO (New Zealand)
XI JIANG (China)
YANGTZE (China)
YENISEI (USSR)

7 —continued
ZAMBEZI (Zambia, Angola, Zimbabwe, Mozambique)

8
AMU DARYA (USSR)
ARAGUAIA (Brazil)
ARKANSAS (USA)
CANADIAN (USA)
CHARENTE (France)
COLORADO (USA)
COLUMBIA (USA)
DEMERARA (Guyana)
DORDOGNE (France)
GODAVARI (India)
MANAWATU (New Zealand)
MENDERES (Turkey)
MISSOURI (USA)
PARAGUAY (Paraguay)

8 —continued
PUTUMAYO (Ecuador)
RIO BRAVO (Mexico)
SAGUENAY (Canada)
SYR DARYA (USSR)
TORRIDGE (England)
TUNGUSKA (USSR)
VOLTURNO (Italy)
WANSBECK (England)
WINDRUSH (England)

9
ATHABASCA (Canada)
CHURCHILL (Canada)
ESSEQUIBO (Guyana)
EUPHRATES (Iraq)
GREAT OUSE (England)
HSI CHIANG (China)
IRRAWADDY (Burma)

9 —continued
MACKENZIE (Australia)
MAGDALENA (Colombia)
RIO GRANDE (Jamaica)
TENNESSEE (USA)

10
CHANG JIANG (China)
CHAO PHRAYA (Thailand)
COPPERMINE (Canada)
HAWKESBURY (Australia)
SHENANDOAH (USA)
ST LAWRENCE (USA)

11
ASSINIBOINE (Canada)

11 —continued
BRAHMAPUTRA (Tibet, India)
MISSISSIPPI (USA)
SHATT AL-ARAB (Iran, Iraq)
SUSQUEHANNA (USA)
YELLOWSTONE (USA)

12
GUADALQUIVIR (Spain)
MURRUMBIDGEE (Australia)
RÍO DE LA PLATA (Argentina, Uruguay)
SASKATCHEWAN (Canada)

MOUNTAINS AND HILLS

MOUNTAIN (Country)

3
ASO (MT) (Japan)
IDA (MT) (Turkey)

4
ALPS (France, Switzerland, Italy, Austria)
BLUE (MTS) (Australia)
COOK (MT) (New Zealand)
ETNA (MT) (Sicily)
HARZ (MTS) (East Germany, West Germany)
JAYA (MT) (Indonesia)
JURA (MTS) (France, Switzerland)
OSSA (MT) (Australia)
RIGI (Switzerland)
URAL (MTS) (Soviet Union)

5
ALTAI (MTS) (Soviet Union, China, Mongolia)
ANDES (South America)
ATHOS (MT) (Greece)

5 —continued
ATLAS (MTS) (Morocco, Algeria)
BLACK (MTS) (Wales)
COAST (MTS) (Canada)
EIGER (Switzerland)
ELGON (MT) (Uganda, Kenya)
GHATS (India)
KAMET (MT) (India)
KENYA (MT) (Kenya)
LENIN (PEAK) (Soviet Union)
LOGAN (MT) (Canada)
PELÉE (MT) (Martinique)
ROCKY (MTS) (USA, Canada)
SAYAN (MTS) (Soviet Union)
SNOWY (MTS) (Australia)
TATRA (MTS) (Poland, Czechoslovakia)
WEALD (THE) (England)

6
ARARAT (MT) (Turkey)
BALKAN (MTS) (Bulgaria)
CARMEL (MT) (Israel)
EGMONT (MT) (New Zealand)
ELBERT (MT) (USA)
ELBRUS (MT) (Soviet Union)
ELBURZ (MTS) (Soviet Union)
EREBUS (MT) (Ross Island)
HERMON (MT) (Syria, Lebanon)
HOGGAR (MTS) (Algeria)
KUNLUN (MTS) (China)
LADAKH (RANGE) (India)
MATOPO (HILLS) (Zimbabwe)
MENDIP (HILLS) (England)
MOURNE (MTS) (Northern Ireland)

6 —continued
OLIVES (MT OF) (Israel)
PAMIRS (Soviet Union, China, Afghanistan)
PINDUS (MTS) (Greece, Albania)
TAURUS (MTS) (Turkey)
VOSGES (France)
ZAGROS (MTS) (Iran)

7
AHAGGAR (MTS) (Algeria)
BERNINA (Switzerland)
BROCKEN (East Germany)
CHEVIOT (HILLS) (United Kingdom)
CHIANTI (Italy)
EVEREST (MT) (Nepal, Tibet)
OLYMPUS (MT) (Greece)
PALOMAR (MT) (USA)
RAINIER (MT) (USA)

7 —continued

RORAIMA (MT)
(Brazil, Guyana,
Venezuela)
RUAPEHU (MT) (New
Zealand)
SKIDDAW (England)
SNOWDON (Wales)
ST ELIAS (MTS)
(Alaska, Yukon)
TIBESTI (MTS) (Chad,
Libya)

8

ARDENNES
(Luxembourg,
Belgium, France)
BEN NEVIS (Scotland)
CAMBRIAN (MTS)
(Wales)
CAUCASUS (MTS)
(Soviet Union)
CÉVENNES (France)
CHILTERN (HILLS)
(England)
COTOPAXI (Ecuador)
COTSWOLD (HILLS)
(England)
FLINDERS (RANGE)
(Australia)
FUJIYAMA (Japan)
HYMETTUS (MT)
(Greece)
JUNGFRAU
(Switzerland)
KAIKOURA (RANGES)
(New Zealand)
MUSGRAVE
(RANGES)
(Australia)
PENNINES (England)
PYRENEES (France,
Spain)
STANOVOI (RANGE)
(Soviet Union)
TIAN SHAN (Soviet
Union, China,
Mongolia)
VESUVIUS (Italy)

9

ACONCAGUA (MT)
(Argentina)

9 —continued

ALLEGHENY (MTS)
(USA)
ANNAPURNA (MT)
(Nepal)
APENNINES (Italy)
CAIRNGORM (MTS)
(Scotland)
DOLOMITES (Italy)
DUNSINANE
(Scotland)
GRAMPIANS
(Scotland)
HAMERSLEY
(RANGE) (Australia)
HELVELLYN
(England)
HIMALAYAS (S Asia)
HINDU KUSH (Central
Asia)
HUASCARÁN (Peru)
KARAKORAM
(RANGE) (China,
Pakistan, India)
KOSCIUSKO (MT)
(Australia)
MONT BLANC
(France, Italy)
NANDA DEVI (MT)
(India)
PACARAIMA (MTS)
(Brazil, Venezuela,
Guyana)
PARNASSUS (MT)
(Greece)
RUWENZORI (MTS)
(Uganda-Zaire)
TIRICH MIR (MT)
(Pakistan)
ZUGSPITZE (West
Germany)

10

ADIRONDACK (MTS)
(USA)
CADER IDRIS (Wales)
CANTABRIAN (MTS)
(Spain)
CARPATHIAN (MTS)
(Czechoslovakia,
Poland, Romania,
Soviet Union)

10 —continued

CHIMBORAZO (MT)
(India)
DHAULAGIRI (MT)
(Nepal)
ERZGEBIRGE
(Czechoslovakia,
East Germany)
KEBNEKAISE
(Sweden)
LAMMERMUIR
(HILLS) (Scotland)
MACDONNELL
(RANGES)
(Australia)
MAJUBA HILL (South
Africa)
MATTERHORN
(Switzerland, Italy)
MIDDLEBACK
(RANGE) (Australia)
MONTSERRAT
(Spain)
MOUNT LOFTY
(RANGES)
(Australia)

11

ANTI-LEBANON
(MTS) (Lebanon,
Syria)
APPALACHIAN (MTS)
(USA)
DRAKENSBERG
(MTS) (South
Africa)
JOTUNHEIMEN
(Norway)
KILIMANJARO (MT)
(Tanzania)
MONADHLIATH (MTS)
(Scotland)
NANGA PARBAT (MT)
(Pakistan)
SCAFELL PIKE
(England)
SIERRA MADRE
(Mexico)

12

CITLALTÉPETL
(Mexico)

12 —continued

GODWIN AUSTEN
(MT) (Pakistan)
GOLAN HEIGHTS
(Syria)
GRAN PARADISO
(Italy)
INGLEBOROUGH
(England)
KANCHENJUNGA
(MT) (Nepal)
PEAK DISTRICT
(England)
POPOCATEPETL
(MT) (Mexico)
SIDING SPRING (MT)
(Australia)
SIERRA MORENA
(Spain)
SIERRA NEVADA
(Spain, USA)
WARRUMBUNGLE
(RANGE) (Australia)

13

CARRANTUOHILL
(Ireland)
COMMUNISM PEAK
(Soviet Union)
GROSSGLOCKNER
(Austria)
KANGCHENJUNGA
(MT) (Nepal)
KOMMUNIZMA PIK
(Soviet Union)
OJOS DEL SALADO
(Argentina, Chile)
SIERRA MAESTRA
(Cuba)

14 +

BERNESE
OBERLAND
(Switzerland)
FICHTELGEBIRGE
(West Germany)
FINSTERAARHORN
(Switzerland)
MACGILLICUDDY'S
REEKS (Ireland)
SHIRE HIGHLANDS
(Malawi)

VOLCANOES

VOLCANO (Country)

3
ASO (Japan)
AWU (Indonesia)
4
ETNA (Sicily)
FOGO (Cape Verde
  Islands)
GEDE (Indonesia)
KABA (Indonesia)
LAKI (Iceland)
NILA (Indonesia)
POAS (Costa Rica)
SIAU (Indonesia)
TAAL (Philippines)
5
AGUNG (Indonesia)
ASAMA (Japan)
ASKJA (Iceland)
DEMPO (Indonesia)
FUEGO (Guatemala)
HEKLA (Iceland)
KATLA (Iceland)
MANAM (Bismarck
  Archipelago)
MAYON (Philippines)
NOYOE (Iceland)
OKMOK (USA)
PALOE (Indonesia)
PELÉE (W. Indies)
SPURR (USA)
6
ALCEDO (Galapagos
  Islands)
AMBRIM (Vanuatu
  Republic)
BIG BEN (Heard
  Island)
BULENG (Indonesia)
COLIMA (Mexico)
DUKONO (Indonesia)
IZALCO (El Salvador)
KATMAI (USA)
LASCAR (Chile)
LASSEN (USA)
LLAIMA (Chile)
LOPEVI (Vanuatu
  Republic)

6 —continued
MARAPI (Indonesia)
MARTIN (USA)
MEAKAN (Japan)
MERAPI (Indonesia)
MIHARA (Japan)
O'SHIMA (Japan)
OSORNO (Chile)
PACAYA (Guatemala)
PAVLOF (USA)
PURACÉ (Colombia)
SANGAY (Ecuador)
SEMERU (Indonesia)
SLAMAT (Indonesia)
TACANA (Guatemala)
UNAUNA (Indonesia)
7
ATITLAN (Guatemala)
BÁRCENA (Mexico)
BULUSAN
  (Philippines)
DIDICAS (Philippines)
EL MISTI (Peru)
GALERAS (Colombia)
JORULLO (Mexico)
KILAUEA (USA)
OMETEPE
  (Nicaragua)
PUYEHUE (Chile)
RUAPEHU (New
  Zealand)
SABRINA (Azores)
SOPUTAN (Indonesia)
SURTSEY (Iceland)
TERNATE (Indonesia)
TJAREME (Indonesia)
TOKACHI (Japan)
TORBERT (USA)
TRIDENT (USA)
VULCANO (Italy)
8
BOGOSLOF (USA)
CAMEROON
  (Cameroon)
COTOPAXI (Ecuador)

8 —continued
DEMAVEND (Iran)
FONUALEI (Tonga
  Islands)
FUJIYAMA (Japan)
HUALALAI (USA)
KERINTJI (Indonesia)
KRAKATAU
  (Indonesia)
KRAKATOA
  (Indonesia)
MAUNA LOA (USA)
NIUAFO'OU (Tonga
  Islands)
RINDJANI (Indonesia)
SANGEANG
  (Indonesia)
TARAWERA (New
  Zealand)
VESUVIUS (Italy)
YAKEDAKE (Japan)
9
AMBUROMBU
  (Indonesia)
BANDAI-SAN (Japan)
CLEVELAND (USA)
COSEGUINA
  (Nicaragua)
COTACACHI
  (Ecuador)
GAMKONORA
  (Indonesia)
GRIMSVÖTN (Iceland)
KORYAKSKY (USSR)
MOMOTOMBO
  (Nicaragua)
MYOZIN-SYO (Japan)
NGAURUHOE (New
  Zealand)
PARICUTIN (Mexico)
RININAHUE (Chile)
SANTORINI (Greece)
STROMBOLI (Italy)
TONGARIRO (New
  Zealand)

10
ACATENANGO
  (Guatemala)
CAPELINHOS
  (Azores)
CERRO NEGRO
  (Nicaragua)
GUALLATIRI (Chile)
HIBOK HIBOK
  (Philippines)
ICHINSKAYA (USSR)
LONG ISLAND
  (Bismarck
  Archipelago)
MIYAKEJIMA (Japan)
NYAMIAGIRA (Zaïre)
NYIRAGONGO (Zaïre)
SANTA MARIA
  (Guatemala)
SHISHALDIN (USA)
TUNGURAHUA
  (Ecuador)
VILLARRICA (Chile)
11
GREAT SITKIN (USA)
KILIMANJARO
  (Tanzania)
LA SOUFRIÈRE (W.
  Indies)
TUPUNGATITO
  (Chile)
WHITE ISLAND (New
  Zealand)
12
HUAINAPUTINA
  (Peru)
POPOCATAPETL
  (Mexico)
SARYCHEV PEAK
  (USSR)
13
KLYUCHEVSKAYA
  (USSR)

DESERTS

4
GILA
GOBI
THAR

5
NAMIB
NEFUD
NEGEV
OLMOS
ORDOS
SINAI
STURT

6
ARUNTA
GIBSON
MOJAVE

6 —continued
NUBIAN
SAHARA
SYRIAN
UST'-URT

7
ALASHAN
ARABIAN
ATACAMA
KARA KUM
MORROPE
PAINTED
SECHURA
SIMPSON

8
COLORADO

8 —continued
KALAHARI
KYZYL KUM
MUYUNKUM
VIZCAINO

9
BLACK ROCK
DASHT-I-LUT
DZUNGARIA

10
AUSTRALIAN
BET-PAK-DALA
GREAT SANDY
PATAGONIAN
RUB'AL KHALI

11
DASHT-I-KAVIR
DASHT-I-MARGO
DEATH VALLEY

13
GREAT SALT LAKE
GREAT VICTORIA

14
BOLSON DE MAPIMI

16
TURFAN
 DEPRESSION

ANIMALS AND PLANTS

ANIMALS

2 & 3	5 —continued	6 —continued	6 —continued
AI	COYPU	AUROCH	SEA COW
APE	DHOLE	AYE-AYE	SERVAL
ASS	DINGO	BABOON	SIFAKA
BAT	DRILL	BADGER	TENREC
CAT	ELAND	BEAVER	VERVET
DOG	FOSSA	BOBCAT	VICUNA
ELK	GAYAL	CATTLE	WALRUS
FOX	GENET	CHITAL	WAPITI
GNU	GORAL	COLUGO	WEASEL
KOB	HINNY	COUGAR	WISENT
PIG	HORSE	COYOTE	WOMBAT
RAT	HUTIA	CUSCUS	**7**
YAK	HYENA	DESMAN	ACOUCHI
4	HYRAX	DIK-DIK	ANT BEAR
ANOA	INDRI	DONKEY	BANTENG
BEAR	KIANG	DUGONG	BIGHORN
CAVY	KOALA	DUIKER	BLESBOK
CONY	LEMUR	ERMINE	BLUE FOX
DEER	LIGER	FENNEC	BUFFALO
GAUR	LLAMA	FERRET	CANE RAT
GOAT	LORIS	FISHER	CARACAL
HARE	MOOSE	GALAGO	CARIBOU
IBEX	MOUSE	GELADA	CHAMOIS
KUDU	NYALA	GERBIL	CHEETAH
LION	OKAPI	GIBBON	COLOBUS
LYNX	ORIBI	GOPHER	DASYURE
MINK	OTTER	GRISON	DOLPHIN
MOLE	OUNCE	GUENON	ECHIDNA
MULE	PANDA	HYAENA	FELIDAE
ORYX	POTTO	IMPALA	GAZELLE
PACA	RATEL	JACKAL	GEMSBOK
PIKA	SABLE	JAGUAR	GERENUK
PUMA	SAIGA	JERBOA	GIRAFFE
SAKI	SEROW	LANGUR	GLUTTON
SEAL	SHEEP	MAMMAL	GORILLA
SIKA	SHREW	MARGAY	GRAMPUS
TAHR	SKUNK	MARMOT	GUANACO
TITI	SLOTH	MARTEN	GYMNURE
VOLE	STOAT	MONKEY	HAMSTER
WOLF	TAPIR	MUSK OX	LEMMING
ZEBU	TIGER	NILGAI	LEOPARD
5	TIGON	NUMBAT	LINSANG
ADDAX	WHALE	NUTRIA	MACAQUE
BISON	ZEBRA	OCELOT	MAMMOTH
BONGO	**6**	OLINGO	MANATEE
CAMEL	AGOUTI	ONAGER	MARKHOR
CHIRU	ALPACA	POSSUM	MEERKAT
CIVET	AOUDAD	RABBIT	MOLE RAT
COATI	ARGALI	RED FOX	
		RODENT	

7 —continued
MOON RAT
MOUFLON
MUSKRAT
NARWHAL
NOCTULE
OPOSSUM
PACK RAT
PANTHER
PECCARY
POLECAT
PRIMATE
RACCOON
RED DEER
ROE DEER
RORQUAL
SEALION
SIAMANG
SOUSLIK
SUN BEAR
TAMARIN
TAMAROU
TARSIER
WALLABY
WARTHOG
WILDCAT
ZORILLA

8
AARDVARK
AARDWOLF
ANTEATER
ANTELOPE
AXIS DEER
BABIRUSA
BONTEBOK
BUSHBABY
BUSHBUCK
CACHALOT
CAPYBARA
CHIPMUNK
DORMOUSE
ELEPHANT
ENTELLUS
FRUIT BAT
HEDGEHOG
IRISH ELK
KANGAROO
KINKAJOU
MANDRILL
MANGABEY
MARMOSET
MONGOOSE
MUSK DEER
MUSQUASH
PANGOLIN
PLATYPUS

8 —continued
PORPOISE
REEDBUCK
REINDEER
RUMINANT
SEA OTTER
SEI WHALE
SQUIRREL
STEINBOK
TALAPOIN
TAMANDUA
VISCACHA
WALLAROO
WATER RAT
WILD BOAR

9
ARCTIC FOX
ARMADILLO
BANDICOOT
BINTURONG
BLACK BEAR
BLACKBUCK
BLUE WHALE
BROWN BEAR
DEER MOUSE
DESERT RAT
DROMEDARY
FLYING FOX
GOLDEN CAT
GROUNDHOG
GUINEA PIG
HAMADRYAS
MARSUPIAL
MONOTREME
MOUSE DEER
ORANG-UTAN
PACHYDERM
PALM CIVET
PAMPAS CAT
PHALANGER
POLAR BEAR
PORCUPINE
PRONGHORN
PROSIMIAN
SILVER FOX
SITATUNGA
SLOTH BEAR
SOLENODON
SPRINGBOK
THYLACINE
TREE SHREW
WATERBUCK
WATER VOLE
WOLVERINE
WOODCHUCK

10
ANGWANTIBO

10 —continued
BARBARY APE
BOTTLENOSE
CACOMISTLE
CHEVROTAIN
CHIMPANZEE
CHINCHILLA
CHIROPTERA
FALLOW DEER
FIELDMOUSE
GOLDEN MOLE
HARTEBEEST
HONEY MOUSE
HOODED SEAL
JAGUARUNDI
KODIAK BEAR
MONA MONKEY
OTTER SHREW
PALLAS'S CAT
PILOT WHALE
PINE MARTEN
POUCHED RAT
PRAIRIE DOG
RACCOON DOG
RHINOCEROS
RIGHT WHALE
SPERM WHALE
SPRINGHAAS
TIMBER WOLF
VAMPIRE BAT
WATER SHREW
WHITE WHALE
WILDEBEEST

11
BARBASTELLE
BARKING DEER
DOUROUCOULI
FLYING LEMUR
GRASS MONKEY
GRIZZLY BEAR
HARBOUR SEAL
HONEY BADGER
KANGAROO RAT
KILLER WHALE
LEOPARD SEAL
PATAS MONKEY
PIPISTRELLE
PRAIRIE WOLF
RAT KANGAROO
RED SQUIRREL
SEROTINE BAT
SNOW LEOPARD

12
ELEPHANT SEAL
HARVEST MOUSE
HIPPOPOTAMUS

12 —continued
HORSESHOE BAT
HOWLER MONKEY
JUMPING MOUSE
KLIPSPRINGER
MOUNTAIN LION
POCKET GOPHER
RHESUS MONKEY
ROAN ANTELOPE
SNOWSHOE HARE
SPIDER MONKEY
TREE KANGAROO
WATER BUFFALO
WOOLLY MONKEY

13
ANTHROPOID APE
CRABEATER SEAL
DORCAS GAZELLE
HUMPBACK WHALE
MARSUPIAL MOLE
ROYAL ANTELOPE
SABLE ANTELOPE
TASMANIAN WOLF

14
CAPUCHIN MONKEY
CLOUDED LEOPARD
FLYING SQUIRREL
GROUND SQUIRREL
MOUNTAIN BEAVER
NEW WORLD
  MONKEY
OLD WORLD
  MONKEY
PÈRE DAVID'S DEER
SPECTACLED BEAR
SQUIRREL MONKEY
TASMANIAN DEVIL

15+
CHINESE WATER
  DEER
DUCK-BILLED
  PLATYPUS
FLYING PHALANGER
PROBOSCIS
  MONKEY
PYGMY
  HIPPOPOTAMUS
SCALY-TAILED
  SQUIRREL
WHITE RHINOCEROS
WOOLLY
  RHINOCEROS
WOOLLY SPIDER
  MONKEY

ANIMALS AND THEIR GENDER

ANIMAL	MALE	FEMALE
ANTELOPE	BUCK	DOE
ASS	JACKASS	JENNYASS
BADGER	BOAR	SOW
BEAR	BOAR	SOW
BOBCAT	TOM	LIONESS
BUFFALO	BULL	COW
CAMEL	BULL	COW
CARIBOU	STAG	DOE
CAT	TOM	QUEEN
CATTLE	BULL	COW
CHICKEN	COCK	HEN
COUGAR	TOM	LIONESS
COYOTE	DOG	BITCH
DEER	STAG	DOE
DOG	DOG	BITCH
DONKEY	JACKASS	JENNYASS
DUCK	DRAKE	DUCK
ELAND	BULL	COW
ELEPHANT	BULL	COW
FERRET	JACK	JILL
FISH	COCK	HEN
FOX	FOX	VIXEN
GIRAFFE	BULL	COW
GOAT	BILLYGOAT	NANNYGOAT
GOOSE	GANDER	GOOSE
HARE	BUCK	DOE
HARTEBEAST	BULL	COW
HORSE	STALLION	MARE
IMPALA	RAM	EWE
JACKRABBIT	BUCK	DOE
KANGAROO	BUCK	DOE
LEOPARD	LEOPARD	LEOPARDESS
LION	LION	LIONESS
MOOSE	BULL	COW
OX	BULLOCK	COW
PEACOCK	PEACOCK	PEAHEN
PHEASANT	COCK	HEN
PIG	BOAR	SOW
RHINOCEROS	BULL	COW
ROEDEER	ROEBUCK	DOEDEER
SEAL	BULL	COW
SHEEP	RAM	EWE
SWAN	COB	PEN
TIGER	TIGER	TIGRESS
WALRUS	BULL	COW
WEASEL	BOAR	COW
WHALE	BULL	COW
WOLF	DOG	BITCH
ZEBRA	STALLION	MARE

ANIMALS AND THEIR YOUNG

ANIMAL	YOUNG	ANIMAL	YOUNG
ANTELOPE	KID	HARE	LEVERET
BADGER	CUB	HARTEBEAST	CALF
BEAR	CUB	HAWK	CHICK
BEAVER	KITTEN	HORSE	FOAL
BOBCAT	KITTEN	JACKRABBIT	KITTEN
BUFFALO	CALF	KANGAROO	JOEY
CAMEL	CALF	LEOPARD	CUB
CARIBOU	FAWN	LION	CUB
CAT	KITTEN	MONKEY	INFANT
CATTLE	CALF	OX	STOT
CHICKEN	CHICK	PHEASANT	CHICK
COUGAR	KITTEN	PIG	PIGLET
COYOTE	PUPPY	RHINOCEROS	CALF
DEER	FAWN	ROEDEER	KID
DOG	PUPPY	SEAL	CALF
DUCK	DUCKLING	SHEEP	LAMB
ELAND	CALF	SKUNK	KITTEN
ELEPHANT	CALF	SWAN	CYGNET
ELK	CALF	TIGER	CUB
FISH	FRY	TOAD	TADPOLE
FROG	TADPOLE	WALRUS	CUB
FOX	CUB	WEASEL	KIT
GIRAFFE	CALF	WHALE	CALF
GOAT	KID	WOLF	CUB
GOOSE	GOSLING	ZEBRA	FOAL

COLLECTIVE TERMS

ANIMAL	COLLECTIVE TERM	ANIMAL	COLLECTIVE TERM
ANTELOPE	HERD	DOG	PACK
APE	SHREWDNESS	DONKEY	DROVE
ASS	DROVE	DUCK	PADDLING
BADGER	CETE	ELAND	HERD
BEAR	SLEUTH	ELEPHANT	HERD
BEAVER	COLONY	ELK	GANG
BLOODHOUND	SUTE	FERRET	BUSINESS
BOAR	SOUNDER	FISH	SCHOOL
BUFFALO	HERD	FOX	TROOP
CAMEL	TRAIN	GELDING	BRACE
CARIBOU	HERD	GIRAFFE	HERD
CAT	CLUSTER	GOAT	FLOCK
CATTLE	HERD	GOOSE	GAGGLE
CHAMOIS	HERD	HARE	HUSKE
CHICKEN	FLOCK	HARTEBEAST	HERD
CHOUGH	CHATTERING	HAWK	CAST
COLT	RAG	HORSE	HERD
COOT	FLEET	IMPALA	COUPLE
COYOTE	PACK	JACKRABBIT	HUSK
DEER	HERD	KANGAROO	TROOP

ANIMAL	COLLECTIVE TERM	ANIMAL	COLLECTIVE TERM
KINE	DROVE	ROEDEER	BEVY
LEOPARD	LEAP	ROOK	BUILDING
LION	PRIDE	SEAL	POD
MOLE	LABOUR	SHEEP	FLOCK
MONKEY	TROOP	SNAKE	KNOT
MOOSE	HERD	TOAD	NEST
MOUSE	NEST	WALRUS	POD
OX	TEAM	WEASEL	PACK
PEACOCK	PRIDE	WHALE	SCHOOL
PHEASANT	BROOD	WOLF	PACK
PIG	TRIP	ZEBRA	HERD
RHINOCEROS	CRASH		

BREEDS OF CATS

3
REX
4
MANX
5
CREAM
SMOKE
TABBY
6
BIRMAN
HAVANA
7
BURMESE
PERSIAN
RED SELF
SIAMESE

7—continued
SPOTTED
TURKISH
8
DEVON REY
RED TABBY
9
BLUE CREAM
10
ABYSSINIAN
BROWN TABBY
CHINCHILLA
CORNISH REY
11
BLUE BURMESE
BRITISH BLUE

11—continued
COLOURPOINT
RUSSIAN BLUE
SILVER TABBY
12
BROWN BURMESE
13
CHESTNUT BROWN
RED ABYSSINIAN
TORTOISESHELL
14
LONG HAIRED BLUE
TORTIE AND WHITE
15
RED-POINT SIAMESE

18
BLUE-POINTED
  SIAMESE
SEAL-POINTED
  SIAMESE
TORTIE-POINT
  SIAMESE
19
LILAC-POINTED
  SIAMESE
TABBY-POINTED
  SIAMESE
20+
CHOCOLATE-
  POINTED SIAMESE

BREEDS OF DOGS

3
PUG
4
PULI
5
BOXER
CORGI
HUSKY
SPITZ
6
BEAGLE
BORZOI
BRIARD
COLLIE
KELPIE
POODLE
SALUKI

6—continued
SETTER
7
BASENJI
BULLDOG
GRIFFON
HARRIER
LOWCHEN
MALTESE
MASTIFF
POINTER
SAMOYED
SHELTIE
SHIH TZU
SPANIEL
TERRIER
WHIPPET

8
ALSATIAN
CHOW CHOW
ELKHOUND
FOXHOUND
KEESHOND
PAPILLON
SHEEPDOG
9
CHIHUAHUA
DACHSHUND
DALMATIAN
DEERHOUND
GREAT DANE
GREYHOUND
LHASA APSO
PEKINGESE

9—continued
RETRIEVER
SCHNAUZER
STAGHOUND
ST BERNARD
10
BLOODHOUND
FOX TERRIER
OTTERHOUND
POMERANIAN
ROTTWEILER
SCHIPPERKE
WEIMARANER
WEIMERANER
WELSH CORGI
11
AFGHAN HOUND

11—continued
BASSET HOUND
BULL MASTIFF
BULL TERRIER
IBIZAN HOUND
IRISH SETTER
SKYE TERRIER

12
CAIRN TERRIER
FINNISH SPITZ
IRISH TERRIER
JAPANESE CHIN
NEWFOUNDLAND
PHARAOH HOUND
SILKY TERRIER
WELSH TERRIER

13
AFFENPINSCHER
BORDER TERRIER
BOSTON TERRIER

13—continued
COCKER SPANIEL
ENGLISH SETTER
HUNGARIAN PULI

14
GERMAN SHEPHERD
IRISH WOLFHOUND

15
AIREDALE TERRIER
ALASKAN
  MALAMUTE
GOLDEN RETRIEVER
HUNGARIAN VIZSLA
LAKELAND TERRIER
SCOTTISH TERRIER
SEALYHAM TERRIER
SPRINGER SPANIEL

16
KERRY BLUE
  TERRIER

16—continued
PYRENEAN
  MOUNTAIN
SHETLAND
  SHEEPDOG
YORKSHIRE
  TERRIER

17
BEDLINGTON
  TERRIER
DOBERMANN
  PINSCHER
LABRADOR
  RETRIEVER

18
JACK RUSSELL
  TERRIER
KING CHARLES
  SPANIEL

18—continued
LARGE
  MUNSTERLANDER
OLD ENGLISH
  SHEEPDOG
RHODESIAN
  RIDGEBACK

20
DANDIE DINMONT
  TERRIER
STAFFORDSHIRE
  BULL TERRIER
WEST HIGHLAND
  WHITE TERRIER
WIREHAIRED
  POINTING
  GRIFFON

BREEDS OF HORSES AND PONIES

3
COB
DON

4
ARAB
BARB
FELL
POLO
RUSS

5
DALES
FJORD
HUCUL
KONIK
LOKAI
ORLOV
PINTO
SHIRE
TERSK
TIMOR
WELSH

6
ALBINO

6—continued
BASUTO
EXMOOR
MERENS
MORGAN
TARPAN
VIATKA

7
CASPIAN
COMTOIS
CRIOLLO
FURIOSA
HACKNEY
JUTLAND
LLANERO
MUSTANG
NORIKER
QUARTER
SORRAIA

8
BUDEONNY
CAMARGUE

8—continued
DARTMOOR
GALICEÑO
HIGHLAND
HOLSTEIN
KABARDIN
KARABAIR
KARABAKH
LUSITANO
PALOMINO
SHETLAND

9
AKHAL-TEKE
ALTER-REAL
APPALOOSA
CONNEMARA
FALABELLA
HAFLINGER
KNABSTRUP
NEW FOREST
OLDENBURG
PERCHERON

9—continued
SCHLESWIG

10
ANDALUSIAN
AVELIGNESE
CLYDESDALE
GELDERLAND
HANOVERIAN
IRISH DRAFT
LIPIZZANER

11
NOVOKIRGHIZ

12
CLEVELAND BAY
SUFFOLK PUNCH
THOROUGHBRED

13
WELSH MOUNTAIN

16
TENNESSEE
  WALKING

BREEDS OF CATTLE

3
GIR

5
DEVON
KERRY
LUING

6
DEXTER
JERSEY
SUSSEX

7
BEEFALO
BRANGUS

8
AYRSHIRE
FRIESIAN
GALLOWAY
GUERNSEY
HEREFORD
HIGHLAND
LIMOUSIN

9
CHAROLAIS
SHORTHORN
SIMMENTAL
10
BROWN SWISS

10—continued
LINCOLN RED
MURRAY GREY
WELSH BLACK
11
JAMAICA HOPE

11—continued
MARCHIGIANA
13
ABERDEEN ANGUS
DROUGHTMASTER
TEXAS LONGHORN

BREEDS OF SHEEP

4
LONK
MULE
SOAY
5
CARDY
CHIOS
JACOB
LLEYN
MORFE
TEXEL
6
AWASSI
MASHAM
MERINO

6—continued
ROMNEY
7
CHEVIOT
GOTLAND
KARAKUL
LACAUNE
SUFFOLK
8
HERDWICK
LONGMYND
POLWARTH
PORTLAND
SHETLAND

9
HEBRIDEAN
LONGWOOLS
OLDENBERG
ROUGH FELL
SWALEDALE
TEESWATER
10
CORRIEDALE
DORSET HORN
EXMOOR HORN
POLL DORSET
11
MANX LOGHTAN

11—continued
WENSLEYDALE
13
WELSH MOUNTAIN
WILTSHIRE HORN
15
FRIES MELKSCHAAP
17
SCOTTISH
  BLACKFACE
18
WHITEFACED
  WOODLAND

BREEDS OF PIGS

5
DUROC
WELSH
8
PIETRAIN
TAMWORTH

9
BERKSHIRE
HAMPSHIRE
10
LARGE WHITE

15
SWEDISH LANDRACE
17
BRITISH
  SADDLEBACK

17—continued
GLOUCESTER OLD
  SPOT

BREEDS OF POULTRY

4
BUFF (goose)
5
MARAN (chicken)
PEARL (guinea fowl)
PEKIN (duck)
ROMAN (goose)
ROUEN (duck)
WHITE (guinea fowl)
6
ANCONA (chicken)
CAYUGA (duck)

6—continued
EMBDEN (goose)
SILKIE (chicken)
7
AFRICAN (goose)
CHINESE (goose)
CRESTED (duck)
DORKING (chicken)
LEGHORN (chicken)
MUSCOVY (duck)
PILGRIM (goose)

8
LAVENDER (guinea
  fowl)
TOULOUSE (goose)
9
AYLESBURY (duck)
WELSUMMER
  (chicken)
10
BARNVELDER
  (chicken)

10—continued
BELTSVILLE (turkey)
BOURBON RED
  (turkey)
INDIAN GAME
  (chicken)
ROSS RANGER
  (chicken)
SEBASTOPOL
  (goose)

11
CUCKOO MARAN
(chicken)
LIGHT SUSSEX
(chicken)
12
BLACK NORFOLK
(turkey)
INDIAN RUNNER
(duck)

12—continued
NARRAGANSETT
(turkey)
PLYMOUTH ROCK
(chicken)
WHITE HOLLAND
(turkey)
13
BUFF ORPINGTON
(duck)

13—continued
KHAKI CAMPBELL
(duck)
MAMMOTH BRONZE
(turkey)
WHITE AUSTRIAN
(turkey)
14
BLACK EAST INDIE
(duck)

14—continued
RHODE ISLAND RED
(chicken)
WELSH HARLEQUIN
(duck)
WHITE WYANDOTTE
(chicken)
15
CAMBRIDGE
BRONZE (turkey)

BIRDS

3
AUK
EMU
JAY
MOA
OWL
TIT
TUI
4
CHAT
COLY
COOT
CROW
DODO
DOVE
DUCK
GULL
HAWK
HUIA
IBIS
KAGU
KITE
KIWI
KNOT
LARK
LORY
RAIL
RHEA
ROOK
RUFF
SHAG
SKUA
SMEW
SWAN
TEAL
TERN
WREN
5
BOOBY
CRAKE
CRANE
DIVER
EAGLE
EGRET

5 —continued
EIDER
FINCH
GOOSE
GREBE
HERON
HOBBY
MACAW
MYNAH
NODDY
OUZEL
PIPIT
PRION
QUAIL
RAVEN
ROBIN
SCAUP
SERIN
SNIPE
STILT
STORK
6
AVOCET
BARBET
BULBUL
CANARY
CHOUGH
CONDOR
CUCKOO
CURLEW
DARTER
DIPPER
DRONGO
DUNLIN
FALCON
FULMAR
GANNET
GODWIT
HOOPOE
JABIRU
JACANA
KAKAPO
LINNET
MAGPIE

6 —continued
MARTIN
MERLIN
MOTMOT
ORIOLE
OSPREY
PARROT
PEEWIT
PETREL
PIGEON
PLOVER
PUFFIN
QUELEA
RATITE
ROLLER
SHRIKE
SISKIN
TAKAHE
THRUSH
TOUCAN
TROGON
TURACO
TURKEY
WHIDAH
WHYDAH
WIGEON
7
ANTBIRD
BABBLER
BARN OWL
BITTERN
BLUETIT
BUNTING
BUSTARD
BUZZARD
COAL TIT
COURSER
DUNNOCK
EMU WREN
FANTAIL
FINFOOT
FISH OWL
GADWALL
GOSHAWK

7 —continued
GRACKLE
HARRIER
HAWK OWL
HOATZIN
JACAMAR
JACKDAW
KESTREL
LAPWING
MALLARD
MANAKIN
MARABOU
MINIVET
MOORHEN
OILBIRD
ORTOLAN
OSTRICH
PEACOCK
PEAFOWL
PELICAN
PENGUIN
PINTAIL
POCHARD
QUETZAL
REDPOLL
REDWING
ROSELLA
SEAGULL
SERIEMA
SKIMMER
SKYLARK
SPARROW
SUNBIRD
SWALLOW
TANAGER
TINAMOU
TOURACO
VULTURE
WAGTAIL
WARBLER
WAXBILL
WAXWING
WRYBILL
WRYNECK

8

ACCENTOR
AVADAVAT
BATELEUR
BEE-EATER
BLACKCAP
BLUEBIRD
BOATBILL
BOBOLINK
CARACARA
CARDINAL
COCKATOO
CURASSOW
DABCHICK
DOTTEREL
EAGLE OWL
FISH HAWK
FLAMINGO
GAMEBIRD
GARGANEY
GREAT TIT
GROSBEAK
HAWFINCH
HORNBILL
LOVEBIRD
LYREBIRD
MANNIKIN
MEGAPODE
MUTE SWAN
NIGHTJAR
NUTHATCH
OVENBIRD
OXPECKER
PARAKEET
PHEASANT
PYGMY OWL
REDSHANK
REDSTART
REEDLING
RIFLEMAN
ROCK DOVE
SCOPS OWL
SCREAMER
SEA EAGLE
SHELDUCK
SHOEBILL
SNOWY OWL
SONGBIRD
STARLING
SWIFTLET
TAWNY OWL
TITMOUSE
TRAGOPAN
WHEATEAR
WHIMBREL
WHINCHAT
WHIPBIRD
WHITE-EYE
WILDFOWL
WOODCHAT
WOODCOCK

9

ALBATROSS
BALD EAGLE
BLACKBIRD
BLACK SWAN
BOWERBIRD
BRAMBLING
BROADBILL
BULLFINCH
CASSOWARY
CHAFFINCH
COCKATIEL
CORMORANT
CORNCRAKE
CROSSBILL
CURRAWONG
FIELDFARE
FIRECREST
FRANCOLIN
FRIARBIRD
FROGMOUTH
GALLINULE
GOLDCREST
GOLDENEYE
GOLDFINCH
GUILLEMOT
GYRFALCON
HILL MYNAH
KITTIWAKE
LITTLE OWL
MERGANSER
MOUSEBIRD
PARTRIDGE
PHALAROPE
PTARMIGAN
RAZORBILL
RED GROUSE
RIFLEBIRD
RING OUZEL
SANDPIPER
SCRUB BIRD
SNAKEBIRD
SNOW GOOSE
SPOONBILL
STONECHAT
THICKHEAD
THORNBILL
TRUMPETER
TURNSTONE

10

ARCTIC TERN
BEARDED TIT
BRENT GOOSE
BUDGERIGAR
CHIFFCHAFF
CRESTED TIT
DEMOISELLE
DIVING DUCK
FLYCATCHER
GRASSFINCH
GREENFINCH

10 —continued

GREENSHANK
GUINEA FOWL
HAMMERHEAD
HARPY EAGLE
HONEYEATER
HONEY GUIDE
HOODED CROW
JUNGLE FOWL
KINGFISHER
KOOKABURRA
MALLEE FOWL
MUTTONBIRD
NIGHT HERON
NUTCRACKER
PRATINCOLE
SACRED IBIS
SADDLEBACK
SAGE GROUSE
SANDERLING
SANDGROUSE
SCREECH OWL
SHEARWATER
SHEATHBILL
SONG THRUSH
SUN BITTERN
TAILORBIRD
TROPIC BIRD
TURTLE DOVE
WEAVERBIRD
WOODPECKER
WOOD PIGEON
ZEBRA FINCH

11

BLACK GROUSE
BRUSH TURKEY
BUTCHERBIRD
BUTTON QUAIL
CANADA GOOSE
CARRION CROW
DIAMONDBIRD
FRIGATE BIRD
GNATCATCHER
GOLDEN EAGLE
HERRING GULL
HUMMINGBIRD
LAMMERGEIER
LAUGHING OWL
MOCKINGBIRD
MUSCOVY DUCK
NIGHTINGALE
REED WARBLER
SNOW BUNTING
SPARROWHAWK
STONE CURLEW
STORM PETREL
TREECREEPER
WALLCREEPER
WEAVERFINCH
WHITETHROAT
WOODCREEPER

11 —continued

WREN BABBLER

12

BURROWING OWL
CAPERCAILLIE
CUCKOO-SHRIKE
DABBLING DUCK
FAIRY PENGUIN
FLOWERPECKER
GREYLAG GOOSE
HEDGE SPARROW
HONEYCREEPER
HOUSE SPARROW
LANNER FALCON
MANDARIN DUCK
MARSH HARRIER
MISTLE THRUSH
MOURNING DOVE
PERCHING DUCK
SHOVELER DUCK
STANDARDWING
UMBRELLA BIRD
WHIPPOORWILL
YELLOWHAMMER

13

ADJUTANT STORK
AMERICAN EAGLE
BARNACLE GOOSE
CROCODILE BIRD
ELEPHANT BIRDS
FAIRY BLUEBIRD
HARLEQUIN DUCK
HAWAIIAN GOOSE
LONG-TAILED TIT
OYSTERCATCHER
PASSERINE BIRD
SECRETARY BIRD
WHISTLING DUCK
WHOOPING CRANE

14

BEARDED VULTURE
BIRD OF PARADISE
DARWIN'S FINCHES
EMPEROR PENGUIN
GOLDEN PHEASANT
GRIFFON VULTURE
OWLET FROGMOUTH
PLAINS-WANDERER

15+

BALTIMORE ORIOLE
GREAT CRESTED
   GREBE
IVORY-BILLED
   WOODPECKER
LAUGHING JACKASS
PASSENGER PIGEON
PEREGRINE FALCON
PHILIPPINE EAGLE
TYRANT
   FLYCATCHER

FISH

3	6 —continued	8 —continued	9 —continued
COD	GUNNEL	BLUEFISH	PILOT FISH
DAB	KIPPER	BRISLING	PLACODERM
EEL	MARLIN	BROTULID	PORBEAGLE
GAR	MINNOW	BULLHEAD	RED MULLET
IDE	MULLET	CAVE FISH	RED SALMON
RAY	PLAICE	CHARACIN	STARGAZER
4	PUFFER	CHIMAERA	STONE BASS
BASS	REMORA	DEVIL RAY	STONEFISH
CARP	SAITHE	DRAGONET	SWORDFISH
CHAR	SALMON	DRUMFISH	SWORDTAIL
CHUB	TARPON	FILEFISH	THREADFIN
DACE	TURBOT	FLATFISH	TIGERFISH
DORY	WEEVER	FLATHEAD	TOP MINNOW
FISH	WRASSE	FLOUNDER	TRUNKFISH
GOBY	**7**	FROGFISH	WHITEBAIT
HAKE	ALEWIFE	GOLDFISH	WHITEFISH
LING	ANCHOVY	GRAYLING	WRECKFISH
OPAH	BATFISH	JOHN DORY	ZEBRA FISH
ORFE	CATFISH	LUNGFISH	**10**
PIKE	CICHLID	MACKEREL	ANGLERFISH
RUDD	CROAKER	MANTA RAY	ARCHER FISH
SHAD	DOGFISH	MONKFISH	BOMBAY DUCK
SOLE	EELPOUT	MOONFISH	COELACANTH
TOPE	GARFISH	MORAY EEL	CORNETFISH
TUNA	GARPIKE	PILCHARD	CYCLOSTOME
5	GOURAMI	PIPEFISH	DAMSELFISH
BLEAK	GROUPER	SAILFISH	DRAGONFISH
BREAM	GUDGEON	SEA BREAM	FLYING FISH
BRILL	GURNARD	SEA HORSE	GHOST SHARK
DANIO	HADDOCK	SEA PERCH	GUITAR FISH
GRUNT	HAGFISH	SEA ROBIN	LUMPSUCKER
GUPPY	HALIBUT	SKIPJACK	MIDSHIPMAN
LOACH	HERRING	STINGRAY	MUDSKIPPER
MOLLY	HOGFISH	STURGEON	NEEDLEFISH
PERCH	ICEFISH	SWAMP EEL	NURSE SHARK
PORGY	LAMPREY	TOADFISH	PADDLEFISH
ROACH	MUDFISH	WOLF FISH	PARROT FISH
SAURY	OARFISH	**9**	PINK SALMON
SHARK	PIRANHA	ANGELFISH	PLACODERMI
SKATE	POLLACK	BARRACUDA	RIBBONFISH
SMELT	POMPANO	BLUE SHARK	SHIELD FERN
SPRAT	RATFISH	CLINGFISH	SILVERSIDE
TENCH	SARDINE	CONGER EEL	TIGER SHARK
TETRA	SAWFISH	GLASSFISH	WHALE SHARK
TROUT	SCULPIN	GLOBEFISH	WHITE SHARK
TUNNY	SEA BASS	GOOSEFISH	**11**
6	SNAPPER	GRENADIER	ELECTRIC EEL
BARBEL	SUNFISH	KILLIFISH	ELECTRIC RAY
BELUGA	TELEOST	LATIMERIA	GOBLIN SHARK
BLENNY	TORPEDO	LEMON SOLE	HATCHETFISH
BONITO	WHITING	MURRAY COD	LANTERN FISH
BOWFIN	**8**	PEARLFISH	MOORISH IDOL
BURBOT	ALBACORE	PIKEPERCH	STICKLEBACK

11 —continued
SURGEONFISH
TRIGGERFISH
12+
BASKING SHARK
CLIMBING PERCH

12+ —continued
FIGHTING FISH
FOUR-EYED FISH
GREENLAND SHARK
HAMMERHEAD
  SHARK

12+ —continued
LABYRINTH FISH
MACKEREL SHARK
MILLER'S THUMB
MOUTHBROODER
PORCUPINE FISH

12+ —continued
REQUIEM SHARK
SCORPION FISH
SOCKEYE SALMON
THRESHER SHARK
YELLOWFIN TUNA

SEASHELLS

3
SUN
4
HARP
5
TULIP
6
NUTMEG
7
JUNONIA
SUNDIAL
8
DYE MUREX
LION'S PAW
NOBLE PEN
PHEASANT
TURK'S CUP
9
ANGEL WING
BAT VOLUTE
BURSA FROG
GIANT CLAM
PINK CONCH
ROTA MUREX
SPINY VASE
TELESCOPE
TENT OLIVE
WEDGE CLAM
10
BLUE MUSSEL
COAT-OF-MAIL
CROWN CONCH
DELPHINULA
DRUPE SNAIL
EYED COWRIE
PAPERY RAPA
QUAHOG CLAM
SCALED WORM
WINGED FROG
11
BEAR PAW CLAM
CAMEO HELMET
CLIONE SNAIL
FRONS OYSTER
GREEN TURBAN
HEART COCKLE
MUSIC VOLUTE

11—continued
ONYX SLIPPER
OSTRICH FOOT
PAPER BUBBLE
PEARL OYSTER
SACRED CHANK
TEXTILE CONE
TIGER COWRIE
12
AMORIA VOLUTE
ATLANTIC CONE
FLORIDA MITER
GAUDY ASAPHIS
GOLDEN COWRIE
GOLDEN TELLIN
LIMA FILE CLAM
MONEY COWRIES
PACIFIC AUGER
PARTRIDGE TUN
PELICAN'S FOOT
SCOTCH BONNET
SPIKED LIMPET
SPINDLE TIBIA
13
ANGULAR VOLUTE
BABLYON TURRID
BLEEDING TOOTH
CARDINAL MITER
COMMERCIAL TOP
COSTATE COCKLE
FIGHTING CONCH
GEOGRAPHY CONE
JACKKNIFE CLAM
JAPANESE CONES
PAPER NAUTILUS
PRICKLY HELMET
RIDGED ABALONE
SPIRAL BABYLON
SUNRISE TELLIN
TURKEY WING ARK
VENUS COMB CLAM
14
CHANNELED WHELK
DISTAFF SPINDLE
ELEGANT FIMBRIA
EPISCOPAL MITER
IMPERIAL VOLUTE

14—continued
INDONESIAN CLAM
LEUCODON COWRIE
LEWIS' MOON SNAIL
LIGHTNING WHELK
PANAMANIAN CONE
PHILIPPINE CONE
POLYNESIAN CONE
TAPESTRY TURBAN
TRITON'S TRUMPET
VENUS COMB
  MUREX
15
BITTERSWEET CLAM
BULL-MOUTH
  HELMET
JAPANESE CARRIER
NEW ENGLAND
  WHELK
PANAMANIAN
  AUGER
PILGRIM'S SCALLOP
SUNBURST CARRIER
TURRITELLA SNAIL
WATERING POT
  CLAM
WEST INDIAN CHANK
WEST AFRICAN
  CONE
16
ASIAN MOON
  SCALLOP
ATLANTIC SURF
  CLAM
DONKEY EAR
  ABALONE
EDIBLE BAY
  SCALLOP
FRILLED
  DOGWINKLE
GLORY-OF-INDIA
  CONE
ORANGE-MOUTH
  OLIVE
PAGODA
  PERIWINKLE

16—continued
PERPLICATE
  VOLUTE
PINK-MOUTHED
  MUREX
ROOSTERTAIL
  CONCH
WEDDING CAKE
  VENUS
17
AUSTRALIAN
  TRUMPET
CHAMBERED
  NAUTILUS
FLORIDA HORSE
  CONCH
PACIFIC WING
  OYSTER
SANTA CRUZ
  LATIAXIS
VIOLET SPIDER
  CONCH
18
ATLANTIC DEER
  COWRIE
GIANT KNOBBED
  CERITH
GLORY-OF-THE-
  SEAS CONE
GREAT KEYHOLE
  LIMPET
PACIFIC GRINNING
  TUN
PRECIOUS
  WENTLETRAP
WHITE-SPOTTED
  MARGIN
19
TANKERVILLE'S
  ANCILLA
20+
ARTHRITIC SPIDER
  CONCH
ATLANTIC THORNY
  OYSTER
COLOURFUL
  ATLANTIC MOON

20+ —continued
ELEPHANT'S SNOUT
 VOLUTE

20+ —continued
IMBRICATE CUP-
 AND-SAUCER

20+ —continued
MIRACULOUS
 THATCHERIA

REPTILES AND AMPHIBIANS

3
ASP
BOA
OLM
4
FROG
NEWT
TOAD
5
ADDER
AGAMA
COBRA
GECKO
KRAIT
MAMBA
SIREN
SKINK
SNAKE
TOKAY
VIPER
6
CAYMAN
GAVIAL
IGUANA
LIZARD
MOLOCH
MUGGER
PYTHON
TAIPAN
TURTLE
ZALTYS

7
AXOLOTL
GHARIAL
REPTILE
TUATARA
8
ANACONDA
BASILISK
BULLFROG
CONGO EEL
MATAMATA
MOCCASIN
MUDPUPPY
PIT VIPER
RINGHALS
SEA SNAKE
SLOWWORM
TERRAPIN
TORTOISE
TREE FROG
9
ALLIGATOR
BLINDWORM
BOOMSLANG
BOX TURTLE
CAECILIAN
CHAMELEON
CROCODILE
HAIRY FROG
PUFF ADDER
TREE SNAKE

9 —continued
VINE SNAKE
WART SNAKE
WHIP SNAKE
10
BLACK SNAKE
BUSHMASTER
CHUCKWALLA
CLAWED FROG
COPPERHEAD
CORAL SNAKE
FER-DE-LANCE
GLASS SNAKE
GRASS SNAKE
HELLBENDER
HORNED TOAD
NATTERJACK
POND TURTLE
SALAMANDER
SAND LIZARD
SIDEWINDER
WATER SNAKE
WORM LIZARD
11
AMPHISBAENA
CONSTRICTOR
COTTONMOUTH
DIAMONDBACK
FLYING SNAKE
GABOON VIPER
GILA MONSTER

11 —continued
GOLIATH FROG
GREEN TURTLE
HORNED VIPER
MIDWIFE TOAD
RATTLESNAKE
SMOOTH SNAKE
12
FLYING LIZARD
HORNED LIZARD
KOMODO DRAGON
13
BEARDED LIZARD
FRILLED LIZARD
GIANT TORTOISE
MANGROVE SNAKE
MONITOR LIZARD
RUSSELL'S VIPER
SPADEFOOT TOAD
WATER MOCCASIN
14+
FIRE SALAMANDER
HAWKSBILL TURTLE
LEATHERBACK
 TURTLE
SNAKE-NECKED
 TURTLE
SOFT-SHELLED
 TURTLE

INSECTS

3
ANT
BEE
BUG
FLY
4
FLEA
GNAT
WASP
5
APHID
DRONE
LOUSE

5 —continued
MIDGE
6
BEDBUG
BEETLE
BOT FLY
CAPSID
CHAFER
CHIGOE
CICADA
EARWIG
GAD FLY
HORNET

6 —continued
IO MOTH
LOCUST
LOOPER
MAGGOT
MANTIS
MAYFLY
SAWFLY
THRIPS
WEEVIL
7
ANTLION
ARMY ANT

7 —continued
BLOWFLY
CRICKET
CUTWORM
DIPTERA
FIRE ANT
FIREFLY
KATYDID
MONARCH (butterfly)
PEACOCK (butterfly)
PROTURA
RINGLET
SANDFLY

7 —continued
SATYRID (butterfly)
SKIPPER (butterfly)
STYLOPS
TERMITE
WAX MOTH

8
ALDERFLY
ARMY WORM
BLACKFLY
BOOKWORM
CINNABAR
CRANEFLY
FIREBRAT
FRUIT FLY
GALL WASP
GLOWWORM
GOAT MOTH
GREENFLY
HAWK MOTH
HONEY ANT
HONEYBEE
HORNTAIL
HORSE FLY
HOUSEFLY
HOVERFLY
LACEWING
LADYBIRD
LUNA MOTH
MASON BEE
MEALWORM
MEALYBUG
MILKWEED (butterfly)
MOSQUITO
PHASMIDA
PLANT BUG
PUSS MOTH
SHEEP KED
SILKWORM
SNAKEFLY
STINK BUG
STONEFLY
WATER BUG
WHITE FLY
WIREWORM
WOODWASP
WOODWORM

9
AMAZON ANT
ANOPHELES
BLOODWORM

9 —continued
BOOKLOUSE
BRIMSTONE
BUMBLEBEE
CADDIS FLY
CHINCH BUG
COCKROACH
CORN BORER
DAMSELFLY
DOBSONFLY
DOR BEETLE
DRAGONFLY
DRIVER ANT
GALL MIDGE
GROUND BUG
GYPSY MOTH
ICHNEUMON
LAC INSECT
NYMPHALID
   (butterfly)
OIL BEETLE
OWLET MOTH
ROBBER FLY
SCREWWORM
SHIELD BUG
SWIFT MOTH
TIGER MOTH
TSETSE FLY
WARBLE FLY
WHIRLIGIG

10
BARK BEETLE
BLUEBOTTLE
BOLL WEEVIL
CACTUS MOTH
COCKCHAFER
COLEOPTERA
DIGGER WASP
DROSOPHILA
DUNG BEETLE
FRITILLARY
FROGHOPPER
HAIRSTREAK
JUNE BEETLE
LEAF BEETLE
LEAF HOPPER
LEAF INSECT
PAPILIONID (butterfly)
PHYLLOXERA
POND SKATER

10 —continued
POTTER WASP
RED ADMIRAL
   (butterfly)
ROVE BEETLE
SILVERFISH
SPANISH FLY
SPIDER WASP
SPITTLEBUG
SPRINGTAIL
STAG BEETLE
TINEID MOTH
TREEHOPPER
WEBSPINNER
WOOLLY BEAR

11
ASSASSIN BUG
BACKSWIMMER
BAGWORM MOTH
BLACK BEETLE
BRISTLETAIL
BUFFALO GNAT
BUSH CRICKET
CANTHARIDIN
CATERPILLAR
CLICK BEETLE
CLOTHES MOTH
CODLING MOTH
EMPEROR MOTH
GRASSHOPPER
MOLE CRICKET
NOCTUID MOTH
PAINTED LADY
   (butterfly)
PLANT HOPPER
PYRALID MOTH
SCALE INSECT
SCORPION FLY
STICK INSECT
SWALLOWTAIL
   (butterfly)
TIGER BEETLE
TUSSOCK MOTH
WATER BEETLE

12
CABBAGE WHITE
   (butterfly)
CACTOBLASTIS
CARPENTER BEE

12 —continued
CARPET BEETLE
CECROPIA MOTH
DIVING BEETLE
GROUND BEETLE
HERCULES MOTH
PEPPERED MOTH
SCARAB BEETLE
SEXTON BEETLE
WATER BOATMAN
WATER STRIDER

13
BLISTER BEETLE
BURYING BEETLE
CLEARWING MOTH
COTTON STAINER
DADDY LONGLEGS
ELM BARK BEETLE
GEOMETRID MOTH
GIANT WATER BUG
GOLIATH BEETLE
LEAFCUTTER ANT
LEAFCUTTER BEE
SATURNIID MOTH
SOLDIER BEETLE
TORTOISESHELL
   (butterfly)
UNDERWING MOTH
WATER SCORPION

14+
AMBROSIA BEETLE
BOMBARDIER
   BEETLE
CABBAGE ROOT FLY
CAMBERWELL
   BEAUTY (butterfly)
COLORADO BEETLE
CUCKOO-SPIT
   INSECT
DARKLING BEETLE
DEATH'S-HEAD
   MOTH
DEATHWATCH
   BEETLE
DEVIL'S COACH
   HORSE
HERCULES BEETLE
SLAVE-MAKING ANT
TORTOISE BEETLE

PLANTS AND FLOWERS

3
ABE
HOP
IVY
RYE
4
DOCK
FERN
FLAG (*Iris*)
FLAX
HEMP
IRIS (flag, sweet flag,
  gladdon)
JUTE
LILY
PINK (carnation)
RAPE
REED
RICE
ROSE
RUSH
TARE
UPAS
WOAD
5
AGAVE
ASTER (Michaelmas
  daisy)
AVENS
BRIAR
CANNA
CYCAD
DAISY
HENNA
JALAP
KUDZU
LOTUS
LUPIN
OXLIP (*Primula*)
PANSY (*Viola*)
PEONY
PHLOX
POPPY
SEDGE
SENNA
SISAL
TULIP
VIOLA (pansy, violet)
6
ALLIUM
ALSIKE (clover)
BALSAM
BLUETS
BRYONY

6 —continued
CACTUS
CLOVER (trefoil)
COLEUS
COTTON
COWPEA
CROCUS
DAHLIA
DARNEL
FESCUE
HYSSOP
MADDER
MEDICK
MILLET
NETTLE (*Urtica*)
ORCHID
PETREA
PEYOTE (cactus)
RATTAN
SALVIA
SPURGE
SQUILL (*Scilla*)
SUNDEW
TEASEL
THRIFT
TWITCH (couch
  grass)
VIOLET (*Viola*)
YARROW
ZINNIA
7
ACONITE
  (monkshood)
ALFALFA
ALKANET
ANEMONE
ASTILBE
BEGONIA
BISTORT (snakeroot)
BRACKEN (fern)
BUGLOSS
BULRUSH (reed
  mace)
BURDOCK
CAMPION
CATMINT
CLARKIA
COWSLIP (*Primula*)
DAY LILY
DOGBANE
DOG ROSE
FIGWORT
FREESIA
FROG-BIT

7 —continued
GENTIAN
GLADDON (*Iris*)
GUARANA
HEMLOCK
HENBANE
HONESTY (*Lunaria*)
JONQUIL (*Narcissus*)
KINGCUP (marsh
  marigold)
LOBELIA
MILFOIL (yarrow)
MULLEIN (Aaron's
  rod)
OPUNTIA (prickly
  pear)
PAPYRUS
PETUNIA
PIGWEED
PRIMULA (cowslip,
  primrose)
RAGWORT
ROSELLE
SAGUARO
SANICLE
SPURREY
THISTLE
TIMOTHY
TOBACCO
TREFOIL (clover)
VERBENA (vervain)
VERVAIN (*Verbena*)
8
ACANTHUS
AGRIMONY
ARUM LILY
  (cuckoopint, lords-
  and-ladies)
ASPHODEL
AURICULA
BEDSTRAW
BERGENIA
BINDWEED
  (*Convolvulus*)
BLUEBELL
CATBRIER
CAT'S TAIL
  (reedmace)
CHARLOCK
CLEAVERS
  (goosegrass)
CLEMATIS (old man's
  beard, traveller's
  joy)

8 —continued
CROWFOOT
CYLCAMEN
DAFFODIL
DIANTHUS
EELGRASS
EUCHARIS (amazon
  lily)
FLEABANE
FLEAWORT
FOXGLOVE (*Digitalis*)
FUMITORY
GERANIUM
  (*Pelargonium*)
GLOXINIA
GOUTWEED (ground
  elder)
HAREBELL
HAWKWEED
HENEQUEN
HIBISCUS (rose of
  China, rose of
  Sharon)
HORNWORT
HYACINTH
ICE PLANT
KNAPWEED
LADY FERN
LARKSPUR
LUNGWORT
MARIGOLD
MILKWEED
MILKWORT
MOSS PINK (*Phlox*)
PLANTAIN
PLUMBAGO
POLYPODY
PRIMROSE (*Primula*)
REEDMACE (bulrush,
  cat's-tail)
ROCK ROSE
SAINFOIN
SALTWORT
SAMPHIRE
SCABIOUS
SEED FERN
SELF HEAL
SHAMROCK (clover,
  medick, wood
  sorrel)
SNOWDROP

8 —continued
SOAPWORT
SWEET PEA
TOAD LILY (fritillary)
TUBEROSE
VALERIAN
VERONICA
(speedwell)
WAXPLANT
WOODBINE (virginia
creeper)
WOODRUSH
WORMWOOD

9
AARON'S ROD
(mullein)
AMARYLLIS
(belladonna lily)
ANTHURIUM
AQUILEGIA
(columbine)
ARROWROOT
BLUEGRASS
BROOMRAPE
BRYOPHYTE
BUCKWHEAT
BUTTERCUP
CAMPANULA
(Canterbury bell)
CANDYTUFT
CARNATION (pink)
CELANDINE
CHICKWEED
CINERARIA
COCKLEBUR
COCKSFOOT
(orchard grass)
COLTSFOOT
COLUMBINE
(Aquilegia)
CORDGRASS
CORN POPPY
CORYDALIS
CYMBIDIUM (orchid)
DANDELION
DEVIL'S FIG (prickly
poppy)
DOG VIOLET
EDELWEISS
EGLANTINE (sweet
briar)
EYEBRIGHT
GERMANDER
GLADIOLUS
GLASSWORT
GOLDENROD
(Solidago)
GOOSEFOOT
(pigweed)
GRASS TREE
GROUND IVY

9 —continued
GROUNDSEL
HELLEBORE
(christmas rose)
HERB PARIS
HOLLYHOCK
HORSETAIL
HOUSELEEK
IMPATIENS (touch-
me-not, busy Lizzie)
JABORANDI
MARE'S TAIL
MONEYWORT
(creeping jenny)
MONKSHOOD
(aconite)
MOSCHATEL
(townhall clock)
NARCISSUS (jonquil)
PATCHOULI
PIMPERNEL
PYRETHRUM
QUILLWORT
ROYAL FERN
SAFFLOWER
SAXIFRAGE (London
pride)
SNAKEROOT (bistort)
SPEEDWELL
(Veronica)
SPIKENARD
STONECROP
SUNFLOWER
SWEET FLAG (Iris)
TORMENTIL
WATER LILY
WITCHWEED
WOUNDWORT

10
AGAPANTHUS
AMARANTHUS (love-
lies-bleeding)
AMAZON LILY
ASPIDISTRA
BELLADONNA
(deadly nightshade)
BUSY LIZZIE
BUTTERWORT
CHARMOMILE
CINQUEFOIL
CITRONELLA
CLIFFBREAK (fern)
CORNCOCKLE
CORNFLOWER
COUCH GRASS
(twitch, quack
grass)
COW PARSLEY
CRANESBILL
CUCKOOPINT (arum
lily)

10 —continued
DAMASK ROSE
DRAGONROOT
DYER'S BROOM
FRITILLARY (snake's
head, leopard lily,
toad lily)
GAILLARDIA (blanket
flowers)
GOATSBEARD
GOOSEGRASS
(cleavers)
GRANADILLA
(passionflower)
GREENBRIER
(catbrier)
HELIOTROPE
HERB ROBERT
JIMSONWEED (thorn
apple)
LADY'S SMOCK
MARGUERITE (oxeye
daisy)
MIGNONETTE
MONTBRETIA
MOONFLOWER
(morning glory)
NASTURTIUM
OPIUM POPPY
OXEYE DAISY
(marguerite)
PENNYROYAL
PERIWINKLE
POLYANTHUS
(Primula)
QUACK GRASS
(couch grass)
SHIELD FERN
SNAKE'S HEAD
SNAPDRAGON
(Antirrhinum)
SOW THISTLE
SPIDERWORT
SPLEENWORT
STITCHWORT
SWEET BRIAR
(eglantine)
THORN APPLE
(jimsonweed)
TOUCH-ME-NOT
WALLFLOWER
WATERCRESS
WELSH POPPY
WILLOWHERB
WOOD SORREL

11
ANTIRRHINUM
(snapdragon)
BISHOP'S WEED
(ground elder)

11 —continued
BITTERSWEET
(woody nightshade)
BLADDERWORT
CALCEOLARIA
CANARY GRASS
CONVOLVULUS
(bindweed)
FIG MARIGOLD
FORGET-ME-NOT
GILLYFLOWER
(gilliflower, pink,
carnation)
GLOBE FLOWER
GROUND ELDER
(goutweed, bishop's
weed)
HELLEBORINE
(orchid)
HONEYSUCKLE
IPECACUANHA
KANGAROO PAW
LADY'S SLIPPER
LEOPARD LILY
(fritillary, blackberry
lily)
LONDON PRIDE
(saxifrage)
LOVE-IN-A-MIST
MARRAM GRASS
MARSH MALLOW
MEADOWSWEET
PAMPAS GRASS
PONTENTILLA
(cinquefoil)
PRICKLY PEAR
(cactus)
RAGGED ROBIN
RED-HOT POKER
ROSE OF CHINA
(Hibiscus)
RUBBER PLANT
SEA LAVENDER
SHRIMP PLANT
SPIDER PLANT
ST JOHN'S WORT
(Hibiscus)
STRAWFLOWER
WELWITSCHIA
WINTERGREEN

12
AUTUMN CROCUS
(meadow saffron)
CENTURY PLANT
COMPASS PLANT
(turpentine plant)
GLOBE THISTLE
MONKEYFLOWER

12 —continued
MORNING GLORY
  (moonflower)
OLD MAN CACTUS
OLD MAN'S BEARD
  (*Clematis*)
ORCHARD GRASS
  (cocksfoot)
PITCHER PLANT
PRICKLY POPPY
  (devil's fig)
QUAKING GRASS
ROSE OF SHARON
  (*Hibiscus*)
SOLOMON'S SEAL
SWEET WILLIAM
VENUS FLYTRAP

13
AFRICAN VIOLET
BIRD'S NEST FERN
BLEEDING HEART
CALYPSO ORCHID
CARRION FLOWER
CHRISTMAS ROSE
  (hellebore)
CHRYSANTHEMUM

13 —continued
CREEPING JENNY
  (moneywort)
ELEPHANT GRASS
GARLIC MUSTARD
  (jack-by-the-hedge)
GRAPE HYACINTH
MARSH MARIGOLD
  (kingcup)
MEADOW SAFFRON
  (autumn crocus)
PASSIONFLOWER
  (granadilla)
RANUNCULACEAE
ROSE OF JERICHO
SLIPPER ORCHID
TOWNHALL CLOCK
  (moschatel)
TRAVELLER'S JOY
  (*Clematis*)
WINTER ACONITE

14
BELLADONNA LILY
  (*Amaryllis*)
BLACKBERRY LILY
  (leopard lily)

14 —continued
BLANKET FLOWERS
CANTERBURY BELL
  (*Campanula*)
CASTOR-OIL PLANT
HEDGEHOG CACTUS
JACK-BY-THE-
  HEDGE (garlic
  mustard)
LORDS-AND-LADIES
  (arum lily)
MAIDENHAIR FERN
TRUMPET CREEPER

15+
BIRD-OF-PARADISE
  FLOWER
BIRD'S NEST
  ORCHID
BLACK NIGHTSHADE
DEADLY
  NIGHTSHADE
  (belladonna)
DOG'S TOOTH
  VIOLET

15+ —continued
ENCHANTER'S
  NIGHTSHADE
GRASS OF
  PARNASSUS
LILY-OF-THE-VALLEY
LOVE-LIES-
  BLEEDING
  (*Amaranthus*)
MICHAELMAS DAISY
  (*Aster*)
ORGAN-PIPE
  CACTUS
SNOW-ON-THE-
  MOUNTAIN
SQUIRTING
  CUCUMBER
STAR OF
  BETHLEHEM
TURPENTINE PLANT
  (compass plant)
WOODY
  NIGHTSHADE
  (bittersweet)

TREES AND SHRUBS

3
ASH
BOX
ELM
FIG
FIR
MAY (hawthorn)
OAK
TEA
YEW

4
ANIL
COCA
DATE (palm)
KAVA
KOLA (cola)
NIPA (palm)
PALM
PINE
TEAK

5
ALDER
ASPEN
BALSA
BEECH (*Fagus*)
BIRCH
BROOM
CACAO

5 —continued
CAPER
CEDAR
EBONY
ELDER
ERICA (heath,
  heather)
FURZE (gorse)
GORSE (furze)
HAZEL
HEATH (*Erica*)
HOLLY
KARRI
LARCH
LILAC
MAPLE
OSIER (willow)
PECAN (hickory)
ROWAN (mountain
  ash)
SAVIN (juniper)
YUCCA

6
ACACIA
AZALEA
BAMBOO
BANYAN
BAOBAB

6 —continued
BONSAI
BO TREE
CASSIA
DAPHNE
DATURA
DEODAR (cedar)
DERRIS
DURIAN
GINKGO (maidenhair
  tree)
GOMUTI (sugar palm)
JARRAH
JINBUL (coolabar)
JUJUBE
LAUREL
LOCUST (carob tree,
  St John's bread)
MIMOSA
MOOLAR (coolabar)
MYRTLE
NUTMEG
ORACHE
POPLAR
PRIVET
PROTEA
REDBUD (judas tree)

6 —continued
RED GUM
  (*Eucalyptus*)
SALLOW (willow)
SALVIA
SAPPAN
SPRUCE
WILLOW

7
AMBOYNA
ARBUTUS
BEBEERU
  (greenheart)
BLUE GUM
  (*Eucalyptus*)
CAMELIA
CORK OAK
CYPRESS
DOGWOOD
DURMAST (oak)
FUCHSIA
GUM TREE
  (*Eucalyptus*)
HEATHER (*Erica*, ling)
HEMLOCK
HICKORY (pecan)
HOLM OAK (holly
  oak)

7 —continued
JASMINE
JUNIPER
MUGWORT
  (wormwood)
OIL PALM
PALMYRA
REDWOOD
ROSEBAY (oleander)
SEQUOIA (redwood,
  wellingtonia, big
  tree)
SOURSOP
SPIRAEA
SYRINGA (lilac, mock
  orange)

8
BARBERRY (*Berberis*)
BASSWOOD
BAYBERRY
BERBERIS (barberry)
BERGAMOT
BLACKBOX
  (coolabar)
BOX ELDER (maple)
CALABASH
CINCHONA
COOLABAR (jinbul,
  moolar, blackbox,
  dwarf box)
CORKWOOD (balsa)
DWARF BOX
  (coolabar)
EUONYMUS (spindle
  tree)
GARDENIA
GUAIACUM
HAWTHORN (may)
HORNBEAM
IRONWOOD
JAPONICA
LABURNUM (golden
  chain, golden rain)
LAVENDER
MAGNOLIA (umbrella
  tree)
OLEANDER (rosebay)
QUANDONG
RAMBUTAN
ROSEWOOD
SAGO PALM

8 —continued
SALTBUSH
SILKY OAK
SWEET GUM
SWEETSOP
SYCAMORE (maple)
TAMARISK
TOLU TREE
VIBURNUM (snowball
  tree)
WISTERIA
WOODBINE (virginia
  creeper)
WORMWOOD
  (mugwort)

9
ARAUCARIA
  (monkey puzzle
  tree)
BEARBERRY
BUCKTHORN
CAROB TREE (locust)
CORAL TREE
EUPHORBIA (crown
  of thorns,
  poinsettia, snow-on-
  the-mountain)
FIRETHORN
  (pyracantha)
FLAME TREE
  (flamboyant)
FORSYTHIA (golden
  bell)
JACARANDA
JUDAS TREE
  (redbud)
KALANCHOE
KAURI PINE
MANGROVES
MISTLETOE
PLANE TREE
POINCIANA
POISON IVY
SASSAFRAS
SATINWOOD
SCREW PINE
STINKWOOD
STONE PINE
SWEETWOOD
  (greenheart)
TULIP TREE

9 —continued
WHITEBEAM

10
ARBOR VITAE
BIRD CHERRY
BRAZILWOOD
COFFEE TREE
COTTONWOOD
DOUGLAS FIR
DRAGON TREE
EUCALYPTUS (blue
  gum, red gum)
FRANGIPANI (pagoda
  tree, temple flower)
GOLDEN BELL
  (forsythia)
GOLDEN RAIN
  (laburnum)
GREENHEART
  (sweetwood,
  bebeeru)
JOSHUA TREE
MANGOSTEEN
MOCK ORANGE
PAGODA TREE
  (frangipani)
POINSETTIA
PYRACANTHA
RAFFIA PALM
RUBBER TREE
WITCH HAZEL
YELLOWWOOD

11
BOTTLEBRUSH
CABBAGE PALM
CAMPHOR TREE
CHAULMOOGRA
COTONEASTER
CYPRESS PINE
DAWN REDWOOD
GOLDEN CHAIN
  (laburnum)
GUELDER ROSE
HONEY LOCUST
JUMPING BEAN
MOUNTAIN ASH
  (rowan)
PENCIL CEDAR
  (juniper)
PHYLLANTHUS

11 —continued
SERVICE TREE
SLIPPERY ELM
SPINDLE TREE
STEPHANOTIS
TALIPOT PALM

12
CHERRY LAUREL
CREOSOTE BUSH
CUCUMBER TREE
CUSTARD APPLE
  (soursop, sweetsop)
INCENSE CEDAR
MONKEY PUZZLE
SNOWBALL TREE
ST JOHN'S BREAD
  (locust)
SWAMP CYPRESS
TEMPLE FLOWER
  (frangipani)
TREE OF HEAVEN
UMBRELLA TREE
  (*Magnolia*)

13
BOUGAINVILLEA
BUTCHER'S BROOM
CROWN OF THORNS
HORSE CHESTNUT
JAPANESE CEDAR
JAPANESE MAPLE
PAPER MULBERRY
PEACOCK FLOWER
  (flamboyant)
WAYFARING TREE

14+
FLAMBOYANT TREE
  (flame tree, peacock
  flower)
FLOWERING
  CURRANT
JERUSALEM
  CHERRY
MAIDENHAIR TREE
  (ginkgo)
STRAWBERRY TREE
TRAVELLER'S TREE
TURPENTINE TREE
VIRGINIA CREEPER
  (woodbine)

FRUIT, VEGETABLES, AND PULSES

3
FIG
PEA

3 —continued
YAM

4
BEET
EDDO (taro)

4 —continued
KALE
KIWI

49   FUNGI

4 —continued
LEEK
LIME (linden)
OKRA (lady's fingers, gumbo)
PEAR
PLUM
SLOE
TARO (eddo, dasheen, elephant's ear)
5
APPLE
CAROB
CHARD (swiss chard)
CRESS
GRAPE
GUAVA
GUMBO (okra)
LEMON
MANGO
MELON (musk, honeydew, canteloupe, water)
OLIVE
ONION (spring onion, scallion)
PEACH
SWEDE
6
ALMOND
BANANA
CARROT
CASHEW
CELERY
CHERRY
CITRON
COB NUT
DAMSON
ENDIVE
LENTIL
LICHEE
LINDEN (lime)
LITCHI
LOQUAT
LYCHEE (litchi, lichee)
MANIOC (cassava)

6 —continued
MARROW
MEDLAR
ORANGE
PAWPAW
PEANUT (groundnut)
POTATO
PRUNUS (plum, almond, apricot, cherry)
QUINCE
RADISH
SQUASH
TOMATO
TURNIP
WALNUT
7
APRICOT
AVOCADO
BRAMBLE (blackberry)
BULLACE (plum)
CABBAGE
CASSAVA (manioc)
CHICORY
CURRANT
DASHEEN (taro)
FILBERT
GENIPAP
GHERKIN
KUMQUAT
LETTUCE
PARSNIP
PUMPKIN
RHUBARB
SALSIFY
SATSUMA (tangerine)
SHALLOT
SPINACH
8
BEETROOT
BILBERRY (blaeberry, huckleberry, whortleberry)
BRASSICA (broccoli, cabbage)
BROCCOLI

8 —continued
CAPSICUM (sweet pepper, chilli, paprika)
CELERIAC (knob celery)
CHESTNUT
CHICK PEA
CUCUMBER
DEWBERRY
EARTHNUT (groundnut)
EGGPLANT (aubergine)
KOHLRABI (cabbage)
MANDARIN (tangerine)
MULBERRY
MUNG BEAN (green gram)
MUSHROOM
OLEASTER (russian olive, trebizond date)
SCALLION
SOYA BEAN
TAMARIND
ZUCCHINI (courgette)
9
ARTICHOKE
ASPARAGUS
AUBERGINE (eggplant)
BLAEBERRY (bilberry)
BROAD BEAN
COCODEMER
COURGETTE (marrow, zucchini)
CRAB APPLE
CRANBERRY
CROWBERRY
GREENGAGE
GROUNDNUT (peanut, earthnut)
MANGETOUT
NECTARINE
PERSIMMON

9 —continued
PINEAPPLE
PISTACHIO
RASPBERRY
SAPODILLA
STAR APPLE
SWEET CORN
TANGERINE
10
BLACKBERRY (bramble)
CLEMENTINE
ELDERBERRY
FRENCH BEAN (kidney bean)
GOOSEBERRY
GRAPEFRUIT (*Citrus Paradisi*)
KIDNEY BEAN
LOGANBERRY
REDCURRANT
RUNNER BEAN
SNAKE GOURD
STRAWBERRY
11
CAULIFLOWER
COCONUT PALM
HORSE-RADISH
HUCKLEBERRY (bilberry)
POMEGRANATE
SWEET POTATO
12+
BLACKCURRANT
BRUSSELS SPROUT
ELEPHANT'S EAR (taro)
JERUSALEM ARTICHOKE
LADY'S FINGERS (okra)
MANGEL-WURZEL (beet)
WATER CHESTNUT
WHORTLEBERRY (bilberry)

FUNGI

4
CEPE
5
MOREL
YEAST

6
AGARIC
INK CAP
7
AMANITA
BLEWITS

7—continued
BOLETUS
CANDIDA
TRUFFLE
8
DEATH CAP

8—continued
MUSHROOM
PUFFBALL
9
CUP FUNGUS
EARTHSTAR

9—continued
FLY AGARIC
PSILOCYBE
RUST FUNGI
STINKHORN
TOADSTOOL

10
BREAD MOULD
CHAMPIGNON

11
ASCOMYCETES
ASPERGILLUS
CHANTERELLE

11—continued
HONEY FUNGUS
PENICILLIUM
SLIME MOULDS

13
BRACKET FUNGUS

14
BASIDIOMYCETES

15
PARASOL
  MUSHROOM

FERNS

4
TREE

5
ROYAL

7
BRACKEN

7—continued
OSMUNDA

8
LADY FERN
POLYPODY
STAGHORN

9
BIRD'S NEST

10
CLIFFBRAKE
DRYOPTERIS

10—continued
MAIDENHAIR
SPLEENWORT

11
HART'S TONGUE

PEOPLE

ARTISTS, SCULPTORS, AND ARCHITECTS

3

ARP, Jean (1887–1966; French sculptor and poet)

DOU, Gerrit (1613–75; Dutch painter)

FRY, Roger (1866–1934; British painter and art critic)

LOW, Sir David (1871–1963; New Zealand-born cartoonist)

4

ADAM, Robert (1728–92; British architect and interior designer)

CAPP, Al (Alfred Caplin, 1909–79; US cartoonist)

CUYP, Aelbert Jacobsz (1620–91; Dutch landscape painter)

DADD, Richard (1817–86; British painter)

DALI, Salvador (1904–89; Spanish surrealist painter)

DIOR, Christian (1905–57; French fashion designer)

DORÉ, Gustave (1832–83; French illustrator, painter, and sculptor)

DUFY, Raoul (1877–1953; French painter)

ERTÉ (Romain de Tirtoff, 1892–   ; French fashion illustrator and designer, born in Russia)

ETTY, William (1787–1849; British painter)

GABO, Naum (Naum Neemia Pevsner, 1890–1977; Russian sculptor)

GOES, Hugo van der (c. 1440–82; Flemish painter)

GOYA, Francesco de (1746–1828; Spanish painter)

GRIS, Juan (José Victoriano González, 1887–1927; Spanish-born cubist painter)

GROS, Antoine Jean, Baron (1771–1835; French painter)

HALS, Frans (c. 1581–1666; Dutch painter)

HILL, David Octavius (1802–70; Scottish painter and photographer)

HUNT, William Holman (1827–1910; British painter)

JOHN, Augustus (1878–1961; British painter)

KAHN, Louis Isadore (1901–74; US architect)

KENT, William (1685–1748; English architect, landscape gardener, and interior designer)

KLEE, Paul (1879–1940; Swiss painter and etcher)

LAMB, Henry (1885–1960; Australian-born British painter)

4—continued

LELY, Sir Peter (Pieter van der Faes, 1618–80; English portrait painter of Dutch descent)

LOOS, Adolph (1870–1933; Austrian architect)

MAES, Nicolas (or N Maas, 1634–93; Dutch painter)

MARC, Franz (1880–1916; German expressionist painter)

MIRÓ, Joan (1893–1983; Spanish painter)

NASH, John (1752–1835; British architect)

NASH, Paul (1889–1946; British painter)

NEER, Aert van der (c. 1603–77; Dutch landscape painter)

OPIE, John (1761–1807; British portrait and history painter)

RENI, Guido (1575–1642; Italian painter)

ROSA, Salvator (1615–73; Italian painter and etcher)

SHAW, Norman (1831–1912; British architect)

WARD, Sir Leslie (1851–1922; British caricaturist)

WEST, Benjamin (1738–1820; British painter of American birth)

WOOD, Christopher (1901–30; English painter)

WOOD, Grant (1892–1942; US painter)

WOOD, John, of Bath (1704–54; English architect)

WREN, Sir Christopher (1632–1723; English architect and scientist)

ZORN, Anders (1860–1920; Swedish artist)

5

AALTO, Alvar (1898–1976; Finnish architect)

ATGET, Eugène (1856–1927; French photographer)

BACON, Francis (1909–   ; British painter, born in Dublin)

BACON, John (1740–99; British neoclassical sculptor)

BAKST, Léon (Lev Samoilovich Rosenberg, 1866–1924; Russian artist)

BALLA, Giacomo (1871–1958; Italian futurist painter)

BARRY, Sir Charles (1795–1860; British architect)

BLAKE, Peter (1932–   ; British painter)

BOSCH, Hieronymus (Jerome van Aeken, c. 1450–c. 1516; Dutch painter)

BOUTS, Dierick (c. 1400–75; Netherlandish painter)

5—continued

BROWN, Capability (Lancelot B, 1716–83; British landscape gardener)

BROWN, Ford Madox (1821–93; British painter, born in Calais)

BURRA, Edward (1905–76; British painter)

CAMPI, Giulio (1502–72; Italian Renaissance architect)

COROT, Jean Baptiste Camille (1796–1875; French landscape painter)

CRANE, Walter (1845–1915; British illustrator, painter, and designer of textiles and wallpaper)

CROME, John (1768–1821; British landscape painter and etcher)

DAGLY, Gerhard (c. 1653–?1714; Belgian artist)

DANBY, Francis (1793–1861; Irish painter)

DANCE, George (c. 1700–68; British architect)

DAVID, Gerard (c. 1460–1523; Netherlandish painter)

DAVID, Jacques Louis (1748–1825; French neoclassical painter)

DEGAS, Edgar (1834–1917; French painter and sculptor)

DENIS, Maurice (1870–1943; French painter, designer, and art theorist)

DÜRER, Albrecht (1471–1528; German painter)

ENSOR, James Sydney, Baron (1860–1949; Belgian painter)

ERNST, Max (1891–1976; German artist)

FOLEY, John Henry (1818–74; British sculptor)

GADDI, Taddeo (c. 1300–?1366; Florentine painter)

GIBBS, James (1682–1754; British architect)

GILES, Carl Ronald (1916– ; British cartoonist)

GORKY, Arshile (Vosdanig Adoian, 1905–48; US painter, born in Armenia)

GOYEN, Jan Josephszoon van (1596–1656; Dutch landscape painter and etcher)

GRANT, Duncan James Corrowr (1885–1978; British painter and designer)

GROSZ, George (1893–1959; German painter and draughtsman)

HOMER, Winslow (1836–1910; US painter)

HOOCH, Pieter de (1629–c. 1684; Dutch painter)

HORTA, Victor (1861–1947; Belgian architect)

JOHNS, Jasper (1930– ; US artist)

JONES, Inigo (1573–1652; English classical architect)

KEENE, Charles Samuel (1823–91; British artist and illustrator)

KLIMT, Gustav (1862–1918; Viennese Art Nouveau artist)

KLINT, Kaare (1888–1954; Danish furniture designer),

5—continued

LEACH, Bernard (1887–1979; British potter, born in Hong Kong)

LEECH, John (1817–64; British caricaturist)

LÉGER, Fernand (1881–1955; French painter)

LE VAU, Louis (1612–70; French baroque architect)

LIPPI, Fra Filippo (c. 1406–69; Florentine painter)

LOTTO, Lorenzo (c. 1480–1556; Venetian painter)

LOWRY, L S (1887–1976; British painter)

MACKE, August (1887–1914; German painter)

MANET, Edouard (1832–83; French painter)

MENGS, Anton Raphael (1728–79; German painter)

METSU, Gabriel (1629–67; Dutch painter)

MONET, Claude (1840–1926; French impressionist painter)

MOORE, Henry (1898–1986; British sculptor)

MOSES, Grandma (Anna Mary Robertson M, 1860–1961; US primitive painter)

MUNCH, Edvard (1863–1944; Norwegian painter and printmaker)

MYRON (5th century BC; Athenian sculptor)

NADAR (Gaspard Felix Tournachon, 1820–1910; French photographer and caricaturist)

NERVI, Pier Luigi (1891–1979; Italian architect)

NOLAN, Sir Sidney (1917– ; Australian painter)

NOLDE, Emil (E Hansen, 1867–1956; German expressionist painter and printmaker)

OUDRY, Jean-Baptiste (1686–1755; French rococo painter and tapestry designer)

PHYFE, Duncan (or Fife, 1768–1854; US cabinetmaker and furniture designer, born in Scotland)

PIPER, John (1903– ; British painter and writer)

PUGIN, Augustus Welby Northmore (1812–52; British architect and theorist)

QUANT, Mary (1934– ; British fashion designer)

REDON, Odilon (1840–1916; French symbolist painter and lithographer)

RICCI, Sebastiano (1659–1734; Venetian painter)

RILEY, Bridget Louise (1931– ; British painter)

RODIN, Auguste (1840–1917; French sculptor)

SCOTT, Sir George Gilbert (1811–78; British architect)

SHAHN, Ben (1898–1969; Lithuanian-born US artist)

SOANE, Sir John (1753–1837; British architect)

STEEN, Jan (c. 1626–79; Dutch painter)

STOSS, Veit (c. 1445–1533; German gothic sculptor and woodcarver)

5—continued

TOBEY, Mark (1890–1976; US painter)

VICKY (Victor Weisz, 1913–66; British cartoonist, born in Berlin)

WATTS, George Frederick (1817–1904; British artist)

WYATT, James (1747–1813; British architect)

6

ALBERS, Josef (1888–1976; German abstract painter)

ARCHER, Thomas (1668–1743; English baroque architect)

BEATON, Sir Cecil (1904–80; British photographer)

BEHZAD (c. 1455–c. 1536; Persian painter)

BENTON, Thomas Hart (1889–1975; US painter)

BEWICK, Thomas (1753–1828; British wood engraver)

BOUDIN, Eugène (1824–98; French painter)

BOULLE, André Charles (or Buhl, 1642–1732; French cabinetmaker)

BRANDT, Bill (1905– ; British photographer)

BRAQUE, Georges (1882–1963; French painter)

BRATBY, John (1928– ; British painter and writer)

BREUER, Marcel Lajos (1902–81; US architect, born in Hungary)

BUFFET, Bernard (1928– ; French painter)

BUTLER, Reg Cotterell (1913–81; British sculptor)

CALDER, Alexander (1898– ; US sculptor)

CALLOT, Jacques (c. 1592–1635; French graphic artist)

CANOVA, Antonio (1757–1822; Italian sculptor)

CARDIN, Pierre (1922– ; French fashion designer)

CASSON, Sir Hugh (1910– ; British architect)

CHANEL, Coco (Gabrielle C, 1883–1971; French fashion designer)

CLOUET, Jean (c. 1485–1540; French portrait painter)

COOPER, Samuel (1609–72; British miniaturist)

COSWAY, Richard (1742–1821; British portrait miniaturist)

COTMAN, John Sell (1782–1842; British landscape watercolourist and etcher)

DERAIN, André (1880–1954; French postimpressionist painter)

DE WINT, Peter (1784–1849; British landscape painter)

EAKINS, Thomas (1844–1916; US painter)

FLORIS, Cornelis (1514–75; Flemish artist)

FLORIS, Frans (c. 1516–70; Flemish artist)

FULLER, Richard Buckminster (1895–1983; US inventor and architect)

6—continued

FUSELI, Henry (Johann Heinrich Füssli, 1741–1825; British painter of Swiss birth)

GÉRARD, François, Baron (1770–1837; French painter)

GIOTTO (Giotto di Bondone, c. 1266–1337; Italian painter and architect)

GIRTIN, Thomas (1775–1802; British landscape painter)

GOUJON, Jean (c. 1510–68; French Renaissance sculptor)

GREUZE, Jean-Baptiste (1725–1805; French painter)

GUARDI, Francesco (1712–93; Venetian painter)

HOLLAR, Wenceslaus (1607–77; Bohemian etcher)

HOUDON, Jean Antoine (1741–1828; French sculptor)

INGRES, Jean-Auguste-Dominique (1780–1867; French painter)

ISABEY, Jean Baptiste (1767–1855; French portrait painter and miniaturist)

JOCHHO (d. 1057; Japanese sculptor)

KNIGHT, Dame Laura (1877–1970; British painter)

LASDUN, Sir Denys (1914– ; British architect)

LA TOUR, Georges de (1593–1652; French painter)

LA TOUR, Maurice-Quentin de (1704–88; French portrait pastellist)

LE BRUN, Charles (1619–90; French history and portrait painter and designer)

LE NAIN, Antoine (c. 1588–1648; French painter)

LE NAIN, Louis (c. 1593–1648; French painter)

LE NAIN, Mathieu (c. 1607–77; French painter)

LESCOT, Pierre (c. 1510–78; French architect)

LONGHI, Pietro (Pietro Falca, 1702–85; Venetian painter)

LURCAT, Jean (1892–1966; French painter)

MARINI, Marino (1901–80; Italian sculptor and painter)

MARTIN, John (1789–1854; British painter)

MASSYS, Quentin (or Matsys, Messys, Metsys, c. 1466–1530; Flemish painter)

MILLET, Jean François (1814–75; French painter)

MOREAU, Gustave (1826–98; French symbolist painter)

MORONI, Giovanni Battista (c. 1525–78; Italian painter)

MORRIS, William (1834–96; British designer and artist)

OLIVER, Isaac (?1556–1617; English portrait miniaturist, born in France)

6—continued

OROZCO, José (1883–1949; Mexican mural painter)

OSTADE, Adrian van (1610–85; Dutch painter and etcher)

PALMER, Samuel (1805–81; British landscape painter and etcher)

PAXTON, Sir Joseph (1801–65; British architect)

PISANO, Andrea (Andrea de Pontedera, c. 1290–1348; Italian sculptor)

PISANO, Nicola (c. 1220–c. 1278; Italian sculptor)

RENOIR, Pierre Auguste (1841–1919; French impressionist painter)

RIBERA, José de (or Jusepe R, 1591–1652; Spanish-born painter and etcher)

RIVERA, Diego (1886–1957; Mexican mural painter)

ROMNEY, George (1734–1802; British portrait painter)

ROTHKO, Mark (Marcus Rothkovitch, 1903–70; Russian-born US painter)

RUBENS, Peter Paul (1577–1640; Flemish painter)

SCARFE, Gerald (1936–   ; British cartoonist)

SEARLE, Ronald William Fordham (1920–   ; British cartoonist)

SESSHU (Sesshu Toyo, 1420–1506; Japanese landscape painter)

SEURAT, Georges (1859–91; French painter)

SIGNAC, Paul (1863–1935; French painter and art theorist)

SISLEY, Alfred (1839–99; Impressionist painter)

SLUTER, Claus (c. 1345–1406; Dutch sculptor)

SPENCE, Sir Basil (1907–   ; British architect)

STUBBS, George (1724–1806; British animal painter)

TANGUY, Yves (1900–55; French surrealist painter)

TISSOT, James Joseph Jacques (1836–1902; French painter and etcher)

TITIAN (Tiziano Vecellio, c. 1488–1576; Venetian painter)

TURNER, Joseph Mallord William (1775–1851; British landscape and marine painter)

VASARI, Giorgio (1511–74; Italian painter, architect, and writer)

VOYSEY, Charles Francis Annesley (1857–1941; British architect and designer)

WARHOL, Andy (Andrew Warhola, 1926–87; US pop artist)

WEYDEN, Rogier van der (c. 1400–64; Flemish painter)

WILKIE, Sir David (1785–1841; Scottish painter)

WILSON, Richard (1714–82; British landscape painter)

6—continued

WRIGHT, Frank Lloyd (1869–1959; US architect)

XIA GUI (or Hsia Knei, c. 1180–c. 1230, Chinese landscape painter)

ZEUXIS (late 5th century BC; Greek painter)

7

ALBERTI, Leon Battista (1404–72; Italian Renaissance architect)

ALLSTON, Washington (1779–1843; US Romantic painter)

ANTENOR (late 6th century BC; Athenian sculptor)

APELLES (4th century BC; Greek painter)

ASTBURY, John (1688–1743; English potter)

BARLACH, Ernst (1870–1938; German expressionist sculptor and playwright)

BASSANO, Jacopo (Jacopo or Giacomo da Ponte, c. 1517–92; Italian painter)

BEHRENS, Peter (1868–1940; German architect)

BELLINI, Jacopo (c. 1400–c. 1470; Venetian painter)

BERNINI, Gian Lorenzo (1598–1680; Italian sculptor and architect)

BONNARD, Pierre (1867–1947; French painter)

BORGLUM, Gutzon (1867–1941; US sculptor)

BOUCHER, François (1703–70; French rococo painter)

BROUWER, Adriaen (c. 1605–38; Flemish painter)

CAMERON, Julia Margaret (1815–79; British photographer, born in Calcutta)

CASSATT, Mary (1844–1926; US painter)

CELLINI, Benvenuto (1500–71; Florentine goldsmith and sculptor)

CENNINI, Cennino (c. 1370–c. 1440; Florentine painter)

CÉZANNE, Paul (1839–1906; French postimpressionist painter)

CHAGALL, Marc (1887–1985; Russian-born painter and printmaker)

CHARDIN, Jean-Baptiste-Siméon (1699–1779; French painter)

CHIRICO, Giorgio de (1888–1978; Italian painter, born in Greece)

CIMABUE, Giovanni (Cenni de Peppi, c. 1240–c. 1302; Florentine painter)

CLODION (Claude Michel, 1738–1814; French rococo sculptor)

COURBET, Gustave (1819–77; French painter)

DAUMIER, Honoré (1808–79; French caricaturist, painter, and sculptor)

DELORME, Philibert (?1510–70; French Renaissance architect)

DELVAUX, Paul (1897–   ; Belgian painter)

DUCHAMP, Marcel (1887–1968; French artist)

7—continued

EL GRECO (Dornenikos Theotokopoulos, 1541–1614; Painter of Greek parentage, born in Crete)

EPSTEIN, Sir Jacob (1880–1959; British sculptor of US birth)

EXEKIAS (6th century BC; Athenian potter and vase painter)

FABERGÉ, Peter Carl (1846–1920; Russian goldsmith and jeweller)

FLAXMAN, John Henry (1755–1826; British sculptor and book illustrator)

FONTANA, Domenico (1543–1607; Italian architect)

FOUQUET, Jean (c. 1420–81; French painter and manuscript illuminator)

GAUGUIN, Paul (1848–1903; French postimpressionist painter)

GIBBONS, Grinling (1648–1721; English wood carver and sculptor)

GILLRAY, James (1756–1815; British caricaturist)

GOZZOLI, Benozzo (Benozzo di Lese, 1420–97; Florentine painter)

GROPIUS, Walter (1883–1969; German architect)

GUARINI, Guarino (1624–83; Italian baroque architect)

HASSALL, John (1868–1948; British artist)

HERRERA, Juan de (1530–97; Spanish architect)

HOBBEMA, Meindert (1638–1709; Dutch landscape painter)

HOCKNEY, David (1937– ; British painter, draughtsman, and printmaker)

HOGARTH, William (1697–1764; British painter and engraver)

HOKUSAI (Katsushika H, 1760–1849; Japanese painter and book illustrator)

HOLLAND, Henry (1745–1806; British architect)

HOPPNER, John (1758–1810; British portrait painter)

ICTINUS (5th century BC; Greek architect)

JOHNSON, Cornelius (Janssen van Ceulen, 1593–1661; English portrait painter)

KNELLER, Sir Godfrey (1646–1723; English portrait painter of German birth)

LALIQUE, René (1860–1945; French Art Nouveau jeweller and glassmaker)

LAMERIE, Paul de (1688–1751; English silversmith)

L'ENFANT, Pierre-Charles (1754–1825; US architect and town planner of French birth)

LE NÔTRE, André (1613–1700; French landscape gardener)

LIMBURG, Pol de (active c. 1400–c. 1416; French manuscript illuminator)

LIMOSIN, Léonard (or Limousin, c. 1505–c. 1577; French artist)

7—continued

LOCHNER, Stefan (c. 1400–51; German painter)

LUTYENS, Sir Edwin Landseer (1869–1944; British architect)

MACLISE, Daniel (1806–70; Irish portrait and history painter)

MADERNA, Carlo (1556–1629; Roman architect)

MAILLOL, Aristide (1861–1944; French sculptor)

MANSART, François (or Mansard, 1596–1666; French classical architect)

MARTINI, Simone (c. 1284–1344; Italian painter)

MATISSE, Henri (1869–1954; French painter and sculptor)

MEMLING, Hans (or Memlinc, c. 1430–1494; German painter)

MILLAIS, Sir John Everett (1829–96; British painter)

MORANDI, Giorgio (1890–1964; Italian still-life painter and etcher)

MORISOT, Berthe (1841–95; French painter)

MORLAND, George (1763–1804; British painter)

MURILLO, Bartolomé Esteban (1617–82; Spanish painter)

NEUMANN, Balthasar (1687–1753; German architect)

O'KEEFFE, Georgia (1887–1986; US painter)

ORCAGNA, Andrea (Andrea di Cione, c. 1308–c. 1368; Florentine artist)

PALISSY, Bernard (1510–89; French potter)

PASMORE, Victor (1908– ; British artist)

PATINIR, Joachim (or Patenier, c. 1485–1524; Flemish painter)

PEVSNER, Antoine (1886–1962; Russian sculptor and painter)

PHIDIAS (c. 490–c. 417 BC; Athenian sculptor)

PICABIA, Francis (1879–1953; French painter and writer)

PICASSO, Pablo (1881–1973; Spanish artist)

POLLOCK, Jackson (1912–56; US painter)

POUSSIN, Nicolas (1594–1665; French painter)

PRUD'HON, Pierre Paul (1758–1823; French painter and draughtsman)

RACKHAM, Arthur (1867–1939; British watercolourist and book illustrator)

RAEBURN, Sir Henry (1756–1823; Scottish portrait painter)

RAPHAEL (Raffaello Sanzio, 1483–1520; Italian Renaissance painter and architect)

REDOUTÉ, Pierre Joseph (1759–1841; French flower painter)

ROBERTS, Tom (1856–1931; Australian painter, born in Britain)

ROUAULT, Georges (1871–1958; French artist)

7—continued

RUBLYOV, Andrey (or A Rublev, c. 1370–
1430; Russian icon painter)

SARGENT, John Singer (1856–1925; US
portrait painter, born in Florence)

SCHIELE, Egon (1890–1918; Austrian
expressionist painter)

SEGHERS, Hercules Pieterzoon (c. 1589–c.
1638; Dutch landscape painter and etcher)

SHEPARD, Ernest Howard (1879–1976; British
artist)

SICKERT, Walter Richard (1860–1942; British
impressionist painter and etcher, born in
Munich)

SNOWDON, Antony Armstrong-Jones, Earl of
(1930–   ; British photographer)

SNYDERS, Frans (1579–1657; Flemish animal
painter)

SOUTINE, Chaim (1893–1943; Lithuanian-
born painter, who emigrated to Paris)

SPENCER, Sir Stanley (1891–1959; British
painter)

TENNIEL, Sir John (1820–1914; British
cartoonist and book illustrator)

TIBALDI, Pellegrino (1527–96; Italian architect
and painter)

TIEPOLO, Giovanni Battista (1696–1770;
Venetian rococo painter)

UCCELLO, Paolo (P di Dono, 1397–1475;
Florentine painter and craftsman)

UTRILLO, Maurice (1883–1955; French
painter)

VAN DYCK, Sir Anthony (or Vandyke, 1599–
1641; Flemish baroque painter)

VAN EYCK, Jan (c. 1390–1441; Flemish
painter)

VAN GOGH, Vincent (1853–90; Dutch
postimpressionist painter)

VERMEER, Jan (1632–75; Dutch painter)

VIGNOLA, Giacomo da (1507–73; Roman
mannerist architect)

WATTEAU, Antoine (1684–1721; French
rococo painter)

ZADKINE, Ossip (1890–1967; French sculptor
of Russian birth)

ZOFFANY, Johann (c. 1733–1810; German-
born English painter)

ZUCCARO, Federico (1543–1609; Italian
painter)

ZUCCARO, Taddeo (1529–66; Italian painter)

8

AALTONEN, Wäinö (1894–1966; Finnish
sculptor)

AMMANATI, Bartolommeo (1511–92;
Florentine mannerist architect and sculptor)

ANGELICO, Fra (Guido di Pietro, c. 1400–55;
Italian painter)

ANNIGONI, Pietro (1910–   ; Italian painter)

ANTELAMI, Benedetto (active 1177–1233;
Italian sculptor)

8—continued

BECKMANN, Max (1884–1950; German
expressionist painter)

BOCCIONI, Umberto (1882–1916; Italian
futurist painter and sculptor)

BRAMANTE, Donato (1444–1514; Italian
Renaissance architect)

BRANCUSI, Constantin (1876–1957;
Romanian sculptor)

BRONZINO, Il (Agnolo di Cosimo, 1503–72;
Florentine mannerist painter)

CARRACCI, Annibale (1560–1609; Italian
painter)

CASTAGNO, Andrea del (Andrea di Bartolo de
Simone, c. 1421–57; Italian painter)

CHAMBERS, Sir William (1723–96; British
architect and interior designer)

CRESSENT, Charles (1685–1768; French
cabinetmaker)

CRIVELLI, Carlo (c. 1430–95; Venetian
painter)

DAUBIGNY, Charles-François (1817–78;
French landscape painter)

DELAUNAY, Robert (1885–1941; French
painter)

DRYSDALE, Sir Russell (1912–81; Australian
painter, born in England)

DUBUFFET, Jean (1901–85; French painter
and sculptor)

FILARETE (Antonio Averlino, c. 1400–c. 1469;
Italian Renaissance architect)

FRAMPTON, Sir George James (1860–1928;
British sculptor)

GHIBERTI, Lorenzo (c. 1378–1455; Florentine
Renaissance sculptor)

GIORDANO, Luca (1632–1705; Neapolitan
painter, nicknamed LUCA FA PRESTO)

GOSSAERT, Jan (c. 1478–c. 1532; Flemish
painter)

GUERCINO (Giovanni Francesco Barbieri,
1591–1666; Italian painter)

HEPWORTH, Dame Barbara (1903–75; British
sculptor)

HILLIARD, Nicholas (1547–1619; English
portrait miniaturist)

JACOBSEN, Arne (1902–71; Danish architect
and designer of furniture and wallpaper)

JONGKIND, Johan Barthold (1819–91; Dutch
landscape painter and etcher)

JORDAENS, Jakob (1593–1678; Flemish
painter)

KIRCHNER, Ernst Ludwig (1880–1938;
German expressionist painter and
printmaker)

LANDSEER, Sir Edwin Henry (1802–73;
British artist)

LAWRENCE, Sir Thomas (1769–1830; British
painter)

LIPCHITZ, Jacques (1891–1973; Lithuanian
cubist sculptor)

8—continued

LOMBARDO, Pietro (c. 1438–1515; Italian sculptor and architect)

LYSIPPUS (4th century BC; Court sculptor of Alexander the Great)

MAGRITTE, René (1898–1967; Belgian surrealist painter)

MALEVICH, Kazimir (1878–1935; Russian painter and art theorist)

MANTEGNA, Andrea (c. 1431–1506; Italian Renaissance painter and engraver)

MASACCIO (Tommaso di Giovanni di Simone Guidi, 1401–28; Florentine painter)

MASOLINO (Tommaso di Cristoforo Fini, 1383–?1447; Italian painter)

MEEGEREN, Hans van (1889–1947; Dutch painter)

MONDRIAN, Piet (Pieter Cornelis Mondriaan, 1872–1944; Dutch painter)

MULREADY, William (1786–1863; British painter)

MUNNINGS, Sir Alfred (1878–1959; British painter)

NIEMEYER, Oscar (1907–   ; Brazilian architect)

PALLADIO, Andrea (1508–80; Italian architect)

PIRANESI, Giambattista (1720–78; Italian etcher)

PISSARRO, Camille (1830–1903; French impressionist painter, born in the West Indies)

PONTORMO, Jacopo da (J Carrucci, 1494–1557; Italian mannerist painter)

REYNOLDS, Sir Joshua (1723–92; British portrait painter)

ROBINSON, William Heath (1872–1944; British cartoonist and book illustrator)

ROUSSEAU, Henri (1844–1910; French painter)

ROUSSEAU, Théodore (1812–67; French Romantic painter)

RUISDAEL, Jacob van (?1628–82; Dutch landscape painter)

SAARINEN, Eero (1910–61; US architect, born in Finland)

SASSETTA (Stefano di Giovanni, c. 1392–c. 1450; Italian painter)

SEVERINI, Gino (1883–1966; Italian painter)

SHERATON, Thomas (1751–1806; British furniture designer)

SOUFFLOT, Jacques Germain (1713–80; French architect)

SULLIVAN, Louis Henry (1856–1924; US architect)

TERBORCH, Gerard (1617–81; Dutch painter)

VANBRUGH, Sir John (1664–1726; English architect)

VASARELY, Victor (1908–   ; Hungarian-born painter)

8—continued

VERONESE, Paolo (P Caliari, 1528–88; Italian painter)

VLAMINCK, Maurice de (1876–1958; French painter)

VUILLARD, Édouard (1868–1940; French artist)

WEDGWOOD, Josiah (1730–95; British potter, industrialist, and writer)

WHISTLER, James McNeill (1834–1903; US painter)

WHISTLER, Rex (1905–44; British artist)

WOOLLETT, William (1735–85; British engraver)

ZURBARÁN, Francisco de (1598–1664; Spanish painter)

9

ALTDORFER, Albrecht (c. 1480–1538; German artist)

BARTHOLDI, Frédéric August (1834–1904; French sculptor)

BEARDSLEY, Aubrey Vincent (1872–98; British illustrator)

BONINGTON, Richard Parkes (1801–28; British painter)

BORROMINI, Francesco (1599–1667; Italian baroque architect)

BOURDELLE, Émile (1861–1929; French sculptor)

CANALETTO (Antonio Canal, 1697–1768; Venetian painter)

CARPACCIO, Vittore (c. 1460–c. 1525; Venetian painter)

CAVALLINI, Pietro (c. 1250–c. 1330; Italian painter)

COCKERELL, Charles Robert (1788–1863; British architect)

CONSTABLE, John (1776–1837; British landscape painter)

CORNELIUS, Peter von (1783–1867; German painter)

CORREGGIO (Antonio Allegri, c. 1494–1534; Italian Renaissance painter)

COURRÈGES, André (1923–   ; French fashion designer)

DE KOONING, Willem (1904–   ; US painter of Dutch birth)

DELACROIX, Eugène (1798–1863; French Romantic painter)

DELAROCHE, Paul (1797–1859; French history and portrait painter)

DONATELLO (Donato de Nicolo di Betti Bardi, c. 1386–1466; Florentine sculptor)

FABRITIUS, Carel (1622–54; Dutch painter)

FEININGER, Lyonel (1871–1956; US painter and illustrator)

FRAGONARD, Jean Honoré (1732–1806; French rococo painter)

FRIEDRICH, Caspar David (1774–1840; German Romantic landscape painter)

9—continued

GÉRICAULT, Théodore (1791–1824; French painter)

GIORGIONE (*c.* 1477–1510; Italian painter)

GREENAWAY, Kate (1846–1901; British artist and book illustrator)

GREENOUGH, Horatio (1805–52; US neoclassical sculptor)

GRUNEWALD, Matthias (Mathis Gothardt, d. 1528; German painter)

HAWKSMOOR, Nicholas (1661–1736; English baroque architect)

HIROSHIGE (Ando Tokitaro, 1797–1858; Japanese colour-print artist)

HONTHORST, Gerrit von (1590–1656; Dutch painter)

JAWLENSKY, Alexey von (1864–1941; Russian expressionist painter)

KANDINSKY, Wassily (1866–1944; Russian expressionist painter and art theorist)

KAUFFMANN, Angelica (1741–1807; Swiss painter)

KOKOSCHKA, Oskar (1886–1980; Austrian expressionist painter and writer)

LISSITZKY, El (Eliezer L, 1890–1941; Russian painter and architect)

MESTROVIĆ, Ivan (1883–1962; US sculptor, born in Yugoslavia)

MUYBRIDGE, Eadweard (Edward James Muggeridge, 1830–1904; US photographer, born in Britain)

NICHOLSON, Ben (1894–1982; British artist)

NOLLEKENS, Joseph (1737–1823; British neoclassical sculptor)

OLDENBURG, Claes; (1929– ; US sculptor, born in Sweden)

PISANELLO (Antonio Pisano, *c.* 1395–*c.* 1455; Italian international gothic painter, draughtsman, and medallist)

ROUBILLAC, Louis François (*or* L F Roubiliac, 1695–1762; French sculptor)

SIQUEIROS, David Alfaro (1896–1974; Mexican painter)

STIEGLITZ, Alfred (1864–1946; US photographer)

THORNHILL, Sir James (1675–1734; English baroque decorative painter)

VELÁZQUEZ, Diego Rodriguez de Silva (1599–1660; Spanish painter)

VITRUVIUS (Marcus Vitruvius Pollio, 1st century BC; Roman architect)

WOUWERMAN, Philips (1619–68; Dutch painter)

10

ALMA-TADEMA, Sir Lawrence (1836–1912; Dutch painter)

ALTICHIERO (*c.* 1330–*c.* 1390; Italian painter)

ARCHIPENKO, Alexander (1887–1964; Russian-born sculptor and painter)

ARCIMBOLDO, Giuseppe (1527–93; Mannerist painter)

10—continued

BERRUGUETE, Alonso (*c.* 1488–1561; Castillian painter)

BERRUGUETE, Pedro (*c.* 1450–*c.* 1504; Castillian painter)

BOTTICELLI, Sandro (Alessandro di Mariano Filipepi, *c.* 1445–1510; Florentine Renaissance painter)

BURLINGTON, Richard Boyle, 3rd Earl of (1694–1753; English architect)

BURNE-JONES, Sir Edward Coley (1833–98; Pre-Raphaelite painter)

CARAVAGGIO (Michelangelo Merisi, 1573–1610; Italian painter)

CHAMPAIGNE, Philippe de (1602–74; French portrait painter)

CRUIKSHANK, George (1792–1872; British caricaturist, painter, and illustrator)

EUPHRONIOS (late 6th–early 5th centuries BC; Athenian potter and vase painter)

GIACOMETTI, Alberto (1901–66; Swiss sculptor and painter)

LORENZETTI, Ambrogio (*c.* 1290–?1348; Italian painter)

MACKINTOSH, Charles Rennie (1868–1928; Scottish architect and designer)

MEISSONIER, Jean-Louis-Ernest (1815–91; French painter)

MODIGLIANI, Amedeo (1884–1920; Italian painter and sculptor)

MOHOLY-NAGY, László (1895–1946; Hungarian artist)

MOTHERWELL, Robert (1915– ; US abstract painter)

POLLAIUOLO, Antonio (*c.* 1432–98; Florentine Renaissance artist)

POLYCLITUS (5th century BC; Greek sculptor)

PRAXITELES (mid-4th century BC; Athenian sculptor)

RICHARDSON, Henry Hobson (1838–86; US architect)

ROWLANDSON, Thomas (1756–1827; British caricaturist)

SCHWITTERS, Kurt (1887–1958; German artist and poet)

SENEFELDER, Aloys (1771–1834; German playwright and engraver)

SIGNORELLI, Luca (*c.* 1441–1523; Italian Renaissance painter)

SUTHERLAND, Graham Vivian (1903–80; British artist)

TANGE KENZO (1913– ; Japanese architect)

TINTORETTO (Jacopo Robusti, 1518–94; Venetian painter)

VAN DE VELDE, Henry (1863–1957; Belgian Art Nouveau architect, interior designer, and painter)

VERROCCHIO, Andrea del (Andrea del Cione, *c.* 1435–88; Italian sculptor, painter, and goldsmith)

10—continued

WATERHOUSE, Alfred (1830–1905; British architect)

ZUCCARELLI, Francesco (1702–88; Italian painter)

11

ABERCROMBIE, Sir Patrick (1879–1957; British architect)

BARTOLOMMEO, Fra (Baccio della Porta, c. 1472–1517; Florentine Renaissance painter)

BUTTERFIELD, William (1814–1900; British architect)

CALLICRATES (5th century BC; Athenian architect)

CALLIMACHUS (late 5th century BC; Greek sculptor)

CHIPPENDALE, Thomas (1718–79; British cabinetmaker)

CHODOWIECKI, Daniel Nikolaus (1726–1801; German painter and engraver)

DELLA ROBBIA, Luca (1400–82; Florentine Renaissance sculptor)

DOMENICHINO (Domenico Zampieri, 1581–1641; Italian painter)

GHIRLANDAIO, Domenico (Domenico di Tommaso Bigordi, 1449–94; Florentine painter)

GIAMBOLOGNA (Giovanni da Bologna or Jean de Boulogne, 1529–1608; Italian mannerist sculptor)

GISLEBERTUS (early 12th century; French romanesque sculptor)

HEPPLEWHITE, George (d. 1786; British furniture designer and cabinetmaker)

LE CORBUSIER (Charles-Édouard Jeanneret, 1887–1965; French architect, born in Switzerland)

TERBRUGGHEN, Hendrik (1588–1629; Dutch painter)

THORVALDSEN, Bertel (or B Thorwaldsen, 1768–1844; Danish sculptor)

12

BRUNELLESCHI, Filippo (1377–1446; Italian architect)

FANTIN-LATOUR, Henri (1836–1904; French painter)

GAINSBOROUGH, Thomas (1727–88; British portrait and landscape painter)

GAUDÍ Y CORNET, Antonio (1852–1926; Spanish architect)

GIULIO ROMANO (Giulio Pippi, c. 1499–1546; Italian mannerist painter and architect)

LICHTENSTEIN, Roy (1923–   ; US painter)

LUCA FA PRESTO (Nickname of Luca Giordano)

PALMA VECCHIO, Jacopo (J Negretti, c. 1480–1528; Italian painter)

PARMIGIANINO (Girolamo Francesco Maria Mazzola, 1503–40; Italian painter)

12—continued

PINTURICCHIO (Bernardino di Betto, c. 1454–1513; Italian Renaissance painter)

RAUSCHENBERG, Robert (1925–   ; US artist)

SAINT-LAURENT, Yves (1936–   ; French fashion designer)

SCHIAPARELLI, Elsa (1896–1973; Italian-born fashion designer)

VIOLLET-LE-DUC, Eugène Emmanuel (1814–79; French architect and author)

WINTERHALTER, Franz Xavier (1806–73; German painter and lithographer)

13

LORENZO MONACO (Piero di Giovanni, c. 1370–1425; Italian painter)

PIERO DI COSIMO (P di Lorenzo, 1462–1521; Florentine Renaissance painter)

WILLIAMS-ELLIS, Sir Clough (1883–1978; Welsh architect)

14

ANDREA DEL SARTO (Andrea d'Agnolo, 1486–1530; Italian painter)

BÉRAIN THE ELDER, Jean (1637–1711; French designer, engraver, and painter)

CARTIER-BRESSON, Henri (1908–   ; French photographer)

CLAUDE LORRAINE (Claude Gellée, 1600–82; French landscape painter)

COUSIN THE ELDER, Jean (1490–1560; French artist and craftsman)

GAUDIER-BRZESKA, Henri (1891–1915; French sculptor)

LUCAS VAN LEYDEN (Lucas Hugensz or Jacobsz, c. 1494–1533; Dutch artist)

MIES VAN DER ROHE, Ludwig (1886–1969; German architect)

15

CRANACH THE ELDER, Lucas (Lucas Müller, 1472–1553; German artist)

HARDOUIN-MANSART, Jules (1646–1708; French baroque architect)

KITAGAWA UTAMARO (1753–1806; Japanese artist)

LEONARDO DA VINCI (1452–1519; Italian artistic and scientific genius of the Renaissance)

TOULOUSE-LAUTREC, Henri de (1864–1901; French artist)

16

BRUEGHEL THE ELDER, Pieter (or Bruegel, 1525–69; Flemish painter)

FISCHER VON ERLACH, Johann Bernhard (1656–1723; Austrian architect)

PUVIS DE CHAVANNES, Pierre (1824–98; French painter)

REMBRANDT VAN RIJN (1606–69; Dutch painter and etcher)

16—continued
UTAGAWA KUNIYOSHI (Igusa Magosaburo, 1797–1861; Japanese painter and printmaker)

17
DOMENICO VENEZIANO (active c. 1438–1461; Italian painter)
GENTILE DA FABRIANO (Niccolo di Giovanni di Massio, c. 1370–1427; Florentine painter)
HERRERA THE YOUNGER, Francisco de (1622–85; Spanish baroque painter and architect)
HOLBEIN THE YOUNGER, Hans (c. 1497–1543; German painter)
TENIERS THE YOUNGER, David (1610–90; Flemish painter)

18
ANTONELLO DA MESSINA (c. 1430–c. 1479; Italian painter)

18—continued
JACOPO DELLA QUERCIA (c. 1374–1438; Italian Renaissance sculptor)
LEIGHTON OF STRETTON, Frederic, Baron (1830–96; British painter and sculptor)

19
DUCCIO DI BUONINSEGNA (c. 1255–c. 1318; Italian painter)
PIERO DELLA FRANCESCA (c. 1420–92; Italian Renaissance painter)

20
DESIDERIO DA SETTIGNANO (c. 1430–64; Italian Renaissance sculptor)
MICHELANGELO BUONARROTI (1475–1564; Italian sculptor, painter, and architect)
MICHELOZZO DI BARTOLOMMEO (1396–1472; Florentine Renaissance sculptor and architect)

WRITERS, PLAYWRIGHTS, AND POETS

3
FRY, Christopher (C Harris, 1907–   ; British dramatist)
GAY, John (1685–1732; British poet and dramatist)
KYD, Thomas (1558–94; English dramatist)
PAZ, Octavio (1914–   ; Mexican poet)
SUE, Eugène (Joseph Marie S, 1804–57; French novelist)

4
AGEE, James (1909–55; US poet and novelist)
AMIS, Kingsley (1922–   ; British novelist and poet)
ASCH, Sholem (1880–1957; Jewish novelist)
BANA (7th century AD; Sanskrit writer)
BAUM, L Frank (1856–1919; US novelist)
BENN, Gottfried (1886–1956; German poet)
BLOK, Aleksandr Aleksandrovich (1880–1921; Russian symbolist poet)
BÖLL, Heinrich (1917–85; German novelist)
BOLT, Robert Oxton (1924–   ; British dramatist)
BUCK, Pearl S (1892–1973; US novelist)
CARY, Joyce (1888–1957; British novelist)
CRUZ, Sor Juana Inéz de la (1651–95; Mexican poet)
DAHL, Roald (1916–   ; British author)
DEUS, João de (1830–96; Portuguese poet)
DU FU (or Tu Fu; 712–70 AD; Chinese poet)
FORD, Ford Madox (Ford Hermann Hueffer, 1873–1939; British novelist)
FORD, John (1586–c. 1640; English dramatist)

4—continued
FOXE, John (1516–87; English religious writer)
GALT, John (1779–1839; Scottish novelist)
GIDE, André (1869–1951; French novelist and critic)
GRAY, Thomas (1716–71; British poet)
GUNN, Thomson W (1929–   ; British poet)
HART, Moss (1904–61; US dramatist)
HOGG, James (1770–1835; Scottish poet and writer)
HOOD, Thomas (1799–1845; British poet)
HOPE, Anthony (Sir Anthony Hope Hawkins; 1863–1933; British novelist)
HUGO, Victor (1802–85; French poet, dramatist, and novelist)
HUNT, Leigh (1784–1859; British poet and journalist)
KIVI, Alexis (A Stenvall, 1834–72; Finnish poet, dramatist, and novelist)
LAMB, Charles (1775–1834; British essayist and critic)
LEAR, Edward (1812–88; British artist and poet)
LIVY (Titus Livius, 59 BC–17 AD; Roman writer)
LOTI, Pierre (Julien Viaud; 1850–1923; French novelist)
LYLY, John (c. 1554–1606; English dramatist and writer)
MANN, Thomas (1875–1955; German novelist)
MUIR, Edwin (1887–1959; Scottish poet)
NASH, Ogden (1902–71; US humorous writer)

4—continued

NEXØ, Martin Andersen (1869–1954; Danish novelist)

OVID (Publius Ovidius Naso 43 BC–17 AD; Roman poet)

OWEN, Wilfred (1893–1918; British poet)

POPE, Alexander (1688–1744; British poet)

READ, Sir Herbert (1893–1968; British poet)

RHYS, Jean (1894–1979; British novelist)

ROTH, Philip (1933–   ; US novelist)

ROWE, Nicholas (1674–1718; British dramatist)

RUIZ, Juan (c. 1283–c. 1350; Spanish poet)

SADE, Donatien Alphonse François, Marquis de (1740–1814; French novelist)

SA'DI (Mosleh al-Din S, c. 1215–92; Persian poet)

SAKI (H H Munro, 1870–1916; British humorous short-story writer)

SAND, George (Aurore Dupin, Baronne Dudevant, 1804–76; French novelist)

SHAW, George Bernard (1856–1950; Irish dramatist)

SNOW, C P, Baron (1905–80; British novelist)

TATE, Allen (1899–   ; US poet and critic)

TATE, Nahum (1652–1715; British poet)

URFÉ, Honoré d' (1568–1625; French novelist)

VEGA, Lope Félix de (1562–1635; Spanish poet and dramatist)

WAIN, John (1925–   ; British novelist and poet)

WARD, Artemus (Charles Farrar Browne, 1834–67; US humorous writer)

WARD, Mrs Humphry (1851–1920; British novelist)

WEBB, Mary (1881–1927; British novelist)

WEST, Dame Rebecca (Cicely Isabel Fairfield, 1892–1983; British novelist and journalist)

WEST, Nathanael (Nathan Weinstein, 1903–40; US novelist)

WOOD, Mrs Henry (1814–87; British novelist)

WREN, P C (1885–1941; British novelist)

WYSS, Johann Rudolph (1782–1830; Swiss writer)

ZOLA, Émile (1840–1902; French novelist)

5

ADAMS, Henry (1838–1918; US historian)

ADAMS, Richard (1920–   ; British novelist)

AGNON, Shmuel Yosef (Samuel Josef Czaczkes, 1888–1970; Jewish novelist)

ALBEE, Edward (1928–   ; US dramatist)

ARANY, János (1817–82; Hungarian poet)

AUDEN, W H (1907–73; British poet)

BABEL, Isaac Emmanuilovich (1894–1941; Russian short-story writer)

BARTH, John (1930–   ; US novelist)

BATES, H E (1905–74; British writer)

BEHAN, Brendan (1923–64; Irish playwright)

BELLO, Andrés (1781–1865; Venezuelan scholar and poet)

5—continued

BELYI, Andrei (Boris Nikolaevich Bugaev, 1880–1934; Russian symbolist poet and critic)

BEMBO, Pietro (1470–1547; Italian scholar)

BENDA, Julien (1867–1956; French novelist and philosopher)

BENÉT, Stephen Vincent (1898–1943; US poet and novelist)

BETTI, Ugo (1892–1953; Italian dramatist)

BOWEN, Elizabeth (1899–1973; British novelist, born in Dublin)

BRANT, Sebastian (?1458–1521; German poet)

BROCH, Hermann (1886–1951; Austrian novelist)

BUNIN, Ivan Alekseevich (1879–1953; Russian poet and novelist)

BURNS, Robert (1759–96; Scottish poet)

BUTOR, Michel (1926–   ; French experimental novelist and critic)

BYRON, George Gordon, Lord (1788–1824; British poet)

CAMUS, Albert (1913–60; French novelist)

CAREW, Thomas (c. 1595–1640; British poet)

CLARE, John (1793–1864; British poet)

COLUM, Padraic (Patrick Colm; 1881–1972; Irish poet)

CRAIK, Dinah Maria Mulock (1826–87; British novelist)

CRANE, Hart (1899–1932; US poet)

CRANE, Stephen (1871–1900; US novelist)

DARÍO, Rubén (Félix García Sarmiento; 1867–1916; Nicaraguan poet)

DEFOE, Daniel (1660–1731; British novelist)

DONNE, John (1572–1631; English poet)

DOYLE, Sir Arthur Conan (1859–1930; British author)

DUMAS, Alexandre (1802–70; French novelist and dramatist)

DURAS, Marguerite (1914–   ; French novelist)

ELIOT, George (Mary Ann Evans, 1819–80; British novelist)

ELIOT, T S (1888–1965; Anglo-American poet, critic, and dramatist)

ELYOT, Sir Thomas (c. 1490–1546; English scholar)

EWALD, Johannes (1743–81; Danish poet and playwright)

FROST, Robert Lee (1874–1963; US poet)

GENET, Jean (1910–86; French novelist and dramatist)

GOGOL, Nikolai Vasilievich (1809–52; Russian novelist and dramatist)

GORKI, Maksim (Aleksei Maksimovich Peshkov; 1868–1936; Russian novelist)

GOSSE, Sir Edmund (1849–1928; British critic)

GOWER, John (c. 1330–1408; English poet)

GRASS, Günter (1927–   ; German novelist and poet)

5—continued

GREEN, Henry (Henry Vincent Yorke; 1905–73; British novelist)

HAFIZ, Shams al-Din Muhammad (?1326–90; Persian lyric poet)

HALLE, Adam de la (c. 1240–90; French poet and musician)

HARDY, Thomas (1840–1928; British novelist and poet)

HARTE, Brett (1836–1902; US short-story writer)

HAŠEK, Jaroslav (1883–1923; Czech novelist)

HEINE, Heinrich (1797–1856; German Jewish poet and writer)

HENRY, O (William Sidney Porter, 1862–1910; US short-story writer)

HESSE, Hermann (1877–1962; German novelist and poet)

HOMER (8th century BC; Greek epic poet)

HOOFT, Pieter Corneliszoon (1581–1647; Dutch poet)

IBSEN, Henrik (1828–1906; Norwegian playwright and poet)

JAMES, Henry (1843–1916; US novelist and critic)

JARRY, Alfred (1873–1907; French dramatist)

JONES, David (1895–1974; Anglo-Welsh writer)

JONES, LeRoi (1934–   ; US dramatist and poet)

JOYCE, James (1882–1941; Irish novelist and poet)

KAFKA, Franz (1883–1924; Czech writer)

KEATS, John (1795–1821; British poet)

KEMAL, Namik (1840–88; Turkish poet, novelist, and dramatist)

KESEY, Ken (1935–   ; US novelist)

LEWIS, C S (1898–1963; British writer)

LEWIS, Matthew Gregory (1775–1818; British novelist)

LEWIS, Sinclair (1885–1951; US novelist)

LEWIS, Wyndham (1882–1957; British novelist)

LODGE, Thomas (1558–1625; English poet, dramatist, and writer)

LOWRY, Malcolm (1909–57; British novelist)

LUCAN (Marcus Annaeus Lucanus, 39–65 AD; Roman poet)

MAROT, Clément (1496–1544; French poet)

MARSH, Dame Ngaio (1899–1981; New Zealand detective-story writer)

MARTÍ, José Julián (1853–95; Cuban poet)

MASON, A E W (1865–1948; British novelist)

MILNE, A A (1882–1956; British novelist and dramatist)

MOORE, Marianne (1887–1972; US poet)

MOORE, Thomas (1779–1852; Irish poet)

MURRY, John Middleton (1889–1957; British literary critic)

MUSIL, Robert (1880–1942; Austrian novelist)

5—continued

MYERS, F W H (1843–1901; British essayist and poet)

NASHE, Thomas (1567–c. 1601; British dramatist)

NOYES, Alfred (1880–1958; British poet)

ODETS, Clifford (1906–63; US dramatist)

O'HARA, John (1905–70; US novelist)

OPITZ, Martin (1597–1639; German poet)

ORCZY, Baroness Emmusca (1865–1947; British novelist)

OTWAY, Thomas (1652–85; British dramatist)

OUIDA (Marie Louise de la Ramée, 1839–1908; British novelist)

PAN GU (or P'an Ku; 32–92 AD; Chinese historian)

PATON, Alan (1903–   ; South African novelist)

PEAKE, Mervyn (1911–68; British novelist)

PEELE, George (1556–96; English dramatist)

PÉGUY, Charles (1873–1914; French poet and essayist)

PERSE, Saint-John (Alexis Saint-Léger, 1887–1975; French poet)

PLATH, Sylvia (1932–63; US poet and writer)

POUND, Ezra (1885–1972; US poet and critic)

POWYS, John Cowper (1872–1963; British novelist)

PRIOR, Matthew (1664–1721; British poet)

PULCI, Luigi (1432–84; Italian poet)

RAINE, Kathleen (1908–   ; British poet)

READE, Charles (1814–84; British novelist)

RILKE, Rainer Maria (1875–1926; Austrian poet)

ROLFE, Frederick William (1860–1913; British novelist)

SACHS, Hans (1494–1576; German poet and folk dramatist)

SACHS, Nelly (1891–1970; German Jewish poet and dramatist)

SAGAN, Françoise (Françoise Quoirez, 1935–   ; French writer)

SCOTT, Sir Walter (1771–1832; Scottish novelist)

SETON, Ernest Thompson (1860–1946; US writer)

SHUTE, Nevil (Nevil Shute Norway, 1899–1960; British novelist)

SIMMS, William Gilmore (1806–70; US novelist)

SMART, Christopher (1722–71; British poet)

SMITH, Stevie (Florence Margaret S, 1902–71; British poet)

SPARK, Muriel (1918–   ; British novelist)

STAËL, Anne Louise Germaine Necker, Madame de (1766–1817; French writer)

STEIN, Gertrude (1874–1946; US writer)

STORM, Theodor Woldsen (1817–1888; German writer)

STOWE, Harriet Beecher (1811–96; US novelist)

5—continued

SVEVO, Italo (Ettore Schmitz, 1861–1928; Italian novelist)

SWIFT, Jonathan (1667–1745; Anglo-Irish poet and satirist)

SYNGE, John Millington (1871–1909; Anglo-Irish dramatist)

TASSO, Torquato (1544–95; Italian poet)

TIECK, Ludwig (1773–1853; German writer)

TWAIN, Mark (Samuel Langhorne Clemens, 1835–1910; US novelist)

UDALL, Nicholas (1505–56; English dramatist)

VARRO, Marcus Terentius (116–27 BC; Roman scholar and poet)

VERNE, Jules (1828–1905; French writer)

VIDAL, Gore (1925– ; US novelist and essayist)

VIGNY, Alfred de (1797–1863; French poet, novelist, and dramatist)

WALEY, Arthur (1889–1966; British translator and poet)

WAUGH, Evelyn (1903–66; British novelist)

WEISS, Peter (1916–82; German dramatist and novelist)

WELLS, H G (1866–1946; British novelist)

WHITE, Patrick (1912– ; Australian novelist)

WHITE, T H (1906–64; British novelist)

WILDE, Oscar (O. Fingal O'Flahertie Wills W, 1854–1900; British dramatist and poet)

WOLFE, Charles (1791–1823; Irish poet)

WOLFE, Thomas (1900–38; US novelist)

WOOLF, Virginia (1882–1941; British novelist)

WYATT, Sir Thomas (1503–42; English poet)

YEATS, William Butler (1865–1939; Irish poet and dramatist)

YONGE, Charlotte (1823–1901; British novelist)

ZWEIG, Arnold (1887–1968; East German-Jewish novelist)

ZWEIG, Stefan (1881–1942; Austrian Jewish writer)

6

ACCIUS, Lucius (170–c. 85 BC; Roman tragic dramatist)

ADAMOV, Arthur (1908–70; French dramatist)

ALCOTT, Louisa May (1832–88; US novelist)

ALDISS, Brian W (1925– ; British novelist)

ALEMÁN, Mateo (1547–?1614; Spanish writer)

ALGREN, Nelson (1909–81; US novelist)

AMBLER, Eric (1909– ; British novelist)

ANDRIĆ, Ivo (1892–1975; Serbian writer)

ARAGON, Louis (1897–1982; French poet, novelist, and journalist)

ASCHAM, Roger (1515–68; English scholar and writer)

ASIMOV, Isaac (1920– ; US science fiction writer, born in Russia)

AUBREY, John (1626–97; English antiquary)

AUSTEN, Jane (1775–1817; British novelist)

AZORÍN (José Martinéz Ruiz, 1874–1967; Spanish novelist, essayist, and critic)

6—continued

AZUELA, Mariano (1873–1952; Mexican novelist)

BALZAC, Honoré de (1799–1850; French novelist)

BARHAM, Richard Harris (1788–1845; British humorous writer)

BARKER, George (1913– ; British poet)

BARNES, William (1801–86; British poet)

BAROJA, Pío (1872–1956; Spanish novelist)

BARRÈS, Maurice (1862–1923; French writer)

BARRIE, Sir James (1860–1937; British dramatist and novelist)

BELLAY, Joachim de (1522–60; French poet)

BELLOC, Hilaire (1870–1953; British poet and essayist)

BELLOW, Saul (1915– ; Canadian-born US novelist)

BESANT, Sir Walter (1836–1901; British novelist)

BIALIK, Chaim Nachman (1873–1934; Jewish poet and translator)

BIERCE, Ambrose Gwinnett (1842–?1914; US writer)

BINYON, Laurence (1869–1943; British poet)

BLYTON, Enid (1897–1968; British writer of children's books)

BORGES, Jorge Luis (1899–1986; Argentinian writer)

BORROW, George Henry (1803–81; British writer)

BRECHT, Bertolt (1898–1956; German dramatist and poet)

BRETON, André (1896–1966; French poet)

BRIDIE, James (Osborne Henry Mavor; 1888–1951; British dramatist)

BRONTË, Anne (1820–49; British novelist)

BRONTË, Charlotte (1816–55; British novelist)

BRONTË, Emily (1818–48; British novelist)

BROOKE, Rupert (1887–1915; British poet)

BROWNE, Sir Thomas (1605–82; English writer)

BRYANT, William Cullen (1794–1878; US poet, journalist, and critic)

BUCHAN, John, 1st Baron Tweedsmuir (1875–1940; British novelist)

BUNYAN, John (1628–88; English writer)

BÜRGER, Gottfried (1747–94; German poet)

BURNEY, Fanny (Mrs Frances Burney D'Arblay; 1752–1840; British novelist)

BUTLER, Samuel (1612–80; British satirical poet)

BUTLER, Samuel (1835–1902; British novelist)

CAMÕES, Luís de (c. 1524–80; Portuguese poet)

CAPOTE, Truman (1924–84; US novelist)

CARSON, Rachel Louise (1907–64; US science writer)

CAVAFY, Constantine (C Kavafis, 1863–1933; Greek poet)

6—continued

CÉLINE, Louis Ferdinand (L F Destouches, 1884–1961; French novelist)

CIBBER, Colley (1671–1757; British dramatist)

CLARKE, Marcus (1846–81; Australian novelist, born in London)

COLMAN, George (1732–94; British dramatist)

CONRAD, Joseph (Teodor Josef Konrad Watęcz Korzeniowski, 1857–1924; Polish-born British novelist)

COOPER, James Fenimore (1789–1851; US novelist)

COWLEY, Abraham (1618–67; English poet)

COWPER, William (1731–1800; British poet)

CRABBE, George (1754–1832; British poet)

CRONIN, A J (1896–1981; British novelist)

DANIEL, Samuel (?1562–1619; English poet, dramatist, and critic)

DAUDET, Alphonse (1840–97; French novelist)

DAVIES, W H (1871–1940; British poet)

DEKKER, Thomas (c. 1572–1632; British dramatist and pamphleteer)

DOWSON, Ernest (1867–1900; British poet)

DRYDEN, John (1631–1700; British poet)

DUNBAR, William (c. 1460–c. 1530; Scots poet)

ÉLUARD, Paul (Eugène Grindel, 1895–1952; French poet)

EMPSON, Sir William (1906–84; British poet and critic)

ENNIUS, Quintus (238–169 BC; Roman poet)

EVELYN, John (1620–1706; English diarist)

FOUQUÉ, Friedrich Heinrich Karl, Baron de la Motte (1777–1843; German novelist and dramatist)

FOWLES, John (1926– ; British novelist)

FRANCE, Anatole (Jacques Anatole François Thibault, 1844–1924; French novelist)

FRISCH, Max (1911– ; Swiss dramatist and novelist)

FUGARD, Athol (1932– ; South African dramatist)

FULLER, Roy (1912– ; British poet and novelist)

FULLER, Thomas (1608–61; British historian)

GEORGE, Stefan (1868–1933; German poet)

GIBBON, Edward (1737–94; British historian)

GIBRAN, Khalil (1883–1931; Lebanese mystic and poet)

GOETHE, Johann Wolfgang von (1749–1832; German poet)

GRAVES, Robert (1895–1985; British poet, critic, and novelist)

GREENE, Graham (1904– ; British novelist)

GREENE, Robert (c. 1558–92; English dramatist)

HAMSUN, Knut (1859–1952; Norwegian novelist)

HARRIS, Joel Chandler (1848–1908; US novelist and short-story writer)

6—continued

HEBBEL, Friedrich (1813–63; German dramatist)

HELLER, Joseph (1923– ; US novelist)

HESIOD (8th century BC; Greek poet)

HILTON, James (1900–54; British novelist)

HOLMES, Oliver Wendell (1809–94; US essayist and poet)

HORACE (Quintus Horatius Flaccus; 65–8 BC; Roman poet)

HUDSON, W H (1841–1922; British naturalist and writer)

HUGHES, Richard (1900–76; British novelist)

HUGHES, Ted (1930– ; British poet)

HUGHES, Thomas (1822–96; British writer)

IRVING, Washington (1783–1859; US short-story writer)

ISAACS, Jorge (1837–95; Colombian novelist)

JENSEN, Johannes (1873–1950; Danish novelist and poet)

JONSON, Ben (1572–1637; English dramatist and poet)

KAISER, Georg (1878–1945; German dramatist)

KELLER, Gottfried (1819–90; German-Swiss poet and novelist)

KLEIST, Heinrich von (1777–1811; German dramatist)

LACLOS, Pierre Choderlos de (1741–1803; French novelist)

LANDOR, Walter Savage (1775–1864; British poet and prose writer)

LANIER, Sidney (1842–81; US poet)

LARKIN, Philip (1922–85; British poet)

LAWLER, Ray (1921– ; Australian dramatist)

LE FANU, Sheridan (1814–73; Irish novelist)

LEONOV, Leonid (1899– ; Soviet novelist and playwright)

LESAGE, Alain-René (1668–1747; French novelist)

LONDON, Jack (1876–1916; US novelist)

LOWELL, Amy (1874–1925; US poet)

LOWELL, James Russell (1819–91; US poet)

LOWELL, Robert (1917–77; US poet)

LU HSÜN (or Chou Shu-jen; 1881–1936; Chinese writer)

MACHEN, Arthur (1863–1947; Welsh novelist)

MAILER, Norman (1923– ; US novelist and journalist)

MALORY, Sir Thomas (?1400–71; English writer)

MERCER, David (1928–80; British dramatist)

MILLAY, Edna St Vincent (1892–1950; US poet)

MILLER, Arthur (1915– ; US dramatist)

MILLER, Henry (1891–1980; US novelist)

MILTON, John (1608–74; English poet)

MOLNÁR, Ferenc (1878–1952; Hungarian dramatist)

MORGAN, Charles (1894–1958; British novelist and dramatist)

6—continued

MÖRIKE, Eduard Friedrich (1804–75; German poet and novelist)

MUNTHE, Axel (1857–1949; Swedish author)

MUSSET, Alfred de (1810–57; French poet and dramatist)

NERUDA, Pablo (Neftali Ricardo Reyes; 1904–73; Chilean poet)

NERVAL, Gérard de (Gérard Labrunie; 1808–55; French poet)

NESBIT, Edith (1858–1924; British children's writer)

O'BRIEN, Flann (Brian O'Nolan; 1911–66; Irish novelist and journalist)

O'CASEY, Sean (1880–1964; Irish dramatist)

O'NEILL, Eugene (1888–1953; US dramatist)

ORWELL, George (Eric Blair; 1903–50; British novelist, born in India)

PARKER, Dorothy Rothschild (1893–1967; US humorous writer)

PAVESE, Cesare (1908–50; Italian novelist and poet)

PETÖFI, Sándor (1823–49; Hungarian poet)

PINDAR (518–438 BC; Greek poet)

PINERO, Sir Arthur Wing (1855–1934; British dramatist)

PINTER, Harold (1930– ; British dramatist)

PIOZZI, Hester Lynch (1741–1821; British writer)

PLOMER, William (1903–73; South African poet and novelist)

PORTER, Katherine Anne (1890–1980; US short-story writer and novelist)

PORTER, Peter (1929– ; British poet)

POTTER, Beatrix (1866–1943; British children's writer)

POTTER, Stephen (1900–70; British writer)

POWELL, Anthony (1905– ; British novelist)

PROUST, Marcel (1871–1922; French novelist)

RACINE, Jean (1639–99; French dramatist)

RAMSAY, Allan (?1685–1758; Scottish poet)

RANSOM, John Crowe (1888–1974; US poet)

RUNYON, Damon (1884–1946; US humorous writer)

SAPPER (H C McNeile, 1888–1937; British novelist)

SAPPHO (c. 612–c. 580 BC; Greek poet)

SARDOU, Victorien (1831–1908; French dramatist)

SARTRE, Jean-Paul (1905–80; French philosopher, novelist, dramatist, and critic)

SAVAGE, Richard (c. 1696–1743; British poet)

SAYERS, Dorothy L (1893–1957; British writer)

SIDNEY, Sir Philip (1554–86; English poet)

SILONE, Ignazio (Secondo Tranquilli, 1900–78; Italian novelist)

SINGER, Isaac Bashevis (1904– ; US novelist and short-story writer)

SMILES, Samuel (1812–1904; British writer)

6—continued

STEELE, Sir Richard (1672–1729; British essayist and dramatist)

STERNE, Laurence (1713–68; British novelist)

STOKER, Bram (Abraham S, 1847–1912; Irish novelist)

STOREY, David (1933– ; British novelist and dramatist)

SURREY, Henry Howard, Earl of (1517–47; English poet)

SYMONS, Arthur (1865–1945; British poet and critic)

TAGORE, Rabindranath (1861–1941; Indian poet)

THOMAS, Dylan (1914–53; Welsh poet)

THOMAS, Edward (1878–1917; British poet)

TOLLER, Ernst (1893–1939; German playwright and poet)

TRAVEN, B (Berick Traven Torsvan, 1890–1969; US novelist)

UHLAND, Ludwig (1787–1862; German poet)

UNDSET, Sigrid (1882–1949; Norwegian novelist)

UPDIKE, John (1932– ; US novelist and short-story writer)

VALÉRY, Paul (1871–1945; French poet, essayist, and critic)

VILLON, François (1431–?1463; French poet)

VIRGIL (Publius Vergilius Maro, 70–19 BC; Roman poet)

VONDEL, Joost van den (1587–1679; Dutch dramatist and poet)

WALLER, Edmund (1606–87; British poet)

WALTON, Izaak (1593–1683; English writer)

WARTON, Joseph (1722–1800; British poet and critic)

WERFEL, Franz (1890–1945; Austrian Jewish poet, dramatist, and novelist)

WESKER, Arnold (1932– ; British dramatist)

WILDER, Thornton (1897–1975; US novelist and dramatist)

WILSON, Colin (1931– ; British critic and novelist)

WILSON, Edmund (1895–1972; US critic and essayist)

WILSON, Sir Angus (1913– ; British novelist)

WOTTON, Sir Henry (1568–1639; English poet)

WRIGHT, Judith (1915– ; Australian poet)

WRIGHT, Richard (1908–60; US novelist and critic)

7

ADDISON, Joseph (1672–1719; British essayist and poet)

AELFRIC (c. 955–c. 1020; Anglo-Saxon prose writer)

ALARCÓN, Pedro Antonio de (1833–91; Spanish novelist)

ALBERTI, Raphael (1902– ; Spanish poet)

ALCAEUS (6th century BC; Greek lyric poet)

7—continued

ALDANOV, Mark (M Aleksandrovich Landau, 1886–1957; Russian novelist)

ALDRICH, Thomas Bailey (1836–1907; US short-story writer and poet)

ALEGRÍA, Ciro (1909–61; Peruvian novelist)

ALFIERI, Vittorio, Count (1749–1803; Italian poet and dramatist)

ANEIRIN (6th century AD; Welsh poet)

ARETINO, Pietro (1492–1556; Italian satirist)

ARIOSTO, Ludovico (1474–1533; Italian poet)

ARRABAL, Fernando (1932– ; Spanish playwright and novelist)

BALCHIN, Nigel (1908–70; British novelist)

BALDWIN, James Arthur (1924–87; US novelist, essayist, and dramatist)

BARBOUR, John (1316–95; Scottish poet)

BECKETT, Samuel (1906– ; Irish novelist, dramatist, and poet)

BEDDOES, Thomas Lovell (1803–49; British poet)

BENNETT, Arnold (1837–1931; British novelist)

BENTLEY, Edmund Clerihew (1875–1956; British writer)

BERGMAN, Hjalmar (1883–1931; Swedish novelist and dramatist)

BLUNDEN, Edmund Charles (1896–1974; British poet and critic)

BOIARDO, Matteo Maria, Conte di Scandiano (1441–94; Italian poet)

BOILEAU(-Despréaux), Nicolas (1636–1711; French poet and critic)

BOSWELL, James (1740–95; Scottish writer)

BO ZHU YI (or Po Chü-i; 772–846; Chinese poet)

BRADLEY, Andrew Cecil (1851–1935; British literary critic)

BRIDGES, Robert Seymour (1844–1930; British poet)

BÜCHNER, Georg (1813–37; German dramatist)

BURGESS, Anthony (John Burgess Wilson; 1917– ; British novelist and critic)

BURNETT, Frances Eliza Hodgson (1849–1924; British novelist)

CAEDMON (d. c. 680 AD; English poet)

CAO CHAN (or Zao Zhan; ?1715–63; Chinese novelist)

CAROSSA, Hans (1878–1956; German novelist)

CARROLL, Lewis (Charles Lutwidge Dodgson; 1832–98; British writer)

CHAPMAN, George (c. 1560–1634; British poet and dramatist)

CHAUCER, Geoffrey (c. 1342–1400; English poet)

CHEKHOV, Anton Pavlovich (1860–1904; Russian dramatist and short-story writer)

CHÉNIER, André de (1762–94; French poet, born in Istanbul)

7—continued

CHU YUAN (c. 343 BC–c. 289 BC, Chinese poet)

CLAUDEL, Paul (1868–1955; French dramatist and poet)

CLELAND, John (1709–89; English novelist)

COCTEAU, Jean (1889–1963; French poet and artist)

COLETTE (Sidonie-Gabrielle C, 1873–1954; French novelist)

COLLINS, William (1721–59; British poet)

COLLINS, William Wilkie (1824–89; British novelist)

CORELLI, Marie (1854–1924; British novelist)

CRASHAW, Richard (c. 1613–49; British poet)

CREELEY, Robert (1926– ; US poet)

DA PONTE, Lorenzo (1749–1838; Italian author)

DELEDDA, Grazia (1871–1936; Italian novelist)

DICKENS, Charles (1812–70; British novelist)

DINESEN, Isak (Karen Blixen, Baroness Blixen-Finecke, 1885–1962; Danish author)

DOUGLAS, Gavin (?1474–1522; Scottish poet)

DOUGLAS, Norman (1868–1952; British novelist)

DRABBLE, Margaret (1939– ; British novelist)

DRAYTON, Michael (1563–1631; English poet)

DREISER, Theodore (1871–1945; US novelist)

DUHAMEL, Georges (1884–1966; French novelist)

DUNSANY, Edward John Moreton Drax Plunkett, 18th Baron (1878–1957; Irish author)

DURRELL, Lawrence George (1912– ; British novelist and poet, born in India)

EMERSON, Ralph Waldo (1803–82; US essayist and poet)

ERCILLA, Alonso de (1533–94; Spanish poet)

EUPOLIS (late 5th century BC; Greek dramatist)

FERRIER, Susan Edmonstone (1782–1854; Scottish novelist)

FEYDEAU, Georges (1862–1921; French playwright)

FIRBANK, Ronald (1886–1926; British novelist)

FLECKER, James Elroy (1884–1915; British poet)

FLEMING, Ian (1908–64; British author)

FLEMING, Paul (1609–40; German poet)

FONTANE, Theodor (1819–98; German novelist)

FORSTER, E M (1879–1970; British novelist)

FOSCOLO, Ugo (1778–1827; Italian poet)

FRENEAU, Philip (1752–1832; US poet)

FRÖDING, Gustaf (1860–1911; Swedish lyric poet)

GASKELL, Elizabeth Cleghorn (1810–65; British novelist)

7—continued

GAUTIER, Théophile (1811–72; French poet)

GILBERT, Sir William Schwenk (1836–1911; British comic dramatist)

GISSING, George Robert (1857–1903; British novelist)

GOLDING, William (1911–   ; British novelist)

GOLDONI, Carlo (1707–93; Italian comic playwright)

GRAHAME, Kenneth (1859–1932; British children's writer)

GUARINI, Giovanni Battista (1538–1612; Italian poet)

HAGGARD, Sir H Rider (1856–1925; British novelist)

HAMMETT, Dashiell (1894–1961; US novelist)

HARTLEY, L P (1895–1972; British novelist)

HELLMAN, Lillian (1905–84; US dramatist)

HERBERT, George (1593–1633; English poet)

HERRICK, Robert (1591–1674; English poet)

HEYWOOD, Thomas (c. 1574–1641; English dramatist)

HOLBERG, Ludvig, Baron (1684–1754; Danish playwright and poet)

HOPKINS, Gerard Manley (1844–89; British poet)

HOUSMAN, A E (1859–1936; British poet and scholar)

IBN EZRA, Abraham Ben Meir (1093–1167; Hebrew poet and scholar)

IONESCO, Eugène (1912–   ; French dramatist)

JEFFERS, Robinson (1887–1962; US poet)

JIMÉNEZ, Juan Ramón (1881–1958; Spanish poet)

JUVENAL (Decimus Junius Juvenalis, c. 60–c. 130 AD; Roman satirist)

KÄSTNER, Erich (1899–1974; German novelist and poet)

KAUFMAN, George S (1889–1961; US dramatist)

KENDALL, Henry (1841–82; Australian poet)

KEROUAC, Jack (1922–69; US novelist)

KIPLING, Rudyard (1865–1936; British writer and poet)

KLINGER, Friedrich Maximilian von (1752–1831; German dramatist)

LABICHE, Eugène (1815–88; French dramatist)

LARDNER, Ring (1885–1933; US short-story writer)

LAXNESS, Halldór (1902–   ; Icelandic novelist and essayist)

LAYAMON (early 13th century; English poet)

LEACOCK, Stephen (1869–1944; English-born Canadian humorist)

LE CARRÉ, John (David Cornwell, 1931–   ; British novelist)

LESSING, Doris (1919–   ; British novelist)

LESSING, Gotthold Ephraim (1729–81; German dramatist and writer)

7—continued

LINDSAY, Vachel (1879–1931; US poet)

LYDGATE, John (c. 1370–c. 1450; English poet)

MACHAUT, Guillaume de (c. 1300–77; French poet)

MALAMUD, Bernard (1914–86; US novelist)

MALRAUX, André (1901–76; French novelist and essayist)

MANZONI, Alessandro (1785–1873; Italian poet and novelist)

MARLOWE, Christopher (1564–93; English dramatist and poet)

MARRYAT, Captain Frederick (1792–1848; British novelist)

MARSTON, John (1576–1634; English dramatist)

MARTIAL (Marcus Valerius Martialis, c. 40–c. 104 AD; Roman poet)

MARVELL, Andrew (1621–78; English poet)

MASTERS, Edgar Lee (1868–1950; US poet)

MAUGHAM, W Somerset (1874–1965; British novelist and dramatist)

MAURIAC, François (1885–1970; French novelist)

MAUROIS, André (Émile Herzog; 1885–1967; French biographer, novelist, and critic)

MÉRIMÉE, Prosper (1803–70; French novelist)

MISHIMA, Yukio (Kimitake Hiraoka; 1925–70; Japanese novelist and playwright)

MISTRAL, Frédéric (1830–1914; French poet)

MISTRAL, Gabriela (Lucila Godoy Alcayaga, 1889–1957; Chilean poet)

MOLIÈRE (Jean-Baptiste Poquelin, 1622–73; French dramatist)

MONTAGU, Lady Mary Wortley (1689–1762; English writer)

MONTALE, Eugenio (1896–1981; Italian poet)

MORAVIA, Alberto (Alberto Pincherle, 1907–   ; Italian novelist)

MURDOCH, Dame Iris (1919–   ; British novelist)

NABOKOV, Vladimir (1899–1977; US novelist)

NAEVIUS, Gnaeus (c. 270–c. 200 BC; Roman poet)

NAIPAUL, V S (1932–   ; West Indian novelist)

NOVALIS (Friedrich Leopold, Freiherr von Hardenberg; 1772–1801; German poet and writer)

O'CONNOR, Frank (Michael O'Donovan; 1903–66; Irish short-story writer)

OSBORNE, John (1929–   ; British dramatist)

PATMORE, Coventry (1823–96; British poet)

PEACOCK, Thomas Love (1785–1866; British satirical novelist)

PLAUTUS, Titus Maccius (c. 254–184 BC; Roman dramatist)

PRÉVERT, Jacques (1900–77; French poet)

PUSHKIN, Aleksandr (1799–1837; Russian poet, novelist, and dramatist)

PYNCHON, Thomas (1937–   ; US novelist)

7—continued

QUENEAU, Raymond (1903–79; French novelist and poet)

RANSOME, Arthur Mitchell (1884–1967; British journalist and children's writer)

REGNIER, Henri François Joseph de (1864–1936; French poet)

RICHLER, Mordecai (1931– ; Canadian novelist)

RIMBAUD, Arthur (1854–91; French poet)

ROLLAND, Romain (1866–1944; French novelist, dramatist, and essayist)

ROMAINS, Jules (Louis Farigoule; 1885–1972; French poet, novelist, and dramatist)

RONSARD, Pierre de (1524–85; French poet)

ROSTAND, Edmond (1868–1918; French dramatist)

ROUSSEL, Raymond (1877–1933; French writer and dramatist)

SAROYAN, William (1908–81; US dramatist and fiction writer)

SASSOON, Siegfried (1886–1967; British poet and writer)

SCARRON, Paul (1610–60; French poet, dramatist, and satirist)

SEFERIS, George (Georgios Seferiadis, 1900–71; Greek poet)

SHAFFER, Peter (1926– ; British dramatist)

SHELLEY, Percy Bysshe (1792–1822; British poet)

SIMENON, Georges (1903– ; Belgian novelist)

SIMONOV, Konstantin (1915–79; Soviet novelist, playwright, poet, and journalist)

SITWELL, Edith (1887–1964; British poet and writer)

SKELTON, John (c. 1460–1529; English poet)

SOUTHEY, Robert (1774–1843; British poet and writer)

SOYINKA, Wole (1934– ; Nigerian dramatist and poet)

SPENDER, Stephen (1909– ; British poet and critic)

SPENSER, Edmund (c. 1552–99; English poet)

STEVENS, Wallace (1879–1955; US poet)

SURTEES, Robert Smith (1803–64; British novelist)

TERENCE (Publius Terentius Afer, c. 185–c. 159 BC; Roman dramatist)

THESPIS (6th century BC; Greek poet)

THOMSON, James (1700–48; British poet)

THURBER, James (1894–1961; US humorous writer and cartoonist)

TOLKIEN, J R R (1892–1973; British scholar and writer)

TOLSTOY, Leo, Count (1828–1910; Russian writer)

TRAVERS, Ben (1886–1980; British dramatist)

TUTUOLA, Amos (1920– ; Nigerian writer)

VAUGHAN, Henry (c. 1622–95; English poet)

7—continued

VICENTE, Gil (c. 1465–1536; Portuguese dramatist)

WALLACE, Edgar (1875–1932; British novelist)

WALPOLE, Sir Hugh (1884–1941; British novelist)

WEBSTER, John (c. 1580–c. 1625; English dramatist)

WHARTON, Edith (1862–1937; US novelist)

WHITMAN, Walt (1819–92; US poet)

WIELAND, Christoph Martin (1733–1813; German novelist and poet)

YESENIN, Sergei Aleksandrovich (1895–1925; Russian poet)

8

ABU NUWAS (c. 762–c. 813 AD; Arab poet)

ANACREON (6th century BC; Greek lyric poet)

ANCHIETA, José de (1534–97; Portuguese poet)

ANDERSEN, Hans Christian (1805–75; Danish author)

ANDERSON, Sherwood (1876–1941; US author)

APULEIUS, Lucius (2nd century AD; Roman writer and rhetorician)

ASTURIAS, Miguel Ángel (1899–1974; Guatemalan novelist and poet)

BANDEIRA, Manuel Carneiró de Sousa (1886–1968; Brazilian poet)

BANVILLE, Théodore Faullain de (1823–89; French poet)

BARBUSSE, Henri (1873–1935; French novelist)

BEAUMONT, Francis (1584–1616; British dramatist)

BEAUVOIR, Simone de (1908–86; French novelist and essayist)

BECKFORD, William (?1760–1844; British writer)

BEERBOHM, Sir Max (1872–1956; British caricaturist and writer)

BELINSKY, Vissarion (1811–48; Russian literary critic)

BENCHLEY, Robert Charles (1889–1945; US humorist)

BERANGER, Pierre Jean de (1780–1857; French poet and songwriter)

BERNANOS, Georges (1888–1948; French novelist)

BETJEMAN, Sir John (1906–84; British poet)

BJØRNSON, Bjørnstjerne (1832–1910; Norwegian novelist, poet, and playwright)

BRADBURY, Ray (1920– ; US science-fiction writer)

BRENTANO, Clemens (1778–1842; German writer)

BROWNING, Robert (1812–89; British poet)

CAMPBELL, Roy (1901–57; South African poet)

8—continued

CAMPBELL, Thomas (1777–1844; British poet)

CARDUCCI, Giosuè (1835–1907; Italian poet and critic)

CASTILHO, Antonio Feliciano de (1800–75; Portuguese poet)

CATULLUS, Valerius (c. 84–c. 54 BC; Roman poet)

CHANDLER, Raymond (1888–1959; US novelist)

CHARTIER, Alain (c. 1385–c. 1440; French poet and prose writer)

CHRISTIE, Dame Agatha (1891–1976; British author of detective fiction and playwright)

CLAUDIAN (c. 370–404 AD; Roman poet)

CONGREVE, William (1670–1729; British dramatist)

CONSTANT, Benjamin (1767–1830; French novelist)

CROMPTON, Richmal (Richmal Crompton Lamburn, 1890–1969; British children's author)

CUMMINGS, e e (1894–1962; US poet)

CYNEWULF (early 9th century AD; Anglo-Saxon religious poet)

DAVENANT, Sir William (1606–68; English dramatist and poet)

DAY LEWIS, C (1904–72; British poet and critic)

DE LA MARE, Walter (1873–1956; British poet, novelist, and anthologist)

DONLEAVY, J P (1926–   ; Irish-American novelist)

ETHEREGE, Sir George (c. 1635–c. 1692; English dramatist)

FARQUHAR, George (1678–1707; Irish dramatist)

FAULKNER, William (1897–1962; US novelist)

FIELDING, Henry (1707–54; British novelist and dramatist)

FIRDAUSI (Abul Qasim Mansur; c. 935–c. 1020; Persian poet)

FLAUBERT, Gustave (1821–80; French novelist)

FLETCHER, John (1579–1625; English dramatist)

FORESTER, C S (1899–1966; British novelist)

GINSBERG, Allen (1926–   ; US poet)

GONCOURT, Edmond de (1822–96; French writer)

HENRYSON, Robert (15th century; Scottish poet)

HOCHHUTH, Rolf (1933–   ; Swiss dramatist)

HUYSMANS, Joris Karl (1848–1907; French novelist)

JEAN PAUL (Johann Paul Friedrich Richter, 1763–1825; German novelist)

KALIDASA (5th century AD; Indian poet)

KINGSLEY, Charles (1819–79; British writer)

KOESTLER, Arthur (1905–83; British writer)

8—continued

KOTZEBUE, August von (1761–1819; German dramatist and novelist)

LAFORGUE, Jules (1860–87; French poet)

LAGERLÖF, Selma Ottiliana Lovisa (1858–1940; Swedish novelist)

LANGLAND, William (c. 1330–c. 1400; English poet)

LAS CASES, Emmanuel, Comte de (1776–1842; French writer)

LAWRENCE, D H (1885–1930; British novelist, poet, and painter)

LEOPARDI, Giacomo (1798–1837; Italian poet)

LOCKHART, John Gibson (1794–1854; Scottish biographer and journalist)

LONGINUS (1st century AD; Greek rhetorician)

LOVELACE, Richard (1618–57; English Cavalier poet)

MACAULAY, Dame Rose (1881–1958; British novelist)

MACLEISH, Archibald (1892–1982; US poet)

MACNEICE, Louis (1907–63; Irish-born British poet)

MALHERBE, François de (1555–1628; French poet and critic)

MALLARMÉ, Stéphane (1842–98; French poet)

MARIVAUX, Pierre Carlet de Chamblain de (1688–1763; French dramatist)

MARQUAND, J P (1893–1960; US novelist)

MCCARTHY, Mary (1912–   ; US novelist)

MELVILLE, Herman (1819–91; US novelist)

MENANDER (c. 341–c. 290 BC; Greek dramatist)

MEREDITH, George (1828–1909; British poet and novelist)

MICHELET, Jules (1798–1874; French historian)

MITCHELL, Margaret (1909–49; US novelist)

NEKRASOV, Nikolai Alekseevich (1821–78; Russian poet)

NICOLSON, Sir Harold (1886–1968; British literary critic)

PALGRAVE, Francis Turner (1824–97; British poet and anthologist)

PERELMAN, S J (1904–79; US humorous writer)

PERRAULT, Charles (1628–1703; French poet and fairytale writer)

PETRARCH (Francesco Petrarca, 1304–74; Italian poet)

PHAEDRUS (1st century AD; Roman writer)

PHILEMON (c. 368–c. 264 BC; Greek dramatist)

PLUTARCH (c. 46–c. 120 AD; Greek biographer and essayist)

RABELAIS, François (1483–1553; French satirist)

RADIGUET, Raymond (1903–23; French novelist)

8—continued

RATTIGAN, Sir Terence (1911–77; British dramatist)

REMARQUE, Erich Maria (1898–1970; German novelist)

RICHARDS, Frank (Charles Hamilton, 1876–1961; British children's writer)

RUNEBERG, Johan Ludvig (1804–77; Finnish poet)

SALINGER, J D (1919–   ; US novelist)

SANDBURG, Carl (1878–1967; US poet)

SARRAUTE, Nathalie (1902–   ; French novelist, born in Russia)

SCALIGER, Julius Caesar (1484–1558; Italian humanist scholar)

SCHILLER, Friedrich (1759–1805; German dramatist, poet, and writer)

SHADWELL, Thomas (c. 1642–92; British dramatist)

SHERIDAN, Richard Brinsley (1751–1816; Anglo-Irish dramatist)

SILLITOE, Alan (1928–   ; British novelist)

SINCLAIR, Upton (1878–1968; US novelist)

SMOLLETT, Tobias (1721–71; British novelist)

SPILLANE, Mickey (Frank Morrison S, 1918–   ; US detective-story writer)

STENDHAL (Henri Beyle, 1783–1842; French novelist)

STOPPARD, Tom (1937–   ; British dramatist)

SUCKLING, Sir John (1609–42; English poet and dramatist)

SU DONG PO (or Su Tung-p'o, 1036–1101; Chinese poet)

TALIESIN (6th century AD; Welsh poet)

TENNYSON, Alfred, Lord (1809–92; British poet)

THOMPSON, Francis (1859–1907; British poet and critic)

TIBULLUS, Albius (c. 55–c. 19 BC; Roman poet)

TOURNEUR, Cyril (c. 1575–1626; English dramatist)

TRAHERNE, Thomas (c. 1637–74; English poet)

TRILLING, Lionel (1905–75; US literary critic)

TROLLOPE, Anthony (1815–82; British novelist)

TULSIDAS (c. 1532–1623; Indian poet)

TURGENEV, Ivan (1818–83; Russian novelist)

VERLAINE, Paul (1844–96; French poet)

VOLTAIRE (François-Marie Arouet, 1694–1778; French writer)

VONNEGUT, Kurt (1922–   ; US novelist)

WEDEKIND, Frank (1864–1918; German dramatist)

WHITTIER, John Greenleaf (1807–92; US poet)

WILLIAMS, Tennessee (1911–83; US dramatist)

WILLIAMS, William Carlos (1883–1963; US poet)

8—continued

ZAMYATIN, Yevgenii Ivanovich (1884–1937; Russian novelist)

9

AESCHYLUS (c. 525–456 BC; Greek tragic dramatist)

AINSWORTH, W Harrison (1805–82; British historical novelist)

AKHMATOVA, Anna (Anna Andreevna Gorenko, 1889–1966; Russian poet)

ALDINGTON, Richard (1892–1962; British poet, novelist, and biographer)

ALLINGHAM, Margery (1904–66; British detective-story writer)

ARBUTHNOT, John (1667–1735; Scottish writer)

AYCKBOURN, Alan (1939–   ; British dramatist)

BLACKMORE, R D (1825–1900; British historical novelist)

BLACKWOOD, Algernon Henry (1869–1951; British novelist and short-story writer)

BOCCACCIO, Giovanni (1313–75; Italian writer and poet)

BURROUGHS, Edgar Rice (1875–1950; US novelist)

BURROUGHS, William (1914–   ; US novelist)

CERVANTES, Miguel de (1547–1616; Spanish novelist)

CHARTERIS, Leslie (L Charles Bowyer Yin, 1907–   ; British novelist)

CHURCHILL, Charles (1731–64; British poet)

COLERIDGE, Samuel Taylor (1772–1834; British poet)

CORNEILLE, Pierre (1606–84; French dramatist)

D'ANNUNZIO, Gabriele (1863–1938; Italian poet, novelist, and dramatist)

DE LA ROCHE, Mazo (1885–1961; Canadian novelist)

DE QUINCEY, Thomas (1785–1859; British essayist and critic)

DICKINSON, Emily (1830–86; US poet)

DOOLITTLE, Hilda (1886–1961; US poet)

DOS PASSOS, John (1896–1970; US novelist)

DU MAURIER, George (1834–96; British caricaturist and novelist)

ECKERMANN, Johann Peter (1792–1854; German writer)

EDGEWORTH, Maria (1767–1849; Anglo-Irish writer)

EHRENBERG, Iliya Grigorievich (1891–1967; Soviet author)

EURIPIDES (c. 480–406 BC; Greek dramatist)

FROISSART, Jean (1337–c. 1400; French chronicler and poet)

GIRAUDOUX, Jean (1882–1944; French dramatist and novelist)

GOLDSMITH, Oliver (1730–74; Anglo-Irish writer)

9—continued

GONCHAROV, Ivan Aleksandrovich (1812–91; Russian novelist)

GOTTSCHED, Johann Christoph (1700–66; German critic)

GREENWOOD, Walter (1903–   ; British novelist)

HAUPTMANN, Gerhart (1862–1946; German dramatist)

HAWTHORNE, Nathaniel (1804–64; US novelist and short-story writer)

HEMINGWAY, Ernest (1899–1961; US novelist)

HIGHSMITH, Patricia (1921–   ; US author of crime fiction)

HÖLDERLIN, Friedrich (1770–1843; German poet)

ISHERWOOD, Christopher (1904–86; British novelist)

JEFFERIES, Richard (1848–87; British novelist and naturalist)

KLOPSTOCK, Friedrich Gottlieb (1724–1803; German poet)

LA BRUYÈRE, Jean de (1645–96; French satirist)

LA FAYETTE, Mme de (Marie Madeleine, Comtesse de L F, 1634–93; French novelist)

LAMARTINE, Alphonse de (1790–1869; French poet)

LAMPEDUSA, Giuseppe Tomasi di (1896–1957; Italian novelist)

LERMONTOV, Mikhail (1814–41; Russian poet and novelist)

LINKLATER, Eric (1889–1974; Scottish novelist)

LLEWELLYN, Richard (R D V L Lloyd, 1907–83; Welsh novelist)

LOMONOSOV, Mikhail Vasilievich (1711–65; Russian poet)

LOVECRAFT, H P (1890–1937; US novelist and short-story writer)

LUCRETIUS (Titus Lucretius Carus, c. 95–c. 55 BC; Roman philosopher and poet)

MACKENZIE, Sir Compton (1883–1972; British novelist)

MALAPARTE, Curzio (Kurt Erich Suckert; 1898–1957; Italian novelist and dramatist)

MANSFIELD, Katherine (Kathleen Mansfield Beauchamp, 1888–1923; New Zealand short-story writer)

MARINETTI, Filippo Tommaso (1876–1944; Italian poet and novelist)

MARTINEAU, Harriet (1802–76; British writer)

MASEFIELD, John (1878–1967; British poet)

MASSINGER, Philip (1583–1640; English dramatist)

MCCULLERS, Carson (1917–67; US novelist and playwright)

MIDDLETON, Thomas (1580–1627; English dramatist)

9—continued

MONSARRAT, Nicholas (John Turney, 1910–79; British novelist)

MONTAIGNE, Michel de (1533–92; French essayist)

MUTANABBI, Abu At-Tayyib Ahmad Ibn Husayn al- (915–65 AD; Arab poet)

O'FLAHERTY, Liam (1897–1984; Irish novelist)

PARKINSON, Northcote (1909–   ; British author)

PASTERNAK, Boris (1890–1960; Russian poet and novelist)

POLIZIANO (or Politian; 1454–94; Italian poet and scholar)

PRITCHETT, V S (1900–   ; British short-story writer and critic)

RADCLIFFE, Ann (1764–1823; British novelist)

ROCHESTER, John Wilmot, 2nd Earl of (1647–80; British poet)

SACKVILLE, Thomas, 1st Earl of Dorset (1536–1608; British poet and dramatist)

SCHREINER, Olive (1855–1920; South African novelist)

SHENSTONE, William (1714–63; British poet)

SHOLOKHOV, Mikhail (1905–   ; Soviet novelist)

SOPHOCLES (c. 496–406 BC; Greek dramatist)

STEINBECK, John (1902–68; US novelist)

STEVENSON, Robert Louis (1850–94; British novelist)

STURLUSON, Snorri (1178–1241; Icelandic poet)

SWINBURNE, Algernon Charles (1837–1909; British poet)

THACKERAY, William Makepeace (1811–63; British novelist)

TSVETAEVA, Marina (1892–1941; Russian poet)

UNGARETTI, Giuseppe (1888–1970; Italian poet)

VERHAEREN, Émile (1844–96; Belgian poet)

VITTORINI, Elio (1908–66; Italian novelist)

WERGELAND, Henrik Arnold (1808–45; Norwegian poet)

WODEHOUSE, Sir P G (1881–1975; US humorous writer)

WYCHERLEY, William (1640–1716; English dramatist)

10

BAUDELAIRE, Charles (1821–67; French poet)

BILDERDIJK, Willem (1756–1831; Dutch poet and dramatist)

CAVALCANTI, Guido (c. 1255–1300; Italian poet)

CHATTERJEE, Bankim Chandra (1838–94; Indian novelist)

CHATTERTON, Thomas (1752–70; British poet)

10—continued

CHESTERTON, G K (1874–1936; British essayist, novelist, and poet)

CONSCIENCE, Hendrik (1812–83; Flemish novelist)

DAZAI OSAMU (Tsushima Shuji; 1909–48; Japanese novelist)

DIO CASSIUS (*c.* 150–235 AD; Roman historian)

DRINKWATER, John (1882–1937; British poet and dramatist)

DÜRRENMATT, Friedrich (1921– ; Swiss dramatist and novelist)

FITZGERALD, Edward (1809–83; British poet)

FITZGERALD, F Scott (1896–1940; US novelist)

GALSWORTHY, John (1867–1933; British novelist and dramatist)

JEAN DE MEUN (*c.* 1240–*c.* 1305; French poet)

KHLEBNIKOV, Velimir (Victor K, 1885–1922; Russian poet)

LA FONTAINE, Jean de (1621–95; French poet)

LAGERKVIST, Pär (1891–1974; Swedish novelist, poet, and dramatist)

LONGFELLOW, Henry Wadsworth (1807–82; US poet)

MACDIARMID, Hugh (Christopher Murray Grieve, 1892–1978; Scottish poet)

MANDELSTAM, Osip (1891–?1938; Russian poet)

MAUPASSANT, Guy de (1850–93; French short-story writer and novelist)

MCGONAGALL, William (1830–1902; Scottish poet)

MICKIEWICZ, Adam (1798–1855; Polish poet)

OSTROVSKII, Aleksandr Nikolaevich (1823–86; Russian dramatist)

PIRANDELLO, Luigi (1867–1936; Italian dramatist and novelist)

PROPERTIUS, Sextus (*c.* 50–*c.* 16 BC; Roman poet)

RICHARDSON, Henry Handel (Ethel Florence R, 1870–1946; Australian novelist)

RICHARDSON, Samuel (1689–1761; British novelist)

RUTHERFORD, Mark (William Hale White, 1831–1913; British novelist)

SCHNITZLER, Arthur (1862–1931; Austrian Jewish dramatist and novelist)

STRINDBERG, August (1849–1912; Swedish dramatist and writer)

TANNHÄUSER (*c.* 1200–*c.* 1270; German poet)

THEOCRITUS (*c.* 310–250 BC; Greek poet)

VAN DER POST, Sir Laurens (1906– ; South African novelist)

10—continued

WILLIAMSON, Henry (1895–1977; British novelist)

WORDSWORTH, William (1770–1850; British poet)

XENOPHANES (6th century BC; Greek poet)

11

ANZENGRUBER, Ludwig (1839–89; Austrian dramatist and novelist)

APOLLINAIRE, Guillaume (Wilhelm de Kostrowitzky, 1880–1918; French poet)

ARCHILOCHUS (*c.* 680–*c.* 640 BC; Greek poet)

BACCHYLIDES (*c.* 516–*c.* 450 BC; Greek lyric poet)

BLESSINGTON, Marguerite, Countess of (1789–1849; Irish author)

CALLIMACHUS (*c.* 305–*c.* 240 BC; Greek poet)

CASTIGLIONE, Baldassare (1478–1529; Italian writer)

DOSTOIEVSKI, Fedor Mikhailovich (1821–81; Russian novelist)

EICHENDORFF, Josef, Freiherr von (1788–1857; German writer)

GARCÍA LORCA, Federico (1898–1936; Spanish poet and dramatist)

GRILLPARZER, Franz (1791–1872; Austrian dramatist)

KAZANTZAKIS, Nikos (1885–1957; Greek novelist and poet)

LAUTRÉAMONT, Comte de (Isidore Ducasse, 1846–70; French writer)

MAETERLINCK, Maurice (1862–1949; Belgian poet and dramatist)

MATSUO BASHO (Matsuo Munefusa, 1644–94; Japanese poet)

MAYAKOVSKII, Vladimir (1893–1930; Russian poet)

MONTHERLANT, Henry de (1896–1972; French novelist and dramatist)

'OMAR KHAYYAM (?1048–?1122; Persian poet)

PÉREZ GALDÓS, Benito (1843–1920; Spanish novelist)

SHAKESPEARE, William (1564–1616; English dramatist)

SIENKIEWICZ, Henryk (1846–1916; Polish novelist)

STIERNHIELM, Georg Olofson (1598–1672; Swedish poet)

YEVTUSHENKO, Yevgenii (1933– ; Soviet poet)

12

ARISTOPHANES (*c.* 450–*c.* 385 BC; Greek comic dramatist)

BEAUMARCHAIS, Pierre-Augustin Caron de (1732–99; French dramatist)

BLASCO IBÁÑEZ, Vicente (1867–1928; Spanish novelist)

12—continued

FERLINGHETTI, Lawrence (1919–   ; US poet)
FEUCHTWANGER, Lion (1884–1958; German novelist and dramatist)
HOFMANNSTHAL, Hugo von (1874–1929; Austrian poet and dramatist)
LÓPEZ DE AYALA, Pero (c. 1332–c. 1407; Spanish poet and chronicler)
MARTIN DU GARD, Roger (1881–1958; French novelist)
MATTHEW PARIS (c. 1200–59; English chronicler)
ROBBE-GRILLET, Alain (1922–   ; French novelist)
SAINT-EXUPÉRY, Antoine de (1900–44; French novelist)
SOLZHENITSYN, Aleksandr (1918–   ; Russian novelist)
VOZNESENSKII, Andrei (1933–   ; Soviet poet)

13

BERTRAN DE BORN (?1140–?1215; French troubadour poet)
CASTELO BRANCO, Camilo (1825–95; Portuguese novelist)
CHATEAUBRIAND, Vicomte de (1768–1848; French writer)
CSOKONAI VITÉZ, Mihaly (1773–1805; Hungarian poet)
HARISHCHANDRA (1850–85; Hindi poet, dramatist, and essayist, also known as Bharatendu)
MARIE DE FRANCE (12th century AD; French poet)
TIRSO DE MOLINA (Gabriel Téllez, c. 1584–1648; Spanish dramatist)
ZEAMI MOTOKIYO (1363–c. 1443; Japanese playwright)

14

BRILLAT-SAVARIN, Anthelme (1755–1826; French writer)
COMPTON-BURNETT, Dame Ivy (1892–1969; British novelist)
DAFYDD AP GWILYM (c. 1320–c. 1380; Welsh poet)
DANTE ALIGHIERI (1265–1321; Italian poet)
DROSTE-HÜLSHOFF, Annette von (1797–1848; German poet and novelist)
GÓNGORA Y ARGOTE, Luis de (1561–1627; Spanish poet)
GRIMMELSHAUSEN, Hans Jacob Christoph von (c. 1625–76; German novelist)
JACOPONE DA TODI (c. 1236–1306; Italian religious poet)
LECONTE DE LISLE, Charles Marie René (1818–94; French poet)
OEHLENSCHLÄGER, Adam (1779–1850; Danish poet and playwright)
PRÉVOST D'EXILES, Antoine François, Abbé (1697–1763; French novelist)

14—continued

SULLY-PRUDHOMME, René François Armand (1839–1907; French poet)
WOLLSTONECRAFT, Mary (1759–97; British writer)
ZORRILLA Y MORAL, José (1817–93; Spanish poet and dramatist)

15

ALARCÓN Y MENDOZA, Juan Ruiz de (1581–1639; Spanish dramatist)
DIODORUS SICULUS (1st century BC; Greek historian)
PLINY THE YOUNGER (Gaius Plinius Caecilius Secundus, c. 61–c. 113 AD; Roman writer)

16

CHRÉTIEN DE TROYES (12th century AD; French poet)
CYRANO DE BERGERAC, Savinien (1619–55; French writer and dramatist)
KAWABATA YASUNARI (1899–1972; Japanese novelist)
PETRONIUS ARBITER (1st century AD; Roman satirist)

17

CALDERÓN DE LA BARCA, Pedro (1600–81; Spanish dramatist)
GUILLAUME DE LORRIS (13th century; French poet and author)
TANIZAKI JUN-ICHIRO (1886–1965; Japanese novelist)

18

APOLLONIUS OF RHODES (3rd century BC; Greek epic poet)
KAKINOMOTO HITOMARO (c. 680–710; Japanese poet)
THOMAS OF ERCELDOUNE (13th century; English poet and prophet)

19

BENOIT DE SAINTE-MAURE (12th century AD; French poet)
CHIKAMATSU MONZAEMON (Sugimori Nobumori; 1653–1724; Japanese dramatist)
VILLIERS DE L'ISLE-ADAM, Philippe Auguste, Comte de (1838–89; French poet, novelist, and dramatist)

20+

BERNARDIN DE SAINT-PIERRE, Jacques Henri (1737–1814; French naturalist and writer)
DIONYSIUS OF HALICARNASSUS (1st century BC; Greek historian)
DRUMMOND OF HAWTHORNDEN, William (1585–1649; Scots poet)
ECHEGARAY Y EIZAGUIRRE, José (1832–1916; Spanish dramatist)
GOTTFRIED VON STRASSBURG (13th century; German poet)

20+—continued
WALTHER VON DER VOGELWEIDE (c. 1170–
   c. 1230; German poet)

20+—continued
WOLFRAM VON ESCHENBACH (c. 1170–
   c. 1220; German poet)

MUSICIANS AND COMPOSERS

3

BAX, Sir Arnold Edward Trevor (1883–1953;
   British composer)

4

ADAM, Adolphe-Charles (1803–56; French
   composer)
ARNE, Thomas Augustine (1710–78; British
   composer)
BACH, Johann Sebastian (1685–1750;
   German composer and keyboard player)
BERG, Alban (1885–1935; Austrian composer)
BING, Sir Rudolf (1902–   ; British opera
   administrator)
BLOW, John (1649–1708; English composer)
BÖHM, Karl (1894–1981; Austrian conductor)
BULL, John (c. 1562–1628; English composer
   and organist)
BUSH, Alan Dudley (1900–   ; British
   composer)
BUTT, Dame Clara (1873–1936; British
   contralto singer)
BYRD, William (?1543–1623; English
   composer)
CAGE, John (1912–   ; US composer)
HESS, Dame Myra (1890–1965; British pianist)
IVES, Charles (1874–1954; US composer)
LALO, Édouard (1823–92; French composer)
LILL, John (1944–   ; British pianist)
LIND, Jenny (1820–87; Swedish soprano)
NONO, Luigi (1924–   ; Italian composer)
ORFF, Carl (1895–1982; German composer
   and conductor)
WOLF, Hugo (1860–1903; Austrian composer)
WOOD, Sir Henry (1869–1944; British
   conductor)

5

ALKAN, Charles Henri Valentin (C H V
   Morhange, 1813–88; French pianist and
   composer)
ARRAU, Claudio (1903–   ; Chilean pianist)
AUBER, Daniel François Esprit (1782–1871;
   French composer)
AURIC, Georges (1899–   ; French composer)
BAKER, Dame Janet (1933–   ; British mezzo-
   soprano)
BERIO, Luciano (1925–   ; Italian composer)
BIZET, Georges (Alexandre César Léopold B,
   1838–75; French composer)
BLISS, Sir Arthur Edward Drummond (1891–
   1975; British composer)

5—continued

BLOCH, Ernest (1880–1959; Swiss-born
   composer)
BOEHM, Theobald (1794–1881; German
   flautist)
BOULT, Sir Adrian (1889–1983; British
   conductor)
BOYCE, William (c. 1710–79; British
   composer)
BREAM, Julian Alexander (1933–   ; British
   guitarist and lutenist)
BRIAN, Havergal (1876–1972; British
   composer)
BRUCH, Max (1838–1920; German composer)
BÜLOW, Hans Guido, Freiherr von (1830–94;
   German pianist and conductor)
DAVIS, Sir Colin (1927–   ; British conductor)
D'INDY, Vincent (1851–1931; French
   composer)
DUFAY, Guillaume (c. 1400–74; Burgundian
   composer)
DUKAS, Paul (1865–1935; French composer)
DUPRÉ, Marcel (1886–1971; French organist
   and composer)
ELGAR, Sir Edward (1857–1934; British
   composer)
EVANS, Sir Geraint (1922–   ; Welsh baritone)
FALLA, Manuel de (1876–1946; Spanish
   composer)
FAURÉ, Gabriel (1845–1924; French
   composer and organist)
FIELD, John (1782–1837; Irish pianist and
   composer)
FRIML, Rudolph (1879–1972; Czech-born
   composer and pianist)
GIGLI, Beniamino (1890–1957; Italian tenor)
GLUCK, Christoph Willibald (1714–87;
   German composer)
GOBBI, Tito (1915–84; Italian baritone)
GRIEG, Edvard Hagerup (1843–1907;
   Norwegian composer)
GROVE, Sir George (1820–1900; British
   musicologist)
HALLÉ, Sir Charles (Karl Hallé, 1819–1895;
   German conductor and pianist)
HAYDN, Franz Joseph (1732–1809; Austrian
   composer)
HENZE, Hans Werner (1926–   ; German
   composer)
HOLST, Gustav (1874–1934; British composer
   and teacher)

5—continued

IBERT, Jacques (1890–1962; French composer)

LEHÁR, Franz (Ferencz L, 1870–1948; Hungarian composer)

LISZT, Franz (Ferencz L, 1811–86; Hungarian pianist and composer)

LOCKE, Matthew (c. 1622–77; English composer)

LULLY, Jean Baptiste (Giovanni Battista Lulli, 1632–87; French composer)

MELBA, Dame Nellie (Helen Porter Armstrong, 1861–1931; Australian soprano)

MOORE, Gerald (1899–1987; British pianist)

MUNCH, Charles (1892–1968; French conductor)

OGDON, John (1937–   ; British pianist)

PARRY, Sir Hubert (1848–1918; British composer)

PATTI, Adelina (Adela Juana Maria, 1843–1919; Italian-born operatic soprano)

PEARS, Sir Peter (1910–86; British tenor)

RAVEL, Maurice (1875–1937; French composer)

REGER, Max (1873–1916; German composer, organist, and teacher)

SATIE, Erik (1866–1925; French composer)

SHARP, Cecil (1859–1924; British musician)

SOLTI, Sir Georg (1912–   ; Hungarian-born British conductor)

SOUSA, John Philip (1854–1933; US composer and bandmaster)

SPOHR, Louis (Ludwig S, 1784–1859; German violinist and composer)

STERN, Isaac (1920–   ; Russian-born US violinist)

SZELL, George (1897–1970; Hungarian conductor)

TEYTE, Dame Maggie (1888–1976; British soprano)

VERDI, Giuseppe (1813–1901; Italian composer)

WEBER, Carl Maria von (1786–1826; German composer)

WEILL, Kurt (1900–50; German composer)

WIDOR, Charles Marie (1844–1937; French organist and composer)

6

ARNOLD, Malcolm (1921–   ; British composer)

BARBER, Samuel (1910–81; US composer)

BARTÓK, Béla (1881–1945; Hungarian composer)

BISHOP, Sir Henry Rowley (1786–1855; British composer and conductor)

BOULEZ, Pierre (1925–   ; French composer and conductor)

BRAHMS, Johannes (1833–97; German composer)

BRIDGE, Frank (1879–1941; British composer)

6—continued

BURNEY, Charles (1726–1814; British musicologist, organist, and composer)

BUSONI, Ferruccio (1866–1924; Italian virtuoso pianist and composer)

CALLAS, Maria (Maria Anna Kalageropoulos, 1923–77; US-born soprano)

CARTER, Elliott (1908–   ; US composer)

CARUSO, Enrico (1873–1921; Italian tenor)

CASALS, Pablo (Pau C, 1876–1973; Spanish cellist, conductor, and composer)

CHOPIN, Frédéric (François, 1810–49; Polish composer)

CLARKE, Jeremiah (?1673–1707; English composer and organist)

CORTOT, Alfred (1877–1962; French pianist and conductor)

COWELL, Henry (1897–1965; US composer)

CURWEN, John (1816–80; British teacher who perfected the Tonic Sol-fa system)

CURZON, Sir Clifford (1907–82; British pianist)

DAVIES, Sir Peter Maxwell (1934–   ; British composer)

DELIUS, Frederick (1862–1934; British composer)

DIBDIN, Charles (1745–1814; British composer, actor, and singer)

DUPARC, Henri (Marie Eugène Henri Foucques D, 1848–1933; French composer)

DVOŘÁK, Antonín (1841–1904; Czech composer)

ENESCO, Georges (G Enescu, 1881–1955; Romanian violinist and composer)

FLOTOW, Friedrich von (1812–83; German composer)

FRANCK, César Auguste (1822–90; Belgian composer, organist, and teacher)

GALWAY, James (1939–   ; Irish flautist)

GLINKA, Mikhail Ivanovich (1804–57; Russian composer)

GOUNOD, Charles François (1818–93; French composer)

GRÉTRY, André Ernest Modeste (1741–1813; Belgian composer)

GROVES, Sir Charles (1915–   ; British conductor)

HALÉVY, Jacques François (Fromental Elias Levy, 1799–1862; French composer)

HANDEL, George Frederick (1685–1759; German composer)

HARRIS, Roy (1898–1979; US composer)

HOTTER, Hans (1909–   ; German baritone)

HUMMEL, Johann Nepomuk (1778–1837; Hungarian pianist and composer)

JOCHUM, Eugen (1902–   ; German conductor)

KODÁLY, Zoltan (1882–1967; Hungarian composer)

KRENEK, Ernst (1900–   ; Austrian composer)

6—continued

LASSUS, Roland de (*c.* 1532–94; Flemish composer)

LIGETI, György (1923–   ; Hungarian composer)

MAAZEL, Lorin (1930–   ; US conductor)

MAHLER, Gustav (1860–1911; Austrian composer and conductor)

MORLEY, Thomas (1557–1603; English composer, music printer, and organist)

MOZART, Wolfgang Amadeus (1756–91; Austrian composer)

PREVIN, André (Andreas Ludwig Priwin, 1929–   ; German-born conductor, pianist, and composer)

RAMEAU, Jean Philippe (1683–1764; French composer)

RUBBRA, Edmund (1901–86; British composer)

SCHÜTZ, Heinrich (1585–1672; German composer)

TALLIS, Thomas (*c.* 1505–85; English composer)

VARÈSE, Edgard (1883–1965; French composer)

WAGNER, Richard (1813–83; German composer)

WALTER, Bruno (B W Schlesinger, 1876–1962; German conductor)

WALTON, Sir William (1902–83; British composer)

WEBERN, Anton von (1883–1945; Austrian composer)

7

ALBÉNIZ, Isaac Manuel Francisco (1860–1909; Spanish composer and pianist)

ALLEGRI, Gregorio (1582–1652; Italian composer)

ANTHEIL, George (1900–59; US composer)

BABBITT, Milton (1916–   ; US composer)

BEECHAM, Sir Thomas (1879–1961; British conductor)

BELLINI, Vincenzo (1801–35; Italian opera composer)

BENNETT, Richard Rodney (1936–   ; British composer)

BENNETT, Sir William Sterndale (1816–75; British pianist)

BERLIOZ, Hector (1803–69; French composer and conductor)

BORODIN, Aleksandr Porfirevich (1833–87; Russian composer)

BRENDEL, Alfred (1931–   ; Austrian pianist)

BRITTEN, Benjamin, Baron (1913–76; British composer and pianist)

CABALLÉ, Montserrat (1933–   ; Spanish soprano)

CACCINI, Giulio (*c.* 1545–*c.* 1618; Italian singer and composer)

CAMPION, Thomas (*or* Campian, 1567–1620; English composer)

7—continued

CAVALLI, Francesco (1602–76; Italian composer)

COPLAND, Aaron (1900–   ; US composer)

CORELLI, Arcangelo (1653–1713; Italian violinist and composer)

DEBUSSY, Claude (1862–1918; French composer)

DELIBES, Leo (1836–91; French composer)

DOMINGO, Placido (1941–   ; Spanish tenor)

DOWLAND, John (1563–1626; English composer and lutenist)

FARNABY, Giles (*c.* 1565–1640; English composer)

FERRIER, Kathleen (1912–53; British contralto)

GALUPPI, Baldassare (1706–85; Venetian composer)

GIBBONS, Orlando (1583–1625; English composer, organist, and virginalist)

GIULINI, Carlo Maria (1914–   ; Italian conductor)

HAMMOND, Dame Joan (1912–   ; British soprano)

HOFMANN, Joseph Casimir (1876–1957; Polish-born pianist)

IRELAND, John Nicholson (1879–1962; British composer)

JANÁČEK, Leoš (1854–1928; Czech composer)

JOACHIM, Joseph (1831–1907; Hungarian violinist and composer)

KARAJAN, Herbert von (1908–   ; Austrian conductor)

KUBELIK, Rafael (1914–   ; Czech conductor)

LAMBERT, Constant (1905–51; British composer and conductor)

LEHMANN, Lilli (1848–1929; German soprano)

LEHMANN, Lotte (1885–1976; German soprano)

MALCOLM, George John (1917–   ; British harpsichordist)

MARTINŮ, Bohuslav (1890–1959; Czech composer)

MENOTTI, Gian Carlo (1911–   ; Italian-born US composer)

MENUHIN, Sir Yehudi (1916–   ; British violinist)

MILHAUD, Darius (1892–1974; French composer)

MONTEUX, Pierre (1875–1964; French conductor)

NICOLAI, Otto Ehrenfried (1810–49; German conductor and composer)

NIELSEN, Carl (1865–1931; Danish composer and conductor)

NIKISCH, Arthur (1855–1922; Hungarian conductor)

NILSSON, Birgit Marta (1918–   ; Swedish soprano)

7—continued

OKEGHEM, Jean d' (*c.* 1425—*c.* 1495; Flemish composer)

ORMANDY, Eugene (E Blau, 1899—1985; Hungarian-born US conductor)

PÉROTIN (Latin name: Perotinus Magnus, *c.* 1155—*c.* 1202; French composer)

POULENC, Francis (1899—1963; French composer)

PUCCINI, Giacomo (1858—1924; Italian opera composer)

PURCELL, Henry (1659—95; English composer and organist)

RICHTER, Hans (1843—1916; Hungarian conductor)

RICHTER, Sviatoslav (1914— ; Soviet pianist)

RODRIGO, Joaquín (1902— ; Spanish composer)

ROSSINI, Gioacchino Antonio (1792—1868; Italian composer)

ROUSSEL, Albert (1869—1937; French composer)

RUGGLES, Carl (1876—1971; US composer)

SALIERI, Antonio (1750—1825; Italian composer and conductor)

SARGENT, Sir Malcolm (1895—1967; British conductor)

SCHUMAN, William (1910— ; US composer)

SMETANA, Bedřich (1824—84; Bohemian composer)

SOLOMON (S Cutner, 1902— ; British pianist)

STAINER, Sir John (1840—1901; British composer and organist)

STAMITZ, Johann (Jan Stamic, 1717—57; Bohemian composer)

STRAUSS, Richard (1864—1949; German composer and conductor)

THIBAUD, Jacques (1880—1953; French violinist)

THOMSON, Virgil (1896— ; US composer and conductor)

TIPPETT, Sir Michael (1905— ; British composer)

VIVALDI, Antonio (1678—1741; Italian composer and violinist)

WARLOCK, Peter (Philip Heseltine, 1894—1930; British composer and music scholar)

WEELKES, Thomas (*c.* 1575—1623; English composer and organist)

WELLESZ, Egon (1885—1974; Austrian composer)

XENAKIS, Yannis (1922— ; Greek composer)

8

ALBINONI, Tomaso (1671—1750; Italian composer)

ANSERMET, Ernest (1883—1969; Swiss conductor)

BERKELEY, Sir Lennox Randal Francis (1903— ; British composer)

8—continued

BRUCKNER, Anton (1824—96; Austrian composer and organist)

CHABRIER, Emmanuel (1841—94; French composer)

CHAUSSON, Ernest (1855—99; French composer)

CIMAROSA, Domenico (1749—1801; Italian composer)

CLEMENTI, Muzio (1752—1832; Italian pianist and composer)

COUPERIN, François (1668—1733; French composer)

DOHNÁNYI, Erno (Ernst von D, 1877—1960; Hungarian composer and pianist)

FLAGSTAD, Kirsten Malfrid (1895—1962; Norwegian soprano)

GERSHWIN, George (Jacob Gershvin, 1898—1937; US composer)

GESUALDO, Carlo, Prince of Venosa (*c.* 1560—1631; Italian composer)

GLAZUNOV, Aleksandr Konstantinovich (1865—1936; Russian composer)

GOOSSENS, Sir Eugene (1893—1962; British conductor and composer)

GRAINGER, Percy Aldridge (1882—1961; Australian composer and pianist)

GRANADOS, Enrique (1867—1916; Spanish composer and pianist)

HONEGGER, Arthur (1892—1955; French composer)

HOROWITZ, Vladimir (1904— ; Russian pianist)

KREISLER, Fritz (1875—1962; Austrian violinist)

MACONCHY, Elizabeth (1907— ; British composer)

MARENZIO, Luca (1553—99; Italian composer)

MASCAGNI, Pietro (1863—1945; Italian composer)

MASSENET, Jules (1842—1912; French composer)

MELCHIOR, Lauritz (1890—1973; Danish tenor)

MESSAGER, André (1853—1929; French composer and conductor)

MESSIAEN, Olivier (1908— ; French composer, organist, and teacher)

MILSTEIN, Nathan (1904— ; US violinist)

MUSGRAVE, Thea (1928— ; Scottish composer)

OISTRAKH, David (1908—75; Russian violinist)

PAGANINI, Niccolò (1782—1840; Italian violinist)

PHILIDOR, André Danican (d. 1730; French musician)

RESPIGHI, Ottorino (1879—1936; Italian composer)

SCHNABEL, Artur (1882—1951; Austrian pianist)

8—continued

SCHUBERT, Franz (1797–1828; Austrian composer)

SCHUMANN, Elisabeth (1885–1952; German-born soprano)

SCHUMANN, Robert (1810–56; German composer)

SCRIABIN, Alexander (1872–1915; Russian composer and pianist)

SESSIONS, Roger (1896–1985; US composer)

SIBELIUS, Jean (Johan Julius Christian S, 1865–1957; Finnish composer)

STANFORD, Sir Charles (1852–1924; Irish composer)

SULLIVAN, Sir Arthur (1842–1900; British composer)

TAVERNER, John (c. 1495–1545; English composer)

TE KANAWA, Dame Kiri (1944– ; New Zealand soprano)

TELEMANN, Georg Philipp (1681–1767; German composer)

VICTORIA, Tomás Luis de (c. 1548–1611; Spanish composer)

WILLIAMS, John (1941– ; Australian guitarist)

ZABALETA, Nicanor (1907– ; Spanish harpist)

9

ADDINSELL, Richard (1904–77; British composer)

ASHKENAZY, Vladimir (1937– ; Russian pianist and conductor)

BALAKIREV, Mili Alekseevich (1837–1910; Russian composer)

BARENBOIM, Daniel (1942– ; Israeli pianist and composer)

BEETHOVEN, Ludwig van (1770–1827; German composer)

BERNSTEIN, Leonard (1918– ; US conductor, composer, and pianist)

BOULANGER, Nadia (1887–1979; French composer, teacher, and conductor)

BUXTEHUDE, Dietrich (1637–1707; Danish organist and composer)

CHALIAPIN, Feodor Ivanovich (1873–1938; Russian bass)

CHERUBINI, Maria Luigi (1760–1842; Italian composer)

CHRISTOFF, Boris (1919– ; Bulgarian singer)

DOLMETSCH, Arnold (1858–1940; British musician and instrument maker)

DONIZETTI, Gaetano (1797–1848; Italian composer)

DUNSTABLE, John (d. 1453; English composer)

HINDEMITH, Paul (1895–1963; German composer and viola player)

HODDINOTT, Alun (1929– ; Welsh composer)

9—continued

KLEMPERER, Otto (1885–1973; German conductor)

LANDOWSKA, Wanda (1877–1959; Polish-born harpsichordist)

MACKERRAS, Sir Charles (1925– ; US-born Australian conductor)

MALIPIERO, Gian Francesco (1882–1973; Italian composer and teacher)

MEYERBEER, Giacomo (Jacob Liebmann Beer, 1791–1864; German composer and pianist)

OFFENBACH, Jacques (J Eberst, 1819–80; French composer)

PAVAROTTI, Luciano (1935– ; Italian tenor)

PERGOLESI, Giovanni (1710–36; Italian composer)

SCARLATTI, Domenico (1685–1757; Italian composer, harpsichordist, and organist)

STOKOWSKI, Leopold (1882–1977; British-born conductor)

TORTELIER, Paul (1914– ; French cellist)

TOSCANINI, Arturo (1867–1957; Italian conductor)

10

BARBIROLLI, Sir John (1899–1970; British conductor)

BIRTWISTLE, Harrison (1934– ; British composer)

BOCCHERINI, Luigi (1743–1805; Italian violoncellist and composer)

GALLI-CURCI, Amelita (1882–1963; Italian soprano)

LOS ANGELES, Victoria de (1923– ; Spanish soprano)

MENGELBERG, William (1871–1951; Dutch conductor)

MONTEVERDI, Claudio (1567–1643; Italian composer)

MUSSORGSKI, Modest Petrovich (1839–81; Russian composer)

PADEREWSKI, Ignacy (1860–1941; Polish pianist and composer)

PALESTRINA, Giovanni Pierluigi da (?1525–94; Italian composer)

PENDERECKI, Krzysztof (1933– ; Polish composer)

PRAETORIUS, Michael (M Schultheiss, 1571–1621; German composer)

RAWSTHORNE, Alan (1905–71; British composer)

RUBINSTEIN, Anton (1829–94; Russian pianist and composer)

RUBINSTEIN, Artur (1888–1982; Polish-born pianist)

SAINT-SAENS, Camille (1835–1921; French composer, conductor, pianist, and organist)

SCHOENBERG, Arnold (1874–1951; Austrian-born composer)

SKALKOTTAS, Nikos (1904–49; Greek composer)

10—continued

STRADIVARI, Antonio (?1644—1737; Italian violin maker)

STRAVINSKY, Igor (1882—1971; Russian-born composer)

SUTHERLAND, Dame Joan (1926— ; Australian soprano)

TETRAZZINI, Luisa (1871—1940; Italian soprano)

VILLA-LOBOS, Heitor (1887—1959; Brazilian composer)

11

CHARPENTIER, Gustave (1860—1956; French composer)

FURTWÄNGLER, Wilhelm (1886—1954; German conductor)

HUMPERDINCK, Engelbert (1854—1921; German composer)

LEONCAVALLO, Ruggiero (1858—1919; Italian composer)

LESCHETIZKY, Theodor (1830—1915; Polish pianist and piano teacher)

LUTOSLAWSKI, Witold (1913— ; Polish composer)

MENDELSSOHN, Felix (Jacob Ludwig Felix Mendelssohn-Bartholdy, 1809—47; German composer)

RACHMANINOV, Sergei (1873—1943; Russian composer, pianist, and conductor)

SCHWARZKOPF, Elisabeth (1915— ; German soprano)

STOCKHAUSEN, Karlheinz (1928— ; German composer)

SZYMANOWSKI, Karol (1882—1937; Polish composer)

11—continued

TCHAIKOVSKY, Peter Ilich (1840—93; Russian composer)

WOLF-FERRARI, Ermanno (1876—1948; Italian composer)

12

DALLAPICCOLA, Luigi (1904—1975; Italian composer and pianist)

GUIDO D'AREZZO (c. 990—c. 1050; Italian monk and musical theorist)

KHACHATURIAN, Aram Ilich (1903—78; Soviet composer)

KOUSSEVITSKY, Sergei (1874—1951; Russian composer)

13

ROUGET DE L'ISLE, Claude Joseph (1760—1836; French composer)

14

FISCHER-DIESKAU, Dietrich (1925— ; German baritone)

JAQUES-DALCROZE, Émile (1865—1950; Swiss composer)

JOSQUIN DES PREZ (c. 1450—1521; Flemish composer)

RIMSKY-KORSAKOV, Nikolai (1844—1908; Russian composer)

15

COLERIDGE-TAYLOR, Samuel (1875—1912; British composer)

VAUGHAN WILLIAMS, Ralph (1872—1958; British composer)

17

STRAUSS THE YOUNGER, Johann (1825—99; Austrian violinist, conductor, and composer)

POPULAR MUSICIANS

2	3—continued	4—continued	4—continued
U2	WHO, The	CHIC	KERN, Jerome
3	YES	COLE, Nat 'King'	KIDD, Johnny
ABC	**4**	COMO, Perry	KING, B B
ANT, Adam	10CC	CURE, The	KING, Carole
DAY, Doris	ABBA	DION	KING, Jonathon
ENO, Brian	AC/DC	DURY, Ian	KISS
JAM, The	ANKA, Paul	EDDY, Duane	KITT, Eartha
LEE, Brenda	BAEZ, Joan	FAME, Georgie	LOWE, Nick
MUD	BAND, The	FORD, Tennessee	LULU
O.M.D. (Orchestral	BART, Lionel	Ernie	LYNN, Vera
Manoeuvres in the	BECK, Jeff	FREE	MANN, Barry
Dark)	BLUE, Barry	FURY, Billy	MAZE
ONO, Yoko	BROS	GAYE, Marvin	MONK, Thelonius
RAY, Johnny	BUSH, Kate	GETZ, Stan	MOST, Mickie
REA, Chris	BYRD, Charlie	IDOL, Billy	MOVE, The
UFO	CARS, The	JOEL, Billy	NICE, The
VEE, Bobby	CASH, Johnny	JOHN, Elton	PAUL, Billy
WAR	CHER	KALE, J J	PIAF, Edith

4—continued
REED, Lou
RICH, Charlie
ROSS, Diana
RUSH
SADE
SHAW, Artie
SHAW, Sandie
STYX
T REX
UB40
WHAM!
WOLF, Howlin'
WOOD, Roy
WRAY, Link

5
ADLER, Larry
ADLER, Lou
ASWAD
BAKER, Peter 'Ginger'
BASIE, Count
BERRY, Chuck
BLACK, Cilla
BOLAN, Marc
BONDS, Gary US
BOONE, Pat
BOWIE, David
BREAD
BROWN, James
BYRDS, The
CHINN, Nicky
CLARK, Dave
CLARK, Petula
CLASH, The
CLIFF, Jimmy
COHEN, Leonard
COOKE, Sam
CREAM, The
CROCE, Jim
DARIN, Bobby
DAVIS, Miles
DAVIS, Sammy, Jnr
DAVIS, Spencer,
  Group
DELLS, The
DOORS, The
DYLAN, Bob
ESSEX, David
FACES, The
FERRY, Bryan
FLACK, Roberta
FREED, Alan
GREEN, Al
HALEY, Bill
HANDY, William
  Christopher
HAYES, Isaac
HEART
HINES, Earl
HOLLY, Buddy
JAMES, Bob

5—continued
JAMES, Tommy, &
  The Shondells
JARRE, Jean-Michel
JONES, Quincy
JONES, Tom
KINKS, The
KLEIN, Allen
LAINE, Frankie
LEWIS, Huey, & The
  News
LEWIS, Jerry Lee
LYMON, Frankie, &
  The Teenagers
MCCOY, Van
MOORE, Gary
MOYET, Alison
NUMAN, Gary
O'JAYS, The
PERRY, Richard
PRICE, Alan
PROBY, P J
QUEEN
REDDY, Helen
SAXON
SAYER, Leo
SCOTT, Ronnie
SEGER, Bob
SIMON, Carly
SLADE
SMITH, Bessie
STARR, Ringo
STING
SWEET, The
TATUM, Art
WHITE, Barry
WYMAN, Bill
YAZOO
YOUNG, Neil
YOUNG, Paul
ZAPPA, Frank
ZZ TOP

6
ALPERT, Herb
ARGENT
ATKINS, Chet
ATWELL, Winifred
AVALON, Frankie
BALDRY, Long John
BASSEY, Shirley
BECHET, Sidney
BENSON, George
BERLIN, Irving
BOLDEN, Buddy
BONEY M
BOSTON
BROWNE, Jackson
BURDON, Eric
CHAPIN, Harry
COCKER, Joe
COODER, Ry

6—continued
COOPER, Alice
COUGAR, John
CREOLE, Kid, & The
  Coconuts
CROSBY, Bing
DAMNED, The
DEKKER, Desmond
DENVER, John
DOMINO, Fats
DR HOOK
EAGLES, The
EASTON, Sheena
EQUALS, The
FABIAN
FAMILY
FISHER, Eddie
GELDOF, Bob
HARRIS, Emmylou
HOOKER, John Lee
HUNTER, Ian
JAGGER, Mick
JOLSON, Al
JOPLIN, Janis
KNIGHT, Gladys, &
  The Pips
KOOPER, Al
KORNER, Alexis
KRAMER, Billy J
LAUPER, Cyndi
LEIBER, Jerry
LENNON, John
LERNER, Alan Jay
MARLEY, Bob, & The
  Wailers
MARTIN, George
MARTIN, John
MATHIS, Johnny
MAYALL, John
MCLEAN, Don
MIDLER, Bette
MILLER, Glenn
MILLER, Steve
MINGUS, Charlie
MONTEZ, Chris
MORTON, Jelly Roll
NELSON, Ricky
NELSON, Willie
NEWMAN, Randy
NUGENT, Ted
OSMOND, Donny
PALMER, Robert
PARKER, Charlie
PARKER, Colonel
  Tom
PARTON, Dolly
PAXTON, Tom
PITNEY, Gene
POLICE, The
PORTER, Cole
PRINCE

6—continued
REEVES, Jim
REVERE, Paul, & The
  Raiders
RICHIE, Lionel
RIVERS, Johnny
ROGERS, Kenny
SEDAKA, Neil
SEEGER, Pete
SIMONE, Nina
SLEDGE, Percy
SUMMER, Donna
TAUPIN, Bernie
TAYLOR, James
THOMAS, B J
TROGGS, The
TURNER, Ike & Tina
TWITTY, Conway
VALENS, Ritchie
VINTON, Bobby
WALLER, Fats
WATERS, Muddy
WEBBER, Andrew
  Lloyd
WILSON, Jackie
WINTER, Edgar
WINTER, Johny
WOMACK, Bobby
WONDER, Stevie

7
AMERICA
ANIMALS, The
BALLARD, Hank
BEATLES
BEE GEES, The
BENNETT, Tony
BLONDIE
BON JOVI
BRUBECK, Dave
CALVERT, Eddie
CASSIDY, David
CHAPMAN, Mike
CHARLES, Ray
CHECKER, Chubby
CLAPTON, Eric
CLOONEY, Rosemary
COCHRAN, Eddie
COLLINS, Judy
COLLINS, Phil
DE BURGH, Chris
DIAMOND, Neil
DIDDLEY, Bo
DONEGAN, Lonnie
DONOVAN
EDMUNDS, Dave
EPSTEIN, Brian
FRANCIS, Connie
GABRIEL, Peter
GENESIS
GLITTER, Gary
GOODMAN, Benny

7—continued
GUTHRIE, Woody
HAMPTON, Lionel
HANCOCK, Herbie
HENDRIX, Jimi
HOLIDAY, Billie
HOLLIES, The
JACKSON, Mahalia
JACKSON, Michael
JACKSON, Millie
JARREAU, Al
LOFGREN, Nils
MADNESS
MADONNA
MANILOW, Barry
MARTINO, Al
MICHAEL, George
MONKEES, The
NILSSON
ORBISON, Roy
OSMONDS, The
PERKINS, Carl
PRESLEY, Elvis
PRESTON, Billy
RAINBOW
REDDING, Otis
RICHARD, Cliff
RICHARD, Keith
RODGERS, Richard
  Charles
RUSSELL, Leon
SANTANA
SCRAGGS, Boz
SEEKERS, The
SHADOWS, The
SHANKAR, Ravi
SHANNON, Del
SINATRA, Frank
SPECTOR, Phil
SQUEEZE
STEVENS, Cat
STEWART, Rod
TRAFFIC
TURTLES, The
VAUGHAN, Sarah
VINCENT, Gene
WAKEMAN, Rick
WARWICK, Dionne
WHITMAN, Slim
WIZZARD
WYNETTE, Tammy
ZOMBIES, The

8
ANDERSEN, Eric
AZNAVOUR, Charles
CAMPBELL, Glen
CHI-LITES, The
COASTERS, The
COLTRANE, John
CRYSTALS, The
DRIFTERS, The

8—continued
FOUR ACES, The
FOUR TOPS, The
FRAMPTON, Peter
FRANKLIN, Aretha
HAMLISCH, Marvin
HARRISON, George
HAWKWIND
HEATWAVE
INK SPOTS
JENNINGS, Waylon
MARSALIS, Wynton
MAYFIELD, Curtis
MEAT LOAF
MINNELLI, Liza
MIRACLES, The
MITCHELL, Joni
MORRISON, Van
OLDFIELD, Mike
OSBOURNE, Ozzy
PETERSON, Oscar
  Emmanuel
PICKETTS, Wilson
PLATTERS, The
RAFFERTY, Gerry
ROBINSON, Smokey
RONETTES, The
RONSTADT, Linda
SONDHEIM, Stephen
SPECIALS, The
STIGWOOD, Robert
STROLLER, Mike
SUPREMES, The
ULTRAVOX
VANDROSS, Luther

9
AIR SUPPLY
ARMSTRONG, Louis
BACHARACH, Burt
BADFINGER
BEACH BOYS, The
BEEFHEART, Captain
BELAFONTE, Harry
BUCKS FIZZ
CHIPMUNKS, The
CRUSADERS, The
ELLINGTON, Duke
FAITHFULL, Marianne
FOGELBERG, Dan
FOREIGNER
GILLESPIE, Dizzy
GOLDSBORO, Booby
GRAPPELLI,
  Stephane
LEADBELLY
LITTLE EVA
LYTTELTON,
  Humphrey
MARMALADE
MCCARTNEY, Paul
MEN AT WORK

9—continued
MOTORHEAD
O'SULLIVAN, Gilbert
PINK FLOYD
REINHARDT, Django
ROSE ROYCE
ROXY MUSIC
SCORPIONS
SEARCHERS, The
SHIRELLES, The
SIMPLY RED
STATUS QUO
STEELY DAN
STREISAND, Barbra
THIN LIZZY
TOWNSHEND, Pete
URIAH HEEP
YARDBIRDS, The

10
AMEN CORNER
BAD COMPANY
BANANARAMA
CARMICHAEL, Hoagy
CARPENTERS, The
COMMODORES, The
DEEP PURPLE
DR FEELGOOD
DURAN DURAN
EURYTHMICS, The
FITZGERALD, Ella
FUNKADELIC
IRON MAIDEN
JETHRO TULL
LITTLE FEAT
LONG RYDERS, The
MOODY BLUES
MUNGO JERRY
NEWTON-JOHN,
  Olivia
PRETENDERS, The
SCOTT-HERON, Gil
SEX PISTOLS, The
SMALL FACES, The
STRANGLERS, The
STYLISTICS, The
WASHINGTON, Dinah
WHITESNAKE
ZAGER & EVANS

11
ARMATRADING, Joan
BEIDERBECKE, Bix
CULTURE CLUB
DIRE STRAITS
FOUNDATIONS
FOUR SEASONS, The
HUMAN LEAGUE
IMPRESSIONS, The
JACKSON FIVE
JOY DIVISION
KING CRIMSON

11—continued
LED ZEPPELIN
LINDISFARNE
MANFRED MANN
MARVELETTES, The
OHIO PLAYERS
PET SHOP BOYS
PROCUL HARUM
SIMPLE MINDS
SPRINGFIELD, Dusty
SPRINGFIELD, Rick
SPRINGSTEEN, Bruce
TEMPTATIONS, The
THEODORAKIS, Mikis
WISHBONE ASH

12
BLACK SABBATH
BOOMTOWN RATS
COCKNEY REBEL
FLEETWOOD MAC
GRATEFUL DEAD
HALL AND OATES
HOT CHOCOLATE
HOUSEMARTINS, The
SONNY AND CHER
STYLE COUNCIL
TALKING HEADS
YOUNG RASCALS,
  The

13
HAMMERSTEIN II,
  Oscar
ISLEY BROTHERS
KRISTOFFERSON,
  Kris
LITTLE RICHARD
LOVIN' SPOONFUL
MAMAS AND PAPAS
MOTT THE HOOPLE
REO SPEEDWAGON
ROLLING STONES,
  The
SPANDAU BALLET
STAPLE SINGERS
TEARS FOR FEARS
THREE DOG NIGHT

14
ALLMAN BROTHERS
BAY CITY ROLLERS
BLUE OYSTER CULT
DOOBIE BROTHERS
FIFTH DIMENSION
HERMAN'S HERMITS
JON AND VANGELIS
KOOL AND THE
  GANG
SEALS AND CROFTS

15
DETROIT SPINNERS
EVERLEY BROTHERS

16
AVERAGE WHITE
  BAND
BOOKER T AND THE
  MG'S
EARTH WIND AND
  FIRE
PETER, PAUL AND
  MARY

17
GRAND FUNK
  RAILROAD
JEFFERSON
  AIRPLANE
RIGHTEOUS
  BROTHERS

17—continued
SIMON AND
  GARFUNKEL
SWINGING BLUE
  JEANS

18
BLOOD SWEAT AND
  TEARS
BUFFALO
  SPRINGFIELD
FAIRPORT
  CONVENTION
PUBLIC IMAGE
  LIMITED

19
BARCLAY JAMES
  HARVEST

20+
BACHMAN-TURNER
  OVERDRIVE
CREEDENCE
  CLEARWATER
  REVIVAL
CROSBY, STILLS,
  NASH AND YOUNG
DEXYS MIDNIGHT
  RUNNERS
ELECTRIC LIGHT
  ORCHESTRA

20+—continued
EMERSON, LAKE
  AND PALMER
FREDDIE AND THE
  DREAMERS
GERRY AND THE
  PACEMAKERS
K C AND THE
  SUNSHINE BAND
SIOUXSIE AND THE
  BANSHEES
SLY AND THE
  FAMILY STONE

STAGE AND SCREEN PERSONALITIES

3
BOW, Clara (US film actress)
COX, Robert (English comic actor)
FOY, Eddie (US actor)
HAY, Will (British comedian)
LEE, Gypsy Rose (US entertainer)
RAY, Satyajit (Indian film director)
RIX, Sir Brian (British actor)
SIM, Alastair (Scottish actor)

4
ARNE, Susanna Maria (British actress)
BIRD, Theophilus (English actor)
BOND, Edward (British dramatist)
CANE, Andrew (English actor)
COBB, Lee J (US actor)
COOK, Peter (British comedy actor)
DALY, Augustin (US theatre manager)
DEAN, James (US film actor)
DUFF, Mrs (US actress)
DUSE, Eleonora (Italian actress)
FORD, John (US film director)
GISH, Lillian (US actress)
GOLD, Jimmy (British comedian)
GRAY, Dulcie (British actress)
GRAY, 'Monsewer' Eddie (British comedian)
HALL, Sir Peter (British theatre director)
HOPE, Bob (US comedian, born in Britain)
KEAN, Edmund (British actor)
KNOX, Teddy (British comedian)
LAHR, Bert (US actor)
LANG, Fritz (German film director)
LEAN, Sir David (British film director)
LUNT, Alfred (US actor)
OWEN, Alun Davies (British dramatist)
PAGE, Geraldine (US actress)
PIAF, Edith (French cabaret and music-hall
  performer)

4—continued
RANK, J Arthur (British industrialist and film
  executive)
REED, Sir Carol (British film director)
REID, Beryl (British actress)
RIGG, Diana (British actress)
SHER, Anthony (British actor)
TATE, Harry (British music-hall comedian)
TREE, Sir Herbert Beerbohm (British actor and
  theatre manager)
WEST, Mae (US actress)

5
ALLEN, Chesney (British comedian)
ALLEN, Woody (US film actor and director)
ARMIN, Robert (British actor)
ASTON, Anthony (Irish actor)
BADEL, Alan (British actor)
BARON, André (French actor)
BARON, Michel (French actor)
BARRY, Elizabeth (English actress)
BARRY, Spranger (Irish actor)
BATES, Alan (British actor)
BETTY, William Henry West (British boy actor)
BLOOM, Claire (British actress)
BOOTH, Barton (British actor)
BOOTH, Edwin Thomas (US actor)
BOOTH, Junius Brutus (US actor)
BOYER, Charles (French film actor)
BRICE, Fanny (US actress)
BROOK, Peter (British theatre director)
BROWN, Pamela (British actor)
BRYAN, Dora (British actress)
CAPRA, Frank (US film director, born in Italy)
CAREY, Joyce (British actress)
CARNÉ, Marcel (French film director)
CLAIR, René (French film director)
CLIVE, Kitty (British actress)
CONTI, Italia (British actress)

5—continued

DAVIS, Bette (US film actress)
DENCH, Dame Judi (British actress)
EDWIN, John (British actor)
EKHOF, Konrad (German actor and director)
EVANS, Dame Edith (British actress)
FLYNN, Errol (Australian actor, born in Tasmania)
FONDA, Henry (US film actor and director)
GABIN, Jean (French film actor)
GABLE, Clark (US film actor)
GARBO, Greta (Swedish actress)
GOZZI, Carlo (Italian dramatist)
GRANT, Cary (US film actor, born in England)
GWYNN, Nell (English actress)
HAIGH, Kenneth (British actor)
HANDL, Dame Irene (British actress)
HAWKS, Howard (US film director)
HICKS, Sir Seymour (British actor-manager)
IRONS, Jeremy (British actor)
KAZAN, Elia (US stage and film director and novelist)
KELLY, Grace (US film actress)
KORDA, Sir Alexander (British film producer and director)
LA RUE, Danny (British female impersonator)
LEIGH, Vivien (British actress)
LENYA, Lotte (German actress and singer)
LIFAR, Serge (Russian ballet dancer and choreographer)
LLOYD, Harold (US film comedian)
LLOYD, Marie (British music-hall entertainer)
LOREN, Sophia (Italian film actress)
LOSEY, Joseph (US film director)
MAYER, Louis B (US film producer, born in Russia)
MILES, Bernard (British theatre director and actor)
MILLS, Sir John (British actor)
MOORE, Dudley (British actor and songwriter)
NERVO, Jimmy (British comedian)
NIVEN, David (British film actor)
PAIGE, Elaine (British actress and singer)
PASCO, Richard (British actor)
PETIT, Roland (French ballet dancer and choreographer)
POLUS (Greek tragic actor)
POPOV, Alexei Dmitrevich (Soviet director)
POPOV, Oleg Konstantinovich (Russian clown)
POWER, Tyrone (US actor)
PRYCE, Jonathan (British actor)
ROBEY, Sir George Edward (British music-hall comedian)
SMITH, Maggie Natalie (British actress)
TERRY, Dame Ellen Alice (British actress)
TOPOL, Chaim (Israeli actor)
TRACY, Spencer (US film actor)
TUTIN, Dorothy (British actress)
WAJDA, Andrzej (Polish film director)
WAYNE, John (US film actor)

6

ADRIAN, Max (British actor)
AINLEY, Henry (British actor)
AITKEN, Maria (British actress)
ALIZON (French actor)
ALLEYN, Edward (English actor)
ARNAUD, Yvonne Germaine (French actress)
ARTAUD, Antonin (French actor, poet, producer, and theoretician of the theatre)
ASHTON, Sir Frederick (British ballet dancer and choreographer, born in Ecuador)
ATKINS, Eileen (British actress)
BALCON, Sir Michael (British film producer)
BARDOT, Brigitte (French film actress)
BARNUM, Phineas Taylor (US showman)
BAYLIS, Lilian (British theatre manager)
BÉJART, Joseph (French actor)
BÉJART, Maurice (French ballet dancer and choreographer)
BENSON, Sir Frank (British actor-manager)
BLASIS, Carlo (Italian dance teacher)
BOCAGE (French actor)
BOGART, Humphrey (US film actor)
BRANDO, Marlon (US actor)
BRIERS, Richard (British actor)
BROOKE, Gustavus Vaughan (British actor)
BROUGH, Lionel (British actor)
BROWNE, Robert (English actor)
BRYANT, Michael (British actor)
BUÑUEL, Luis (Spanish film director)
BURTON, Richard Walter (British actor, born in Wales)
CAGNEY, James (US actor)
CALLOW, Simon (British actor)
CANTOR, Eddie (US singer and actor)
CASSON, Sir Lewis (British actor and director)
CIBBER, Colley (British actor-manager)
COLMAN, Ronald (British actor)
CONWAY, William Augustus (British actor)
COOPER, Dame Gladys (British actress)
COOPER, Gary (US film actor)
COWARD, Sir Noël (British dramatist, composer, and actor)
COWELL, Joe Leathley (British actor)
CRANKO, John (British choreographer, born in South Africa)
CROSBY, Bing (US popular singer and film actor)
CURTIS, Tony (US film actor)
DE SICA, Vittorio (Italian film director)
DEVINE, George Alexander Cassady (British theatre manager, director, and actor)
DIGGES, Dudley (British actor)
DISNEY, Walt (US film producer and animator)
DRAPER, Ruth (US actress)
DREYER, Carl Theodor (Danish film director)
DUNCAN, Isadora (US dancer)
FIELDS, Gracie (British popular entertainer)
FIELDS, W C (US actor)
FINLAY, Frank (British actor)
FINNEY, Albert (British actor)

6—continued

FLEURY (French actor)
FOKINE, Michel (Russian ballet dancer and choreographer)
FORMAN, Miloš (Czech film director)
FORMBY, George (British music hall singer)
GODARD, Jean-Luc (French film director)
GORING, Marius (British actor)
GRAHAM, Martha (US ballet dancer and choreographer)
GUITRY, Sacha (French actor and dramatist)
HARLOW, Jean (US film actress)
HERZOG, Werner (German film director)
HILLER, Dame Wendy (British actress)
HOWARD, Leslie (British actor of Hungarian descent)
IRVING, Sir Henry (British actor and manager)
JACOBI, Derek (British actor)
JOLSON, Al (US actor and singer)
JORDAN, Dorothy (British actress)
JOUVET, Louis (French actor and theatre director)
KEATON, Buster (US comedian of silent films)
KEMBLE, John Philip (British actor and manager)
KENDAL, Felicity (British actress)
KOONEN, Alisa Georgievna (Soviet actress)
LANDEN, Dinsdale (British actor)
LAUDER, Sir Harry (Scottish singer and music-hall comedian)
LEMMON, Jack (US actor)
LESSER, Anton (British actor)
LILLIE, Beatrice Gladys (British actress, born in Canada)
LIPMAN, Maureen (British actress)
MARTIN, Mary (US actress)
MASSEY, Daniel (British actor)
MASSEY, Raymond Hart (Canadian actor)
MCEWAN, Geraldine (British actress)
MCKERN, Leo (Australian actor)
MERMAN, Ethel (US actress)
MONROE, Marilyn (US film actress)
MORLEY, Robert (British actor)
O'TOOLE, Peter (British actor)
PETIPA, Marius (French dancer and choreographer)
PORTER, Eric (British actor)
QUAYLE, Sir Anthony (British actor)
RACHEL (French actress)
RÉJANE (French actress)
ROBSON, Dame Flora (British actress)
ROGERS, Ginger (US actress and singer)
ROWLEY, Thomas (English dramatist and actor)
SHUTER, Ned (British actor)
SINDEN, Donald (British actor)
STEELE, Tommy (British singer and actor)
STREEP, Meryl (US actress)
SUZMAN, Janet (British actress)
TAYLOR, Elizabeth (US film actress, born in England)

6—continued

TEARLE, Godfrey Seymour (British actor)
TEMPLE, Shirley (US film actress)
TILLEY, Vesta (British music-hall entertainer)
WARREN, William (US actor, born in Britain)
WELLES, Orson (US film actor and director)
WILDER, Billy (US film director, born in Austria)
WOLFIT, Sir Donald (British actor and manager)

7

ACHURCH, Janet (British actress)
ACKLAND, Joss (British actor)
AESOPUS, Claudius (Roman tragic actor)
ALLGOOD, Sara (Irish actress)
ANTOINE, André (French actor, director, and theatre manager)
BEAUVAL (French actor)
BELLAMY, George Anne (British actress)
BENNETT, Hywel (British actor, born in Wales)
BENNETT, Jill (British actress)
BERGMAN, Ingmar (Swedish film and stage director)
BERGMAN, Ingrid (Swedish actress)
BERGNER, Elisabeth (Austrian actress)
BLAKELY, Colin (British actor)
BOGARDE, Dirk (British film actor of Dutch descent)
BRANAGH, Kenneth (British actor)
BRESSON, Robert (French film director)
BURBAGE, Richard (English actor)
CALVERT, Louis (British actor)
CASARÉS, Maria (French actress)
CELESTE, Céline (French actress)
CHABROL, Claude (French film director)
CHAPLIN, Charlie (US film actor, born in Britain)
COLBERT, Claudette (US film actress, born in France)
COLLIER, Constance (British actress)
COMPTON, Fay (British actress)
CONDELL, Henry (English actor)
CORALLI, Jean (Italian ballet dancer and choreographer)
CORNELL, Katharine (US actress)
DEBURAU, Jean-Gaspard (French pantomimist, born in Bohemia)
DÉJAZET, Pauline-Virginie (French actress)
DELYSIA, Alice (French actress and singer)
DE MILLE, Cecil B (US film producer and director)
DENISON, Michael (British actor)
DOGGETT, Thomas (British actor)
DOTRICE, Roy (British actor)
DOUGLAS, Kirk (US film actor)
DURANTE, Jimmy (US actor and singer, known as 'Schnozzle')
ELLIOTT, Denholm (British actor)
FELLINI, Federico (Italian film director)
FONTEYN, Dame Margot (British ballet dancer)

7—continued

GARLAND, Judy (US singer and film actress)
GARRICK, David (English actor)
GIELGUD, Sir John (British actor)
GINGOLD, Hermione (British actress)
GOLDWYN, Samuel (US film producer)
GREGORY, Lady Augusta (Irish theatre patron and dramatist)
GUTHRIE, Tyrone (British theatre director)
HANCOCK, Sheila (British actress)
HANCOCK, Tony (British comedian)
HAWTREY, Sir Charles (British actor-manager)
HEPBURN, Audrey (British actress)
HEPBURN, Katharine (US actress)
HOFFMAN, Dustin (US film actor)
HORDERN, Sir Michael (British actor)
HOUDINI, Harry (US magician)
IFFLAND, August Wilhelm (German actor)
JACKSON, Glenda (British actress)
JOHNSON, Dame Celia (British actress)
KARLOFF, Boris (British character actor)
KUBRICK, Stanley (US film writer, director, and producer)
LACKAYE, Wilton (US actor)
LANGTRY, Lillie (British actress, known as the 'Jersey Lily')
LAROQUE (French actor)
LÉOTARD, Jules (French acrobat and music-hall performer)
MARCEAU, Marcel (French mime)
MARKOVA, Dame Alicia (British ballet dancer)
MASSINE, Léonide (Russian ballet dancer and choreographer)
MCKENNA, Siobhán (Irish actress)
MCQUEEN, Steve (US film actor)
MICHELL, Keith (Australian actor)
NUREYEV, Rudolf (Russian ballet dancer)
OLIVIER, Laurence Kerr, Lord (British actor)
OXBERRY, William (British actor)
PAVLOVA, Anna (Russian ballet dancer)
PAXINOU, Katina (Greek actress)
PLUMMER, Christopher (Canadian actor)
PORTMAN, Eric (British actor)
QUILLEY, Denis (British actor)
RAMBERT, Dame Marie (British ballet dancer and choreographer)
REDFORD, Robert (US film actor)
RISTORI, Adelaide (Italian actress)
ROBARDS, Jason (US actor)
ROBBINS, Jerome (US ballet dancer and choreographer)
ROBESON, Paul Bustil (US Black actor)
RUSSELL, Ken (British film director)
SALVINI, Tommaso (Italian actor)
SELLERS, Peter (British comic actor)
SIDDONS, Sarah (English actress)
STEWART, James (US film actor)
STRITCH, Elaine (US actress)
TEMPEST, Dame Marie (British actress)
ULANOVA, Galina (Russian ballet dancer)

7—continued

USTINOV, Peter Alexander (British actor, director, and dramatist)
VESTRIS, Madame (British actress)
WITHERS, Googie (British actress)

8

ABINGTON, Frances (British actress)
ALDRIDGE, Ira Frederick (US actor)
ANDERSON, Dame Judith (Australian actress)
ANDREINI, Francesco (Italian actor-manager and playwright)
ANDREINI, Giovanni Battista (Italian actor)
ANDREINI, Isabella (Italian actress)
ASHCROFT, Dame Peggy (British actress)
BADDELEY, Hermione (British actress)
BANCROFT, Anne (US actress)
BANKHEAD, Tallulah (US actress)
BARRAULT, Jean-Louis (French actor and director)
BERKELEY, Busby (US dance director)
BORISOVA, Yulia Konstantinovna (Soviet actress)
BRASSEUR, Pierre (French actor)
BUCHANAN, Jack (Scottish actor-manager)
CALDWELL, Zoë (Australian actress)
CAMPBELL, Mrs Patrick (British actress)
CHANNING, Carol (US actress and singer)
CLEMENTS, Sir John (British actor-manager)
CRAWFORD, Joan (US film actress)
CRAWFORD, Michael (British actor)
DANCOURT, Florent (French actor and playwright)
DE LA TOUR, Frances (British actress)
DE VALOIS, Dame Ninette (British ballet dancer and choreographer, born in Ireland)
DEVRIENT, Ludwig (German actor)
DIETRICH, Marlene (German film actress and singer)
DUFRESNE (French actor)
ESTCOURT, Richard (English actor)
FLAHERTY, Robert (US film director)
FLANAGAN, Bud (British comedian)
FLORENCE, William Jermyn (US actor)
FLORIDOR (French actor)
GRENFELL, Joyce (British actress)
GRIERSON, John (British film director)
GRIMALDI, Joseph (British clown)
GUINNESS, Sir Alec (British actor)
HARRISON, Rex (British actor)
HELPMANN, Sir Robert Murray (Australian ballet dancer, choreographer, and actor)
KUROSAWA, Akira (Japanese film director)
KYNASTON, Ned (English actor)
LANSBURY, Angela (US actress)
LAUGHTON, Charles (British actor)
LAWRENCE, Gertrude (British actress)
LEIGHTON, Margaret (British actress)
MACREADY, William Charles (British actor and theatre manager)
MATTHEWS, Jessie (British actress)
MCKELLEN, Ian (British actor)

8—continued

MERCOURI, Melina (Greek actress and politician)
NAUGHTON, Charlie (British comedian)
NAZIMOVA, Alla (Russian actress)
NIJINSKY, Vaslav (Russian ballet dancer)
PICKFORD, Mary (Canadian-born US film actress)
POLANSKI, Roman (Polish film director, born in Paris)
REDGRAVE, Corin (British actor)
REDGRAVE, Lynn (British actress)
REDGRAVE, Sir Michael (British actor)
REDGRAVE, Vanessa (British actress)
ROBINSON, Edward G (US film actor, born in Romania)
SCOFIELD, Paul (British actor)
SELZNICK, David O (US film producer)
STROHEIM, Erich von (US film director and actor)
THOMPSON, Emma (British actress)
VISCONTI, Luchino (Italian film director)
WHITELAW, Billie (British actress)
WILLIAMS, Kenneth (British comic actor)
WILLIAMS, Michael (British actor)
ZIEGFELD, Florenz (US theatrical producer)

9

ANTONIONI, Michelangelo (Italian film maker)
BARKWORTH, Peter (British actor)
BARRYMORE, Ethel (US actress)
BARRYMORE, John (US actor)
BARRYMORE, Lionel (US actor)
BARRYMORE, Maurice (British actor)
BELLECOUR (French actor)
BELLEROSE (French actor-manager)
BERIOSOVA, Svetlana (Russian ballet dancer)
BERNHARDT, Sarah (French actress)
BETTERTON, Thomas (English actor)
CHEVALIER, Maurice (French singer and actor)
COURTENAY, Tom (British actor)
DIAGHILEV, Sergei (Russian ballet impresario)
DU MAURIER, Sir Gerald (British actor-manager)
FAIRBANKS, Douglas (US film actor)
FAVERSHAM, William (US actor)
FERNANDEL (French comedian)
FEUILLÈRE, Edwige (French actress)
GRAMATICA, Irma (Italian actress)
GROSSMITH, George (British actor)
GRÜNDGENS, Gustav (German actor)
LAPOTAIRE, Jane (British actress)
MACMILLAN, Sir Kenneth (British ballet dancer and choreographer)
MONCRIEFF, Gladys (Australian actress)
NICHOLSON, Jack (US film actor)
PECKINPAH, Sam (US film director)
PLEASENCE, Donald (British actor)
PLOWRIGHT, Joan Anne (British actress)
PREMINGER, Otto (US film director, born in Austria)

9—continued

REINHARDT, Max (Austrian theatre director)
STERNBERG, Josef von (US film director, born in Austria)
STREISAND, Barbra (US singer and actress)
THORNDIKE, Dame Sybil (British actress)
VALENTINO, Rudolf (US film actor, born in Italy)

10

BALANCHINE, George (US ballet dancer and choreographer, born in Russia)
BASSERMANN, Albert (German actor)
BELLEROCHE (French actor)
BERTOLUCCI, Bernardo (Italian film director)
BOUCICAULT, 'Dot' (British actor-manager)
BOUCICAULT, Nina (British actress)
CARTWRIGHT, William (English actor)
CUNNINGHAM, Merce (US dancer and choreographer)
D'OYLY CARTE, Richard (British theatre impresario and manager)
EISENSTEIN, Sergei (Russian film director)
FASSBINDER, Rainer Werner (German film director)
LITTLE TICH (British music-hall comedian)
LITTLEWOOD, Joan (British theatre director)
MONTFLEURY (French actor)
RICHARDSON, Ian (British actor)
RICHARDSON, Sir Ralph (British actor)
ROSSELLINI, Roberto (Italian film director)
RUTHERFORD, Dame Margaret (British actress)
WOFFINGTON, Peg (Irish actress)
ZEFFIRELLI, G Franco (Italian director and stage designer)

11

BEAUCHÂTEAU (French actor)
BIANCOLELLI, Giuseppe Domenico (French actor)
BRACEGIRDLE, Anne (English actress)
BRAITHWAITE, Dame Lilian (British actress)
COURTNEIDGE, Dame Cicely (British actress)
DAUVILLIERS (French actor)
MACLIAMMÓIR, Micheál (Irish actor and dramatist)
MASTROIANNI, Marcello (Italian actor)
MISTINGUETT (French singer and comedienne)
SCHLESINGER, John (British film and theatre director)

12

BRUSCAMBILLE (French actor)
MARX BROTHERS (US family of comic film actors)
STANISLAVSKY, Konstantin (Russian actor and theatre director)

13

ROSCIUS GALLUS, Quintus (Roman comic actor)

14
MIZOGUCHI KENJI (Japanese film director)
15
FFRANGCON-DAVIES, Gwen (British actress)
FORBES-ROBERTSON, Sir Johnston (British actor-manager)

15—continued
GRANVILLE-BARKER, Harley (British theatre director)
KOBAYASHI MASAKI (Japanese film director)

SCIENTISTS AND INVENTORS

3
DAM, Carl Peter Henrik (1895–1976; Danish biochemist)
KAY, John (1704–c. 1764; British inventor)
LEE, Tsung-Dao (1926– ; US physicist)
OHM, Georg Simon (1787–1854; German physicist)
RAY, John (1627–1705; English naturalist)
4
ABEL, Niels Henrik (1802–29; Norwegian mathematician)
ABEL, Sir Frederick Augustus (1827–1902; British chemist)
ADER, Clément (1841–1926; French engineer and inventor)
AIRY, Sir George Biddell (1801–92; British astronomer)
BAER, Karl Ernest von (1792–1876; Russian embryologist)
BELL, Alexander Graham (1847–1922; Scottish scientist and inventor)
BENZ, Karl (1844–1929; German engineer)
BIRÓ, Laszlo (1900–85; Hungarian inventor)
BOHR, Niels Henrik David (1885–1962; Danish physicist)
BORN, Max (1882–1970; British physicist)
BOSE, Sir Jagadis Chandra (1858–1937; Indian plant physiologist and physicist)
COHN, Ferdinand Julius (1839–1884; German botanist)
COKE, Thomas William, of Holkham, Earl of Leicester (1752–1842; British agriculturalist)
CORT, Henry (1740–1800; British inventor)
DAVY, Sir Humphry (1778–1829; British chemist and inventor)
EADS, John Buchanan (1820–87; US civil engineer)
FUST, Johann (1400–66; German printer)
GOLD, Thomas (1920– ; Austrian-born astronomer)
GRAY, Asa (1810–88; US botanist)
HAHN, Otto (1879–1968; German chemist and physicist)
HESS, Victor Francis (1883–1964; US physicist)
HOWE, Elias (1819–67; US inventor)
KOCH, Robert (1843–1910; German bacteriologist)

4—continued
LAND, Edwin Herbert (1909– ; US inventor)
LAUE, Max Theodor Felix Von (1879–1960; German physicist)
LOEB, Jacques (1859–1924; US zoologist)
MACH, Ernst (1838–1916; Austrian physicist)
MAYO (family of US medical researchers)
OTIS, Elisha Graves (1811–61; US inventor)
OTTO, Nikolaus August (1832–91; German engineer)
RABI, Isidor Isaac (1898– ; US physicist)
RYLE, Sir Martin (1918–84; British astronomer)
SWAN, Sir Joseph Wilson (1828–1914; British physicist)
TODD, Alexander Robertus, Baron (1907– ; British biochemist)
TULL, Jethro (1674–1741; English agriculturalist and inventor of the seed drill)
UREY, Harold Clayton (1893–1981; US physicist)
WATT, James (1736–1819; British engineer)
YANG, Chen Ning (1922– ; US physicist)
5
ADAMS, John Couch (1819–92; English astronomer)
AIKEN, Howard Hathaway (1900–73; US mathematician)
AMICI, Giovanni Battista (1786–1863; Italian astronomer, microscopist, and optical instrument maker)
ASTON, Francis William (1877–1945; British chemist)
AVERY, Oswald Theodore (1877–1955; Canadian bacteriologist)
BACON, Roger (c. 1214–c. 1292; English scientist)
BAILY, Francis (1774–1844; British amateur astronomer)
BAIRD, John Logie (1888–1946; British electrical engineer)
BAKER, Sir Benjamin (1840–1907; British civil engineer)
BANKS, Sir Joseph (1743–1820; British botanist and explorer)
BATES, Henry Walter (1825–92; British naturalist and explorer)

5—continued

BEEBE, Charles William (1877–1962; US explorer and naturalist)

BETHE, Hans Albrecht (1906– ; US physicist)

BLACK, Joseph (1728–99; Scottish physician and chemist)

BLOCH, Felix (1905– ; US physicist)

BONDI, Sir Hermann (1919– ; British cosmologist and mathematician)

BOOLE, George (1815–64; British mathematician)

BOSCH, Carl (1874–1940; German chemist)

BOTHE, Walther Wilhelm Georg Franz (1891–1957; German experimental physicist)

BOVET, Daniel (1907– ; Swiss pharmacologist)

BOWEN, Norman Levi (1887–1956; Canadian experimental petrologist)

BOWER, Frederick Orpen (1855–1948; British botanist)

BOYLE, Robert (1627–91; British physicist and chemist)

BRAGG, Sir William Henry (1862–1942; British physicist)

BRAHE, Tycho (1546–1601; Danish astronomer)

BROWN, Robert (1773–1858; Scottish botanist)

BÜRGE, Joost (1552–1632; Swiss mathematician)

CHAIN, Sir Ernst Boris (1906–79; British biochemist)

CREED, Frederick (1871–1957; Canadian inventor)

CRICK, Francis Harry Compton (1916– ; British biophysicist)

CURIE, Marie (1867–1934; Polish chemist)

CURIE, Pierre (1859–1906; French physicist)

DEBYE, Peter Joseph Wilhelm (1884–1966; Dutch physicist and chemist)

DIELS, Otto Paul Hermann (1876–1954; German chemist)

DIRAC, Paul Adrien Maurice (1902–84; British physicist)

ELTON, Charles (1900– ; British zoologist)

EULER, Leonhard (1707–83; Swiss mathematician)

EVANS, Oliver (1755–1819; American engineer)

FABRE, Jean Henri (1823–1915; French entomologist)

FABRY, Charles (1867–1945; French physicist)

FERMI, Enrico (1901–54; US physicist)

FREGE, Gottlob (1848–1925; German mathematician and logician)

GABOR, Dennis (1900–79; British electrical engineer)

GALLE, Johann Gottfried (1812–1910; German astronomer)

5—continued

GAUSS, Karl Friedrich (1777–1855; German mathematician)

GEBER (14th century; Spanish alchemist)

GIBBS, Josiah Willard (1839–1903; US physicist)

GÖDEL, Kurt (1906–78; US mathematician)

HABER, Fritz (1868–1934; German chemist and inventor)

HARDY, Godfrey Harold (1877–1947; British mathematician)

HENRY, Joseph (1797–1878; US physicist)

HERTZ, Heinrich Rudolf (1857–94; German physicist)

HOOKE, Robert (1635–1703; British physicist)

HOYLE, Sir Fred (1915– ; British astronomer)

JEANS, Sir James Hopwood (1877–1946; British mathematician and astronomer)

JOULE, James Prescott (1818–89; British physicist)

KOLBE, Hermann (1818–84; German chemist)

KREBS, Sir Hans Adolf (1900–81; British biochemist)

LAWES, Sir John Bennet (1814–1900; British agriculturalist)

LIBBY, Willard Frank (1908–80; US chemist)

LODGE, Sir Oliver Joseph (1851–1940; British physicist)

LYELL, Sir Charles (1797–1875; British geologist)

MAXIM, Sir Hiram Stevens (1840–1916; British inventor)

MAYER, Julius Robert Von (1814–78; German physicist)

MONGE, Gaspard (1746–1818; French mathematician)

MONOD, Jacques-Lucien (1910–76; French biochemist)

MORSE, Samuel Finley Breese (1791–1872; US inventor)

NOBEL, Alfred Bernhard (1833–96; Swedish chemist)

NOBLE, Sir Andrew (1831–1915; British physicist)

PAULI, Wolfgang (1900–58; US physicist)

POPOV, Aleksandr Stepanovich (1859–1905; Russian physicist)

PROUT, William (1785–1850; British chemist and physiologist)

RAMAN, Sir Chandrasekhara Venkata (1888–1970; Indian physicist)

REBER, Grote (1911– ; US astronomer)

RHINE, Joseph Banks (1895–1980; US psychologist)

ROSSE, William Parsons, 3rd Earl Of (1800–67; Irish astronomer)

SEGRÈ, Emilio (1905– ; US physicist)

SMITH, Sir Keith Macpherson (1890–1955; Australian aviator)

5—continued

SODDY, Frederick (1877–1956; British chemist)

STAHL, Georg Ernst (1660–1734; German physician and chemist)

TATUM, Edward Lawrie (1909–75; US geneticist)

TESLA, Nikola (1856–1943; US electrical engineer)

VOLTA, Alessandro Giuseppe Antonio Anastasio, Count (1745–1827; Italian physicist)

WEBER, Ernst Heinrich (1795–1878; German physiologist)

WHITE, Gilbert (1720–93; English naturalist)

YOUNG, Thomas (1773–1829; British physician and physicist)

6

ACHARD, Franz Karl (1753–1821; German chemist)

ADRIAN, Edgar Douglas, 1st Baron (1889–1977; British physiologist)

AGNESI, Maria Gaetana (1718–99; Italian mathematician and philosopher)

ALFVÉN, Hannes Olof Gösta (1908– ; Swedish astrophysicist)

AMPÈRE, André Marie (1775–1836; French physicist)

APPERT, Nicolas (1750–1841; French inventor)

ARCHER, Frederick Scott (1813–57; British inventor and sculptor)

BAEYER, Adolf Von (1835–1917; German chemist)

BEADLE, George Wells (1903– ; US geneticist)

BODONI, Giambattista (1740–1813; Italian printer)

BOLYAI, János (1802–60; Hungarian mathematician)

BONNET, Charles (1720–93; Swiss naturalist)

BORDET, Jules Jean Baptiste Vincent (1870–1961; Belgian bacteriologist)

BOVERI, Theodor Heinrich (1862–1915; German cell biologist)

BRAMAH, Joseph (1748–1814; British engineer and inventor)

BRIGGS, Henry (1561–1630; English mathematician)

BRUNEL, Isambard Kingdom (1806–59; British engineer)

BUFFON, Georges Louis Leclerc, Comte de (1707–88; French naturalist)

BUNSEN, Robert Wilhelm (1811–99; German chemist)

CALVIN, Melvin (1911– ; US biochemist)

CANTOR, Georg (1845–1918; Russian mathematician)

CARNOT, Sadi (1796–1832; French scientist and soldier)

CARREL, Alexis (1873–1944; French surgeon)

6—continued

CARVER, George Washington (1864–1943; US agriculturalist)

CAUCHY, Augustin Louis, Baron (1789–1857; French mathematician)

CAXTON, William (c. 1422–91; first English printer)

CAYLEY, Arthur (1821–95; British mathematician)

CAYLEY, Sir George (1773–1857; British engineer and pioneer designer of flying machines)

CUVIER, Georges, Baron (1769–1832; French zoologist)

DALTON, John (1766–1844; British chemist)

DARWIN, Charles Robert (1809–1882; British naturalist)

DE BARY, Heinrich Anton (1831–88; German botanist)

DE DUVE, Christian (1917– ; Belgian biochemist)

DREYER, Johan Ludvig Emil (1852–1926; Danish astronomer)

DU MONT, Allen Balcom (1901–65; US engineer)

DUNLOP, John Boyd (1840–1921; Scottish inventor)

ECKERT, John Presper (1919– ; US electronics engineer)

EDISON, Thomas Alva (1847–1931; US inventor)

ENDERS, John Franklin (1897– ; US microbiologist)

ENGLER, Gustav Heinrich Adolf (1844–1930; German botanist)

EUCLID (c. 300 BC; Greek mathematician)

FERMAT, Pierre de (1601–65; French mathematician)

FINSEN, Niels Ryberg (1860–1904; Danish physician)

FOKKER, Anthony Hermann Gerard (1890–1939; Dutch aircraft manufacturer)

FRANCK, James (1882–1964; US physicist)

FRISCH, Karl Von (1886–1982; Austrian zoologist)

FRISCH, Otto Robert (1904–79; Austrian-born physicist)

FULTON, Robert (1765–1815; American inventor)

GALOIS, Évariste (1811–32; French mathematician)

GALTON, Sir Francis (1822–1911; British scientist)

GEIGER, Hans (1882–1945; German physicist)

GESNER, Conrad (1516–65; Swiss physician)

GRAHAM, Thomas (1805–69; British physicist)

HALLEY, Edmund (1656–1742; British astronomer)

HEVESY, George Charles Von (1885–1966; Hungarian-born chemist)

6—continued

HOOKER, Sir William Jackson (1785–1865; British botanist)

HUBBLE, Edwin Powell (1889–1953; US astronomer)

HUTTON, James (1726–97; Scottish physician)

HUXLEY, Thomas Henry (1825–95; British biologist)

JANSKY, Karl Guthe (1905–50; US radio engineer)

JENSON, Nicolas (c. 1420–80; French printer)

JOLIOT, Frédéric (1900–59; French physicist)

KELVIN, William Thomson, 1st Baron (1824–1907; Scottish physicist)

KEPLER, Johannes (1571–1630; German astronomer)

KINSEY, Alfred (1894–1956; US zoologist and sociologist)

LANDAU, Lev Davidovich (1908–68; Soviet physicist)

LARTET, Édouard Armand Isidore Hippolyte (1801–71; French archaeologist)

LIEBIG, Justus, Baron Von (1803–73; German chemist)

LORENZ, Konrad (1903– ; Austrian zoologist)

LOVELL, Sir Bernard (1913– ; British astronomer)

LOWELL, Percival (1855–1916; US astronomer)

MARKOV, Andrei Andreevich (1856–1922; Russian mathematician)

MARTIN, Archer John Porter (1910– ; British biochemist)

MARTIN, Pierre-Émile (1824–1915; French engineer)

MCADAM, John Loudon (1756–1836; British inventor)

MENDEL, Gregor Johann (1822–84; Austrian botanist)

MORGAN, Thomas Hunt (1866–1945; US geneticist)

MORLEY, Edward Williams (1838–1923; US chemist)

MORRIS, Desmond John (1928– ; British zoologist)

MULLER, Hermann Joseph (1890–1967; US geneticist)

MÜLLER, Paul Hermann (1899–1965; Swiss chemist)

NAPIER, John (1550–1617; Scottish mathematician)

NERNST, Walther Hermann (1864–1941; German physical chemist)

NEWTON, Sir Isaac (1642–1727; British physicist and mathematician)

OLBERS, Heinrich Wilhelm Matthäus (1758–1840; German astronomer)

PASCAL, Blaise (1623–62; French mathematician and physicist)

6—continued

PENNEY, William George, Baron (1909– ; British mathematician)

PERKIN, Sir William Henry (1838–1907; British chemist)

PERRIN, Jean-Baptiste (1870–1942; French physicist)

PLANCK, Max Karl Ernst Ludwig (1858–1947; German physicist)

POWELL, Cecil Frank (1903–69; British physicist)

PROUST, Joseph-Louis (1754–1826; French chemist)

RAMSAY, Sir William (1852–1916; Scottish chemist)

RENNIE, John (1761–1821; British civil engineer)

SANGER, Frederick (1918– ; British biochemist)

SAVERY, Thomas (c. 1650–1715; English engineer)

SHOLES, Christopher Latham (1819–90; US inventor)

SINGER, Isaac Merrit (1811–75; US inventor)

SLOANE, Sir Hans (1660–1753; British physician and naturalist)

STOKES, Sir George Gabriel (1819–1903; British physicist and mathematician)

STRUVE, Otto (1897–1963; US astronomer)

SUTTON, Walter Stanborough (1877–1916; US geneticist)

TALBOT, William Henry Fox (1800–77; British botanist and physicist)

TAYLOR, Brook (1685–1737; English mathematician)

TAYLOR, Frederick Winslow (1856–1915; US engineer)

TELLER, Edward (1908– ; US physicist)

TOWNES, Charles Hard (1915– ; US physicist)

VAUBAN, Sébastian Le Prestre de (1633–1707; French military engineer)

WALLIS, Sir Barnes (1887–1979; British aeronautical engineer)

WALTON, Ernest Thomas Sinton (1903– ; Irish physicist)

WATSON, James Dewey (1928– ; US geneticist)

WIENER, Norbert (1894–1964; US mathematician)

WIGNER, Eugene Paul (1902– ; US physicist)

WILSON, Charles Thomson Rees (1869–1959; British physicist)

WILSON, Edmund Beecher (1856–1939; US biologist)

WÖHLER, Friedrich (1800–82; German chemist)

WRIGHT, Orville (1871–1948; US aviator)

YUKAWA, Hideki (1907–81; Japanese physicist)

91 SCIENTISTS AND INVENTORS

6—continued

ZEEMAN, Pieter (1865–1943; Dutch physicist)

7

AGASSIZ, Jean Louis Rodolphe (1807–73; Swiss natural historian)

ALVAREZ, Luis Walter (1911–   ; US physicist)

AUDUBON, John James (1785–1851; US naturalist)

BABBAGE, Charles (1792–1871; British mathematician and inventor)

BARDEEN, John (1908–   ; US physicist)

BARNARD, Edward Emerson (1857–1923; US astronomer)

BATESON, William (1861–1926; British biologist)

BATTANI, Al- (c. 858–929; Islamic astronomer)

BERGIUS, Friedrich (1884–1949; German chemist)

BORLAUG, Norman (1914–   ; US plant breeder)

BRAILLE, Louis (1809–52; French inventor of system of writing and printing for the blind)

BROUWER, Luitzen Egbertus Jan (1881–1966; Dutch mathematician)

BURBANK, Luther (1849–1926; US plant breeder)

CANDELA, Felix (1910–   ; Mexican engineer)

CARDANO, Girolamo (1501–76; Italian mathematician)

COMPTON, Arthur Holly (1892–1962; US physicist)

CORRENS, Carl Erich (1864–1933; German botanist and geneticist)

COULOMB, Charles Augustin de (1736–1806; French physicist)

CROOKES, Sir William (1832–1919; British physicist)

CURTISS, Glenn (1878–1930; US aviator and aeronautical engineer)

DAIMLER, Gottlieb (1834–1900; German inventor)

DANIELL, John Frederic (1790–1845; British chemist)

DE LA RUE, Warren (1815–89; British astronomer)

DE VRIES, Hugo Marie (1848–1935; Dutch botanist)

DOPPLER, Christian Johann (1803–53; Austrian physicist)

DRIESCH, Hans Adolf Eduard (1867–1941; German zoologist)

EICHLER, August Wilhelm (1839–87; German botanist)

FARADAY, Michael (1791–1867; British chemist and physicist)

FEYNMAN, Richard Phillips (1918–   ; US physicist)

FISCHER, Emil Hermann (1852–1919; German chemist)

7—continued

FLEMING, Sir John Ambrose (1849–1945; British electrical engineer)

FOURIER, Jean Baptiste Joseph, Baron (1768–1830; French mathematician and physicist)

FRESNEL, Augustin Jean (1788–1827; French physicist)

GAGARIN, Yuri Alekseevich (1934–68; Soviet cosmonaut)

GALVANI, Luigi (1737–98; Italian physician)

GILBERT, William (1544–1603; English physicist)

GODDARD, Robert Hutchings (1882–1945; US physicist)

GREGORY, James (1638–75; Scottish mathematician and astronomer)

HAECKEL, Ernst Heinrich (1834–1919; German zoologist)

HAWORTH, Sir Walter Norman (1883–1950; British biochemist)

HELMONT, Jan Baptist van (1580–1644; Belgian alchemist and physician)

HERMITE, Charles (1822–1901; French mathematician)

HILBERT, David (1862–1943; German mathematician)

HODGKIN, Alan Lloyd (1914–   ; British physiologist)

HODGKIN, Dorothy Mary Crowfoot (1910–   ; British biochemist)

HOPKINS, Sir Frederick Gowland (1861–1947; British biochemist)

HUGGINS, Sir William (1824–1910; British astronomer)

HUYGENS, Christiaan (1629–95; Dutch astronomer and physicist)

JUSSIEU (French family of botanists)

KAPITZA, Peter Leonidovich (1894–1984; Soviet physicist)

KENDALL, Edward Calvin (1886–1972; US biochemist)

KENDREW, Sir John Cowdery (1917–   ; British biochemist)

KHORANA, Har Gobind (1922–   ; US biochemist)

KIDINNU (4th century BC; Babylonian mathematician and astronomer)

KOZIREV, Nikolai Aleksandrovich (1908–   ; Soviet astronomer)

LALANDE, Joseph-Jérôme le Français de (1732–1807; French astronomer)

LAMARCK, Jean-Baptiste de Monet, Chevalier de (1744–1829; French naturalist)

LAMBERT, Johann Heinrich (1728–77; German mathematician and astronomer)

LANGLEY, Samuel Pierpont (1834–1906; US astronomer)

LAPLACE, Pierre Simon, Marquis de (1749–1827; French mathematician and astronomer)

92

7—continued

LESSEPS, Ferdinand de (1805–94; French diplomat)

LOCKYER, Sir Joseph Norman (1836–1920; British astronomer)

LORENTZ, Hendrick Antoon (1853–1928; Dutch physicist)

LUMIÈRE, Auguste (1862–1954; French photographer and inventor)

LYSENKO, Trofim Denisovich (1898–1976; Soviet biologist)

MARCONI, Guglielmo (1874–1937; Italian electrical engineer)

MAXWELL, James Clerk (1831–79; Scottish physicist)

MEITNER, Lise (1878–1968; Austrian physicist)

MESSIER, Charles (1730–1817; French astronomer)

MOSELEY, Henry Gwyn Jeffries (1887–1915; British physicist)

NEUMANN, John Von (1903–57; US mathematician)

OERSTED, Hans Christian (1777–1851; Danish physicist)

ONSAGER, Lars (1903–76; US chemist)

OSTWALD, Wilhelm (1853–1932; German chemist)

PARSONS, Sir Charles Algernon (1854–1931; British engineer)

PASTEUR, Louis (1822–95; French chemist and microbiologist)

PAULING, Linus Carl (1901– ; US chemist)

PICCARD (family of Swiss scientists)

POISSON, Siméon Dénis (1781–1840; French mathematician)

PRANDTL, Ludwig (1875–1953; German physicist)

PTOLEMY (or Claudius Ptolemaeus, 2nd century AD; Egyptian mathematician, astronomer, and geographer)

PURCELL, Edward Mills (1912– ; US physicist)

RÉAUMUR, René-Antoine Ferchault de (1683–1757; French physicist)

RIEMANN, Georg Friedrich Bernhard (1826–66; German mathematician)

RUMFORD, Benjamin Thompson, Count (1753–1814; American-born scientist)

SANDAGE, Allan Rex (1926– ; US astronomer)

SCHEELE, Carl Wilhelm (1742–86; Swedish chemist)

SCHWANN, Theodor (1810–82; German physiologist)

SEABORG, Glenn Theodore (1912– ; US physicist)

SHEPARD, Jr, Allan Bartlett (1923– ; US astronaut)

SIEMENS, Ernst Werner von (1816–92; German electrical engineer)

7—continued

SIMPSON, George Gaylord (1902– ; US palaeontologist)

SZILARD, Leo (1898–1964; US physicist)

TELFORD, Thomas (1757–1834; British civil engineer)

THENARD, Louis-Jacques (1777–1857; French chemist)

THOMSON, Sir Joseph John (1856–1940; British physicist)

TUPOLEV, Andrei Niklaievich (1888–1972; Soviet designer)

TYNDALL, John (1820–93; Irish physicist)

VAVILOV, Nikolai Ivanovich (1887–1943; Soviet plant geneticist)

WAKSMAN, Selman Abraham (1888–1973; US microbiologist)

WALLACE, Alfred Russel (1823–1913; British naturalist)

WEGENER, Alfred Lothar (1880–1930; German geologist)

WHITNEY, Eli (1765–1825; American inventor)

WHITTLE, Sir Frank (1907– ; British aeronautical engineer)

WILKINS, Maurice Hugh Frederick (1916– ; New Zealand physicist)

ZIEGLER, Karl (1898–1973; German chemist)

8

AGRICOLA, Georgius (1494–1555; German physician and mineralogist)

ANDERSON, Carl David (1905– ; US physicist)

ÅNGSTRÖM, Anders Jonas (1814–74; Swedish physicist and astronomer)

AVOGADRO, Amedeo, Conte di Quaregna e Ceretto (1776–1856; Italian physicist)

BAKEWELL, Robert (1725–95; British agriculturalist)

BESSEMER, Sir Henry (1813–98; British engineer and inventor)

BIRKHOFF, George David (1864–1944; US mathematician)

BJERKNES, Vilhelm Friman Koren (1862–1951; Norwegian meteorologist and physicist)

BLACKETT, Patrick Maynard Stuart, Baron (1897–1974; British physicist)

BRATTAIN, Walter Houser (1902– ; US physicist)

BREWSTER, Sir David (1781–1868; Scottish physicist)

BRIDGMAN, Percy Williams (1882–1961; US physicist)

BRINDLEY, James (1716–72; British canal builder)

BUSHNELL, David (1742–1824; US inventor; built the first submarine)

CALMETTE, Albert Léon Charles (1863–1933; French bacteriologist)

CHADWICK, Sir James (1891–1974; British physicist)

8—continued

CLAUSIUS, Rudolf Julius Emanuel (1822–88; German physicist)

CROMPTON, Samuel (1753–1827; British inventor)

CULPEPER, Nicholas (1616–54; English physician)

DAGUERRE, Louis-Jacques-Mandé (1789–1851; French inventor)

DEDEKIND, Richard (1831–1916; German mathematician)

DE FOREST, Lee (1873–1961; US electrical engineer)

DE MORGAN, Augustus (1806–71; British mathematician and logician)

EINSTEIN, Albert (1879–1955; German physicist)

ERICSSON, John (1803–89; US naval engineer and inventor)

FOUCAULT, Jean Bernard Léon (1819–68; French physicist)

GASSENDI, Pierre (1592–1655; French physicist)

GELL-MANN, Murray (1929– ; US physicist)

GUERICKE, Otto Von (1602–86; German physicist)

HAMILTON, Sir William Rowan (1805–65; Irish mathematician)

HERSCHEL, Sir William (1738–1822; British astronomer)

ILYUSHIN, Sergei Vladimirovich (1894–1977; Soviet aircraft designer)

IPATIEFF, Vladimir Nikolaievich (1867–1952; US physicist)

JACQUARD, Joseph-Marie (1752–1834; French inventor)

KENNELLY, Arthur Edwin (1861–1939; US electrical engineer)

KLAPROTH, Martin Heinrich (1743–1817; German chemist)

KOROLIOV, Sergei Pavlovich (1906–66; Soviet aeronautical engineer)

LAGRANGE, Joseph Louis, Comte de (1736–1813; French mathematician and astronomer)

LANGMUIR, Irving (1881–1957; US chemist)

LAWRENCE, Ernest Orlando (1901–58; US physicist)

LEGENDRE, Adrien Marie (1752–1833; French mathematician)

LEMAÎTRE, Georges Édouard, Abbé (1894–1966; Belgian priest and astronomer)

LEUCKART, Karl Georg Friedrich Rudolph (1822–98; German zoologist)

LINNAEUS, Carolus (Carl Linné; 1707–78; Swedish botanist)

LIPSCOMB, William Nunn (1919– ; US chemist)

LONSDALE, Dame Kathleen (1903–71; Irish physicist)

8—continued

MAUDSLAY, Henry (1771–1831; British engineer)

MCMILLAN, Edwin Mattison (1907– ; US physicist)

MERCATOR, Gerardus (1512–94; Flemish geographer)

MEYERHOF, Otto Fritz (1884–1951; US biochemist)

MILLIKAN, Robert Andrews (1868–1953; US physicist)

MITCHELL, Reginald Joseph (1895–1937; British aeronautical engineer)

MULLIKEN, Robert Sanderson (1896–1986; US chemist and physicist)

NEWCOMEN, Thomas (1663–1729; English blacksmith and inventor of steam engine)

OLIPHANT, Sir Mark Laurence Elwin (1901– ; Australian physicist)

POINCARÉ, Jules Henri (1854–1912; French mathematician)

RAYLEIGH, John William Strutt, 3rd Baron (1842–1919; British physicist)

RHETICUS (1514–76; German mathematician)

ROBINSON, Sir Robert (1886–1975; British chemist)

ROEBLING, John Augustus (1806–69; US engineer)

ROENTGEN, Wilhelm Konrad (1845–1923; German physicist)

SABATIER, Paul (1854–1941; French chemist)

SAKHAROV, Andrei Dimitrievich (1921– ; Soviet physicist)

SHOCKLEY, William Bradfield (1910– ; US physicist)

SHRAPNEL, Henry (1761–1842; British army officer, who invented the shrapnel shell)

SIKORSKY, Igor Ivan (1889–1972; US aeronautical engineer)

STIRLING, James (1692–1770; Scottish mathematician)

VAN ALLEN, James Alfred (1914– ; US physicist)

VAN'T HOFF, Jacobus Henricus (1852–1911; Dutch chemist)

WEISMANN, August Friedrich Leopold (1834–1914; German biologist)

WOODWARD, Robert Burns (1917– ; US chemist)

ZERNICKE, Frits (1888–1966; Dutch physicist)

ZWORYKIN, Vladimir Kosma (1889–1982; US physicist)

9

ABU AL-WAFA (940–98 AD; Persian mathematician and astronomer)

ARKWRIGHT, Sir Richard (1732–92; British inventor)

ARMSTRONG, Edwin Howard (1890–1954; US electrical engineer)

ARMSTRONG, William George, Baron (1810–1900; British engineer)

9—continued

ARRHENIUS, Svante August (1859–1927; Swedish physicist and chemist)

BECQUEREL, Henri (1852–1908; French physicist)

BERNOULLI (family of Swiss mathematicians and physicists)

BERTHELOT, Marcelin (1827–1907; French chemist)

BERZELIUS, Jöns Jakob, Baron (1779–1848; Swedish chemist)

BOLTZMANN, Ludwig Eduard (1844–1906; Austrian physicist)

BRONOWSKI, Jacob (1908–74; British mathematician)

CAVENDISH, Henry (1731–1810; British physicist)

CHEBISHEV, Pafnuti Lvovich (1821–94; Russian mathematician)

CHERENKOV, Pavel Alekseievich (1904– ; Soviet physicist)

COCKCROFT, Sir John Douglas (1897–1967; British physicist)

CORNFORTH, Sir John Warcup (1917– ; Australian chemist)

D'ALEMBERT, Jean Le Rond (1717–83; French mathematician)

DAUBENTON, Louis Jean Marie (1716–1800; French naturalist)

DAVENPORT, Charles Benedict (1866–1944; US zoologist)

EDDINGTON, Sir Arthur Stanley (1882–1944; British theoretical astronomer)

ENDLICHER, Stephan Ladislaus (1804–49; Hungarian botanist)

FIBONACCI, Leonardo (*c.* 1170–*c.* 1230; Italian mathematician)

FLAMSTEED, John (1646–1719; English astronomer)

GAY-LUSSAC, Joseph Louis (1778–1850; French chemist and physicist)

GUTENBERG, Johann (*c.* 1400–*c.* 1468; German printer)

HEAVISIDE, Oliver (1850–1925; British physicist)

HELMHOLTZ, Hermann Ludwig Ferdinand Von (1821–94; German physicist and physiologist)

HOPKINSON, John (1849–98; British physicist and electrical engineer)

JOHANNSEN, Wilhelm Ludvig (1857–1927; Danish geneticist)

JOSEPHSON, Brian David (1940– ; British physicist)

KIRCHHOFF, Gustav Robert (1824–87; German physicist)

KURCHATOV, Igor Vasilievich (1903–60; Soviet physicist)

LANKESTER, Sir Edwin Ray (1847–1929; British zoologist)

9—continued

LAVOISIER, Antoine Laurent (1743–94; French chemist)

LEDERBERG, Joshua (1925– ; US geneticist)

LEVERRIER, Urbain Jean Joseph (1811–77; French astronomer)

LIOUVILLE, Joseph (1809–82; French mathematician)

MACINTOSH, Charles (1766–1843; Scottish chemist)

MACMILLAN, Kirkpatrick (d. 1878; Scottish inventor)

MICHELSON, Albert Abraham (1852–1931; US physicist)

NICHOLSON, William (1753–1815; British chemist)

NIRENBERG, Marshall Warren (1927– ; US biochemist)

PELLETIER, Pierre Joseph (1788–1842; French chemist)

PRIESTLEY, Joseph (1733–1804; British chemist)

REMINGTON, Eliphalet (1793–1863; US inventor)

SCHLEIDEN, Matthias Jakob (1804–81; German botanist)

STEINMETZ, Charles Proteus (1865–1923; US electrical engineer)

TINBERGEN, Nikolaas (1907– ; Dutch zoologist and pioneer ethologist)

ZSIGMONDY, Richard Adolph (1865–1929; Austrian chemist)

ZUCKERMAN, Solly, Baron (1904–84; British anatomist)

10

ARCHIMEDES (*c.* 287–*c.* 212 BC; Greek mathematician and inventor)

ARROWSMITH, Aaron (1750–1823; British cartographer)

BARKHAUSEN, Heinrich (1881–1956; German physicist)

BERTHOLLET, Claude Louis, Comte (1748–1822; French chemist and physician)

BLENKINSOP, John (1783–1831; British engineer)

CANNIZZARO, Stanislao (1826–1910; Italian chemist)

CARTWRIGHT, Edmund (1743–1823; British inventor)

COPERNICUS, Nicolaus (1473–1543; Polish astronomer)

DOBZHANSKY, Theodosius (1900–75; US geneticist)

FITZGERALD, George Francis (1851–1901; Irish physicist)

FOURNEYRON, Benoît (1802–67; French engineer)

FRAUNHOFER, Joseph Von (1787–1826; German physicist)

10—continued

HARGREAVES, James (d. 1778; English inventor)

HEISENBERG, Werner Karl (1901–76; German physicist)

HIPPARCHUS (*c*. 190–*c*. 120 BC; Greek astronomer)

HOFMEISTER, Wilhelm Friedrich Benedict (1824–77; German botanist)

INGENHOUSZ, Jan (1730–99; Dutch physician and plant physiologist)

KOLMOGOROV, Andrei Nikolaevich (1903– ; Soviet mathematician)

LILIENTHAL, Otto (1848–96; German aeronautical engineer)

LIPPERSHEY, Hans (d. *c*. 1619; Dutch lens grinder)

MAUPERTUIS, Pierre Louis Moreau de (1698–1759; French mathematician)

MENDELEYEV, Dimitrii Ivanovich (1834–1907; Russian chemist)

METCHNIKOV, Ilya Ilich (1845–1916; Russian zoologist)

RUTHERFORD, Ernest, 1st Baron (1871–1937; English physicist)

SOMMERFELD, Arnold Johannes Wilhelm (1868–1951; German physicist)

STAUDINGER, Hermann (1881–1965; German chemist)

STEPHENSON, George (1781–1848; British engineer)

SWAMMERDAM, Jan (1637–80; Dutch naturalist and microscopist)

TORRICELLI, Evangelista (1608–47; Italian physicist)

TOURNEFORT, Joseph Pitton de (1656–1708; French botanist)

TREVITHICK, Richard (1771–1833; British engineer)

WATSON-WATT, Sir Robert Alexander (1892–1973; Scottish physicist)

WHEATSTONE, Sir Charles (1802–75; British physicist)

11

AL-KHWARIZMI, Muhammed Ibn Musa (*c*. 780–*c*. 850 AD; Arabic mathematician)

BASKERVILLE, John (1706–75; British printer)

BHOSKHARA II (1114–*c*. 1185; Indian mathematician)

CHAMBERLAIN, Owen (1920– ; US physicist)

GOLDSCHMIDT, Richard Benedict (1878–1958; US geneticist)

HINSHELWOOD, Sir Cyril Norman (1897–1967; British chemist)

JOLIOT-CURIE, Irène (1896–1956; French physicist)

LE CHÂTELIER, Henri-Louis (1850–1936; French chemist)

11—continued

LEEUWENHOEK, Antonie van (1632–1723; Dutch scientist)

LOBACHEVSKI, Nikolai Ivanovich (1793–1856; Russian mathematician)

MONTGOLFIER, Jacques-Étienne (1745–99; French balloonist and inventor)

NOSTRADAMUS (1503–66; French physician and astrologer)

OPPENHEIMER, J Robert (1904–67; US physicist)

SCHRÖDINGER, Erwin (1887–1961; Austrian physicist)

SHERRINGTON, Sir Charles Scott (1857–1952; British physiologist)

SPALLANZANI, Lazzaro (1729–99; Italian physiologist)

TSIOLKOVSKI, Konstantin Eduardovich (1857–1935; Russian aeronautical engineer)

VAN DER WAALS, Johannes Diderik (1837–1923; Dutch physicist)

12

AMBARTSUMIAN, Viktor Amazaspovich (1908– ; Soviet astrophysicist)

SZENT-GYÖRGYI, Albert (1893–1986; US biochemist)

13

ARAGO FRANÇOIS (1786–1853; French astronomer and physicist)

CHANDRASEKHAR, Subrahmanyan (1910– ; US astronomer)

REGIOMONTANUS (1436-76; German astronomer and mathematician)

14

GALILEO GALILEI (1564–1642; Italian mathematician, physicist, and astronomer)

15

EUDOXUS OF CNIDUS (*c*. 408–*c*. 355 BC; Greek astronomer and mathematician)

16

HERO OF ALEXANDRIA (mid-1st century AD; Greek engineer and mathematician)

17

APOLLONIUS OF PERGA (*c*. 261–*c*. 190 BC; Greek mathematician)

18

ARISTARCHUS OF SAMOS (*c*. 310–230 BC; Greek astronomer)

LECOQ DE BOISBAUDRAN, Paul-Émile (1838–1912; French chemist)

PAPPUS OF ALEXANDRIA (3rd century BC; Greek mathematician)

19

DIOSCORIDES PEDANIUS (*c*. 40–*c*. 90 AD; Greek physician)

KEKULÉ VON STRADONITZ, Friedrich August (1829–96; German chemist)

20+
BOYD-ORR OF BRECHIN MEARNS, John, 1st
  Baron (1880–1971; Scottish scientist)
DIOPHANTUS OF ALEXANDRIA (mid-3rd
  century AD; Greek mathematician)
ERATOSTHENES OF CYRENE (c. 276–c. 194
  BC; Greek astronomer)

20+—continued
GEOFFROY SAINT-HILAIRE, Étienne (1772–
  1844; French naturalist)
SOSIGENES OF ALEXANDRIA (1st century BC;
  Greek astronomer)

EXPLORERS, PIONEERS, AND ADVENTURERS

4
BYRD, Richard E (1888–1957; US explorer)
CANO, Juan Sebastián del (c. 1460–1526;
  Spanish navigator)
COOK, Captain James (1728–79; British
  navigator)
DIAS, Bartolomeu (c. 1450–c. 1500;
  Portuguese navigator)
EYRE, Edward John (1815–1901; British
  explorer)
GAMA, Vasco da (c. 1469–1524; Portuguese
  navigator)
HUME, Hamilton (1797–1873; Australian
  explorer)
HUNT, John, Baron (1910–   ; British
  mountaineer)
KIDD, William (c. 1645–1701; Scottish sailor)
PARK, Mungo (1771–c. 1806; Scottish
  explorer)
POLO, Marco (c. 1254–1324; Venetian
  traveller)
ROSS, Sir James Clark (1800–62; British
  explorer)
SOTO, Hernando de (?1496–1542; Spanish
  explorer)

5
BAKER, Sir Samuel White (1821–93; British
  explorer)
BARTH, Heinrich (1821–65; German explorer
  and geographer)
BOONE, Daniel (1734–1820; American
  pioneer)
BRUCE, James (1730–94; British explorer)
BURKE, Robert O'Hara (1820–61; Irish
  explorer)
CABOT, John (Giovanni Caboto,
  c. 1450–c. 1499; Italian explorer)
DAVIS, John (or J Davys, c. 1550–1605)
  English navigator)
FUCHS, Sir Vivian (1908–   ; British explorer)
LAIRD, Macgregor (1808–61; Scottish
  explorer)
OATES, Lawrence Edward Grace (1880–1912;
  British explorer)
OÑATE, Juan de (d. 1630; Spanish
  conquistador)

5—continued
PARRY, Sir William Edward (1790–1855;
  British navigator)
PEARY, Robert Edwin (1856–1920; US
  explorer)
SCOTT, Robert Falcon (1868–1912; British
  explorer)
SPEKE, John Hanning (1827–64; British
  explorer)
STURT, Charles (1795–1869; British explorer)
TEACH, Edward (d. 1718; British pirate)

6
ALCOCK, Sir John (1892–1919; British
  aviator)
BAFFIN, William (c. 1584–1622; English
  navigator)
BALBOA, Vasco Núñez de (c. 1475–1517;
  Spanish explorer)
BERING, Vitus Jonassen (1681–1741; Danish
  navigator)
BRAZZA, Pierre Paul François Camille
  Savorgnan de (1852–1905; French explorer)
BROOKE, Sir James (1803–68; British
  explorer)
BURTON, Sir Richard (1821–90; British
  explorer)
CABRAL, Pedro Álvares (?1467–1520;
  Portuguese navigator)
CARSON, Kit (Christopher C, 1809–68; US
  frontiersman)
CORTÉS, Hernán (1485–1547; Spanish
  conquistador)
HUDSON, Henry (d. 1611; English navigator)
MORGAN, Sir Henry (c. 1635–88; Welsh
  buccaneer)
NANSEN, Fridtjof (1861–1930; Norwegian
  explorer)
NOBILE, Umberto (1885–1978; Italian aviator)
STUART, John McDouall (1815–66; Scottish
  explorer)
TASMAN, Abel Janszoon (c. 1603–c. 1659;
  Dutch navigator)

7
BARENTS, Willem (c. 1550–97; Dutch
  navigator)
BLÉRIOT, Louis (1872–1936; French aviator)

7—continued

CARPINI, Giovanni da Pian del (c. 1180– c. 1252; Italian traveller)

CARTIER, Jacques (1491–1557; French navigator)

CÓRDOBA, Francisco Fernández de (d. 1518; Spanish explorer)

COVILHÃ, Pêro da (c. 1460–c. 1526; Portuguese explorer)

DAMPIER, William (c. 1652–1715; English explorer)

EARHART, Amelia (1898–1937; US aviator)

FRÉMONT, John C (1813–90; US explorer)

GILBERT, Sir Humphrey (c. 1539–83; English navigator)

HAWKINS, Sir John (1532–95; English navigator)

HILLARY, Sir Edmund (1919– ; New Zealand mountaineer and explorer)

HINKLER, Herbert John Lewis (1892–1933; Australian aviator)

LA SALLE, Robert Cavelier, Sieur de (1643– 87; French explorer)

MCCLURE, Sir Robert John Le Mesurier (1807–73; Irish explorer)

PIZARRO, Francisco (c. 1475–1541; Spanish conquistador)

PYTHEAS (4th century BC; Greek navigator)

RALEIGH, Sir Walter (1554–1618; British explorer)

SELKIRK, Alexander (1676–1721; Scottish sailor)

STANLEY, Sir Henry Morton (1841–1904; British explorer)

WILKINS, Sir George Hubert (1888–1958; British explorer)

WRANGEL, Ferdinand Petrovich, Baron von (1794–1870; Russian explorer)

8

AMUNDSEN, Roald (1872–1928; Norwegian explorer)

COLUMBUS, Christopher (1451–1506; Italian navigator)

COUSTEAU, Jacques Yves (1910– ; French underwater explorer)

FLINDERS, Matthew (1774–1814; British navigator and hydrographer)

FRANKLIN, Sir John (1786–1847; British explorer)

MAGELLAN, Ferdinand (c. 1480–1521; Portuguese explorer)

MARCHAND, Jean Baptiste (1863–1934; French explorer)

VESPUCCI, Amerigo (1454–1512; Italian navigator)

9

BLANCHARD, Jean Pierre François (1753– 1809; French balloonist)

CHAMPLAIN, Samuel de (1567–1635; French explorer)

FROBISHER, Sir Martin (c. 1535–94; English navigator)

HEYERDAHL, Thor (1914– ; Norwegian ethnologist)

IBERVILLE, Pierre Le Moyne, Sieur d' (1661– 1706; French-Canadian explorer)

LEICHARDT, Ludwig (1813–48; German explorer)

LINDBERGH, Charles A (1902–74; US aviator)

MARQUETTE, Jacques (1637–75; French explorer)

PAUSANIAS (2nd century AD; Greek traveller)

RASMUSSEN, Knud Johan Victor (1879–1933; Danish explorer)

VANCOUVER, George (c. 1758–98; British navigator)

VELÁSQUEZ, Diego (?1465–1522; Spanish explorer)

10

BARBAROSSA (Khayr ad-Din, d. 1546; Turkish pirate)

ERIC THE RED (late 10th century; Norwegian explorer)

SHACKLETON, Sir Ernest Henry (1874–1922; British explorer)

11

IBN BATTUTAH (1304–?1368; Arab traveller)

LA CONDAMINE, Charles Marie de (1701–74; French geographer)

LIVINGSTONE, David (1813–73; Scottish missionary and explorer)

PONCE DE LEON, Juan (1460–1521; Spanish explorer)

12

BOUGAINVILLE, Louis Antoine de (1729– 1811; French navigator)

LEIF ERIKSSON (11th century; Icelandic explorer)

NORDENSKJÖLD, Nils Adolf Erik, Baron (1832–1901; Swedish navigator)

14

BELLINGSHAUSEN, Fabian Gottlieb, Baron von (1778–1852; Russian explorer)

DUMONT D'URVILLE, Jules Sébastien César (1790–1842; French navigator)

17

HENRY THE NAVIGATOR (1394–1460; Portuguese navigator and patron of explorers)

WORLD LEADERS

3

FOX, Charles James (1749–1806; British Whig politician)

LIE, Trygve (Halvdan) (1896–1968; Norwegian Labour politician)

4

BENN, Anthony Neil Wedgwood (1925– ; British Labour politician)

BLUM, Léon (1872–1950; French socialist)

BOSE, Subhas Chandra (c. 1897–c. 1945; Indian nationalist leader)

COOK, Sir Joseph (1860–1947; Australian statesman)

DÍAZ, Porfirio (1830–1915; Mexican soldier)

FOOT, Michael (Mackintosh) (1913– ; British Labour politician)

HILL, Sir Rowland (1795–1879; British postal expert)

HOLT, Harold Edward (1908–67; Australian statesman)

HOWE, Sir Richard Edward Geoffrey (1926– ; British Conservative politician)

HULL, Cordell (1871–1955; US Democratic politician)

KING, Jr, Martin Luther (1929–68; US Black civil-rights leader)

KING, William Lyon Mackenzie (1874–1950; Canadian statesman)

KIRK, Norman Eric (1923–74; New Zealand statesman)

MEIR, Golda (1898–1978; Israeli stateswoman)

NAGY, Imre (1896–1958; Hungarian statesman)

OWEN, Dr David (1938– ; British Social Democrat politician)

RHEE, Syngman (1875–1965; Korean statesman)

RUSK, David Dean (1909– ; US statesman)

TOJO (Hideki) (1884–1948; Japanese general)

TONE, Theobald Wolfe (1763–98; Irish nationalist)

TUTU, Desmond (1931– ; South African clergyman)

WARD, Sir Joseph George (1856–1930; New Zealand statesman)

5

AGNEW, Spiro Theodore (1918– ; US Republican politician)

ASTOR, Nancy Witcher, Viscountess (1879–1964; British politician)

BANDA, Hastings Kamuzu (1905– ; Malawi statesman)

5—continued

BEGIN, Menachem (1913– ; Israeli statesman)

BERIA, Lavrenti Pavlovich (1899–1953; Soviet politician)

BEVAN, Aneurin (1897–1960; British Labour politician)

BEVIN, Ernest (1881–1951; British politician)

BOTHA, Louis (1862–1919; South African statesman)

BOTHA, Pieter Willem (1916– ; South African statesman)

CLARK, Charles Joseph (1939– ; Canadian statesman)

DAYAN, Moshe (1915–81; Israeli general)

DEBRÉ, Michel (1912– ; French statesman)

DESAI, Shri Morarji Ranchhodji (1896– ; Indian statesman)

DE WET, Christian Rudolf (1854–1922; Afrikaner politician and soldier)

EBERT, Friedrich (1871–1925; German statesman)

EMMET, Robert (1778–1803; Irish nationalist)

FLOOD, Henry (1732–91; Irish politician)

LAVAL, Pierre (1883–1945; French statesman)

LENIN, Vladimir Ilich (V I Ulyanov, 1870–1924; Russian revolutionary)

LODGE, Henry Cabot (1850–1924; US Republican politician)

LYNCH, Jack (1917– ; Irish statesman)

LYONS, Joseph Aloysius (1879–1939; Australian statesman)

MANIN, Daniele (1804–57; Italian patriot)

MBOYA, Tom (1930–69; Kenyan politician)

MENON, Krishna (Vengalil Krishnan Krishna Menon, 1896–1974; Indian diplomat)

NEHRU, Jawaharlal (1889–1964; Indian statesman)

NKOMO, Joshua (1917– ; Zimbabwean politician)

OBOTE, Apollo Milton (1925– ; Ugandan statesman)

PERÓN, Juan Domingo (1895–1974; Argentine statesman)

SADAT, Anwar (1918–81; Egyptian statesman)

SMITH, Ian Douglas (1919– ; Rhodesian prime minister)

SMUTS, Jan Christiaan (1870–1950; South African statesman and general)

SPAAK, Paul Henri (1899–1972; Belgian statesman)

STEEL, David Martin Scott (1938– ; British politician)

VANCE, Cyrus (1917– ; US statesman)

5—continued

VILLA, Pancho (Francesco V, 1878–1923; Mexican revolutionary)

6

ARAFAT, Yassir (1929–   ; Palestinian leader)

BARTON, Sir Edmund (1849–1920; Australian statesman)

BHUTTO, Benazir (1953–   ; Pakistani politician)

BHUTTO, Zulfikar Ali (1928–79; Pakistani statesman)

BORDEN, Sir Robert Laird (1854–1937; Canadian statesman)

BRANDT, Willy (1913–   ; West German statesman)

BRIGHT, John (1811–89; British radical politician)

BUTLER, Richard Austen, Baron (1902–82; British Conservative politician)

CHIRAC, Jacques (1932–   ; French statesman)

COATES, Joseph Gordon (1878–1943; New Zealand statesman)

COBDEN, Richard (1804–65; British politician and economist)

CRIPPS, Sir Richard Stafford (1889–1952; British Labour politician)

CURTIN, John Joseph (1885–1945; Australian statesman)

CURZON, George Nathaniel, 1st Marquess (1859–1925; British politician)

DAVITT, Michael (1846–1906; Irish nationalist)

DEAKIN, Alfred (1856–1919; Australian statesman)

DJILAS, Milovan (1911–   ; Yugoslav politician)

DUBČEK, Alexander (1921–   ; Czechoslovak statesman)

DULLES, John Foster (1888–1959; US Republican politician and diplomat)

ERHARD, Ludwig (1897–1977; German statesman)

FADDEN, Sir Arthur William (1895–1973; Australian statesman)

FISHER, Andrew (1862–1928; Australian statesman)

FLEURY, André Hercule de, Cardinal (1653–1743; French statesman)

FORBES, George William (1869–1947; New Zealand statesman)

FRANCO, Francisco (1892–1975; Spanish general and statesman)

FRASER, John Malcolm (1930–   ; Australian statesman)

FRASER, Peter (1884–1950; New Zealand statesman)

GANDHI, Indira (1917–84; Indian stateswoman)

GANDHI, Mohandas Karamchand (1869–1948; Indian nationalist leader)

6—continued

GÖRING, Hermann Wilhelm (1893–1946; German Nazi politician)

GORTON, John Grey (1911–   ; Australian statesman)

GRIVAS, Georgios (1898–1974; Greek general)

HEALEY, Denis Winston (1917–   ; British Labour politician)

HUGHES, William Morris (1864–1952; Australian statesman)

JUÁREZ, Benito Pablo (1806–72; Mexican statesman)

KAUNDA, Kenneth David (1924–   ; Zambian statesman)

KRUGER, Stephanus Johannes Paulus (1825–1904; Afrikaner statesman)

MARCOS, Ferdinand Edralin (1917–   ; Philippine statesman)

MASSEY, William Ferguson (1856–1925; New Zealand statesman)

MOBUTU, Sese Seko (Joseph Désiré M, 1930–   ; Zaïrese statesman)

MOSLEY, Sir Oswald Ernald (1896–1980; British fascist)

NASSER, Gamal Abdel (1918–70; Egyptian statesman)

O'BRIEN, Conor Cruise (1917–   ; Irish diplomat)

O'NEILL, Terence, Baron (1914–   ; Northern Irish statesman)

PÉTAIN, Henri Philippe (1856–1951; French general and statesman)

POWELL, John Enoch (1912–   ; British politician)

QUAYLE, Dan (1947–   ; US politician)

REVERE, Paul (1735–1818; American revolutionary)

RHODES, Cecil John (1853–1902; South African financier and statesman)

SAVAGE, Michael Joseph (1872–1940; New Zealand statesman)

SEDDON, Richard John (1845–1906; New Zealand statesman)

STALIN, Joseph (1879–1953; Soviet statesman)

SUÁREZ, Adolfo, Duke of (1932–   ; Spanish statesman)

THORPE, John Jeremy (1929–   ; British Liberal politician)

WATSON, John Christian (1867–1941; Australian statesman)

WILKES, John (1725–97; British journalist and politician)

ZAPATA, Emiliano (?1877–1919; Mexican revolutionary)

7

ACHESON, Dean Gooderham (1893–1971; US lawyer and statesman)

ASHDOWN, Paddy (1941–   ; Social and Liberal Democrat politician)

7—continued

ATATÜRK, Kemal (Mustafa Kemal, 1881–1938; Turkish statesman)

BATISTA (y Zaldivar), Fulgencio (1901–73; Cuban statesman)

BENNETT, Richard Bedford, Viscount (1870–1947; Canadian statesman)

BOLÍVAR, Simón (1783–1830; South American statesman)

BORMANN, Martin (1900–45; German Nazi leader)

CLINTON, de Witt (1769–1828; US statesman)

COLLINS, Michael (1890–1922; Irish nationalist)

GADDAFI, Moammar Al- (or Qaddafi, 1942– ; Libyan colonel and statesman)

GRATTAN, Henry (1746–1820; Irish politician)

GRIMOND, Joseph (1913– ; British politician)

GROMYKO, Andrei (1909– ; Soviet statesman)

HIMMLER, Heinrich (1900–45; German Nazi politician)

HOLLAND, Sir Sidney George (1893–1961; New Zealand statesman)

HUSSEIN (ibn Talal) (1935– ; King of Jordan

JENKINS, Roy Harris (1920– ; British politician and historian)

KINNOCK, Neil (1942– ; Labour politician)

KOSYGIN, Aleksei Nikolaevich (1904–80; Soviet statesman)

LUMUMBA, Patrice Hemery (1925–61; Congolese statesman)

MACLEOD, Iain Norman (1913–70; British Conservative politician)

MANDELA, Nelson (Rolihlahla) (1918– ; South African lawyer and politician)

MAZZINI, Giuseppe (1805–72; Italian patriot)

MCMAHON, William (1908– ; Australian statesman)

MENZIES, Sir Robert Gordon (1894–1978; Australian statesman)

MINTOFF, Dominic (1916– ; Maltese statesman)

MOLOTOV, Vyacheslav Mikhailovich (1890–1986; Soviet statesman)

NYERERE, Julius Kambarage (1922– ; Tanzanian statesman)

PAISLEY, Ian (1926– ; Northern Irish politician)

PARNELL, Charles Stewart (1846–91; Irish politician)

PEARSON, Lester Bowles (1897–1972; Canadian statesman)

RAFFLES, Sir Thomas Stamford (1781–1826; British colonial administrator)

SALAZAR, António de Oliveira (1889–1970; Portuguese dictator)

SCHMIDT, Helmut (1918– ; West German statesman)

7—continued

SCULLIN, James Henry (1876–1953; Australian statesman)

SHASTRI, Shri Lal Bahadur (1904–66; Indian statesman)

SUHARTO (1921– ; Indonesian statesman and general)

TROTSKY, Leon (1879–1940; Russian revolutionary)

TRUDEAU, Pierre Elliott (1919– ; Canadian statesman)

VORSTER, Balthazar Johannes (1915–83; South African statesman)

WHITLAM, Edward Gough (1916– ; Australian statesman)

8

ADENAUER, Konrad (1876–1967; German statesman)

AMIN DADA, Idi (c. 1925– ; Ugandan politician and president)

AYUB KHAN, Mohammad (1907–74; Pakistani statesman)

BEN BELLA, Ahmed (1916– ; Algerian statesman)

BISMARCK, Otto Eduard Leopold, Prince Von (1815–98; Prussian statesman)

BREZHNEV, Leonid Ilich (1906–82; Soviet statesman)

BUKHARIN, Nikolai Ivanovich (1888–1938; Soviet politician)

BULGANIN, Nikolai Aleksandrovich (1895–1975; Soviet statesman)

COSGRAVE, William Thomas (1880–1965; Irish statesman)

CROSSMAN, Richard Howard Stafford (1907–74; British Labour politician)

DALADIER, Édouard (1884–1970; French statesman)

DE GAULLE, Charles André Joseph Marie (1890–1970; French general and statesman)

DE VALERA, Eamon (1882–1975; Irish statesman)

DOLLFUSS, Engelbert (1892–1934; Austrian statesman)

DUVALIER, François (1907–71; Haitian politician)

EICHMANN, Adolf (1906–62; German Nazi politician)

FRANKLIN, Benjamin (1706–90; US diplomat)

GOEBBELS, Paul Joseph (1897–1945; German Nazi politician)

GRIFFITH, Arthur (1872–1922; Irish journalist and nationalist)

HARRIMAN, William Averell (1891–1986; US diplomat)

HASTINGS, Warren (1732–1818; British colonial administrator)

HIROHITO (1901–89; Emperor of Japan)

HOLYOAKE, Sir Keith Jacka (1904–83; New Zealand statesman)

8—continued

HONECKER, Erich (1912–   ; East German statesman)

HUMPHREY, Hubert Horatio (1911–1978; US Democratic politician)

IBARRURI, Dolores (1895–   ; Spanish politician)

KENYATTA, Jomo (c. 1891–1978; Kenyan statesman)

KHOMEINI, Ayatollah Ruholla (1900–   ; Iranian Shiite Muslim leader)

MALENKOV, Georgi Maksimilianovich (1902–88; Soviet statesman)

MCCARTHY, Joseph Raymond (1908–57; US Republican senator)

MORRISON, Herbert Stanley, Baron (1888–1965; British Labour politician)

MUZOREWA, Bishop Abel Tendekayi (1925–   ; Zimbabwean statesman)

O'CONNELL, Daniel (1775–1847; Irish politician)

O'HIGGINS, Bernardo (?1778–1842; Chilean national hero)

PINOCHET, Augusto (1915–   ; Chilean general)

PODGORNY, Nikolai (1903–   ; Soviet statesman)

POINCARÉ, Raymond (1860–1934; French statesman)

POMPIDOU, Georges Jean Raymond (1911–74; French statesman)

QUISLING, Vidkun Abraham Lauritz Jonsson (1887–1945; Norwegian army officer and Nazi collaborator)

RASPUTIN, Grigori Yefimovich (c. 1872–1916; Russian mystic)

SIHANOUK, Norodim, Prince (1923–   ; King of Cambodia)

SIKORSKI, Władysław (1881–1943; Polish general and statesman)

ULBRICHT, Walter (1893–1973; East German statesman)

VERWOERD, Hendrik Frensch (1901–66; South African statesman)

WALDHEIM, Kurt (1918–   ; Austrian diplomat and statesman)

WEIZMANN, Chaim Azriel (1874–1952; Israeli statesman)

WELENSKY, Sir Roy (1907–   ; Rhodesian statesman)

WILLIAMS, Shirley Vivien Teresa Brittain (1930–   ; British politician)

9

AGA KHAN IV (1936–   ; Imam (of the Ismaili sect of Muslims)

BEN-GURION, David (1886–1973; Israeli statesman)

CASTRO RUZ, Fidel (1926–   ; Cuban statesman)

CHOU EN-LAI (or Zhou En Lai, 1898–1976; Chinese communist statesman)

9—continued

CHURCHILL, Lord Randolph Henry Spencer (1849–95; British Conservative politician)

GAITSKELL, Hugh (1906–63; British politician)

GARIBALDI, Giuseppe (1807–82; Italian soldier)

GORBACHOV, Mikhail Sergeevich (1931–   ; Soviet statesman)

HENDERSON, Arthur (1863–1935; British Labour politician)

HO CHI MINH (Nguyen That Thanh, 1890–1969; Vietnamese statesman)

KISSINGER, Henry Alfred (1923–   ; US diplomat and political scientist)

LA GUARDIA, Fiorello Henry (1882–1947; US politician

LUXEMBURG, Rosa (1871–1919; German revolutionary)

MACDONALD, James Ramsay (1866–1937; British statesman)

MACDONALD, Sir John Alexander (1815–91; Canadian statesman)

MUSSOLINI, Benito Amilcare Andrea (1883–1945; Italian fascist dictator)

PANKHURST, Emmeline (1858–1928; British suffragette)

STEVENSON, Adlai Ewing (1900–65; US Democratic politician)

10

BERNADOTTE, Jean Baptiste Jules (c. 1763–1844; French marshal)

CARRINGTON, Peter Alexander Rupert, 6th Baron (1919–   ; British Conservative politician)

CLEMENCEAU, Georges (1841–1929; French statesman)

KHRUSHCHEV, Nikita Sergeevich (1894–1971; Soviet statesman)

LEE KUAN YEW (1923–   ; Singaporean statesman)

MAO TSE-TUNG (or Mao Ze Dong, 1893–1976; Chinese communist statesman)

MITTERRAND, François Maurice (1916–   ; French socialist politician)

RIBBENTROP, Joachim von (1893–1946; German Nazi politician)

VOROSHILOV, Kliment Yefremovich (1881–1969; Soviet marshal and statesman)

11

ABDUL RAHMAN, Tunku (1903–73; Malaysian statesman)

CASTLEREAGH, Robert Stewart, Viscount (1769–1822; British statesman)

DIEFENBAKER, John George (1895–1979; Canadian statesman)

HORE-BELISHA, Isaac Leslie, 1st Baron (1893–1957; British politician)

11—continued

MAKARIOS III, Mikhail Khristodolou Mouskos (1913–77; Cypriot churchman and statesman)

MOUNTBATTEN (of Burma), Louis, 1st Earl (1900–79; British admiral and colonial administrator)

SELWYN LLOYD, John, Baron (1904–78; British Conservative politician)

WILBERFORCE, William (1759–1833; British philanthropist)

12

BANDARANAIKE, Solomon (1899–1959; Sri Lankan statesman)

FREI MONTALVA, Eduardo (1911–82; Chilean statesman)

HAMMARSKJÖLD, Dag (1905–61; Swedish international civil servant)

MENDÈS-FRANCE, Pierre (1907–82; French statesman)

PAPADOPOULOS, George (1919–   ; Greek colonel)

13

CHIANG KAI-SHEK (or Jiang Jie Shi, 1887–1975; Nationalist Chinese soldier and statesman)

14

ALLENDE GOSSENS, Salvador (1908–73; Chilean statesman)

CLIVE OF PLASSEY, Robert, Baron (1725–74; British soldier and colonial administrator)

15

GISCARD D'ESTAING, Valéry (1926–   ; French statesman)

20+

AYATOLLAH RUHOLLA KHOMEINI. See KHOMEINI, Ayatollah Ruholla.

HAILSHAM OF ST MARYLEBONE, Baron (Quintin Mcgarel Hogg, 1907–   )

MILITARY LEADERS

3

LEE, Robert E (1807–70; US Confederate commander)

NEY, Michel, Prince of Moscow (1769–1815; French marshal)

4

ALBA, Fernando Alvarez de Toledo, Duke of (1507–83; Spanish general)

BART, Jean (1650–1702; French admiral)

BYNG, George, Viscount Torrington (1663–1733; English admiral)

DIAZ, Porfirio (1830–1915; Mexican soldier)

FOCH, Ferdinand (1851–1929; French marshal)

HAIG, Douglas, 1st Earl (1861–1928; British field marshal)

HOOD, Samuel, 1st Viscount (1724–1816; British admiral)

HOWE, Richard, Earl (1726–99; British admiral)

JODL, Alfred (1890–1946; German general)

RAIS, Gilles de (or G de Retz, 1404–40; French marshal)

RÖHM, Ernst (1887–1934; German soldier)

ROON, Albrecht, Graf von (1803–79; Prussian general)

SAXE, Maurice, Comte de (1696–1750; Marshal of France)

SLIM, William Joseph, 1st Viscount (1891–1970; British field marshal)

TOGO (Heihachiro) (1847–1934; Japanese admiral)

5

ANDRÉ, John (1751–80; British soldier)

ANSON, George Anson, Baron (1697–1762; British admiral)

BLAKE, Robert (1599–1657; English admiral)

BLIGH, William (1754–1817; British admiral)

CIMON (d. c. 450 BC; Athenian general and politician)

DEWEY, George (1837–1917; US admiral)

DRAKE, Sir Francis (1540–96; English navigator and admiral)

EL CID (Rodrigo Diáz de Vivar, c. 1040–99; Spanish warrior)

GATES, Horatio (?1728–1806; American general)

HAWKE, Edward, 1st Baron (1705–81; British admiral)

JONES, John Paul (1747–92; American naval commander)

LALLY, Thomas, Comte de (1702–66; French general)

LEVEN, Alexander Leslie, 1st Earl of (1580–1661; Scottish general)

MOORE, Sir John (1761–1809; British general)

MURAT, Joachim (1767–1815; French marshal)

PERRY, Matthew C (1794–1858; US naval officer)

PRIDE, Thomas (d. 1658; English parliamentary soldier)

5—continued

SULLA, Lucius Cornelius (c. 138–78 BC; Roman dictator)

TILLY, Johan Tserclaes, Graf von (1559–1632; Bavarian general)

TROMP, Maarten (1598–1653; Dutch admiral)

WOLFE, James (1727–59; British soldier)

6

AETIUS, Flavius (d. 454 AD; Roman general)

ARNOLD, Benedict (1741–1801; American general)

BAYARD, Pierre Terrail, Seigneur de (c. 1473–1524; French soldier)

BEATTY, David, 1st Earl (1871–1936; British admiral)

BENBOW, John (1653–1702; English naval officer)

CRONJE, Piet Arnoldus (c. 1840–1911; South African general)

CUSTER, George Armstrong (1839–76; US cavalry general)

DARLAN, Jean (Louis Xavier) François (1881–1942; French admiral)

DÖNITZ, Karl (1891–1981; German admiral)

DUNDEE, John Graham of Claverhouse, 1st Viscount (c. 1649–89; Scottish soldier)

DUNOIS, Jean d'Orléans, Comte de (1403–68; French general)

FISHER, John Arbuthnot, 1st Baron (1841–1920; British admiral)

FRENCH, John, 1st Earl of Ypres (1852–1925; British field marshal)

FULLER, J F C (1878–1966; British soldier)

GINKEL, Godert de, 1st Earl of Athlone (1644–1703; Dutch general)

GORDON, Charles George (1833–85; British general)

GRANBY, John Manners, Marquess of (1721–70, British soldier)

GREENE, Nathaneal (1742–86; American general)

HALSEY, William F (1882–1959; US admiral)

JOFFRE, Joseph Jacques Césaire (1852–1931; French marshal)

KEITEL, Wilhelm (1882–1946; German field marshal)

KLÉBER, Jean Baptiste (1753–1800; French general)

KONIEV, Ivan Stepanovich (1897–1973; Soviet marshal)

MARIUS, Gaius (c. 157–86 BC; Roman general)

MOLTKE, Helmuth, Graf von (1800–91; Prussian field marshal)

MOREAU, Jean Victor (1763–1813; French general)

NAPIER (of Magdala), Robert Cornelis, 1st Baron (1810–90; British field marshal)

NAPIER, Sir Charles James (1782–1853; British general)

NARSES (c. 480–574 AD; Byzantine general)

6—continued

NELSON, Horatio, Viscount (1758–1805; British admiral)

NIMITZ, Chester W (1885–1966; US admiral)

OUTRAM, Sir James (1803–63; British soldier)

PATTON, George S (1885–1945; US general)

PAULUS, Friedrich (1890–1957; German field marshal)

PÉTAIN, (Henri) Philippe (1856–1951; French general and statesman)

RAEDER, Erich (1876–1960; German admiral)

RAGLAN, Fitzroy James Henry Somerset, 1st Baron (1788–1855; British field marshal)

RODNEY, George Brydges, 1st Baron (1719–92; British admiral)

ROMMEL, Erwin (1891–1944; German general)

RUPERT, Prince (1619–82; Cavalry officer)

RUYTER, Michiel Adriaanszoon de (1607–76; Dutch admiral)

TEDDER, Arthur William, 1st Baron (1890–1967; British air marshal)

VERNON, Edward (1684–1757; British admiral)

WAVELL, Archibald Percival, 1st Earl (1883–1950; British field marshal)

WILSON, Henry Maitland, 1st Baron (1881–1964; British field marshal)

WILSON, Sir Henry Hughes (1864–1922; British field marshal)

ZHUKOV, Georgi Konstantinovich (1896–1974; Soviet marshal)

7

AGRIPPA, Marcus Vipsanius (?63–12 BC; Roman general)

ALLENBY, Edmund Henry Hynman, 1st Viscount (1861–1936; British field marshal)

ARTIGAS, José Gervasio (1764–1850; national hero of Uruguay)

ATHLONE, Alexander Cambridge, 1st Earl of (1874–1957; British soldier)

BAZAINE, Achille François (1811–88; French marshal)

BERWICK, James Fitzjames, Duke of (1670–1734; Marshal of France)

BLÜCHER, Gebhard Leberecht von, Prince of Wahlstatt (1742–1819; Prussian general)

BRADLEY, Omar Nelson (1893–1981; US general)

DECATUR, Stephen (1779–1820; US naval officer)

DENIKIN, Anton Ivanovich (1872–1947; Russian general)

DOWDING, Hugh Caswall Tremenheere, 1st Baron (1882–1970; British air chief marshal)

FAIRFAX, Thomas, 3rd Baron (1612–71; English general)

JACKSON, Andrew (1767–1845; US statesman and general)

JACKSON, Stonewall (Thomas Jonathan J. 1824–63; US Confederate general)

7—continued

KOLCHAK, Alexander Vasilievich (1874–1920; Russian admiral)

LAMBERT, John (1619–83; English parliamentary general)

LYAUTEY, Louis Hubert Gonzalve (1854–1934; French marshal)

MASSÉNA, André (?1756–1817; French marshal)

METAXAS, Ioannis (1871–1941; Greek general)

MORTIER, Édouard Adolphe Casimir Joseph, Duc de Trévise (1768–1835; French marshal)

PHILLIP, Arthur (1738–1814; British admiral)

REGULUS, Marcus Attilus (d. c. 251 BC; Roman general)

ROBERTS, Frederick Sleigh, 1st Earl (1832–1914; British field marshal)

SHERMAN, William Tecumseh (1820–91; US Federal general)

SHOVELL, Sir Cloudesley (1650–1707; English admiral)

SUVOROV, Aleksandr Vasilievich, Count (1729–1800; Russian field marshal)

TANCRED (c. 1078–1112; Norman Crusader)

TIRPITZ, Alfred von (1849–1930; German admiral)

TURENNE, Henri de la Tour d'Auvergne, Vicomte de (1611–75; French marshal)

VENDÔME, Louis Joseph, Duc de (1654–1712; French marshal)

VILLARS, Claude Louis Hector, Duc de (1653–1734; French marshal)

WALLACE, Lew (1827–1905; US soldier)

WINGATE, Orde Charles (1903–44; British soldier)

WRANGEL, Peter Nikolaievich, Baron (1878–1928; Russian general)

8

AGRICOLA, Gnaeus Julius (40–93 AD; Roman governor)

ANGLESEY, Henry William Paget, 1st Marquess of (1768–1854; British field marshal)

AUGEREAU, Pierre François Charles, Duc de Castiglione (1757–1816; French marshal)

BADOGLIO, Pietro (1871–1956; Italian general)

BERTRAND, Henri Gratien, Comte (1773–1844; French marshal)

BOURMONT, Louis Auguste Victor de Ghaisnes, Comte de (1773–1846; French marshal)

BURGOYNE, John (1722–92; British general)

CAMPBELL, Colin, Baron Clyde (1792–1863; British field marshal)

CARDIGAN, James Thomas Brudenell, 7th Earl of (1797–1868; British cavalry officer)

CARRANZA, Venustiano (1859–1920; Mexican statesman and soldier)

8—continued

COCHRANE, Thomas, 10th Earl of Dundonald (1775–1860; British admiral)

CROMWELL, Oliver (1599–1658; English soldier and statesman)

GUESCLIN, Bertrand du (c. 1320–80; French commander)

HANNIBAL (247–c. 183 BC; Carthaginian general)

IRONSIDE, William Edmund, 1st Baron (1880–1959; British field marshal)

JELLICOE, John Rushworth, 1st Earl (1859–1935; British admiral)

KORNILOV, Lavrentia Georgievich (1870–1918; Russian general)

LUCULLUS, Lucius Licinius (d. c. 57 BC; Roman general)

LYSANDER (d. 395 BC; Spartan general)

MARSHALL, George C (1880–1959; US general)

MONTCALM, Louis Joseph de Montcalm-Grozon, Marquis de (1712–59; French general)

O'HIGGINS, Bernardo (?1778–1842; Chilean national hero)

PERSHING, John J (1860–1948; US general)

SANDWICH, John Montagu, 4th Earl of (1718–92; first lord of the admiralty)

SHERIDAN, Philip H (1831–88; US Federal general)

STILICHO, Flavius (d. 408 AD; Roman general)

STILWELL, Joseph W (1883–1946; US general)

WOLSELEY, Garnet Joseph, 1st Viscount (1833–1913; British field marshal)

9

ANGOULÊME, Charles de Valois, Duc d' (1573–1650; French soldier)

ANTIPATER (397–319 BC; Macedonian general)

ANTONESCU, Ion (1882–1946; Romanian general)

ARISTIDES (the Just) (c. 520–c. 468 BC; Athenian statesman)

BONAPARTE, Napoleon (1769–1821; French emperor)

DUMOURIEZ, Charles François Du Périer (1739–1823; French general)

GNEISENAU, August, Graf Neithardt von (1760–1831; Prussian field marshal)

GRENVILLE, Sir Richard (?1541–91; British sailor)

HASDRUBAL (d. 207 BC; Carthaginian general)

KITCHENER (of Khartoum), Horatio Herbert, 1st Earl (1850–1916; British field marshal)

LAFAYETTE, Marie Joseph Gilbert Motier, Marquis de (1757–1834; French general and politician)

MACARTHUR, Douglas (1880–1964; US general)

9—continued

MARCELLUS, Marcus Claudius (d. 208 BC; Roman general)

MCCLELLAN, George B (1826–85; Federal general)

MILTIADES (c. 550–489 BC; Athenian general)

NEWCASTLE, William Cavendish, Duke of (1592–1676; English soldier)

OLDCASTLE, Sir John (c. 1378–1417; English soldier)

PRETORIUS, Andries (1799–1853; Afrikaner leader)

RUNDSTEDT, Gerd von (1875–1953; German field marshal)

SANTA ANNA, Antonio López de (1794–1876; Mexican soldier)

TRENCHARD, Hugh Montague, 1st Viscount (1873–1956; The first British air marshal)

10

ABERCROMBY, Sir Ralph (1734–1801; British general)

ALANBROOKE, Alan Francis Brooke, 1st Viscount (1883–1963; British field marshal)

ALCIBIADES (c. 450–404 BC; Athenian general and politician)

ANTIGONUS I (c. 382–301 BC; Macedonian general)

AUCHINLECK, Sir Claude (1884–1981; British field marshal)

BELISARIUS (c. 505–65 AD; Byzantine general)

BERNADOTTE, Jean Baptiste Jules (1763–1844)

CORNWALLIS, Charles, 1st Marquess (1738–1805; British general)

CUMBERLAND, William Augustus, Duke of (1721–65; British general)

ENVER PASHA (1881–1922; Turkish soldier)

FLAMININUS, Titus Quinctius (c. 230–c. 174 BC; Roman general)

HINDENBURG, Paul von Beneckendorff und von (1847–1934; German general)

KESSELRING, Albert (1885–1960; German general)

KUBLAI KHAN (1215–94; Mongol conqueror of China)

MANNERHEIM, Carl Gustaf Emil, Baron von (1867–1951; Finnish general)

MONTGOMERY (of Alamein), Bernard Law, 1st Viscount (1887–1976; British field marshal)

OGLETHORPE, James Edward (1696–1785; English general)

RICHTHOFEN, Manfred, Freiherr von (1892–1918; German air ace)

SCHLIEFFEN, Alfred, Graf von (1833–1913; German general)

TIMOSHENKO, Semyon Konstantinovich (1895–1970; Soviet marshal)

VILLENEUVE, Pierre (1763–1806; French admiral)

10—continued

WELLINGTON, Arthur Wellesley, Duke of (1769–1852; British general)

11

ALBUQUERQUE, Alfonso de (1453–1515; Portuguese governor in India)

BADEN-POWELL, Robert Stephenson Smyth, 1st Baron (1857–1941; British general)

BEAUHARNAIS, Alexandre, Vicomte de (1760–94; French general)

BRAUCHITSCH, Walther von (1881–1948; German general)

COLLINGWOOD, Cuthbert, 1st Baron (1750–1810; British admiral)

EPAMINONDAS (c. 418–362 BC; Theban general)

LIDDELL HART, Sir Basil Henry (1895–1970; British soldier)

MARLBOROUGH, John Churchill, 1st Duke of (1650–1722; British general)

MÜNCHHAUSEN, Karl Friedrich, Freiherr von (1720–97; German soldier)

PONIATOWSKI, Józef (1763–1813; Marshal of France)

WALLENSTEIN, Albrecht Wenzel von (1583–1634; Bohemian-born general)

12

IBRAHIM PASHA (1789–1848; Ottoman general)

13

EUGÈNE OF SAVOY, Prince (1663–1736; Austrian general)

FABIUS MAXIMUS, Quintus (d. 203 BC; Roman general)

HAMILCAR BARCA (d. c. 229 BC; Carthaginian general)

14

BARCLAY DE TOLLY, Mikhail Bogdanovich, Prince (1761–1818; Russian field marshal)

CLIVE OF PLASSEY, Robert, Baron (1725–74; British soldier and colonial administrator)

15

CASSIUS LONGINUS, Gaius (d. 42 BC; Roman general)

SCIPIO AFRICANUS (236–183 BC; Roman general)

16

ALEXANDER OF TUNIS, Harold, 1st Earl (1891–1969; British field marshal)

17

HOWARD OF EFFINGHAM, Charles, 2nd Baron (1536–1624; English Lord High Admiral)

20+

BERNHARD OF SAXE-WEIMAR, Duke (1604–39; German general)

SCIPIO AEMILIANUS AFRICANUS (c. 185–129 BC; Roman general)

PRIME MINISTERS OF GREAT BRITAIN (FROM 1721)

NAME (TERM)

ROBERT WALPOLE (1721–42)
SPENCER COMPTON, EARL OF WILMINGTON (1742–43)
HENRY PELHAM (1743–54)
THOMAS PELHAM-HOLLES, DUKE OF NEWCASTLE (1754–56)
WILLIAM CAVENDISH, DUKE OF DEVONSHIRE (1756–57)
THOMAS PELHAM-HOLLES, DUKE OF NEWCASTLE (1757–62)
JOHN STUART, EARL OF BUTE (1762–63)
GEORGE GRENVILLE (1763–65)
CHARLES WATSON-WENTWORTH, MARQUIS OF ROCKINGHAM (1765–66)
WILLIAM PITT, EARL OF CHATHAM (1766–68)
AUGUSTUS HENRY FITZROY, DUKE OF GRAFTON (1768–70)
FREDERICK NORTH (1770–82)
CHARLES WATSON-WENTWORTH, MARQUIS OF ROCKINGHAM (1782)
WILLIAM PETTY, EARL OF SHELBURNE (1782–83)
WILLIAM HENRY CAVENDISH BENTINCK, DUKE OF PORTLAND (1783)
WILLIAM PITT (SON OF EARL OF CHATHAM) (1783–1801)
HENRY ADDINGTON (1801–04)
WILLIAM PITT (1804–06)
WILLIAM WYNDHAM GRENVILLE, BARON GRENVILLE (1806–07)
WILLIAM BENTINCK, DUKE OF PORTLAND (1807–09)
SPENCER PERCEVAL (1809–12)
ROBERT BANKS JENKINSON, EARL OF LIVERPOOL (1812–27)
GEORGE CANNING (1827)
FREDERICK JOHN ROBINSON, VISCOUNT GODERICH (1827–28)
ARTHUR WELLESLEY, DUKE OF WELLINGTON (1828–30)
CHARLES GREY, EARL GREY (1830–34)
WILLIAM LAMB, VISCOUNT MELBOURNE (1834)
ROBERT PEEL (1834–35)
WILLIAM LAMB, VISCOUNT MELBOURNE (1835–41)
ROBERT PEEL (1841–46)
JOHN RUSSELL (1846–52)
EDWARD GEORGE GEOFFREY SMITH STANLEY, EARL OF DERBY (1852)

GEORGE HAMILTON GORDON, EARL OF ABERDEEN (1852–55)
HENRY JOHN TEMPLE, VISCOUNT PALMERSTON (1855–58)
EDWARD STANLEY, EARL OF DERBY (1858–59)
HENRY TEMPLE, VISCOUNT PALMERSTON (1859–65)
JOHN RUSSELL, EARL RUSSELL (1865–66)
EDWARD STANLEY, EARL OF DERBY (1866–68)
BENJAMIN DISRAELI (1868)
WILLIAM EWART GLADSTONE (1868–74)
BENJAMIN DISRAELI, EARL (1876) OF BEACONSFIELD (1874–80)
WILLIAM EWART GLADSTONE (1880–85)
ROBERT A. T. GASCOYNE-CECIL, MARQUIS OF SALISBURY (1885–86)
WILLIAM EWART GLADSTONE (1886)
ROBERT GASCOYNE-CECIL, MARQUIS OF SALISBURY (1886–92)
WILLIAM EWART GLADSTONE (1892–94)
ARCHIBALD PHILIP PRIMROSE, EARL OF ROSEBERY (1894–95)
ROBERT GASCOYNE-CECIL, MARQUIS OF SALISBURY (1895–1902)
ARTHUR JAMES BALFOUR (1902–05)
HENRY CAMPBELL-BANNERMAN (1905–08)
HERBERT HENRY ASQUITH (1908–16)
DAVID LLOYD GEORGE (1916–22)
ANDREW BONAR LAW (1922–23)
STANLEY BALDWIN (1923–24)
JAMES RAMSAY MACDONALD (1924)
STANLEY BALDWIN (1924–29)
JAMES RAMSAY MACDONALD (1929–35)
STANLEY BALDWIN (1935–37)
NEVILLE CHAMBERLAIN (1937–40)
WINSTON CHURCHILL (1940–45)
CLEMENT RICHARD ATTLEE (1945–51)
WINSTON CHURCHILL (1951–55)
ANTHONY EDEN (1955–57)
HAROLD MACMILLAN (1957–63)
ALEC DOUGLAS-HOME (1963–64)
HAROLD WILSON (1964–70)
EDWARD HEATH (1970–74)
HAROLD WILSON (1974–76)
JAMES CALLAGHAN (1976–79)
MARGARET THATCHER (1979–   )

THE PRESIDENTS OF THE UNITED STATES OF AMERICA

NAME (TERM)

GEORGE WASHINGTON (1789–97)
JOHN ADAMS (1797–1801)
THOMAS JEFFERSON (1801–09)
JAMES MADISON (1809–17)
JAMES MONROE (1817–25)
JOHN QUINCY ADAMS (1825–29)
ANDREW JACKSON (1829–37)
MARTIN VAN BUREN (1837–41)
WILLIAM HENRY HARRISON (1841)
JOHN TYLER (1841–45)
JAMES KNOX POLK (1845–49)
ZACHARY TAYLOR (1849–50)
MILLARD FILLMORE (1850–53)
FRANKLIN PIERCE (1853–57)
JAMES BUCHANAN (1857–61)
ABRAHAM LINCOLN (1861–65)
ANDREW JOHNSON (1865–69)
ULYSSES SIMPSON GRANT (1869–77)
RUTHERFORD BIRCHARD HAYES (1877–81)
JAMES ABRAM GARFIELD (1881)
CHESTER ALAN ARTHUR (1881–85)

GROVER CLEVELAND (1885–89)
BENJAMIN HARRISON (1889–93)
GROVER CLEVELAND (1893–97)
WILLIAM MCKINLEY (1897–1901)
THEODORE ROOSEVELT (1901–09)
WILLIAM HOWARD TAFT (1909–13)
WOODROW WILSON (1913–21)
WARREN GAMALIEL HARDING (1921–23)
CALVIN COOLIDGE (1923–29)
HERBERT CLARK HOOVER (1929–33)
FRANKLIN DELANO ROOSEVELT (1933–45)
HARRY S TRUMAN (1945–53)
DWIGHT DAVID EISENHOWER (1953–61)
JOHN FITZGERALD KENNEDY (1961–63)
LYNDON BAINES JOHNSON (1963–69)
RICHARD MILHOUS NIXON (1969–74)
GERALD RUDOLPH FORD (1974–77)
JAMES EARL CARTER (1977–81)
RONALD WILSON REAGAN (1981–89)
GEORGE HERBERT WALKER BUSH (1989–   )

RULERS OF ENGLAND

KINGS OF KENT

HENGEST (c. 455–488)
GERIC surnamed OISC (488–?512)
OCTA (?512–?)
EORMENRIC (?–560)
ETHELBERT I (560–616)
EADBALD (616–640)
EARCONBERT (640–664)
EGBERT I (664–673)
HLOTHERE* (673–685)
EADRIC* (685–686)
SUAEBHARD* (676–692)
OSWINI* (?688–?690)
WIHTRED* (690–725)
ETHELBERT II* (725–762)
EADBERT* (?725–?762)
ALRIC* (c. 750s)
EARDWULF* (747–762)
SIGERED* (?762)
EANMUND* (c. 759–765)
HEABERHT* (764–765)
EGBERT II (c. 765–780)
EALHMUND (784–786)
EADBERT (PRAEN) (796–798)
EADWALD (?798 or 807)

CUTHRED (798–807)
BALDRED (?–825)

KINGS OF DEIRA

AELLI (c. 560–590)
EDWIN (?590–592)
ETHELFRITH (592–616)
EDWIN (616–632)
OSRIC (632–633)
OSWALD (ST.) (633–641)
OSWINE (644–651)
ETHELWALD (651–654)

KINGS OF NORTHUMBRIA

ETHELFRITH (592–616)
EDWIN (616–632)
OSWALD (ST.) (633–641)
OSWIU (654–670)
EGFRITH (670–685)
ALDFRITH (685–704)
OSRED I (704–716)
COENRED (716–718)
OSRIC (718–729)
CEOLWULF (729–737)

EADBERT (737–758)
OSWULF (c. 758)
ETHELWALD MOLL (758–765)
ALCHRED (765–774)
ETHELRED I (774–778)
ELFWALD I (778–788)
OSRED II (788–790)
ETHELRED I (790–796)
OSBALD (796)
EARDWULF (796–806)
ELFWALD II (806–808)
EARDWULF (?808)
EANRED (808–840)
ETHELRED II (840–844)
REDWULF (844)
ETHELRED II (844–849)
OSBERT (849–862)
AELLE (862–867)
EGBERT I (867–873)
RICSIG (873–876)
EGBERT II (876–?878)

KINGS OF MERCIA

CEARL (c. 600)
PENDA (632–654)
WULFHERE (657–674)
ETHELRED (674–704)
COENRED (704–709)
CEOLRED (709–716)
ETHELBALD (716–?757)
BEORNRED (757)
OFFA (757–796)
EGFRITH (796)
COENWULF (796–?821)
CEOLWULF I (821–823)
BEORNWULF (823–825)
LUDECAN (825–827)
WIGLAF (827–840)
BEORHTWULF (840–852)
BURGRED (852–874)
CEOLWULF II (874–?883)

KINGS OF THE WEST SAXONS

CERDIC (519–534)
CYNRIC (534–560)
CEAWLIN (560–591)
CEOL (591–597)
CEOLWULF (597–611)
CYNEGILS (611–643)
CENWALH (643–672)
SEAXBURH (Queen) (?672–?674)
AESCWINE (674–676)
CENTWINE (676–685)
CAEDWALLA (685–688)
INI (688–726)
AETHELHEARD (726–?740)
CUTHRED (740–756)
SIGEBERHT (756–757)
CYNEWULF (757–786)
BEORHTRIC (786–802)
EGBERT (802–839)

ETHELWULF (839–855)
ETHELBALD (855–860)
ETHELBERT (860–866)
ETHELRED (866–871)
ALFRED (871–899)
EDWARD THE ELDER (899–925)
ATHELSTAN (925–939)
EDMUND (939–946)
EDRED (946–955)

RULERS OF ENGLAND

EDWY (955–959)
EDGAR (959–975)
EDWARD THE MARTYR (975–979)
ETHELRED (979–1013)
SWEGN FORKBEARD (1013–14)
ETHELRED (1014–16)
EDMUND IRONSIDE (1016)
CANUTE (1016–35)
HAROLD HAREFOOT (1035–40)
HARTACNUT (1040–42)
EDWARD THE CONFESSOR (1042–66)
HAROLD GODWINSON (1066)
EDGAR ETHELING (1066)
WILLIAM I (THE CONQUEROR) (1066–87)
WILLIAM II (RUFUS) (1087–1100)
HENRY I (1100–35)
STEPHEN (1135–54)
HENRY II (1154–89)
RICHARD I (1189–99)
JOHN (1199–1216)
HENRY III (1216–72)
EDWARD I (1272–1307)
EDWARD II (1307–27)
EDWARD III (1327–77)
RICHARD II (1377–99)
HENRY IV (1399–1413)
HENRY V (1413–22)
HENRY VI (1422–61; 1470–71)
EDWARD IV (1461–83)
EDWARD V (1483)
RICHARD III (1483–85)
HENRY VII (1485–1509)
HENRY VIII (1509–47)
EDWARD VI (1547–53)
JANE (LADY JANE GREY) (1553)
MARY (1553–58)
PHILIP* (1554–58)
ELIZABETH I (1558–1603)
JAMES I (1603–25)
CHARLES I (1625–49)
THE COMMONWEALTH (1649–60; OLIVER
  CROMWELL (LORD PROTECTOR, 1653–
  58); RICHARD CROMWELL (LORD
  PROTECTOR, 1658–59))
CHARLES II (1660–85)
JAMES II (1685–88)
WILLIAM AND MARY (1689–1694)
WILLIAM III (1694–1702)
ANNE (1702–14)
GEORGE I (1714–27)

GEORGE II (1727–60)
GEORGE III (1760–1820)
GEORGE IV (1820–30)
WILLIAM IV (1830–37)
VICTORIA (1837–1901)
EDWARD VII (1901–10)

GEORGE V (1910–36)
EDWARD VIII (DUKE OF WINDSOR) (1936)
GEORGE VI (1936–52)
ELIZABETH II (1952–   )

* Joint rulers

NOBEL PRIZE WINNERS

PHYSICS

1901	W RÖNTGEN (GER)
1902	H ANTOON LORENTZ (NETH)
	P ZEEMAN (NETH)
1903	A BECQUEREL (FR)
	P CURIE (FR)
	M CURIE (FR)
1904	LORD RAYLEIGH (GB)
1905	P LENARD (GER)
1906	SIR J J THOMSON (GB)
1907	A A MICHELSON (US)
1908	G LIPPMANN (FR)
1909	G MARCONI (ITALY)
	K BRAUN (GER)
1910	J VAN DER WAALS (NETH)
1911	W WIEN (GER)
1912	N G DALÉN (SWED)
1913	H KAMERLINGH ONNES (NETH)
1914	M VON LAUE (GER)
1915	SIR W BRAGG (GB)
	SIR L BRAGG (GB)
1916	(NO AWARD)
1917	C BARKLA (GB)
1918	M PLANCK (GER)
1919	J STARK (GER)
1920	C GUILLAUME (SWITZ)
1921	A EINSTEIN (SWITZ)
1922	N BOHR (DEN)
1923	R MILLIKAN (US)
1924	K SIEGBAHN (SWED)
1925	J FRANCK (GER)
	G HERTZ (GER)
1926	J PERRIN (FR)
1927	A H COMPTON (US)
	C WILSON (GB)
1928	SIR O RICHARDSON (GB)
1929	PRINCE L DE BROGLIE (FR)
1930	SIR C RAMAN (INDIA)
1931	(NO AWARD)
1932	W HEISENBERG (GER)
1933	P A M DIRAC (GB)
	E SCHRÖDINGER (AUSTRIA)
1934	(NO AWARD)
1935	SIR J CHADWICK (GB)
1936	V HESS (AUSTRIA)
	C ANDERSON (US)
1937	C DAVISSON (US)
	SIR G P THOMSON (GB)

1938	E FERMI (ITALY)
1939	E LAWRENCE (US)
1943	O STERN (US)
1944	I RABI (US)
1945	W PAULI (AUSTRIA)
1946	P BRIDGMAN (US)
1947	SIR E APPLETON (GB)
1948	P BLACKETT (GB)
1949	H YUKAWA (JAPAN)
1950	C POWELL (GB)
1951	SIR J COCKCROFT (GB)
	E WALTON (IRE)
1952	F BLOCH (US)
	E PURCELL (US)
1953	F ZERNIKE (NETH)
1954	M BORN (GB)
	W BOTHE (GER)
1955	W LAMB, JR (US)
	P KUSCH (US)
1956	W SHOCKLEY (US)
	J BARDEEN (US)
	W BRATTAIN (US)
1957	TSUNG-DAO LEE (CHINA)
	C N YANG (CHINA)
1958	P A CHERENKOV (USSR)
	I M FRANK (USSR)
	I Y TAMM (USSR)
1959	E SEGRÈ (US)
	O CHAMBERLAIN (US)
1960	D GLASER (US)
1961	R HOFSTADTER (US)
	R MÖSSBAUER (GER)
1962	L D LANDAU (USSR)
1963	J H D JENSEN (GER)
	M G MAYER (US)
	E P WIGNER (US)
1964	C H TOWNES (US)
	N G BASOV (USSR)
	A M PROKHOROV (USSR)
1965	J S SCHWINGER (US)
	R P FEYNMAN (US)
	S TOMONAGA (JAPAN)
1966	A KASTLER (FR)
1967	H A BETHE (US)
1968	L W ALVAREZ (US)
1969	M GELL-MANN (US)
1970	H ALVÉN (SWED)

	L NÉEL (FR)	1919	(NO AWARD)	
1971	D GABOR (GB)	1920	W NERNST (GER)	
1972	J BARDEEN (US)	1921	F SODDY (GB)	
	L N COOPER (US)	1922	F ASTON (GB)	
	J R SCHRIEFFER (US)	1923	F PREGL (AUSTRIA)	
1973	L ESAKI (JAPAN)	1924	(NO AWARD)	
	I GIAEVER (US)	1925	R ZSIGMONDY (AUSTRIA)	
	B JOSEPHSON (GB)	1926	T SVEDBERG (SWED)	
1974	SIR M RYLE (GB)	1927	H WIELAND (GER)	
	A HEWISH (GB)	1928	A WINDAUS (GER)	
1975	J RAINWATER (US)	1929	SIR A HARDEN (GB)	
	A BOHR (DEN)		H VON EULER-CHELPIN (SWED)	
	B MOTTELSON (DEN)	1930	H FISCHER (GER)	
1976	B RICHTER (US)	1931	K BOSCH (GER)	
	S TING (US)		F BERGIUS (GER)	
1977	P W ANDERSON (US)	1932	I LANGMUIR (US)	
	SIR N F MOTT (GB)	1933	(NO AWARD)	
	J H VAN VLECK (US)	1934	H UREY (US)	
1978	P L KAPITSA (USSR)	1935	F JOLIOT-CURIE (FR)	
	A A PENZIAS (US)		I JOLIOT-CURIE (FR)	
	R W WILSON (US)	1936	P DEBYE (NETH)	
1979	S L GLASHOW (US)	1937	SIR W HAWORTH (GB)	
	A SALAM (PAK)		P KARRER (SWITZ)	
	S WEINBERG (US)	1938	R KUHN (GER)	
1980	J CRONIN (US)	1939	A BUTENANDT (GER)	
	V FITCH (US)		L RUZICKA (SWITZ)	
1981	K SIEGBAHN (SWED)	1943	G DE HEVESY (HUNG)	
	N BLOEMBERGEN (US)	1944	O HAHN (GER)	
	A SCHAWLOW (US)	1945	A VIRTANEN (FIN)	
1982	K G WILSON (US)	1946	J SUMNER (US)	
1983	S CHANDRASEKHAR (US)		J NORTHROP (US)	
	W FOWLER (US)		W STANLEY (US)	
1984	C RUBBIA (ITALY)	1947	SIR R ROBINSON (GB)	
	S VAN DER MEER (NETH)	1948	A TISELIUS (SWED)	
1985	K VON KLITZING (GER)	1949	W GIAUQUE (US)	
1986	E RUSKA (GER)	1950	O DIELS (GER)	
	G BINNIG (GER)		K ALDER (GER)	
	H ROHRER (SWITZ)	1951	E MCMILLAN (US)	
1987	A MÜLLER (SWITZ)		G SEABORG (US)	
	G BEDNORZ (GER)	1952	A MARTIN (GB)	
			R SYNGE (GB)	

CHEMISTRY

		1953	H STAUDINGER (GER)	
1901	J V HOFF (NETH)	1954	L C PAULING (US)	
1902	E FISCHER (GER)	1955	V DU VIGNEAUD (US)	
1903	S ARRHENIUS (SWED)	1956	N SEMYONOV (USSR)	
1904	SIR W RAMSAY (GB)		SIR C HINSHELWOOD (GB)	
1905	A VON BAEYER (GER)	1957	SIR A TODD (GB)	
1906	H MOISSAN (FR)	1958	F SANGER (GB)	
1907	E BUCHNER (GER)	1959	J HEYROVSKY (CZECH)	
1908	LORD RUTHERFORD (GB)	1960	W LIBBY (US)	
1909	W OSTWALD (GER)	1961	M CALVIN (US)	
1910	O WALLACH (GER)	1962	J C KENDREW (GB)	
1911	M CURIE (FR)		M F PERUTZ (GB)	
1912	V GRIGNARD (FR)	1963	G NATTA (ITALY)	
	P SABATIER (FR)		K ZIEGLER (GER)	
1913	A WERNER (SWITZ)	1964	D M C HODGKIN (GB)	
1914	T RICHARDS (US)	1965	R B WOODWARD (US)	
1915	R WILLSTÄTTER (GER)	1966	R S MULLIKEN (US)	
1916	(NO AWARD)	1967	M EIGEN (GER)	
1917	(NO AWARD)		R G W NORRISH (GB)	
1918	F HABER (GER)		G PORTER (GB)	

1968	L ONSAGER (US)		J J R MACLEOD (GB)
1969	D H R BARTON (GB)	1924	W EINTHOVEN (NETH)
	O HASSEL (NOR)	1925	(NO AWARD)
1970	L F LELOIR (ARG)	1926	J FIBIGER (DEN)
1971	G HERZBERG (CAN)	1927	J WAGNER VON JAUREGG
1972	C B ANFINSEN (US)		(AUSTRIA)
	S MOORE (US)	1928	C NICOLLE (FR)
	W H STEIN (US)	1929	C EIJKMAN (NETH)
1973	E FISCHER (GER)		SIR F HOPKINS (GB)
	G WILKINSON (GB)	1930	K LANDSTEINER (US)
1974	P J FLORY (US)	1931	O WARBURG (GER)
1975	J W CORNFORT (AUSTR)	1932	E D ADRIAN (GB)
	V PRELOG (SWITZ)		SIR C SHERRINGTON (GB)
1976	W M LIPSCOMB (US)	1933	T H MORGAN (US)
1977	I PRIGOGINE (BELGIUM)	1934	G R MINOT (US)
1978	P MITCHELL (GB)		W P MURPHY (US)
1979	H C BROWN (US)		G H WHIPPLE (US)
	G WITTIG (GER)	1935	H SPEMANN (GER)
1980	P BERG (US)	1936	SIR H H DALE (GB)
	W GILBERT (US)		O LOEWI (GER)
	F SANGER (GB)	1937	A SZENT-GYÖRGYI (HUNG)
1981	K FUKUI (JAPAN)	1938	C HEYMANS (BELG)
	R HOFFMANN (POL)	1939	G DOMAGK (GER)
1982	A KLUG (GB)	1943	H DAM (DEN)
1983	H TAUBE (US)		E A DOISY (US)
1984	R B MERRIFIELD (US)	1944	J ERLANGER (US)
1985	H HAUPTMAN (US)		H S GASSER (US)
	J KARLE (US)	1945	SIR A FLEMING (GB)
1986	D HERSCHBACH (US)		E B CHAIN (GB)
	Y TSEH LEE (US)		LORD FLOREY (AUSTR)
	J POLANYI (CAN)	1946	H J MULLER (US)
1987	D CRAM (US)	1947	C F CORI (US)
	J LEHN (FR)		G T CORI (US)
	C PEDERSEN (US)		B HOUSSAY (ARG)

PHYSIOLOGY OR MEDICINE

		1948	P MÜLLER (SWITZ)
		1949	W R HESS (SWITZ)
1901	E VON BEHRING (GER)		A E MONIZ (PORT)
1902	SIR R ROSS (GB)	1950	P S HENCH (US)
1903	N R FINSEN (DEN)		E C KENDALL (US)
1904	I PAVLOV (RUSS)		T REICHSTEIN (SWITZ)
1905	R KOCH (GER)	1951	M THEILER (S AF)
1906	C GOLGI (ITALY)	1952	S A WAKSMAN (US)
	S RAMÓN Y CAJAL (SPAIN)	1953	F A LIPMANN (US)
1907	A LAVERAN (FR)		SIR H A KREBS (GB)
1908	P EHRLICH (GER)	1954	J F ENDERS (US)
	I MECHNIKOV (RUSS)		T H WELLER (US)
1909	E KOCHER (SWITZ)		F ROBBINS (US)
1910	A KOSSEL (GER)	1955	A H THEORELL (SWED)
1911	A GULLSTRAND (SWED)	1956	W FORSSMANN (GER)
1912	A CARREL (FR)		D RICHARDS (US)
1913	C RICHET (FR)		A F COURNAND (US)
1914	R BÁRÁNY (AUSTRIA)	1957	D BOVET (ITALY)
1915	(NO AWARD)	1958	G W BEADLE (US)
1916	(NO AWARD)		E L TATUM (US)
1917	(NO AWARD)		J LEDERBERG (US)
1919	J BORDET (BELG)	1959	S OCHOA (US)
1920	A KROGH (DEN)		A KORNBERG (US)
1921	(NO AWARD)	1960	SIR F MACFARLANE BURNET
1922	A V HILL (GB)		(AUSTR)
	O MEYERHOF (GER)		P B MEDAWAR (GB)
1923	SIR F G BANTING (CAN)	1961	G VON BÉKÉSY (US)

1962	F H C CRICK (GB)		M BROWN (US)
	J D WATSON (US)	1986	S COHEN (US)
	M WILKINS (GB)		R LEVI-MONTALCINI (ITALY)
1963	SIR J C ECCLES (AUSTR)	1987	S TONEGAWA (JAPAN)
	A L HODGKIN (GB)		
	A F HUXLEY (GB)		**LITERATURE**
1964	K BLOCH (US)	1901	S PRUDHOMME (FR)
	F LYNEN (GER)	1902	T MOMMSEN (GER)
1965	F JACOB (FR)	1903	B BJØRNSON (NOR)
	A LWOFF (FR)	1904	F MISTRAL (FR)
	J MONOD (FR)		J ECHEGARAY Y EIZAGUIRRE
1966	C B HUGGINS (US)		(SPAIN)
	F P ROUS (US)	1905	H SIENKIEWICZ (POL)
1967	H K HARTLINE (US)	1906	G CARDUCCI (ITALY)
	G WALD (US)	1907	R KIPLING (GB)
	R A GRANIT (SWED)	1908	R EUCKEN (GER)
1968	R W HOLLEY (US)	1909	S LAGERLÖF (SWED)
	H G KHORANA (US)	1910	P VON HEYSE (GER)
	M W NIRENBERG (US)	1911	M MAETERLINCK (BELG)
1969	M DELBRÜCK (US)	1912	G HAUPTMANN (GER)
	A D HERSHEY (US)	1913	SIR R TAGORE (INDIA)
	S E LURIA (US)	1914	(NO AWARD)
1970	J AXELROD (US)	1915	R ROLLAND (FR)
	SIR B KATZ (GB)	1916	V VON HEIDENSTAM (SWED)
	U VON EULER (SWED)	1917	K GJELLERUP (DEN)
1971	E W SUTHERLAND, JR (US)		H PONTOPPIDAN (DEN)
1972	G M EDELMAN (US)	1919	C SPITTELER (SWITZ)
	R R PORTER (GB)	1920	K HAMSUN (NOR)
1973	K VON FRISCH (GER)	1921	A FRANCE (FR)
	K LORENZ (GER)	1922	J BENAVENTE Y MARTINEZ (SPAIN)
	N TINBERGEN (NETH)	1923	W B YEATS (IRE)
1974	A CLAUDE (US)	1924	W S REYMONT (POL)
	C DE DUVE (BELG)	1925	G B SHAW (IRE)
	G E PALADE (BELG)	1926	G DELEDDA (ITALY)
1975	D BALTIMORE (US)	1927	H BERGSON (FR)
	R DULBECCO (US)	1928	S UNDSET (NOR)
	H M TEMIN (US)	1929	T MANN (GER)
1976	B S BLUMBERG (US)	1930	S LEWIS (US)
	D G GAJDUSEK (US)	1931	E A KARLFELDT (SWED)
1977	R S YALOW (US)	1932	J GALSWORTHY (GB)
	R GUILLEMIN (US)	1933	I BUNIN (USSR)
	A V SCHALLY (US)	1934	L PIRANDELLO (ITALY)
1978	W ARBER (SWITZ)	1935	(NO AWARD)
	D NATHANS (US)	1936	E O'NEILL (US)
	H SMITH (US)	1937	R M DU GARD (FR)
1979	A M CORMACK (US)	1938	P BUCK (US)
	G N HOUNSFIELD (GB)	1939	F E SILLANPÄÄ (FIN)
1980	G SNELL (US)	1943	(NO AWARD)
	J DAUSSET (FR)	1944	J V JENSEN (DEN)
	B BENACERRAF (US)	1945	G MISTRAL (CHILE)
1981	R SPERRY (US)	1946	H HESSE (SWITZ)
	D HUBEL (US)	1947	A GIDE (FR)
	T WIESEL (SWED)	1948	T S ELIOT (GB)
1982	S K BERGSTROM (SWED)	1949	W FAULKNER (US)
	B I SAMUELSON (SWED)	1950	B RUSSELL (GB)
	J R VANE (GB)	1951	P F LAGERKVIST (SWED)
1983	B MCCLINTOCK (US)	1952	F MAURIAC (FR)
1984	N K JERNE (DEN)	1953	SIR WINSTON CHURCHILL (GB)
	G J F KÖHLER (GER)	1954	E HEMINGWAY (US)
	C MILSTEIN (GB)	1955	H K LAXNESS (ICE)
1985	J GOLDSTEIN (US)	1956	J R JIMÉNEZ (SPAIN)

1957	A CAMUS (FR)	1916	(NO AWARD)
1958	B L PASTERNAK (DECLINED	1917	INTERNATIONAL RED CROSS
	AWARD) (USSR)		COMMITTEE (FOUNDED, 1863)
1959	S QUASIMODO (ITALY)	1919	W WILSON (US)
1960	S J PERSE (FR)	1920	L BOURGEOIS (FR)
1961	I ANDRIĆ (YUGOS)	1921	K BRANTING (SWED)
1962	J STEINBECK (US)		C L LANGE (NOR)
1963	G SEFERIS (GR)	1922	F NANSEN (NOR)
1964	J P SARTRE (DECLINED AWARD)	1923	(NO AWARD)
	(FR)	1924	(NO AWARD)
1965	M SHOLOKHOV (USSR)	1925	SIR A CHAMBERLAIN (GB)
1966	S Y AGNON (ISR)		C G DAWES (US)
	N SACHS (SWED)	1926	A BRIAND (FR)
1967	M A ASTURIAS (GUAT)		G STRESEMANN (GER)
1968	K YASUNARI (JAPAN)	1927	F BUISSON (FR)
1969	S BECKETT (IRE)		L QUIDDE (GER)
1970	A I SOLZHENITSYN (USSR)	1928	(NO AWARD)
1971	P NERUDA (CHILE)	1929	F B KELLOGG (US)
1972	H BÖLL (GER)	1930	N SÖDERBLOM (SWED)
1973	P WHITE (AUSTR)	1931	J ADDAMS (US)
1974	E JOHNSON (SWED)		N M BUTLER (US)
	H MARTINSON (SWED)	1932	(NO AWARD)
1975	E MONTALE (ITALY)	1933	SIR N ANGELL (GB)
1976	S BELLOW (US)	1934	A HENDERSON (GB)
1977	S ALEIXANDRE (SPAIN)	1935	C VON OSSIETZKY (GER)
1978	I B SINGER (US)	1936	C S LAMAS (ARG)
1979	O ALEPOUDELLIS (GREECE)	1937	VISCOUNT CECIL OF CHELWOOD
1980	C MILOSZ (US)		(GB)
1981	E CANETTI (BULG)	1938	NANSEN INTERNATIONAL OFFICE
1982	G GARCIA MARQUEZ (COLOMBIA)		FOR REFUGEES (FOUNDED, 1931)
1983	W GOLDING (GB)	1939	(NO AWARD)
1984	J SEIFERT (CZECH)	1943	(NO AWARD)
1985	C SIMON (FR)	1944	INTERNATIONAL RED CROSS
1986	W SOYINKA (NIGERIA)		COMMITTEE (FOUNDED, 1863)
1987	J BRODSKY (US)	1945	C HULL (US)
		1946	E G BALCH (US)

PEACE

			J R MOTT (US)
1901	J H DUNANT (SWITZ)	1947	AMERICAN FRIENDS' SERVICE
	F PASSY (FR)		COMMITTEE (US)
1902	E DUCOMMUN (SWITZ)		FRIENDS' SERVICE COUNCIL
	C A GOBAT (SWITZ)		(LONDON)
1903	SIR W CREMER (GB)	1948	(NO AWARD)
1904	INSTITUTE OF INTERNATIONAL	1949	LORD BOYD-ORR (GB)
	LAW (FOUNDED, 1873)	1950	R BUNCHE (US)
1905	BARONESS VON SUTTNER	1951	L JOUHAUX (FR)
	(AUSTRIA)	1952	A SCHWEITZER (ALSATIAN)
1906	T ROOSEVELT (US)	1953	G C MARSHALL (US)
1907	E TEODORO MONETA (ITALY)	1954	OFFICE OF THE UNITED NATIONS
	L RENAULT (FR)		HIGH COMMISSIONER FOR
1908	K P ARNOLDSON (SWED)		REFUGEES (FOUNDED, 1951)
1909	BARON D'ESTOURNELLES DE	1955	(NO AWARD)
	CONSTANT (FR)	1956	(NO AWARD)
	A BEERNAERT (BELG)	1957	L B PEARSON (CAN)
1910	INTERNATIONAL PEACE BUREAU	1958	D G PIRE (BELG)
	(FOUNDED, 1891)	1959	P J NOEL-BAKER (GB)
1911	T ASSER (NETH)	1960	A J LUTHULI (S AF)
	A FRIED (AUSTRIA)	1961	D HAMMARSKJÖLD (SWED)
1912	E ROOT (US)	1962	L C PAULING (US)
1913	H LAFONTAINE (BELG)	1963	INTERNATIONAL RED CROSS
1914	(NO AWARD)		COMMITTEE (FOUNDED, 1863)
1915	(NO AWARD)		

	LEAGUE OF RED CROSS SOCIETIES (GENEVA)	1977	MISS M CORRIGAN (N IRE) AMNESTY INTERNATIONAL (FOUNDED IN UK, 1961)
1964	M LUTHER KING, JR (US)	1978	A SADAT (EGYPT)
1965	UNITED NATIONS CHILDREN'S FUND (FOUNDED, 1946)		M BEGIN (ISR)
1966	(NO AWARD)	1979	MOTHER TERESA (YUGOS)
1967	(NO AWARD)	1980	A P ESQUIVEL (ARG)
1968	R CASSIN (FR)	1981	OFFICE OF THE U N HIGH COMMISSION FOR REFUGEES (FOUNDED, 1951)
1969	INTERNATIONAL LABOUR ORGANISATION (FOUNDED, 1919)	1982	A GARCIA ROBLES (MEX)
1970	N E BORLAUG (US)		MRS A MYRDAL (SWED)
1971	W BRANDT (GER)	1983	L WALESA (POL)
1972	(NO AWARD)	1984	BISHOP D TUTU (S AF)
1973	H KISSINGER (US)	1985	INTERNATIONAL PHYSICIANS FOR THE PREVENTION OF NUCLEAR WAR (FOUNDED, 1980)
	LE DUC THO (DECLINED AWARD) (N VIET)	1986	E WIESEL (US)
1974	S MACBRIDE (IRE)	1987	OSCAR ARIAS SÁNCHEZ (COSTA RICA)
	E SATO (JAPAN)		
1975	A S SAKHAROV (USSR)		
1976	MRS B WILLIAMS (N IRE)		

SPORTSMEN

3

ALI, Muhammad (Cassius Marcellus Clay, 1942– ; US boxer)

COE, Sebastian (1956– ; British middle-distance runner)

LEE, Bruce (1940–73; US kungfu expert)

4

ASHE, Arthur (1943– ; US tennis player)

BORG, Bjorn (1956– ; Swedish tennis player)

CLAY, Cassius. *See* Ali, Muhammed

CRAM, Steve (1960– ; British middle-distance runner)

DUKE, Geoffrey E (1923– ; British racing motorcyclist)

GRAF, Steffi (1969– ; W German tennis player)

HILL, Graham (1929–75; British motor-racing driver)

HOAD, Lewis Alan (1934– ; Australian tennis player)

HUNT, James (1947– ; British motor-racing driver)

JOHN, Barry (1945– ; Welsh Rugby Union footballer)

KING, Billie Jean (*born* Moffitt, 1943– ; US tennis player)

MILO (late 6th century BC; Greek wrestler)

MOSS, Stirling (1929– ; British motor-racing driver)

PELÉ (1940– ; Brazilian Association footballer)

WADE, Virginia (1945– ; British tennis player)

5

BRUNO, Frank (1961– ; British heavyweight boxer)

BUDGE, Don (1916– ; US tennis player)

BUENO, Maria (1939– ; Brazilian tennis player)

BUSBY, Matt (1909– ; British Association footballer)

CLARK, Jim (1937–68; British motor-racing driver)

COURT, Margaret (*born* Smith, 1942– ; Australian tennis player)

CURRY, John Anthony (1949– ; British ice skater)

EVERT, Christine (1954– ; US tennis player)

GRACE, William Gilbert (1848–1915; British cricketer)

GREIG, Tony (1946– ; Rhodesian-born cricketer)

HAGEN, Walter Charles (1892–1969; US professional golfer)

HOBBS, Jack (1882–1963; British cricketer)

HOGAN, Ben (1912– ; US professional golfer)

HOYLE, Edmond (1672–1769; British authority on card games)

JEEPS, Dickie (1931– ; British Rugby Union footballer)

JONES, Bobby (1902–71; US amateur golfer)

LAUDA, Niki (1949– ; Austrian motor-racing driver)

LAVER, Rod (1938– ; Australian tennis player)

LEWIS, Carl (1961– ; US athlete)

5—continued

LLOYD, Clive (1944— ; West Indian cricketer)
LOUIS, Joe (1914—81; US boxer)
MEADE, Richard (1938— ; British three-day-event horse rider)
MEADS, Colin Earl (1935— ; New Zealand Rugby Union footballer)
MOORE, Bobby (1941— ; British Association footballer)
NURMI, Paavo Johannes (1897—1973; Finnish middle-distance and long-distance runner)
OVETT, Steve (1955— ; British middle-distance runner)
OWENS, Jesse (1913—80; US sprinter, long jumper, and hurdler)
PERRY, Fred (1909— ; British tennis and table-tennis player)
SMITH, Harvey (1938— ; British showjumper and equestrian)
SPITZ, Mark Andrew (1950— ; US swimmer)
VIREN, Lasse Artturi (1949— ; Finnish middle-distance and long-distance runner)

6

BORDER, Allan (1955— ; Australian cricketer)
BOTHAM, Ian (1955— ; British cricketer)
BROOME, David (1940— ; British show-jumper)
BROUGH, Louise (1923— ; US tennis player)
CAWLEY, Evonne (*born* Goolagong, 1951— ; Australian tennis player)
CRUYFF, Johann (1947— ; Dutch Association footballer)
D'INZEO, Colonel Piero (1923— ; Italian show jumper and equestrian)
EDBERG, Stefan (1966— ; Swedish tennis player)
FANGIO, Juan Manuel (1911— ; Argentinian motor-racing driver)
HUTTON, Len (1916— ; British cricketer)
KARPOV, Anatoly (1951— ; Soviet chess player)
KEEGAN, Kevin (1951— ; British footballer)
LASKER, Emanuel (1868—1941; German chess player)
MORPHY, Paul Charles (1837—84; US chess player)
PALMER, Arnold (1929— ; US professional golfer)
RAMSEY, Alf (1922— ; British Association footballer)
RHODES, Wilfred (1877—1973; British cricketer)
SHEENE, Barry (1950— ; British racing motorcyclist)
SMYTHE, Pat (1928— ; British showjumper and equestrian)
SOBERS, Gary (1936— ; West Indian cricketer)
TUNNEY, Gene (1897—1978; US boxer)

7

BRABHAM, Jack (1926— ; Australian motor-racing driver)
BRADMAN, Donald George (1908— ; Australian cricketer)
CARNERA, Primo (1906—67; Italian boxer)
COMPTON, Denis (1918— ; British cricketer)
CONNORS, Jimmy (1952— ; US tennis player)
COWDREY, Colin (1932— ; British cricketer)
DEMPSEY, Jack (1895— ; US boxer)
FISCHER, Bobby (1943— ; US chess player)
FRAZIER, Joe (1944— ; US boxer)
HAMMOND, Wally (1903—65; British cricketer)
LENGLEN, Suzanne (1899—1938; French tennis player)
MCBRIDE, Willie John (1939— ; Irish Rugby Union footballer)
MCENROE, John (1959— ; US tennis player)
SPASSKY, Boris (1937— ; Soviet chess player)
STEWART, Jackie (1939— ; British motor-racing driver)
SURTEES, John (1934— ; British racing motorcyclist and motor-racing driver)
TREVINO, Lee (1939— ; US golfer)
TRUEMAN, Fred (1931— ; British cricketer)
WHYMPER, Edward (1840—1911; British mountaineer)
WINKLER, Hans Günter (1926— ; West German showjumper)
ZÁTOPEK, Emil (1922— ; Czech long-distance runner)

8

AGOSTINI, Giacomo (1944— ; Italian racing motorcyclist)
ALEKHINE, Alexander (1892—1946; French chess player)
CAMPBELL, Sir Malcolm (1885—1949; British land- and water-speed racing driver)
CHARLTON, Bobby (1937— ; British Association footballer)
COMANECI, Nadia (1961— ; Romanian gymnast)
HAILWOOD, Mike (1940—81; British racing motorcyclist)
HAWTHORN, Mike (1929—58; British motor-racing driver)
JOSELITO (1895—1920; Spanish matador)
KORCHNOI, Victor (1931— ; Soviet chess player)
LINDWALL, Raymond Russell (1921— ; Australian cricketer)
MATTHEWS, Stanley (1915— ; British Association footballer)
NEWCOMBE, John (1944— ; Australian tennis player)
NICKLAUS, Jack William (1940— ; US golfer)
RICHARDS, Sir Gordon (1904—86; British jockey)

8—continued

RICHARDS, Viv (1952— ; West Indian cricketer)

ROBINSON, Sugar Ray (1920— ; US boxer)

ROSEWALL, Ken (1934— ; Australian tennis player)

SULLIVAN, John Lawrence (1858—1918; US boxer)

THOMPSON, Daley (1958— ; British decathlete)

WILLIAMS, J P R (1949— ; Welsh Rugby Union footballer)

9

BANNISTER, Roger (1929— ; British middle distance runner)

BONINGTON, Chris (1934— ; British mountaineer)

BOTVINNIK, Mikhail Moiseivich (1911— ; Soviet chess player)

D'OLIVIERA, Basil Lewis (1931— ; South African-born cricketer)

GOOLAGONG, Evonne. *See* Cawley, Evonne

LLEWELLYN, Harry (1911— ; British show-jumper and equestrian)

PETROSIAN, Tigran Vartanovich (1929—84; Soviet chess player)

SCHMELING, Max (1905— ; German boxer)

SUTCLIFFE, Herbert (1894—1978; British cricketer)

SZEWINSKA, Irena (1946— ; Polish athlete)

10

CARPENTIER, Georges (1894—1975; French boxer)

CULBERTSON, Ely (1891—1955; US bridge authority)

IMRAN KHAN (1952— ; Pakistani cricketer)

JUANTORENA, Alberto (1951— ; Cuban middle-distance runner)

WILLS MOODY, Helen (1905— ; US tennis player)

11

BALLESTEROS, Severiano (1957— ; Spanish golfer)

CONSTANTINE, Learie Nicholas, Baron (1902—71; West Indian cricketer)

FITZSIMMONS, Bob (1862—1917; New Zealand boxer)

NAVRATILOVA, Martina (1956— ; Czech-born US tennis player)

TURISHCHEVA, Ludmilla (1952— ; Soviet gymnast)

WEISSMULLER, Johnny (1904—84; US swimmer)

13

TENZING NORGAY (*c.* 1914—86; Sherpa mountaineer)

19

CAPABLANCA Y GRAUPERA, José Raúl (1888—1942; Cuban chess player)

RANJITSINHJI VIBHAJI, Kumar Shri, Maharajah Jam Sahib of Nawanagar (1872—1933; Indian cricketer)

THE ARTS

ART TERMS

2
OP

3
FEC
INC
OIL
POP

4
BODY
BUST
CAST
DADA
HERM
KORE
SIZE
SWAG
TERM
WASH

5
BRUSH
BURIN
CHALK
EASEL
FECIT
GESSO
GLAZE
MODEL
NAIVE
PIETÀ
PUTTO
SALON
SCULP
SECCO
SEPIA
STYLE
TONDO

6
ASHCAN
BISTRE
CANVAS
CUBISM
FRESCO
GOTHIC
GROUND
KIT-CAT
KITSCH
KOUROS
LIMNER
MAESTÀ

6 —continued
MEDIUM
MOBILE
MOSAIC
PASTEL
PATINA
PENCIL
PURISM
RELIEF
ROCOCO
SCHOOL
SKETCH
STUCCO
STYLUS
TUSCAN
VEDUTA
VERISM

7
ACADEMY
ARCHAIC
ATELIER
BAROQUE
BAUHAUS
BITUMEN
BODEGÓN
CABINET
CAMAÏEU
CARTOON
COLLAGE
COSMATI
DIPTYCH
DRAWING
ECORCHÉ
ETCHING
GOUACHE
IMPASTO
INCIDIT
LINOCUT
LOST WAX
MODELLO
MONTAGE
PALETTE
PIGMENT
POCHADE
REALISM
SCUMBLE
SFUMATO
SINOPIA
TEMPERA
VANITAS

7 —continued
VARNISH
WOODCUT

8
ABSTRACT
AIR-BRUSH
ALLEGORY
ANCIENTS
AQUATINT
ARMATURE
ARRICCIO
BARBIZON
BOZZETTO
CARYATID
CHARCOAL
DRÔLERIE
DRYPOINT
EMULSION
FIXATIVE
FROTTAGE
FUTURISM
GRAFFITI
HATCHING
INTAGLIO
INTONACO
MANDORLA
MAQUETTE
PASTICHE
PLEURANT
POUNCING
PREDELLA
REPOUSSÉ
SCULPSIT
STAFFAGE
TACHISME
TESSERAE
TRECENTO
TRIPTYCH
VENETIAN

9
ALLA PRIMA
ANTI-CERNE
AQUARELLE
AUTOGRAPH
BRUSHWORK
BYZANTINE
CAPRICCIO
COLOURIST
DISTEMPER
ENGRAVING

9 —continued
GRISAILLE
GROTESQUE
INTIMISME
LANDSCAPE
MAHLSTICK
MAULSTICK
MEZZOTINT
MINIATURE
POLYPTYCH
PRIMITIVE
SCULPTURE
STILL LIFE
STIPPLING
SYMBOLISM
TENEBRISM
VORTICISM

10
ARRICCIATO
ART NOUVEAU
ASSEMBLAGE
AUTOMATISM
AVANTGARDE
BIOMORPHIC
CARICATURE
CIRE-PERDUE
CRAQUELURE
FLORENTINE
METALPOINT
MONOCHROME
MORBIDEZZA
NATURALISM
PENTIMENTO
PROVENANCE
QUADRATURA
REPOUSSOIR
ROMANESQUE
SURREALISM
SYNTHETISM
TURPENTINE
XYLOGRAPHY

11
BAMBOCCANTI
BIEDERMEIER
CAROLINGIAN
CHIAROSCURO
CONTÉ CRAYON
DIVISIONISM
ECLECTICISM
ILLUSIONISM

11 —continued	11 —continued	12 —continued	13 —continued
IMPRIMATURA	STYLIZATION	CONTRAPPOSTO	EXPRESSIONISM
LITHOGRAPHY	SUPREMATISM	COUNTERPROOF	FÊTE CHAMPÊTRE
MASTERPIECE	TROMPE L'OEIL	ILLUMINATION	IMPRESSIONISM
PERSPECTIVE	WATERCOLOUR	PRECISIONISM	PAPIERS COLLES
PICTURESQUE	**12**	QUATTROCENTO	**14**
POINTILLISM	ACRYLIC PAINT	SUPERREALISM	CONSTRUCTIVISM
PORTRAITURE	ANAMORPHOSIS	**13**	
RENAISSANCE	CLOISONNISME	ARCHITECTONIC	
RETROUSSAGE			

ARCHITECTURAL TERMS

3	5 —continued	6 —continued	7 —continued
BAY	SHANK	METOPE	FESTOON
CAP	TALON	MUTULE	FLEURON
DIE	TENIA	NORMAN	FLUTING
EYE	TUDOR	OCULUS	GADROON
KEY	VERGE	PAGODA	GALILEE
4	**6**	PATERA	GALLERY
AMBO	ABACUS	PLINTH	LACUNAR
ANTA	ACCESS	PULPIT	LANTERN
APSE	ALCOVE	QUADRA	LATTICE
ARCH	ARCADE	REGULA	LEQUEAR
BAND	ATRIUM	ROCOCO	LUNETTE
BEAD	ATTICK	SCAPUS	NARTHEX
BELL	AUMBRY	SCROLL	NULLING
BOSS	BELFRY	SEDILE	OBELISK
DADO	BONNET	SOFFIT	ORATORY
DAIS	BROACH	TROPHY	PARVISE
DOME	CANOPY	URELLA	PORTAIL
FRET	CHEVET	VESTRY	PORTICO
FROG	COLUMN	VOLUTE	POSTERN
FUST	CORONA	WREATH	PTEROMA
NAVE	CRENEL	XYSTUS	REEDING
PELE	CUPOLA	ZIG-ZAG	REGENCY
STOA	DAGGER	**7**	REREDOS
5	DENTIL	ANNULET	ROSETTE
AISLE	DIAPER	ARCH RIB	ROTUNDA
AMBRY	FAÇADE	ASTYLAR	ROUNDEL
ARRIS	FILLET	BALCONY	SCALLOP
ATTIC	FINIAL	BAROQUE	SPANISH
CONGE	FLÉCHE	BASTION	SYSTYLE
CROWN	FRESCO	BOULTIN	TESSARA
CRYPT	FRIEZE	BUTMENT	TONDINO
DORIC	GABLET	CAPITAL	TRACERY
FOILS	GAZEBO	CAVETTO	TRUMEAU
GABLE	GOTHIC	CHANCEL	**8**
GLYPH	GUTTAE	CHEVRON	ABUTMENT
HELIX	HEROIC	CORNICE	ACANTHUS
INLAY	LESENE	CROCHET	AEDICULA
IONIC	LINTEL	CROCKET	APOPHYGE
LOBBY	LINTOL	DISTYLE	ASTRAGAL
NEWEL	LOGGIA	ECHINUS	ATLANTES
ROMAN	LOUVRE	ENCARPA	BALUSTER
SCAPE	MANTEL	ENTASIS	BARTIZAN
SHAFT	MERLON	EUSTYLE	BASILICA

8 —continued	8 —continued	9 —continued	10 —continued
BEAK HEAD	VIGNETTE	PALLADIAN	QUATREFOIL
CARYATID	WAINSCOT	REFECTORY	ROMANESQUE
CIMBORIO	**9**	SGRAFFITO	ROOD SCREEN
CINCTURE	ACROPOLIS	STRAPWORK	ROSE WINDOW
CRENELLE	ANTEFIXAE	STYLOBATE	SEXPARTITE
CRESTING	ANTHEMION	TRABEATED	TETRASTYLE
CYMATIUM	APEX STONE	TRIFORIUM	TRACHELION
DIASTYLE	ARABESQUE	TRILITHON	**11**
DIPTERAL	ARCH BRICK	VESTIBULE	CASTELLATED
DOG-TOOTH	ARCHIVOLT	ZOOPHORUS	ENTABLATURE
EDGE ROLL	ATTIC BASE	**10**	FAN VAULTING
EXTRADOS	BIRD'S BEAK	ACROTERION	HARELIP ARCH
FORMERET	BYZANTINE	AMBULATORY	LEADED LIGHT
GARGOYLE	CAMPANILE	ARAEOSTYLE	MANTELPIECE
INTRADOS	CANEPHORA	ARCHITRAVE	MANTELSHELF
KEEL ARCH	CARTOUCHE	BALDACHINO	ORIEL WINDOW
KEYSTONE	CAULICOLI	BALL FLOWER	RENAISSANCE
LICH GATE	CLOISTERS	BALUSTRADE	RETICULATED
LYCH GATE	COLONNADE	BATTLEMENT	**12**
MISERERE	COMPOSITE	CINQUEFOIL	AMPHITHEATRE
PAVILION	DRIPSTONE	COLONNETTE	BLIND TRACERY
PEDESTAL	FOLIATION	CORINTHIAN	COCKLE STAIRS
PEDIMENT	GROTESQUE	EGG AND DART	EGG AND TONGUE
PILASTER	HEXASTYLE	ENRICHMENT	LANCET WINDOW
PREDELLA	HYPOCAUST	HAGIOSCOPE	PORTE-COCHÈRE
PULPITUM	HYPOSTYLE	LADY CHAPEL	**13**
ROCAILLE	INGLE NOOK	LANCET ARCH	AMPHI-PROSTYLE
SPANDREL	LABEL STOP	MISERICORD	**14**
SPANDRIL	LACUNARIA	MODILLIONS	ANGULAR CAPITAL
TORCHING	LINENFOLD	PIETRA DURA	FLYING BUTTRESS
TRANSEPT	MEZZANINE	PRESBYTERY	HYPOTRACHELION
TRIGLYPH	MOULDINGS	PYCNOSTYLE	
TYMPANUM	OCTASTYLE		
VERANDAH			

LITERARY TERMS

3	5 —continued	6 —continued	7 —continued
ODE	RHYME	SEPTET	HUMOURS
WIT	STYLE	SESTET	IMAGERY
4	THEME	SIMILE	NEMESIS
EPIC	VERSE	SONNET	PARADOX
FOOT	**6**	STANZA	PROSODY
IAMB	BALLAD	STRESS	PYRRHIC
MYTH	BATHOS	SYMBOL	REALISM
5	CESURA	**7**	SPONDEE
ELEGY	CLICHÉ	CAESURA	SUBPLOT
FABLE	DACTYL	CONCEIT	TRAGEDY
GENRE	HUBRIS	COUPLET	TROCHEE
ICTUS	LAMENT	DICTION	**8**
IRONY	MONODY	ELISION	ALLEGORY
LYRIC	OCTAVE	EPIGRAM	ANAPAEST
METRE	PARODY	EPISTLE	AUGUSTAN
NOVEL	PATHOS	EPITAPH	DIDACTIC
OCTET	SATIRE	EUPHONY	ELEMENTS
PROSE	SCHOOL	FABLIAU	EXEMPLUM

8 —continued
EYE RHYME
METAPHOR
OXYMORON
PASTORAL
QUATRAIN
RHETORIC
SCANSION
SYLLABLE
TRIMETER

9
AMBIGUITY
ASSONANCE
BURLESQUE
CATHARSIS
CLASSICAL
EUPHEMISM
FREE VERSE
HALF RHYME
HEXAMETER
HYPERBOLE

9 —continued
MONOMETER
OCTAMETER
PARARHYME

10
BLANK VERSE
CARICATURE
DENOUEMENT
EPIC SIMILE
HEPTAMETER
MOCK HEROIC
NATURALISM
PENTAMETER
PICARESQUE
SPOONERISM
SUBJECTIVE
TETRAMETER

11
ANACHRONISM
COURTLY LOVE
END STOPPING

11 —continued
ENJAMBEMENT
GOTHIC NOVEL
HORATIAN ODE
MALAPROPISM
NOBLE SAVAGE
OBJECTIVITY
TRAGICOMEDY

12
ALLITERATION
ONOMATOPOEIA

13
ANTHROPOMORPH
HEROIC COUPLET
INTERNAL RHYME

14
EXISTENTIALISM
FEMININE ENDING
MILTONIC SONNET
ROMANTIC POETRY
SENTIMENTALITY

15
MASCULINE ENDING
PATHETIC FALLACY
PERSONIFICATION

16
PETRARCHAN
  SONNET

18
METAPHYSICAL
  POETRY
NEGATIVE
  CAPABILITY
OMNISCIENT
  NARRATOR

20+
STREAM OF
  CONSCIOUSNESS

MUSICAL TERMS

TERM — definition

1 & 2
F — loud
FF - very loud
MF — half loud
P — soft
PP — very soft
SF — strongly accented

3
BIS — repeat
DIM — becoming softer
PED — abbr. for pedal
PIÙ — more
PIZ — plucked
RFZ — accentuated
RIT — slowing down, holding back
SFZ — strongly accented
TEN — held
VIF — lively (Fr.)

4
CODA — final part of a movement
MOTO — motion
RALL — slowing down
SINO — up to; until
TIEF — deep; low (Ger.)

5
AD LIB — at will
ASSAI — very
BUFFO — comic
DOLCE — sweet
FORTE — loud
LARGO — very slow

5 —continued
LENTO — slowly
MESTO — sad, mournful
MEZZO — half
MOLTO — very much
MOSSO — moving, fast
PIANO — soft
QUASI — almost, as if
SEGNO — sign
SENZA — without
SOAVE — sweet; gentle
STARK — strong, loud (Ger.)
TACET — instrument is silent
TANTO — so much
TEMPO — the speed of a composition
TUTTI — all
ZOPPA — in syncopated rhythm

6
ADAGIO — slow
AL FINE — to the end
CHIUSO — stopped (of a note); closed
DA CAPO — from the beginning
DEHORS — outside; prominent
DIVISI — divided
DOPPIO — double
FACILE — easy, fluent
LEGATO — bound, tied (of notes), smoothly
MARCIA — march
NIENTE — nothing
NOBILE — noble
RETENU — held back

6 —continued
SEMPRE – always, still
SUBITO – immediately
TENUTO – held
7
AGITATO – agitated; rapid tempo
ALLEGRO – lively, brisk
AL SEGNO – as far as the sign
AMOROSO – loving, emotional
ANIMATO – spirited
ATTACCA – attack; continue without a pause
CALANDO – ebbing; lessening of tempo
CODETTA – small coda; to conclude a
   passage
CON BRIO – with vigour
DOLENTE – sorrowful
ESTINTO – extremely softly, almost without
   tone
GIOCOSO – merry; playful
MARCATO – accented
MORBIDO – soft, delicate
PESANTE – heavily, firmly
SCHNELL – fast (Ger.)
SFOGATO – effortless; in a free manner
SORDINO – mute
STRETTO – accelerating or intensifying;
   overlapping of entries of fugue
8
A BATTUTA – return to strict time
A PIACERE – as you please
BRILLANT – brilliant
COL CANTO – accompaniment to follow solo
   line
COL LEGNO – to strike strings with stick of
   the bow
CON FUOCO – fiery; vigorous
DAL SEGNO – from the sign
IN MODO DI – in the manner of
MAESTOSO – majestic
MODERATO – moderately
PORTANDO – carrying one note into the next
RITENUTO – slowing down, holding back
SOURDINE – mute (Fr.)
STACCATO – detached
VIVEMENT – lively (Fr.)
9
ADAGIETTO – quite slow
CANTABILE – in a singing fashion

9 —continued
CANTILENA – lyrical, flowing
FIORITURA – decoration of a melody
GLISSANDO – sliding scale played on
   instrument
MENO MOSSO – slower pace
MEZZA VOCE – at half power
OBBLIGATO – not to be omitted
PIUTTOSTO – somewhat
PIZZICATO – plucked
SCHNELLER – faster (Ger.)
SFORZANDO – strongly accented
SIN'AL FINE – up to the end
SLENTANDO – slowing down
SOSTENUTO – sustained
SOTTO VOCE – quiet subdued tone
10
AFFETTUOSO – tender
ALLA CACCIA – in hunting style
ALLARGANDO – broadening; more dignified
ALLEGRETTO – quite lively, brisk
DIMINUENDO – becoming softer
FORTISSIMO – very loud
MEZZOFORTE – half loud
NOBILMENTE – nobly
PERDENDOSI – dying away gradually
PIANISSIMO – very soft
PORTAMENTO – carrying one note into the
   next
RAVVIVANDO – quickening
RITARDANDO – slowing down, holding back
SCHERZANDO – joking; playing
SCHLEPPEND – dragging; deviating from
   correct speed (Ger.)
SCORREVOLE – gliding; fluent
STRINGENDO – tightening; intensification
11
ACCELERANDO – accelerating
AFFRETTANDO – hurrying
MINACCIANDO – menacing
RALLENTANDO – slowing down
RINFORZANDO – accentuated
12
ALLA CAPPELLA – in church style
LEGGERAMENTE – lightly
13
LEGGIERAMENTE – lightly

TONIC SOL-FA

| DOH | ME | SOH | TE |
| RAY | FAH | LAH | |

MUSICAL INSTRUMENTS

2
UD (lute)
YU (scraper)
3
BIN (vina)
KIT (fiddle)
LUR (horn)
OUD (ud)
SAZ (lute)
SHŌ (mouth organ)
TAR (drum; lute)
UTI (lute)
4
BATA (drum)
BIWA (lute)
CH'IN (zither)
DRUM
FIFE
FUYE (flute)
GONG
HARP
HORN
KENA (quena)
KHEN (mouth organ)
KOTO (zither)
LIRA (fiddle)
LUTE
LYRA (lyre)
LYRE
MU YÜ (drum)
MVET (zither)
OBOE
OUTI (lute)
P'I P'A (lute)
PIPE
ROTE (lyre)
RUAN (lute)
SONA (shawm)
TRO-U (fiddle)
URUA (clarinet)
VINA (stringed
   instrument related
   to sitar)
VIOL
WHIP (percussion)
ZOBO (mirliton)
5
AULOI (shawm)
BANJO
BELLS
BHAYA (kettledrum)
BUGLE
BUMPA (clarinet)
CELLO

5 —continued
CHANG (dulcimer)
CHIME
CLAVE
COBZA (lute)
CORNU (trumpet)
CRWTH (lyre)
DAULI (drum)
DHOLA (drum)
DOBRO (guitar)
ERH-HU (fiddle)
FIDEL (fiddle)
FIDLA (zither)
FLUTE
GAITA (bagpipe)
GAJDY (bagpipe)
GUSLE (fiddle)
HURUK (drum)
KAKKO (drum)
KANUN (qanun)
KAZOO (mirliton)
KERAR (lyre)
KO-KIU (fiddle)
MBILA (xylophone)
NGOMA (drum)
NGURU (flute)
OKEDO (drum)
ORGAN
PIANO
PI NAI (shawm)
PU-ILU (clappers)
QANUN (zither)
QUENA (flute)
RASPA (scraper)
REBAB (fiddle)
REBEC (fiddle)
SARON
   (metallophone)
SHAWM
SHENG (mouth organ)
SITAR (lute)
TABLA (drum)
TABOR (drum)
TAIKO (drum)
TIBIA (shawm)
TIPLE (shawm)
TI-TZU (flute)
TUDUM (drum)
TUMYR (drum)
TUPAN (drum)
VIOLA
YUN LO (gong)
ZURLA (shawm)
ZURNA (shawm)

6
ALBOKA (hornpipe)
ARGHUL (clarinet)
BAGANA (lyre)
BINIOU (bagpipe)
CARNYX (trumpet)
CHAKAY (zither)
CHA PEI (lute)
CORNET
CURTAL (double
   reed)
DARBUK (drum)
FANDUR (fiddle)
FIDDLE
FUJARA (flute)
GEKKIN (lute)
GENDER
   (metallophone)
GONGUE
   (percussion)
GUITAR
HU CH'IN (fiddle)
HUMMEL (zither)
KENONG (gong)
KISSAR (lyre)
KOBORO (drum)
LIRICA (fiddle)
LIRONE (fiddle)
LITUUS (trumpet)
LONTAR (clappers)
MAYURI (lute)
MOROPI (drum)
NAKERS (drums)
NAQARA (drums)
NTENGA (drum)
O-DAIKO (drum)
OMBGWE (flute)
P'AI PAN (clappers)
POMMER (shawm)
RACKET (double
   reed)
RAMKIE (lute)
RATTLE
SANTIR (dulcimer)
SHAING (horn)
SHAKER
SHANAI (shawm)
SHIELD (percussion)
SHOFAR (horn)
SOPILE (shawm)
SPINET
SPOONS (clappers)
SRALAY (shawm)
SURNAJ (shawm)

6 —continued
SWITCH (percussion)
SYRINX (panpipe)
TAM-TAM (gong)
TOM-TOM (drum)
TXISTU (flute)
VALIHA (zither)
VIELLE (fiddle)
VIOLIN
YANGUM (dulcimer)
ZITHER
7
ADENKUM (stamping
   tube)
ALPHORN (trumpet)
ANKLUNG (rattle)
ATUMPAN
   (kettledrum)
BAGPIPE
BARYTON (viol)
BASSOON
BODHRAN (drum)
BONNANG (gong)
BOW HARP
BOX LYRE
BUCCINA (trumpet)
BUISINE (trumpet)
BUMBASS
CELESTE
CHANGKO (drum)
CITTERN
CORNETT
COWBELL
CROTALS
   (percussion)
CYMBALS
DA-DAIKO (drum)
DIPLICE (clarinet)
DUGDUGI (drum)
ENZENZE (zither)
FITHELE (fiddle)
GADULKA (fiddle)
GITTERN
GLING-BU (flute)
HULA IPU
   (percussion)
INGUNGU (drum)
ISIGUBU (drum)
KACHAPI (zither)
KALUNGU (talking
   drum)
KAMANJE (fiddle)
KANTELE (zither)
KEMANAK (clappers)

7 —continued
KITHARA (lyre)
KOMUNGO (zither)
MACHETE (lute)
MANDOLA (lute)
MARACAS
 (percussion)
MASENQO (fiddle)
MIGYAUN (zither)
MOKUGYO (drum)
MURUMBU (drum)
MUSETTE (bagpipe)
MUSETTE (shawm)
OBUKANO (lyre)
OCARINA (flute)
OCTAVIN (wind)
ORPHICA (piano)
PANDORA (cittern)
PANPIPE
PIANINO
PIBCORN (hornpipe)
PICCOLO
PIFFARO (shawm)
QUINTON (viol)
RESHOTO (drum)
RINCHIK (cymbals)
SACKBUT (trombone)
SALPINX (trumpet)
SAMISEN (lute)
SANTOOR (dulcimer)
SARANGI (fiddle)
SARINDA (fiddle)
SAW-THAI (fiddle)
SAXHORN
SAXTUBA
SERPENT
SHIWAYA (flute)
SISTRUM (rattle)
SORDINE (kit)
SORDONE (double
 reed)
SPAGANE (clappers)
TAM ÁM LA (gong)
TAMBURA (lute)
TERBANG (drum)
THEORBO (lute)
TIKTIRI (clarinet)
TIMPANI
TRUMPET
TSUZUMI (drum)
UJUSINI (flute)
UKULELE
VIHUELA (guitar)
VIOLONE (viol)
WHISTLE
YUN NGAO (gong)
ZUMMARA (clarinet)

8
ALGHAITA (shawm)
ALTOHORN
AUTOHARP

8 —continued
BANDOURA (lute)
BASS DRUM
BASS HORN
BOMBARDE (shawm)
BOUZOUKI (lute)
BOWL LYRE
BUZZ DISK
CALLIOPE
 (mechanical organ)
CARILLON
CHIME BAR
CIMBALOM (dulcimer)
CIPACTLI (flute)
CLAPPERS
CLARINET
CLAVICOR (brass
 family)
CLAW BELL
COURTAUT (double
 reed)
CRECELLE (cog
 rattle)
CRUMHORN (double
 reed)
DULCIMER
DVOYNICE (flute)
GONG DRUM
HANDBELL
HAND HORN
HAWKBELL
JEW'S HARP
KAYAKEUM (zither)
KHUMBGWE (flute)
LANGLEIK (zither)
LANGSPIL (zither)
LAP ORGAN
 (melodeon)
MANDOLIN (lute)
MELODEON
MELODICA
MIRLITON (kazoo)
MRIDANGA (drum)
OLIPHANT (horn)
O-TSUZUMI (drum)
OTTAVINO (virginal)
P'AI HSIAO (panpipe)
PENORCON (cittern)
POCHETTE (kit)
PSALTERY (zither)
PUTORINO (trumpet)
RECORDER
RKAN-DUNG
 (trumpet)
RKAN-LING (horn)
RONÉAT-EK
 (xylophone)
SAN HSIEN (lute)
SIDE DRUM
SLIT DRUM
SONAJERO (rattle)

8 —continued
SRINGARA (fiddle)
SURBAHAR (lute)
TALAMBAS (drum)
TARABUKA (drum)
TAROGATO (clarinet;
 shawm)
TIMBALES (drum)
TRIANGLE
TRO-KHMER (fiddle)
TROMBONE
VIOLETTA (viol)
VIRGINAL
YANGCHIN (dulcimer)
YUEH CH'IN (lute)
ZAMPOGNA
 (bagpipe)

9
ACCORDION
ANGLE HARP
ARPANETTA (zither)
BALALAIKA (lute)
BANDURRIA (lute)
BANJOLELE
BASSONORE
 (bassoon)
BOMBARDON (tuba)
CASTANETS
CHALUMEAU
 (clarinet)
COG RATTLE
COMPONIUM
 (mechanical organ)
CORNEMUSE
 (bagpipe)
CORNOPEAN (brass
 family)
CROOK HORN
DAIBYOSHI (drum)
DARABUKKE (drum)
DJUNADJAN (zither)
DUDELSACK
 (bagpipes)
DVOJACHKA (flute)
EUPHONIUM (brass
 family)
FLAGEOLET (flute)
FLEXATONE
 (percussion)
GONG AGENG
HACKBRETT
 (dulcimer)
HARMONICA
HARMONIUM
HYDRAULIS (organ)
KELONTONG (drum)
KONIGHORN (brass
 family)
LAUNEDDAS
 (clarinet)
MANDOBASS (lute)

9 —continued
MANDOLONE (lute)
MORIN-CHUR (fiddle)
ORPHARION (cittern)
PICCO PIPE (flute)
PIEN CH'ING
 (lithophone)
ROMMELPOT (drum)
SAXOPHONE
TALLHARPA (lyre)
TOTOMBITO (zither)
TUBA-DUPRÉ
WOOD BLOCK
WURLITZER
XYLOPHONE
XYLORIMBA
 (xylophone)

10
BANANA DRUM
BARREL DRUM
BASSANELLO
 (double reed)
BASSET HORN
BIBLE REGAL (organ)
BICITRABIN (vina)
BIRD SCARER
BONGO DRUMS
BULL-ROARER
CHENGCHENG
 (cymbals)
CHITARRONE (lute)
CLAVICHORD
CLAVIORGAN
COLASCIONE (lute)
CONTRABASS
 (double bass)
COR ANGLAIS
DIDGERIDOO
 (trumpet)
DOUBLE BASS
FLUGELHORN
FRENCH HORN
GEIGENWERK
 (mechanical
 harpsichord)
GONG CHIMES
GRAND PIANO
HANDLE DRUM
HURDY GURDY
KETTLEDRUM
LITHOPHONE
 (percussion)
MANDOCELLO (lute)
MELLOPHONE (horn)
MOSHUPIANE (drum)
MOUTH ORGAN
OPHICLEIDE (brass
 family)
RANASRINGA (horn)
SAXOTROMBA
SHAKUHACHI (flute)

10 —continued
SOUSAPHONE
SPITZHARFE (zither)
SYMPHONIUM (mouth organ)
TAMBOURINE (drum)
TEPONAZTLI (drum)
THUMB PIANO (jew's harp)
TIN WHISTLE
TLAPIZTALI (flute)
TSURI DAIKO (drum)

11
AEOLIAN HARP
ANGEL CHIMES
BARREL ORGAN
BELL CITTERN
BIVALVE BELL
BLADDER PIPE
BOARD ZITHER
CLAPPER BELL
FIPPLE FLUTE
GAMBANG KAYA (xylophone)
GUITAR-BANJO
HAND TRUMPET
HARPSICHORD
HECKELPHONE (oboe)
NYCKELHARPA
PAIMENSARVI (horn)

11 —continued
PANHUEHUETL (drum)
SARON DEMONG (metallophone)
SLEIGH BELLS
SPIKE FIDDLE
THEORBO-LUTE
UCHIWA DAIKO (drum)
VIOLA D'AMORE (viol)
VIOLONCELLO

12
DIPLO-KITHARA (zither)
GANSA GAMBANG (metallophone)
GANSA JONGKOK (metallophone)
GLOCKENSPIEL (metallophone)
GUITAR-VIOLIN
HI-HAT CYMBALS
KANTELEHARPE (lyre)
MANDOLINETTO (ukulele)
PEACOCK SITAR (lute)

12 —continued
RAUSCHPFEIFE (double reed)
SARRUSOPHONE (brass)
SHOULDER HARP
STOCK-AND-HORN (hornpipe)
TIPPOO'S TIGER (organ)
TUBULAR BELLS
VIOLA DA GAMBA (viol)
WHISTLE FLUTE

13
COCKTAIL DRUMS
CONTRABASSOON
DOUBLE BASSOON (contrabassoon)
HARDANGERFELE (fiddle)
HECKELCLARINA (clarinet)
SAVERNAKE HORN
SCHRILLPFEIFE (flute)
SLIDE TROMBONE
VIOLA BASTARDA (viol)

14
CLARINET D'AMORE
CLAVICYTHERIUM (harpsichord)
CYTHARA ANGLICA (harp)
JINGLING JOHNNY
TLAPANHUÉHUETL (drum)
TRICCABALLACCA (clappers)

15
CLASSICAL GUITAR
MOOG SYNTHESIZER
TURKISH CRESCENT (jingling johnny)

16
CHINESE WOOD BLOCK
CHITARRA BATTENTE (guitar)
CYLINDRICAL DRUMS
DEUTSCHE SCHALMEI (double reed)
STRUMENTO DI PORCO (zither)

THEATRICAL TERMS

2
OP
SM

3
ACT
ARC
ASM
GEL
HAM
LEG
PIT
RUN
SET

4
BLUE
BOOK
BOOM
DROP
EXIT
FLAT
GAFF
GOBO
GODS

4 —continued
GRID
IRIS
LEKO
MASK
OLIO
PIPE
PROP
RAIL
RAKE
SOCK
TABS
TAIL
WING

5
ABOVE
ACTOR
AD LIB
AGENT
APRON
ARENA
ASIDE
BELOW

5 —continued
BRACE
CLOTH
CLOUD
FLIES
FLOAT
FOYER
GAUZE
GLORY
HALLS
HEAVY
HOIST
INSET
LYRIC
MANET
ODEUM
PERCH
SCENE
SCRIM
SKENE
SLIPS
SLOTE
SOUND

5 —continued
STAGE
STALL
STILE
TRAPS
TRUCK
VISOR

6
BARREL
BATTEN
BOARDS
BORDER
BOX SET
BRIDGE
BUSKER
CELLAR
CENTRE
CIRCLE
CRITIC
DIMMER
GEGGIE
GROOVE
MAKE-UP

6 —continued	8 —continued	9 —continued	11 —continued
NEUMES	JUVENILE	SKY BORDER	ROLL CEILING
OLD MAN	LASHLINE	SLAPSTICK	SCENE RELIEF
POSTER	LIBRETTO	SLIP STAGE	SPIELTREPPE
PUPPET	LIGHTING	SOUBRETTE	STAGE-KEEPER
RETURN	OFF STAGE	SPOTLIGHT	STROBE LIGHT
RUNWAY	OLD WOMAN	STAGE CREW	SWITCHBOARD
SCRUTO	PANORAMA	STAGE DOOR	TRITAGONIST
SEA ROW	PARADISO	STAGE PROP	UPPER CIRCLE
TEASER	PARALLEL	STAGE RAKE	WAGGON STAGE
TELARI	PASS DOOR	THREE-FOLD	WIND MACHINE
TOGGLE	PLATFORM	THROWLINE	**12**
WALK-ON	PLAYBILL	THYRISTOR	ACTOR-MANAGER
7	PRODUCER	TORMENTOR	AMPHITHEATRE
ACT DROP	PROLOGUE	TRAVELLER	AUTHOR'S NIGHT
ACTRESS	PROMPTER	TRICKWORK	CAULDRON TRAP
AULAEUM	SCENARIO	WATER ROWS	CEILING-CLOTH
BALCONY	SET PIECE	**10**	CHOREOGRAPHY
BENEFIT	SILL IRON	ANTI-MASQUE	CONCERT PARTY
CALL BOY	SIPARIUM	AUDITORIUM	CORSICAN TRAP
CATWALK	SKY CLOTH	AVANT-GARDE	COSTUME DRAMA
CIRCUIT	STAR TRAP	BUILT STUFF	CURTAIN-MUSIC
CURTAIN	VAMP TRAP	CORNER TRAP	FLYING EFFECT
DIORAMA	WARDROBE	CURTAIN SET	FRONT OF HOUSE
FLIPPER	**9**	DRAG ARTIST	LIGHT CONSOLE
GALLERY	ACOUSTICS	FLOODLIGHT	LOBSTERSCOPE
JORNADA	BACKCLOTH	FOLLOW SPOT	MASKING PIECE
MANAGER	BACKSTAGE	GHOST GLIDE	PEPPER'S GHOST
MATINÉE	BOAT TRUCK	HALL KEEPER	PROFILE BOARD
ON STAGE	BOX OFFICE	HOUSE LIGHT	REVERBERATOR
PINSPOT	CALL BOARD	IMPRESARIO	RUNDHORIZONT
RAIN BOX	CARPET CUT	INNER STAGE	SCISSOR CROSS
ROLL-OUT	CYCLORAMA	LYCOPODIUM	SOUND EFFECTS
ROSTRUM	DOWNSTAGE	MARIONETTE	STAGE MANAGER
ROYALTY	FAN EFFECT	PIPE BATTEN	STAGE SETTING
SCENERY	FOOTLIGHT	PROMPT SIDE	STEREOPTICON
SKY DOME	GRAVE TRAP	SADDLE-IRON	STICHOMYTHIA
SPOT BAR	GREEN ROOM	SCIOPTICON	STOCK COMPANY
TABLEAU	GROUNDROW	SHOW PORTAL	THUNDERSHEET
TOP DROP	HAND-PROPS	SPECTATORY	TRANSPARENCY
TRILOGY	HEMP HOUSE	STAGE CLOTH	TWOPENNY GAFF
TUMBLER	LIGHT PIPE	STRIP LIGHT	**13**
TWO-FOLD	LIMELIGHT	THUNDER RUN	DETAIL SCENERY
UPSTAGE	LOFT BLOCK	TREE BORDER	DEUS EX MACHINA
VALANCE	NOISES OFF	UNDERSTUDY	IMPROVISATION
8	OPEN STAGE	**11**	LATERNA MAGICA
AUDITION	ORCHESTRA	BACKING FLAT	MAZARINE FLOOR
BLACKOUT	PENNY GAFF	BOOK CEILING	PLATFORM STAGE
BOOK FLAT	PERIAKTOI	BORDER LIGHT	PORTAL OPENING
BOOK WING	PROJECTOR	BRISTLE TRAP	SAFETY CURTAIN
CALL DOOR	PROMENADE	CURTAIN CALL	STAGE LIGHTING
CHAIRMAN	PROVINCES	DRESS CIRCLE	SUPERNUMERARY
CUT-CLOTH	REFLECTOR	FALLING FLAP	WORD REHEARSAL
DESIGNER	REHEARSAL	FORMAL STAGE	**14**
DIRECTOR	REPERTORY	FRESNEL SPOT	CONTOUR CURTAIN
DUMB SHOW	ROD-PUPPET	LIGHT BATTEN	COURTROOM
ELEVATOR	ROPE HOUSE	LOW COMEDIAN	DRAMA
EPILOGUE	SAND-CLOTH	OFF-BROADWAY	DRAPERY SETTING
FAUTEUIL	SCENE DOCK	PROFILE SPOT	DRESS REHEARSAL
FOX WEDGE	SET WATERS	RISE-AND-SINK	FOOTLIGHTS TRAP
	SIGHT LINE		

BALLET TERMS

14 —continued
GENERAL UTILITY
JACKKNIFE STAGE
KUPPELHORIZONT
MEZZANINE FLOOR
OFF-OFF-
  BROADWAY
PAGEANT LANTERN
PRIVATE THEATRE
PROSCENIUM ARCH
REVOLVING STAGE
STAGE DIRECTION

15
BARN DOOR
  SHUTTER
FLEXIBLE STAGING
HAND WORKED
  HOUSE
INCIDENTAL MUSIC
MULTIPLE SETTING
PROSCENIUM
  DOORS

15 —continued
QUICK-CHANGE
  ROOM
STAGE-DOOR
  KEEPER
TRAVERSE CURTAIN

16
ALIENATION EFFECT
ASPHALEIAN
  SYSTEM
COMPOSITE
  SETTING
DRAMATIS
  PERSONAE
DRAWING-ROOM
  DRAMA
PROSCENIUM
  BORDER
TOURING
  COMPANIES

17
CUP-AND-SAUCER
  DRAMA

18
BESPEAK
  PERFORMANCE
CARBON ARC
  SPOTLIGHT
DRUM-AND-SHAFT
  SYSTEM
FEMALE
  IMPERSONATOR
GRAND MASTER
  CONTROL
LINSEN-
  SCHEINWERFER
TECHNICAL
  REHEARSAL

19
COUNTERWEIGHT
  SYSTEM

19 —continued
SIMULTANEOUS
  SETTING
TRANSFORMATION
  SCENE

20
ADVERTISEMENT
  CURTAIN
ASSISTANT STAGE
  MANAGER
CARRIAGE-AND-
  FRAME SYSTEM
CHARIOT-AND-POLE
  SYSTEM
PROMENADE
  PRODUCTIONS
SILICON
  CONTROLLED
  RECTIFIER
SYNCHRONOUS
  WINCH SYSTEM

BALLET TERMS

4
BRAS
DEMI
JETÉ
PLIÉ
POSÉ
SAUT
TUTU
VOLÉ

5
ARQUÉ
BARRE
BATTU
BEATS
BRISÉ
COLLÉ
COUPÉ
DÉCOR
ÉLÈVE
FONDU
LIGNE
PASSÉ
PIQUÉ
PIVOT
PORTÉ
ROSIN
SAUTÉ
SERRÉ
TOMBÉ

6
APLOMB
À TERRE

6 —continued
ATTACK
BAISSÉ
BALLON
CAMBRÉ
CHAINÉ
CHANGÉ
CHASSÉ
CROISÉ
DÉGAGÉ
DÉTIRÉ
DEVANT
ÉCARTÉ
ÉFFACÉ
ÉLANCÉ
ENTRÉE
ÉPAULÉ
ÉTENDU
ÉTOILE
FAILLI
JARRET
MONTER
PENCHÉ
POINTE
RELEVÉ
RETIRÉ
VOYAGÉ

7
ALLONGÉ
ARRONDI
ATTAQUE
BALANCÉ

7 —continued
DANSEUR
DÉBOITÉ
ÉCHAPPÉ
EMBOITÉ
ÉTENDRE
FOUETTÉ
JARRETÉ
LEOTARD
MAILLOT
MARQUER
POISSON
RAMASSÉ
RETOMBÉ
SISSONE
SOUTENU
TAQUETÉ

8
ASSEMBLÉ
ATTITUDE
BACK BEND
BALLONNÉ
BALLOTTÉ
BATTERIE
CABRIOLE
CAGNEAUX
CORYPHÉE
DANSEUSE
DÉBOULÉS
DERRIÈRE
DÉTOURNE
GLISSADE

8 —continued
PISTOLET
RENVERSÉ
SERPETTE
SPOTTING
STULCHIK
TONNELET

9
ARABESQUE
BALLABILE
COU DE PIED
DÉVELOPPÉ
ÉLÉVATION
ENTRECHAT
ENVELOPPÉ
ÉQUILIBRE
HORTENSIA
JUPONNAGE
LIMBERING
MARCHEUSE
PAS DE DEUX
PIROUETTE
RACCOURCI
RÉVÉRENCE
REVOLTADE

10
BATTEMENTS
ENLÈVEMENT
ÉPAULEMENT
SOUBRESAUT
TAQUETERIE

11	13	14 —continued	17
CONTRETEMPS	CHOREOGRAPHER	PRIMA BALLERINA	RÉGISSEUR-
PAS DE BASQUE	CORPS DE BALLET	**15**	GÉNÉRALE
12	**14**	AUTOUR DE LA	
CHOREOGRAPHY		SALLE	
ENCHAÎNEMENT	CLOSED POSITION		
GARGOUILLADE	DIVERTISSEMENT		

NOVEL TITLES

NOVEL (Author)

3
SHE (H Rider Haggard)
4
DR NO (Ian Fleming)
EMMA (Jane Austen)
GIGI (Colette)
NANA (Émile Zola)
5
CHÉRI (Colette)
KIPPS (H G Wells)
SCOOP (Evelyn Waugh)
SYBIL (Benjamin Disraeli)
ZADIG (Voltaire)
6
AMELIA (Henry Fielding)
BEN HUR (Lew Wallace)
CHOCKY (John Wyndham)
LOLITA (Vladimir Nabokov)
PAMELA (Henry Fielding)
ROB ROY (Walter Scott)
7
CAMILLA (Fanny Burney)
CANDIDE (Voltaire)
CECILIA (Fanny Burney)
DRACULA (Bram Stoker)
EREWHON (Samuel Butler)
EVELINA (Fanny Burney)
IVANHOE (Walter Scott)
REBECCA (Daphne Du Maurier)
SHIRLEY (Charlotte Brontë)
THE FALL (Albert Camus)
ULYSSES (James Joyce)
8
ADAM BEDE (George Eliot)
CRANFORD (Mrs Gaskell)
JANE EYRE (Charlotte Brontë)
LUCKY JIM (Kingsley Amis)
SWAN SONG (John Galsworthy)
THE IDIOT (Fyodor Mikhailovich Dostoevsky)
THE MAGUS (John Fowles)
THE REBEL (Albert Camus)
TOM JONES (Henry Fielding)
VILLETTE (Charlotte Brontë)
WAVERLEY (Walter Scott)

9
AGNES GREY (Anne Brontë)
BILLY LIAR (Keith Waterhouse)
CONINGSBY (Benjamin Disraeli)
DUBLINERS (James Joyce)
GLENARVON (Lady Caroline Lamb)
HARD TIMES (Charles Dickens)
I CLAUDIUS (Robert Graves)
KIDNAPPED (R L Stevenson)
LOVE STORY (Erich Segal)
ROGUE MALE (Geoffrey Household)
THE CHIMES (Charles Dickens)
THE DEVILS (Fyodor Mikhailovich
    Dostoevsky)
THE HEROES (Charles Kingsley)
THE HOBBIT (J R R Tolkien)
THE PLAGUE (Albert Camus)
VICE VERSA (F Anstey)
10
ANIMAL FARM (George Orwell)
BLEAK HOUSE (Charles Dickens)
CANCER WARD (Alexander Solzhenitsyn)
CLAYHANGER (Arnold Bennett)
DON QUIXOTE (Cervantes)
GOLDFINGER (Ian Fleming)
IN CHANCERY (John Galsworthy)
KENILWORTH (Walter Scott)
LORNA DOONE (R D Blackmore)
PERSUASION (Jane Austen)
THE RAINBOW (D H Lawrence)
TITUS ALONE (Mervyn Peake)
TITUS GROAN (Mervyn Peake)
VANITY FAIR (William Makepeace Thackeray)
11
BLACK BEAUTY (Anna Sewell)
BURMESE DAYS (George Orwell)
CAKES AND ALE (W Somerset Maugham)
COUSIN BETTE (Honoré de Balzac)
DAISY MILLER (Henry James)
GORMENGHAST (Mervyn Peake)
LITTLE WOMEN (Louisa M Alcott)
LOST HORIZON (James Hilton)
MIDDLEMARCH (George Eliot)
MRS DALLOWAY (Virginia Woolf)
OLIVER TWIST (Charles Dickens)

11 —continued
SILAS MARNER (George Eliot)
THE BIG SLEEP (Raymond Chandler)
THE OUTSIDER (Albert Camus)
WAR AND PEACE (Leo Tolstoy)
WOMEN IN LOVE (D H Lawrence)

12
ANNA KARENINA (Leo Tolstoy)
A SEVERED HEAD (Iris Murdoch)
BARNABY RUDGE (Charles Dickens)
BRIGHTON ROCK (Graham Greene)
CASINO ROYALE (Ian Fleming)
DOMBEY AND SON (Charles Dickens)
FRANKENSTEIN (Mary Shelley)
GUY MANNERING (Walter Scott)
HEADLONG HALL (Thomas Love Peacock)
LITTLE DORRIT (Charles Dickens)
MADAME BOVARY (Gustave Flaubert)
MOLL FLANDERS (Daniel Defoe)
OF MICE AND MEN (John Steinbeck)
ROGUE JUSTICE (Geoffrey Household)
ROOM AT THE TOP (John Braine)
THE DECAMERON (Boccaccio)
THE GO-BETWEEN (L P Hartley)
THE LOST WORLD (Arthur Conan Doyle)
THE MOONSTONE (Wilkie Collins)
THE PROFESSOR (Charlotte Brontë)

13
A KIND OF LOVING (Stan Barstow)
A MODERN COMEDY (John Galsworthy)
BRAVE NEW WORLD (Aldous Huxley)
DANIEL DERONDA (George Eliot)
DOCTOR ZHIVAGO (Boris Pasternak)
FANNY AND ZOOEY (J D Salinger)
JACOB FAITHFUL (Captain Marryat)
JUST-SO STORIES (Rudyard Kipling)
LES MISÉRABLES (Victor Hugo)
LIVE AND LET DIE (Ian Fleming)
LIZA OF LAMBETH (W Somerset Maugham)
MANSFIELD PARK (Jane Austen)
NORTH AND SOUTH (Mrs Gaskell)
PINCHER MARTIN (William Golding)
SKETCHES BY BOZ (Charles Dickens)
SMILEY'S PEOPLE (John Le Carré)
SONS AND LOVERS (D H Lawrence)
TARKA THE OTTER (Henry Williamson)
THE BLUE LAGOON (H de Vere Stacpoole)
THE CHRYSALIDS (John Wyndham)
THE GOLDEN BOWL (Henry James)
THE HISTORY MAN (Malcolm Bradbury)
THE LAST TYCOON (F Scott Fitzgerald)
THÉRÈSE RAQUIN (Émile Zola)
ZULEIKA DOBSON (Max Beerbohm)

14
A MAN OF PROPERTY (John Galsworthy)
A ROOM OF ONE'S OWN (Virginia Woolf)
A ROOM WITH A VIEW (E M Forster)
A TOWN LIKE ALICE (Neville Shute)
CHANGING PLACES (David Lodge)
CIDER WITH ROSIE (Laurie Lee)

14 —continued
CROTCHET CASTLE (Thomas Love Peacock)
DEATH ON THE NILE (Agatha Christie)
DECLINE AND FALL (Evelyn Waugh)
GOODBYE, MR CHIPS (James Hilton)
JUDE THE OBSCURE (Thomas Hardy)
LORD OF THE FLIES (William Golding)
NIGHTMARE ABBEY (Thomas Love Peacock)
OUR MAN IN HAVANA (Graham Greene)
PICKWICK PAPERS (Charles Dickens)
RITES OF PASSAGE (William Golding)
ROBINSON CRUSOE (Daniel Defoe)
THE AMBASSADORS (Henry James)
THE CORAL ISLAND (R M Ballantyne)
THE FIRST CIRCLE (Alexander Solzhenitsyn)
THE FORSYTE SAGA (John Galsworthy)
THE GREAT GATSBY (F Scott Fitzgerald)
THE KRAKEN WAKES (John Wyndham)
THE LONG GOODBYE (Raymond Chandler)
THE SECRET AGENT (Joseph Conrad)
THE SILVER SPOON (John Galsworthy)
THE TIME MACHINE (H G Wells)
THE WATER-BABIES (Charles Kingsley)
THE WHITE MONKEY (John Galsworthy)
THE WOODLANDERS (Thomas Hardy)
TREASURE ISLAND (R L Stevenson)
TRISTRAM SHANDY (Laurence Sterne)
WHAT MAISIE KNEW (Henry James)

15
A CHRISTMAS CAROL (Charles Dickens)
A FAREWELL TO ARMS (Ernest Hemingway)
A PASSAGE TO INDIA (E M Forster)
COLD COMFORT FARM (Stella Gibbons)
EUSTACE AND HILDA (L P Hartley)
GONE WITH THE WIND (Margaret Mitchell)
GOODBYE TO BERLIN (Christopher
  Isherwood)
NORTHANGER ABBEY (Jane Austen)
OUR MUTUAL FRIEND (Charles Dickens)
PORTRAIT OF A LADY (Henry James)
PORTRAIT OF CLARE (Francis Brett Young)
STRAIT IS THE GATE (André Gide)
THE COUNTRY GIRLS (Edna O'Brien)
THE INVISIBLE MAN (H G Wells)
THE SECRET GARDEN (Frances Hodgson
  Burnett)
THE SILMARILLION (J R R Tolkien)
THE TRUMPET MAJOR (Thomas Hardy)
THE WHITE COMPANY (Arthur Conan Doyle)
THE WOMAN IN WHITE (Wilkie Collins)
THREE MEN IN A BOAT (Jerome K Jerome)

16
A CLOCKWORK ORANGE (Anthony Burgess)
A TALE OF TWO CITIES (Charles Dickens)
DAVID COPPERFIELD (Charles Dickens)
GULLIVER'S TRAVELS (Jonathan Swift)
MARTIN CHUZZLEWIT (Charles Dickens)
MR MIDSHIPMAN EASY (Captain Marryat)
NICHOLAS NICKLEBY (Charles Dickens)
TENDER IS THE NIGHT (F Scott Fitzgerald)

16 —continued

TEN LITTLE NIGGERS (Agatha Christie)
THE GRAPES OF WRATH (John Steinbeck)
THE PLUMED SERPENT (D H Lawrence)
THE SCARLET LETTER (Nathaniel
  Hawthorne)
WUTHERING HEIGHTS (Emily Bronte)

17

ALICE IN WONDERLAND (Lewis Carroll)
DR JEKYLL AND MR HYDE (R L Stevenson)
GREAT EXPECTATIONS (Charles Dickens)
KING SOLOMON'S MINES (H Rider Haggard)
MY BROTHER JONATHAN (Francis Brett
  Young)
POINT COUNTER POINT (Aldous Huxley)
PRIDE AND PREJUDICE (Jane Austen)
THE DEVILS OF LOUDUN (Aldous Huxley)
THE DIARY OF A NOBODY (G and W
  Grossmith)
THE LORD OF THE RINGS (J R R Tolkien)
THE MIDWICH CUCKOOS (John Wyndham)
THE MILL ON THE FLOSS (George Eliot)
THE WAR OF THE WORLDS (H G Wells)
THE WINGS OF THE DOVE (Henry James)
WIVES AND DAUGHTERS (Mrs Gaskell)

18

A HIGH WIND IN JAMAICA (Richard Hughes)
ANNA OF THE FIVE TOWNS (Arnold Bennett)
CRIME AND PUNISHMENT (Fyodor
  Dostoevsky)
NINETEEN EIGHTY-FOUR (George Orwell)
SWALLOWS AND AMAZONS (Arthur
  Ransome)
THE CATCHER IN THE RYE (J D Salinger)
THE MOON AND SIXPENCE (W Somerset
  Maugham)
THE OLD MAN AND THE SEA (Ernest
  Hemingway)
THE PRISONER OF ZENDA (Anthony Hope)
THE THIRTY-NINE STEPS (John Buchan)
THE THREE MUSKETEERS (Alexandre
  Dumas)

19

BRIDESHEAD REVISITED (Evelyn Waugh)
FOR WHOM THE BELL TOLLS (Ernest
  Hemingway)
SENSE AND SENSIBILITY (Jane Austen)
THE DAY OF THE TRIFFIDS (John Wyndham)
THE GULAG ARCHIPELAGO (Alexander
  Solzhenitsyn)
THE HISTORY OF MR POLLY (H G Wells)
THE MAN IN THE IRON MASK (Alexandre
  Dumas)
THE OLD CURIOSITY SHOP (Charles
  Dickens)
THE PILGRIM'S PROGRESS (John Bunyan)
THE RIDDLE OF THE SANDS (Erskine
  Childers)
THE SCARLET PIMPERNEL (Baroness Orczy)
THE SCREWTAPE LETTERS (C S Lewis)

19 —continued

THE VICAR OF WAKEFIELD (Oliver
  Goldsmith)
THE WIND IN THE WILLOWS (Kenneth
  Grahame)
TOM BROWN'S SCHOOLDAYS (Thomas
  Hughes)

20+

A CONNECTICUT YANKEE IN KING
  ARTHUR'S COURT (Mark Twain)
A DANCE TO THE MUSIC OF TIME (Anthony
  Powell)
AS I WALKED OUT ONE MIDSUMMER
  MORNING (Laurie Lee)
CHILDREN OF THE NEW FOREST (Captain
  Marryat)
FAR FROM THE MADDING CROWD (Thomas
  Hardy)
JOHN HALIFAX, GENTLEMAN (Mrs Craik)
KEEP THE ASPIDISTRA FLYING (George
  Orwell)
LADY CHATTERLEY'S LOVER (D H
  Lawrence)
LARK RISE TO CANDLEFORD (Flora
  Thompson)
LITTLE LORD FAUNTLEROY (Frances
  Hodgson Burnett)
MURDER ON THE ORIENT EXPRESS (Agatha
  Christie)
OUT OF THE SILENT PLANET (C S Lewis)
AROUND THE WORLD IN EIGHTY DAYS
  (Jules Verne)
TESS OF THE D'URBERVILLES (Thomas
  Hardy)
THE ADVENTURES OF HUCKLEBERRY FINN
  (Mark Twain)
THE ADVENTURES OF TOM SAWYER (Mark
  Twain)
THE BEAUTIFUL AND DAMNED (F Scott
  Fitzgerald)
THE BRIDE OF LAMMERMOOR (Walter Scott)
THE BROTHERS KARAMAZOV (Fyodor
  Mikhailovich Dostoevsky)
THE CRICKET ON THE HEARTH (Charles
  Dickens)
THE FRENCH LIEUTENANT'S WOMAN (John
  Fowles)
THE HEART OF MIDLOTHIAN (Walter Scott)
THE HISTORY OF HENRY ESMOND (William
  Makepeace Thackeray)
THE HONOURABLE SCHOOLBOY (John Le
  Carré)
THE INNOCENCE OF FATHER BROWN (G K
  Chesterton)
THE ISLAND OF DOCTOR MOREAU (H G
  Wells)
THE LAST OF THE MOHICANS (James
  Fenimore Cooper)
THE MEMOIRS OF SHERLOCK HOLMES
  (Arthur Conan Doyle)

PLAY TITLES

TITLE (Playwright)

11 —continued

LOVE FOR LOVE (William Congreve)
PANDORA'S BOX (Frank Wedekind)
ROOKERY NOOK (Ben Travers)
THE BANKRUPT (Alexander Ostrovsky)
THE CONTRAST (Royall Tyler)
THE CRUCIBLE (Arthur Miller)
THE WILD DUCK (Henrik Ibsen)

12

AFTER THE FALL (Arthur Miller)
ANNA CHRISTIE (Eugene O'Neill)
BEDROOM FARCE (Alan Ayckbourn)
BLITHE SPIRIT (Noël Coward)
BLOOD WEDDING (García Lorca)
CHARLEY'S AUNT (Brandon Thomas)
DUEL OF ANGELS (Jean Giraudoux)
JULIUS CAESAR (William Shakespeare)
MAJOR BARBARA (G B Shaw)
PRIVATE LIVES (Noël Coward)
THE ALCHEMIST (Ben Jonson)
THE ANATOMIST (James Bridie)
THE APPLE CART (G B Shaw)
THE BROKEN JUG (Heinrich von Kleist)
THE CARETAKER (Harold Pinter)
THE MOUSETRAP (Agatha Christie)
THREE SISTERS (Anton Chekhov)
TWELFTH NIGHT (William Shakespeare)

13

ARMS AND THE MAN (G B Shaw)
A TASTE OF HONEY (Shelagh Delaney)
HOBSON'S CHOICE (Harold Brighouse)
LE MISANTHROPE (Molière)
QUALITY STREET (J M Barrie)
THE ACHARNIANS (Aristophanes)
THE DUMB WAITER (Harold Pinter)
THE JEW OF MALTA (Christopher Marlowe)
THE LINDEN TREE (J B Priestley)
THE MAGISTRATE (Pinero)
THE MATCHMAKER (Thornton Wilder)
THE WHITE DEVIL (John Webster)
THE WINSLOW BOY (Terence Rattigan)
TIMON OF ATHENS (William Shakespeare)
UNDER MILK WOOD (Dylan Thomas)

14

AN IDEAL HUSBAND (Oscar Wilde)
MAN AND SUPERMAN (G B Shaw)
ROMEO AND JULIET (William Shakespeare)
SEPARATE TABLES (Terence Rattigan)
THE CORN IS GREEN (Emlyn Williams)
THE COUNTRY GIRL (Clifford Odets)
THE DEEP BLUE SEA (Terence Rattigan)
THE FIRE-RAISERS (Max Frisch)
THE GHOST SONATA (August Strindberg)
THE OLD BACHELOR (William Congreve)
THE PHILANDERER (G B Shaw)
THE TROJAN WOMEN (Euripides)
THE WINTER'S TALE (William Shakespeare)
THIS HAPPY BREED (Noel Coward)

15

BARTHOLOMEW FAIR (Ben Jonson)

15 —continued

DANGEROUS CORNER (J B Priestley)
DESIGN FOR LIVING (Noël Coward)
HEARTBREAK HOUSE (G B Shaw)
LOOK BACK IN ANGER (John Osborne)
MARRIAGE À LA MODE (John Dryden)
PRESENT LAUGHTER (Noël Coward)
THE CONSTANT WIFE (W Somerset Maugham)
THE ICEMAN COMETH (Eugene O'Neill)
TITUS ANDRONICUS (William Shakespeare)
TWO NOBLE KINSMEN (William Shakespeare)
VENICE PRESERVED (Thomas Otway)
WAITING FOR GODOT (Samuel Beckett)

16

A CUCKOO IN THE NEST (Ben Travers)
AN INSPECTOR CALLS (J B Priestley)
CAT ON A HOT TIN ROOF (Tennessee Williams)
DEATH OF A SALESMAN (Arthur Miller)
LOVE'S LABOUR'S LOST (William Shakespeare)
PILLARS OF SOCIETY (Henrik Ibsen)
RING ROUND THE MOON (Jean Anouilh)
THE ADDING MACHINE (Elmer Rice)
THE AMERICAN DREAM (Edward Albee)
THE BIRTHDAY PARTY (Harold Pinter)
THE CHERRY ORCHARD (Anton Chekhov)
THE COCKTAIL PARTY (T S Eliot)
THE FAMILY REUNION (T S Eliot)
THE MASTER BUILDER (Henrik Ibsen)
WHAT THE BUTLER SAW (Joe Orton)

17

A MAN FOR ALL SEASONS (Robert Bolt)
AN ITALIAN STRAW HAT (Eugène Labiche)
ARSENIC AND OLD LACE (Joseph Kesselring)
BAREFOOT IN THE PARK (Neil Simon)
JUNO AND THE PAYCOCK (Sean O'Casey)
MEASURE FOR MEASURE (William Shakespeare)
ROMANOFF AND JULIET (Peter Ustinov)
THE BEAUX' STRATAGEM (George Farquhar)
THE COMEDY OF ERRORS (William Shakespeare)
THE DEVIL'S DISCIPLE (G B Shaw)
THE DOCTOR'S DILEMMA (G B Shaw)
THE DUCHESS OF MALFI (John Webster)
THE GLASS MENAGERIE (Tennessee Williams)
THE GOOD-NATURED MAN (Oliver Goldsmith)
THE SCHOOL FOR WIVES (Molière)
THE SUPPLIANT WOMEN (Aeschylus)
'TIS PITY SHE'S A WHORE (John Ford)

18

AN ENEMY OF THE PEOPLE (Henrik Ibsen)
ANTONY AND CLEOPATRA (William Shakespeare)
CAESAR AND CLEOPATRA (G B Shaw)
FIVE FINGER EXERCISE (Peter Shaffer)

18 —continued

FRENCH WITHOUT TEARS (Terence Rattigan)
LADY WINDERMERE'S FAN (Oscar Wilde)
SHE STOOPS TO CONQUER (Oliver Goldsmith)
SUDDENLY LAST SUMMER (Tennessee Williams)
THE BROWNING VERSION (Terence Rattigan)
THE ROMANS IN BRITAIN (Howard Brenton)
TROILUS AND CRESSIDA (William Shakespeare)

19

ANDROCLES AND THE LION (G B Shaw)
CHIPS WITH EVERYTHING (Arnold Wesker)
MUCH ADO ABOUT NOTHING (William Shakespeare)
TAMBURLAINE THE GREAT (Christopher Marlowe)
THE MERCHANT OF VENICE (William Shakespeare)
THE SCHOOL FOR SCANDAL (Sheridan)
THE TAMING OF THE SHREW (William Shakespeare)
WHAT EVERY WOMAN KNOWS (J M Barrie)

20+

ACCIDENTAL DEATH OF AN ANARCHIST (Dario Fo)
ALL GOD'S CHILLUN GOT WINGS (Eugene O'Neill)
ALL'S WELL THAT ENDS WELL (William Shakespeare)
A MIDSUMMER NIGHT'S DREAM (William Shakespeare)

20+ —continued

A STREETCAR NAMED DESIRE (Tennessee Williams)
A WOMAN OF NO IMPORTANCE (Oscar Wilde)
CAPTAIN BRASSBOUND'S CONVERSION (G B Shaw)
ENTERTAINING MR SLOANE (Joe Orton)
INADMISSIBLE EVIDENCE (John Osborne)
MOURNING BECOMES ELECTRA (Eugene O'Neill)
MURDER IN THE CATHEDRAL (T S Eliot)
ROSENCRANTZ AND GUILDENSTERN ARE DEAD (Tom Stoppard)
THE ADMIRABLE CRICHTON (J M Barrie)
THE BARRETTS OF WIMPOLE STREET (Rudolf Besier)
THE CAUCASIAN CHALK CIRCLE (Bertolt Brecht)
THE GOVERNMENT INSPECTOR (Nikolai Gogol)
THE IMPORTANCE OF BEING EARNEST (Oscar Wilde)
THE LADY'S NOT FOR BURNING (Christopher Fry)
THE MERRY WIVES OF WINDSOR (William Shakespeare)
THE SECOND MRS TANQUERAY (Pinero)
THE TWO GENTLEMEN OF VERONA (William Shakespeare)
WHO'S AFRAID OF VIRGINIA WOOLF? (Edward Albee)

FICTIONAL CHARACTERS

CHARACTER (*Title*, Author)

3

FOX, Brer (*Uncle Remus*, J. C. Harris)
GOG (*The Tower of London*, W. H. Ainsworth)
HUR, Judah (*Ben Hur*, L. Wallace)
JIM, 'Lord' (*Lord Jim*, J. Conrad)
KIM (*Kim*, Rudyard Kipling)
LEE, General Robert E. (*Abraham Lincoln*, J. Drinkwater)
LEE, Lorelei (*Gentlemen Prefer Blondes*, Anita Loos)
OWL (*Winnie the Pooh*, A. A. Milne)
ROO (*Winnie the Pooh*, A. A. Milne)
TOM (*The Water Babies*, C. Kingsley)
TOM, 'Uncle' (*Uncle Tom's Cabin*, Harriet B. Stowe)

4

ABEL (*Middlemarch*, George Eliot)
CASS, Eppie (*Silas Marner*, George Eliot)

4 —continued

CASY, Rev. Jim (*The Grapes of Wrath*, J. Steinbeck)
CUFF, Sergeant (*The Moonstone*, W. Collins)
DEAN, Ellen (*Wuthering Heights*, Emily Brontë)
EAST (*Tom Brown's Schooldays*, T. Hughes)
EASY, John (*Mr Midshipman Easy*, Captain Marryat)
EYRE, Jane (*Jane Eyre*, Charlotte Brontë)
FAWN, Lord Frederic (*Phineas Finn*, A. Trollope)
FELL, Dr Gideon (*The Black Spectacles*, J. Dickson Carr)
FINN, Huckleberry (*Huckleberry Finn*, Tom Sawyer*, M. Twain)
FINN, Phineas (*Phineas Finn*, A. Trollope)

4 —continued

GRAY, Dorian (*The Picture of Dorian Gray*, Oscar Wilde)

GRAY, Nelly (*Faithless Nelly Gray*, T. Hood)

GUNN, Ben (*Treasure Island*, R. L. Stevenson)

HOOK, Captain James (*Peter Pan*, J. M. Barrie)

HYDE, Edward (*Dr Jekyll and Mr Hyde*, R. L. Stevenson)

JUDY (*Wee Willie Winkie*, R. Kipling)

LAMB, Leonard (*Middlemarch*, George Eliot)

MOLE, Mr (*The Wind in the Willows*, K. Grahame)

NANA (*Peter Pan*, J. M. Barrie)

NASH, Richard (Beau) (*Monsieur Beaucaire*, Booth Tarkington)

PUCK (Robin Goodfellow) (*Puck of Pook's Hill*, R. Kipling)

RAMA (Tiger Tiger) (*The Jungle Book*, R. Kipling)

REED, Mrs (*Jane Eyre*, Charlotte Brontë)

RIDD, John (*Lorna Doone*, R. D. Blackmore)

SEAL, Basil (*Put Out More Flags*, E. Waugh)

SMEE (*Peter Pan*, J. M. Barrie)

TOAD, Mr (*The Wind in the Willows*, K. Grahame)

TROY, Sergeant Francis (*Far from the Madding Crowd*, T. Hardy)

VANE, Harriet (*Strong Poison*, Dorothy L. Sayers)

VANE, Lady Isabel (*East Lynne*, Mrs Henry Wood)

WOLF, 'Brer' (*Uncle Remus*, J. C. Harris)

5

ADLER, Irene (*The Adventures of Sherlock Holmes*, A. Conan Doyle)

AKELA (*The Jungle Book*, R. Kipling)

ALIBI, Tom (*Waverley*, W. Scott)

ATHOS (*The Three Musketeers*, Alexandre Dumas)

BALOO (*The Jungle Book*, R. Kipling)

BLAKE, Franklin (*The Moonstone*, W. Collins)

BONES, Captain Billy (*Treasure Island*, R. L. Stevenson)

BOOBY, Sir Thomas (*Joseph Andrews*, H. Fielding)

BRUFF (*The Moonstone*, W. Collins)

BULBO, Prince (*The Rose and the Ring*, W. M. Thackeray)

CHANT, Mercy (*Tess of the D'Urbervilles*, T. Hardy)

CLACK, Drusilla (*The Moonstone*, W. Collins)

CLARE, Angel (*Tess of the D'Urbervilles*, T. Hardy)

DARCY, Fitzwilliam (*Pride and Prejudice*, Jane Austen)

DEANS, Effie/Jeanie (*The Heart of Midlothian*, W. Scott)

DIXON, James (*Lucky Jim*, K. Amis)

DOONE, Lorna (*Lorna Doone*, R. D. Blackmore)

5 —continued

EAGER, Rev. Cuthbert (*Room with a View*, E. M. Forster)

FANNY (*Fanny's First Play*, G. B. Shaw)

FLYNN, Father James (*The Dubliners*, J. Joyce)

GESTE, Beau (*Beau Geste*, P. C. Wren)

GWYNN, Nell (*Simon Dale*, A. Hope)

HANDS, Israel (*Treasure Island*, R. L. Stevenson)

HATCH, Bennet (*The Black Arrow*, R. L. Stevenson)

JONES, Tom (*Tom Jones*, H. Fielding)

KANGA (*Winnie the Pooh*, A. A. Milne)

KIPPS, Arthur (*Kipps*, H. G. Wells)

LEIGH, Captain Sir Amyas (*Westward Ho!*, C. Kingsley)

MAGOG (*The Tower of London*, W. H. Ainsworth)

MARCH, Amy/Beth/Josephine (Jo)/Meg (*Little Women*, etc., Louisa M. Alcott)

MERCY (*Pilgrim's Progress*, J. Bunyan)

MITTY, Walter (*The Secret Life of Walter Mitty*, J. Thurber)

MOORE, Mrs (*A Passage to India*, E. M. Forster)

O'HARA, Kimball (*Kim*, Rudyard Kipling)

O'HARA, Scarlett (*Gone with the Wind*, Margaret Mitchell)

OTTER, Mr (*The Wind in the Willows*, K. Grahame)

PAGET, Jean (*A Town like Alice*, N. Shute)

POLLY, Alfred (*The History of Mr Polly*, H. G. Wells)

POOLE, Grace (*Jane Eyre*, Charlotte Brontë)

PORGY (*Porgy*, Du Bose Heyward)

PRISM, Miss Laetitia (*The Importance of Being Earnest*, Oscar Wilde)

PUNCH (*Wee Willie Winkie*, R. Kipling)

READY, Masterman (*Masterman Ready*, F. Marryat)

REMUS, Uncle (*Uncle Remus* series, J. C. Harris)

RYDER, Charles (*Brideshead Revisited*, E. Waugh)

SALLY (*Sally in Our Alley*, H. Carey)

SAMBO (*Just So Stories*, R. Kipling)

SHARP, Rebecca (Becky) (*Vanity Fair*, W. M. Thackeray)

SLOPE, Rev. Obadiah (*Barchester Towers*, A. Trollope)

SLOTH (*Pilgrim's Progress*, J. Bunyan)

SMITH, Winston (*1984*, G. Orwell)

SNOWE, Lucy (*Villette*, Charlotte Brontë)

TARKA (*Tarka the Otter*, H. Williamson)

THUMB, Tom (*The Tale of Two Bad Mice*, Beatrix Potter)

TOPSY (*Uncle Tom's Cabin*, Harriet B. Stowe)

UNCAS (*The Last of the Mohicans*, J. Fennimore Cooper)

6

AITKEN (*Prester John*, J. Buchan)
ARAMIS (*The Three Musketeers*, Alexandre Dumas)
AYESHA (*She*, H. Rider Haggard)
BENNET, Catherine/Elizabeth/Jane/Lydia/ Mary (*Pride and Prejudice*, Jane Austen)
BESSIE (*Jane Eyre*, Charlotte Brontë)
BINKIE, Lady Grizzel (*Vanity Fair*, W. M. Thackeray)
BOVARY, Emma (*Madame Bovary*, G. Flaubert)
BUTLER, Rhett (*Gone with the Wind*, Margaret Mitchell)
CACKLE (*Vanity Fair*, W. M. Thackeray)
CARDEW, Cecily (*The Importance of Being Earnest*, Oscar Wilde)
CRUSOE, Robinson (*Robinson Crusoe*, D. Defoe)
DANGLE (*The Critic*, R. B. Sheridan)
EEYORE (*Winnie the Pooh*, A. A. Milne)
ELAINE (*Idylls of the King*, Lord Tennyson)
'FRIDAY' (*Robinson Crusoe*, D. Defoe)
FRITHA (*The Snow Goose*, P. Gallico)
GARTER, Polly (*Under Milk Wood*, D. Thomas)
GATSBY, Major Jay (*The Great Gatsby*, F. Scott Fitzgerald)
GEORGE (*Three Men in a Boat*, J. K. Jerome)
GERARD, Etienne (*The Exploits of Brigadier Gerard*, A. Conan Doyle)
GILPIN, John (*John Gilpin*, W. Cowper)
GLOVER, Catherine (*The Fair Maid of Perth*, W. Scott)
GORDON, Squire (*Black Beauty*, A. Sewell)
GRIMES (*The Water Babies*, C. Kingsley)
HANNAY, Richard (*The Thirty-Nine Steps*, J. Buchan)
HARKER, Jonathan/Minna (*Dracula*, Bram Stoker)
HARMAN, Joe (*A Town like Alice*, N. Shute)
HAROLD, Childe (*Childe Harold's Pilgrimage*, Lord Byron)
HEARTS, King of/Knave of/Queen of (*Alice in Wonderland*, L. Carroll)
HOLMES, Mycroft (*The Return of Sherlock Holmes*, A. Conan Doyle)
HOLMES, Sherlock (*A Study in Scarlet, The Sign of Four, The Hound of the Baskervilles*, etc., A. Conan Doyle)
HOOPER, Fanny (*Fanny by Gaslight*, M. Sadleir)
JEEVES (*Thank you, Jeeves*, P. G. Wodehouse)
JEKYLL, Henry (*Dr Jekyll and Mr Hyde*, R. L. Stevenson)
LAURIE (*Little Women*, Louisa M. Alcott)
LAURIE, Annie (*Annie Laurie*, Douglass)
LEGREE, Simon (*Uncle Tom's Cabin*, Harriet B Stowe)
LINTON, Edgar (*Wuthering Heights*, Emily Brontë)

6 —continued

MANGAN, Boss (*Heartbreak House*, G. B. Shaw)
MANSON, Dr Andrew (*The Citadel*, A. J. Cronin)
MARPLE, Jane (*A Pocket Full of Rye*, Agatha Christie)
MERLIN (*Idylls of the King*, Lord Tennyson)
MODRED, Sir (*Idylls of the King*, Lord Tennyson)
MOREAU, André-Louis (*Scaramouche*, R. Sabatini)
MOREAU, Dr (*The Island of Dr Moreau*, H. G. Wells)
MORGAN, Angharad/Huw (*How Green Was My Valley*, R. Llewellyn)
MORGAN, Organ (*Under Milk Wood*, D. Thomas)
MOWGLI (*The Jungle Book*, R. Kipling)
NUTKIN, Squirrel, (*The Tale of Squirrel Nutkin*, Beatrix Potter)
OMNIUM, Duke of (Family name Palliser) (*The Barsetshire series*, Angela Thirkell)
PICKLE, Peregrine (*Peregrine Pickle*, T. Smollett)
PIGLET, Henry Pootel (*Winnie the Pooh*, A. A. Milne)
POIROT, Hercule (*The Mysterious Affair at Styles*, Agatha Christie)
RABBIT (*Winnie the Pooh*, A. A. Milne)
RABBIT, 'Brer' (*Uncle Remus*, J. C. Harris)
RABBIT, The White (*Alice in Wonderland*, L. Carroll)
RIVERS, St John (*Jane Eyre*, Charlotte Brontë)
RUSTUM (*Sohrab and Rustum*, M. Arnold)
SAWYER, Tom (*The Adventures of Tom Sawyer*, M. Twain)
SHANDY, Tristram (*Tristram Shandy*, L. Sterne)
SILVER, Long John (*Treasure Island*, R. L. Stevenson)
SIMNEL, Lambert (*Perkin Warbeck*, John Ford)
SOHRAB (*Sohrab and Rustum*, M. Arnold)
TEMPLE, Miss (*Jane Eyre*, Charlotte Brontë)
THORNE, Dr Thomas (*Doctor Thorne*, A. Trollope)
THORPE, Isabella (*Northanger Abbey*, Jane Austen)
TILNEY, Henry (*Northanger Abbey*, Jane Austen)
TURNER, Jim (Captain Flint) (*Swallows and Amazons*, A. Ransome)
UMPOPA (*King Solomon's Mines*, H. Rider Haggard)
WALKER, John/Roger/Susan/Titty/Vicky (*Swallows and Amazons*, A. Ransome)
WESTON, Mrs (*Emma*, Jane Austen)
WILKES, Ashley/India (*Gone with the Wind*, Margaret Mitchell)

6 —continued

WIMSEY, Lord Peter Death Bredon (*Whose Body?*, Dorothy L. Sayers)

7

AISGILL, Alice (*Room at the Top*, J. Braine)

BAGSTER (*Middlemarch*, George Eliot)

BEESLEY (*Lucky Jim*, Kingsley Amis)

BINGLEY, Charles (*Pride and Prejudice*, Jane Austen)

BRANDON, Colonel (*Sense and Sensibility*, Jane Austen)

CANDOUR, Mrs (*The School for Scandal*, R. B. Sheridan)

CHESNEY, Jack (*Charley's Aunt*, Brandon Thomas)

COLLINS, Rev. William (*Pride and Prejudice*, Jane Austen)

CYPRESS, Mr (*Nightmare Abbey*, T. L. Peacock)

DANVERS, Mrs (*Rebecca*, Daphne du Maurier)

DESPAIR, Giant (*Pilgrim's Progress*, J. Bunyan)

DRACULA, Count (*Dracula*, Bram Stoker)

EPICENE (*Epicene*, B. Jonson)

FAIRFAX, Gwendolen (*The Importance of Being Earnest*, Oscar Wilde)

FAIRFAX, Jane (*Emma*, J. Austen)

FAIRFAX, Mrs (*Jane Eyre*, Charlotte Brontë)

FAIRLIE, Frederick (*Woman in White*, W. Collins)

FAUSTUS (*The History of Dr Faustus*, C. Marlowe)

FORSYTE, Fleur/Irene/Jolyon/Jon/Soames (*The Forsyte Saga*, J. Galsworthy)

GALAHAD (*Idylls of the King*, Lord Tennyson)

GERAINT (*Idylls of the King*, Lord Tennyson)

GRANTLY, Bishop of Barchester (*The Warden, Barchester Towers*, A. Trollope)

HAWKINS, Jim (*Treasure Island*, R. L. Stevenson)

HENTZAU, Rupert of (*The Prisoner of Zenda*, A. Hope)

HERRIES, Francis (*Rogue Herries*, H. Walpole)

HIGGINS, Henry (*Pygmalion*, G. B. Shaw)

IVANHOE, Wilfred, Knight of (*Ivanhoe*, W. Scott)

JENKINS, Rev. Eli (*Under Milk Wood*, D. Thomas)

KEELDAR, Shirley (*Shirley*, Charlotte Brontë)

LAMPTON, Joe (*Room at the Top*, J. Braine)

LATIMER, Darsie (*Redgauntlet*, W. Scott)

LAWLESS (*The Black Arrow*, R. L. Stevenson)

LINCOLN, Abraham (*Abraham Lincoln*, J. Drinkwater)

LUCIFER (*Faustus*, C. Marlowe)

MESSALA (*Ben Hur*, L. Wallace)

MICHAEL, Duke of Strelsau (*The Prisoner of Zenda*, A. Hope)

MINIVER, Mrs Caroline (*Mrs Miniver*, Jan Struther)

7 —continued

MORLAND, Catherine (*Northanger Abbey*, Jane Austen)

NOKOMIS (*Song of Hiawatha*, H. W. Longfellow)

PORTHOS (*The Three Musketeers*, Alexandre Dumas)

PROUDIE, Dr/Mrs (*Framley Parsonage*, A. Trollope)

RAFFLES, A. J. (*Raffles* series; E. W. Hornung)

RANDALL, Rebecca (*Rebecca of Sunnybrook Farm*, Kate D. Wiggin)

RATTLER, Martin (*Martin Rattler*, R. M. Ballantyne)

REBECCA (*Rebecca*, Daphne du Maurier)

REBECCA (*Rebecca of Sunnybrook Farm*, Kate D. Wiggin)

RED KING (*Alice Through the Looking Glass*, L. Carroll)

ROBSART, Amy (*Kenilworth*, W. Scott)

SANDERS (Sandi) (*Sanders of the River*, E. Wallace)

SHELTON, Richard (*The Black Arrow*, R. L. Stevenson)

SHIPTON, Mother (*The Luck of Roaring Camp*, Bret Harte)

SMOLLET, Captain (*Treasure Island*, R. L. Stevenson)

SORRELL, Christopher (Kit) (*Sorrell and Son*, W. Deeping)

ST CLARE, Evangeline (Little Eva) (*Uncle Tom's Cabin*, Harriet B. Stowe)

TIDDLER, Tom (*Adam's Opera*, Clemence Dane)

WARBECK, Perkin (*Perkin Warbeck*, John Ford)

WESTERN, Mrs/Sophia/Squire, (*Tom Jones*, H. Fielding)

WILLIAM (*Just William*, Richmal Crompton)

WINSLOW, Ronnie (*The Winslow Boy*, T. Rattigan)

WOOSTER, Bertie (*Thank You, Jeeves*, P. G. Wodehouse)

8

ABSOLUTE, Sir Anthony (*The Rivals*, R. B. Sheridan)

ANGELICA (*The Rose and the Ring*, W. M. Thackeray)

APOLLYON (*Pilgrim's Progress*, J. Bunyan)

ARMITAGE, Jacob (*The Children of the New Forest*, Captain Marryat)

BACKBITE, Sir Benjamin (*The School for Scandal*, R. B. Sheridan)

BAGHEERA (*The Jungle Book*, R. Kipling)

BLACK DOG (*Treasure Island*, R. L. Stevenson)

CARRAWAY, Nick (*The Great Gatsby*, F. Scott Fitzgerald)

CASAUBON, Rev. Edward, (*Middlemarch*, George Eliot)

8 —continued

CRAWFURD, David (*Prester John*, J. Buchan)

CRICHTON, Bill (*The Admirable Crichton*, J. M. Barrie)

DASHWOOD, Henry (*Sense and Sensibility*, Jane Austen)

DE BOURGH, Lady Catherine (*Pride and Prejudice*, Jane Austen)

DE WINTER, Maximilian (*Rebecca*, Daphne du Maurier)

EARNSHAW, Catherine (*Wuthering Heights*, Emily Brontë)

EVERDENE, Bathsheba (*Far from the Madding Crowd*, T. Hardy)

FFOULKES, Sir Andrew (*The Scarlet Pimpernel*, Baroness Orczy)

FLANDERS, Moll (*Moll Flanders*, D. Defoe)

FLASHMAN (*Tom Brown's Schooldays*, T. Hughes)

GLORIANA (*The Faërie Queen*, E. Spenser)

GOLLANTZ, Emmanuel (*Young Emmanuel*, N. Jacob)

GULLIVER, Lemuel (*Gulliver's Travels*, J. Swift)

GUNGA DIN (*Barrack-room Ballads*, R. Kipling)

HIAWATHA (*The Song of Hiawatha*, H. W. Longfellow)

KNIGHTLY, George (*Emma*, J. Austen)

LANCELOT, Sir (*Idylls of the King*, Lord Tennyson)

LANGUISH, Lydia (*The Rivals*, R. B. Sheridan)

LAURENCE, Theodore (*Little Women*, Louisa M. Alcott)

LESSWAYS, Hilda (*The Clayhanger Trilogy*, Arnold Bennett)

LESTRADE, of Scotland Yard (*A Study in Scarlet*, A. Conan Doyle)

LOCKWOOD (*Wuthering Heights*, Emily Brontë)

MACAVITY (*Old Possum's Book of Practical Cats*, T. S. Eliot)

MALAPROP, Mrs (*The Rivals*, R. B. Sheridan)

MARY JANE (*When We Were Very Young*, A. A. Milne)

MORIARTY, Professor James (*Memoirs of Sherlock Holmes*, A. Conan Doyle)

O'FERRALL, Trilby (*Trilby*, George du Maurier)

OLIFAUNT, Nigel (*The Fortunes of Nigel*, W. Scott)

O'TRIGGER, Sir Lucius (*The Rivals*, R. B. Sheridan)

PALLISER, Lady Glencora/Plantagenet (*Phineas Finn*, A. Trollope)

PRIMROSE, Dr Charles (*The Vicar of Wakefield*, O. Goldsmith)

QUANTOCK, Mrs Daisy (*Queen Lucia*, E. F. Benson)

RED QUEEN (*Alice Through the Looking Glass*, L. Carroll)

8 —continued

SHOTOVER, Captain (*Heartbreak House*, G. B. Shaw)

ST BUNGAY, Duke of (*Phineas Finn*, A. Trollope)

SVENGALI (*Trilby*, George du Maurier)

THATCHER, Becky (*The Adventures of Tom Sawyer*, M. Twain)

TRISTRAM (*Idylls of the King*, Lord Tennyson)

TULLIVER, Maggie/Tom (*The Mill on the Floss*, George Eliot)

VERINDER, Lady Julia (*The Moonstone*, W. Collins)

WATER RAT (Ratty) (*The Wind in the Willows*, K. Grahame)

WAVERLEY, Edward (*Waverley*, W. Scott)

WHITEOAK (family) (*The Whiteoak Chronicles*, Mazo de la Roche)

WHITE-TIP (*Tarka the Otter*, Henry Williamson)

WHITTIER, Pollyanna (*Pollyanna*, Eleanor H. Porter)

WILLIAMS, Percival William (*Wee Willie Winkie*, R. Kipling)

WORTHING, John (*The Importance of Being Earnest*, Oscar Wilde)

9

ABBEVILLE, Horace (*Cannery Row*, J. Steinbeck)

ABLEWHITE, Godfrey (*The Moonstone*, W. Collins)

ALLWORTHY, Squire (*Tom Jones*, H. Fielding)

BABBERLEY, Lord Fancourt (*Charley's Aunt*, Brandon Thomas)

BARRYMORE (*The Hound of the Baskervilles*, A. Conan Doyle)

BRACKNELL, Lady (*The Importance of Being Earnest*, Oscar Wilde)

BULSTRODE, Nicholas (*Middlemarch*, George Eliot)

CHAINMAIL (*Crotchet Castle*, T. L. Peacock)

CHRISTIAN (*Pilgrim's Progress*, J. Bunyan)

CHURCHILL, Frank (*Emma*, Jane Austen)

D'ARTAGNAN (*The Three Musketeers*, Alexandre Dumas)

DOOLITTLE, Eliza (*Pygmalion*, G. B. Shaw)

GREYSTOKE, Lord (*Tarzan* series, E. R. Burroughs)

GUINEVERE (*Idylls of the King*, Lord Tennyson)

INDIAN JOE (*The Adventures of Tom Sawyer*, M. Twain)

LEICESTER, Earl of (*Kenilworth*, W. Scott)

MACGREGOR, Robin (*Rob Roy*, W. Scott)

MARCH HARE, The (*Alice in Wonderland*, L. Carroll)

MARCHMAIN, Lady Cordelia/Lady Julia/Lord Sebastian/Marquis of/Teresa/The Earl of Brideshead (*Brideshead Revisited*, E Waugh)

9 —continued

MEHITABEL, the cat (*Archy and Mehitabel*, D. Marquis)

MERRILIES, Meg (*Guy Mannering*, W. Scott)

MINNEHAHA (*The Song of Hiawatha*, H. W. Longfellow)

MONCRIEFF, Algernon (*The Importance of Being Earnest*, Oscar Wilde)

PENDENNIS, Arthur (Pen) (*Pendennis*, W. M. Thackeray)

PERCIVALE (*Idylls of the King*, Lord Tennyson)

RED KNIGHT (*Alice Through the Looking Glass*, L. Carroll)

ROCHESTER, Bertha/Edward Fairfax (*Jane Eyre*, Charlotte Brontë)

SHERE KHAN (Lungri) (*The Jungle Book*, R. Kipling)

SOUTHDOWN, Earl of (*Vanity Fair*, W. M. Thackeray)

TAMERLANE (*Tamerlane*, N. Rowe)

TANQUERAY, Aubrey (*The Second Mrs Tanqueray*, A. W. Pinero)

TIGER LILY (*Peter Pan*, J. M. Barrie)

TRELAWNEY, Rose (*Trelawney of the Wells*, A. W. Pinero)

TRELAWNEY, Squire (*Treasure Island*, R. L. Stevenson)

TWITCHETT, Mrs Tabitha (*The Tale of Tom Kitten*, Beatrix Potter)

VIRGINIAN, The (*The Virginian*, O. Wister)

WAYNFLETE, Lady Cicely (*Captain Brassbound's Conversion*, G. B. Shaw)

WOODHOUSE, Emma/Isabella (*Emma*, Jane Austen)

10

ABRAMS MOSS (*Pendennis*, W. M. Thackeray)

ALLAN-A-DALE (*Ivanhoe*, W. Scott)

ARROWPOINT (*Daniel Deronda*, George Eliot)

BELLADONNA (*Vanity Fair*, W. M. Thackeray)

CHALLENGER, Professor (*The Lost World*, A. Conan Doyle)

CRIMSWORTH, William (*The Professor*, Charlotte Brontë)

EVANGELINE (*Evangeline*, H. W. Longfellow)

FAUNTLEROY, Lord Cedric Errol (*Little Lord Fauntleroy*, F. H. Burnett)

GOODFELLOW, Robin (*St Ronan's Well*, W. Scott)

HEATHCLIFF (*Wuthering Heights*, Emily Bronte)

HORNBLOWER, Horatio (The *Hornblower* series, C. S. Forester)

HUNCA MUNCA (*The Tale of Two Bad Mice*, Beatrix Potter)

HUNTER-DUNN, Joan (*A Subaltern's Love Song*, J. Betjeman)

JACKANAPES (*Jackanapes*, Juliana H. Ewing)

LETHBRIDGE, Daphne (*The Dark Tide*, Vera Brittain)

10 —continued

MAN IN BLACK (*A Citizen of the World*, O. Goldsmith)

MAULEVERER, Lord (*Cranford*, Mrs Gaskell)

MOCK TURTLE, THE (*Alice in Wonderland*, L. Carroll)

PUDDLEDUCK, Jemima (*The Tale of Jemima Puddleduck*, Beatrix Potter)

QUATERMAIN, Allan (*King Solomon's Mines*, H. Rider Haggard)

RASSENDYLL, Rudolf (*The Prisoner of Zenda*, A. Hope)

STARKADDER, Judith/Old Mrs (*Cold Comfort Farm*, Stella Gibbons)

TINKER BELL (*Peter Pan*, J. M. Barrie)

TWEEDLEDEE (*Alice Through the Looking-Glass*, L. Carroll)

TWEEDLEDUM (*Alice Through the Looking-Glass*, L. Carroll)

UNDERSHAFT, Barbara (*Major Barbara*, G. B. Shaw)

WILLOUGHBY, John (*Sense and Sensibility*, Jane Austen)

WINDERMERE, Lord Arthur/Margaret (*Lady Windermere's Fan*, Oscar Wilde)

11

ADDENBROOKE, Bennett (*Raffles*, E. W. Hornung)

DURBEYFIELD, Tess (*Tess of the D'Urbervilles*, T. Hardy)

JABBERWOCKY (*Alice Through the Looking-Glass*, L. Carroll)

MACCROTCHET (*Crotchet Castle*, T. L. Peacock)

MONTMORENCY, the dog (*Three Men in a Boat*, J. K. Jerome)

REDGAUNTLET, Sir Arthur Darsie (*Redgauntlet*, W. Scott)

TAMBURLAINE (*Tamburlaine*, C. Marlowe)

TAM O'SHANTER (*Tam O'Shanter*, R. Burns)

TIGGY-WINKLE, Mrs (*The Tale of Mrs Tiggy-Winkle*, Beatrix Potter)

TITTLEMOUSE, Mrs Thomasina (*The Tale of Mrs Tittlemouse*, Beatrix Potter)

TRUMPINGTON, Lady (*The Virginians*, W. M. Thackeray)

12

BROCKLEHURST (*Jane Eyre*, Charlotte Brontë)

CAPTAIN FLINT (*Swallows and Amazons*, A. Ransome)

FRANKENSTEIN, Victor (*Frankenstein*, M. W. Shelley)

HUMPTY-DUMPTY (*Alice Through the Looking-Glass*, L. Carroll)

PENNYFEATHER, Paul (*Decline and Fall*, E. Waugh)

13

WINNIE-THE-POOH (Edward Bear) (*Winnie-the-Pooh*, A. A. Milne)

14

MARKHAM, Gilbert (*The Tenant of Wildfell Hall*, Anne Brontë)

MEPHISTOPHELES (*Doctor Faustus*, C. Marlowe)

RIKKI-TIKKI-TAVI (*The Jungle Book*, R. Kipling)

SAMUEL WHISKERS (*The Tale of Samuel Whiskers*, Beatrix Potter)

14 —continued

WORDLY-WISEMAN (*Pilgrim's Progress*, J. Bunyan)

15

OGMORE-PRITCHARD, Mrs (*Under Milk Wood*, D. Thomas)

VALIANT-FOR-TRUTH (*Pilgrim's Progress*, J. Bunyan)

VIOLET ELIZABETH (*Just William*, Richmal Crompton)

DICKENSIAN CHARACTERS

CHARACTER (Novel)

2
JO (Bleak House)

3
AMY (Oliver Twist)
BET, Betsy (Oliver Twist)
BUD, Rosa (Edwin Drood)
CLY (A Tale of Two Cities)
GAY, Walter (Dombey and Son)
JOE (Pickwick Papers)
TOX, Miss (Dombey and Son)

4
ANNE (Dombey and Son)
BAPS (Dombey and Son)
BEGS, Mrs Ridger (David Copperfield)
BRAY, Madeline (Nicholas Nickleby)
BRAY, Walter (Nicholas Nickleby)
DICK, Mr (Oliver Twist)
DUFF (Oliver Twist)
FIPS, Mr (Martin Chuzzlewit)
FOGG (Pickwick Papers)
GAMP, Mrs Sarah (Martin Chuzzlewit)
GRIP (Barnaby Rudge)
HAWK, Sir Mulberry (Nicholas Nickleby)
HEEP, Uriah (David Copperfield)
HUGH (Barnaby Rudge)
JOWL, Mat (The Old Curiosity Shop)
JUPE, Cecilia (Hard Times)
KAGS (Oliver Twist)
KNAG, Miss (Nicholas Nickleby)
LIST, Isaac (The Old Curiosity Shop)
MANN, Mrs (Oliver Twist)
MARY (Pickwick Papers)
MELL, Charles (David Copperfield)
MIFF, Mrs (Dombey and Son)
OMER (David Copperfield)
PEAK (Barnaby Rudge)
PELL, Solomon (Pickwick Papers)
PEPS, Dr Parker (Dombey and Son)
POTT, Minverva (Pickwick Papers)
'RIAH (Our Mutual Friend)
RUGG, Anastasia (Little Dorrit)
TIGG, Montague (Martin Chuzzlewit)

4 —continued
WADE, Miss (Little Dorrit)
WEGG, Silas (Our Mutual Friend)

5
ADAMS, Jack (Dombey and Son)
ALLEN, Arabella/Benjamin (Pickwick Papers)
BATES, Charley (Oliver Twist)
BETSY (Pickwick Papers)
BRASS, Sally/Sampson (The Old Curiosity Shop)
BRICK, Jefferson (Martin Chuzzlewit)
BROWN, Alice/Mrs (Dombey and Son)
BUZUZ, Sergeant (Pickwick Papers)
CASBY, Christopher (Little Dorrit)
CHICK, John/Louisa (Dombey and Son)
CLARE, Ada (Bleak House)
CLARK (Dombey and Son)
CLIVE (Little Dorrit)
CROWL (Nicholas Nickleby)
CRUPP, Mrs (David Copperfield)
DAISY, Solomon (Barnaby Rudge)
DAVID (Nicholas Nickleby)
DAWES, Mary (Dombey and Son)
DINGO, Professor (Bleak House)
DIVER, Colonel (Martin Chuzzlewit)
DONNY, Mrs (Bleak House)
DOYCE, Daniel (Little Dorrit)
DUMPS, Nicodemus (Pickwick Papers)
FAGIN (Oliver Twist)
FLITE, Miss (Bleak House)
GILES (Oliver Twist)
GILLS, Solomon (Dombey and Son)
GOWAN, Harry (Little Dorrit)
GREEN, Tom (Barnaby Rudge)
GRIDE, Arthur (Nicholas Nickleby)
GUPPY, William (Bleak House)
HEXAM, Charlie/Jesse/Lizzie (Our Mutual Friend)
JANET (David Copperfield)
JONES, Mary (Barnaby Rudge)
KROOK (Bleak House)

5 —continued

LOBBS, Maria/'Old' (Pickwick Papers)
LORRY, Jarvis (A Tale of Two Cities)
LUCAS, Solomon (Pickwick Papers)
LUPIN, Mrs (Martin Chuzzlewit)
MEALY (David Copperfield)
'MELIA (Dombey and Son)
MIGGS, Miss (Barnaby Rudge)
MILLS, Julia (David Copperfield)
MOLLY (Great Expectations)
MOULD (Martin Chuzzlewit)
NANCY (Oliver Twist)
NANDY, John Edward (Little Dorrit)
NOGGS, Newman (Nicholas Nickleby)
PERCH (Dombey and Son)
PINCH, Ruth/Tom (Martin Chuzzlewit)
PRICE, 'Tilda (Nicholas Nickleby)
PROSS, Miss/Solomon (A Tale of Two Cities)
QUALE (Bleak House)
QUILP, Daniel (The Old Curiosity Shop)
RUDGE, Barnaby/Mary (Barnaby Rudge)
SALLY, Old (Oliver Twist)
SCOTT, Tom (The Old Curiosity Shop)
SHARP (David Copperfield)
SIKES, Bill (Oliver Twist)
SLURK (Pickwick Papers)
SLYME, Chevy (Martin Chuzzlewit)
SMIKE (Nicholas Nickleby)
SNOBB, The Hon (Nicholas Nickleby)
SQUOD, Phil (Bleak House)
STAGG (Barnaby Rudge)
TOOTS, Mr P (Dombey and Son)
TRABB (Great Expectations)
TRENT, Frederick/Nellie (The Old Curiosity Shop)
TWIST, Oliver (Oliver Twist)
VENUS, Mr (Our Mutual Friend)
WATTY (Pickwick Papers)

6

BADGER, Dr Bayham/Laura/Malta/Matthew/Quebec/Woolwich (Bleak House)
BAILEY, Benjamin (Martin Chuzzlewit)
BAILEY, Captain (David Copperfield)
BAMBER, Jack (Pickwick Papers)
BANTAM, Angelo Cyrus (Pickwick Papers)
BARKER, Phil (Oliver Twist)
BARKIS (David Copperfield)
BARLEY, Clara (Great Expectations)
BARNEY (Oliver Twist)
BEDWIN, Mrs (Oliver Twist)
BETSEY, Jane (Dombey and Son)
BITZER (Hard Times)
BOFFIN, Henrietta/Nicodemus (Our Mutual Friend)
BONNEY (Nicholas Nickleby)
BRIGGS (Dombey and Son)
BUMBLE (Oliver Twist)
BUNSBY, Captain (Dombey and Son)
CARKER, Harriet/James/John (Dombey and Son)
CARTON, Sydney (A Tale of Two Cities)

6 —continued

CHEGGS, Alick (The Old Curiosity Shop)
CLARKE (Pickwick Papers)
CODGER, Mrs (Martin Chuzzlewit)
CODLIN, Thomas (The Old Curiosity Shop)
CONWAY, General (Barnaby Rudge)
CORNEY, Mrs (Oliver Twist)
CURDLE (Nicholas Nickleby)
CUTLER, Mr/Mrs (Nicholas Nickleby)
CUTTLE, Captain Ned (Dombey and Son)
DARNAY, Charles (A Tale of Two Cities)
DARTLE, Rosa (David Copperfield)
DENNIS, Ned (Barnaby Rudge)
DIBABS, Mrs (Nicholas Nickleby)
DODSON (Pickwick Papers)
DOMBEY, Fanny/Florence/Louisa/Paul (Dombey and Son)
DORKER (Nicholas Nickleby)
DORRIT, Amy/Edward/Fanny/Frederick/William (Little Dorrit)
DOWLER, Captain (Pickwick Papers)
FEEDER (Dombey and Son)
FEENIX (Dombey and Son)
FIZKIN, Horatio (Pickwick Papers)
FOLIAR (Nicholas Nickleby)
GEORGE (The Old Curiosity Shop)
GEORGE (Pickwick Papers)
GEORGE, Mr (Bleak House)
GORDON, Lord George (Barnaby Rudge)
GRAHAM, Mary (Martin Chuzzlewit)
GROVES, 'Honest' James (The Old Curiosity Shop)
GUNTER (Pickwick Papers)
HARMON, John (Our Mutual Friend)
HARRIS, Mrs (Martin Chuzzlewit)
HAWDON, Captain (Bleak House)
HIGDEN, Betty (Our Mutual Friend)
HOMINY, Major (Martin Chuzzlewit)
HOWLER, Rev M (Dombey and Son)
JARLEY, Mrs (The Old Curiosity Shop)
JASPER, Jack (Edwin Drood)
JINGLE, Alfred (Pickwick Papers)
KETTLE, La Fayette (Martin Chuzzlewit)
LAMMLE, Alfred (Our Mutual Friend)
LOBLEY (Edwin Drood)
LUMLEY, Dr (Nicholas Nickleby)
MAGNUS, Peter (Pickwick Papers)
MALDEN, Jack (David Copperfield)
MARLEY, Jacob (A Christmas Carol)
MARTON (The Old Curiosity Shop)
MAYLIE, Harrie/Mrs/Rose (Oliver Twist)
MERDLE, Mr (Little Dorrit)
MILVEY, Rev Frank (Our Mutual Friend)
MIVINS (Pickwick Papers)
MODDLE, Augustus (Martin Chuzzlewit)
MORFIN (Dombey and Son)
MULLET, Professor (Martin Chuzzlewit)
NIPPER, Susan (Dombey and Son)
PANCKS (Little Dorrit)
PERKER (Pickwick Papers)
PHUNKY (Pickwick Papers)

6 —continued

PIPKIN, Nathaniel (Pickwick Papers)
PIRRIP, Philip (Great Expectations)
POCKET, Herbert/Matthew/Sarah (Great Expectations)
POGRAM, Elijah (Martin Chuzzlewit)
RADDLE, Mr and Mrs (Pickwick Papers)
RIGAUD, Monsieur (Little Dorrit)
SAPSEA, Thomas (Edwin Drood)
SAWYER, Bob (Pickwick Papers)
SCALEY (Nicholas Nickleby)
SLEARY, Josephine (Hard Times)
'SLOPPY' (Our Mutual Friend)
SOWNDS (Dombey and Son)
STRONG, Dr (David Copperfield)
TACKER (Martin Chuzzlewit)
TAPLEY, Mark (Martin Chuzzlewit)
TARTAR (Edwin Drood)
TIPPIN, Lady (Our Mutual Friend)
TISHER, Mrs (Edwin Drood)
TOODLE (Dombey and Son)
TUPMAN, Tracy (Pickwick Papers)
VARDEN, Dolly/Gabriel (Barnaby Rudge)
VHOLES (Bleak House)
VUFFIN (The Old Curiosity Shop)
WALKER, Mick (David Copperfield)
WARDLE, Emily/Isabella/Mr/Rachel (Pickwick Papers)
WELLER, Sam/Tony (Pickwick Papers)
WILFER, Bella/Lavinia/Reginald (Our Mutual Friend)
WILLET, Joe/John (Barnaby Rudge)
WINKLE, Nathaniel (Pickwick Papers)
WOPSLE (Great Expectations)

7

BAILLIE, Gabriel (Pickwick Papers)
BANGHAM, Mrs (Little Dorrit)
BARBARA (The Old Curiosity Shop)
BARBARY, Miss (Bleak House)
BARDELL, Mrs Martha/Tommy (Pickwick Papers)
BAZZARD (Edwin Drood)
BELLING, Master (Nicholas Nickleby)
BLIMBER, Dr (Dombey and Son)
BLOTTON (Pickwick Papers)
BOBSTER, Cecilia/Mr (Nicholas Nickleby)
BOLDWIG, Captain (Pickwick Papers)
BROGLEY (Dombey and Son)
BROOKER (Nicholas Nickleby)
BROWDIE, John (Nicholas Nickleby)
BULLAMY (Martin Chuzzlewit)
CHARLEY (David Copperfield)
CHESTER, Edward/Sir John (Barnaby Rudge)
CHILLIP, Dr (David Copperfield)
CHIVERY, John (Little Dorrit)
CHOLLOP, Hannibal (Martin Chuzzlewit)
CHUFFEY (Martin Chuzzlewit)
CLEAVER, Fanny (Our Mutual Friend)
CLENNAM, Arthur (Little Dorrit)
CLUBBER, Sir Thomas (Pickwick Papers)
CRACKIT, Toby (Oliver Twist)

7 —continued

CRAWLEY, Young Mr (Pickwick Papers)
CREAKLE (David Copperfield)
CREWLER, Mrs/Rev Horace/Sophy (David Copperfield)
CRIMPLE, David (Martin Chuzzlewit)
CROOKEY (Pickwick Papers)
DAWKINS, Jack (Oliver Twist)
DEDLOCK, Sir Leicester/Volumnia (Bleak House)
DEFARGE, Madame (A Tale of Two Cities)
DOLLOBY (David Copperfield)
DRUMMLE, Bentley (Great Expectations)
DUBBLEY (Pickwick Papers)
DURDLES (Edwin Drood)
EDMUNDS, John (Pickwick Papers)
ESTELLA (Great Expectations)
FLEMING, Agnes (Oliver Twist)
GABELLE, Theophile (A Tale of Two Cities)
GARGERY, Biddy/Joe/Pip (Great Expectations)
GARLAND, Abel/Mrs/Mr (The Old Curiosity Shop)
GASPARD (A Tale of Two Cities)
GAZINGI, Miss (Nicholas Nickleby)
GENERAL, Mrs (Little Dorrit)
GILBERT, Mark (Barnaby Rudge)
GRANGER, Edith (Dombey and Son)
GRIDLEY (Bleak House)
GRIMWIG (Oliver Twist)
GRUDDEN, Mrs (Nicholas Nickleby)
HAGGAGE, Dr (Little Dorrit)
HEYLING, George (Pickwick Papers)
JAGGERS (Great Expectations)
JELLYBY, Caddy/Mrs/Peepy (Bleak House)
JINKINS (Martin Chuzzlewit)
JOBLING, Dr John (Martin Chuzzlewit)
JOBLING, Tony (Bleak House)
JOHNSON, Mr (Nicholas Nickleby)
JORKINS (David Copperfield)
KEDGICK, Captain (Martin Chuzzlewit)
KENWIGS, Morleena (Nicholas Nickleby)
LARKINS, Mr (David Copperfield)
LEEFORD, Edward (Oliver Twist)
LEWSOME (Martin Chuzzlewit)
MALLARD (Pickwick Papers)
MANETTE, Dr/Lucie (A Tale of Two Cities)
MEAGLES (Little Dorrit)
MINERVA (Pickwick Papers)
MOWCHER, Miss (David Copperfield)
NADGETT (Martin Chuzzlewit)
NECKETT, Charlotte/Emma/Tom (Bleak House)
NUBBLES, Christopher (The Old Curiosity Shop)
NUPKINS, George (Pickwick Papers)
PAWKINS, Major (Martin Chuzzlewit)
PILKINS, Dr (Dombey and Son)
PIPCHIN, Mrs (Dombey and Son)
PODSNAP, Georgiana/Mr (Our Mutual Friend)
QUINION (David Copperfield)

7 —continued

SAMPSON, George (Our Mutual Friend)
SCADDER, Zephaniah (Martin Chuzzlewit)
SCROOGE, Ebenezer (A Christmas Carol)
SIMMONS, William (Martin Chuzzlewit)
SKEWTON, Hon Mrs (Dombey and Son)
SKYLARK, Mr (David Copperfield)
SLAMMER, Dr (Pickwick Papers)
SLUMKEY, Hon Samuel (Pickwick Papers)
SNAGSBY (Bleak House)
SNAWLEY (Nicholas Nickleby)
SNUBBIN, Sergeant (Pickwick Papers)
SPARSIT, Mrs (Hard Times)
SPENLOW, Dora (David Copperfield)
SQUEERS, Fanny/Wackford (Nicholas
  Nickleby)
STARTOP (Great Expectations)
STRYVER, C J (A Tale of Two Cities)
TAMAROO, Miss (Martin Chuzzlewit)
TODGERS, Mrs (Martin Chuzzlewit)
TROTTER, Job (Pickwick Papers)
TRUNDLE (Pickwick Papers)
WACKLES, Jane/Melissa/Sophie (The Old
  Curiosity Shop)
WATKINS (Nicholas Nickleby)
WEMMICK (Great Expectations)
WICKHAM, Mrs (Dombey and Son)
WITHERS (Dombey and Son)

8

AKERSHEM, Sophronia (Our Mutual Friend)
BAGSTOCK, Major (Dombey and Son)
BARNWELL, B B (Martin Chuzzlewit)
BILLIKIN, Mrs (Edwin Drood)
BLATHERS (Oliver Twist)
BOYTHORN, Lawrence (Bleak House)
BRAVASSA, Miss (Nicholas Nickleby)
BROWNLOW, Mr (Oliver Twist)
CLAYPOLE, Noah (Oliver Twist)
CLUPPINS (Pickwick Papers)
CRADDOCK, Mrs (Pickwick Papers)
CRATCHIT, Belinda/Bob/Tiny Tim (A
  Christmas Carol)
CRIPPLES, Mr (Little Dorrit)
CRUMMLES, Ninetta/Vincent (Nicholas
  Nickleby)
CRUNCHER, Jeremiah/Jerry (A Tale of Two
  Cities)
CRUSHTON, Hon Mr (Pickwick Papers)
DATCHERY, Dick (Edwin Drood)
D'AULNAIS (A Tale of Two Cities)
FINCHING, Mrs Flora (Little Dorrit)
FLEDGEBY, Old/Young (Our Mutual Friend)
GASHFORD (Barnaby Rudge)
HAREDALE, Emma/Geoffrey/Reuben
  (Barnaby Rudge)
HAVISHAM, Miss (Great Expectations)
HORTENSE (Bleak House)
JARNDYCE, John (Bleak House)
LA CREEVY, Miss (Nicholas Nickleby)
LANDLESS, Helena/Neville (Edwin Drood)
LANGDALE (Barnaby Rudge)

8 —continued

LENVILLE (Nicholas Nickleby)
LITTIMER (David Copperfield)
LOSBERNE (Oliver Twist)
MAGWITCH, Abel (Great Expectations)
MARY ANNE (David Copperfield)
MATTHEWS (Nicholas Nickleby)
MICAWBER, Wilkins (David Copperfield)
MUTANHED, Lord (Pickwick Papers)
NICKLEBY, Godfrey/Kate/Nicholas/Ralph
  (Nicholas Nickleby)
PEGGOTTY, Clara/Daniel/Ham/Little Em'ly
  (David Copperfield)
PICKWICK, Samuel (Pickwick Papers)
PLORNISH, Thomas (Little Dorrit)
POTATOES (David Copperfield)
SCADGERS, Lady (Hard Times)
SKIFFINS, Miss (Great Expectations)
SKIMPOLE, Arethusa/Harold/Kitty/Laura
  (Bleak House)
SKITTLES, Sir Barnet (Dombey and Son)
SMIGGERS, Joseph (Pickwick Papers)
SPARKLER, Edmund (Little Dorrit)
STIGGINS (Pickwick Papers)
TRADDLES, Tom (David Copperfield)
TROTWOOD, Betsey (David Copperfield)
WESTLOCK, John (Martin Chuzzlewit)
WRAYBURN, Eugene (Our Mutual Friend)

9

BELVAWNEY, Miss (Nicholas Nickleby)
BERINTHIA (Dombey and Son)
BLACKPOOL, Stephen (Hard Times)
BOUNDERBY, Josiah (Hard Times)
CHARLOTTE (Oliver Twist)
CHEERYBLE, Charles/Frank/Ned (Nicholas
  Nickleby)
CHICKWEED, Conkey (Oliver Twist)
CHUCKSTER (The Old Curiosity Shop)
COMPEYSON (Great Expectations)
FIBBITSON, Mrs (David Copperfield)
GRADGRIND, Louisa/Thomas (Hard Times)
GREGSBURY (Nicholas Nickleby)
GREWGIOUS (Edwin Drood)
HARTHOUSE, James (Hard Times)
HEADSTONE, Bradley (Our Mutual Friend)
LIGHTWOOD, Mortimer (Our Mutual Friend)
LILLYVICK (Nicholas Nickleby)
MANTALINI, Mr (Nicholas Nickleby)
MURDSTONE, Edward/Jane (David
  Copperfield)
OLD BARLEY (Great Expectations)
PARDIGGLE, Francis/O A (Bleak House)
PECKSNIFF, Charity/Mercy/Seth (Martin
  Chuzzlewit)
PRISCILLA (Bleak House)
RIDERHOOD, Pleasant/Roger (Our Mutual
  Friend)
SMALLWEED, Bartholomew/Joshua/Judy
  (Bleak House)
SMORLTORK, Count (Pickwick Papers)
SNODGRASS, Augustus (Pickwick Papers)

9 —continued
SUMMERSON, Esther (Bleak House)
SWIVELLER, Richard (The Old Curiosity Shop)
TAPPERTIT, Simon (Barnaby Rudge)
VENEERING, Anastasia/Hamilton (Our Mutual Friend)
VERISOPHT, Lord Frederick (Nicholas Nickleby)
WICKFIELD, Agnes/Mr (David Copperfield)
WITHERDEN, Mr (The Old Curiosity Shop)
WOODCOURT, Allan (Bleak House)

10
AYRESLEIGH, Mr (Pickwick Papers)
CHUZZLEWIT, Anthony/Diggory/George/ Jonas/Martin/Mrs Ned/Toby (Martin Chuzzlewit)
CRISPARKLE, Rev Septimus (Edwin Drood)
FLINTWINCH, Affery/Ephraim/Jeremiah (Little Dorrit)
MACSTINGER, Mrs (Dombey and Son)
ROUNCEWELL, Mrs (Bleak House)
SNEVELLICI, Miss (Nicholas Nickleby)
SOWERBERRY (Oliver Twist)
STARELEIGH, Justice (Pickwick Papers)
STEERFORTH, James (David Copperfield)
TATTYCORAM (Little Dorrit)

10 —continued
TURVEYDROP, Prince (Bleak House)
TWINKLETON, Miss (Edwin Drood)
WATERBROOK (David Copperfield)
WITITTERLY, Julia (Nicholas Nickleby)

11
COPPERFIELD, Clara/David (David Copperfield)
'DISMAL JIMMY' (Pickwick Papers)
'GAME CHICKEN', The (Dombey and Son)
MARCHIONESS, The (The Old Curiosity Shop)
PUMBLECHOOK (Great Expectations)
SPOTTLETOES, Mrs (Martin Chuzzlewit)
ST EVREMONDE, Marquis de/Marquise de (A Tale of Two Cities)
SWEEDLEPIPE, Paul (Martin Chuzzlewit)
TULKINGHORN (Bleak House)

12
HONEYTHUNDER, Luke (Edwin Drood)
'SHINY WILLIAM' (Pickwick Papers)
SWEET WILLIAM (The Old Curiosity Shop)
TITE-BARNACLE, Clarence/Ferdinand/ Junior/Lord Decimus/Mr (Little Dorrit)

15
VON KOELDWETHOUT (Nicholas Nickleby)

SHAKESPEAREAN CHARACTERS

CHARACTER (Play)

3
HAL (1 Henry IV)
NYM (Henry V, The Merry Wives of Windsor)

4
ADAM (As You Like It)
AJAX (Troilus and Cressida)
EROS (Antony and Cleopatra)
FORD, Mistress (The Merry Wives of Windsor)
GREY (Henry V)
HERO (Much Ado About Nothing)
IAGO (Othello)
IRAS (Antony and Cleopatra)
LEAR (King Lear)
PAGE, Mistress (The Merry Wives of Windsor)
PETO (2 Henry IV)
PUCK (A Midsummer Night's Dream)
SNUG (A Midsummer Night's Dream)

5
AARON (Titus Andronicus)
ARIEL (The Tempest)
BELCH, Sir Toby (Twelfth Night)
BLUNT (2 Henry IV)
CAIUS, Doctor (The Merry Wives of Windsor)
CELIA (As You Like It)
CLEON (Pericles)

5 —continued
CORIN (As You Like It)
DIANA (All's Well that Ends Well)
EDGAR (King Lear)
ELBOW (Measure for Measure)
FESTE (Twelfth Night)
FLUTE (A Midsummer Night's Dream)
FROTH (Measure for Measure)
GOBBO, Launcelot (The Merchant of Venice)
JULIA (The Two Gentlemen of Verona)
LAFEW (All's Well That Ends Well)
MARIA (Love's Labour's Lost, Twelfth Night)
PARIS (Troilus and Cressida)
PERCY (1 Henry IV)
PHEBE (As You Like It)
PINCH (The Comedy of Errors)
POINS (1 Henry IV, 2 Henry IV)
PRIAM (Troilus and Cressida)
REGAN (King Lear)
ROMEO (Romeo and Juliet)
SNOUT (A Midsummer Night's Dream)
TIMON (Timon of Athens)
TITUS (Titus Andronicus)
VIOLA (Twelfth Night)

6

AEGEON (The Comedy of Errors)
ALONSO (The Tempest)
ANGELO (Measure for Measure)
ANTONY (Antony and Cleopatra)
ARCITE (The Two Noble Kinsmen)
ARMADO (Love's Labour's Lost)
AUDREY (As You Like It)
BANQUO (Macbeth)
BIANCA (The Taming of the Shrew, Othello)
BOTTOM (A Midsummer Night's Dream)
BRUTUS (Coriolanus, Julius Caesar)
CASSIO (Othello)
CHIRON (Titus Andronicus)
CLOTEN (Cymbeline)
DENNIS (As You Like It)
DROMIO (The Comedy of Errors)
DUMAIN (Love's Labour's Lost)
DUNCAN (Macbeth)
EDMUND (King Lear)
EMILIA (Othello, The Two Noble Kinsmen)
FABIAN (Twelfth Night)
FENTON (The Merry Wives of Windsor)
FULVIA (Antony and Cleopatra)
HAMLET (Hamlet)
HECATE (Macbeth)
HECTOR (Troilus and Cressida)
HELENA (A Midsummer Night's Dream, All's
   Well That Ends Well)
HERMIA (A Midsummer Night's Dream)
IMOGEN (Cymbeline)
JULIET (Romeo and Juliet, Measure for
   Measure)
LUCIUS (Titus Andronicus)
MARINA (Pericles)
MUTIUS (Titus Andronicus)
OBERON (A Midsummer Night's Dream)
OLIVER (As You Like It)
OLIVIA (Twelfth Night)
ORSINO (Twelfth Night)
OSWALD (King Lear)
PISTOL (2 Henry IV, Henry V, The Merry Wives
   of Windsor)
POMPEY (Measure for Measure, Antony and
   Cleopatra)
PORTIA (The Merchant of Venice)
QUINCE (A Midsummer Night's Dream)
RUMOUR (2 Henry IV)
SCROOP (2 Henry IV, 2 Henry V)
SILVIA (The Two Gentlemen of Verona)
TAMORA (Titus Andronicus)
THASIA (Pericles)
THURIO (The Two Gentlemen of Verona)
TYBALT (Romeo and Juliet)
VERGES (Much Ado About Nothing)

7

ADRIANA (The Comedy of Errors)
AEMILIA (The Comedy of Errors)
AGRIPPA (Antony and Cleopatra)
ALARBUS (Titus Andronicus)

7 —continued

ANTONIO (The Merchant of Venice, The
   Tempest)
BEROWNE (Love's Labour's Lost)
BERTRAM (All's Well That Ends Well)
CALCHAS (Troilus and Cressida)
CALIBAN (The Tempest)
CAPULET (Romeo and Juliet)
CESARIO (Twelfth Night)
CLAUDIO (Much Ado About Nothing, Measure
   for Measure)
COSTARD (Love's Labour's Lost)
DIONYZA (Pericles)
DOUGLAS (1 Henry IV)
ESCALUS (Measure for Measure)
FLAVIUS (Timon of Athens)
FLEANCE (Macbeth)
GONERIL (King Lear)
GONZALO (The Tempest)
HORATIO (Hamlet)
HOTSPUR (1 Henry IV)
IACHIMO (Cymbeline)
JACQUES (As You Like It)
JESSICA (The Merchant of Venice)
LAERTES (Hamlet)
LAVINIA (Titus Andronicus)
LEONTES (The Winter's Tale)
LORENZO (The Merchant of Venice)
LUCIANA (The Comedy of Errors)
MACBETH (Macbeth)
MACDUFF (Macbeth)
MALCOLM (Macbeth)
MARIANA (Measure for Measure, All's Well
   That Ends Well)
MARTIUS (Titus Andronicus)
MIRANDA (The Tempest)
NERISSA (The Merchant of Venice)
OCTAVIA (Antony and Cleopatra)
OPHELIA (Hamlet)
ORLANDO (As You Like It)
OTHELLO (Othello)
PALAMON (The Two Noble Kinsmen)
PAULINA (The Winter's Tale)
PERDITA (The Winter's Tale)
PISANIO (Cymbeline)
PROTEUS (The Two Gentlemen of Verona)
QUICKLY, Mistress (1 Henry IV, 2 Henry IV,
   The Merry Wives of Windsor)
QUINTUS (Titus Andronicus)
SHALLOW, Justice (2 Henry IV, The Merry
   Wives of Windsor)
SHYLOCK (The Merchant of Venice)
SILENCE (2 Henry IV)
SILVIUS (As You Like It)
SLENDER (The Merry Wives of Windsor)
SOLINUS (The Comedy of Errors)
THESEUS (A Midsummer Night's Dream,
   The Two Noble Kinsmen)
TITANIA (A Midsummer Night's Dream)
TROILUS (Troilus and Cressida)
ULYSSES (Troilus and Cressida)

7 —continued

WILLIAM (As You Like It)

8

ACHILLES (Troilus and Cressida)
AUFIDIUS (Coriolanus)
BAPTISTA (The Taming of the Shrew)
BARDOLPH (Henry IV, Henry V, The Merry
  Wives of Windsor)
BASSANIO (The Merchant of Venice)
BEATRICE (Much Ado About Nothing)
BELARIUS (Cymbeline)
BENEDICK (Much Ado About Nothing)
BENVOLIO (Romeo and Juliet)
CHARMIAN (Antony and Cleopatra)
CLAUDIUS (Hamlet)
COMINIUS (Coriolanus)
CORDELIA (King Lear)
CRESSIDA (Troilus and Cressida)
DIOMEDES (Antony and Cleopatra, Troilus
  and Cressida)
DOGBERRY (Much Ado About Nothing)
DON PEDRO (Much Ado About Nothing)
FALSTAFF (The Merry Wives of Windsor,
  Henry IV)
FLORIZEL (The Winter's Tale)
GERTRUDE (Hamlet)
GRATIANO (The Merchant of Venice)
HERMIONE (The Winter's Tale)
ISABELLA (Measure for Measure)
LUCENTIO (The Taming of the Shrew)
LYSANDER (A Midsummer Night's Dream)
MALVOLIO (Twelfth Night)
MENENIUS (Coriolanus)
MERCUTIO (Romeo and Juliet)
MONTAGUE (Romeo and Juliet)
MORTIMER (1 Henry IV)
OCTAVIUS (Antony and Cleopatra)
PANDARUS (Troilus and Cressida)
PAROLLES (All's Well That Ends Well)
PERICLES (Pericles)
PHILOTEN (Pericles)
POLONIUS (Hamlet)
PROSPERO (The Tempest)
RODERIGO (Othello)
ROSALIND (As You Like It)
ROSALINE (Love's Labour's Lost)
SICINIUS (Coriolanus)
STEPHANO (The Tempest)
TRINCULO (The Tempest)
VIOLENTA (All's Well That Ends Well)
VOLUMNIA (Coriolanus)

9

ANTIOCHUS (Pericles)

9 —continued

ARVIRAGUS (Cymbeline)
AUGECHEEK, Sir Andrew (Twelfth Night)
BASSIANUS (Titus Andronicus)
BRABANTIO (Othello)
CAMBRIDGE (Henry V)
CLEOPATRA (Antony and Cleopatra)
CYMBELINE (Cymbeline)
DEMETRIUS (A Midsummer Night's Dream,
  Antony and Cleopatra, Titus Andronicus)
DESDEMONA (Othello)
ENOBARBUS (Antony and Cleopatra)
FERDINAND (Loves Labours Lost, The
  Tempest)
FREDERICK (As You Like It)
GLENDOWER, Owen (1 Henry IV)
GUIDERIUS (Cymbeline)
HELICANUS (Pericles)
HIPPOLYTA (A Midsummer Night's Dream,
  The Two Noble Kinsmen)
HORTENSIO (The Taming of the Shrew)
KATHARINA (The Taming of the Shrew)
KATHERINE (Henry V, Love's Labour's Lost)
MAMILLIUS (The Winter's Tale)
PATROCLUS (Troilus and Cressida)
PETRUCHIO (The Taming of the Shrew)
POLIXENES (The Winter's Tale)
SEBASTIAN (The Tempest, Twelfth Night)
TEARSHEET, Doll (2 Henry IV)
VALENTINE (The Two Gentlemen of Verona)
VINCENTIO (Measure for Measure, The
  Taming of the Shrew)

10

ALCIBIADES (Timon of Athens)
ANTIPHOLUS (The Comedy of Errors)
CORIOLANUS (Coriolanus)
FORTINBRAS (Hamlet)
JAQUENETTA (Love's Labour's Lost)
LONGAVILLE (Love's Labour's Lost)
LYSIMACHUS (Pericles)
POSTHUMOUS (Cymbeline)
SATURNINUS (Titus Andronicus)
TOUCHSTONE (As You Like It)

11

ROSENCRANTZ (Hamlet)

12

GUILDENSTERN (Hamlet)

14

CHRISTOPHER SLY (The Taming of the
  Shrew)

GILBERT AND SULLIVAN

OPERAS

THESPIS (The Gods Grown Old)
TRIAL BY JURY
THE SORCERER
HMS PINAFORE (The Lass that Loved a Sailor)
THE PIRATES OF PENZANCE (The Slave of Duty)
PATIENCE (Bunthorne's Bride)
IOLANTHE (The Peer and the Peri)
PRINCESS IDA (Castle Adamant)
THE MIKADO (The Town of Titipu)
RUDDIGORE (The Witch's Curse)
THE YEOMEN OF THE GUARD (The Merryman and his Maid)
THE GONDOLIERS (The King of Barataria)
UTOPIA, LIMITED (The Flowers of Progress)
THE GRAND DUKE (The Statutory Duel)

CHARACTERS (Operas)

4
ADAM (Ruddigore)
ELLA (Patience)
GAMA (Princess Ida)
INEZ (The Gondoliers)
JANE (Patience)
KATE (The Pirates of Penzance)
KO-KO (The Mikado)
LUIZ (The Gondoliers)
RUTH (The Pirates of Penzance)

5
ALINE (The Sorcerer)
CELIA (Iolanthe)
CYRIL (Princess Ida)
EDITH (The Pirates of Penzance)
EDWIN (Trial by Jury)
FLETA (Iolanthe)
LEILA (Iolanthe)
MABEL (The Pirates of Penzance)
TESSA (The Gondoliers)

6
ALEXIS (The Sorcerer)
ANGELA (Patience)
ISABEL (The Pirates of Penzance)
PEEP-BO (The Mikado)
SAPHIR (Patience)
YUM-YUM (The Mikado)

7
CASILDA (The Gondoliers)
FLORIAN (Princess Ida)
KATISHA (The Mikado)
LEONARD (The Yeomen of the Guard)

7 —continued
MELISSA (Princess Ida)
PHYLLIS (Iolanthe)
POOH-BAH (The Mikado)

8
ANGELINA (Trial by Jury)
FREDERIC (The Pirates of Penzance)
GIANETTA (The Gondoliers)
HILARION (Princess Ida)
IOLANTHE (Iolanthe)
NANKI-POO (The Mikado)
PATIENCE (Patience)
PISH-TUSH (The Mikado)
SERGEANT (The Pirates of Penzance)
STREPHON (Iolanthe)

9
BUNTHORNE (Patience)
JACK POINT (The Yeomen of the Guard)
JOSEPHINE (HMS Pinafore)
PITTI-SING (The Mikado)

10
DAME HANNAH (Ruddigore)
HILDEBRAND (Princess Ida)
LADY PSYCHE (Princess Ida)
PIRATE KING (The Pirates of Penzance)
ROSE MAYBUD (Ruddigore)
SIR RODERIC (Ruddigore)

11
DICK DEADEYE (HMS Pinafore)
LADY BLANCHE (Princess Ida)
MAD MARGARET (Ruddigore)
MOUNTARARAT (Iolanthe)
PRINCESS IDA (Princess Ida)

12
ELSIE MAYNARD (The Yeomen of the Guard)
PHOEBE MERYLL (The Yeomen of the Guard)
SIR MARMADUKE (The Sorcerer)

13
LADY SANGAZURE (The Sorcerer)
MARCO PALMIERI (The Gondoliers)
ROBIN OAKAPPLE (Ruddigore)

14
COLONEL FAIRFAX (The Yeomen of the Guard)
DAME CARRUTHERS (The Yeomen of the Guard)
RALPH RACKSTRAW (HMS Pinafore)

15
CAPTAIN CORCORAN (HMS Pinafore)
DUKE OF DUNSTABLE (Patience)
DUKE OF PLAZA TORO (The Gondoliers)

15 —continued
EARL OF TOLLOLLER (*Iolanthe*)
LITTLE BUTTERCUP (*HMS Pinafore*)
SIR JOSEPH PORTER (*HMS Pinafore*)
WILFRED SHADBOLT (*The Yeomen of the Guard*)

16
COLONEL CALVERLEY (*Patience*)
GIUSEPPE PALMIERI (*The Gondoliers*)
RICHARD DAUNTLESS (*Ruddigore*)

18
ARCHIBALD GROSVENOR (*Patience*)

19
JOHN WELLINGTON WELLS (*The Sorcerer*)
MAJOR-GENERAL STANLEY (*The Pirates of Penzance*)

20
SIR DESPARD MURGATROYD (*Ruddigore*)
SIR RICHARD CHOLMONDELEY (*The Yeomen of the Guard*)

SCIENCE AND TECHNOLOGY

WEIGHTS AND MEASURES

2	4 —continued	5 —continued	7 —continued
CM	HAND	NEPER	DIOPTER
DR	HIDE	OUNCE	FARADAY
FT	HOUR	PERCH	FURLONG
GR	INCH	POINT	GILBERT
HL	KILO	POISE	HECTARE
IN	KNOT	POUND	KILOBAR
KG	LINE	QUART	KILOTON
KM	LINK	QUIRE	LAMBERT
LB	MILE	STADE	MAXWELL
MG	MOLE	STERE	MEGATON
ML	NAIL	STILB	OERSTED
MM	PECK	STOKE	POUNDAL
OZ	PHON	STONE	QUARTER
YD	PHOT	TESLA	QUINTAL
3	PICA	THERM	RÖNTGEN
AMP	PINT	TOISE	SCRUPLE
ARE	PIPE	TONNE	SIEMENS
BAR	POLE	WEBER	**8**
BEL	REAM	**6**	ÅNGSTROM
BIT	ROOD	AMPERE	CHALDRON
CWT	SLUG	BARREL	HOGSHEAD
DWT	SPAN	BUSHEL	KILOGRAM
ELL	TORR	CANDLE	KILOWATT
ERG	TROY	CENTAL	QUADRANT
LUX	VOLT	DEGREE	MEGAWATT
MHO	WATT	DENIER	MICROOHM
MIL	YARD	DRACHM	WATT-HOUR
MIM	**5**	FATHOM	**9**
NIT	CABLE	FIRKIN	BOARD-FOOT
OHM	CARAT	GALLON	CENTIGRAM
RAD	CHAIN	GRAMME	CUBIC FOOT
REM	CRITH	KELVIN	CUBIC INCH
ROD	CUBIT	LEAGUE	CUBIC YARD
TON	CURIE	MEGOHM	DECALITRE
TUN	CUSEC	MICRON	DECAMETRE
4	CYCLE	MINUTE	DECILITRE
ACRE	DEBYE	NEWTON	DECIMETRE
BALE	FARAD	PARSEC	FOOT-POUND
BARN	FERMI	PASCAL	HECTOGRAM
BOLT	GAUGE	RADIAN	KILOCYCLE
BYTE	GAUSS	RÉAUMUR	KILOHERTZ
CASK	GRAIN	SECOND	KILOLITRE
CORD	HENRY	STOKES	KILOMETRE
CRAN	HERTZ	**7**	LIGHT-YEAR
DRAM	JOULE	CALORIE	MEGACYCLE
DYNE	LITRE	CANDELA	MEGAFARAD
FOOT	LUMEN	CENTNER	MEGAHERTZ
GILL	METRE	COULOMB	METRIC TON
GRAM	MINIM	DECIBEL	MICROGRAM

9 —continued
MICROWATT
MILLIGRAM
NANOMETRE
SCANTLING
STERADIAN
10+
BARLEYCORN
CENTILITRE

10+ —continued
CENTIMETRE
CUBIC METRE
DECAGRAMME
DECIGRAMME
FLUID OUNCE
HECTOLITRE
HORSEPOWER
HUNDREDWEIGHT

10+ —continued
KILOGRAMME
MICROFARAD
MILLILITRE
MILLIMETRE
MILLISTERES
NANOSECOND
PENNYWEIGHT

10+ —continued
RUTHERFORD
SQUARE
  CENTIMETRE
SQUARE INCH
SQUARE KILOMETRE
SQUARE MILE
SQUARE YARD

PAPER MEASURES

4
BALE
COPY
DEMY
POST
POTT
REAM
5
ATLAS
BRIEF
CROWN
DRAFT
QUIRE
ROYAL

6
BAG CAP
BUNDLE
CASING
MEDIUM
7
EMPEROR
KENT CAP
8
ELEPHANT
FOOLSCAP
HAVEN CAP

8—continued
IMPERIAL
9
CARTRIDGE
COLOMBIER
LARGE POST
MUSIC DEMY
10
DOUBLE DEMY
DOUBLE POST
GRAND EAGLE
SUPER ROYAL

11
ANTIQUARIAN
IMPERIAL CAP
PINCHED POST
14
DOUBLE ELEPHANT
15
DOUBLE LARGE
  POST

ELEMENTARY PARTICLES

2
XI
3
ETA
PHI
PSI
4
KAON
MUON
PION
5
BOSON

5—continued
GLUON
MESON
OMEGA
QUARK
SIGMA
6
BARYON
HADRON
LAMBDA
LEPTON
PHOTON

6—continued
PROTON
7
FERMION
HYPERON
NEUTRON
TACHYON
8
DEUTERON
ELECTRON
GRAVITON

8—continued
NEUTRINO
POSITRON
9
NEUTRETTO
12
ANTIPARTICLE
BETA PARTICLE
13
ALPHA PARTICLE

THE CHEMICAL ELEMENTS

NAME (SYMBOL)

ACTINIUM (AC)
ALUMINIUM (AL)
AMERICIUM (AM)
ANTIMONY (SB)

ARGON (AR)
ARSENIC (AS)
ASTATINE (AT)
BARIUM (BA)

BERKELIUM (BK)
BERYLLIUM (BE)
BISMUTH (BI)
BORON (B)

BROMINE (BR)
CADMIUM (CD)
CAESIUM (CS)
CALCIUM (CA)

CALIFORNIUM (CF)	HYDROGEN (H)	OSMIUM (OS)	SILVER (AG)
CARBON (C)	INDIUM (IN)	OXYGEN (O)	SODIUM (NA)
CERIUM (CE)	IODINE (I)	PALLADIUM (PD)	STRONTIUM (SR)
CHLORINE (CL)	IRIDIUM (IR)	PHOSPHORUS (P)	SULPHUR (S)
CHROMIUM (CR)	IRON (FE)	PLATINUM (PT)	TANTALUM (TA)
COBALT (CO)	KRYPTON (KR)	PLUTONIUM (PU)	TECHNETIUM (TC)
COLUMBIUM (CB)	LANTHANUM (LA)	POLONIUM (PO)	TELLURIUM (TE)
COPPER (CU)	LAWRENCIUM (LR)	POTASSIUM (K)	TERBIUM (TB)
CURIUM (CM)	LEAD (PB)	PRASEODYMIUM	THALLIUM (TL)
DYSPROSIUM (DY)	LITHIUM (LI)	(PR)	THORIUM (TH)
EINSTEINIUM (ES)	LUTETIUM (LU)	PROMETHIUM (PM)	THULIUM (TM)
ERBIUM (ER)	MAGNESIUM (MG)	PROTACTINIUM (PA)	TIN (SN)
EUROPIUM (EU)	MANGANESE (MN)	RADIUM (RA)	TITANIUM (TI)
FERMIUM (FM)	MENDELEVIUM (MD)	RADON (RN)	TUNGSTEN (W)
FLUORINE (F)	MERCURY (HG)	RHENIUM (RE)	URANIUM (U)
FRANCIUM (FR)	MOLYBDENUM (MO)	RHODIUM (RH)	VANADIUM (V)
GADOLINIUM (GD)	NEODYMIUM (ND)	RUBIDIUM (RB)	WOLFRAM (W)
GALLIUM (GA)	NEON (NE)	RUTHENIUM (RU)	XENON (XE)
GERMANIUM (GE)	NEPTUNIUM (NP)	SAMARIUM (SM)	YTTERBIUM (YB)
GOLD (AU)	NICKEL (NI)	SCANDIUM (SC)	YTTRIUM (Y)
HAFNIUM (HF)	NIOBIUM (NB)	SELENIUM (SE)	ZINC (ZN)
HELIUM (HE)	NITROGEN (N)	SILICON (SI)	ZIRCONIUM (ZR)
HOLMIUM (HO)	NOBELIUM (NO)		

ALLOYS

ALLOY – main components

4
ALNI – iron, nickel, aluminium, copper
BETA – titanium, aluminium, vanadium, chromium

5
ALPHA – titanium, aluminium, tin, copper, zirconium, niobium, molybdenum
BRASS – copper, zinc
INVAR – iron, nickel
MAZAC – zinc, aluminium, magnesium, copper
MONEL – nickel, cobalt, iron
STEEL – iron, carbon

6
ALNICO – aluminium, nickel, cobalt
BABBIT – tin, lead, antimony, copper
BRONZE – copper, tin
CUNICO – iron, cobalt, copper, nickel
CUNIFE – iron, cobalt, nickel
FEROBA – iron, barium oxide, iron oxide
PEWTER – tin, lead
SOLDER – lead, tin (soft), copper, zinc (brazing)

7
ALCOMAX – aluminium, cobalt, nickel, copper, lead, niobium
ALUMNEL – aluminium, chromium
AMALGAM – mercury, various
CHROMEL – nickel, chromium

7—continued
COLUMAN – iron, chromium, nickel, aluminium, nobium, copper
ELINVAR – iron, nickel, chromium, tungsten
INCONEL – nickel, chromium, iron
KANTHAL – chromium, aluminium, iron
MUMETAL – iron, nickel, copper, chromium
NIMONIC – nickel, chromium, iron, titanium, aluminium, manganese, silicon

8
CAST IRON – carbon, iron
DOWMETAL – magnesium, aluminium, zinc, manganese
GUNMETAL – copper, tin, zinc
HIPERNIK – nickel, iron
KIRKSITE – zinc, aluminium, copper
MANGANIN – copper, manganese, nickel
NICHROME – nickel, iron, chromium
VICALLOY – iron, cobalt, vanadium
ZIRCALOY – zirconium, tin, iron, nickel, chromium

9
DURALUMIN – aluminium, copper, silicon, magnesium, manganese, zinc
HASTELLOY – nickel, molybdenum, iron, chromium, cobalt, tungsten
PERMALLOY – nickel, iron
PERMINVAR – nickel, iron, cobalt
TYPE METAL – lead, tin, antimony

10
CONSTANTAN – copper, nickel
MISCH METAL – cerium, various
MUNTZ METAL – copper, zinc
ROSE'S METAL – bismuth, lead, tin
SUPERALLOY – type of stainless steel
WOOD'S METAL – lead, tin, bismuth,
  cadmium

11
CUPRONICKEL – copper, nickel
ELECTROTYPE – lead, tin, antimony
SUPERMALLOY – iron, nickel
SUPERMENDUR – iron, cobalt

12
FERROSILICON – iron, silicon
GERMAN SILVER – copper, nickel, zinc, lead,
  tin

12—continued
SILVER SOLDER – copper, silver, zinc

13
FERROCHROMIUM – iron, chromium
FERROTUNGSTEN – iron, tungsten
FERROVANADIUM – iron, vanadium

14
ADMIRALTY METAL – copper, zinc
BRITANNIA METAL – tin, antimony, copper
FERROMANGANESE – iron, manganese
PHOSPHOR BRONZE – copper, tin,
  phosphorus
STAINLESS STEEL – iron, chromium,
  vanadium

GEOMETRIC FIGURES AND CURVES

3	6—continued	8—continued	10—continued
ARC	SECTOR	FRUSTRUM	ANCHOR RING
4	SPHERE	GEODESIC	CYLINDROID
CONE	SPIRAL	HEPTAGON	EPICYCLOID
CUBE	SPLINE	INCIRCLE	HEMISPHERE
KITE	SQUARE	INVOLUTE	HEXAHEDRON
LINE	**7**	PARABOLA	KAPPA CURVE
LOOP	ANNULUS	PENTAGON	LEMNISCATE
LUNE	CISSOID	PRISMOID	OCTAHEDRON
OVAL	CYCLOID	QUADRANT	PARABOLOID
ROSE	DECAGON	RHOMBOID	PEANO CURVE
ZONE	ELLIPSE	ROULETTE	POLYHEDRON
5	EVOLUTE	SPHEROID	PRISMATOID
CHORD	FRACTAL	TRACTRIX	QUADRANGLE
CONIC	HEXAGON	TRIANGLE	QUADREFOIL
HELIX	LIMACON	TROCHOID	RIGHT ANGLE
LOCUS	OCTAGON	**9**	SEMICIRCLE
NAPPE	PERIGON	ANTIPRISM	SERPENTINE
OGIVE	POLYGON	CRUCIFORM	TRISECTRIX
PLANE	PYRAMID	DIRECTRIX	**11**
PRISM	RHOMBUS	DODECAGON	CORNU SPIRAL
RHOMB	SEGMENT	ELLIPSOID	EPITROCHOID
SHEET	SURFACE	HYPERBOLA	HEPTAHEDRON
SOLID	TANGENT	ISOCHRONE	HYPERBOLOID
TORUS	TREFOIL	KOCH CURVE	HYPOCYCLOID
WEDGE	TRIDENT	LOXODROME	ICOSAHEDRON
WITCH	**8**	MULTIFOIL	KLEIN BOTTLE
6	CARDIOID	PENTAGRAM	LATUS RECTUM
CIRCLE	CATENARY	PENTANGLE	MÖBIUS STRIP
CONOID	CATENOID	RHUMB LINE	OBTUSE ANGLE
FOLIUM	CONCHOID	SINE CURVE	PENTAHEDRON
LAMINA	CONICOID	STROPHOID	REFLEX ANGLE
NORMAL	CYLINDER	TRAPEZIUM	TAUTOCHRONE
OCTANT	ENVELOPE	TRAPEZOID	TETRAHEDRON
PENCIL	EPICYCLE	**10**	**12**
RADIUS	EXCIRCLE	ACUTE ANGLE	HYPOTROCHOID

12—continued	13—continued	15	19
PSEUDOSPHERE	PARALLELOTOPE	BRACHISTOCHRONE	EQUILATERAL
RHOMBOHEDRON	PEDAL TRIANGLE	SCALENE TRIANGLE	TRIANGLE
SIGMOID CURVE	PERPENDICULAR	**17**	
13	QUADRILATERAL	ICOSIDODECAHEDRON	
CIRCUMFERENCE	**14**	ISOSCELES	
CUBOCTAHEDRON	SNOWFLAKE CURVE	TRIANGLE	
PARALLELOGRAM			

COMPUTER PROGRAMMING LANGUAGES

1	4	5—continued	6—continued
C	BCPL	COBOL	PROLOG
3	FRED	COMAL	SIMULA
ADA	LISP	CORAL	SNOBOL
AED	LOGO	FORTH	**7**
APL	REXX	KAPSE	BABBAGE
AWK	YACC	MOHLL	FORTRAN
CPL	**5**	**6**	MACLISP
CSL	ALGOL	EDISON	**9**
IAL	BASIC	JOVIAL	FRANZLISP
LEX	CHILL	MODULA	SMALLTALK
POL	CLEAR	PASCAL	
POP			
RPG			

PLANETS AND SATELLITES

MAIN PLANETS (NAMED SATELLITES)	MINOR PLANETS
MERCURY	ACHILLES
VENUS	ADONIS
EARTH (MOON)	AMOR
MARS (PHOBOS, DEIMOS)	APOLLO
JUPITER (METIS, ADRASTEA, AMALTHEA, THEBE, IO, EUROPA, GANYMEDE, CALLISTO, LEDA, MILALIA, LYSITHEA, ELARA, ANANKE, CARME, PASIPHAE, SINOPE)	ASTRAEA ATEN CERES CHIRON EROS
SATURN (MIMAS, ENCELADUS, TETHYS, DIONE, RHEA, TITAN, HYPERION, IAPETUS, PHOEBE, JANUS)	EUNOMIA EUPHROSYNE HEBE
URANUS (MIRANDA, ARIEL, UMBRIEL, TITANIA, OBERON)	HERMES HIDALGO
NEPTUNE (TRITON, NEREID)	HYGIEA
PLUTO (CHARON)	ICARUS
	IRIS
	JUNO
	PALLAS
	VESTA

COMETS

4	7	9	13
FAYE	BENNETT	COMAS SOLÀ	STEPHAN-OTERMA
5	D'ARREST	CROMMELIN	**14**
BIELA	VÄISÄLÄ	**10**	BRONSEN-METCALF
ENCKE	WHIPPLE	PONS-BROOKS	**15**
KOPFF	**8**	SCHAUMASSE	GIACOBINI-ZINNER
6	BORRELLY	**11**	GRIGG-SKIELLERUP
HALLEY	DAYLIGHT	AREND-ROLAND	
OLBERS	KOHOUTEK	**12**	
TUTTLE	WESTPHAL	PONS-WINNECKE	

NAMED NEAREST AND BRIGHTEST STARS

4	6 —continued	7 —continued	9
ROSS	ALTAIR	CAPELLA	ALDEBARAN
VEGA	CASTOR	LALANDE	BELLATRIX
WOLF	CRUCIS	PROCYON	FOMALHAUT
5	KRUGER	REGULUS	**10+**
CYGNI	LUYTEN	TAU CETI	BETELGEUSE
DENEB	POLLUX	**8**	EPSILON INDI
RIGEL	SHAULA	ACHERNAR	ALPHA CENTAURI
SIRUS	SIRIUS	ARCTURUS	EPSILON ERIDANI
SPICA	**7**	BARNARD'S	PROXIMA CENTAURI
6	ANTARES	CENTAURI	
ADHARA	CANOPUS	KAPTEYN'S	

THE CONSTELLATIONS

3	5 —continued	6 —continued	7 —continued
ARA	LIBRA	CRATER	LACERTA
LEO	LUPUS	CYGNUS	PEGASUS
4	MENSA	DORADO	PERSEUS
APUS	MUSCA	FORNAX	PHOENIX
CRUX	NORMA	GEMINI	SAGITTA
GRUS	ORION	HYDRUS	SERPENS
LYNX	PYXIS	OCTANS	SEXTANS
LYRA	VIRGO	PICTOR	**8**
PAVO	**6**	PISCES	AQUARIUS
VELA	ANTLIA	PUPPIS	CIRCINUS
5	AQUILA	SCUTUM	EQUULEUS
ARIES	AURIGA	TAURUS	ERIDANUS
CETUS	BOÖTES	TUCANA	HERCULES
DRACO	CAELUM	VOLANS	LEO MINOR
HYDRA	CANCER	**7**	SCORPIUS
INDUS	CARINA	CEPHEUS	SCULPTOR
LEPUS	CORVUS	COLUMBA	

9	**9 —continued**	**11**	**12+ —continued**
ANDROMEDA	VULPECULA	CAPRICORNUS	CORONA AUSTRALIS
CENTAURUS	**10**	SAGITTARIUS	CORONA BOREALIS
CHAMELEON	CANIS MAJOR	TELESCOPIUM	MICROSCOPIUM
DELPHINUS	CANIS MINOR	**12+**	PISCIS AUSTRINUS
MONOCEROS	CASSIOPEIA	CAMELOPARDALIS	TRIANGULUM
OPHIUCHUS	HOROLOGIUM	CANES VENATICI	AUSTRALE
RETICULUM	TRIANGULUM	COMA BERENICES	
URSA MAJOR			
URSA MINOR			

METEOR SHOWERS

6	**7—continued**	**8—continued**	**11**
LYRIDS	TAURIDS	PERSEIDS	QUADRANTIDS
URSIDS	**8**	**10**	**12**
7	CEPHEIDS	AUSTRALIDS	CAPRICORNIDS
CYGNIDS	GEMINIDS	OPHIUCHIDS	
LEONIDS	ORIONIDS	PHOENICIDS	

ASTRONOMERS ROYAL

JOHN FLAMSTEED (1675–1719)
EDMUND HALLEY (1720–42)
JAMES BRADLEY (1742–62)
NATHANIEL BLISS (1762–64)
NEVIL MASKELYNE (1765–1811)
JOHN POND (1811–35)
SIR GEORGE BIDDELL AIRY (1835–81)

SIR WILLIAM H. M. CHRISTIE (1881–1910)
SIR FRANK WATSON DYSON (1910–33)
SIR HAROLD SPENCER JONES (1933–55)
SIR RICHARD WOOLLEY (1955–71)
SIR MARTIN RYLE (1972–82)
PROF. E. GRAHAM SMITH (1982–   )

GEOLOGICAL TIME SCALE

CENOZOIC	QUATERNARY	HOLOCENE
		PLEISTOCENE
	TERTIARY	PLIOCENE
		MIOCENE
		OLIGOCENE
		EOCENE
		PALAEOCENE
MESOZOIC	CRETACEOUS	
	JURASSIC	
	TRIASSIC	
PALAEOZOIC	PERMIAN	
	CARBONIFEROUS	
	DEVONIAN	
	SILURIAN	
	ORDOVICIAN	
	CAMBRIAN	
PRECAMBRIAN	PRECAMBRIAN	

CLOUDS

ALTOCUMULUS
ALTOSTRATUS
CIRROCUMULUS

CIRROSTRATUS
CIRRUS
CUMULONIMBUS

CUMULUS
NIMBOSTRATUS

STRATOCUMULUS
STRATUS

PREHISTORIC ANIMALS

8
EOHIPPUS
RUTIODON
SMILODON
9
IGUANODON
TRACHODON
10
ALLOSAURUS
ALTISPINAX
BAROSAURUS
DIPLODOCUS
DRYOSAURUS
EUPARKERIA
MESOHIPPUS
ORTHOMERUS
PLIOHIPPUS
PTERANODON
STEGOCERAS
11
ANATOSAURUS
ANCHISAURUS
APATOSAURUS
APHANERAMMA
CETIOSAURUS
COELOPHYSIS

11—continued
DEINONYCHUS
KRITOSAURUS
MANDASUCHUS
MERYCHIPPUS
MONOCLONIUS
POLACANTHUS
PTERODACTYL
RIOJASAURUS
SAUROLOPHUS
SCOLOSAURUS
SPINOSAURUS
STEGOSAURUS
TARBOSAURUS
TRICERATOPS
12
ANKYLOSAURUS
BRONTOSAURUS
CAMPTOSAURUS
CERATOSAURUS
CHASMOSAURUS
DEINOCHEIRUS
HYLAEOSAURUS
KENTROSAURUS
LAMBEOSAURUS

12—continued
MEGALOSAURUS
ORNITHOMIMUS
OURANOSAURUS
PLATEOSAURUS
TICINOSUCHUS
13
BRACHIOSAURUS
COMPSOGNATHUS
CORYTHOSAURUS
DESMATOSUCHUS
DILOPHOSAURUS
EDMONTOSAURUS
ERYTHROSUCHUS
HYPSELOSAURUS
HYPSILOPHODON
LESOTHOSAURUS
PANOPLOSAURUS
PENTACERATOPS
PROTOCERATOPS
PTERODACTYLUS
SCELIDOSAURUS
SCLEROMOCHLUS
STYRACOSAURUS
TENONTOSAURUS

13—continued
TYRANNOSAURUS
14
BALUCHITHERIUM
CETIOSAURISCUS
CHASMATOSAURUS
EUOPLOCEPHALUS
MASSOSPONDYLUS
PSITTACOSAURUS
THESCELOSAURUS
15
PARASAUROLOPHUS
PROCHENE-
  OSAURUS
16
PACHYRHI-
  NOSAURUS
PROCOMP-
  SOGNATHUS
17
HETERO-
  DONTOSAURUS
18
PACHYCEPHALOSAURUS

ROCKS AND MINERALS

4
GOLD
MICA
OPAL
RUBY
TALC
5
AGATE
BERYL
BORAX
EMERY
FLINT
SHALE

5—continued
SHARD
SKARN
TOPAZ
TRONA
6
ACMITE
ALBITE
ARKOSE
AUGITE
BARITE
BASALT
COPPER

6—continued
DACITE
DUNITE
GABBRO
GALENA
GARNET
GNEISS
GYPSUM
HALITE
HAÜYNE
HUMITE
ILLITE
LEVYNE

6—continued
MINIUM
NORITE
NOSEAN
PELITE
PYRITE
PYROPE
QUARTZ
RUTILE
SALITE
SCHIST
SCHORL
SILICA

6—continued
SILVER
SPHENE
SPINEL
URTITE
ZIRCON

7
ALNOITE
ALTAITE
ALUNITE
ANATASE
APATITE
ARSENIC
AXINITE
AZURITE
BARYTES
BAUXITE
BIOTITE
BISMUTH
BORNITE
BRECCIA
BRUCITE
CALCITE
CALOMEL
CELSIAN
CITRINE
COESITE
CUPRITE
DIAMOND
DIORITE
EMERALD
EPIDOTE
FELSITE
FOYAITE
GAHNITE
GEDRITE
GRANITE
GUMMITE
HELVITE
HESSITE
HOPEITE
HUNTITE
IJOLITE
JADEITE
KAINITE
KERNITE
KYANITE
LEUCITE
LIGNITE
MELLITE
MULLITE
OLIVINE
ORTHITE
RASPITE
REALGAR
SPARITE
SYENITE
SYLVITE
THORITE
THULITE
ZEOLITE

7—continued
ZINCITE
ZOISITE

8
AEGIRINE
ALLANITE
ALUNOGEN
ANALCIME
ANALCITE
ANDESINE
ANDORITE
ANKERITE
ANTIMONY
ARCANITE
AUGELITE
AUTUNITE
BASANITE
BIXBYITE
BLOEDITE
BLUE JOHN
BOEHMITE
BORACITE
BRAGGITE
BRAUNITE
BRAVOITE
BRONZITE
BROOKITE
CALAMINE
CHIOLITE
CHLORITE
CHROMITE
CINNABAR
CORUNDUM
CROCOITE
CRYOLITE
CUBANITE
DATOLITE
DIALLAGE
DIASPORE
DIGENITE
DIOPSIDE
DIOPTASE
DOLERITE
DOLOMITE
ECLOGITE
ENARGITE
EPSOMITE
ESSEXITE
EULYTITE
EUXENITE
FAYALITE
FELDSPAR
FLUORITE
GIBBSITE
GOETHITE
GRAPHITE
HANKSITE
HAWAIITE
HEMATITE
HYACINTH
IDOCRASE

8—continued
ILMENITE
IODYRITE
JAROSITE
LAZURITE
LIMONITE
LITHARGE
MARSHITE
MEIONITE
MELANITE
MELILITE
MESOLITE
MIERSITE
MIMETITE
MONAZITE
MONETITE
MYLONITE
NEPHRITE
ORPIMENT
PARISITE
PERIDOTE
PERTHITE
PETALITE
PLATINUM
PORPHYRY
PREHNITE
PSAMMITE
PYRIBOLE
PYROXENE
RHYOLITE
ROCKSALT
SANIDINE
SAPPHIRE
SELLAITE
SIDERITE
SMECTITE
SODALITE
STANNITE
STEATITE
STIBNITE
STILBITE
STOLSITE
STRUVITE
TITANITE
TONALITE
TRACHYTE
VARISITE
VATERITE
WEHRLITE
WURTZITE
XENOTIME

9
ACANTHITE
ALMANDINE
ALUMINITE
AMPHIBOLE
ANDRADITE
ANGLESITE
ANHYDRITE
ANORTHITE
ARAGONITE

9—continued
ARGENTITE
ATACAMITE
BENITOITE
BRIMSTONE
BROMYRITE
BUNSENITE
BYTOWNITE
CARNALITE
CARNOTITE
CELESTITE
CERUSSITE
CHABAZITE
CHINACLAY
COBALTITE
COLUMBITE
COPIAPITE
COTUNNITE
COVELLITE
DANBURITE
DERBYLITE
DIATOMITE
ENSTATITE
ERYTHRITE
EUCAIRITE
EUCLASITE
EUDIALITE
FERBERITE
FIBROLITE
FLUORSPAR
GEHLENITE
GMELINITE
GOSLARITE
GRANULITE
GREYWACKE
GROSSULAR
GRUNERITE
HARMOTOME
HERCYNITE
HERDERITE
HORNSTONE
KAOLINITE
KIESERITE
LANARKITE
LAWSONITE
LEUCITITE
LIMESTONE
LODESTONE
MAGNESITE
MAGNETITE
MALACHITE
MALIGNITE
MANGANITE
MARCASITE
MARGARITE
MARIALITE
MENDIPITE
MICROLITE
MIGMATITE
MILLERITE
MISPICKEL

9—continued	10—continued	10—continued	11—continued
MONZONITE	CACOXENITE	PYROCHLORE	GLAUBER SALT
MORDENITE	CALEDONITE	PYROLUSITE	GLAUCOPHANE
MUGEARITE	CANCRINITE	PYRRHOTITE	GREENOCKITE
MUSCOVITE	CERVANTITE	RHYODACITE	HARZBURGITE
NANTOKITE	CHALCEDONY	RICHTERITE	HASTINGSITE
NATROLITE	CHALCOCITE	RIEBECKITE	HAUSMANNITE
NEPHELINE	CHLORITOID	SAFFLORITE	HYPERSTHENE
NICCOLITE	CHRYSOLITE	SAMARSKITE	ICELAND SPAR
OLDHAMITE	CLAUDETITE	SAPPHIRINE	KATOPHORITE
OLIVENITE	CLINTONITE	SERPENTINE	LAPIS LAZULI
PECTOLITE	COLEMANITE	SHONKINITE	LEADHILLITE
PENNINITE	CONNELLITE	SPERRYLITE	LOELLINGITE
PERCYLITE	COQUIMBITE	SPHALERITE	MANGANOSITE
PERICLASE	CORDIERITE	STAUROLITE	MELANTERITE
PHENAKITE	DOUGLASITE	STERCORITE	MOLYBDENITE
PHONOLITE	DYSCRASITE	STISHOVITE	MONTROYDITE
PIGEONITE	EMPLECTITE	TESCHENITE	NEPHELINITE
PISTACITE	EMPRESSITE	THENARDITE	NORDMARKITE
POLLUCITE	EPIDIORITE	THOMSONITE	PENFIELDITE
POWELLITE	FORSTERITE	THORIANITE	PENTLANDITE
PROUSTITE	GANOMALITE	TORBERNITE	PHILLIPSITE
PULASKITE	GARNIERITE	TOURMALINE	PITCHBLENDE
QUARTZITE	GAYLUSSITE	TRAVERTINE	PLAGIOCLASE
RHODONITE	GEIKIELITE	TROEGERITE	PSILOMELANE
SANDSTONE	GLAUBERITE	ULLMANNITE	PUMPELLYITE
SCAPOLITE	GLAUCONITE	ULVÖSPINEL	PYRARGYRITE
SCHEELITE	GREENSTONE	VANADINITE	PYROCHROITE
SCOLECITE	HAMBERGITE	VITROPHYRE	RADIOLARITE
SCORODITE	HEULANDITE	WEBSTERITE	ROCK CRYSTAL
SMALLTITE	HORNBLENDE	WHEWELLITE	SILLIMANITE
SOAPSTONE	HUEBNERITE	WOLFRAMITE	SMITHSONITE
SPODUMENE	IGNIMBRITE	ZINCBLENDE	SPESSARTITE
STRENGITE	JAMESONITE	**11**	TITANAUGITE
SYLVANITE	KIMBERLITE	ALLEMONTITE	TRIPHYLLITE
TACHYLITE	LANTHANITE	AMBLYGONITE	VALENTINITE
TANTALITE	LAUMONTITE	ANORTHOSITE	VERMICULITE
TAPIOLITE	LAURIONITE	APOPHYLLITE	VESUVIANITE
THERALITE	LEPIDOLITE	BADDELEYITE	VILLIAUMITE
THOLEIITE	LHERZOLITE	BERTRANDITE	ZINNWALDITE
TREMOLITE	LIMBURGITE	BERYLLONITE	**12**
TRIDYMITE	MASCAGNITE	BROCHANTITE	ANORTHOCLASE
TURQUOISE	MATLOCKITE	CALCARENITE	ARSENOPYRITE
URANINITE	MEERSCHAUM	CALCILUTITE	BISMUTHINITE
VIVIANITE	MELILITITE	CALCIRUDITE	BOULANGERITE
WAGNERITE	MELTEIGITE	CARBONATITE	CALCISILTITE
WAVELLITE	MICROCLINE	CARBORUNDUM	CHALCANTHITE
WILLEMITE	MIRABILITE	CASSITERITE	CHALCOPYRITE
WITHERITE	MOISSANITE	CERARGYRITE	CLAY MINERALS
WULFENITE	NEWBERYITE	CHARNOCKITE	CLINOPTOLITE
ZEUNERITE	OLIGOCLASE	CHIASTOLITE	CLINOZOISITE
10	ORTHOCLASE	CHLOANTHITE	CRISTOBALITE
ACTINOLITE	PARAGONITE	CHONDRODITE	EDDINGTONITE
AKERMANITE	PEKOVSKITE	CHRYSOBERYL	FELDSPATHOID
ALABANDITE	PERIDOTITE	CHRYSOCOLLA	FERGUSSONITE
ANDALUSITE	PERTHOSITE	CLINOCHLORE	FLUORAPATITE
ANKARAMITE	PHLOGOPITE	COBALTBLOOM	GROSSULARITE
ARSENOLITE	PHOSGENITE	DAUBREELITE	HEDENBERGITE
BOROLONITE	PIEMONTITE	EGLESTONITE	HEMIMORPHITE
BOURNONITE	POLYBASITE	FERROAUGITE	LUXULLIANITE
BRONZITITE	PYRALSPITE	FRANKLINITE	METACINNABAR

12—continued	13	14	16
MONTICELLITE	ANTHOPHYLLITE	CRYOLITHIONITE	GALENABISMUTHITE
PYROMORPHITE	BREITHAUPTITE	HYDROMAGNESITE	ORTHOFERROSILITE
PYROPHYLLITE	CLINOPYROXENE	LECHATELIERITE	PHARMACOSIDERITE
RHODOCROSITE	CUMMINGTONITE	LITHIOPHYLLITE	17
SENARMONTITE	JACUPIRANGITE	ORTHOQUARTZITE	HYDROGROSSU-
SKUTTERUDITE	KALIOPHYLLITE	PSEUDOBROOKITE	LARITE
STRONTIANITE	LEPIDOCROCITE	RAMMELSBERGITE	TELLUROBIS-
SYENODIORITE	LITCHFIELDITE	TRACHYANDESITE	MUTHITE
TERLINGUAITE	ORTHOPYROXENE	XANTHOPHYLLITE	
TETRAHEDRITE	QUARTZARENITE	15	
THOMSENOLITE	RHODOCHROSITE	MONTMORILLONITE	
TRACHYBASALT	STILPNOMELANE	PSEUDOTACHYLITE	
WOLLASTONITE	THERMONATRITE	STIBIOTANTALITE	
	UNCOMPAHGRITE		

ORES

ELEMENT – ore(s)

3
TIN – cassiterite
4
IRON – haematite, magnetite
LEAD – galena
ZINC – sphalerite, smithsonite, calamine
5
BORON – kernite
6
BARIUM – barite, witherite
CERIUM – monazite, bastnaesite
COBALT – cobaltite, smaltite, erythrite
COPPER – malachite, azurite, chalcopyrite, bornite, cuprite
ERBIUM – monazite, bastnaesite
INDIUM – sphalerite, smithsonite, calamine
NICKEL – pentlandite, pyrrhotite
OSMIUM – iridosime
RADIUM – pitchblende, carnotite
SILVER – argentite, horn silver
SODIUM – salt
7
ARSENIC – realgar, orpiment, arsenopyrite
CADMIUM – greenockite
CAESIUM – lepidolite, pollucite
CALCIUM – limestone, gypsum, fluorite
GALLIUM
HAFNIUM – zircon
HOLMIUM – monazite
IRIDIUM
LITHIUM – lepidolite, spodumene
MERCURY – cinnabar
NIOBIUM – columbite-tantalite, pyrochlore, euxenite
RHENIUM – molybdenite
RHODIUM
SILICON – silica

7—continued
THORIUM – monazite
THULIUM – monazite
URANIUM – pitchblende, uraninite, carnotite
YTTRIUM – monazite
8
ANTIMONY – stibnite
CHROMIUM – chromite
LUTETIUM – monazite
PLATINUM – sperrylite
RUBIDIUM – lepidolite
SAMARIUM – monazite, bastnaesite
SCANDIUM – thortveitite, davidite
SELENIUM – pyrites
TANTALUM – columbite-tantalite
THALLIUM – pyrites
TITANIUM – rutile, ilmenite, sphere
TUNGSTEN – wolframite, scheelite
VANADIUM – carnotite, roscoelite, vanadinite
9
ALUMINIUM – bauxite
BERYLLIUM – beryl
GERMANIUM – germanite, argyrodite
LANTHANUM – monazite, bastnaesite
MAGNESIUM – magnesite, dolomite
MANGANESE – pyrolusite, rhodochrosite
NEODYMIUM – monazite, bastnaesite
PALLADIUM
POTASSIUM – sylvite, carnallite, polyhalite
RUTHENIUM – pentlandite, pyroxinite
STRONTIUM – celestite, strontianite
TELLURIUM
YTTERBIUM – monazite
10
DYSPROSIUM – monazite, bastnaesite
GADOLINIUM – monazite, bastnaesite
MOLYBDENUM – molybdenite, wulfenite
PHOSPHORUS – apatite

12
PRASEODYMIUM − monazite, bastnaesite

12—continued
PROTACTINIUM − pitchblende

GEMSTONES

STONE (colour)

4
JADE (green, mauve, brown)
ONYX (various colours, banded)
OPAL (white, milky blue, or black with rainbow-coloured reflections)
RUBY (red)

5
AGATE (brown, red, blue, green, yellow)
BERYL (green, blue, pink)
TOPAZ (usually yellow or colourless)

6
GARNET (red)
ZIRCON (all colours)

7
CITRINE (yellow)
DIAMOND (colourless)
EMERALD (green)

8
AMETHYST (purple)

8—continued
SAPPHIRE (blue and other colours except red)
SUNSTONE (whitish-red-brown flecked with gold)

9
MALACHITE (dark green banded)
MOONSTONE (white with bluish tinge)
SOAPSTONE (white or greenish)
TURQUOISE (greenish-blue)

10
AQUAMARINE (turquoise, greenish-blue)
BLOODSTONE (green with red spots)
CHALCEDONY (red, brown, grey, or black)
SERPENTINE (usually green or white)
TOURMALINE (all colours)

11
LAPIS LAZULI (deep blue)

MEDICAL TERMS

3	5—continued	5—continued	6—continued
GUT	FEMUR	TIBIA	PELVIS
HIP	FOVEA	UVULA	PEPSIN
JAW	HEART	VALVE	RADIUS
RIB	HYOID	VOMER	RECTUM
4	ILEUM	WRIST	REFLEX
ANUS	ILIUM	**6**	RENNET
BILE	INCUS	ARTERY	RETINA
CUSP	JOINT	ATRIUM	SACRUM
GALL	LIVER	BICEPS	SALIVA
HEEL	MALAR	CAECUM	SCLERA
IRIS	MEDIA	CARDIA	SQUAMA
LENS	NARES	CARPAL	STAPES
NOSE	NASAL	CARPUS	TARSUS
ULNA	NERVE	COCCYX	TENDON
VEIN	OPTIC	CORNEA	TONGUE
5	PUBIS	CUBOID	TUNICA
ANKLE	PULSE	DERMIS	URETER
AORTA	PUPIL	FIBULA	VASTUS
BOLUS	SENSE	GULLET	VENULE
BOWEL	SINEW	KIDNEY	VESSEL
CHYLE	SINUS	LUNATE	**7**
CHYME	SKULL	MUSCLE	AURICLE
COLON	SPINE	MYELIN	BLADDER
	TALUS		

7—continued
CAROTID
CHOROID
COCHLEA
CRANIUM
CUTICLE
DELTOID
ECCRINE
ETHMOID
FRONTAL
GEMMULE
GLOTTIS
HUMERUS
INGESTA
JEJUNUM
JUGULAR
LACTEAL
MALLEUS
MAMMARY
MEDULLA
NEPHRON
NEURONE
NOSTRIL
PATELLA
PHALANX
PHARYNX
PTYALIN
PYLORUS
SAPHENA
SCAPULA
SENSORY
STERNUM
STOMACH
SYNAPSE
SYSTOLE
THYROID
TRICEPS
URETHRA

8
ADDUCTOR
APOCRINE
APPENDIX
BACKBONE
BILE DUCT
CEREBRUM

8—continued
CLAVICLE
CORONARY
DIASTOLE
DUODENUM
EXOCRINE
GANGLION
LIGAMENT
MANDIBLE
MENINGES
PALATINE
PANCREAS
PARIETAL
PERINEUM
PISIFORM
RECEPTOR
SACCULUS
SALIVARY
SCAPHOID
SPHENOID
TEMPORAL
TUBINATE
TYMPANUM
UNCIFORM
VENA CAVA
VERTEBRA

9
ARTERIOLE
BILIRUBIN
BRAINSTEM
CAPILLARY
CUNEIFORM
DIAPHRAGM
DIGESTION
ENDOCRINE
ENDORPHIN
EPICARDIA
EPIDERMIS
GOLGI BODY
HAMSTRING
INGESTION
INTESTINE
LACHRYMAL
LYMPHATIC
LYMPH NODE

9—continued
MAXILLARY
NAVICULAR
OCCIPITAL
PACEMAKER
SPHINCTER
TASTE BUDS
TRAPEZIUM
TRAPEZIUS
TRAPEZOID
UTRICULUS
VENTRICLE

10
ADAM'S APPLE
ADRENALINE
ASTRAGALUS
BILIVERDIN
BREASTBONE
CEREBELLUM
COLLAR BONE
EPICARDIUM
EPIGLOTTIS
GREY MATTER
HEMISPHERE
HENLE'S LOOP
INNOMINATE
METACARPAL
METACARPUS
METATARSAL
METATARSUS
MYOCARDIUM
QUADRICEPS
SUPRARENAL

11
CONJUNCTIVA
ENDOCARDIUM
GALL BLADDER
PERICARDIUM
PERISTALSIS
VASA VASORUM

12
ADRENAL GLAND
HAIR FOLLICLE
MOTOR NEURONE

12—continued
PELVIC GIRDLE
RECEPTACULUM
SCHWANN CELLS
SCIATIC NERVE
SPINAL COLUMN
SUBMAXILLARY

13
AQUEOUS HUMOUR
BICUSPID VALVE
BLOOD PRESSURE
KUPFFER'S CELLS
NERVOUS SYSTEM
NODE OF RANVIER
NORADRENALINE
PEYER'S PATCHES
PURKINJE CELLS
SUBMANDIBULAR

14
ACHILLES TENDON
BOWMAN'S
  CAPSULE
BRUNNER'S GLANDS
EUSTACHIAN TUBE
PURKINJE FIBRES
VITREOUS HUMOUR

15
ALIMENTARY CANAL
MALPIGHIAN LAYER
OBTURATOR
  MUSCLE
ORGAN OF
  JACOBSON
PECTORAL
  MUSCLES

16
MEDULLA
  OBLONGATA

18
ISLETS OF
  LANGERHANS
SEMICIRCULAR
  CANALS

RELIGION AND MYTHOLOGY

BOOKS OF THE BIBLE

OLD TESTAMENT

GENESIS
EXODUS
LEVITICUS
NUMBERS
DEUTERONOMY
JOSHUA
JUDGES
RUTH
1 SAMUEL
2 SAMUEL
1 KINGS
2 KINGS
1 CHRONICLES
2 CHRONICLES
EZRA
NEHEMIAH
ESTHER
JOB
PSALMS
PROVERBS
ECCLESIASTES
SONG OF SOLOMON
ISAIAH

JEREMIAH
LAMENTATIONS
EZEKIEL
DANIEL
HOSEA
JOEL
AMOS
OBADIAH
JONAH
MICAH
NAHUM
HABAKKUK
ZEPHANIAH
HAGGAI
ZECHARIAH
MALACHI

APOCRYPHA

I ESDRAS
II ESDRAS
TOBIT
JUDITH
THE REST OF
ESTHER

WISDOM
ECCLESIASTICUS
BARUCH, WITH
EPISTLE OF
JEREMIAH
SONG OF THE
THREE CHILDREN
SUSANNA
BEL AND THE
DRAGON
PRAYER OF
MANASSES
I MACCABEES
II MACCABEES

NEW TESTAMENT

MATTHEW
MARK
LUKE
JOHN
THE ACTS
ROMANS
1 CORINTHIANS

2 CORINTHIANS
GALATIANS
EPHESIANS
PHILIPPIANS
COLOSSIANS
1 THESSALONIANS
2 THESSALONIANS
1 TIMOTHY
2 TIMOTHY
TITUS
PHILEMON
HEBREWS
JAMES
1 PETER
2 PETER
1 JOHN
2 JOHN
3 JOHN
JUDE
REVELATION

BIBLICAL CHARACTERS

OLD TESTAMENT

AARON – elder brother of Moses; 1st high priest of Hebrews

ABEL – second son of Adam and Eve; murdered by brother Cain

ABRAHAM – father of Hebrew nation

ABSALOM – David's spoilt third son; killed after plotting against his father

ADAM – the first man created; husband of Eve

BAAL – fertility god of Canaanites and Phoenicians

BATHSHEBA – mother of Solomon

BELSHAZZAR – last king of Babylon, son of Nebuchadnezzar; Daniel interpreted his vision of writing on the wall as foretelling the downfall of his kingdom

BENJAMIN – youngest son of Jacob and Rachel. His descendants formed one of the 12 tribes of Israel

CAIN – first son of Adam and Eve; murdered his brother Abel

DANIEL – prophet at the court of Nebuchadnezzar with a gift for interpreting dreams

DAVID – slayed the giant Goliath

DELILAH – a Philistine seducer and betrayer of Samson

ELIJAH – Hebrew prophet, taken into heaven in a fiery chariot

ELISHA – prophet and disciple of Elijah

ENOCH – father of Methuselah

EPHRAIM – son of Joseph; founded one of the 12 tribes of Israel

ESAU – elder of Isaac's twin sons; tricked out of his birthright by his younger brother Jacob

ESTHER – beautiful Israelite woman; heroically protected her people

EVE – first woman; created as companion for Adam in Garden of Eden

EZEKIEL – prophet of Israel captured by Babylonians

GIDEON – Israelite hero and judge

GOLIATH – Philistine giant killed by David

HEZEKIAH – king of Judah (c. 715–686 BC)

ISAAC – son of Abraham and Sarah, conceived in their old age; father of Jacob and Esau

ISAIAH – the greatest old testament prophet

ISHMAEL – Abraham's son by Hagar, hand-maiden to his wife, Sarah; rival of Isaac

ISRAEL – new name given to Jacob after his reconciliation with Esau

JACOB – second son of Isaac and Rebekah, younger twin of Esau whom he tricked out of his inheritance. The 12 tribes of Israel were named after his 12 descendents

JEREMIAH – one of the great prophets; foretold destruction of Jerusalem

JEZEBEL – cruel and lustful wife of Ahab, king of Israel

JOB – long-suffering and pious inhabitant of Uz

JONAH – after ignoring God's commands he was swallowed by a whale

JONATHAN – eldest son of Saul and close friend of David

JOSEPH – favourite son of Jacob and Rachel with his "coat of many colours"; sold into slavery by his jealous brothers

JOSHUA – succeeded Moses and led Israelites against Canaan. He defeated Jericho where the walls fell down

JUDAH – son of Jacob and Leah; founded tribe of Judah

LOT – nephew of Abraham; he escaped the destruction of Sodom, but his wife was turned into a pillar of salt for looking back

METHUSELAH – son of Enoch, the oldest person ever (969 years)

MIRIAM – sister of Aaron and Moses whom she looked after as a baby; prophetess and leader of Israelites

MOSES – Israel's great leader and lawgiver, he led the Israelites out of captivity in Egypt to the promised land of Canaan. Received ten commandments from Jehovah on Mt Sinai

NATHAN – Hebrew prophet at courts of David and Solomon

NEBUCHADNEZZAR – king of Babylon

NOAH – grandson of Methuselah, father of Shem, Ham, and Japheth; built ark to save his family and all animal species from the great flood

REBEKAH – wife of Isaac, mother of Jacob and Esau

RUTH – Moabite who accompanied her mother-in-law Naomi to Bethlehem. Remembered for her loyalty

SAMSON – Israelite judge of great physical strength; seduced and betrayed by Delilah

SAMUEL – prophet and judge of Israel

SARAH – wife of Abraham, mother of Isaac

SAUL – first king of Israel

SOLOMON – son of David and Bathsheba; remembered for his great wisdom and wealth

NEW TESTAMENT

ANDREW – fisherman and brother of Peter; one of 12 Apostles

BARABAS – Cypriot missionary; introduced Paul to the Church

BARABBAS – robber and murderer; in prison with Jesus and released instead of him

BARTHOLOMEW – possibly same person as Nathaniel, one of the 12 Apostles

CAIAPHAS – high priest of the Jews; Jesus brought to him after arrest

GABRIEL – angel who announced birth of Jesus to Mary; and of John the Baptist to Zechariah

HEROD – 1. the Great, ruled when Jesus was born 2. Antipas, son of Herod the Great, ruled when John the Baptist was murdered 3. Agrippa, killed James (brother of John) 4. Agrippa II, before whom Paul was tried

JAMES – 1. the Greater, one of 12 Apostles, brother of John 2. the Less, one of 12 Apostles 3. leader of the Church in Jerusalem and author of the New Testament epistle

JESUS – founder of Christianity

JOHN – youngest of 12 Apostles

JOHN THE BAPTIST – announced coming of Jesus, and baptized him

JOSEPH – 1. husband of Mary the mother of Jesus 2. of Arimathea, a secret disciple of Jesus

JUDAS ISCARIOT – the disciple who betrayed Jesus

LAZARUS – brother of Mary and Martha, raised from the dead by Jesus

LUKE – companion of Paul, author of Luke and Acts

MARK – author of the gospel; companion of Paul, Barnabas, and Peter

MARTHA – sister of Mary and Lazarus, friend of Jesus

MARY – 1. mother of Jesus 2. sister of Martha and Lazarus 3. Magdalene, cured by Jesus and the first to see him after the resurrection

MATTHEW – one of 12 Apostles, author of the gospel

MATTHIAS – chosen to replace the apostle Judas

MICHAEL – a chief archangel

NATHANIEL – *see* Bartholomew

NICODEMUS – a Pharisee who had a secret meeting with Jesus

PAUL – formerly Saul of Tarsus, persecutor of Christians; renamed after his conversion. Apostle to the Gentiles and author of epistles

PETER – Simon, one of 12 Apostles; denied Jesus before the crucifixion but later became leader of the Church

PHILIP – one of 12 Apostles

PILATE – Roman procurator of Judea; allowed Jesus to be crucified

SALOME – 1. wife of Zebedee, mother of James and John 2. daughter of Herodias; danced before Herod for the head of John the Baptist

SAUL – *see* Paul

SIMON – 1. Simon Peter *see* Peter 2. the Canaanite, one of 12 Apostles 3. one of Jesus' four brothers 4. the leper, in whose house Jesus was anointed 5. of Cyrene, carried the cross of Jesus 6. the tanner, in whose house Peter had his vision

STEPHEN – Christian martyr, stoned to death

THOMAS – one of 12 Apostles, named 'Doubting' because he doubted the resurrection

TIMOTHY – Paul's fellow missionary; two of Paul's epistles are to him

TITUS – convert and companion of Paul, who wrote him one epistle

PATRON SAINTS

NAME (Patron of)

AGATHA (bell-founders)
ALBERT THE GREAT (students of natural sciences)
ANDREW (Scotland)
BARBARA (gunners and miners)
BERNARD OF MONTJOUX (mountaineers)
CAMILLUS (nurses)
CASIMIR (Poland)
CECILIA (musicians)
CHRISTOPHER (wayfarers)
CRISPIN (shoemakers)
DAVID (Wales)
DIONYSIUS (DENIS) OF PARIS (France)
DUNSTAN (goldsmiths, jewellers, and locksmiths)
DYMPNA (insane)
ELIGIUS *or* ELOI (metalworkers)
ERASMUS (sailors)
FIACRE (gardeners)
FRANCES CABRINI (emigrants)
FRANCES OF ROME (motorists)
FRANCIS DE SALES (writers)
FRANCIS XAVIER (foreign missions)

FRIDESWIDE (Oxford)
GEORGE (England)
GILES (cripples)
HUBERT (huntsmen)
JEROME EMILIANI (orphans and abandoned children)
JOHN OF GOD (hospitals and booksellers)
JUDE (hopeless causes)
JULIAN (innkeepers, boatmen, travellers)
KATHERINE OF ALEXANDRIA (students, philosophers, and craftsmen)
LUKE (physicians and surgeons)
MARTHA (housewives)
NICHOLAS (children, sailors, unmarried girls, merchants, pawnbrokers, apothecaries, and perfumeries)
PATRICK (Ireland)
PETER NOLASCO (midwives)
SAVA (Serbian people)
VALENTINE (lovers)
VITUS (epilepsy and nervous diseases)
WENCESLAS (Czechoslovakia)
ZITA (domestic servants)

RELIGIOUS MOVEMENTS

3	3—continued	4	5
BON	ZEN	AINU	BOSCI
I AM			ISLAM

5—continued
KEGON
THAGS
THUGS

6
BABISM
PARSIS
QUAKER
SHINTO
TAOISM
VOODOO

7
AJIVIKA
BAHAISM
GIDEONS
JAINISM
JUDAISM
JUMPERS
LAMAISM
MORMONS
PARSEES
SHAKERS
SIKHISM
WAHABIS
ZIONISM

8
ABELIANS
ABELITES
ACOEMETI
ADAMITES
ADMADIYA
AHMADIYA
AMARITES
BAPTISTS
BUDDHISM
CATHOLIC
HINDUISM
HUMANISM
MAR THOMA
NICHIREN
NOSAIRIS
PURITANS
STUDITES

9
CALVINISM
CHUNTOKYO
FRANKISTS
HICKSITES
HUGUENOTS
JANSENISM
METHODIST

9—continued
PANTHEISM

10
ABSTINENTS
ADVENTISTS
AGONIZANTS
AMBROSIANS
BUCHANITES
CALIXTINES

11
ABODE OF LOVE
ABRAHAMITES
ANABAPTISTS
ANGLICANISM
ARMINIANISM
BASILIDEANS
BERNARDINES
COVENANTERS

12
ABECEDARIANS
BENEDICTINES
CHRISTIANITY
PRESBYTERIAN
SPIRITUALISM
UNITARIANISM

13
MOHAMMEDANISM
PROTESTANTISM
REDEMPTORISTS
ROMAN CATHOLIC
SALVATION ARMY

14
CONGREGATIONAL
FUNDAMENTALISM

16
ABYSSINIAN
  CHURCH
CHRISTIAN SCIENCE
MORAVIAN
  BRETHREN
PLYMOUTH
  BRETHREN

17
ANTIPAEDOBAP-
  TISTS
JEHOVAH'S
  WITNESSES

RELIGIOUS ORDERS

AUGUSTINIAN
BARNABITE
BENEDICTINE
BRIGITTINE
CAMALDOLESE
CAPUCHINS
CARMELITE

CARTHUSIAN
CISTERCIAN
DOMINICAN
FRANCISCAN
HOSPITALLERS
JERONYMITE
MINIMS

POOR CLARES
PREMONSTRATEN-
  SIAN
SALESIAN
SERVITE
SYLVESTRINE
TEMPLARS

THEATINE
TRAPPIST
TRINITARIAN
URSULINE
VISITANDINE,
  VISITATION

CLERGY

ARCHBISHOP
ARCHDEACON
BISHOP
CANON
CARDINAL

CHAPLAIN
CURATE
DEACON
DEAN

ELDER
MINISTER
PARSON
POPE

PRIEST
RECTOR
VICAR
VICAR-FORANE

POPES

POPE (DATE OF ACCESSION)

ST PETER (42)
ST LINUS (67)

ST ANACLETUS
  (Cletus) (76)

ST CLEMENT I (88)
ST EVARISTUS (97)

ST ALEXANDER I
  (105)

ST SIXTUS I (115)
ST TELESPHORUS (125)
ST HYGINUS (136)
ST PIUS I (140)
ST ANICETUS (155)
ST SOTERUS (166)
ST ELEUTHERIUS (175)
ST VICTOR I (189)
ST ZEPHYRINUS (199)
ST CALLISTUS I (217)
ST URBAN I (222)
ST PONTIAN (230)
ST ANTERUS (235)
ST FABIAN (236)
ST CORNELIUS (251)
ST LUCIUS I (253)
ST STEPHEN I (254)
ST SIXTUS II (257)
ST DIONYSIUS (259)
ST FELIX I (269)
ST EUTYCHIAN (275)
ST CAIUS (283)
ST MARCELLINUS (296)
ST MARCELLUS I (308)
ST EUSEBIUS (309)
ST MELCHIADES (311)
ST SYLVESTER I (314)
ST MARCUS (336)
ST JULIUS I (337)
LIBERIUS (352)
ST DAMASUS I (366)
ST SIRICIUS (384)
ST ANASTASIUS I (399)
ST INNOCENT I (401)
ST ZOSIMUS (417)
ST BONIFACE I (418)
ST CELESTINE I (422)
ST SIXTUS III (432)
ST LEO I (the Great) (440)
ST HILARY (461)
ST SIMPLICIUS (468)
ST FELIX III (483)
ST GELASIUS I (492)
ANASTASIUS II (496)
ST SYMMACHUS (498)
ST HORMISDAS (514)
ST JOHN I (523)
ST FELIX IV (526)
BONIFACE II (530)
JOHN II (533)
ST AGAPETUS I (535)

ST SILVERIUS (536)
VIGILIUS (537)
PELAGIUS I (556)
JOHN III (561)
BENEDICT I (575)
PELAGIUS II (579)
ST GREGORY I (the Great) (590)
SABINIANUS (604)
BONIFACE III (607)
ST BONIFACE IV (608)
ST DEUSDEDIT (Adeodatus I) (615)
BONIFACE V (619)
HONORIUS I (625)
SEVERINUS (640)
JOHN IV (640)
THEODORE I (642)
ST MARTIN I (649)
ST EUGENE I (654)
ST VITALIAN (657)
ADEODATUS II (672)
DONUS (676)
ST AGATHO (678)
ST LEO II (682)
ST BENEDICT II (684)
JOHN V (685)
CONON (686)
ST SERGIUS I (687)
JOHN VI (701)
JOHN VII (705)
SISINNIUS (708)
CONSTANTINE (708)
ST GREGORY II (715)
ST GREGORY III (731)
ST ZACHARY (741)
STEPHEN II (III)* (752)
ST PAUL I (757)
STEPHEN III (IV) (768)
ADRIAN I (772)
ST LEO III (795)
STEPHEN IV (V) (816)
ST PASCHAL I (817)
EUGENE II (824)
VALENTINE (827)
GREGORY IV (827)
SERGIUS II (844)
ST LEO IV (847)
BENEDICT III (855)
ST NICHOLAS I (858)
ADRIAN II (867)
JOHN VIII (872)
MARINUS I (882)
ST ADRIAN III (884)
STEPHEN V (VI) (885)
FORMOSUS (891)
BONIFACE VI (896)
STEPHEN VI (VII) (896)

ROMANUS (897)
THEODORE II (897)
JOHN IX (898)
BENEDICT IV (900)
LEO V (903)
SERGIUS III (904)
ANASTASIUS III (911)
LANDUS (913)
JOHN X (914)
LEO VI (928)
STEPHEN VII (VIII) (928)
JOHN XI (931)
LEO VII (936)
STEPHEN VIII (IX) (939)
MARINUS II (942)
AGAPETUS II (946)
JOHN XII (955)
LEO VIII (963)
BENEDICT V (964)
JOHN XIII (965)
BENEDICT VI (973)
BENEDICT VII (974)
JOHN XIV (983)
JOHN XV (985)
GREGORY V (996)
SYLVESTER II (999)
JOHN XVII (1003)
JOHN XVIII (1004)
SERGIUS IV (1009)
BENEDICT VIII (1012)
JOHN XIX (1024)
BENEDICT IX (1032)
GREGORY VI (1045)
CLEMENT II (1046)
BENEDICT IX (1047)
DAMASUS II (1048)
ST LEO IX (1049)
VICTOR II (1055)
STEPHEN IX (X) (1057)
NICHOLAS II (1059)
ALEXANDER II (1061)
ST GREGORY VII (1073)
VICTOR III (1086)
URBAN II (1088)
PASCHAL II (1099)
GELASIUS II (1118)
CALLISTUS II (1119)
HONORIUS II (1124)
INNOCENT II (1130)
CELESTINE II (1143)
LUCIUS II (1144)
EUGENE III (1145)
ANASTASIUS IV (1153)
ADRIAN IV (1154)
ALEXANDER III (1159)
LUCIUS III (1181)

URBAN III (1185)
GREGORY VIII (1187)
CLEMENT III (1187)
CELESTINE III (1191)
INNOCENT III (1198)
HONORIUS III (1216)
GREGORY IX (1227)
CELESTINE IV (1241)
INNOCENT IV (1243)
ALEXANDER IV (1254)
URBAN IV (1261)
CLEMENT IV (1265)
GREGORY X (1271)
INNOCENT V (1276)
ADRIAN V (1276)
JOHN XXI (1276)
NICHOLAS III (1277)
MARTIN IV (1281)
HONORIUS IV (1285)
NICHOLAS IV (1288)
ST CELESTINE V (1294)
BONIFACE VIII (1294)
BENEDICT XI (1303)
CLEMENT V (1305)
JOHN XXII (1316)
BENEDICT XII (1334)
CLEMENT VI (1342)
INNOCENT VI (1352)
URBAN V (1362)
GREGORY XI (1370)
URBAN VI (1378)
BONIFACE IX (1389)
INNOCENT VII (1404)
GREGORY XII (1406)
MARTIN V (1417)
EUGENE IV (1431)
NICHOLAS V (1447)
CALLISTUS III (1455)
PIUS II (1458)
PAUL II (1464)
SIXTUS IV (1471)
INNOCENT VIII (1484)
ALEXANDER VI (1492)
PIUS III (1503)
JULIUS II (1503)
LEO X (1513)
ADRIAN VI (1522)
CLEMENT VII (1523)
PAUL III (1534)
JULIUS III (1550)
MARCELLUS II (1555)
PAUL IV (1555)
PIUS IV (1559)
ST PIUS V (1566)
GREGORY XIII (1572)
SIXTUS V (1585)
URBAN VII (1590)
GREGORY XIV (1590)

INNOCENT IX (1591)
CLEMENT VIII (1592)
LEO XI (1605)
PAUL V (1605)
GREGORY XV (1621)
URBAN VIII (1623)
INNOCENT X (1644)
ALEXANDER VII
  (1655)
CLEMENT IX (1667)
CLEMENT X (1670)
INNOCENT XI (1676)

ALEXANDER VIII
  (1689)
INNOCENT XII (1691)
CLEMENT XI (1700)
INNOCENT XIII (1721)
BENEDICT XIII (1724)
CLEMENT XII (1730)
BENEDICT XIV (1740)
CLEMENT XIII (1758)
CLEMENT XIV (1769)
PIUS VI (1775)

PIUS VII (1800)
LEO XII (1823)
PIUS VIII (1829)
GREGORY XVI (1831)
PIUS IX (1846)
LEO XIII (1878)
ST PIUS X (1903)
BENEDICT XV (1914)
PIUS XI (1922)
PIUS XII (1939)
JOHN XXIII (1958)

PAUL VI (1963)
JOHN PAUL I (1978)
JOHN PAUL II (1978)

*Stephen II died
  before consecration
  and was dropped
  from the list of
  popes in 1961;
  Stephen III became
  Stephen II

ARCHBISHOPS OF CANTERBURY

ARCHBISHOP (DATE OF ACCESSION)

AUGUSTINE (597)
LAURENTIUS (604)
MELLITUS (619)
JUSTUS (624)
HONORIUS (627)
DEUSDEDIT (655)
THEODORUS (668)
BEORHTWEALD (693)
TATWINE (731)
NOTHELM (735)
CUTHBEORHT (740)
BREGUWINE (761)
JAENBEORHT (765)
ÆTHELHEARD (793)
WULFRED (805)
FEOLOGILD (832)
CEOLNOTH (833)
ÆTHELRED (870)
PLEGMUND (890)
ÆTHELHELM (914)
WULFHELM (923)
ODA (942)
ÆLFSIGE (959)
BEORHTHELM (959)
DUNSTAN (960)
ÆTHELGAR (988)
SIGERIC SERIO (990)
ÆLFRIC (995)
ÆLFHEAH (1005)
LYFING (1013)
ÆTHELNOTH (1020)
EADSIGE (1038)
ROBERT OF
  JUMIÈGES (1051)
STIGAND (1052)
LANFRANC (1070)
ANSELM (1093)
RALPH D'ESCURES
  (1114)
WILLIAM OF
  CORBEIL (1123)

THEOBALD OF BEC
  (1139)
THOMAS BECKET
  (1162)
RICHARD OF DOVER
  (1174)
BALDWIN (1184)
REGINALD
  FITZJOCELIN
  (1191)
HUBERT WALTER
  (1193)
REGINALD (1205)
JOHN DE GRAY
  (1205)
STEPHEN LANGTON
  (1213)
WALTER OF
  EVESHAM (1128)
RICHARD GRANT
  (Wethershed) (1229)
RALPH NEVILL (1231)
JOHN OF
  SITTINGBOURNE
  (1232)
JOHN BLUND (1232)
EDMUND RICH (1234)
BONIFACE OF
  SAVOY (1245)
ADAM OF
  CHILLENDEN
  (1270)
ROBERT KILWARDBY
  (1273)
ROBERT BURNELL
  (1278)
JOHN PECHAM
  (1279)
ROBERT
  WINCHELSEY
  (1295)

THOMAS COBHAM
  (1313)
WALTER REYNOLDS
  (1314)
SIMON MEPHAM
  (1328)
JOHN STRATFORD
  (1334)
JOHN OFFORD (1348)
THOMAS
  BRADWARDINE
  (1349)
SIMON ISLIP (1349)
SIMON LANGHAM
  (1366)
WILLIAM
  WHITTLESEY
  (1369)
SIMON SUDBURY
  (1375)
WILLIAM
  COURTENAY
  (1381)
THOMAS ARUNDEL
  (1397)
ROGER WALDEN
  (1398)
THOMAS ARUNDEL
  (1399)
HENRY CHICHELE
  (1414)
JOHN STAFFORD
  (1443)
JOHN KEMPE (1452)
THOMAS
  BOURGCHIER
  (1454)
JOHN MORTON
  (1486)
HENRY DEANE
  (1501)

WILLIAM WARHAM
  (1504)
THOMAS CRANMER
  (1533)
REGINALD POLE
  (1556)
MATTHEW PARKER
  (1559)
EDMUND GRINDAL
  (1576)
JOHN WHITGIFT
  (1583)
RICHARD BANCROFT
  (1604)
GEORGE ABBOT
  (1611)
WILLIAM LAUD (1633)
WILLIAM JUXON
  (1660)
GILBERT SHELDON
  (1663)
WILLIAM SANCROFT
  (1678)
JOHN TILLOTSON
  (1691)
THOMAS TENISON
  (1695)
WILLIAM WAKE
  (1716)
JOHN POTTER (1737)
THOMAS HERRING
  (1747)
MATTHEW HUTTON
  (1757)
THOMAS SECKER
  (1758)
FREDERICK
  CORNWALLIS
  (1768)
JOHN MOORE (1783)

CHARLES MANNERS SUTTON (1805)

WILLIAM HOWLEY (1828)

JOHN BIRD SUMNER (1848)

CHARLES THOMAS LONGLEY (1862)

ARCHIBALD CAMPBELL TAIT (1868)

EDWARD WHITE BENSON (1883)

FREDERICK TEMPLE (1896)

RANDALL THOMAS DAVIDSON (1903)

COSMO GORDON LANG (1928)

GEOFFREY FRANCIS FISHER (1945)

ARTHUR MICHAEL RAMSEY (1961)

FREDERICK DONALD COGGAN (1974)

ROBERT ALEXANDER KENNEDY RUNCIE (1980)

RELIGIOUS TERMS

2	5	5—continued	6—continued
BA	ABBOT	SYNOD	MANTRA
HO	ABYSS	TOTEM	MATINS
OM	AGATI	USHER	MISSAL
3	AISLE	VEDAS	NIGGUN
ALB	ALLEY	WAFER	NIMBUS
ARA	ALTAR	**6**	ORATIO
AUM	AMBRY	ABBACY	ORISON
HAJ	AMICE	ABODAH	PARVIS
PEW	ANGEL	ADVENT	PESACH
PIX	APRON	AGUNAH	PRAYER
PYX	ARMOR	AHIMSA	PULPIT
YAD	BANNS	AKASHA	ROCHET
4	BASON	AKEDAH	ROSARY
AMBO	BEADS	AL CHET	SANGHA
APSE	BIBLE	ANOINT	SERMON
AZAN	BIMAH	ANTHEM	SERVER
BEMA	BODHI	AUMBRY	SHARI'A
BUJI	BRIEF	AVODAH	SHRIVE
BULL	BUGIA	BARSOM	SPIRIT
COPE	BURSE	BAT KOL	SUTRAS
COWL	COTTA	BEADLE	TAUHID
FONT	CREED	BELFRY	TIPPET
HADJ	CROSS	CANTOR	VERGER
HAJJ	CRUET	CHOHAN	VESTRY
HALO	DIKKA	CHOVAH	**7**
HELL	EMETH	CHRISM	ACCIDIA
HOOD	EPHOD	CLERGY	ACCIDIE
HOST	FALDA	DHARMA	ACOLYTE
HYMN	GOHEI	DHYANA	AGRAPHA
JUBE	HYLIC	DITTHI	AMPULLA
KAMA	IHRAM	DOSSAL	ANGELUS
KNOP	KALPA	DUCHAN	APOSTIL
LENT	KARMA	EASTER	APOSTLE
MACE	LAVER	FLECHE	APPAREL
MASS	LIMBO	FRATER	ASHAMNU
NAOS	MOTZI	GLORIA	ATHEISM
NAVE	NICHE	HEAVEN	AUREOLE
OLAH	PASCH	HEKHAL	BADCHAN
RAMA	PESAH	HESPED	BANKERS
SOMA	PESHA	KAIROS	BAPTISM
TIEN	PSALM	KIBLAH	BATHING
VOID	ROSHI	KISMET	BELL COT
WAKE	SHIVA	KITTEL	BERAKAH
YOGA	STOUP	LITANY	BIRETTA

7—continued
CASSOCK
CHALICE
CHAMETZ
CHANCEL
CHANTRY
CHAPTER
CHAZZAN
CHRISOM
COLLECT
COMPLIN
CORNICE
CROSIER
CROZIER
DHARANI
DIOCESE
DIPTYCH
EILETON
FISTULA
GAYATRI
GELILAH
GEULLAH
GRADINE
GREMIAL
HASSOCK
HEATHEN
HEKDESH
INTROIT
KHEREBU
LECTERN
LOCULUS
MANIPLE
MINARET
MOZETTA
NARTHEX
NIRVANA
NOCTURN
PALLIUM
PENANCE
PILGRIM
PURUSHA
REQUIEM
REREDOS
SAMSARA
STHIBEL
TALLITH
TONSURE

7—continued
TRINITY
TZADDIK
VESPERS
WORSHIP

8
ABLUTION
ABSTEMII
A CAPELLA
AFFLATUS
AFFUSION
AFIKOMEN
AGNUS DEI
ANTIPHON
ARMORIUM
AUTO DA FE
AVE MARIA
BEADROLL
BELL COTE
BEMIDBAR
BENEFICE
BREVIARY
BUTSUDEN
CANCELLI
CANTICLE
CIBORIUM
CINCTURE
COMPLINE
CONCLAVE
CORPORAL
CRUCIFIX
DALMATIC
DIKERION
DISCIPLE
DOXOLOGY
EPIPHANY
EVENSONG
FRONTLET
HABDALAH
MANIPULE
NATIVITY
NER TAMID
NIVARANA
OBLATION
PAROKHET
PASSOVER
PREDELLA

8—continued
RESPONSE
SACRISTY
SURPLICE
TASHLICH
TRIPTYCH
VESTMENT

9
ADIAPHORA
ANAMNESIS
APOCRYPHA
ARBA KOSOT
ARCHANGEL
ASPERSION
CANDLEMAS
CARTOUCHE
CATACOMBS
CATECHISM
CERECLOTH
CHALITZAH
CHRISTMAS
COLLATION
COMMUNION
EPHPHETHA
EUCHARIST
FALDSTOOL
FLABELLUM
FORMULARY
MUNDATORY
OFFERTORY
PACE-AISLE
PURGATORY
SANCTUARY
YOM KIPPUR

10
ABSOLUTION
AGATHOLOGY
ALLOCUTION
AMBULATORY
ANTECHAPEL
APOCALYPSE
BALDACHINO
BAR MITZVAH
BAS MITZVAH
BAT MITZVAH
BENEDICTUS

10—continued
CATAFALQUE
CLERESTORY
CUTTY STOOL
HAGIOSCOPE
INDULGENCE
INTINCTION
INVOCATION
LADY CHAPEL
PRESBYTERY
SEXAGESIMA

11
ABBREVIATOR
ABOMINATION
AGNOSTICISM
ALITURGICAL
ANTEPENDIUM
ANTIMINSION
ASPERGILLUM
BENEDICTION
CHRISTENING
HUMERAL VEIL
INQUISITION
INVESTITURE
SCRIPTORIUM

12
ANTILEGOMENA
ARON HA-KODESH
ASH WEDNESDAY
CONFIRMATION
CONGREGATION
SEPTUAGESIMA

13
BEATIFICATION
BIRKAT HA-MAZON
EPITRACHELION

14
FOLDED CHASUBLE
MAUNDY THURSDAY

17
CONSUBSTANTIA-
  TION

RELIGIOUS BUILDINGS

3
WAT
4
CELL
KIRK
5
ABBEY

5—continued
BET AM
CELLA
DUOMO
HONDO
JINGU
JINJA

6
CHAPEL
CHURCH
MOSQUE
PAGODA
PRIORY

7
CHANTRY
CONVENT
DEANERY
MINSTER
8
BASILICA

8—continued	9	12	13
CLOISTER	BADRINATH	BET HA-KNESSET	ANGELUS TEMPLE
HOUNFORT	CATHEDRAL	BET HA-MIDRASH	
LAMASERY	MONASTERY	CHAPTER HOUSE	
	SYNAGOGUE	MEETINGHOUSE	

HINDU DEITIES

BRAHMA - the Creator
SHIVA - the Destroyer
VISHNU - the Preserver
INDRA - king of the gods; god of war and storm
AGNI - god of fire
AHI or IHI - the Sistrum Player
AMRITA - water of life
YAMA - king of the dead
VARUNA - god of water
SURYA - the sun-god
VAYU - god of the wind
KUBERA - god of wealth; guardian of the north
KARTTIKEYA - war-god; god of bravery
VISVAKARMA - architect for the gods
KAMA - god of desire
SARASVATI - goddess of speech
LAKSHMI - goddess of fortune

DEVI - a mother goddess
ADITI - goddess of heaven; mother of the gods
SARANYU - goddess of the clouds
PRITHIVI - earth-goddess; goddess of fertility
DITI - mother of the demons
MANASA - sacred mountain and lake
SHITALA - goddess of smallpox
GANESHA - god of literature, wisdom, and prosperity
GARUDA - the devourer, identified with fire and the sun
HANUMAN - a monkey chief
SUGRIVA - monkey king
BALI - demon who became king of heaven and earth
AMARAVATI - city of the gods
GANDHARVAS - celestial musicians
JYESTHA - goddess of misfortune
SOMA - ambrosial offering to the gods

GREEK AND ROMAN MYTHOLOGY

Mythological Characters

ACHILLES – Greek hero; invulnerable except for his heel
ADONIS – renowned for his beauty
AGAMEMNON – king of Mycenae
AJAX – Greek warrior
ATLAS – bore heaven on his shoulders
BELLEROPHON – Corinthian hero who rode winged horse Pegasus
BOREAS – the north wind
CERBERUS – three-headed dog, guarded Hades
CHARON – boatman who rowed dead across river Styx
CHARYBDIS – violent whirlpool
CIRCE – sorceress who had the power to turn men into beasts
CYCLOPS – one of a race of one-eyed giants (cyclopes)
DAEDALUS – craftsman; designed and built the labyrinth in Crete

GORGONS – three sisters (Stheno, Euryale, and Medusa) who had snakes for hair and whose appearance turned people to stone
HADES – the Underworld
HELEN OF TROY – famed for her beauty; cause of Trojan war
HERACLES – famed for his courage and strength; performed the twelve labours
HERCULES – Roman name for HERACLES
HYDRA – many-headed snake
JASON – led the Argonauts in search of the Golden Fleece
LETHE – river in Hades whose water caused forgetfulness
MIDAS – King of Phrygia whose touch turned everything to gold
MINOTAUR – monster with the head of a bull and the body of a man. It was kept in the Cretan labyrinth and fed with human flesh
NARCISSUS – beautiful youth who fell in love with his own reflection
ODYSSEUS – Greek hero of the Trojan war

OEDIPUS – king of Thebes; married his mother

OLYMPUS – a mountain; the home of the gods

ORPHEUS – skilled musician

PANDORA – the first woman; opened the box that released all varieties of evil

PERSEUS – Greek hero who killed the Gorgon Medusa.

POLYPHEMUS – leader of the Cyclopes

ROMULUS – founder of Rome

SATYRS – hoofed spirits of forests, fields, and streams

SCYLLA – six-headed sea monster

SIBYL – a prophetess

SIRENS – creatures depicted as half women, half birds, who lured sailors to their deaths

STYX – main river of Hades, across which Charon ferried the souls of the dead

THESEUS – Greek hero who killed the Cretan Minotaur

ULYSSES – Roman name for ODYSSEUS

GREEK GODS (ROMAN EQUIVALENT)

APHRODITE – goddess of beauty and love (VENUS)

APOLLO – god of poetry, music, and prophecy (APOLLO)

ARES – god of war (MARS)

ARTEMIS – goddess of the moon (DIANA)

ASCLEPIUS – god of medical art (AESCULAPIUS)

ATHENE – goddess of wisdom (MINERVA)

CHARITES – 3 daughters of Zeus: Euphrosyne, Aglaia, and Thalia; personified grace, beauty, and charm (GRACES)

CRONOS – god of agriculture (SATURN)

DEMETER – goddess of agriculture (CERES)

DIONYSUS – god of wine and fertility (BACCHUS)

EOS – goddess of dawn (AURORA)

EROS – god of love (CUPID)

FATES – 3 goddesses who determine man's destiny: Clotho, Lachesis, and Atropos

HEBE – goddess of youth (JUVENTAS)

HECATE – goddess of witchcraft (HECATE)

HELIOS – god of the sun (SOL)

HEPHAESTUS – god of destructive fire (VULCAN)

HERA – queen of heaven, goddess of women and marriage (JUNO)

HERMES – messenger of gods (MERCURY)

HESTIA – goddess of the hearth (VESTA)

HYPNOS – god of sleep (SOMNUS)

NEMESIS – goddess of retribution

PAN – god of woods and fields (FAUNUS)

PERSEPHONE – goddess of the Underworld (PROSERPINE)

PLUTO – god of the Underworld (PLUTO)

PLUTUS – god of wealth

POSEIDON – god of the sea (NEPTUNE)

RHEA – goddess of nature (CYBELE)

SELENE – goddess of the moon (LUNA)

THANATOS – god of death (MORS)

ZEUS – supreme god; god of sky and weather (JUPITER)

ROMAN GODS (GREEK EQUIVALENT)

AESCULAPIUS (ASCLEPIUS)

APOLLO (APOLLO)

AURORA (EOS)

BACCHUS (DIONYSUS)

CERES (DEMETER)

CUPID (EROS)

CYBELE (RHEA)

DIANA (ARTEMIS)

FAUNUS (PAN)

GRACES (CHARITES)

HECATE (HECATE)

JUNO (HERA)

JUPITER (ZEUS)

JUVENTAS (HEBE)

LUNA (SELENE)

MARS (ARES)

MERCURY (HERMES)

MINERVA (ATHENE)

MORS (THANATOS)

NEPTUNE (POSEIDON)

PLUTO (PLUTO)

PROSERPINE (PERSEPHONE)

SATURN (CRONOS)

SOL (HELIOS)

SOMNUS (HYPNOS)

VENUS (APHRODITE)

VESTA (HESTIA)

VULCAN (HEPHAESTUS)

THE NINE MUSES

CALLIOPE (EPIC POETRY)

CLIO (HISTORY)

ERATO (LOVE POETRY)

EUTERPE (LYRIC POETRY)

MELPOMENE (TRAGEDY)

POLYHYMNIA (SACRED SONG)

TERPSICHORE (DANCING)

THALIA (COMEDY)

URANIA (ASTRONOMY)

THE TWELVE LABOURS OF HERCULES

THE NEMEAN LION

THE LERNAEAN HYDRA

THE WILD BOAR OF ERYMANTHUS

THE STYMPHALIAN BIRDS

THE CERYNEIAN HIND

THE AUGEAN STABLES

THE CRETAN BULL

THE MARES OF DIOMEDES

THE GIRDLE OF HIPPOLYTE

THE CATTLE OF GERYON

THE GOLDEN APPLES OF THE HESPERIDES

THE CAPTURE OF CERBERUS

NORSE MYTHOLOGY

AEGIR – god of the sea

ALFHEIM – part of Asgard inhabited by the light elves

ASGARD – the home of the gods

ASK – name of the first man created, from a fallen tree

BALDER – god of the summer sun

BRAGI – god of poetry

EIR – goddess of healing

EMBLA – name of first woman, created from a fallen tree

FORSETI – god of justice

FREY – god of fertility and crops

FREYJA – goddess of love and night

FRIGG – Odin's wife; supreme goddess

GUNGNIR – Odin's magic spear

HEIMDAL – guardian of Asgard

HEL – goddess of the dead

HODUR – god of night

IDUN – wife of Bragi; guardian of the golden apples of youth

LOKI – god of evil

MIDGARD – the world of men

NORNS – three goddesses of destiny: Urd (Fate), Skuld (Being), and Verdandi (Necessity)

ODIN – supreme god; god of battle, inspiration, and death

RAGNAROK – final battle between gods and giants, in which virtually all life is destroyed

SIF – wife of Thor; her golden hair was cut off by Loki

SLEIPNIR – Odin's eight-legged horse

THOR – god of thunder

TYR – god of war

VALHALLA – hall in Asgard where Odin welcomed the souls of heroes killed in battle

VALKYRIES – nine handmaidens of Odin who chose men doomed to die in battle

YGGDRASILL – the World Tree, an ash linking all the worlds

YMIR – giant from whose body the world was formed

EGYPTIAN MYTHOLOGY

AMON-RA – supreme god

ANUBIS – jackel-headed son of Osiris; god of the dead

BES – god of marriage

GED – earth-god

HATHOR – cow-headed goddess of love

HORUS – hawk-headed god of light

ISIS – goddess of fertility

MAAT – goddess of law, truth, and justice

MONT – god of war

MUT – wife of Amon-Ra

NEHEH – god of eternity

NUN or NU – the primordial Ocean

NUT – goddess of the sky

OSIRIS – ruler of the afterlife

PTAH – god of the arts

RA – the sun god

RENPET – goddess of youth

SEKHMET – goddess of war

SET or SETH – god of evil

SHU – god of air

TEFNUT – goddess of dew and rain

THOTH – god of wisdom

UPUAUT – warrior-god; god of the dead

ARTHURIAN LEGEND

ARTHUR – legendary British leader of the Knights of the Round Table

AVALON – paradise

CAMELOT – capital of Arthur's kingdom

EXCALIBUR – Arthur's magic sword

GALAHAD – son of Lancelot; purest of the Knights of the Round Table; succeeded in the quest of the Grail

GAWAIN – nephew of Arthur, son of Morgan Le Fay; searched for the Grail

GRAIL (SANGREAL, THE HOLY GRAIL) —
said to be the vessel of the Last Supper; in
the custody of the Fisher King

GUINEVERE — wife of Arthur, lover of
Lancelot

KAY — foster brother of Arthur

LANCELOT or LAUNCELOT — knight and
lover of Queen Guinevere

MERLIN — magician and bard who prepared
Arthur for kingship

MODRED or MORDRED — nephew of Arthur,
son of Morgan Le Fay

MORGAN LE FAY — sorceress and healer;
sister of Arthur

PERCIVAL or PERCEVAL —knight who vowed
to seek the Grail

UTHER PENDRAGON — father of Arthur

VIVIANE — the Lady of the Lake

WORK

PROFESSIONS, TRADES, AND OCCUPATIONS

2	5—continued	5—continued	6—continued
GP	BAKER	QUILL	BUSKER
MD	BONZE	RABBI	BUTLER
MO	BOOTS	RATER	CABBIE
PA	BOSUN	REEVE	CABMAN
PM	CADDY	RUNER	CALKER
3	CHOIR	SCOUT	CANNER
DOC	CLERK	SEWER	CARTER
DON	CLOWN	SHOER	CARVER
GYP	COACH	SLAVE	CASUAL
PRO	COMIC	SMITH	CENSOR
REP	CRIER	SOWER	CLERGY
SPY	CRIMP	STAFF	CLERIC
VET	CURER	SWEEP	CODIST
4	DAILY	TAMER	COINER
AMAH	ENVOY	TAWER	COMBER
AYAH	EXTRA	TAXER	CONDER
BABU	FAKIR	TILER	COOLIE
BARD	FENCE	TUNER	COOPER
BOSS	FIFER	TUTOR	COPPER
CHAR	FILER	TYLER	CO-STAR
CHEF	FINER	USHER	COSTER
COOK	FLIER	VALET	COWBOY
CREW	GIPSY	VINER	COWMAN
DIVA	GLUER	**6**	CRITIC
DYER	GROOM	AIRMAN	CUTLER
GANG	GUARD	ARCHER	CUTTER
GRIP	GUIDE	ARTIST	DANCER
HACK	GUILD	AURIST	DEALER
HAND	HAKIM	AUTHOR	DIGGER
HEAD	HARPY	BAGMAN	DOCKER
HERD	HELOT	BAILER	DOCTOR
HIND	HIRER	BAILOR	DOWSER
MAGI	HIVER	BALKER	DRAPER
MAID	HOPPO	BANKER	DRAWER
MATE	LAMIA	BARBER	DRIVER
MIME	LEECH	BARGEE	DROVER
PAGE	LUTER	BARKER	EDITOR
PEON	MASON	BARMAN	FABLER
POET	MEDIC	BATMAN	FACTOR
SEER	MINER	BEARER	FARMER
SERF	NAVVY	BINDER	FELLER
SYCE	NURSE	BOFFIN	FICTOR
TOUT	OILER	BOOKIE	FISHER
WARD	OWLER	BOWMAN	FITTER
WHIP	PILOT	BREWER	FLAYER
5	PIPER	BROKER	FORGER
ACTOR	PLYER	BUGLER	FOWLER
AD-MAN	PUPIL	BURLER	FRAMER
AGENT	QUACK	BURSAR	FULLER

6—continued	6—continued	6—continued	6—continued
GAFFER	MUMPER	SERVER	WEEDER
GANGER	MYSTIC	SETTER	WELDER
GAOLER	NAILER	SEXTON	WHALER
GAUCHO	NOTARY	SHROFF	WORKER
GAUGER	NURSER	SINGER	WRIGHT
GIGOLO	OBOIST	SIRCAR	WRITER
GILDER	OILMAN	SKIVVY	**7**
GILLIE	ORATOR	SLATER	ABACIST
GLAZER	OSTLER	SLAVER	ABIGAIL
GLOVER	PACKER	SLAVEY	ACOLYTE
GRAVER	PARSON	SLEUTH	ACOLYTH
GROCER	PASTOR	SNARER	ACROBAT
GUIDER	PAVIER	SOCMAN	ACTRESS
GUIDON	PAVIOR	SORTER	ACTUARY
GUNMAN	PEDANT	SOUTER	ALEWIFE
GUNNER	PEDLAR	SPICER	ALMONER
HARPER	PENMAN	SQUIRE	ANALYST
HATTER	PICKER	STAGER	APPOSER
HAWKER	PIEMAN	STOKER	ARABIST
HEALER	PIRATE	STORER	ARBITER
HEAVER	PITMAN	SUTLER	ARTISAN
HODMAN	PLATER	TABLER	ARTISTE
HOOPER	PLAYER	TAILOR	ASSAYER
HORNER	PORTER	TAMPER	ASSIZER
HOSIER	POTBOY	TANNER	ASSURED
HUNTER	POTTER	TASKER	ASSURER
INTERN	PRIEST	TASTER	AUDITOR
ISSUER	PRUNER	TELLER	AVIATOR
JAILER	PURSER	TERMER	AWARDER
JAILOR	QUERRY	TESTER	BAILIFF
JOBBER	RABBIN	TILLER	BANDMAN
JOCKEY	RAGMAN	TINKER	BARMAID
JOINER	RANGER	TINMAN	BELLBOY
JOWTER	RATTER	TINNER	BELLHOP
JURIST	READER	TOLLER	BEST BOY
KEELER	REAPER	TOUTER	BIRDMAN
KEEPER	REAVER	TRACER	BLASTER
KILLER	RECTOR	TRADER	BLENDER
LACKEY	REGENT	TUBMAN	BOATMAN
LANDER	RELIEF	TURNER	BONDMAN
LASCAR	RENTER	TYCOON	BOOKMAN
LAWYER	RIGGER	TYPIST	BOTTLER
LECTOR	RINGER	USURER	BRIGAND
LENDER	ROBBER	VACHER	BUILDER
LOADER	ROOFER	VALUER	BURGLAR
LOGMAN	ROOTER	VAMPER	BUTCHER
LUMPER	SACKER	VANMAN	BUTTONS
MARKER	SAILOR	VASSAL	CALLBOY
MATRON	SALTER	VENDER	CAMBIST
MEDICO	SALVOR	VENDOR	CARRIER
MENDER	SAPPER	VERGER	CASEMAN
MENIAL	SARTOR	VERSER	CASHIER
MENTOR	SAWYER	VIEWER	CATERER
MERCER	SCRIBE	WAITER	CAULKER
MILKER	SEA-DOG	WALLER	CELLIST
MILLER	SEALER	WARDEN	CHANTER
MINTER	SEAMAN	WARDER	CHAPMAN
MONGER	SEINER	WARPER	CHEMIST
MORISK	SEIZOR	WASHER	CHORIST
MUMMER	SELLER	WEAVER	CLEANER

7—continued

CLICKER
CLIPPIE
COALMAN
COBBLER
COCKLER
COLLIER
CO-PILOT
COPYIST
CORONER
CORSAIR
COUNSEL
COURIER
COWHERD
COWPOKE
CROFTER
CROPPER
CURATOR
CURRIER
CUSTODE
DANSEUR
DENTIST
DIALIST
DIETIST
DITCHER
DOMINIE
DOORMAN
DRAGMAN
DRAPIER
DRAWBOY
DRAYMAN
DREDGER
DRESSER
DROGMAN
DRUMMER
DUSTMAN
FARRIER
FASCIST
FIDDLER
FIREMAN
FLESHER
FLORIST
FLUNKEY
FLUTIST
FOOTBOY
FOOTMAN
FOOTPAD
FOREMAN
FOUNDER
FRISEUR
FROGMAN
FUELLER
FURRIER
GATEMAN
GIRDLER
GLAZIER
GLEANER
GLEEMAN
GLOSSER
GRAFFER
GRAFTER

7—continued

GRAINER
GRANGER
GRANTEE
GRANTOR
GRAZIER
GRINDER
GYMNAST
HACKLER
HARPIST
HAULIER
HELOTRY
HERBIST
HERDMAN
HERITOR
HIGGLER
HOGHERD
HOSTLER
INDEXER
INLAYER
IRONIST
JANITOR
JUGGLER
JUNKMAN
JURYMAN
KEELMAN
KNACKER
KNITTER
LACEMAN
LINKBOY
LINKMAN
LOCKMAN
LOMBARD
MALTMAN
MANAGER
MANGLER
MARBLER
MARCHER
MARINER
MARSHAL
MATADOR
MATELOT
MEALMAN
MEATMAN
MIDWIFE
MILKMAN
MODISTE
MONEYER
MONITOR
MOOTMAN
MOULDER
NEWSBOY
OCULIST
OFFICER
ORDERER
ORDERLY
PACKMAN
PAGEBOY
PAINTER
PALMIST
PANTLER

7—continued

PEDDLER
PIANIST
PICADOR
PLANNER
PLANTER
PLEADER
PLUMBER
POACHER
POSTBOY
POSTMAN
PRESSER
PRESTOR
PRINTER
PUDDLER
RANCHER
REALTOR
REFINER
RIVETER
ROADMAN
ROASTER
RUSTLER
SACRIST
SADDLER
SAMPLER
SAMURAI
SCOURER
SCRAPER
SERVANT
SETTLER
SHARPER
SHEARER
SHIPPER
SHOPBOY
SHOWMAN
SHUNTER
SILKMAN
SIMPLER
SKINNER
SKIPPER
SLIPPER
SMELTER
SNIPPER
SOCAGER
SOLDIER
SOLOIST
SPENCER
SPINNER
SPOTTER
STAINER
STAMPER
STAPLER
STATIST
STEERER
STEWARD
SURGEON
SWABBER
SWEEPER
TABORER
TALLIER
TAPSTER

7—continued

TAXI-MAN
TEACHER
TIPSTER
TRACKER
TRAINER
TRAPPER
TRAWLER
TRIMMER
TRUCKER
TRUSTEE
TUMBLER
TURNKEY
VINTNER
VIOLIST
WAGONER
WARRIOR
WEBSTER
WEIGHER
WHEELER
WHETTER
WIREMAN
WOODMAN
WOOLMAN
WORKMAN
WRAPPER

8

ADSCRIPT
AERONAUT
ALGERINE
ANALYSER
APHORIST
APIARIST
APRON-MAN
ARBORIST
ARMORIST
ARMOURER
ARRESTOR
ASSESSOR
ATTORNEY
BAGMAKER
BAGPIPER
BANDSMAN
BARGEMAN
BEARHERD
BEDESMAN
BEDMAKER
BIT-MAKER
BLEACHER
BOATSMAN
BONDMAID
BONDSMAN
BOTANIST
BOWMAKER
BOXMAKER
BREWSTER
BROACHER
CABIN BOY
CELLARER
CERAMIST
CHANDLER

8—continued	8—continued	8—continued	8—continued
CHOIRBOY	GANGSTER	MILLHAND	RIVETTER
CIDERIST	GARDENER	MILLINER	ROMANCER
CLAQUEUR	GAVELMAN	MINISTER	RUGMAKER
CLOTHIER	GENDARME	MINSTREL	RUMOURER
COACHMAN	GLASSMAN	MODELLER	SALESMAN
CO-AUTHOR	GOATHERD	MULETEER	SATIRIST
CODIFIER	GODSMITH	MURALIST	SAWBONES
COISTRIL	GOSSIPER	MUSICIAN	SCULLION
COLLATOR	GOVERNOR	NEWSHAWK	SCULPTOR
COMEDIAN	GUARDIAN	NOVELIST	SEAMSTER
COMPILER	GUNSMITH	ONION-MAN	SEA-ROVER
COMPOSER	HAMMERER	OPERATOR	SEASONER
CONCLAVE	HANDMAID	OPTICIAN	SEEDSMAN
CONJURER	HANDYMAN	ORDAINER	SEMPSTER
CONVEYOR	HATMAKER	ORDINAND	SERVITOR
COURTIER	HAYMAKER	ORGANIST	SHEARMAN
COW-LEECH	HEAD COOK	OUTRIDER	SHEPHERD
COXSWAIN	HEADSMAN	OVERSEER	SHIPMATE
CROUPIER	HELMSMAN	PARGETER	SHIP'S BOY
CUTPURSE	HENCHMAN	PARODIST	SHOPGIRL
DAIRYMAN	HERDSMAN	PENMAKER	SHOWGIRL
DANSEUSE	HIRELING	PERFUMER	SIDESMAN
DECKHAND	HISTRION	PETERMAN	SIMPLIST
DEFENDER	HOME HELP	PEWTERER	SKETCHER
DESIGNER	HOTELIER	PICAROON	SMUGGLER
DIRECTOR	HOUSEBOY	PLOUGHER	SOLDIERY
DOG-LEECH	HUCKSTER	POLISHER	SPACEMAN
DOMESTIC	HUNTSMAN	PORTRESS	SPEARMAN
DOUGHBOY	IMPORTER	POSTILER	SPEEDCOP
DRAGOMAN	IMPROVER	POTMAKER	SPURRIER
DRUGGIST	INKMAKER	PREACHER	STARCHER
EDUCATOR	INVENTOR	PREFACER	STITCHER
EMBALMER	JAPANNER	PRELUDER	STOCKMAN
EMISSARY	JET PILOT	PRESSMAN	STOREMAN
ENGINEER	JEWELLER	PROBATOR	STRIPPER
ENGRAVER	JONGLEUR	PROCURER	STRUMMER
ENROLLER	KIPPERER	PROMOTER	STUNTMAN
EPIC POET	LABOURER	PROMPTER	SUPPLIER
ESSAYIST	LANDGIRL	PROSAIST	SURVEYOR
ESSOINER	LANDLADY	PROVIDER	SWINDLER
EXORCIST	LANDLORD	PSALMIST	TABOURER
EXPLORER	LAPIDARY	PUBLICAN	TALLYMAN
EXPORTER	LARCENER	PUGILIST	TAVERNER
FABULIST	LARDERER	PURVEYOR	TEAMSTER
FACTOTUM	LEADSMAN	QUARRIER	THATCHER
FALCONER	LECTURER	RAFTSMAN	THESPIAN
FAMULIST	LINESMAN	RANCHERO	THRESHER
FARMHAND	LUMBERER	RAPPEREE	TIN MINER
FERRYMAN	MAGICIAN	RECEIVER	TINSMITH
FIGURANT	MAGISTER	REGRATER	TORTURER
FILMSTAR	MALTSTER	RELESSEE	TOYMAKER
FINISHER	MASSEUSE	RELESSOR	TRIPEMAN
FISHWIFE	MEASURER	REPAIRER	TRUCKMAN
FLATFOOT	MECHANIC	REPORTER	TURNCOCK
FLAUTIST	MEDALIST	RESETTER	TURNSPIT
FLETCHER	MELODIST	RESTORER	TUTORESS
FODDERER	MERCATOR	RETAILER	UNIONIST
FORESTER	MERCHANT	RETAINER	VALUATOR
FORGEMAN	METAL-MAN	REVIEWER	VINTAGER
FUGLEMAN	MILKMAID	REWRITER	VIRTUOSO

8—continued	9—continued	9—continued	9—continued
VOCALIST	CELLARMAN	EXCHANGER	HYGIENIST
VOLUMIST	CHARWOMAN	EXCISEMAN	HYPNOTIST
WAITRESS	CHAUFFEUR	EXECUTIVE	INCUMBENT
WALKER-ON	CHEAPJACK	EXERCITOR	INGRAFTER
WARDRESS	CHORISTER	EXORCISER	INNHOLDER
WARRENER	CLARIFIER	FABRICANT	INNKEEPER
WATCHMAN	CLERGYMAN	FASHIONER	INSCRIBER
WATERMAN	CLINICIAN	FELT-MAKER	INSPECTOR
WET NURSE	CLOGMAKER	FIGURANTE	INTENDANT
WHALEMAN	COALMINER	FILM ACTOR	IRONSMITH
WHITENER	COALOWNER	FILM EXTRA	ITINERANT
WHITSTER	COLLECTOR	FILM-MAKER	JACK-SMITH
WIGMAKER	COLOURIST	FINANCIER	JOB-MASTER
WINNOWER	COLUMNIST	FIRE-EATER	KENNEL-MAN
WOOL-DYER	COMPRADOR	FISH-CURER	LACEMAKER
WRESTLER	CONCIERGE	FISHERMAN	LACQUERER
9	CONDUCTOR	FISH-WOMAN	LADY'S MAID
ALCHEMIST	CONSERVER	FLAG-MAKER	LAND AGENT
ALLUMINOR	COSMONAUT	FLAX-WENCH	LANDREEVE
ANATOMIST	COST CLERK	FLYFISHER	LARCENIST
ANNOTATOR	COSTUMIER	FREELANCE	LAUNDERER
ANNOUNCER	COURTESAN	FREIGHTER	LAUNDRESS
ARBORATOR	COUTURIER	FRIPPERER	LEGIONARY
ARCHERESS	COWFEEDER	FRUITERER	LIBRARIAN
ARCHITECT	COWKEEPER	FURBISHER	LINOTYPER
ARCHIVIST	CRACKSMAN	FURNISHER	LIONTAMER
ART CRITIC	CRAFTSMAN	GALVANIST	LIVERYMAN
ART DEALER	CRAYONIST	GASFITTER	LOAN AGENT
ARTIFICER	CYMBALIST	GAZETTEER	LOCKMAKER
ASTRONAUT	DAILY HELP	GEM-CUTTER	LOCKSMITH
ATTENDANT	DAIRYMAID	GEOLOGIST	LOG-ROLLER
AUTHORESS	DECORATOR	GLADIATOR	LUMBERMAN
BALLADIST	DECRETIST	GLUEMAKER	MACHINIST
BALLERINA	DESK CLERK	GOLDSMITH	MAGNETIST
BANK AGENT	DETECTIVE	GONDOLIER	MAJORDOMO
BARRISTER	DICE-MAKER	GOSPELLER	MALE MODEL
BARROW BOY	DIE-SINKER	GOVERNESS	MALE NURSE
BEEFEATER	DIETETIST	GROUNDMAN	MAN-AT-ARMS
BEEKEEPER	DIETITIAN	GUARDSMAN	MANNEQUIN
BIOLOGIST	DIRECTRIX	GUERRILLA	MECHANIST
BOATSWAIN	DISPENSER	GUITARIST	MEDALLIST
BODYGUARD	DISSECTOR	GUN-RUNNER	MEMOIRIST
BOILERMAN	DISTILLER	HARLEQUIN	MERCENARY
BONDSLAVE	DOCTORESS	HARMONIST	MESMERIST
BONDWOMAN	DRAFTSMAN	HARPOONER	MESSENGER
BOOKMAKER	DRAMATIST	HARVESTER	METALLIST
BOOTBLACK	DRAWLATCH	HELLENIST	METRICIAN
BOOTMAKER	DRUM-MAKER	HERBALIST	MILL-OWNER
BUCCANEER	DRYSALTER	HERBARIAN	MODELGIRL
BURNISHER	ECOLOGIST	HERBORIST	MORTICIAN
BUS DRIVER	EMBEZZLER	HERB-WOMAN	MUFFIN-MAN
CAB DRIVER	ENAMELLER	HIRED HAND	MUSKETEER
CAFÉ OWNER	ENGINEMAN	HIRED HELP	MUSKETOON
CAMERAMAN	ENGROSSER	HISTORIAN	MYOLOGIST
CAR DRIVER	EPITOMIST	HOG-RINGER	NAVIGATOR
CARETAKER	ERRAND BOY	HOMEOPATH	NEGOTIANT
CARPENTER	ESTIMATOR	HOP-PICKER	NEOLOGIAN
CARVANEER	EXAMINANT	HOSTELLER	NEOLOGIST
CASEMAKER	EXCAVATOR	HOUSEMAID	NEWSAGENT
CATECHIST	EXCERPTOR	HOUSEWIFE	NURSEMAID

9—continued

ODD JOB MAN
OFFICE BOY
OPERATIVE
ORDINATOR
OSTEOPATH
OTOLOGIST
OUTFITTER
PASQUILER
PAYMASTER
PEDAGOGUE
PERFORMER
PHYSICIAN
PHYSICIST
PINKMAKER
PITSAWYER
PLANISHER
PLASTERER
PLOUGHBOY
PLOUGHMAN
PLURALIST
POETASTER
POINTSMAN
POLICEMAN
POP ARTIST
PORTERESS
PORTRAYER
PORTREEVE
POSTILION
POSTWOMAN
POULTERER
PRACTISER
PRECENTOR
PRECEPTOR
PREDICANT
PRELECTOR
PRIESTESS
PRIVATEER
PROFESSOR
PROFILIST
PROVEDORE
PUBLICIST
PUBLISHER
PULPITEER
PUPPETEER
PYTHONESS
QUALIFIER
QUARRYMAN
RACKETEER
RAILMAKER
RECRUITER
REFORMIST
REHEARSER
RIBBONMAN
ROADMAKER
ROPEMAKER
ROUNDSMAN
RUM-RUNNER
SACRISTAN
SAFEMAKER
SAILMAKER

9—continued

SCARIFIER
SCAVENGER
SCENARIST
SCHOLIAST
SCHOOLMAN
SCIENTIST
SCRIVENER
SCYTHEMAN
SEA-ROBBER
SECRETARY
SHIPOWNER
SHIP'S MATE
SHOEBLACK
SHOEMAKER
SIGHTSMAN
SIGNALMAN
SINOLOGUE
SOAPMAKER
SOLICITOR
SONNETEER
SORCERESS
STABLEBOY
STABLEMAN
STAGEHAND
STATIONER
STAY-MAKER
STEERSMAN
STEVEDORE
SUBEDITOR
SUCCENTOR
SUR-MASTER
SWAN-UPPER
SWINEHERD
SWITCHMAN
SWORDSMAN
SYNDICATE
SYNOPTIST
TABLEMAID
TACTICIAN
TAILORESS
TEATASTER
TENTMAKER
TEST PILOT
THERAPIST
THEURGIST
THROWSTER
TIMBERMAN
TIRE-WOMAN
TOOLSMITH
TOWN CLERK
TOWNCRIER
TRADESMAN
TRAGEDIAN
TRAVELLER
TREASURER
TREPANNER
TRIBUTARY
TRUMPETER
TYMPANIST
USHERETTE

9—continued

VARNISHER
VERSIFIER
VETTURINO
VEXILLARY
VIOLINIST
VOLCANIST
VOLTIGEUR
WADSETTER
WARRANTEE
WARRANTER
WASHERMAN
WAXWORKER
WHITESTER
WINEMAKER
WOOD-REEVE
WORKWOMAN
ZOOKEEPER
ZOOLOGIST
ZOOTOMIST

10

ABLE SEAMAN
ACCOMPTANT
ACCOUCHEUR
ACCOUNTANT
ACOLOTHIST
ADVERTISER
AEROLOGIST
AGROLOGIST
AGRONOMIST
AIR HOSTESS
AIR STEWARD
ALGEBRAIST
AMANUENSIS
APOTHECARY
APPRENTICE
ARBALISTER
ARBITRATOR
ASTROLOGER
ASTRONOMER
ATMOLOGIST
AUCTIONEER
AUDIT CLERK
BALLOONIST
BALLPLAYER
BANDMASTER
BASEBALLER
BASSOONIST
BEADSWOMAN
BEAUTICIAN
BELL-HANGER
BELL-RINGER
BIOCHEMIST
BIOGRAPHER
BLACKSMITH
BLADESMITH
BLOCKMAKER
BLUEJACKET
BOMBARDIER
BONDSWOMAN
BONESETTER

10—continued

BOOKBINDER
BOOKHOLDER
BOOKKEEPER
BOOKSELLER
BOOTLEGGER
BRICKLAYER
BRICKMAKER
BRUSHMAKER
BUREAUCRAT
BUTTERWIFE
CAREER GIRL
CARTOONIST
CARTWRIGHT
CASH-KEEPER
CAT BREEDER
CAT BURGLAR
CERAMICIST
CHAIR-MAKER
CHARGEHAND
CHARIOTEER
CHIRURGEON
CHORUS GIRL
CHRONICLER
CIRCUITEER
CLAIM AGENT
CLAPPER BOY
CLOCKMAKER
CLOG DANCER
CLOTH MAKER
COACHMAKER
COAL-BACKER
COAL-FITTER
COALHEAVER
COAL-MASTER
CO-ASSESSOR
COASTGUARD
COLLOCUTOR
COLLOQUIST
COLPORTEUR
COMEDIENNE
COMPOSITOR
COMPOUNDER
CONCORDIST
CONTRACTOR
CONTROLLER
COPYHOLDER
COPYWRITER
CORDWAINER
COUNSELLOR
CULTIVATOR
CUSTOMS MAN
CYTOLOGIST
DELINEATOR
DIRECTRESS
DISC JOCKEY
DISCOUNTER
DISCOVERER
DISHWASHER
DISPATCHER
DISTRAINER

10—continued

10—continued	10—continued	10—continued	10—continued
DISTRAINOR	HOROLOGIST	PASQUILANT	SIGNWRITER
DOCKMASTER	HORSECOPER	PASTRY-COOK	SILENTIARY
DOG BREEDER	HORSE-LEECH	PATHFINDER	SILK-MERCER
DOG-FANCIER	HOUSE AGENT	PAWNBROKER	SILK-WEAVER
DOORKEEPER	HUCKSTRESS	PEARL-DIVER	SINOLOGIST
DRAMATURGE	HUSBANDMAN	PEDIATRIST	SKIRMISHER
DRESSMAKER	INOCULATOR	PEDICURIST	SLOP SELLER
DRUMMER-BOY	INSTITUTOR	PELTMONGER	SNEAK THIEF
DRY CLEANER	INSTRUCTOR	PENOLOGIST	SOAP-BOILER
EMBLAZONER	INTERAGENT	PERRUQUIER	SPECIALIST
EMBOWELLER	IRONMONGER	PHARMACIST	STAFF NURSE
ENAMELLIST	IRONWORKER	PHILOLOGER	STEERSMATE
EPHEMERIST	JOURNALIST	PIANO TUNER	STEWARDESS
EPITAPHIST	JOURNEYMAN	PICKPOCKET	STIPULATOR
EPITOMIZER	KENNELMAID	PLATELAYER	STOCKTAKER
EVANGELIST	KEYBOARDER	PLAYWRIGHT	STONE-BORER
EXAMINATOR	LAUNDRYMAN	POLITICIAN	STONEMASON
EXPLORATOR	LAW OFFICER	PORTIONIST	STRATEGIST
EYE-SERVANT	LEGISLATOR	POSTILLION	STREET-WARD
FELL-MONGER	LIBRETTIST	POSTMASTER	SUPERCARGO
FILE-CUTTER	LIGHTERMAN	PRESCRIBER	SUPERVISER
FILIBUSTER	LIME-BURNER	PRIMA DONNA	SURCHARGER
FILM EDITOR	LINOTYPIST	PRIVATE EYE	SURFACE-MAN
FIREMASTER	LIQUIDATOR	PROCURATOR	SWAN-KEEPER
FIRE-WORKER	LOBSTERMAN	PROGRAMMER	SYMPHONIST
FISHMONGER	LOCK-KEEPER	PRONOUNCER	TALLY CLERK
FLIGHT CREW	LUMBERJACK	PROPRIETOR	TASKMASTER
FLOWERGIRL	MAGISTRATE	PROSPECTOR	TAXI-DRIVER
FLUVIALIST	MANAGERESS	PROTRACTOR	TEA-BLENDER
FOLK-DANCER	MANICURIST	PROVEDITOR	TEA PLANTER
FOLK-SINGER	MANSERVANT	PUNCTURIST	TECHNICIAN
FORECASTER	MATCHMAKER	PYROLOGIST	TECHNOCRAT
FRAME-MAKER	MEAT-HAWKER	QUIZ-MASTER	THEOGONIST
FREEBOOTER	MEDICAL MAN	RAILWAYMAN	THEOLOGIAN
FUND RAISER	MILITIAMAN	RAT-CATCHER	THEOLOGIST
GAMEKEEPER	MILLWRIGHT	RECITALIST	THRENODIST
GAME WARDEN	MINERALIST	RESEARCHER	TIMEKEEPER
GEAR-CUTTER	MINISTRESS	RINGMASTER	TRACTARIAN
GEISHA GIRL	MINTMASTER	ROADMENDER	TRADE UNION
GENETICIST	MISSIONARY	ROPEDANCER	TRAFFIC COP
GEOGRAPHER	MOONSHINER	ROUGHRIDER	TRAFFICKER
GLEE-SINGER	NATURALIST	SAFEBLOWER	TRAM-DRIVER
GLOSSARIST	NAUTCH GIRL	SALES FORCE	TRANSACTOR
GLUE-BOILER	NEGOTIATOR	SALESWOMAN	TRANSLATOR
GOLD-BEATER	NEWSCASTER	SCHOOLMARM	TRAWLERMAN
GOLD-DIGGER	NEWS EDITOR	SCRUTINEER	TREASURESS
GOLD-WASHER	NEWSVENDOR	SCULPTRESS	TROUBADOUR
GOVERNANTE	NEWSWRITER	SEA-CAPTAIN	TYPESETTER
GRAMMARIAN	NIGHT NURSE	SEAMSTRESS	UNDERTAKER
GUNSLINGER	NOSOLOGIST	SECOND MATE	VETERINARY
HACKNEY-MAN	NURSERYMAN	SEMINARIST	VICTUALLER
HALL PORTER	OBITUARIST	SERVING-MAN	VIVANDIÈRE
HANDMAIDEN	OIL PAINTER	SEXOLOGIST	VOCABULIST
HARVESTMAN	ORCHARDIST	SHIP-BROKER	WAINWRIGHT
HATCHELLER	OSTEOLOGER	SHIP-HOLDER	WARRIORESS
HEAD PORTER	OVERLOOKER	SHIPMASTER	WATCHMAKER
HEAD WAITER	PANEGYRIST	SHIPWRIGHT	WATERGUARD
HIEROPHANT	PANTRYMAID	SHOPFITTER	WHARFINGER
HIGHWAYMAN	PARK-KEEPER	SHOPKEEPER	WHITESMITH
HORN PLAYER	PARK-RANGER	SHOPWALKER	WHOLESALER

10—continued	11—continued	11—continued	11—continued
WINEGROWER	CHIROMANCER	GLASS-BENDER	MUSIC MASTER
WINE-WAITER	CHIROPODIST	GLASS-BLOWER	MYOGRAPHIST
WIREWORKER	CHOIRMASTER	GLASS-CUTTER	MYSTERIARCH
WOODCARVER	CHRONOLOGER	GLASS-WORKER	MYTHOLOGIST
WOODCUTTER	CINDER-WENCH	GRAVE-DIGGER	NECROLOGIST
WOOD-MONGER	CLOCK-SETTER	GREENGROCER	NECROMANCER
WOODWORKER	CLOTH-WORKER	HABERDASHER	NEEDLEWOMAN
WOOL-CARDER	COAL-WHIPPER	HAGIOLOGIST	NEUROLOGIST
WOOL-COMBER	COFFIN-MAKER	HAIRDRESSER	NEUROTOMIST
WOOL-DRIVER	COGNOSCENTE	HAIR STYLIST	NIGHT PORTER
WOOL-GROWER	COLLAR-MAKER	HARDWAREMAN	NIGHTWORKER
WOOL-SORTER	CONDISCIPLE	HEDGE-PRIEST	NOMENCLATOR
WOOL-TRADER	CONDOTTIERE	HEDGE-WRITER	NUMISMATIST
WOOL-WINDER	CONDUCTRESS	HIEROLOGIST	OFFICE STAFF
YARDMASTER	CONFEDERATE	HISTOLOGIST	ONION-SELLER
ZINC-WORKER	CONGRESSMAN	HORSE DOCTOR	OPERA SINGER
ZOOGRAPHER	CONSECRATOR	HORSE TRADER	OPHIOLOGIST
ZYMOLOGIST	CONSERVATOR	HOSPITALLER	ORIENTALIST
11	CONSTITUENT	HOTEL-KEEPER	ORTHOPEDIST
ACCOMPANIST	CONVEYANCER	HOUSEMASTER	OSTEOLOGIST
ACCOUCHEUSE	COPPERSMITH	HOUSEMOTHER	PAMPHLETEER
ACOUSTICIAN	COSMOGONIST	HYMNOLOGIST	PANEL-BEATER
ADJUDICATOR	COSMOLOGIST	ILLUMINATOR	PANTOMIMIST
ALLOPATHIST	CRANE DRIVER	ILLUSIONIST	PAPERHANGER
ANNUNCIATOR	CRIMEWRITER	ILLUSTRATOR	PARLOURMAID
ANTIQUARIAN	CUB REPORTER	INFANTRYMAN	PATHOLOGIST
APPLE-GROWER	CYPHER CLERK	INSTITUTIST	PATTENMAKER
ARBITRATRIX	DELIVERY MAN	INTERPRETER	PEARLFISHER
ARMY OFFICER	DEMOGRAPHER	INTERVIEWER	PETROLOGIST
ARQUEBUSIER	DISPENSATOR	IRON-FOUNDER	PETTIFOGGER
ARTILLERIST	DRAUGHTSMAN	IVORY-CARVER	PHILATELIST
AUDIO TYPIST	DUTY OFFICER	IVORY-TURNER	PHILOLOGIST
AUSCULTATOR	ELECTRICIAN	IVORY-WORKER	PHONOLOGIST
BANK CASHIER	EMBLEMATIST	KITCHENMAID	PHYTOLOGIST
BANK MANAGER	EMBROIDERER	LAMPLIGHTER	POLYPHONIST
BARGEMASTER	ENTERTAINER	LAND STEWARD	PORK BUTCHER
BASKETMAKER	ESTATE AGENT	LAUNDRYMAID	PORTRAITIST
BATTI-WALLAH	ETHNOLOGIST	LEADING LADY	PRECEPTRESS
BATTOLOGIST	ETYMOLOGIST	LEDGER CLERK	PRINT-SELLER
BEACHCOMBER	EXECUTIONER	LIFEBOATMAN	PROBATIONER
BELL-FOUNDER	EXTORTIONER	LIGHTKEEPER	PROMULGATOR
BILL-STICKER	FACE-PAINTER	LINEN DRAPER	PROOFREADER
BIRD-CATCHER	FACTORY HAND	LITHOLOGIST	PROPERTY MAN
BIRD-FANCIER	FAITH HEALER	LITHOTOMIST	PROPRIETRIX
BIRD-WATCHER	FANCY-MONGER	LORRY DRIVER	QUESTIONARY
BOATBUILDER	FIELD WORKER	MADRIGALIST	RADIOLOGIST
BODY SERVANT	FIGURE-MAKER	MAIDSERVANT	RAG MERCHANT
BOILERSMITH	FILING CLERK	MAMMALOGIST	REPRESENTER
BONDSERVANT	FINESTILLER	MASTER BAKER	REPUBLISHER
BOOT-CATCHER	FIRE BRIGADE	MECHANICIAN	RHETORICIAN
BROADCASTER	FIRE INSURER	MEDICINE MAN	ROADSWEEPER
BULLFIGHTER	FLAX-DRESSER	MEMORIALIST	SAFEBREAKER
CANDLEMAKER	FLESH-MONGER	MERCHANTMAN	SANDWICH MAN
CAR SALESMAN	FOURBISSEUR	METAL WORKER	SANSCRITIST
CAT'S-MEAT-MAN	FRINGE-MAKER	MINIATURIST	SAXOPHONIST
CHAIR-MENDER	FRUIT PICKER	MONEY-BROKER	SCOUTMASTER
CHALK-CUTTER	FUNAMBULIST	MONEY-LENDER	SCRAPDEALER
CHAMBERMAID	GALLEY-SLAVE	MONOGRAPHER	SCRIP-HOLDER
CHIFFONNIER	GENEALOGIST	MULE-SPINNER	SECRET AGENT
CHIROLOGIST	GHOSTWRITER	MUSIC CRITIC	SEDITIONARY

11—continued

SERVANT GIRL
SERVING-MAID
SHARE-BROKER
SHEEPFARMER
SHEPHERDESS
SHIPBREAKER
SHIPBUILDER
SHIP'S MASTER
SHOPSTEWARD
SILK-THROWER
SILVERSMITH
SLAUGHTERER
SLAVE-DRIVER
SLAVE-HOLDER
SMALLHOLDER
SOCIOLOGIST
STAGE-DRIVER
STEEPLEJACK
STOCKBROKER
STOCKJOBBER
STONECUTTER
STOREKEEPER
SUNDRIESMAN
SYSTEM-MAKER
TAXIDERMIST
TELEGRAPHER
TELEPHONIST
TICKET AGENT
TOASTMASTER
TOBACCONIST
TOOTH-DRAWER
TOPOGRAPHER
TORCH-BEARER
TOWN PLANNER
TOXOPHILITE
TRAIN-BEARER
TRANSCRIBER
TRANSPORTER
TRAVEL AGENT
TYPE-FOUNDER
TYPOGRAPHER
UNDERBEARER
UNDERLETTER
UNDERWRITER
UPHOLSTERER
VERSEMONGER
VINE-DRESSER
WASHERWOMAN
WATCHKEEPER
WAX-CHANDLER
WHEEL-CUTTER
WHEELWRIGHT
WHITEWASHER
WITCH-DOCTOR
WOOL-STAPLER
XYLOPHONIST
ZOOGRAPHIST

12

ACCORDIONIST
ACTOR MANAGER

12—continued

AMBULANCE MAN
ANAESTHETIST
ANIMALCULIST
ARCHEOLOGIST
ARTILLERYMAN
BALLET DANCER
BALLET MASTER
BANTAMWEIGHT
BELLOWS-MAKER
BIBLIOLOGIST
BIBLIOPEGIST
BIBLIOPOLIST
BOOKING CLERK
BUS CONDUCTOR
CABINET-MAKER
CALLIGRAPHER
CARICATURIST
CARPET-FITTER
CARTOGRAPHER
CATACLYSMIST
CEROGRAPHIST
CHEESEMONGER
CHIEF CASHIER
CHIMNEY-SWEEP
CHIROPRACTOR
CHRONOLOGIST
CHURCHWARDEN
CIRCUIT RIDER
CIVIL SERVANT
CLARINETTIST
CLERK OF WORKS
CLOTH-SHEARER
COACH-BUILDER
COLEOPTERIST
COMMISSIONER
CONCHOLOGIST
CONFECTIONER
CORN CHANDLER
COSMOGRAPHER
COSTERMONGER
CRAFTS-MASTER
CRANIOLOGIST
CRYPTOGAMIST
DANCE HOSTESS
DEEP-SEA DIVER
DEMONOLOGIST
DEMONSTRATOR
DENDROLOGIST
DRAMATURGIST
ECCLESIASTIC
EGYPTOLOGIST
ELECUTIONIST
ENGASTRIMUTH
ENGINE-DRIVER
ENTOMOLOGIST
ENTOMOTOMIST
ENTREPRENEUR
ESCAPOLOGIST
ETHNOGRAPHER
EXPERIMENTER

12—continued

FAMILY DOCTOR
FARM LABOURER
FILM DIRECTOR
FILM PRODUCER
FIRST OFFICER
FLYING DOCTOR
FOOTPLATEMAN
GEOMETRICIAN
GERIATRICIAN
GLASS-GRINDER
GLOSSOLOGIST
GREASEMONKEY
GUILD BROTHER
GYMNOSOPHIST
GYNECOLOGIST
HAGIOGRAPHER
HALIOGRAPHER
HARNESS-MAKER
HEAD GARDENER
HOMEOPATHIST
HORSE-BREAKER
HORSE-COURSER
HORSE-KNACKER
HOTEL MANAGER
HOUSEBREAKER
HOUSEPAINTER
HOUSE STEWARD
HOUSE SURGEON
HYDROGRAPHER
HYDROPATHIST
HYPOTHECATOR
IMMUNOLOGIST
IMPROPRIATOR
INSTRUCTRESS
INVOICE CLERK
JERRY-BUILDER
JOINT-TRUSTEE
JURISCONSULT
JUVENILE LEAD
KING'S COUNSEL
KNIFE-GRINDER
KNIFE-THROWER
LABOURING MAN
LAND SURVEYOR
LATH-SPLITTER
LEADER-WRITER
LEXICOLOGIST
LITHOGRAPHER
LONGSHOREMAN
LOSS ADJUSTER
LUMBER-DEALER
MAITRE D'HOTEL
MAKE-UP ARTIST
MALACOLOGIST
MANUAL WORKER
MANUFACTURER
MASS PRODUCER
MEAT-SALESMAN
METALLURGIST
MEZZO SOPRANO

12—continued

MICROSCOPIST
MINERALOGIST
MISCELLANIST
MONEY-CHANGER
MONOGRAPHIST
MORRIS-DANCER
MOSAIC-ARTIST
MOSAIC-WORKER
MYTHOGRAPHER
NEWSPAPERMAN
NUTRITIONIST
OBSTETRICIAN
OFFICE JUNIOR
ONEIROCRITIC
ORCHESTRATOR
ORGAN-BUILDER
ORGAN-GRINDER
ORTHODONTIST
ORTHOGRAPHER
OVARIOTOMIST
PAPER-STAINER
PATTERN-MAKER
PEDIATRICIAN
PHONOGRAPHER
PHOTOGRAPHER
PHRENOLOGIST
PHYSIOLOGIST
PLANT MANAGER
PLOUGHWRIGHT
PLUMBER'S MATE
PLYER-FOR-HIRE
POSTMISTRESS
PRACTITIONER
PRESS OFFICER
PRESTIGIATOR
PRISON WARDER
PRIZE-FIGHTER
PROFESSIONAL
PROPAGANDIST
PROPRIETRESS
PSYCHIATRIST
PSYCHOLOGIST
PUBLICITY MAN
PUPIL-TEACHER
PUPPET-PLAYER
QUARRY MASTER
RACING DRIVER
RADIOGRAPHER
RECEPTIONIST
REMEMBRANCER
RESTAURATEUR
RIDING-MASTER
RIGHT-HAND MAN
RUBBER-GRADER
SALES MANAGER
SCENE-PAINTER
SCENE-SHIFTER
SCHOOLMASTER
SCREENWRITER
SCRIPTWRITER

12—continued
SCULLERY-MAID
SEED-MERCHANT
SEISMOLOGIST
SHARECROPPER
SHARPSHOOTER
SHIP CHANDLER
SHIP'S HUSBAND
SHOE-REPAIRER
SILVER-BEATER
SLAUGHTERMAN
SNAKE-CHARMER
SOCIAL WORKER
SOIL MECHANIC
SPECIAL AGENT
SPEECHWRITER
SPICE-BLENDER
SPORTSCASTER
SPORTSWRITER
STAGE MANAGER
STATISTICIAN
STENOGRAPHER
STONEBREAKER
STONEDRESSER
STONESQUARER
STREET-TRADER
STREET-WALKER
SUGAR-REFINER
TAX-COLLECTOR
TECHNOLOGIST
TELEGRAPH BOY
TELEGRAPHIST
TEST ENGINEER
THERAPEUTIST
THIEF-CATCHER
TICKET-PORTER
TIMBER TRADER
TOLL-GATHERER
TOURIST AGENT
TOXICOLOGIST
TRADESPEOPLE
TRANSPLANTER
TRICHOLOGIST
UNDERMANAGER
UNDERSERVANT
VETERINARIAN
WAITING-WOMAN
WAREHOUSEMAN
WATER DIVINER
WINE MERCHANT
WOOD-ENGRAVER
WORKS MANAGER
ZINCOGRAPHER

13
ADMINISTRATOR
AGRICULTURIST
ANTIQUE DEALER
ARACHNOLOGIST
ARCHAEOLOGIST
ARITHMETICIAN
ARTICLED CLERK

13—continued
ASSYRIOLOGIST
BARBER-SURGEON
BIBLIOGRAPHER
CALICO-PRINTER
CAMPANOLOGIST
CARTOGRAPHIST
CHARTOGRAPHER
CHICKEN-FARMER
CHIROGRAPHIST
CHOREOGRAPHER
CHRONOGRAPHER
CIVIL ENGINEER
CLEARSTARCHER
COFFEE-PLANTER
COMETOGRAPHER
CONTORTIONIST
CONTRABANDIST
COTTON-SPINNER
COUNTER-CASTER
COUNTERFEITER
CRANIOSCOPIST
CRYPTOGRAPHER
DANCING MASTER
DEIPNOSOPHIST
DERMATOLOGIST
DIAGNOSTICIAN
DIAMOND-CUTTER
DRAUGHTSWOMAN
DRAWING-MASTER
DRESS DESIGNER
DRILL SERGEANT
ELECTROPLATER
ELECTROTYPIST
EMIGRATIONIST
ENCYCLOPEDIST
ENTOZOOLOGIST
EPIGRAMMATIST
ESTATE MANAGER
EXHIBITIONIST
FENCING-MASTER
FORTUNE-TELLER
FRIEGHT-BROKER
GALVANOLOGIST
GASTRILOQUIST
GLOSSOGRAPHER
GLYPHOGRAPHER
GROUND-BAILIFF
GYNAECOLOGIST
HARBOUR MASTER
HIEROGLYPHIST
HORSE-MILLINER
HOSPITAL NURSE
ICHTHYOLOGIST
INDUSTRIALIST
INTELLIGENCER
JOINT-EXECUTOR
LETTER-CARRIER
LETTER-FOUNDER
LEXICOGRAPHER
LIGHTHOUSE-MAN

13—continued
MAID-OF-ALL-WORK
MASTER-BUILDER
MASTER MARINER
MATHEMATICIAN
MELODRAMATIST
METAPHYSICIAN
METEOROLOGIST
METOPOSCOPIST
MUSIC MISTRESS
NIGHT-WATCHMAN
OLD-CLOTHES-MAN
ORNITHOLOGIST
ORTHOGRAPHIST
PARK ATTENDANT
PERIODICALIST
PHARMACEUTIST
PHYSIOGNOMIST
PHYSIOGRAPHER
POSTURE-MASTER
POULTRY FARMER
PRIVATEERSMAN
PROCESS-SERVER
PSALMOGRAPHER
PSYCHOANALYST
PTERIDOLOGIST
PUBLIC SPEAKER
QUEEN'S COUNSEL
RACING-TIPSTER
REVOLUTIONARY
REVOLUTIONIST
RUBBER-PLANTER
SAILING MASTER
SCHOOLTEACHER
SCIENCE MASTER
SHOP ASSISTANT
SILK-THROWSTER
SINGING-MASTER
STATION-MASTER
STENOGRAPHIST
STEREOSCOPIST
STETHOSCOPIST
STREET-SWEEPER
SUB-CONTRACTOR
SUPERINTENDER
SUPERNUMERARY
THAUMATURGIST
THIMBLE-RIGGER
TOLL COLLECTOR
TRADE UNIONIST
TRAMCAR-DRIVER
TRAM CONDUCTOR
VENTRILOQUIST
VIOLONCELLIST
WINDOW-CLEANER
WINDOW-DRESSER
WOOLLEN-DRAPER
WRITING-MASTER

14
ADMINISTRATRIX
ANTHROPOLOGIST

14—continued
AUTOBIOGRAPHER
BACTERIOLOGIST
BALLET MISTRESS
BILLIARD-MARKER
BILLIARD-PLAYER
CHAMBER-COUNSEL
CHIMNEY-SWEEPER
CITIZEN-SOLDIER
CLASSICS MASTER
COLOUR SERGEANT
COMMISSIONAIRE
DANCING PARTNER
DISCOUNT-BROKER
ECCLESIOLOGIST
EDUCATIONALIST
ENCYCLOPAEDIST
EXCHANGE-BROKER
GRAMMATICASTER
HANDICRAFTSMAN
HERESIOGRAPHER
HORTICULTURIST
HOUSE DECORATOR
HOUSE FURNISHER
LANGUAGE MASTER
LEATHER-DRESSER
MANUAL LABOURER
MARKET-GARDENER
MEDICAL OFFICER
MERCHANT-TAILOR
MISCELLANARIAN
MONEY-SCRIVENER
MOTHER-SUPERIOR
MUSIC PUBLISHER
NAVAL PENSIONER
OPTHALMOLOGIST
PAINTER-STAINER
PHARMACOLOGIST
PNEUMATOLOGIST
PSALMOGRAPHIST
RECEPTION CLERK
REPRESENTATIVE
SCHOOLMISTRESS
SHIP'S-CARPENTER
SIDEROGRAPHIST
SPECTACLE-MAKER
SPECTROSCOPIST
SUPERINTENDENT
SYSTEMS ANALYST
TALLOW CHANDLER
WATER-COLOURIST
WEATHER PROPHET

15
ARBORICULTURIST
ASSISTANT MASTER
BOW STREET
  RUNNER
CROSSING-
  SWEEPER
CRUSTACEOLOGIST
DANCING MISTRESS

15—continued	15—continued	15—continued	15—continued
DIAMOND	HEART SPECIALIST	PALAEONTOLOGIST	RAILWAY ENGINEER
MERCHANT	HELMINTHOLOGIST	PLATFORM-	RESURRECTIONIST
DOMESTIC SERVANT	HIEROGRAMMATIST	SPEAKER	SCRIPTURE-READER
FORWARDING	HISTORIOGRAPHER	PORTRAIT-PAINTER	SLEEPING PARTNER
AGENT	INSTRUMENTALIST	PROFESSIONAL MAN	STRETCHER-
GENTLEMAN-	INSURANCE BROKER	PROGRAMME	BEARER
FARMER	MUSICAL DIRECTOR	SELLER	TICKET COLLECTOR
HACKNEY	NUMISMATOLOGIST	PROVISION DEALER	TIGHTROPE WALKER
COACHMAN			

TOOLS

3	4—continued	5—continued	6—continued
AWL	TOOL	LEVER	DIBBLE
AXE	TRUG	MOWER	DOFFER
BIT	VICE	PARER	DREDGE
DIE	WHIM	PLANE	DRIVER
FAN	**5**	PLUMB	FANNER
GAD	ANVIL	PREEN	FAUCET
GIN	AUGER	PRISE	FERRET
HOD	BEELE	PRONG	FOLDER
HOE	BENCH	PUNCH	GIMLET
JIG	BESOM	QUERN	GRAVER
LOY	BETTY	QUOIN	HACKLE
SAW	BEVEL	RATCH	HAMMER
ZAX	BLADE	RAZOR	HARROW
4	BORER	SARSE	JAGGER
ADZE	BRACE	SCREW	JIGGER
BILL	BURIN	SPADE	JIG SAW
BORE	CHUCK	SPIKE	LADDER
BROG	CHURN	SPILE	MALLET
BURR	CLAMP	SPILL	MORTAR
CART	CLAMS	SWAGE	MULLER
CELT	CLASP	TEMSE	OLIVER
CRAB	CLEAT	TOMMY	PALLET
FILE	CRAMP	TONGS	PENCIL
FORK	CRANE	TROMP	PESTLE
FROW	CROOM	TRONE	PITSAW
GAGE	CROZE	WEDGE	PLANER
HINK	CUPEL	WINCH	PLIERS
HOOK	DOLLY	**6**	PLOUGH
JACK	DRILL	BARROW	PONTEE
LAST	FLAIL	BENDER	POOLER
LOOM	FLANG	BLOWER	RAMMER
MALL	FORGE	BODKIN	RASPER
MAUL	GAUGE	BORCER	REAPER
MULE	GAVEL	BOW-SAW	RIDDLE
NAIL	GOUGE	BRAYER	RIPSAW
PICK	HOIST	BROACH	RUBBER
PIKE	INCUS	BURTON	SANDER
PLOW	JACKS	CHASER	SAW-SET
RAKE	JEMMY	CHISEL	SCREEN
RASP	JIMMY	COLTER	SCYTHE
RULE	KNIFE	CREVET	SEGGER
SOCK	LATHE	CRUSET	SHEARS
SPUD	LEVEL	DIBBER	SHOVEL

6—continued

SICKLE
SIFTER
SKEWER
SLEDGE
SLICER
SQUARE
STIDDY
STITHY
STRIKE
TACKLE
TENTER
TREPAN
TROWEL
TUBBER
TURREL
WIMBLE
WRENCH

7

BOASTER
BRADAWL
CAPSTAN
CATLING
CAUTERY
CHAMFER
CHIP-AXE
CHOPPER
CLEAVER
COULOIR
COULTER
CRAMPON
CRISPER
CROWBAR
CUVETTE
DERRICK
DIAMOND
DOG-BELT
DRUDGER
FISTUCA
FORCEPS
FRETSAW
FRUGGIN
GRADINE
GRAINER
GRAPNEL
GRUB AXE
HACKSAW
HANDSAW
HATCHET
HAY FORK
JOINTER
MANDREL
MATTOCK
NIPPERS
NUT HOOK
PICKAXE
PIERCER
PINCERS
PLUMMET
POLE AXE

7—continued

POUNDER
PRICKER
SALT-PAN
SCALPEL
SCAUPER
SCRAPER
SCREWER
SCRIBER
SEED LOP
SPADDLE
SPANNER
SPITTLE
SPRAYER
STROCAL
TENONER
THIMBLE
TRESTLE
TRIBLET
T-SQUARE
TWIBILL
TWISTER
WHIP-SAW
WHITTLE
WOOLDER

8

BARK MILL
BAR SHEAR
BEAKIRON
BENCH PEG
BILL HOOK
BISTOURY
BLOOMARY
BLOWLAMP
BLOWPIPE
BOATHOOK
BOWDRILL
BULL NOSE
BUTTERIS
CALIPERS
CANTHOOK
CHOPNESS
CROW MILL
CRUCIBLE
DIE STOCK
DOWEL BIT
DRILL BOW
EDGE TOOL
FILATORY
FIRE KILN
FLAME GUN
FLAX COMB
GAVELOCK
GEE CRAMP
HANDLOOM
HANDMILL
HAND VICE
HAY KNIFE
HORSE HOE
LAPSTONE

8—continued

LEAD MILL
MITRE BOX
MOLEGRIP
MUCK RAKE
NUT SCREW
OILSTONE
PAINT PAD
PANEL SAW
PICKLOCK
PINCHERS
PLUMB BOB
POLISHER
POWER SAW
PRONG-HOE
PUNCHEON
REAP HOOK
SAW WREST
SCISSORS
SCUFFLER
SLATE AXE
STILETTO
STRICKLE
TENON SAW
THROSTLE
TOOTH KEY
TWEEZERS
TWIST BIT
WATERCAN
WATER RAM
WEED HOOK
WINDLASS
WINDMILL

9

BELT PUNCH
BENCH HOOK
BOLT AUGER
BOOT CRIMP
CANKER BIT
CANNIPERS
CAN OPENER
CENTRE BIT
COMPASSES
CORKSCREW
COTTON GIN
CRAMP IRON
CURRY COMB
CUTTER BAR
DOG CLUTCH
DRAW KNIFE
DRAW-PLATE
EXCAVATOR
EYELETEER
FILLISTER
FINING POT
FORK CHUCK
GAS PLIERS
HAMMER AXE
HANDBRACE
HANDSCREW

9—continued

HANDSPIKE
HOLING AXE
HUMMELLER
IMPLEMENT
JACKKNIFE
JACKPLANE
JACKSCREW
LACE FRAME
LAWNMOWER
NAIL PUNCH
NUT WRENCH
PITCH FORK
PLANE IRON
PLANISHER
PLUMBLINE
PLUMBRULE
SCREWJACK
SCRIBE AWL
SHEARLEGS
SHEEP HOOK
STEELYARD
SUGAR MILL
TIN OPENER
TRY SQUARE
TURF SPADE
TURN BENCH
TURNSCREW
WATERMILL

10

BUSH HARROW
CLASPKNIFE
CLAWHAMMER
COLD CHISEL
CRANE'S BILL
CULTIVATOR
DRAY PLOUGH
DRIFT BOLTS
DRILLPRESS
DRILLSTOCK
EMERY WHEEL
FIRE ENGINE
FIRING IRON
GRINDSTONE
INSTRUMENT
MASONRY BIT
MASTICATOR
MITRE BLOCK
MOTOR MOWER
MOULD BOARD
NAIL DRAWER
PAINTBRUSH
PERFORATOR
PIPE WRENCH
POINTED AWL
SAFETY LAMP
SCREW PRESS
SLEEK STONE
SNOWPLOUGH
SPOKESHAVE

10—continued
STEAM PRESS
STEPLADDER
TENTERHOOK
THUMBSCREW
THUMBSTALL
TILT HAMMER
TRIP HAMMER
TURF CUTTER
TURNBUCKLE
WATERCRANE
WATERGAUGE
WATERLEVEL
WHEEL BRACE

11
BRACE-AND-BIT
BREAST DRILL
CHAFF CUTTER
CHAIN BLOCKS
CHAIN WRENCH
CHEESE PRESS
COUNTERSINK
CRAZING MILL
CRISPING PIN
CROSSCUT SAW
DRILL BARROW
DRILL HARROW
DRILL PLOUGH
FANNING MILL
GRUBBING HOE
HELVEHAMMER
JAGGING IRON
MACHINE TOOL
MONKEY BLOCK
PAINT ROLLER
PLOUGHSHARE
PRUNING HOOK

11—continued
RABBET PLANE
REAPING-HOOK
SAWING STOOL
SCREWDRIVER
SINGLE-EDGED
SKIM COULTER
SNATCH BLOCK
SPIRIT LEVEL
SQUARING ROD
STEAM HAMMER
STONE HAMMER
STRAW CUTTER
STRIKE BLOCK
STUBBLE RAKE
SWARD CUTTER
SWINGPLOUGH
TAPEMEASURE
TURFING IRON
TWO-FOOT RULE
WARPING HOOK
WARPING POST
WEEDING FORK
WEEDING HOOK
WEEDING RHIM
WHEELBARROW

12
BARKING IRONS
BELT ADJUSTER
BRANDING IRON
BREASTPLOUGH
CAULKING TOOL
COUNTER GAUGE
CRADEL SCYTHE
CRAMPING IRON
CRIMPING IRON
CRISPING IRON

12—continued
CURLING TONGS
DRILL GRUBBER
DRIVING SHAFT
DRIVING WHEEL
EMERY GRINDER
FLOUR DRESSER
GLASS FURNACE
HYDRAULIC RAM
MANDREL LATHE
MARLINE SPIKE
MONKEY WRENCH
PRUNING KNIFE
PULLEY BLOCKS
RUNNING BLOCK
SCRIBING IRON
SLEDGE HAMMER
SLIDING BEVEL
SOCKET CHISEL
STONE BREAKER
STRAIGHTEDGE
SWINGLE KNIFE
TOUCH NEEDLES
TRENCH PLOUGH
TURFING SPADE
TURNING LATHE
WATER BELLOWS
WEEDING TONGS

13
BUTCHER'S BROOM
CHOPPING BLOCK
CHOPPING KNIFE
CYLINDER PRESS
ELECTRIC DRILL
GRAPPLING-IRON
HYDRAULIC JACK
PACKING NEEDLE

13—continued
SCRIBING BLOCK
SEWING MACHINE
SOLDERING BOLT
SOLDERING IRON
SOWING MACHINE
SPINNING JENNY
SPINNING WHEEL
STOCKING FRAME
SUBSOIL PLOUGH
TWO-HOLE PLIERS
WEEDING CHISEL

14
BLOWING MACHINE
CARDING MACHINE
DRAINING ENGINE
DRAINING PLOUGH
PENUMATIC DRILL
REAPING MACHINE
SMOOTHING PLANE
SWINGLING KNIFE
THRUSTING SCREW
WEEDING FORCEPS

15
CARPENTER'S
  BENCH
CRIMPING MACHINE
DREDGING MACHINE
DRILLING MACHINE
ENTRENCHING TOOL
PESTLE AND
  MORTAR
PUMP
  SCREWDRIVER
WEIGHING MACHINE

MILITARY TERMS

TITLES

ARMY RANKS

FIELD MARSHAL
GENERAL
LIEUTENANT-
  GENERAL
MAJOR-GENERAL
BRIGADIER
COLONEL
LIEUTENANT-
  COLONEL
MAJOR
CAPTAIN
LIEUTENANT
SECOND-
  LIEUTENANT
SERGEANT-MAJOR
QUARTERMASTER-
  SERGEANT
SERGEANT
CORPORAL
LANCE-CORPORAL
BOMBARDIER
PRIVATE

ROYAL NAVY RANKS

ADMIRAL OF THE
  FLEET
ADMIRAL
VICE-ADMIRAL
REAR-ADMIRAL
COMMODORE
CAPTAIN
COMMANDER
LIEUTENANT-
  COMMANDER
LIEUTENANT
SUB-LIEUTENANT
CHIEF PETTY
  OFFICER
PETTY OFFICER
LEADING SEAMAN
ABLE SEAMAN
ORDINARY SEAMAN
JUNIOR SEAMAN

ROYAL AIR FORCE RANKS

MARSHAL OF THE
  ROYAL AIR FORCE
AIR CHIEF MARSHAL
AIR MARSHAL
AIR VICE-MARSHAL
AIR COMMODORE
GROUP CAPTAIN
WING COMMANDER
SQUADRON LEADER
FLIGHT LIEUTENANT
FLYING OFFICER
PILOT OFFICER
MASTER AIR
  LOADMASTER
MASTER AIR
  ELECTRONIC
  OPERATOR

MASTER ENGINEER
MASTER NAVIGATOR
MASTER SIGNALLER
MASTER PILOT
WARRANT OFFICER
CHIEF TECHNICIAN
FLIGHT SERGEANT
SERGEANT
CORPORAL
JUNIOR TECHNICIAN
SENIOR
  AIRCRAFTMAN
LEADING
  AIRCRAFTMAN
AIRCRAFTMAN 1ST
  CLASS
AIRCRAFTMAN 2ND
  CLASS

DECORATIONS AND MEDALS

AIR FORCE CROSS (AFC)
AIR FORCE MEDAL (AFM)
ALBERT MEDAL (AM)
CONSPICUOUS GALLANTRY MEDAL (CGM)
DISTINGUISHED FLYING CROSS (DFC)
DISTINGUISHED FLYING MEDAL (DFM)
DISTINGUISHED SERVICE CROSS (DSC)
DISTINGUISHED SERVICE MEDAL (DSM)
GEORGE CROSS (GC)

GEORGE MEDAL (GM)
MEDAL FOR DISTINGUISHED CONDUCT IN
  THE FIELD (DCM)
MILITARY CROSS (MC)
MILITARY MEDAL (MM)
THE DISTINGUISHED SERVICE ORDER
  (DSO)
VICTORIA CROSS (VC)

BATTLES

2
RE, ÎLE DE (1627, Anglo-French Wars)
3
ACS (1849, Hungarian Rising)
AIX, ÎLE D' (1758, Seven Years' War)
DEE, BRIG OF (1639, Bishops' War)

3—continued
DIU (1537, 1545, Portuguese in India)
GOA (1511, 1570, Portuguese Conquest)
HUE (1968, Vietnam War)
UJI (1180, Taira War)
ULM (1805, Napoleonic Wars)

3—continued

ZAB, THE (590, Bahram's Revolt)

4

ACRE (1189–1191, Third Crusade; 1291, Crusader-Turkish Wars; 1799, French Revolutionary Wars; 1840, Egyptian Revolt)

AGRA (1713, Farrukhsiyar's Rebellion; 1803, Second British-Maratha War; 1857, Indian Mutiny)

ALMA (1854, Crimean War)

AONG (1857, Indian Mutiny)

ARAS (1775, First British-Maratha War)

AVUS (198 B.C., Second Macedonian War)

BAZA (1489, Spanish-Muslim Wars)

BEDR (623, Islamic Wars)

BEGA (1696, Ottoman Wars)

CUBA (1953, Castro Revolt)

CYME (474 B.C., Etruscan-Greek Wars)

DEEG (1780, First British-Maratha War; 1804, Second British-Maratha War)

DYLE (896, German States' Wars)

GAZA (332 B.C., Alexander's Asiatic Campaigns; 312 B.C., Wars of Alexander's Successors; 1917, World War I)

GELT, THE (1570, Anglo-Scottish Wars)

GUAM (1944, World War II)

IRUN (1837, First Carlist War)

ISLY (1844, Abd-el-Kader's Rebellion)

IVRY (1590, French Religious Wars)

JENA (1806, Napoleonic Wars)

KARS (1855, Crimean War; 1877, Russo-Turkish War)

KIEV (1941, World War II)

KISO (1180, Taira War)

KULM (1813, Napoleonic Wars)

LADE (494 B.C., Ionian War; 201 B.C., Macedonian Wars)

LAON (1814, Napoleonic Wars)

LECK, THE (1632, Thirty Years' War)

LENS (1648, Thirty Years' War)

LÓDŹ (1914, World War I)

LOJA (1482, Spanish-Muslim Wars)

MAIN, THE (9 B.C., Germanic War)

MAYA, COLDE (1813, Peninsular War)

METZ (1870, Franco-Prussian War)

MUTA (636, Muslim Invasion of Syria)

NEON (354 B.C., Sacred War)

NILE (1798, French Revolutionary Wars)

NIVE (1813, Peninsular War)

NOVI (1799, French Revolutionary Wars)

OFEN (1849, Hungarian Rising)

OHUD (623, Mohammed's War with the Koreish)

ONAO (1857, Indian Mutiny)

ORAN (1509, Spanish Invasion of Morocco; 1940, World War II)

OREL (1943, World War II)

ORUO (1862, Bolivian Civil War)

POLA (1380, War of Chioggia)

RAAB (1809, Napoleonic Wars)

RIGA (1621, Swedish-Polish Wars)

4—continued

ROME (387 B.C., First Invasion of the Gauls; 408, Wars of the Western Roman Empire, 472, Ricimer's Rebellion; 537, 546, Wars of the Byzantine Empire; 1082, Norman Seizure; 1527, Wars of Charles V, 1849, Italian Wars of Independence)

SCIO (1769, Ottoman Wars)

SETA (1183, Yoshinaka's Rebellion)

SOHR (1745, War of the Austrian Succession)

ST LÔ (1944, World War II)

TOBA (1868, Japanese Revolution)

TORO (1476, War of the Castilian Succession)

TROY (1100 B.C.)

TRUK (1944, World War II)

TYRE (332 B.C., Alexander's Asiatic Campaigns)

VEII (405 B.C., Rise of Rome)

ZAMA (202 B.C., Second Punic War)

ZEIM (1877, Russo-Turkish War)

ZELA (67 B.C., Third Mithridatic War; 47 B.C., Wars of the First Triumvirate)

5

ACCRA (1824, 1825, First British-Ashanti War)

ADUWA (1896, Italian Invasion of Ethiopia)

ALAMO, STORMING OF THE (1836, Texan Rising)

ALAND (1714, Great Northern War)

ALLIA, THE (390 B.C., The First Invasion of the Gauls)

ALSEN (1864, Schleswig-Holstein War)

AMBUR (1749, Carnatic War; 1767, First British-Mysore War)

AMIDA (359, Roman-Persian Wars)

ANZIO (1944, World War II)

ARCOT (1751, Carnatic War)

ARGOS (195 B.C., Roman Invasion of Greece)

ARIUS (214 B.C., The Wars of the Hellenistic Monarchies)

ARNEE (1751, Carnatic War; 1782, First British-Mysore War)

ARRAH (1857, Indian Mutiny)

ARRAS (1654, Wars of Louis XIV; 1917, World War I)

A SHAU (1966, Vietnam War)

AURAY (1364, Hundred Years' War)

BAHUR (1752, Seven Years' War)

BANDA (1858, Indian Mutiny)

BANDS, THE (961, Danish Invasion of Scotland)

BASRA (665, Islamic Wars)

BAVAY (57 B.C., Gallic Wars)

BEREA (1852, Kaffir Wars)

BETWA, THE (1858, Indian Mutiny)

BOSRA (632, Muslim Invasion of Syria)

BOYNE, THE (1690, War of the Grand Alliance)

BREST (1512, War of the Holy League)

BRILL (1572, Netherlands War of Independence)

BURMA (1942, 1943, World War II)

5—continued

BUXAR (1764, British Conquest of Bengal)
CADIZ (1587, Anglo-Spanish War)
CAIRO (1517, Ottoman Wars)
CANEA (1644, Candian War)
CAPUA (212 B.C., Second Punic War)
CARPI (1701, War of the Spanish Succession)
CESME (1770, Ottoman Wars)
CHIOS (357 B.C., Social War; 201 B.C., Wars of
  the Hellenistic Monarchies)
CRÉCY (1346, Hundred Years' War)
CRETE (1941, World War II)
CUZCO (1536, Conquest of Peru)
DAK TO (1967, Vietnam War)
DAMME (1213, Wars of Philip Augustus)
DELHI (1297, First Tatar Invasion of India;
  1398, Second Tatar Invasion; 1803, Second
  British-Maratha War; 1804, Second British-
  Maratha War; 1857, Indian Mutiny)
DOUAI (1710, War of the Spanish Succession)
DOURO (1809, Peninsular War)
DOVER (1652, Anglo-Dutch Wars)
DOWNS, THE (1666, Anglo-Dutch Wars)
DREUX (1562, French Religious Wars)
DUBBA (1843, Sind Campaign)
DUNES (1658, Wars of Louis XIV)
DWINA, THE (1701, Swedish-Polish War)
ELENA (1877, Russo-Turkish War)
EL TEB (1884, British-Sudan Campaigns)
EMESA (272, Wars of the Roman Empire)
ENGEN (1800, French Revolutionary Wars)
EYLAU (1807, Napoleonic Wars)
GENOA (1746, Patriotic Rising; 1795, 1800,
  French Revolutionary Wars)
GIHON, THE (1362, Wars of Tamerlane)
GINGI (1689, Mughal Invasion of the Deccan)
GOITS (1848, Italian Wars of Independence)
GUBAT (1885, British Sudan Campaigns)
HANAU (1813, Napoleonic Wars)
HERAT (1220, Tatar Invasion of Afghanistan;
  1837, Persian-Afghan Wars)
HIPPO (430, Wars of the Western Roman
  Empire)
IMMAC (218, Revolt of Elagabalus)
IMOLA (1797, French Revolutionary Wars)
INDUS, THE (1221, Tatar Invasion of Central
  Asia)
IPSUS (306 B.C., Wars of Alexander's
  Successors)
ISSUS (333 B.C., Alexander's Asiatic
  Campaigns; 1488, Ottoman Wars)
JASSY (1620, Ottoman Wars)
JIRON (1829, Peruvian-Colombian War)
JUNÍN (1824, Peruvian War of Independence)
KAGUL (1770, Ottoman Wars)
KALPI (1858, Indian Mutiny)
KAREE (1900, Second Boer War)
KAZAN (1774, Cossack Rising)
KIÖGE (1677, Northern War)
KOLIN (1757, Seven Years' War)
KOTAH (1858, Indian Mutiny)

5—continued

KUMAI (1355, Moronoshi's Rebellion)
LAGOS (1693, War of the Grand Alliance)
LA PAZ (1865, Bolivian Civil War)
LARGS (1263, Norse Invasion of Scotland)
LESNO (1708, Russo-Swedish War)
LEWES (1264, Barons' Wars)
LEYTE (1944, World War II)
LIÈGE (1914, World War I)
LIGNY (1815, Napoleonic Wars)
LILLE (1708, War of the Spanish Succession)
LIPPE (11 B.C., Germanic Wars)
LISSA (1866, Seven Weeks' War)
LUZON (1945, World War II)
LYONS (197, Civil Wars of the Roman Empire)
MAIDA (1806, Napoleonic Wars)
MALTA (1565, Ottoman Wars; 1798, French
  Revolutionary Wars; 1942, World War II)
MARNE (1914, 1918, World War I)
MAXEN (1759, Seven Years' War)
MAYPO (1818, Chilean War of Independence)
MERTA (1561, Mughal Invasion of the Deccan)
MORAT (1476, Burgundian Wars)
MOTYA (398 B.C., Carthaginian Invasion of
  Sicily)
MUDKI (1845, First British-Sikh War)
MUNDA (45 B.C., Civil War of Caesar and
  Pompey)
MURET (1213, Albigensian Crusade)
MURSA (351, Civil Wars of the Roman Empire)
MYLAE (260 B.C., First Punic War)
MYLEX (36 B.C., Wars of the Second
  Triumvirate)
NAMUR (1914, World War I)
NARVA (1700, Great Northern War)
NAXOS (376 B.C., Wars of the Greek City
  States)
NIKKO (1868, Japanese Revolution)
NISSA (1064, Scandinavian Wars)
NIZIB (1839, Mehmet Ali's Second Rebellion)
OLPAE (426 B.C., Great Peloponnesian War)
OSTIA (1500, Italian Wars)
OTRAR (1219, Tatar Invasion of Khorezm)
PARIS (1814, Napoleonic Wars; 1870, Franco-
  Prussian War)
PARMA (1734, War of the Polish Succession)
PATAY (1429, Hundred Years' War)
PAVIA (271, Invasion of the Alemanni; 568,
  Lombard Conquest of Italy; 1431, Italian
  Wars; 1525, Wars of Charles V)
PERED (1849, Hungarian Rising)
PETRA (549, Persian Wars)
PIROT (1885, Serbo-Bulgarian War)
PODOL (1866, Seven Weeks' War)
POONA (1802, Maratha Wars)
PRUTH, THE (1770, Ottoman Wars)
PYDNA (168 B.C., Third Macedonian War)
RAMLA (1177, Crusader-Turkish Wars)
REBEC (1524, Wars of Charles V)
REDAN, THE GREAT (1855, Crimean War)
REIMS (1814, Napoleonic Wars)

5—continued

REVAL (1790, Russo-Swedish Wars)
RIETI (1821, Italian Wars of Independence)
ROUEN (1418, Hundred Years' War)
SEDAN (1870, Franco-Prussian War)
SELBY (1644, English Civil War)
SEOUL (1950, Korean War)
SLUYS (1340, Hundred Years' War)
SOMME (1916, 1918, World War I)
SPIRA (1703, War of the Spanish Succession)
SPURS (1302, Flemish War; 1513, Anglo-
   French Wars)
STOKE (1487, Lambert Simnel's Rebellion)
SUERO, THE (75 B.C., Civil War of Sertorius)
TACNA (1880, Peruvian-Chilean War)
TAMAI (1884, British Sudan Campaigns)
TEGEA (473 B.C., Wars of Sparta)
TEXEL (1653, Anglo-Dutch Wars)
THALA (22, Numidian Revolt)
THORN (1702, Great Northern War)
TOURS (732, Muslim Invasion of France)
TUNIS (255 B.C., First Punic War; 1270, Eighth
   Crusade)
TURIN (312, Civil Wars of the Roman Empire;
   1706, War of the Spanish Succession)
UCLES (1109, Spanish-Muslim Wars)
UTICA (49 B.C., Civil War of Caesar and
   Pompey; 694, Muslim Conquest of Africa)
VALMY (1792, French Revolutionary Wars)
VARNA (1444, Anti-Turkish Crusade; 1828,
   Ottoman Wars)
VARUS, DEFEAT OF (A.D. 9, Wars of the
   Roman Empire)
VASAQ (1442, Ottoman Wars)
WAVRE (1815, Napoleonic Wars)
WISBY (1613, Danish-Swedish Wars)
WÖRTH (1870, Franco-Prussian War)
XERES (711, Spanish-Muslim Wars)
YPRES (1914, 1915, 1917, World War I)
ZENTA (1679, Ottoman Wars)
ZNAIM (1809, Napoleonic Wars)

6

AACHEN (1944, World War II)
ABUKIR (1799, 1801, French Revolutionary
   Wars)
ABU KRU (1885, British Sudan Campaigns)
ACTIUM (31 B.C., Wars of the Second
   Triumvirate)
ÆGINA (458 B.C., Third Messenian War)
ÆGUSA (241 B.C., First Punic War)
ALEPPO (638, Muslim Invasion of Syria; 1400,
   Tatar Invasion of Syria; 1516, Ottoman
   Wars)
ALESIA (52 B.C., Gallic Wars)
ALFORD (1645, English Civil War)
ALHAMA (1482, Spanish-Muslim Wars)
ALIWAL (1846, First British-Sikh War)
AMBATE (1532, Conquest of Peru)
AMIENS (1870, Franco-Prussian War)
ANCONA (1860, Italian Wars of Independence)
ANGORA (1402, Tatar Invasion of Asia Minor)

6—continued

ANTIUM (1378, War of Chioggia)
ARBELA (331 B.C., Alexander's Asiatic
   Campaigns)
ARCOLA (1796, French Revolutionary Wars)
ARGAON (1803, Second British-Maratha War)
ARKLOW (1798, Irish Rebellion)
ARNHEM (1944, World War II)
ARQUES (1589, French Religious Wars)
ARSOUF (1191, Third Crusade)
ARTOIS (1915, World War I)
ASHTEE (1818, Third British-Maratha War)
ASIAGO (1916, World War I)
ASPERN (1809, Napoleonic Wars)
ASSAYE (1803, Second British-Maratha War)
ATBARA (1898, British Sudan Campaigns)
AZORES (1591, Anglo-Spanish War)
BAMIAN (1221, Tatar Invasion of Kharismia)
BARDIA (1941, World War II)
BARNET (1471, Wars of the Roses)
BASING (871, Danish Invasion of Britain)
BAYLEN (1808, Peninsular War)
BEAUGÉ (1421, Hundred Years' War)
BENDER (1768, Ottoman Wars)
BERGEN (1759, Seven Years' War)
BEYLAN (1831, Egyptian Revolt)
BILBAO (1836, First Carlist War; 1937, Spanish
   Civil War)
BINGEN (70, Gallic Revolt)
BIRUAN (1221, Tatar Invasion of Kharismia)
BOYACÁ (1819, Colombian War of
   Independence)
BUSACO (1810, Peninsular War)
CABALA (379 B.C., Second Carthaginian
   Invasion of Sicily)
CABRIA (72 B.C., Third Mithridatic War)
CALAIS (1346, Hundred Years' War; 1558,
   Anglo-French Wars)
CALLAO (1866, Peruvian War of
   Independence)
CALVEN, THE (1499, Swiss-Swabian War)
CAMDEN (1780, American Revolutionary War)
CAMPEN (1759, Seven Years' War)
CANDIA (1648, Candian War)
CANNAE (216 B.C., Second Punic War)
CEPEDA (1859, Argentine Civil War)
CHANDA (1818, Third British-Maratha War)
CHIARI (1701, War of the Spanish Succession)
CHILOE (1826, Chilean War of Independence)
CHIZAI (1372, Hundred Years' War)
CHUNAR (1538, Hindu-Mughal Wars)
CNIDUS (394 B.C., Wars of Greek City States)
CONCON (1891, Chilean Civil War)
CUNAXA (401 B.C., Expedition of Cyrus the
   Younger)
CYSSUS (191 B.C., Wars of the Hellenistic
   Monarchies)
DANZIG (1627, Thirty Years' War: 1807, 1813,
   Napoleonic Wars)

6—continued

DARGAI (1897, British Northwest Frontier Campaign)

DELIUM (424 B.C., Peloponnesian War)

DELPHI (355 B.C., Sacred War)

DENAIN (1712, War of the Spanish Succession)

DESSAU (1626, Thirty Years' War)

DIEPPE (1942, World War II)

DIPAEA (471 B.C., Arcadian War)

DJERBA (1560, Ottoman Wars)

DOLLAR (875, Danish Invasions of Scotland)

DUNBAR (1296, 1339, Wars of Scottish Independence; 1650, Cromwell's Scottish Campaign)

DUNDEE (1899, Second Boer War)

DUPPEL (1864, Schleswig-Holstein War)

EDESSA (259, Persian Wars)

ELINGA (206 B.C., Second Punic War)

EMBATA (356 B.C., Social War)

ERBACH (1800, French Revolutionary Wars)

FAENZA (541, Wars of the Byzantine Empire)

FERKEH (1896, British Sudan Campaigns)

GAZALA (1942, World War II)

GEBORA (1811, Peninsular War)

GERONA (1809, Peninsular War)

GHAZNI (1839, First British-Afghan War)

GISORS (1197, Anglo-French Wars)

GROZKA (1739, Ottoman Wars)

HALLUE (1870, Franco-Prussian War)

HARLAW (1411, Scottish Civil Wars)

HASHIN (1885, British Sudan Campaigns)

HATVAN (1849, Hungarian Rising)

HAVANA (1748, War of the Austrian Succession; 1762, Seven Years' War)

HEXHAM (1464, Wars of the Roses)

HIMERA (480 B.C., First Carthaginian Invasion of Sicily; 409 B.C., Second Carthaginian Invasion of Sicily)

HOCHST (1622, Thirty Years' War)

HONAIN (629, Muslim Conquest of Arabia)

HUESCA (1105, Spanish-Muslim Wars; 1837, First Carlist War)

HYSIAE (668 B.C., Sparta against Argos)

INCHON (1950, Korean War)

INGAVI (1841, Bolivian-Peruvian War)

INGOGO (1881, First Boer War)

ISMAIL (1790, Ottoman Wars)

ISONZO (1915, World War I)

JALULA (637, Muslim Invasion of Persia)

JARNAC (1569, Third French Religious War)

JERSEY (1550, Anglo-French Wars)

JHANSI (1857, Indian Mutiny) ·

KAPPEL (1531, Swiss Religious Wars)

KARAKU (1218, Tatar Invasion of Khwarizm)

KHELAT (1839, First British-Afghan War)

KIRKEE (1817, Third British-Maratha War)

KOKEIN (1824, First Burma War)

KOMORN (1849, Hungarian Rising)

KONIAH (1831, Mehemet Ali's First Rebellion)

KOTZIN (1622, 1673, Ottoman Wars)

6—continued

KRONIA (1738, Ottoman Wars)

LAHORE (1296, First Tatar Invasion of India)

LANDAU (1702, War of the Spanish Succession)

LANDEN (1693, War of the Grand Alliance)

LANNOY (1567, Netherlands War of Independence)

LARCAY (1829, Chilean Revolution)

LAUPEN (1339, Burgundian Wars)

LAWARI (1803, Second British-Maratha War)

LE MANS (1871, Franco-Prussian War)

LERIDA (1642, 1647, Thirty Years' War)

LEYDEN (1574, Netherlands War of Independence)

LONATO (1796, French Revolutionary Wars)

LUCENA (1483, Spanish-Muslim Wars)

LUNDEN (1676, Danish-Swedish Wars)

LUTTER (1626, Thirty Years' War)

LUTZEN (1632, Thirty Years' War; 1813, Napoleonic Wars)

MACALO (1427, Italian Wars)

MADRAS (1746, War of the Austrian Succession; 1758, Seven Years' War)

MADRID (1936, Spanish Civil War)

MAIDAN (1842, First British-Afghan War)

MAJUBA (1881, First Boer War)

MALAGA (1487, Spanish-Muslim Wars; 1704, War of the Spanish Succession)

MALAYA (1941, World War II)

MALDON (991, Danish Invasions of Britain)

MANILA (1898, Spanish-American War)

MANTUA (1797, French Revolutionary Wars)

MARDIS (315, War of the Two Empires)

MARGUS (285, Civil Wars of the Roman Empire)

MEDINA (625, Muslim Conquest of Arabia)

MEDOLA (1796, French Revolutionary Wars)

MEERUT (1398, Second Tatar Invasion of India)

MERIDA (712, Spanish-Muslim Wars)

MERTON (871, Danish Invasions of Britain)

MEXICO (1520, Conquest of Mexico)

MINDEN (1759, Seven Years' War)

MIYAKO (1353, Moronoshi's Rebellion; 1391, Mitsuyakis' Revolt)

MOHACZ (1526, 1687, Ottoman Wars)

MORAWA (1443, Ottoman Wars)

MOSCOW (1941, World War II)

MUKDEN (1905, Russo-Japanese War; 1948, Chinese Civil War)

MULTAN (1848, Second British-Sikh War)

MUTHUL, THE (108 B.C., Jugurthine War)

MUTINA (43 B.C., Roman Civil Wars)

MYCALE (479 B.C., Persian-Greek Wars)

MYTTON (1319, Wars of Scottish Independence)

NACHOD (1866, Seven Weeks' War)

NAJARA (1367, Hundred Years' War)

NANHAN (1904, Russo-Japanese War)

NASEBY (1645, English Civil War)

6—continued

NICAEA (1097, First Crusade)
NORWAY (1940, World War II)
NOTIUM (407 B.C., Peloponnesian War)
NOVARA (1513, Italian Wars; 1849, Italian Wars of Independence)
OCKLEY (851, Danish Invasions of Britain)
OLMEDO (1467, War of the Castilian Succession)
OLMÜTZ (1758, Seven Years' War)
OPORTO (1809, Peninsular War)
ORTHEZ (1814, Peninsular War)
OSTEND (1601, Netherlands War of Independence)
OSWEGO (1756, Seven Years' War)
OTUMBA (1520, Spanish Conquest of Mexico)
PANION (198 B.C., Wars of the Hellenistic Monarchies)
PARANA (1866, Paraguayan War)
PATILA (1394, Tatar Invasion of Persia)
PEKING (1214, Tatar Invasion of China)
PLEI ME (1965, Vietnam War)
PLEVNA (1877, Russo-Turkish War)
POLAND (1939, World War II)
PONANI (1780, First British-Mysore War)
POTOSI (1825, Bolivian War of Independence)
PRAGUE (1620, Thirty Years' War; 1757, Seven Years' War)
PUENTE (1816, Colombian War of Independence)
QUEBEC (1759, 1760, Seven Years' War)
RABAUL (1943, World War II)
RAGATZ (1446, Armagnac War)
RAPHIA (217 B.C., Wars of the Hellenistic Monarchies)
RASZYN (1809, Napoleonic Wars)
RHODES (1480, Ottoman Wars)
RIVOLI (1797, French Revolutionary Wars)
ROCROI (1643, Thirty Years' War)
ROLICA (1808, Peninsular War)
RUMANI (1915, World War I)
SACILE (1809, Napoleonic Wars)
SADOWA (1866, Seven Weeks' War)
SAIGON (1968, Vietnam War)
SAINTS, THE (1782, American Revolutionary War)
SALADO (1340, Spanish-Muslim Wars)
SANGRO (1943, World War II)
SARDIS (280 B.C., Wars of Alexander's Successors)
SEPEIA (494 B.C., Argive War)
SESKAR (1790, Russo-Swedish Wars)
SHILOH (1862, American Civil War)
SICILY (1943, World War II)
SIFFIN (657, Muslim Civil Wars)
SILPIA (206 B.C., Second Punic War)
SINOPE (1853, Crimean War)
SON-TAI (1883, Tongking War)
SORATA (1780, Inca Rising)
STE FOY (1760, Seven Years' War)
ST KITS (1667, Anglo-Dutch Wars)

6—continued

SYBOTA (433 B.C., Peloponnesian Wars)
TAURIS (47 B.C., Civil War of Caesar and Pompey)
TEGYRA (373 B.C., Boeotian War)
TERTRY (687, Rise of the Franks)
TETUAN (1860, Spanish-Moroccan War)
THEBES (335 B.C., Macedonian Conquest)
THURII (282 B.C., Roman Civil Wars)
TIFLIS (1386, Tatar Invasion of the Caucasus)
TIGRIS (363, Persian Wars)
TOBRUK (1941, 1942, World War II)
TOFREK (1885, British-Sudan Campaigns)
TORGAU (1760, Seven Years' War)
TOULON (1707, War of the Spanish Succession; 1744, War of the Austrian Succession; 1793, French Revolutionary Wars)
TOWTON (1461, Wars of the Roses)
TSINAN (1948, Chinese Civil War)
TUDELA (1808, Peninsular War)
ULUNDI (1879, Zulu-British War)
UROSAN (1595, Japanese Invasion of Korea)
USHANT (1794, French Revolutionary Wars)
VARESE (1859, Italian Wars of Independence)
VARMAS (1813, Colombian War of Independence)
VENICE (1848, Italian Wars of Independence)
VERDUN (1916, World War I)
VERONA (312, Civil Wars of the Roman Empire)
VIENNA (1529, 1683, Ottoman Wars)
VYBORG (1918, Russo-Finnish War)
WAGRAM (1809, Napoleonic Wars)
WAIZAN (1849, Hungarian Rising)
WARSAW (1831, Second Polish Rising; 1914, World War I; 1918, Russo-Polish War; 1939, 1944, World War II)
WERBEN (1631, Thirty Years' War)
WIAZMA (1812, Napoleonic Wars)
YARMUK (636, Muslim Invasion of Syria)
YAWATA (1353, War of the Northern and Southern Empires)
ZALAKA (1086, Moorish against Castile)
ZAMORA (901, Spanish-Muslim Wars)
ZÜRICH (1799, French Revolutionary Wars)

7

ABRAHAM, PLAINS OF (1759, Seven Years' War)
ABU KLEA (1885, British Sudan Campaigns)
ACRAGAS (406 B.C., Second Carthaginian Invasion of Sicily)
AGORDAT (1893, Italian Sudan Campaigns)
ALARCOS (1195, Spanish-Muslim Wars)
ALBUERA (1811, Peninsular War)
ALCOLEA (1868, Isabel II of Spain Deposed)
ALGHERO (1353, Aragonese Conquest of Sardinia)
ALGIERS (1775, Spanish-Algerian War; 1816, Bombardment of)
ALIGARH (1803, First British-Maratha War)

7—continued

ALKMAAR (1573, Netherlands War of
Independence; 1799, French Revolutionary
Wars)
ALMANSA (1707, War of the Spanish
Succession)
ALMORAH (1815, British-Gurkha War)
ALNWICK (1093, Anglo-Scottish Wars)
AMAKUSA (1638, Revolt of the Christians in
Japan)
AMOAFUL (1874, Second British-Ashanti War)
AMORIUM (838, Muslim Invasion of Asia
Minor)
ANCYRAE (242 B.C., Hierax's Rebellion)
ANTIOCH (244 BC., Syrian Wars; 1097, First
Crusade)
ANTWERP (1576, Netherlands War of
Independence; 1832, Liberation of Belgium;
1914, World War I)
ARAUSIO (105 B.C., Fourth Gallic Invasion)
ARIKERA (1791, Second British-Mysore War)
ASCALON (1099, First Crusade)
ASCULUM (279 B.C., Pyrrhus' Invasion of Italy;
89 B.C., Social War)
ASHDOWN (871, Danish Invasion of Britain)
ATHENRY (1316, Conquest of Ireland)
AUGHRIM (1691, War of the English
Succession)
BAGHDAD (1401, Mongul Invasion of
Mesopotamia)
BALKANS (1940, 1944, World War II)
BAPAUME (1871, Franco-Prussian War)
BAROSSA (1811, Peninsular War)
BASSANO (1796, French Revolutionary Wars)
BASSEIN (1780, First British-Maratha War)
BATAVIA (1811, Napoleonic Wars)
BATOCHE (1885, Riel's Second Rebellion)
BAUTZEN (1813, Napoleonic Wars)
BELMONT (1899, Second Boer War)
BENBURB (1646, Great Irish Rebellion)
BÉTHUNE (1707, War of the Spanish
Succession)
BETIOCA (1813, Colombian War of
Independence)
BEZETHA (66, Jewish Wars of Roman Empire)
BIBERAC (1796, French Revolutionary Wars)
BITONTO (1734, War of the Polish
Succession)
BOKHARA (1220, Tatar Invasion of Kharismia)
BOURBON (1810, Napleonic Wars)
BRESCIA (1849, Italian Rising)
BRESLAU (1757, Seven Years' War)
BRIENNE (1814, Napoleonic Wars)
BULL RUN (1861, 1862, American Civil War)
CADESIA (636, Muslim Invasion of Persia)
CADSAND (1357, Hundred Years' War)
CALAFAT (1854, Crimean War)
CALICUT (1790, Second British-Mysore War)
CARACHA (1813, Colombian War of
Independence)
CARIGAT (1791, Second British-Mysore War)

7—continued

CARNOUL (1739, Persian Invasion of India)
CARRHAE (53 B.C., Parthian War)
CASSANO (1705, War of the Spanish
Succession)
CASSINO (1944, World War II)
CHÂLONS (271, Revolt of the Legions of
Aquitaine; 366, Invasion of the Alemanni;
451, Wars of the Western Roman Empire)
CHETATE (1854, Crimean War)
CHOCZIM (1769, Ottoman Wars)
CHONG-JU (1904, Russo-Japanese War)
CIBALIS (315, War of the Two Empires)
CLISSAU (1702, Swedish-Polish Wars)
CLUSIUM (225 B.C., Conquest of Cisalpine
Gaul)
COLENSO (1899, Second Boer War)
COLOMBO (1796, French Revolutionary Wars)
CORDOVA (1010, Spanish-Muslim Wars)
CORINTH (429 B.C., Peloponnesian War; 394
B.C., Corinthian War; 1862, American Civil
War)
CORONEA (447 B.C., First Peloponnesian War;
394 B.C., Corinthian War)
CORONEL (1914, World War I)
CORUMBA (1877, Paraguayan War)
CORUNNA (1809, Peninsular War)
COUTRAS (1587, French Religious Wars)
CRAONNE (1814, Napoleonic Wars)
CRAVANT (1423, Hundred Years' War)
CREFELD (1758, Seven Years' War)
CREMONA (198 B.C., Second Gallic Invasion;
69, Civil Wars of the Roman Empire; 1702,
War of the Spanish Succession)
CRONION (379 B.C., Second Carthaginian
Invasion of Sicily)
CROTONE (982, German Invasion of Italy)
CROTOYE (1347, Hundred Years' War)
CUASPAD (1862, Ecuador-Colombia War)
CURICTA (49 B.C., Civil War of Caesar and
Pompey)
CUSTOZA (1866, Italian Wars of
Independence)
CYZICUS (410 B.C., Peloponnesian War; 88
B.C., First Mithridatic War)
CZASLAU (1742, War of the Austrian
Succession)
DAZAIFU (1281, Chinese Invasion of Japan)
DEORHAM (577, Wessex against the Welsh)
DODOWAH (1826, First British-Ashanti War)
DONABEW (1825, First Burma War)
DRESDEN (1813, Napleonic Wars)
DRISTEN (973, Wars of the Byzantine Empire)
DUNDALK (1318, Scottish Invasion of Ireland)
DUNKELD (1689, Jacobite Rising)
DUNKIRK (1940, World War II)
DUPPLIN (1332, Baliol's Rising)
DURAZZO (1081, Norman Invasion of Italy)
ECKMÜHL (1809, Napoleonic Wars)
ECNOMUS (256 B.C., First Punic War)
EL CANEY (1898, Spanish-American War)

7—continued

ELK HORN (1862, American Civil War)
ENTHOLM (1676, Northern Wars)
EPHESUS (499 B.C., Ionian War; 262 B.C., Gallic Invasion of Asia)
ESSLING (1809, Napoleonic Wars)
ETAMPES (604, Burgundians against Neustrians)
EVESHAM (1265, Barons' War)
FALKIRK (1298, Wars of Scottish Independence; 1746, The Forty-five Rebellion)
FERRARA (1815, Napoleon's Hundred Days)
FLEURUS (1622, Thirty Years' War; 1690, War of the Grand Alliance; 1794, French Revolutionary Wars)
FLODDEN (1513, Anglo-Scottish Wars)
FOCSANI (1789, Ottoman Wars)
FORNOVO (1495, Italian Wars)
FRANLIN (1864, American Civil War)
FULFORD (1066, Norse Invasion of England)
FUSHIMI (1868, Japanese Revolution)
GALICIA (1914, World War I)
GATE PAH (1864, Maori-British War)
GHERAIN (1763, British Conquest of Bengal)
GHOAINE (1842, First British-Afghan War)
GORARIA (1857, Indian Mutiny)
GORLICE (1915, World War I)
GRANADA (1319, 1491, Spanish-Muslim Wars)
GRANGAM (1721, Great Northern War)
GRANSON (1476, Burgundian Wars)
GRASPAN (1899, Second Boer War)
GRENADA (1779, American Revolutionary War; 1983, American Invasion)
GROCHOW (1831, Second Polish Rising)
GUJERAT (1849, Second British-Sikh War)
GWALIOR (1780, First British-Maratha War; 1858, Indian Mutiny)
HAARLEM (1572, Netherlands War of Independence)
HASLACH (1805, Napoleonic Wars)
HELORUS (492 B.C., Wars of Sicily)
HERNANI (1836, 1837, First Carlist War)
HERRERA (1837, First Carlist War)
HILL 875 (1967, Vietnam War)
HILL 881 (1967, Vietnam War)
HOGLAND (1789, Russo-Swedish Wars)
HOOGHLY, THE (1759, Anglo-Dutch Wars in India)
HUMAITA (1866, 1868, Paraguayan War)
HWAI-HAI (1948, Chinese Civil War)
ISASZCQ (1849, Hungarian Rising)
IWO-JIMA (1945, World War II)
JAMAICA (1655, Anglo-Spanish Wars)
JAVA SEA (1942, World War II)
JITGURH (1815, British Gurkha War)
JUTLAND (1916, World War I)
KAIPING (1895, Sino-Japanese War)
KALISCH (1706, Great Northern War)
KALUNGA (1814, British-Gurkha War)
KAMARUT (1824, First Burma War)

7—continued

KAMBULA (1879, Zulu War)
KAPOLNA (1849, Hungarian Rising)
KASHGAL (1883, British Sudan Campaigns)
KHARKOV (1942, 1943, World War II)
KHE SANH (1968, Vietnam War)
KILSYTH (1645, English Civil War)
KINEYRI (1848, Second British-Sikh War)
KINLOSS (1009, Danish Invasion of Scotland)
KINSALE (1601, O'Neill's Rebellion)
KIUCHAU (1904, Russo-Japanese War)
KOJENDE (1219, Tatar Invasion of Central Asia)
KOMATSU (1062, Japanese Nine Years' War)
KOSSOVA (1398, 1448, Ottoman Wars)
KRASNOI (1812, Napoleonic Wars)
KROTZKA (1739, Ottoman Wars)
KURDLAH (1795, Maratha Wars)
LA HOGUE (1692, War of the Grand Alliance)
LARISSA (171 B.C., Third Macedonian War)
L'ECLUSE (1340, Hundred Years' War)
LEGHORN (1653, Anglo-Dutch Wars)
LEGNANO (1176, Wars of the Lombard League)
LEIPZIG (1631, Thirty Years' War; 1813, Napoleonic Wars)
LEPANTO (1571, Cyprus War)
LEUCTRA (371 B.C., Wars of the Greek City States)
LEUTHEN (1757, Seven Years' War)
LINCOLN, FAIR OF (1217, First Barons' War)
LINDLEY (1900, Second Boer War)
LOCNINH (1967, Vietnam War)
LOFTCHA (1877, Russo-Turkish War)
LUCKNOW (1857, Indian Mutiny)
LUZZARA (1702, War of the Spanish Succession)
MAGENTA (1859, Italian Wars of Independence)
MAIWAND (1880, Second British-Afghan War)
MALACCA (1513, Portuguese Conquests)
MALAKOV (1855, Crimean War)
MALNATE (1859, Italian Wars of Independence)
MANSURA (1250, Seventh Crusade)
MARENGO (1800, French Revolutionary Wars)
MARGATE (1387, Hundred Years' War)
MAROSCH, THE (101, Roman Empire Wars)
MATAPAN, CAPE (1941, World War II)
MATCHIN (1791, Ottoman Wars)
MEEANEE (1843, Sind Campaign)
MEMPHIS (459 B.C., Athenian Expedition to Egypt; 638, Muslim Conquest of Egypt; 1862, American Civil War)
MENTANA (1867, Italian Wars of Independence)
MESSINA (1284, Aragonese Conquest of Sicily; 1718, War of the Quadruple Alliance)
METHVEN (1306, Wars of Scottish Independence)

7—continued

MILAZZO (1860, Italian Wars of Independence)
MINORCA (1756, Seven Years' War; 1762, American Revolutionary War)
MOGILEV (1812, Napoleonic Wars)
MONARDA (1501, Moorish Insurrection)
MONTIEL (1369, Castilian Civil War)
MORELLA (1840, First Carlist War)
MORTARA (1849, Italian Wars of Independence)
MOSKOWA (1812, Napoleonic Wars)
NAEFELS (1388, Swiss-Austrian Wars)
NAISSUS (269, Gothic Invasion of the Roman Empire)
NAM DONG (1964, Vietnam War)
NANKING (1949, Chinese Civil War)
NEUWIED (1797, French Revolutionary Wars)
NEWBURN (1640, Anglo-Scottish Wars)
NEWBURY (1643, 1644, English Civil War)
NEW ROSS (1798, Irish Rebellion)
NIAGARA (1759, Seven Years' War)
NINEVEH (627, Persian Wars)
NISIBIS (338, 346, 350, Persian Wars of the Roman Empire)
NIVELLE (1813, Peninsular War)
OCZAKOV (1737, Ottoman Wars)
ODAWARA (1590, Hojo Rebellion)
OKINAWA (1945, World War II)
OOSCATA (1768, First British-Mysore War)
OPEQUAN (1864, American Civil War)
ORLÉANS (1428, Hundred Years' War)
PAGAHAR (1825, First Burma War)
PALERMO (1848, Italian Wars of Independence)
PALMYRA (272, Roman Empire Wars)
PANIPAT (1526, Third Mughal Invasion of India; 1556, Hindu Revolt; 1759, Afghan Maratha Wars)
PARKANY (1663, Ottoman Wars)
PLASSEY (1757, Seven Years' War)
PLATAEA (479 B.C., Third Persian Invasion; 429 B.C., Great Peloponnesian War)
PLESCOW (1615, Russo-Swedish Wars)
PLOVDIV (1878, Russo-Turkish War)
POLOTSK (1812, Napoleonic Wars)
PRESTON (1648, English Civil War; 1715, The Fifteen Rebellion)
PULTAVA (1709, Great Northern War)
PULTUSK (1703, Great Northern War; 1806, Napoleonic Wars)
PUNNIAR (1843, Gwalior Campaign)
RASTADT (1796, French Revolutionary Wars)
RAVENNA (729, Byzantine Empire Wars; 1512, War of the Holy League)
READING (871, Danish Invasions of Britain)
REVOLAX (1808, Russo-Swedish Wars)
RIMNITZ (1789, Ottoman Wars)
RIO SECO (1808, Peninsular War)
ROSTOCK (1677, Danish-Swedish Wars)

7—continued

ROUCOUX (1746, War of the Austrian Succession)
RUMANIA (1916, World War I)
RUSPINA (46 B.C., Civil War of Caesar and Pompey)
SABUGAL (1811, Peninsular War)
SAGUNTO (1811, Peninsular War)
SALAMIS (480 B.C., Third Persian Invasion; 307 B.C., Wars of Alexander's Successors)
SALERNO (1943, World War II)
SAN JUAN (1898, Spanish-American War)
SÁRKÁNY (1848, Hungarian Rising)
SCUTARI (1474, Ottoman Wars)
SEALION, OPERATION (1940, World War II)
SECCHIA, THE (1734, War of the Polish Succession)
SEGEWÁR (1849, Hungarian Rising)
SELINUS (409 B.C., Second Carthaginian Invasion of Sicily)
SEMPACH (1386, Swiss War of Independence)
SENEFFE (1674, Wars of Louis XIV)
SENEKAL (1900, Second Boer War)
SHARQAT (1918, World War I)
SIMGARA (348, 360, Persian Wars of the Roman Empire)
SINNACA (53 B.C., Parthian War)
SINUIJU (1951, Korean War)
SKALITZ (1866, Seven Weeks' War)
SOBRAON (1846, First Sikh-Sikh War)
SOCZAWA (1676, Ottoman Wars)
SOMNATH (1024, Mahmud's Twelfth Invasion of India)
ST DENIS (1567, French Religious Wars; 1837, French-Canadian Rising)
ST LUCIA (1794, French Revolutionary Wars)
SURINAM (1804, Napoleonic Wars)
SURSUTI, THE (1191, 1192, Mohammed Ghori's Invasion)
SVISTOV (1877, Russo-Turkish War)
SZIGETH (1566, Ottoman Wars)
TABRACA (398, Revolt of Gildon)
TAGINAE (552, Byzantine Empire Wars)
TALKHAN (1221, Tatar Invasion of Khorassan)
TALNEER (1818, Third British-Maratha War)
TANAGRA (457 B.C., Peloponnesian Wars)
TANJORE (1758, Seven Years' War; 1773, First British-Mysore War)
TARANTO (1501, Italian Wars; 1940, World War II)
TELAMON (225 B.C., Conquest of Cisalpine Gaul)
TE-LI-SSU (1904, Russo-Japanese War)
TERGOES (1572, Netherlands War of Independence)
THAPSUS (46 B.C., Civil War of Caesar and Pompey)
TICINUS (218 B.C., Second Punic War)
TOLBIAC (496, Rise of the Franks)
TOLENUS (90 B.C., Social War)

7—continued

TOURNAI (1581, Netherlands War of Independence; 1709, War of the Spanish Succession)
TREBBIA (218 B.C., Second Punic War; 1799, French Revolutionary Wars)
TREVERI (55 B.C., Gallic Wars)
TRIPOLI (643, Muslim Conquest of Africa)
TUNISIA (1942, World War II)
TURBIGO (1859, Italian Wars of Independence)
UKRAINE (1943, World War II)
UPPSALA (1520, 1521, Danish-Swedish Wars)
VESERIS (339 B.C., Latin War)
VIGO BAY (1702, War of the Spanish Succession)
VILLACH (1492, Ottoman Wars)
VILLETA (1868, Paraguayan War)
VIMEIRO (1808, Peninsular War)
VINAROZ (1938, Spanish Civil War)
VITORIA (1813, Peninsular War)
VOUILLÉ (507, Rise of the Franks)
WARBURG (1760, Seven Years' War)
WARGAOM (1779, First British-Maratha War)
WEPENER (1900, Second Boer War)
WIMPFEN (1622, Thirty Years' War)
WINKOVO (1812, Napoleonic Wars)
YASHIMA (1184, Taira War)
ZLOTSOW (1676, Ottoman Wars)
ZURAKOW (1676, Ottoman Wars)
ZUTPHEN (1586, Netherlands War of Independence)

8

ABERDEEN (1644, English Civil War)
ABU HAMED (1897, British Sudan Campaigns)
ACAPULCO (1855, Mexican Liberal Rising)
ADUATUCA (52 B.C., Gallic Wars)
AIZNADIN (634, Muslim Invasion of Syria)
ALICANTE (1706, War of the Spanish Succession)
ALMENARA (1710, War of the Spanish Succession)
AMALINDE (1818, Kaffir Wars)
ANAQUITO (1546, Conquest of Peru)
ANTIETAM (1862, American Civil War)
AQUILEIA (394, Roman Civil Wars)
ARRETIUM (283 B.C., Etruscan War)
ASIRGHAR (1819, Third British-Maratha War)
ASPENDUS (191 B.C., Wars of the Hellenistic Monarchies)
ASSUNDUN (1016, Danish Invasions of Britain)
ATLANTIC (1917, World War I)
AUGSBURG (900, Germans verus Hungarians)
AULDEARN (1645, English Civil War)
AVARICUM (53 B.C., Gallic Wars)
AXARQUIA (1483, Spanish-Muslim Wars)
AYACUCHO (1824, Peruvian War of Independence)
AZIMGHUR (1858, Indian Mutiny)

8—continued

BAGRADAS (49 B.C., Wars of the First Triumvirate)
BASTOGNE (1944, World War II)
BEAUMONT (1870, Franco-Prussian War)
BEDA FOMM (1941, World War II)
BELGRADE (1456, 1717, 1789, Ottoman Wars)
BELLEVUE (1870, Franco-Prussian War)
BEREZINA (1812, Napoleonic War)
BEYMAROO (1841, First British-Afghan War)
BIBRACTE (58 B.C., Gallic Wars)
BISMARCK (1941, World War II)
BLENHEIM (1704, War of the Spanish Succession)
BLUEBERG (1806, Napoleonic Wars)
BORNHOLM (1676, Northern War)
BORODINO (1812, Napoleonic Wars)
BOULOGNE (1544, Anglo-French Wars)
BOUVINES (1214, Anglo-French Wars)
BOVIANUM (305 B.C., Second Samnite War)
BRIHUEGA (1710, War of the Spanish Succession)
BROOKLYN (1776, American Revolutionary War)
BUZENVAL (1871, Franco-Prussian War)
CALCUTTA (1756, Seven Years' War)
CALDIERO (1796, French Revolutionary Wars; 1805, Napoleonic Wars)
CAPE BONA (468, Wars of the Western Roman Empire)
CARABOBO (1821, Venezuelan War of Independence)
CARLISLE (1745, The Forty-five Rebellion)
CARRICAL (1758, Seven Years' War)
CARTHAGE (152 B.C., Third Punic War; 533, Byzantine Empire Wars)
CASTELLA (1813, Peninsular War)
CAWNPORE (1857, Indian Mutiny)
CHERITON (1644, English Civil War)
CHEVILLY (1870, Franco-Prussian War)
CHIOGGIA (1380, War of Chioggia)
CHIPPEWA (1814, War of 1812)
CLONTARF (1014, Norse Invasion of Ireland)
COCHEREL (1364, Hundred Years' War)
COLOMBEY (1870, Franco-Prussian War)
COPRATUS, THE (316 B.C., Wars of Alexander's Successors)
CORAL SEA (1942, World War II)
COURTRAI (1302, Flemish War)
CRAYFORD (456, Jutish Invasion)
CRIMISUS (341 B.C., Third Carthaginian Invasion of Sicily)
CULLODEN (1746, The Forty-five Rebellion)
CZARNOVO (1806, Napoleonic Wars)
DAMASCUS (635, Muslim Invasion of Syria; 1401, Tatar Invasion of Syria; 1918, World War I)
DAN-NO-URA (1185, Taira War)
DNIESTER (1769, Ottoman Wars)
DOMINICA (1782, American Revolutionary War)

8—continued

DREPANUM (249 B.C., First Punic Wars)
DROGHEDA (1641, Great Irish Rebellion; 1649, Cromwell's Campaign in Ireland)
DRUMCLOG (1679, Covenanters' Rising)
EDGEHILL (1642, English Civil War)
ESPINOSA (1808, Peninsular War)
ETHANDUN (878, Danish Invasions of Britain)
FAIR OAKS (1862, American Civil War)
FAVENTIA (82 B.C., Civil War of Marius and Sulla)
FLANDERS (1940, World War II)
FLORENCE (406, Wars of the Western Roman Empire)
FLUSHING (1809, Napoleonic Wars)
FONTENOY (1745, War of the Austrian Succession)
FORMIGNY (1450, Hundred Years' War)
FRASTENZ (1499, Swiss-Swabian War)
FREIBURG (1644, Thirty Years' War)
FRETEVAL (1194, Anglo-French Wars)
GADEBESK (1712, Great Northern War)
GAULAULI (1858, Indian Mutiny)
GEMBLOUX (1578, Netherlands War of Independence)
GEOK TEPE (1878, Russian Conquest of Central Asia)
GERBEROI (1080, Norman Revolt)
GERGOVIA (52 B.C., Gallic Wars)
GISLIKON (1847, War of the Sonderbund)
GITSCHIN (1866, Seven Weeks' War)
GOODWINS, THE (1666, Anglo-Dutch Wars)
GRAF SPEE (1939, World War II)
GRANICUS, THE (334 B.C., Alexander's Asiatic Campaigns)
GÜNZBURG (1805, Napoleonic Wars)
HADRANUM (344 B.C., Sicilian Wars)
HAHOZAKI (1274, Tatar Invasion of Japan)
HASTINGS (1066, Norman Conquest)
HERACLEA (280 B.C., Pyrrhus' Invasion of Italy; 313, Roman Civil Wars)
HERDONEA (210 B.C., Second Punic War)
HERRINGS, THE (1429, Hundred Years' War)
HONG KONG (1941, World War II)
HYDASPES, THE (326 B.C., Alexander's Asiatic Campaigns)
INKERMAN (1854, Crimean War)
ITABITSU (740, Hirotsuke's Rebellion)
JEMAPPES (1792, French Revolutionary Wars)
JIDBALLI (1904, Somali Expedition)
JOTAPATA (67 A.D., Jewish Wars of Roman Empire)
KANDAHAR (1221, Tatar Invasion of Afghanistan; 1545, Mughal Invasion of Afghanistan; 1648, Perso-Afghan Wars; 1834, Afghan Tribal Wars; 1880, Second British-Afghan War)
KATZBACH (1813, Napoleonic Wars)
KHARTOUM (1884, British-Sudan Campaigns)
KIRBEKAN (1885, British Sudan Campaigns)

8—continued

KLUSHINO (1610, Russo-Polish Wars)
KORYGAOM (1818, Third British-Maratha War)
KULEVCHA (1829, Ottoman Wars)
KUMAMOTO (1876, Satsuma Rebellion)
KUMANOVO (1912, 1st Balkan War)
LANGPORT (1645, English Civil War)
LANGSIDE (1568, Scottish Civil Wars)
LA PUEBLA (1862, 1863, Franco-Mexican War)
LARISSUS, THE (209 B.C., Wars of the Achaean League)
LAUFFELD (1747, War of the Austrian Succession)
LAUTULAE (316 B.C., Second Samnite War)
LE CATEAU (1914, World War I)
LEITSKAU (1813, Napoleonic Wars)
LEONTINI (211 B.C., Second Punic War)
LIAOYANG (1904, Russo-Japanese War)
LIEGNITZ (1760, Seven Years' War)
LOBOSITZ (1756, Seven Years' War)
LUNCARTY (980, Danish Invasions of Scotland)
LYS RIVER (1918, World War I)
MAFEKING (1899, Second Boer War)
MAGNESIA (190 B.C., Wars of the Hellenistic Monarchies)
MAHIDPUR (1817, Third British-Maratha War)
MANDONIA (338 B.C., Macedonian Wars)
MANTINEA (418 B.C., Peloponnesian War; 362 B.C., Wars of the Greek City States; 208 B.C., Wars of the Achaean League)
MARATHON (490 B.C., Persian-Greek Wars)
MEDELLIN (1809, Peninsular War)
MEDENINE (1943, World War II)
MELITENE (578, Persian-Byzantine Wars)
MESSINES (1917, World War I)
METAURUS (207 B.C., Second Punic War)
MOLLWITZ (1741, War of the Austrian Succession)
MONTREAL (1760, Seven Years' War)
MORTLACK (1010, Danish Invasions of Scotland)
MORTMANT (1814, Napoleonic Wars)
MÖSKIRCH (1800, French Revolutionary Wars)
MOUSCRON (1794, French Revolutionary Wars)
MÜHLBERG (1547, German Reformation Wars)
MÜHLDORF (1322, Civil War of the Holy Roman Empire)
MUSA BAGH (1858, Indian Mutiny)
MYTILENE (428 B.C., 406 B.C., Great Peloponnesian War)
NAVARINO (1827, Greek War of Independence)
NEHAVEND (A.D. 641, Muslim Invasion of Persia)
NIQUITAS (1813, Colombian War of Independence)

8—continued

NUMANTIA (142 B.C., Lusitanian War)
OBLIGADO (1845, Uruguayan Civil War)
OMDURMAN (1898, British-Sudan Campaigns)
ONESSANT (1778, American Revolutionary War)
OSTROWNO (1812, Napoleonic Wars)
OVERLORD, OPERATION (1944, World War II)
PALESTRO (1859, Italian Wars of Independence)
PALO ALTO (1846, American-Mexican War)
PANDOSIA (331 B.C., Macedonian Wars)
PANORMUS (251 B.C., First Punic War)
PEA RIDGE (1862, American Civil War)
PELUSIUM (525 B.C., Persian Conquest of Egypt; 321 B.C., War of Alexander's Successors)
PESHAWAR (1001, Afghan Invasion of India)
PHILIPPI (42 B.C., Roman Civil Wars)
PODHAJCE (1667, Polish-Turkish Wars)
POITIERS (507, Gothic Invasion of France; 1356, Hundred Years' War)
PORTLAND (1653, Anglo-Dutch Wars)
PYRAMIDS (1798, French Revolutionary Wars)
PYRENEES (1813, Peninsular War)
RATHENOW (1675, Swedish Invasion of Brandenburg)
RICHMOND (1862, American Civil War)
ROSSBACH (1757, Seven Years' War)
ROVEREDO (1796, French Revolutionary Wars)
SAALFELD (1806, Napoleonic Wars)
SAMAGHAR (1658, Rebellion of Aurungzebe)
SANTAREM (1834, Portuguese Civil War)
SAPIENZA (1490, Ottoman Wars)
SARATOGA (1777, American Revolutionary War)
SAUCOURT (861, Norse Invasion of France)
SEMINARA (1495, French Wars in Italy)
SENTINUM (298 B.C., Third Samnite War)
SHANGHAI (1937, Sino-Japanese War)
SHOLAPUR (1818, Third British-Maratha War)
SIDASSIR (1799, Third British-Mysore War)
SIKAJOKI (1808, Russo-Swedish Wars)
SILISTRA (1854, Crimean War)
SINSHEIM (1674, Wars of Louis XIV)
SLIVNICA (1885, Serbo-Bulgarian War)
SMOLENSK (1708, Great Northern War; 1812, Napoleonic Wars; 1941, World War II)
SOISSONS (486, Rise of the Franks)
SORAUREN (1813, Peninsular War)
SPION KOP (1900, Second Boer War)
SPLITTER (1679, Swedish Invasion of Brandenburg)
ST ALBANS (1455, 1461, Wars of the Roses)
STANDARD, THE (1138, Anglo-Scottish Wars)
STE CROIX (1807, Napoleonic Wars)
ST GEORGE (1500, Ottoman Wars)
ST MIHIEL (1918, World War I)
STOCKACH (1799, French Revolutionary Wars)

8—continued

ST PRIVAT (1870, Franco-Prussian War)
STRATTON (1643, English Civil War)
ST THOMAS (1807, Napoleonic Wars)
SYRACUSE (415 B.C., Peloponnesian Wars; 387 B.C., Second Carthaginian Invasion of Sicily; 213 B.C., Second Punic War)
TACUBAYA (1859, Mexican Liberal Rising)
TALAVERA (1809, Peninsular War)
TARAPACA (1879, Peruvian-Chilean War)
TAYEIZAN (1868, Japanese Revolution)
TEMESVAR (1849, Hungarian Rising)
THETFORD (870, Danish Invasions of England)
TIBERIAS (1187, Crusader-Saracen Wars)
TOULOUSE (1814, Napoleonic Wars)
TRINIDAD (1797, French Revolutionary Wars)
TSINGTAO (1914, World War I)
TSUSHIMA (1419, Mongol Invasion of Japan)
TURNHOUT (1597, Netherlands War of Independence)
VALLETTA (1798, French Revolutionary Wars)
VALUTINO (1812, Napoleonic Wars)
VELENEZE (1848, Hungarian Rising)
VELLETRI (1849, Italian Wars of Independence)
VERNEUIL (1424, Hundred Years' War)
VILLIERS (1870, Franco-Prussian War)
VOLTURNO (1860, Italian Wars of Independence)
WATERLOO (1815, Napoleonic Wars)
WATIGAON (1825, First Burma War)
WIESLOCH (1622, Thirty Years' War)
YAMAZAKI (1582, Mitsuhide Rebellion)
YENIKALE, GULF OF (1790, Ottoman Wars)
YORKTOWN (1781, American Revolutionary War; 1862, American Civil War)
ZENDECAN (1039, Turkish Invasion of Afghanistan)
ZORNDORF (1758, Seven Years' War)

9

ABENSBERG (1809, Napoleonic Wars)
AGENDICUM (52 B.C., Gallic Wars)
AGINCOURT (1415, Hundred Years' War)
AGNADELLO (1509, War of the League of Cambrai)
AHMADABAD (1780, First British-Maratha War)
AHMED KHEL (1880, Second British-Afghan War)
AIGUILLON (1347, Hundred Years' War)
ALCANTARA (1580, Spanish Conquest of Portugal; 1706, War of the Spanish Succession)
ALHANDEGA (939, Spanish-Muslim Wars)
ALRESFORD (1644, English Civil War)
ALTENDORF (1632, Thirty Years' War)
AMSTETTEN (1805, Napoleonic Wars)
ANGOSTURA (1847, American-Mexican War; 1868, Paraguayan War)
AQUIDABAN (1870, Paraguayan War)

9—continued

ARGINUSAE (406 B.C.. Great Peloponnesian War)

ARKENHOLM (1455, Douglas Rebellion)

ASKULTSIK (1828, Ottoman Wars)

ASTRAKHAN (1569, Turkish Invasion of Russia)

ATAHUALPA (1531, Conquest of Peru)

AUERSTADT (1806, Napoleonic Wars)

AYLESFORD (456, Jutish Invasion of Britain)

BALACLAVA (1854, Crimean War)

BALLYMORE (1798, Irish Rebellion)

BANGALORE (1791, Second British-Mysore War)

BARCELONA (1705, War of the Spanish Succession; 1938, Spanish Civil War)

BEDRIACUM (69, Civil Wars of the Roman Empire)

BENEVENTO (1266, Franco-Italian Wars)

BERGFRIED (1807, Napleonic Wars)

BHURTPORE (1805, Second British-Maratha War; 1827, Second Siege of)

BLACK ROCK (1812, War of 1812)

BLUFF COVE (1982, Falkland Isles)

BOIS-LE-DUC (1794, French Revolutionary Wars)

BORGHETTO (1796, French Revolutionary Wars)

BORNHOVED (1227, War of Scandinavia)

BRENTFORD (1642, English Civil War)

BRIG OF DEE (1639, Bishops' Wars)

BUCHAREST (1771, Ottoman Wars)

BURNS HILL (1847, Kaffir Wars)

BYZANTIUM (318 B.C., Wars of Alexander's Successors; 323, Civil Wars of the Roman Empire)

CAMERINUM (298 B.C., Third Samnite War)

CAPE HENRY (1781, American Revolutionary War)

CAPORETTO (1917, World War I)

CAPRYSEMA (743 B.C., First Messenian War)

CASILINUM (554, Byzantine Empire Wars)

CASTILLON (1453, Hundred Years' War)

CERIGNOLA (1503, Italian Wars)

CHACABUCO (1817, Chilean War of Independence)

CHAERONEA (338 B.C., Amphictyonic War; 86 B.C., First Mithridatic War)

CHALCEDON (74 B.C., Third Mithridatic War)

CHAMPAGNE (1915, World War I)

CHARASIAB (1879, Second British-Afghan War)

CHARENTON (1649, War of the Fronde)

CHE-MUL-PHO (1904, Russo-Japanese War)

CHORILLOS (1861, Peruvian-Chilean War)

CHOTUSITZ (1742, War of the Austrian Succession)

CIVITELLA (1033, Norman Invasion of Italy)

CORRICHIE (1562, Huntly's Rebellion)

COULMIERS (1870, Franco-Prussian War)

CROSSKEYS (1862, American Civil War)

9—continued

CUDDALORE (1783, American Revolutionary War)

CURUPAYTI (1866, Paraguayan War)

CYNOSSEMA (411 B.C., Peloponnesian War)

DENNEWITZ (1813, Napoleonic Wars)

DETTINGEN (1743, War of the Austrian Succession)

DEVICOTTA (1749, Carnatic War)

DORYLAEUM (1097, First Crusade)

DUNSINANE (1054, Anglo-Scottish Wars)

EBRO RIVER (1938, Spanish Civil War)

EDERSBERG (1809, Napoleonic Wars)

EDGEWORTH (1469, Wars of the Roses)

EL ALAMEIN (1942, World War II)

ELCHINGEN (1805, Napoleonic Wars)

ELLANDUNE (825, Wessex versus Mercia)

ELLEPORUS (389 B.C., Italiot Invasion of Sicily)

EMPINGHAM (1470, Wars of the Roses)

EURYMEDON, THE (466 B.C., Third Persian Invasion)

FAMAGUSTA (1570, Cyprus War)

FISH CREEK (1855, Riel's Second Rebellion)

FIVE FORKS (1865, American Civil War)

FRIEDLAND (1807, Napoleonic Wars)

FRONTIERS, BATTLE OF THE (1914, World War I)

GALLIPOLI (1915, World War I)

GERMAGHAH (1193, Tatar Conquest of Central Asia)

GIBRALTAR (1704, War of the Spanish Succession; 1779, American Revolutionary War)

GLADSMUIR (1745, The Forty-five Rebellion)

GLEN FRUIN (1604, Scottish Civil Wars)

GLENLIVET (1594, Huntly's Rebellion)

GRAMPIANS, THE (Roman Invasion of Scotland)

GRANDELLA (1266, Italian Wars)

GUAL-EL-RAS (1860, Spanish-Moroccan War)

GUINEGATE (1513, Anglo-French Wars)

GUMBINNEN (1914, World War I)

HALIARTUS (395 B.C., Wars of Greek City-States)

HEILSBERG (1807, Napoleonic Wars)

HEMUSHAGU (1595, Japanese Invasion of Korea)

HERICOURT (1474, Burgundian Wars)

HOCHKIRCH (1758, Seven Years' War)

HOCHSTADT (1800, French Revolutionary Wars)

HYDERABAD (1843, Conquest of Sind)

JERUSALEM (70 A.D., Jewish Wars of Roman Empire; 637, Muslim Invasion of Syria; 1099, First Crusade; 1187, Crusader-Turkish Wars; 1917, World War I; 1948, Israeli-Arab Wars)

JUGDULLUK (1842, First British-Afghan War)

KAGOSHIMA (1877, Satsuma Rebellion)

KARA BURUR (1791, Ottoman Wars)

KARAGAULA (1774, Cossack Rising)

9—continued

KARAMURAN (1225, Tatar Conquest of Central Asia)
KASSASSIN (1882, Egyptian Revolt)
KEMENDINE (1824, First Burma War)
KERESZTES (1596, Ottoman Wars)
KHARISMIA (1220, Tatar Invasion of Central Asia)
KIMBERLEY (1899, Second Boer War)
KISSINGEN (1866, Seven Weeks' War)
KIZIL-TEPE (1877, Russo-Turkish War)
KRAKOVICZ (1475, Ottoman Wars)
KUNOBITZA (1443, Ottoman Wars)
LADYSMITH (1899, Second Boer War)
LANG'S NECK (1881, First Boer War)
LANSDOWNE (1643, English Civil Wars)
LE BOURGET (1870, Franco-Prussian War)
LENINGRAD (1944, World War II)
LEXINGTON (1775, American Revolutionary War; 1861, American Civil War)
LEYTE GULF (1944, World War II)
LILYBAEUM (250 B.C., First Punic War)
LINKÖPING (1598, Swedish-Polish Wars)
LÖWENBERG (1813, Napoleonic Wars)
MAGDEBURG (1631, Thirty Years' War)
MALAVILLY (1799, Third British-Mysore War)
MALEGNANO (1859, Italian Wars of Independence)
MANGALORE (1783, First British-Mysore War)
MANSFIELD (1864, American Civil War)
MARIA ZELL (1805, Napoleonic Wars)
MARIGNANO (1515, Italian Wars)
MARSAGLIA (1693, War of the Grand Alliance)
MERSEBURG (934, Germans against Hungarians)
MILLESIMO (1796, French Revolutionary Wars)
MIOHOSAKI (764, Oshikatsa's Rebellion)
MITA CABAN (1362, Tatar Wars)
MOHRUNGEN (1807, Napoleonic Wars)
MONTEREAU (1814, Napoleonic Wars)
MONTERREY (1846, Amercian-Mexican War)
MONTLHÉRY (1465, Franco-Burgundian War)
MORAZZONE (1848, Italian Wars of Independence)
MUKWANPUR (1816, British-Gurkha War)
MYONNESUS (190 B.C., Wars of the Hellenistic Monarchies)
NAGY-SARLO (1849, Hungarian Rising)
NASHVILLE (1863, American Civil War)
NAULOCHUS (36 B.C., Wars of the Second Triumvirate)
NAUPACTUS (429 B.C., Great Peloponnesian War)
NAVARRETE (1367, Hundred Years' War)
NEGAPATAM (1746, War of the Austrian Succession; 1781, Second British Mysore War; 1782, American Revolutionary War)
NEW GUINEA (1942, World War II)
NEW MARKET (1864, American Civil War)

9—continued

NICOPOLIS (66 B.C., 47 B.C., Third Mithridatic War; 1396, Ottoman Wars; 1877, Russo-Turkish War)
NUJUFGHUR (1857, Indian Mutiny)
OCEAN POND (1864, American Civil War)
OENOPHYTA (457 B.C., First Peloponnesian War)
OLTENITZA (1853, Crimean War)
OTTERBURN (1388, Wars of Scottish Independence)
OUDENARDE (1708, War of the Spanish Succession)
PELEKANON (1329, Ottoman Wars)
PELISCHAT (1877, Russo-Turkish War)
PERISABOR (363, Persian Wars)
PERPIGNAN (1474, Franco-Spanish War)
PHARSALUS (48 B.C., Civil War of Caesar and Pompey; 1897, Greco-Turkish Wars)
PLACENTIA (271, Invasion of the Alemanni)
POLLENTIA (402, Wars of the Western Roman Empire)
POLLICORE (1781, First British-Mysore War)
PONTEVERT (57 B.C., Gallic Wars)
PORTO NOVO (1781, First British-Mysore War)
PRIMOLANO (1796, French Revolutionary Wars)
PRINCETON (1777, American Revolutionary War)
PYONGYANG (1894, Sino-Japanese War)
QUISTELLO (1734, War of the Polish Succession)
RAMILLIES (1706, War of the Spanish Succession)
RAMNUGGUR (1849, Second British-Sikh War)
RATHMINES (1649, Cromwell's Campaign in Ireland)
RHINELAND, THE (1945, World War II)
RIACHUELA (1865, Paraguayan War)
ROSBECQUE (1382, Flemish-French Wars)
ROSEBURGH (1460, Anglo-Scottish Wars)
RYNEMANTS (1578, Netherlands War of Independence)
SADULAPUR (1848, Second British-Sikh War)
SALAMANCA (1812, Peninsular War; 1858, Mexican Liberal Rising)
SAMARKAND (1220, Tatar Invasion of Khorezm)
SAN LAZARO (1746, War of the Austrian Succession)
SANTANDER (1937, Spanish Civil War)
SARAGOSSA (1700, War of the Spanish Succession; 1808, Peninsular War)
SAXA RUBRA (312, Revolt of Maxentius)
SCARPHEIA (146 B.C., War of the Achaean League)
SCHWECHAT (1848, Hungarian Rising)
SEDGEMOOR (1685, Monmouth's Rebellion)
SERINGHAM (1753, Carnatic War)

9—continued

SEVENOAKS (1450, Cade's Rebellion)
SHAHJEHAN (1221, Tatar Invasion of Khorezm)
SHALDIRAN (1514, Ottoman Wars)
SHEERNESS (1667, Anglo-Dutch Wars)
SHERSTONE (1016, Danish Invasion of England)
SHINOWARA (1183, Yoshinaka's Rebellion)
SHIROGAWA (1876, Satsuma Rebellion)
SHOLINGUR (1781, First British-Mysore War)
SINGAPORE (1942, World War II)
SITABALDI (1817, Third British-Maratha War)
SOLFERINO (1859, Italian Wars of Independence)
SOUTHWARK (1450, Cade's Rebellion)
SPICHEREN (1870, Franco-Prussian War)
STADTLOHN (1623, Thirty Years' War)
STAFFARDA (1690, War of the Grand Alliance)
ST CHARLES (1837, French-Canadian Rising)
ST GOTHARD (1664, Ottoman Wars)
STORMBERG (1899, Second Boer War)
ST QUENTIN (1557, Franco-Spanish Wars; 1871, Franco-Prussian War)
STRALSUND (1628, Thirty Years' War; 1715, Great Northern War)
SUDDASAIN (1848, Second British-Sikh War)
TAKASHIMA (1281, Chinese Invasion of Japan)
TAKU FORTS (1859, Second China War)
TARRAGONA (1811, Peninsular War)
TCHERNAYA (1855, Crimean War)
TOLENTINO (1815, Napoleonic Wars)
TOU MORONG (1966, Vietnam War)
TOURCOING (1794, French Revolutionary Wars)
TRAFALGAR (1805, Napoleonic Wars)
TRAUTENAU (1866, Seven Weeks' War)
TREBIZOND (1461, Ottoman Wars)
TRINKITAT (1884, British-Sudan Campaigns)
VAALKRANZ (1900, Second Boer War)
VARAVILLE (1058, Rise of Normandy)
VAUCHAMPS (1814, Napoleonic Wars)
VERCELLAE (101 B.C., Cimbric War)
VICKSBURG (1862, American Civil War)
VIMY RIDGE (1917, World War I)
VIONVILLE (1870, Franco-Prussian War)
WAKAMATSU (1868, Japanese Revolution)
WAKEFIELD (1460, Wars of the Roses)
WANDIWASH (1760, Seven Years' War; 1780, First British-Mysore War)
WEI-HAI-WEI (1895, Sino-Japanese War)
WORCESTER (1651, English Civil War)
WURTZBURG (1796, French Revolutionary Wars)
WYNANDAEL (1708, War of the Spanish Succession)
YALU RIVER (1894, Sino-Japanese War; 1904, Russo-Japanese War)
ZEUGMINUM (1168, Hungarian Wars)

9—continued

ZUYDER ZEE (1573, Netherlands War of Indpendence)

10

ACULTZINGO (1862, Franco-Mexican War)
ADRIANOPLE (1205, Fourth Crusade; 1913, First Balkan War)
AHMADNAGAR (1593, Mughal Invasion of the Deccan)
ALADJA DAGH (1877, Russo-Turkish War)
ALEXANDRIA (642, Muslim Invasion of Egypt; 1801, British Invasion of Egypt; 1881, Egyptian Revolt)
ALTO PASCIO (1325, Guelfs and Ghibellines)
AMPHIPOLIS (422 B.C., Great Peloponnesian War)
ANCRUM MOOR (1545, Anglo-Scottish Wars)
ARGENTARIA (378, Invasion of the Alemanni)
ARTOIS-LOOS (1915, World War I)
ASPROMONTE (1862, Italian Wars of Independence)
AUSTERLITZ (1805, Napoleonic Wars)
BALL'S BLUFF (1861, American Civil War)
BEACHY HEAD (1690, War of the Grand Alliance)
BEAUSÉJOUR (1755, Seven Year's War)
BENEVENTUM (275 B.C., Pyrrhus' Invasion of Italy; 214 B.C., 212 B.C., Second Punic War)
BENNINGTON (1777, American Revolutionary War)
BERESTECKO (1651, Polish-Cossack War)
BLACKHEATH (1497, Flammock's Rebellion)
BLACKWATER (1598, O'Neill's Rebellion)
BLORE HEATH (1459, Wars of the Roses)
BRANDYWINE (1777, American Revolutionary War)
BRUNANBURH (937, Danish Invasion)
BUENA VISTA (1846, American-Mexican War)
CALATAFIMI (1860, Italian Wars of Independence)
CAMPALDINO (1289, Guelfs and Ghibellines)
CAMPERDOWN (1797, French Revolutionary Wars)
CAMPO SANTO (1743, War of the Austrian Succession)
CARAGUATAY (1869, Paraguayan War)
CARTHAGENA (1741, War of the Austrian Succession)
CEDAR CREEK (1864, American Civil War)
CERISOLLES (1544, Wars of Charles V)
CHARLESTON (1863, American Civil War)
CHEVY CHASE (1388, Wars of Scottish Independence)
CHINGLEPUT (1752, Carnatic War)
CHIPPENHAM (878, Danish Invasions of Britain)
COPENHAGEN (1801, French Revolutionary Wars; 1807, Napoleonic Wars)
CORTE NUOVA (1237, Guelfs and Ghibellines)
CORUPEDION (281 B.C., Wars of the Hellenistic Monarchies)

10—continued

DALMANUTHA (1900, Second Boer War)
DOGGER BANK (1781, American
  Revolutionary War; 1915, World War I)
DONAUWÖRTH (1704, War of the Spanish
  Succession)
DUFFINDALE (1549, Kett's Rebellion)
DUNGANHILL (1647, Great Irish Rebellion)
DYRRACHIUM (48 B.C., Civil War of Caesar
  and Pompey)
ENGLEFIELD (871, Danish Invasion of Britain)
FEHRBELLIN (1675, Swedish Invasion of
  Brandenburg)
FEROZESHAH (1845, First British-Sikh War)
FETHANLEAG (584, Saxon Conquests)
FUTTEYPORE (1857, Indian Mutiny)
GAINES' MILL (1862, American Civil War)
GARIGLIANO (1503, Italian Wars; 1850, Italian
  Wars of Independence)
GERMANTOWN (1777, American
  Revolutionary War)
GETTYSBURG (1863, American Civil War)
GLEN MALONE (1580, Colonization of Ireland)
GOLDEN ROCK (1753, Carnatic War)
GORODECZNO (1812, Napoleonic Wars)
GOTHIC LINE (1944, World War II)
GRANT'S HILL (1758, Seven Years' War)
GRAVELINES (1558, Franco-Spanish Wars)
GRAVELOTTE (1870, Franco-Prussian War)
GUADELOUPE (1794, French Revolutionary
  Wars)
HABBANIYAH (1941, World War II)
HARDENBERG (1580, Netherlands War of
  Independence)
HASTENBECK (1757, Seven Years' War)
HEATHFIELD (633, Mercia against
  Northumbria)
HEKITAI-KAN (1595, Japanese Invasion of
  Korea)
HELIGOLAND (1807, Napoleonic Wars)
HELIOPOLIS (1800, French Revolutionary
  Wars)
HELLESPONT (323, War of the Two Empires)
HOLLABRUNN (1805, Napleonic Wars)
HUMBLEBECK (1700, Great Northern War)
ICHINOTANI (1189, Taira War)
INVERLOCHY (1645, English Civil War)
JELLALABAD (1842, First British-Afghan War)
KHOJAH PASS (1842, First British-Afghan
  War)
KÖNIGGRÄTZ (1866, Seven Weeks' War)
KORNSPRUIT (1900, Second Boer War)
KRINGELLEN (1612, Danish-Swedish Wars)
KUNERSDORF (1759, Seven Years' War)
KUT-EL-AMARA (1915, World War I)
LA FAVORITA (1797, French Revolutionary
  Wars)
LAKE GEORGE (1755, Seven Years' War)
LANDSKRONE (1676, Danish-Swedish Wars)
LA PLACILLA (1891, Chilean Civil War)

10—continued

LA ROCHELLE (1372, Hundred Years' War;
  1627, French Religious Wars)
LA ROTHIERE (1814, Napoleonic Wars)
LAS SALINAS (1538, Conquest of Peru)
LEUCOPETRA (146 B.C., Wars of the Achaean
  League)
LOUDON HILL (1307, Wars of Scottish
  Independence)
LOUISBOURG (1745, War of the Austrian
  Succession; 1758, Seven Years' War)
LÜLEBÜRGAZ (1912, Balkan Wars)
LUNDY'S LANE (1814, War of 1812)
MAASTRICHT (1579, Netherlands War of
  Independence)
MAHARAJPUR (1843, Gwalior Campaign;
  1857, Indian Mutiny)
MALPLAQUET (1709, War of the Spanish
  Succession)
MARETH LINE (1943, World War II)
MARIENDAHL (1645, Thirty Years' War)
MARS-LA-TOUR (1870, Franco-Prussian War)
MARTINESTI (1789, Ottoman Wars)
MARTINIQUE (1794, French Revolutionary
  Wars; 1809, Napoleonic Wars)
MASERFIELD (642, Northumbria against
  Mercia)
MELANTHIAS (559, Wars of the Byzantine
  Empire)
MICHELBERG (1805, Napoleonic Wars)
MIDDELBURG (1593, Netherlands War of
  Independence)
MIRAFLORES (1881, Peruvian-Chilean War)
MONTEBELLO (1800, French Revolutionary
  Wars; 1859, Italian Wars of Independence)
MONTENOTTE (1796, French Revolutionary
  Wars)
MONTEVIDEO (1807, Napoleonic Wars; 1843,
  1851, 1863, Uruguayan Civil War)
MONTFAUCON (886, Norman Invasion of
  France)
MONTMIRAIL (1814, Napoleonic Wars)
MORTGARTEN (1315, First Swiss-Austrian
  War)
MOUNT TABOR (1799, French Revolutionary
  Wars)
MÜHLHAUSEN (58 B.C., Gallic War)
NAROCH LAKE (1916, World War I)
NEERWINDEN (1693, War of the Grand
  Alliance; 1793, French Revolutionary Wars)
NEW ORLEANS (1814, War of 1812; 1862,
  American Civil War)
NIEUWPOORT (1600, Netherlands War of
  Independence)
NÖRDLINGEN (1634, 1645, Thirty Year's War)
ORCHOMENUS (85 B.C., First Mithridatic War)
OSTROLENKA (1853, Crimean War)
PAARDEBERG (1900, Second Boer War)
PALESTRINA (1849, Italian Wars of
  Independence)
PANDU NADDI (1857, Indian Mutiny)

10—continued

PEN SELWOOD (1016, Danish Invasions of Britain)

PEREMBACUM (1780, First British-Mysore War)

PERRYVILLE (1862, American Civil War)

PERSEPOLIS (316 B.C., Wars of Alexander's Successors)

PETERSBURG (1864, American Civil War)

PIAVE RIVER (1918, World War I)

PONT VALAIN (1370, Hundred Years' War)

PORT ARTHUR (1894, Sino-Japanese War; 1904, Russo-Japanese War)

PORT HUDSON (1863, American Civil War)

PORTO BELLO (1740, War of the Austrian Succession)

QUATRE BRAS (1815, Napoleonic Wars)

QUIPUAYPAN (1532, Conquest of Peru)

RAKERSBERG (1416, Ottoman Wars)

ROMERSWAEL (1574, Netherlands War of Independence)

RUHR POCKET (1945, World War II)

RUMERSHEIM (1709, War of the Spanish Successsion)

SALANKEMEN (1691, Ottoman Wars)

SAN ISODORO (1870, Paraguayan War)

SAN JACINTO (1836, Texan Rising; 1867, Franco-Mexican War)

SANNA'S POST (1900, Second Boer War)

SANTA LUCIA (1842, Rio Grande Rising)

SAVANDROOG (1791, Second British-Mysore War)

SEINE MOUTH (1416, Hundred Years' War)

SEKIGAHARA (1600, Rebellion of Hideyori)

SEVASTOPOL (1854, Crimean War)

SEVEN PINES (1862, American Civil War)

SHREWSBURY (1403, Percy's Rebellion)

SHROPSHIRE (A.D. 50, Roman Conquest of Britain)

SIDI REZEGH (1941, World War II)

SOLWAY MOSS (1542, Anglo-Scottish Wars)

SPHACTERIA (425 B.C., Great Peloponnesian War)

STALINGRAD (1942, World War II)

STEENKERKE (1692, War of the Grand Alliance)

ST EUSTACHE (1837, French-Canadian Rising)

STILLWATER (1777, American Revolutionary War)

STOLHOFFEN (1707, War of the Spanish Succession)

STONE RIVER (1862, American Civil War)

TAIKEN GATE (1157, Hogen Insurrection)

TALANA HILL (1899, Second Boer War)

TANNENBERG (1410, German-Polish Wars; 1914, World War I)

TASHKESSEN (1877, Russo-Turkish War)

TEL-EL-KEBIR (1882, Egyptian Revolt)

TETTENHALL (910, Danish Invasions of England)

10—continued

TEWKESBURY (1471, Wars of the Roses)

TINCHEBRAI (1106, Norman Civil War)

TIPPERMUIR (1644, English Civil War)

TRAVANCORE (1789, Second British-Mysore War)

TRICAMERON (533, Invasion of the Vandals)

UTSONOMIYA (1868, Japanese Revolution)

VAL-ES-DUNES (1047, Rise of Normandy)

VELESTINOS (1897, Greco-Turkish War)

WARTEMBERG (1813, Napoleonic Wars)

WATTIGNIES (1793, French Revolutionary Wars)

WILDERNESS, THE (1864, American Civil War)

WINCHESTER (1863, American Civil War)

ZIEZICKSEE (1302, Flemish War)

11

ÆGOSPOTAMI (405 B.C., Peloponnesian War)

ALAM EL HALFA (1942, World War II)

ALESSANDRIA (1799, French Revolutionary Wars)

ALJUBAROTTA (1385, Spanish-Portuguese Wars)

AN LAO VALLEY (1966, Vietnam War)

AQUAE SEXTIA (102 B.C., Cimbric War)

BANNOCKBURN (1314, Wars of Scottish Independence)

BELLEAU WOOD (1918, World War I)

BISMARCK SEA (1943, World War II)

BLADENSBURG (1814, War of 1812)

BLANQUEFORT (1450, Hundred Years' War)

BORYSTHENES, THE (1512, Russo-Polish Wars)

BRAMHAM MOOR (1408, Northumberland's Rebellion)

BREITENFELD (1642, Thirty Years' War)

BRENNEVILLE (1119, Anglo-French Wars)

BUENOS AIRES (1806, 1807, Napoleonic Wars; 1874, Mitre's Rebellion)

BUNKER'S HILL (1775, American Revolutionary War)

CALPULALPAM (1860, Mexican Liberal Rising)

CAMELODUNUM (43, Roman Invasion of Britain)

CAPE PASSERO (1718, War of the Quadruple Alliance)

CARBIESDALE (1650, English Civil War)

CARENAGE BAY (1778, American Revolutionary War)

CASTIGLIONE (1706, War of the Spanish Succession; 1796, French Revolutionary Wars)

CASTILLEJOS (1860, Spanish-Moroccan War)

CECRYPHALEA (458 B.C., Third Messenian War)

CHAMPAUBERT (1814, Napoleonic Wars)

CHAPULTEPEC (1847, American-Mexican War)

CHATEAUGUAY (1813, War of 1812)

11—continued

CHATTANOOGA (1863, American Civil War)
CHICKAMAUGA (1863, American Civil War)
CHILIANWALA (1849, Second British-Sikh War)
CHRYSOPOLIS (324, War of the Two Empires)
COLDHARBOUR (1864, American Civil War)
COLLINE GATE (82 B.C., Civil War of Marius and Sulla)
CONSTANTINE (1836, Conquest of Algeria)
DEUTSCHBROD (1422, Hussite War)
DIAMOND HILL (1900, Second Boer War)
DINGAAN'S DAY (1838, Afrikaner-Zulu War)
DOLNI-DUBNIK (1877, Russo-Turkish War)
DRIEFONTEIN (1900, Second Boer War)
DÜRRENSTEIN (1805, Napoleonic Wars)
ELANDS RIVER (1900, Second Boer War)
FARRUKHABAD (1804, Second British-Maratha War)
FERRYBRIDGE (1461, Wars of the Roses)
FISHER'S HILL (1864, American Civil War)
FORT ST DAVID (1758, Seven Years' War)
FRAUBRUNNEN (1376, Invasion of the 'Guglers')
FRAUENSTADT (1706, Great Northern War)
GIBBEL RUTTS (1798, Irish Rebellion)
GORNI-DUBNIK (1877, Russo-Turkish War)
GROSS-BEEREN (1813, Napoleonic Wars)
GUADALAJARA (1937, Spanish Civil War)
GUADALCANAL (1942, World War II)
HADRIANOPLE (323, War of the Two Empires; 378, Second Gothic Invasion of the East)
HALIDON HILL (1333, Wars of Scottish Independence)
HEAVENFIELD (634, Northumbria against the British)
HEILIGERLEE (1568, Netherlands War of Independence)
HELSINGBORG (1710, Great Northern War)
HENNERSDORF (1745, War of the Austrian Succession)
HERMANSTADT (1442, Ottoman Wars)
HOHENLINDEN (1800, French Revolutionary Wars)
HONDSCHOOTE (1793, French Revolutionary Wars)
ÎLE DE FRANCE (1810, Napoleonic Wars)
ISANDHLWANA (1879, Zulu-British War)
KLAUSENBURG (1660, Ottoman Wars)
LAKE KERGUEL (1391, Tatar Invasion of Russia)
LAKE VADIMON (283 B.C., Gallic Invasion of Italy)
LANGENSALZA (1866, Seven Weeks' War)
LONDONDERRY (1689, War of the Grand Alliance)
LOSTWITHIEL (1644, English Civil War)
MACIEJOWICE (1794, First Polish Rising)
MALVERN HILL (1862, American Civil War)
MAOGAMALCHA (363, Persian Wars)
MARSTON MOOR (1644, English Civil War)

11—continued

MASULIPATAM (1759, Seven Years' War)
MEGALOPOLIS (331 B.C., Macedonian Wars; 226 B.C., Wars of the Achaean League)
MERSA MATRÜH (1942, World War II)
MILETOPOLIS (86 B.C., First Mithridatic War)
MILL SPRINGS (1862, American Civil War)
MISSOLONGHI (1821, Greek War of Independence)
MODDER RIVER (1899, Second Boer War)
MONTCONTOUR (1569, Third French Religious War)
MONTE APERTO (1260, Guelfs and Ghibellines)
MONTE LEZINO (1796, French Revolutionary Wars)
MONTMORENCI (1759, Seven Years' War)
MOOKERHEIDE (1574, Netherlands War of Independence)
MORSHEDABAD (1763, British Conquest of Bengal)
MOUNT TAURUS (804, Muslim Invasion of Asia Minor)
MOUNT TIFATA (83 B.C., Civil War of Marius and Sulla)
NOISSEVILLE (1870, Franco-Prussian War)
NORTHAMPTON (1460, Wars of the Roses)
PEARL HARBOR (1941, World War II)
PEIWAR KOTAL (1878, Second British-Afghan War)
PENA CERRADA (1838, First Carlist War)
PHILIPHAUGH (1645, English Civil War)
PIETER'S HILL (1900, Second Boer War)
PONDICHERRY (1748, War of the Austrian Succession; 1760, Seven Years' War; 1778, 1783, American Revolutionary War)
PRESTONPANS (1745, The Forty-five Rebellion)
QUIBERON BAY (1759, Seven Years' War)
RAJAHMUNDRY (1758, Seven Years' War)
REDDERSBERG (1900, Second Boer War)
RHEINFELDEN (1638, Thirty Years' War)
RIETFONTEIN (1899, Second Boer War)
RORKE'S DRIFT (1879, Zulu-British War)
ROTTO FREDDO (1746, War of the Austrian Succession)
ROWTON HEATH (1645, English Civil War)
SACRIPONTUS (82 B.C., Civil War of Marius and Sulla)
SALDANHA BAY (1796, French Revolutionary Wars)
SAN GIOVANNI (1799, French Revolutionary Wars)
SAUCHIE BURN (1488, Rebellion of the Scottish Barons)
SCHIPKA PASS (1877, Russo-Turkish War)
SHERIFFMUIR (1715, The Fifteen Rebellion)
SHIJO NAWATE (1339, War of the Northern and Southern Empires)
SIDI BARRÂNI (1940, World War II)
STAVRICHANI (1739, Ottoman Wars)

11—continued

TAGLIACOZZO (1268, Guelfs and Ghibellines)
TAILLEBOURG (1242, Anglo-French Wars)
TANSARA SAKA (1876, Satsuma Rebellion)
TARAWA-MAKIN (1943, World War II)
TEL-EL-MAHUTA (1882, Egyptian Revolt)
TELLICHERRY (1780, First British-Mysore
  War)
TEUTTLINGEN (1643, Thirty Years' War)
THERMOPYLAE (480 B.C., Third Persian
  Invasion; 191 B.C., Wars of the Hellenistic
  Monarchies)
TICONDEROGA (1758, Seven Years' War;
  1777, American Revolutionary War)
TRINCOMALEE (1759, Seven Years' War;
  1767, First British-Mysore War; 1782,
  American Revolutionary War)
VINEGAR HILL (1798, Irish Rebellion)
VÖGELINSECK (1402, Appenzel Rebellion)
WALTERSDORF (1807, Napoleonic Wars)
WEDNESFIELD (911, Danish Invasions of
  England)
WEISSENBURG (1870, Franco-Prussian War)
WHITE RUSSIA (1943, World War II)

12

ADWALTON MOOR (1643, English Civil War)
ALGECIRAS BAY (1801, French Revolutionary
  Wars)
ARCIS-SUR-AUBE (1814, Napoleonic Wars)
ARGENTORATUM (357, Invasion of the
  Alemanni)
ARROYO GRANDE (1842, Uruguayan Civil
  War)
ATHERTON MOOR (1643, English Civil War)
BANDA ISLANDS (1796, French Revolutionary
  Wars)
BARQUISIMETO (1813, Colombian War of
  Independence)
BERGEN-OP-ZOOM (1747, War of the
  Austrian Succession; 1799, French
  Revolutionary Wars)
BLOEMFONTEIN (1900, Second Boer War)
BRADDOCK DOWN (1643, English Civil War)
CAUDINE FORKS (321 B.C., Second Samnite
  War)
CHICKAHOMINY (1864, American Civil War)
CONCHA RAYADA (1818, Chilean War of
  Independence)
ELANDSLAAGTE (1899, Second Boer War)
EUTAW SPRINGS (1781, American
  Revolutionary War)
FORT DONELSON (1862, American Civil War)
FREDRIKSHALD (1718, Great Northern War)
HAMPTON ROADS (1862, American Civil War)
HARPER'S FERRY (1862, American Civil War)
HEDGELEY MOOR (1464, Wars of the Roses)
HENGESTESDUN (837, Danish Invasions of
  Britain)
HOMILDON HILL (1402, Anglo-Scottish Wars)
ICLISTAVISUS (16 A.D., Germanic Wars)

12—continued

KIRCH-DENKERN (1761, Seven Years' War)
KIU-LIEN-CHENG (1904, Russo-Japanese
  War)
KONIGSWARTHA (1813, Napoleonic Wars)
KURSK SALIENT (1943, World War II)
LAKE REGILLUS (497 B.C., Roman Civil Wars)
LYNN HAVEN BAY (1781, American
  Revolutionary War)
MALAKAND PASS (1895, Chitral Campaign)
MIDWAY ISLAND (1942, World War II)
MONS-EN-PÉVÈLE (1304, Flemish War)
MONTE CASEROS (1852, Argentine Civil War)
MONT VALÉRIEN (1871, Franco-Prussian
  War)
MÜNCHENGRÄTZ (1866, Seven Weeks' War)
MURFREESBORO (1862, American Civil War)
NECHTAN'S MERE (685, Northumbrian
  Invasion of Scotland)
NOVA CARTHAGO (209 B.C., Second Punic
  War)
OONDWA NULLAH (1763, British Conquest of
  Bengal)
PENOBSCOT BAY (1779, American
  Revolutionary War)
PETERWARDEIN (1716, Ottoman Wars)
PHILIPPSBURG (1734, War of the Polish
  Succession)
PINKIE CLEUGH (1547, Anglo-Scottish Wars)
PORT REPUBLIC (1862, American Civil War)
PRAIRIE GROVE (1862, American Civil War)
RADCOT BRIDGE (1387, Appellants'
  Rebellion)
RICH MOUNTAIN (1861, American Civil War)
RONCESVALLES (778, Charlemagne's
  Conquests; 1813, Peninsular War)
ROUNDWAY DOWN (1643, English Civil War)
RULLION GREEN (1666, Covenanters' Rising)
SAN SEBASTIAN (1813, Peninsular War; 1836,
  First Carlist War)
SECUNDERBAGH (1857, Indian Mutiny)
SERINGAPATAM (1792, Second British-
  Mysore War; 1799, Third British-Mysore
  War)
SOUTHWOLD BAY (1672, Anglo-Dutch Wars)
SPOTSYLVANIA (1864, American Civil War)
ST MARY'S CLYST (1549, Arundel's
  Rebellion)
SUNGARI RIVER (1947, Chinese Civil War)
TET OFFENSIVE, THE (1968, Vietnam War)
TIGRANOCERTA (69 B.C., Third Mithridatic
  War)
VALENCIENNES (1566, Netherlands War of
  Independence; 1656, Franco-Spanish Wars)
VILLA VICIOSA (1710, War of the Spanish
  Succession)
WILLIAMSBURG (1862, American Civil War)
WILSON'S CREEK (1861, American Civil War)
WROTHAM HEATH (1554, Wyatt's
  Insurrection)

13

ADMAGETOBRIGA (61 B.C., Gallic Tribal
Wars)
AIX-LA-CHAPELLE (1795, French
Revolutionary Wars)
AMBRACIAN GULF (435 B.C., Corcyrean-
Corinthian War)
BADULI-KI-SERAI (1857, Indian Mutiny)
BELLE-ÎLE-EN-MER (1759, 1761, Seven Years'
War; 1795, French Revolutionary Wars)
BOROUGHBRIDGE (1322, Rebellion of the
Marches)
BOSWORTH FIELD (1485, Wars of the Roses)
CAPE ST VINCENT (1797, French
Revolutionary Wars)
CASTELFIDARDO (1860, Italian Wars of
Independence)
CASTELNAUDARY (1632, French Civil Wars)
CEDAR MOUNTAIN (1862, American Civil
War)
CHANDERNAGORE (1757, Seven Years' War)
CHRISTIANOPLE (1611, Danish-Swedish
Wars)
CHRYSLER'S FARM (1813, War of 1812)
CIUDAD RODRIGO (1812, Peninsular War)
CYNOSCEPHALAE (364 B.C., Wars of Greek
City States; 197 B.C., Second Macedonian
War)
FALKLAND ISLES (1914, World War I; 1982,
Falklands War)
FARQUHAR'S FARM (1899, Second Boer War)
FORT FRONTENAC (1758, Seven Years' War)
FRANKENHAUSEN (1525, Peasants' War)
GLENMARRESTON (683, Angles' Invasion of
Britain)
HORNS OF HATTIN (1187, Crusader-Saracen
Wars)
INVERKEITHING (1317, Anglo-Scottish Wars)
KASSERINE PASS (1943, World War II)
KILLIECRANKIE (1689, Jacobite Rising)
LITTLE BIG HORN (1876, Sioux Rising)
LOIGNY-POUPREY (1870, Franco-Prussian
War)
MAGERSFONTEIN (1899, Second Boer War)
MARCIANOPOLIS (376, Gothic Invasion of
Thrace)
MASURIAN LAKES (1914, 1915, World War I)
MEGALETAPHRUS (740 B.C., First Messenian
War)
MOLINOS DEL REY (1808, Peninsular War)
MOUNT SELEUCUS (353, Civil Wars of the
Roman Empire)
NEVILLE'S CROSS (1346, Anglo-Scottish
Wars)
NEWTOWN BUTLER (1689, War of the Grand
Alliance)
NORTHALLERTON (1138, Anglo-Scottish
Wars)
NORTH FORELAND (1666, Anglo-Dutch Wars)
PAGASAEAN GULF (352 B.C., Sacred War)
PALAIS GALLIEN (1649, War of the Fronde)

13—continued

PASSCHENDAELE (1917, World War I)
PELELIU-ANGAUR (1944, World War II)
PHILIPPINE SEA (1944, World War II)
PHILIPPOPOLIS (251, First Gothic Invasion of
the Roman Empire; 1878, Russo-Turkish
War)
PORTO PRAIA BAY (1781, American
Revolutionary War)
ROANOKE ISLAND (1862, American Civil War)
SANTA VITTORIA (1702, War of the Spanish
Succession)
SIEVERSHAUSEN (1553, German Reformation
Wars)
SOUTH MOUNTAIN (1862, American Civil
War)
SPANISH ARMADA (1588, Anglo-Spanish
War)
SUDLEY SPRINGS (1862, American Civil War)
SUGAR-LOAF ROCK (1753, Carnatic War)
WHITE OAK SWAMP (1862, American Civil
War)
YOUGHIOGHENNY (1754, Seven Years' War)
ZUSMARSHAUSEN (1647, Thirty Years' War)

14

BERWICK-ON-TWEED (1296, Wars of Scottish
Independence)
BOTHWELL BRIDGE (1679, Covenanters'
Rising)
BRISTOE STATION (1863, American Civil War)
CAMPUS CASTORUM (69, Revolt of Vitellius)
CAPE FINISTERRE (1747, War of the Austrian
Succession; 1805, Napoleonic Wars)
CHALGROVE FIELD (1643, English Civil War)
CHÂTEAU-THIERRY (1814, Napoleonic Wars)
CONSTANTINOPLE (668, Muslim Invasion of
Europe; 1203–04, Fourth Crusade; 1261,
Reconquest by Byzantines; 1422, Ottoman
Invasion of Europe; 1453, Turkish Conquest)
CROPREDY BRIDGE (1644, English Civil War)
DRUMMOSSIE MOOR (1746, The Forty-five
Rebellion)
FREDERICKSBURG (1862, American Civil
War)
FUENTES DE OÑORO (1811, Peninsular War)
HOHENFRIEDBERG (1745, War of the
Austrian Succession)
KOVEL-STANISLAV (1916, World War I)
LA BELLE FAMILLE (1759, Seven Years' War)
LOOSECOAT FIELD (1470, Wars of the Roses)
MARIANA ISLANDS (1944, World War II)
MORTIMER'S CROSS (1461, Wars of the
Roses)
MOUNT LACTARIUS (553, Wars of the
Byzantine Empire)
NICHOLSON'S NECK (1899, Second Boer
War)
PASO DE LA PATRIA (1866, Paraguayan War)
PEACH TREE CREEK (1864, American Civil
War)

14—continued

PORTE ST ANTOINE (1652, War of the
Fronde)
PUSAN PERIMETER (1950, Korean War)
ROUVRAY-ST-DENIS (1429, Hundred Years'
War)
SANTIAGO DE CUBA (1898, Spanish-
American War)
SAVAGE'S STATION (1862, American Civil
War)
SECESSIONVILLE (1862, American Civil War)
SINAI PENINSULA (1956, Israeli-Arab War)
SOLOMON ISLANDS (1942, World War II)
STAMFORD BRIDGE (1066, Norse Invasion of
Britain; 1453, Wars of the Roses)
STIRLING BRIDGE (1297, Wars of Scottish
Independence)
TEARLESS BATTLE (368 B.C., Wars of Sparta)
TONDEMAN'S WOODS (1754, Carnatic War)
TSUSHIMA STRAIT (1905, Russo-Japanese
War)
VITTORIO VENETO (1918, World War I)

15

ALEUTIAN ISLANDS (1943, World War II)
AMATOLA MOUNTAIN (1846, Kaffir Wars)
APPOMATTOX RIVER (1865, American Civil
War)
BATTLE OF BRITAIN (1940, World War II)
BEAUNE-LA-ROLANDE (1870, Franco-
Prussian War)
BEAVER'S DAM CREEK (1862, American Civil
War)
FORUM TEREBRONII (251, First Gothic
Invasion of the Roman Empire)
FRANKFURT-ON-ODER (1631, Thirty Years'
War)
GROSS-JÄGERSDORF (1757, Seven Years'
War)
HELIGOLAND BIGHT (1914, World War I)
KHOORD KABUL PASS (1842, First British-
Afghan War)
MALOYAROSLAVETS (1812, Napoleonic
Wars)
MISSIONARY RIDGE (1863, American Civil
War)
PLAINS OF ABRAHAM (1759, Seven Years'
War)
PUENTE DE LA REYNA (1872, Second Carlist
War)
SEVEN DAYS' BATTLE (1862, American Civil
War)
SPANISH GALLEONS (1702, War of the
Spanish Succession)

16

BATAAN-CORREGIDOR (1941, World War II)
BRONKHORST SPRUIT (1880, First Boer War)
CAMBRAI-ST QUENTIN (1918, World War I)
CHANCELLORSVILLE (1863, American Civil
War)

16—continued

FARRINGTON BRIDGE (1549, Arundel's
Rebellion)
FORT WILLIAM HENRY (1757, Seven Years'
War)
KINNESAW MOUNTAIN (1864, American Civil
War)
LAS NAVAS DE TOLOSA (1212, Spanish-
Muslim Wars)
LIPARAEAN ISLANDS (257 B.C., First Punic
War)
MADONNA DELL'OLENO (1744, War of the
Austrian Succession)
MONONGAHELA RIVER (1755, Seven Years'
War)
QUEENSTON HEIGHTS (1812, War of 1812)
SALUM-HALFAYA PASS (1941, World War II)
SAMPFORD COURTNEY (1549, Arundel's
Rebellion)
ST JAKOB AN DER BIRS (1444, Armagnac
War)

17

BURLINGTON HEIGHTS (1813, War of 1812)
DODECANESE ISLANDS (1943, World War II)
GUSTAV-CASSINO LINE (1943, World War II)
INHLOBANE MOUNTAIN (1879, Zulu War)
KWAJALEIN-ENIWETOK (1944, World War II)
LA FÈRE CHAMPENOISE (1814, Napoleonic
Wars)
PITTSBURGH LANDING (1862, American Civil
War)
POLAND-EAST PRUSSIA (1944, World War II)
VAN TUONG PENINSULA (1965, Vietnam War)

18

FORNHAM ST GENEVIÈVE (1173, Rebellion of
the Princes)
GUILFORD COURTHOUSE (1781, American
Revolutionary War)
MEUSE-ARGONNE FOREST (1918, World War
I)
PYLOS AND SPHACTERIA (425 B.C., Great
Peloponnesian War)

19

CHU PONG-IA DRANG RIVER (1965, Vietnam
War)
'GLORIOUS FIRST OF JUNE' (1794, French
Revolutionary Wars)

20+

BARBOSTHENIAN MOUNTAINS (192 B.C.,
Wars of the Achaean League)
PARAETAKENE MOUNTAINS (316 B.C., Wars
of Alexander's Successors)
RHINE AND THE RUHR POCKET, THE (1945,
World War II)
SHANNON AND CHESAPEAKE (1813, War of
1812)
THIRTY-EIGHTH PARALLEL (1951, Korean
War)

ARMOUR

4	6 —continued	8	9 —continued
JACK	MASCLE	ALLECRET	CHAIN MAIL
MAIL	MESAIL	BARDINGS	CHAMPFRON
5	MORIAN	BASCINET	CHAUSSONS
ARMET	MORION	BAUDRICK	EPAULETTE
BACYN	SALADE	BRASSARD	HAUSSE-COL
BUFFE	SHIELD	BRAYETTE	JACK BOOTS
CREST	TABARD	BUFF COAT	POURPOINT
CULET	UMBRIL	BURGINOT	REREBRACE
GIPON	**7**	BURGONET	SABATYNES
IMBER	AILETES	CABASSET	**10**
JUPEL	BACINET	CHAMPONS	AVENTAILLE
JUPON	BALDRIC	CHANFRON	BANDED MAIL
LAMES	BARBUTE	CHAUCHES	BARREL HELM
SALET	BASINET	CHAUSSES	BRICHETTES
VISOR	BUCKLER	COD PIECE	BRIGANDINE
6	CHAUCES	COLLERET	CROISSANTS
ALETES	CORSLET	COLLETIN	ECREVISSES
BASNET	CRUPPER	CORSELET	EMBOITMENT
BHANJU	CUIRASS	CRINIERE	FLANCHARDS
BRACER	CUISSES	GAUNTLET	LAMBREQUIN
BRIDLE	CULESET	HALECRET	**11**
BRUGNE	FENDACE	JAMBEAUX	BREASTPLATE
CALOTE	FRONTAL	JAZERANT	BREASTSTRAP
CAMAIL	GAUCHET	PAULDRON	BRIGANDYRON
CASQUE	GOUCHET	PECTORAL	BRIGANTAYLE
CASSIS	GREAVES	PLASTRON	CHAPEL DE FER
CELATE	HAUBERK	SABATONS	ESPALLIERES
CHEEKS	HOGUINE	SOLARETS	PLATE ARMOUR
CRENEL	LANIERS	SOLERETS	**13**
CRINET	MURSAIL	TESTIERE	ARMING DOUBLET
CUELLO	PANACHE	**9**	**15**
GORGET	PLACARD	BAINBERGS	IMBRICATE ARMOUR
GUSSET	POITRAL	BEINBERGS	
HEAUME	SURCOAT		
HELMET	VISIERE		

WEAPONS

2	3 —continued	4 —continued	4 —continued
NU	TNT	FANG	TUCK
V1	**4**	FOIL	**5**
V2	ADZE	KORA	A-BOMB
3	BARB	KRIS	ANCUS
AXE	BILL	MACE	ANKUS
BOW	BOLO	MINE	ANLAS
DAG	BOLT	PIKE	ARROW
DAS	BOMB	SHOT	ASWAR
GUN	CLUB	TANK	BATON
GYN	DIRK	TOCK	BIDAG

5 —continued	6 —continued	8 —continued	9 —continued
BILBO	PETARD	ARBALEST	GRAPESHOT
BOLAS	PISTOL	ARBALETE	GUNPOWDER
BOSON	POP GUN	ARQUEBUS	HARQUEBUS
BRAND	QILLIJ	ATOM BOMB	KNOBSTICK
ESTOC	QUIVER	AXE-KNIFE	MATCHLOCK
FLAIL	RAMROD	BASELARD	MAZZUELLE
FUSEE	RAPIER	BASILARD	MILLS BOMB
FUSIL	ROCKET	BLOWPIPE	MUSKETOON
GUPTI	SCYTHE	CALTHORP	POM-POM GUN
H-BOMB	SEMTEX	CANISTER	SLUNG SHOT
KERIS	SUMPIT	CARABINE	TRUNCHEON
KHORA	TALWAR	CATAPULT	**10**
KILIG	VGO GUN	CHACHEKA	ARTILLATOR
KILIJ	**7**	CLADIBAS	BANDEROLLE
KNIFE	ASSEGAI	CLAYMORE	BRANDESTOC
KUKRI	AWL-PIKE	CROSSBOW	BROAD ARROW
KYLIE	BALASAN	DERINGER	BROADSWORD
LANCE	BALISTA	DESTRIER	CANNON BALL
LATCH	BALISTA	FALCHION	FIRE-STICKS
PILUM	BAYONET	FALCONET	FLICK KNIFE
PRODD	BELFREY	FAUCHARD	GATLING GUN
RIFLE	BILIONG	FIRELOCK	KNOBKERRIE
SABRE	BOMBARD	HACKBUTT	LETTER BOMB
SHELL	BOURDON	HAIL SHOT	LIMPET MINE
SLING	BREN GUN	HAQUEBUT	MACHINE GUN
SPEAR	CALIVER	HASSEGAI	PEA-SHOOTER
STAKE	CALTRAP	HOWITZER	POWDERHORN
STAVE	CARABEN	PETRONEL	SIDEWINDER
SWORD	CARBINE	POIGNARD	SMALL SWORD
TACHI	CARREAU	QUERQUER	SWORD STICK
WADDY	CHAKRAM	REPEATER	**11**
6	CHALCOS	REVOLVER	ANTI-TANK GUN
AMUKTA	CHOPPER	SCIMITAR	ARMOURED CAR
ARMLET	CURRIER	SHAMSHIR	BLUNDERBUSS
BARKAL	CUTLASS	SHRAPNEL	HAND GRENADE
BARONG	DUDGEON	SPONTOON	KHYBER KNIFE
BASTON	DUSSACK	SUMPITAN	MISERICORDE
BODKIN	FAUCHON	TOMAHAWK	NEUTRON BOMB
BULLET	FIRE-POT	TOMMY GUN	**12**
CANNON	GRENADE	**9**	BATTERING RAM
CARCAS	HALBARD	ACK-ACK GUN	BREECH LOADER
CEMTEX	HALBART	ARTILLERY	BRIDLE CUTTER
CUDGEL	HALBERD	BADELAIRE	FIRE CARRIAGE
DAGGER	HAND GUN	BANDELEER	FLAME-THROWER
DAISHO	HARPOON	BANDOLIER	HYDROGEN BOMB
DRAGON	KASTANE	BANNEROLE	**13**
DUM-DUM	KINDJAL	BATTLE-AXE	BRASS KNUCKLES
DUSACK	LONG BOW	BIG BERTHA	DUELLING SWORD
EXOCET	MISSILE	BOOMERANG	GUIDED MISSILE
KATANA	MUSQUET	CARRONADE	KNUCKLE DUSTER
KERRIE	PONIARD	CARTOUCHE	THROWING KNIFE
KHANDA	PUNT GUN	CARTRIDGE	**14**
KIKUKI	QUARREL	CHAIN SHOT	DUELLING PISTOL
KODOGU	SHASHQA	DETONATOR	INCENDIARY BOMB
MASSUE	SHINKEN	DOODLE-BUG	NUCLEAR WEAPONS
MAZULE	STEN GUN	FALCASTRA	ROCKET LAUNCHER
MORTAR	TORPEDO	FLAGELLUM	SAWN-OFF
MUSKET	TRIDENT	FLAMBERGE	SHOTGUN
NAPALM	**8**	FLINTLOCK	
PARANG	AMUSETTE	GELIGNITE	

14 —continued
TWO-HANDED
  SWORD
15
ANTI-AIRCRAFT GUN

16
BALLISTIC MISSILE
18
HEAT-SEEKING
  MISSILE

20+
DOUBLE-
  BARRELLED
  SHOTGUN

TRANSPORT

VEHICLES

3
BMX
BUS
CAB
CAR
FLY
GIG
VAN

4
AUTO
BIKE
CART
DRAG
DRAY
EKKA
HACK
JEEP
LUGE
SHAY
SLED
TAXI
TRAM
TRAP
TUBE
WAIN

5
ARABA
BRAKE
BUGGY
COACH
COUPÉ
CRATE
CYCLE
DANDY
DOOLY
LORRY
METRO
MOPED
MOTOR
PALKI
SEDAN
SULKY
TONGA
TRAIN
TRUCK
WAGON

6
BERLIN
CALASH
CHAISE
DIESEL

6—continued
FIACRE
GO-CART
HANSOM
HEARSE
HOTROD
HURDLE
JALOPY
JITNEY
LANDAU
LIMBER
LITTER
MAGLEV
MODEL-T
ROCKET
SALOON
SLEDGE
SLEIGH
SNOCAT
SURREY
TANDEM
TANKER
TOURER
TRICAR
WEASEL

7
AUTOBUS
AUTOCAR
BICYCLE
BOB-SLED
BRITZKA
BROWSER
CALÈCHE
CARAVAN
CAROCHE
CHARIOT
COASTER
DOG-CART
DROSHKY
FLIVVER
GROWLER
HACKERY
HARD-TOP
OMNIBUS
OPEN-CAR
PHÆTON
PULLMAN
SCOOTER
SHUNTER
SIDE-CAR
TALLY-HO

7—continued
TAXI-CAB
TILBURY
TRACTOR
TRAILER
TROLLEY
TUMBRIL
TWO-DOOR
UNICORN
VIS-À-VIS
WHISKEY

8
BAROUCHE
BRANCARD
BROUGHAM
CABLE-CAR
CAPE-CART
CARRIAGE
CARRIOLE
CLARENCE
CURRICLE
DEAD-CART
DORMEUSE
FOUR-DOOR
HORSE-BUS
HORSE-CAB
HORSE-VAN
ICE-YACHT
KIBITZKA
MONORAIL
MOTOR-CAR
MOTOR-VAN
OLD CROCK
PONY-CART
PUSH-BIKE
QUADRIGA
RICKSHAW
ROADSTER
RUNABOUT
SOCIABLE
STAFF CAR
STEAM-CAR
TOBOGGAN
TRICYCLE
UNICYCLE
VICTORIA

9
AMBULANCE
BOAT-TRAIN
BOB-SLEIGH
BUBBLECAR

9—continued
BUCKBOARD
CABRIOLET
CHAR-À-BANC
DILIGENCE
ESTATE-CAR
FUNICULAR
HORSE-CART
LIMOUSINE
MAIL-COACH
MILKFLOAT
MILK TRAIN
MONOCYCLE
MOTOR-BIKE
PALANKEEN
PALANQUIN
RACING CAR
SPORTS CAR
STREET-CAR
STRETCHER
TARANTASS
TIN LIZZIE
TWO-SEATER
WAGONETTE

10
AUTOMOBILE
BAIL GHARRY
BEACHWAGON
BLACK MARIA
FIRE-ENGINE
FOUR-IN-HAND
GOODS TRAIN
JINRICKSHA
LOCAL TRAIN
LOCOMOTIVE
MOTOR-COACH
MOTOR-CYCLE
NIGHT TRAIN
OUTSIDE CAR
PADDYWAGON
PEDAL-CYCLE
PONY-ENGINE
POST-CHAISE
RATTLETRAP
SEDAN-CHAIR
SHANDRYDAN
SINCLAIR C5
SNOWPLOUGH
STAGE-COACH
STAGE-WAGON

10—continued
STATE COACH
TROLLEY-BUS
TROLLEY-CAR
TWO-WHEELER
VELOCIPEDE

11
BONE-BREAKER
BULLOCK-CART
CONVERTIBLE
DIESEL TRAIN
FOUR-WHEELER
GUN-CARRIAGE
JAUNTING-CAR
JINRICKSHAW
LANDAULETTE
MAIL-PHÆTON
QUADRICYCLE

11—continued
SIT-UP-AND-BEG
SOUPED-UP CAR
STEAM-ENGINE
STEAM-ROLLER
THIKA-GHARRY
WHITECHAPEL

12
COACH AND FOUR
DÉSOBLIGEANT
DOUBLE-DECKER
EXPRESS TRAIN
FREIGHT TRAIN
HORSE-AND-CART
LUGGAGE TRAIN
PANTECHNICON
PUFFING BILLY
RAILWAY TRAIN

12—continued
SINGLE-DECKER
STATION-WAGON
STEAM-OMNIBUS
THROUGH TRAIN

13
CYCLE-RICKSHAW
ELECTRIC TRAIN
GOVERNESS-CART
HORSE-CARRIAGE
PENNYFARTHING
RACING CHARIOT
SHOOTING-BRAKE

14
PASSENGER TRAIN
RIDING-CARRIAGE
TRACTION ENGINE

15
HACKNEY-CARRIAGE
PRAIRIE-SCHOONER

16
MOTORIZED
  BICYCLE
UNDERGROUND
  TRAIN

17
HORSELESS
  CARRIAGE

18
TRAVELLING
  CARRIAGE

SHIPS AND BOATS

3
ARK
COG
HOY
TUG

4
ARGO
BARK
BOAT
BRIG
BUSS
DHOW
DORY
GRAB
JUNK
PROA
PUNT
RAFT
SAIC
SNOW
TROW
YAWL

5
BARGE
CANOE
COBLE
DANDY
FERRY
FUNNY
KAYAK
KETCH
LINER
NOBBY
PRAHU
SHELL
SKIFF

5—continued
SLOOP
SMACK
TRAMP
U-BOAT
UMIAK
XEBEC
YACHT

6
BARQUE
BAWLEY
BIREME
CAIQUE
CARVEL
CUTTER
DINGHY
DOGGER
DUG-OUT
GALLEY
HOOKER
HOPPER
LAUNCH
LORCHA
LUGGER
PACKET
RANDAN
SAMPAN
SEALER
SLAVER
TANKER
TENDER
WHALER

7
BUMBOAT
CARAVEL
CARRACK

7—continued
CLIPPER
COASTER
COLLIER
CORACLE
CORSAIR
CURRACH
DREDGER
DRIFTER
DROMOND
FELUCCA
FLY-BOAT
FRIGATE
GABBARD
GALLEON
GONDOLA
JANGADA
PINNACE
PIRAGUA
POLACCA
POLACRE
ROWBOAT
SCULLER
STEAMER
TARTANE
TOWBOAT
TRAWLER
TRIREME
WAR SHIP

8
BILANDER
BUDGEROW
COCKBOAT
CORVETTE
CRUMSTER
DAHABIYA

8—continued
FIRESHIP
FOLDBOAT
GALLIVAT
LIFEBOAT
LONG-BOAT
MAIL-SHIP
NOAH'S ARK
OUTBOARD
SAILBOAT
SCHOONER
SHOWBOAT

9
BUCENTAUR
CARGO-BOAT
CATAMARAN
CRIS-CRAFT
FREIGHTER
HOUSE BOAT
JOLLY-BOAT
LIGHTSHIP
MOTORBOAT
MOTORSHIP
MUD-HOPPER
OUTRIGGER
RIVER-BOAT
ROTOR SHIP
SHIP'S BOAT
SLAVE-SHIP
SPEEDBOAT
STEAMBOAT
STEAMSHIP
STORESHIP
SUBMARINE

10
BANANA-BOAT

10—continued
BRIGANTINE
PADDLE-BOAT
PICKET BOAT
PIRATE-SHIP
PRISON-SHIP
QUADRIREME
ROWING BOAT
TEA-CLIPPER
TRAIN-FERRY
VIKING-SHIP
WIND-JAMMER

11
BARQUENTINE
CHASSE-MARÉE
COCKLE-SHELL
DOUBLE-CANOE
FISHING-BOAT
HOPPER-BARGE
MAIL-STEAMER
PENTECONTER
PILOT VESSEL
QUINQUEREME
SAILING-SHIP

11—continued
THREE-MASTER
12
CABIN-CRUISER
ESCORT VESSEL
FISHING SMACK
HOSPITAL SHIP
MERCHANT SHIP
PLEASURE BOAT
SAILING BARGE
STERN-WHEELER

13
HERRING-FISHER
PASSENGER SHIP
TRANSPORT SHIP
14
CHANNEL STEAMER
COASTING VESSEL
FLOATING PALACE
OCEAN GREYHOUND

AIRCRAFT

3
JET
4
KITE
5
PLANE
6
AIR CAR
BOMBER
GLIDER
7
AIRSHIP
BALLOON
BIPLANE
CLIPPER

7—continued
FIGHTER
JUMP-JET
SHUTTLE
8
AEROSTAT
AIRPLANE
AUTOGIRO
CONCORDE
JUMBO-JET
ROTODYNE
SEA-PLANE
TRIPLANE
TURBO-JET
WARPLANE
ZEPPELIN

9
AEROPLANE
DIRIGIBLE
MAIL-PLANE
MONOPLANE
SAILPLANE
TURBO-PROP
10
FLYING-BOAT
GAS-BALLOON
HELICOPTER
HOVERCRAFT
HYDROPLANE
11
FIRE-BALLOON

12
FREIGHT-PLANE
13
STRATOCRUISER
14
FLYING BEDSTEAD
PASSENGER PLANE
18
MONTGOLFIER
  BALLOON

MOTORING TERMS

2
C.C.
3
BHP
CAM
FAN
HUB
JET
REV
ROD
4
AXLE
BOOT
BUSH
COIL
GEAR
HORN
LOCK
SUMP

4—continued
TYRE
5
BRAKE
CHOKE
SERVO
SHAFT
VALVE
WHEEL
6
BIG END
BONNET
CAMBER
CLUTCH
DAMPER
DECOKE
DYNAMO
ENGINE
FILTER

6—continued
GASKET
HEATER
HUB CAP
IDLING
PISTON
REBORE
STROKE
TAPPET
TORQUE
TUNING
7
BATTERY
BEARING
BRACKET
CHASSIS
DYNAMIC
EXHAUST
FAN BELT

7—continued
GEARBOX
OIL SEAL
8
ADHESION
BRAKE PAD
BULKHEAD
CALLIPER
CAMSHAFT
CROSS-PLY
CYLINDER
DIPSTICK
FLYWHEEL
FUEL PUMP
IGNITION
KICK-DOWN
KNOCKING
LIVE AXLE
MANIFOLD

8—continued
MOUNTING
RADIATOR
ROTOR ARM
SELECTOR
SILENCER
SMALL END
STEERING
THROTTLE
TRACK ROD

9
BRAKESHOE
CONDENSER
DISC BRAKE
DRUM BRAKE
GEAR STICK
GENERATOR
HALF-SHAFT
HANDBRAKE
INDUCTION
MISFIRING
OVERDRIVE
OVERSTEER
PROP SHAFT
RADIAL-PLY
SIDE VALVE
SPARK PLUG

9—continued
TWO-STROKE
UNDERSEAL
WHEELBASE

10
AIR CLEANER
ALTERNATOR
BRAKE FLUID
CRANKSHAFT
DETONATION
DRIVE SHAFT
FOUR-STROKE
GUDGEON PIN
HORSEPOWER
PISTON RING
REV COUNTER
SUSPENSION
TACHOMETER
THERMOSTAT
UNDERSTEER
WINDSCREEN

11
ANTI-ROLL BAR
CARBURETTER
CARBURETTOR
COMPRESSION

11—continued
CROSSMEMBER
DISTRIBUTOR
SERVO SYSTEM
SYNCHROMESH

12
ACCELERATION
CYLINDER HEAD
DIESEL ENGINE
DIFFERENTIAL
SPARKING PLUG
SUPERCHARGER
TRANSMISSION
TURBOCHARGER
VISCOUS DRIVE

13
COOLING SYSTEM
DECARBONIZING
FUEL INJECTION
OVERHEAD VALVE
POWER STEERING
RACK-AND-PINION
SHOCK ABSORBER
SLAVE CYLINDER
SPARK IGNITION

14
FOUR-WHEEL DRIVE
PROPELLER SHAFT
UNIVERSAL JOINT

15
FRONT-WHEEL
  DRIVE
HYDRAULIC SYSTEM
PETROL INJECTION

17
INDUCTION
  MANIFOLD
REVOLUTION
  COUNTER

19
CROWN WHEEL AND
  PINION

20+
AUTOMATIC
  TRANSMISSION
INDEPENDENT
  SUSPENSION
POWER ASSISTED
  STEERING

NAUTICAL TERMS

3
AFT
BOW
FID
LEE

4
ALEE
BEAM
BITT
BOOM
FORE
HOLD
HULL
KEEL
KNOT
LIST
MATE
POOP
PORT
PROW
STAY
STEM
WAKE
WARP

5
ABAFT
ABEAM

5—continued
ABOUT
ALOFT
AVAST
BELAY
BELLS
BILGE
BOSUN
CABLE
CAULK
CLEAT
DAVIT
HATCH
HAWSE
STERN
TRICK
TRUCK
WAIST
WEIGH
WINCH

6
BRIDGE
BUNKER
FATHOM
FENDER
FLUKES
FO'C'SLE

6—continued
GALLEY
HAWSER
JETSAM
LEAGUE
LEEWAY
OFFING
PURSER
SHROUD
YAWING

7
ADMIRAL
BALLAST
BOLLARD
BULWARK
CAPSTAN
CATWALK
COAMING
DRAUGHT
FLOTSAM
GANGWAY
GRAPNEL
GUNWALE
INBOARD
LANYARD
MOORING
QUARTER

7—continued
RIGGING
SEA MILE
TONNAGE
TOPSIDE
WATCHES

8
BINNACLE
BOWSPRIT
BULKHEAD
COXSWAIN
DOG WATCH
HALYARDS
HATCHWAY
LARBOARD
PITCHING
RATLINES
SCUPPERS
SPLICING
TAFFRAIL
WINDLASS
WINDWARD

9
AMIDSHIPS
COMPANION
CROW'S NEST
FREEBOARD

9—continued
SHIP'S BELL
STARBOARD
WATER-LINE

10
BATTEN DOWN
DEADLIGHTS
DEADWEIGHT
FIRST WATCH

10—continued
FORE-AND-AFT
FORECASTLE
NIGHT WATCH

11
MIDDLE WATCH
QUARTER-DECK
WEATHER SIDE

12
DISPLACEMENT
JACOB'S LADDER
MARLINE SPIKE
NAUTICAL MILE
PLIMSOLL LINE

13
QUARTERMASTER

14
SUPERSTRUCTURE

15
COMPANION-
  LADDER
DAVY JONES'
  LOCKER

CLOTHES AND MATERIALS

CLOTHES

3	4 —continued	5 —continued	5 —continued
ABA	MITT	CHAPS	SHIRT
ALB	MUFF	CHOGA	SKIRT
BAL	MULE	CHOLI	SMOCK
BAS	PUMP	CLOAK	SNOOD
BAT	ROBE	CORDY	STOCK
BIB	RUFF	COTTA	STOLA
BRA	SARI	COTTE	STOLE
COP	SASH	CREST	TAILS
FEZ	SAYA	CROWN	TEDDY
HAT	SHOE	CURCH	TIARA
LEI	SLIP	CYLAS	TONGS
OBI	SLOP	CYMAR	TOPEE
TAM	SOCK	DERBY	TOQUE
4	SPAT	DHOTI	TREWS
ABBA	SUIT	EPHOD	TUNIC
AGAL	TABI	FICHU	VISOR
ALBA	TOGA	FROCK	VIZOR
APEX	TOGS	GANSY	WEEDS
BAJU	TOPI	GILET	**6**
BARB	TUTU	GIPPO	ABOLLA
BECK	VAMP	GLOVE	ALMUCE
BELT	VEIL	HABIT	ANADEM
BENN	VEST	HULLS	ANALAV
BOTA	WRAP	IHRAM	ANKLET
BUSK	**5**	JABOT	ANORAK
CACK	ABNET	JAMAH	ARCTIC
CAPE	ACTON	JEANS	ARTOIS
CLOG	AEGIS	JELAB	BALKAN
COAT	AMICE	JUPON	BANYAN
COPE	AMPYX	LAMMY	BARRET
COTE	APRON	LODEN	BARVEL
COWL	ARCAN	LUNGI	BASQUE
DAPS	ARMET	MIDDY	BAUTTA
DIDO	ARMOR	MUFTI	BEANIE
DISK	ASCOT	NUBIA	BEAVER
GARB	BARBE	PAGNE	BEQUIN
GETA	BARRY	PAGRI	BERTHA
GOWN	BENJY	PALLA	BICORN
HAIK	BERET	PANTS	BIETLE
HOOD	BLAKE	PARKA	BIGGIN
HOSE	BLUEY	PILCH	BIKINI
IZAR	BOINA	PIRNY	BIRRUS
JAMA	BOOTS	PUMPS	BISHOP
KEPI	BURKA	SABOT	BLAZER
KILT	BUSBY	SAREE	BLIAUD
MASK	CABAS	SCARF	BLOUSE
MAXI	CADET	SHAKO	BOATER
MIDI	CAPPA	SHAWL	BODICE
MINI	CHALE	SHIFT	BOLERO

6 —continued	6 —continued	6 —continued	7 —continued
BONNET	GAUCHO	TWEEDS	CHRISOM
BOOTEE	GILLIE	ULSTER	CHUDDAR
BOWLER	GUIMPE	UNDIES	CHUDDER
BOXERS	HALTER	UPLIFT	COMMODE
BRACAE	HENNIN	VAMPAY	CORONEL
BRACES	HUIPIL	VESTEE	CORONET
BRAGAS	JACKET	WIMPLE	COSSACK
BRAIES	JERKIN	WOOLLY	COXCOMB
BRETON	JERSEY	ZOUAVE	CREPIDA
BRIEFS	JUBBAH	**7**	CRISPIN
BROGAN	JUMPER	AMICTUS	CUCULLA
BROGUE	KABAYA	APPAREL	CUIRASS
BUSKIN	KIMONO	ARISARD	CULOTTE
BYRNIE	KIRTLE	ARM BAND	CURCHEF
BYRRUS	KITTEL	BABOOSH	CUTAWAY
CABAAN	LAMMIE	BALDRIC	DOPATTA
CADDIE	LOAFER	BALTEUS	DOUBLET
CAFTAN	LUNGEE	BANDEAU	DRAWERS
CALASH	MAGYAR	BANDORE	DULBAND
CALCEI	MANTEE	BARBUTE	DUL HOSE
CALIGA	MANTLE	BAROQUE	EARMUFF
CALPAC	MANTUA	BASHLYK	ETON CAP
CAMAIL	MITTEN	BASINET	EVERETT
CAMISA	MOBCAP	BAVETTE	FANCHON
CAMISE	MOGGAN	BAVOLET	FASHION
CAPOTE	OUTFIT	BEDIZEN	FILIBEG
CAPUCE	PEG-TOP	BELCHER	FLATCAP
CAPUTI	PEPLOS	BERDASH	GARMENT
CARACO	PEPLUM	BERETTA	GHILLIE
CASQUE	PILEUS	BETSIES	G STRING
CASTOR	PINNER	BIRETTA	GUM BOOT
CAUSIA	PIRNIE	BOTTINE	GUM SHOE
CESTUS	PONCHO	BOX CAPE	GYM SHOE
CHADAR	PUGREE	BOX COAT	HANDBAG
CHITON	PUTTEE	BRIMMER	HIGH-LOW
CHOKER	RAGLAN	BROGINE	HOMBURG
CILICE	REEFER	BURNOUS	HOSIERY
CIMIER	RUFFLE	BUSSKIN	JODHPUR
CLAQUE	SANDAL	CALEÇON	KLOMPEN
CLOCHE	SARONG	CALOTTE	LAYETTE
COBCAB	SERAPE	CAMOURO	LEOTARD
COCKET	SHIMMY	CANEZOU	MAILLOT
CORNET	SHORTS	CAPE HAT	MANTEAU
CORONA	SHROUD	CAPUCHE	MONTERA
CORSET	SLACKS	CAPULET	MONTERO
COTHUM	SONTAG	CASAQUE	MUFFLER
COVERT	STEP-IN	CASSOCK	OLIVERS
CRAVAT	SUN HAT	CATSKIN	OVERALL
DIADEM	TABARD	CAUBEEN	OXFORDS
DICKEY	TAMISE	CEREVIS	PANTIES
DIRNDL	TIGHTS	CHAINSE	PARASOL
DOLMAN	TIPPET	CHALWAR	PATTERN
DOMINO	TOP HAT	CHAPLET	PELISSE
DUSTER	TOPPER	CHEMISE	PETASOS
EARCAP	TRILBY	CHEVRON	PIERROT
FEDORA	TRUNKS	CHIMERE	PILLBOX
FILLET	T-SHIRT	CHIP HAT	PLUVIAL
GAITER	TUCKER	CHLAMYS	PUGGREE
GANSEY	TURBAN	CHOPINE	PYJAMAS
GARTER	TUXEDO	CHOU HAT	RAIMENT

7 —continued	8 —continued	8 —continued	9 —continued
REGALIA	BOTTEKIN	LINGERIE	BILLYCOCK
ROMPERS	BREECHES	LIRIPIPE	BLOUSETTE
RUBBERS	BURGONET	MANTELET	BODY LINEN
SARAFAN	BURNOOSE	MANTILLA	BOURRELET
SCOGGER	BYCOCKET	MOCCASIN	BRASSIÈRE
SHALWAR	CABASSET	NECKLACE	BROADBRIM
SILK HAT	CAMISOLE	NIGHTCAP	BRODEQUIN
SINGLET	CANOTIER	OPERA HAT	BRUNSWICK
SKI BOOT	CAPE COAT	OVERALLS	BYZANTINE
SLIPPER	CAPELINE	OVERCOAT	CABRIOLET
SLYDERS	CAPRIOLE	OVERSHOE	CAPE DRESS
SMICKET	CAPUCINE	PARAMENT	CAPE STOLE
SNEAKER	CAPUTIUM	PEASECOD	CARTWHEEL
SOUTANE	CARCANET	PEIGNOIR	CASENTINO
SPENCER	CARDIGAN	PHILIBEG	CASQUETTE
SPORRAN	CARDINAL	PILEOLUS	CASSIMERE
SULTANE	CAROLINE	PINAFORE	CHEMILOON
SUN SUIT	CASAQUIN	PLASTRON	CHIN-CLOTH
SURCOAT	CATERCAP	PLATINUM	CHIVARRAS
SURTOUT	CHANDAIL	PLIMSOLL	CHOLO COAT
SWEATER	CHAPERON	PULLOVER	COAT DRESS
TANK TOP	CHAQUETA	SABOTINE	COAT SHIRT
TEA GOWN	CHASUBLE	SKULL-CAP	COCKED HAT
TOP BOOT	CHAUSSES	SLIP-OVER	COOLIE HAT
TOP COAT	CHONGSAM	SNOWSHOE	COPINTANK
TRAHEEN	COLOBIUM	SOMBRERO	CORNERCAP
TRICORN	COPATAIN	STOCKING	COVERSLUT
TUNICLE	CORSELET	SURPLICE	COWBOY HAT
TWIN SET	COUCH HAT	SWIM SUIT	CREEDMORE
UNIFORM	COVERALL	TAIL COAT	CRINOLINE
VEILING	CRUSH HAT	TAILLEUR	DOG COLLAR
WATTEAU	CUCULLUS	TARBOOSH	DOMINICAL
WEDGIES	DANCE SET	TOQUETTE	DRESS COAT
WING TIE	DANDY HAT	TRAINERS	DRESS SHOE
WOOLLEN	DJELLABA	TRENCHER	DRESS SUIT
WRAPPER	DOM PEDRO	TRICORNE	DUNGAREES
YASHMAK	DORMEUSE	TROUSERS	DUNSTABLE
Y-FRONTS	DUCK-BILL	TWO-PIECE	ESCOFFIAN
ZIMARRA	DUNCE CAP	WOOLLENS	FORAGE CAP
8	DUST COAT	WOOLLIES	FROCK COAT
ABBÉ CAPE	DUTCH CAP	ZOOT SUIT	FULL DRESS
ALL-IN-ONE	FALDETTA	**9**	GABARDINE
ANALABOS	FLANNELS	AFTERWELT	GABERDINE
ANTELOPE	FLIMSIES	ALPARGATA	GARIBALDI
BABUSHKA	FOOTWEAR	ALPINE HAT	GLENGARRY
BALADRAN	GAMASHES	ANKLE BOOT	GREATCOAT
BALMORAL	GAUNTLET	APON DRESS	HEADDRESS
BANDANNA	GUERNSEY	ARMILAUSA	HEADPIECE
BARBETTE	HALF-HOSE	BABY SKIRT	HELMET CAP
BASQUINE	HALF SLIP	BALAYEUSE	HOURI-COAT
BATH ROBE	HEADGEAR	BALL DRESS	HOUSE-COAT
BEARSKIN	JACK BOOT	BALMACAAN	HULA SKIRT
BED SOCKS	JUDO COAT	BAMBIN HAT	INVERNESS
BENJAMIN	JUMP SUIT	BANDOLEER	JOCKEY CAP
BIGGONET	KERCHIEF	BARCELONA	JULIET CAP
BINNOGUE	KNICKERS	BEAVERTOP	LOINCLOTH
BLOOMERS	KNITWEAR	BED JACKET	MILLINERY
BODY COAT	LARRIGAN	BEEGUM HAT	NECKCLOTH
BOMBARDS	LAVA-LAVA	BELL SKIRT	NIGHTGOWN
BOOT-HOSE	LEGGINGS	BILLICOCK	OUTERWEAR

9 —continued

OVERDRESS
OVERSHIRT
OVERSKIRT
PANAMA HAT
PANTALETS
PANTOFFLE
PANTY HOSE
PEA JACKET
PETTICOAT
PILOT COAT
PLUS FOURS
POLONAISE
QUAKER HAT
REDINGOTE
SANBENITO
SHAKSHEER
SHINTIYAN
SHOVEL HAT
SLOPPY JOE
SLOUCH HAT
SNEAKERS
SOU'WESTER
STOMACHER
STRING TIE
SUNBONNET
SURCINGLE
TENT DRESS
THIGH BOOT
TROUSSEAU
TRUNK-HOSE
UNDERCOAT
UNDERGOWN
UNDERVEST
UNDERWEAR
VESTMENTS
VICTORINE
WAISTCOAT
WATCH COAT
WIDE-AWAKE
WITCH'S HAT
WYLIECOAT

10

ANGELUS CAP
APRON TUNIC
BABY BONNET
BASIC DRESS
BATHING CAP
BEER JACKET
BELLBOY CAP
BERRETTINO
BIBI BONNET
BICYCLE BAL
BLOUSE COAT
BOBBY SOCKS
BOSOM SHIRT
BOUDOIR CAP
BRIGANDINE
BRUNCH COAT
BUCKET TOPS
BUMPER BRIM

10 —continued

BUSH JACKET
BUSK JACKET
CALZONERAS
CANVAS SHOE
CAPE COLLAR
CAPPA MAGNA
CARMAGNOLE
CERVELIÈRE
CHARTREUSE
CHATELAINE
CHEMISETTE
CHIGNON CAP
CHOUQUETTE
CLOCK-MUTCH
COOLIE COAT
COQUELUCHE
CORPS PIQUÉ
COSSACK CAP
COTE-HARDIE
COUVRE-CHEF
COVERCHIEF
COVERT COAT
CROSSCLOTH
CUMMERBUND
DANCE DRESS
DESHABILLE
DINNER SUIT
DIPLOIDIAN
DOUILLETTE
DRESS PLAID
DRESS SHIRT
DUFFEL COAT
ECLIPSE TIE
ESPADRILLE
ETON JACKET
EUGÉNIE HAT
FANCY DRESS
FASCINATOR
FLYING SUIT
FORE-AND-AFT
FUSTANELLA
GARMENTURE
GRASS SKIRT
HAREM SKIRT
HUG-ME-TIGHT
JIGGER COAT
LIRIPIPIUM
LOUNGE SUIT
LUMBERJACK
MESS JACKET
NIGHTDRESS
NIGHTSHIRT
OPERA CLOAK
OVERBLOUSE
OVERGAITER
OXFORD BAGS
OXFORD GOWN
PANTALOONS
PICTURE HAT
PITH HELMET

10 —continued

POKE BONNET
PORK PIE HAT
RIDING-HOOD
SERVICE CAP
SHIRTWAIST
SPORTS COAT
SPORT SHIRT
SPORTSWEAR
STICHARION
STRING VEST
SUNDAY BEST
SUSPENDERS
SWEAT SHIRT
THREE-PIECE
TRENCH COAT
UNDERDRESS
UNDERLINEN
UNDERPANTS
UNDERSHIRT
UNDERSKIRT
VELDSCHOEN
WINDSOR TIE
WING COLLAR

11

ALSATIAN BOW
BATHING SUIT
BIB-AND-BRACE
BOILED SHIRT
BOXER SHORTS
BRACONNIÈRE
BREECHCLOTH
BRITISH WARM
CANCAN DRESS
CAVALIER HAT
CHAPEAU BRAS
CHAPEL DE FER
CIRCASSIENE
COMBINATION
CORSET COVER
COWBOY BOOTS
DANCING CLOG
DEERSTALKER
DINNER DRESS
EMPIRE SKIRT
ESPADRILLES
EVENING GOWN
EVENING SLIP
FORMAL DRESS
FORTUNY GOWN
GALLIGASKIN
HOBBLE SKIRT
HOSTESS GOWN
HOUPPELANDE
HUNTING BOOT
MIDDY BLOUSE
NECKERCHIEF
OVERGARMENT
PANTY GIRDLE
RIDING HABIT
RUBBER APRON

11 —continued

RUNNING SHOE
RUSSIAN BOOT
SEWING APRON
SNAP-BRIM HAT
SOUP-AND-FISH
SOUTHWESTER
SPATTERDASH
STOCKING CAP
STRING GLOVE
SWAGGER COAT
TAM-O'SHANTER
TYROLEAN HAT
UNDERGIRDLE
UNDERTHINGS
WALKING SHOE
WEDDING GOWN
WEDDING VEIL
WELLINGTONS
WINDBREAKER
WINDCHEATER

12

AMISH COSTUME
BALKAN BLOUSE
BALLOON SKIRT
BASEBALL BOOT
BATTLE JACKET
BELLY DOUBLET
BLOOMER DRESS
BUSINESS SUIT
CAMICIA ROSSA
CAVALIER BOOT
CHEMISE DRESS
CHEMISE FROCK
CHESTERFIELD
CHUKKER SHIRT
CIGARETTE MIT
CORSET BODICE
COTTAGE CLOAK
CRUSADER HOOD
DINNER JACKET
DIVIDED SKIRT
DORIC CHILTON
DRESS CLOTHES
DRESSING GOWN
EASTER BONNET
ENGLISH DRAPE
EVENING DRESS
EVENING SHOES
EVENING SKIRT
HANDKERCHIEF
HEADKERCHIEF
HELMET BONNET
KNEE BREECHES
LOUNGING ROBE
MANDARIN COAT
MONKEY JACKET
MORNING DRESS
MOTORING VEIL
PEDAL PUSHERS
PENITENTIALS

12 —continued
QUAKER BONNET
ROLL-ON GIRDLE
SCOTCH BONNET
SHIRTWAISTER
SLEEPING COAT
SLEEPING SUIT
SMALLCLOTHES
STOVEPIPE HAT
SUGAR-LOAF HAT
TAILORED SUIT
TEN-GALLON HAT
TROUSERETTES
UNDERCLOTHES
UNDERGARMENT
WIDE-AWAKE HAT
ZOUAVE JACKET

13
ACROBATIC SHOE
AFTER-SKI SOCKS
BACK-STRAP SHOE
BEEFEATER'S HAT
BELLBOY JACKET
BUNGALOW APRON
COACHMAN'S COAT
COMBING JACKET
COTTAGE BONNET
DRESSING SAQUE
ELEVATOR SHOES

13 —continued
HAWAIIAN SKIRT
MOTHER HUBBARD
MOURNING DRESS
NORFOLK JACKET
PEEK-A-BOO WAIST
PRINCESS DRESS
SAM BROWNE BELT
SMOKING JACKET
SPORTS CLOTHES
SUSPENDER-BELT
TEDDYBEAR COAT
TRUNK-BREECHES
UNDERCLOTHING

14
AFTERNOON DRESS
BAREFOOT SANDAL
BATHING COSTUME
BICYCLE CLIP HAT
CABBAGE-TREE HAT
CACHE-POUSSIÈRE
CAMOUFLAGE SUIT
CARDIGAN BODICE
CONGRESS GAITOR
CONTINENTAL HAT
DRESSING JACKET
DRESSMAKER SUIT
EGYPTIAN SANDAL
EVENING SWEATER

14 —continued
KNICKERBOCKERS
SHOOTING JACKET

15
BOUDOIR SLIPPERS
CARDIGAN
  SWEATER
CHAPEAU FRANÇAIS
CHEMISE À LA REINE
CHEVALIER BONNET
DOUBLE-DUTY
  DRESS
ENVELOPE CHEMISE
FAIR ISLE SWEATER
MONTGOMERY
  BERET

16
BALLERINA
  COSTUME
BUTCHER BOY
  BLOUSE
CALMEL'S HAIR
  SHAWL
CHICKEN SKIN
  GLOVE
EISENHOWER
  JACKET

16 —continued
ELBERT HUBBARD
  TIE
GOING-AWAY
  COSTUME
SWADDLING
  CLOTHES

17
CHEMISE À
  L'ANGLAISE
COAL SCUTTLE
  BONNET
CONFIRMATION
  DRESS
FOUNDATION
  GARMENT
SWALLOW-TAILED
  COAT

18
BETHLEHEM
  HEADDRESS
CHARLOTTE
  CORDAY CAP

19
SALVATION ARMY
  BONNET

MATERIALS

3
ABB
BAN
FUR
NET
REP

4
ACCA
ALMA
BAKU
BRIN
BURE
CALF
CORD
CREA
FELT
FUJI
GROS
HEMP
HIDE
JEAN
LACE
LAMÉ
LAWN
LYNX

4 —continued
MULL
PELT
ROAN
SILK
SKIN
VAIR
WOOL

5
ABACA
ACELE
ACETA
ARDIL
BAIZE
BASCO
BASIN
CADIS
CAFFA
CASHA
CLOTH
CRAPE
CRASH
CRISP
CROWN
DENIM

5 —continued
DORIA
FITCH
GAUZE
GENET
GUNNY
HONAN
JUPON
KAPOK
LAINE
LAPIN
LINEN
LINON
LISLE
LLAMA
LUREX
MOIRE
NINON
NYLON
ORLON
OTTER
PEKIN
PIQUÉ
PLUSH
PRINT

5 —continued
RAYON
SATIN
SCRIM
SERGE
SISAL
SISOL
SKUNK
STRAW
STUFF
SUEDE
SURAH
TAMMY
TISSU
TOILE
TULLE
TWEED
TWILL
UNION
VOILE

6
ALACHA
ALASKA
ALPACA
AMAZON

6 —continued	6 —continued	7 —continued	7 —continued
ANGORA	MANTUA	CARACAL	PIGSKIN
ARALAC	MARMOT	CARACUL	RACCOON
ARIDEX	MARTEN	CATALIN	RAWHIDE
ARMURE	MELTON	CHALLIS	RAW SILK
BALINE	MERINO	CHAMOIS	ROMAINE
BARÉGE	MILIUM	CHARVET	SACKING
BEAVER	MOHAIR	CHEKMAK	SAFFIAN
BENGAL	MOUTON	CHEVIOT	SATINET
BERBER	MULMUL	CHEYNEY	SUITING
BIRETZ	MUSLIN	CHIFFON	TAFFETA
BLATTA	NAPERY	COOTHAY	TEXTILE
BOTANY	NUTRIA	COWHIDE	TICKING
BUREAU	OCELOT	DAMMASÉ	TIE SILK
BURLAP	OSPREY	DELAINE	TIFFANY
BURNET	OXFORD	DOESKIN	TUSSORE
BURRAH	PAILLE	DORNICK	VALENCE
BYSSUS	PONGEE	DRABBET	VELOURS
CAFFOY	POPLIN	DRUGGET	VISCOSE
CALICO	PYTHON	DUCHESS	VIYELLA
CAMACA	RABBIT	DURANCE	WEBBING
CAMLET	RED FOX	DUVETYN	WOOLLEN
CANGAN	RIBBON	EARL GLO	WORSTED
CANVAS	RUBBER	ÉPINGLÉ	8
CASTOR	SAMITE	ESPARTO	AGA BANEE
CATGUT	SATEEN	ETAMINE	ALOE LACE
CHILLO	SAXONY	FAKE FUR	ANTELOPE
CHINTZ	SENNIT	FISHNET	ARMOZEEN
CHROME	SHODDY	FITCHEW	ARMOZINE
CHUNAN	SISSOL	FLANNEL	ART LINEN
COBURG	SKIVER	FOULARD	ASBESTOS
CONTRO	SOUPLE	FUR FELT	BAGHEERA
COSSAS	TARTAN	FUSTIAN	BARATHEA
CÔTELÉ	TINSEL	GALATEA	BARRACAN
CREPON	TISSUE	GINGHAM	BATSWING
CROISE	TRICOT	GOBELIN	BAUDEKIN
CUBICA	TUSSAH	GROGRAM	BEUTANOL
DAMASK	TUSSEH	GUANACO	BLANCARD,
DIAPER	VELURE	GUIPURE	BOBBINET
DIMITY	VELVET	HESSIAN	BOMBAZET
DJERSA	VICUNA	HOLLAND	BOX CLOTH
DOMETT	WINCEY	JACONET	BUCKSKIN
DOWLAS	WITNEY	JAP SILK	BUFFSKIN
DUCAPE	7	KASHMIR	CALFSKIN
ÉPONGE	ACRILON	KIDSKIN	CAPESKIN
ERMINE	ACRYLIC	LEATHER	CASHMERE
FABRIC	ALAMODE	LEGHORN	CELANESE
FAILLE	ART SILK	LEOPARD	CELENESE
FISHER	BAGGING	LIBERTY	CHAMBRAY
FORFAR	BATISTE	MINIVER	CHARMEEN
FRIEZE	BATTING	MOROCCO	CHENILLE
GALYAC	BEMBERG	NANKEEN	CHIRIMEN
GALYAK	BLUE FOX	NETTING	CHIVERET
GRENAI	BRABANT	OILSKIN	CIVET CAT
GURRAH	BRUNETE	ORGANDY	CORDUROY
KERSEY	BUNTING	ORGANZA	COTELINE
LAMPAS	BUSTIAN	OTTOMAN	CRETONNE
LASTEX	CAMBAYE	PAISLEY	CROSS FOX
LINENE	CAMBRIC	PARAGON	DIAPHANE
LIZARD	CANTOON	PECCARY	DRAP D'ÉTÉ
MADRAS	CAPENET	PERCALE	DUCHESSE

8 —continued	9 —continued	10 —continued	11 —continued
ÉCRU SILK	BOOK CLOTH	BOUCLÉ YARN	LEATHERETTE
EOLIENNE	BOOK LINEN	BROADCLOTH	MARQUISETTE
ESTAMENE	BROCATELL	BROAD GOODS	NAPA LEATHER
EVERFAST	BYRD CLOTH	CADET CLOTH	NUN'S VEILING
FARADINE	CALAMANCO	CAMBRESINE	OVERCOATING
FLORENCE	CANNEQUIN	CHINCHILLA	PANNE VELVET
GOATSKIN	CATALOWNE	CHINO CLOTH	PERSIAN LAMB
GOSSAMER	CHARMEUSE	CIRCASSIAN	POODLE CLOTH
HOMESPUN	CHINA SILK	CONGO CLOTH	POULT-DE-SOIE
INDIENNE	COTTONADE	CREPE LISSE	SCOTCH PLAID
KOLINSKY	COTTON REP	DRESS LINEN	SPONGE CLOTH
LAMBSKIN	CREPELINE	GRASS CLOTH	STONE MARTEN
LUSTRINE	CRINOLINE	HOP SACKING	TOILE DE JOUY
LUSTRING	CUT VELVET	HORSECLOTH	WAFFLE CLOTH
MARABOUT	DACCA SILK	INDIAN LAMB	
MARCELLA	ÉCRU CLOTH	IRISH LINEN	**12**
MAROCAIN	ÉLASTIQUE	MARSEILLES	ACETATE RAYON
MATERIAL	FLANNELET	MOUSSELINE	BALLOON CLOTH
MILANESE	FUR FABRIC	PEAU DE SOIE	BERLIN CANVAS
MOGADORE	GABARDINE	PIECE GOODS	BOLIVIA CLOTH
MOLESKIN	GEORGETTE	PILOT CLOTH	BOLTING CLOTH
MOQUETTE	GRENADINE	SEERSUCKER	BRILLIANTINE
MUSLINET	GROSGRAIN	SUEDE CLOTH	BROWN HOLLAND
MUSQUASH	HAIRCLOTH	TERRY CLOTH	BRUSHED RAYON
NAINSOOK	HORSEHAIR	TOILINETTE	BUTCHER LINEN
OILCLOTH	HUCKABACK	WINCEYETTE	CARACUL CLOTH
ORGANDIE	LONGCLOTH		CAVALRY TWILL
PURE SILK	MARCELINE	**11**	CONVENT CLOTH
SARCENET	MESSALINE	ABRADED YARN	COTTON VELVET
SARSENET	MOSS CREPE	AERATED YARN	CRINKLE CLOTH
SEALSKIN	ORGANZINE	ALBERT CREPE	CROISÉ VELVET
SHAGREEN	PATCHWORK	ARABIAN LACE	DENMARK SATIN
SHANTUNG	PETERSHAM	ARMURE-LAINE	DOUBLE DAMASK
SHIRTING	RANCH MINK	BABY FLANNEL	DRESS FLANNEL
SHOT SILK	SACKCLOTH	BAG SHEETING	ELEMENT CLOTH
SQUIRREL	SAIL CLOTH	BANDLE LINEN	EMPRESS CLOTH
TAPESTRY	SATINETTE	BASKET CLOTH	GLAZED CHINTZ
TARLATAN	SHARKSKIN	BATH COATING	MUTATION MINK
TARLETAN	SHEEPSKIN	BEDFORD CORD	SHETLAND WOOL
TOILINET	SILVER FOX	BOMBER CLOTH	SLIPPER SATIN
VALENCIA	SNAKESKIN	BRUSHED WOOL	SUMMER ERMINE
WAX CLOTH	STOCKINET	CANTON CREPE	VISCOSE RAYON
WHIPCORD	SWANSDOWN	CANTON LINEN	WELSH FLANNEL
WHITE FOX	TARPAULIN	CHAMOISETTE	
WILD MINK	TOWELLING	CHEESECLOTH	**13**
WILD SILK	TRICOTINE	CHESS CANVAS	AIRPLANE CLOTH
ZIBELINE	VELVETEEN	CHINA COTTON	AMERICAN CLOTH
9	WOLVERINE	CLAY WORSTED	ARMURE-SATINÉE
ADA CANVAS	WORCESTER	COTTON CREPE	BRITTANY CLOTH
AGRA GAUZE	**10**	DACCA MUSLIN	CANTON FLANNEL
ALBATROSS	ABBOT CLOTH	DIAPER CLOTH	CARDINAL CLOTH
ALLIGATOR	AIDA CANVAS	DOTTED SWISS	CASEMENT CLOTH
ASBESTALL	ANGOLA YARN	DRAP DE BERRY	CLOISTER CLOTH
ASTRAKHAN	AUSTINIZED	DREADNOUGHT	COSTUME VELVET
ASTRAKHAN	BALBRIGGAN	DRUID'S CLOTH	COTTON FLANNEL
BARK CLOTH	BARLEYCORN	DU PONT RAYON	COTTON SUITING
BARK CREPE	BAUM MARTEN	ESKIMO CLOTH	COTTON WORSTED
BENGALINE	BEAVERETTE	EVERLASTING	CRUSHED VELVET
BOMBAZINE	BEAVERTEEN	FLANNELETTE	DIAGONAL CLOTH
BOMBYCINE	BOOK MUSLIN	HARRIS TWEED	DIAPER FLANNEL
		IRISH POPLIN	EGYPTIAN CLOTH

13 —continued
END-TO-END CLOTH
LINSEY-WOOLSEY
PATENT LEATHER
RUSSIA LEATHER
14
ALGERIAN STRIPE
AMERICAN COTTON
ARGENTINE CLOTH
BANDOLIER CLOTH
BARONETTE SATIN
BROADTAIL CLOTH
CORKSCREW TWILL
EGYPTIAN COTTON

14 —continued
ELECTORAL CLOTH
FRUIT OF THE LOOM
HONEYCOMB CLOTH
JACQUARD FABRIC
SHEPHERD'S PLAID
15
ABSORBENT
  COTTON
ADMIRALITY CLOTH
CACHEMIRE DE SOIE
CAMEL'S HAIR
  CLOTH

15 —continued
EMBROIDERY LINEN
OSTRICH FEATHERS
PARACHUTE FABRIC
SEA-ISLAND
  COTTON
SHIRTING FLANNEL
TATTERSALL CHECK
TATTERSALL PLAID
TROPICAL SUITING
16
CANDLEWICK
  FABRIC

16 —continued
CONSTITUTION
  CORD
MERCERIZED
  COTTON
TURKISH
  TOWELLING
17
CROSS-STITCH
  CANVAS
CUPRAMMONIUM
  RAYON

FOOD AND DRINK

COOKERY TERMS

4
BARD
BEAT
BLEU (AU)
BOIL
BONE
CHOP
COAT
HANG
HASH
LARD
PIPE
RARE
TOSS

5
BASTE
BERNY
BLANC (À)
BLANC (AU)
BROIL
BROWN
BRULÉ
CARVE
CHILL
CROWN
DAUBE
DRAIN
DRESS
GLAZE
GRILL
KNEAD
MELBA
PLUCK
POACH
POINT (À)
PROVE
PURÉE
REINE (À LA)

5—continued
ROAST
RUB IN
SAUTÉ
SCALD
STEAM
SWEAT
TRUSS

6
AURORE
BRAISE
CONFIT
CRÉOLE (À LA)
DECANT
DESALT
DIABLE (À LA)
FILLET
FONDUE
GRATIN
GREASE
MAISON
MIGNON
NATURE
REDUCE
SIMMER
ZEPHYR

7
AL DENTE
ARRÊTER
BLANCHE
BLONDIR
CHEMISE (EN)
COLBERT
CROUTON.
DEGLAZE
EMINCER
FLAMBER
GRECQUE (À LA)

7—continued
MARENGO
MÉDICIS
NICOISE (À LA)
REFRESH
SUPRÊME
TARTARE (À LA)

8
ALLONGER
ANGLAISE (À L')
APPAREIL
ASSATION
BARBECUE
BELLEVUE (EN)
BRETONNE (À LA)
CATALANE (À LA)
CHAMBORD
CHASSEUR
CHEMISER
CRUDITÉS
DAUPHINE (À LA)
DEVILLED
DUCHESSE (À LA)
EMULSION
ESCALOPE
FERMIÈRE (À LA)
FLAMANDE (ÀLA)
INFUSION
JULIENNE
MACERATE
MARINATE
MEUNIÈRE (À LA)
PISTACHE
POT-ROAST
SURPRISE (EN)

9
ACIDULATE
BAKE BLIND

9—continued
CANELLING
DETAILLER
DIEPPOISE (À LA)
ESPAGNOLE (À L')
FRICASSÉE
KNOCK BACK
LIÉGEOISE (À LA)
LYONNAISE (À LA)
MARINIÈRE (À LA)
MEDALLION
MILANAISE (À LA)

10
ANTILLAISE (À L')
BALLOTTINE
BLANQUETTE
BONNE FEMME
BORDELAISE (À LA)
BOULANGÈRE (À LA)
CHAUD-FROID
DIJONNAISE (À LA)
FLORENTINE (À LA)
PROVENCALE (À LA)

11
BELLE-HÉLÈNE
BOURGUIGNON
CHARCUTERIE
DAUPHINOISE (À LA)
HOLLANDAISE (À LA)

13
BOURGUIGNONNE (À LA)
CLARIFICATION
DEEP-FAT FRYING

KITCHEN UTENSILS AND TABLEWARE

3
CUP
HOB
JAR
JUG

3—continued
LID
MUG
PAN
POT

3—continued
TIN
WOK

4
BOWL

4—continued
DISH
EWER
FORK
MILL

4—continued	6—continued	8—continued	10—continued
RACK	SHAKER	SCISSORS	SLOW COOKER
SPIT	SHEARS	STOCKPOT	STERILIZER
TIAN	SIPHON	STRAINER	WAFFLE IRON
TRAY	SKEWER	TART RING	**11**
5	STRING	TASTE-VIN	BAKING SHEET
BAHUT	TAJINE	TRENCHER	BRAISING PAN
BASIN	TOUPIN	**9**	CANDISSOIRE
BOARD	TUREEN	ALCARRAZA	CHAFING DISH
CHOPE	**7**	AUTOCLAVE	CHEESECLOTH
CHURN	ALEMBIC	BAIN-MARIE	COFFEE MAKER
FLUTE	ATTELET	BAKING TIN	DOUGH TROUGH
GRILL	BLENDER	CAFETIÈRE	DRIPPING PAN
KNIFE	BROILER	CASSEROLE	FRUIT STONER
LADLE	CAISSES	COMPOTIER	GARGOULETTE
MIXER	CHINOIS	CORKSCREW	JAMBONNIÈRE
MOULD	CHIP PAN	CRUMB TRAY	NUTCRACKERS
PELLE	CHOPPER	DÉCOUPOIR	PASTRY BRUSH
PLATE	COCOTTE	FISH SLICE	PASTRY WHEEL
PRESS	DRAINER	FRYING-PAN	SERVING DISH
RUSSE	DREDGER	KILNER JAR	THERMOMETER
SIEVE	ÉCUELLE	MANDOLINE	YOGURT-MAKER
SPOON	GRINDER	MIJOTEUSE	**12**
STEEL	MARMITE	PASTRY BAG	CARVING KNIFE
STRAW	PITCHER	PIPING BAG	DEEP-FAT FRYER
TONGS	RAMEKIN	RING MOULD	MEASURING JUG
WHISK	RONDEAU	SALAD BOWL	PALETTE KNIFE
6	SALT BOX	SAUCEBOAT	PASTRY CUTTER
BASKET	SAMOVAR	SHARPENER	TURBOT KETTLE
BUCKET	SKILLET	STEAK BATT	**13**
CARAFE	SKIMMER	TISANIÈRE	BUTCHER'S BLOCK
CLOCHE	SPATULA	TOURTIÈRE	FOOD PROCESSOR
COOLER	SYRINGE	**10**	ICE-CREAM MAKER
CRIBLE	TÂTE-VIN	APPLE-CORER	KITCHEN SCALES
DIABLE	TOASTER	CAISSETTES	LARDING NEEDLE
EGG CUP	**8**	CASSOLETTE	PRESERVING JAR
FUNNEL	CAQUELON	CHOPSTICKS	SACCHAROMETER
GOBLET	CAULDRON	CRUET STAND	VEGETABLE DISH
GRADIN	COLANDER	DIPPING PIN	**14**
GRATER	CRÊPE PAN	FISH KETTLE	JUICE EXTRACTOR
KETTLE	CROCKERY	LIQUIDISER	KNEADING TROUGH
MINCER	DAUBIÈRE	MUSTARD POT	KNIFE SHARPENER
MORTAR	EGG TIMER	PERCOLATOR	PRESSURE COOKER
MUSLIN	FLAN RING	ROLLING PIN	TRUSSING NEEDLE
PESTLE	HOTPLATE	ROTISSERIE	**16**
PICHET	MAZAGRAN	SALAMANDER	MEAT-CARVING
PITTER	MOUVETTE	SALT CELLAR	TONGS
POÊLON	SAUCEPAN	SALTING TUB	
SAUCER	SAUTÉ PAN		

BAKING

3	3—continued	4—continued	5
BAP	PIE	FLAN	BAGEL
BUN	**4**	PAVÉ	BÂTON
COB	BABA	RUSK	BREAD
FAR	CHOU	TART	CRÊPE

CEREALS

5—continued
FLÛTE
ICING
PLAIT
SABLÉ
SCONE
STICK
TOAST
6
COOKIE
CORNET
ÉCLAIR
LEAVEN
MUFFIN
OUBLIE
ROCHER
TOURTE
WAFFLE
7
BAKLAVA
BANNOCK
BISCUIT
BLOOMER
BRIOCHE

7—continued
CHAPATI
COTTAGE
CRACKER
CRUMPET
FICELLE
FRITTER
GALETTE
PALMIER
PANCAKE
PRALINE
PRETZEL
STOLLEN
STRUDEL
TARTINE
TARTLET
8
AMANDINE
BAGUETTE
BARM CAKE
BÂTONNET
BISCOTTE
DOUGHNUT
DUCHESSE

8—continued
DUMPLING
EMPANADA
FROSTING
GRISSINI
SANDWICH
SPLIT TIN
TORTILLA
TURNOVER
9
ALLUMETTE
BARQUETTE
CROISSANT
FEUILLETÉ
FRIANDISE
KUGELHOPF
PETIT FOUR
VOL-AU-VENT
10
CRISPBREAD
FRANGIPANE
PÂTISSERIE

10—continued
PUFF PASTRY
RELIGIEUSE
SHORTBREAD
SPONGE CAKE
11
CHOUX PASTRY
LINZERTORTE
PETIT-BEURRE
PROFITEROLE
12
LANGUE-DE-CHAT
PUMPERNICKEL
SPONGE FINGER
13
GENOESE SPONGE
14
PAIN AU CHOCOLAT
15
SAVOY SPONGE
  CAKE

CEREALS

3
RYE
4
BRAN
CORN
OATS
RICE

5
MAIZE
SPELT
WHEAT
6
BARLEY
BULGUR

6—continued
MÉTEIL
MILLET
7
BURGHUL
FROMENT
SORGHUM

9
BUCKWHEAT
12
CRACKED WHEAT

CHEESES

4
BRIE (France)
CURD (CHEESE)
EDAM (Netherlands)
FETA (Greece)
TOME (France)
5
BANON (France)
BRICK (US)
CABOC (Scotland)
COMTÉ (France)
DANBO (Denmark)
DERBY (England)
FETTA (Greece)
GOUDA (Netherlands)
HERVE (Belgium)

5—continued
LEIGH (England)
MOLBO (Denmark)
MUROL (France)
NIOLO (Corsica)
TAMIÉ (France)
6
ASIAGO (Italy)
BAGNES (Switzerland)
BRESSE (France)
CACHAT (France)
CANTAL (France)
CENDRÉ (France)
DUNLOP (Scotland)
FOURME (France)
GAPRON (France)

6—continued
GÉROMÉ (France)
HALUMI (Greece)
HRAMSA (Scotland)
LEIDEN (Netherlands)
MORVEN (Scotland)
OLIVET (France)
POURLY (France)
ROLLOT (France)
SALERS (France)
SAMSOË (Denmark)
SBRINZ (Switzerland)
SURATI (India)
TILSIT (Switzerland; Germany; Austria)
VENACO (Corsica)

7
BONDARD (France)
BRINZEN (Hungary)
BROCCIO (Corsica)
BROCCIU (Corsica)
BROUSSE (France)
BRUCCIU (Corsica)
BRYNDZA (Hungary)
CABÉCOU (France)
CHEDDAR (England)
CROWDIE (Scotland)
DAUPHIN (France)
DEMI-SEL (France)
FONTINA (Italy)
GAPERON (France)
GJETÖST (Norway)
GRUYÈRE (France; Switzerland)
JONCHÉE (France)
LANGRES (France)
LEVROUX (France)
LIMBURG (Belgium)
LIVAROT (France)
MACQUÉE (France)
MONT-D'OR (France)
MORBIER (France)
MÜNSTER (France)
NANTAIS (France)
PICODON (France)
QUARGEL (Austria)
RICOTTA (Italy)
SAPSAGO (Switzerland)
STILTON (England)
VENDÔME (France)

8
AUVERGNE (France)
AYRSHIRE (Scotland)
BEAUFORT (France)
BEL PAESE (Italy)
BERGKÄSE (Austria)
BOULETTE (France)
CHAOURCE (France)
CHESHIRE (England)
EDELPILZ (Germany)
EMMENTAL (Switzerland)
EPOISSES (France)

8—continued
MANCHEGO (Spain)
PARMESAN (Italy)
PECORINO (Italy)
PÉLARDON (France)
REMOUDOU (Belgium)
SCAMORZE (Italy)
TALEGGIO (Italy)
VACHERIN (Switzerland)
VALENCAY (France)

9
APPENZELL (Switzerland)
BROODKAAS (Netherlands)
CAITHNESS (Scotland)
CAMBOZOLA (Italy; Germany)
CAMEMBERT (France)
CHABICHOU (France)
CHEVRETON (France)
EMMENTHAL (Switzerland)
EXCELSIOR (France)
GAMMELÖST (Norway)
LA BOUILLE (France)
LEICESTER (England)
LIMBURGER (Belgium)
MAROILLES (France)
MIMOLETTE (France)
PAVÉ D'AUGE (France)
PORT-SALUT (France)
PROVOLONE (Italy)
REBLOCHON (France)
ROQUEFORT (France)
SOVIETSKI (USSR)

10
CAERPHILLY (Wales)
DANISH BLUE (Denmark)
DOLCELATTE (Italy)
GLOUCESTER (England)
GORGONZOLA (Italy)
LANCASHIRE (England)
MOZZARELLA (Italy)
NEUFCHÂTEL (Switzerland)
PITHIVIERS (France)
RED WINDSOR (England)
SAINGORLON (France)
STRACCHINO (Italy)

11
CARRÉ DE L'EST (France)
COEUR DE BRAY (France)
COULOMMIERS (France)
KATSHKAWALJ (Bulgaria)
PETIT-SUISSE (France)
PONT-L'ÉVÊQUE (France)
SAINTE-MAURE (France)
SAINT-PAULIN (France)
SCHABZIEGER (Switzerland)
SCHLOSSKÄSE (Austria)
TÊTE-DE-MOINE (Switzerland)
WEISSLACKER (Germany)
WENSLEYDALE (England)

12
CACIOCAVALLO (Italy)
RED LEICESTER (England)
SOUMAINTRAIN (France)

13
SAINT-NECTAIRE (France)
SELLES-SUR-CHER (France)

14
BRILLAT-SAVARIN (France)
FEUILLE DE DREUX (France)
LAGUIOLE-AUBRAC (France)
SAINT-FLORENTIN (France)
SAINT-MARCELLIN (France)
TRAPPISTENKÄSE (Germany)

15
BOUTON-DE-CULOTTE (France)

16
DOUBLE GLOUCESTER (England)

17
RIGOTTE DE PELUSSIN (France)

18
CHEVROTIN DES ARAVIS (France)
CROTTIN DE CHAVIGNOL (France)

19
POULIGNY-SAINT-PIERRE (France)

HERBS AND SPICES

3
BAY
RUE
4
BALM
DILL
MINT
SAGE
5
ANISE
BASIL
CHIVE
CLOVE
CUMIN
TANSY
THYME
6
BETONY
BORAGE
BURNET

6 —continued
CICELY
FENNEL
GARLIC
GINGER
LOVAGE
PEPPER
SAVORY
SESAME
SORREL
7
BONESET
CARAWAY
CHERVIL
COMFREY
DITTANY
MUSTARD
OREGANO
PAPRIKA

7 —continued
PARSLEY
PERILLA
PIMENTO
SAFFRON
SALSIFY
TABASCO
VANILLA
8
ALLSPICE
ANGELICA
CAMOMILE
CARDAMOM
CARDAMON
CINNAMON
DROPWORT
FEVERFEW
MARJORAM
ROSEMARY

8 —continued
TARRAGON
TURMERIC
9
CHAMOMILE
CORIANDER
FENUGREEK
SPEARMINT
10+
ASAFOETIDA
BLACK-EYED SUSAN
HERB OF GRACE
HORSERADISH
HOTTENTOT FIG
OYSTER PLANT
PEPPERMINT
POT MARIGOLD
VEGETABLE OYSTER

DRINKS

WINES AND APERITIFS

4
FINO
HOCK
PORT
5
BYRRH
CRÉPY
FITOU
MÉDOC
MOSEL
RIOJA

5—continued
TAVEL
TOKAY
6
ALSACE
BANDOL
BAROLO
BARSAC
BEAUNE
CAHORS
CASSIS

6—continued
CHINON
CLARET
FRANGY
GRAVES
MÁLAGA
SAUMUR
SHERRY
VOLNAY
7
ALIGOTÉ

7—continued
CAMPARI
CHABLIS
CHIANTI
CLAIRET
CRÉMANT
FALERNO
GAILLAC
MADEIRA
MARGAUX
MARSALA

7—continued
MARTINI
MOSELLE
ORVIETO
POMMARD
RETSINA
VOUVRAY
8
BORDEAUX
BROUILLY
DUBONNET
GIGONDAS
MERCUREY
MONTAGNY
MONTILLA
MUSCADET
PAUILLAC
RIESLING
ROSÉ WINE
SANCERRE
SANTENAY
VALENCAY
VERMOUTH
VIN JAUNE
9
BOURGUEIL
CHAMPAGNE

9—continued
CLAIRETTE
CÔTE-RÔTIE
HERMITAGE
LAMBRUSCO
MEURSAULT
MONTLOUIS
SAUTERNES
10
BARBARESCO
BEAUJOLAIS
BULL'S BLOOD
MANZANILLA
MONTRACHET
RICHEBOURG
RIVESALTES
VINHO VERDE
11
ALOXE-CORTON
AMONTILLADO
MONBAZILLAC
POUILLY-FUMÉ
SAINT JULIEN
VIN DE PAILLE
12
CÔTES-DU-RHÔNE
ROMANÉE-CONTI

12—continued
SAINT-EMILION
SAINT ESTEPHE
VALPOLICELLA
VOSNE-ROMANÉE
13
CHÂTEAU D'YQUEM
CHÂTEAU LAFITE
CHÂTEAU LATOUR
ENTRE-DEUX-MERS
POUILLY-FUISSÉ
14
CHÂTEAU MARGAUX
CÔTES-DU-VENTOUX
GEWÜRZTRAMINER
LACRIMA CHRISTI
15
CÔTES-DE-
  PROVENCE
CÔTES-DU-VIVARAIS
CROZES-HERMITAGE
HAUT POITOU WINES
MOREY-SAINT-DENIS
16
CHAMBOLLE-
  MUSIGNY

16—continued
CHÂTEAU HAUT-
  BRION
GEVREY-
  CHAMBERTIN
SAVIGNY-LÈS-
  BEAUNE
17
CORTON-
  CHARLEMAGNE
CÔTES-DU-
  ROUSSILLON
NUITS-SAINT-
  GEORGES
18
BLANQUETTE DE
  LIMOUX
19
CHASSAGNE-
  MONTRACHET
20
CHÂTEAU MOUTON-
  ROTHSCHILD

COCKTAILS AND MIXED DRINKS

3
FIX
KIR
NOG
4
FIZZ
FLIP
GROG
RAKI
SOUR
5
JULEP
NEGUS
PUNCH
TODDY
6
BEADLE
BISHOP
GIMLET
POSSET
7
BACARDI

7—continued
MARTINI
SANGRIA
SIDECAR
WALDORF
8
APPLE CAR
DAIQUIRI
GIN AND IT
GIN SLING
HIGHBALL
NIGHTCAP
PINK LADY
WHIZ BANG
9
ALEXANDER
APPLEJACK
BEE'S KNEES
BUCK JONES
BUCKS FIZZ
COMMODORE
MANHATTAN

9—continued
MINT JULEP
MOONLIGHT
MOONSHINE
MULLED ALE
WHITE LADY
10
ANGEL'S KISS
ARCHBISHOP
BLACK MARIA
BLOODY MARY
HORSE'S NECK
MERRY WIDOW
MULLED WINE
PINA COLADA
RUM COLLINS
TOM COLLINS
11
BEACHCOMBER
BLACK VELVET
FALLEN ANGEL
JOHN COLLINS

11—continued
WASSAIL BOWL
12
CHURCHWARDEN
ELEPHANT'S EAR
FINE AND DANDY
OLD-FASHIONED
WHITE GIN SOUR
13
CHAMPAGNE BUCK
CORPSE REVIVER
KNICKERBOCKER
MAIDEN'S PRAYER
PLANTER'S PUNCH
PRAIRIE OYSTER
16
BETWEEN THE
  SHEETS
HARVEY
  WALLBANGER

BEERS AND BEVERAGES

3
ALE

4
MEAD

4—continued
MILD

5
CIDER

5—continued
KVASS
LAGER
PERRY
STOUT

6
BITTER
LAMBIC
SHANDY

8
GUINNESS
HYDROMEL

10
BARLEY BEER
BARLEY WINE

SPIRITS

3
GIN
RUM
4
ARAK
MARC
OUZO
5
CHOUM
VODKA
6
BOUKHA
BRANDY

6—continued
CHICHA
COGNAC
GRAPPA
KIRSCH
MESCAL
METAXA
PASTIS
PERNOD
PULQUE
WHISKY
7
AKVAVIT

7—continued
AQUAVIT
BACARDI
BOUKHRA
BOURBON
SCHNAPS
TEQUILA
WHISKEY
8
ARMAGNAC
CALVADOS

8—continued
FALERNUM
SCHNAPPS
9
FRAMBOISE
SLIVOVITZ
10
RYE WHISKEY
11
AGUARDIENTE

LIQUEURS

4
SAKÉ
SAKI
5
ANISE
ANRAM
6
CASSIS
KÜMMEL
MÊLISS
QETSCH
SCUBAC
STREGA
7
ALCAMAS

7—continued
ALLASCH
BAILEYS
CURACAO
ESCUBAC
RATAFIA
SAMBUCA
8
ABSINTHE
ADVOCAAT
ANISETTE
DRAMBUIE
PERSICOT
PRUNELLE

9
ARQUEBUSE
COINTREAU
FRAMBOISE
GUIGNOLET
MIRABELLE
TRIPLE SEC
10
BROU DE NOIX
CHARTREUSE
MARASCHINO
11
BENEDICTINE
TRAPPISTINE

12
CHERRY BRANDY
CRÈME DE CACAO
GRAND MARNIER
13
CRÈME DE MENTHE
15
SOUTHERN
  COMFORT
17
AMARETTO DI
  SARANNO

NON-ALCOHOLIC DRINKS

3
CHA (TEA)
TEA
4
CHAR (TEA)
COLA
MATÉ
SODA
5
LASSI

5—continued
WATER
6
COFFEE
ORGEAT
TISANE
7
BEEF TEA

7—continued
DIABOLO
SELTZER
8
LEMONADE
9
GRENADINE

9—continued
MILKSHAKE
ORANGEADE
10
GINGER BEER
TONIC WATER

SPORT AND RECREATION

SPORTS

4
GOLF
JUDO
PATO
POLO

5
BOWLS
FIVES
KENDO
RALLY
RODEO

6
AIKIDO
BOULES
BOXING
HOCKEY
KARATE
KUNG FU
PELOTA
ROWING
SHINTY
SKIING
TENNIS

7
ANGLING
ARCHERY
BOWLING
CRICKET
CROQUET
CURLING
FENCING
HURLING
JUJITSU
KABADDI
KARTING

7—continued
NETBALL
RACKETS
SHOT PUT

8
BASEBALL
BIATHLON
CANOEING
COURSING
DRESSAGE
FALCONRY
GYMKHANA
HANDBALL
HURDLING
LACROSSE
LONG JUMP
MARATHON
PETANQUE
PING-PONG
ROUNDERS
SHOOTING
SPEEDWAY
SWIMMING
TUG OF WAR

9
ATHLETICS
BADMINTON
DECATHLON
ICE HOCKEY
MOTO-CROSS
POLE VAULT
SKYDIVING
TAE KWON-DO
WATER POLO
WRESTLING

10
BASKETBALL
DRAG RACING
FLAT RACING
FOXHUNTING
GYMNASTICS
ICE SKATING
REAL TENNIS
RUGBY UNION
TRIPLE JUMP
VOLLEYBALL

11
BEARBAITING
BLOOD SPORTS
BOBSLEDDING
BULLBAITING
DISCUS THROW
HAMMER THROW
HAND-GLIDING
HORSE RACING
HORSE TRAILS
MARTIAL ARTS
MOTOR RACING
PARACHUTING
PENTHATHLON
RUGBY LEAGUE
SEPAK TAKRAW
TABLE TENNIS
TOBOGGANING
WATER SKIING

12
BULLFIGHTING
CABER TOSSING
COCKFIGHTING

12—continued
ETON WALL GAME
JAVELIN THROW
ORIENTEERING
PIGEON RACING
POINT-TO-POINT
STEEPLECHASE

13
EQUESTRIANISM
HARNESS RACING
SKATEBOARDING
SQUASH RACKETS
WEIGHT LIFTING

14
FOOTBALL LEAGUE
MOUNTAINEERING
STOCK-CAR RACING

15
GREYHOUND
  RACING

16
AMERICAN
  FOOTBALL
MOTORCYCLE
  RACING

18
CLAY-PIGEON
  SHOOTING
FREESTYLE
  WRESTLING

19
ASSOCIATION
  FOOTBALL

GAMES

2
GO

4
BRAG
POOL
SNAP

5
BINGO
CAVES
CHESS

5—continued
CRAPS
DARTS
FIVES
POKER
RUMMY
SHOGI
SPOOF
WHIST

6
CLUEDO
PAC-MAN
QUOITS
TIPCAT

7
BEZIQUE
CANASTA

7—continued
DOBBERS
MAHJONG
MARBLES
MATADOR
OLD MAID
PACHISI
PONTOON

DANCES (games continued at top)

7—continued
SNOOKER
YAHTZEE

8
BACCARAT
BIRD CAGE
CRIBBAGE
DADDLUMS
DOMINOES
DRAUGHTS
LIAR DICE
MONOPOLY
PATIENCE
ROULETTE

8—continued
SCRABBLE
SKITTLES

9
AUNT SALLY
BILLIARDS
BLACKJACK
POKER DICE
SNAKE-EYES
VINGT-ET-UN

10
BACKGAMMON
BAT AND TRAP

10—continued
CASABLANCA
RUNNING OUT

11
CHEMIN DE FER
TIDDLYWINKS

12
BAR BILLIARDS
KNUR AND SPELL
SHOVE HA'PENNY

13
HAPPY FAMILIES

13—continued
SPACE INVADERS

14
CONTRACT BRIDGE
TRIVIAL PURSUIT

16
SNAKES AND
    LADDERS

20
DEVIL AMONG THE
    TAILORS

DANCES

3
DOG
GIG
JIG
OLE

4
AHIR
BUMP
CANA
HAKA
HORA
JIVE
JOTA
POGO
SHAG
VIRA

5
BARIS
BULBA
CAROL
CONGA
CUECA
DANSA
DEBKA
GAVOT
GIGUE
GOPAK
HALOA
HOPAK
KUMMI
L'AG-YA
LIMBO
LOURE
MAMBO
NAZUN
NUMBA
OKINA
POLKA
RUEDA

5—continued
RUMBA
SAMBA
SARBA
SHAKE
SIBEL
SIBYL
STOMP
TANGO
TRATA
TWIST
VELAL
WALTZ

6
ABUANG
AMENER
ATINGA
BATUTA
BOLERO
BOOGIE
CALATA
CANARY
CAN-CAN
CAROLE
CEBELL
CHA CHA
DJOGED
EIXIDA
GANGAR
GIENYS
HUSTLE
JACARA
JARABE
JARANA
KAGURA
KALELA
MINUET
PAVANE
PESSAH
POLSKA

6—continued
SHIMMY
TIRANA
VALETA
VELETA
YUMARI

7
ABRASAX
ABRAXAS
AHIDOUS
APARIMA
ARNAOUT
BABORÁK
BALL PLA
BAMBUCO
BANJARA
BATUQUE
BHARANG
BOURRÉE
CANARIE
CANARIO
CINQ PAS
CSARDAS
FORLANA
FOX-TROT
FURIANT
FURLANA
GAVOTTE
GERANOS
GLOCSEN
GOMBEYS
GONDHAL
GOSHIKI
HIMINAU
JABADAO
JON-NUK.E
LAMENTO
LANCERS
LANDLER
LLORONA

7—continued
MADISON
MAYPOLE
MAZURKA
MEASURE
MILONGA
MUNEIRA
PASILLO
PERICON
PLANXTY
PURPURI
SARDANA
SATACEK
SIKINIK
TANDAVA
TANTARA
TRAIPSE
WAKAMBA

8
ALEGRIAS
À MOLESON
AURRESKU
BALZTANZ
BULL-FOOT
CACHUCHA
CAKEWALK
CANACUAS
CANDIOTE
CHARRADA
COURANTE
FANDANGO
GALLIARD
GYMNASKA
HABANERA
HAND JIVE
HORNPIPE
HUAPANGO
MAILEHEN
MOHOBELO
MOONWALK

8—continued
MUTCHICO
OXDANSEN
PERICOTE
RIGAUDON
RUTUBURI
TSAMIKOS

9
BAGUETTES
BAILECITO
BARN DANCE
BOULANGER
CARDADORA
CLOG DANCE
COTILLION
ECOSSAISE
FARANDOLE
GALLEGADA
HAJDUTÂNC
HORN DANCE
JITTERBUG
KOLOMEJKA
MISTLETOE
MOKOROTLO
PASSEPIED
POLONAISE
QUADRILLE

9—continued
QUICKSTEP
RENNINGEN
ROCK 'N' ROLL
SARABANDE
SATECKOVA
TAMBORITO
TROYANATS

10
ATNUMOKITA
BANDLTANTZ
BATON DANCE
BERGERETTA
CHANIOTIKO
CHARLESTON
ESPRINGALE
FACKELTANZ
FARANDOULO
FURRY DANCE
GAY GORDONS
HOKEY-COKEY
KYNDELDANS
LAUTERBACH
LOCOMOTION
RUNNING SET
STRATHSPEY
STRIP TEASE

10—continued
SURUVAKARY
TARANTELLA
TRENCHMORE
TURKEY TROT

11
BABORASCHKA
BLACKBOTTOM
DANSURINGUR
DITHYRAMBOS
FLORAL DANCE
GHARBA DANCE
LAMBETH WALK
MORRIS DANCE
PALAIS GLIDE
PAMPERRUQUE
ROCK AND ROLL
SCHOTTISCHE
SQUARE DANCE
TEWRDANNCKH

12
BREAKDANCING
CREUX DE VERVI
DAMHSA NAM BOC
DANSE MACABRE

12—continued
FUNKY CHICKEN
GREEN GARTERS
REEL O'TULLOCH

13
EIGHTSOME REEL
GHILLIE CALLUM
HIGHLAND FLING

14
BABBITY BOWSTER
MILKMAIDS' DANCE
STRIP THE WILLOW

15
COUNTRY BUMPKIIN
MILITARY TWO-STEP
SELLINGER'S
  ROUND

17
HASTE TO THE
  WEDDING

18
SIR ROGER DE
  COVERLEY

HOBBIES AND CRAFTS

3
DIY

5
BATIK
BINGO

6
BONSAI
SEWING

7
COLLAGE
COOKERY
CROCHET
KEEP FIT
MACRAMÉ
MOSAICS
ORIGAMI
POTTERY
READING
TATTING
TOPIARY
WEAVING

8
AEROBICS
APPLIQUÉ
BASKETRY
CANEWORK

8—continued
FRETWORK
KNITTING
LAPIDARY
PAINTING
QUILTING
SPINNING
TAPESTRY
WOODWORK

9
ASTROLOGY
ASTRONOMY
DÉCOUPAGE
GARDENING
GENEALOGY
MARQUETRY
PALMISTRY
PATCHWORK
PHILATELY
RUG MAKING

10
BEE-KEEPING
BEER MAKING
CROSSWORDS
EMBROIDERY
ENAMELLING
KITE FLYING

10—continued
LACE MAKING
UPHOLSTERY
WINE MAKING

11
ARCHAEOLOGY
BARK RUBBING
BOOK BINDING
CALLIGRAPHY
DRESS MAKING
HANG GLIDING
LEPIDOPTERY
MODEL MAKING
PHOTOGRAPHY
STENCILLING
VINTAGE CARS

12
BEACH COMBING
BIRD WATCHING
BRASS RUBBING
CANDLE-MAKING
FLOWER DRYING
TROPICAL FISH

13
FOSSIL HUNTING
JIG-SAW PUZZLES

13—continued
MODEL RAILWAYS
TRAIN SPOTTING

14
BADGER WATCHING
CAKE DECORATING
COIN COLLECTING
FLOWER PRESSING
GLASS ENGRAVING
PIGEON FANCYING

15
FLOWER
  ARRANGING
LAMPSHADE MAKING
SHELL COLLECTING
STAMP COLLECTING

16
AMATEUR
  DRAMATICS
AUTOGRAPH
  HUNTING

19
BUTTERFLY
  COLLECTING

STADIUMS AND VENUES

AINTREE (horse racing)
ANAHEIM STADIUM, CALIFORNIA (baseball)
ASCOT (horse racing)
AZTECA STADIUM, MEXICO CITY (olympics, football)
BELFRY, THE (golf)
BELMONT PARK, LONG ISLAND (horse racing)
BERNABAU STADIUM, MADRID (football)
BIG FOUR CURLING RINK (curling)
BRANDS HATCH (motor racing)
BROOKLANDS (motor racing)
CAESAR'S PALACE, LAS VEGAS (boxing)
CARDIFF ARMS PARK (rugby union)
CENTRAL STADIUM, KIEV (football)
CLEVELAND MUNICIPAL STADIUM (baseball)
CORPORATION STADIUM, CALICUR (cricket)
CROKE PARK, DUBLIN (Gaelic football, hurling)
CRUCIBAL, SHEFFIELD (snooker)
CRYSTAL PALACE (athletics)
DAYTONA INTERNATIONAL SPEEDWAY (motor racing, motor cycling)
EDEN GARDENS, CALCUTTA (cricket)
EDGBASTON (cricket)
EPSOM DOWNS (horse racing)
FORUM, THE (gymnastics)
FRANCORCHAMPS, BELGIUM (motor racing)
HAMPDEN PARK, GLASGOW (football)
HEADINGLEY (cricket)
HEYSEL STADIUM, BRUSSELS (football)
LAHORE (cricket)

LANDSDOWNE ROAD, BELFAST (rugby union)
LENIN STADIUM, MOSCOW (football)
LORDS CRICKET GROUND (cricket)
LOUISIANA SUPERDOME (most sports)
MARACANA STADIUM, BRAZIL (football)
MEADOWBANK (athletics)
MEMORIAL COLISEUM, LOS ANGELES (most sports)
MOOR PARK, RICKMANSWORTH (golf)
MUNICH OLYMPIC STADIUM (athletics, football)
MURRAYFIELD (rugby union)
NEWMARKET (horse racing)
NOU CAMP, BARCELONA (football)
ODSAL STADIUM, BRADFORD (rugby league)
OLD TRAFFORD (cricket)
OVAL, THE (cricket)
ROYAL AND ANCIENT GOLF CLUB OF ST ANDREWS (golf)
SENAYAN MAIN STADIUM, JAKARTA (cricket)
SHANGHAI STADIUM (gymnastics)
SILVERSTONE (motor racing)
STAHOV STADIUM, PRAGUE (gymnastics)
TEXAS STADIUM (most sports)
TWICKENHAM (rugby union)
WEMBLEY CONFERENCE CENTRE (darts)
WEMBLEY STADIUM (football, rugby)
WHITE CITY (greyhound racing)
WIMBLEDON (tennis)
WINDSOR PARK, BELFAST (football)

TROPHIES, EVENTS, AND AWARDS

ADMIRAL'S CUP (sailing)
AFRICAN NATIONS CUP (football)
AIR CANADA SILVER BROOM (curling)
ALL-IRELAND CHAMPIONSHIP (Gaelic football)
ALL-IRELAND CHAMPIONSHIPS (hurling)
ALPINE CHAMPIONSHIPS (skiing)
AMERICA'S CUP (sailing)
ASHES (cricket)
BADMINTON THREE DAY EVENT (equestrian)
BBC SPORTS PERSONALITY OF THE YEAR (all-round)
BENSON HEDGES CUP (cricket)
BOAT RACE (rowing)
BRITISH OPEN CHAMPIONSHIP (golf)
BRONZE MEDAL (most sports)

CAMANACHD ASSOCIATION CHALLENGE CUP (shinty)
CHELTENHAM GOLD CUP (horse racing)
CLASSICS (horse racing)
COMMONWEALTH GAMES (athletics)
CORNHILL TEST (cricket)
DAVIS CUP (tennis)
DAYTONA 500 (motor racing)
DECATHLON (athletics)
DERBY (horse racing)
EMBASSY WORLD INDOOR BOWLS CROWN (bowls)
EMBASSY WORLD PROFESSIONAL SNOOKER CHAMPIONSHIP (snooker)
ENGLISH GREYHOUND DERBY (greyhound racing)

EUROPEAN CHAMPION CLUBS CUP
(football)
EUROPEAN CHAMPIONS CUP (basketball)
EUROPEAN CHAMPIONSHIPS (football)
EUROPEAN CUP WINNERS' CUP (football)
EUROPEAN FOOTBALLER OF THE YEAR
(football)
EUROPEAN SUPER CUP (football)
FEDERATION CUP (tennis)
FOOTBALL ASSOCIATION CHALLENGE CUP
(football)
FOOTBALL ASSOCIATION CHARITY SHIELD
(football)
FOOTBALL LEAGUE CHAMPIONSHIP
(football)
FOOTBALL LEAGUE CUP (football)
FULL CAP (football, rugby)
FWA FOOTBALLER OF THE YEAR (football)
GILLETTE CUP (cricket)
GOLDEN BOOT AWARD (football)
GOLD MEDAL (most sports)
GORDEN INTERNATIONAL MEDAL (curling)
GRAND NATIONAL (greyhound racing)
GRAND NATIONAL STEEPLECHASE (horse
racing)
GRAND PRIX (motor racing)
GUINNESS TROPHY (tiddlywinks)
HARMSWORTH TROPHY (power boat racing)
HENLEY REGATTA (rowing)
HENRI DELANEY TROPHY (football)
HIGHLAND GAMES
ICY SMITH CUP (ice hockey)
INDIANAPOLIS 500 (motor racing)
INTERNATIONAL CHAMPIONSHIP (bowls)
INTERNATIONAL CROSS-COUNTRY
CHAMPIONSHIP (athletics)
INTERNATIONAL INTER-CITY INDUSTRIAL
FAIRS CUP (football)
IROQUOIS CUP (lacrosse)
ISLE OF MAN TT (motorcycle racing)
JOHN PLAYER CUP (rugby league)
JOHN PLAYER LEAGUE (cricket)
JULES RIMET TROPHY (football)
KING GEORGE V GOLD CUP (equestrian)
KINNAIRD CUP (fives)
LE MANS 24 HOUR (motor racing)
LITTLEWOODS CHALLENGE CUP (football)
LOMBARD RALLY (motor racing)
LONSDALE BELT (boxing)
MACROBERTSON INTERNATIONAL SHIELD
(croquet)
MAN OF THE MATCH (football)
MARATHON (athletics)
MIDDLESEX SEVENS (rugby union)
MILK CUP (football)
MILK RACE (cycling)
MONTE CARLO RALLY (motor racing)
MOST VALUABLE PLAYER (American
football)

NATIONAL ANGLING CHAMPIONSHIP (horse
racing)
NATIONAL HUNT JOCKEY CHAMPIONSHIP
(horse racing)
NATIONAL WESTMINSTER BANK TROPHY
(cricket)
NORDIC CHAMPIONSHIPS (skiing)
OAKS (horse racing)
OLYMPIC GAMES (most sports)
ONE THOUSAND GUINEAS (horse racing)
OPEN CROQUET CHAMPIONSHIP (croquet)
OXFORD BLUE (most sports)
PALIO
PENTATHLON
PFA FOOTBALLER OF THE YEAR (football)
PRUDENTIAL WORLD CUP (cricket)
PYONGYANG
QUEEN ELIZABETH II CUP (equestrian)
RAC TOURIST TROPHY (motor racing)
ROSE BOWL (American football)
ROYAL HUNT CUP (horse racing)
RUGBY LEAGUE CHALLENGE CUP (rugby
league)
RUNNERS-UP MEDAL (most sports)
RYDER CUP (golf)
SCOTTISH FOOTBALL ASSOCIATION CUP
(football)
SILVER MEDAL (most sports)
SIMOD CUP (football)
SKOL CUP (football)
SOUTH AMERICAN CHAMPIONSHIP (football)
STANLEY CUP (ice hockey)
ST LEGER (horse racing)
STRATHCONA CUP (curling)
SUPER BOWL (American football)
SUPER CUP (handball)
SWAYTHLING CUP (table tennis)
THOMAS CUP (badminton)
TOUR DE FRANCE (cycling)
TRIPLE CROWN (rugby union)
TWO THOUSAND GUINEAS (horse racing)
UBER CUP (badminton)
U.E.F.A. CUP (Union of European Football
Associations) (football)
UNIROYAL WORLD JUNIOR
CHAMPIONSHIPS (curling)
WALKER CUP (golf)
WIGHTMAN CUP (sailing)
WIMBLEDON (tennis)
WINGFIELD SKULLS (rowing)
WINNERS MEDAL (most sports)
WOODEN SPOON! (most sports)
WORLD CLUB CHAMPIONSHIP (football)
WORLD MASTERS CHAMPIONSHIPS (darts)
WORLD SERIES (baseball)
YELLOW JERSEY (cycling)

FOOTBALL TEAMS

TEAM	GROUND	NICKNAME
ABERDEEN	PITTODRIE STADIUM	DONS
AIRDRIEONIANS	BROOMFIELD PARK	DIAMONDS; WAYSIDERS
ALBION ROVERS	CLIFTON HALL	WEE ROVERS
ALDERSHOT	RECREATION GROUND	SHOTS
ALLOA	RECREATION PARK	WASPS
ARBROATH	GAYFIELD PARK	RED LICHTIES
ARSENAL	HIGHBURY	GUNNERS
ASTON VILLA	VILLA PARK	VILLANS
AYR UNITED	SOMERSET PARK	HONEST MEN
BARNSLEY	OAKWELL GROUND	TYKES; REDS; COLLIERS
BERWICK RANGERS	SHIELFIELD PARK	BORDERERS
BIRMINGHAM CITY	ST ANDREWS	BLUES
BLACKBURN ROVERS	EWOOD PARK	BLUE WHITES; ROVERS
BLACKPOOL	BLOMMFIELD ROAD	SEASIDERS
BOLTON WANDERERS	BURNDEN PARK	TROTTERS
BOURNEMOUTH	DEAN COURT	CHERRIES
BRADFORD CITY	VALLEY PARADE	BANTAMS
BRECHIN CITY	GLEBE PARK	CITY
BRENTFORD	GRIFFIN PARK	BEES
BRIGHTON HOVE ALBION	GOLDSTONE GROUND	SEAGULLS
BRISTOL CITY	ASHTON GATE	ROBINS
BRISTOL ROVERS	TWERTON PARK	PIRATES
BURNLEY	TURF MOOR	CLARETS
BURY	GIGG LANE	SHAKERS
CAMBRIDGE UNITED	ABBEY STADIUM	UNITED
CARDIFF CITY	NINIAN PARK	BLUEBIRDS
CARLISLE UNITED	BRUNTON PARK	CUMBRIANS; BLUES
CELTIC	CELTIC PARK	BHOYS
CHARLTON ATHLETIC	SELHURST PARK	HADDICKS; ROBINS; VALIANTS
CHELSEA	STAMFORD BRIDGE	BLUES
CHESTER CITY	SEALAND ROAD	BLUES
CHESTERFIELD	RECREATION GROUND	BLUES; SPIREITES
CLYDEBANK	KILBOWIE PARK	BANKIES
CLYDE	FIRHILL PARK	BULLY WEE
COLCHESTER UNITED	LAYER ROAD	U'S
COVENTRY CITY	HIGHFIELD ROAD	SKY BLUES
COWDENBEATH	CENTRAL PARK	COWDEN
CREWE ALEXANDRA	GRESTY ROAD	RAILWAYMEN
CRYSTAL PALACE	SELHURST PARK	EAGLES
DARLINGTON	FEETHAMS GROUND	QUAKERS
DERBY COUNTY	BASEBALL GROUND	RAMS
DONCASTER ROVERS	BELLE VUE GROUND	ROVERS
DUMBARTON	BOGHEAD PARK	SONS
DUNDEE	DENS PARK	DARK BLUES; DEE
DUNDEE UNITED	TANNADICE PARK	TERRORS
DUNFERMLINE ATHLETIC	EAST END PARK	PARS
EAST FIFE	BAYVIEW PARK	FIFERS
EAST STIRLINGSHIRE	FIRS PARK	SHIRE
EVERTON	GOODISON PARK	TOFFEES
EXETER CITY	ST JAMES PARK	GRECIANS
FALKIRK	BROCKVILLE PARK	BAIRNS
FORFAR ATHLETIC	STATION PARK	SKY BLUES

FULHAM	CRAVEN COTTAGE	COTTAGERS
GILLINGHAM	PRIESTFIELD STADIUM	GILLS
GRIMSBY TOWN	BLUNDELL PARK	MARINERS
HALIFAX TOWN	SHAY GROUND	SHAYMEN
HAMILTON ACADEMICAL	DOUGLAS PARK	ACCES
HARTLEPOOL UNITED	VICTORIA GROUND	POOL
HEART OF MIDLOTHIAN	TYNECASTLE PARK	HEARTS
HEREFORD UNITED	EDGAR STREET	UNITED
HIBERNIAN	EASTER ROAD	HIBEES
HUDDERSFIELD TOWN	LEEDS ROAD	TERRIERS
HULL CITY	BOOTHFERRY PARK	TIGERS
IPSWICH TOWN	PORTMAN ROAD	BLUES; TOWN
KILMARNOCK	RUGBY PARK	KILLIE
LEEDS UNITED	ELLAND ROAD	UNITED
LEICESTER CITY	FILBERT STREET	FILBERTS; FOXES
LEYTON ORIENT	BRISBANE ROAD	O'S
LINCOLN CITY	SINCIL BANK	RED IMPS
LIVERPOOL	ANFIELD	REDS; POOL
LUTON TOWN	KENILWORTH ROAD	HATTERS
MANCHESTER CITY	MAINE ROAD	BLUES
MANCHESTER UNITED	OLD TRAFFORD	RED DEVILS
MANSFIELD TOWN	FIELD MILL GROUND	STAGS
MEADOWBANK THISTLE	MEADOWBANK STADIUM	THISTLE; WEE JAGS
MIDDLESBROUGH	AYRESOME PARK	BORO
MILLWALL	THE DEN	LIONS
MONTROSE	LINKS PARK	GABLE ENDERS
MORTON	CAPPIELOW PARK	TON
MOTHERWELL	FIR PARK	WELL
NEWCASTLE UNITED	ST JAMES PARK	MAGPIES
NORTHAMPTON TOWN	COUNTY GROUND	COBBLERS
NORWICH CITY	CARROW ROAD	CANARIES
NOTTINGHAM FOREST	CITY GROUND	REDS; FOREST
NOTTS COUNTY	MEADOW LANE	MAGPIES
OLDHAM ATHLETIC	BOUNDARY PARK	LATICS
OXFORD UNITED	MANOR GROUND	U'S
PARTICK THISTLE	FIRHILL PARK	JAGS
PETERBOROUGH UNITED	LONDON ROAD	POSH
PLYMOUTH ARGYLE	HOME PARK	PILGRIMS
PORTSMOUTH	FRATTON PARK	POMPEY
PORT VALE	VALE PARK	VALIANTS
PRESTON NORTH END	DEEPDALE	LILYWHITES; NORTH END
QUEEN OF THE SOUTH	PALMERSTON PARK	DOONHAMERS
QUEEN'S PARK	HAMPDEN PARK	SPIDERS
QUEEN'S PARK RANGERS	LOFTUS ROAD	RANGERS; R'S
RAITH ROVERS	STARK'S PARK	ROVERS
RANGERS	IBROX STADIUM	GERS
READING	ELM PARK	ROYALS
ROCHDALE	SPOTLAND	DALE
ROTHERHAM UNITED	MILLMOOR GROUND	MERRY MILLERS
SCARBOROUGH	SEAMER ROAD	BORO
SCUNTHORPE UNITED	GLANFORD PARK	IRON
SHEFFIELD UNITED	BRAMALL LANE	BLADES
SHEFFIELD WEDNESDAY	HILLSBOROUGH	OWLS
SHREWSBURY TOWN	GAY MEADOW	SHREWS; TOWN
SOUTHAMPTON	DELL	SAINTS
SOUTHEND UNITED	ROOTS HALL	SHRIMPERS
STENHOUSEMUIR	OCHILVIEW PARK	WARRIORS
STIRLING ALBION	ANNFIELD PARK	ALBION
ST JOHNSTONE	MUIRTON PARK	SAINTS
ST MIRREN	LOVE STREET	BUDDIES; PAISLEY SAINTS
STOCKPORT COUNTY	EDGELEY PARK	COUNTY; HATTERS

STOKE CITY	VICTORIA GROUND	POTTERS
STRANRAER	STAIR PARK	BLUES
SUNDERLAND	ROKER PARK	ROKERITES
SWANSEA CITY	VETCH FIELD	SWANS
SWINDON TOWN	COUNTY GROUND	ROBINS
TORQUAY UNITED	PLAINMOOR GROUND	GULLS
TOTTENHAM HOTSPUR	WHITE HART LANE	SPURS
TRANMERE ROVERS	PRENTON PARK	ROVERS
WALSALL	FELLOWS PARK	SADDLERS
WATFORD	VICARAGE ROAD	HORNETS
WEST BROMWICH ALBION	HAWTHORNS	THROSTLES; BAGGIES; ALBION
WEST HAM UNITED	UPTON PARK	HAMMERS
WIGAN ATHLETIC	SPRINGFIED PARK	LATICS
WIMBLEDON	PLOUGH LANE	DONS
WOLVERHAMPTON WANDERERS	MOLINEUX	WOLVES
WREXHAM	RACECOURSE GROUND	ROBINS
YORK CITY	BOOTHAM CRESCENT	MINSTERMEN

MISCELLANEOUS

COLOURS

3	5 —continued	6 —continued	7 —continued
AAL	GREEN	MADDER	OLD ROSE
ABA	GRÈGE	MAROON	PEARLED
DUN	HAZEL	MATARA	PLATINA
JET	HENNA	MOTLEY	SAFFRON
RED	IVORY	ORANGE	SCARLET
TAN	JASPÉ	ORCHID	SEA BLUE
4	JAUNE	OYSTER	SKY BLUE
BLEU	JEWEL	PASTEL	TEA ROSE
BLUE	KHAKI	PEARLY	THISTLE
BOIS	LODEN	PIRNED	TILE RED
BURE	MAIZE	PURPLE	TILLEUL
CUIR	MAUVE	RACHEL	TUSSORE
DRAB	OCHRE	RAISIN	VIOLINE
EBON	OLIVE	RESEDA	**8**
ÉCRU	OMBRÉ	RUSSET	ABSINTHE
GOLD	PEACH	SALMON	ALIZARIN
GREY	PEARL	SHRIMP	AMARANTH
GRIS	PÉCHE	SILVER	AURULENT
HOPI	PRUNE	TITIAN	BABY BLUE
IRIS	ROUGE	VIOLET	BABY PINK
JADE	SEPIA	YELLOW	BORDEAUX
LAKE	SHADE	ZIRCON	BURGUNDY
LARK	TAUPE	**7**	CAPUCINE
NAVY	TOPAZ	ANAMITE	CHALDERA
NOIR	UMBER	APRICOT	CHÂTAINE
ONYX	WHITE	ARDOISE	CHESTNUT
OPAL	**6**	AUREATE	CIEL BLUE
PIED	ACAJOU	BISCUIT	CINNAMON
PINK	ALESAN	CALDRON	CREVETTE
PLUM	ARGENT	CARAMEL	CYCLAMEN
PUCE	AUBURN	CARMINE	EAU DE NIL
ROSE	BASANÉ	CHAMOIS	ÉCARLATE
RUBY	BISTRE	CORBEAU	EGGPLANT
SAND	BLONDE	CRIMSON	EGGSHELL
SHOT	BRONZE	EMERALD	GRIZZLED
VERT	BURNET	FILBERT	GUN METAL
5	CASTOR	FUCHSIA	HAZEL NUT
AMBER	CENDRÉ	GRIZZLE	HYACINTH
BEIGE	CERISE	HEATHER	LARKSPUR
BLACK	CHERRY	INGÉNUE	LAVENDER
BROWN	CHROMA	JACINTH	MAHOGANY
CAMEL	CITRON	JONQUIL	MOLE GREY
CAPRI	CLARET	LACQUER	MULBERRY
CHAIR	COPPER	LAVANDE	NAVY BLUE
COCOA	DORADO	MAGENTA	PEA GREEN
CORAL	FLAXEN	MOTTLED	PISTACHE
CREAM	GARNET	MUSTARD	POPPY RED
CYMAR	GOLDEN	NACARAT	PRIMROSE
DELFT	INDIGO	NATURAL	SAPPHIRE
FLESH	JASPER	NEUTRAL	SEA GREEN

8 —continued
SHAGREEN
SPECTRUM
VIRIDIAN

9
ALICE BLUE
AUBERGINE
AZURE BLUE
BLUE-GREEN
CADET BLUE
CADET GREY
CARNATION
CARNELIAN
CHAMPAGNE
CHOCOLATE
COCHINEAL
DELPH BLUE
DUTCH BLUE
FLESH PINK
GREEN-BLUE
HARLEQUIN
LEAF GREEN
LIME GREEN
MOONSTONE
MOSS GREEN
NILE GREEN
OLIVE DRAB
PARCHMENT
PEARL GREY
RASPBERRY
ROYAL BLUE

9 —continued
TANGERINE
TOMATO RED
TURKEY RED
VERDIGRIS
VERMILION
WALLY BLUE

10
AQUAMARINE
AURICOMOUS
BOIS DE ROSE
CAFÉ AU LAIT
CASTOR GREY
COBALT BLUE
CONGO BROWN
ENSIGN BLUE
LIVER BROWN
MARINA BLUE
MARINE BLUE
OXFORD BLUE
PETROL BLUE
POLYCHROME
POWDER BLUE
TERRACOTTA
ZENITH BLUE

11
BOTTLE GREEN
BURNT ALMOND
CARDINAL RED
CLAIR DE LUNE

11 —continued
FOREST GREEN
GOBELIN BLUE
HORIZON BLUE
HUNTER'S PINK
LAPIS LAZULI
LEMON YELLOW
LIPSTICK RED
PARROT GREEN
PEACOCK BLUE
POMEGRANATE
SMOKED PEARL
SOLID COLOUR
ULTRAMARINE
VERSICOLOUR
WALNUT BROWN
YELLOW OCHRE

12
BALL PARK BLUE
CANARY YELLOW
CARROT COLOUR
CASTILIAN RED
CELADON GREEN
HUNTER'S GREEN
HYACINTH BLUE
LOGWOOD BROWN
MIDNIGHT BLUE
OVERSEAS BLUE
SAPPHIRE BLUE
SOLFERINO RED

12 —continued
TYRIAN PURPLE
VERDANT GREEN

13
BISHOP'S PURPLE
BISHOP'S VIOLET
CAMBRIDGE BLUE
MOTHER-OF-PEARL
MULTICOLOURED
PARTI-COLOURED
PEPPER-AND-SALT
PRIMARY COLOUR
TORTOISE SHELL
TURQUOISE BLUE

14
HEATHER MIXTURE
PERIWINKLE BLUE
PISTACHIO GREEN
TURQUOISE GREEN

15
CALEDONIAN
  BROWN
CHARTREUSE
  GREEN
SECONDARY
  COLOUR

16
CHARTREUSE
  YELLOW

CALENDARS

GREGORIAN
JANUARY
FEBRUARY
MARCH
APRIL
MAY
JUNE
JULY
AUGUST
SEPTEMBER
OCTOBER
NOVEMBER
DECEMBER

HEBREW
SHEVAT (Jan/Feb)
ADAR (Feb/Mar)
NISAN (Mar/Apr)
IYAR (Apr/May)
SIVAN (May/June)
TAMMUZ (June/July)
AV (July/Aug)
ELUL (Aug/Sept)
TISHRI (Sept/Oct)

HESHVAN (Oct/Nov)
KISLEV (Nov/Dec)
TEVET (Dec/Jan)

ISLAMIC
MUHARRAN (Jan)
SAFAR (Feb)
RAB I (Mar)
RAB II (Apr)
JUMĀDĀ I (May)
JUMĀDĀ II (June)
RAJAB (July)
SHA'BAN (Aug)
RAMADĀN (Sept)
SHAWWĀL (Oct)
DHŪAL-QA'DAH (Nov)
DHŪAL-HIJJAH (Dec)

CHINESE
XIAO HAN (Jan)
DA HAN (Jan/Feb)
LI CHUN (Feb)
YU SHUI (Feb/Mar)
JING ZHE (Mar)
CHUN FEN (Mar/Apr)

QING MING (Apr)
GU YU (Apr/May)
LI XIA (May)
XIAO MAN (May/
  June)
MANG ZHONG (June)
XIA ZHI (June/July)
XIAO SHU (July)
DA SHU (July/Aug)
LI QUI (Aug)
CHU SHU (Aug/Sept)
BAI LU (Sept)
QUI FEN (Sept/Oct)
HAN LU (Oct)
SHUANG JIANG (Oct/
  Nov)
LI DONG (Nov)
XIAO XUE (Nov/Dec)
DA XUE (Dec)
DONG ZHI (Dec/Jan)

FRENCH REVOLUTIONARY
VENDÉMIAIRE —
  Vintage (Sept)

BRUMAIRE — Fog
  (Oct)
FRIMAIRE — Sleet
  (Nov)
NIVÔSE — Snow
  (Dec)
PLUVIÔSE — Rain
  (Jan)
VENTÔSE — Wind
  (Feb)
GERMINAL — Seed
  (Mar)
FLOREAL — Blossom
  (Apr)
PRAIRIAL — Pasture
  (May)
MESSIDOR — Harvest
  (June)
THERMIDOR — Heat
  (July)
FRUCTIDOR — Fruit
  (Aug)

THE SIGNS OF THE ZODIAC

SIGN (Symbol; Dates)

ARIES (Ram; 21 Mar–19 Apr)
TAURUS (Bull; 20 Apr–20 May)
GEMINI (Twins; 21 May–21 June)
CANCER (Crab; 22 June–22 July)
LEO (Lion; 23 July–22 Aug)
VIRGO (Virgin; 23 Aug–22 Sept)

LIBRA (Scales; 23 Sept–23 Oct)
SCORPIO (Scorpion; 24 Oct–21 Nov)
SAGITTARIUS (Archer; 22 Nov–21 Dec)
CAPRICORN (Goat; 22 Dec–19 Jan)
AQUARIUS (Water-carrier; 20 Jan–18 Feb)
PISCES (Fish; 19 Feb–20 Mar)

THE TWELVE SIGNS OF THE CHINESE ZODIAC

RAT	RABBIT	HORSE	ROOSTER
OX	DRAGON	SHEEP	DOG
TIGER	SNAKE	MONKEY	BOAR

BIRTHSTONES

Month – STONE

January – GARNET
February – AMETHYST
March – BLOODSTONE/AQUAMARINE
April – DIAMOND
May – EMERALD
June – PEARL

July – RUBY
August – SARDONYX/PERIDOT
September – SAPPHIRE
October – OPAL
November – TOPAZ
December – TURQUOISE

WEDDING ANNIVERSARIES

1st – PAPER
2nd – COTTON
3rd – LEATHER
4th – FRUIT/FLOWERS
5th – WOOD
6th – IRON
7th – WOOL/COPPER
8th – BRONZE/POTTERY
9th – POTTERY/WILLOW
10th – TIN/ALUMINIUM
11th – STEEL
12th – SILK/LINEN

13th – LACE
14th – IVORY
15th – CRYSTAL
20th – CHINA
25th – SILVER
30th – PEARL
35th – CORAL
40th – RUBY
45th – SAPPHIRE
50th – GOLD
55th – EMERALD
60th – DIAMOND

PEERAGE

DUKE	DUCHESS	MARQUIS	MARCHIONESS
EARL	BARONESS	MARQUESS	VISCOUNTESS
BARON	COUNTESS	VISCOUNT	

HERALDIC TERMS

TINCTURES
OR (gold)
ARGENT (silver)
ERMINE
VAIR
POTENT
AZURE (blue)
GULES (red)
SABLE (black)
VERT (green)
PURPURE (purple)

**DIVISIONS OF
FIELDS**

PER PALE
PER FESS
PER CROSS
PER BEND
PER SALTIRE
PER CHEVRON

**DESCRIPTIONS OF
FIELDS**

PARTY
BARRY
BURELY
BENDY
QUARTERLY
ENTY
FRETTY
GIRONNY
BEZANTY

**PARTS OF THE
ESCUTCHEON**

DEXTER (right)
SINISTER (left)
MIDDLE
CHIEF (top)
FLANK (side)
BASE
NOMBRIL
FESS POINT
HONOUR POINT

TRESSURE (border)

LINES

ENGRAILED
EMBATTLED
INDENTED
INVECTED
WAVY, UNDY
NEBULY
DANCETTY
RAGULY
POTENTÉ
DOVETAILED
URDY

CROSSES

FORMY
PATY
FLORY
MOLINE
BOTONNY

CROSLETTED
FITCHY
SALTIRE

**OTHER OBJECTS
AND DECORATIONS**

LOZENGES
ROUNDELS (circles)
ANNELETS (rings)
FOUNTAINS (wavey
  lines on a circle)
BILLETS (upright
  objects)
MOLET (star)
RAMPANT (rearing
  up)
COUCHANT (sleeping
  or sitting)
PASSANT (standing)
BAR

SEVEN DEADLY SINS

PRIDE	LUST	GLUTTONY	SLOTH
COVETOUSNESS	ENVY	ANGER	

SEVEN WONDERS OF THE WORLD

THE PYRAMIDS OF EGYPT
THE COLOSSUS OF RHODES
THE HANGING GARDENS OF BABYLON
THE MAUSOLEUM OF HALICARNASSUS

THE STATUE OF ZEUS AT OLYMPIA
THE TEMPLE OF ARTEMIS AT EPHESUS
THE PHAROS OF ALEXANDRIA

SEVEN VIRTUES

FAITH	HOPE	LOVE (CHARITY)	TEMPERANCE
FORTITUDE	JUSTICE	PRUDENCE	

MONEY

1 & 2	4 —continued	6	7 —continued
AS	UNIK	AMANIA	UNICORN
D	**5**	AUREUS	**8**
L	ANGEL	BAUBEE	AMBROSIN
P	ASPER	BAWBEE	DENARIUS
S	BELGA	BEZART	DIDRACHM
3	BETSO	CONDOR	DOUBLOON
BIT	BROAD	COPANG	DUCATOON
BOB	CONTO	COPPER	FARTHING
COB	COPEC	DÉCIME	FLORENCE
DAM	CROWN	DOBLON	JOHANNES
ECU	DARIC	FLORIN	KREUTZER
FAR	DUCAT	FUORTE	LOUIS D'OR
KIP	EAGLE	GUINEA	MARAVEDI
LAT	GROAT	GULDEN	NAPOLEON
MIL	LIARD	KOPECK	PICAYUNE
MNA	LIBRA	MONKEY	QUETZALE
PIE	LITAS	NICKEL	SESTERCE
REE	LIVRE	PAGODE	SHILLING
REI	LOCHO	SCEATT	SIXPENCE
SHO	LOUIS	SEQUIN	**9**
SOL	MEDIO	STATER	BOLIVIANO
SOU	MOHAR	STIVER	CUARTILLO
4	MOHUR	TALARI	DIDRACHMA
ANNA	NOBLE	TALENT	DUPONDIUS
BEKA	OBANG	TANNER	GOLD BROAD
BIGA	PAOLO	TESTER	GOLD NOBLE
BUCK	PENCE	TESTON	GOLD PENNY
CASH	PENGO	THALER	HALFPENNY
DAUM	PENNY	TOMAUN	PISTAREEN
DIME	PLACK	ZECHIN	RIXDOLLAR
DOIT	QURSH	**7**	ROSE-NOBLE
JOEY	SCEAT	ANGELOT	SESTERTII
KRAN	SCUDI	CAROLUS	SOVEREIGN
MAIL	SCUDO	CENTAVA	SPUR ROYAL
MERK	SEMIS	DENARII	YELLOW BOY
MITE	SOLDO	GUILDER	**10**
OBOL	STICA	JACOBUS	EASTERLING
PEAG	STYCA	MILREIS	FIRST BRASS
PICE	SYCEE	MOIDORE	GOLD STATER
PONY	TICAL	NGUSANG	QUADRUSSIS
QUID	TICCY	PISTOLE	SESTERTIUM
REAL	TOMAN	QUARTER	SILVERLING
RYAL	UNCIA	SEXTANS	STOUR-ROYAL
TAEL	UNITE	STOOTER	THREEPENCE
		TESTOON	

10 —continued	11 —continued	12 —continued	13
TRIPONDIUS	MILL SIXPENCE	TETRADRACHMA	THREEPENNY BIT
VENEZOLANO	SILVER PENNY	TRIBUTE PENNY	
	SPADE GUINEA		
11			
HONG KONG	**12**		
DOLLAR	SILVER-STATER		

COLLECTIVE NAMES

ACROBATS – troupe
APES – shrewdness
ASSES – pace
BABOONS – troop
BAKERS – tabernacle
BARBERS – babble
BARMEN – promise
BAYONETS – grove
BEES – erst, swarm
BELLS – change
BISHOPS – bench, psalter
BISON – herd
BREWERS – feast
BUFFALOES – obstinacy
BULLFINCHES – bellowing
BULLOCKS – drove
BUTCHERS – goring
BUTLERS – sneer
CANONS – chapter, dignity
CATERPILLARS – army
CATTLE – herd
CHOUGHS – chattering
COBBLERS – cutting
CROCODILES – bask
CROWS – murder
DEANS – decanter, decorum
DONS – obscuration
DUCKS – paddling, safe
ELEPHANTS – herd, parade
FERRETS – busyness
FLIES – swarm
GAMBLERS – talent
GEESE – gaggle
GOLDFINCHES – charm
GOVERNESSES – galaxy
GRAMMARIANS – conjunction
HARES – down
HARPISTS – melody
HERONS – serge
HIPPOPOTOMI – bloat
HUNTERS – blast
JELLYFISH – fluther, smack
JUGGLERS – neverthriving

KITTENS – litter
LAPWING – desert
LARKS – exaltation
LEOPARDS – leap, lepe
LIONS – pride, sawt, sowse
LOCUSTS – swarm
MAGPIES – tittering
MERCHANTS – faith
MESSENGERS – diligence
MOLES – labour
MULES – span
NIGHTINGALES – watch
ORCHIDS – coterie
OWLS – parliament, stare
PAINTERS – curse, illusion
PARROTS – pandemonium
PEKINGESE – pomp
PENGUINS – parcel
PIGS – litter
PIPERS – skirl
PORPOISES – turmoil
PREACHERS – converting
RABBITS – bury
RHINOCEROS – crash
ROBBERS – band
SHEEP – flock
SHERIFFS – posse
SHIPS – fleet, armada
SHOEMAKERS – blackening
STARLINGS – murmuration
SWALLOWS – gulp
SWINE – doylt
TAILORS – disguising
TAVERNERS – closing
TROUT – hover
TURKEY – rafter
TURTLES – turn
UNDERTAKERS – unction
WIDOWS – ambush
WILDCATS – destruction, dout
WOODPECKERS – descent
WRITERS – worship
ZEBRAS – zeal

TYPEFACES

3	6—continued	7—continued	8—continued
DOW	FUTURA	MADISON	SOUVENIR
4	GLYPHA	MEMPHIS	**9**
BELL	GOTHIC	NEUZEIT	AMERICANA
GILL	HORLEY	PLANTIN	ATHENAEUM
ZAPF	ITALIA	RALEIGH	BARCELONA
5	JANSON	SPARTAN	BRITANNIC
ASTER	LUCIAN	STEMPEL	CALEDONIA
BEMBO	MELIOR	TIFFANY	CLARENDON
BLOCK	MODERN	UNIVERS	CLEARFACE
DORIC	OLIVER	WEXFORD	CRITERION
ERBAR	ONDINE	WINDSOR	DOMINANTE
FOLIO	OPTIMA	**8**	EUROSTILE
GOUDY	ROMANA	BENGUIAT	EXCELSIOR
IONIC	**7**	BERKELEY	FAIRFIELD
KABEL	ANTIQUE	BREUGHEL	GROTESQUE
LOTUS	BASILIA	CLOISTER	HELVETICA
MITRA	BAUHAUS	CONCORDE	WORCESTER
SABON	BERNARD	EGYPTIAN	**10**
TIMES	BOOKMAN	EHRHARDT	AVANT GARDE
6	BRAMLEY	FOURNIER	CHELTENHAM
AACHEN	CANDIDA	FRANKLIN	CHURCHWARD
ADROIT	CENTURY	FRUTIGER	DEVANAGARI
AURIGA	CORONET	GALLIARD	EGYPTIENNE
BECKET	CUSHING	GARAMOND	LEAMINGTON
BODONI	ELECTRA	KENNERLY	**11**
BULMER	FLOREAL	NOVARESE	BASKERVILLE
CASLON	IMPRINT	OLYMPIAN	COPPERPLATE
COCHIN	IRIDIUM	PALATINO	**14**
COOPER	KORINNA	PERPETUA	TRUMP MEDIAEVAL
CORONA	LUBALIN	ROCKWELL	
FENICE			

AMERICAN INDIANS

3	5 —continued	6 —continued	6 —continued
FOX	CREEK	APACHE	PAIUTE
OTO	HAIDA	ATSINA	PAWNEE
UTE	HURON	CAYUGA	QUAPAW
4	KASKA	DAKOTA	SALISH
CREE	KIOWA	DOGRIB	SANTEE
CROW	OMAHA	MANDAN	SENECA
HOPI	OSAGE	MICMAC	TANANA
HUPA	SIOUX	MIXTEC	TOLTEC
IOWA	SLAVE	MOHAWK	YAKIMA
SAUK	TETON	NAVAJO	**7**
TUPI	WAPPO	NOOTKA	ARIKARA
5	YUROK	OJIBWA	BEOTHUK
AZTEC	**6**	ONEIDA	CATAWBA
CADDO	ABNAKI	OTTAWA	CHINOOK

7 —continued
CHOKTAW
HIDATSA
INGALIK
KUTCHIN
NATCHEZ
SHAWNEE
SHUSWAP
TLINGIT
WICHITA
WYANDOT

8
CHEROKEE
CHEYENNE
COMANCHE
DELAWARE
ILLINOIS
IROQUOIS
KICKAPOO
NEZ PERCÉ
OKANOGAN
ONONDAGA
SHOSHONI

8 —continued
TUTCHONE
9
ALGONQUIN
BLACKFOOT
CHICKASAW
CHIPEWYAN
CHIPPEWAY
MENOMINEE
PENOBSCOT
TAHAGMIUT
TILLAMOOK

9 —continued
TSIMSHIAN
TUSCARORA
WINNEBAGO
10+
KAVIAGMIUT
PASAMAQUODDY
POTAWATOMI

LANGUAGE

LANGUAGES OF THE WORLD

2
WU
3
MIN
4
URDU
5
DUTCH
GREEK
HINDI
IRISH
MALAY
ORIYA
TAMIL
WELSH
6
ARABIC
BIHARI

6 —continued
BRETON
DANISH
FRENCH
GAELIC
GERMAN
KOREAN
PAHARI
POLISH
ROMANY
SINDHI
SLOVAK
TELUGU
7
BENGALI
CATALAN
ENGLISH
FRISIAN

7 —continued
ITALIAN
LATVIAN
MARATHI
PUNJABI
RUSSIAN
SLOVENE
SORBIAN
SPANISH
SWEDISH
TURKISH
8
ASSAMESE
GUJARATI
JAPANESE
JAVANESE
KASHMIRI
MANDARIN

8 —continued
ROMANSCH
RUMANIAN
UKRANIAN
9
AFRIKAANS
BULGARIAN
CANTONESE
ICELANDIC
NORWEGIAN
SINHALESE
10
LITHUANIAN
PORTUGUESE
RAJASTHANI
SERBO-CROAT

THE GREEK ALPHABET

ALPHA
BETA
GAMMA
DELTA
EPSILON
ZETA
ETA
THETA
IOTA
KAPPA
LAMBDA
MU

NU
XI
OMICRON
PI
RHO
SIGMA
TAU
UPSILON
PHI
CHI
PSI
OMEGA

THE HEBREW ALPHABET

ALEPH
BETH
GIMEL
DALETH
HE
VAV
ZAYIN

CHETH
TETH
YOD
KAPH
LAMED
MEM
NUN

SAMEKH	RESH
AYIN	SHIN
PE	SIN
SADI	TAV
KOPH	

FOREIGN WORDS

ENGLISH	FRENCH	GERMAN	ITALIAN	SPANISH	LATIN
AND	ET	UND	E, ED	E	ET
BUT	MAIS	ABER	MA	PERO	SED
FOR	POUR	FÜR	PER	PARA, POR	PER
TO	À	AUF, NACH	A	A	AD
WITH	AVEC	MIT	CON	CON	CUM
MISTER, MR.	MONSIEUR, M.	HERR, HR., HRN.	SIGNOR, SIG.	SEÑOR, SR.	DOMINUS
MADAME, MRS.	MADAME, MME.	FRAU, FR.	SIGNORA, SIG.A., SIG.RA.	SEÑORA, SRA.	DOMINA
MISS, MS.	MADEMOI-SELLE, MLLE.	FRÄULEIN, FRL.	SIGNORINA, SIG.NA.	SEÑORITA, SRTA.	
FROM	DE	AUS, VON	DA	DE	AB
OF	DE	VON	DI	DE	DE
GIRL	FILLE	MÄDCHEN	RAGAZZA	CHICA, NIÑA	PUELLA
BOY	GARÇON	JUNGE	RAGAZZO	CHICO, NIÑO	PUER
BIG	GRAND	GROSS	GRANDE	GRANDE	MAGNUS
LITTLE	PETIT	KLEIN	PICCOLO	PEQUENO, CHICO, POCO	PAUCUS
VERY	TRÈS	SEHR	MOLTO	MUCHO	
FASHIONABLE	À LA MODE	MODISCH	DI MODA	DE MODA	
GENTLEMAN	MONSIEUR	HERR	SIGNORE	CABALLERO	DOMINUS
LADY	DAME	DAME	SIGNORA	SEÑORA	DOMINA
MAN	HOMME	MANN	UOMO	HOMBRE	HOMO
WOMAN	FEMME	FRAU	DONNA	DOÑA	MULIER
WHO	QUI	WER	CHI	QUIÉN, QUE	QUIS
I	JE	ICH	IO	YO	EGO
YOU	TU, VOUS	DU, SIE, IHR	TU, VOI, LEI	TU, VOSOTROS/AS	TU, VOS
WHAT	QUOI, QUEL	WAS	CHE COSA	QUE	QUOD
HE	IL	ER	EGLI	EL	IS
SHE	ELLE	SIE	ELLA	ELLA	EA
WE	NOUS	WIR	NOI	NOSOTROS/AS	NOS
THEY	ILS, ELLES	SIE	ESSI/E, LORO	ELLOS, ELLAS	EI, EAE
AT HOME	CHEZ MOI/NOUS OR À LA MAISON	ZU HAUSE	A CASA	EN CASA	DOMO
HOUSE	MAISON	HAUS	CASA	CASA	VILLA, DOMUS
STREET	RUE	STRASSE	STRADA	CALLE	VIA
ROAD	ROUTE	WEG	VIA	CAMINO	VIA
BY	PAR	BEI	PER	POR	PER
BEFORE	AVANT	VOR	PRIMA	(DEL) ANTE	ANTE
AFTER	APRÈS	NACH	DOPO	DESPUES	POST

ENGLISH	FRENCH	GERMAN	ITALIAN	SPANISH	LATIN
UNDER	SOUS	UNTER	SOTTO	(DE)BAJO	SUB
OVER	SUR	OBER	SOPRA, SU	SOBRE	SUPER
NEAR	PRÈS DE	NAHE, BEI	VICINO	CERCA	PROPE
OUT	DEHORS	AUS	VIA, FUORI	FUERA	EX
IN	DANS	IN	IN	EN	IN
HOW	COMMENT	WIE	COME	COMO	QUO MODO
WHY	POURQUOI	WARUM	PERCHE	POR QUÉ	CUR
THE	LE, LA, LES	DER, DIE, DAS	IL, LO, LA, I, GLI, LE	EL, LA, LO, LOS, LAS	
A	UN, UNE	EIN, EINE	UN, UNO, UNA	UN, UNA	
RED	ROUGE	ROT	ROSSO	ROJO	RUBER
BLUE	BLEU	BLAU	AZZURRO	AZUL	CAERULEUS
YELLOW	JAUNE	GELB	GIALLO	AMARILLO	FULVUS
GREEN	VERT	GRÜN	VERDE	VERDE	VIRIDIS
BLACK	NOIR	SCHWARZ	NERO	NEGRO	NIGER
WHITE	BLANC OR BLANCHE	WEISS	BIANCO	BLANCO	ALBUS
SHORT	COURT	KURZ	CORTO, BREVE	CORTO	BREVIS
LONG	LONG	LANG	LUNGO	LARGO	LONGUS

NUMBERS

ENGLISH	ROMAN NUMERALS	FRENCH	GERMAN	ITALIAN	SPANISH
ONE	I	UN	EIN	UNO	UNO
TWO	II	DEUX	ZWEI	DUE	DOS
THREE	III	TROIS	DREI	TRE	TRES
FOUR	IV	QUATRE	VIER	QUATTRO	CUATRO
FIVE	V	CINQ	FÜNF	CINQUE	CINCO
SIX	VI	SIX	SECHS	SEI	SEIS
SEVEN	VII	SEPT	SIEBEN	SETTE	SIETE
EIGHT	VIII	HUIT	ACHT	OTTO	OCHO
NINE	IX	NEUF	NEUN	NOVE	NUEVE
TEN	X	DIX	ZEHN	DIECI	DIEZ
TWENTY	XX	VINGT	ZWANZIG	VENTI	VEINTE
TWENTY-FIVE	XV	VINGT-CINQ	FÜNF UND ZWANZIG	VENTICINQUE	VEINTICINCO
THIRTY	XXX	TRENTE	DREISSIG	TRENTA	TREINTA
FORTY	XL	QUARANTE	VIERZIG	QUARANTA	CUARENTA
FIFTY	L	CINQUANTE	FÜNFZIG	CINQUANTA	CINCUENTA
SIXTY	LX	SOIXANTE	SECHZIG	SESSANTA	SESENTA
SEVENTY	LXX	SOIXANTE-DIX	SIEBZIG	SETTANTA	SETENTA
EIGHTY	LXXX	QUATRE-VINGT	ACHTZIG	OTTANTA	OCHENTA
NINETY	XC	QUANTRE-VINGT-DIX	NEUNZIG	NOVANTA	NOVENTA
ONE HUNDRED	C	CENT	HUNDERT	CENTO	CIEN (CIENTO)
FIVE HUNDRED	D	CINQ CENTS	FÜNFHUNDERT	CINQUECENTO	QUINIENTOS
ONE THOUSAND	M	MILLE	TAUSEND	MILLE	MIL

FRENCH PHRASES

5
MÊLÉE – brawl
ON DIT – piece of gossip, rumour
6
DE TROP – unwelcome
7
À LA MODE – fashionable
À PROPOS – to the point
CAP-À-PIE – from head to foot
DE RÈGLE – customary
EN MASSE – all together
EN ROUTE – on the way
8
BÈTE NOIR – person or thing particularly
  disliked
IDÉE FIXE – obsession
MAL DE MER – seasickness
MOT JUSTE – the appropriate word
9
DE RIGUEUR – required by custom
EN PASSANT – by the way
EN RAPPORT – in harmony
ENTRE NOUS – between you and me
10
À BON MARCHÉ – cheap
BILLET DOUX – love letter
DERNIER CRI – latest fashion, the last word
NOM DE PLUME – writer's assumed name
PENSE À BIEN – think for the best
11
AMOUR PROPRE – self-esteem
GARDEZ LA FOI – keep the faith

11 –continued
LÈSE MAJESTÉ – treason
NOM DE GUERRE – assumed name
RAISON D'ÊTRE – justification for existence
SAVOIR FAIRE – address, tact
TOUR DE FORCE – feat or accomplishment
  of great strength
12
FORCE MAJEURE – irresistible force or
  compulsion
HORS DE COMBAT – out of the fight,
  disabled
SANS DIEU RIEN – nothing without God
VENTRE À TERRE – at great speed
14
DOUBLE ENTENDRE – double meaning
ENFANT TERRIBLE – child who causes
  embarrassment
NOBLESSE OBLIGE – privilege entails
  responsibility
PREUX CHEVALIER – gallant knight
VÉRITÉ SANS PEUR – truth without fear
15
AMENDE HONORABLE – reparation
CHERCHEZ LA FEMME – look for the woman
17
PIÈCE DE RÉSISTANCE – most outstanding
  item; main dish at a meal
20+
AUTRE TEMPS, AUTRES MOEURS – other
  times, other manners

LATIN PHRASES

4
FIAT – let it be done or made
IN RE – concerning
STET – let it stand
5
AD HOC – for this special purpose
AD LIB – to speak off the cuff, without notes
AD REM – to the point
CIRCA – about
FECIT – he did it
6
AD USUM – as customary
IN SITU – in its original situation
IN TOTO – entirely

6 –continued
IN VIVO – in life, describing biological
  occurrences within living bodies
PRO TEM – temporary, for the time being
7
AD FINEM – to the end
A PRIORI – by deduction
CUI BONO? – whom does it benefit?
DE FACTO – in fact
FIAT LUX – let there be light
IN VITRO – in glass, describing biological
  experiments outside a body
PECCAVI – a confession of guilt (I have
  sinned)

7 —continued
PER DIEM — by the day
SINE DIE — without a day being appointed
SUB ROSA — confidential
UNA VOCE — with one voice, unanimously

8
ALTER EGO — another self
BONA FIDE — in good faith
EMERITUS — one retired from active official duties
MEA CULPA — an acknowledgement of guilt (I am to blame)
NOTA BENE — observe or note well
PRO FORMA — for the sake of form
UT PROSIM — that I may be of use

9
AD INTERIM — meanwhile
AD LITERAM — to the letter
AD NAUSEAM — to a disgusting, sickening degree
DEI GRATIA — by the grace of God
ET TU, BRUTE — and you, Brutus
EXCELSIOR — still higher
EX OFFICIO — by right of position or office
HIC ET NUNC — here and now
INTER ALIA — among other things
PRO PATRIA — for our country
STATUS QUO — the existing situation or state of affairs
SUB JUDICE — under consideration
VICE VERSA — the terms being exchanged, the other way round
VOX POPULI — popular opinion

10
ANNO DOMINI — in the year of our Lord
DEO GRATIAS — thanks be to God
EX CATHEDRA — with authority
IN EXTREMIS — in dire straits, at the the point of death
IN MEMORIAM — to the memory of
LOCO CITATO — in the place quoted
POST MORTEM — after death
PRIMA FACIE — at first sight
SINE QUA NON — something indispensable
TERRA FIRMA — solid ground

11
AD INFINITUM — endlessly, to infinity
ANIMO ET FIDE — by courage and faith
DE DIE IN DIEM — from day to day
DE PROFUNDIS — from the depths of misery
EX POST FACTO — after the event
GLORIA PATRI — glory to the Father
LOCUS STANDI — the right to be heard (in a law case)
NON SEQUITUR — an unwarranted conclusion
PAX VOBISCUM — peace be with you
TEMPUS FUGIT — time flies

12
ANTE MERIDIEM — before noon

12 —continued
CAVEAT EMPTOR — let the buyer beware
COMPOS MENTIS — of sane mind
FESTINA LENTE — hasten slowly, be quick without impetuosity
JACTA EST ALEA — the die is cast
PERSEVERANDO — by perseverance
POST MERIDIEM — after noon
SERVABO FIDEM — I will keep faith
VENI, VIDI, VICI — I came, I saw, I conquered
VOLO NON VALEO — I am willing but unable

13
CORPUS DELICTI — body of facts that constitute an offence
DUM SPIRO, SPERO — while I breathe, I hope
IN VINO VERITAS — there is truth in wine, that is, the truth comes out
MODUS OPERANDI — a method of operating
NE FRONTI CREDE — trust not to appearances
VINCIT VERITAS — truth conquers
VIRTUTIS AMORE — By love of virtue

14
CETERIS PARIBUS — other things being equal
EDITIO PRINCEPS — the original edition
IN LOCO PARENTIS — in place of a parent
NIL DESPERANDUM — never despair
PRO BONO PUBLICO — for the public good

15
ANIMO NON ASTUTIA — by courage not by craft
FORTITER ET RECTE — courageously and honourably
FORTUNA SEQUATUR — let fortune follow
INFRA DIGNITATEM — beneath one's dignity
NON COMPOS MENTIS — mentally unsound
OMNIA VINCIT AMOR — love conquers all things
PERSONA NON GRATA — an unacceptable person

16
GLORIA IN EXCELSIS — glory to God in the highest

17
LABOR IPSE VOLUPTAS — labour itself is pleasure
NUNQUAM NON PARATUS — always ready
PROBUM NON PAENITET — honesty repents not
VER NON SEMPER VIRET — Spring does not always flourish

18
NEC TEMERE NEC TIMIDE — neither rashly nor timidly
PRO REGE, LEGE, ET GREGE — for the king, the law, and the people
REDUCTIO AD ABSURDAM — reducing to absurdity

19

CANDIDE ET CONSTANTER – fairly and firmly

SOLA NOBILITAS VIRTUS – virtue alone is true nobility

VIRTUTI NON ARMIS FIDO – I trust to virtue and not to arms

20+

DE MORTUIS NIL NISI BONUM – speak only good of the dead

DULCE ET DECORUM EST PRO PATRIA MORI – it is sweet and seemly to die for one's country

20+ —continued

FORTUNA FAVET FORTIBUS – fortune favours the brave

PATRIA CARA CARIOR LIBERTAS – my country is dear, but liberty is dearer

QUOD ERAT DEMONSTRANDUM – which was to be demonstrated

SIC TRANSIT GLORIA MUNDI – thus passes the glory from the world

TIMEO DANAOS ET DONA FERENTES – I fear the Greeks, even when bearing gifts

VIVIT POST FUNERA VIRTUS – virtue survives the grave

AMERICANISMS

BRITISH	AMERICAN	BRITISH	AMERICAN
ACTION REPLAY	INSTANT REPLAY	DEMISEMIQUAVER	THIRTY-SECOND NOTE
ADRENALINE	EPINEPHRINE		
AERODROME	AIRDROME	DICKY	RUMBLE SEAT
AEROFOIL	AIRFOIL	DINNER JACKET	TUXEDO
AEROPLANE	AIRPLANE	DOSSHOUSE	FLOPHOUSE
ANAESTHETIST	ANESTHESIOLOGIST	DOWNPIPE	DOWNSPOUT
ANAESTHETICS	ANESTHESIOLOGY	DRAUGHTS	CHECKERS
ARMISTICE DAY	VETERANS DAY	DRAWING PIN	THUMBTACK
AUBERGINE	EGGPLANT	DUAL CARRIAGEWAY	DIVIDED HIGHWAY
AUTOCUE	TELEPROMPTER	DUMBWAITER	LAZY SUSAN
BACK BOILER	WATER BACK	DUSTBIN	GARBAGE CAN; TRASH CAN
BARYTES	BARITE		
BEETROOT	RED BEET	DUSTCART	GARBAGE TRUCK
BILL	CHECK	DUSTER	DUST CLOTH
BISCUIT	COOKIE	ÉTRIER	STIRRUP
BLACK PUDDING	BLOOD SAUSAGE	FANLIGHT	TRANSOM
BLOWLAMP	BLOWTORCH	FLAT	APARTMENT
BLUE-EYED BOY	FAIR-HAIRED BOY	FLEX	CORD
BONNET	HOOD	FLY-PAST	FLYOVER
BOOT	TRUNK	FOUR-STROKE	FOUR-CYCLE
BOWLER	DERBY	FRENCH WINDOWS	FRENCH DOORS
BRACES	SUSPENDER	FRIESIAN	HOLSTEIN
BREATHALYZER	DRUNKOMETER	FUNERAL PARLOUR	FUNERAL HOME
BREEZE BLOCK	CINDER BLOCK	FUNNY BONE	CRAZY BONE
CAMBERWELL BEAUTY	MOURNING CLOAK	GRAMOPHONE	PHONOGRAPH
		GREY MULLET	MULLET
CANDYFLOSS	COTTON CANDY	GUDGEON PIN	WRIST PIN
CARAVAN	TRAILER	HAIRSLIDE	BARRETTE
CATAPULT	SLINGSHOT	HEMIDEMISEMI- QUAVER	SIXTY-FOURTH NOTE
CATCH PIT	CATCH BASIN		
CENTRAL RESERVE	MEDIAN STRIP	HEMLOCK	POISON HEMLOCK
CORNFLOUR	CORNSTARCH	HEN HARRIER	MARSH HAWK; MARSH HARRIER
COS	ROMAINE		
COURGETTE	ZUCCHINI	HOLDALL	CARRYALL
CREEPING THISTLE	CANADA THISTLE	INSULATING TAPE	FRICTION TAPE
CROTCHET	QUARTER NOTE	JELLY	JELLO
CURRENT ACCOUNT	CHECKING ACCOUNT	JUMP LEADS	JUMPER CABLES
CUTTHROAT	STRAIGHT RAZOR	KENNEL	DOGHOUSE
DELIVERY VAN		LADYBIRD	
	PANEL TRUCK		LADYBUG

BRITISH	AMERICAN	BRITISH	AMERICAN
LEFT-LUGGAGE OFFICE	CHECKROOM	RING ROAD	BELTWAY
		ROOF RACK	CARRIER
LEVEL CROSSING	GRADE CROSSING	ROUNDABOUT	TRAFFIC CIRCLE
LIFT	ELEVATOR	RUBBER	ERASER
LIGNOCAINE	LIDOCAINE	RUCKSACK	BACKPACK
LOOSE COVER	SLIPCOVER	SEASON TICKET	COMMUTATION TICKET
LORRY	TRUCK		
LOUD-HAILER	BULLHORN	SEMIBREVE	WHOLE NOTE
LOUDSPEAKER VAN	SOUND TRUCK	SEMIQUAVER	SIXTEENTH NOTE
LUGGAGE VAN	BAGGAGE CAR	SHOPWALKER	FLOORWALKER
MAIZE	CORN	SHORTHAND TYPIST	STENOGRAPHER
MERRY-GO-ROUND	CAROUSEL	SILENCER	MUFFLER
MILEOMETER	ODOMETER	SKIRTING BOARD	BASEBOARD; MOPBOARD
MILLEFEUILLE	NAPOLEON		
MINIM	HALF-NOTE	SLEEVE	JACKET
MUDGUARD	FENDER	SOCKET	OUTLET
MUSIC HALL	VAUDEVILLE	STEAM ORGAN	CALLIOPE
NAPPY	DIAPER	STOCKBROKER BELT	EXURBIA
NORADRENALINE	NOREPINEPHRINE	SUSPENDER BELT	GARTER BELT
NOSEBAG	FEEDBAG	SWALLOW DIVE	SWAN DIVE
NOTICE BOARD	BULLETIN BOARD	SWEDE	RUTABAGA
OPEN DAY	OPEN HOUSE	TAP	FAUCET
ORDINARY SHARES	COMMON STOCK	TEA TOWEL	DISHTOWEL
OVERHEAD-VALVE ENGINE	VALVE-IN-HEAD ENGINE	TERYLENE	DACRON
		THORN APPLE	JIMSON WEED
PATIENCE	SOLITAIRE	TIE	NECKTIE
PAVEMENT	SIDEWALK	TIEPIN	STICK PIN
PEDESTRIAN CROSSING	CROSSWALK	TORSK	CUSK
		TRAM	STREETCAR; TROLLEY CAR
PENNY-FARTHING	ORDINARY		
PEPPERWORT	PEPPERGRASS	TRAPEZIUM	TRAPEZOID
PETROL	GASOLINE	TREACLE	MOLASSES
PLOUGH	BIG DIPPER	TRUNCHEON	NIGHT STICK
PRAM	BABY CARRIAGE	TURN UP	CUFF
PREFERENCE SHARES	PREFERRED STOCK	UNDERGROUND	SUBWAY
		UNDERSEAL	UNDERCOAT
PROTEOSE	ALBUMOSE	URSA MINOR	LITTLE DIPPER
QUAVER	EIGHTH NOTE	VALVE	VACUUM TUBE
RAGWORM	CLAMWORM	VIRGINIA CREEPER	BOSTON IVY
REAR LIGHT	TAILLIGHT; TAIL LAMP	WAISTCOAT	VEST
		WINDMILL	PINWHEEL
RED MULLET	GOATFISH	WINDSCREEN	WINDSHIELD
REPERTORY COMPANY	STOCK COMPANY	WINDSCREEN WIPER	WINDSHIELD WIPER
		WING	FENDER
REVERSING LIGHT	BACK-UP LIGHT	WINTERGREEN	SHINLEAF
RIGHT-ANGLED TRIANGLE	RIGHT TRIANGLE		

COMMON SAYINGS

PROVERBS

A bad penny always turns up.
A bad workman always blames his tools.
A bird in the hand is worth two in the bush.
Absence makes the heart grow fonder.
A cat has nine lives.
A cat may look at a king.
Accidents will happen in the best regulated families.
A chain is no stronger than its weakest link.
Actions speak louder than words.
A drowning man will clutch at a straw.
A fool and his money are soon parted.
A fool at forty is a fool indeed.
A friend in need is a friend indeed.
All cats are grey in the dark.
All good things must come to an end.
All is fair in love and war.
All roads lead to Rome.
All's grist that comes to the mill.
All's well that ends well.
All that glitters is not gold.
All the world loves a lover.
All work and no play makes Jack a dull boy.
A miss is as good as a mile.
An apple a day keeps the doctor away.
An Englishman's home is his castle.
An Englishman's word is his bond.
A nod is as good as a wink to a blind horse.
Any port in a storm.
Any publicity is good publicity.
A trouble shared is a trouble halved.
Attack is the best form of defence.
A watched pot never boils.
A woman's work is never done.
A young physician fattens the churchyard.
Bad news travels fast.
Beauty is in the eye of the beholder.
Beauty is only skin-deep.
Beggars can't be choosers.
Better be an old man's darling than a young man's slave.
Better be safe than sorry.
Better late than never.
Birds of a feather flock together.
Blood is thicker than water.
Books and friends should be few but good.
Caesar's wife must be above suspicion.
Charity begins at home.
Christmas comes but once a year.
Civility costs nothing.

Cold hands, warm heart.
Constant dripping wears away the stone.
Curiosity killed the cat.
Cut your coat according to your cloth.
Dead men tell no tales.
Death is the great leveller.
Divide and rule.
Do as I say, not as I do.
Do as you would be done by.
Dog does not eat dog.
Don't count your chickens before they are hatched.
Don't cross the bridge till you get to it.
Don't cut off your nose to spite your face.
Don't meet troubles half-way.
Don't put all your eggs in one basket.
Don't spoil the ship for a ha'porth of tar.
Don't teach your grandmother to suck eggs.
Don't throw the baby out with the bathwater.
Don't wash your dirty linen in public.
Early to bed and early to rise, makes a man healthy, wealthy and wise.
Easier said than done.
East, west, home's best.
Easy come, easy go.
Empty vessels make the greatest sound.
Even a worm will turn.
Every cloud has a silver lining.
Every dog has his day.
Every dog is allowed one bite.
Every man for himself, and the devil take the hindmost.
Everything comes to him who waits.
Experience is the best teacher.
Faith will move mountains.
Familiarity breeds contempt.
Fight fire with fire.
Fine feathers make fine birds.
Fine words butter no parsnips.
Fish and guests smell in three days.
Forewarned is forearmed.
Forgive and forget.
For want of a nail the shoe was lost; for want of a shoe the horse was lost; for want of a horse the rider was lost.
From clogs to clogs in only three generations.
Give a dog a bad name and hang him.
Give him an inch and he'll take a yard.
Great minds think alike.
Great oaks from little acorns grow.

Handsome is as handsome does.

He that fights and runs away, may live to fight another day.

He travels fastest who travels alone.

He who hesitates is lost.

He who lives by the sword dies by the sword.

He who pays the piper calls the tune.

He who sups with the devil should have a long spoon.

History repeats itself.

Honesty is the best policy.

If a job's worth doing, it's worth doing well.

If at first you don't succeed, try, try, try again.

If the mountain will not come to Mahomet, Mahomet must go to the mountain.

If you don't like the heat, get out of the kitchen.

Imitation is the sincerest form of flattery.

In for a penny, in for a pound.

In the country of the blind, the one-eyed man is king.

It is no use crying over spilt milk.

It never rains but it pours.

It's an ill wind that blows nobody any good.

It's too late to shut the stable door after the horse has bolted.

It will all come right in the wash.

It will be all the same in a hundred years.

Jack of all trades, master of none.

Keep something for a rainy day.

Kill not the goose that lays the golden egg.

Least said soonest mended.

Let bygones be bygones.

Let sleeping dogs lie.

Let the cobbler stick to his last.

Life begins at forty.

Life is just a bowl of cherries.

Life is not all beer and skittles.

Look before you leap.

Love is blind.

Love laughs at locksmiths.

Lucky at cards, unlucky in love.

Many a true word is spoken in jest.

Many hands make light work.

March comes in like a lion and goes out like a lamb.

March winds and April showers bring forth May flowers.

Marry in haste, and repent at leisure.

More haste, less speed.

Necessity is the mother of invention.

Needs must when the devil drives.

Ne'er cast a clout till May be out.

Never look a gift horse in the mouth.

No time like the present.

Old habits die hard.

Old sins cast long shadows.

One for sorrow, two for joy; three for a girl, four for a boy; five for silver, six for gold; seven for a secret, not to be told; eight for heaven, nine for hell; and ten for the devil's own sel.

One good turn deserves another.

One man's meat is another man's poison.

One swallow does not make a summer.

Out of sight, out of mind.

Patience is a virtue.

Penny wise, pound foolish.

Prevention is better than cure.

Red sky at night, shepherd's delight; red sky in the morning, shepherd's warning.

Revenge is a dish that tastes better cold.

Revenge is sweet.

See a pin and pick it up, all the day you'll have good luck; see a pin and let it lie, you'll want a pin before you die.

Seeing is believing.

See Naples and die.

Silence is golden.

Spare the rod and spoil the child.

Sticks and stones may break my bones, but words will never hurt me.

Still waters run deep.

St. Swithin's Day, if thou dost rain, for forty days it will remain; St. Swithin's Day, if thou be fair, for forty days 'twill rain no more.

Take a hair of the dog that bit you.

The darkest hour is just before the dawn.

The devil finds work for idle hands to do.

The devil looks after his own.

The early bird catches the worm.

The end justifies the means.

The exception proves the rule.

The hand that rocks the cradle rules the world.

Time is a great healer.

There is honour among thieves.

There is more than one way to skin a cat.

There is no accounting for tastes.

There is safety in numbers.

There's many a good tune played on an old fiddle.

There's many a slip' twixt the cup and the lip.

There's no place like home.

There's no smoke without fire.

The road to hell is paved with good intentions.

Time and tide wait for no man.

Time is a great healer.

Too many cooks spoil the broth.

Truth is stranger than fiction.

Two heads are better than one.

Two wrongs do not make a right.

United we stand, divided we fall.

Waste not, want not.

We must learn to walk before we can run.

What you lose on the swings you gain on the roundabouts.

When poverty comes in at the door, love flies out of the window.

When the cat's away, the mice will play.

When the wine is in, the wit is out.

Where there's a will there's a way.
Why keep a dog and bark yourself?
You can lead a horse to the water, but you
  can't make him drink.
You cannot run with the hare and hunt with
  the hounds.

You can't make an omelette without breaking
  eggs.
You can't teach an old dog new tricks.
You can't tell a book by its cover.

SIMILES

as bald as a coot
as black as pitch
as black as the ace of spades
as blind as a bat
as blind as a mole
as bold as brass
as bright as a button
as busy as a bee
as calm as a millpond
as cheap as dirt
as chirpy as a cricket
as clean as a whistle
as clear as a bell
as clear as crystal
as clear as mud
as cold as charity
as common as muck
as cool as a cucumber
as cross as two sticks
as daft as a brush
as dead as a dodo
as dead as a doornail
as dead as mutton
as deaf as a post
as different as chalk and cheese
as drunk as a lord
as dry as a bone
as dry as dust
as dull as dishwater
as easy as falling off a log
as easy as pie
as fit as a flea
as flat as a pancake
as free as a bird
as free as air
as free as the wind
as fresh as a daisy
as good as gold
as green as grass
as happy as a lark
as happy as a sandboy
as happy as Larry
as happy as the day is long
as hard as nails
as keen as mustard
as large as life
as light as a feather
as like as two peas in a pod

as lively as a cricket
as mad as a hatter
as mad as a March hare
as meek as a lamb
as merry as a cricket
as neat as a new pin
as nutty as a fruitcake
as obstinate as a mule
as old as the hills
as pale as death
as plain as a pikestaff
as plain as the nose on your face
as pleased as Punch
as poor as a church mouse
as poor as Lazarus
as pretty as a picture
as proud as a peacock
as pure as the driven snow
as quick as a flash
as quick as lightning
as quick as thought
as quiet as a mouse
as quiet as the grave
as red as a beetroot
as regular as clockwork
as rich as Croesus
as right as rain
as safe as houses
as sharp as a needle
as sick as a dog
as simple as falling off a log
as slippery as an eel
as snug as a bug in a rug
as sound as a bell
as steady as a rock
as stiff as a board
as stiff as a poker
as stiff as a ramrod
as straight as a die
as straight as an arrow
as stubborn as a mule
as sure as eggs is eggs
as sure as hell
as thick as thieves
as thick as two short planks
as thin as a lath
as thin as a rake
as thin as a stick

as tough as nails
as tough as old boots
as ugly as sin
as warm as toast

as weak as a kitten
as weak as dishwater
as welcome as the flowers in May
as white as a sheet

NURSERY RHYMES

A frog he would a-wooing go,
Heigh ho! says Rowley,
A frog he would a-wooing go,
Whether his mother would let him or no.
With a rowley, powley, gammon and spinach,
Heigh ho! says Anthony Rowley.

As I was going to St Ives,
I met a man with seven wives.
Each wife had seven sacks
Each sack had seven cats,
Each cat had seven kits,
How many were going to St Ives?

Baa, baa, black sheep,
Have you any wool?
Yes, sir, yes, sir,
Three bags full;
One for the master,
And one for the dame,
And one for the little boy
Who lives down the lane.

Bobby Shafto's gone to sea,
Silver buckles on his knee;
He'll come back and marry me,
Bonny Bobby Shafto!

Come, let's to bed
Says Sleepy-head;
Tarry a while, says Slow;
Put on the pan;
Says Greedy Nan,
Let's sup before we go.

Ding dong, bell,
Pussy's in the well.
Who put her in?
Little Johnny Green.
Who pulled her out?
Little Tommy Stout.

Doctor Foster went to Gloucester
In a shower of rain:
He stepped in a puddle,
Right up to his middle,
And never went there again.

Georgie Porgie, pudding and pie,
Kissed the girls and made them cry;
When the boys came out to play,
Georgie Porgie ran away.

Goosey, goosey gander,
Whither shall I wander?

Upstairs and downstairs
And in my lady's chamber.

Hey diddle diddle,
The cat and the fiddle,
The cow jumped over the moon;
The little dog laughed
To see such sport,
And the dish ran away with the spoon.

Hickory, dickory, dock,
The mouse ran up the clock.
The clock struck one,
The mouse ran down,
Hickory, dickory, dock.

Jack and Jill went up the hill
To fetch a pail of water;
Jack fell down and broke his crown,
And Jill came tumbling after.

Little Bo-peep has lost her sheep,
And can't tell where to find them;
Leave them alone, and they'll come home,
Bringing their tails behind them.

Little Boy Blue,
Come blow your horn,
The sheep's in the meadow,
The cow's in the corn.

Little Jack Horner
Sat in the corner,
Eating a Christmas pie;
He put in his thumb,
And pulled out a plum,
And said, What a good boy am I!

Little Miss Muffet
Sat on a tuffet,
Eating her curds and whey;
There came a big spider,
Who sat down beside her
And frightened Miss Muffet away.

Little Tommy Tucker,
Sings for his supper:
What shall we give him?
White bread and butter
How shall he cut it
Without a knife?
How will he be married
Without a wife?

Mary, Mary, quite contrary,

How does your garden grow?
With silver bells and cockle shells,
And pretty maids all in a row.

Monday's child is fair of face,
Tuesday's child is full of grace,
Wednesday's child is full of woe,
Thursday's child has far to go,
Friday's child is loving and giving,
Saturday's child works hard for his living,
And the child that is born on the Sabbath day
Is bonny and blithe, and good and gay.

Oh! the grand old Duke of York
He had ten thousand men;
He marched them up to the top of the hill,
And he marched them down again.
And when they were up they were up,
And when they were down they were down,
And when they were only half way up,
They were neither up nor down.

Old King Cole
Was a merry old soul,
And a merry old soul was he;
He called for his pipe,
And he called for his bowl,
And he called for his fiddlers three.

Old Mother Hubbard
Went to the cupboard,
To fetch her poor dog a bone;
But when she got there
The cupboard was bare
And so the poor dog had none.

One, two,
Buckle my shoe;
Three, four,
Knock at the door.
Five, six,
Pick up sticks;
Seven, eight,
Close the gate.
Nine, ten,
Big fat hen;
Eleven, twelve,
Dig and delve.
Thirteen, fourteen,
Maid's a'courting;
Fifteen, sixteen,
Maids in the kitchen.
Seventeen, eighteen,
Maids a'waiting;
Nineteen, twenty,
My plate's empty.

Oranges and lemons,
Say the bells of St Clement's.
You owe me five farthings,
Say the bells of St Martin's.
When will you pay me?
Say the bells of Old Bailey.
When I grow rich,

Say the bells of Shoreditch.
When will that be?
Say the bells of Stepney.
I'm sure I don't know,
Says the great bell at Bow.
Here comes a candle to light you to bed,
Here comes a chopper to chop off your head.

Peter Piper picked a peck of pickled pepper;
A peck of pickled pepper Peter Piper picked;
If Peter Piper picked a peck of pickled pepper,
Where's the peck of pickled pepper Peter
    Piper picked?

Polly put the kettle on,
Polly put the kettle on,
Polly put the kettle on,
We'll all have tea.
Sukey take it off again,
Sukey take it off again,
Sukey take it off again,
They've all gone away.

Pussy cat, pussy cat, where have you been?
I've been to London to look at the queen.
Pussy cat, pussy cat, what did you there?
I frightened a little mouse under her chair.

Ride a cock-horse to Banbury Cross,
To see a fine lady upon a white horse;
Rings on her fingers and bells on her toes,
And she shall have music wherever she goes.

Ring-a-ring o'roses,
A pocket full of posies,
A-tishoo! A-tishoo!
We all fall down.

Rub-a-dub-dub,
Three men in a tub,
And who do you think they be?
The butcher, the baker,
The candlestick-maker,
And they all sailed out to sea.

See-saw, Margery Daw,
Jacky shall have a new master;
Jacky shall have but a penny a day,
Because he can't work any faster.

Simple Simon met a pieman,
Going to the fair;
Says Simple Simon to the pieman,
Let me taste your ware.
Says the pieman to Simple Simon,
Show me first your penny;
Says Simple Simon to the pieman,
Indeed I have not any.

Sing a song of sixpence,
A pocket full of rye;
Four and twenty blackbirds,
Baked in a pie.
When the pie was opened,
The birds began to sing;
Was not that a dainty dish,

To set before the king?
The king was in his counting-house,
Counting out his money;
The queen was in the parlour,
Eating bread and honey.
The maid was in the garden,
Hanging out the clothes,
When down came a blackbird,
And pecked off her nose.

Solomon Grundy,
Born on a Monday,
Christened on Tuesday,
Married on Wednesday,
Took ill on Thursday,
Worse on Friday,
Died on Saturday,
Buried on Sunday.
This is the end
Of Solomon Grundy.

The lion and the unicorn
Were fighting for the crown;
The lion beat the unicorn
All round about the town.

There was a crooked man, and he walked a
    crooked mile,
He found a crooked sixpence against a
    crooked stile:
He bought a crooked cat, which caught a
    crooked mouse,
And they all lived together in a little crooked
    house.

There was an old woman who lived in a shoe,
She had so many children she didn't know
    what to do;
She gave them some broth without any bread;
She whipped them all soundly and put them to
    bed.

The twelfth day of Christmas,
My true love sent to me
Twelve lords a-leaping,
Eleven ladies dancing,
Ten pipers piping,
Nine drummers drumming,
Eight maids a-milking,
Seven swans a-swimming,
Six geese a-laying,
Five gold rings,
Four colly birds,
Three French hens,
Two turtle doves, and
A partridge in a pear tree.

Thirty days hath September,
April, June, and November;
All the rest have thirty-one,
Excepting February alone
And that has twenty-eight days clear
And twenty-nine in each leap year.

This little piggy went to market,

This little piggy stayed at home,
This little piggy had roast beef,
This little piggy had none,
And this little piggy cried, Wee-wee-wee-wee-
    wee,
I can't find my way home.

Three blind mice, see how they run!
They all run after the farmer's wife,
Who cut off their tails with a carving knife,
Did you ever see such a thing in your life,
As three blind mice?

Tinker,
Tailor,
Soldier,
Sailor,
Rich man,
Poor man,
Beggarman,
Thief.

Tom, Tom, the piper's son,
Stole a pig and away he run;
The pig was eat
And Tom was beat,
And Tom went howling down the street.

Two little dicky birds,
Sitting on a wall;
One named Peter,
The other named Paul,
Fly away, Peter!
Fly away, Paul!
Come back, Peter!
Come back, Paul!

Wee Willie Winkie runs through the town
Upstairs and downstairs and in his nightgown,
Rapping at the window, crying through the
    lock,
Are the children all in bed? It's past eight
    o'clock.

What are little boys made of?
Frogs and snails
And puppy-dogs' tails,
That's what little boys are made of.
What are little girls made of?
Sugar and spice
And all that's nice,
That's what little girls are made of.

Who killed Cock Robin?
I, said the Sparrow,
With my bow and arrow,
I killed Cock Robin.
Who saw him die?
I, said the Fly,
With my little eye,
I saw him die.

Jack Sprat could eat no fat,
His wife could eat no lean,
And so between them both you see,

They licked the platter clean.

How many miles to Babylon?
Three score miles and ten.
Can I get there by candle-light?
Yes, and back again.
If your heels are nimble and light,

You may get there by candle-light.

Humpty Dumpty sat on a wall,
Humpty Dumpty had a great fall.
All the king's horses and
All the king's men,
Couldn't put Humpty together again.

MOTTOES

A DEO ET REGE — By God and the King (Earl of Chesterfield)
AD MAJOREM DEI GLORIAM — to the greater glory of God (The Jesuits)
A MARI USQUE AD MARE — from sea to sea (Canada)
APRES NOUS LE DELUGE — after us the deluge (617 Squadron, 'The Dam Busters', RAF)
ARS LONGA, VITA BREVIS — art is long, life is short (Millais)
AUDI, VIDE, TACE — hear, see, keep silence (United Grand Lodge of Freemasons)
AUSPICIUM MELIORIS AEVI — the sign of a better age (Duke of St Albans, Order of St Michael and St George)
BE PREPARED — Scout Association, 1908
CAVENDO TUTUS — safe by being cautious (Duke of Devonshire)
CHE SERA SERA — what will be will be (Duke of Bedford)
DARE QUAM ACCIPERE — to give rather than to receive (Guy's Hospital)
DE PRAESCIENTIA DEI — from the foreknowledge of God (Barbers' Company, 1461)
DICTUM MEUM PACTUM — my word is my bond (Stock Exchange)
DIEU ET MON DROIT — God and my right (British Sovereigns)
DILIGENT AND SECRET (College of Arms, 1484)
DOMINE DIRIGE NOS — Lord, guide us (City of London)
DOMINUS ILLUMINATIO MEA — the Lord is my light (Oxford University)
DONORUM DEI DISPENSATIO FIDELIS — faithful dispensation of the gifts of God (Harrow School)
ENTALENTÉ À PARLER D'ARMES — equipped to speak of arms (The Heraldry Society, 1957)
ESPÉRANCE EN DIEU — hope in God (Duke of Northumberland)
FIDES ATQUE INTEGRITAS — faith and integrity (Society of Incorporated Accountants and Auditors)

FLOREAT ETONA — may Eton flourish (Eton College)
FOR COUNTRY NOT FOR SELF (226 Squadron, RAF)
GARDEZ BIEN — watch well (Montgomery)
HEAVEN'S LIGHT OUR GUIDE (Order of the Star of India)
HELP (Foundling Hospital, London)
HINC LUCEM ET POCULA SACRA — hence light and sacred cups (Cambridge University)
HONI SOIT QUI MAL Y PENSE — evil be to him who evil thinks (Order of the Garter)
HONNEUR ET PATRIE — honour and country (Order of the Legion of Honour)
ICH DIEN — I serve (Prince of Wales)
IMPERATRICUS AUSPICIIS — imperial in its auspices (Order of the Indian Empire)
IN ACTION FAITHFUL AND IN HONOUR CLEAR (Order of the Companions of Honour, 1917)
IN FIDE SALUS — safety in faith (Star of Rumania)
IN SOMNO SECURITAS — security in sleep (Association of Anaesthetists of Great Britain and Ireland)
JUSTITA VIRTUTUM REGINA — justice is queen of the virtues (Goldsmiths' Company)
LABORARE EST ORARE — to labour is to pray (Benedictine Order)
LABOR VIRIS CONVENIT — labour becomes men (Richard I)
LIFE IN OUR HANDS (Institute of Hospital Engineers)
MIHI ET MEA — to me and mine (Anne Boleyn)
NATION SHALL SPEAK PEACE UNTO NATION (British Broadcasting Corporation)
NEC ASPERA TERRENT — difficulties do not daunt (3rd Foot, 'The Buffs', East Kent Regiment)
NEC CUPIAS NEC METUAS — neither desire nor fear (Earl of Hardwicke)
NEMO ME IMPUNE LACESSIT — no one injures me with impunity (Order of the Thistle)
NOLI ME TANGERE — touch me not (Graeme of Garvock, 103 Squadron, RAF)

NON EST VIVERE SED VALERE VITA — life is not living, but health is life (Royal Society of Medicine)

NON SIBI, SED PATRIAE — not for himself, but for his country (Earl of Romney)

NULLIUS IN VERBA — in no man's words (Royal Society)

PAX IN BELLO — peace in war (Godolphin, Duke of Leeds)

PEACE THROUGH UNDERSTANDING (President Eisenhower)

PER ARDUA AD ASTRA — through endeavour to the stars (RAF motto)

PER CAELUM VIA NOSTRA — our way through heaven (Guild of Air Pilots and Navigators)

PISCATORES HOMINUM — fishers of men (National Society)

POWER IN TRUST (Central Electricity Generating Board)

QUIS SEPARABIT? — who shall separate? (Order of St Patrick)

QUOD PETIS HIC EST — here is what you seek (Institute of British Engineers)

RATIONE ET CONCILIO — by reason and counsel (Magistrates Association)

RERUM COGNOSCERE CAUSAS — to know the causes of things (Institute of Brewing)

SEMPER FIDELIS — always faithful (Devonshire regiment, East Devon Militia)

SEMPER PARATUS — always prepared (207 Squadron, RAF)

SOLA VIRTUS INVICTA — virtue alone is invincible (Duke of Norfolk)

TOUCH NOT THE CAT BOT A GLOVE (Macpherson Clan)

TRIA JUNCTA IN UNO — three joined in one (Order of the Bath)

UNITATE FORTIOR — stronger by union (Building Societies Association; Army and Navy Club)

VER NON SEMPER VIRET — the spring does not always flourish

VERNON SEMPER VIRET — Vernon always flourishes (Lord Lyveden)

WHO DARES WINS (Special Air Service)

WORDS

PALINDROMES

3	3—continued	4—continued	5—continued
AHA	NUN	DEED	SAGAS
BIB	OHO	KOOK	SEXES
BOB	PAP	MA'AM	SHAHS
DAD	PEP	NOON	SOLOS
DID	PIP	PEEP	TENET
DUD	POP	POOP	**6**
ERE	PUP	SEES	DENNED
EVE	SIS	TOOT	HALLAH
EWE	SOS	**5**	HANNAH
EYE	TAT	CIVIC	REDDER
GAG	TIT	KAYAK	TERRET
GIG	TNT	LEVEL	TUT-TUT
HAH	TOT	MADAM	**9**
HEH	TUT	MINIM	MALAYALAM
HUH	WOW	RADAR	ROTAVATOR
MAM	**4**	REFER	
MOM	BOOB	ROTOR	
MUM			

BACK WORDS

2	3—continued	3—continued	3—continued
AH – HA	BOY – YOB	GUT – TUG	PAR – RAP
AM – MA	BUD – DUB	HOD – DOH	PAT – TAP
AT – TA	BUN – NUB	JAR – RAJ	PAY – YAP
EH – HE	BUS – SUB	LAG – GAL	PER – REP
HA – AH	BUT – TUB	LAP – PAL	PIN – NIP
HE – EH	DAB – BAD	LEE – EEL	PIT – TIP
HO – OH	DAM – MAD	LEG – GEL	POT – TOP
IT – TI	DEW – WED	MAD – DAM	PUS – SUP
MA – AM	DIM – MID	MAR – RAM	RAJ – JAR
MP – PM	DNA – AND	MAY – YAM	RAM – MAR
NO – ON	DOG – GOD	MID – DIM	RAP – PAR
OH – HO	DOH – HOD	MUG – GUM	RAT – TAR
ON – NO	DON – NOD	NAB – BAN	RAW – WAR
PM – MP	DOT – TOD	NAP – PAN	REP – PER
TA – AT	DUB – BUD	NET – TEN	ROT – TOR
TI – IT	EEL – LEE	NIB – BIN	SAG – GAS
3	GAB – BAG	NIP – PIN	SUB – BUS
AND – DNA	GAL – LAG	NIT – TIN	SUP – PUS
BAD – DAB	GAS – SAG	NOD – DON	TAB – BAT
BAG – GAB	GEL – LEG	NOT – TON	TAP – PAT
BAN – NAB	GOB – BOG	NOW – WON	TAR – RAT
BAT – TAB	GOD – DOG	NUB – BUN	TEN – NET
BIN – NIB	GOT – TOG	PAL – LAP	TIN – NIT
BOG – GOB	GUM – MUG	PAN – NAP	TIP – PIT

3—continued	4—continued	4—continued	5—continued
TOD – DOT	LEEK – KEEL	STAR – RATS	RECAP – PACER
TOG – GOT	LEER – REEL	STEP – PETS	REGAL – LAGER
TON – NOT	LIAR – RAIL	STEW – WETS	REMIT – TIMER
TOP – POT	LIVE – EVIL	STOP – POTS	REPEL – LEPER
TOR – ROT	LOOP – POOL	STUB – BUTS	REVEL – LEVER
TUB – BUT	LOOT – TOOL	STUN – NUTS	SALTA – ATLAS
TUG – GUT	MACS – SCAM	SWAM – MAWS	SERAC – CARES
WAR – RAW	MADE – EDAM	SWAP – PAWS	SERIF – FIRES
WAY – YAW	MAPS – SPAM	SWAY – YAWS	SLEEK – KEELS
WED – DEW	MAWS – SWAM	SWOT – TOWS	SLOOP – POOLS
WON – NOW	MEET – TEEM	TANG – GNAT	SMART – TRAMS
YAM – MAY	MOOD – DOOM	TAPS – SPAT	SNIPS – SPINS
YAP – PAY	MOOR – ROOM	TEEM – MEET	SPINS – SNIPS
YAW – WAY	NAPS – SPAN	TIDE – EDIT	SPOOL – LOOPS
YOB – BOY	NIPS – SPIN	TIME – EMIT	SPOTS – STOPS
4	NUTS – STUN	TIPS – SPIT	STOPS – SPOTS
ABLE – ELBA	OGRE – ERGO	TONS – SNOT	STRAP – PARTS
ABUT – TUBA	PALS – SLAP	TOOL – LOOT	STRAW – WARTS
BARD – DRAB	PANS – SNAP	TOPS – SPOT	STROP – PORTS
BATS – STAB	PART – TRAP	TORT – TROT	TIMER – REMIT
BRAG – GARB	PAWS – SWAP	TOWS – SWOT	TRAMS – SMART
BUNS – SNUB	PEEK – KEEP	TRAP – PART	TUBER – REBUT
BUTS – STUB	PETS – STEP	TROT – TORT	WARTS – STRAW
DEER – REED	PINS – SNIP	TUBA – ABUT	**6**
DIAL – LAID	PLUG – GULP	WARD – DRAW	ANIMAL – LAMINA
DOOM – MOOD	POOH – HOOP	WETS – STEW	DELIAN – NAILED
DOOR – ROOD	POOL – LOOP	WOLF – FLOW	DENIER – REINED
DRAB – BARD	POTS – STOP	YAPS – SPAY	DIAPER – REPAID
DRAW – WARD	RAIL – LIAR	YARD – DRAY	DRAWER – REWARD
DRAY – YARD	RAPS – SPAR	YAWS – SWAY	HARRIS – SIRRAH
DUAL – LAUD	RATS – STAR	**5**	LAMINA – ANIMAL
EDAM – MADE	REED – DEER	ANNAM – MANNA	LOOTER – RETOOL
EDIT – TIDE	REEL – LEER	ATLAS – SALTA	NAILED – DELIAN
ELBA – ABLE	RIAL – LAIR	CARES – SERAC	PUPILS – SLIP-UP
EMIR – RIME	RIME – EMIR	DARAF – FARAD	RECAPS – SPACER
EMIT – TIME	ROOD – DOOR	DECAL – LACED	REINED – DENIER
ERGO – OGRE	ROOM – MOOR	DENIM – MINED	RENNET – TENNER
ET AL – LATE	SCAM – MACS	DEVIL – LIVED	REPAID – DIAPER
EVIL – LIVE	SLAG – GALS	FARAD – DARAF	RETOOL – LOOTER
FLOG – GOLF	SLAP – PALS	FIRES – SERIF	REWARD – DRAWER
FLOW – WOLF	SMUG – GUMS	KEELS – SLEEK	SERVES – SEVRES
GALS – SLAG	SNAP – PANS	LACED – DECAL	SEVRES – SERVES
GARB – BRAG	SNIP – PINS	LAGER – REGAL	SIRRAH – HARRIS
GNAT – TANG	SNOT – TONS	LEPER – REPEL	SLIP-UP – PUPILS
GOLF – FLOG	SNUB – BUNS	LEVER – REVEL	SNOOPS – SPOONS
GULP – PLUG	SNUG – GUNS	LIVED – DEVIL	SPACER – RECAPS
GUMS – SMUG	SPAM – MAPS	LOOPS – SPOOL	SPOONS – SNOOPS
GUNS – SNUG	SPAN – NAPS	MANNA – ANNAM	TENNER – RENNET
HOOP – POOH	SPAR – RAPS	MINED – DENIM	**8**
KEEL – LEEK	SPAT – TAPS	PACER – RECAP	DESSERTS –
KEEP – PEEK	SPAY – YAPS	PARTS – STRAP	STRESSED
LAID – DIAL	SPIN – NIPS	POOLS – SLOOP	STRESSED –
LAIR – RIAL	SPIT – TIPS	PORTS – STROP	DESSERTS
LATE – ET AL	SPOT – TOPS	REBUT – TUBER	
LAUD – DUAL	STAB – BATS		

HOMOPHONES

ACCESSARY – ACCESSORY
ACCESSORY – ACCESSARY
AERIAL – ARIEL
AERIE – AIRY
AIL – ALE
AIR – AIRE, E'ER, ERE, EYRE, HEIR
AIRE – AIR, E'ER, ERE, EYRE, HEIR
AIRSHIP – HEIRSHIP
AIRY – AERIE
AISLE – I'LL, ISLE
AIT – EIGHT, ATE
ALE – AIL
ALL – AWL, ORLE
ALMS – ARMS
ALTAR – ALTER
ALTER – ALTAR
AMAH – ARMOUR
ANTE – ANTI
ANTI – ANTE
ARC – ARK
AREN'T – AUNT
ARES – ARIES
ARIEL – AERIAL
ARIES – ARES
ARK – ARC
ARMOUR – AMAH
ARMS – ALMS
ASCENT – ASSENT
ASSENT – ASCENT
ATE – AIT, EIGHT
AUK – ORC
AUNT – AREN'T
AURAL – ORAL
AUSTERE – OSTIA
AWAY – AWEIGH
AWE – OAR, O'ER, ORE
AWEIGH – AWAY
AWL – ALL, ORLE
AXEL – AXLE
AXLE – AXEL
AY – AYE, EYE, I
AYAH – IRE
AYE – AY, EYE, I
AYES – EYES
BAA – BAH, BAR
BAAL – BASLE
BAH – BAA, BAR
BAIL – BALE
BALE – BAIL
BALL – BAWL
BALM – BARM
BALMY – BARMY
BAR – BAA, BAH
BARE – BEAR

BARM – BALM
BARMY – BALMY
BARON – BARREN
BARREN – BARON
BASE – BASS
BASLE – BAAL
BASS – BASE
BAUD – BAWD, BOARD
BAWD – BAUD, BOARD
BAWL – BALL
BAY – BEY
BEACH – BEECH
BEAN – BEEN
BEAR – BARE
BEAT – BEET
BEATER – BETA
BEAU – BOH, BOW
BEECH – BEACH
BEEN – BEAN
BEER – BIER
BEET – BEAT
BEL – BELL, BELLE
BELL – BEL, BELLE
BELLE – BEL, BELL
BERRY – BURY
BERTH – BIRTH
BETA – BEATER
BEY – BAY
BHAI – BI, BUY, BY, BYE
BI – BHAI, BUY, BY, BYE
BIER – BEER
BIGHT – BITE, BYTE
BIRTH – BERTH
BITE – BIGHT, BYTE
BLEW – BLUE
BLUE – BLEW
BOAR – BOER, BOOR, BORE
BOARD – BAUD, BAWD
BOARDER – BORDER
BOART – BOUGHT
BOER – BOAR, BOOR, BORE
BOH – BEAU, BOW
BOLE – BOWL
BOLT – BOULT
BOOR – BOAR, BOER, BORE
BOOTIE – BOOTY
BOOTY – BOOTIE
BORDER – BOARDER
BORE – BOAR, BOER, BOOR
BORN – BORNE
BORNE – BORN
BOUGH – BOW
BOUGHT – BOART
BOULT – BOLT

BOW – BEAU, BOH
BOW – BOUGH
BOWL – BOLE
BOY – BUOY
BRAKE – BREAK
BREAD – BRED
BREAK – BRAKE
BRED – BREAD
BREDE – BREED, BREID
BREED – BREDE, BREID
BREID – BREDE, BREED
BRIDAL – BRIDLE
BRIDLE – BRIDAL
BROACH – BROOCH
BROOCH – BROACH
BUNION – BUNYAN
BUNYAN – BUNION
BUOY – BOY
BURGER – BURGHER
BURGHER – BURGER
BURY – BERRY
BUS – BUSS
BUSS – BUS
BUY – BHAI, BI, BY, BYE
BUYER – BYRE
BY – BHAI, BI, BUY, BYE
BYE – BHAI, BI, BUY, BY
BYRE – BUYER
BYTE – BIGHT, BITE
CACHE – CASH
CACHOU – CASHEW
CAIN – CANE, KAIN
CALL – CAUL
CALLAS – CALLOUS, CALLUS
CALLOUS – CALLAS, CALLUS
CALLUS – CALLAS, CALLOUS
CANAPÉ – CANOPY
CANE – CAIN, KAIN
CANOPY – CANAPÉ
CARAT – CARROT, KARAT
CARROT – CARAT, KARAT
CART – CARTE, KART
CARTE – CART, KART
CASH – CACHE
CASHEW – CACHOU
CASHMERE – KASHMIR
CAST – CASTE, KARST
CASTE – CAST, KARST
CAUGHT – COURT
CAUL – CALL
CAW – COR, CORE, CORPS
CEDAR – SEEDER
CEDE – SEED
CEIL – SEEL, SEAL
CELL – SELL, SZELL
CELLAR – SELLER
CENSER – CENSOR, SENSOR
CENSOR – CENSER, SENSOR
CENT – SCENT, SENT
CERE – SEAR, SEER
CEREAL – SERIAL

CESSION – SESSION
CHAW – CHORE
CHEAP – CHEEP
CHECK – CZECH
CHEEP – CHEAP
CHOIR – QUIRE
CHOLER – COLLAR
CHORD – CORD
CHORE – CHAW
CHOTT – SHOT, SHOTT
CHOU – SHOE, SHOO
CHOUGH – CHUFF
CHUFF – CHOUGH
CHUTE – SHOOT, SHUTE
CITE – SIGHT, SITE
CLACK – CLAQUE
CLAQUE – CLACK
CLIMB – CLIME
CLIME – CLIMB
COAL – COLE, KOHL
COARSE – CORSE, COURSE
COLE – COAL, KOHL
COLLAR – CHOLER
COLONEL – KERNEL
COLOUR – CULLER
COME – CUM
COMPLEMENTARY – COMPLIMENTARY
COMPLIMENTARY – COMPLEMENTARY
COO – COUP
COOP – COUPE
COR – CAW, CORE, CORPS
CORD – CHORD
CORE – CAW, COR, CORPS
CORNFLOUR – CORNFLOWER
CORNFLOWER – CORNFLOUR
CORPS – CAW, COR, CORE
CORSE – COARSE, COURSE
COUNCIL – COUNSEL
COUNSEL – COUNCIL
COUP – COO
COUPE – COOP
COURSE – COARSE, CORSE
COURT – CAUGHT
CREAK – CREEK
CREEK – CREAK
CULLER – COLOUR
CUM – COME
CURB – KERB
CURRANT – CURRENT
CURRENT – CURRANT
CYGNET – SIGNET
CYMBAL – SYMBOL
CZECH – CHECK
DAM – DAMN
DAMN – DAM
DAW – DOOR, DOR
DAYS – DAZE
DAZE – DAYS
DEAR – DEER
DEER – DEAR
DESCENT – DISSENT

DESERT – DESSERT
DESSERT – DESERT
DEW – DUE
DINAH – DINER
DINE – DYNE
DINER – DINAH
DISSENT – DESCENT
DOE – DOH, DOUGH
DOH – DOE, DOUGH
DONE – DONNE, DUN
DONNE – DONE, DUN
DOOR – DAW, DOR
DOR – DAW, DOOR
DOST – DUST
DOUGH – DOE, DOH
DRAFT – DRAUGHT
DRAUGHT – DRAFT
DROOP – DRUPE
DRUPE – DROOP
DUAL – DUEL
DUCKS – DUX
DUE – DEW
DUEL – DUAL
DUN – DONE, DONNE
DUST – DOST
DUX – DUCKS
DYEING – DYING
DYING – DYEING
DYNE – DINE
EARN – URN
EATEN – ETON
E'ER – AIR, AIRE, ERE, EYRE, HEIR
EERIE – EYRIE
EIDER – IDA
EIGHT – AIT, ATE
EIRE – EYRA
ELATION – ILLATION
ELICIT – ILLICIT
ELUDE – ILLUDE
ELUSORY – ILLUSORY
EMERGE – IMMERGE
EMERSED – IMMERSED
EMERSION – IMMERSION
ERE – AIR, AIRE, E'ER, EYRE, HEIR
ERK – IRK
ERR – UR
ESTER – ESTHER
ESTHER – ESTER
ETON – EATEN
EWE – YEW, YOU
EYE – AY, AYE, I
EYED – I'D, IDE
EYELET – ISLET
EYES – AYES
EYRA – EIRE
EYRE – AIR, AIRE, E'ER, ERE, HEIR
EYRIE – EERIE
FA – FAR
FAIN – FANE, FEIGN
FAINT – FEIGNT
FAIR – FARE

FANE – FAIN, FEIGN
FAR – FA
FARE – FAIR
FARO – PHARAOH
FARTHER – FATHER
FATE – FÊTE
FATHER – FARTHER
FAUGH – FOR, FOUR, FORE
FAUN – FAWN
FAWN – FAUN
FAZE – PHASE
FEAT – FEET
FEET – FEAT
FEIGN – FAIN, FANE
FEIGNT – FAINT
FELLOE – FELLOW
FELLOW – FELLOE
FELT – VELD, VELDT
FETA – FETTER
FÊTE – FATE
FETTER – FETA
FEU – FEW, PHEW
FEW – FEU, PHEW
FIR – FUR
FISHER – FISSURE
FISSURE – FISHER
FIZZ – PHIZ
FLAIR – FLARE
FLARE – FLAIR
FLAW – FLOOR
FLEA – FLEE
FLEE – FLEA
FLEW – FLU, FLUE
FLOE – FLOW
FLOOR – FLAW
FLOUR – FLOWER
FLOW – FLOE
FLOWER – FLOUR
FLU – FLEW, FLUE
FLUE – FLEW, FLU
FOR – FAUGH, FOUR, FORE
FORE – FAUGH, FOR, FOUR
FORT – FOUGHT
FORTE – FORTY
FORTH – FOURTH
FORTY – FORTE
FOUGHT – FORT
FOUL – FOWL
FOUR – FAUGH, FOR, FORE
FOURTH – FORTH
FOWL – FOUL
FRIAR – FRIER
FRIER – FRIAR
FUR – FIR
GAIL – GALE
GAIT – GATE
GALE – GAIL
GALLOP – GALLUP
GALLUP – GALLOP
GAMBLE – GAMBOL
GAMBOL – GAMBLE

GATE – GAIT
GAWKY – GORKY
GENE – JEAN
GIN – JINN
GLADDEN – GLADDON
GLADDON – GLADDEN
GNASH – NASH
GNAT – NAT
GNAW – NOR
GORKY – GAWKY
GRATER – GREATER
GREATER – GRATER
GROAN – GROWN
GROWN – GROAN
HAE – HAY, HEH, HEY
HAIL – HALE
HAIR – HARE
HALE – HAIL
HALL – HAUL
HANDEL – HANDLE
HANDLE – HANDEL
HANGAR – HANGER
HANGER – HANGAR
HARE – HAIR
HART – HEART
HAUD – HOARD, HORDE
HAUL – HALL
HAW – HOARE, WHORE
HAY – HAE, HEH, HEY
HEAR – HERE
HEART – HART
HEH – HAE, HAY, HEY
HEIR – AIR, AIRE, E'ER, ERE, EYRE
HEIRSHIP – AIRSHIP
HERE – HEAR
HEROIN – HEROINE
HEROINE – HEROIN
HEW – HUE
HEY – HAE, HAY, HEH
HIE – HIGH
HIGH – HIE
HIGHER – HIRE
HIM – HYMN
HIRE – HIGHER
HO – HOE
HOAR – HAW, WHORE
HOARD – HAUD, HORDE
HOARSE – HORSE
HOE – HO
HOLE – WHOLE
HOO – WHO
HORDE – HAUD, HOARD
HORSE – HOARSE
HOUR – OUR
HOURS – OURS
HUE – HEW
HYMN – HIM
I – AY, AYE, EYE
I'D – EYED, IDE
IDA – EIDER
IDE – EYED, I'D

IDLE – IDOL
IDOL – IDLE
I'LL – AISLE, ISLE
ILLATION – ELATION
ILLICIT – ELICIT
ILLUDE – ELUDE
ILLUSORY – ELUSORY
IMMERGE – EMERGE
IMMERSED – EMERSED
IMMERSION – EMERSION
IN – INN
INCITE – INSIGHT
INDICT – INDITE
INDITE – INDICT
INN – IN
INSIGHT – INCITE
INSOLE – INSOUL
INSOUL – INSOLE
ION – IRON
IRE – AYAH
IRK – ERK
IRON – ION
ISLE – AISLE, I'LL
ISLET – EYELET
JAM – JAMB, JAMBE
JAMB – JAM, JAMBE
JAMBE – JAM, JAMB
JEAN – GENE
JINKS – JINX
JINN – GIN
JINX – JINKS
KAIN – CAIN, CANE
KARAT – CARAT, CARROT
KARST – CAST, CASTE
KART – CART, CARTE
KASHMIR – CASHMERE
KERB – CURB
KERNEL – COLONEL
KEW – KYU, QUEUE
KEY – QUAY
KNAVE – NAVE
KNEAD – NEED
KNEW – NEW, NU
KNIGHT – NIGHT
KNIGHTLY – NIGHTLY
KNIT – NIT
KNOW – NOH, NO
KNOWS – NOES, NOSE
KOHL – COAL, COLE
KYU – KEW, QUEUE
LACKER – LACQUER
LACQUER – LACKER
LAIN – LANE
LANCE – LAUNCE
LANE – LAIN
LAUD – LORD
LAUNCE – LANCE
LAW – LORE
LAY – LEI, LEY
LAYS – LAZE

LAZE – LAYS
LEAD – LED
LEAF – LIEF
LEAH – LEAR, LEER, LEHR
LEAK – LEEK
LEANT – LENT
LEAR – LEAH, LEER, LEHR
LED – LEAD
LEEK – LEAK
LEER – LEAH, LEAR, LEHR
LEHR – LEAH, LEAR, LEER
LEI – LAY, LEY
LEMAN – LEMON
LEMON – LEMAN
LENT – LEANT
LESSEN – LESSON
LESSON – LESSEN
LEY – LAY, LEI
LIAR – LYRE
LIEF – LEAF
LINCS – LINKS, LYNX
LINKS – LINCS, LYNX
LOAD – LODE
LOAN – LONE
LODE – LOAD
LONE – LOAN
LORD – LAUD
LORE – LAW
LUMBAR – LUMBER
LUMBER – LUMBAR
LYNX – LINCS, LINKS
LYRE - LIAR
MA – MAAR, MAR
MAAR – MA, MAR
MADE – MAID
MAID – MADE
MAIL – MALE
MAIN – MAINE, MANE
MAINE – MAIN, MANE
MAIZE – MAZE
MALE – MAIL
MALL – MAUL
MANE – MAIN, MAINE
MANNA – MANNER, MANOR
MANNER – MANNA, MANOR
MANOR – MANNA, MANNER
MAQUIS – MARQUEE
MAR – MA, MAAR
MARC – MARK, MARQUE
MARE – MAYOR
MARK – MARC, MARQUE
MARQUE – MARC, MARK
MARQUEE – MAQUIS
MAUL – MALL
MAW – MOR, MORE, MOOR
MAYOR – MARE
MAZE – MAIZE
MEAN – MESNE, MIEN
MEAT – MEET, METE
MEDAL – MEDDLE
MEDDLE – MEDAL

MEET – MEAT, METE
MESNE – MIEN, MEAN
METAL – METTLE
METE – MEAT, MEET
METTLE – METAL
MEWS – MUSE
MIEN – MESNE, MEAN
MIGHT – MITE
MINER – MINOR
MINOR – MINER
MITE – MIGHT
MOAN – MOWN
MOAT – MOTE
MOCHA – MOCKER
MOCKER – MOCHA
MOOR – MAW, MOR, MORE
MOOSE – MOUSSE
MOR – MAW, MORE, MOOR
MORE – MAW, MOR, MOOR
MORN – MOURN
MORNING – MOURNING
MOTE – MOAT
MOURN – MORN
MOURNING – MORNING
MOUSSE – MOOSE
MOWN – MOAN
MUSCLE – MUSSEL
MUSE – MEWS
MUSSEL – MUSCLE
NAE – NAY, NEAGH, NEIGH, NEY
NASH – GNASH
NAT – GNAT
NAUGHT – NOUGHT
NAVAL – NAVEL
NAVE – KNAVE
NAVEL – NAVAL
NAY – NAE, NEAGH, NEIGH, NEY
NEAGH – NAE, NAY, NEIGH, NEY
NEED – KNEAD
NEIGH – NAE, NAY, NEAGH, NEY
NEUK – NUKE
NEW – KNEW, NU
NEY – NAE, NAY, NEAGH, NEIGH
NIGH – NYE
NIGHT – KNIGHT
NIGHTLY – KNIGHTLY
NIT – KNIT
NO – KNOW, NOH
NOES – KNOWS, NOSE
NOH – KNOW, NO
NONE – NUN
NOR – GNAW
NOSE – KNOWS, NOES
NOUGHT – NAUGHT
NU – KNEW, NEW
NUKE – NEUK
NUN – NONE
NYE – NIGH
OAR – AWE, O'ER, ORE
O'ER – AWE, OAR, ORE
OFFA – OFFER

OFFER – OFFA
OH – OWE
ORAL – AURAL
ORC – AUK
ORE – AWE, OAR, O'ER
ORLE – ALL, AWL
OSTIA – AUSTERE
OUR – HOUR
OURS – HOURS
OUT – OWT
OVA – OVER
OVER – OVA
OWE – OH
OWT – OUT
PA – PAH, PAR, PARR, PAS
PACKED – PACT
PACT – PACKED
PAH – PA, PAR, PARR, PAS
PAIL – PALE
PAIR – PARE, PEAR
PALATE – PALETTE, PALLET
PALE – PAIL
PALETTE – PALATE, PALLET
PALLET – PALATE, PALETTE
PANDA – PANDER
PANDER – PANDA
PAR – PA, PAH, PARR, PAS
PARE – PEAR, PAIR
PARR – PA, PAH, PAR, PAS
PAS – PA, PAH, PAR, PARR
PAW – POOR, PORE, POUR
PAWKY – PORKY
PAWN – PORN
PEA – PEE
PEACE – PIECE
PEAK – PIQUE
PEAKE – PEEK, PEKE
PEAL – PEEL
PEAR – PARE, PAIR
PEARL – PURL
PEARLER – PURLER
PEDAL – PEDDLE
PEDDLE – PEDAL
PEE – PEA
PEEK – PEAKE, PEKE
PEEL – PEAL
PEKE – PEAKE, PEEK
PER – PURR
PETREL – PETROL
PETROL – PETREL
PHARAOH – FARO
PHASE – FAZE
PHEW – FEU, FEW
PHIZ – FIZZ
PI – PIE, PYE
PIE – PI, PYE
PIECE – PEACE
PILATE – PILOT
PILOT – PILATE
PIQUE – PEAK
PLACE – PLAICE

PLAICE – PLACE
PLAIN – PLANE
PLANE – PLAIN
POLE – POLL
POLL – POLE
POMACE – PUMICE
POMMEL – PUMMEL
POOR – PAW, PORE, POUR
POPULACE – POPULOUS
POPULOUS – POPULACE
PORE – PAW, POOR, POUR
PORKY – PAWKY
PORN – PAWN
POUR – PAW, POOR, PORE
PRAY – PREY
PREY – PRAY
PRINCIPAL – PRINCIPLE
PRINCIPLE – PRINCIPAL
PROFIT – PROPHET
PROPHET – PROFIT
PSALTER – SALTER
PUCKA – PUCKER
PUCKER – PUCKA
PUMICE – POMACE
PUMMEL – POMMEL
PURL – PEARL
PURLER – PEARLER
PURR – PER
PYE – PI, PIE
QUAY – KEY
QUEUE – KEW, KYU
QUIRE – CHOIR
RACK – WRACK
RACKET – RACQUET
RACQUET – RACKET
RAIN – REIGN, REIN
RAINS – REINS
RAISE – RASE
RAP – WRAP
RAPT – WRAPPED
RASE – RAISE
RAW – ROAR
READ – REDE, REED
RECK – WRECK
REDE – READ, REED
REED – READ, REDE
REEK – WREAK
REIGN – RAIN, REIN
REIN – RAIN, REIGN
REINS – RAINS
RENNES – WREN
RETCH – WRETCH
REVERE – REVERS
REVERS – REVERE
RHEUM – ROOM
RHEUMY – ROOMY
RHO – ROW, ROE
RHÔNE – ROAN, RONE
RIGHT – RITE, WRIGHT, WRITE
RING – WRING
RINGER – WRINGER

RITE – RIGHT, WRIGHT, WRITE
ROAM – ROME
ROAN – RHÔNE, RONE
ROAR – RAW
ROE – RHO, ROW
ROLE – ROLL
ROLL – ROLE
ROME – ROAM
RONE – RHÔNE, ROAN
ROOD – RUDE
ROOM – RHEUM
ROOMY – RHEUMY
ROOSE – RUSE
ROOT – ROUTE
RORT – WROUGHT
ROTE – WROTE
ROUGH – RUFF
ROUTE – ROOT
ROW – RHO, ROE
RUDE – ROOD
RUFF – ROUGH
RUNG – WRUNG
RUSE – ROOSE
RYE – WRY
SAIL – SALE
SAIN – SANE, SEINE
SALE – SAIL
SALTER – PSALTER
SANE – SAIN, SEINE
SAUCE – SOURCE
SAUT – SORT, SOUGHT
SAW – SOAR, SORE
SAWN – SORN
SCENE – SEEN
SCENT – CENT, SENT
SCULL – SKULL
SEAL – CEIL, SEEL
SEAM – SEEM
SEAR – CERE, SEER
SEED – CEDE
SEEDER – CEDAR
SEEK – SEIK, SIKH
SEEL – CEIL, SEAL
SEEM – SEAM
SEEN – SCENE
SEER – CERE, SEAR
SEIK – SEEK, SIKH
SEINE – SAIN, SANE
SELL – CELL, SZELL
SELLER – CELLAR
SENSOR – CENSER, CENSOR
SENT – CENT, SCENT
SERF – SURF
SERGE – SURGE
SERIAL – CEREAL
SESSION – CESSION
SEW – SO, SOH, SOW
SEWN – SONE, SOWN
SHAKE – SHEIK
SHEIK – SHAKE
SHIER – SHYER, SHIRE

SHIRE – SHIER, SHYER
SHOE – CHOU, SHOO
SHOO – CHOU, SHOE
SHOOT – SHUTE, CHUTE
SHOT – SHOTT, CHOTT
SHOTT – SHOT, CHOTT
SHUTE – SHOOT, CHUTE
SHYER – SHIER, SHIRE
SIGHT – CITE, SITE
SIGN – SYN
SIGNET – CYGNET
SIKH – SEEK, SEIK
SIOUX – SOU
SITE – CITE, SIGHT
SKULL – SCULL
SKY – SKYE
SKYE – SKY
SLAY – SLEIGH
SLEAVE – SLEEVE
SLEEVE – SLEAVE
SLEIGH – SLAY
SLOE – SLOW
SLOW – SLOE
SO – SEW, SOH, SOW
SOAR – SAW, SORE
SOH – SEW, SO, SOW
SOLE – SOUL
SOME – SUM
SON – SUN, SUNN
SONE – SEWN, SOWN
SONNY – SUNNI, SUNNY
SORE – SAW, SOAR
SORN – SAWN
SORT – SAUT, SOUGHT
SOU – SIOUX
SOUGHT – SAUT, SORT
SOUL – SOLE
SOURCE – SAUCE
SOW – SEW, SO, SOH
SOWN – SEWN, SONE
STAIR – STARE
STAKE – STEAK
STALK – STORK
STARE – STAIR
STEAK – STAKE
STEAL – STEEL
STEEL – STEAL
STOREY – STORY
STORK – STALK
STORY – STOREY
SUITE – SWEET
SUM – SOME
SUN – SON, SUNN
SUNDAE – SUNDAY
SUNDAY – SUNDAE
SUNN – SON, SUN
SUNNI – SONNY, SUNNY
SUNNY – SONNY, SUNNI
SURF – SERF
SURGE – SERGE
SWAT – SWOT

SWEET – SUITE
SWOT – SWAT
SYMBOL – CYMBAL
SYN – SIGN
SZELL – CELL, SELL
TACIT – TASSET
TAI – TAILLE, THAI, TIE
TAIL – TALE
TAILLE – TAI, THAI, TIE
TALE – TAIL
TALK – TORC, TORQUE
TARE – TEAR
TASSET – TACIT
TAUGHT – TAUT, TORT, TORTE
TAUT – TAUGHT, TORT, TORTE
TEA – TEE, TI
TEAM – TEEM
TEAR – TARE
TEE – TEA, TI
TEEM – TEAM
TENNER – TENOR
TENOR – TENNER
TERNE – TURN
THAI – TAI, TAILLE, TIE
THAW – THOR
THEIR – THERE, THEY'RE
THERE – THEIR, THEY'RE
THEY'RE – THEIR, THERE
THOR – THAW
THREW – THROUGH, THRU
THROE – THROW
THRONE – THROWN
THROUGH – THREW, THRU
THROW – THROE
THROWN – THRONE
THRU – THREW, THROUGH
THYME – TIME
TI – TEA, TEE
TIC – TICK
TICK – TIC
TIDE – TIED
TIE – TAI, TAILLE, THAI
TIED – TIDE
TIER – TIRE, TYRE
TIGHTEN – TITAN
TIMBER – TIMBRE
TIMBRE – TIMBER
TIME – THYME
TIRE – TIER, TYRE
TITAN – TIGHTEN
TO – TOO, TWO
TOAD – TOED, TOWED
TOE – TOW
TOED – TOAD, TOWED
TOO – TO, TWO
TOR – TORE
TORC – TALK, TORQUE
TORE – TOR
TORQUE – TALK, TORC
TORT – TAUGHT, TAUT, TORTE
TORTE – TAUGHT, TAUT, TORT

TOW – TOE
TOWED – TOAD, TOED
TROOP – TROUPE
TROUPE – TROOP
TUNA – TUNER
TUNER – TUNA
TURN – TERNE
TWO – TO, TOO
TYRE – TIER, TIRE
UR – ERR
URN – EARN
VAIL – VALE, VEIL
VAIN – VANE, VEIN
VALE – VAIL, VEIL
VANE – VAIN, VEIN
VEIL – VAIL, VALE
VEIN – VAIN, VANE
VELD – FELT, VELDT
VELDT – FELT, VELD
WAE – WAY, WHEY
WAIL – WHALE
WAIN – WANE. WAYNE
WAIST – WASTE
WAIT – WEIGHT
WAIVE – WAVE
WANE – WAIN, WAYNE
WAR – WAUGH, WAW, WORE
WARE – WEAR, WHERE
WARN – WORN
WASTE – WAIST
WATT – WHAT, WOT
WAUGH – WAR, WAW, WORE
WAVE – WAIVE
WAW – WAR, WAUGH, WORE
WAY – WAE, WHEY
WAYNE – WAIN, WANE
WEAK – WEEK
WEAKLY – WEEKLY
WEAR – WARE, WHERE
WEAVE – WE'VE
WE'D – WEED
WEED – WE'D
WEEK – WEAK
WEEKLY – WEAKLY
WEEL – WE'LL, WHEAL, WHEEL
WEIGHT – WAIT
WE'LL – WEEL, WHEAL, WHEEL
WEN – WHEN
WERE – WHIRR
WE'VE – WEAVE
WHALE – WAIL
WHAT – WATT, WOT
WHEAL – WEEL, WE'LL, WHEEL
WHEEL – WEEL. WE'LL, WHEAL
WHEN – WEN
WHERE – WARE, WEAR
WHEY – WAE, WAY
WHICH – WITCH
WHINE – WINE
WHIRR – WERE
WHITE – WIGHT, WITE

WHITHER – WITHER
WHO – HOO
WHOA – WO, WOE
WHOLE – HOLE
WHORE – HAW, HOAR
WIGHT – WHITE, WITE
WINE – WHINE
WITCH – WHICH
WITE – WHITE, WIGHT
WITHER – WHITHER
WO – WHOA, WOE
WOE – WHOA, WO
WORE – WAR, WAUGH, WAW
WORN – WARN
WOT – WATT, WHAT
WRACK – RACK
WRAP – RAP
WRAPPED – RAPT
WREAK – REEK
WRECK – RECK
WREN – RENNES

WRETCH – RETCH
WRIGHT – RIGHT, RITE. WRITE
WRING – RING
WRINGER – RINGER
WRITE – RIGHT, RITE, WRIGHT
WROTE – ROTE
WROUGHT – RORT
WRUNG – RUNG
WRY – RYE
YAW – YORE, YOUR
YAWS – YOURS
YEW – EWE, YOU
YOKE – YOLK
YOLK – YOKE
YORE – YAW, YOUR
YOU – EWE, YEW
YOU'LL – YULE
YOUR – YAW, YORE
YOURS – YAWS
YULE – YOU'LL

TWO-WORD PHRASES

FIRST WORD

ABERDEEN – ANGUS, TERRIER
ABLE – BODIED, RATING, SEAMAN
ABSOLUTE – ALCOHOL, HUMIDITY, JUDGMENT, MAGNITUDE, MAJORITY, MONARCHY, MUSIC, PITCH, TEMPERATURE, THRESHOLD, UNIT, VALUE, ZERO
ABSTRACT – EXPRESSIONISM, NOUN
ACCESS – ROAD, TIME
ACCOMMODATION – ADDRESS, BILL, LADDER, PLATFORM
ACHILLES – HEEL, TENDON
ACID – DROP, RAIN, ROCK, SOIL, TEST, VALUE
ACT – AS, FOR, ON, OUT, UP
ACTION – COMMITTEE, GROUP, PAINTING, POTENTIAL, REPLAY, STATIONS
ACTIVE – CENTRE, LIST, SERVICE, TRANSPORT, VOCABULARY, VOLCANO
ADMIRALTY – BOARD, HOUSE, ISLANDS, MILE, RANGE
ADVANCE – BOOKING, COPY, GUARD, MAN, NOTICE, POLL, RATIO
AEOLIAN – DEPOSITS, HARP, ISLANDS, MODE
AFRICAN – LILY, MAHOGANY, TIME, VIOLET
AGONY – AUNT, COLUMN
AIR – ALERT, BAG, BED, BLADDER, BRAKE, BRIDGE, COMMODORE, CONDITIONING, CORRIDOR, COVER, CURTAIN, CUSHION, CYLINDER, DAM, EMBOLISM, FORCE, GAS, GUN, HARDENING, HOLE, HOSTESS, JACKET, LETTER, MAIL, MARSHAL, MASS, MILE, OFFICER, PLANT, POCKET, POWER, PUMP, RAID, RIFLE, SAC, SCOOP, SCOUT, SHAFT, SHOT, SOCK, SPRAY, SPRING, STATION, TERMINAL, TRAFFIC, TURBINE, VALVE, VICE-MARSHAL

ALL – BLACK, CLEAR, FOURS, HAIL, IN, ONE, OUT, RIGHT, SQUARE, THERE, TOLD
ALPHA – CENTAURI, HELIX, IRON, PARTICLE, PRIVATIVE, RAY, RHYTHM
ALTAR – BOY, CLOTH, -PIECE
AMERICAN – ALOE, CHAMELEON, CHEESE, CLOTH, EAGLE, FOOTBALL, INDIAN, PLAN, REVOLUTION, SAMOA, WAKE
ANCHOR – MAN, PLATE, RING
ANCIENT – GREEK, HISTORY, LIGHTS, MONUMENT
ANGEL – CAKE, DUST, FALLS, FOOD, SHARK
ANGLE – BRACKET, DOZER, IRON, PLATE
ANIMAL – HUSBANDRY, KINGDOM, MAGNETISM, RIGHTS, SPIRITS, STARCH
ANT – BEAR, BIRD, COW, EATER, HEAP, HILL
APPLE – BLIGHT, BOX, BRANDY, BUTTER, GREEN, ISLE, JACK, MAGGOT, POLISHER, SAUCE
ARCTIC – CHAR, CIRCLE, FOX, HARE, OCEAN, TERN, WILLOW
ART – DECO, FORM, NOUVEAU, PAPER
ARTIFICIAL – INSEMINATION, INTELLIGENCE, RESPIRATION
ASH – BLOND. CAN, WEDNESDAY
ATOMIC – AGE, CLOCK, COCKTAIL, ENERGY, HEAT, MASS, NUMBER, PILE, POWER, STRUCTURE, THEORY, VOLUME, WEIGHT
AUTOMATIC – CAMERA, PILOT, REPEAT, TRANSMISSION, TYPESETTING
BABY – BOOM, BUGGY, CARRIAGE, GRAND, SNATCHER, TALK, TOOTH

BACK — BOILER, BURNER, COUNTRY, DOOR, DOWN, END, LIGHT, LIST, MARKER, MATTER, OUT, PASSAGE, PAY, REST, ROOM, SEAT, STRAIGHT, UP, YARD

BAD — BLOOD, FAITH LANDS, NEWS

BALL — BEARING, BOY, COCK, GAME, VALVE

BANANA — OIL, REPUBLIC, SKIN, SPLIT

BANK — ACCEPTANCE, ACCOUNT, ANNUITIES, BILL, CARD, CLERK, DISCOUNT, HOLIDAY, MANAGER, ON, RATE, STATEMENT

BAR — BILLIARDS, CHART, CODE, DIAGRAM, FLY, GIRL, GRAPH, LINE, MITZVAH, SINISTER

BARLEY — SUGAR, WATER, WINE

BARN — DANCE, DOOR, OWL, SWALLOW

BASE — LOAD, METAL, RATE

BASKET — CASE, CHAIR, HILT, MAKER, WEAVE

BATH — BUN, CHAIR, CHAP, CUBE, OLIVER, SALTS, STONE

BATTLE — CRUISER, CRY, FATIGUE, ROYAL

BAY — LEAF, LYNX, RUM, STREET, TREE, WINDOW

BEACH — BALL, BOYS, BUGGY, FLEA, PLUM

BEAR — DOWN, GARDEN, HUG, OFF, OUT, UP, WITH

BEAUTY — QUEEN, SALON, SLEEP, SPOT

BED — JACKET, LINEN

BELL — BRONZE, BUOY, GLASS, HEATHER, JAR, MAGPIE, METAL, MOTH, PULL, PUNCH, PUSH, SHEEP, TENT

BELLY — DANCE, FLOP, LANDING, LAUGH

BERMUDA — GRASS, RIG, SHORTS, TRIANGLE

BEST — BOY, END, GIRL, MAN, SELLER

BICYCLE — CHAIN, CLIP, PUMP

BIG — APPLE, BAND, BANG, BEN, BERTHA, BROTHER, BUSINESS, CHEESE, CHIEF, DEAL, DIPPER, END, SCREEN, SHOT, STICK, TIME, TOP, WHEEL

BINARY — CODE, DIGIT, FISSION, FORM, NOTATION, NUMBER, STAR, WEAPON

BIRD — CALL, CHERRY, DOG, PEPPER, SPIDER, STRIKE, TABLE

BIRTH — CERTIFICATE, CONTROL, RATE

BIRTHDAY — HONOURS, SUIT

BIT — PART, RATE, SLICE

BITTER — APPLE, END, LAKES, ORANGE, PRINCIPLE

BLACK — ART, BEAN, BEAR, BEETLE, BELT, BILE, BODY, BOOK, BOTTOM, BOX, COUNTRY, DEATH, DIAMOND, ECONOMY, EYE, FLY, FOREST, FRIAR, FROST, HILLS, HOLE, ICE, MAGIC, MARIA, MARK, MARKET, MASS, MONK, MOUNTAINS, PANTHER, PEPPER, PRINCE, PUDDING, ROD, ROT, SEA, SHEEP, SPOT, SWAN, TIE, TREACLE, VELVET, WATCH, WIDOW

BLANK — CARTRIDGE, CHEQUE, ENDORSEMENT, VERSE

BLANKET — BATH, FINISH, STITCH

BLIND — ALLEY, DATE, FREDDIE, GUT, SNAKE, SPOT, STAGGERS, STAMPING

BLISTER — BEETLE, COPPER, PACK, RUST

BLOCK — DIAGRAM, IN, LETTER, OUT, PRINTING, RELEASE, SAMPLING, TIN, VOTE

BLOOD — BANK, BATH, BROTHER, CELL, COUNT, DONOR, FEUD, FLUKE, GROUP, HEAT, MONEY, ORANGE, POISONING, PRESSURE, PUDDING, RED, RELATION, SPORT, TEST, TYPE, VESSEL

BLUE — BABY, BAG, BILLY, BLOOD, CHEESE, CHIP, DEVILS, ENSIGN, FUNK, GUM, JAY, MOON, MOUNTAINS, MURDER, NILE, PENCIL, PETER, RIBAND, RIBBON, VEIN

BOARDING — HOUSE, OUT, SCHOOL

BOAT — DECK, DRILL, NECK, PEOPLE, RACE, TRAIN

BOBBY — CALF, PIN, SOCKS

BODY — BLOW, BUILDING, CAVITY, CORPORATE, IMAGE, LANGUAGE, POPPING, SHOP, SNATCHER, STOCKING, WARMER

BOG — ASPHODEL, COTTON, DEAL, DOWN, IN, MOSS, MYRTLE, OAK, ORCHID, RUSH, STANDARD

BON — MOT, TON, VIVANT, VOYAGE

BONE — ASH, CHINA, IDLE, MEAL, OIL, UP

BOOBY — HATCH, PRIZE, TRAP

BOOK — CLUB, END, IN, INTO, OUT, SCORPION, TOKEN, UP

BOTTLE — GOURD, GREEN, OUT, PARTY, TREE, UP

BOTTOM — DRAWER, END, HOUSE, LINE, OUT

BOW — LEGS, OUT, TIE, WINDOW

BOWLING — ALLEY, CREASE, GREEN

BOX — CAMERA, COAT, ELDER, GIRDER, JELLYFISH, NUMBER, OFFICE, PLEAT, SEAT, SPANNER, SPRING

BRAIN — CORAL, DEATH, DRAIN, FEVER, STEM, WAVE

BRAKE — BAND, DRUM, FLUID, HORSEPOWER, LIGHT, LINING, PARACHUTE, SHOE, VAN

BRAND — IMAGE, LEADER, NAME

BRANDY — BOTTLE, BUTTER, SNAP

BRASS — BAND, FARTHING, HAT, NECK, RUBBING, TACKS

BREAK — DANCE, DOWN, EVEN, IN, INTO, OFF, OUT, THROUGH, UP, WITH

BRING — ABOUT, DOWN, FORWARD, IN, OFF, ON, OUT, OVER, ROUND, TO, UP

BRISTOL — BOARD, CHANNEL, FASHION

BROAD — ARROW, BEAN, CHURCH, GAUGE, JUMP, SEAL

BROWN — BEAR, BOMBER, FAT, OWL, PAPER, RICE, SHIRT, SNAKE, STUDY, SUGAR

BRUSSELS — CARPET, LACE, SPROUT

BUBBLE — BATH, CAR, CHAMBER, FLOAT, GUM, MEMORY, PACK

BUCK — FEVER, RABBIT, UP

BUILDING — BLOCK, LINE, PAPER, SOCIETY

BULL — MASTIFF, NOSE, RUN, SESSION, SNAKE, TERRIER, TONGUE, TROUT

BURNT — ALMOND, OFFERING, SHALE, SIENNA, UMBER

BUS — BOY, LANE, SHELTER, STOP

BUTTER — BEAN, MUSLIN, UP

BUZZ — BOMB, OFF, SAW, WORD

CABBAGE — BUG, LETTUCE, MOTH, PALM, PALMETTO, ROSE, TREE, WHITE

CABIN — BOY, CLASS, CRUISER, FEVER

CABLE — CAR, RAILWAY, RELEASE, STITCH, TELEVISION

CALL — ALARM, BOX, DOWN, FORTH, GIRL, IN, LOAN, MONEY, NUMBER, OFF, OUT, RATE, SIGN, SLIP, UP

CAMP — DAVID, FOLLOWER, MEETING, OVEN, SITE

CANARY — CREEPER, GRASS, ISLANDS, SEED, YELLOW

CANTERBURY — BELL, LAMB, PILGRIMS

CAPE — BUFFALO, CART, COD, COLONY, COLOURED, DOCTOR, DUTCH, FLATS, GOOSEBERRY, HORN, JASMINE, PENINSULA, PIGEON, PRIMROSE, PROVINCE, SPARROW, TOWN, VERDE, YORK

CAPITAL — ACCOUNT, ALLOWANCE, ASSETS, EXPENDITURE, GAIN, GOODS, LEVY, MARKET, PUNISHMENT, SHIP, STOCK, SURPLUS

CARD — FILE, INDEX, PUNCH, READER, VOTE

CARDINAL — BEETLE, FLOWER, NUMBER, POINTS, SPIDER, VIRTUES

CARPET — BEETLE, KNIGHT, MOTH, PLOT, SHARK, SLIPPER, SNAKE, TILES

CARRIAGE — BOLT, CLOCK, DOG, LINE, TRADE

CARRIER — BAG, PIGEON, WAVE

CARRY — AWAY, BACK, FORWARD, OFF, ON, OUT, OVER, THROUGH

CARTRIDGE — BELT, CLIP, PAPER, PEN

CASH — CROP, DESK, DISCOUNT, DISPENSER, FLOW, IN, LIMIT, RATIO, REGISTER, UP

CAST — ABOUT, BACK, DOWN, IRON, ON, OUT, STEEL, UP

CAT — BURGLAR, DOOR, HOLE, LITTER, RIG, SCANNER

CATCH — BASIN, CROP, ON, OUT, PHRASE, PIT, POINTS, UP

CAULIFLOWER — CHEESE, EAR

CENTRE — BIT, FORWARD, HALF, PUNCH, SPREAD, THREE-QUARTER

CHAIN — DRIVE, GANG, GRATE, LETTER, LIGHTNING, MAIL, PRINTER, REACTION, RULE, SAW, SHOT, STITCH, STORE

CHAMBER — COUNSEL, MUSIC, ORCHESTRA, ORGAN, POT

CHARGE — ACCOUNT, DENSITY, HAND, NURSE, SHEET

CHEESE — CUTTER, MITE, SKIPPER, STRAW

CHICKEN — BREAST, FEED, LOUSE, OUT, WIRE

CHILD — ABUSE, BENEFIT, CARE, GUIDANCE, LABOUR, MINDER

CHIMNEY — BREAST, CORNER, STACK, SWALLOW, SWEEP, SWIFT

CHINA — ASTER, BARK, CLAY, INK, ROSE, SEA, TREE

CHINESE — BLOCK, CABBAGE, CHEQUERS, CHIPPENDALE, EMPIRE, GOOSEBERRY, INK, LANTERN, LEAVES, PUZZLE, WALL, WAX, WHITE, WINDLASS

CHIP — BASKET, HEATER, IN, LOG, PAN, SHOT

CHRISTMAS — BEETLE, BOX, CACTUS, CARD, DISEASE, EVE, ISLAND, PUDDING, ROSE, STOCKING, TREE

CIGARETTE — CARD, END, HOLDER, LIGHTER, PAPER

CIRCUIT — BINDING, BOARD, BREAKER, JUDGE, RIDER, TRAINING

CITY — BLUES, COMPANY, DESK, EDITOR, FATHER, HALL, MANAGER, PLANNING, SLICKER

CIVIL — DEFENCE, DISOBEDIENCE, ENGINEER, LAW, LIBERTY, LIST, MARRIAGE, RIGHTS, SERVANT, SERVICE, WAR

CLAW — BACK, HAMMER, HATCHET, OFF, SETTING

CLOCK — GOLF, OFF, ON, UP

CLOSE — CALL, COMPANY, DOWN, HARMONY, IN, OUT, PUNCTUATION, QUARTERS, SEASON, SHAVE, WITH

CLOSED — BOOK, CHAIN, CIRCUIT, CORPORATION, GAME, PRIMARY, SCHOLARSHIP, SENTENCE, SET, SHOP

CLOTHES — MOTH, PEG, POLE, PROP

CLUB — FOOT, HAND, MOSS, ROOT, SANDWICH

COAL — GAS, HEAVER, HOLE, MEASURES, OIL, POT, SACK, SCUTTLE, TAR, TIT

COCONUT — BUTTER, ICE, MATTING, OIL, PALM, SHY

COFFEE — BAG, BAR, CUP, HOUSE, MILL, MORNING, NUT, SHOP, TABLE, TREE

COLD — CALL, CHISEL, CREAM, CUTS, DUCK, FEET, FRAME, FRONT, SHOULDER, SNAP, SORE, STORAGE, SWEAT, TURKEY, WAR, WARRIOR, WAVE, WORK

COLLECTIVE — AGREEMENT, BARGAINING, FARM, FRUIT, NOUN, OWNERSHIP, SECURITY, UNCONSCIOUS

COLORADO — BEETLE, DESERT, SPRINGS

COLOUR — BAR, CODE, CONTRAST, FILTER, GUARD, INDEX, LINE, PHASE, SCHEME, SERGEANT, SUPPLEMENT, TEMPERATURE

COME — ABOUT, ACROSS, ALONG, AT, AWAY, BETWEEN, BY, FORWARD, IN, INTO, OF, OFF, OUT, OVER, ROUND, THROUGH, TO, UP, UPON

COMIC — OPERA, STRIP

COMMAND — GUIDANCE, MODULE, PAPER, PERFORMANCE, POST

COMMERCIAL — ART, BANK, COLLEGE, PAPER, TRAVELLER, VEHICLE

COMMON — COLD, DENOMINATOR, ENTRANCE, ERA, FACTOR, FEE, FRACTION, GOOD, GROUND, KNOWLEDGE, LAW, MARKET, NOUN, ROOM, SENSE, STOCK, TIME

COMMUNITY — CARE, CENTRE, CHEST, SERVICE, SINGING

COMPOUND — EYE, FLOWER, FRACTION, FRACTURE, INTEREST, LEAF, NUMBER, SENTENCE, TIME

CON — AMORE, BRIO, DOLORE, ESPRESSIONE, FUOCO, MAN, MOTO, ROD, SORDINO, SPIRITO, TRICK

CONTINENTAL — BREAKFAST, CLIMATE, DIVIDE, DRIFT, QUILT, SHELF, SYSTEM

CORAL — FERN, REEF, SEA, SNAKE, TREE

CORN — BORER, BREAD, BUNTING, DOLLY, EXCHANGE, FACTOR, LAWS, LILY, MARIGOLD, MEAL, OIL, PONE, POPPY, ROSE, ROW, SALAD, SHOCK, SHUCK, SILK, WHISKY

CORONA — AUSTRALIS, BOREALIS, DISCHARGE

COTTAGE — CHEESE, FLAT, HOSPITAL, INDUSTRY, LOAF, PIANO, PIE

COTTON — BELT, BUSH, CAKE, CANDY, FLANNEL, GRASS, ON, PICKER, SEDGE, STAINER, TO, WASTE, WOOL

COUGH — DROP, MIXTURE, UP

COUNTRY — CLUB, CODE, COUSIN, DANCE, HOUSE, MUSIC, SEAT

COURT — CARD, CIRCULAR, DRESS, MARTIAL, ROLL, SHOE

COVER — CROP, GIRL, NOTE, POINT, VERSION

CRASH — BARRIER, DIVE, HELMET, OUT, PAD

CREAM — CHEESE, CRACKER, PUFF, SAUCE, SODA, TEA

CREDIT — ACCOUNT, CARD, LINE, RATING, SQUEEZE, STANDING

CROCODILE — BIRD, CLIP, RIVER, TEARS
CRYSTAL — BALL, GAZING, MICROPHONE, PALACE, PICK-UP, SET, VIOLET
CUCKOO — BEE, CLOCK, SHRIKE, SPIT
CURTAIN — CALL, LECTURE, SPEECH, WALL
CUSTARD — APPLE, PIE, POWDER
CUT — ACROSS, ALONG, DOWN, GLASS, IN, OFF, OUT, STRING, UP
CUTTY — GRASS, SARK, STOOL
DANISH — BLUE, LOAF, PASTRY
DARK — AGES, CONTINENT, GLASSES, HORSE, LANTERN, REACTION, STAR
DAVY — JONES, LAMP
DAY — BED, LILY, NAME, NURSERY, RELEASE, RETURN, ROOM, SCHOOL, SHIFT, TRIP
DE — FACTO, FIDE, LUXE, PROFUNDIS, RIGUEUR, TROP
DEAD — BEAT, CENTRE, DUCK, END, FINISH, HAND, HEART, HEAT, LETTER, LOSS, MARCH, SEA, SET, WEIGHT
DEATH — ADDER, CAP, CELL, CERTIFICATE, DUTY, GRANT, KNELL, MASK, PENALTY, RATE, RATTLE, RAY, ROW, SEAT, VALLEY, WARRANT, WISH
DECIMAL — CLASSIFICATION, CURRENCY, FRACTION, PLACE, POINT, SYSTEM
DECK — CHAIR, HAND, OVER, TENNIS
DENTAL — CLINIC, FLOSS, HYGIENE, HYGIENIST, NURSE, PLAQUE, SURGEON
DESERT — BOOTS, COOLER, ISLAND, LYNX, OAK, PEA, RAT, SOIL
DIAMOND — ANNIVERSARY, BIRD, JUBILEE, POINT, SNAKE, WEDDING, WILLOW
DINNER — JACKET, LADY, SERVICE
DIPLOMATIC — BAG, CORPS, IMMUNITY, SERVICE
DIRECT — ACCESS, ACTION, EVIDENCE, LABOUR, METHOD, OBJECT, QUESTION, SPEECH
DISC — BRAKE, FLOWER, HARROW, JOCKEY, PLOUGH, WHEEL
DISPATCH — BOX, CASE, RIDER
DOG — BISCUIT, BOX, COLLAR, DAYS, FENNEL, HANDLER, LATIN, PADDLE, ROSE, STAR, TAG, VIOLET
DONKEY — DERBY, ENGINE, JACKET, VOTE
DOUBLE — AGENT, BACK, BAR, BASS, BASSOON, BILL, BOND, CHIN, CREAM, CROSS, DUTCH, ENTENDRE, ENTRY, EXPOSURE, FAULT, FIRST, GLAZING, GLOUCESTER, KNIT, KNITTING, NEGATION, NEGATIVE, PNEUMONIA, STANDARD, TAKE, TALK, TIME, UP
DOWN — PAYMENT, TIME, UNDER
DRAWING — BOARD, CARD, PIN, ROOM
DRESS — CIRCLE, COAT, DOWN, PARADE, REHEARSAL, SHIELD, SHIRT, SUIT, UNIFORM, UP
DRESSING — CASE, GOWN, ROOM, STATION, TABLE
DROP — AWAY, CANNON, CURTAIN, FORGE, GOAL, HAMMER, KICK, LEAF, OFF, SCONE, SHOT, TANK
DRUM — BRAKE, MAJOR, MAJORETTE, OUT, UP
DRY — BATTERY, CELL, DISTILLATION, DOCK, ICE, MARTINI, MEASURE, NURSE, OUT, ROT, RUN, UP
DUST — BOWL, COAT, COVER, DEVIL, DOWN, JACKET, SHOT, STORM
DUTCH — AUCTION, BARN, CAP, CHEESE, COURAGE, DOLL, DOOR, ELM, MEDICINE, OVEN, TREAT, UNCLE
EAR — LOBE, PIERCING, SHELL, TRUMPET

EARLY — BIRD, CLOSING, WARNING
EARTH — CLOSET, MOTHER, PILLAR, RETURN, SCIENCE, UP, WAX
EASTER — CACTUS, EGG, ISLAND, LILY
EASY — CHAIR, GAME, MEAT, MONEY, STREET
EGG — CUP, ROLL, SLICE, SPOON, TIMER, TOOTH, WHITE
ELECTRIC — BLANKET, BLUE, CHAIR, CHARGE, CONSTANT, CURRENT, EEL, EYE, FIELD, FIRE, FURNACE, GUITAR, HARE, NEEDLE, ORGAN, POTENTIAL, RAY, SHOCK, STORM
ELEPHANT — BIRD, GRASS, SEAL, SHREW
EVENING — CLASS, DRESS, PRIMROSE, STAR
EX — CATHEDRA, DIVIDEND, GRATIA, LIBRIS, OFFICIO
EYE — CONTACT, DOG, RHYME, SHADOW, SOCKET, SPLICE
FACE — CLOTH, OUT, PACK, POWDER, VALUE
FAIR — COPY, GAME, ISLE, PLAY, RENT, SEX
FAIRY — CYCLE, GODMOTHER, LIGHTS, PENGUIN, RING, SHRIMP, SWALLOW, TALE
FALL — ABOUT, AMONG, AWAY, BACK, BEHIND, DOWN, FOR, GUY, IN, OFF, ON, OVER, THROUGH, TO
FALSE — ALARM, COLOURS, DAWN, IMPRISONMENT, PRETENCES, STEP, TEETH
FAMILY — ALLOWANCE, BENEFIT, BIBLE, CIRCLE, DOCTOR, MAN, NAME, PLANNING, SKELETON, TREE
FAN — BELT, DANCE, HEATER, MAIL, VAULTING
FANCY — DRESS, GOODS, MAN, WOMAN
FAST — FOOD, LANE, MOTION, TALK
FATHER — CHRISTMAS, CONFESSOR, TIME
FIELD — ARMY, ARTILLERY, BATTERY, CENTRE, DAY, EMISSION, EVENT, GLASSES, HOSPITAL, MARSHAL, OFFICER, SPORTS, STUDY, TRIP, WORK
FIGURE — ON, OUT, SKATING
FILM — LIBRARY, PACK, SET, STAR, STRIP
FILTER — BED, OUT, PAPER, PRESS, PUMP, TIP
FINGER — BOWL, PAINTING, POST, WAVE
FIRE — ALARM, ANT, AWAY, BRIGADE, CLAY, CONTROL, DEPARTMENT, DOOR, DRILL, ENGINE, ESCAPE, HYDRANT, INSURANCE, IRONS, RAISER, SCREEN, SHIP, STATION, WALKING, WALL, WATCHER
FIRING — LINE, ORDER, PARTY, PIN, SQUAD
FIRST — AID, BASE, CLASS, FLOOR, FRUITS, LADY, LANGUAGE, LIEUTENANT, LIGHT, MATE, NAME, NIGHT, OFFENDER, OFFICER, PERSON, POST, PRINCIPLE, READING, REFUSAL, SCHOOL, WATER
FIVE — HUNDRED, KS, NATIONS, STONES, TOWNS
FLAKE — OUT, WHITE
FLASH — BURN, CARD, ELIMINATOR, FLOOD, GUN, PHOTOGRAPHY, PHOTOLYSIS, POINT, SET, SMELTING
FLAT — CAP, KNOT, RACING, SPIN, TUNING
FLIGHT — ARROW, DECK, ENGINEER, FEATHER, FORMATION, LIEUTENANT, LINE, PATH, PLAN, RECORDER, SERGEANT, SIMULATOR, STRIP, SURGEON
FLYING — BOAT, BOMB, BRIDGE, BUTTRESS, CIRCUS, COLOURS, DOCTOR, DUTCHMAN, FISH, FOX, FROG, JIB, LEMUR, LIZARD, MARE, OFFICER, PICKET, SAUCER, SQUAD, SQUIRREL, START, WING
FOLK — DANCE, MEDICINE, MEMORY, MUSIC, SINGER, SONG, TALE, WEAVE
FOOD — ADDITIVE, CHAIN, POISONING, PROCESSOR

FOOT — BRAKE, FAULT, ROT, RULE, SOLDIER

FOREIGN — AFFAIRS, AID, BILL, CORRESPONDENT, EXCHANGE, LEGION, MINISTER, MISSION, OFFICE, SERVICE

FOUL — PLAY, SHOT, UP

FOURTH — DIMENSION, ESTATE, INTERNATIONAL, REPUBLIC, WORLD

FREE — AGENT, ASSOCIATION, CHURCH, ELECTRON, ENERGY, ENTERPRISE, FALL, FLIGHT, FORM, GIFT, HAND, HOUSE, KICK, LOVE, SPACE, SPEECH, STATE, THOUGHT, THROW, TRADE, VERSE, WILL, ZONE

FRENCH — ACADEMY, BEAN, BREAD, CHALK, CRICKET, CUFF, CURVE, DOORS, DRESSING, HORN, KISS, KNICKERS, KNOT, LEAVE, LETTER, MUSTARD, PLEAT, POLISH, SEAM, STICK, TOAST, WINDOWS

FRONT — BENCH, DOOR, LINE, MAN, MATTER

FRUIT — BAT, BODY, COCKTAIL, CUP, FLY, KNIFE, MACHINE, SALAD, SUGAR, TREE

FULL — BLOOD, BOARD, DRESS, HOUSE, MOON, NELSON, PITCH, STOP, TIME, TOSS

GALLEY — PROOF, SLAVE

GALLOWS — BIRD, HUMOUR, TREE

GAME — BIRD, CHIPS, FISH, FOWL, LAWS, PARK, POINT, THEORY, WARDEN

GARDEN — CENTRE, CITY, CRESS, FLAT, FRAME, PARTY, SNAIL, SUBURB, WARBLER

GAS — BURNER, CHAMBER, CONSTANT, ENGINE, EQUATION, FIXTURE, GANGRENE, LAWS, LIGHTER, MAIN, MANTLE, MASK, METER, OIL, OVEN, POKER, RING, STATION, TURBINE

GENERAL — ANAESTHETIC, ASSEMBLY, DELIVERY, ELECTION, HOSPITAL, PRACTITIONER, STAFF, STRIKE, SYNOD, WILL

GIN — PALACE, RUMMY, SLING

GINGER — ALE, BEER, GROUP, SNAP, UP, WINE

GIRL — FRIDAY, GUIDE, SCOUT

GIVE — AWAY, IN, OFF, ONTO, OUT, OVER, UP

GLAD — EYE, HAND, RAGS

GLOVE — BOX, COMPARTMENT, PUPPET

GOLD — BASIS, BEETLE, BRICK, CERTIFICATE, COAST, DUST, FOIL, LEAF, MEDAL, MINE, NOTE, PLATE, POINT, RECORD, RESERVE, RUSH, STANDARD, STICK

GOLDEN — AGE, ASTER, CALF, CHAIN, DELICIOUS, EAGLE, FLEECE, GATE, GOOSE, HANDSHAKE, NUMBER, OLDIE, RETRIEVER, RULE, SECTION, SYRUP

GOLF — BALL, CLUB, COURSE, LINKS

GOOD — AFTERNOON, DAY, EVENING, FRIDAY, MORNING, NIGHT, SAMARITAN, SORT, TURN

GOOSE — BARNACLE, FLESH, STEP

GRAND — CANARY, CANYON, DUCHESS, DUCHY, DUKE, FINAL, GUIGNOL, JURY, LARCENY, MAL, MARNIER, MASTER, NATIONAL, OPERA, PIANO, PRIX, SEIGNEUR, SIÈCLE, SLAM, TOUR

GRANNY — BOND, FLAT, KNOT, SMITH

GRASS — BOX, CLOTH, COURT, HOCKEY, MOTH, ROOTS, SNAKE, TREE, WIDOW

GRAVY — BOAT, TRAIN

GREASE — CUP, GUN, MONKEY

GREAT — AUK, BEAR, BRITAIN, DANE, DIVIDE, LAKES, OUSE, PLAINS, SEAL, TIT, TREK, WAR,

GREEN — BEAN, BELT, BERET, CARD, DRAGON, FINGERS, LIGHT, MONKEY, MOULD, PAPER, PEPPER, PLOVER, THUMB, TURTLE, WOODPECKER

GREGORIAN — CALENDAR, CHANT, TELESCOPE, TONE

GREY — AREA, EMINENCE, FOX, FRIAR, MARKET, MATTER, SQUIRREL, WARBLER, WHALE, WOLF

GROUND — CONTROL, COVER, ENGINEER, FLOOR, GLASS, ICE, IVY, PLAN, PLATE, PROVISIONS, RENT, RULE, SWELL

GROW — BAG, INTO, ON, UP

GUIDE — DOG, ROPE

HAIR — DRYER, FOLLICLE, GEL, LACQUER, RESTORER, SHIRT, SLIDE, SPRAY, TRIGGER

HAPPY — EVENT, HOUR, MEDIUM, RELEASE

HARD — CASH, CHEESE, COPY, CORE, COURT, DISK, FEELING, HAT, HITTER, LABOUR, LINES, ROCK, SELL, SHOULDER, STANDING

HARVEST — HOME, MITE, MOON, MOUSE

HAT — STAND, TRICK

HATCHET — JOB, MAN

HEALTH — CENTRE, FOOD, SALTS, VISITOR

HEN — HARRIER, PARTY, RUN

HIGH — ALTAR, CHURCH, COMEDY, COMMAND, COMMISSIONER, COUNTRY, COURT, DAY, EXPLOSIVE, FASHION, FIDELITY, GERMAN, HAT, HOLIDAYS, JINKS, JUMP, POINT, PRIEST, SCHOOL, SEAS, SEASON, SOCIETY, SPOT, STREET, TABLE, TEA, TECH, TECHNOLOGY, TIDE, TIME, TREASON, WATER, WIRE, WYCOMBE

HIGHLAND — CATTLE, DRESS, FLING, REGION

HIP — BATH, FLASK, JOINT, POCKET

HIT — LIST, MAN, OFF, ON, OUT, PARADE

HOLD — BACK, DOWN, FORTH, IN, OFF, ON, OUT, OVER, TOGETHER, WITH

HOLY — BIBLE, CITY, COMMUNION, DAY, FATHER, GHOST, GRAIL, ISLAND, JOE, LAND, MARY, OFFICE, ORDERS, PLACE, ROLLER, ROOD, SCRIPTURE, SEE, SEPULCHRE, SPIRIT, WAR, WATER, WEEK, WRIT

HOME — AID, COUNTIES, ECONOMICS, FARM, GROUND, GUARD, HELP, LOAN, OFFICE, PLATE, RANGE, RULE, RUN, SECRETARY, STRAIGHT, TEACHER, TRUTH, UNIT

HORSE — AROUND, BEAN, BRASS, CHESTNUT, GUARDS, LAUGH, MACKEREL, MARINE, MUSHROOM, NETTLE, OPERA, PISTOL, SENSE, TRADING

HOT — AIR, DOG, LINE, METAL, MONEY, PEPPER, POTATO, ROD, SEAT, SPOT, SPRING, STUFF, UP, ZONE

HOUSE — ARREST, GUEST, LIGHTS, MARTIN, MOTH, ORGAN, PARTY, PHYSICIAN, PLANT, SPARROW, SPIDER

HUMAN — BEING, CAPITAL, INTEREST, NATURE, RESOURCES, RIGHTS

HURRICANE — DECK, LAMP

ICE — AGE, AXE, BAG, BLOCK, CREAM, FISH, HOCKEY, HOUSE, LOLLY, MACHINE, MAN, PACK, PICK, PLANT, POINT, SHEET, SHELF, SHOW, SKATE, STATION, WATER, YACHT

ILL — FEELING, HUMOUR, TEMPER, WILL

IN — ABSENTIA, AETERNUM, CAMERA, ESSE, EXTENSO, EXTREMIS, MEMORIAM, NOMINE, PERPETUUM, PERSONAM, RE, REM, SITU, TOTO, UTERO, VACUO, VITRO, VIVO

INDIA — PAPER, PRINT, RUBBER
INDIAN — CLUB, EMPIRE, FILE, HEMP, INK, MALLOW,
  MILLET, MUTINY, OCEAN, RED, RESERVE, ROPE-TRICK,
  SUMMER
INNER — CITY, EAR, HEBRIDES, LIGHT, MAN,
  MONGOLIA, TUBE
INSIDE — FORWARD, JOB, LANE, TRACK
IRISH — COFFEE, MOSS, POTATO, REPUBLIC, SEA,
  SETTER, STEW, TERRIER, WHISKEY, WOLFHOUND
IRON — AGE, CHANCELLOR, CROSS, CURTAIN, FILINGS,
  GUARD, HAND, HORSE, LUNG, MAIDEN, MAN, OUT,
  PYRITES, RATIONS
JACK — FROST, IN, PLANE, RABBIT, ROBINSON,
  RUSSELL, TAR, UP
KICK — ABOUT, IN, OFF, OUT, PLEAT, TURN, UP,
  UPSTAIRS
KIDNEY — BEAN, MACHINE, STONE, VETCH
KNIFE — EDGE, GRINDER, PLEAT, SWITCH
LADY — BOUNTIFUL, CHAPEL, DAY, FERN, MAYORESS,
  MUCK, ORCHID
LAND — AGENT, BANK, BRIDGE, CRAB, FORCES, GIRL,
  GRANT, LINE, MINE, OFFICE, RAIL, REFORM, TAX, UP,
  WITH
LAST — JUDGMENT, NAME, OUT, POST, QUARTER,
  RITES, STRAW, SUPPER, THING
LATIN — AMERICA, CROSS, QUARTER, SQUARE
LAY — ASIDE, AWAY, BROTHER, DAYS, DOWN, FIGURE,
  IN, INTO, OFF, ON, OUT, OVER, READER, TO, UP
LEADING — AIRCRAFTMAN, ARTICLE, DOG, EDGE,
  LIGHT, MAN, NOTE, QUESTION, REINS
LEAVE — BEHIND, OFF, OUT
LEFT — BANK, WING
LEMON — BALM, CHEESE, DROP, FISH, GERANIUM,
  GRASS, SOLE, SQUASH, SQUEEZER, VERBENA
LETTER — BOMB, BOX, CARD
LIBERTY — BODICE, CAP, HALL, HORSE, ISLAND, SHIP
LIE — DETECTOR, DOWN, IN, TO
LIFE — ASSURANCE, BELT, BUOY, CYCLE,
  EXPECTANCY, FORM, GUARDS, HISTORY, INSURANCE,
  INTEREST, JACKET, PEER, PRESERVER, RAFT,
  SCIENCE, SPAN, STYLE
LIGHT — BULB, FACE, FLYWEIGHT, HEAVYWEIGHT,
  HORSE, INTO, METER, MIDDLEWEIGHT, MUSIC, OPERA,
  OUT, SHOW, UP, WELTERWEIGHT, YEAR
LIVER — FLUKE, SALTS, SAUSAGE
LIVING — DEATH, FOSSIL, PICTURE, ROOM, WAGE
LOBSTER — MOTH, NEWBURG, POT, THERMIDOR
LOCAL — ANAESTHETIC, AUTHORITY, COLOUR,
  GOVERNMENT, TIME
LONE — HAND, WOLF
LONG — ARM, BEACH, FACE, HAUL, HOP, ISLAND,
  JENNY, JOHNS, JUMP, PARLIAMENT, SHOT, SUIT, TOM,
  VACATION, WEEKEND
LOOK — AFTER, BACK, DOWN, ON, OVER, THROUGH,
  UP
LOOSE — CHANGE, COVER, END
LORD — ADVOCATE, CHAMBERLAIN, CHANCELLOR,
  LIEUTENANT, MAYOR, MUCK, PROTECTOR, PROVOST
LOUNGE — LIZARD, SUIT
LOVE — AFFAIR, APPLE, CHILD, FEAST, GAME, KNOT,
  LETTER, LIFE, MATCH, NEST, POTION, SEAT, SET

LOW — CHURCH, COMEDY, COUNTRIES, FREQUENCY,
  PROFILE, TECH, TECHNOLOGY, TIDE
LUNAR — CAUSTIC, ECLIPSE, MODULE, MONTH, YEAR
LUNCHEON — CLUB, MEAT, VOUCHER
MACHINE — BOLT, GUN, HEAD, SHOP, TOOL
MACKEREL — BREEZE, SHARK, SKY
MAGIC — CARPET, EYE, LANTERN, MUSHROOM,
  NUMBER, SQUARE
MAGNETIC — CIRCUIT, COMPASS, CONSTANT, DISK,
  EQUATOR, FIELD, FLUX, INDUCTION, INK, LENS,
  MOMENT, NEEDLE, NORTH, PICK-UP, POLE, STORM,
  TAPE
MAIDEN — NAME, OVER, VOYAGE
MAIL — DROP, ORDER
MAKE — AFTER, AWAY, BELIEVE, FOR, OF, OFF, OUT,
  OVER, WITH
MALT — EXTRACT, LIQUOR, WHISKY
MANDARIN — CHINESE, COLLAR, DUCK
MARCH — BROWN, HARE, PAST
MARKET — GARDEN, GARDENING, ORDER, PRICE,
  RENT, RESEARCH, SHARE, TOWN, VALUE
MARRIAGE — BUREAU, GUIDANCE
MARSH — ELDER, FERN, FEVER, GAS, HARRIER, HAWK,
  HEN, MALLOW, MARIGOLD, ORCHID, TIT
MASTER — BUILDER, CYLINDER, KEY, RACE,
  SERGEANT
MATINÉE — COAT, IDOL
MAUNDY — MONEY, THURSDAY
MAY — APPLE, BEETLE, BLOBS, BLOSSOM, DAY,
  QUEEN, TREE
MECHANICAL — ADVANTAGE, DRAWING,
  ENGINEERING, INSTRUMENT
MEDICAL — CERTIFICATE, EXAMINATION, EXAMINER,
  JURISPRUDENCE
MEDICINE — BALL, CHEST, LODGE, MAN
MELBA — SAUCE, TOAST
MEMORY — BANK, MAPPING, SPAN, TRACE
MENTAL — AGE, BLOCK, CRUELTY, DISORDER,
  HANDICAP
MERCHANT — BANK, NAVY, PRINCE
MERCY — FLIGHT, KILLING, SEAT
MESS — ABOUT, HALL, JACKET, KIT
MICHAELMAS — DAISY, TERM
MICKEY — FINN, MOUSE
MIDDLE — AGE, AGES, C, CLASS, EAR, EAST,
  MANAGEMENT, NAME, SCHOOL, TEMPLE
MIDNIGHT — BLUE, SUN
MIDSUMMER — DAY, MADNESS
MILITARY — ACADEMY, HONOURS, LAW, ORCHID,
  PACE, POLICE
MILK — BAR, CHOCOLATE, FEVER, FLOAT, LEG,
  PUDDING, PUNCH, ROUND, RUN, SHAKE, STOUT,
  TOOTH
MINT — BUSH, JULEP, SAUCE
MINUTE — GUN, HAND, MARK, STEAK
MIRROR — CANON, CARP, FINISH, IMAGE, LENS,
  SYMMETRY, WRITING
MITRE — BLOCK, BOX, GEAR, JOINT, SQUARE
MIXED — BAG, BLESSING, DOUBLES, ECONOMY,
  FARMING, GRILL, MARRIAGE, METAPHOR
MONEY — MARKET, ORDER, SPIDER, SUPPLY

MONKEY — BREAD, BUSINESS, CLIMB, FLOWER, JACKET, NUT, ORCHID, PUZZLE, SUIT, TRICKS, WRENCH

MORNING — COAT, DRESS, SICKNESS, STAR, TEA, WATCH

MOSQUITO — BOAT, HAWK, NET

MOSS — AGATE, LAYER, PINK, ROSE, STITCH

MOTHER — COUNTRY, GOOSE, HUBBARD, LODE, SHIP, SHIPTON, SUPERIOR, TONGUE, WIT

MOTOR — CARAVAN, DRIVE, GENERATOR, SCOOTER, VEHICLE, VESSEL

MOUNTAIN — ASH, CAT, CHAIN, DEVIL, GOAT, LAUREL, LION, RANGE, SHEEP, SICKNESS

MUD — BATH, DAUBER, FLAT, HEN, MAP, PIE, PUPPY, TURTLE

MUSTARD — GAS, OIL, PLASTER

MYSTERY — PLAY, TOUR

NANSEN — BOTTLE, PASSPORT

NARROW — BOAT, GAUGE, SEAS

NATIONAL — ACCOUNTING, AGREEMENT, ANTHEM, ASSEMBLY, ASSISTANCE, DEBT, FRONT, GALLERY, GRID, SERVICE, TRUST

NERVE — CELL, CENTRE, FIBRE, GAS, IMPULSE

NEW — BROOM, FOREST, GUINEA, LOOK, MATHS, MOON, PENNY, TESTAMENT, TOWN, WAVE, WORLD, YEAR, YORK, ZEALAND

NEWS — AGENCY, CONFERENCE, VENDOR

NIGHT — BLINDNESS, DANCER, FIGHTER, NURSE, OWL, ROBE, SAFE, SCHOOL, SHIFT, WATCH, WATCHMAN

NINETEENTH — HOLE, MAN

NOBLE — ART, GAS, SAVAGE

NORFOLK — ISLAND, JACKET, TERRIER

NOSE — CONE, DIVE, OUT, RAG, RING

NUCLEAR — BOMB, ENERGY, FAMILY, FISSION, FUEL, FUSION, ISOMER, PHYSICS, POWER, REACTION, REACTOR, THRESHOLD, WINTER

NURSERY — RHYME, SCHOOL, SLOPES, STAKES

OFF — CHANCE, COLOUR, KEY, LIMITS, LINE, SEASON

OIL — BEETLE, CAKE, DRUM, HARDENING, PAINT, PAINTING, PALM, RIG, RIVERS, SHALE, SLICK, VARNISH, WELL

OLD — BAILEY, BILL, BIRD, BOY, CONTEMPTIBLES, COUNTRY, GIRL, GOLD, GUARD, HAND, HAT, LADY, MAID, MAN, MOON, NICK, PRETENDER, SCHOOL, STYLE, TESTAMENT, WORLD

OLIVE — BRANCH, BROWN, CROWN, DRAB, GREEN, OIL

ON — DIT, KEY, LINE

OPEN — AIR, BOOK, CHAIN, CIRCUIT, COURT, DAY, DOOR, HOUSE, LETTER, MARKET, PRISON, PUNCTUATION, SANDWICH, SESAME, UNIVERSITY, UP, VERDICT

OPERA — BUFFA, CLOAK, GLASSES, HAT, HOUSE, SERIA

OPIUM — DEN, POPPY, WARS

ORANGE — BLOSSOM, PEEL, PEKOE, STICK

ORDINARY — LEVEL, RATING, RAY, SEAMAN, SHARES

OXFORD — ACCENT, BAGS, BLUE, ENGLISH, FRAME, GROUP, MOVEMENT

OYSTER — BED, CRAB, PINK, PLANT, WHITE

PACK — ANIMAL, DRILL, ICE, IN, RAT, UP

PALM — BEACH, CIVET, OFF, OIL, SUGAR, SUNDAY, VAULTING, WINE

PANAMA — CANAL, CITY, HAT

PANIC — BOLT, BUTTON, BUYING, GRASS, STATIONS

PAPER — CHASE, FILIGREE, MONEY, MULBERRY, NAUTILUS, OVER, TAPE, TIGER

PAR — AVION, EXCELLENCE, VALUE

PARISH — CLERK, COUNCIL, PUMP, REGISTER

PARTY — LINE, MAN, POLITICS, WALL

PASSING — BELL, NOTE, SHOT

PASSION — FRUIT, PLAY, SUNDAY, WEEK

PATCH — BOARD, POCKET, QUILT, TEST

PAY — BACK, BED, DIRT, DOWN, FOR, IN, OFF, OUT, TELEVISION, UP

PEACE — CORPS, OFFERING, PIPE, RIVER, SIGN

PEG — CLIMBING, DOWN, LEG, OUT, TOP

PEN — FRIEND, NAME, PAL

PENNY — ARCADE, BLACK, WHISTLE

PER — ANNUM, CAPITA, CENT, CONTRA, DIEM, MENSEM, MILL, PRO, SE

PERSIAN — BLINDS, CARPET, CAT, EMPIRE, GREYHOUND, GULF, LAMB, MELON

PETIT — BOURGEOIS, FOUR, JURY, LARCENY, MAL, POINT

PETROL — BOMB, PUMP, STATION

PETTY — CASH, JURY, LARCENY, OFFICER, SESSIONS

PICTURE — CARD, HAT, HOUSE, MOULDING, PALACE, WINDOW, WRITING

PIECE — GOODS, OUT, RATE

PILLOW — BLOCK, FIGHT, LACE, LAVA, SHAM, TALK

PILOT — BALLOON, BIRD, BISCUIT, CLOTH, ENGINE, FILM, FISH, HOUSE, LAMP, LIGHT, OFFICER, PLANT, STUDY, WHALE

PIN — CURL, DOWN, JOINT, MONEY, RAIL, TUCK, WRENCH

PINE — CONE, END, MARTEN, NEEDLE, TAR

PINK — ELEPHANTS, GIN, NOISE, SALMON, SLIP

PIPE — CLEANER, DOWN, DREAM, MAJOR, ORGAN, ROLL, UP

PLACE — CARD, KICK, NAME, SETTING

PLAIN — CHOCOLATE, CLOTHES, FLOUR, SAILING, TEXT

PLAY — ALONG, DOWN, OFF, ON, OUT, UP, WITH

PLYMOUTH — BRETHREN, COLONY, ROCK

POCKET — BATTLESHIP, BILLIARDS, BOROUGH, GOPHER, MONEY, MOUSE

POETIC — JUSTICE, LICENCE

PONY — EXPRESS, TREKKING

POOR — BOX, LAW, MOUTH, RELATION, WHITE

POP — ART, OFF, SHOP

POST — CHAISE, HOC, HORN, HOUSE, MERIDIEM, OFFICE, ROAD, TOWN

POT — CHEESE, LIQUOR, MARIGOLD, ON, PLANT, ROAST, SHOT, STILL

POTATO — BEETLE, BLIGHT, CHIP, CRISP

POWDER — BLUE, BURN, COMPACT, FLASK, HORN, KEG, MONKEY, PUFF, ROOM

POWER — CUT, DIVE, DRILL, FACTOR, LINE, PACK, PLANT, POINT, POLITICS, STATION, STEERING, STRUCTURE

PRAIRIE — DOG, OYSTER, PROVINCES, SCHOONER, SOIL, TURNIP, WOLF

PRAYER — BEADS, BOOK, MEETING, RUG, SHAWL, WHEEL

PRESS — AGENCY, AGENT, BOX, CONFERENCE, GALLERY, GANG, RELEASE, STUD

PRESSURE — CABIN, COOKER, DRAG, GAUGE, GRADIENT, GROUP, HEAD, POINT, SUIT

PRICE — COMMISSION, CONTROL, DISCRIMINATION, RING, SUPPORT, TAG, WAR

PRICKLY — ASH, HEAT, PEAR, POPPY

PRIME — COST, MERIDIAN, MINISTER, MOVER, NUMBER, RATE, TIME, VERTICAL

PRIVATE — BAR, BILL, COMPANY, DETECTIVE, ENTERPRISE, EYE, HOTEL, INCOME, LANGUAGE, LIFE, MEMBER, PARTS, PATIENT, PRACTICE, PRESS, PROPERTY, SCHOOL, SECRETARY, SECTOR

PRIVY — CHAMBER, COUNCIL, PURSE, SEAL

PRIZE — COURT, MONEY, RING

PRO — FORMA, PATRIA, RATA, TEMPORE

PUBLIC — BAR, BILL, COMPANY, CONVENIENCE, CORPORATION, DEBT, DEFENDER, ENEMY, ENTERPRISE, EXPENDITURE, FOOTPATH, GALLERY, HOLIDAY, HOUSE, LAW, NUISANCE, OPINION, OWNERSHIP, PROSECUTOR, RELATIONS, SCHOOL, SECTOR, SERVANT, SERVICE, SPEAKING, SPENDING, TRANSPORT

PUFF — ADDER, PASTRY

PULL — ABOUT, BACK, DOWN, IN, OFF, ON, OUT, THROUGH, TOGETHER, UP

PURPLE — EMPEROR, GALLINULE, HEART, MEDIC, PATCH

PUSH — ABOUT, ALONG, BUTTON, IN, OFF, ON, THROUGH

PUT — ABOUT, ACROSS, ASIDE, AWAY, BACK, BY, DOWN, FORTH, FORWARD, IN, OFF, ON, OUT, OVER, THROUGH, UP, UPON

QUANTUM — LEAP, MECHANICS, NUMBER, STATE, STATISTICS, THEORY

QUARTER — CRACK, DAY, GRAIN, HORSE, NOTE, PLATE, ROUND, SECTION, SESSIONS, TONE

QUEEN — BEE, CONSORT, DOWAGER, MAB, MOTHER, OLIVE, POST, REGENT, REGNANT, SUBSTANCE

QUEER — FISH, STREET

QUESTION — MARK, MASTER, TIME

RAIN — CHECK, GAUGE, SHADOW, TREE

REAL — ALE, ESTATE, LIFE, NUMBER, PART, PRESENCE, PROPERTY, TENNIS, WAGES

RED — ADMIRAL, ALGAE, BAG, BARK, BEDS, BIDDY, CARPET, CEDAR, CROSS, DUSTER, DWARF, ENSIGN, FLAG, HAT, HEAT, HERRING, INDIAN, MEAT, MULLET, PEPPER, RAG, RIVER, ROSE, SALMON, SEA, SETTER, SHANK, SHIFT, SNAPPER, SPIDER, SQUIRREL, TAPE

RES — ADJUDICATA, GESTAE, JUDICATA, PUBLICA

RIGHT — ABOUT, ANGLE, ASCENSION, AWAY, HONOURABLE, OFF, ON, REVEREND, WING

ROCK — BOTTOM, CAKE, CLIMBING, GARDEN, PLANT, SALT, STEADY

ROLLER — BEARING, CAPTION, COASTER, DERBY, SKATE, TOWEL

ROMAN — ARCH, CALENDAR, CANDLE, CATHOLIC, CATHOLICISM, COLLAR, EMPIRE, HOLIDAY, LAW, MILE, NOSE, NUMERALS

ROOF — GARDEN, RACK

ROOM — SERVICE, TEMPERATURE

ROOT — BEER, CANAL, CROP, NODULE, OUT, POSITION, UP

ROTARY — CLOTHESLINE, CLUB, ENGINE, PLOUGH, PRESS, PUMP

ROUGH — COLLIE, DIAMOND, OUT, PASSAGE, SPIN, STUFF, UP

ROUND — ANGLE, CLAM, DANCE, DOWN, HAND, OFF, ON, OUT, ROBIN, TABLE, TOP, TRIP, UP

ROYAL — ACADEMY, ASSENT, BLUE, BURGH, COMMISSION, DUKE, ENGINEERS, FLUSH, HIGHNESS, ICING, JELLY, MARINES, NAVY, PURPLE, ROAD, STANDARD, TENNIS, WARRANT, WORCESTER

RUBBER — BAND, BRIDGE, CEMENT, CHEQUE, GOODS, PLANT, STAMP, TREE

RUN — ACROSS, AFTER, ALONG, AROUND, AWAY, DOWN, IN, INTO, OFF, ON, OUT, OVER, THROUGH, TO, UP

RUNNING — BOARD, COMMENTARY, HEAD, LIGHT, MATE, REPAIRS, RIGGING, STITCH

RUSSIAN — DRESSING, EMPIRE, REVOLUTION, ROULETTE, SALAD, WOLFHOUND

SAFETY — BELT, CATCH, CHAIN, CURTAIN, FACTOR, FILM, FUSE, GLASS, LAMP, MATCH, NET, PIN, RAZOR, VALVE

SALAD — DAYS, DRESSING

SALLY — ARMY, LUNN

SALT — AWAY, BATH, CAKE, DOME, FLAT, LAKE, LICK, MARSH, OUT, PORK

SAND — BAR, CASTLE, EEL, FLEA, HOPPER, LANCE, LEEK, LIZARD, MARTIN, PAINTING, SHRIMP, TABLE, TRAP, VIPER, WASP, WEDGE, YACHT

SANDWICH — BOARD, CAKE, COURSE, ISLANDS, MAN

SAUSAGE — DOG, ROLL

SCARLET — FEVER, HAT, LETTER, PIMPERNEL, RUNNER, WOMAN

SCATTER — DIAGRAM, PIN, RUG

SCOTCH — BROTH, EGG, MIST, PANCAKE, SNAP, TAPE, TERRIER

SCRAPE — IN, THROUGH, TOGETHER

SCRATCH — PAD, SHEET, TEST, TOGETHER, VIDEO

SECOND — CHILDHOOD, CLASS, COMING, COUSIN, FIDDLE, FLOOR, GENERATION, GROWTH, HAND, LANGUAGE, LIEUTENANT, MATE, NAME, NATURE, READING, SIGHT, STRING, THOUGHT, WIND

SECONDARY — COLOUR, EMISSION, PICKET, PROCESSES, QUALITIES, SCHOOL, STRESS

SECRET — AGENT, POLICE, SERVICE, SOCIETY

SEE — ABOUT, INTO, OF, OFF, OUT, OVER, THROUGH

SENIOR — AIRCRAFTMAN, CITIZEN, MANAGEMENT, SERVICE

SERVICE — AREA, CHARGE, INDUSTRY, MODULE, ROAD, STATION

SET — ABOUT, AGAINST, ASIDE, BACK, DOWN, FORTH, IN, OFF, ON, OUT, PIECE, POINT, SQUARE, THEORY, TO, UP, UPON

SETTLE — DOWN, FOR, IN, WITH

SHAKE — DOWN, OFF, UP
SHEET — ANCHOR, BEND, DOWN, LIGHTNING, METAL, MUSIC
SHOP — AROUND, ASSISTANT, FLOOR, STEWARD
SHORE — BIRD, LEAVE, PATROL
SHORT — CIRCUIT, CUT, FUSE, HEAD, LIST, ODDS, SHRIFT, STORY, STRAW, TIME, WAVE
SHOW — BILL, BUSINESS, CARD, COPY, OFF, STOPPER, TRIAL, UP
SIAMESE — CAT, TWINS
SICK — LEAVE, LIST, NOTE, PAY
SIGN — AWAY, IN, LANGUAGE, MANUAL, OFF, ON, OUT, UP
SINGLE — BOND, CREAM, DENSITY, ENTRY, FILE, TAX, THREAD, TICKET
SIT — BACK, DOWN, ON, OUT, OVER, UNDER, UP
SITTING — BULL, ROOM, TARGET, TENANT
SKI — JUMP, LIFT, PANTS, RUN, STICK, TOW
SKIN — DIVING, EFFECT, FLICK, FOOD, FRICTION, GAME, GRAFT, TEST
SLAVE — ANT, COAST, CYLINDER, DRIVER, SHIP, STATE, TRADE
SLIDE — FASTENER, GUITAR, OVER, REST, RULE, TROMBONE, VALVE
SLIP — GAUGE, RAIL, RING, ROAD, STEP, STITCH, UP
SLOW — BURN, HANDCLAP, MARCH, MOTION, TIME
SMALL — ARMS, BEER, CHANGE, FRY, HOURS, INTESTINE, SLAM, TALK
SMART — ALECK, CARD, MONEY, SET
SMOKE — BOMB, OUT, SCREEN, TREE
SNEAK — PREVIEW, THIEF
SOB — SISTER, STORY, STUFF
SOCIAL — CLIMBER, SCIENCE, SECRETARY, SECURITY, SERVICES, STUDIES, WELFARE, WORK
SODA — ASH, BISCUIT, BREAD, FOUNTAIN, JERK, LIME, NITRE, POP, SIPHON, WATER
SOFT — DRINK, FRUIT, FURNISHINGS, GOODS, LANDING, LINE, OPTION, PORN, SELL, SOAP, SPOT, TOP, TOUCH
SOLAR — ECLIPSE, FLARE, FURNACE, HEATING, MONTH, MYTH, PANEL, PLEXUS, POWER, SYSTEM, WIND, YEAR
SOUND — BARRIER, BOW, CHECK, EFFECT, HEAD, HOLE, MIXER, OFF, OUT, WAVE
SOUR — CHERRY, CREAM, GOURD, GRAPES, GUM, MASH
SPACE — AGE, BLANKET, CADET, CAPSULE, CHARACTER, HEATER, INVADERS, OPERA, PLATFORM, PROBE, SHUTTLE, STATION
SPAGHETTI — JUNCTION, WESTERN
SPARK — CHAMBER, COIL, EROSION, GAP, OFF, PLUG, TRANSMITTER
SPEAK — FOR, OUT, TO, UP
SPECIAL — ASSESSMENT, BRANCH, CASE, CONSTABLE, DELIVERY, EFFECTS, JURY, LICENCE, PLEADING, PRIVILEGE, SCHOOL, SORT
SPEED — LIMIT, TRAP, UP
SPINNING — JENNY, MULE, TOP, WHEEL
SPIRIT — GUM, LAMP, LEVEL, VARNISH
SPLIT — CANE, DECISION, INFINITIVE, PEA, PERSONALITY, SECOND, SHIFT, TIN, UP

SPONGE — BAG, BATH, CAKE, CLOTH, DOWN
SPORTS — CAR, COAT, JACKET, SHIRT
SPRING — BALANCE, CHICKEN, FEVER, LOCK, MATTRESS, ONION, ROLL, TIDE
SPUN — SILK, SUGAR, YARN
SQUARE — AWAY, BRACKET, DANCE, LEG, MEAL, NUMBER, OFF, ROOT, UP
STABLE — DOOR, FLY, LAD
STAFF — ASSOCIATION, COLLEGE, CORPORAL, NURSE, OFFICER, SERGEANT
STAG — BEETLE, PARTY
STAGE — DIRECTION, DOOR, EFFECT, FRIGHT, LEFT, MANAGER, RIGHT, WHISPER
STAMP — ACT, COLLECTING, DUTY, MILL, OUT
STAND — BY, DOWN, FOR, IN, OIL, ON, OUT, OVER, PAT, TO, UP
STAR — CHAMBER, CONNECTION, GRASS, SAPPHIRE, SHELL, STREAM, SYSTEM, THISTLE, WARS
STATUS — QUO, SYMBOL
STEEL — BAND, BLUE, GREY, GUITAR, WOOL
STICK — AROUND, AT, BY, DOWN, INSECT, OUT, TO, TOGETHER, WITH
STICKY — END, WICKET
STIRRUP — BONE, CUP, PUMP
STOCK — CAR, CERTIFICATE, COMPANY, EXCHANGE, FARM, MARKET
STOCKING — CAP, FILLER, FRAME, MASK, STITCH
STORAGE — BATTERY, CAPACITY, DEVICE, HEATER
STORM — BELT, CENTRE, CLOUD, COLLAR, CONE, DOOR, GLASS, LANTERN, PETREL, WARNING, WINDOW
STRAIGHT — BAT, FACE, FIGHT, FLUSH, MAN, OFF, UP
STRAWBERRY — BLONDE, BUSH, MARK, TOMATO, TREE
STREET — ARAB, CREDIBILITY, CRY, DOOR, PIANO, THEATRE, VALUE
STRIKE — DOWN, FAULT, NOTE, OFF, OUT, PAY, THROUGH, UP
STRING — ALONG, BAND, BASS, BEAN, COURSE, LINE, ORCHESTRA, QUARTET, TIE, VARIABLE
STRIP — CARTOON, CLUB, CROPPING, LIGHTING, MILL, MINING, OUT, POKER
SUGAR — BEET, CANDY, CANE, CORN, DADDY, DIABETES, LOAF, MAPLE
SUMMER — HOLIDAY, PUDDING, SCHOOL, SOLSTICE, TIME
SUN — BATH, BEAR, BITTERN, BLIND, BLOCK, DANCE, DECK, DISC, KING, LAMP, LOUNGE
SUPREME — BEING, COMMANDER, COURT, SACRIFICE
SURFACE — MAIL, NOISE, PLATE, STRUCTURE, TENSION
SWAN — DIVE, MAIDEN, NECK, SONG
SWEAT — GLAND, OFF, OUT, SHIRT, SUIT
SWEET — BASIL, BAY, CHERRY, CHESTNUT, CICELY, CIDER, CLOVER, CORN, FERN, FLAG, GALE, GUM, MARJORAM, MARTEN, OIL, PEA, PEPPER, POTATO, SHOP, TOOTH, WILLIAM, WOODRUFF
SWISS — CHARD, CHEESE, GUARD, MUSLIN, ROLL, TOURNAMENT
TABLE — BAY, D'HOTE, LICENCE, MONEY, MOUNTAIN, NAPKIN, SALT, TALK, TENNIS, WINE
TAIL — COAT, COVERT, END, FAN, GATE, OFF, OUT

TAKE — ABACK, AFTER, APART, AWAY, BACK, DOWN, FOR, IN, OFF, ON, OUT, OVER, TO, UP

TALK — ABOUT, AT, BACK, DOWN, INTO, OUT, ROUND, SHOW

TANK — ENGINE, FARMING, TOP, TRAP, UP, WAGON

TAX — AVOIDANCE, DISC, EVASION, EXILE, HAVEN, RATE, RETURN, SHELTER

TEA — BAG, BISCUIT, CLOTH, COSY, GARDEN, GOWN, LEAF, PARTY, ROSE, SERVICE, TOWEL, TROLLEY

TEAR — AWAY, DOWN, DUCT, GAS, INTO, OFF, SHEET

TELEPHONE — BOX, DIRECTORY, NUMBER

TERRA — ALBA, COTTA, FIRMA, INCOGNITA, SIGILLATA

TEST — ACT, BAN, CASE, MARKETING, MATCH, PAPER, PILOT, TUBE

THIRD — CLASS, DEGREE, DIMENSION, ESTATE, EYELID, MAN, PARTY, PERSON, READING, REICH, WORLD

THROW — ABOUT, IN, OFF, OUT, OVER, TOGETHER, UP, WEIGHT

TIME — BOMB, CAPSULE, CLOCK, IMMEMORIAL, MACHINE, SERIES, SHARING, SHEET, SIGNATURE, SWITCH, TRIAL, ZONE

TIN — CAN, GOD, HAT, LIZZIE, PLATE, SOLDIER, WHISTLE

TITLE — DEED, PAGE, ROLE

TOILET — PAPER, SET, SOAP, TRAINING, WATER

TONE — CLUSTER, COLOUR, CONTROL, DOWN, LANGUAGE, POEM, ROW, UP

TOP — BOOT, BRASS, DOG, DRAWER, END, GEAR, HAT, MANAGEMENT, OFF, OUT, UP

TORQUE — CONVERTER, METER, SPANNER, WRENCH

TOUCH — FOOTBALL, JUDGE, OFF, UP

TOWN — CLERK, CRIER, GAS, HALL, HOUSE, MEETING, PLANNING

TRACK — DOWN, EVENT, MEET, RECORD, ROD, SHOE

TRADE — ACCEPTANCE, CYCLE, DISCOUNT, GAP, JOURNAL, NAME, ON, PLATE, SCHOOL, SECRET, UNION, WIND

TRAFFIC — COP, COURT, ISLAND, JAM, LIGHT, OFFICER, PATTERN, WARDEN

TREASURY — BENCH, BILL, BOND, CERTIFICATE, NOTE, TAG

TRENCH — COAT, FEVER, FOOT, KNIFE, MORTAR, MOUTH, WARFARE

TRIPLE — ALLIANCE, BOND, ENTENTE, JUMP, POINT, TIME

TURKISH — BATH, COFFEE, DELIGHT, EMPIRE, TOBACCO, TOWEL

TURN — AGAINST, AWAY, BRIDGE, DOWN, IN, OFF, ON, OUT, OVER, TO, UP

TWELFTH — DAY, MAN, NIGHT

TWIN — BED, BILL, TOWN

UMBRELLA — BIRD, PINE, PLANT, STAND, TREE

UNION — CARD, JACK

UNIT — COST, FACTOR, PRICE, TRUST

UNITED — KINGDOM, NATIONS, PARTY, PROVINCES

VACUUM — CLEANER, FLASK

VALUE — ADDED, DATE, JUDGMENT

VENETIAN — BLIND, GLASS, RED

VENTURE — CAPITAL, SCOUT

VICAR — APOSTOLIC, FORANE, GENERAL

VICE — ADMIRAL, CHANCELLOR, PRESIDENT, SQUAD, VERSA

VIDEO — CASSETTE, GAME, NASTY, TAPE

VIRGIN — BIRTH, ISLANDS, MARY, WOOL

VIRGINIA — BEACH, CREEPER, DEER, REEL, STOCK

VOX — ANGELICA, HUMANA, POP, POPULI

VULGAR — FRACTION, LATIN

WALK — AWAY, INTO, OFF, OUT

WAR — BABY, BONNET, BRIDE, CHEST, CORRESPONDENT, CRIME, CRY, DANCE, GAME, MEMORIAL, OFFICE, PAINT, WHOOP

WASHING — MACHINE, POWDER, SODA

WATCH — CAP, CHAIN, COMMITTEE, FIRE, NIGHT, OUT

WEATHER — EYE, HOUSE, MAP, STATION, STRIP, VANE, WINDOW

WEDDING — BREAKFAST, CAKE, RING

WEIGH — DOWN, IN, UP

WELSH — CORGI, DRESSER, HARP, MOUNTAIN, POPPY, RABBIT, TERRIER

WET — BLANKET, CELL, DREAM, FISH, FLY, LOOK, NURSE, PACK, ROT, STEAM, SUIT

WHITE — ADMIRAL, AREA, BEAR, BIRCH, ELEPHANT, ENSIGN, FEATHER, FISH, FLAG, GOLD, HEAT, HORSE, HOUSE, KNIGHT, LADY, LEAD, LIE, LIGHT, MEAT, OUT, PAPER, PEPPER, SLAVE, SPIRIT, STICK, TIE, WHALE

WINDOW — BOX, ENVELOPE, SASH, SEAT, TAX

WINE — BAR, BOX, CELLAR, COOLER, TASTING

WING — CHAIR, COLLAR, COMMANDER, COVERT, LOADING, NUT, SHOT, TIP

WITCH — DOCTOR, HAZEL

WOLF — CUB, SPIDER, WHISTLE

WORD — ASSOCIATION, BLINDNESS, ORDER, PICTURE, PROCESSING, PROCESSOR, SQUARE

WORK — BACK, CAMP, ETHIC, FUNCTION, IN, OFF, ON, OUT, OVER, SHEET, STATION, THROUGH, UP

WORKING — BEE, CAPITAL, CLASS, DAY, DOG, DRAWING, PAPERS, PARTY, SUBSTANCE, WEEK

WRITE — DOWN, IN, OFF, OUT, UP

YELLOW — BELLY, CARD, FEVER, JACKET, PAGES, PERIL, RIVER, STREAK

YORKSHIRE — DALES, FOG, PUDDING, TERRIER

YOUNG — BLOOD, FOGEY, LADY, MAN, PRETENDER, TURK

YOUTH — CLUB, CUSTODY, HOSTEL

SECOND WORD

ABOUT — BRING, CAST, COME, FALL, HANG, KICK, KNOCK, MESS, MUCK, PUSH, PUT, RIGHT, SET, TALK, THROW

ABSOLUTE — ABLATIVE, DECREE

ACADEMY — FRENCH, MILITARY, ROYAL

ACCESS — DIRECT, RANDOM, SEQUENTIAL

ACCOUNT — BANK, BUDGET, CAPITAL, CHARGE, CONTROL, CREDIT, CURRENT, DEPOSIT, DRAWING, EXPENSE, JOINT, SAVINGS, SHORT, SUSPENSE, TRUST

ACCOUNTANT — CHARTERED, TURF

ACROSS — COME, CUT, GET, PUT, RUN

ACT — ENABLING, HOMESTEAD, JURISTIC, LOCUTIONARY, RIOT, SPEECH, STAMP, TEST

ADMIRAL — FLEET, REAR, RED, VICE, WHITE

ADVOCATE — DEVIL'S, JUDGE, LORD

AGAINST — COUNT, GO, SET, STACK, TURN

AGENCY — ADVERTISING, EMPLOYMENT, MERCANTILE, NEWS, PRESS, TRAVEL

AGENT — CROWN, DISCLOSING, DOUBLE, ESTATE, FORWARDING, FREE, HOUSE, LAND, LAW, OXIDIZING, PRESS, REDUCING, SECRET, SHIPPING, WETTING

AGREEMENT — COLLECTIVE, GENTLEMEN'S, NATIONAL, PROCEDURAL, STANDSTILL, TECHNOLOGY

AID — ARTIFICIAL, FIRST, FOREIGN, HEARING, HOME, LEGAL, TEACHING

ALARM — CALL, FALSE, FIRE

ALCOHOL — ABSOLUTE, ALLYL, AMYL, BUTYL, ETHYL, GRAIN, LAURYL, METHYL, RUBBING, WOOD

ALE — GINGER, REAL

ALLEY — BLIND, BOWLING

ALLIANCE — DUAL, HOLY, TRIPLE

ALONG — COME, CUT, GET, GO, MUDDLE, PLAY, PUSH, RUB, RUN, SING, STRING

ANGEL — DESTROYING, HELL'S, RECORDING

ANGLE — CENTRAL, COMPLEMENTARY, CRITICAL, EXTERIOR, FACIAL, HOUR, INTERIOR, OBLIQUE, PLANE, RIGHT, STRAIGHT

ANT — AMAZON, ARMY, BULLDOG, DRIVER, FIRE, LEAFCUTTER, LEGIONARY, PHARAOH, SLAVE, VELVET, WHITE, WOOD

APPLE — ADAM'S, BALSAM, BIG, BITTER, CRAB, CUSTARD, LOVE, MAY, OAK, ROSE, SUGAR, THORN

ARCADE — AMUSEMENT, PENNY

ARCH — ACUTE, FALLEN, GOTHIC, HORSESHOE, KEEL, LANCET, NORMAN, OGEE, POINTED, ROMAN, SKEW, TRIUMPHAL, ZYGOMATIC

AREA — CATCHMENT, DEVELOPMENT, GOAL, GREY, MUSH, NO-GO, PENALTY, SERVICE

ARMS — CANTING, ORDER, SIDE, SMALL

ARMY — CHURCH, FIELD, SALLY, SALVATION, STANDING, TERRITORIAL

AROUND — BAT, GET, GO, HORSE, RUN, SHOP, SLEEP, SLOP, STICK

ART — BLACK, COMMERCIAL, FINE, NOBLE, OP, PERFORMANCE, POP

ARTS — GRAPHIC, LIBERAL, PERFORMING, VISUAL

ASH — BONE, FLY, MOUNTAIN, PEARL, PRICKLY, SODA

ASIDE — BRUSH, LAY, PUT, SET

ASSEMBLY — GENERAL, LEGISLATIVE, NATIONAL, UNLAWFUL

ATTORNEY — CROWN, DISTRICT, PROSECUTING

AWAY — BLOW, BOIL, CARRY, CLEAR, COME, EXPLAIN, FALL, FIRE, GET, GIVE, GO, KEEP, LAUGH, LAY, MAKE, PUT, RIGHT, RUN, SALT, SIGN, SOCK, SQUARE, TAKE, TEAR, TRAIL, TUCK, TURN, WALK, WHILE

BABY — BLUE, JELLY, PLUNKET, RHESUS, TEST-TUBE, WAR

BACK — ANSWER, BITE, BOUNCE, CARRY, CAST, CHOKE, CLAW, DOUBLE, FALL, FIGHT, GET, GO, HANG, HARK, HOLD, KEEP, KNOCK, LADDER, LOOK, PAY, PLOUGH, PULL, PUT, RING, SET, SIT, TAKE, TALK

BAG — AIR, BLUE, BODY, CARRIER, COFFEE, COOL, DIPLOMATIC, DOGGY, DUFFEL, GLADSTONE, GROW, ICE, JELLY, JIFFY, LAVENDER, MIXED, SAG, SLEEPING, SPONGE, TEA, TOTE

BALLOON — BARRAGE, HOT-AIR, PILOT, TRIAL

BAND — BIG, BRAKE, BRASS, CITIZENS', CONDUCTION, ELASTIC, ENERGY, FREQUENCY, RUBBER, STEEL

BANK — BLOOD, CENTRAL, CLEARING, COMMERCIAL, COOPERATIVE, DATA, DOGGER, FOG, JODRELL, LAND, LEFT, MEMORY, MERCHANT, NATIONAL, PIGGY, RESERVE, SAVINGS, SOIL, SPERM

BAR — CAPSTAN, COFFEE, COLOUR, DOUBLE, HEEL, HORIZONTAL, INNER, MILK, OUTER, PINCH, PRIVATE, PUBLIC, SAND, SINGLES, SNACK, TORSION, WINE

BARRIER — CRASH, CRUSH, HEAT, SONIC, SOUND, THERMAL, TRANSONIC

BASE — AIR, DATA, FIRST, LEWIS, PRISONER'S, PYRIMIDINE

BASKET — CHIP, MOSES, POLLEN, WASTEPAPER

BASS — BLACK, DOUBLE, FIGURED, GROUND, LARGEMOUTH, ROCK, SEA, SMALLMOUTH, STONE, STRING, THOROUGH, WALKING

BAT — FRUIT, HORSESHOE, INSECTIVOROUS, STRAIGHT, VAMPIRE

BATH — BLANKET, BLOOD, BUBBLE, HIP, MUD, SALT, SPONGE, STEAM, SUN, SWIMMING, TURKISH

BEACON — BELISHA, LANDING, RADAR, RADIO

BEAN — ADSUKI, ADZUKI, BLACK, BROAD, BUTTER, CALABAR, CASTOR, COCOA, DWARF, FRENCH, GREEN, HORSE, JACK, JUMPING, KIDNEY, LIMA, MUNG, PINTO, RUNNER, SHELL, SNAP, SOYA, STRING, TONKA, WAX

BEAR — ANT, BLACK, BROWN, CINNAMON, GREAT, GRIZZLY, HONEY, KOALA, KODIAK, LITTLE, NATIVE, POLAR, SLOTH, SUN, TEDDY, WATER, WHITE, WOOLLY

BEAT — DEAD, MERSEY, WING

BEAUTY — BATHING, CAMBERWELL, SPRING

BED — AIR, APPLE-PIE, BUNK, FEATHER, OYSTER, PAY, SOFA, TRUCKLE, TRUNDLE, TWIN, WATER

BEE — CARPENTER, CUCKOO, HIVE, LEAFCUTTER, MASON, MINING, QUEEN, SPELLING, WORKING

BEER — BOCK, GINGER, KAFFIR, ROOT, SMALL, SPRUCE

BELL — CANTERBURY, DIVING, LUTINE, PASSING, SACRING, SANCTUS, SHARK, SILVER

BELT — BIBLE, BLACK, CARTRIDGE, CHASTITY, CONVEYOR, COPPER, COTTON, FAN, GREEN, LIFE, LONSDALE, SAFETY, SEAT, SHELTER, STOCKBROKER, STORM, SUSPENDER, SWORD

BENCH — FRONT, KING'S, OPTICAL, TREASURY

BENEFIT — CHILD, DISABLEMENT, FAMILY, FRINGE, HOUSING, INJURY, INVALIDITY, MATERNITY, SICKNESS, SUPPLEMENTARY, UNEMPLOYMENT, WIDOW'S

BILL — ACCOMMODATION, BUFFALO, DEMAND, DOUBLE, FINANCE, FOREIGN, OLD, PRIVATE, PUBLIC, REFORM, TREASURY, TRUE, TWIN

BIRD — ADJUTANT, ANT, BRAIN-FEVER, CROCODILE, DIAMOND, EARLY, ELEPHANT, GALLOWS, GAME, PARSON, WATER

BISCUIT — BOURBON, CAPTAIN'S, DIGESTIVE, DOG, PILOT, SEA, SHIP'S, SODA, TARARUA, TEA, WATER

BLACK — ALL, CARBON, GAS, IVORY, JET, LARGE, PENNY, PLATINUM

BLOCK — BREEZE, BUILDING, CAVITY, CYLINDER, HEART, ICE, MENTAL, OFFICE, PSYCHOLOGICAL, SADDLE, STARTING, STUMBLING, SUN, WOOD

BLOOD – BAD, BLUE, BULL'S, DRAGON'S, FULL, WHOLE, YOUNG

BOARD – ABOVE, ADMIRALTY, BULLETIN, CATCHMENT, CIRCUIT, CRIBBAGE, DIVING, DRAFT, DRAINING, DRAWING, EMERY, FULL, HALF, IDIOT, IRONING, NOTICE, PATCH, RUNNING, SANDWICH, SCHOOL, SKIRTING, SOUNDING, WOBBLE

BOAT – CANAL, FLYING, GRAVY, JOLLY, MOSQUITO, NARROW, ROWING, SAILING, SAUCE, SWAMP, TORPEDO

BOMB – ATOM, BORER, BUZZ, CLUSTER, COBALT, FISSION, FLYING, FUSION, HYDROGEN, LETTER, MILLS, NEUTRON, NUCLEAR, PETROL, SMOKE, STINK, TIME, VOLCANIC

BOND – BAIL, CHEMICAL, COORDINATE, COVALENT, DATIVE, DOUBLE, ELECTROVALENT, ENGLISH, FLEMISH, GRANNY, HERRINGBONE, HYDROGEN, INCOME, IONIC, METALLIC, PAIR, PEPTIDE, SINGLE, TREASURY, TRIPLE

BONE – CANNON, CARTILAGE, COFFIN, CRAZY, FETTER, FRONTAL, FUNNY, HAUNCH, HEEL, INNOMINATE, MEMBRANE, OCCIPITAL, PARIETAL, SPHENOID, SPLINT, STIRRUP, TEMPORAL, TYMPANIC, ZYGOMATIC

BOOK – BLACK, CLOSED, COMMONPLACE, COOKERY, DOMESDAY, DOOMSDAY, HYMN, OPEN, PHRASE, PRAYER, REFERENCE, STATUTE, TALKING

BOTTLE – BRANDY, FEEDING, HOT-WATER, KLEIN, NANSEN, WATER

BOWL – BEGGING, DUST, FINGER, GOLDFISH, RICE

BOX – APPLE, BALLOT, BLACK, CHRISTMAS, COIN, DEED, DISPATCH, FUSE, FUZZ, GLOVE, JUNCTION, JURY, LETTER, MUSIC, PENALTY, PILLAR, POOR, PRESS, SENTRY, SHOOTING, SIGNAL, TELEPHONE, VOICE, WINDOW, WINE, WITNESS

BOY – ALTAR, BALL, BARROW, BEST, BEVIN, BLUE-EYED, CABIN, ERRAND, OFFICE, OLD, PRINCIPAL, RENT, TAR, TEDDY, WHIPPING

BRAKE – AIR, CENTRIFUGAL, DISC, DRUM, FOOT, HYDRAULIC, SHOOTING

BRETHREN – BOHEMIAN, ELDER, EXCLUSIVE, OPEN, PLYMOUTH, TRINITY

BRIDGE – AIR, AUCTION, BAILEY, BALANCE, BOARD, CABLE-STAYED, CANTILEVER, CLAPPER, CONTRACT, COUNTERPOISE, DUPLICATE, FLYING, FOUR-DEAL, LAND, PIVOT, RAINBOW, RUBBER, SNOW, SUSPENSION, SWING, TRANSPORTER, TRUSS, TURN, WHEATSTONE

BRIGADE – BOYS', FIRE, FUR, INTERNATIONAL

BROTHER – BIG, BLOOD, LAY

BUG – ASSASSIN, CABBAGE, CHINCH, CROTON, DAMSEL, DEBRIS, FLOWER, GROUND, HARLEQUIN, JUNE, KISSING, LACE, LIGHTNING, MAORI, MEALY, PILL, RHODODENDRON, SHIELD, SOW, SQUASH, WATER, WHEEL

BUGGY – BABY, BEACH, SWAMP

BUOY – BELL, BREECHES, CAN, LIFE, NUN, SPAR

BURNER – BACK, BUNSEN, GAS, LIME, WELSBACH

BUSH – BURNING, BUTTERFLY, CALICO, COTTON, CRANBERRY, CREOSOTE, DAISY, EMU, GOOSEBERRY, MINT, NATIVE, NEEDLE, ORCHARD, STRAWBERRY, SUGAR

BUSINESS – BIG, MONKEY, SHOW

BY – COME, DO, GET, GO, PASS, PUT, STAND, STICK

CAKE – ANGEL, BANBURY, BARM, COTTON, DUNDEE, ECCLES, FISH, GENOA, JOHNNY, LARDY, LAYER, MADEIRA, MARBLE, OIL, PONTEFRACT, POUND, ROCK, SALT, SANDWICH, SIMNEL, SPONGE, TIPSY, UPSIDE-DOWN, WEDDING

CALL – BIRD, CLOSE, COLD, CURTAIN, LINE, PHOTO, ROLL, TOLL, TRUNK

CAMERA – AUTOMATIC, BOX, CANDID, CINE, COMPACT, GAMMA, IN, MINIATURE, MOVIE, PINHOLE, REFLEX

CAMP – CONCENTRATION, HEALTH, HIGH, HOLIDAY, LABOUR, LOW, MOTOR, TRANSIT, WORK

CANAL – ALIMENTARY, ANAL, CALEDONIAN, ERIE, GRAND, HAVERSIAN, MITTELLAND, PANAMA, ROOT, SEMICIRCULAR, SPINAL, SUEZ, WELLAND

CAP – BATHING, CLOTH, CROWN, DEATH, DUNCE, DUTCH, FILLER, FLAT, FOOL'S, FUNNEL, JOCKEY, JULIET, LEGAL, LIBERTY, MILK, PERCUSSION, ROOT, SHAGGY, STOCKING, WATCH, WAX

CAPITAL – BLOCK, HUMAN, RISK, SMALL, VENTURE, WORKING

CAPSULE – SEED, SPACE, TIME

CARD – BANK, BANKER'S, CALLING, CHEQUE, CHRISTMAS, CIGARETTE, COURT, CREDIT, DONOR, DRAWING, FLASH, GREEN, ID, LASER, LETTER, PICTURE, PLACE, PLAYING, POSTAL, PUNCHED, SHOW, SMART, UNION, VISITING, YELLOW

CASE – ATTACHÉ, BASKET, COT, DISPATCH, DRESSING, LOWER, SPECIAL, SPORE, STATED, TEST, UPPER, WARDIAN, WORST, WRITING

CELL – BLOOD, CADMIUM, CLARK, COLLAR, CONDEMNED, DANIELL, DEATH, DRY, ELECTROLYTIC, FLAME, FUEL, GERM, GRAVITY, GUARD, LYMPH, MAST, NERVE, PADDED, PARIETAL, PHOTOELECTRIC, PRIMARY, SECONDARY, SELENIUM, SOLAR, SOMATIC, STANDARD, STEM, SWARM, UNIT, VOLTAIC, WET

CENTRE – ACTIVE, ATTENDANCE, CIVIC, COMMUNITY, COST, DAYCARE, DEAD, DETENTION, GARDEN, HEALTH, MUSIC, NERVE, REMAND, SHOPPING, STORM

CHAIN – BICYCLE, BRANCHED, CLOSED, DAISY, FOOD, GOLDEN, GRAND, GUNTER'S, LEARNER'S, MARKOV, MOUNTAIN, OPEN, SAFETY, SIDE, SNIGGING, STRAIGHT, SURVEYOR'S, WATCH

CHAIR – BATH, BOATSWAIN'S, DECK, EASY, ELECTRIC, ROCKING, SEDAN, STRAIGHT, SWIVEL, WINDSOR, WING

CHAMBER – BUBBLE, CLOUD, COMBUSTION, DECOMPRESSION, ECHO, FLOAT, GAS, INSPECTION, IONIZATION, LOWER, MAGMA, PRESENCE, PRIVY, SECOND, SPARK, STAR, UPPER

CHART – BAR, BREAKEVEN, CONTROL, FLOW, ORGANIZATION, PIE, PLANE

CHASE – PAPER, WILD-GOOSE

CHEST – COMMUNITY, HOPE, MEDICINE, SEA, SLOP, WAR, WIND

CHILD – FOSTER, LATCHKEY, LOVE, MOON

CHINA – BONE, COCHIN, COMMUNIST, DRESDEN, NATIONALIST, RED, WORCESTER

CHIP – BLUE, LOG, POTATO, SILICON

CIRCLE — ANTARCTIC, ARCTIC, DIP, DRESS, EQUINOCTIAL, FAMILY, GREAT, HOUR, HUT, MERIDIAN, PARQUET, PITCH, POLAR, TURNING, VERTICAL, VICIOUS

CLASS — CABIN, CRYSTAL, EVENING, FIRST, LOWER, MIDDLE, SECOND, THIRD, UNIVERSAL, UPPER, WORKING

CLAY — BOULDER, CHINA, FIRE, PORCELAIN

CLEF — ALTO, BASS, C, F, G, SOPRANO, TENOR, TREBLE, VIOLA

CLERK — ARTICLED, BANK, DESK, FILING, PARISH, SHIPPING, TALLY, TOWN

CLIP — BICYCLE, BULLDOG, CARTRIDGE, CROCODILE, WOOL

CLOCK — ALARM, ANALOGUE, ATOMIC, BIOLOGICAL, CAESIUM, CARRIAGE, CUCKOO, DIGITAL, GRANDFATHER, GRANDMOTHER, LONGCASE, QUARTZ, SETTLER'S, SPEAKING, TIME, TOWNHALL, WATER

CLOTH — AEROPLANE, AIRCRAFT, ALTAR, BARK, COVERT, FACE, GRASS, MONK'S, NUN'S, SPONGE, TEA, WIRE

CLUB — BOOK, CHARTERED, COUNTRY, GLEE, GOLF, INDIAN, JOCKEY, LIONS, LUNCHEON, MONDAY, PROVIDENT, PUDDING, ROTARY, STRIP, SUPPER, TRAMPING, YOUTH

COAL — BITUMINOUS, BROWN, CANNEL, GAS, HARD, SOFT, STEAM, WHITE, WOOD

COCKTAIL — ATOMIC, FRUIT, MOLOTOV

CODE — AREA, BAR, BINARY, CHARACTER, CLARENDON, COLOUR, COUNTRY, DIALLING, GENETIC, GRAY, HIGHWAY, JUSTINIAN, MORSE, NAPOLEONIC, NATIONAL, PENAL, STD, TIME, ZIP

COLLAR — CLERICAL, DOG, ETON, HEAD, MANDARIN, ROMAN, SHAWL, STORM, VANDYKE, WING

COLOUR — ACHROMATIC, CHROMATIC, COMPLEMENTARY, CROSS, LOCAL, OFF, PRIMARY, SECONDARY, TONE

COLUMN — AGONY, CORRESPONDENCE, FIFTH, PERSONAL, SPINAL, STEERING, VERTEBRAL

COMPANY — CLOSE, FINANCE, FIRE, FREE, HOLDING, JOINT-STOCK, LIMITED, PARENT, PRIVATE, PUBLIC, REPERTORY, STOCK

COMPLEX — ELECTRA, INFERIORITY, LAUNCH, OEDIPUS, PERSECUTION, SUPERIORITY

CONE — ICE-CREAM, NOSE, PINE, STORM, WIND

CORD — COMMUNICATION, SASH, SPERMATIC, SPINAL, UMBILICAL

COUNTER — CRYSTAL, GEIGER, PROPORTIONAL, REV, SCINTILLATION

COURSE — ASSAULT, BARGE, GOLF, MAGNETIC, MAIN, REFRESHER, SANDWICH

COURT — CLAY, COUNTY, CROWN, DISTRICT, DOMESTIC, GRASS, HARD, HIGH, INFERIOR, JUSTICE, JUVENILE, KANGAROO, MAGISTRATES', MOOT, OPEN, POLICE, PRIZE, PROVOST, SHERIFF, SUPERIOR, SUPREME, TERRITORIAL, TOUT, TRAFFIC, TRIAL, WORLD

COVER — AIR, DUST, EXTRA, FIRST-DAY, GROUND, LOOSE

CREAM — BARRIER, BAVARIAN, CLOTTED, COLD, DEVONSHIRE, DOUBLE, GLACIER, ICE PASTRY, SINGLE, SOUR, VANISHING, WHIPPING

CROP — CASH, CATCH, COVER, ETON, RIDING, ROOT

CROSS — CALVARY, CELTIC, CHARING, DOUBLE, FIERY, GEORGE, GREEK, IRON, JERUSALEM, LATIN, LORRAINE, MALTESE, NORTHERN, PAPAL, PATRIARCHAL, RED, SOUTHERN, TAU, VICTORIA

CROSSING — LEVEL, PEDESTRIAN, PELICAN, ZEBRA

CROW — CARRION, HOODED, JIM

CUP — AMERICA'S, CLARET, COFFEE, DAVIS, EGG, FA, FRUIT, GRACE, GREASE, LOVING, MOUSTACHE, STIRRUP, WORLD

CURRENCY — DECIMAL, FRACTIONAL, MANAGED, RESERVE

CURRENT — ALTERNATING, CROMWELL, DARK, DIRECT, EDDY, ELECTRIC, FOUCAULT, HUMBOLDT, JAPAN, LABRADOR, PERU, THERMIONIC, TURBIDITY

CURTAIN — AIR, BAMBOO, DROP, IRON, SAFETY

CUT — BASTARD, CREW, CULEBRA, GAILLARD, NAVY, OPEN, POWER, SHORT

DASH — EM, EN, PEBBLE, SWUNG

DAYS — DOG, EMBER, HUNDRED, JURIDICAL, LAY, ROGATION, SALAD

DEATH — BLACK, BRAIN, CIVIL, COT, CRIB, HEAT, LIVING, SUDDEN

DECK — 'TWEEN, BOAT, FLIGHT, HURRICANE, LOWER, MAIN, POOP, PROMENADE, SUN, TAPE

DELIVERY — BREECH, FORWARD, GENERAL, JAIL, RECORDED, RURAL, SPECIAL

DERBY — CROWN, DONKEY, KENTUCKY, ROLLER, SAGE

DESK — CASH, CITY, COPY, ROLL-TOP, WRITING

DEVIL — DUST, MOUNTAIN, PRINTER'S, SNOW, TASMANIAN

DIAGRAM — BAR, BLOCK, INDICATOR, RUSSELL, SCATTER, VENN

DIVE — CRASH, NOSE, POWER, SWALLOW, SWAN

DOCTOR — ANGELIC, BAREFOOT, CAPE, FAMILY, FLYING, SAW, WITCH

DOG — BACKING, BIRD, CARRIAGE, COACH, ESKIMO, EYE, GREAT, GUIDE, GUN, HEADING, HOT, KANGAROO, LEADING, LITTLE, NATIVE, PARIAH, PIG, POLICE, PRAIRIE, RACCOON, SAUSAGE, SEA, SHEPHERD, SLED, SNIFFER, SPOTTED, TOP, TRACKER, WORKING

DOOR — BACK, BARN, CAT, DUTCH, FIRE, FOLDING, FRONT, NEXT, OPEN, OVERHEAD, REVOLVING, STABLE, STAGE, STORM, STREET, SWING, TRAP

DOWN — BACK, BEAR, BEAT, BOG, BOIL, BREAK, BRING, BUCKET, BUCKLE, CALL, CAST, CHANGE, CLAMP, CLIMB, CLOSE, CRACK, CRY, CUT, DIE, DO, DRAG, DRESS, DUST, FALL, GET, GO, HAND, HOLD, HUNT, KEEP, KNOCK, LAY, LET, LIE, LIVE, LOOK, MOW, NAIL, PAY, PEG, PIN, PIPE, PLAY, PULL, PUT, RIDE, ROUND, RUB, RUN, SEND, SET, SETTLE, SHAKE, SHOOT, SHOUT, SIMMER, SIT, SLAP, SPONGE, STAND, STEP, STICK, STOP, STRIKE, TAKE, TALK, TEAR, TONE, TRACK, TURN, UPSIDE, VOTE, WASH, WEAR, WEIGH, WIND, WRITE

DRESS — ACADEMIC, COAT, COURT, EVENING, FANCY, FULL, HIGHLAND, MORNING, PINAFORE, TENT

DRESSING — FRENCH, ORE, RUSSIAN, SALAD, TOP, WELL

DRILL — BOAT, FIRE, HAMMER, KERB, PACK, POWER, TWIST

DRIVE — BEETLE, CHAIN, DISK, FLUID, FOUR-WHEEL, MOTOR, WHIST

DROP — ACID, COUGH, DELAYED, DOLLY, KNEE, LEMON, MAIL

DUCK — BLUE, BOMBAY, COLD, DEAD, HARLEQUIN, LAME, MANDARIN, MUSCOVY, MUSK, PARADISE, RUDDY, SEA, TUFTED, WOOD

DUST — ANGEL, BULL, COSMIC, GOLD

DUTY — DEATH, ESTATE, POINT, STAMP

EDGE — DECKLE, KNIFE, LEADING, TRAILING

EGG — CURATE'S, DARNING, EASTER, NEST, SCOTCH

END — BACK, BEST, BIG, BITTER, BOOK, BOTTOM, BUSINESS, CIGARETTE, COD, DEAD, EAST, FAG, GABLE, LAND'S, LOOSE, ROPE'S, STICKY, TAG, TAIL, TOP, WEST

ENGINE — AERO, BEAM, BYPASS, COMPOUND, DIESEL, DONKEY, EXTERNAL-COMBUSTION, FIRE, GAS, HEAT, INTERNAL-COMBUSTION, ION, JET, LIGHT, OVERHEAD-VALVE, PILOT, PLASMA, RADIAL, REACTION, RECIPROCATING, ROCKET, ROTARY, SIDE-VALVE, STATIONARY, STIRLING, TANK, TRACTION, TURBOJET, V-TYPE, VALVE-IN-HEAD, WANKEL

ENSIGN — BLUE, RED, WHITE

EVENT — FIELD, HAPPY, MEDIA, THREE-DAY, TRACK

EVIDENCE — CIRCUMSTANTIAL, CUMULATIVE, DIRECT, HEARSAY, KING'S, PRIMA-FACIE, QUEEN'S, STATE'S

EXCHANGE — CORN, EMPLOYMENT, FOREIGN, ION, LABOUR, PART, POST, STOCK

EYE — BEADY, BLACK, COMPOUND, ELECTRIC, EVIL, GLAD, MAGIC, MIND'S, PHEASANT'S, PINEAL, POPE'S, PRIVATE, RED, SCREW, WEATHER

FACE — BOLD, EN, LIGHT, LONG, OLD, POKER, STRAIGHT

FACTOR — COMMON, CORN, GROWTH, HOUSE, LOAD, POWER, QUALITY, RH, RHESUS, SAFETY, UNIT

FEATHER — COCK, CONTOUR, FLIGHT, SHAFT, SICKLE, WHITE

FILE — CARD, CROSSCUT, INDIAN, SINGLE

FINGER — INDEX, LADY'S, RING

FINISH — BLANKET, DEAD, MIRROR, PHOTO

FIRE — BRUSH, ELECTRIC, GREEK, LIQUID, QUICK, RAPID, RED, WATCH

FLAT — ADOBE, ALKALI, COTTAGE, DOUBLE, GARDEN, GRANNY, MUD, SALT, STUDIO

FOOD — CONVENIENCE, FAST, HEALTH, JUNK, SKIN, SOUL

FORTH — CALL, GO, HOLD, PUT, SET

FORWARD — BRING, CARRY, CENTRE, COME, INSIDE, PUT

FRACTION — COMMON, COMPLEX, COMPOUND, CONTINUED, DECIMAL, IMPROPER, PACKING, PARTIAL, PROPER, SIMPLE, VULGAR

FRACTURE — COLLES', COMMINUTED, COMPOUND, GREENSTICK, POTT'S, SIMPLE

FRAME — CLIMBING, COLD, GARDEN, HALF, OXFORD, PORTAL, SAMPLING, STILL, STOCKING

FRIDAY — GIRL, GOOD, MAN

FRONT — COLD, EYES, NATIONAL, OCCLUDED, PEOPLE'S, POLAR, POPULAR, RHODESIAN, WARM, WAVE

FROST — BLACK, JACK, SILVER, WHITE

FRUIT — ACCESSORY, COLLECTIVE, FALSE, FORBIDDEN, KEY, KIWI, MULTIPLE, PASSION, SIMPLE, SOFT, STONE, WALL

GALLERY — LADIES', NATIONAL, PRESS, PUBLIC, ROGUES', SHOOTING, STRANGER'S, TATE, WHISPERING, WINNING

GAP — CREDIBILITY, DEFLATIONARY, ENERGY, GENERATION, INFLATIONARY, SPARK, TRADE, WATER, WIND

GARDEN — BEAR, BOTANICAL, COVENT, KITCHEN, KNOT, MARKET, PEBBLE, ROCK, ROOF, TEA, WINTER, ZOOLOGICAL

GAS — AIR, BOTTLED, CALOR, COAL, CS, ELECTROLYTIC, IDEAL, INERT, LAUGHING, MARSH, MUSTARD, NATURAL, NERVE, NOBLE, NORTH-SEA, PERFECT, POISON, PRODUCER, RARE, SEWAGE, TEAR, TOWN, WATER

GATE — GOLDEN, HEAD, IRON, KISSING, LICH, LYCH, MORAVIAN, STARTING, TAIL, TARANAKI, WATER

GIRL — BACHELOR, BAR, BEST, CALL, CAREER, CHORUS, CONTINUITY, COVER, DANCING, FLOWER, GIBSON, LAND, MARCHING, OLD, SWEATER

GLASS — BELL, BURNING, CHEVAL, CROWN, CUPPING, CUT, FAVRILE, FIELD, FLINT, FLOAT, GREEN, GROUND, HAND, LEAD, LIQUID, LOOKING, MAGNIFYING, MILK, MURRHINE, OBJECT, OPTICAL, PIER, PLATE, QUARTZ, REDUCING, RUBY, SAFETY, SILICA, SOLUBLE, STAINED, STORM, TIFFANY, VENETIAN, VOLCANIC, WATER, WIRE

GLASSES — DARK, FIELD, OPERA

GOAT — ANGORA, BILLY, KASHMIR, MOUNTAIN, NANNY

GOLD — FILLED, FOOL'S, FREE, MOSAIC, OLD, ROLLED, WHITE

GREEN — APPLE, BACK, BOTTLE, BOWLING, CHROME, CROWN, GRETNA, JADE, KENDAL, LIME, LINCOLN, NILE, OLIVE, PARIS, PEA, PUTTING, RIFLE, SEA

GROUND — BURIAL, CAMPING, COMMON, HOME, HUNTING, MIDDLE, PROVING, RECREATION, STAMPING, VANTAGE

GUARD — ADVANCE, COLOUR, HOME, IRON, NATIONAL, OLD, PRAETORIAN, PROVOST, RED, SECURITY, SWISS

GUIDE — BROWNIE, GIRL, HONEY, QUEEN'S

GUM — ACAROID, BLUE, BUBBLE, CHEWING, COW, FLOODED, GHOST, KAURI, RED, SNOW, SOUR, SPIRIT, SUGAR, SWEET, WATER, WHITE

HALF — BETTER, CENTRE, FLY, SCRUM

HALL — CARNEGIE, CITY, FESTIVAL, LIBERTY, MESS, MUSIC, TAMMANY, TOWN

HAND — CHARGE, CLUB, COURT, DAB, DEAD, DECK, FARM, FREE, GLAD, HELPING, HOUR, IRON, LONE, MINUTE, OLD, ROUND, SECOND, SHED, SWEEP, UPPER, WHIP

HAT — BRASS, COCKED, COSSACK, HARD, HIGH, OLD, OPERA, PANAMA, PICTURE, PORKPIE, RED, SAILOR, SCARLET, SHOVEL, SILK, SLOUCH, TEN-GALLON, TIN, TOP

HEART — BLEEDING, BULLOCK'S, DEAD, FLOATING, PURPLE, SACRED

HEAT — ATOMIC, BLACK, BLOOD, DEAD, LATENT, PRICKLY, RADIANT, RED, TOTAL, WHITE

HISTORY — ANCIENT, CASE, LIFE, NATURAL, ORAL

HITCH — BLACKWALL, CLOVE, HARNESS, MAGNUS, ROLLING, TIMBER, WEAVER'S

HOLE — AIR, BEAM, BLACK, BOLT, COAL, FUNK, GLORY, KETTLE, LUBBER'S, NINETEENTH, SOUND, SPIDER, SWALLOW, WATER, WATERING

HOLIDAY — BANK, BUSMAN'S, HALF, LEGAL, PUBLIC, ROMAN

HOME — EVENTIDE, HARVEST, MOBILE, NURSING, REMAND, STATELY, VILLA

HORSE — CHARLEY, DARK, IRON, LIBERTY, LIGHT, NIGHT, POLE, POST, QUARTER, RIVER, ROCKING, SADDLE, SEA, SHIRE, TROJAN, WHEEL, WHITE, WILLING, WOODEN

HOUR — ELEVENTH, HAPPY, LUNCH, RUSH, SIDEREAL, WITCHING, ZERO

HOUSE — ACCEPTING, ADMIRALTY, BOARDING, BROILER, BUSH, CHARNEL, CHATTEL, CLEARING, COACH, COFFEE, COUNTING, COUNTRY, CUSTOM, DISCOUNT, DISORDERLY, DOWER, FASHION, FORCING, FREE, FULL, HALFWAY, ICE, ISSUING, LODGING, MANOR, MANSION, MEETING, OPEN, OPERA, PICTURE, POST, PUBLIC, ROOMING, SAFE, SOFTWARE, SPORTING, STATE, STATION, STOREY, TERRACED, THIRD, TOWN, TRINITY, UPPER, WASH, WENDY, WHITE

HUMOUR — AQUEOUS, GALLOWS, ILL, VITREOUS

HUNT — DRAG, FOX, SCAVENGER, STILL, TREASURE

ICE — BLACK, CAMPHOR, COCONUT, DRIFT, DRY, GLAZE, GROUND, PACK, PANCAKE, SHELF, SLOB, WATER

IN — ALL, BLOCK, BLOW, BOOK, BREAK, BRING, BUILD, BURN, BUY, CALL, CASH, CAVE, CHECK, CHIP, CLOSE, COME, DIG, DO, DRAG, DRAW, FALL, FILL, FIT, GET, GIVE, GO, HAND, HANG, HOLD, HORN, INK, JACK, KEEP, KEY, KICK, LAY, LET, LIE, LISTEN, LIVE, LOG, MOVE, MUCK, PACK, PAY, PHASE, PITCH, PLUG, PULL, PUSH, PUT, RAKE, REIN, RING, ROLL, ROPE, RUB, RUN, SCRAPE, SET, SETTLE, SIGN, SINK, SLEEP, STAND, START, STEP, SUCK, SWEAR, TAKE, THROW, TIE, TUCK, TUNE, TURN, WEIGH, WELL, WHIP, WORK, WRITE, ZERO, ZOOM

INTEREST — COMPOUND, CONTROLLING, HUMAN, LIFE, SIMPLE, VESTED

IRON — ALPHA, ANGLE, BETA, CAST, CHANNEL, CORRUGATED, DELTA, GAMMA, GEM, GRAPPLING, GROZING, INGOT, LILY, MALLEABLE, PIG, PUMP, SHOOTING, SMOOTHING, SOLDERING, STEAM, TOGGLE, WROUGHT

IVY — BOSTON, GRAPE, GROUND, JAPANESE, POISON, WEEPING

JACK — JUMPING, MAN, SCREW, UNION, YELLOW

JACKET — AIR, BED, BOMBER, BUSH, DINNER, DONKEY, DUST, ETON, FLAK, HACKING, LIFE, MESS, MONKEY, NORFOLK, PEA, REEFING, SAFARI, SHELL, SMOKING, SPORTS, STEAM, WATER, YELLOW

JELLY — CALF'S-FOOT, COMB, MINERAL, PETROLEUM, ROYAL

JOE — GI, HOLY, SLOPPY

JUDGMENT — ABSOLUTE, COMPARATIVE, LAST, VALUE

JUMP — BROAD, HIGH, LONG, SKI, TRIPLE, WATER

KEY — ALLEN, CHROMA, CHURCH, CONTROL, DEAD, FUNCTION, IGNITION, MASTER, MINOR, NUT, OFF, ON, PRONG, SHIFT, SKELETON, TUNING

KICK — DROP, FLUTTER, FREE, FROG, GOAL, PENALTY, PLACE, SCISSORS, STAB

KNIFE — BOWIE, CARVING, CASE, CLASP, FLICK, FRUIT, HUNTING, PALLET, SHEATH, TRENCH

KNOT — BLACK, FISHERMAN'S, FLAT, FRENCH, GORDIAN, GRANNY, LOOP, LOVE, OVERHAND, REEF, SQUARE, STEVEDORE'S, SURGEON'S, SWORD, THUMB, TRUELOVE, WALL, WINDSOR

LACE — ALENCON, BOBBIN, BRUSSELS, CHANTILLY, CLUNY, MECHLIN, PILLOW, POINT, SEA, TORCHON

LADY — BAG, DINNER, FIRST, NAKED, OLD, OUR, PAINTED, WHITE, YOUNG

LAMP — ALDIS, DAVY, FLUORESCENT, GLOW, HURRICANE, INCANDESCENT, NEON, PILOT, SAFETY, SPIRIT, SUN, TUNGSTEN

LANGUAGE — BODY, COMPUTER, FIRST, FORMAL, MACHINE, NATURAL, PROGRAMMING, SECOND, SIGN

LANTERN — CHINESE, DARK, FRIAR'S, JAPANESE, MAGIC, STORM

LEAVE — FRENCH, MASS, MATERNITY, SHORE, SICK

LETTER — AIR, BEGGING, BLACK, CHAIN, COVERING, DEAD, DOMINICAL, FORM, FRENCH, LOVE, OPEN, POISON-PEN, SCARLET

LIBRARY — CIRCULATING, FILM, LENDING, MOBILE, SUBSCRIPTION

LICENCE — DRIVING, OCCASIONAL, POETIC, SPECIAL, TABLE

LIFE — FUTURE, LOVE, MEAN, PRIVATE, REAL, SHELF, STILL

LIGHT — ARC, BACK, BACK-UP, BENGAL, BRAKE, COURTESY, FIRST, GREEN, INNER, KLIEG, LEADING, PILOT, REAR, RED, REVERSING, RUSH, TRAFFIC, WHITE

LIGHTING — INDIRECT, STRIP, STROBE

LIGHTNING — CHAIN, FORKED, HEAT, SHEET

LIGHTS — ANCIENT, BRIGHT, FAIRY, HOUSE, NORTHERN, POLAR, SOUTHERN

LINE — ASSEMBLY, BAR, BOTTOM, BRANCH, CLEW, CONTOUR, DATE, FALL, FIRING, FLIGHT, FRONT, GOAL, HARD, HINDENBURG, HOT, LAND, LEAD, LEDGER, MAGINOT, MAIN, MASON-DIXON, NUMBER, ODER-NEISSE, OFF, ON, PARTY, PICKET, PLIMSOLL, PLUMB, POWER, PRODUCTION, PUNCH, SIEGFRIED, SNOW, STORY, TIMBER, WATER

LINK — CUFF, DRAG, MISSING

LION — MOUNTAIN, NEMEAN, SEA

LIST — BACK, CHECK, CIVIL, CLASS, HIT, HONOURS, MAILING, RESERVED, SHORT, SICK, TRANSFER, WAITING

LOCK — COMBINATION, FERMENTATION, MAN, MORTISE, PERCUSSION, SCALP, SPRING, STOCK, VAPOUR, WHEEL, YALE

LOVE — CALF, COURTLY, CUPBOARD, FREE, PUPPY

MACHINE — ADDING, ANSWERING, BATHING, FRUIT, KIDNEY, SEWING, SLOT, TIME, VENDING, WASHING

MAIL — AIR, CHAIN, ELECTRONIC, FAN, SURFACE

MAIN — RING, SPANISH, WATER

MAN — ADVANCE, ANCHOR, BEST, COMPANY, CON, CONFIDENCE, ENLISTED, FAMILY, FANCY, FRONT, HATCHET, HIT, ICE, INNER, IRON, LADIES', LEADING, MEDICINE, MUFFIN, NEANDERTHAL, PALAEOLITHIC, PARTY, PILTDOWN, RAG-AND-BONE, SANDWICH, STRAIGHT, TWELFTH, YES

MARCH — DEAD, FORCED, HUNGER, LONG, QUICK, SLOW

MARIA — AVE, BLACK, HENRIETTA, SANTA, TIA

MARK — BENCH, BLACK, EXCLAMATION, KITE, PUNCTUATION, QUESTION, QUOTATION

MARKET — BLACK, BUYERS', CAPITAL, CAPTIVE, COMMON, FLEA, KERB, MONEY, OPEN, SELLERS', SPOT, STOCK

MARRIAGE — CIVIL, COMMON-LAW, GROUP, MIXED

MASK — DEATH, GAS, LIFE, LOO, OXYGEN, SHADOW, STOCKING

MASTER — CAREERS, GRAND, HARBOUR, INTERNATIONAL, OLD, PAST, QUESTION

MATCH — FRICTION, LOVE, SAFETY, SHIELD, SLANGING, SLOW, TEST

MATE — FIRST, FOOL'S, RUNNING, SCHOLAR'S, SECOND, SOUL

MATTER — BACK, END, FRONT, GREY, SUBJECT, WHITE

MEDICINE — ALTERNATIVE, COMPLEMENTARY, DUTCH, FOLK, FORENSIC, PATENT

MILE — ADMIRALTY, AIR, GEOGRAPHICAL, NAUTICAL, ROMAN, SEA, STATUTE, SWEDISH

MILL — COFFEE, PEPPER, ROLLING, SMOCK, STAMP, STRIP, WATER

MITE — BULB, CHEESE, FLOUR, FOWL, GALL, HARVEST, ITCH, SPIDER, WIDOW'S

MONEY — BIG, BLOOD, CALL, CAUTION, COB, CONSCIENCE, DANGER, EASY, FOLDING, GATE, HEAD, HOT, HUSH, KEY, MAUNDY, NEAR, PAPER, PIN, PLASTIC, POCKET, PRIZE, READY, SEED, SHIP

MOON — BLUE, FULL, HARVEST, HUNTER'S, MOCK, NEW, OLD

MOTHER — EARTH, FOSTER, NURSING, QUEEN, REVEREND, SOLO

MOTION — FAST, HARMONIC, LINK, PERPETUAL, PROPER, SLOW

NAME — BRAND, CHRISTIAN, DAY, FAMILY, FIRST, GIVEN, HOUSEHOLD, LAST, MAIDEN, MIDDLE, PEN, PLACE, PROPRIETARY, SECOND, TRADE

NECK — BOAT, BRASS, CREW, SCOOP, SWAN, V

NEEDLE — CLEOPATRA'S, DARNING, DIP, ELECTRIC, ICE, MAGNETIC, PINE, SHEPHERD'S

NET — DRIFT, GILL, LANDING, MOSQUITO, POUND, SAFETY, SHARK

NIGHT — FIRST, GOOD, TWELFTH, WALPURGIS, WATCH

NOTE — ADVICE, AUXILIARY, BLUE, COVER, CURRENCY, DEMAND, EIGHTH, GOLD, GRACE, LEADING, PASSING, POSTAL, PROMISSORY, QUARTER, SICK, TREASURY, WHOLE

NUMBER — ACCESSION, ALGEBRAIC, ATOMIC, BACK, BINARY, BOX, CALL, CARDINAL, COMPLEX, COMPOSITE, COMPOUND, CONCRETE, E, GOLDEN, INDEX, MACH,

MAGIC, OPPOSITE, ORDINAL, PERFECT, PRIME, REAL, REGISTRATION, SERIAL, SQUARE, TELEPHONE, WHOLE, WRONG

OFFERING — BURNT, PEACE

OFFICE — BOX, CROWN, DIVINE, ELECTRONIC, EMPLOYMENT, FOREIGN, HOLY, HOME, LAND, LEFT-LUGGAGE, PATENT, POST, REGISTER, WAR

OIL — CAMPHORATED, CASTOR, COCONUT, COD-LIVER, CORN, CRUDE, DIESEL, ESSENTIAL, FATTY, GAS, LINSEED, MACASSAR, MINERAL, MUSTARD, NUT, OLIVE, PALM, PEANUT, RAPE, SASSAFRAS, SHALE, SPERM, VEGETABLE, WHALE

OPERA — BALLAD, COMIC, GRAND, HORSE, LIGHT, SOAP, SPACE

ORANGE — AGENT, BITTER, BLOOD, MOCK, NAVEL, OSAGE, SEVILLE

ORDER — AFFILIATION, APPLE-PIE, ATTIC, BANKER'S, COMMUNITY-SERVICE, COMPENSATION, ENCLOSED, FIRING, LOOSE, MAIL, MARKET, MONEY, PECKING, POSSESSION, POSTAL, RECEIVING, SHORT, STANDING, SUPERVISION, TEUTONIC, THIRD, WORD

ORDERS — HOLY, MAJOR, MARCHING, MINOR, SEALED

ORGAN — BARREL, ELECTRIC, ELECTRONIC, END, GREAT, HAMMOND, HAND, HOUSE, MOUTH, PIPE, PORTATIVE, REED, SENSE, STEAM

OVER — BIND, BLOW, BOIL, BOWL, BRING, CARRY, CHEW, DO, FALL, GET, GIVE, GLOSS, GO, HAND, HOLD, KEEL, LAY, LOOK, MAIDEN, MAKE, PAPER, PASS, PUT, ROLL, RUN, SEE, SKATE, SLIDE, SMOOTH, SPILL, STAND, TAKE, THINK, THROW, TICK, TIDE, TURN, WARM, WORK

OYSTER — BUSH, PEARL, PRAIRIE, SEED, VEGETABLE

PACK — BLISTER, BUBBLE, COLD, FACE, FILM, ICE, POWER, WET

PAD — CRASH, HARD, LAUNCHING, LILY, SCRATCH, SHOULDER

PAINT — GLOSS, OIL, POSTER, WAR

PALACE — BUCKINGHAM, CRYSTAL, GIN, PICTURE

PAPER — ART, BALLOT, BLOTTING, BOND, BROMIDE, BROWN, BUILDING, CARBON, CARTRIDGE, CIGARETTE, COMMERCIAL, CREPE, FILTER, FLOCK, GRAPH, GREEN, INDIA, LAVATORY, LINEN, MANILA, MERCANTILE, MUSIC, ORDER, RICE, TISSUE, TOILET, TRACING, WAX, WRITING

PARK — AMUSEMENT, CAR, COUNTRY, FOREST, GAME, HYDE, NATIONAL, SAFARI, SCIENCE, THEME

PARTY — BOTTLE, COMMUNIST, CONSERVATIVE, FIRING, GARDEN, HEN, HOUSE, LABOUR, LIBERAL, NATIONAL, NATIONALIST, PEOPLE'S, REPUBLICAN, SEARCH, STAG, TEA, THIRD, WORKING

PASSAGE — BACK, BRIDGE, DRAKE, MIDDLE, MONA, NORTHEAST, NORTHWEST, ROUGH, WINDWARD

PATH — BRIDLE, FLARE, FLIGHT, GLIDE, PRIMROSE, TOWING

PAY — BACK, EQUAL, SEVERANCE, SICK, STRIKE, TAKE-HOME

PEA — BLACK-EYED, DESERT, PIGEON, SPLIT, SUGAR, SWEET

PEAR — ALLIGATOR, ANCHOVY, CONFERENCE, PRICKLY, WILLIAMS

PEN – CARTRIDGE, CATCHING, DATA, FELT-TIP, FOUNTAIN, QUILL, SEA

PENSION – EN, OCCUPATIONAL, RETIREMENT

PIANO – COTTAGE, GRAND, PLAYER, PREPARED, SQUARE, STREET, UPRIGHT

PIE – COTTAGE, CUSTARD, HUMBLE, MINCE, MUD, PORK, SHEPHERD'S

PIN – BOBBY, COTTER, DRAWING, END, FIRING, GUDGEON, PANEL, ROLLING, SAFETY, SCATTER, SHEAR, STICK, SWIVEL, TAPER, WREST, WRIST

PIPE – CORNCOB, ESCAPE, FLUE, INDIAN, JET, PEACE, PITCH, RAINWATER, REED, SOIL, WASTE

PITCH – ABSOLUTE, CONCERT, FEVER, PERFECT, WOOD

PLACE – DECIMAL, HIGH, HOLY, RESTING, WATERING

PLASTER – COURT, MUSTARD, STICKING

PLATE – ANGLE, ARMOUR, BATTEN, BUTT, ECHO, FASHION, FUTTOCK, GLACIS, GOLD, GROUND, HOME, LICENSE, NICKEL, QUARTER, REGISTRATION, SCREW, SILVER, SOUP, SURFACE, SWASH, TIN, TRADE, WALL, WOBBLE

PLAY – CHILD'S, DOUBLE, FAIR, FOUL, MATCH, MIRACLE, MORALITY, MYSTERY, PASSION, SHADOW, STROKE

PLEAT – BOX, FRENCH, INVERTED, KICK, KNIFE

POCKET – AIR, HIP, PATCH, SLASH, SLIT

POINT – BOILING, BREAKING, BROWNIE, CHANGE, CLOVIS, COVER, CRITICAL, CURIE, DEAD, DECIMAL, DEW, DIAMOND, DRY, END, EQUINOCTIAL, FESSE, FIXED, FLASH, FOCAL, FREEZING, GALLINAS, GAME, GOLD, HIGH, ICE, LIMIT, MATCH, MELTING, OBJECTIVE, PETIT, POWER, PRESSURE, SAMPLE, SATURATION, SET, SPECIE, STEAM, STRONG, SUSPENSION, TRANSITION, TRIG, TRIPLE, TURNING, VANISHING, VANTAGE, WEST, YIELD

POLE – BARBER'S, CELESTIAL, MAGNETIC, NORTH, SOUTH, TOTEM

POLL – ADVANCE, DEED, GALLUP, OPINION, RED, STRAW

POST – COMMAND, FINGER, FIRST, GOAL, GRADED, GRADIENT, HITCHING, LAST, LISTENING, NEWEL, OBSERVATION, REGISTERED, STAGING, TOOL, TRADING, WINNING

POT – CHAMBER, COAL, LOBSTER, MELTING, PEPPER, WATERING

POTATO – HOT, IRISH, SEED, SWEET, WHITE

POWDER – BAKING, BLACK, BLEACHING, CHILLI, CURRY, CUSTARD, FACE GIANT, TALCUM, TOOTH, WASHING

PRESS – DRILL, FILTER, FLY, FOLDING, GUTTER, HYDRAULIC, PRINTING, PRIVATE, RACKET, STOP

PRESSURE – ATMOSPHERIC, BAROMETRIC, BLOOD, CRITICAL, FLUID, OSMOTIC, PARTIAL, VAPOUR

PRICE – ASKING, BID, BRIDE, INTERVENTION, LIST, MARKET, OFFER, RESERVE, STARTING, UNIT

PROFESSOR – ASSISTANT, ASSOCIATE, FULL, REGIUS, VISITING

PUDDING – BLACK, BLOOD, CABINET, CHRISTMAS, COLLEGE, EVE'S, HASTY, MILK, PEASE, PLUM, SUET, SUMMER, WHITE, YORKSHIRE

PUMP – AIR, BICYCLE, CENTRIFUGAL, ELECTROMAGNETIC, FILTER, FORCE, HEAT, LIFT, PARISH, PETROL, ROTARY, STIRRUP, STOMACH, SUCTION, VACUUM

PUNCH – BELL, CARD, CENTRE, KEY, MILK, PLANTER'S, RABBIT, SUFFOLK, SUNDAY

PURSE – LONG, MERMAID'S, PRIVY, SEA

PUZZLE – CHINESE, CROSSWORD, JIGSAW, MONKEY

QUARTER – EMPTY, FIRST, LAST, LATIN

QUESTION – DIRECT, INDIRECT, LEADING, RHETORICAL

RABBIT – ANGORA, BUCK, JACK, ROCK, WELSH

RACE – ARMS, BOAT, BUMPING, CLAIMING, DRAG, EGG-AND-SPOON, MASTER, OBSTACLE, RAT, RELAY, SACK, THREE-LEGGED

RACK – CLOUD, ROOF, TOAST

RATE – BANK, BASE, BASIC, BIRTH, BIT, DEATH, EXCHANGE, LAPSE, MORTALITY, MORTGAGE, PIECE, POOR, PRIME, TAX

RECORDER – FLIGHT, INCREMENTAL, TAPE, WIRE

RED – BLOOD, BRICK, CHINESE, CHROME, CONGO, INDIAN, TURKEY, VENETIAN

RELATIONS – COMMUNITY, INDUSTRIAL, LABOUR, PUBLIC, RACE

RELIEF – HIGH, LOW, OUTDOOR, PHOTO

RENT – COST, ECONOMIC, FAIR, GROUND, MARKET, PEPPERCORN

RESERVE – CENTRAL, GOLD, INDIAN, NATURE, SCENIC

REVOLUTION – AMERICAN, BLOODLESS, CHINESE, CULTURAL, FEBRUARY, FRENCH, GLORIOUS, GREEN, INDUSTRIAL, OCTOBER, PALACE, RUSSIAN

RING – ANCHOR, ANNUAL, BENZENE, ENGAGEMENT, ETERNITY, EXTENSION, FAIRY, GAS, GROWTH, GUARD, KEEPER, NOSE, PISTON, PRICE, PRIZE, RETAINING, SEAL, SIGNET, SLIP, SNAP, TEETHING, TREE, VORTEX, WEDDING

ROAD – ACCESS, CLAY, CONCESSION, DIRT, ESCAPE, POST, RING, SERVICE, SLIP, TRUNK

ROD – AARON'S, BLACK, BLUE, CON, CONNECTING, CONTROL, DIVINING, DOWSING, DRAIN, FISHING, FLY, HOT, PISTON, STAIR, TIE, TRACK, WELDING

ROLL – BARREL, BRIDGE, COURT, DANDY, EGG, FORWARD, MUSIC, MUSTER, PIANO, PIPE, SAUSAGE, SNAP, SPRING, SWISS, VICTORY, WESTERN

ROOM – BACK, COMBINATION, COMMON, COMPOSING, CONSULTING, DAY, DINING, DRAWING, DRESSING, ENGINE, GUN, LIVING, MEN'S, OPERATIONS, ORDERLY, POWDER, PUMP, RECEPTION, RECREATION, REST, ROBING, RUMPUS, SITTING, SMOKING, STILL, TIRING, UTILITY, WAITING, WITHDRAWING

ROOT – BUTTRESS, CLUB, CUBE, CULVER'S, MALLEE, PLEURISY, PROP, SQUARE

ROT – BLACK, BROWN, DRY, FOOT, SOFT, WET

ROUND – BRING, CHANGE, COME, MILK, RALLY, SCRUB, TALK

ROW – CORN, DEATH, NOTE, SKID, TONE

ROYAL – ANNAPOLIS, BATTLE, PAIR, PORT, PRINCE, PRINCESS, RHYME

RUBBER – COLD, CREPE, HARD, INDIA, PARÁ, SMOKED, SORBO, SYNTHETIC, WILD

RULE — CHAIN, FOOT, GLOBAL, GOLDEN, GROUND, HOME, PARALLELOGRAM, PHASE, PLUMB, SETTING, SLIDE

RUN — BOMBING, BULL, DRY, DUMMY, GROUND, HEN, HOME, MILK, MOLE, SKI, TRIAL

SALAD — CORN, FRUIT, RUSSIAN, WALDORF

SALE — BOOT, BRING-AND-BUY, CAR-BOOT, JUMBLE, RUMMAGE, WHITE

SALTS — BATH, EPSOM, HEALTH, LIVER, SMELLING

SAUCE — APPLE, BÉCHAMEL, BREAD, CHILLI, CREAM, HARD, HOLLANDAISE, MELBA, MINT, MOUSSELINE, SOY, TARTAR, WHITE, WORCESTER

SAW — BACK, BAND, BUZZ, CHAIN, CIRCULAR, COMPASS, COPING, CROSSCUT, CROWN, FLOORING, FRET, GANG, PANEL, SCROLL, STONE, TENON

SCHOOL — APPROVED, BOARD, BOARDING, CHOIR, COMPREHENSIVE, CORRESPONDENCE, DAME, DAY, DIRECT-GRANT, ELEMENTARY, FINISHING, FIRST, GRAMMAR, HIGH, INDEPENDENT, INFANT, JUNIOR, LOWER, MIDDLE, NIGHT, NURSERY, PREP, PREPARATORY, PRIMARY, PRIVATE, PUBLIC, RESIDENTIAL, SECONDARY, SPECIAL, STATE, SUMMER, SUNDAY, UPPER

SCIENCE — BEHAVIOURAL, CHRISTIAN, COGNITIVE, DOMESTIC, EARTH, HARD, INFORMATION, LIFE, NATURAL, PHYSICAL, POLICY, POLITICAL, RURAL, SOCIAL, VETERINARY

SCOUT — AIR, BOY, CUB, GIRL, KING'S, QUEEN'S, SEA, TALENT, VENTURE

SCREEN — BIG, FIRE, ORGAN, ROOD, SILVER, SMALL, SMOKE

SCREW — ARCHIMEDES', CAP, COACH, GRUB, ICE, INTERRUPTED, LAG, LEAD, LEVELLING, LUG, MACHINE, MICROMETER, PHILLIPS

SEASON — CLOSE, HIGH, OFF, SILLY

SEAT — BACK, BOX, BUCKET, COUNTRY, COUNTY, DEATH, EJECTION, HOT, JUMP, LOVE, MERCY, RUMBLE, SAFE, SLIDING, WINDOW

SECRETARY — COMPANY, HOME, PARLIAMENTARY, PRIVATE, SOCIAL

SERVICE — ACTIVE, CIVIL, COMMUNITY, DINNER, DIPLOMATIC, DIVINE, FOREIGN, LIP, NATIONAL, PUBLIC, ROOM, SECRET, SENIOR, SILVER, TEA

SET — CLOSED, COMPANION, CRYSTAL, DATA, DEAD, FILM, FLASH, JET, LOVE, NAIL, OPEN, ORDERED, PERMANENT, POWER, SAW, SMART, SOLUTION, TOILET, TRUTH

SHAFT — AIR, BUTT, DRIVE, ESCAPE, PROPELLER

SHEET — BALANCE, CHARGE, CRIME, DOPE, FLOW, FLY, ICE, SCRATCH, SWINDLE, TEAR, THUNDER, TIME, WINDING, WORK

SHIFT — BACK, BLUE, DAY, EINSTEIN, FUNCTION, NIGHT, RED, SOUND, SPLIT, SWING

SHIRT — BOILED, BROWN, DRESS, HAIR, SPORTS, STUFFED, SWEAT, TEE

SHOE — BLOCKED, BRAKE, COURT, GYM, HOT, LAUNCHING, PILE, TENNIS, TRACK

SHOP — BETTING, BODY, BUCKET, CLOSED, COFFEE, DUTY-FREE, FISH-AND-CHIP, JUNK, MACHINE, OPEN, PRINT, SEX, SWAP, SWEET, TALKING, TUCK, UNION

SHOT — APPROACH, BIG, BOOSTER, DIRECT-MAIL, DROP, FOUL, JUMP, LONG, PARTHIAN, PASSING, POT

SHOW — CHAT, DUMB, FLOOR, ICE, LIGHT, MINSTREL, RAREE, ROAD, TALK

SICKNESS — ALTITUDE, BUSH, DECOMPRESSION, FALLING, MILK, MORNING, MOTION, MOUNTAIN, RADIATION, SERUM, SLEEPING, SWEATING

SIDE — DISTAFF, FLIP, PROMPT, SPEAR, SUNNY

SLEEVE — BALLOON, BATWING, BISHOP, DOLMAN

SOAP — CASTILE, GREEN, JOE, METALLIC, SADDLE, SOFT, SUGAR, TOILET

SODA — CAUSTIC, CREAM, ICE-CREAM, WASHING

SOLDIER — FOOT, GALLANT, OLD, RETURNED, TIN, UNKNOWN, WAGON, WATER

SONG — FOLK, PART, PATTER, PRICK, SWAN, THEME, TORCH

SPEECH — CURTAIN, DIRECT, FREE, INDIRECT, KING'S, QUEEN'S, REPORTED

SPIRIT — HOLY, PROOF, SURGICAL, TEAM, WHITE, WOOD

SPOT — BEAUTY, BLACK, BLIND, HIGH, HOT, LEAF, SOFT, TROUBLE

SQUAD — FIRING, FLYING, FRAUD, SNATCH, VICE

SQUARE — ALL, BEVEL, LATIN, MAGIC, MITRE, SET, TIMES, WORD

STAMP — DATE, POSTAGE, RUBBER, TRADING

STAND — HALL, HAT, MUSIC, ONE-NIGHT, UMBRELLA

STANDARD — DOUBLE, GOLD, LAMP, ROYAL, SILVER

STAR — BINARY, BLAZING, DARK, DOG, DOUBLE, DWARF, EVENING, EXPLODING, FALLING, FEATHER, FILM, FIXED, FLARE, GIANT, MORNING, MULTIPLE, NEUTRON, NORTH, POLE, PULSATING, RADIO, SHOOTING

START — BUMP, FLYING, HEAD

STEAK — MINUTE, T-BONE, TARTAR

STICK — BIG, CANCER, COCKTAIL, CONTROL, FRENCH, JOSS, POGO, SHOOTING, SKI, SWAGGER, SWIZZLE, WALKING, WHITE

STITCH — BLANKET, BUTTONHOLE, CABLE, CHAIN, GARTER, LOCK, MOSS, RUNNING, SATIN, SLIP, STOCKING, TENT

STOCK — CAPITAL, COMMON, DEAD, JOINT, LAUGHING, PREFERRED, ROLLING, VIRGINIA

STONE — BATH, BLARNEY, CINNAMON, COPING, FOUNDATION, IMPOSING, KIDNEY, MOCHA, OAMARU, PAVING, PHILOSOPHER'S, PRECIOUS, ROSETTA, STEPPING

STOOL — CUCKING, CUTTY, DUCKING, MILKING, PIANO

STRAW — CHEESE, LAST, SHORT

STRIKE — BIRD, GENERAL, HUNGER, OFFICIAL, SIT-DOWN, SYMPATHY, TOKEN, WILDCAT

STUDY — BROWN, CASE, FEASIBILITY, FIELD, MOTION, NATURE, PILOT, TIME

STUFF — HOT, KIDS', ROUGH, SMALL, SOB

SUGAR — BARLEY, BEET, BROWN, CANE, CASTER, CONFECTIONERS', FRUIT, GRANULATED, GRAPE, ICING, INVERT, LOAF, MAPLE, MILK, PALM, SPUN, WOOD

SUIT — BATHING, BIRTHDAY, BOILER, DIVING, DRESS, JUMP, LONG, LOUNGE, MAJOR, MAO, MINOR, MONKEY, PATERNITY, PRESSURE, SAFARI, SAILOR, SLACK, TROUSER, WET, ZOOT

TABLE — BIRD, COFFEE, DRESSING, GATE-LEG, GLACIER, HIGH, LEAGUE, LIFE, MULTIPLICATION, OCCASIONAL, OPERATING, PEMBROKE, PERIODIC, POOL, REFECTORY, ROUND, SAND, TIDE, WATER, WOOL, WRITING

TALK — BABY, DOUBLE, PEP, PILLOW, SALES, SMALL

TAPE — CHROME, FRICTION, GAFFER, GRIP, IDIOT, INSULATING, MAGNETIC, MASKING, PAPER, PERFORATED, PUNCHED, RED, SCOTCH, TICKER, VIDEO

TAR — COAL, JACK, MINERAL, PINE, WOOD

TENNIS — COURT, DECK, LAWN, REAL, ROYAL, TABLE

TERM — HALF, HILARY, INKHORN, LAW, LENT, MICHAELMAS, TRINITY

THROUGH — BREAK, CARRY, COME, FOLLOW, MUDDLE, PULL, PUSH, PUT, ROMP, RUN, SCRAPE, SEE, WALK, WORK

TICKET — MEAL, ONE-WAY, PARKING, PAWN, PLATFORM, RETURN, ROUND-TRIP, SEASON, SINGLE

TIDE — HIGH, LOW, NEAP, RED, SPRING

TIE — BLACK, BOW, CUP, ENGLISHMAN'S, STRING, WHITE, WINDSOR

TIME — BIG, BORROWED, CLOSING, COMMON, COMPOUND, CORE, DAYLIGHT-SAVING, DOUBLE, DOWN, DRINKING-UP, EXTRA, FATHER, FOUR-FOUR, FULL, HIGH, IDLE, INJURY, LIGHTING-UP, LOCAL, MEAN, OPENING, PRIME, QUADRUPLE, QUESTION, QUICK, RESPONSE, SHORT, SIX-EIGHT, SLOW, STANDARD, SUMMER, THREE-FOUR, TRIPLE, TWO-FOUR, UNIVERSAL

TO — BRING, COME, FALL, GO, HEAVE, KEEP, RISE, RUN, SET, SPEAK, STAND, STICK, TAKE, TUMBLE, TURN

TOGETHER — GO, HANG, HOLD, LIVE, PULL, SCRAPE, SCRATCH, STICK, THROW

TOM — LONG, PEEPING, UNCLE

TOOTH — BABY, EGG, MILK, SWEET, WISDOM

TOP — BIG, DOUBLE, FIGHTING, HUMMING, PEG, ROUND, SCREW, SOFT, SPINNING, TANK

TOWN — BOOM, CAPE, COUNTY, GEORGE, GHOST, MARKET, NEW, POST, TWIN

TRADE — CARRIAGE, FREE, RAG, SLAVE

TRAIN — BOAT, DOG, GRAVY, WAGON, WAVE

TRAP — BOOBY, LIVE, POVERTY, RADAR, SAND, SPEED, STEAM, STENCH, STINK, TANK

TRIANGLE — BERMUDA, CIRCULAR, ETERNAL, PASCAL'S, RIGHT, RIGHT-ANGLED, SPHERICAL

TRICK — CON, CONFIDENCE, DIRTY, HAT, THREE-CARD

TRIP — DAY, EGO, FIELD, ROUND

TROT — JOG, RISING, SITTING, TURKEY

TUBE — CAPILLARY, CATHODE-RAY, DRIFT, ELECTRON, EUSTACHIAN, FALLOPIAN, GEISSLER, INNER, NIXIE, PICTURE, PITOT, POLLEN, SHOCK, SIEVE, SPEAKING, STATIC, TELEVISION, TEST, VACUUM

TURN — ABOUT, GOOD, KICK, LODGING, PARALLEL, STEM, THREE-POINT

UNDER — DOWN, GO, KEEP, KNUCKLE, SIT

WALL — ANTONINE, CAVITY, CELL, CHINESE, CLIMBING, CURTAIN, FIRE, HADRIAN'S, HANGING, PARTY, RETAINING, SEA, WAILING, WESTERN—

WATCH — BLACK, MIDDLE, MORNING, NIGHT

WAVE — BRAIN, ELECTROMAGNETIC, FINGER, GROUND, HEAT, LONG, LONGITUDINAL, MEDIUM, NEW, PERMANENT, RADIO, SEISMIC, SHOCK, SHORT, SKY, SOUND, STANDING, STATIONARY, TIDAL

WAX — CHINESE, COBBLER'S, EARTH, JAPAN, MINERAL, MONTAN, PARAFFIN, SEALING, VEGETABLE

WAY — APPIAN, EACH, FLAMINIAN, FLY, FOSSE, MILKY, PENNINE, PERMANENT, UNDER

WHEEL — BALANCE, BIG, BUFFING, CATHERINE, CROWN, DISC, DRIVING, EMERY, ESCAPE, FERRIS, GRINDING, PADDLE, POTTER'S, PRAYER, SPINNING, STEERING, STITCH, TAIL, WATER, WIRE

WHISKEY — IRISH, CORN, MALT

WHISTLE — PENNY, STEAM, TIN, WOLF

WINDOW — BAY, BOW, COMPASS, GABLE, JESSE, LANCET, LAUNCH, PICTURE, RADIO, ROSE, SASH, STORM, WEATHER, WHEEL

WIRE — BARBED, CHICKEN, FENCING, HIGH, LIVE, RAZOR

WITH — BEAR, BREAK, CLOSE, DEAL, GO, LIVE, PLAY, SETTLE, SLEEP, STICK

WOMAN — FANCY, LITTLE, OLD, PAINTED, SCARLET, WIDOW

WORK — FIELD, NUMBER, OUTSIDE, SOCIAL

YARD — BACK, MAIN, SCOTLAND

YEAR — ASTRONOMICAL, CALENDAR, CIVIL, EQUINOCTIAL, FINANCIAL, FISCAL, GREAT, HOLY, LEAP, LIGHT, LUNAR, NEW, SABBATICAL, SCHOOL, SIDEREAL, SOLAR, TROPICAL

ZONE — ECONOMIC, ENTERPRISE, FREE, FRIGID, HOT, NUCLEAR-FREE, SKIP, SMOKELESS, TEMPERATE, TIME, TORRID, TWILIGHT

ABBREVIATIONS

AA (Alcoholics Anonymous; Automobile Association)
AAA (Amateur Athletic Association)
AB (able seaman)
ABA (Amateur Boxing Association)
ABP (archbishop)
ABTA (Association of British Travel Agents)
AC (alternating current; account)

ACA (Associate of the Institute of Chartered Accountants)
ACAS (Advisory Conciliation and Arbitration Service)
ACIS (Associate of the Chartered Institute of Secretaries)
AD (anno domini)
ADC (aide-de-camp; amateur dramatic club)

ADJ (adjective)
ADM (Admiral)
ADV (adverb)
AD VAL (ad valorem)
AFA (Amateur Football Association)
AFC (Air Force Cross)
AFM (Air Force Medal)
AGM (annual general meeting)
AI (artificial insemination; artificial intelligence)
AIB (Associate of the Institute of Bankers)
AIDS (Acquired Immune Deficiency Syndrome)
ALA (Alabama)
AM (ante meridiem)
AMU (atomic mass unit)
ANON (anonymous)
AOB (any other business)
AOC (Air Officer Commanding)
APEX (Association of Professional, Executive, Clerical, and Computer Staff)
APOCR (Apocrypha)
APPROX (approximate)
APT (Advanced Passenger Train)
ARA (Associate of the Royal Academy)
ARAM (Associate of the Royal Academy of Music)
ARCM (Associate of the Royal College of Music)
ARCS (Associate of the Royal College of Science)
ARIBA (Associate of the Royal Institute of British Architects)
ARIZ (Arizona)
ARK (Arkansas)
ASA (Advertising Standards Authority)
ASAP (as soon as possible)
ASH (Action on Smoking and Health)
ASLEF (Associated Society of Locomotive Engineers and Firemen)
AT (atomic)
ATC (air traffic control; Air Training Corps)
ATS (Auxiliary Territorial Service)
ATTN (for the attention of)
ATTRIB (attributive)
AT WT (atomic weight)
AU (Angstrom unit; astronomical unit)
AUEW (Amalgamated Union of Engineering Workers)
AUG (August)
AV (ad valorem; Authorized Version)
AVDP (avoirdupois)
AVE (avenue)
AWOL (absent without leave)
BA (Bachelor of Arts; British Academy; British Airways; British Association)
BAA (British Airports Authority)
BAFTA (British Academy of Film and Television Arts)
B ARCH (Bachelor of Architecture)
BART (baronet)
BBC (British Broadcasting Corporation)
BC (before Christ)

BCH (Bachelor of Surgery)
BCL (Bachelor of Civil Law)
BCOM (Bachelor of Commerce)
BD (Bachelor of Divinity)
BDA (British Dental Association)
BDS (Bachelor of Dental Surgery)
BE (bill of exchange)
B ED (Bachelor of Education)
B ENG (Bachelor of Engineering)
BHP (brake horsepower)
BIM (British Institute of Management)
B LITT (Bachelor of Letters)
BMA (British Medical Association)
BMC (British Medical Council)
BMJ (British Medical Journal)
BMUS (Bachelor of Music)
BN (billion)
BOC (British Oxygen Company)
BP (bishop)
BPAS (British Pregnancy Advisory Service)
BPHARM (Bachelor of Pharmacy)
BPHIL (Bachelor of Philosophy)
BR (British Rail)
BRCS (British Red Cross Society)
BROS (brothers)
BSC (Bachelor of Science)
BSI (British Standards Institution)
BST (British Standard Time; British Summer Time)
BT (Baronet)
BTA (British Tourist Authority)
BVA (British Veterinary Association)
C (centigrade; circa)
CA (chartered accountant)
CAA (Civil Aviation Authority)
CAD (computer-aided design)
CADCAM (computer-aided design and manufacture)
CAL (California; calorie)
CAM (computer-aided manufacture)
CAMRA (Campaign for Real Ale)
C AND G (City and Guilds)
C AND W (country and western)
CANT (canticles)
CANTAB (of Cambridge – used with academic awards)
CAP (capital)
CAPT (captain)
CARD (Cardinal)
CB (Citizens' Band; Companion of the Bath)
CBE (Commander of the British Empire)
CBI (Confederation of British Industry)
CC (County Council; Cricket Club; cubic centimetre)
CDR (Commander)
CDRE (Commodore)
CE (Church of England; civil engineer)
CEGB (Central Electricity Generating Board)
C ENG (Chartered Engineer)
CENTO (Central Treaty Organization)
CERT (certificate; certified; certify)

CET (Central European Time)
CF (compare)
CFE (College of Further Education)
CFI (cost, freight, and insurance)
CGM (Conspicuous Gallantry Medal)
CH (chapter; church; Companion of Honour)
CHAS (Charles)
CI (curie; Order of the Crown of India)
CIA (Central Intelligence Agency)
CID (Criminal Investigation Department)
CIE (Companion of the Indian Empire)
CIF (cost, insurance, and freight)
CII (Chartered Insurance Institute)
C IN C (Commander in Chief)
CIS (Chartered Institute of Secretaries)
CL (centilitre)
CLLR (councillor)
CM (centimetre)
CMG (Companion of St Michael and St
    George)
CNAA (Council for National Academic Awards)
CND (Campaign for Nuclear Disarmament)
CO (commanding officer; company; county)
COD (cash on delivery)
C OF E (Church of England)
C OF S (Church of Scotland)
COHSE (Confederation of Health Service
    Employees)
COL (colonel; Colorado; Colossians)
CONN (Connecticut)
CONT (continued)
COR (Corinthians)
COS (cosine)
CR (credit)
CRO (cathode ray oscilloscope; Criminal
    Records Office)
CSE (Certificate of Secondary Education)
CSI (Companion of the Star of India)
CSM (Company Sergeant Major)
CU (cubic)
CV (curriculum vitae)
CVO (Commander of the Victorian Order)
CWT (hundredweight)
D (daughter; died; penny)
DA (District Attorney)
DAK (Dakota)
DAN (Daniel)
DBE (Dame Commander of the British Empire)
DC (Detective Constable; direct current; from
    the beginning)
DCB (Dame Commander of the Bath)
DCL (Doctor of Civil Law)
DCM (Distinguished Conduct Medal)
DCMG (Dame Commander of St Michael and
    St George)
DCVO (Dame Commander of the Victorian
    Order)
DD (direct debit; Doctor of Divinity)
DDS (Doctor of Dental Surgery)
DEL (Delaware)
DEPT (department)

DES (Department of Education and Science)
DEUT (Deuteronomy)
DF (Defender of the Faith)
DFC (Distinguished Flying Cross)
DFM (Distinguished Flying Medal)
DG (by the grace of God)
DHSS (Department of Health and Social
    Security)
DI (Detective Inspector)
DIAL (dialect)
DIP (Diploma)
DIP ED (Diploma in Education)
DIY (do-it-yourself)
D LITT (Doctor of Literature)
DM (Doctor of Medicine)
D MUS (Doctor of Music)
DNB (Dictionary of National Biography)
DO (ditto)
DOA (dead on arrival)
DOB (date of birth)
DOE (Department of the Environment)
DOM (to God, the best and greatest)
DOZ (dozen)
DPHIL (Doctor of Philosophy)
DPP (Director of Public Prosecutions)
DR (debtor; doctor; drive)
DSC (Distinguished Service Cross; Doctor of
    Science)
DSM (Distinguished Service Medal)
DSO (Distinguished Service Order)
DT (delirium tremens)
DV (God willing)
DVLC (Driver and Vehicle Licensing Centre)
E (East; Easterly; Eastern)
EA (each)
EC (East Central — London postal district)
ECCLES (Ecclesiastes)
ECCLUS (Ecclesiasticus)
ECG (electrocardiogram)
ECS (European Communication Satellite)
EE (Early English)
EEC (European Economic Community)
EEG (electroencephalogram)
EFTA (European Free Trade Association)
EG (for example)
EMA (European Monetary Agreement)
EMF (electromotive force)
ENC (enclosed; enclosure)
ENE (east-northeast)
ENSA (Entertainments National Service
    Association)
ENT (ear, nose and throat)
EOC (Equal Opportunities Commission)
EOF (end of file)
EP (electroplate; epistle)
EPH (Ephesians)
EPNS (electroplated nickel silver)
EPROM (erasable programmable read only
    memory)
ER (Edward Rex; Elizabeth Regina)
ESE (east-southeast)

ESN (educationally subnormal)
ESQ (esquire)
ESTH (Esther)
ETA (estimated time of arrival)
ETC (etcetera)
ETD (estimated time of departure)
ET SEQ (and the following one)
EX DIV (without dividend)
EX LIB (from the books)
EXOD (Exodus)
EZEK (Ezekiel)
F (Fahrenheit; franc)
FA (Football Association)
FANY (First Aid Nursing Yeomanry)
FAS (free alongside ship)
FBA (Fellow of the British Academy)
FBI (Federal Bureau of Investigation)
FC (Football Club)
FCA (Fellow of the Institute of Chartered
    Accountants)
FCII (Fellow of the Chartered Insurance
    Institute)
FCIS (Fellow of the Chartered Institute of
    Secretaries)
FCO (Foreign and Commonwealth Office)
FIFA (International Football Federation)
FL (flourished)
FLA (Florida)
FO (Field Officer; Flying Officer; Foreign
    Office)
FOB (free on board)
FOC (Father of the Chapel; free of charge)
FPA (Family Planning Association)
FRAM (Fellow of the Royal Academy of Music)
FRAS (Fellow of the Royal Astronomical
    Society)
FRCM (Fellow of the Royal College of Music)
FRCO (Fellow of the Royal College of
    Organists)
FRCOG (Fellow of the Royal College of
    Obstetricians and Gynaecologists)
FRCP (Fellow of the Royal College of
    Physicians)
FRCS (Fellow of the Royal College of
    Surgeons)
FRCVS (Fellow of the Royal College of
    Veterinary Surgeons)
FRGS (Fellow of the Royal Geographical
    Society)
FRIBA (Fellow of the Royal Institute of British
    Architects)
FRIC (Fellow of the Royal Institute of
    Chemistry)
FRICS (Fellow of the Royal Institution of
    Chartered Surveyors)
FRPS (Fellow of the Royal Photographic
    Society)
FRS (Fellow of the Royal Society)
FRSA (Fellow of the Royal Society of Arts)
FSA (Fellow of the Society of Antiquaries)
FZS (Fellow of the Zoological Society)

G (gram)
GA (Georgia)
GAL (Galatians)
GATT (General Agreement on Tariffs and
    Trade)
GB (Great Britain)
GBE (Knight/Dame Grand Cross of the British
    Empire)
GBH (grievous bodily harm)
GC (George Cross)
GCB (Knight/Dame Grand Cross of the Bath)
GCE (General Certificate of Education)
GCHQ (Government Communications
    Headquarters)
GCIE (Grand Commander of the Indian
    Empire)
GCMG (Knight/Dame Grand Cross of St
    Michael and St George)
GCSE (General Certificate of Secondary
    Education)
GCVO (Knight/Dame Grand Cross of the
    Victorian Order)
GDP (gross domestic product)
GDR (German Democratic Republic)
GEO (George)
GER (German)
GHQ (general headquarters)
GIB (Gibraltar)
GLC (Greater London Council)
GM (George Medal; gram)
GMT (Greenwich Mean Time)
GNP (gross national product)
GOM (grand old man)
GP (general practitioner)
GPO (general post office)
H (hour)
HCF (highest common factor)
HEB (Hebrews)
HF (high frequency)
HGV (heavy goods vehicle)
HIH (His/Her Imperial Highness)
HIM (His/Her Imperial Majesty)
HM (headmaster; headmistress; His/Her
    Majesty)
HMI (His/Her Majesty's Inspector)
HMS (His/Her Majesty's Ship)
HMSO (His/Her Majesty's Stationery Office)
HNC (Higher National Certificate)
HND (Higher National Diploma)
HO (Home Office; house)
HON (honorary; honour; honourable)
HONS (honours)
HON SEC (Honorary Secretary)
HOS (Hosea)
HP (hire purchase; horsepower)
HQ (headquarters)
HR (holiday route; hour)
HRH (His/Her Royal Highness)
HSH (His/Her Serene Highness)
HT (height)
HV (high velocity; high-voltage)

IA (Institute of Actuaries; Iowa)
IAAF (International Amateur Athletic Federation)
IABA (International Amateur Boxing Association)
IATA (International Air Transport Association)
IB (ibidem; Institute of Bankers)
IBA (Independent Broadcasting Authority)
IBID (ibidem)
IC (in charge; integrated circuit)
ICE (Institution of Civil Engineers)
ICHEME (Institute of Chemical Engineers)
ID (idem; identification)
IE (that is)
IEE (Institution of Electrical Engineers)
IHS (Jesus)
ILL (Illinois)
I MECH E (Institution of Mechanical Engineers)
IMF (International Monetary Fund)
INC (incorporated)
INCL (included; including; inclusive)
IND (Indiana)
INST (instant)
IOM (Isle of Man)
IOW (Isle of Wight)
IPA (International Phonetic Alphabet)
IQ (intelligence quotient)
IR (Inland Revenue)
IRA (Irish Republican Army)
IS (Isaiah)
ISO (Imperial Service Order)
ITA (initial teaching alphabet)
ITAL (italic; italicized)
ITV (Independent Television)
JAM (James)
JC (Jesus Christ; Julius Caesar)
JER (Jeremiah)
JP (Justice of the Peace)
JR (junior)
KAN (Kansas)
KB (King's Bench)
KBE (Knight Commander of the British Empire)
KC (King's Counsel)
KCB (Knight Commander of the Bath)
KCIE (Knight Commander of the Indian Empire)
KCMG (Knight Commander of St Michael and St George)
KCSI (Knight Commander of the Star of India)
KCVO (Knight Commander of the Victorian Order)
KG (kilogram; Knight of the Garter)
KGB (Soviet State Security Committee)
KKK (Ku Klux Klan)
KM (kilometre)
KO (knock-out)
KP (Knight of St Patrick)
KSTJ (Knight of St John)
KT (Knight of the Thistle)

KY (Kentucky)
L (Latin; learner; pound)
LA (Louisiana)
LA I (latitude)
LB (pound)
LBW (leg before wicket)
LCD (liquid crystal display; lowest common denominator)
LCJ (Lord Chief Justice)
LEA (Local Education Authority)
LEV (Leviticus)
LF (low frequency)
LIEUT (Lieutenant)
LITT D (Doctor of Letters; Doctor of Literature)
LJ (Lord Justice)
LJJ (Lords Justices)
LLB (Bachelor of Laws)
LLD (Doctor of Laws)
LLM (Master of Laws)
LOC CIT (in the place cited)
LOQ (he/she speaks)
LPG (liquefied petroleum gas)
LPO (London Philharmonic Orchestra)
LPS (Lord Privy Seal)
LRAM (Licentiate of the Royal Academy of Music)
LS (locus sigilli)
LSD (pounds, shillings, and pence)
LSE (London School of Economics)
LSO (London Symphony Orchestra)
LTD (limited)
LW (long wave)
M (male; married; motorway; thousand)
MA (Master of Arts)
MACC (Maccabees)
MAJ (Major)
MAL (Malachi)
MASH (mobile army surgical hospital)
MASS (Massachusetts)
MATT (Matthew)
MB (Bachelor of Medicine)
MBE (Member of the British Empire)
MC (Master of Ceremonies)
MCC (Marylebone Cricket Club)
MCP (male chauvinist pig)
MD (Doctor of Medicine; Managing Director; Maryland)
ME (Maine)
MEP (Member of the European Parliament)
MET (meteorological; meteorology; metropolitan)
MF (medium frequency)
MG (milligram)
MIC (Micah)
MICH (Michigan)
MINN (Minnesota)
MISS (Mississippi)
ML (millilitre)
M LITT (Master of Letters)
MLR (minimum lending rate)
MM (millimetre)

MO (Medical Officer; Missouri)
MOC (Mother of the Chapel)
MOD (Ministry of Defence)
MOH (Medical Officer of Health)
MONT (Montana)
MP (Member of Parliament; Metropolitan
  Police; Military Police)
MPG (miles per gallon)
MPH (miles per hour)
MPHIL (Master of Philosophy)
MR (Master of the Rolls)
MRCOG (Member of the Royal College of
  Obstetricians and Gynaecologists)
MRCP (Member of the Royal College of
  Physicians)
MRCS (Member of the Royal College of
  Surgeons)
MRCVS (Member of the Royal College of
  Veterinary Surgeons)
MS (manuscript; multiple sclerosis)
MSC (Master of Science)
MSM (Meritorious Service Medal)
MSS (manuscripts)
MT (Mount)
MVO (Member of the Victorian Order)
N (North)
NA (North America; not applicable)
NAAFI (Navy, Army, and Air Force Institutes)
NALGO (National and Local Government
  Officers Association)
NASA (National Aeronautics and Space
  Administration)
NAT (Nathaniel)
NATO (North Atlantic Treaty Organization)
NATSOPA (National Society of Operative
  Printers, Graphical and Media Personnel)
NB (note well)
NCB (National Coal Board)
NCO (non-commissioned officer)
NCP (National Car Parks)
NCT (National Childbirth Trust)
NCV (no commercial value)
NDAK (North Dakota)
NE (Northeast)
NEB (Nebraska)
NEC (National Executive Committee)
NEH (Nehemiah)
NEV (Nevada)
NFU (National Farmers' Union)
NGA (National Graphical Association)
NHS (National Health Service)
NI (National Insurance; Northern Ireland)
NNE (north-northeast)
NNW (north-northwest)
NO (not out; number)
NORM (normal)
NOS (numbers)
NP (new paragraph)
NR (near; Northern Region)
NSB (National Savings Bank)

NSPCC (National Society for the Prevention of
  Cruelty to Children)
NT (National Trust; New Testament)
NUBE (National Union of Bank Employees)
NUGMW (National Union of General and
  Municipal Workers)
NUJ (National Union of Journalists)
NUM (National Union of Mineworkers)
NUPE (National Union of Public Employees)
NUR (National Union of Railwaymen)
NUS (National Union of Seamen; National
  Union of Students)
NUT (National Union of Teachers)
NW (Northwest)
NY (New York)
O (Ohio)
OAP (old-age pensioner)
OB (outside broadcast)
OBAD (Obadiah)
OBE (Officer of the British Empire)
OCTU (Officer Cadets Training Unit)
OFM (Order of Friars Minor)
OHMS (On His/Her Majesty's Service)
OKLA (Oklahoma)
OM (Order of Merit)
ONC (Ordinary National Certificate)
OND (Ordinary National Diploma)
ONO (or near offer)
OP (opus)
OP CIT (in the work cited)
OPEC (Organization of Petroleum Exporting
  Countries)
OPS (operations)
OREG (Oregon)
OS (ordinary seaman; Ordnance Survey)
OSA (Order of St Augustine)
OSB (Order of St Benedict)
OSF (Order of St Francis)
OT (occupational therapy; Old Testament)
OTC (Officers' Training Corps)
OU (Open University)
OUDS (Oxford University Dramatic Society)
OXFAM (Oxford Committee for Famine Relief)
OZ (ounce)
P (page; penny; purl)
PA (Pennsylvania; per annum; personal
  assistant; public address system)
PAYE (pay as you earn)
PC (per cent; personal computer; police
  constable)
PD (paid)
PDSA (People's Dispensary for Sick Animals)
PE (physical education)
PEI (Prince Edward Island)
PER PRO (by the agency of)
PG (paying guest; postgraduate)
PHD (Doctor of Philosophy)
PHIL (Philippians)
PL (place; plural)
PLC (public limited company)
PLO (Palestine Liberation Organization)

PM (post meridiem; Prime Minister)
PO (Petty Officer; Pilot Officer; postal order; Post Office)
POW (prisoner of war)
PP (pages; per pro)
PPS (further postscript; Parliamentary Private Secretary)
PR (public relations)
PRAM (programmable random access memory)
PRO (Public Records Office; public relations officer)
PROM (programmable read-only memory)
PROV (Proverbs)
PS (postscript; Private Secretary)
PT (physical training)
PTA (Parent-Teacher Association)
PTO (please turn over)
PVA (polyvinyl acetate)
PVC (polyvinyl chloride)
QB (Queen's Bench)
QC (Queen's Counsel)
QED (which was to be demonstrated)
QM (quartermaster)
QR (quarter; quire)
QT (quart)
QV (which see)
R (king; queen; right; river)
RA (Royal Academy; Royal Artillery)
RAC (Royal Automobile Club)
RADA (Royal Academy of Dramatic Art)
RAF (Royal Air Force)
RAM (random access memory; Royal Academy of Music)
RAMC (Royal Army Medical Corps)
R AND D (research and development)
RBA (Royal Society of British Artists)
RBS (Royal Society of British Sculptors)
RC (Roman Catholic)
RCA (Royal College of Art)
RCM (Royal College of Music)
RCN (Royal College of Nursing)
RCP (Royal College of Physicians)
RCS (Royal College of Surgeons)
RCVS (Royal College of Veterinary Surgeons)
RD (road)
RE (religious education; Royal Engineers)
REME (Royal Electrical and Mechanical Engineers)
REV (Reverend)
RFC (Royal Flying Corps)
RH (Royal Highness; right hand)
RHA (Royal Horse Artillery)
RI (religous instruction)
RIBA (Royal Institute of British Architects)
RIC (Royal Institute of Chemistry)
RICS (Royal Institution of Chartered Surveyors)
RIP (may he rest in peace)
RK (religious knowledge)

RM (Resident Magistrate; Royal Mail; Royal Marines)
RMA (Royal Military Academy)
RN (Royal Navy)
RNIB (Royal National Institute for the Blind)
RNLI (Royal National Lifeboat Institution)
ROM (read only memory)
ROSPA (Royal Society for the Prevention of Accidents)
RPM (revolutions per minute)
RS (Royal Society)
RSA (Royal Society of Arts)
RSC (Royal Shakespeare Company)
RSM (Regimental Sergeant Major; Royal Society of Medicine)
RSPB (Royal Society for the Protection of Birds)
RSPCA (Royal Society for the Prevention of Cruelty to Animals)
RSVP (please answer)
RT HON (Right Honourable)
RT REV (Right Reverend)
RU (Rugby Union)
RUC (Royal Ulster Constabulary)
S (second; shilling; South)
SA (Salvation Army; sex appeal)
SAE (stamped addressed envelope)
SALT (Strategic Arms Limitation Talks)
SAS (Special Air Service)
SATB (soprano, alto, tenor, bass)
SAYE (save-as-you-earn)
SCD (Doctor of Science)
SE (southeast)
SEC (second; secretary)
SEN (senior; State Enrolled Nurse)
SEQ (the following)
SF (science fiction)
SGT (Sergeant)
SHAPE (Supreme Headquarters Allied Powers Europe)
SI (International System of Units)
SIN (sine)
SLADE (Society of Lithographic Artists, Designers, and Etchers)
SLR (single lens reflex)
SNCF (French National Railways)
SNP (Scottish National Party)
SNR (senior)
SOGAT (Society of Graphical and Allied Trades)
SOP (soprano)
SQ (square)
SRN (State Registered Nurse)
SSE (south-southeast)
SSW (south-southwest)
ST (saint; street)
STD (subscriber trunk dialling)
SW (southwest)
TA (Territorial Army)
TAN (tangent)

TASS (official news agency of the Soviet Union)
TB (tubercle bacillus)
TCCB (Test and County Cricket Board)
TEFL (teaching English as a foreign language)
TENN (Tennessee)
TEX (Texas)
TGWU (Transport and General Workers' Union)
THESS (Thessalonians)
THOS (Thomas)
TM (trademark; transcendental meditation)
TOPS (Training Opportunities Scheme)
TSB (Trustee Savings Bank)
TT (teetotal; teetotaller)
TU (trade union)
TUC (Trades Union Congress)
TV (television)
UC (upper case)
UCATT (Union of Construction, Allied Trades, and Technicians)
UCCA (Universities Central Council on Admissions)
UCL (University College, London)
UDI (unilateral declaration of independence)
UEFA (Union of European Football Associations)
UHF (ultrahigh frequency)
UHT (ultrahigh temperature)
UK (United Kingdom)
ULT (ultimo)
UN (United Nations)
UNCTAD (United Nations Commission for Trade and Development)
UNESCO (United Nations Educational, Scientific, and Cultural Organization)
UNO (United Nations Organization)
UPOW (Union of Post Office Workers)
US (United States)
USA (United States of America)
USDAW (Union of Shop, Distributive, and Allied Workers)
USSR (Union of Soviet Socialist Republics)
V (verse; versus; volt)
VA (Order of Victoria and Albert; Virginia)

VAT (value-added tax)
VB (verb)
VC (Vice Chancellor; Victoria Cross)
VD (venereal disease)
VDU (visual display unit)
VE (Victory in Europe)
VG (very good)
VHF (very high frequency)
VIP (very important person)
VIZ (namely)
VLF (very low frequency)
VR (Victoria Regina; Volunteer Reserve)
VS (verse)
VSO (Voluntary Service Overseas)
VT (Vermont)
W (west)
WAAC (Women's Army Auxiliary Corps)
WAAF (Women's Auxiliary Air Force)
WC (water closet; West Central)
WI (West Indies; Women's Institute)
WIS (Wisconsin)
WK (week)
WM (William)
WNW (west-northwest)
WO (Warrant Officer)
WP (word processor)
WPC (Woman Police Constable)
WPM (words per minute)
WRAC (Women's Royal Army Corps)
WRAF (Women's Royal Air Force)
WRNS (Women's Royal Naval Service)
WRVS (Women's Royal Voluntary Service)
WSW (west-southwest)
WT (weight)
WW (Word War)
WWF (World Wildlife Fund)
WYO (Wyoming)
XL (extra large)
YHA (Youth Hostels Association)
YMCA (Young Men's Christian Association)
YR (year)
YWCA (Young Women's Christian Association)
ZECH (Zechariah)
ZEPH (Zephania)

FIRST NAMES

GIRLS' NAMES

2	3—continued	4—continued	4—continued
DI	MEL	CARY	HOPE
EM	MIA	CASS	ILMA
JO	NAN	CATH	ILSE
VI	NAT	CERI	IMMY
3	ONA	CISS	INEZ
ADA	PAM	CLEM	IOLA
AMY	PAT	CLEO	IONA
ANN	PEG	CORA	IRIS
AUD	PEN	DAFF	IRMA
AVA	PIA	DALE	ISLA
BAB	PRU	DANA	IVAH
BEA	RAE	DAPH	JADE
BEE	RIA	DAWN	JAEL
BEL	ROS	DOLL	JANE
CIS	SAL	DORA	JEAN
DEB	SAM	EDEN	JESS
DEE	SIB	EDIE	JILL
DOT	SUE	EDNA	JOAN
EDA	UNA	EILY	JODI
ENA	VAL	EIRA	JODY
ETH	VIV	ELLA	JOSS
EVA	WIN	ELMA	JUDI
EVE	ZOË	ELSA	JUDY
FAN	**4**	EMMA	JUNE
FAY	ABBY	ENID	KARA
FLO	ADAH	ERIN	KATE
GAY	ADDY	ERYL	KATH
GUS	AINE	ESME	KATY
IDA	ALDA	ETTA	KERI
INA	ALEX	ETTY	KYLE
ISA	ALIX	EVIE	LANA
ITA	ALLY	FAYE	LELA
IVY	ALMA	FERN	LENA
JAN	ALVA	FIFI	LETA
JAY	ALYS	FLOY	LILA
JEN	ANIS	FRAN	LILI
JOY	ANNA	GABI	LILY
KAY	ANNE	GABY	LINA
KIM	ANYA	GAIL	LISA
KIT	AVIS	GALE	LISE
LEE	BABS	GAYE	LITA
LES	BEAT	GERT	LIZA
LIL	BELL	GILL	LOIS
LIZ	BESS	GINA	LOLA
LOU	BETA	GLAD	LORA
LYN	BETH	GWEN	LORI
MAE	BINA	GWYN	LORN
MAY	CARA	HEBE	LUCE
MEG		HEDY	LUCY

4—continued	4—continued	5—continued	5—continued
LULU	TRIX	BETSY	ERICA
LYNN	TYRA	BETTE	ERIKA
LYRA	VERA	BETTY	ESMEE
MAIR	VIDA	BIDDY	ESSIE
MARA	VINA	BONNY	ETHEL
MARY	VITA	BRIDE	ETHNE
MAUD	VIVA	BRITA	ETTIE
META	WYNN	BRITT	EVITA
MIMA	ZANA	CANDY	FAITH
MIMI	ZARA	CAREY	FANNY
MINA	ZENA	CARLA	FARON
MIRA	ZITA	CARLY	FIONA
MOLL	ZOLA	CAROL	FLEUR
MONA	ZORA	CARYL	FLORA
MYRA	5	CARYS	FLOSS
NADA	ABBEY	CASEY	FREDA
NELL	ABBIE	CATHY	FREYA
NEST	ADDIE	CELIA	GABBY
NEVA	ADELA	CERYS	GAYLE
NINA	ADELE	CHLOE	GEMMA
NITA	ADLAI	CHRIS	GERDA
NOLA	AGGIE	CILLA	GERRY
NONA	AGNES	CINDY	GILDA
NORA	AILIE	CISSY	GINNY
NOVA	AILIS	CLARA	GRACE
OLGA	AILSA	CLARE	GRETA
OONA	AIMEE	CORAL	GUSTA
OPAL	ALANA	DAISY	HAGAR
OZZY	ALEXA	DARCY	HATTY
PETA	ALICE	DEBRA	HAZEL
PHIL	ALINA	DELIA	HEDDA
POLL	ALINE	DELLA	HEIDI
PRUE	ALLIE	DELMA	HELEN
RENA	ALVIE	DERYN	HELGA
RENE	AMATA	DIANA	HENNY
RHEA	AMBER	DIANE	HEPSY
RICA	AMICE	DILYS	HETTY
RIKA	ANGEL	DINAH	HILDA
RINA	ANGIE	DIONE	HOLLY
RITA	ANITA	DODIE	HORRY
ROMA	ANNIE	DOLLY	HULDA
RONA	ANNIS	DONNA	HYLDA
ROSA	ANONA	DORIA	ILONA
ROSE	ANWEN	DORIS	IRENE
ROXY	APHRA	DREDA	ISMAY
RUBY	APRIL	DULCE	JACKY
RUTH	ASTRA	EDITH	JANET
SARA	AUDRA	EFFIE	JANEY
SIAN	AUREA	ELAIN	JANIE
SILE	AVICE	ELENA	JANIS
SINE	AVRIL	ELISE	JAYNE
SUZY	BEATA	ELIZA	JEMMA
TACY	BECKY	ELLEN	JENNA
TARA	BELLA	ELLIE	JENNY
TESS	BELLE	ELROY	JEWEL
THEA	BERNY	ELSIE	JINNY
TINA	BERRY	ELVIE	JODIE
TONI	BERTA	EMILY	JOSIE
TRIS	BERYL	EMMIE	JOYCE
	BESSY	EPPIE	JUDOC

5—continued	5—continued	5—continued	5—continued
JULIA	MARTI	PEGGY	TILDA
JULIE	MARTY	PENNY	TILLY
KAREN	MATTY	PETRA	TISHA
KARIN	MAUDE	PHEBE	TONIA
KATHY	MAURA	PIPPA	TONYA
KATIE	MAVIS	POLLY	TOPSY
KELDA	MEAVE	POPPY	TOTTY
KELLY	MEGAN	RAINA	TRACY
KEREN	MEGGY	RAINE	TRINA
KERRI	MELBA	REINE	TRUDI
KERRY	MELVA	RENÉE	TRUDY
KEZIA	MERCY	RENIE	UNITY
KIRBY	MERLE	RHIAN	VALDA
KITTY	MERRY	RHODA	VANDA
KYLIE	MERYL	RHONA	VELDA
LAURA	MILLY	ROBYN	VELMA
LAURI	MINNA	RONNA	VENUS
LEIGH	MINTY	ROSIE	VERNA
LEILA	MITZI	ROWAN	VICKI
LENNY	MOIRA	SADIE	VICKY
LEONA	MOLLY	SALLY	VIKKI
LETTY	MORAG	SAMMY	VILMA
LIANA	MORNA	SANDY	VINNY
LIBBY	MOYNA	SARAH	VIOLA
LIDDY	MOYRA	SARAI	VIVIA
LIESL	MYRNA	SARRA	WANDA
LILAC	MYSIE	SELMA	WENDA
LILLA	NADIA	SENGA	WENDY
LINDA	NAHUM	SHANI	WILLA
LINDY	NANCE	SHARI	WILMA
LIZZY	NANCY	SHEBA	WYNNE
LOLLY	NANNY	SHENA	XENIA
LOREN	NAOMI	SHIRL	ZELDA
LORNA	NELLY	SHONA	ZELMA
LORNE	NERYS	SIBBY	ZORAH
LOTTY	NESSA	SIBYL	6
LUCIA	NESTA	SISSY	AGACIA
LUCIE	NETTA	SONIA	AGATHA
LUCKY	NICKY	SONJA	AGNETA
LYDIA	NIKKI	SONYA	AILEEN
LYNDA	NOELE	SOPHY	AILITH
LYNNE	NORAH	STACY	AITHNE
MABEL	NORMA	SUKEY	ALANNA
MABLE	NUALA	SUSAN	ALBINA
MADDY	NYREE	SUSIE	ALDITH
MADGE	ODILE	SYBIL	ALEXIA
MAEVE	OLIFF	TACEY	ALEXIS
MAGDA	OLIVE	TAMAR	ALICIA
MAIRE	OLLIE	TAMMY	ALISON
MAMIE	OLWEN	TANIA	ALTHEA
MANDY	OLWYN	TANSY	ALVINA
MARAH	ORIEL	TANYA	AMABEL
MARCY	OWENA	TEGAN	AMALIA
MARGE	PANSY	TERRI	AMALIE
MARGO	PATSY	TERRY	AMANDA
MARIA	PATTI	TESSA	AMELIA
MARIE	PATTY	TETTY	AMICIA
MARLA	PAULA	THORA	AMINTA
MARNI	PEACE	THYRA	ANDREA
MARTA	PEARL	TIBBY	ANDRÉE

6—continued	6—continued	6—continued	6—continued
ANEIRA	CECILY	EVELYN	ISOLDE
ANGELA	CELINA	EVONNE	JACKIE
ANNICE	CELINE	FARRAN	JACOBA
ANNIKA	CHARIS	FARREN	JACQUI
ANNORA	CHERIE	FEDORA	JANICE
ANSTEY	CHERRY	FELICE	JANINE
ANTHEA	CHERYL	FINOLA	JANSIS
ARIANE	CICELY	FLAVIA	JEANIE
ARLEEN	CISSIE	FLOWER	JEANNE
ARLENE	CLAIRE	FOSTER	JEHANE
ARLINE	COLINA	FRANCA	JEMIMA
ARMINA	CONNIE	FRANNY	JENNIE
ARMINE	DAGMAR	FRIEDA	JESSIE
ASHLEY	DANITA	GABBIE	JOANNA
ASTRID	DANUTA	GAENOR	JOANNE
ATHENE	DAPHNE	GARNET	JOLEEN
AUDREY	DAVIDA	GAYNOR	JOLENE
AURIEL	DAVINA	GERTIE	JUDITH
AURIOL	DEANNA	GINGER	JULIET
AURORA	DEANNE	GISELA	KARINA
AURORE	DEBBIE	GLADYS	KEELEY
AVERIL	DECIMA	GLENDA	KELLIE
BARBIE	DELWEN	GLENIS	KENDRA
BARBRA	DELWYN	GLENNA	KERRIE
BAUBIE	DELYTH	GLENYS	KEZIAH
BEATTY	DENISE	GLINYS	KIRSTY
BENITA	DENNIE	GLORIA	LALAGE
BERNIE	DIANNE	GLYNIS	LAUREL
BERTHA	DIONNE	GOLDIE	LAUREN
BESSIE	DORCAS	GRACIE	LAURIE
BETHAN	DOREEN	GRANIA	LAVENA
BETHIA	DORICE	GRETEL	LAVINA
BEULAH	DORITA	GRIZEL	LEANNE
BIANCA	DORRIE	GUSSIE	LEILAH
BILLIE	DOTTIE	GWENDA	LENNIE
BIRDIE	DULCIE	HAIDEE	LENORE
BIRGIT	DYMPNA	HANNAH	LEONIE
BLANCH	EARTHA	HATTIE	LESLEY
BLODYN	EASTER	HAYLEY	LESLIE
BLYTHE	EDWINA	HEDWIG	LETTIE
BOBBIE	EILEEN	HELENA	LIANNE
BONITA	EILWEN	HELENE	LIESEL
BONNIE	EIRIAN	HENNIE	LILIAN
BRENDA	EITHNE	HEPSEY	LILIAS
BRIDIE	ELAINE	HEPSIE	LILITH
BRIGID	ELINED	HERMIA	LILLAH
BRIGIT	ELINOR	HESTER	LILLIE
BRIONY	ELISHA	HILARY	LINNET
BRYONY	ELISSA	HONORA	LIZZIE
CANICE	ELOISA	HOWARD	LLINOS
CARINA	ELOISE	HULDAH	LOLITA
CARITA	ELSPIE	IANTHE	LOREEN
CARMEL	ELUNED	IDONEA	LOTTIE
CARMEN	ELVINA	IMOGEN	LOUISA
CAROLA	ELVIRA	INGRID	LOUISE
CAROLE	EMELYN	ISABEL	LUCINA
CARRIE	EMILIA	ISEULT	LUELLA
CASSIE	ESTHER	ISHBEL	MADDIE
CATRIN	EUNICE	ISOBEL	MAGGIE
CECILE	EVADNE	ISOLDA	MAHALA

6—continued	6—continued	6—continued	7—continued
MAIDIE	QUEENA	THELMA	ARIANNA
MAIRIN	QUEENY	THIRSA	ARLETTA
MAISIE	RACHEL	THIRZA	ARLETTE
MARCIA	RAMONA	TIRZAH	ASPASIA
MARCIE	REGINA	TRACEY	AUGUSTA
MARGIE	RENATA	TRICIA	AURELIA
MARGOT	RHONDA	TRISHA	AUREOLA
MARIAM	ROBINA	TRIXIE	AUREOLE
MARIAN	ROISIN	TRUDIE	AVELINE
MARIEL	ROSINA	ULRICA	BABETTE
MARINA	ROSITA	URSULA	BARBARA
MARION	ROSLYN	VASHTI	BARBARY
MARISA	ROWENA	VERENA	BASILIA
MARITA	ROXANA	VERITY	BASILIE
MARLIN	ROXANE	VERONA	BASILLA
MARLYN	RUBINA	VICKIE	BEATRIX
MARNIE	RUTHIE	VINNIE	BEATTIE
MARSHA	SABINA	VIOLET	BEDELIA
MARTHA	SALENA	VIVIAN	BELINDA
MARTIE	SALINA	VIVIEN	BERNICE
MATTIE	SALOME	VYVYAN	BETHANY
MAUDIE	SANDIE	WALLIS	BETTINA
MAXINE	SANDRA	WINNIE	BETTRYS
MEGGIE	SARINA	XANTHE	BEVERLY
MEGHAN	SARITA	YASMIN	BLANCHE
MEHALA	SELENA	YVETTE	BLODWEN
MELODY	SELINA	YVONNE	BLOSSOM
MERCIA	SERENA	ZANDRA	BRANWEN
MERIEL	SHARON	ZILLAH	BRIDGET
MIGNON	SHAUNA	ZINNIA	BRIGHID
MILLIE	SHEENA	**7**	BRONWEN
MINNIE	SHEILA	ABIGAIL	BRONWYN
MIRIAM	SHELLY	ADAMINA	CAITLIN
MONICA	SHERRI	ADELINA	CAMILLA
MURIEL	SHERRY	ADELINE	CAMILLE
MYRTLE	SHERYL	ADRIANA	CANDACE
NADINE	SIBBIE	AINSLEY	CANDICE
NELLIE	SIDONY	AINSLIE	CANDIDA
NERINA	SILVIA	AISLING	CARLEEN
NESSIE	SIMONA	AISLINN	CARLENE
NETTIE	SIMONE	ALBERTA	CARMELA
NICOLA	SINEAD	ALBINIA	CAROLYN
NICOLE	SISLEY	ALBREDA	CECILIA
NOELLE	SISSIE	ALDREDA	CECILIE
NOREEN	SOPHIA	ALEDWEN	CEINWEN
ODETTE	SOPHIE	ALETHEA	CELESTE
ODILIA	SORCHA	ALFREDA	CHARITY
OLIVET	STACEY	ALLEGRA	CHARLEY
OLIVIA	STELLA	ALLISON	CHARLIE
OONAGH	STEVIE	ALOISIA	CHATTIE
ORIANA	SYLVIA	ALOYSIA	CHRISSY
PAMELA	SYLVIE	ANNABEL	CHRISTY
PATTIE	TAMARA	ANNAPLE	CLARICE
PEPITA	TAMSIN	ANNETTE	CLARRIE
PETULA	TANITH	ANOUSKA	CLAUDIA
PHEMIE	TEGWEN	ANSELMA	CLODAGH
PHOEBE	TERESA	ANSTICE	COLETTE
PORTIA	TESSIE	ANTOINE	COLLEEN
PRISCA	THECLA	ANTONIA	CORALIE
PRISSY	THEKLA	ARIADNE	

7—continued	7—continued	7—continued	7—continued
CORINNA	GWYNETH	LORINDA	PANDORA
CORINNE	HALCYON	LOUELLA	PASCALE
CRYSTAL	HARRIET	LOVEDAY	PAULINE
CYNTHIA	HEATHER	LUCASTA	PEARLIE
DAMARIS	HÉLOÏSE	LUCETTA	PERDITA
DANETTE	HEULWEN	LUCETTE	PERONEL
DARLENE	HILLARY	LUCIANA	PETRINA
DAVINIA	HONORIA	LUCILLA	PHILLIS
DEBORAH	HORATIA	LUCILLE	PHYLLIS
DEIRDRE	HYPATIA	LUCINDA	QUEENIE
DELILAH	ISADORA	LUCRECE	RACHAEL
DEMELZA	ISIDORA	LYNETTE	RAELENE
DESIREE	JACINTA	MABELLA	RAFAELA
DIAMOND	JACINTH	MABELLE	REBECCA
DOLORES	JANETTA	MAHALAH	REBEKAH
DONALDA	JANETTE	MAHALIA	RHONWEN
DORETTE	JASMINE	MALVINA	RICARDA
DORINDA	JEANNIE	MANUELA	RICHMAL
DOROTHY	JENIFER	MARILYN	ROBERTA
DYMPHNA	JESSICA	MARISSA	ROMAINE
EILUNED	JILLIAN	MARLENE	RONALDA
ELDREDA	JOCASTA	MARTINA	ROSABEL
ELEANOR	JOCELYN	MARTINE	ROSALIA
ELFREDA	JOHANNA	MATILDA	ROSALIE
ELFRIDA	JONQUIL	MAUREEN	ROSALYN
ELSPETH	JOSEPHA	MEHALAH	ROSANNA
EMELINE	JOSETTE	MEHALIA	ROSANNE
EMERALD	JUANITA	MEIRION	ROSEANN
ESTELLA	JULIANA	MELANIA	ROSELYN
ESTELLE	JULITTA	MELANIE	ROSETTA
EUGENIA	JUSTINA	MELINDA	ROSSLYN
EUGENIE	JUSTINE	MELIORA	ROXANNA
EULALIA	KATHRYN	MELISSA	ROXANNE
EULALIE	KATRINA	MELODIE	RUPERTA
EVELEEN	KATRINE	MELVINA	SABRINA
EVELINA	KETURAH	MERILYN	SAFFRON
EVELINE	KIRSTEN	MERRION	SANCHIA
FABIANA	KRISTEN	MICHELE	SARANNA
FELICIA	KRISTIN	MILDRED	SCARLET
FENELLA	LARAINE	MINERVA	SEPTIMA
FEODORA	LARISSA	MIRABEL	SHANNON
FIDELIA	LAUREEN	MIRANDA	SHARRON
FLORRIE	LAURINA	MODESTY	SHEILAH
FLOSSIE	LAVERNE	MONIQUE	SHELAGH
FORTUNE	LAVINIA	MYFANWY	SHELLEY
FRANCES	LEONORA	NANETTE	SHIRLEY
FRANCIE	LETITIA	NATALIA	SIBELLA
FRANKIE	LETTICE	NATALIE	SIBILLA
FRANNIE	LILLIAN	NATASHA	SIBYLLA
GENEVRA	LILLIAS	NERISSA	SIDONIA
GEORGIA	LINDSAY	NICHOLA	SIDONIE
GEORGIE	LINDSEY	NINETTE	SILVANA
GILLIAN	LINETTE	NOELEEN	SIOBHAN
GINETTE	LISBETH	NOELINE	SUSANNA
GINEVRA	LISETTE	OCTAVIA	SUSANNE
GISELLE	LIZANNE	OLYMPIA	SUZANNA
GRAINNE	LIZBETH	OPHELIA	SUZANNE
GRIZZEL	LORAINE	OTTILIA	SUZETTE
GWLADYS	LORETTA	OTTILIE	SYBELLA
GWYNEDD	LORETTE	PAMELIA	

7—continued	8—continued	8—continued	8—continued
SYBILLA	CORDELIA	LAETITIA	ROSEMARY
TABITHA	CORNELIA	LARRAINE	SAMANTHA
TALITHA	COURTNEY	LAURAINE	SAPPHIRA
TATIANA	CRESSIDA	LAURETTA	SAPPHIRE
THERESA	CYTHEREA	LAURETTE	SCARLETT
THÉRÈSE	DANIELLA	LAURINDA	SHEELAGH
TIFFANY	DANIELLE	LORRAINE	SHUSHANA
TRISSIE	DELPHINE	LUCIENNE	STEFANIE
VALERIA	DIONYSIA	LUCRETIA	SUSANNAH
VALERIE	DOMINICA	LUCREZIA	TALLULAH
VANESSA	DOROTHEA	LYNNETTE	TAMASINE
VENETIA	DOWSABEL	MADELINA	THEODORA
VIVIANA	DRUSILLA	MADELINE	THERESIA
YOLANDA	ELEANORA	MAGDALEN	THOMASIN
YOLANDE	ELEONORA	MAGNOLIA	TIMOTHEA
ZENOBIA	EMANUELA	MARCELLA	TRYPHENA
ZULEIKA	EMMELINE	MARCELLE	VERONICA
8	EUPHEMIA	MARGARET	VICTORIA
ADELAIDE	EUSTACIA	MARIAMNE	VIOLETTA
ADELHEID	FAUSTINA	MARIANNE	VIOLETTE
ADRIANNE	FELICITY	MARIETTA	VIRGINIA
ADRIENNE	FLORENCE	MARIETTE	VIVIENNE
ANGELICA	FLORETTA	MARIGOLD	WALBURGA
ANGELINA	FLORETTE	MARJORIE	WILFREDA
ANGELINE	FLORINDA	MELICENT	WILFRIDA
ANGHARAD	FRANCINE	MELISENT	WINEFRED
ANNALISA	FREDRICA	MELLONEY	WINIFRED
ANTONINA	FREDRIKA	MERCEDES	**9**
ANTONNIA	GEORGINA	MEREDITH	ALBERTINA
APPOLINA	GERMAINE	MERRILYN	ALBERTINE
APPOLINE	GERTRUDE	MICHAELA	ALEXANDRA
ARABELLA	GILBERTA	MICHELLE	AMARYLLIS
ARAMINTA	GRETCHEN	MORWENNA	AMBROSINA
BEATRICE	GRISELDA	MYRTILLA	AMBROSINE
BERENICE	GULIELMA	PATIENCE	ANASTASIA
BEVERLEY	GWYNNETH	PATRICIA	ANGELIQUE
BIRGITTA	HADASSAH	PAULETTE	ANNABELLA
BRIGITTA	HELEWISE	PENELOPE	ANNABELLE
BRIGITTE	HEPZIBAH	PERPETUA	ANNELIESE
BRUNETTA	HERMIONE	PHILIPPA	APOLLONIA
CARLOTTA	HORTENSE	PHILLIDA	ARTEMISIA
CAROLINA	HYACINTH	PHILLIPA	ARTHURINA
CAROLINE	INGEBORG	PHYLLIDA	ARTHURINE
CATHLEEN	IOLANTHE	PRIMROSE	AUGUSTINA
CATRIONA	ISABELLA	PRUDENCE	BATHSHEBA
CERIDWEN	ISABELLE	PRUNELLA	BENEDICTA
CHARISSA	JACOBINA	RAPHAELA	BERNADINA
CHARLENE	JAMESINA	RAYMONDE	BERNADINE
CHARMIAN	JEANETTE	RHIANNON	BRITANNIA
CHRISSIE	JEANNINE	RICHENDA	CARMELITA
CHRISTIE	JENNIFER	ROCHELLE	CASSANDRA
CLARIBEL	JESSAMYN	RONNETTE	CATHARINE
CLARINDA	JOSCELIN	ROSALEEN	CATHERINE
CLARISSA	JULIANNE	ROSALIND	CELESTINA
CLAUDINE	JULIENNE	ROSALINE	CELESTINE
CLEMENCE	JULIETTE	ROSAMOND	CHARLOTTE
CLEMENCY	KATHLEEN	ROSAMUND	CHARMAINE
CLOTILDA	KIMBERLY	ROSEANNA	CHRISTIAN
CONCEPTA	KRISTINA	ROSEANNE	CHRISTINA
CONCETTA	KRISTINE	ROSELINE	CHRISTINE

9—continued	9—continued	9—continued	10—continued
CHRISTMAS	GWENLLIAN	PHILOMENA	CLEMENTINA
CLAUDETTE	HARRIETTE	PLEASANCE	CLEMENTINE
CLEMENTIA	HENRIETTA	POLLYANNA	CONSTANTIA
CLEOPATRA	HENRIETTE	PRISCILLA	DULCIBELLA
COLUMBINA	HEPHZIBAH	ROSABELLA	ERMINTRUDE
COLUMBINE	HILDEGARD	ROSABELLE	ERMYNTRUDE
CONSTANCE	HIPPOLYTA	ROSALINDA	ETHELDREDA
CONSTANCY	HORTENSIA	ROSEMARIE	EVANGELINA
COURTENAY	HYACINTHA	SERAPHINA	EVANGELINE
DESDEMONA	JACQUELYN	SHUSHANNA	GILBERTINE
DOMINIQUE	JACQUETTA	SOPHRONIA	GWENDOLINE
DONALDINA	JEANNETTE	STEPHANIE	HILDEGARDE
ELISABETH	JESSAMINE	THEODOSIA	JACQUELINE
ELIZABETH	JOSEPHINE	THEOPHILA	KINBOROUGH
EMMANUELA	KATHARINE	THOMASINA	MARGARETTA
ERNESTINE	KATHERINE	THOMASINE	MARGUERITA
ESMERALDA	KIMBERLEY	VALENTINA	MARGUERITE
ETHELINDA	LAURENCIA	VALENTINE	MARIABELLA
FIONNUALA	LAURENTIA	VÉRONIQUE	MILBOROUGH
FRANCESCA	MADELEINE	VICTORINE	PETRONELLA
FRANCISCA	MAGDALENA	VINCENTIA	PETRONILLA
FREDERICA	MAGDALENE	WINNIFRED	TEMPERANCE
FREDERIKA	MARGARETA	**10**	THEOPHANIA
GABRIELLA	MARGARITA	ALEXANDRIA	WILHELMINA
GABRIELLE	MEHETABEL	ALPHONSINE	WILLIAMINA
GENEVIEVE	MEHITABEL	ANTOINETTE	**11**
GEORGETTE	MÉLISANDE	ARTHURETTA	ALEXANDRINA
GEORGIANA	MILLICENT	BERENGARIA	CHRISTIANIA
GERALDINE	MIRABELLA	BERNADETTE	FIONNGHUALA
GHISLAINE	MIRABELLE	BERNARDINA	**12**
GUENDOLEN	NICOLETTE	BERNARDINE	KERENHAPPUCH
GUINEVERE	PARTHENIA	CHRISTABEL	PHILADELPHIA
GWENDOLEN	PHILLIPPA	CHRISTIANA	
GWENDOLYN		CINDERELLA	

BOYS' NAMES

2	3—continued	3—continued	3—continued
AL	DEE	IRA	LEW
CY	DEL	IVO	LEX
ED	DES	JAN	LOU
TY	DON	JAY	LYN
3	DUD	JED	MAT
ABE	ELI	JEM	MAX
ALF	ERN	JIM	MEL
ART	GIB	JOB	NAT
ASA	GIL	JOE	NED
BAS	GUS	JON	NYE
BAT	GUY	KAY	ODO
BAZ	HAL	KEN	PAT
BEN	HAM	KIM	PIP
BOB	HEW	KIT	RAB
BUD	HOB	LEE	RAY
CAI	HUW	LEN	REG
DAI	IAN	LEO	REX
DAN	IKE	LES	ROB

3—continued	4—continued	4—continued	4—continued
ROD	DAVE	JUDE	SEAN
RON	DAVY	KANE	SETH
ROY	DEAN	KARL	SHAW
SAM	DEWI	KEIR	SHEM
SEB	DICK	KENT	STAN
SID	DION	KING	STEW
SIM	DIRK	KIRK	THEO
STU	DOUG	KRIS	THOM
SYD	DREW	KURT	TOBY
TAM	DUKE	KYLE	TODD
TED	EARL	LARS	TONY
TEL	EBEN	LEON	TREV
TEX	EDDY	LEVI	TROY
TIM	EDEN	LIAM	VERE
TOM	EDOM	LORI	VICK
VIC	EMIL	LORN	WADE
VIN	ENOS	LUDO	WALT
WAL	ERIC	LUKE	WARD
WAT	ERIK	LYLE	WILF
WIN	ERLE	MARC	WILL
ZAK	ESAU	MARK	WYNN
4	ESME	MATT	YVES
ABEL	EVAN	MERV	ZACK
ADAM	EWAN	MICK	ZANE
ALAN	EWEN	MIKE	ZEKE
ALDO	EZRA	MILO	**5**
ALEC	FRED	MORT	AARON
ALED	GARY	MOSS	ABNER
ALEX	GENE	MUIR	ABRAM
ALGY	GLEN	NEAL	ADAIR
ALUN	GLYN	NEIL	ADOLF
ALVA	GREG	NICK	AIDAN
AMOS	GWYN	NOAH	ALAIN
ANDY	HAMO	NOEL	ALBAN
ARTY	HANK	NORM	ALBIN
AXEL	HANS	OLAF	ALDEN
BART	HERB	OLAV	ALDIS
BEAU	HUEY	OMAR	ALDUS
BERT	HUGH	OSSY	ALFIE
BILL	HUGO	OTHO	ALGAR
BING	IAGO	OTIS	ALGER
BOAZ	IAIN	OTTO	ALGIE
BOYD	IFOR	OWEN	ALICK
BRAD	IGOR	PAUL	ALLAN
BRAM	IOLO	PETE	ALLEN
BRET	IVAN	PHIL	ALVAH
BRYN	IVES	RAFE	ALVAR
BURT	IVOR	RENÉ	ALVIE
CARL	JACK	RHYS	ALVIN
CARY	JAGO	RICH	ALVIS
CERI	JAKE	RICK	ALWYN
CHAD	JEFF	ROLF	AMIAS
CHAS	JOCK	ROLY	AMYAS
CHAY	JOEL	RORY	ANCEL
CLEM	JOEY	ROSS	ANDRÉ
COLM	JOHN	RUDI	ANGEL
CONN	JOSÉ	RUDY	ANGUS
CURT	JOSH	RUSS	ANSEL
DALE	JUAN	RYAN	ANTON
DANA	JUDD	SAUL	ARCHY

5—continued	5—continued	5—continued	5—continued
ARMIN	CYRIL	GLENN	LLOYD
ARTIE	CYRUS	GRANT	LOREN
ASHER	DAMON	GREGG	LORIN
ATHOL	DANNY	GUIDO	LORNE
AULAY	DANTE	GYLES	LOUIE
AVERY	DARBY	HAMON	LOUIS
BARON	DARCY	HARDY	LUCAS
BARRY	DARYL	HARRY	LYULF
BASIE	DAVID	HAYDN	MADOC
BASIL	DENIS	HEATH	MANNY
BENET	DENNY	HEBER	MANUS
BENJY	DENYS	HENRI	MARCO
BENNY	DERBY	HENRY	MARIO
BERNY	DEREK	HERVÉ	MARTY
BERRY	DERRY	HIRAM	MICAH
BEVIS	DERYK	HOMER	MICKY
BILLY	DICKY	HONOR	MILES
BJORN	DIGBY	HORRY	MITCH
BLAIR	DONAL	HOWEL	MONTE
BLAKE	DONNY	HUMPH	MONTY
BLANE	DORAN	HYMAN	MORAY
BLASE	DROGO	HYMIE	MORTY
BOBBY	DUANE	HYWEL	MOSES
BONAR	DYLAN	IDRIS	MOSHE
BORIS	EAMON	INIGO	MUNGO
BOYCE	EDDIE	IRVIN	MYLES
BRENT	EDGAR	IRWIN	MYRON
BRETT	EDWIN	ISAAC	NEDDY
BRIAN	EDWYN	ITHEL	NEILL
BRICE	ELDON	IZAAK	NEVIL
BROCK	ELIAS	JABEZ	NIALL
BRUCE	ELIHU	JACKY	NICKY
BRUNO	ELIOT	JACOB	NICOL
BRYAN	ELLIS	JAMES	NIGEL
BRYCE	ELMER	JAMIE	NIKKI
BYRON	ELTON	JARED	NOLAN
CADEL	ELVIN	JASON	OGDEN
CAIUS	ELVIS	JEMMY	OLAVE
CALEB	ELWYN	JERRY	OLLIE
CALUM	EMERY	JESSE	ORSON
CAREY	EMILE	JESUS	ORVAL
CARLO	EMLYN	JIMMY	OSCAR
CAROL	EMRYS	JONAH	OSSIE
CASEY	ENOCH	JONAS	OSWIN
CECIL	EPPIE	JUDAH	OWAIN
CHRIS	ERNIE	JUDAS	OZZIE
CHUCK	ERROL	JULES	PABLO
CLARK	ETHAN	KAROL	PADDY
CLAUD	FARON	KEITH	PAOLO
CLIFF	FELIX	KENNY	PARRY
CLINT	FIDEL	KEVIN	PEDRO
CLIVE	FLOYD	KIRBY	PERCE
CLYDE	FRANK	LABAN	PERCY
COLIN	GAIUS	LANCE	PERRY
COLUM	GARRY	LANTY	PETER
CONAN	GARTH	LARRY	PIERS
CONOR	GAVIN	LAURI	PIRAN
COSMO	GEOFF	LEIGH	QUINN
CRAIG	GERRY	LEROY	RALPH
CUDDY	GILES	LEWIS	RAMON

5—continued

RANDY
RAOUL
RICKI
RICKY
RIKKI
ROALD
ROBIN
RODDY
RODGE
ROGER
ROLLO
ROLLY
ROLPH
ROWAN
ROYAL
RUFUS
SACHA
SAMMY
SAXON
SCOTT
SELBY
SERGE
SHANE
SHAUN
SHAWN
SILAS
SIMON
SOLLY
STEVE
TAFFY
TEDDY
TERRI
TERRY
TIMMY
TITUS
TOLLY
TOMMY
TUDOR
ULRIC
UPTON
URBAN
URIAH
VINCE
VITUS
WALDO
WALLY
WAYNE
WILLY
WYATT
WYNNE

6

ADOLPH
ADRIAN
AENEAS
ALARIC
ALBANY
ALBERT
ALDOUS
ALDRED
ALDWIN

6—continued

ALDWYN
ALEXIS
ALFRED
ALONSO
ALONZO
ALURED
ANDREW
ANGELO
ANSELL
ANSELM
ANTONY
AQUILA
ARCHER
ARCHIE
ARMAND
ARNAUD
ARNOLD
ARTHUR
ASHLEY
AUBERT
AUBREY
AUGUST
AUSTEN
AUSTIN
AYLMER
AYLWIN
BALDIE
BARNET
BARNEY
BARRIE
BARRON
BARTLE
BENITO
BENNET
BERNIE
BERTIE
BETHEL
BILLIE
BLAINE
BLAISE
BOBBIE
BONAMY
BOTOLF
BOTULF
BUSTER
CADELL
CAESAR
CALLUM
CALVIN
CARLOS
CAROLE
CARTER
CASPAR
CEDRIC
CERDIC
CLAUDE
COLLEY
CONNOR
CONRAD
CORMAC

6—continued

CORNEY
COSIMO
CUDDIE
CURTIS
DAFYDD
DAMIAN
DAMIEN
DANIEL
DARREL
DARREN
DARRYL
DECLAN
DENNIS
DENZIL
DERMOT
DERYCK
DEXTER
DICKIE
DICKON
DILLON
DONALD
DORIAN
DOUGAL
DOUGIE
DUDLEY
DUGALD
DUGGIE
DUNCAN
DURAND
DUSTIN
DWAYNE
DWIGHT
EAMONN
EASTER
EDMOND
EDMUND
EDWARD
EGBERT
ELDRED
ELIJAH
ELLERY
ELLIOT
EOGHAN
ERNEST
ESMOND
EUGENE
EVELYN
FABIAN
FARRAN
FARREN
FERGIE
FERGUS
FINLAY
FLURRY
FRANCO
FRASER
FRAZER
FREDDY
GARETH
GARNET

6—continued

GARRET
GASPAR
GAWAIN
GEORGE
GERALD
GERARD
GERWYN
GETHIN
GIDEON
GILROY
GODWIN
GORDON
GRAEME
GRAHAM
GREGOR
GROVER
GUNTER
GUSSIE
GUSTAF
GUSTAV
GWILYM
GWYLIM
HAMISH
HAMLET
HAMLYN
HAMNET
HARLEY
HAROLD
HARVEY
HAYDEN
HAYDON
HECTOR
HEDLEY
HERBIE
HERMAN
HERVEY
HILARY
HOBART
HOLDEN
HONOUR
HORACE
HOWARD
HOWELL
HUBERT
HUGHIE
INGRAM
IRVINE
IRVING
ISAIAH
ISRAEL
JACKIE
JACQUI
JARRED
JARROD
JARVIS
JASPER
JEREMY
JEROME
JETHRO
JOHNNY

6—continued	6—continued	6—continued	7—continued
JOLYON	MURRAY	SHAMUS	BALDWIN
JORDAN	NATHAN	SHELLY	BARCLAY
JOSEPH	NEDDIE	SHOLTO	BARNABY
JOSHUA	NELSON	SIDNEY	BARNARD
JOSIAH	NEWTON	SIMEON	BARRETT
JOSIAS	NINIAN	STEVEN	BARTLET
JOTHAM	NORMAN	STEVIE	BASTIAN
JULIAN	NORRIS	ST JOHN	BEDFORD
JULIUS	NORTON	STUART	BENNETT
JUNIOR	NOWELL	SYDNEY	BENTLEY
JUSTIN	OBERON	TALBOT	BERNARD
KELVIN	OLIVER	TAYLOR	BERTRAM
KENDAL	ORRELL	TEDDIE	BETHELL
KENELM	OSBERT	THOMAS	BOTOLPH
KENTON	OSBORN	TOBIAS	BRADLEY
KESTER	OSMOND	TRAVIS	BRANDAN
KIERAN	OSMUND	TREFOR	BRANDON
LAUNCE	OSWALD	TREVOR	BRENDAN
LAUREN	PALMER	TYBALT	CAMERON
LAURIE	PARKER	TYRONE	CARADOC
LAWRIE	PASCAL	VAUGHN	CARADOG
LAYTON	PASCOE	VERNON	CARLTON
LEMUEL	PELHAM	VICTOR	CAROLUS
LENNOX	PHILIP	VIRGIL	CEDRYCH
LESLIE	PIERRE	WALLIS	CHARLES
LESTER	POLDIE	WALTER	CHARLEY
LIONEL	PRINCE	WARNER	CHARLIE
LONNIE	QUINCY	WARREN	CHAUNCY
LOVELL	RABBIE	WESLEY	CHESTER
LOWELL	RAFAEL	WILBUR	CHRISTY
LUCIAN	RAINER	WILLIE	CLAYTON
LUCIEN	RAMSAY	WILLIS	CLEDWYN
LUCIUS	RAMSEY	WILMER	CLEMENT
LUTHER	RANALD	WILMOT	CLIFTON
LYNDON	RANDAL	WINNIE	CLINTON
LYULPH	RAYNER	WYBERT	COLUMBA
MAGNUS	RAYNOR	WYSTAN	CRISPIN
MALISE	REGGIE	XAVIER	CRYSTAŁ
MALORY	REUBEN	YEHUDI	CYPRIAN
MALVIN	RICHIE	7	DARRELL
MANLEY	ROBBIE	ABRAHAM	DECIMUS
MANSEL	ROBERT	ABSALOM	DENHOLM
MANUEL	RODGER	ABSOLON	DERRICK
MARCEL	RODNEY	ADAMNAN	DESMOND
MARCUS	ROLAND	ADOLPHE	DIGGORY
MARIUS	RONALD	AINSLEY	DOMINIC
MARTIN	RONNIE	AINSLIE	DONOVAN
MARTYN	RUDOLF	ALBERIC	DOUGLAS
MARVIN	RUPERT	ALDHELM	DUNSTAN
MARVYN	RUSSEL	ALFONSO	EARNEST
MELVIN	SAMSON	AMBROSE	ELEAZAR
MELVYN	SAMUEL	ANDREAS	ELKANAH
MERLIN	SEAMUS	ANEIRIN	ELLIOTT
MERTON	SEFTON	ANEURIN	EMANUEL
MERVIN	SELWYN	ANTHONY	EPHRAIM
MERVYN	SERGEI	ANTONIO	ERASMUS
MICKEY	SERGIO	ARTEMAS	EUSTACE
MILTON	SEUMAS	ARTEMUS	EVERARD
MORGAN	SEWARD	AUBERON	EZEKIEL
MORRIS	SEXTUS	AZARIAH	FEARGUS

7—continued

FITZROY
FLORIAN
FRANCIS
FRANKIE
FREDDIE
FREDRIC
FULBERT
GABRIEL
GARRETT
GARRICK
GAYLORD
GEORDIE
GEORGIE
GERAINT
GERRARD
GERSHOM
GERVAIS
GERVASE
GILBERT
GILLEAN
GILLIAN
GODFREY
GOLDWIN
GOLDWYN
GRAHAME
GREGORY
GUNTHER
GUSTAVE
GWYNFOR
HADRIAN
HAMMOND
HARTLEY
HERBERT
HERMANN
HILLARY
HORATIO
HUMBERT
ICHABOD
ISIDORE
JACQUES
JAPHETH
JEFFERY
JEFFREY
JILLIAN
JOACHIM
JOCELYN
JOHNNIE
KENDALL
KENNETH
KENRICK
KIMBALL
LACHLAN
LAMBERT
LAZARUS
LEANDER
LEOFRIC
LEOLINE
LEONARD
LEOPOLD
LINCOLN

7—continued

LINDSAY
LORENZO
LUDOVIC
MALACHI
MALACHY
MALCOLM
MALLORY
MANFRED
MANSELL
MATTHEW
MAURICE
MAXWELL
MAYNARD
MEIRION
MERRION
MICHAEL
MILBURN
MONTAGU
MURDOCH
MURTAGH
NEVILLE
NICOLAS
NORBERT
OBADIAH
OLIVIER
ORLANDO
ORVILLE
OSBORNE
PADRAIG
PATRICK
PHILLIP
PHINEAS
PRESTON
QUENTIN
QUINTIN
RANDALL
RAPHAEL
RAYMOND
RAYMUND
REDVERS
REYNARD
REYNOLD
RICARDO
RICHARD
RODOLPH
RODRIGO
ROWLAND
ROYSTON
RUDOLPH
RUSSELL
SALAMON
SAMPSON
SERGIUS
SEYMOUR
SHANNON
SHELDON
SHELLEY
SIGMUND
SOLOMON
SPENCER

7—continued

STANLEY
STEPHEN
STEWART
SWITHIN
TANCRED
TERENCE
TERTIUS
THORLEY
TIMOTHY
TORQUIL
TRAVERS
TRISTAN
ULYSSES
VAUGHAN
VINCENT
WALLACE
WARWICK
WENDELL
WILBERT
WILFRED
WILFRID
WILLARD
WILLIAM
WINDSOR
WINFRED
WINFRID
WINSTON
WOODROW
WYNDHAM
WYNFORD
ZACHARY

8

ADOLPHUS
ALASDAIR
ALASTAIR
ALGERNON
ALISTAIR
ALOYSIUS
ALPHONSE
ALPHONSO
AUGUSTIN
AUGUSTUS
AURELIAN
BARDOLPH
BARNABAS
BARTLETT
BENEDICK
BENEDICT
BENJAMIN
BERENGER
BERKELEY
BERNHARD
BERTHOLD
BERTRAND
BEVERLEY
BONIFACE
CAMILLUS
CAMPBELL
CARLETON
CARTHACH

8—continued

CHARLTON
CHAUNCEY
CHRISTIE
CHRYSTAL
CLARENCE
CLAUDIUS
CLIFFORD
CONSTANT
COURTNEY
CRISPIAN
CUTHBERT
DIARMAIT
DIARMUID
DOMINICK
EBENEZER
EMMANUEL
ETHELRED
FARQUHAR
FERNANDO
FLETCHER
FLORENCE
FLUELLEN
FRANKLIN
FREDERIC
FREDRICK
GAMALIEL
GARFIELD
GEOFFREY
GRAYBURN
GRIFFITH
GUSTAVUS
HAMILTON
HANNIBAL
HARRISON
HERCULES
HEREWARD
HEZEKIAH
HUMPHREY
IGNATIUS
IORWERTH
JEDIDIAH
JEPHTHAH
JEREMIAH
JEREMIAS
JERMAINE
JOHANNES
JONATHAN
JOSCELIN
KIMBERLY
KINGSLEY
LANCELOT
LAURENCE
LAWRENCE
LEIGHTON
LLEWELYN
MANASSEH
MANASSES
MARSHALL
MATTHIAS
MELVILLE

8—continued
MEREDITH
MITCHELL
MONTAGUE
MORDECAI
MORTIMER
NAPOLEON
NEHEMIAH
NICHOLAS
OCTAVIAN
OCTAVIUS
PERCEVAL
PERCIVAL
PHILEMON
PHINEHAS
RADCLIFF
RANDOLPH
REGINALD
RODERICK
SALVADOR
SEPTIMUS
SHERIDAN
SILVANUS
SINCLAIR
STAFFORD
STANFORD
STIRLING
SYLVANUS
TALIESIN
TERRENCE

8—continued
THADDEUS
THEOBALD
THEODORE
THORNTON
THURSTAN
THURSTON
TRISTRAM
TURLOUGH
WINTHROP
ZEDEKIAH

9
ALEXANDER
ALPHONSUS
AMBROSIUS
ARCHELAUS
ARCHIBALD
ATHELSTAN
AUGUSTINE
BALTHASAR
BALTHAZAR
BRODERICK
CADWALADR
CHRISTIAN
CHRISTMAS
CORNELIUS
COURTENAY
DIONYSIUS
ETHELBERT

9—continued
FERDINAND
FRANCESCO
FRANCISCO
FREDERICK
GERONTIUS
GRANVILLE
GRENVILLE
JEFFERSON
KENTIGERN
KIMBERLEY
LAUNCELOT
LLEWELLYN
MARCELLUS
MARMADUKE
NATHANAEL
NATHANIEL
NICODEMUS
ONUPHRIUS
PEREGRINE
PHILIBERT
RADCLIFFE
SALVATORE
SEBASTIAN
SIEGFRIED
SIGISMUND
SILVESTER
STANISLAS
SYLVESTER

9—continued
THEODORIC
VALENTINE
ZACCHAEUS
ZACHARIAH
ZACHARIAS
ZECHARIAH
ZEPHANIAH

10
BARRINGTON
CARACTACUS
FORTUNATUS
HIERONYMUS
HILDEBRAND
HIPPOLYTUS
MAXIMILIAN
MONTGOMERY
STANISLAUS
THEOPHILUS
WASHINGTON
WILLOUGHBY

11
BARTHOLOMEW
CADWALLADER
CHRISTOPHER
CONSTANTINE
SACHEVERELL

INDEX

Entries in bold face type (e.g. **COUNTRIES OF THE WORLD** 1) refer to tables or lists in the text, with their page numbers. Other index entries suggest tables that might be useful (e.g., SHELLS *see* SEASHELLS, or CHARACTER *try* DICKENSIAN CHARACTERS; GILBERT AND SULLIVAN; FICTIONAL CHARACTERS). We have also included a selection of cue words for cryptic clues (e.g., the word ZERO often indicates the letter O).

CROSSWORD SOLVER

INTRODUCTION

This book consists of a set of lists of words specifically designed to help crossword-puzzle solvers. We have included over 100,000 English words organized into words with two letters, words with three letters, four letters etc, up to fifteen letters. Within each section, the words are arranged alphabetically.

The words chosen include proper nouns, names of people and places, as well as common two- and three-word phrases. We have also given, in many cases, plurals of nouns, comparatives and superlatives of adjectives, and inflections of verbs. In general, '–ize' endings have been used for verbs. It should be noted that '–ise' endings are also possible for these.

At the back of the dictionary are a number of tables and word lists. A list of contents is given overleaf. In addition, there is a list of over 1000 'special words' for word-game enthusiasts. These are unusual in containing combinations of uncommon letters - such as Q, J, K, and Z. They should prove useful to people who play games such as *Scrabble* ®.

We hope that the book will prove useful, and helpful to all who enjoy doing crossword puzzles – and, in particular, to those who enjoy solving them.

CONTENTS

Ⓨ

A	DJ	HO	ME	PE	TO
AB	DO	HQ	MI	PH	TV
AC			MO	PI	
AD	**E**	**I**	MP	PM	**U**
AH	EH	ID	MR	PR	UK
AI	ER	IF	MS	PS	UM
AM	EX	IN	MY	PT	UN
AN		IQ		PX	UP
AS	**F**	IT	**N**		US
AT	FA		NO	**Q**	
	FM	**J**		QC	**V**
B		JP	**O**	QT	VC
BE	**G**		OF		VD
BO	GI	**K**	OH	**R**	VS
BY	GO	KC	ON	RE	
	GP	KO	OP		**W**
C	GS		OR	**S**	WC
CB		**L**	OW	SH	WE
CD		LA	OX	SO	
CO	**H**	LO			**X**
CV	HA	LP			
	HE		**P**	**T**	**Y**
D	HI	**M**	PA	TA	YE
DA	H'M	MA	PC	TI	

A	BID	CUP	ELT	GAY	HOB
ABC	BIG	CUR	EMU	GCE	HOD
ABO	BIN	CUT	END	GDP	HOE
ACE	BIO-	CVS	EON	GEE	HOG
ACT	BIT	CWM	ERA	GEL	HOM
ADD	BOA		ERE	GEM	HOO
ADJ	BOB	**D**	ERG	GEN	HOP
ADO	BOD	DAB	ERR	GET	HOT
ADS	BOG	DAD	ESP	GIG	HOW
ADV	BOO	DAM	ESQ	GIN	HOY
AFT	BOP	DAY	ETC	GIS	HQS
AGE	BOW	DDT	EVE	GNP	HSI
AGM	BOX	DEB	EWE	GNU	HUB
AGO	BOY	DEM	EYE	GOB	HUE
AHA	BRA	DEN		GOD	HUG
AID	BUB	DEP	**F**	GOO	HUH
AIL	BUD	DEW	FAB	GOP	HUM
AIM	BUG	DID	FAD	GOT	HUN
AIR	BUM	DIE	FAG	GPS	HUT
A LA	BUN	DIG	FAN	GUM	
ALE	BUR	DIM	FAR	GUN	**I**
ALL	BUS	DIN	FAT	GUT	ICE
AMP	BUT	DIP	FAX	GUV	ICY
AND	BUY	DIY	FAY	GUY	IDS
ANT	BYE	DJS	FBI	GYM	IFS
ANY		DNA	FED	GYP	ILK
APE	**C**	DOC	FEE		ILL
APT	CAB	DOE	FEN	**H**	IMP
ARC	CAD	DOG	FEW	HAD	INC
ARK	CAM	DOH	FEY	HAE	INK
ARM	CAN	DON	FEZ	HAG	INN
ART	CAP	DOS	FIB	HAH	ION
ASH	CAR	DOT	FIE	HAM	IOU
ASK	CAT	DRY	FIG	HAN	IPA
ASP	CAW	DTS	FIN	HAP	IQS
ASS	CDS	DUB	FIR	HAS	IRA
ATE	CIA	DUD	FIT	HAT	IRE
AUK	CID	DUE	FIX	HAW	IRK
AWE	CND	DUG	FLU	HAY	ISM
AWL	COB	DUN	FLY	HE'D	ITS
AXE	COD	DUO	FOB	HEH	ITV
AYE	COG	DYE	FOE	HEL	IUD
	COL		FOG	HEM	IVY
B	CON	**E**	FOP	HEN	
BAA	COO	EAR	FOR	HEP	**J**
BAD	COP	EAT	FOX	HER	JAB
BAG	COS	EBB	FRO	HE'S	JAG
BAH	COT	ECG	FRY	HET	JAM
BAN	COW	ECT	FUG	HEW	JAR
BAR	COX	EEC	FUN	HEX	JAW
BAT	COY	EEK	FUR	HEY	JAY
BAY	CPA	EEL		HIC	JET
BBC	CPU	EFF	**G**	HID	JEW
BED	CRY	EGG	GAB	HIE	JIB
BEE	CSE	EGO	GAD	HIM	JIG
BEG	CUB	EKG	GAG	HIN	JOB
BEN	CUD	ELF	GAL	HIP	JOG
BET	CUE	ELK	GAP	HIS	JOT
BIB	CUM	ELM	GAS	HIT	JOY

JPS	MAY	OIL	PUG	SEA	TOD
JUG	MEN	OLD	PUN	SEC	TOE
JUT	MET	ONE	PUP	SEE	TOG
	MEW	OOF	PUS	SET	TON
K	MID	OPS	PUT	SEW	TOO
KEG	MIX	OPT	PVC	SEX	TOP
KEN	MOB	ORB	PYX	SHE	TOR
KEY	MOD	ORE		SHY	TOT
KID	MOM	OUR	**Q**	SIC	TOW
KIN	MOO	OUT	QCS	SIN	TOY
KIP	MOP	OVA	QUA	SIP	TRY
KIT	MOS	OWE		SIR	TUB
	MOT	OWL	**R**	SIS	TUC
L	MOW	OWN	RAF	SIT	TUG
LAB	MPS		RAG	SIX	TUT
LAD	MRS	**P**	RAJ	SKI	TVS
LAG	MSC	PAD	RAM	SKY	TWO
LAN	MUD	PAL	RAN	SLY	
LAP	MUG	PAN	RAP	SOB	**U**
LAW	MUM	PAP	RAT	SOD	UFO
LAX		PAR	RAW	SOH	UGH
LAY	**N**	PAS	RAY	SOL	UHF
LCD	NAB	PAT	RED	SON	UNI–
LCM	NAG	PAW	REF	SOP	URN
LEA	NAP	PAY	REP	SOS	USE
LED	NAY	PCS	REV	SOT	
LEE	NCO	PEA	REX	SOU	**V**
LEG	NEE	PEE	RIB	SOW	VAC
LEI	NET	PEG	RID	SOX	VAN
LEO	NEW	PEN	RIG	SOY	VAT
LET	NHS	PEP	RIM	SPA	VCR
LIB	NIB	PER	RIP	SPY	VCS
LID	NIL	PET	RNA	STD	VDU
LIE	NIP	PEW	ROB	STY	VEG
LIP	NIT	PHD	ROC	SUB	VET
LIT	NIX	PHS	ROD	SUE	VEX
LOB	NOB	PIE	ROE	SUM	VHF
LOG	NOD	PIG	ROM	SUN	VIA
LOO	NON–	PIN	ROT	SUP	VIE
LOP	NOR	PIP	ROW		VIM
LOT	NOT	PIS	RUB	**T**	VIP
LOW	NOW	PIT	RUE	TAB	VIZ
LOX	NTH	PIX	RUG	TAG	VOW
LPS	NUB	PLC	RUM	TAN	
LSD	NUN	PLY	RUN	TAP	**W**
LUG	NUT	PMS	RUT	TAR	WAD
LUV		POD	RYE	TAT	WAG
	O	POP		TAX	WAN
M	OAF	POT	**S**	TEA	WAR
MAC	OAK	POW	SAC	TEE	WAX
MAD	OAP	POX	SAD	TEN	WAY
MAG	OAR	PPS	SAE	THE	WEB
MAM	ODD	PRE–	SAG	THY	WED
MAN	ODE	PRO	SAP	TIC	WEE
MAP	O'ER	PRY	SAT	TIE	WET
MAR	OFF	PTA	SAW	TIN	WHO
MAS	OFT	PTO	SAY	TIP	WHY
MAT	OHM	PUB	SDI	TIT	WIG
MAW	OHO	PUD	SDP	TNT	WIN

WIT	WOT	YAM	YES	YOB	ZED
WOE	WOW	YAP	YET	YOU	ZEN
WOG	WPC	YAW	YEW		ZIP
WOK	WRY	YEA	YID	Z	ZOO
WON		YEN	YIN	ZAP	
WOO	Y				
WOP	YAK				

A	ANTE	BAKU	BIKE	BRAE	CAME
ABCS	ANTI-	BALD	BILE	BRAG	CAMP
ABED	ANTS	BALE	BILK	BRAN	CAMS
ABET	ANUS	BALI	BILL	BRAS	CANE
ABLE	APED	BALK	BIND	BRAT	CANS
ABLY	APES	BALL	BINS	BRAY	CANT
ABOS	APEX	BALM	BIRD	BRIM	CAPE
ABUT	APSE	BAND	BIRO	BRIT	CAPS
ACCT	AQUA	BANE	BITE	BRNO	CARD
ACDC	ARAB	BANG	BITS	BROW	CARE
ACES	ARCH	BANK	BLAB	BUBO	CARP
ACHE	ARCS	BANS	BLAH	BUBS	CARS
ACID	AREA	BARB	BLED	BUCK	CART
ACME	AREG	BARD	BLEW	BUDS	CASE
ACNE	ARIA	BARE	BLIP	BUFF	CASH
ACRE	ARID	BARK	BLOB	BUGS	CASK
ACTS	ARKS	BARN	BLOC	BULB	CAST
ADAM	ARMS	BARS	BLOT	BULK	CATS
ADEN	ARMY	BASE	BLOW	BULL	CAUL
ADZE	ARSE	BASH	BLUE	BUMF	CAVE
AEON	ARTS	BASK	BLUR	BUMP	CAVY
AERO-	ARTY	BASS	BOAR	BUMS	CAWS
AFAR	ASHY	BAST	BOAS	BUNA	CEDE
AFRO	ASIA	BATH	BOAT	BUNG	CELL
AGED	ASPS	BATS	BOBS	BUNK	CENT
AGES	ATOM	BAUD	BODE	BUNS	CERT
AGMS	ATOP	BAWD	BODS	BUOY	CHAP
AGOG	AUBE	BAWL	BODY	BURK	CHAR
AGRA	AUDE	BAYS	BOER	BURN	CHAT
AGUE	AUKS	BEAD	BOGS	BURP	CHEF
AHEM	AUNT	BEAK	BOIL	BURR	CHER
AHOY	AURA	BEAM	BOLD	BURS	CHEW
AIDE	AUTO	BEAN	BOLE	BURY	CHIC
AIDS	AVER	BEAR	BOLL	BUSH	CHID
AIMS	AVID	BEAT	BOLT	BUSK	CHIN
AINU	AVOW	BEAU	BOMB	BUSS	CHIP
AIRS	AWAY	BECK	BOND	BUST	CHIT
AIRY	AWED	BEDS	BONE	BUSY	CHOP
AJAR	AWLS	BEEF	BONN	BUTS	CHOU
AKIN	AWOL	BEER	BONY	BUTT	CHOW
ALAS	AWRY	BEES	BOOB	BUYS	CHUG
ALIT	AXED	BEET	BOOK	BUZZ	CHUM
ALLY	AXES	BELL	BOOM	BYES	C-IN-C
ALMS	AXIS	BELT	BOON	BYRE	CINE-
ALOE	AXLE	BEND	BOOR	BYTE	CITE
ALPS	AYAH	BENS	BOOS		CITY
ALSO	AYES	BENT	BOOT	C	CLAD
ALTO		BERK	BOPS	CABS	CLAM
ALUM	B	BERN	BORE	CADS	CLAN
AMBO	BAAS	BEST	BORN	CAEN	CLAP
AMEN	BABE	BETA	BORT	CAFE	CLAW
AMID	BABU	BETS	BOSH	CAGE	CLAY
AMIR	BABY	BEVY	BOSS	CAKE	CLEF
AMOK	BACK	BIAS	BOTH	CALF	CLEW
AMPS	BADE	BIBS	BOUT	CALI	CLIP
ANAL	BAGS	BIDE	BOWL	CALK	CLOD
ANEW	BAIL	BIDS	BOWS	CALL	CLOG
ANKH	BAIT	BIER	BOYS	CALM	CLOP
ANON	BAKE	BIFF	BOZO	CALX	CLOT

CLOY	CROP	DEAR	DORY	EAST	FADS
CLUB	CROW	DEBS	DOSE	EASY	FAGS
CLUE	CRUS	DEBT	DOSS	EATS	FAIL
COAL	CRUX	DECK	DOTE	EBBS	FAIN
COAT	CSES	DEED	DOTS	ECGS	FAIR
COAX	CUBA	DEEM	DOUR	ECHO	FAKE
COBS	CUBE	DEEP	DOVE	ECRU	FALL
COCK	CUBS	DEER	DOWN	EDAM	FAME
CODA	CUED	DEFT	DOZE	EDDY	FANG
CODE	CUES	DEFY	DOZY	EDEN	FANS
CODS	CUFF	DELE	DRAB	EDGE	FARE
COED	CULL	DELL	DRAG	EDGY	FARM
COGS	CULM	DEMO	DRAM	EDIT	FART
COIF	CULT	DENS	DRAT	EELS	FAST
COIL	CUNT	DENT	DRAW	EFIK	FATE
COIN	CUPS	DENY	DRAY	EGGS	FATS
COIR	CURB	DERV	DREW	EGOS	FAUN
COKE	CURD	DESK	DRIP	EIRE	FAWN
COLA	CURE	DEWY	DROP	ELAN	FAZE
COLD	CURL	DHAK	DRUB	ELBA	FEAR
COLS	CURS	DHOW	DRUG	ELBE	FEAT
COLT	CURT	DIAL	DRUM	ELIA	FEED
COMA	CUSP	DICE	DUAL	ELKS	FEEL
COMB	CUSS	DICK	DUCK	ELMS	FEES
COME	CUTE	DIED	DUCT	ELSE	FEET
CONE	CUTS	DIET	DUDE	EMIR	FELL
CONK	CYAN	DIGS	DUDS	EMIT	FELT
CONS	CYST	DIKE	DUEL	EMUS	FEND
CONY	CZAR	DILL	DUES	ENDS	FENS
COOK		DIME	DUET	ENVY	FERN
COOL	D	DINE	DUFF	EONS	FETE
COON	DABS	DINS	DUGS	EPEE	FEUD
COOP	DADO	DINT	DUKE	EPIC	FIAT
COOS	DADS	DIPS	DULL	ERAS	FIBS
COOT	DAFT	DIRE	DULY	ERGO	FIFE
COPE	DAGO	DIRK	DUMB	ERGS	FIGS
COPS	DAIS	DIRT	DUMP	ERIE	FIJI
COPY	DALE	DISC	DUNE	ERSE	FILE
CORD	DAME	DISH	DUNG	ESPY	FILL
CORE	DAMN	DISK	DUNK	ET AL	FILM
CORK	DAMP	DIVE	DUNS	ETCH	FIND
CORM	DAMS	DOCK	DUOS	EURE	FINE
CORN	DANK	DOCS	DUPE	EVEN	FINN
COSH	DARE	DODO	DUSK	EVER	FINS
COST	DARK	DOER	DUST	EVES	FIRE
COSY	DARN	DOES	DUTY	EVIL	FIRM
COTS	DART	DOFF	DYAD	EWER	FIRS
COUP	DASH	DOGE	DYED	EWES	FISH
COVE	DATA	DOGS	DYER	EXAM	FIST
COWL	DATE	DOHA	DYES	EXES	FITS
COWS	DAUB	DOLE	DYKE	EXIT	FIVE
COXA	DAWN	DOLL	DYNE	EYED	FIZZ
COZY	DAYS	DOLT		EYES	FLAB
CRAB	DAZE	DOME	E	EYOT	FLAG
CRAG	D-DAY	DONE	EACH		FLAK
CRAM	DEAD	DONS	EARL	F	FLAN
CRAP	DEAF	DOOM	EARN	FACE	FLAP
CREW	DEAL	DOOR	EARS	FACT	FLAT
CRIB	DEAN	DOPE	EASE	FADE	FLAW

FLAX	FURS	GIST	GUTS	HEAR	HOKE
FLAY	FURY	GIVE	GUVS	HEAT	HOLD
FLEA	FUSE	GIZA	GUYS	HEBE	HOLE
FLED	FUSS	GLAD	GYBE	HECK	HOLM
FLEE	FUZZ	GLEE	GYMS	HEED	HOLP
FLEW		GLEN		HEEL	HOLS
FLEX	G	GLIB	H	HEFT	HOLT
FLIP	GAFF	GLOW	HAAF	HEIR	HOLY
FLIT	GAGA	GLUE	HAAR	HELA	HOMA
FLOE	GAGE	GLUM	HABU	HELD	HOME
FLOG	GAGS	GLUT	HACK	HELL	HOMO
FLOP	GAIN	GNAT	HADE	HELM	HOMS
FLOW	GAIT	GNAW	HADJ	HELP	HOMY
FLUE	GALA	GNUS	HAEM	HEMP	HONE
FLUX	GALE	GOAD	HAFT	HEMS	HONG
FOAL	GALL	GOAL	HAGS	HENS	HONK
FOAM	GALS	GOAT	HA-HA	HENT	HOOD
FOBS	GAME	GOBI	HAIG	HERA	HOOF
FOCI	GAMY	GOBO	HAIK	HERB	HOOK
FOES	GANG	GOBS	HAIL	HERD	HOOP
FOGS	GAOL	GODS	HAIR	HERE	HOOT
FOGY	GAPE	GOER	HAJJ	HERL	HOPE
FOHN	GAPS	GOES	HAKE	HERM	HOPI
FOIL	GARB	GO-GO	HALE	HERN	HOPS
FOLD	GARD	GOLD	HALF	HERO	HORA
FOLK	GASH	GOLF	HALL	HERR	HORN
FOND	GASP	GONE	HALM	HERS	HOSE
FONT	GATE	GONG	HALO	HESS	HOST
FOOD	GAVE	GOOD	HALT	HEST	HOTS
FOOL	GAWK	GOOF	HAMA	HETH	HOUR
FOOT	GAWP	GOON	HAME	HEWN	HOVE
FOPS	GAYS	GORE	HAMS	HICK	HOWE
FORA	GAZA	GORY	HAND	HIDE	HOWF
FORD	GAZE	GOSH	HANG	HIED	HOWL
FORE	GCES	GOUT	HANK	HI-FI	HOYA
FORK	GCSE	GOWN	HARD	HIGH	HUBS
FORM	G'DAY	GRAB	HARE	HIKE	HUED
FORT	GEAR	GRAM	HARK	HILL	HUES
FOUL	GELD	GRAN	HARL	HILT	HUFF
FOUR	GELS	GRAY	HARM	HIND	HUGE
FOWL	GEMS	GREW	HARP	HINT	HUGO
FOXY	GENE	GREY	HART	HIPS	HUGS
FRAP	GENT	GRID	HARZ	HIRE	HULA
FRAU	GENU	GRIM	HASA	HISS	HULK
FRAY	GERM	GRIN	HASH	HIST	HULL
FREE	GHAT	GRIP	HASK	HITS	HUME
FRET	GHEE	GRIT	HASP	HIVE	HUMP
FROE	GIBE	GROG	HAST	HOAD	HUMS
FROG	GIFT	GROW	HATE	HOAR	HUNG
FROM	GIGS	GRUB	HATH	HOAX	HUNK
FUCK	GILD	GUFF	HATS	HOBO	HUNT
FUEL	GILL	GULF	HAUL	HOBS	HUON
FUJI	GILT	GULL	HAVE	HOCK	HURL
FULL	GIMP	GULP	HAWK	HODS	HURT
FUME	GINS	GUMS	HAZE	HOED	HUSH
FUMY	GIRD	GUNS	HAZY	HOER	HUSK
FUND	GIRL	GURU	HEAD	HOES	HUSS
FUNK	GIRO	GUSH	HEAL	HOGG	HUTS
FURL	GIRT	GUST	HEAP	HOGS	HUTU

HWAN	JAMS	KIEL	LATE	LIPS	LUVS
HWYL	JAPE	KIEV	LATH	LIRA	LYNX
HYDE	JARS	KIKE	LAUD	LIRE	LYON
HYMN	JAWS	KILL	LAVA	LISP	LYRE
HYPE	JAYS	KILN	LAWN	LIST	
HYPO	JAZZ	KILO	LAWS	LIVE	**M**
	JEEP	KILT	LAYS	LOAD	MA'AM
I	JEER	KIND	LAZE	LOAF	MACE
IAMB	JELL	KINE	LAZY	LOAM	MACH
IBEX	JERK	KING	LEAD	LOAN	MACS
IBID	JEST	KINK	LEAF	LOBE	MADE
IBIS	JETS	KIPS	LEAK	LOBS	MAGI
ICBM	JEWS	KIRK	LEAN	LOCH	MAGS
ICED	JIBE	KISS	LEAP	LOCI	MAID
ICES	JIBS	KITE	LEAS	LOCK	MAIL
ICON	JIGS	KITS	LEEK	LOCO	MAIM
IDEA	JILT	KIWI	LEER	LODE	MAIN
IDEM	JINN	KNAP	LEES	LODZ	MAKE
IDES	JINX	KNEE	LEFT	LOFT	MALE
IDLE	JIVE	KNEW	LEGS	LOGO	MALI
IDLY	JOBS	KNIT	LEIS	LOGS	MALL
IDOL	JOCK	KNOB	LEND	LOGY	MALM
IFFY	JOGS	KNOT	LENS	LOIN	MALT
IKBS	JOHN	KNOW	LENT	LOLL	MAMA
IKON	JOIN	KOBE	LEOS	LONE	MAMS
ILEX	JOKE	KOHL	LESS	LONG	MANE
ILLS	JOLT	KOOK	LEST	LOOK	MANX
IMAM	JOSH	KRIS	LETS	LOOM	MANY
IMPS	JOVE	KUDU	LEVY	LOON	MAPS
INCA	JOWL		LEWD	LOOP	MARE
INCH	JOYS	**L**	LIAR	LOOS	MARK
INDO-	JUDO	LABS	LIAS	LOOT	MARL
INFO	JUGS	LACE	LICE	LOPE	MARS
INKS	JUJU	LACK	LICK	LORD	MASH
INKY	JULY	LACY	LIDO	LORE	MASK
INNS	JUMP	LADE	LIDS	LORN	MASS
INTO	JUNE	LADS	LIED	LOSE	MAST
IONS	JUNK	LADY	LIEF	LOSS	MATE
IOTA	JURA	LAGS	LIEN	LOST	MATS
IOUS	JURY	LAID	LIES	LOTH	MATT
IOWA	JUST	LAIN	LIEU	LOTS	MAUL
IPOH	JUTE	LAIR	LIFE	LOUD	MAWS
IRAN		LAKE	LIFT	LOUR	MAYA
IRAQ	**K**	LAKH	LIKE	LOUT	MAYS
IRIS	KALE	LAMA	LILO	LOVE	MAZE
IRON	KEEL	LAMB	LILT	LOWS	MAZY
ISLE	KEEN	LAME	LILY	LUCK	MEAD
ISMS	KEEP	LAMP	LIMA	LUDO	MEAL
ITCH	KEGS	LAND	LIMB	LUFF	MEAN
ITEM	KELP	LANE	LIME	LUGS	MEAT
IUDS	KENS	LANK	LIMN	LULL	MEEK
	KENT	LAOS	LIMP	LUMP	MEET
J	KEPT	LAPP	LIMY	LUNG	MEGA-
JABS	KERB	LAPS	LINE	LUNY	MELT
JACK	KERN	LARD	LING	LURE	MEMO
JADE	KEYS	LARK	LINK	LURK	MEND
JAGS	KHAN	LASH	LINT	LUSH	MENU
JAIL	KICK	LASS	LINZ	LUST	MEOW
JAMB	KIDS	LAST	LION	LUTE	MERE

MESH	MUCK	NOEL	ORAL	PEAR	PLUG
MESS	MUFF	NOES	ORAN	PEAS	PLUM
METE	MUGS	NONE	ORBS	PEAT	PLUS
MEWS	MULE	NON-U	ORES	PECK	PODS
MICA	MULL	NOOK	ORGY	PEED	POEM
MICE	MUMS	NOON	ORLY	PEEK	POET
MICK	MUON	NOPE	ORYX	PEEL	POKE
MIDI	MURK	NORM	OSLO	PEEP	POKY
MIEN	MUSE	NOSE	OUCH	PEER	POLE
MIKE	MUSH	NOSH	OURS	PEGS	POLL
MILD	MUSK	NOSY	OUST	PELT	POLO
MILE	MUSS	NOTE	OUZO	PENS	POLY
MILK	MUST	NOUN	OVAL	PERK	POMP
MILL	MUTE	NOUS	OVEN	PERM	POND
MILT	MUTT	NOVA	OVER	PERT	PONG
MIME	MYNA	NUBS	OVUM	PERU	PONY
MIND	MYTH	NUDE	OWED	PESO	POOF
MINE		NUKE	OWLS	PEST	POOH
MINI	N	NULL	OXEN	PETS	POOL
MINK	NAFF	NUMB	OYEZ	PEWS	POOP
MINT	NAGS	NUNS		PHEW	POOR
MINX	NAIL	NUTS	P	PHON	POPE
MIRE	NAME		PACE	PHOT	POPS
MIRY	NAPE	O	PACK	PHUT	PORE
MISS	NAPS	OAFS	PACT	PICA	PORK
MIST	NARK	OAKS	PADS	PICK	PORN
MITE	NASA	OAPS	PAGE	PIED	PORT
MITT	NATO	OARS	PAID	PIER	POSE
MOAN	NAVE	OATH	PAIL	PIES	POSH
MOAT	NAVY	OATS	PAIN	PIGS	POST
MOBS	NAYS	OBEY	PAIR	PIKE	POSY
MOCK	NAZI	OBOE	PALE	PILE	POTS
MODE	NCOS	ODDS	PALL	PILL	POUF
MODS	NEAR	ODES	PALM	PIMP	POUR
MOKE	NEAT	OGLE	PALP	PINE	POUT
MOLD	NECK	OGRE	PALS	PING	POWS
MOLE	NEED	OHIO	PANE	PINK	PRAM
MOLL	NE'ER	OHMS	PANG	PINS	PRAT
MOLT	NEJD	OILS	PANS	PINT	PRAY
MOMS	NEON	OILY	PANT	PINY	PREP
MONK	NERD	OINK	PAPA	PION	PREY
MONO	NEST	OKAY	PAPS	PIPE	PRIG
MOOD	NETS	OKRA	PARA-	PIPS	PRIM
MOON	NETT	OMEN	PARE	PISA	PROD
MOOR	NEWS	OMIT	PARK	PISH	PROF
MOOS	NEWT	OMNI-	PARS	PISS	PROM
MOOT	NEXT	ONCE	PART	PITH	PROP
MOPE	NIBS	ONES	PASS	PITS	PROS
MOPS	NICE	ONLY	PAST	PITY	PROW
MORE	NICK	ONTO	PATE	PLAN	PSST
MORN	NIFF	ONUS	PATH	PLAY	PUBS
MOSS	NIGH	ONYX	PATS	PLEA	PUCE
MOST	NINE	OOPS	PAVE	PLEB	PUCK
MOTE	NIPS	OOZE	PAWL	PLED	PUDS
MOTH	NISI	OOZY	PAWN	PLOD	PUFF
MOTS	NITS	OPAL	PAWS	PLOP	PUGS
MOVE	NOBS	OPEC	PAYE	PLOT	PUKE
MOWN	NODE	OPEN	PEAK	PLOW	PULL
MUCH	NODS	OPUS	PEAL	PLOY	PULP

PUMA	REAP	ROOK	SASH	SHOW	SLUT
PUMP	REAR	ROOM	SASS	SHUN	SMOG
PUNK	RECK	ROOT	SATE	SHUT	SMUG
PUNS	REDO	ROPE	SAVE	SIAN	SMUT
PUNT	REDS	ROPY	SAWN	SICK	SNAG
PUNY	REED	ROSE	SAWS	SIDE	SNAP
PUPA	REEF	ROSY	SAYS	SIFT	SNIP
PUPS	REEK	ROTA	SCAB	SIGH	SNOB
PURE	REEL	ROTE	SCAG	SIGN	SNOG
PURL	REFS	ROTS	SCAM	SIKH	SNOT
PURR	REIN	ROUE	SCAN	SILK	SNOW
PUSH	RELY	ROUT	SCAR	SILL	SNUB
PUSS	REND	ROUX	SCAT	SILO	SNUG
PUTT	RENT	ROVE	SCUD	SILT	SOAK
PYRE	REPS	ROWS	SCUM	SIND	SOAP
	REST	RUBS	SEAL	SINE	SOAR
	REVS	RUBY	SEAM	SING	SOBS
Q	RHEA	RUCK	SEAR	SINH	SOCK
QUAD	RIAL	RUDE	SEAS	SINK	SODA
QUAY	RIBS	RUED	SEAT	SINO-	SODS
QUID	RICE	RUFF	SECS	SINS	SOFA
QUIN	RICH	RUGS	SECT	SIPS	SOFT
QUIP	RICK	RUHR	SEED	SIRE	SOIL
QUIT	RIDE	RUIN	SEEK	SIRS	SOLD
QUIZ	RIFE	RULE	SEEM	SITE	SOLE
QUOD	RIFF	RUMP	SEEN	SIZE	SOLO
	RIFT	RUMS	SEEP	SKEW	SOMA
R	RIGS	RUNE	SEER	SKID	SOME
RACE	RILE	RUNG	SEES	SKIM	SONG
RACK	RILL	RUNS	SELF	SKIN	SONS
RACY	RIME	RUNT	SELL	SKIP	SOON
RAFT	RIMS	RUSE	SEME	SKIS	SOOT
RAGA	RIMY	RUSH	SEMI	SKIT	SOPS
RAGE	RIND	RUSK	SEND	SKUA	SORE
RAGS	RING	RUST	SENT	SKYE	SORT
RAID	RINK	RUTS	SERA	SLAB	SO-SO
RAIL	RIOT	RYES	SERE	SLAG	SOTS
RAIN	RIPE		SERF	SLAM	SOUL
RAKE	RIPS	S	SETA	SLAP	SOUP
RAMP	RISE	SACK	SETS	SLAT	SOUR
RAMS	RISK	SACS	SEWN	SLAV	SOWN
RAND	RITE	SAFE	SEXY	SLAY	SOWS
RANG	RIVE	SAGA	SHAD	SLED	SPAM
RANI	ROAD	SAGE	SHAG	SLEW	SPAN
RANK	ROAM	SAGO	SHAH	SLID	SPAR
RANT	ROAN	SAGS	SHAM	SLIM	SPAS
RAPE	ROAR	SAID	SHAT	SLIP	SPAT
RAPS	ROBE	SAIL	SHED	SLIT	SPAY
RAPT	ROCK	SAKE	SHEW	SLOB	SPEC
RARE	ROCS	SALE	SHIM	SLOE	SPED
RASH	RODE	SALT	SHIN	SLOG	SPEW
RASP	RODS	SAME	SHIP	SLOP	SPIC
RATE	ROES	SAN'A	SHIT	SLOT	SPIK
RATS	ROLE	SAND	SHOA	SLOW	SPIN
RAVE	ROLL	SANE	SHOD	SLUB	SPIT
RAYS	ROMP	SANG	SHOE	SLUE	SPIV
RAZE	ROMS	SANK	SHOO	SLUG	SPOT
READ	ROOD	SAPS	SHOP	SLUM	SPRY
REAL	ROOF	SARI	SHOT	SLUR	SPUD
REAM					

SPUN	TAKE	TIDE	TRIM	VARY	WARY
SPUR	TALC	TIDY	TRIO	VASE	WASH
STAB	TALE	TIED	TRIP	VAST	WASP
STAG	TALK	TIER	TROD	VATS	WATT
STAR	TALL	TIES	TROT	VAUD	WAUL
STAY	TAME	TIFF	TRUE	VDUS	WAVE
STEM	TAMP	TILE	TRUG	VEAL	WAVY
STEP	TANG	TILL	TSAR	VEER	WAXY
STET	TANH	TILT	TUBA	VEIL	WAYS
STEW	TANK	TIME	TUBE	VEIN	WEAK
STIR	TANS	TINE	TUBS	VELD	WEAL
STOL	TAPE	TING	TUCK	VEND	WEAN
STOP	TAPS	TINS	TUFT	VENT	WEAR
STOW	TARE	TINT	TUGS	VERB	WEBS
STUB	TARN	TINY	TUNA	VERY	WEED
STUD	TARO	TIPS	TUNE	VEST	WEEK
STUM	TARS	TIRE	TURD	VETO	WEEP
STUN	TART	TIRO	TURF	VETS	WEFT
SUBS	TASK	TITS	TURN	VIAL	WEIR
SUCH	TA-TA	TOAD	TUSH	VICE	WELD
SUCK	TATS	TO-DO	TUSK	VIED	WELL
SUDS	TAUT	TODS	TUTU	VIEW	WELT
SUED	TAXI	TOED	TWAT	VILE	WEND
SUER	TEAK	TOES	TWEE	VINE	WENT
SUET	TEAL	TOFF	TWIG	VINO	WEPT
SUEZ	TEAM	TOGA	TWIN	VIOL	WEST
SUIT	TEAR	TOGO	TWIT	VIPS	WETS
SULK	TEAS	TOGS	TWOS	VISA	WHAM
SUMP	TEAT	TOIL	TYPE	VISE	WHAT
SUMS	TEED	TOLD	TYRE	VOID	WHEN
SUNG	TEEM	TOLL	TYRO	VOLE	WHET
SUNK	TEES	TOMB	TZAR	VOLT	WHEW
SUNS	TELE-	TOME		VOTE	WHEY
SUPS	TELL	TONE	U	VOWS	WHIG
SURD	TEMP	TONS	UCCA	VTOL	WHIM
SURE	TEND	TOOK	UFOS		WHIP
SURF	TENS	TOOL	UGLY	W	WHIR
SUSS	TENT	TOOT	ULNA	WADE	WHIT
SWAB	TERM	TOPS	UNDO	WADI	WHIZ
SWAG	TERN	TORE	UNIT	WADS	WHOA
SWAM	TEST	TORN	UNTO	WAFT	WHOM
SWAN	TEXT	TORS	UPON	WAGE	WHOP
SWAP	THAN	TORT	URDU	WAGS	WHYS
SWAT	THAT	TORY	URGE	WAIF	WICK
SWAY	THAW	TOSS	URIC	WAIL	WIDE
SWIG	THEE	TOTE	URNS	WAIT	WIFE
SWIM	THEM	TOTO	USED	WAKE	WIGS
SWOP	THEN	TOTS	USER	WALK	WILD
SWOT	THEO-	TOUR	USES	WALL	WILL
SWUM	THEY	TOUT	UTAH	WAND	WILT
SYNC	THIN	TOWN	UVEA	WANE	WILY
	THIS	TOWS		WANK	WIMP
T	THOU	TOYS	V	WANT	WIND
TABS	THRU	TRAD	VACS	WARD	WINE
TACK	THUD	TRAM	VAIN	WARM	WING
TACO	THUG	TRAP	VALE	WARN	WINK
TACT	THUS	TRAY	VAMP	WARP	WINS
TAGS	TICK	TREE	VANE	WARS	WINY
TAIL	TICS	TREK	VANS	WART	WIPE

WIRE	WONT	X	YAWS	YOKE	ZEDS
WIRY	WOOD	XMAS	YEAH	YOLK	ZEIN
WISE	WOOF	X-RAY	YEAR	YORE	ZERO
WISH	WOOL		YEAS	YOUR	ZEST
WISP	WOPS	Y	YELL	YOWL	ZINC
WITH	WORD	YAKS	YELP	YOYO	ZION
WITS	WORE	YAMS	YENS	YUAN	ZIPS
WOAD	WORK	YANG	YETI	YUCK	ZITS
WOES	WORM	YANK	YEWS	YULE	ZIZZ
WOGS	WORN	YAPS	YIDS		ZOND
WOKE	WOVE	YARD	YLEM	Z	ZONE
WOKS	WPCS	YARN	YOBS	ZANY	ZOOM
WOLD	WRAP	YAWL	YOGA	ZEAL	ZOOS
WOLF	WREN	YAWN	YOGI	ZEBU	ZULU
WOMB	WRIT				

A	AEDES	ALIVE	ANNAM	ARROW
AALII	AEGIS	ALKYD	ANNEX	ARSES
ABACA	AEONS	ALKYL	ANNOY	ARSIS
ABACK	AFFIX	ALLAH	ANNUL	ARSON
ABAFT	AFIRE	ALLAY	ANODE	ARTEL
ABASE	AFOOT	ALLEY	ANOLE	ARYAN
ABASH	AFOUL	ALLOT	ANTED	ASCII
ABATE	AFROS	ALLOW	ANTES	ASCOT
ABBEY	AFTER	ALLOY	ANTIC	ASCUS
ABBOT	AGAIN	ALLYL	ANVIL	ASDIC
ABEAM	AGAMA	ALOFT	ANZAC	ASHEN
ABELE	AGAPE	ALOIN	ANZIO	ASHES
ABHOR	AGATE	ALONE	AORTA	ASIAN
ABIDE	AGAVE	ALONG	APACE	ASIDE
ABODE	AGENT	ALOOF	APART	ASKED
ABOHM	AGGER	ALOUD	APEAK	ASKER
ABORT	AGGRO	ALPHA	APERY	ASKEW
ABOUT	AGILE	ALTAI	APHID	ASPEN
ABOVE	AGING	ALTAR	APHIS	ASPER
ABUSE	AGISM	ALTER	APIAN	ASPIC
ABYSS	AGIST	ALTOS	A PIED	ASSAI
ACCRA	AGLET	AMASS	APING	ASSAM
ACHED	AGLOW	AMAZE	APISH	ASSAY
ACHES	AGONY	AMBER	APORT	ASSES
ACIDS	AGORA	AMBIT	APPAL	ASSET
ACKEE	AGREE	AMBLE	APPEL	ASTER
ACORN	AGUES	AMBRY	APPLE	ASTIR
ACRES	AHEAD	AMEBA	APPLY	ASTRO-
ACRID	AHWAZ	AMEND	APRIL	ASWAN
ACTED	AIDED	AMENT	APRON	ATLAS
ACTIN	AIDES	AMICE	APSES	ATOLL
ACTOR	AILED	AMIDE	APSIS	ATOMS
ACUTE	AIMED	AMINE	APTLY	ATONE
ADAGE	AIRED	AMINO	AQABA	ATONY
ADAMS	AISLE	AMIRS	ARABS	ATRIA
ADANA	AISNE	AMISS	ARBOR	ATRIP
ADAPT	AITCH	AMITY	AREAL	ATTAR
ADDAX	AJMER	AMMAN	AREAS	ATTIC
ADDED	ALACK	AMONG	ARECA	AUDIO
ADDER	ALAMO	AMOUR	ARENA	AUDIT
ADDLE	ALARM	AMPLE	ARETE	AUGER
ADD-ON	ALARY	AMPLY	ARGIL	AUGHT
ADEPT	ALATE	AMUCK	ARGOL	AUGUR
A DEUX	ALBUM	AMUSE	ARGON	AUNTS
AD HOC	ALDER	ANCON	ARGOT	AURAL
ADIEU	ALDOL	ANDES	ARGUE	AURAS
ADIOS	ALECK	ANGEL	ARIAN	AURIC
AD-LIB	ALERT	ANGER	ARIAS	AUTOS
ADMAN	ALGAE	ANGLE	ARIEL	AUXIN
ADMEN	ALGAL	ANGLO-	ARIEN	AVAIL
ADMIT	ALGID	ANGRY	ARIES	AVENS
ADMIX	ALGIN	ANGST	ARISE	AVERT
ADOBE	ALGOL	ANILE	ARMCO	AVIAN
ADOPT	ALGOR	ANIMA	ARMED	AVOID
ADORE	ALIAS	ANION	AROID	AWAIT
ADORN	ALIBI	ANISE	AROMA	AWAKE
AD REM	ALIEN	ANJOU	AROSE	AWARD
ADULT	ALIGN	ANKLE	ARRAY	AWARE
ADZES	ALIKE	ANNAL	ARRIS	AWASH

AWFUL	BARER	BEGET	BIRTH	BOERS
AWOKE	BARGE	BEGIN	BISON	BOGEY
AXIAL	BARIC	BEGOT	BITCH	BOGGY
AXILE	BARKS	BEGUM	BITES	BOGIE
AXING	BARMY	BEGUN	BITTY	BOGOR
AXIOM	BARNS	BEIGE	BIYSK	BOGUS
AXLES	BARON	BEING	BLACK	BOHEA
AYAHS	BARYE	BEIRA	BLADE	BOHOL
AZIDE	BASAL	BELAY	BLAIN	BOILS
AZINE	BASED	BELCH	BLAME	BOLES
AZOIC	BASEL	BELEM	BLANC	BOLLS
AZOLE	BASER	BELIE	BLAND	BOLTS
AZOTE	BASES	BELLE	BLANK	BOLUS
AZTEC	BASIC	BELLS	BLARE	BOMBE
AZURE	BASIL	BELLY	BLASE	BOMBS
	BASIN	BELOW	BLAST	BONDS
B	BASIS	BELTS	BLAZE	BONED
BAAED	BASRA	BEMBA	BLEAK	BONES
BABEL	BASSO	BENCH	BLEAR	BONGO
BABES	BASTE	BENDS	BLEAT	BONNY
BABUL	BATCH	BENIN	BLEED	BONUS
BABUS	BATED	BENTS	BLEEP	BOOBS
BACCY	BATHE	BERET	BLEND	BOOBY
BACKS	BATHS	BERKS	BLESS	BOOED
BACON	BATIK	BERRY	BLEST	BOOKS
BADGE	BATON	BERTH	BLIMP	BOOMS
BADLY	BATTY	BERYL	BLIND	BOONS
BAGEL	BATUM	BESET	BLINI	BOORS
BAGGY	BAULK	BESOM	BLINK	BOOST
BAHAI	BAWDS	BETAS	BLIPS	BOOTH
BAHIA	BAWDY	BETEL	BLISS	BOOTS
BAILS	BAYED	BEVEL	BLITZ	BOOTY
BAIRN	BAYOU	BEZEL	BLOAT	BOOZE
BAIZE	BEACH	BHANG	BLOBS	BOOZY
BAKED	BEADS	BIBLE	BLOCK	BORAX
BAKER	BEADY	BIDED	BLOCS	BORED
BALAS	BEAKS	BIDET	BLOKE	BORER
BALED	BEAKY	BIERS	BLOND	BORES
BALER	BEAMS	BIFFS	BLOOD	BORIC
BALES	BEANO	BIFID	BLOOM	BORNE
BALKS	BEANS	BIGHT	BLOTS	BORNU
BALLS	BEARD	BIGOT	BLOWN	BORON
BALLY	BEARS	BIHAR	BLOWS	BOSKY
BALMS	BEAST	BIJOU	BLOWY	BOSOM
BALMY	BEATS	BIKED	BLUER	BOSON
BALSA	BEAUS	BIKES	BLUES	BOSSY
BANAL	BEAUT	BILGE	BLUFF	BOSUN
BANDS	BEAUX	BILLS	BLUNT	BOTCH
BANDY	BEBOP	BILLY	BLURB	BOUGH
BANES	BECKS	BINAL	BLURT	BOULE
BANFF	BEECH	BINGE	BLUSH	BOUND
BANGS	BEEFY	BINGO	BOARD	BOURN
BANJO	BEERS	BIOME	BOARS	BOUSE
BANKS	BEERY	BIOTA	BOAST	BOUTS
BANNS	BEETS	BIPED	BOATS	BOVID
BANTU	BEFIT	BIPOD	BOBBY	BOWED
BARBS	BEFOG	BIRCH	BOCHE	BOWEL
BARDS	BEGAN	BIRDS	BODED	BOWER
BARED	BEGAT	BIROS	BODGE	BOWLS

BOXED	BRUSH	BYLAW	CARET	CHEAT
BOXER	BRUTE	BYRES	CARGO	CHECK
BOXES	B-SIDE	BYTES	CARNE	CHEEK
BOZOS	BUBAL	BYTOM	CAROB	CHEEP
BRACE	BUCHU	BYWAY	CAROL	CHEER
BRACT	BUCKS		CARPS	CHEFS
BRAES	BUDDY	**C**	CARRY	CHELA
BRAGA	BUDGE	CABAL	CARTS	CHERT
BRAID	BUFFS	CABBY	CARVE	CHESS
BRAIL	BUGGY	CABER	CASED	CHEST
BRAIN	BUGLE	CABIN	CASES	CHEWS
BRAKE	BUILD	CABLE	CASKS	CHEWY
BRAND	BUILT	CACAO	CASTE	CHIBA
BRASH	BULBS	CACHE	CASTS	CHICK
BRASS	BULGE	CACTI	CATCH	CHIDE
BRATS	BULGY	CADDY	CATER	CHIEF
BRAVE	BULKS	CADET	CATTY	CHILD
BRAVO	BULKY	CADGE	CAULK	CHILE
BRAWL	BULLA	CADIZ	CAUSE	CHILL
BRAWN	BULLS	CADRE	CAVED	CHIME
BRAXY	BULLY	CAFES	CAVES	CHINA
BRAYS	BUMPH	CAGED	CAVIL	CHINE
BRAZE	BUMPS	CAGES	CAWED	CHING
BREAD	BUMPY	CAGEY	CD-ROM	CHINK
BREAK	BUNCH	CAIRN	CEARA	CHINS
BREAM	BUNDU	CAIRO	CEASE	CHIPS
BREDA	BUNGS	CAJUN	CEDAR	CHIRM
BREED	BUNKS	CAKED	CEDED	CHIRP
BRENT	BUNNY	CAKES	CEDER	CHIRR
BREST	BUOYS	CALIX	CEIBA	CHITA
BREVE	BURGH	CALLA	CELLA	CHITS
BRIAR	BURIN	CALLS	CELLE	CHIVY
BRIBE	BURKE	CALOR	CELLO	CHOCK
BRICK	BURKS	CALVE	CELLS	CHOIR
BRIDE	BURLY	CALYX	CENSE	CHOKE
BRIEF	BURMA	CAMEL	CENTO	CHOKY
BRIER	BURNS	CAMEO	CENTS	CHOMP
BRILL	BURNT	CAMPO	CERES	CHOPS
BRINE	BURPS	CAMPS	CERIC	CHORD
BRING	BURRO	CANAL	CERTS	CHORE
BRINK	BURRS	CANDY	CETUS	CHOSE
BRINY	BURRY	CANED	CHAFE	CHOUX
BRISK	BURSA	CANER	CHAFF	CHOWS
BRITS	BURSE	CANES	CHAIN	CHRON-
BROAD	BURST	CANNA	CHAIR	CHUCK
BROIL	BUSBY	CANNY	CHALK	CHUFA
BROKE	BUSED	CANOE	CHAMP	CHUFF
BROME	BUSES	CANON	CHANT	CHUMP
BRONX	BUSHY	CANTO	CHAOS	CHUMS
BROOD	BUSTS	CANTS	CHAPS	CHUNK
BROOK	BUSTY	CAPER	CHARD	CHURL
BROOM	BUTCH	CAPES	CHARM	CHURN
BROTH	BUTTE	CAPON	CHARS	CHUTE
BROWN	BUTTS	CAPRI	CHART	CHYLE
BROWS	BUTTY	CAPUT	CHARY	CHYME
BRUIN	BUTYL	CARAT	CHASE	CIDER
BRUIT	BUXOM	CARDS	CHASM	CIGAR
BRUME	BUYER	CARED	CHATS	CIMEX
BRUNT	BWANA	CARES	CHEAP	CINCH

CIRCA	COALS	CORAL	CREAM	CULLS
CISCO	COALY	CORDS	CREDO	CULPA
CISSY	COAST	CORED	CREED	CULTS
CITED	COATS	CORER	CREEK	CUMIN
CIVET	COBIA	CORES	CREEL	CUNTS
CIVIC	COBRA	CORGI	CREEP	CUPEL
CIVIL	COCKS	CORKS	CREME	CUPID
CLACK	COCKY	CORMS	CREPE	CUPPA
CLAIM	COCOA	CORNS	CREPT	CURBS
CLAMP	CODAS	CORNU	CRESS	CURCH
CLAMS	CODED	CORNY	CREST	CURDY
CLANG	CODER	CORPS	CRETE	CURED
CLANK	CODES	CORSE	CREWS	CURES
CLANS	CODEX	COSTA	CRIBS	CURET
CLAPS	CODON	COSTS	CRICK	CURIA
CLARO	COEDS	COTTA	CRIED	CURIE
CLARY	COGON	COUCH	CRIER	CURIO
CLASH	COIFS	COUDE	CRIES	CURLS
CLASP	COIGN	COUGH	CRIME	CURLY
CLASS	COILS	COULD	CRIMP	CURRY
CLAWS	COINS	COUNT	CRISP	CURSE
CLEAN	COKES	COUPE	CROAK	CURVE
CLEAR	COLDS	COUPS	CROAT	CUSEC
CLEAT	COLEY	COURT	CROCK	CUSHY
CLEEK	COLIC	COVEN	CROFT	CUSPS
CLEFS	COLON	COVER	CRONE	CUTER
CLEFT	COLTS	COVES	CRONY	CUTIN
CLERK	COLZA	COVET	CROOK	CUTIS
CLEWS	COMAL	COVEY	CROON	CUT UP
CLICK	COMAS	COVIN	CROPS	CUZCO
CLIFF	COMBO	COWED	CRORE	CYCAD
CLIMB	COMBS	COWER	CROSS	CYCLE
CLIME	COMER	COWES	CROUP	CYDER
CLINE	COMET	COWLS	CROWD	CYMAR
CLING	COMFY	COWRY	CROWN	CYMRY
CLINK	COMIC	COXAL	CROWS	CYNIC
CLIPS	COMMA	COXED	CROZE	CYSTS
CLOAK	COMPO	COXES	CRUDE	CYTON
CLOCK	CONCH	COYLY	CRUEL	CZARS
CLODS	CONES	COYPU	CRUET	CZECH
CLOGS	CONEY	COZEN	CRUMB	
CLONE	CONGA	CRABS	CRUMP	D
CLOSE	CONGE	CRACK	CRURA	DACCA
CLOTH	CONGO	CRAFT	CRUSE	DADDY
CLOTS	CONIC	CRAGS	CRUSH	DAGGA
CLOUD	CONKS	CRAKE	CRUST	DAGOS
CLOUT	CONTE	CRAMP	CRYPT	DAILY
CLOVE	COOED	CRANE	CUBAN	DAIRY
CLOWN	COOKS	CRANK	CUBEB	DAISY
CLUBS	COOLS	CRAPE	CUBED	DAKAR
CLUCK	COONS	CRAPS	CUBES	DALES
CLUES	COOPS	CRASH	CUBIC	DALLY
CLUMP	CO-OPT	CRASS	CUBIT	DAMAN
CLUNG	COOTS	CRATE	CUDDY	DAMES
CLUNK	COPAL	CRAVE	CUFFS	DANCE
CLUNY	COPED	CRAWL	CUING	DANDY
CLWYD	COPES	CRAZE	CULCH	DANIO
CLYDE	COPRA	CRAZY	CULET	DARAF
COACH	COPSE	CREAK	CULEX	DARED

DARER	DEPTH	DODOS	DRANK	DUNGY
DARES	DERBY	DOERS	DRAPE	DUNKS
DARKS	DERMA	DOGES	DRAWL	DUPED
DARKY	DESKS	DOGGO	DRAWN	DUPER
DARNS	DETER	DOGGY	DRAWS	DUPES
DARTS	DEUCE	DOGIE	DRAYS	DUPLE
DATED	DEVIL	DOGMA	DREAD	DUREX
DATER	DHOLE	DOILY	DREAM	DUROC
DATES	DHOTI	DOING	DREAR	DURRA
DATUM	DHOWS	DOLBY	DREGS	DURUM
DAUBS	DIALS	DOLCE	DRESS	DUSKY
DAUBY	DIARY	DOLED	DRIBS	DUSTY
DAUNT	DIAZO	DOLLS	DRIED	DUTCH
DAVIT	DICED	DOLLY	DRIER	DUVET
DAWNS	DICER	DOLTS	DRIFT	DWARF
DAZED	DICEY	DOMED	DRILL	DWELL
DAZES	DICKS	DOMES	DRILY	DWELT
DEALS	DICKY	DONEE	DRINK	DYERS
DEALT	DICTA	DONNA	DRIPS	DYFED
DEANS	DIETS	DONOR	DRIVE	DYING
DEARS	DIGIT	DOOMS	DROIT	DYKES
DEARY	DIJON	DOORS	DROLL	DYULA
DEATH	DIKES	DOPED	DROME	
DEBAR	DILDO	DOPES	DRONE	E
DEBIT	DIMER	DOPEY	DROOL	EAGER
DEBTS	DIMES	DORIC	DROOP	EAGLE
DEBUG	DIMLY	DOSED	DROPS	EAGRE
DEBUT	DINAR	DOSER	DROSS	EARED
DECAL	DINED	DOSES	DROVE	EARLS
DECAY	DINER	DOTED	DROWN	EARLY
DECKS	DINGO	DOTER	DRUGS	EARTH
DECOR	DINGY	DOTTY	DRUID	EASED
DECOY	DINKA	DOUBS	DRUMS	EASEL
DECRY	DINKY	DOUBT	DRUNK	EASER
DEEDS	DIODE	DOUGH	DRUPE	EASTS
DEFER	DIRER	DOURO	DRUSE	EATEN
DEGAS	DIRGE	DOUSE	DRYAD	EATER
DE-ICE	DIRKS	DOVES	DRYER	EAVES
DEIFY	DIRTY	DOWDY	DUALA	EBBED
DEIGN	DISCO	DOWEL	DUBAI	EBONY
DEISM	DISCS	DOWER	DUCAL	ECLAT
DEIST	DISHY	DOWNS	DUCAT	EDEMA
DEITY	DISKS	DOWNY	DUCHY	EDGED
DEKKO	DITCH	DOWRY	DUCKS	EDGER
DELAY	DITTO	DOWSE	DUCKY	EDGES
DELFT	DITTY	DOYEN	DUCTS	EDICT
DELHI	DIVAN	DOZED	DUDES	EDIFY
DELLS	DIVED	DOZEN	DUELS	EDUCE
DELOS	DIVER	DOZER	DUETS	EDUCT
DELTA	DIVES	D PHIL	DUFFS	EERIE
DELVE	DIVOT	DRABS	DUKES	EFFED
DEMOB	DIXIE	DRAFF	DULIA	EGEST
DEMON	DIZZY	DRAFT	DULLY	EGGER
DEMOS	DJINN	DRAGS	DULSE	EGRET
DEMUR	DOBBY	DRAIL	DUMMY	EGYPT
DENIM	DOBRO	DRAIN	DUMPS	EIDER
DENSE	DOCKS	DRAKE	DUMPY	EIGER
DENTS	DODGE	DRAMA	DUNCE	EIGHT
DEPOT	DODGY	DRAMS	DUNES	EIKON

EILAT	EROSE	FAKER	FETCH	FJORD
EJECT	ERRED	FAKES	FETED	FLACK
ELAND	ERROR	FAKIR	FETES	FLAGS
ELATE	ERUCT	FALLS	FETID	FLAIL
ELBOW	ERUPT	FALSE	FETOR	FLAIR
ELDER	ESKER	FAMED	FETUS	FLAKE
ELECT	ESSAY	FANCY	FEUDS	FLAKY
ELEGY	ESSEN	FANGO	FEVER	FLAME
ELEMI	ESTER	FANGS	FEZES	FLAMY
ELFIN	ESTOP	FANNY	FIATS	FLANK
ELIDE	ETHER	FANON	FIBRE	FLANS
ELITE	ETHIC	FANTI	FICHU	FLAPS
ELOPE	ETHOS	FARAD	FIELD	FLARE
ELUDE	ETHYL	FARCE	FIEND	FLASH
ELUTE	ETUDE	FARCI	FIERY	FLASK
ELVER	EVADE	FARCY	FIFER	FLATS
ELVES	EVENS	FARED	FIFES	FLAWS
EMBAY	EVENT	FARER	FIFTH	FLAWY
EMBED	EVERT	FARES	FIFTY	FLEAM
EMBER	EVERY	FARLE	FIGHT	FLEAS
EMBOW	EVICT	FARMS	FILAR	FLECK
EMCEE	EVILS	FARTS	FILCH	FLEER
EMEND	EVOKE	FASTS	FILED	FLEET
EMERY	EWERS	FATAL	FILER	FLESH
EMIRS	EXACT	FATED	FILES	FLEWS
EMMER	EXALT	FATES	FILET	FLICK
EMOTE	EXAMS	FATTY	FILLY	FLIER
EMPTY	EXCEL	FAUGH	FILMS	FLIES
ENACT	EXERT	FAULT	FILMY	FLING
ENATE	EXILE	FAUNA	FILTH	FLINT
ENDED	EXIST	FAUNS	FILUM	FLIPS
ENDER	EXITS	FAVUS	FINAL	FLIRT
ENDOW	EXPEL	FAWNS	FINCH	FLOAT
ENDUE	EXTOL	FAXED	FINDS	FLOCK
ENEMA	EXTRA	FAZED	FINED	FLOES
ENEMY	EXUDE	FEARS	FINER	FLONG
ENJOY	EXULT	FEAST	FINES	FLOOD
ENNUI	EYING	FEATS	FINGO	FLOOR
ENROL	EYOTS	FEAZE	FINIS	FLOPS
ENSUE	EYRIE	FECAL	FINNY	FLORA
ENTER		FECES	FIORD	FLORY
ENTRY	F	FECIT	FIRED	FLOSS
ENUGU	FABLE	FED UP	FIRER	FLOUR
ENURE	FACED	FEEDS	FIRES	FLOUT
ENVOY	FACER	FEIGN	FIRMS	FLOWN
EOSIN	FACES	FEINT	FIRRY	FLUED
EPACT	FACET	FELLS	FIRST	FLUES
EPEES	FACIA	FELON	FIRTH	FLUFF
EPICS	FACTS	FEMUR	FISHY	FLUID
EPOCH	FADDY	FENCE	FISTS	FLUKE
EPODE	FADED	FENNY	FITCH	FLUKY
EPOXY	FADER	FERAL	FITLY	FLUME
EQUAL	FAERY	FERIA	FIVER	FLUNG
EQUIP	FAILS	FERMI	FIVES	FLUNK
ERASE	FAINT	FERNS	FIXED	FLUOR
ERBIL	FAIRS	FERNY	FIXER	FLUSH
ERECT	FAIRY	FERRY	FIXES	FLUTE
ERGOT	FAITH	FESSE	FIZZY	FLUTY
ERODE	FAKED	FETAL	FJELD	FLYBY

FLYER	FRISE	GAINS	GERMS	GNATS
FOALS	FRISK	GAITS	GESSO	GNOME
FOAMY	FRITT	GALAH	GETUP	GOADS
FOCAL	FRIZZ	GALAS	GHANA	GOALS
FOCUS	FROCK	GALEA	GHATS	GOATS
FOGGY	FROGS	GALES	GHENT	GODLY
FOILS	FROND	GALLA	GHOST	GOERS
FOISM	FRONS	GALLS	GHOUL	GOFER
FOIST	FRONT	GAMED	GHYLL	GOIAS
FOLDS	FROST	GAMES	GIANT	GOING
FOLIC	FROTH	GAMEY	GIBER	GOLDS
FOLIO	FROWN	GAMIC	GIBES	GOLEM
FOLKS	FROZE	GAMIN	GIDDY	GOLLY
FOLLY	FRUIT	GAMMA	GIFTS	GOMEL
FONTS	FRUMP	GAMMY	GIGOT	GONAD
FOODS	FRYER	GAMUT	GIGUE	GONDI
FOOLS	FRY-UP	GANDA	GIJON	GONER
FOOTS	FUCKS	GANGS	GILET	GONGS
FORAY	FUCUS	GANJA	GILLS	GOODS
FORCE	FUDGE	GAOLS	GILTS	GOODY
FORDS	FUELS	GAPED	GIPSY	GOOEY
FORGE	FUGAL	GAPER	GIRLS	GOOFS
FORGO	FUGGY	GAPES	GIRON	GOOFY
FORKS	FUGUE	GARDA	GIRTH	GOONS
FORLI	FULLY	GASES	GIVEN	GOOSE
FORME	FUMED	GASPS	GIVER	GOOSY
FORMS	FUMER	GASSY	GLACE	GORAL
FORTE	FUMES	GATED	GLADE	GORED
FORTH	FUNDS	GATES	GLAIR	GORES
FORTS	FUNGI	GAUDY	GLAND	GORGE
FORTY	FUNKS	GAUGE	GLANS	GORKI
FORUM	FUNKY	GAUNT	GLARE	GORSE
FOSSA	FUNNY	GAUSS	GLARY	GOUDA
FOSSE	FURAN	GAUZE	GLASS	GOUGE
FOULS	FURRY	GAUZY	GLAZE	GOURD
FOUND	FURZE	GAVEL	GLEAM	GOUTY
FOUNT	FURZY	GAVLE	GLEAN	GOWNS
FOURS	FUSED	GAWKY	GLEBE	GRABS
FOVEA	FUSEE	GAYER	GLEES	GRACE
FOWLS	FUSEL	GAZED	GLEET	GRADE
FOXED	FUSES	GAZER	GLENS	GRAFT
FOXES	FUSIL	GCSES	GLIDE	GRAIL
FOYER	FUSSY	GEARS	GLINT	GRAIN
FRAIL	FUSTY	GECKO	GLITZ	GRAMA
FRAME	FUTON	GEESE	GLOAT	GRAMS
FRANC	FUZZY	GEEST	GLOBE	GRAND
FRANK	FYLDE	GELID	GLOGG	GRANS
FRAUD		GEMMA	GLOOM	GRANT
FREAK	G	GENES	GLORY	GRAPE
FREED	GABBY	GENET	GLOSS	GRAPH
FREER	GABES	GENIC	GLOVE	GRASP
FREON	GABLE	GENIE	GLUED	GRASS
FRESH	GABON	GENII	GLUER	GRATE
FRETS	GADID	GENOA	GLUEY	GRAVE
FRIAR	GAFFE	GENRE	GLUME	GRAVY
FRIED	GAFFS	GENTS	GLUTS	GRAYS
FRIER	GAGED	GENUS	GLYPH	GRAZE
FRIES	GAGES	GEODE	GNARL	GREAT
FRILL	GAILY	GEOID	GNASH	GREBE

GRECO-	GUSTY	HAPPY	HELLS	HIVED
GREED	GUTSY	HARAR	HELMS	HIVES
GREEK	GUTTA	HARDS	HELOT	HOARD
GREEN	GUYED	HARDY	HELPS	HOARY
GREET	GUYOT	HARED	HELVE	HOBBS
GREYS	GWENT	HAREM	HE-MAN	HOBBY
GRIDS	GYPSY	HARES	HE-MEN	HOBOS
GRIEF	GYRAL	HARPS	HENCE	HOCKS
GRILL		HARPY	HENGE	HOCUS
GRIME	H	HARRY	HENIE	HOFEI
GRIMY	HABER	HARSH	HENNA	HOFUF
GRIND	HABIT	HARTS	HENRY	HOGAN
GRINS	HACEK	HASN'T	HERAT	HOICK
GRIPE	HACKS	HASPS	HERBS	HOIST
GRIPS	HADAL	HASTE	HERBY	HOKKU
GRIST	HADES	HASTY	HERDS	HOKUM
GRITS	HADJI	HATCH	HERES	HOLDS
GROAN	HADN'T	HATED	HEROD	HOLES
GROAT	HADST	HATES	HERON	HOLEY
GROIN	HAFIZ	HAUGH	HERTZ	HOLLA
GROOM	HAFTS	HAULM	HESSE	HOLLO
GROPE	HAGAR	HAULS	HET UP	HOLLY
GROSS	HAGEN	HAUNT	HEWED	HOLST
GROUP	HAGUE	HAUSA	HEWER	HOMER
GROUT	HA-HAS	HAVEN	HEXAD	HOMES
GROVE	HAIDA	HAVER	HEXED	HOMEY
GROWL	HAIFA	HAVES	HEXER	HONAN
GROWN	HAIKU	HAVOC	HEXES	HONDO
GRUBS	HAILS	HAVRE	HEXYL	HONED
GRUEL	HAIN'T	HAWES	HICKS	HONEY
GRUFF	HAIRS	HAWKS	HIDER	HONKS
GRUNT	HAIRY	HAWSE	HIDES	HONKY
GUACO	HAITI	HAYDN	HI-FIS	HONOR
GUANO	HAJJI	HAZED	HIGHS	HOOCH
GUARD	HAKEA	HAZEL	HIGHT	HOODS
GUAVA	HAKES	HAZER	HIJAZ	HOOEY
GUESS	HAKIM	HAZES	HIKED	HOO-HA
GUEST	HALAL	H-BOMB	HIKER	HOOKE
GUIDE	HALER	HEADS	HIKES	HOOKS
GUILD	HALIC	HEADY	HILAR	HOOKY
GUILE	HALID	HEAPS	HILLA	HOOPS
GUILT	HALLO	HEARD	HILLS	HOOTS
GUISE	HALLS	HEART	HILLY	HOPED
GULAG	HALMA	HEATH	HILTS	HOPEH
GULAR	HALOS	HEAVE	HILUM	HOPER
GULCH	HALTS	HEAVY	HILUS	HOPES
GULES	HALVE	HEDGE	HINDI	HORAE
GULFS	HAMAL	HEDGY	HINDS	HORAL
GULLS	HAMMY	HEELS	HINDU	HORDE
GULLY	HAMZA	HEFTY	HINES	HOREB
GULPS	HANCE	HEGEL	HINGE	HORME
GUMBO	HANDS	HEIRS	HINNY	HORNS
GUMMA	HANDY	HEIST	HINTS	HORNY
GUMMY	HANKY	HEJAZ	HIPPO	HORSA
GUNGE	HANOI	HEKLA	HIPPY	HORSE
GUPPY	HANSA	HELEN	HIRAM	HORST
GURUS	HANSE	HELIX	HIRED	HORSY
GUSTO	HANTS	HELLE	HIRER	HORUS
GUSTS	HAPLY	HELLO	HITCH	HOSEA

HOSED	I	INTER	JERKY	KANSU
HOSES	IAMBS	INTRO	JESTS	KAPOK
HOSTA	I-BEAM	INUIT	JESUS	KAPUT
HOSTS	IBIZA	INURE	JETTY	KARAT
HOTEL	ICIER	INURN	JEWEL	KAREN
HOTLY	ICILY	INVAR	JEWRY	KARMA
HOUGH	ICING	IODIC	JIBED	KAROO
HOUND	ICONS	IONIC	JIBES	KARST
HOURI	ICTIC	IOTAS	JIDDA	KASAI
HOURS	ICTUS	IRAQI	JIFFY	KAURI
HOUSE	IDAHO	IRATE	JIHAD	KAYAK
HOVEL	IDEAL	IRBID	JIMMY	KAZAN
HOVER	IDEAS	IRISH	JINGO	KAZOO
HOWDY	IDIOM	IRKED	JINKS	KEBAB
HOWLS	IDIOT	IRONS	JINNI	KEDAH
HOYLE	IDLED	IRONY	JIVED	KEDGE
HSIAN	IDLER	ISERE	JOCKS	KEELS
HUBBY	IDOLS	ISLAM	JOINS	KEENS
HUBLI	IDYLL	ISLES	JOINT	KEEPS
HUFFY	IGLOO	ISLET	JOIST	KENYA
HUFUF	IKONS	ISSUE	JOKED	KERBS
HUGER	ILEAC	ISTLE	JOKER	KERCH
HULKS	ILEUM	ITALO-	JOKES	KERRY
HULLO	ILEUS	ITALY	JOLLY	KETCH
HULLS	ILIAC	ITCHY	JOLTS	KEVEL
HULME	ILIAD	ITEMS	JONAH	KEYED
HUMAN	ILIUM	IVIED	JORUM	KHAKI
HUMIC	IMAGE	IVIES	JOULE	KHANS
HUMID	IMAGO	IVORY	JOUST	KHMER
HUMPH	IMAMS	IZMIR	JOVES	KIANG
HUMPS	IMBED	IZMIT	JOWLS	KICKS
HUMPY	IMBUE		JOYED	KIKES
HUMUS	IMIDE	J	JUDAS	KILLS
HUNAN	IMINE	JABOT	JUDGE	KILNS
HUNCH	IMPEL	JACKS	JUGAL	KILOS
HUNKS	IMPLY	JADED	JUGUM	KILTS
HUNTS	INANE	JADES	JUICE	KINDS
HUPEH	INAPT	JAFFA	JUICY	KINGS
HURDS	INCUR	JAILS	JUJUS	KININ
HURON	INCUS	JALAP	JULEP	KINKS
HURRY	INDEX	JAMBS	JUMBO	KINKY
HURST	INDIA	JAMMU	JUMPS	KIOSK
HURTS	INDIC	JAMMY	JUMPY	KIRIN
HUSKS	INDRE	JAPAN	JUNCO	KIRKS
HUSKY	INDUS	JAPER	JUNES	KIROV
HUSSY	INEPT	JAPES	JUNKS	KITES
HUTCH	INERT	JAUNT	JUNTA	KITTY
HYADS	INFER	JAWED	JUNTO	KITWE
HYDRA	INFIX	JAZZY	JURAL	KIWIS
HYDRO	INGOT	JEANS	JURAT	KNACK
HYENA	INION	JEEPS	JUREL	KNAVE
HYING	INKED	JEERS	JUROR	KNEAD
HYMEN	INKLE	JEHOL	JURUA	KNEED
HYMNS	IN-LAW	JELLO		KNEEL
HYPED	INLAY	JELLY	K	KNEES
HYPER	INLET	JEMMY	KABUL	KNELL
HYPOS	INNER	JENNY	KALAT	KNELT
	INPUT	JEREZ	KANDY	KNIFE
	INSET	JERKS	KANGA	KNOBS

KNOCK	LA PAZ	LEVEE	LLANO	LUCKY
KNOLL	LAPEL	LEVEL	LOACH	LUCRE
KNOTS	LAPSE	LEVER	LOADS	LUFFA
KNOWN	LARCH	LEVIS	LOAMY	LUGER
KNOWS	LARGE	LEWIS	LOANS	LUMEN
KNURL	LARGO	LEXIS	LOATH	LUMME
KOALA	LARKS	LHASA	LOBAR	LUMPS
KOCHI	LAROS	LIANA	LOBBY	LUMPY
KOINE	LARVA	LIARS	LOBED	LUNAR
KONGO	LASER	LIBEL	LOBES	LUNCH
KONYA	LASSO	LIBRA	LOCAL	LUNGE
KOOKS	LASTS	LIBYA	LOCHS	LUNGS
KOOKY	LATCH	LICIT	LOCKS	LUPIN
KORAN	LATER	LICKS	LOCUM	LUPUS
KOREA	LATEX	LIDOS	LOCUS	LURCH
KRAAL	LATHE	LIEGE	LODEN	LURED
KRAFT	LATHS	LIE-IN	LODES	LURER
KRAIT	LATIN	LIENS	LODGE	LURES
KRILL	LAUGH	LIEUS	LOESS	LUREX
KRONA	LAVAL	LIFER	LOFTS	LURGY
KRONE	LAVER	LIFTS	LOFTY	LURID
KROON	LAWNS	LIGER	LOGIC	LUSTS
KUDOS	LAWNY	LIGHT	LOGOS	LUSTY
KUDZU	LAXLY	LIKED	LOINS	LUTES
KUFIC	LAY-BY	LIKEN	LOIRE	LUXOR
KUKRI	LAYER	LIKES	LOLLY	LUZON
KULAK	LAZED	LILAC	LONER	LYCEE
KURIL	LEACH	LILLE	LOOKS	LYING
KURSK	LEADS	LILOS	LOOMS	LYMPH
KUTCH	LEADY	LILTS	LOONS	LYNCH
KWELA	LEAFY	LIMBO	LOONY	LYRES
KYOTO	LEAKS	LIMBS	LOOPS	LYRIC
	LEAKY	LIMED	LOOPY	LYSIN
L	LEANT	LIMEN	LOOSE	LYSIS
LABEL	LEAPS	LIMES	LOPED	LYSOL
LACED	LEAPT	LIMEY	LOPER	LYTIC
LACER	LEARN	LIMIT	LORAN	LYTTA
LACES	LEASE	LINED	LORDS	
LADEN	LEASH	LINEN	LORIS	M
LADER	LEAST	LINER	LORRY	MACAO
LADLE	LEAVE	LINES	LOSER	MACAW
LAGAN	LEDGE	LINGO	LOSSY	MACES
LAGER	LEDGY	LININ	LOTIC	MACHO
LAGOS	LEECH	LINKS	LOTUS	MACLE
LAHTI	LEEKS	LINTY	LOUGH	MACON
LAIRD	LEERS	LIONS	LOUPE	MADAM
LAIRS	LEERY	LIPID	LOUSE	MADLY
LAITY	LEFTY	LIRAS	LOUSY	MAFIA
LAKER	LEGAL	LISLE	LOUTS	MAGIC
LAKES	LEGER	LISTS	LOVAT	MAGMA
LAMAS	LEGGY	LITER	LOVED	MAGUS
LAMBS	LEGIT	LITHE	LOVER	MAIDS
LAMED	LEMMA	LITRE	LOVES	MAINE
LAMER	LEMON	LIVED	LOVEY	MAINS
LAMPS	LEMUR	LIVEN	LOWED	MAINZ
LANCE	LENIS	LIVER	LOWER	MAIZE
LANDS	LENTO	LIVES	LOWLY	MAJOR
LANES	LEPER	LIVID	LOYAL	MAKER
LANKY	LETUP	LLAMA	LUCID	MAKES

MALAR	MEANS	MIMIC	MONZA	MULLS
MALAY	MEANT	MINCE	MOOCH	MULTI-
MALES	MEATH	MINDS	MOODS	MUMMY
MALLS	MEATY	MINED	MOODY	MUMPS
MALMO	MECCA	MINER	MOOED	MUNCH
MALTA	MEDAL	MINES	MOONS	MUNGO
MALTY	MEDAN	MINGY	MOONY	MURAL
MAMAS	MEDIA	MINIM	MOORS	MUREX
MAMBA	MEDIC	MINIS	MOOSE	MURKY
MAMBO	MEDOC	MINOR	MOPED	MUSED
MAMEY	MEETS	MINSK	MOPER	MUSER
MAMMA	MELEE	MINTS	MOP-UP	MUSES
MAMMY	MELON	MINUS	MORAL	MUSHY
MANDE	MEMOS	MIRED	MORAY	MUSIC
MANED	MENAI	MIRES	MOREL	MUSKY
MANES	MENDS	MIRTH	MORES	MUSTH
MANGE	MENUS	MISER	MORNS	MUSTY
MANGO	MEOWS	MISSY	MORON	MUTED
MANGY	MERCY	MISTS	MORPH	MUTES
MANIA	MERES	MISTY	MOSEY	MUTTS
MANIC	MERGE	MITES	MOSSI	MUZAK
MANLY	MERIT	MITIS	MOSSO	MUZZY
MANNA	MERRY	MITRE	MOSSY	MYNAH
MANOR	MESIC	MITTS	MOSUL	MYOMA
MANSE	MESNE	MIXED	MOTEL	MYOPE
MANTA	MESON	MIXER	MOTES	MYRRH
MANUS	MESSY	MIXES	MOTET	MYTHS
MAORI	METAL	MIX-UP	MOTHS	
MAPLE	METED	MIZAR	MOTHY	N
MARCH	METER	MOANS	MOTIF	NAAFI
MARES	METHS	MOATS	MOTOR	NABOB
MARKS	METOL	MOCHA	MOTTO	NACRE
MARNE	ME-TOO	MOCKS	MOULD	NADIR
MARRY	METRE	MODAL	MOULT	NAIAD
MARSH	METRO	MODEL	MOUND	NAILS
MASAI	MEUSE	MODEM	MOUNT	NAIVE
MASAN	MEWED	MODES	MOURN	NAKED
MASER	MEZZO	MOGGY	MOUSE	NAMED
MASKS	MIAMI	MOGUL	MOUSY	NAMES
MASON	MIAOW	MOIRE	MOUTH	NAMUR
MASTS	MICKS	MOIST	MOVED	NANCY
MATCH	MICRO	MOKES	MOVER	NANNY
MATED	MIDDY	MOKPO	MOVES	NAPES
MATER	MIDGE	MOLAL	MOVIE	NAPPA
MATES	MID-ON	MOLAR	MOWED	NAPPE
MATEY	MIDST	MOLDS	MOWER	NAPPY
MATIN	MIENS	MOLDY	MUCIN	NARES
MATTE	MIFFY	MOLES	MUCKY	NARKS
MAUVE	MIGHT	MOLLS	MUCRO	NARKY
MAXIM	MIKES	MOLLY	MUCUS	NASAL
MAYAN	MILAN	MOLTO	MUDDY	NASTY
MAYBE	MILCH	MOLTS	MUFFS	NATAL
MAYN'T	MILER	MOMMA	MUFTI	NATES
MAYOR	MILES	MOMMY	MUGGY	NATTY
MAYST	MILKY	MONAD	MULCH	NAURU
MAZES	MILLS	MONAL	MULCT	NAVAL
MEADS	MIMED	MONEY	MULES	NAVAR
MEALS	MIMER	MONKS	MULEY	NAVEL
MEALY	MIMES	MONTH	MULGA	NAVES

NAVVY	NONCE	OILED	OVERS	PAPPY
NAZIS	NOOKS	OILER	OVERT	PAPUA
'NEATH	NO ONE	OINKS	OVINE	PARAS
NECKS	NOOSE	OKAPI	OVOID	PARCH
NEEDS	NOPAL	OKAYS	OVOLO	PARED
NEEDY	NO-PAR	OLDEN	OVULE	PARER
NEGEV	NORMS	OLDER	OWING	PARIS
NEGRO	NORSE	OLEUM	OWLET	PARKA
NEGUS	NORTH	OLIVE	OWNED	PARKS
NEIGH	NOSED	OMAHA	OWNER	PARKY
NELLY	NOSES	OMEGA	OXBOW	PARMA
NEPAL	NOTCH	OMENS	OXEYE	PAROL
NEPER	NOTED	OMUTA	OXFAM	PARRY
NERDS	NOTES	ON-AIR	OXIDE	PARSE
NERVE	NOTUM	ONION	OXIME	PARTS
NERVY	NOUNS	ONSET	OXLIP	PARTY
NESTS	NOVAE	OOMPH	OZONE	PASHA
NEURO-	NOVAS	OOTID		PASSE
NEUSS	NOVEL	OOZED	P	PASTA
NEVER	NO WAY	OPALS	PACED	PASTE
NEWEL	NUCHA	OP ART	PACER	PASTS
NEWER	NUDES	OPERA	PACES	PASTY
NEWLY	NUDGE	OPINE	PACKS	PATCH
NEWSY	NUKED	OPIUM	PACTS	PATEN
NEWTS	NURSE	OPTED	PADDY	PATER
NEXUS	NUTTY	OPTIC	PADRE	PATES
NICER	NYALA	ORACH	PADUA	PATHS
NICHE	NYLON	ORATE	PAEAN	PATIO
NICKS	NYMPH	ORBIT	PAEON	PATNA
NIDAL		ORDER	PAGAN	PATTY
NIDUS	O	ORGAN	PAGED	PAUSE
NIECE	OAKEN	ORIBI	PAGES	PAVED
NIFFY	OAKUM	ORIEL	PAILS	PAWED
NIFTY	OARED	ORION	PAINS	PAWKY
NIGER	OASES	ORIYA	PAINT	PAWNS
NIGHT	OASIS	ORLON	PAIRS	PAYEE
NIHIL	OATEN	ORLOP	PALEA	PEACE
NIMBI	OATHS	ORMER	PALED	PEACH
NIMES	OBESE	ORRIS	PALER	PEAKS
NINES	OBOES	ORURO	PALES	PEAKY
NINNY	OCCUR	OSAKA	PALLS	PEALS
NINON	OCEAN	OSCAR	PALLY	PEARL
NINTH	OCHRE	OSIER	PALMA	PEARS
NIPPY	OCREA	OSMIC	PALMS	PEATS
NISUS	OCTAD	OTHER	PALMY	PEATY
NITRE	OCTAL	OTTER	PALSY	PECAN
NITTY	OCTET	OUGHT	PANDA	PECKS
NIVAL	ODDER	OUIJA	PANEL	PEDAL
NIXED	ODDLY	OUJDA	PANES	PEEPS
NOBLE	ODEUM	OUNCE	PANGS.	PEERS
NOBLY	ODIUM	OUTDO	PANIC	PEEVE
NODAL	ODOUR	OUTER	PANNE	PEKOE
NODDY	OFFAL	OUTGO	PANSY	PELTS
NODES	OFFER	OUTRE	PANTS	PENAL
NODUS	OFTEN	OUZEL	PANTY	PENCE
NOHOW	OGIVE	OVALS	PAPAL	PENIS
NOISE	OGLED	OVARY	PAPAS	PENNA
NOISY	OGLER	OVATE	PAPAW	PENNY
NOMAD	OGRES	OVENS	PAPER	PENZA

PEONY	PIPED	POINT	PRATO	PUKED
PERAK	PIPER	POISE	PRATS	PUKKA
PERCH	PIPES	POKED	PRAWN	PULER
PERIL	PIPIT	POKER	PREEN	PULLS
PERKS	PIQUE	POKES	PREPS	PULPS
PERKY	PISTE	POLAR	PRESA	PULPY
PERRY	PITCH	POLED	PRESS	PULSE
PER SE	PITHY	POLES	PRICE	PUMAS
PESKY	PITON	POLIO	PRICK	PUMPS
PESOS	PIURA	POLJE	PRICY	PUNCH
PESTS	PIVOT	POLKA	PRIDE	PUNKA
PETAL	PIXEL	POLLS	PRIED	PUNKS
PETER	PIXIE	POLYP	PRIER	PUNTS
PETIT	PIZZA	POLYS	PRIGS	PUNTY
PETTY	PLACE	POMMY	PRILL	PUPAE
PEWEE	PLAID	PONCE	PRIME	PUPAL
PEWIT	PLAIN	PONCY	PRIMO	PUPAS
PHASE	PLAIT	PONDS	PRIMP	PUPIL
PHIAL	PLANE	PONGS	PRINK	PUPPY
PHLOX	PLANK	PONGY	PRINT	PUREE
PHONE	PLANS	POOCH	PRIOR	PURER
PHOTO	PLANT	POOFS	PRISE	PURGE
PHUTS	PLASH	POOFY	PRISM	PURRS
PHYLA	PLASM	POOLE	PRIVY	PURSE
PHYLE	PLATE	POOLS	PRIZE	PUSAN
PIANO	PLATY	POONA	PRO-AM	PUSHY
PIAUI	PLAYS	POOPS	PROBE	PUSSY
PICKS	PLAZA	POPES	PRODS	PUT-ON
PICKY	PLEAD	POPPA	PROEM	PUTTO
PICOT	PLEAS	POPPY	PROFS	PUTTS
PIECE	PLEAT	POPSY	PROLE	PUTTY
PIERS	PLEBS	POP-UP	PROMO	PYGMY
PIETA	PLICA	PORCH	PROMS	PYLON
PIETY	PLIED	PORED	PRONE	PYOID
PIGGY	PLIER	PORES	PRONG	PYRAN
PIGMY	PLONK	PORGY	PROOF	PYRES
PIING	PLOTS	PORKY	PROPS	PYREX
PIKES	PLOWS	PORNO	PROSE	PYXES
PILAF	PLOYS	PORTS	PROSY	PYXIE
PILED	PLUCK	POSED	PROTO-	PYXIS
PILES	PLUGS	POSER	PROUD	
PILLS	PLUMB	POSES	PROVE	Q
PILOT	PLUME	POSIT	PROWL	QATAR
PIMPS	PLUMP	POSSE	PROWS	QUACK
PINCH	PLUMS	POSTS	PROXY	QUADS
PINED	PLUMY	POTTO	PRUDE	QUAFF
PINES	PLUNK	POTTY	PRUNE	QUAIL
PINEY	PLUSH	POUCH	PSALM	QUAKE
PINGO	PLUTO	POUFS	PSEUD	QUAKY
PINKO	PLZEN	POULT	PSKOV	QUALE
PINKS	POACH	POUND	PSOAS	QUALM
PINNA	PO BOX	POUTS	PSYCH	QUANT
PINNY	PODGY	POWAN	PUBES	QUARK
PINTA	PODIA	POWER	PUBIC	QUART
PINTO	POEMS	POXES	PUBIS	QUASH
PINTS	POESY	PRAMS	PUCKS	QUASI-
PINUP	POETS	PRANK	PUDGY	QUAYS
PIOUS	POGGE	PRASE	PUFFS	QUEEN
PIPAL	POILU	PRATE	PUFFY	QUEER

QUELL	R AND B	REINS	RIPER	ROVER
QUERN	R AND D	REJIG	RISEN	ROWAN
QUERY	RANDY	RELAX	RISER	ROWDY
QUEST	RANEE	RELAY	RISES	ROWED
QUEUE	RANGE	RELIC	RISKS	ROWEL
QUICK	RANGY	REMEX	RISKY	ROWER
QUIET	RANKS	REMIT	RITES	ROYAL
QUIFF	RAPED	RENAL	RITZY	RUBLE
QUILL	RAPES	RENEW	RIVAL	RUCHE
QUILT	RAPHE	RENIN	RIVEN	RUCKS
QUINS	RAPID	RENTE	RIVER	RUDDY
QUINT	RARER	RENTS	RIVET	RUDER
QUIPS	RASHT	REPAY	RIYAL	RUFFE
QUIRE	RASPS	REPEL	ROACH	RUFFS
QUIRK	RATAL	REPLY	ROADS	RUGBY
QUITE	RATED	RERAN	ROANS	RUING
QUITO	RATEL	RERUN	ROARS	RUINS
QUITS	RATES	RESAT	ROAST	RULED
QUOIN	RATIO	RESET	ROBED	RULER
QUOIT	RATTY	RESIN	ROBES	RULES
QUOTA	RAVED	RESIT	ROBIN	RUMBA
QUOTE	RAVEL	RESTS	ROBLE	RUMEN
QUOTH	RAVEN	RETCH	ROBOT	RUMMY
QUR'AN	RAVER	RETRO-	ROCKS	RUMPS
	RAWER	RETRY	ROCKY	RUNES
R	RAWLY	REUSE	RODEO	RUNGS
RABAT	RAYON	REVEL	ROGER	RUNIC
RABBI	RAZED	REVET	ROGUE	RUN-IN
RABIC	RAZER	REVUE	ROLES	RUNNY
RABID	RAZOR	REXES	ROLLS	RUNTS
RACED	REACH	RHEAS	ROMAN	RUNTY
RACER	REACT	RHEUM	ROMEO	RUN-UP
RACES	READY	RHINE	ROMPS	RUPEE
RACKS	REALM	RHINO	RONDO	RURAL
RADAR	REAMS	RHONE	ROODS	RUSES
RADII	REARM	RHUMB	ROOFS	RUSHY
RADIO	REARS	RHYME	ROOKS	RUSKS
RADIX	REBEL	RIALS	ROOMS	RUSSO-
RADOM	REBUS	RICIN	ROOMY	RUSTY
RADON	REBUT	RICKS	ROOST	RUTTY
RAFTS	RECAP	RIDER	ROOTS	
RAGAS	RECTO	RIDES	ROPED	S
RAGED	RECUR	RIDGE	ROPES	SABAH
RAGES	REDAN	RIDGY	ROPEY	SABER
RAIDS	REDIA	RIFFS	ROSES	SABIN
RAILS	REDID	RIFLE	ROSIN	SABLE
RAINS	REEDS	RIFTS	ROTAS	SABOT
RAINY	REEDY	RIGHT	ROTOR	SABRA
RAISE	REEFS	RIGID	ROUEN	SABRE
RAJAH	REEKY	RIGOR	ROUES	SACKS
RAKED	REELS	RILED	ROUGE	SADHU
RAKER	REEVE	RILEY	ROUGH	SADLY
RAKES	REFER	RILLS	ROUND	SAFER
RALLY	REFIT	RINDS	ROUPY	SAFES
RAMIE	REGAL	RINGS	ROUSE	SAGAS
RAMPS	REICH	RINKS	ROUST	SAGES
RAMUS	REIFY	RINSE	ROUTE	SAGGY
RANCE	REIGN	RIOTS	ROUTS	SAHIB
RANCH	REIMS	RIPEN	ROVED	SAIGA

SAILS	SCALL	SEGNO	SHEAR	SIDED
SAINT	SCALP	SEINE	SHEDS	SIDES
SAKAI	SCALY	SEISE	SHEEN	SIDLE
SAKER	SCAMP	SEISM	SHEEP	SIEGE
SAKES	SCAMS	SEIZE	SHEER	SIENA
SALAD	SCANS	SELVA	SHEET	SIEVE
SALEM	SCANT	SEMEN	SHEIK	SIGHS
SALEP	SCAPE	SEMIS	SHELF	SIGHT
SALES	SCARE	SENNA	SHELL	SIGLA
SALIC	SCARF	SENOR	SHERD	SIGMA
SALLY	SCARP	SENSE	SHEWN	SIGNS
SALOL	SCARS	SENZA	SHIED	SIKHS
SALON	SCARY	SEOUL	SHIER	SILEX
SALOP	SCAUP	SEPAL	SHIES	SILKS
SALPA	SCEND	SEPIA	SHIFT	SILKY
SALTA	SCENE	SEPOY	SHILY	SILLS
SALTS	SCENT	SERAC	SHINE	SILLY
SALTY	SCHWA	SERFS	SHINS	SILOS
SALVE	SCION	SERGE	SHINY	SILTY
SALVO	SCOFF	SERIF	SHIPS	SINAI
SAMBA	SCOLD	SERIN	SHIRE	SINCE
SAMEY	SCONE	SEROW	SHIRK	SINES
SAMOA	SCOOP	SERUM	SHIRR	SINEW
SANDS	SCOOT	SERVE	SHIRT	SINGE
SANDY	SCOPE	SERVO	SHITS	SINKS
SANER	SCORE	SETAL	SHIVE	SINUS
SAPID	SCORN	SET-TO	SHLUH	SIOUX
SAPPY	SCOTS	SET-UP	SHOAL	SIRED
SARAN	SCOUR	SEVEN	SHOAT	SIREN
SARGE	SCOUT	SEVER	SHOCK	SIRES
SARIS	SCOWL	SEWED	SHOED	SISAL
SARKY	SCRAG	SEWER	SHOES	SISSY
SAROS	SCRAM	SEXED	SHONA	SITAR
SASSY	SCRAP	SEXES	SHONE	SITED
SATAN	SCREE	SHACK	SHOOK	SITES
SATED	SCREW	SHADE	SHOOT	SIT IN
SATEM	SCRIM	SHADY	SHOPS	SIT-UP
SATIN	SCRIP	SHAFT	SHORE	SITUS
SATYR	SCRUB	SHAGS	SHORN	SIVAS
SAUCE	SCRUM	SHAHS	SHORT	SIXES
SAUCY	SCUBA	SHAKE	SHOTS	SIXMO
SAUNA	SCUFF	SHAKO	SHOTT	SIXTE
SAURY	SCULL	SHAKY	SHOUT	SIXTH
SAUTE	SCURF	SHALE	SHOVE	SIXTY
SAVED	SCUTE	SHALL	SHOWN	SIZAR
SAVER	SEALS	SHALT	SHOWS	SIZED
SAVES	SEAMS	SHALY	SHOWY	SIZES
SAVIN	SEAMY	SHAME	SHRED	SKATE
SAVOY	SEATS	SHAMS	SHREW	SKEET
SAVVY	SEBUM	SHANK	SHRUB	SKEIN
SAWED	SECCO	SHAN'T	SHRUG	SKELP
SAWER	SECTS	SHAPE	SHUCK	SKEWS
SAXON	SEDAN	SHARD	SHUNT	SKIDS
SAYER	SEDGE	SHARE	SHUSH	SKIED
SAY-SO	SEDGY	SHARK	SHYED	SKIER
SCABS	SEDUM	SHARP	SHYER	SKIES
SCADS	SEEDS	SHAVE	SHYLY	SKIFF
SCALD	SEEDY	SHAWL	SIBIU	SKILL
SCALE	SEERS	SHEAF	SIBYL	SKIMP

SKINK	SLUSH	SOCHI	SPECK	SQUAD
SKINS	SLUTS	SOCIO-	SPECS	SQUAT
SKINT	SLYER	SOCKS	SPEED	SQUAW
SKIPS	SLYPE	SOCLE	SPELL	SQUIB
SKIRL	SMACK	SODAS	SPELT	SQUID
SKIRT	SMALL	SOFAR	SPEND	STABS
SKITS	SMALT	SOFAS	SPENT	STACK
SKIVE	SMARM	SOFIA	SPERM	STAFF
SKUAS	SMART	SOFTA	SPICA	STAGE
SKULK	SMASH	SOFTY	SPICE	STAGS
SKULL	SMEAR	SOGGY	SPICS	STAGY
SKUNK	SMELL	SOILS	SPICY	STAID
SLABS	SMELT	SOLAR	SPIED	STAIN
SLACK	SMILE	SOLED	SPIEL	STAIR
SLAGS	SMIRK	SOLES	SPIES	STAKE
SLAIN	SMITE	SOL-FA	SPIKE	STALE
SLAKE	SMITH	SOLID	SPIKS	STALK
SLANG	SMOCK	SOLOS	SPIKY	STALL
SLANT	SMOKE	SOLUM	SPILE	STAMP
SLAPS	SMOKY	SOLVE	SPILL	STAND
SLASH	SMOLT	SOMME	SPILT	STANK
SLATE	SMOTE	SONAR	SPINE	STARE
SLATS	SMUTS	SONDE	SPINS	STARK
SLATY	SNACK	SONGS	SPINY	STARS
SLAVE	SNAFU	SONIC	SPIRE	START
SLAVS	SNAGS	SONNY	SPIRY	STASH
SLEDS	SNAIL	SOOTY	SPITE	STATE
SLEEK	SNAKE	SOPOR	SPITS	STAVE
SLEEP	SNAKY	SOPPY	SPITZ	STAYS
SLEET	SNAPS	SORES	SPIVS	STEAD
SLEPT	SNARE	SORGO	SPLAT	STEAK
SLEWS	SNARL	SORRY	SPLAY	STEAL
SLICE	SNATH	SORTS	SPLIT	STEAM
SLICK	SNEAK	SORUS	SPODE	STEED
SLIDE	SNECK	SOTHO	SPOIL	STEEL
SLILY	SNEER	SOUGH	SPOKE	STEEP
SLIME	SNICK	SOULS	SPOOF	STEER
SLIMY	SNIDE	SOUND	SPOOK	STEIN
SLING	SNIFF	SOUPS	SPOOL	STELE
SLINK	SNIPE	SOUPY	SPOON	STEMS
SLIPS	SNIPS	SOUSE	SPOOR	STEPS
SLITS	SNOBS	SOUTH	SPORE	STERE
SLOBS	SNOGS	SOWED	SPORT	STERN
SLOES	SNOOD	SOWER	SPOTS	STEWS
SLOGS	SNOOK	SOYUZ	SPOUT	STICH
SLOOP	SNOOP	SPACE	SPRAG	STICK
SLOPE	SNORE	SPADE	SPRAT	STIES
SLOPS	SNORT	SPAIN	SPRAY	STIFF
SLOSH	SNOUT	SPALL	SPREE	STILE
SLOTH	SNOWS	SPANK	SPRIG	STILL
SLOTS	SNOWY	SPARE	SPRIT	STILT
SLUED	SNUBS	SPARK	SPRUE	STING
SLUGS	SNUFF	SPARS	SPUDS	STINK
SLUMP	SNUGS	SPASM	SPUME	STINT
SLUMS	SOAKS	SPATE	SPUNK	STIPE
SLUNG	SOAPS	SPATS	SPURN	STIRK
SLUNK	SOAPY	SPAWN	SPURS	STIRS
SLURP	SOBER	SPEAK	SPURT	STOAT
SLURS	SOCHE	SPEAR	SQUAB	STOCK

STOIC	SUN-UP	T	TAXER	THESE
STOKE	SUPER	TABBY	TAXES	THETA
STOLE	SUPRA	TABES	TAXIS	THEWS
STOMA	SURAH	TABLE	TAXON	THICK
STOMP	SURAL	TABOO	TAYRA	THIEF
STONE	SURAT	TABOR	TAZZA	THIGH
STONY	SURDS	TACET	T-BONE	THINE
STOOD	SURER	TACIT	TEACH	THING
STOOK	SURFY	TACKS	TEAKS	THINK
STOOL	SURGE	TACKY	TEAMS	THIOL
STOOP	SURLY	TACOS	TEARS	THIRD
STOPE	SUSHI	TAEGU	TEASE	THOLE
STOPS	SWABS	TAFFY	TEATS	THONG
STORE	SWAGE	TAIGA	TECHY	THORN
STORK	SWAIN	TAILS	TEENS	THOSE
STORM	SWAMI	TAINT	TEENY	THREE
STORY	SWAMP	TAKEN	TEETH	THREW
STOSS	SWANK	TAKER	TELEX	THROB
STOUP	SWANS	TAKES	TELIC	THROW
STOUT	SWAPS	TAKIN	TELLY	THRUM
STOVE	SWARD	TALES	TEMPI	THUDS
STRAP	SWARF	TALKS	TEMPO	THUGS
STRAW	SWARM	TALLY	TEMPS	THUJA
STRAY	SWASH	TALON	TEMPT	THUMB
STREW	SWATH	TALUS	TENCH	THUMP
STRIA	SWATS	TAMED	TENET	THYME
STRIP	SWAZI	TAMER	TENON	TIARA
STROP	SWEAR	TAMMY	TENOR	TIBET
STRUM	SWEAT	TAMPA	TENSE	TIBIA
STRUT	SWEDE	TANGO	TENTH	TICAL
STUBS	SWEEP	TANGY	TENTS	TICKS
STUCK	SWEET	TANKS	TEPEE	TIDAL
STUDS	SWELL	TANSY	TEPIC	TIDED
STUDY	SWEPT	TANTA	TEPID	TIDES
STUFF	SWIFT	TANTO	TERMS	TIE-IN
STULL	SWIGS	TAPED	TERNE	TIE-ON
STUMP	SWILL	TAPER	TERNI	TIERS
STUNG	SWIMS	TAPES	TERNS	TIE-UP
STUNK	SWINE	TAPIR	TERRA	TIFFS
STUNT	SWING	TAPIS	TERRY	TIGER
STUPE	SWIPE	TARDY	TERSE	TIGHT
STYLE	SWIRL	TARES	TESLA	TIGON
SUAVE	SWISH	TARNS	TESOL	TIGRE
SUDAN	SWISS	TAROS	TESTA	TILDE
SUDOR	SWOON	TAROT	TESTS	TILED
SUDSY	SWOOP	TARRY	TESTY	TILER
SUEDE	SWOPS	TARSI	TETRA	TILES
SUETY	SWORD	TARTS	TEXAS	TILLS
SUGAR	SWORE	TASKS	TEXTS	TILTH
SUING	SWORN	TASTE	THANE	TILTS
SUINT	SWOTS	TASTY	THANK	TIMED
SUITE	SWUNG	TATAR	THAWS	TIMER
SUITS	SYLPH	TATRA	THECA	TIMES
SULKS	SYLVA	TATTY	THEFT	TIMID
SULKY	SYNOD	TAUNT	THEGN	TINEA
SULLY	SYRIA	TAUPE	THEIR	TINES
SUMPS	SYRUP	TAWER	THEME	TINGE
SUNNI		TAWNY	THERE	TINGS
SUNNY		TAXED	THERM	TINNY

TINTS	TORUS	TROLL	TWAIN	UNITS
TIPSY	TOTAL	TRONA	TWANG	UNITY
TIRED	TOTED	TROOP	TWATS	UNLAY
TIRES	TOTEM	TROPE	TWEAK	UNMAN
TIROS	TOTER	TROTH	TWEED	UNPEG
TITAN	TOTES	TROTS	'TWEEN	UNPIN
TITHE	TOUCH	TROUT	TWEET	UNRIG
TITLE	TOUGH	TROVE	TWERP	UNRIP
TITRE	TOURS	TRUCE	TWICE	UNSAY
TITTY	TOUTS	TRUCK	TWIGS	UNSET
TIZZY	TOWED	TRUER	TWILL	UNSEX
TOADS	TOWEL	TRUES	TWINE	UNTIE
TOADY	TOWER	TRUGS	TWINS	UNTIL
TOAST	TOWNS	TRULY	TWIRL	UNZIP
TODAY	TOXIC	TRUMP	TWIRP	UP-BOW
TODDY	TOXIN	TRUNK	TWIST	UPEND
TO-DOS	TOYED	TRURO	TWITE	UPPER
TOE-IN	TOYER	TRUSS	TWITS	UPSET
TOFFS	TRACE	TRUST	TWIXT	URALS
TOGAS	TRACK	TRUTH	TYING	URATE
TOILE	TRACT	TRYMA	TYPED	URBAN
TOILS	TRADE	TRY-ON	TYPES	UREAL
TOKAY	TRAIL	TRYST	TYRES	UREDO
TOKEN	TRAIN	TSARS	TYROL	URGED
TOKYO	TRAIT	TUBAL	TYROS	URGER
TOLAN	TRAMP	TUBAS	TZARS	URGES
TOLLS	TRAMS	TUBBY	TZU-PO	URINE
TOLYL	TRANS-	TUBER		USAGE
TOMBS	TRAPS	TUBES	U	USERS
TOMES	TRASH	TUCKS	U-BOAT	USHER
TOMMY	TRASS	TUDOR	UDDER	USING
TOMSK	TRAVE	TUFTS	UDINE	USUAL
TONAL	TRAWL	TUFTY	UGRIC	USURP
TONDO	TRAYS	TULIP	UHURU	USURY
TONED	TREAD	TULLE	UIGUR	UTERI
TONER	TREAT	TULSA	ULCER	UTTER
TONES	TREEN	TUMID	ULNAR	U-TURN
TONGA	TREES	TUMMY	ULNAS	UVEAL
TONGS	TREKS	TUNAS	ULTRA-	UVULA
TONIC	TREND	TUNED	UMBEL	UZBEK
TONNE	TRESS	TUNER	UMBER	
TON-UP	TREWS	TUNES	UMBRA	V
TONUS	TRIAD	TUNIC	UMIAK	VADUZ
TOOLS	TRIAL	TUNIS	UNAPT	VAGAL
TOOTH	TRIBE	TUNNY	UNARY	VAGUE
TOOTS	TRICE	TURDS	UNBAR	VAGUS
TOPAZ	TRICK	TURFS	UNCAP	VALES
TOPEE	TRIED	TURFY	UNCLE	VALET
TOPER	TRIER	TURIN	UNCUS	VALID
TOPIC	TRIES	TURKI	UNCUT	VALUE
TOPOS	TRIKE	TURKU	UNDER	VALVE
TOQUE	TRILL	TURNS	UNDID	VAMPS
TORAH	TRIMS	TURPS	UNDUE	VANDA
TORCH	TRINE	TUSKS	UNFIT	VANES
TORIC	TRIOL	TUTEE	UNFIX	VAPID
TORSK	TRIOS	TUTOR	UNIAT	VARIA
TORSO	TRIPE	TUTTI	UNIFY	VARIX
TORTS	TRIPS	TUTTY	UNION	VARNA
TORUN	TRITE	TUTUS	UNITE	VARUS

VARVE	VITAL	WANTS	WHINY	WOMEN
VASES	VITTA	WARDS	WHIPS	WONKY
VAULT	VIVID	WARES	WHIRL	WOODS
VAUNT	VIXEN	WARPS	WHIRR	WOODY
VEDDA	V-NECK	WARTS	WHIRS	WOOED
VEDIC	VOCAB	WARTY	WHISK	WOOER
VEERY	VOCAL	WASHY	WHIST	WOOFS
VEGAN	VODKA	WASPS	WHITE	WOOZY
VEILS	VOGUE	WASTE	WHITS	WORDS
VEINS	VOGUL	WATCH	WHIZZ	WORDY
VEINY	VOICE	WATER	WHOLE	WORKS
VELAR	VOIDS	WATTS	WHOOP	WORLD
VELUM	VOILE	WAVED	WHORE	WORMS
VENAL	VOLAR	WAVER	WHORL	WORMY
VENDA	VOLES	WAVES	WHOSE	WORRY
VENIN	VOLTA	WAXED	WICKS	WORSE
VENOM	VOLTS	WAXEN	WIDEN	WORST
VENTS	VOLVA	WAXER	WIDER	WORTH
VENUE	VOMER	WEALD	WIDES	WOULD
VENUS	VOMIT	WEALS	WIDOW	WOUND
VERBS	VOTED	WEARY	WIDTH	WOVEN
VERGE	VOTER	WEAVE	WIELD	WOWED
VERSE	VOTES	WEBBY	WIGHT	WRACK
VERSO	VOUCH	WEBER	WILCO	WRAPS
VERVE	VOWED	WEDGE	WILDS	WRATH
VESTA	VOWEL	WEDGY	WILES	WREAK
VESTS	VOWER	WEEDS	WILLS	WRECK
VETCH	V-SIGN	WEEDY	WIMPS	WRENS
VEXED	VULVA	WEEKS	WIMPY	WREST
VEXER	VYING	WEENY	WINCE	WRIED
VIALS		WEEPY	WINCH	WRIER
VIAND	W	WEIGH	WINDS	WRING
VIBES	WACKY	WEIRD	WINDY	WRIST
VICAR	WADED	WEIRS	WINED	WRITE
VICES	WADER	WELCH	WINES	WRITS
VICHY	WADGE	WELDS	WINGE	WRONG
VIDEO	WADIS	WELLS	WINGS	WROTE
VIEWS	WAFER	WELLY	WINKS	WROTH
VIGIL	WAGED	WELSH	WINZE	WRUNG
VILER	WAGER	WELTS	WIPED	WRYER
VILLA	WAGES	WENCH	WIPER	WRYLY
VIMEN	WAGON	WETLY	WIPES	WUHAN
VINES	WAHOO	WHACK	WIRED	WURST
VINIC	WAIFS	WHALE	WIRER	WUSIH
VINYL	WAIST	WHAMS	WIRES	
VIOLA	WAIVE	WHANG	WISER	X
VIOLS	WAKED	WHARF	WISPS	X-AXIS
VIPER	WAKEN	WHEAL	WISPY	XENIA
VIRAL	WAKER	WHEAT	WITCH	XENON
VIREO	WAKES	WHEEL	WITHE	XERIC
VIRGA	WALKS	WHELK	WITHY	XEROX
VIRGO	WALLS	WHELP	WITTY	XHOSA
VIRTU	WALLY	WHERE	WIVES	X-RAYS
VIRUS	WALTZ	WHICH	WIZEN	X-UNIT
VISAS	WANDS	WHIFF	WOKEN	XYLAN
VISES	WANED	WHIGS	WOLDS	XYLEM
VISIT	WANES	WHILE	WOLOF	XYLOL
VISOR	WANEY	WHIMS	WOMAN	XYLYL
VISTA	WANLY	WHINE	WOMBS	

Y	YEARN	YOKEL	YUCKY	ZEIST
YACHT	YEARS	YOKES	YUKON	ZENIC
YAHOO	YEAST	YOLKS	YULAN	ZEROS
YAKUT	YELLS	YOLKY	YUMAN	ZESTY
YALTA	YELPS	YONKS		ZIBET
YANKS	YEMEN	YONNE	Z	ZINGY
YAPOK	YERBA	YOUNG	ZAIRE	ZIPPY
YARDS	YETIS	YOURS	ZAMIA	ZLOTY
YARNS	YIELD	YOUTH	ZAPPY	ZONAL
YAWED	YODEL	YOWLS	ZARGA	ZONED
YAWLS	YOGIC	YOYOS	Z-AXIS	ZONES
YAWNS	YOGIS	YUCCA	ZEBRA	ZOOID
Y-AXIS	YOKED			

A	ACHING	AFFECT	ALECKS	AMIDOL
AACHEN	ACIDIC	AFFINE	ALEGAR	AMIDST
AARGAU	ACINIC	AFFIRM	ALEPPO	AMIENS
AARHUS	ACINUS	AFFLUX	ALERTS	AMMINE
ABACUS	ACK-ACK	AFFORD	A LEVEL	AMNION
ABADAN	ACNODE	AFFRAY	ALGOID	AMOEBA
ABASED	ACORNS	AFGHAN	AL HASA	AMORAL
ABATED	ACQUIT	AFIELD	ALIBIS	AMOUNT
ABATIS	ACROSS	AFLAME	ALIENS	AMOURS
ABATOR	ACTING	AFL-CIO	ALIGHT	AMPERE
ABBACY	ACTION	AFLOAT	ALIPED	AMPULE
ABBESS	ACTIVE	AFRAID	ALKALI	AMRITA
ABBEYS	ACTORS	AFRESH	ALKANE	AMULET
ABBOTS	ACTUAL	AFRICA	ALKENE	AMUSED
ABDUCT	ACUITY	AFTERS	ALKYNE	AMYLUM
ABIDED	ACUMEN	AGADIR	ALLEGE	AMYTAL
ABIDER	ADAGES	AGAMIC	ALLELE	ANABAS
ABJECT	ADAGIO	AGARIC	ALLEYS	ANALOG
ABJURE	ADDEND	AGATES	ALLIED	ANCHOR
ABKHAZ	ADDERS	AGEING	ALLIER	ANCONA
ABLAUT	ADDICT	AGEISM	ALLIES	ANDEAN
ABLAZE	ADDING	AGEIST	ALLIUM	ANEMIA
ABOARD	ADDLED	AGENCY	ALLOYS	ANEMIC
ABODES	ADD-ONS	AGENDA	ALLUDE	ANERGY
ABORAL	ADDUCE	AGENTS	ALLURE	ANGARY
ABOUND	ADDUCT	AGHAST	ALMADA	ANGELS
ABRADE	ADEPTS	AGNATE	ALMOND	ANGERS
ABROAD	ADHERE	AGOGIC	ALMOST	ANGINA
ABRUPT	ADIEUS	AGONIC	ALMUCE	ANGKOR
ABSEIL	ADIEUX	AGOUTI	ALNICO	ANGLED
ABSENT	ADJOIN	AGREED	ALPACA	ANGLER
ABSORB	ADJURE	AIDING	ALPHAS	ANGLES
ABSURD	ADJUST	AIKIDO	ALPINE	ANGOLA
ABULIA	ADMIRE	AILING	ALSACE	ANGORA
ABULIC	ADNATE	AIMING	ALSIKE	ANHALT
ABUSED	ADNOUN	AIRBED	ALTAIC	ANHWEI
ABUSER	ADORED	AIRBUS	ALTAIR	ANIMAL
ABUSES	ADRIFT	AIR-DRY	ALTARS	ANIMUS
ABVOLT	ADROIT	AIRGUN	ALTONA	ANKARA
ABWATT	ADSORB	AIRIER	ALUDEL	ANKING
ACACIA	ADULTS	AIRILY	ALUMNA	ANKLES
ACADIA	ADVENT	AIRING	ALUMNI	ANKLET
ACAJOU	ADVERB	AIRMAN	ALVINE	ANLAGE
ACARID	ADVERT	AIRMEN	ALWAYS	ANNABA
ACARUS	ADVICE	AIRWAY	AMADOU	ANNALS
ACCEDE	ADVISE	AISLES	AMATOL	ANNEAL
ACCENT	ADYGEI	AKIMBO	AMAZED	ANNECY
ACCEPT	ADYTUM	ALARMS	AMAZON	ANNEXE
ACCESS	ADZHAR	ALASKA	AMBALA	ANNUAL
ACCORD	AECIUM	ALBANY	AMBARY	ANODES
ACCOST	AEDILE	ALBEDO	AMBITS	ANODIC
ACCRUE	AEGEAN	ALBEIT	AMBLED	ANOINT
ACCUSE	AERATE	ALBINO	AMBLER	ANOMIC
ACETAL	AERIAL	ALBION	AMBUSH	ANOMIE
ACETIC	AERIFY	ALBITE	AMEBAS	ANORAK
ACETUM	AEROBE	ALBUMS	AMEBIC	ANOXIA
ACETYL	AERUGO	ALCOVE	AMENDS	ANOXIC
ACHAEA	AETHER	ALDOSE	AMHARA	ANSATE
ACHENE	AFFAIR	ALDRIN	AMIDIC	ANSHAN

ANSWER	ARCTIC	ASMARA	AUROUS	BALBOA
ANTEED	ARDENT	ASPECT	AUSSIE	BALDLY
ANTHEM	ARDOUR	ASPIRE	AUSTRO-	BALEEN
ANTHER	ARENAS	ASSAIL	AUTEUR	BALING
ANTICS	AREOLA	ASSAYS	AUTHOR	BALKAN
ANTLER	ARETES	ASSENT	AUTISM	BALKED
ANTRUM	ARGALI	ASSERT	AUTUMN	BALKER
ANTUNG	ARGENT	ASSESS	AVATAR	BALLAD
ANURAN	ARGOSY	ASSETS	AVENGE	BALLET
ANURIA	ARGOTS	ASSIGN	AVENUE	BALLOT
ANUSES	ARGUED	ASSIST	AVERSE	BALSAM
ANVILS	ARGUER	ASSIZE	AVIARY	BALSAS
ANYANG	ARGYLE	ASSORT	AVIATE	BALTIC
ANYHOW	ARGYLL	ASSUME	AVIDIN	BAMAKO
ANYONE	ARIEGE	ASSURE	AVIDLY	BAMBOO
ANYWAY	ARIGHT	ASTERN	AVOCET	BANANA
AORIST	ARIOSO	ASTHMA	AVOWAL	BANDED
AORTAS	ARISEN	ASTRAL	AVOWED	BANDIT
AORTIC	ARISTA	ASTRAY	AVOWER	BANGED
AOUDAD	ARKOSE	ASTUTE	AWAKED	BANGER
APACHE	ARMADA	ASWARM	AWAKEN	BANGLE
APATHY	ARMAGH	ASYLUM	AWARDS	BANGUI
APEMAN	ARMFUL	ATAXIA	AWEIGH	BANISH
APERCU	ARMIES	ATAXIC	AWHILE	BANJOS
APEXES	ARMING	ATHENS	AWNING	BANKED
APHIDS	ARMLET	AT-HOME	AWOKEN	BANKER
APHTHA	ARMOUR	ATOLLS	AXENIC	BANNED
APIARY	ARMPIT	ATOMIC	AXILLA	BANNER
APICAL	ARMURE	ATONAL	AXIOMS	BANTAM
APICES	ARNHEM	ATONED	AYMARA	BANTER
APIECE	ARNICA	ATONER	AZALEA	BANYAN
APLITE	AROMAS	ATONIC	AZORES	BAOBAB
APLOMB	AROUND	ATRIUM	AZOTIC	BARBED
APNOEA	AROUSE	ATTACH		BARBEL
APODAL	ARRACK	ATTACK	B	BARBER
APOGEE	ARRANT	ATTAIN	BAAING	BARBET
APOLLO	ARRAYS	ATTEND	BABBLE	BARDIC
APPEAL	ARREST	ATTEST	BABIED	BARELY
APPEAR	ARRIVE	ATTICA	BABIES	BAREST
APPEND	ARROBA	ATTICS	BABOON	BARGED
APPLES	ARROWS	ATTIRE	BACKED	BARGEE
APPOSE	ARSINE	ATTORN	BACKER	BARGES
APRILS	ARTERY	ATTUNE	BACKUP	BARING
APRONS	ARTFUL	AUBADE	BADGER	BARIUM
APULIA	ARTIER	AUBURN	BADGES	BARKED
AQUILA	ARTIST	AUDILE	BAFFLE	BARKER
ARABIA	ARTOIS	AUDITS	BAGELS	BARLEY
ARABIC	ASARUM	AU FAIT	BAGGED	BARMAN
ARABLE	ASCEND	AU FOND	BAILED	BARMEN
ARAGON	ASCENT	AUGEND	BAILEE	BARNEY
ARARAT	ASCOTS	AUGERS	BAILER	BARODA
ARBOUR	ASHIER	AUGITE	BAILEY	BARONS
ARCADE	ASHLAR	AUGURY	BAILOR	BARONY
ARCANA	ASHORE	AUGUST	BAIRNS	BARQUE
ARCANE	ASIANS	AUKLET	BAITED	BARRED
ARCHED	ASIDES	AU LAIT	BAKERS	BARREL
ARCHER	ASKING	AU PAIR	BAKERY	BARREN
ARCHES	ASLANT	AUREUS	BAKING	BARROW
ARCHLY	ASLEEP	AURORA	BALATA	BARTER

BARYON	BEDECK	BETIDE	BIPEDS	B-MOVIE
BASALT	BEDLAM	BETONY	BIRDIE	BOARDS
BASELY	BEDPAN	BETOOK	BIRTHS	BOASTS
BASEST	BEEFED	BETRAY	BISCAY	BOATED
BASHED	BEETLE	BETTED	BISECT	BOATER
BASHES	BEFALL	BETTER	BISHOP	BOBBED
BASICS	BEFELL	BEVELS	BISONS	BOBBIN
BASIFY	BEFOOL	BEVIES	BISQUE	BOBBLE
BASING	BEFORE	BEWAIL	BISSAU	BOBCAT
BASINS	BEFOUL	BEWARE	BISTRE	BOCHUM
BASION	BEGGAR	BEYOND	BISTRO	BODEGA
BASKED	BEGGED	BEZOAR	BITCHY	BODICE
BASKET	BEGONE	BHOPAL	BITING	BODIES
BASQUE	BEGUMS	BHUTAN	BITTEN	BODILY
BASSES	BEHALF	BIAFRA	BITTER	BODING
BASSET	BEHAVE	BIASED	BLACKS	BODKIN
BASTED	BEHEAD	BIASES	BLADES	BOFFIN
BATHED	BEHELD	BIBLES	BLAMED	BOGEYS
BATHER	BEHEST	BICEPS	BLANCH	BOGGED
BATHOS	BEHIND	BICKER	BLANKS	BOGGLE
BATMAN	BEHOLD	BICORN	BLARED	BOGIES
BATMEN	BEHOVE	BIDDEN	BLASTS	BOGOTA
BATONS	BEINGS	BIDETS	BLAZED	BOILED
BATTED	BEIRUT	BIDING	BLAZER	BOILER
BATTEN	BELFRY	BIFFED	BLAZES	BOLAND
BATTER	BELIED	BIFFIN	BLAZON	BOLDER
BATTLE	BELIEF	BIGAMY	BLEACH	BOLDLY
BATTUE	BELIER	BIG CAT	BLEARY	BOLERO
BAUBLE	BELIZE	BIG END	BLEATS	BOLIDE
BAULKS	BELLES	BIGGER	BLEEPS	BOLSHY
BAWLED	BELLOW	BIGGIE	BLENCH	BOLSON
BAWLER	BELONG	BIGHTS	BLENDE	BOLTED
BAYEUX	BELSEN	BIGOTS	BLENDS	BOLTER
BAYING	BELTED	BIG TOP	BLENNY	BOMBAY
BAYOUS	BELUGA	BIGWIG	BLIGHT	BOMBED
BAZAAR	BEMOAN	BIHARI	BLIMEY	BOMBER
BEACON	BEMUSE	BIKING	BLIMPS	BONBON
BEADED	BENGAL	BIKINI	BLINDS	BONDED
BEADLE	BENIGN	BILBAO	BLINKS	BONGOS
BEAGLE	BENONI	BILGES	BLINTZ	BONIER
BEAKER	BENUMB	BILKED	BLITHE	BONILY
BEAMED	BENZOL	BILKER	BLOCKS	BONING
BEARDS	BENZYL	BILLED	BLOKES	BONITO
BEARER	BERATE	BILLET	BLONDE	BON MOT
BEASTS	BEREFT	BILLON	BLOODS	BONNET
BEATEN	BERETS	BILLOW	BLOODY	BONSAI
BEATER	BERGEN	BILLY-O	BLOOMS	BONZER
BEAUNE	BERING	BINARY	BLOTCH	BOOBED
BEAUTS	BERLIN	BINATE	BLOTTO	BOOHOO
BEAUTY	BERTHS	BINDER	BLOUSE	BOOING
BEAVER	BERYLS	BINGES	BLOWER	BOOKED
BECAME	BESEEM	BINGOS	BLOW-UP	BOOKIE
BECKET	BESIDE	BINNED	BLOWZY	BOOMED
BECKON	BESOMS	BIOGEN	BLUEST	BOOSTS
BECOME	BESTED	BIONIC	BLUFFS	BOOTED
BEDAUB	BESTIR	BIOPIC	BLUISH	BOOTEE
BEDBUG	BESTOW	BIOPSY	BLUNGE	BOOTHS
BEDDED	BETAKE	BIOTIC	BLURBS	BOOZED
BEDDER	BETHEL	BIOTIN	BLURRY	BOOZER

				C
BOPPED	BRACER	BROOMS	BURGLE	CABALS
BORAGE	BRACES	BROWNS	BURIAL	CABANA
BORANE	BRAIDS	BROWSE	BURIED	CABERS
BORATE	BRAINS	BRUGES	BURIER	CABINS
BORDER	BRAINY	BRUISE	BURLAP	CABLED
BOREAL	BRAISE	BRUMAL	BURLER	CABLES
BORERS	BRAKED	BRUNCH	BURLEY	CABLET
BORIDE	BRAKES	BRUNEI	BURNED	CABMAN
BORING	BRANCH	BRUTAL	BURNER	CACHES
BORNEO	BRANDS	BRUTES	BURNET	CACHET
BORROW	BRANDY	BRYONY	BURPED	CACHOU
BORZOI	BRASHY	BUBBLE	BURRED	CACKLE
BOSKET	BRASOV	BUBBLY	BURROS	CACTUS
BOSNIA	BRASSY	BUCCAL	BURROW	CADCAM
BOSOMS	BRAVED	BUCKED	BURSAL	CADDIE
BOSOMY	BRAVER	BUCKET	BURSAR	CADDIS
BOSSED	BRAVES	BUCKLE	BURSTS	CADENT
BOSSES	BRAVOS	BUDDED	BURTON	CADETS
BOSTON	BRAWLS	BUDDHA	BURYAT	CADGED
BOSUNS	BRAWNY	BUDDLE	BUSBAR	CADGER
BOTANY	BRAYED	BUDGED	BUS BOY	CADRES
BOTCHY	BRAYER	BUDGET	BUSHED	CAECUM
BOTFLY	BRAZEN	BUFFED	BUSHEL	CAELUM
BOTHER	BRAZER	BUFFER	BUSHES	CAEOMA
BOTTLE	BRAZIL	BUFFET	BUSIED	CAESAR
BOTTOM	BREACH	BUGGED	BUSIER	CAFTAN
BOUAKE	BREAKS	BUGGER	BUSILY	CAGIER
BOUCLE	BREAST	BUGLER	BUSING	CAGILY
BOUGHS	BREECH	BUGLES	BUSKED	CAGING
BOUGHT	BREEZE	BUILDS	BUSKER	CAHIER
BOUGIE	BREEZY	BULBAR	BUSKIN	CAICOS
BOULES	BREGMA	BULBIL	BUSSED	CAIQUE
BOULLE	BREMEN	BULBUL	BUSTED	CAIRNS
BOUNCE	BRETON	BULGED	BUSTER	CAJOLE
BOUNCY	BREVET	BULGES	BUSTLE	CAKING
BOUNDS	BREWER	BULKED	BUST-UP	CALAIS
BOUNTY	BRIBER	BULLET	BUTANE	CALASH
BOURNS	BRIDAL	BUMBLE	BUTENE	CALCAR
BOURSE	BRIDGE	BUMMED	BUTLER	CALCES
BOVINE	BRIDLE	BUMPED	BUTTED	CALCIC
BOVVER	BRIERY	BUMPER	BUTTER	CALCICO
BOWELS	BRIGHT	BUNCHY	BUTTES	CALICO
BOWERS	BRITON	BUNDLE	BUTTON	CALIPH
BOWERY	BROACH	BUNGED	BUYERS	CALKED
BOWFIN	BROADS	BUNGLE	BUYING	CALKIN
BOWING	BROCHE	BUNION	BUYOUT	CALLAO
BOWLED	BROCHE	BROGUE	BUNKED	CALLED
BOWLER	BROKEN	BUNKER	BUZZER	CALLER
BOWMAN	BROKER	BUNKUM	BUZZES	CALL-IN
BOWMEN	BROLLY	BUNK-UP	BY-BLOW	CALLOW
BOWSAW	BROMAL	BUOYED	BYGONE	CALL-UP
BOW TIE	BROMIC	BURBLE	BYLAWS	CALLUS
BOW-WOW	BRONCO	BURBOT	BY-LINE	CALMED
BOWYER	BRONZE	BURDEN	BYPASS	CALMER
BOXCAR	BRONZY	BUREAU	BYPLAY	CALMLY
BOXERS	BROOCH	BURGAS	BYROAD	CALPAC
BOXING	BROODS	BURGEE	BYSSUS	CALQUE
BOYISH	BROODY	BURGER	BYWAYS	CALVED
BRACED	BROOKS	BURGHS	BYWORD	CALVES

CAMASS	CAREER	CAUDLE	CHAMPS	CHITON
CAMBER	CARESS	CAUGHT	CHANCE	CHIVES
CAMELS	CARETS	CAUSAL	CHANCY	CHOCKS
CAMEOS	CARGOS	CAUSED	CHANGE	CHOICE
CAMERA	CARHOP	CAUSES	CHANTS	CHOIRS
CAMION	CARIES	CAVEAT	CHANTY	CHOKED
CAMISE	CARINA	CAVE-IN	CHAOAN	CHOKER
CAMLET	CARING	CAVERN	CHAPEL	CHOKES
CAMPED	CARMAN	CAVIAR	CHARDS	CHOLER
CAMPER	CARMEL	CAVING	CHARGE	CHOLLA
CAMPOS	CARNAL	CAVITY	CHARMS	CHONJU
CAMPUS	CARNES	CAVORT	CHARTS	CHOOSE
CANADA	CARNET	CAWING	CHASED	CHOOSY
CANALS	CAROBS	CAXTON	CHASER	CHOPPY
CANAPE	CAROLS	CAYMAN	CHASES	CHORAL
CANARD	CARPAL	CD-ROMS	CHASMS	CHORDS
CANARY	CARPED	CEASED	CHASSE	CHOREA
CANCAN	CARPEL	CEDARS	CHASTE	CHORES
CANCEL	CARPET	CEDING	CHATTY	CHORIC
CANCER	CARPUS	CELAYA	CHEATS	CHORUS
CANDID	CARREL	CELERY	CHECKS	CHOSEN
CANDLE	CARROT	CELLAR	CHECKY	CHOUGH
CANINE	CARTED	CELLOS	CHEEKS	CHRISM
CANING	CARTEL	CELTIC	CHEEKY	CHRIST
CANKER	CARTER	CEMENT	CHEEPS	CHROMA
CANNED	CARTON	CENSER	CHEERS	CHROME
CANNEL	CARVED	CENSOR	CHEERY	CHUBBY
CANNES	CARVER	CENSUS	CHEESE	CHUCKS
CANNON	CASABA	CENTAL	CHEESY	CHUKAR
CANNOT	CASEFY	CENTER	CHEQUE	CHUKKA
CANOED	CASEIN	CENTRE	CHERRY	CHUMMY
CANOES	CASERN	CENTUM	CHERTY	CHUMPS
CANONS	CASHED	CERATE	CHERUB	CHUNKS
CANOPY	CASHEW	CERCAL	CHESTS	CHUNKY
CANTAL	CASING	CERCIS	CHESTY	CHURCH
CANTED	CASINO	CERCUS	CHEWED	CHURLS
CANTER	CASKET	CEREAL	CHEWER	CHURNS
CANTIC	CASLON	CEREUS	CHICHI	CHUTES
CANTLE	CASQUE	CERISE	CHICKS	CICADA
CANTON	CASSIA	CERIUM	CHICLE	CICERO
CANTOR	CASSIS	CERMET	CHICLY	CIDERS
CANTOS	CASTER	CEROUS	CHIDED	CIGARS
CANTUS	CASTES	CERUSE	CHIDER	CILICE
CANVAS	CASTLE	CERVID	CHIEFS	CILIUM
CANYON	CASTOR	CERVIX	CHIGOE	CINDER
CAPERS	CASUAL	CETANE	CHILES	CINEMA
CAPIAS	CATCHY	CEYLON	CHILLI	CINEOL
CAPONS	CATENA	CHA-CHA	CHILLS	CINQUE
CAPOTE	CATGUT	CHACMA	CHILLY	CIPHER
CAPPED	CATION	CHAETA	CHIMED	CIRCLE
CAPPER	CATKIN	CHAFED	CHIMES	CIRCUM-
CAPSID	CATNAP	CHAFER	CHINES	CIRCUS
CAPTOR	CATNIP	CHAFFY	CHINKS	CIRQUE
CARAFE	CATSUP	CHAINS	CHINTZ	CIRRUS
CARATS	CATTLE	CHAIRS	CHIPPY	CITIES
CARBON	CAUCUS	CHAISE	CHIRPS	CITIFY
CARBOY	CAUDAD	CHALET	CHIRPY	CITING
CARDED	CAUDAL	CHALKS	CHISEL	CITRAL
CAREEN	CAUDEX	CHALKY	CHITIN	CITRIC

CITRIN	CLOUDY	COLDLY	CONVOY	COSTAL
CITRON	CLOUTS	COLEUS	COOING	CO-STAR
CITRUS	CLOVEN	COLEYS	COOKED	COSTLY
CIVETS	CLOVER	COLIMA	COOKER	COTTER
CIVICS	CLOVES	COLLAR	COOKIE	COTTON
CIVIES	CLOWNS	COLLET	COOLED	COUCAL
CLAIMS	CLOYED	COLLIE	COOLER	COUGAR
CLAMMY	CLUBBY	COLONS	COOLIE	COUGHS
CLAMPS	CLUCKS	COLONY	COOLLY	COULEE
CLAQUE	CLUMPS	COLOUR	COOPED	COUNTS
CLARET	CLUMPY	COLUMN	COOPER	COUNTY
CLASPS	CLUMSY	COLURE	COPALM	COUPES
CLASSY	CLUTCH	COMATE	COPIED	COUPLE
CLAUSE	COALED	COMBAT	COPIER	COUPON
CLAWED	COALER	COMBED	COPIES	COURSE
CLAWER	COARSE	COMBER	COPING	COURTS
CLAYEY	COASTS	COMBOS	COP-OUT	COUSIN
CLEATS	COATED	COMEDO	COPPED	COVENS
CLEAVE	COAXED	COMEDY	COPPER	COVERS
CLEFTS	COAXER	COMELY	COPSES	COVERT
CLENCH	COBALT	COME-ON	COPTIC	COVEYS
CLEOME	COBBER	COMERS	COPULA	COWAGE
CLERGY	COBBLE	COMETS	COQUET	COWARD
CLERIC	COBNUT	COMFIT	CORALS	COWBOY
CLERKS	COBRAS	COMICS	CORBAN	COWING
CLEVER	COBWEB	COMING	CORBEL	COWMAN
CLEVIS	COCCID	COMITY	CORDED	COWMEN
CLICHE	COCCUS	COMMAS	CORDON	COWPAT
CLICKS	COCCYX	COMMIS	CORERS	COWPEA
CLIENT	COCHIN	COMMIT	CORFAM	COWPOX
CLIFFS	COCKED	COMMON	CORGIS	COWRIE
CLIMAX	COCKLE	COMORO	CORING	COXING
CLIMBS	COCK-UP	COMOSE	CORIUM	COYOTE
CLIMES	COCOON	COMPEL	CORKED	COYPUS
CLINAL	CODDLE	COMPLY	CORKER	COZIER
CLINCH	CODGER	CONCHA	CORMEL	COZILY
CLINES	CODIFY	CONCHY	CORNEA	CRABBY
CLINGY	CODING	CONCUR	CORNEL	CRACKS
CLINIC	COELOM	CONDOM	CORNER	CRACOW
CLIP-ON	COERCE	CONDOR	CORNET	CRADLE
CLIQUE	COEVAL	CONEYS	CORONA	CRAFTS
CLITIC	COFFEE	CONFER	CORPSE	CRAFTY
CLOACA	COFFER	CONGAS	CORPUS	CRAGGY
CLOAKS	COFFIN	CONGER	CORRAL	CRAMBO
CLOCHE	COGENT	CONGES	CORSES	CRAMPS
CLOCKS	COGGED	CONGOU	CORSET	CRANED
CLODDY	COGNAC	CONICS	CORTEX	CRANES
CLOGGY	COHEIR	CONIES	CORYMB	CRANIA
CLONAL	COHERE	CONIUM	CORYZA	CRANKS
CLONES	COHORT	CONKED	COSECH	CRANKY
CLONIC	COHOSH	CONKER	COSHED	CRANNY
CLONUS	COHUNE	CONMAN	COSHES	CRAPPY
CLOSED	COILED	CONMEN	COSIER	CRASIS
CLOSER	COILER	CONNED	COSIES	CRATED
CLOSES	COINED	CONOID	COSILY	CRATER
CLOSET	COINER	CONSUL	COSINE	CRATES
CLOTHE	COITAL	CONTRA-	COSMIC	CRAVAT
CLOTHS	COITUS	CONVEX	COSMOS	CRAVED
CLOUDS	COLDER	CONVEY	COSSET	CRAVEN

CRAWLS	CRUETS	CURSOR	DAMMED	DEATHS
CRAYON	CRUISE	CURTLY	DAMNED	DEBARK
CRAZED	CRUMBS	CURTSY	DAMPED	DEBASE
CRAZES	CRUMBY	CURVED	DAMPEN	DEBATE
CREAKS	CRUMMY	CURVES	DAMPER	DEBITS
CREAKY	CRUNCH	CURVET	DAMPLY	DEBRIS
CREAMS	CRURAL	CUSCUS	DAMSEL	DEBTOR
CREAMY	CRUSES	CUSPID	DAMSON	DEBUNK
CREASE	CRUSTS	CUSSED	DANCED	DEBUTS
CREATE	CRUSTY	CUSSES	DANCER	DECADE
CRECHE	CRUTCH	CUSTOM	DANCES	DECALS
CREDIT	CRUXES	CUTELY	DANDER	DECAMP
CREDOS	CRYING	CUTEST	DANDLE	DECANE
CREEDS	CRYPTS	CUTLER	DANGER	DECANT
CREEKS	CUBANE	CUTLET	DANGLE	DECARE
CREELS	CUBBED	CUTOFF	DANISH	DECCAN
CREEPS	CUBING	CUTOUT	DANKER	DECEIT
CREEPY	CUBISM	CUTTER	DANUBE	DECENT
CRENEL	CUBIST	CUTUPS	DANZIG	DECIDE
CREOLE	CUBITS	CYANIC	DAPHNE	DECILE
CRESOL	CUBOID	CYCLED	DAPPED	DECKED
CRESTS	CUCKOO	CYCLES	DAPPER	DECKLE
CRETAN	CUCUTA	CYCLIC	DAPPLE	DECOCT
CRETIC	CUDDLE	CYDERS	DARDIC	DECODE
CRETIN	CUDDLY	CYGNET	DARFUR	DECOKE
CREUSE	CUDGEL	CYGNUS	DARING	DECORS
CREWED	CUESTA	CYMBAL	DARKEN	DECOYS
CREWEL	CUFFED	CYMENE	DARKER	DECREE
CRICKS	CUIABA	CYMOID	DARKLY	DEDUCE
CRIERS	CULLED	CYMOSE	DARNED	DEDUCT
CRIKEY	CULLER	CYMRIC	DARNEL	DEEMED
CRIMEA	CULLET	CYNICS	DARNER	DEEPEN
CRIMES	CULLIS	CYPHER	DARTED	DEEPER
CRINGE	CULTIC	CYPRUS	DARTER	DEEPLY
CRINUM	CUMANA	CYSTIC	DASHED	DEFACE
CRIPES	CUMBER		DASHER	DEFAME
CRISES	CUNEAL	D	DASHES	DEFEAT
CRISIS	CUPIDS	DABBED	DATARY	DEFECT
CRISPS	CUPOLA	DABBER	DATING	DEFEND
CRISPY	CUPPAS	DABBLE	DATIVE	DEFIED
CRISTA	CUPPED	DACRON	DATURA	DEFIER
CRITIC	CUPRIC	DACTYL	DAUBED	DEFILE
CROAKS	CUP TIE	DADOES	DAUBER	DEFINE
CROCKS	CUPULE	DAEMON	DAVITS	DEFORM
CROCUS	CURACY	DAFTER	DAWDLE	DEFRAY
CROFTS	CURARE	DAFTLY	DAWNED	DEFTLY
CRONES	CURATE	DAGGER	DAYBOY	DEFUSE
CROOKS	CURBED	DAGOES	DAYGLO	DEGAGE
CRORES	CURDLE	DAHLIA	DAYTON	DEGREE
CROSSE	CURFEW	DAINTY	DAZING	DEHORN
CROTCH	CURIAE	DAISES	DAZZLE	DE-ICED
CROTON	CURING	DAKOTA	DEACON	DE-ICER
CROUCH	CURIOS	DALASI	DEADEN	DEIFIC
CROUPS	CURIUM	DALLAS	DEADLY	DEISTS
CROWDS	CURLED	DALTON	DEAFEN	DEIXIS
CROWED	CURLER	DAMAGE	DEALER	DEJAVU
CROWER	CURLEW	DAMARA	DEARER	DEJECT
CROWNS	CURSED	DAMASK	DEARLY	DE JURE
CRUDER	CURSES	DAMMAR	DEARTH	DELAYS

DELETE	DESMID	DIMPLE	DODDER	DOUBLY
DELIAN	DESORB	DIMPLY	DODDLE	DOUBTS
DELICT	DESPOT	DIM SUM	DODGED	DOUCHE
DELPHI	DESSAU	DIMWIT	DODGEM	DOUGHY
DELTAS	DETACH	DINARS	DODGER	DOURLY
DELUDE	DETAIL	DINERS	DODGES	DOUSED
DELUGE	DETAIN	DINGHY	DODOES	DOUSER
DE LUXE	DETECT	DINGLE	DOFFED	DOVISH
DELVED	DETENT	DINING	DOFFER	DOWNED
DELVER	DETEST	DINKUM	DOG-EAR	DOWNER
DEMAND	DETOUR	DINNED	DOGGED	DOWSED
DEMEAN	DE TROP	DINNER	DOGGER	DOWSER
DEMISE	DEUCED	DIOXAN	DOGIES	DOYENS
DEMIST	DEVICE	DIOXIN	DOGLEG	DOYLEY
DEMODE	DEVILS	DIPLEX	DOGMAS	DOZENS
DEMONS	DEVISE	DIPLOE	DOG TAG	DOZIER
DEMOTE	DEVOID	DIPODY	DOINGS	DOZILY
DEMURE	DEVOTE	DIPOLE	DOLINE	DOZING
DEMURS	DEVOUR	DIPPED	DOLING	DRABLY
DENARY	DEVOUT	DIPPER	DOLLAR	DRACHM
DENGUE	DEWIER	DIRECT	DOLLED	DRAFFY
DENIAL	DEWILY	DIREST	DOLLOP	DRAFTS
DENIED	DEWLAP	DIRGES	DOLMAN	DRAFTY
DENIER	DEXTER	DIRHAM	DOLMAS	DRAGEE
DENIMS	DHOTIS	DIRNDL	DOLMEN	DRAGGY
DENNED	DIACID	DISARM	DOLOUR	DRAGON
DENOTE	DIADEM	DISBAR	DOMAIN	DRAINS
DENSER	DIALED	DISBUD	DOMINO	DRAKES
DENTAL	DIAPER	DISCOS	DONATE	DRAMAS
DENTED	DIAPIR	DISCUS	DONJON	DRAPED
DENTEX	DIARCH	DISEUR	DONKEY	DRAPER
DENTIL	DIATOM	DISHED	DONNED	DRAPES
DENTIN	DIBBED	DISHES	DONORS	DRAWEE
DENUDE	DIBBER	DISMAL	DOODLE	DRAWER
DENVER	DIBBLE	DISMAY	DOOMED	DRAWLS
DEODAR	DICIER	DISOWN	DOPANT	DRAWLY
DEPART	DICING	DISPEL	DOPIER	DREADS
DEPEND	DICKER	DISTAL	DOPING	DREAMS
DEPICT	DICTUM	DISTIL	DORIAN	DREAMT
DEPLOY	DIDDLE	DISUSE	DORIES	DREAMY
DEPORT	DIEPPE	DITHER	DORMER	DREARY
DEPOSE	DIESEL	DITTOS	DORMIE	DREDGE
DEPOTS	DIESIS	DIVANS	DORSAD	DREGGY
DEPTHS	DIETED	DIVERS	DORSAL	DRENCH
DEPUTE	DIETER	DIVERT	DORSUM	DRESSY
DEPUTY	DIFFER	DIVEST	DOSAGE	DRIERS
DERAIL	DIGAMY	DIVIDE	DO-SI-DO	DRIEST
DERIDE	DIGEST	DIVINE	DOSING	DRIFTS
DERIVE	DIGGER	DIVING	DOSSAL	DRIFTY
DERMAL	DIGITS	DJAMBI	DOSSED	DRILLS
DERMIC	DIGLOT	DJINNS	DOSSER	DRINKS
DERMIS	DIK-DIK	DOABLE	DOTAGE	DRIPPY
DERRIS	DIKTAT	DOBBIN	DOTARD	DRIVEL
DESCRY	DILATE	DOCENT	DOTING	DRIVEN
DESERT	DILDOS	DOCILE	DOTTED	DRIVER
DESIGN	DILUTE	DOCKED	DOTTER	DRIVES
DESIRE	DIMITY	DOCKER	DOTTLE	DROGUE
DESIST	DIMMED	DOCKET	DOUALA	DROLLY
DESMAN	DIMMER	DOCTOR	DOUBLE	DRONED

Ⓔ

DRONES	DUSTER	EGESTA	ENCODE	EQUALS
DRONGO	DUSTUP	EGGCUP	ENCORE	EQUATE
DROOPY	DUTIES	EGGNOG	ENCYST	EQUINE
DROPSY	DUVETS	EGOISM	ENDEAR	EQUITY
DROSSY	DWARFS	EGOIST	ENDING	ERASED
DROVER	DYABLE	EGRESS	ENDIVE	ERASER
DROVES	DYADIC	EGRETS	ENDUED	ERBIUM
DROWSE	DYEING	EIGHTH	ENDURE	ERFURT
DROWSY	DYNAMO	EIGHTS	ENEMAS	ERLANG
DRUDGE	DYNAST	EIGHTY	ENERGY	ERMINE
DRUIDS	DYNODE	EITHER	ENFACE	ERODED
DRUNKS		EJECTA	ENFOLD	EROTIC
DRYADS	E	ELANDS	ENGAGE	ERRAND
DRYERS	EAGLES	ELAPID	ENGINE	ERRANT
DRY ICE	EAGLET	ELAPSE	ENGRAM	ERRATA
DRYING	EARFUL	ELATED	ENGULF	ERRING
DRY ROT	EARING	ELATER	ENIGMA	ERRORS
DUBBED	EARNED	ELBOWS	ENJOIN	ERSATZ
DUBBIN	EARNER	ELDERS	ENLACE	ERYNGO
DUBLIN	EARTHS	ELDEST	ENLIST	ESCAPE
DUCATS	EARTHY	ELEGIT	ENMESH	ESCARP
DUCKED	EARWAX	ELEVEN	ENMITY	ESCHAR
DUCKER	EARWIG	ELEVON	ENNAGE	ESCHEW
DUDEEN	EASELS	ELFISH	ENNEAD	ESCORT
DUELED	EASIER	EL GIZA	ENOSIS	ESCROW
DUELLO	EASILY	ELICIT	ENOUGH	ESCUDO
DUENNA	EASING	ELIDED	ENRAGE	ESKIMO
DUFFEL	EASTER	ELIXIR	ENRICH	ESPIAL
DUFFER	EATERS	ELOPED	ENROBE	ESPIED
DUGONG	EATING	ELOPER	ENROOT	ESPIER
DUGOUT	EBBING	EL PASO	ENSIGN	ESPRIT
DUIKER	ECARTE	ELUDED	ENSILE	ESSAYS
DULCET	ECESIS	ELUDER	ENSOUL	ESTATE
DULLED	ECHARD	ELYSEE	ENSUED	ESTEEM
DULLER	ECHOED	EMBALM	ENSURE	ESTRAY
DULUTH	ECHOES	EMBANK	ENTAIL	ETALON
DUMBER	ECHOIC	EMBARK	ENTICE	ETCHED
DUMBLY	ECLAIR	EMBERS	ENTIRE	ETCHER
DUMDUM	ECTYPE	EMBLEM	ENTITY	ETHANE
DUMPED	ECURIE	EMBODY	ENTOMB	ETHENE
DUMPER	ECZEMA	EMBOLY	ENTRAP	ETHICS
DUNCES	EDDIED	EMBOSS	ENTREE	ETHNIC
DUNDEE	EDDIES	EMBRYO	ENVIED	ETHYNE
DUNITE	EDGIER	EMERGE	ENVIER	ETYMON
DUNKED	EDGILY	EMESIS	ENVIES	EUBOEA
DUNKER	EDGING	EMETIC	ENVOYS	EUCHRE
DUNLIN	EDIBLE	EMIGRE	ENWIND	EULOGY
DUNNED	EDICTS	EMOTER	ENWOMB	EUNUCH
DUNNER	EDITED	EMPALE	ENWRAP	EUREKA
DUPERY	EDITOR	EMPIRE	ENZYME	EUROPE
DUPING	EERILY	EMPLOY	EOCENE	EVADED
DUPLET	EFFACE	ENABLE	EOGENE	EVADER
DUPLEX	EFFECT	ENAMEL	EOLITH	EVENLY
DURBAN	EFFETE	ENATIC	EONISM	EVENTS
DURBAR	EFFIGY	EN BLOC	EOZOIC	EVILER
DURESS	EFFING	ENCAGE	EPARCH	EVILLY
DURIAN	EFFLUX	ENCAMP	EPIRUS	EVINCE
DURING	EFFORT	ENCASE	EPONYM	EVOKED
DUSTED	EFFUSE	ENCASH	EPOPEE	EVOKER

EVOLVE	FACULA	FAUNAL	FIACRE	FIRTHS
EVZONE	FADE-IN	FAUNAS	FIANCE	FISCAL
EXAMEN	FADING	FAVOUR	FIASCO	FISHED
EXARCH	FAECAL	FAWNED	FIBBED	FISHER
EXCEED	FAECES	FAWNER	FIBBER	FISHES
EXCEPT	FAENZA	FAXING	FIBRED	FISTIC
EXCESS	FAERIE	FAZING	FIBRES	FITFUL
EXCISE	FAG END	FEALTY	FIBRIL	FITTED
EXCITE	FAGGED	FEARED	FIBRIN	FITTER
EXCUSE	FAGGOT	FEARER	FIBULA	FIVERS
EXEDRA	FAILED	FEASTS	FICKLE	FIXATE
EXEMPT	FAILLE	FECULA	FIDDLE	FIXERS
EXEUNT	FAINTS	FECUND	FIDDLY	FIXING
EXHALE	FAIRER	FEDORA	FIDGET	FIXITY
EXHORT	FAIRLY	FEEBLE	FIELDS	FIZGIG
EXHUME	FAITHS	FEEBLY	FIENDS	FIZZED
EXILED	FAKERS	FEEDER	FIERCE	FIZZER
EXILES	FAKING	FEELER	FIESTA	FIZZLE
EXILIC	FAKIRS	FEINTS	FIFTHS	FJORDS
EXITED	FALCON	FEISTY	FIGHTS	FLABBY
EXODUS	FALLAL	FELINE	FIGURE	FLACON
EXONYM	FALLEN	FELLED	FIJIAN	FLAGGY
EXOTIC	FALLER	FELLER	FILETS	FLAGON
EXPAND	FALLOW	FELLOE	FILIAL	FLAILS
EXPECT	FALSER	FELLOW	FILING	FLAKED
EXPEND	FALTER	FELONS	FILLED	FLAKER
EXPERT	FAMILY	FELONY	FILLER	FLAKES
EXPIRE	FAMINE	FEMALE	FILLET	FLAMBE
EXPIRY	FAMISH	FEMORA	FILL-IN	FLAMED
EXPORT	FAMOUS	FEMURS	FILLIP	FLAMER
EXPOSE	FANGED	FENCED	FILMED	FLAMES
EXSERT	FANION	FENCER	FILMIC	FLANGE
EXTANT	FANJET	FENCES	FILOSE	FLANKS
EXTEND	FANNED	FENDED	FILTER	FLARED
EXTENT	FANNER	FENDER	FILTHY	FLARES
EXTERN	FAN-TAN	FENIAN	FIMBLE	FLASHY
EXTINE	FARCES	FENNEC	FINALE	FLASKS
EXTORT	FARINA	FENNEL	FINALS	FLATLY
EXTRAS	FARING	FERBAM	FINDER	FLATUS
EXUDED	FARMED	FERIAL	FINELY	FLAUNT
EYEFUL	FARMER	FERMAT	FINERY	FLAVIN
EYEING	FAR-OFF	FERRET	FINEST	FLAWED
EYELET	FAR-OUT	FERRIC	FINGAL	FLAXEN
EYELID	FARROW	FERULA	FINGER	FLAYED
EYRIES	FARTED	FERULE	FINIAL	FLAYER
	FASCIA	FERVID	FINING	FLECHE
F	FASTED	FESCUE	FINISH	FLECKS
FABIAN	FASTEN	FESTAL	FINITE	FLEDGE
FABLED	FASTER	FESTER	FINNED	FLEECE
FABLER	FAT CAT	FETIAL	FINNIC	FLEECY
FABLES	FATHER	FETING	FIORDS	FLEETS
FABRIC	FATHOM	FETISH	FIORIN	FLENSE
FACADE	FATTEN	FETTER	FIPPLE	FLESHY
FACETS	FATTER	FETTLE	FIRING	FLETCH
FACIAL	FAUCAL	FEUDAL	FIRKIN	FLEXED
FACIES	FAUCES	FEUDED	FIRMED	FLEXES
FACILE	FAUCET	FEZZAN	FIRMER	FLEXOR
FACING	FAULTS	FEZZED	FIRMLY	FLICKS
FACTOR	FAULTY	FEZZES	FIRSTS	FLIERS

FLIGHT	FOLLOW	FRANCS	FUCK-UP	GADGET
FLIMSY	FOLSOM	FRAPPE	FUCOID	GADOID
FLINCH	FOMENT	FRATER	FUDDLE	GAELIC
FLINTS	FONDER	FRAUDS	FUDGED	GAFFER
FLINTY	FONDLE	FRAUEN	FUELED	GAFFES
FLIRTS	FONDLY	FRAYED	FUGATO	GAGGED
FLITCH	FONDUE	FRAZIL	FUGING	GAGGER
FLOATS	FONTAL	FREAKS	FUGUES	GAGGLE
FLOATY	FOODIE	FREAKY	FUHRER	GAGING
FLOCKS	FOOLED	FREELY	FUKIEN	GAIETY
FLOCKY	FOOTER	FREEST	FULANI	GAINED
FLOODS	FOOTLE	FREEZE	FULCRA	GAINER
FLOORS	FOOZLE	FRENCH	FULFIL	GAINLY
FLOOZY	FORAGE	FRENZY	FULLER	GAITER
FLOPPY	FORAYS	FRESCO	FULMAR	GALATA
FLORAL	FORBAD	FRESNO	FUMBLE	GALATI
FLORET	FORBID	FRIARS	FUMING	GALAXY
FLORID	FORCED	FRIARY	FUNDED	GALENA
FLORIN	FORCER	FRIDAY	FUNDIC	GALERE
FLOSSY	FORCES	FRIDGE	FUNDUS	GALIBI
FLOURY	FORDED	FRIEND	FUNGAL	GALIOT
FLOWED	FOREGO	FRIERS	FUNGIC	GALLED
FLOWER	FOREST	FRIEZE	FUNGUS	GALLEY
FLUENT	FORGED	FRIGHT	FUNKED	GALLIC
FLUFFY	FORGER	FRIGID	FUNKER	GALLON
FLUIDS	FORGES	FRIJOL	FUNNEL	GALLOP
FLUKES	FORGET	FRILLS	FUN RUN	GALORE
FLUKEY	FORGOT	FRILLY	FURFUR	GALOSH
FLUNKY	FORKED	FRINGE	FURIES	GALWAY
FLURRY	FORMAL	FRINGY	FURLED	GALYAK
FLUTED	FORMAT	FRISKS	FURLER	GAMBIA
FLUTER	FORMED	FRISKY	FURORE	GAMBIT
FLUTES	FORMER	FRIULI	FURRED	GAMBLE
FLYBYS	FORMIC	FRIVOL	FURROW	GAMBOL
FLYERS	FORMYL	FRIZZY	FUSAIN	GAMELY
FLYING	FORNIX	FROCKS	FUSHUN	GAMETE
FLYSCH	FORTES	FROGGY	FUSILE	GAMIER
FOALED	FORTIS	FROLIC	FUSING	GAMINE
FOAMED	FORUMS	FRONDS	FUSION	GAMING
FOBBED	FOSSIL	FRONTS	FUSSED	GAMMAS
FO'C'SLE	FOSTER	FROSTS	FUSSER	GAMMED
FODDER	FOUGHT	FROSTY	FUSSES	GAMMON
FOETAL	FOULED	FROTHS	FUSTIC	GANDER
FOETID	FOULER	FROTHY	FUTILE	GANGED
FOETOR	FOULLY	FROWNS	FUTONS	GANGER
FOETUS	FOUL-UP	FROWZY	FUTURE	GANGES
FOGBOW	FOUNTS	FROZEN	FUZZED	GANGUE
FOGDOG	FOURTH	FRUGAL		GANNET
FOGGED	FOVEAL	FRUITS	G	GANOID
FOGGIA	FOWLER	FRUITY	GABBED	GANTRY
FOGIES	FOXIER	FRUMPS	GABBER	GAOLED
FOIBLE	FOXILY	FRUMPY	GABBLE	GAOLER
FOILED	FOXING	FRUNZE	GABBRO	GAPING
FOLDED	FOYERS	FRYERS	GABION	GAPPED
FOLDER	FRACAS	FRYING	GABLED	GARAGE
FOLIAR	FRAMED	FRY-UPS	GABLES	GARBED
FOLIOS	FRAMER	FU-CHOU	GADDED	GARBLE
FOLIUM	FRAMES	FUCKED	GADDER	GARCON
FOLKSY	FRANCE	FUCKER	GADFLY	GARDEN

GARGET	GENTLE	GLIDED	GORGER	GRIFFE
GARGLE	GENTLY	GLIDER	GORGES	GRIGRI
GARISH	GENTRY	GLIDES	GORGON	GRILLE
GARLIC	GEODIC	GLINTS	GORIER	GRILLS
GARNER	GERBIL	GLIOMA	GORILY	GRILSE
GARNET	GERMAN	GLITCH	GORING	GRIMLY
GARRET	GERMEN	GLITZY	GO-SLOW	GRINDS
GARTER	GERUND	GLOATS	GOSPEL	GRINGO
GASBAG	GETTER	GLOBAL	GOSSIP	GRIPED
GASCON	GETUPS	GLOBES	GOTHIC	GRIPER
GASHED	GEYSER	GLOBIN	GOUGED	GRIPES
GASHES	GEZIRA	GLOOMY	GOUGER	GRISLY
GASIFY	GHETTO	GLORIA	GOUGES	GRISON
GASKET	GHIBLI	GLOSSA	GOURDS	GRISTS
GASKIN	GHOSTS	GLOSSY	GOVERN	GRITTY
GASMAN	GHOULS	GLOVED	GRABEN	GRIVET
GASMEN	GHYLLS	GLOVER	GRACED	GROANS
GASPED	GIANTS	GLOVES	GRACES	GROATS
GASPER	GIAOUR	GLOWED	GRADED	GROCER
GASSED	GIBBED	GLOWER	GRADER	GRODNO
GASSER	GIBBER	GLUING	GRADES	GROGGY
GASSES	GIBBET	GLUMLY	GRADIN	GROINS
GATEAU	GIBBON	GLUTEN	GRADUS	GROOMS
GATHER	GIBE AT	GLYCOL	GRAECO-	GROOVE
GAUCHE	GIFTED	GNAWED	GRAFTS	GROOVY
GAUCHO	GIGGLE	GNAWER	GRAINS	GROPED
GAUGED	GIGGLY	GNEISS	GRAINY	GROPER
GAUGER	GIGOLO	GNOMES	GRAMME	GROPES
GAUGES	GILDED	GNOMIC	GRANDS	GROTTO
GAVAGE	GILDER	GNOMON	GRANGE	GROTTY
GAVELS	GILLED	GNOSIS	GRANNY	GROUCH
GAVIAL	GILLIE	GOADED	GRANTS	GROUND
GAWKED	GIMLET	GOATEE	GRAPES	GROUPS
GAWKER	GIMMAL	GOBBET	GRAPHS	GROUSE
GAWPED	GINGER	GOBBLE	GRASSY	GROUTS
GAYEST	GINKGO	GOBIAN	GRATED	GROVEL
GAZEBO	GIRDED	GOBLET	GRATER	GROVES
GAZING	GIRDER	GOBLIN	GRATES	GROWER
GAZUMP	GIRDLE	GODSON	GRATIS	GROWLS
GDYNIA	GIRLIE	GODWIT	GRAVEL	GROWTH
GEARED	GIRTHS	GOFERS	GRAVEN	GROYNE
GECKOS	GIUSTO	GOFFER	GRAVER	GROZNY
GEDACT	GIVING	GOGGLE	GRAVES	GRUBBY
GEE-GEE	GLACIS	GOITRE	GRAVID	GRUDGE
GEEZER	GLADES	GO-KART	GRAYED	GRUGRU
GEISHA	GLADLY	GOLDEN	GRAYER	GRUMPY
GELADA	GLAIRY	GOLFER	GRAZED	GRUNTS
GELDED	GLANCE	GOLLOP	GRAZER	GUARDS
GELLED	GLANDS	GOMUTI	GRAZES	GUAVAS
GEMINI	GLARED	GONADS	GREASE	GUENON
GEMMED	GLARES	GONERS	GREASY	GUESTS
GENDER	GLASSY	GONION	GREATS	GUFFAW
GENERA	GLAZED	GOODLY	GREBES	GUIANA
GENEVA	GLAZER	GOOFED	GREECE	GUIDED
GENIAL	GLAZES	GOOGLY	GREEDY	GUIDER
GENIES	GLEAMS	GOOGOL	GREENS	GUIDES
GENIUS	GLEBES	GOOIER	GREYED	GUIDON
GENOME	GLEETY	GOPHER	GREYER	GUILDS
GENRES	GLIBLY	GORGED	GRIEVE	GUILTY

GUIMPE	HAGGIS	HARD-ON	HEAD-ON	HEMMED
GUINEA	HAGGLE	HARD UP	HEALED	HEMMER
GUISES	HAIDAN	HAREEM	HEALER	HEMPEN
GUITAR	HAIDUK	HAREMS	HEALEY	HENBIT
GULDEN	HAILED	HARING	HEALTH	HENLEY
GULLAH	HAILER	HARKED	HEAPED	HEPCAT
GULLED	HAINAN	HARKEN	HEAPER	HEPTAD
GULLET	HAIRDO	HARLEM	HEARER	HERALD
GULPED	HAIRIF	HARLEY	HEARSE	HERBAL
GULPER	HAJJES	HARLOT	HEARST	HERDED
GUMBOS	HAJJIS	HARLOW	HEARTH	HERDER
GUMMED	HAKIMS	HARMED	HEARTS	HERDIC
GUNDOG	HALEST	HARMER	HEARTY	HEREAT
GUNG-HO	HALIDE	HARNEY	HEATED	HEREBY
GUNMAN	HALITE	HAROLD	HEATER	HEREIN
GUNMEN	HALLAH	HARPED	HEATHS	HEREOF
GUNNED	HALLEL	HARPER	HEATHY	HEREON
GUNNEL	HALLEY	HARRAR	HEAUME	HERERO
GUNNER	HALLOO	HARRIS	HEAVED	HERESY
GUNSHY	HALLOS	HARROW	HEAVEN	HERETO
GUNTUR	HALLOW	HARTAL	HEAVER	HERIOT
GURGLE	HALLUX	HARVEY	HEAVES	HERMES
GURJUN	HALOES	HASHED	HEBREW	HERMIT
GURKHA	HALOID	HASHES	HEBRON	HERMON
GUSHED	HALTED	HASLET	HECATE	HERNIA
GUSHER	HALTER	HASSAN	HECKLE	HEROES
GUSSET	HALVAH	HASSLE	HECTIC	HEROIC
GUSTED	HALVED	HASTEN	HECTOR	HEROIN
GUTTED	HALVES	HATBOX	HECUBA	HERONS
GUTTER	HAMATE	HATHOR	HEDDLE	HERPES
GUVNOR	HAMITE	HATING	HEDGED	HERREN
GUYANA	HAMLET	HATPIN	HEDGER	HESIOD
GUYING	HAMMED	HATRED	HEDGES	HESTIA
GUZZLE	HAMMER	HATTER	HEDJAZ	HETMAN
GYPPED	HAMPER	HAULED	HEEDED	HEWERS
GYPSUM	HANDED	HAULER	HEEDER	HEWING
GYRATE	HANDEL	HAUNCH	HEE-HAW	HEXANE
GYROSE	HANDLE	HAUNTS	HEELED	HEXING
	HANGAR	HAVANA	HEELER	HEXONE
H	HANGER	HAVANT	HEENAN	HEXOSE
HAAKON	HANG-UP	HAVENS	HEFTER	HEYDAY
HABANA	HANKER	HAVEN'T	HEGIRA	HIATAL
HABILE	HANKIE	HAVING	HEIDUC	HIATUS
HABITS	HANKOW	HAWAII	HEIFER	HICCUP
HACKED	HANNAH	HAWHAW	HEIGHT	HICKEY
HACKER	HANSEL	HAWICK	HEJIRA	HICKOK
HACKLE	HANSEN	HAWKED	HEKATE	HIDDEN
HADEAN	HANSOM	HAWKER	HELENA	HIDING
HADITH	HAPPEN	HAWSER	HELIOS	HIEING
HADJES	HAPTEN	HAYBOX	HELIUM	HIEMAL
HADJIS	HAPTIC	HAYMOW	HELLAS	HIGGLE
HADRON	HARALD	HAZARD	HELLEN	HIGHER
HAEMAL	HARASS	HAZELS	HELLER	HIGHLY
HAEMIC	HARBIN	HAZIER	HELLES	HIJACK
HAEMIN	HARD BY	HAZILY	HELLOS	HIKERS
HAERES	HARDEN	HAZING	HELMET	HIKING
HAFTER	HARDER	H-BOMBS	HELPED	HILARY
HAGBUT	HARDIE	HEADED	HELPER	HILLEL
HAGGAI	HARDLY	HEADER	HELVES	HILLER

HIMEJI	HOMAGE	HOUDAN	HURTLE	ILL-USE
HINDER	HOMBRE	HOUNDS	HUSAIN	IMAGES
HINDOO	HOMELY	HOURIS	HUSHED	IMBIBE
HINDUS	HOMIER	HOURLY	HUSH-UP	IMBRUE
HINGED	HOMILY	HOUSED	HUSKER	IMBUED
HINGER	HOMING	HOUSEL	HUSSAR	IMIDIC
HINGES	HOMINY	HOUSES	HUSTLE	IMMUNE
HINTED	HONEST	HOVELS	HUSTON	IMMURE
HINTER	HONIED	HOWARD	HUXLEY	IMPACT
HIPPED	HONING	HOWDAH	HUZZAH	IMPAIR
HIPPER	HONKED	HOWE'ER	HYADES	IMPALA
HIPPIE	HONKER	HOWLED	HYAENA	IMPALE
HIRING	HONOUR	HOWLER	HYALIN	IMPART
HISPID	HONSHU	HOWLET	HYBRID	IMPEDE
HISSED	HOODED	HOWRAH	HYBRIS	IMPEND
HISSER	HOODOO	HOYDEN	HYDRAS	IMPHAL
HISSES	HOOFED	HSIANG	HYDRIA	IMPISH
HI-TECH	HOOKAH	HUBBLE	HYDRIC	IMPORT
HITHER	HOOKED	HUBBUB	HYENAS	IMPOSE
HITLER	HOOKER	HUBCAP	HYMENS	IMPOST
HIT MAN	HOOKUP	HUBRIS	HYMNAL	IMPUGN
HIT MEN	HOOPED	HUCKLE	HYMNED	IMPURE
HITTER	HOOPER	HUDDLE	HYPHEN	IMPUTE
HIVING	HOOP-LA	HUDSON	HYPING	INARCH
HOARDS	HOOPOE	HUFFED		INBORN
HOARSE	HOORAH	HUGELY	I	INBRED
HOAXED	HOORAY	HUGEST	IAMBIC	INCEPT
HOAXER	HOOTED	HUGGED	IAMBUS	INCEST
HOAXES	HOOTER	HUGGER	IBADAN	INCHED
HOBART	HOOVER	HUGHES	IBAGUE	INCHES
HOBBES	HOOVES	HUGHIE	IBERIA	INCHON
HOBBLE	HOPING	HULLED	IBEXES	INCISE
HOBNOB	HOPPED	HULLER	IBIBIO	INCITE
HOBOES	HOPPER	HULLOS	IBISES	INCOME
HOCKED	HOPPLE	HUMANE	ICE AGE	INCUBI
HOCKER	HOPPUS	HUMANS	ICEBOX	INCUSE
HOCKEY	HORACE	HUMBER	ICE CAP	INDEED
HODDEN	HORARY	HUMBLE	ICEMAN	INDENE
HODDIN	HORDES	HUMBLY	ICEMEN	INDENT
HODMAN	HORMIC	HUMBUG	ICHANG	INDIAN
HOEING	HORMUZ	HUMISM	ICICLE	INDICT
HOGGED	HORNED	HUMMED	ICIEST	INDIGO
HOGGER	HORNET	HUMMEL	ICONIC	INDIUM
HOGNUT	HORRID	HUMMER	ID CARD	INDOLE
HOGTIE	HORROR	HUMOUR	IDEALS	INDOOR
HOICKS	HOSIER	HUMPED	IDEATE	INDORE
HOIDEN	HOSING	HUMPTY	IDIOCY	INDRIS
HOISTS	HOSTED	HUNGER	IDIOMS	INDUCE
HOLDEN	HOSTEL	HUNGRY	IDIOTS	INDUCT
HOLDER	HOSTIE	HUNTED	IDLEST	INDULT
HOLDUP	HOT AIR	HUNTER	IDLING	INFAMY
HOLIER	HOTBED	HUPPAH	IDYLLS	INFANT
HOLILY	HOT DOG	HURDLE	IGLOOS	INFECT
HOLISM	HOTELS	HURLED	IGNITE	INFEST
HOLLER	HOTIEN	HURLER	IGNORE	INFIRM
HOLLOW	HOTPOT	HURLEY	IGUACU	INFLOW
HOLMES	HOT ROD	HURRAH	IGUANA	INFLUX
HOLMIC	HOTTER	HURRAY	ILESHA	INFORM
HOLPEN	HOTTIE	HURTER	ILEXES	INFUSE

INGEST	INVOKE	JALOPY	JOGGED	K
INGOTS	INWARD	JAMMED	JOGGER	KABYLE
INHALE	IODATE	JAMMER	JOGGLE	KADUNA
INHAUL	IODIDE	JANGLE	JOHNNY	KAFFIR
INHERE	IODINE	JAPERY	JOHORE	KAFTAN
INHUME	IODISM	JAPURA	JOINED	KAISER
INJECT	IODIZE	JARGON	JOINER	KAKAPO
INJURE	IODOUS	JARRAH	JOINTS	KALMIA
INJURY	IONIAN	JARRED	JOISTS	KALONG
INK-CAP	IONIZE	JASPER	JOKERS	KALUGA
INKIER	IONONE	JAUNTS	JOKING	KAMALA
INKING	IPECAC	JAUNTY	JOLTED	KANARA
INKPAD	IREFUL	JAWING	JORDAN	KANGAS
INLAID	IRENIC	JAZZED	JOSHED	KANPUR
INLAND	IRIDIC	JEERED	JOSHES	KANSAS
IN-LAWS	IRISES	JEERER	JOSTLE	KAOLIN
INLAYS	IRITIC	JEJUNE	JOTTED	KARATE
INLETS	IRITIS	JELLED	JOTTER	KARATS
INLIER	IRKING	JENNET	JOULES	KARIBA
INMATE	IRONED	JERBOA	JOUNCE	KARMIC
INMOST	IRONER	JERKED	JOURNO	KASBAH
INNATE	IRONIC	JERKER	JOVIAL	KASSEL
INNING	IRRUPT	JERKIN	JOYFUL	KAUNAS
INNUIT	IRTYSH	JERSEY	JOYING	KAYAKS
INROAD	ISATIN	JESTED	JOYOUS	KAZAKH
INRUSH	ISCHIA	JESTER	JUDAEA	KEBABS
INSANE	ISLAND	JESUIT	JUDAIC	KEDIRI
INSECT	ISLETS	JET LAG	JUDDER	KEELED
INSERT	ISOBAR	JETSAM	JUDGED	KEENED
INSETS	ISOGON	JET SET	JUDGER	KEENER
INSIDE	ISOHEL	JETTED	JUDGES	KEENLY
INSIST	ISOLEX	JETTON	JUDOGI	KEEPER
IN SITU	ISOMER	JEWELS	JUDOKA	KELOID
INSOLE	ISOPOD	JEWESS	JUGATE	KELPIE
INSTAR	ISRAEL	JEWISH	JUGGED	KELTIC
INSTEP	ISSUED	JHANSI	JUGGLE	KELVIN
INSTIL	ISSUER	JIBBED	JUICED	KENNED
INSULA	ISSUES	JIBBER	JUICES	KENNEL
INSULT	ISTRIA	JIBING	JUJUBE	KENYAN
INSURE	ITALIC	JIGGED	JULEPS	KERALA
INTACT	ITCHED	JIGGER	JULIES	KERMAN
INTAKE	ITCHES	JIGGLE	JUMBLE	KERMES
INTEND	ITHACA	JIGGLY	JUMPED	KERNEL
INTENT	ITSELF	JIGSAW	JUMPER	KERSEY
INTERN		JIHADS	JUNEAU	KETENE
INTIMA	J	JILTED	JUNGLE	KETONE
INTINE	JABBED	JILTER	JUNGLY	KETOSE
INTONE	JABBER	JINGLE	JUNIOR	KETTLE
IN TOTO	JABIRU	JINGLY	JUNKED	KEYING
INTROS	JACANA	JINXED	JUNKET	KEYWAY
INTUIT	JACKAL	JINXES	JUNKIE	KHALIF
INUITS	JACKED	JITTER	JUNTAS	KHULNA
INULIN	JACKET	JIVING	JURIES	KHYBER
INURED	JAFFNA	JOBBED	JURIST	KIBOSH
INVADE	JAGGED	JOBBER	JURORS	KICKED
INVENT	JAGUAR	JOB LOT	JUSTLY	KICKER
INVERT	JAILED	JOCKEY	JUTTED	KIDDED
INVEST	JAILER	JOCOSE	JUTTER	KIDDER
INVITE	JAIPUR	JOCUND		KIDDIE

KIDNAP	KUMMEL	LANDED	LAUNCH	LENITY
KIDNEY	KUNG FU	LANDES	LAUREL	LENSES
KIELCE	KUNLUN	LANGUE	LAVABO	LENTEN
KIKUYU	KURGAN	LANGUR	LAVAGE	LENTIC
KILLED	KUWAIT	LANKER	LAVISH	LENTIL
KILLER	KWACHA	LANKLY	LAWFUL	LEONID
KILTED	KYUSHU	LANNER	LAWYER	LEPERS
KILTER		LANUGO	LAXITY	LEPTON
KIMONO	L	LAPDOG	LAY-BYS	LESION
KINASE	LAAGER	LAPELS	LAYERS	LESSEE
KINDER	LABELS	LAPPED	LAYING	LESSEN
KINDLE	LABIAL	LAPPER	LAYMAN	LESSER
KINDLY	LABILE	LAPPET	LAYMEN	LESSON
KINGLY	LABIUM	LAPSED	LAY-OFF	LESSOR
KIOSKS	LABLAB	LAPSER	LAYOUT	LETHAL
KIPPED	LABOUR	LAPSES	LAZIER	LETTER
KIPPER	LABRET	LAPSUS	LAZILY	LETUPS
KIRKUK	LABRUM	LAP-TOP	LAZING	LEVANT
KIRMAN	LACHES	LARDED	LEADEN	LEVEES
KIRSCH	LACIER	LARDER	LEADER	LEVELS
KISMET	LACILY	LARDON	LEAD-IN	LEVERS
KISSED	LACING	LARGER	LEAGUE	LEVIED
KISSER	LACKED	LARGOS	LEAKED	LEVIER
KISSES	LACKEY	LARIAT	LEAKER	LEVIES
KIT BAG	LACTAM	LARINE	LEANED	LEVITY
KITSCH	LACTIC	LARKED	LEANER	LEWDLY
KITTED	LACUNA	LARKER	LEAN-TO	LIABLE
KITTEN	LADDER	LARNAX	LEAPED	LIAISE
KLAXON	LADDIE	LARVAE	LEAPER	LIBBER
KNAVES	LA-DI-DA	LARVAL	LEARNT	LIBELS
KNAWEL	LADIES	LARYNX	LEASED	LIBIDO
KNELLS	LADING	LASCAR	LEASER	LIBRAN
KNIFED	LADINO	LASERS	LEASES	LIBYAN
KNIFER	LADLED	LASHED	LEAVED	LICHEN
KNIGHT	LADLER	LASHER	LEAVEN	LICKED
KNIVES	LADLES	LASHES	LEAVER	LICKER
KNOCKS	LAGENA	LASH-UP	LEAVES	LIDDED
KNOLLS	LAGERS	LASKET	LECHER	LIEGES
KNOTTY	LAGGED	LASSES	LECTOR	LIE-INS
KNOWER	LAGOON	LASSOS	LEDGER	LIENAL
KOALAS	LAHORE	LASTED	LEDGES	LIERNE
KOHIMA	LAICAL	LASTER	LEERED	LIFERS
KOKAND	LAIRDS	LASTLY	LEEWAY	LIFTED
KOLYMA	LALANG	LATEEN	LEGACY	LIFTER
KOPECK	LAMBDA	LATELY	LEGATE	LIGAND
KOREAN	LAMBED	LATENT	LEGATO	LIGATE
KORUNA	LAMELY	LATEST	LEGEND	LIGHTS
KOSHER	LAMENT	LATHER	LEGERS	LIGNIN
KOSICE	LAMEST	LATHES	LEGGED	LIGULA
KOVROV	LAMINA	LATINS	LEGION	LIGULE
KOWTOW	LAMING	LATISH	LEGIST	LIKASI
KRAALS	LAMMAS	LATIUM	LEGUME	LIKELY
KRISES	LAMPAS	LATRIA	LEIDEN	LIKING
KRONER	LANATE	LATTEN	LE MANS	LILACS
KRONOR	LANCED	LATTER	LEMONS	LILIES
KRUGER	LANCER	LATVIA	LEMONY	LIMBER
KUKRIS	LANCES	LAUDED	LEMURS	LIMBIC
KUMASI	LANCET	LAUDER	LENDER	LIMBOS
KUMISS	LANDAU	LAUGHS	LENGTH	LIMBUS

LIMEYS	LOANER	LOQUAT	LUSTED	MALEIC
LIMIER	LOATHE	LORDED	LUSTRE	MALICE
LIMING	LOAVES	LORDLY	LUTEAL	MALIGN
LIMITS	LOBATE	LORICA	LUXATE	MALLEE
LIMNED	LOBBED	LOSERS	LUXURY	MALLET
LIMNER	LOBITO	LOSING	LYCEES	MALLOW
LIMPED	LOBULE	LOSSES	LYCEUM	MALTED
LIMPER	LOCALE	LOTION	LYCHEE	MALTHA
LIMPET	LOCALS	LOTTED	LYNXES	MAMBAS
LIMPID	LOCATE	LOUDEN	LYRATE	MAMMAL
LIMPLY	LOCHIA	LOUDER	LYRICS	MAMMON
LINAGE	LOCKED	LOUDLY	LYRIST	MANAGE
LINDEN	LOCKER	LOUGHS	LYSINE	MANAMA
LINEAL	LOCKET	LOUISE		MANANA
LINEAR	LOCKUP	LOUNGE	M	MANAUS
LINERS	LOCULE	LOURED	MACACO	MANCHE
LINEUP	LOCUMS	LOUSED	MACAWS	MANCHU
LINGER	LOCUST	LOUVAR	MACEIO	MANEGE
LINGUA	LODGED	LOUVRE	MACKLE	MANFUL
LINING	LODGER	LOVAGE	MACRON	MANGER
LINKED	LODGES	LOVELY	MACULA	MANGLE
LINKUP	LOFTED	LOVERS	MADAME	MANGOS
LINNET	LOFTER	LOVEYS	MADAMS	MANIAC
LINTEL	LOGGED	LOVING	MADCAP	MANIAS
LINTER	LOGGER	LOWEST	MADDEN	MANILA
LIPASE	LOGGIA	LOWING	MADDER	MANNED
LIPIDS	LOGIER	LOW-KEY	MADE-UP	MANNER
LIPOID	LOGION	LOYANG	MADMAN	MANORS
LIPOMA	LOGJAM	LOZERE	MADMEN	MANQUE
LIQUID	LOGLOG	L-PLATE	MADRAS	MANTEL
LIQUOR	LOIRET	LUANDA	MADRID	MANTIC
LISBON	LOITER	LUBBER	MADURO	MANTIS
LISPED	LOLLED	LUBECK	MAENAD	MANTLE
LISPER	LOLLER	LUBLIN	MAGGOT	MANUAL
LISSOM	LOLLOP	LUCENT	MAGIAN	MANURE
LISTED	LOMENT	LUDLOW	MAGNET	MAOISM
LISTEN	LONDON	LUFFED	MAGNUM	MAOIST
LITANY	LONELY	LUGGED	MAGPIE	MAPLES
LITCHI	LONERS	LUGGER	MAGUEY	MAPPED
LITERS	LONGAN	LULLED	MAGYAR	MAQUIS
LITHER	LONGED	LUMBAR	MAHOUT	MARACA
LITHIA	LONGER	LUMBER	MAIDEN	MARAUD
LITHIC	LOOFAH	LUMMOX	MAIKOP	MARBLE
LITMUS	LOOKED	LUMPED	MAILED	MARBLY
LITRES	LOOKER	LUMPEN	MAILER	MARCHE
LITTER	LOOK-IN	LUNACY	MAIMED	MARGAY
LITTLE	LOOMED	LUNATE	MAIMER	MARGIN
LIVE-IN	LOONEY	LUNGED	MAINLY	MARIAN
LIVELY	LOOPED	LUNGER	MAJORS	MARINA
LIVERS	LOOPER	LUNGES	MAKALU	MARINE
LIVERY	LOOSED	LUNULA	MAKERS	MARKED
LIVING	LOOSEN	LUPINE	MAKE-UP	MARKER
LIZARD	LOOSER	LUPINS	MAKING	MARKET
LLAMAS	LOOSES	LURING	MALADY	MARKKA
LOADED	LOOTED	LURKED	MALAGA	MARKUP
LOADER	LOOTER	LURKER	MALANG	MARLIN
LOAFED	LOPING	LUSAKA	MALATE	MARMOT
LOAFER	LOPPED	LUSHES	MALAWI	MAROON
LOANED	LOPPER	LU-SHUN	MALAYA	MARQUE

MARRED	MEDICO	METIER	MINION	MOHAWK
MARRER	MEDICS	METING	MINIUM	MOHOLE
MARRON	MEDINA	METOPE	MINNOW	MOIETY
MARROW	MEDIUM	METRES	MINOAN	MOLARS
MARSHY	MEDLAR	METRIC	MINORS	MOLDED
MARTEN	MEDLEY	METROS	MINTED	MOLDER
MARTIN	MEEKER	METTLE	MINTER	MOLEST
MARTYR	MEEKLY	MEWING	MINUET	MOLISE
MARVEL	MEERUT	MEWLER	MINUTE	MOLOCH
MASCLE	MEETER	MEXICO	MINXES	MOLTED
MASCON	MEGILP	MEZZOS	MIOSIS	MOLTEN
MASCOT	MEGOHM	MIAOWS	MIOTIC	MOMENT
MASERS	MEKNES	MIASMA	MIRAGE	MOMISM
MASERU	MEKONG	MICKEY	MIRING	MOMMAS
MASHED	MELEES	MICMAC	MIRROR	MONACO
MASHER	MELLOW	MICRON	MISCUE	MONDAY
MASHES	MELODY	MICROS	MISERE	MONEYS
MASHIE	MELOID	MIDAIR	MISERS	MONGER
MASJID	MELONS	MIDDAY	MISERY	MONGOL
MASKED	MELTED	MIDDEN	MISFIT	MONIES
MASKER	MELTER	MIDDLE	MISHAP	MONISM
MASONS	MELTON	MIDGES	MISHIT	MONIST
MASQUE	MEMBER	MIDGET	MISLAY	MONKEY
MASSED	MEMOIR	MIDGUT	MISLED	MONTHS
MASSES	MEMORY	MID-OFF	MISSAL	MOOING
MASSIF	MENACE	MIDRIB	MISSED	MOONED
MASTER	MENADO	MIDSTS	MISSES	MOORED
MASTIC	MENAGE	MIDWAY	MISSIS	MOOTED
MATADI	MENDED	MIFFED	MISSUS	MOOTER
MATING	MENDER	MIGHTY	MISTED	MOPEDS
MATINS	MENHIR	MIKADO	MISTER	MOPING
MATRIX	MENIAL	MILADY	MISUSE	MOPOKE
MATRON	MENSES	MILDER	MITRAL	MOPPED
MATTED	MENTAL	MILDEW	MITRES	MOPPET
MATTER	MENTON	MILDLY	MITTEN	MORALE
MATURE	MENTOR	MILERS	MIXERS	MORALS
MAULED	MEOWED	MILIEU	MIXING	MORASS
MAULER	MERCER	MILIUM	MIX-UPS	MORBID
MAUNDY	MERELY	MILKED	MIZZEN	MOREEN
MAUSER	MERGED	MILKER	MOANED	MORGUE
MAXIMA	MERGER	MILLED	MOANER	MORION
MAXIMS	MERINO	MILLER	MOATED	MORMON
MAY DAY	MERITS	MILLET	MOBBED	MORNAY
MAYFLY	MERLIN	MILORD	MOBBER	MORONS
MAYHEM	MERLON	MILTER	MOBILE	MOROSE
MAYORS	MERMAN	MIMICS	MOCKED	MORROW
MAZILY	MERSIN	MIMING	MOCKER	MORSEL
MEADOW	MESCAL	MIMOSA	MOCK-UP	MORTAL
MEAGRE	MESHED	MINCED	MOD CON	MORTAR
MEANER	MESHES	MINCER	MODELS	MORULA
MEANLY	MESSED	MINDED	MODEMS	MOSAIC
MEASLY	MESSES	MINDEL	MODENA	MOSCOW
MEATUS	MESS-UP	MINDER	MODERN	MOSLEM
MECCAS	METAGE	MINERS	MODEST	MOSQUE
MEDALS	METALS	MINGLE	MODIFY	MOSTLY
MEDDLE	METEOR	MINIFY	MODISH	MOTELS
MEDIAL	METERS	MINIMA	MODULE	MOTETS
MEDIAN	METHOD	MINIMS	MOGULS	MOTHER
MEDICK	METHYL	MINING	MOHAIR	MOTIFS

MOTILE	MUSING	NAPPER	NEWEST	NOSHED
MOTION	MUSKET	NARIAL	NEWISH	NOSH-UP
MOTIVE	MUSLIM	NARKED	NEWTON	NO-SIDE
MOTLEY	MUSLIN	NARROW	NIBBLE	NOSIER
MOTMOT	MUSSED	NARVIK	NICELY	NOSILY
MOTORS	MUSSEL	NASALS	NICEST	NOSING
MOTOWN	MUSTEE	NASIAL	NICETY	NOSTOC
MOTTLE	MUSTER	NASION	NICHES	NOTARY
MOTTOS	MUSTN'T	NASSAU	NICKED	NOTICE
MOULDS	MUTANT	NATANT	NICKEL	NOTIFY
MOULDY	MUTATE	NATION	NICKER	NOTING
MOULIN	MUTELY	NATIVE	NIDIFY	NOTION
MOULTS	MUTING	NATRON	NIECES	NOUGAT
MOUNDS	MUTINY	NATTER	NIELLO	NOUGHT
MOUNTS	MUTISM	NATURE	NIEVRE	NOUNAL
MOUSER	MUTTER	NAUGHT	NIGGER	NOVARA
MOUSSE	MUTTON	NAUSEA	NIGGLE	NOVELS
MOUTHS	MUTUAL	NAUTCH	NIGHTS	NOVICE
MOUTON	MUTULE	NAVAHO	NILGAI	NOWISE
MOVERS	MUZZLE	NAVELS	NIMBLE	NOZZLE
MOVIES	MYELIN	NAVIES	NIMBLY	NUANCE
MOVING	MYNAHS	NAZISM	NIMBUS	NUBBLE
MOWERS	MYOPIA	NEARBY	NINETY	NUBBLY
MOWING	MYOPIC	NEARED	NINGPO	NUBILE
MUCKED	MYOSIN	NEARER	NINTHS	NUCHAL
MUCKER	MYRIAD	NEARLY	NIOBIC	NUCLEI
MUCOID	MYRICA	NEATEN	NIPPED	NUDGED
MUCOUS	MYRTLE	NEATER	NIPPER	NUDGER
MUDCAT	MYSELF	NEATLY	NIPPLE	NUDGES
MUDDED	MYSORE	NEBULA	NIPPON	NUDISM
MUDDLE	MYSTIC	NECKED	NITRIC	NUDIST
MUD PIE	MYTHOS	NECKER	NITWIT	NUDITY
MUESLI	MYXOMA	NECTAR	NIXING	NUGGET
MUFFED		NEEDED	NO BALL	NUKING
MUFFIN	N	NEEDLE	NOBBLE	NUMBAT
MUFFLE	NAAFIS	NEEDN'T	NOBLER	NUMBED
MUFTIS	NABBED	NEGATE	NOBLES	NUMBER
MUGGED	NABLUS	NEIGHS	NOBODY	NUMBLY
MUGGER	NABOBS	NEKTON	NODDED	NUNCIO
MUKLUK	NACHOS	NELSON	NODDLE	NURSED
MULISH	NACRED	NEM CON	NODOSE	NURSES
MULLAH	NADIRS	NEPALI	NODULE	NUTANT
MULLED	NAEVUS	NEPHEW	NOESIS	NUTLET
MULLER	NAGANA	NEREID	NOETIC	NUTMEG
MULLET	NAGANO	NEREIS	NOGGIN	NUTRIA
MULTAN	NAGGED	NERVED	NOISES	NUTTED
MUMBLE	NAGGER	NERVES	NOMADS	NUTTER
MUMMER	NAGOYA	NESTED	NOMISM	NUZZLE
MUNICH	NAGPUR	NESTER	NONAGE	NYLONS
MURALS	NAIADS	NESTLE	NONCES	NYMPHA
MURDER	NAILED	NETHER	NONEGO	NYMPHS
MURINE	NAILER	NETTED	NOODLE	
MURMUR	NAMELY	NETTLE	NOOSES	O
MUSCAT	NAMING	NETTLY	NORDIC	OAFISH
MUSCID	NANTES	NEURAL	NORITE	OAXACA
MUSCLE	NAPALM	NEURON	NORMAL	OBELUS
MUSCLY	NAPKIN	NEUTER	NORMAN	OBEYED
MUSEUM	NAPLES	NEVADA	NORTHS	OBEYER
MUSHES	NAPPED	NEWARK	NORWAY	OBJECT

OBLAST	OLEATE	ORIENT	OWLETS	PANNED
OBLATE	O LEVEL	ORIGAN	OWLISH	PANTED
OBLIGE	OLIVES	ORIGIN	OWNERS	PANTRY
OBLONG	OMASUM	ORIOLE	OWNING	PANZER
OBOIST	OMEGAS	ORISON	OXALIS	PAOTOW
OBSESS	ONAGER	ORISSA	OXCART	PAPACY
OBTAIN	ONCOST	ORMOLU	OXIDES	PAPAIN
OBTECT	ONE-OFF	ORNATE	OXTAIL	PAPAYA
OBTUSE	ONE-WAY	ORNERY	OXYGEN	PAPERS
OBVERT	ONIONS	OROIDE	OYSTER	PAPERY
OCCULT	ONLINE	ORPHAN	OZALID	PAPIST
OCCUPY	ONRUSH	ORPINE		PAPPUS
OCEANS	ONSIDE	ORRERY	P	PAPUAN
OCELOT	ONWARD	OSCARS	PACIFY	PAPULE
O'CLOCK	OOCYTE	OSCINE	PACING	PAPYRI
OCTANE	OODLES	OSIERS	PACKED	PARADE
OCTANT	OOGAMY	OSMIUM	PACKER	PARAMO
OCTAVE	OOLITE	OSMOSE	PACKET	PARANA
OCTAVO	OOLOGY	OSMOUS	PADAUK	PARANG
OCTETS	OOLONG	OSPREY	PADDED	PARAPH
OCTOPI	OOZIER	OSSEIN	PADDLE	PARCEL
OCULAR	OOZILY	OSSIFY	PADRES	PARDON
ODDEST	OOZING	OSTEAL	PAEANS	PARENT
ODDITY	OPAQUE	OSTEND	PAELLA	PARGET
ODDS-ON	OPENED	OSTIUM	PAEONY	PARIAH
ODENSE	OPENER	OSTLER	PAGANS	PARIAN
ODESSA	OPENLY	OTHERS	PAGING	PARIES
ODIOUS	OPERAS	OTIOSE	PAGODA	PARING
ODOURS	OPERON	OTITIS	PAHANG	PARISH
OEDEMA	OPHITE	OTTAVA	PAID-UP	PARITY
OEUVRE	OPIATE	OTTAWA	PAINED	PARKAS
OFFEND	OPINED	OTTERS	PAINTS	PARKED
OFFERS	OPORTO	OUNCES	PAIRED	PARKIN
OFFICE	OPPOSE	OUSTED	PAJAMA	PARLEY
OFFING	OPPUGN	OUSTER	PALACE	PARODY
OFFSET	OPTICS	OUTAGE	PALAIS	PAROLE
OGDOAD	OPTING	OUTBID	PALATE	PARREL
OGIVAL	OPTION	OUTCRY	PALELY	PARROT
OGLING	OPUSES	OUTDID	PALEST	PARSEC
OGRESS	ORACLE	OUTFIT	PALING	PARSED
OHMAGE	ORADEA	OUTFOX	PALISH	PARSEE
OIDIUM	ORALLY	OUTGAS	PALLAS	PARSER
OILCAN	ORANGE	OUTING	PALLED	PARSON
OILCUP	ORATOR	OUTLAW	PALLET	PARTED
OILIER	ORBITS	OUTLAY	PALLID	PARTLY
OILILY	ORCEIN	OUTLET	PALLOR	PARTON
OILING	ORCHID	OUTMAN	PALMAR	PARURE
OILMAN	ORCHIL	OUTPUT	PALMED	PASHTO
OILMEN	ORCHIS	OUTRAN	PALTER	PASSED
OILRIG	ORDAIN	OUTRUN	PALTRY	PASSES
OINKED	ORDEAL	OUTSET	PAMPAS	PASSIM
OKAYED	ORDERS	OUTWIT	PAMPER	PASTED
OLD AGE	ORDURE	OVERDO	PANADA	PASTEL
OLD BOY	OREBRO	OVERLY	PANAMA	PASTES
OLDEST	OREGON	OVIEDO	PANDAS	PASTOR
OLD HAT	ORGANS	OVISAC	PANDER	PASTRY
OLDISH	ORGASM	OVOIDS	PANDIT	PATCHY
OLD LAG	ORGEAT	OVULAR	PANELS	PATENT
OLD MAN	ORGIES	OWELTY	PANICS	PATERS

PATHAN	PEERED	PETREL	PILEUP	PIVOTS
PATHOS	PEEVED	PETROL	PILEUS	PIXELS
PATINA	PEEWIT	PETTED	PILFER	PIXIES
PATIOS	PEGGED	PETTER	PILING	PIZZAS
PATOIS	PEG LEG	PEWITS	PILLAR	PLACED
PATRAS	PEKING	PEWTER	PILLOW	PLACER
PATROL	PELAGE	PHASED	PILOSE	PLACES
PATRON	PELITE	PHASES	PILOTS	PLACET
PATTED	PELLET	PHASIC	PILULE	PLACID
PATTEN	PELMET	PHENOL	PIMPED	PLAGAL
PATTER	PELOTA	PHENYL	PIMPLE	PLAGUE
PAUCAL	PELTED	PHIALS	PIMPLY	PLAGUY
PAUNCH	PELTER	PHILAE	PINCER	PLAICE
PAUPER	PELTRY	PHIZOG	PINEAL	PLAIDS
PAUSED	PELVES	PHLEGM	PINENE	PLAINS
PAUSER	PELVIC	PHLOEM	PINERY	PLAINT
PAUSES	PELVIS	PHOBIA	PINGED	PLAITS
PAVANE	PENANG	PHOBIC	PINIER	PLANAR
PAVING	PENCHI	PHOBOS	PINING	PLANED
PAWING	PENCIL	PHOEBE	PINION	PLANER
PAWNED	PENGPU	PHONED	PINITE	PLANES
PAWPAW	PENMAN	PHONES	PINKED	PLANET
PAXWAX	PENNED	PHONEY	PINKER	PLANKS
PAYBED	PENNON	PHONIC	PINKIE	PLANTS
PAYDAY	PEN PAL	PHONON	PINKOS	PLAQUE
PAYEES	PENTAD	PHOOEY	PINNED	PLASHY
PAYING	PENT UP	PHOTIC	PINNER	PLASMA
PAYOFF	PENTYL	PHOTON	PINTAS	PLATAN
PAYOLA	PENULT	PHOTOS	PINTLE	PLATED
PAYOUT	PENURY	PHRASE	PINUPS	PLATEN
PEACES	PEOPLE	PHYLUM	PINXIT	PLATER
PEACHY	PEORIA	PHYSIC	PIPAGE	PLATES
PEAHEN	PEPLUM	PHYSIO	PIPALS	PLAYED
PEAKED	PEPPED	PHYTON	PIPERS	PLAYER
PEALED	PEPPER	PIAFFE	PIPING	PLAZAS
PEANUT	PEPSIN	PIANOS	PIPITS	PLEACH
PEARLS	PEPTIC	PIAZZA	PIPKIN	PLEASE
PEARLY	PERILS	PICKED	PIPPED	PLEATS
PEBBLE	PERIOD	PICKER	PIPPIN	PLEBBY
PEBBLY	PERISH	PICKET	PIQUED	PLEDGE
PECANS	PERKED	PICKLE	PIQUES	PLEIAD
PECKED	PERLIS	PICK-UP	PIQUET	PLENTY
PECKER	PERMED	PICNIC	PIRACY	PLENUM
PECTEN	PERMIT	PIDDLE	PIRATE	PLEURA
PECTIC	PERNOD	PIDGIN	PISCES	PLEXOR
PECTIN	PERRON	PIECED	PISSED	PLEXUS
PEDALS	PERSIA	PIECER	PISSES	PLIANT
PEDANT	PERSON	PIECES	PISS-UP	PLICAL
PEDATE	PERTLY	PIERCE	PISTIL	PLIERS
PEDDLE	PERUKE	PIFFLE	PISTOL	PLIGHT
PEDLAR	PERUSE	PIGEON	PISTON	PLINTH
PEEING	PESADE	PIGGED	PITCHY	PLISSE
PEEKED	PESETA	PIGGIN	PITHOS	PLOUGH
PEELED	PESTER	PIGLET	PITIED	PLOVER
PEELER	PESTLE	PIGNUS	PITIES	PLOWED
PEEPBO	PETALS	PIGNUT	PITMAN	PLUCKS
PEEPED	PETARD	PIGSTY	PITMEN	PLUCKY
PEEPER	PETERS	PILAFS	PITSAW	PLUMED
PEEPUL	PETITE	PILEUM	PITTED	PLUMES

PLUMMY	POORER	PRANKS	PROPEL	PUPPED
PLUNGE	POORLY	PRATED	PROPER	PUPPET
PLURAL	POP ART	PRATER	PROPYL	PUPPIS
PLUSES	POPERY	PRAWNS	PROSES	PURDAH
PLUTON	POPGUN	PRAXIS	PROTEA	PUREED
PLYING	POPISH	PRAYED	PRO TEM	PUREES
PNEUMA	POPLAR	PRAYER	PROTON	PURELY
POCKED	POPLIN	PREACH	PROVED	PUREST
POCKET	POPPAS	PRECIS	PROVEN	PURFLE
PODDED-	POPPED	PREFAB	PROWLS	PURGED
PODIUM	POPPER	PREFER	PRUDES	PURGER
PODZOL	POPPET	PREFIX	PRUNED	PURGES
POETIC	POPPLE	PREPAY	PRUNER	PURIFY
POETRY	PORING	PREPPY	PRUNES	PURINE
POGROM	PORISM	PRESET	PRYING	PURISM
POINTE	PORKER	PRESTO	PSALMS	PURIST
POINTS	POROUS	PRETTY	PSEUDO-	PURITY
POISED	PORTAL	PREWAR	PSEUDS	PURLED
POISON	PORTED	PREYED	PSEUDY	PURLER
POKERS	PORTER	PREYER	PSYCHE	PURLIN
POKIER	PORTLY	PRICED	PSYCHO-	PURPLE
POKILY	POSERS	PRICES	PTISAN	PURRED
POKING	POSEUR	PRICEY	PTOSIS	PURSED
POLAND	POSHER	PRICKS	PUBLIC	PURSER
POLDER	POSIES	PRIDED	PUCKER	PURSES
POLEYN	POSING	PRIDES	PUDDLE	PURSUE
POLICE	POSSES	PRIEST	PUDDLY	PURVEY
POLICY	POSSET	PRIMAL	PUEBLA	PUSHED
POLING	POSSUM	PRIMED	PUEBLO	PUSHER
POLISH	POSTAL	PRIMER	PUFFED	PUSHES
POLITE	POSTED	PRIMES	PUFFER	PUSH-UP
POLITY	POSTER	PRIMLY	PUFFIN	PUSSES
POLKAS	POSTIE	PRIMUS	PUGGED	PUTLOG
POLLAN	POSTIL	PRINCE	PUKING	PUT-OFF
POLLED	POTAGE	PRINTS	PULLED	PUT-ONS
POLLEN	POTASH	PRIORS	PULLET	PUTRID
POLLEX	POTATO	PRIORY	PULLEY	PUTSCH
POLLUX	POTBOY	PRISED	PULL-IN	PUTTED
POLONY	POTEEN	PRISMS	PULL-ON	PUTTEE
POLYPS	POTENT	PRISON	PULPED	PUTTER
POMACE	POTFUL	PRISSY	PULPIT	PUZZLE
POMADE	POTHER	PRIVET	PULSAR	PYKNIC
POMMEL	POTION	PRIZED	PULSED	PYLONS
POMPOM	POTTED	PRIZES	PULSES	PYOSIS
POMPON	POTTER	PRO-AMS	PUMICE	PYRENE
PONCES	POUCHY	PROBED	PUMMEL	PYRITE
PONCEY	POUNCE	PROBER	PUMPED	PYRONE
PONCHO	POUNDS	PROBES	PUNCHY	PYROPE
PONDER	POURED	PROFIT	PUNDIT	PYTHON
PONGED	POURER	PROJET	PUNIER	PYURIA
PONGEE	POUTED	PROLEG	PUNISH	
PONGID	POUTER	PROLES	PUNJAB	Q
PONIES	POWDER	PROLIX	PUNKAH	QATARI
PONTIC	POWERS	PROLOG	PUNNED	QINTAR
PONTIL	POWWOW	PROMOS	PUNNET	QUACKS
POODLE	POZNAN	PROMPT	PUNTED	QUAGGA
POOLED	PRAGUE	PRONGS	PUNTER	QUAGGY
POOPED	PRAISE	PRONTO	PUPATE	QUAHOG
POOPER	PRANCE	PROOFS	PUPILS	QUAILS

QUAINT	RADDLE	RAPIDS	REBELS	REGARD
QUAKED	RADIAL	RAPIER	REBIND	REGENT
QUAKER	RADIAN	RAPINE	REBORN	REGGAE
QUAKES	RADIOS	RAPING	REBUFF	REGIME
QUALMS	RADISH	RAPIST	REBUKE	REGINA
QUANGO	RADIUM	RAPPED	RECALL	REGION
QUANTA	RADIUS	RAPPEL	RECANT	REGLET
QUARKS	RADOME	RAPPER	RECAPS	REGRET
QUARRY	RADULA	RAPTOR	RECAST	REGULO
QUARTO	RAFFIA	RAREFY	RECEDE	REHASH
QUARTS	RAFFLE	RARELY	RECENT	REHEAR
QUARTZ	RAFTED	RAREST	RECEPT	REHEAT
QUASAR	RAFTER	RARING	RECESS	REIGNS
QUAVER	RAGBAG	RARITY	RECIFE	REINED
QUEASY	RAGGED	RASCAL	RECIPE	REJECT
QUEBEC	RAGING	RASHER	RECITE	REJIGS
QUEENS	RAGLAN	RASHES	RECKED	REJOIN
QUEERS	RAGMAN	RASHLY	RECKON	RELAID
QUENCH	RAGOUT	RASPED	RECOIL	RELATE
QUESTS	RAGTAG	RASPER	RECORD	RELAYS
QUEUED	RAIDED	RASTER	RECOUP	RELENT
QUEUES	RAIDER	RATBAG	RECTAL	RELICS
QUICHE	RAILED	RATHER	RECTOR	RELICT
QUIFFS	RAILER	RATIFY	RECTOS	RELIED
QUILLS	RAILEX	RATINE	RECTUM	RELIEF
QUILTS	RAINED	RATING	RECTUS	RELINE
QUINCE	RAISED	RATION	REDACT	RELISH
QUINOL	RAISER	RATIOS	REDBUD	RELIVE
QUINSY	RAISES	RATITE	REDCAP	RELOAD
QUIRES	RAISIN	RATLAM	REDDEN	REMADE
QUIRKS	RAJAHS	RATOON	REDDER	REMAIN
QUIRKY	RAJKOT	RATTAN	REDEEM	REMAKE
QUIVER	RAJPUT	RAT-TAT	REDFIN	REMAND
QUOITS	RAKING	RATTED	RED-HOT	REMARK
QUORUM	RAKISH	RATTER	REDONE	REMEDY
QUOTAS	RAMBLE	RATTLE	REDOWA	REMIND
QUOTED	RAMIFY	RATTLY	REDUCE	REMISE
QUOTES	RAMJET	RAVAGE	REECHO	REMISS
QWERTY	RAMMED	RAVENS	REEFED	REMORA
	RAMMER	RAVERS	REEFER	REMOTE
	RAMOSE	RAVE-UP	REEKED	REMOVE
R	RAMPUR	RAVINE	REELED	RENAME
RABATO	RAMROD	RAVING	REELER	RENDER
RABBIS	RAMTIL	RAVISH	REEVES	RENEGE
RABBIT	RANCHI	RAWEST	REFACE	RENNES
RABBLE	RANCID	RAZING	REFILL	RENNET
RABIES	RANDAN	RAZORS	REFINE	RENNIN
RACEME	RANDOM	RAZZLE	REFITS	RENOWN
RACERS	RANEES	READER	REFLET	RENTAL
RACHIS	RANGED	REALLY	REFLEX	RENTED
RACIAL	RANGER	REALMS	REFLUX	RENTER
RACIER	RANGES	REAMED	REFORM	RENVOI
RACILY	RANKED	REAMER	REFUEL	REOPEN
RACING	RANKER	REAPED	REFUGE	REPAID
RACISM	RANKLE	REAPER	REFUND	REPAIR
RACIST	RANKLY	REARED	REFUSE	REPAND
RACKED	RANSOM	REARER	REFUTE	REPAST
RACKER	RANTED	REASON	REGAIN	REPEAL
RACKET	RANTER	REBATE	REGALE	REPEAT

REPENT	REVVED	RIP-OFF	ROPILY	RUMBLY
REPINE	REWARD	RIPPED	ROPING	RUMMER
REPLAN	REWIND	RIPPER	ROQUET	RUMOUR
REPLAY	REWIRE	RIPPLE	ROSARY	RUMPLE
REPONE	REWORD	RIPPLY	ROSIER	RUMPLY
REPORT	REWORK	RIPSAW	ROSILY	RUMPUS
REPOSE	RHEBOK	RISERS	ROSINY	RUNDLE
REPUTE	RHESUS	RISING	ROSTER	RUNNEL
REREAD	RHEUMY	RISKED	ROSTOV	RUNNER
RERUNS	RHEYDT	RISKER	ROSTRA	RUN-OFF
RESALE	RHINAL	RISQUE	ROTARY	RUN-OUT
RESCUE	RHODIC	RITUAL	ROTATE	RUNWAY
RESEAT	RHYMED	RIVALS	ROTGUT	RUPEES
RESEAU	RHYMES	RIVERS	ROTORS	RUPIAH
RESECT	RHYTHM	RIVETS	ROTTED	RUSHED
RESEDA	RHYTON	RIYADH	ROTTEN	RUSHER
RESENT	RIALTO	RIYALS	ROTTER	RUSHES
RESHIP	RIBALD	ROAMED	ROTUND	RUSSET
RESIDE	RIBBED	ROAMER	ROUBLE	RUSSIA
RESIGN	RIBBON	ROARED	ROUGED	RUSTED
RESILE	RIBOSE	ROARER	ROUNDS	RUSTIC
RESINS	RICHER	ROASTS	ROUSED	RUSTLE
RESIST	RICHES	ROBALO	ROUSER	RUTILE
RESITS	RICHLY	ROBAND	ROUTED	RUTTED
RESORB	RICKED	ROBBED	ROUTER	RWANDA
RESORT	RICTAL	ROBBER	ROUTES	RYAZAN
RESTED	RICTUS	ROBBIN	ROVERS	
RESTER	RIDDED	ROBING	ROVING	S
RESULT	RIDDEN	ROBINS	ROWANS	SABBAT
RESUME	RIDDER	ROBOTS	ROWERS	SABERS
RETAIL	RIDDLE	ROBUST	ROWING	SABLES
RETAIN	RIDERS	ROCHET	ROYALS	SABRAS
RETAKE	RIDGED	ROCKED	ROZZER	SABRES
RETARD	RIDGES	ROCKER	RUBATO	SACHET
RETELL	RIDING	ROCKET	RUBBED	SACKED
RETENE	RIFFLE	ROCOCO	RUBBER	SACKER
RETIAL	RIFLED	RODENT	RUBBLE	SACRAL
RETINA	RIFLER	RODEOS	RUBBLY	SACRED
RETIRE	RIFLES	ROGUES	RUBIES	SACRUM
RETOLD	RIGGED	ROLLED	RUBLES	SADDEN
RETOOK	RIGGER	ROLLER	RUBRIC	SADDER
RETOOL	RIGHTS	ROLL-ON	RUCKED	SADDLE
RETORT	RIGOUR	ROMAIC	RUCKUS	SADHUS
RETURN	RIG-OUT	ROMANO	RUDDER	SADISM
RETUSE	RIJEKA	ROMANS	RUDDLE	SADIST
REUSED	RILEYS	ROMANY	RUDELY	SAFARI
REVAMP	RILING	ROMEOS	RUDEST	SAFELY
REVEAL	RILLET	ROMPED	RUEFUL	SAFEST
REVERE	RIMINI	RONDEL	RUFFLE	SAFETY
REVERS	RIMMED	RONDOS	RUFFLY	SAGELY
REVERT	RIMOSE	ROOFED	RUFOUS	SAGGAR
REVEST	RINGED	ROOKED	RUGGED	SAGGED
REVIEW	RINGER	ROOKIE	RUGOSE	SAHARA
REVILE	RINSED	ROOMED	RUINED	SAHIBS
REVISE	RINSER	ROOMER	RUINER	SAIGON
REVIVE	RINSES	ROOSTS	RULERS	SAILED
REVOKE	RIOTED	ROOTED	RULING	SAILER
REVOLT	RIOTER	ROOTER	RUMBAS	SAILOR
REVUES	RIPEST	ROPIER	RUMBLE	SAINTS

SAITHE	SATINY	SCOFFS	SEATER	SEPTUM
SALAAM	SATIRE	SCOLDS	SEAWAY	SEQUEL
SALADS	SATURN	SCOLEX	SECANT	SEQUIN
SALAMI	SATYRS	SCONCE	SECEDE	SERAPH
SALARY	SAUCED	SCONES	SECOND	SERBIA
SALIFY	SAUCER	SCOOPS	SECRET	SEREIN
SALINE	SAUCES	SCORCH	SECTOR	SERENE
SALIVA	SAUGER	SCORED	SECUND	SERIAL
SALLEE	SAUNAS	SCORER	SECURE	SERIES
SALLOW	SAVAGE	SCORES	SEDANS	SERIFS
SALMON	SAVANT	SCORIA	SEDATE	SERINE
SALONS	SAVERS	SCORNS	SEDILE	SERMON
SALOON	SAVING	SCOTCH	SEDUCE	SEROSA
SALOOP	SAVOIE	SCOTER	SEEDED	SEROUS
SALTED	SAVORY	SCOTIA	SEEDER	SERUMS
SALTER	SAVOUR	SCOUSE	SEEING	SERVAL
SALTUS	SAVOYS	SCOUTS	SEEKER	SERVED
SALUKI	SAWFLY	SCOWLS	SEEMED	SERVER
SALUTE	SAWING	SCRAPE	SEEMER	SERVES
SALVED	SAWYER	SCRAPS	SEEMLY	SERVOS
SALVER	SAXONS	SCRAWL	SEEPED	SESAME
SALVES	SAXONY	SCREAM	SEESAW	SESTET
SALVIA	SAYING	SCREED	SEETHE	SET-OFF
SALVOR	SCABBY	SCREEN	SEICHE	SETOSE
SALVOS	SCALAR	SCREWS	SEINES	SETTEE
SALYUT	SCALDS	SCREWY	SEISER	SETTER
SAMARA	SCALED	SCRIBE	SEISIN	SETTLE
SAMBAR	SCALER	SCRIMP	SEIZED	SET-UPS
SAMBAS	SCALES	SCRIPT	SEIZER	SEVENS
SAMITE	SCALPS	SCROLL	SEJANT	SEVERE
SAMOAN	SCAMPI	SCROOP	SELDOM	SEVRES
SAMOSA	SCAMPS	SCROTA	SELECT	SEWAGE
SAMPAN	SCANTY	SCRUBS	SELLER	SEWERS
SAMPLE	SCARAB	SCRUFF	SELVES	SEWING
SAMSUN	SCARCE	SCRUMP	SEMEME	SEXIER
SANDAL	SCARED	SCRUMS	SEMITE	SEXILY
SANDED	SCARER	SCUBAS	SEMPRE	SEXING
SANDER	SCARES	SCUFFS	SENARY	SEXISM
SANDHI	SCAREY	SCULPT	SENATE	SEXIST
SANELY	SCARFS	SCUMMY	SENDAI	SEXPOT
SANEST	SCARPS	SCURFY	SENDER	SEXTET
SANIES	SCATTY	SCURRY	SEND-UP	SEXTON
SANITY	SCENES	SCURVY	SENECA	SEXUAL
SANTOS	SCENIC	SCUTCH	SENEGA	SHABBY
SAPELE	SCENTS	SCUTUM	SENILE	SHACKS
SAPOTA	SCHEMA	SCUZZY	SENIOR	SHADED
SAPPED	SCHEME	SCYTHE	SENNAR	SHADES
SAPPER	SCHISM	SEABED	SENNIT	SHADOW
SARGES	SCHIST	SEA DOG	SENORA	SHAFTS
SARNIE	SCHLEP	SEALED	SENORS	SHAGGY
SARONG	SCHOOL	SEALER	SENSED	SHAKEN
SARTHE	SCHORL	SEAMAN	SENSES	SHAKER
SASEBO	SCHUSS	SEAMEN	SENSOR	SHAKES
SASHAY	SCHWAS	SEAMER	SENTRY	SHALOM
SASHES	SCHWYZ	SEANCE	SEPALS	SHAMAN
SASSED	SCILLA	SEARCH	SEPSIS	SHAMED
SASSES	SCIONS	SEARED	SEPTAL	SHAMMY
SATEEN	SCLAFF	SEASON	SEPTET	SHANDY
SATING	SCLERA	SEATED	SEPTIC	SHANKS

SHANNY	SHOUTS	SIKKIM	SKIBOB	SLOPPY
SHANSI	SHOVED	SILAGE	SKIERS	SLOSHY
SHANTY	SHOVEL	SILENT	SKIFFS	SLOTHS
SHAPED	SHOVER	SILICA	SKIING	SLOUCH
SHAPES	SHOVES	SILKEN	SKILLS	SLOUGH
SHARDS	SHOWED	SILTED	SKIMPY	SLOVAK
SHARED	SHOWER	SILVAN	SKINNY	SLOVEN
SHARER	SHRANK	SILVER	SKIRTS	SLOWED
SHARES	SHREDS	SIMIAN	SKIVED	SLOWER
SHARIA	SHREWD	SIMILE	SKIVER	SLOWLY
SHARKS	SHREWS	SIMMER	SKIVVY	SLUDGE
SHARPS	SHRIEK	SIMNEL	SKOPJE	SLUDGY
SHAVED	SHRIFT	SIMONY	SKULLS	SLUICE
SHAVEN	SHRIKE	SIMOOM	SKUNKS	SLUING
SHAVER	SHRILL	SIMPER	SKYCAP	SLUMMY
SHAVES	SHRIMP	SIMPLE	SKYLAB	SLUMPS
SHAWLS	SHRINE	SIMPLY	SLACKS	SLURRY
SHEARS	SHRINK	SINDHI	SLAGGY	SLUSHY
SHEATH	SHRIVE	SINEWS	SLAKED	SLYEST
SHEAVE	SHROUD	SINEWY	SLAKER	SMACKS
SHEETS	SHRUBS	SINFUL	SLALOM	SMALLS
SHEIKH	SHRUGS	SINGED	SLANGY	SMALTO
SHEILA	SHRUNK	SINGER	SLANTS	SMARMY
SHEKEL	SHUCKS	SINGES	SLAP-UP	SMEARS
SHELLS	SHUFTI	SINGLE	SLATED	SMEARY
SHELVE	SHUFTY	SINGLY	SLATER	SMEGMA
SHENSI	SHUNTS	SINING	SLATES	SMELLS
SHERDS	SHYEST	SINKER	SLAVED	SMELLY
SHERIA	SHYING	SINNED	SLAVER	SMELTS
SHERPA	SIALIC	SINNER	SLAVES	SMILAX
SHERRY	SIBYLS	SINTER	SLAVIC	SMILED
SHEWED	SICILY	SIOUAN	SLAYER	SMILER
SHIELD	SICKED	SIPHON	SLEAVE	SMILES
SHIEST	SICKEN	SIPPED	SLEAZY	SMIRCH
SHIFTS	SICKER	SIPPER	SLEDGE	SMIRKS
SHIFTY	SICKLE	SIPPET	SLEEPY	SMITER
SHIITE	SICKLY	SIRENS	SLEETY	SMITHS
SHINER	SIDE-ON	SIRING	SLEEVE	SMITHY
SHINNY	SIDING	SIRIUS	SLEIGH	SMOCKS
SHINTO	SIDLED	SIRRAH	SLEUTH	SMOGGY
SHIRAZ	SIDLER	SISKIN	SLEWED	SMOKED
SHIRES	SIECLE	SISTER	SLICED	SMOKER
SHIRTS	SIEGES	SITARS	SLICER	SMOKES
SHIRTY	SIENNA	SITCOM	SLICES	SMOOCH
SHITTY	SIERRA	SITING	SLICKS	SMOOTH
SHIVER	SIESTA	SIT-INS	SLIDES	SMUDGE
SHOALS	SIEVED	SITTER	SLIGHT	SMUDGY
SHOALY	SIEVES	SIT-UPS	SLIMLY	SMUGLY
SHOCKS	SIFAKA	SIXTHS	SLINGS	SMUTCH
SHODDY	SIFTED	SIZING	SLINKY	SMUTTY
SHOGUN	SIFTER	SIZZLE	SLIP-ON	SNACKS
SHOOED	SIGHED	SKATED	SLIPPY	SNAFUS
SHOOTS	SIGHER	SKATER	SLIP-UP	SNAGGY
SHORAN	SIGHTS	SKATES	SLIVER	SNAILS
SHORED	SIGNAL	SKEINS	SLOGAN	SNAKED
SHORES	SIGNED	SKELLY	SLOOPS	SNAKES
SHORTS	SIGNER	SKETCH	SLOPED	SNAPPY
SHORTY	SIGNET	SKEWED	SLOPER	SNARED
SHOULD	SIGNOR	SKEWER	SLOPES	SNARER

SNARES	SOILED	SPATHE	SPOTTY	STALER
SNARLS	SOIREE	SPAVIN	SPOUSE	STALKS
SNARLY	SOLACE	SPAYED	SPOUTS	STALKY
SNATCH	SOLDER	SPEARS	SPRAIN	STALLS
SNAZZY	SOLELY	SPECIE	SPRANG	STAMEN
SNEAKS	SOLEMN	SPECKS	SPRATS	STAMPS
SNEAKY	SOLIDI	SPEECH	SPRAWL	STANCE
SNEERS	SOLIDS	SPEEDS	SPRAYS	STANCH
SNEEZE	SOLING	SPEEDY	SPREAD	STANDS
SNEEZY	SOLUTE	SPEISS	SPREES	STANZA
SNICKS	SOLVED	SPELLS	SPRIER	STAPES
SNIDER	SOLVER	SPERMS	SPRIGS	STAPLE
SNIFFS	SOMALI	SPEWED	SPRING	STARCH
SNIFFY	SOMBRE	SPEWER	SPRINT	STARED
SNIPED	SOMITE	SPHENE	SPRITE	STARER
SNIPER	SONANT	SPHERE	SPROUT	STARES
SNIPES	SONATA	SPHINX	SPRUCE	STARRY
SNIPPY	SONNET	SPICED	SPRUNG	STARTS
SNITCH	SONORA	SPICER	SPRYLY	STARVE
SNIVEL	SOONER	SPICES	SPUNKY	STASIS
SNOOPS	SOOTHE	SPIDER	SPURGE	STATED
SNOOPY	SOPPED	SPIELS	SPURRY	STATER
SNOOTY	SORBET	SPIGOT	SPURTS	STATES
SNOOZE	SORBIC	SPIKED	SPUTUM	STATIC
SNOOZY	SORDID	SPIKES	SPYING	STATOR
SNORED	SORELY	SPILLS	SQUABS	STATUE
SNORER	SORREL	SPINAL	SQUADS	STATUS
SNORES	SORROW	SPINEL	SQUALL	STAVED
SNORTS	SORTED	SPINES	SQUAMA	STAVES
SNOTTY	SORTER	SPINET	SQUARE	STAYED
SNOUTS	SORTIE	SPIRAL	SQUASH	STAYER
SNOWED	SOTHIC	SPIRES	SQUATS	STEADS
SNUBBY	SOUGHS	SPIRIT	SQUAWK	STEADY
SNUFFY	SOUGHT	SPITAL	SQUAWS	STEAKS
SNUGLY	SOUNDS	SPITED	SQUEAK	STEAMY
SOAKED	SOURCE	SPLAKE	SQUEAL	STEEDS
SOAKER	SOURED	SPLASH	SQUIBS	STEELS
SOAPED	SOURER	SPLEEN	SQUIDS	STEELY
SOARED	SOURLY	SPLICE	SQUILL	STEERS
SOARER	SOUSED	SPLINE	SQUINT	STEEVE
SOBBED	SOVIET	SPLINT	SQUIRE	STEINS
SOBBER	SOWERS	SPLITS	SQUIRM	STELAR
SOCAGE	SOWETO	SPLOSH	SQUIRT	STENCH
SOCCER	SOWING	SPOILS	SQUISH	STEPPE
SOCIAL	SPACED	SPOILT	STABLE	STEREO
SOCKED	SPACER	SPOKEN	STABLY	STERIC
SOCKET	SPACES	SPOKES	STACKS	STERNA
SOCMAN	SPADER	SPONGE	STADIA	STERNS
SODDED	SPADES	SPONGY	STAFFS	STEROL
SODDEN	SPADIX	SPOOFS	STAGED	STEWED
SODIUM	SPANKS	SPOOKS	STAGER	STICKS
SODOMY	SPARED	SPOOKY	STAGES	STICKY
SOEVER	SPARER	SPOOLS	STAGEY	STIFFS
SOFFIT	SPARES	SPOONS	STAINS	STIFLE
SOFTEN	SPARID	SPOORS	STAIRS	STIGMA
SOFTER	SPARKS	SPORES	STAKED	STILES
SOFTIE	SPARRY	SPORTS	STAKES	STILLS
SOFTLY	SPARSE	SPORTY	STALAG	STILLY
SOIGNE	SPASMS	SPOT-ON	STALED	STILTS

STINGS	STRIPE	SUITES	SWARDS	TACKLE
STINGY	STRIPS	SUITOR	SWARMS	TACOMA
STINKS	STRIPY	SULCUS	SWATCH	TACTIC
STINTS	STRIVE	SULKED	SWATHE	TAEJON
STIPEL	STROBE	SULKER	SWATHS	TAGGED
STIPES	STRODE	SULLEN	SWATOW	TAHITI
STIRPS	STROKE	SULTAN	SWAYED	TAILED
STITCH	STROLL	SULTRY	SWAYER	TAILOR
STOATS	STROMA	SUMACH	SWEATS	TAINAN
STOCKS	STRONG	SUMMAT	SWEATY	TAIPAN
STOCKY	STROPS	SUMMED	SWEDEN	TAIPEI
STODGE	STROUD	SUMMER	SWEDES	TAIWAN
STODGY	STROVE	SUMMIT	SWEENY	TAKERS
STOICS	STRUCK	SUMMON	SWEEPS	TAKEUP
STOKED	STRUMA	SUNBED	SWEETS	TAKING
STOKER	STRUNG	SUNBOW	SWELLS	TALCUM
STOKES	STRUTS	SUNDAE	SWERVE	TALENT
STOLEN	STUBBY	SUNDAY	SWIFTS	TALION
STOLES	STUCCO	SUNDER	SWILLS	TALKED
STOLID	STUDIO	SUNDEW	SWINES	TALKER
STOLON	STUFFY	SUNDRY	SWINGE	TALKIE
STONED	STUMER	SUN GOD	SWINGS	TALLER
STONER	STUMPS	SUNKEN	SWIPED	TALLOW
STONES	STUMPY	SUNLIT	SWIPES	TALMUD
STOOGE	STUNTS	SUNNED	SWIRLS	TALONS
STOOLS	STUPID	SUNNIS	SWIRLY	TAMBOV
STOP-GO	STUPOR	SUNRAY	SWITCH	TAMELY
STORAX	STURDY	SUNSET	SWIVEL	TAMERS
STORED	STYLAR	SUNTAN	SWOONS	TAMEST
STORES	STYLED	SUPERB	SWOOPS	TAMING
STOREY	STYLER	SUPINE	SWOOSH	TAMPED
STORKS	STYLES	SUPPED	SWORDS	TAMPER
STORMS	STYLET	SUPPER	SYDNEY	TAMPON
STORMY	STYLUS	SUPPLE	SYLVAN	TANDEM
STOUPS	STYMIE	SUPPLY	SYMBOL	TANGLE
STOVER	STYRAX	SURELY	SYNCOM	TANGLY
STOVES	STYRIA	SUREST	SYNDIC	TANGOS
STOWED	SUABLE	SURETY	SYNODS	TANKER
STRAFE	SUBBED	SURFED	SYNTAX	TANNED
STRAIN	SUBDUE	SURFER	SYPHER	TANNER
STRAIT	SUBITO	SURGED	SYPHON	TANNIC
STRAKE	SUBLET	SURGER	SYRIAN	TANNIN
STRAND	SUBMIT	SURGES	SYRINX	TANNOY
STRAPS	SUBORN	SURREY	SYRUPY	TAOISM
STRATA	SUBSET	SURTAX	SYSTEM	TAOIST
STRAWS	SUBTLE	SURVEY	SYZRAN	TAPERS
STRAWY	SUBTLY	SUSLIK	SYZYGY	TAPING
STRAYS	SUBURB	SUSSED	SZEGED	TAPIRS
STREAK	SUBWAY	SUTTEE		TAPPED
STREAM	SUCHOU	SUTURE	T	TAPPER
STREET	SUCKED	SVELTE	TABARD	TAPPET
STRESS	SUCKER	SWABIA	TABBED	TARGET
STREWN	SUCKLE	SWAGER	TABLED	TARIFF
STRICK	SUDDEN	SWAINS	TABLES	TARMAC
STRICT	SUFFER	SWAMIS	TABLET	TAROTS
STRIDE	SUFFIX	SWAMPS	TABOOS	TARPAN
STRIFE	SUGARS	SWAMPY	TABRIZ	TARPON
STRIKE	SUGARY	SWANKS	TACKED	TARRED
STRING	SUITED	SWANKY	TACKER	TARSAL

TARSUS	TEMUCO	THEMES	TICKLE	TITANS
TARTAN	TENACE	THENAR	TIDBIT	TITBIT
TARTAR	TENANT	THENCE	TIDDLY	TITCHY
TARTLY	TENDED	THEORY	TIDIED	TITFER
TASKER	TENDER	THERMS	TIDIER	TITHER
TASMAN	TENDON	THESES	TIDILY	TITHES
TASSEL	TENETS	THESIS	TIDING	TITLED
TASTED	TENNER	THETIC	TIE-DYE	TITLES
TASTER	TENNIS	THIEVE	TIE-INS	TITTER
TASTES	TENONS	THIGHS	TIEPIN	TITTLE
TATARY	TENORS	THINGS	TIERCE	TITTUP
TATTED	TENPIN	THINLY	TIE-UPS	TMESIS
TATTER	TENREC	THIRDS	TIFFIN	TOASTS
TATTLE	TENSED	THIRST	TIFLIS	TOBAGO
TATTOO	TENSER	THIRTY	TIGERS	TOBRUK
TAUGHT	TENSES	THOLOS	TIGHTS	TOCSIN
TAUNTS	TENSOR	THONGS	TIGRIS	TODDLE
TAURUS	TENTER	THORAX	TILDES	TOE CAP
TAUTEN	TENTHS	THORIC	TILERS	TOEING
TAUTER	TENURE	THORNS	TILING	TOFFEE
TAUTLY	TENUTO	THORNY	TILLED	TOGGED
TAUTOG	TEPEES	THORON	TILLER	TOGGLE
TAVERN	TEPEFY	THOUGH	TILTED	TOILED
TAWDRY	TERBIC	THRALL	TILTER	TOILER
TAXEME	TERCEL	THRASH	TIMBAL	TOILET
TAXIED	TERCET	THREAD	TIMBER	TOKENS
TAXING	TEREDO	THREAT	TIMBRE	TOLLED
TAXMAN	TERETE	THREES	TIMELY	TOLUCA
TAXMEN	TERGAL	THRESH	TIMERS	TOLUYL
T-BONES	TERGUM	THRICE	TIMING	TOMATO
TEABAG	TERMED	THRIFT	TINCAL	TOMBAC
TEACUP	TERMLY	THRILL	TINDER	TOMBOY
TEAMED	TERMOR	THRIPS	TINEAL	TOMCAT
TEAPOT	TERRET	THRIVE	TINEID	TOM-TOM
TEAPOY	TERROR	THROAT	TINGED	TONGAN
TEARER	TESTED	THROBS	TINGLE	TONGUE
TEASED	TESTER	THROES	TINGLY	TONICS
TEASEL	TESTES	THRONE	TIN GOD	TONING
TEASER	TESTIS	THRONG	TIN HAT	TONKIN
TEASES	TETCHY	THROVE	TINIER	TONNES
TEDDER	TETHER	THROWN	TINKER	TONSIL
TEDIUM	TETRAD	THROWS	TINKLE	TOOLED
TEEING	TETRYL	THRUSH	TINKLY	TOOLER
TEEMED	TETTER	THRUST	TINNED	TOOTED
TEEPEE	TETUAN	THUMBS	TIN-POT	TOOTER
TEETER	TEUTON	THUMPS	TINSEL	TOOTHY
TEETHE	THAMES	THWACK	TINTED	TOOTLE
TEFLON	THANES	THWART	TIP-OFF	TOP DOG
TEGMEN	THANKS	THYMIC	TIPPED	TOPEES
TELEDU	THATCH	THYMOL	TIPPER	TOPEKA
TELIAL	THAWED	THYMUS	TIPPET	TOP HAT
TELIUM	THAWER	THYRSE	TIPPLE	TOPHUS
TELLER	THECAL	TIARAS	TIPTOE	TOPICS
TELPAL	THEFTS	TIBIAE	TIP-TOP	TOPPED
TELSON	THEGNS	TIBIAS	TIRADE	TOPPER
TEMPED	THEINE	TICINO	TIRANA	TOPPLE
TEMPER	THEIRS	TICKED	TIRING	TORBAY
TEMPLE	THEISM	TICKER	TISANE	TORERO
TEMPOS	THEIST	TICKET	TISSUE	TORIES

TOROID	TREATY	TRUDGE	TURN-ON	ULCERS
TOROSE	TREBLE	TRUEST	TURN-UP	ULLAGE
TORPID	TREBLY	TRUISM	TURRET	ULSTER
TORPOR	TREMOR	TRUMPS	TURTLE	ULTIMA
TORQUE	TRENCH	TRUNKS	TURVES	UMBRAL
TORRID	TRENDS	TRUSTS	TUSCAN	UMBRIA
TORSOS	TRENDY	TRUSTY	TUSCHE	UMLAUT
TOSSED	TREPAN	TRUTHS	TUSHES	UMPIRE
TOSSER	TRESSY	TRYING	TUSKER	UNABLE
TOSSES	TRIADS	TRY-OUT	TUSSAH	UNBELT
TOSS-UP	TRIALS	TRYSTS	TUSSIS	UNBEND
TOTALS	TRIBAL	T-SHIRT	TUSSLE	UNBENT
TOTEMS	TRIBES	TSINAN	TUTORS	UNBIND
TOTING	TRICES	TSONGA	TUTSAN	UNBOLT
TOTTED	TRICKS	TSWANA	TUT-TUT	UNBORN
TOTTER	TRICKY	TUAREG	TUXEDO	UNCIAL
TOUCAN	TRICOT	TUBBED	TUYERE	UNCLAD
TOUCHE	TRIERS	TUBERS	TWANGS	UNCLES
TOUCHY	TRIFID	TUBING	TWANGY	UNCLOG
TOULON	TRIFLE	TUBULE	TWEAKS	UNCOIL
TOUPEE	TRIGER	TUCKED	TWEEDS	UNCORK
TOURED	TRIKES	TUCKER	TWEEDY	UNCURL
TOURER	TRILBY	TUCK-IN	TWEETS	UNDIES
TOUSLE	TRILLS	TUCSON	TWELVE	UNDOER
TOUTED	TRIMER	TUFFET	TWENTY	UNDONE
TOWAGE	TRIMLY	TUFTED	TWERPS	UNDULY
TOWBAR	TRINAL	TUFTER	TWIGGY	UNEASE
TOWELS	TRIODE	TUGGED	TWILIT	UNEASY
TOWERS	TRIOSE	TUGGER	TWINED	UNESCO
TOWHEE	TRIPLE	TULIPS	TWINER	UNEVEN
TOWING	TRIPOD	TUMBLE	TWINGE	UNFAIR
TOWNEE	TRIPOS	TUMEFY	TWIRLS	UNFOLD
TOXINS	TRITON	TUMOUR	TWIRLY	UNFURL
TOXOID	TRIUNE	TUMULI	TWIRPS	UNGUAL
TOYAMA	TRIVET	TUMULT	TWISTS	UNGUIS
TOYING	TRIVIA	TUNDRA	TWISTY	UNGULA
TRACED	TROCAR	TUNERS	TWITCH	UNHAIR
TRACER	TROCHE	TUNE-UP	TWO-BIT	UNHAND
TRACES	TROGON	TUNGUS	TWO-PLY	UNHOLY
TRACKS	TROIKA	TUNICA	TWO-WAY	UNHOOK
TRACTS	TROJAN	TUNICS	TYCOON	UNICEF
TRADED	TROLLS	TUNING	TYMPAN	UNIONS
TRADER	TROMPE	TUNNEL	TYPHUS	UNIPOD
TRADES	TROOPS	TUPELO	TYPIFY	UNIQUE
TRAGAL	TROPES	TUPPED	TYPING	UNISEX
TRAGIC	TROPHY	TURBAN	TYPIST	UNISON
TRAGUS	TROPIC	TURBID	TYRANT	UNITED
TRAILS	TROPPO	TURBIT	TYRONE	UNITER
TRAINS	TROTHS	TURBOT	TYUMEN	UNJUST
TRAITS	TROTYL	TUREEN		UNKIND
TRAMPS	TROUGH	TURFED	U	UNKNIT
TRANCE	TROUPE	TURGID	U-BOATS	UNLACE
TRANNY	TROUTS	TURGOR	UDDERS	UNLAID
TRASHY	TROVER	TURION	UDMURT	UNLASH
TRAUMA	TROVES	TURKEY	UGANDA	UNLEAD
TRAVEL	TROWEL	TURKIC	UGLIER	UNLESS
TRAWLS	TRUANT	TURNED	UGLIFY	UNLIKE
TREADS	TRUCES	TURNER	UGRIAN	UNLIVE
TREATS	TRUCKS	TURNIP	UJJAIN	UNLOAD

UNLOCK	UPSHOT	VALUER	VERSES	VITALS
UNMADE	UPSIDE	VALUES	VERSOS	VITRIC
UNMAKE	UPTAKE	VALVES	VERSUS	VIVACE
UNMASK	UPTILT	VANDAL	VERTEX	VIVIFY
UNMOOR	UPTOWN	VANISH	VERVET	VIXENS
UNPACK	UPTURN	VANITY	VESICA	VIZIER
UNPAID	UPWARD	VAPOUR	VESPER	V-NECKS
UNPICK	UPWIND	VARIED	VESPID	VOCABS
UNPLUG	URACIL	VARLET	VESSEL	VOCALS
UNREAD	URALIC	VASSAL	VESTAL	VOGUES
UNREAL	URANIC	VASTLY	VESTED	VOICED
UNREST	URANUS	VAULTS	VESTRY	VOICER
UNRIPE	URANYL	VAUNTS	VETOED	VOICES
UNROLL	URATIC	VECTOR	VETOER	VOIDED
UNRULY	URBANE	VEERED	VETOES	VOIDER
UNSAFE	URCHIN	VEGANS	VETTED	VOLANT
UNSAID	UREASE	VEILED	VEXING	VOLLEY
UNSEAL	UREIDE	VEILER	VIABLE	VOLUME
UNSEAM	URETER	VEINAL	VIABLY	VOLUTE
UNSEAT	URETIC	VEINED	VIANDS	VOLVOX
UNSEEN	URGENT	VELARS	VIBIST	VOODOO
UNSHIP	URGING	VELATE	VIBRIO	VORTEX
UNSNAP	URINAL	VELCRO	VICARS	VOSGES
UNSTEP	UROPOD	VELLUM	VICTIM	VOSTOK
UNSTOP	URSINE	VELOCE	VICTOR	VOTARY
UNSUNG	URTEXT	VELOUR	VICUNA	VOTERS
UNSURE	USABLE	VELURE	VIDEOS	VOTING
UNTIDY	USAGES	VELVET	VIENNA	VOTIVE
UNTIED	USANCE	VENDED	VIENNE	VOTYAK
UNTOLD	USEFUL	VENDEE	VIEWED	VOWELS
UNTRUE	USHERS	VENDOR	VIEWER	VOWING
UNTUCK	USURER	VENEER	VIGILS	VOX POP
UNUSED	UTAHAN	VENERY	VIGOUR	VOYAGE
UNVEIL	UTERUS	VENETO	VIKING	VOYEUR
UNWARY	UTMOST	VENIAL	VILELY	V-SIGNS
UNWELL	UTOPIA	VENICE	VILEST	VULGAR
UNWEPT	U-TURNS	VENIRE	VILIFY	VULVAE
UNWIND	UVULAE	VENOSE	VILLAS	VULVAL
UNWISE	UVULAR	VENOUS	VILLUS	VULVAS
UNWRAP	UVULAS	VENTED	VINERY	
UNYOKE		VENTER	VINOUS	W
UPBEAT	V	VENUES	VINYLS	WADDLE
UPCAST	VACANT	VENULE	VIOLAS	WADERS
UPDATE	VACATE	VERBAL	VIOLET	WADGES
UPHELD	VACUUM	VERBID	VIOLIN	WADING
UPHILL	VADOSE	VERDIN	VIPERS	WAFERS
UPHOLD	VAGARY	VERGED	VIRAGO	WAFFLE
UPHROE	VAGINA	VERGER	VIRGIN	WAFTED
UPKEEP	VAINER	VERGES	VIRGOS	WAFTER
UPLAND	VAINLY	VERIFY	VIRILE	WAGERS
UPLIFT	VALAIS	VERILY	VIRTUE	WAGGED
UPPERS	VALETS	VERISM	VISAED	WAGGLE
UPPISH	VALGUS	VERIST	VISAGE	WAGGLY
UPPITY	VALINE	VERITY	VISCID	WAGING
UPREAR	VALISE	VERMIN	VISION	WAGONS
UPRISE	VALIUM	VERMIS	VISITS	WAILED
UPROAR	VALLEY	VERNAL	VISORS	WAILER
UPROOT	VALOUR	VERONA	VISTAS	WAISTS
UPSETS	VALUED	VERSED	VISUAL	WAITED

WAITER	WATUSI	WHIFFY	WINGER	WRISTS
WAIVED	WAVIER	WHILED	WINGES	WRISTY
WAIVER	WAVILY	WHILST	WINING	WRITER
WAKING	WAVING	WHIMSY	WINKED	WRITHE
WALKED	WAXIER	WHINED	WINKER	WRONGS
WALKER	WAXILY	WHINER	WINKLE	WRYEST
WALK-IN	WAXING	WHINES	WINNER	WRYING
WALK-ON	WAYLAY	WHINGE	WINNOW	WYVERN
WALK-UP	WAY-OUT	WHINNY	WINTER	
WALLAH	WEAKEN	WHIPPY	WINTRY	X
WALLED	WEAKER	WHIRLS	WIPING	XENIAL
WALLET	WEAKLY	WHISKS	WIRIER	XEROMA
WALLOP	WEALTH	WHISKY	WIRILY	XHOSAN
WALLOW	WEANED	WHITEN	WIRING	XMASES
WALNUT	WEAPON	WHITER	WIRRAL	X-RAYED
WALRUS	WEARER	WHITES	WISDOM	XYLENE
WAMPUM	WEASEL	WHOLLY	WISELY	XYLOID
WANDER	WEAVER	WHOOPS	WISEST	XYLOSE
WANGLE	WEAVES	WHOOSH	WISHED	XYSTER
WANING	WEBBED	WHORES	WISHER	
WANKED	WEDDED	WHORLS	WISHES	Y
WANKER	WEDELN	WHYDAH	WITHAL	YACHTS
WANNED	WEDGED	WICKED	WITHER	YAKKED
WANNER	WEDGES	WICKER	WITHIN	YAMMER
WANT AD	WEEDED	WICKET	WIZARD	YANKED
WANTED	WEEDER	WIDELY	WOBBLE	YANKEE
WANTER	WEEING	WIDEST	WOBBLY	YAPPED
WANTON	WEEKLY	WIDGET	WOEFUL	YAPPER
WAPITI	WEEPER	WIDISH	WOLFED	YARNED
WARBLE	WEEVER	WIDOWS	WOLVER	YARROW
WAR CRY	WEEVIL	WIDTHS	WOLVES	YAUPON
WARDED	WEE-WEE	WIELDY	WOMBAT	YAUTIA
WARDEN	WEIGHT	WIFELY	WONDER	YAWING
WARDER	WEIRDO	WIGEON	WONSAN	YAWNED
WARIER	WELDED	WIGGED	WONTED	YAWNER
WARILY	WELDER	WIGGLE	WOODED	YEARLY
WARMED	WELKIN	WIGGLY	WOODEN	YEASTY
WARMER	WELKOM	WIGHTS	WOOERS	YELLED
WARMLY	WELLED	WIGWAG	WOOFER	YELLER
WARMTH	WELTER	WIGWAM	WOOING	YELLOW
WARM-UP	WENDED	WILDER	WOOLLY	YELPED
WARNED	WESTER	WILDLY	WORDED	YELPER
WARNER	WETHER	WILFUL	WORKED	YEMENI
WARPED	WETTED	WILIER	WORKER	YENTAI
WARPER	WETTER	WILLED	WORLDS	YEOMAN
WARRED	WHACKS	WILLER	WORMED	YEOMEN
WARREN	WHALER	WILLET	WORMER	YES-MAN
WARSAW	WHALES	WILLOW	WORSEN	YES-MEN
WARTED	WHARFS	WILTED	WORTHY	YIELDS
WASHED	WHARVE	WIMBLE	WOUNDS	YIPPEE
WASHER	WHEELS	WIMPLE	WOWING	YODELS
WASHES	WHEEZE	WINCED	WRAITH	YOGISM
WASHIN	WHEEZY	WINCER	WRASSE	YOKELS
WASTED	WHELKS	WINCES	WREATH	YOKING
WASTER	WHELPS	WINCEY	WRECKS	YONDER
WASTES	WHENCE	WINDED	WRENCH	YORKER
WATERS	WHERRY	WINDER	WRETCH	YORUBA
WATERY	WHEYEY	WINDOW	WRIEST	YOUTHS
WATTLE	WHIFFS	WINGED	WRIGHT	YOWLED

YOWLER	ZAGREB	ZEPHYR	ZIPPER	ZOOMED
YTTRIA	ZAMBIA	ZEROED	ZIRCON	ZOSTER
YTTRIC	ZANIER	ZEROES	ZITHER	ZOYSIA
YUCCAS	ZANILY	ZEUGMA	ZODIAC	ZURICH
YUNNAN	ZAPPED	ZIGZAG	ZOMBIE	ZYGOMA
YUPPIE	ZAREBA	ZINCIC	ZONATE	ZYGOSE
	ZEALOT	ZINCKY	ZONING	ZYGOTE
Z	ZEBRAS	ZINNIA	ZONKED	ZYMASE
ZABRZE	ZENIST	ZIPPED	ZONULE	ZYRIAN
ZAFFER	ZENITH			

A	ACCUSER	ADJURED	AIRBASE	ALIQUOT
AALBORG	ACERATE	ADJURER	AIRBEDS	ALIUNDE
ABALONE	ACERBIC	ADMIRAL	AIR-COOL	ALKALIC
ABANDON	ACEROSE	ADMIRED	AIRCREW	ALKALIS
ABASHED	ACETATE	ADMIRER	AIRDROP	ALKANET
ABASING	ACETIFY	ADOPTED	AIRFLOW	ALLAYED
ABATING	ACETONE	ADORING	AIRGLOW	ALLEGED
ABAXIAL	ACETOUS	ADORNED	AIRGUNS	ALLEGRO
ABDOMEN	ACHAEAN	ADRENAL	AIRIEST	ALLELIC
ABETTED	ACHIEVE	ADULATE	AIRINGS	ALLERGY
ABETTOR	ACICULA	ADVANCE	AIRLANE	ALLHEAL
ABEYANT	ACIDIFY	ADVENTS	AIRLESS	ALLONYM
ABFARAD	ACIDITY	ADVERBS	AIRLIFT	ALLOWED
ABHENRY	ACNODAL	ADVERSE	AIRLINE	ALLOYED
ABIDING	ACOLYTE	ADVICES	AIRLOCK	ALLSEED
ABIDJAN	ACONITE	ADVISED	AIRMAIL	ALL-STAR
ABILITY	ACOUCHI	ADVISER	AIRPORT	ALL-TIME
ABIOSIS	ACQUIRE	AEGISES	AIR RAID	ALLUDED
ABJURED	ACREAGE	AEONIAN	AIRSHIP	ALLURED
ABJURER	ACRILAN	AERATED	AIRSICK	ALLURER
ABLATOR	ACROBAT	AERATOR	AIRWAYS	ALLUVIA
ABOLISH	ACROGEN	AERIALS	AITCHES	ALLYING
ABORTED	ACRONYM	AEROBIC	AJACCIO	ALMA-ATA
ABRADED	ACROTER	AEROGEL	ALABAMA	ALMANAC
ABRADER	ACRYLIC	AEROSOL	ALAGOAS	ALMERIA
ABREACT	ACRYLYL	AETOLIA	A LA MODE	ALMONDS
ABREAST	ACTABLE	AFFABLE	ALANINE	ALMONER
ABRIDGE	ACTINAL	AFFABLY	ALARMED	ALOETIC
ABRUZZI	ACTINIA	AFFAIRE	ALASKAN	ALOOFLY
ABSCESS	ACTINIC	AFFAIRS	ALBANIA	ALPACAS
ABSCISE	ACTINON	AFFIXED	ALBERTA	ALPHORN
ABSCOND	ACTIONS	AFFIXES	ALBINIC	ALREADY
ABSENCE	ACTRESS	AFFLICT	ALBINOS	ALRIGHT
ABSINTH	ACTUARY	AFFRAYS	ALBITIC	ALSO-RAN
ABSOLVE	ACTUATE	AFFRONT	ALBUMEN	ALTERED
ABSTAIN	ACULEUS	AFGHANS	ALBUMIN	ALTHAEA
ABUSING	ACUTELY	AFRICAN	ALCAZAR	ALTHING
ABUSIVE	ACYCLIC	AGAINST	ALCHEMY	ALTHORN
ABUTTAL	ADAGIOS	AGAMETE	ALCOHOL	ALUMNAE
ABUTTED	ADAMANT	AGEISTS	ALCOVES	ALUMNUS
ABUTTER	ADAMAWA	AGELESS	AL DENTE	ALUNDUM
ABYSMAL	ADAPTED	AGENDAS	ALEMBIC	ALUNITE
ABYSSAL	ADAPTER	AGENDUM	ALERTED	ALYSSUM
ABYSSES	ADAXIAL	AGGRADE	ALERTLY	AMALGAM
ACACIAS	ADDENDA	AGGRESS	A LEVELS	AMANITA
ACADEMY	ADDICTS	AGILELY	ALFALFA	AMASSED
ACADIAN	ADDRESS	AGILITY	ALGEBRA	AMASSER
ACAROID	ADDUCED	AGITATE	ALGERIA	AMATEUR
ACAUDAL	ADENINE	AGITATO	ALGIERS	AMATORY
ACCEDED	ADENOID	AGNOMEN	AL HUFUF	AMAZING
ACCEDER	ADENOMA	AGONIES	ALIASES	AMAZONS
ACCENTS	ADEPTLY	AGONIST	ALIDADE	AMBIENT
ACCLAIM	ADHERED	AGONIZE	ALIENEE	AMBLING
ACCORDS	ADIPOSE	AGRAFFE	ALIENOR	AMBOYNA
ACCOUNT	ADIVASI	AGRAPHA	ALIFORM	AMENDED
ACCRETE	ADJOINT	AGROUND	ALIGARH	AMENDER
ACCRUAL	ADJOURN	AILERON	ALIGNED	AMENITY
ACCRUED	ADJUDGE	AILMENT	ALIMENT	AMENTIA
ACCUSED	ADJUNCT	AIMLESS	ALIMONY	AMERICA

AMHARIC	ANGLIAN	ANYWISE	ARCADES	ASCENTS
AMIABLE	ANGLIFY	APAGOGE	ARCADIA	ASCETIC
AMIABLY	ANGLING	APATITE	ARCANUM	ASCITES
AMMETER	ANGOLAN	APELIKE	ARCHAIC	ASCITIC
AMMONAL	ANGORAS	APETALY	ARCHERS	ASCRIBE
AMMONIA	ANGRIER	APHAGIA	ARCHERY	ASEPSIS
AMMONIC	ANGRILY	APHASIA	ARCHINE	ASEPTIC
AMNESIA	ANGUINE	APHESIS	ARCHING	ASEXUAL
AMNESTY	ANGUISH	APHONIA	ARCHIVE	ASHAMED
AMOEBAE	ANGULAR	APHONIC	ARCHWAY	ASHANTI
AMOEBAS	ANILINE	APHOTIC	ARCUATE	ASHIEST
AMOEBIC	ANILITY	APHYLLY	ARDECHE	ASHTRAY
AMORIST	ANIMALS	APIEZON	ARDENCY	ASIATIC
AMOROSO	ANIMATE	APLASIA	ARDUOUS	ASININE
AMOROUS	ANIMATO	APLENTY	AREAWAY	ASKANCE
AMOUNTS	ANIMISM	APLITIC	ARENITE	ASOCIAL
AMPHORA	ANIMIST	APOCARP	AREOLAR	ASPECTS
AMPLIFY	ANIONIC	APOCOPE	ARGONNE	ASPERSE
AMPOULE	ANISEED	APOGAMY	ARGOTIC	ASPHALT
AMPULLA	ANISOLE	APOGEES	ARGUING	ASPIRED
AMPUTEE	ANKLETS	APOLOGY	ARIDITY	ASPIRER
AMULETS	ANNATES	APOLUNE	ARIETTA	ASPIRIN
AMUSING	ANNATTO	APOMICT	ARISING	ASSAULT
AMYLASE	ANNELID	APOSTIL	ARIZONA	ASSAYED
AMYLENE	ANNEXED	APOSTLE	ARMADAS	ASSAYER
AMYLOID	ANNEXES	APOTHEM	ARMBAND	ASSEGAI
AMYLOSE	ANNOYED	APPAREL	ARMENIA	ASSHOLE
ANAEMIA	ANNUALS	APPEALS	ARMFULS	ASSIZES
ANAEMIC	ANNUITY	APPEASE	ARMHOLE	ASSUAGE
ANAGOGE	ANNULAR	APPLAUD	ARMIGER	ASSUMED
ANAGRAM	ANNULET	APPLIED	ARMLESS	ASSUMER
ANAHEIM	ANNULUS	APPLIER	ARMOIRE	ASSURED
ANALOGY	ANODIZE	APPOINT	ARMOURY	ASSURER
ANALYSE	ANODYNE	APPRISE	ARMPITS	ASSYRIA
ANALYST	ANOMALY	APPROVE	ARMREST	ASTATIC
ANAPEST	ANORAKS	APPULSE	AROUSAL	ASTOUND
ANARCHY	ANOSMIA	APRAXIA	AROUSED	ASTRIDE
ANATASE	ANOTHER	APRAXIC	AROUSER	ASTROID
ANATOMY	ANSWERS	APRICOT	ARRAIGN	ASTYLAR
ANCHORS	ANTACID	A PRIORI	ARRANGE	ASUNDER
ANCHOVY	ANTEFIX	APROPOS	ARRAYAL	ASYLUMS
ANCHUSA	ANTEING	APSIDAL	ARRAYED	ATACTIC
ANCIENT	ANTENNA	APTERAL	ARREARS	ATAVISM
ANCONAL	ANTHEMS	APTNESS	ARRESTS	ATAVIST
ANDANTE	ANTHERS	AQUARIA	ARRIVAL	ATELIER
ANDIRON	ANTHILL	AQUATIC	ARRIVED	ATHEISM
ANDORRA	ANTHRAX	AQUAVIT	ARRIVER	ATHEIST
ANDROID	ANTIBES	AQUEOUS	ARROWED	ATHLETE
ANEMONE	ANTIGEN	AQUIFER	ARSENAL	ATHWART
ANERGIC	ANTIGUA	ARABIAN	ARSENIC	ATLANTA
ANEROID	ANTIQUE	ARABIST	ART DECO	ATLASES
ANEURIN	ANTLERS	ARACAJU	ARTICLE	ATOMISM
ANGARSK	ANTLION	ARAMAIC	ARTIEST	ATOMIST
ANGELIC	ANTONYM	ARANEID	ARTISAN	ATOMIZE
ANGELUS	ANTWERP	ARAPAHO	ARTISTE	ATONING
ANGERED	ANUROUS	ARAROBA	ARTISTS	ATROPHY
ANGEVIN	ANXIETY	ARBITER	ARTLESS	ATTACHE
ANGINAL	ANXIOUS	ARBOURS	ARTWORK	ATTACKS
ANGIOMA	ANYBODY	ARBUTUS	ASCARID	ATTAINT

ATTEMPT	AWESOME	BALEFUL	BARKING	BAWDILY
ATTIRED	AWFULLY	BALKING	BARMAID	BAWLING
ATTRACT	AWKWARD	BALLADE	BARMIER	BAYAMON
ATTUNED	AWLWORT	BALLADS	BARNAUL	BAYONET
AUBERGE	AWNINGS	BALLAST	BARNEYS	BAYWOOD
AUCTION	AXOLOTL	BALLETS	BARONET	BAZAARS
AUDIBLE	AZIMUTH	BALLOON	BAROQUE	BAZOOKA
AUDIBLY	AZURITE	BALLOTS	BAROTSE	BEACHED
AUDITED	AZYGOUS	BALLS-UP	BARQUES	BEACHES
AUDITOR		BALMIER	BARRACK	BEACONS
AUGITIC	B	BALMILY	BARRAGE	BEADIER
AUGMENT	BABASSU	BALNEAL	BARRELS	BEADILY
AUGURAL	BABBITT	BALONEY	BARRIER	BEADING
AUGURED	BABBLED	BALSAMS	BARRING	BEADLES
AU PAIRS	BABBLER	BALUCHI	BARROWS	BEAGLES
AURALLY	BABOONS	BAMBARA	BARYTES	BEAKERS
AUREATE	BABYING	BAMBINO	BASCULE	BEAMING
AUREOLE	BABYISH	BAMBOOS	BASENJI	BEARDED
AURICLE	BABY-SAT	BANANAS	BASHFUL	BEARERS
AURORAE	BABY-SIT	BANDAGE	BASHING	BEAR HUG
AURORAL	BACCATE	BANDBOX	BASHKIR	BEARING
AURORAS	BACILLI	BANDEAU	BASILAR	BEARISH
AUSPICE	BACKERS	BANDIED	BASILIC	BEASTLY
AUSSIES	BACKING	BANDIER	BASKETS	BEATERS
AUSTERE	BACKLOG	BANDING	BASKING	BEATIFY
AUSTRAL	BACKSAW	BANDITS	BASOTHO	BEATING
AUSTRIA	BACKUPS	BANDUNG	BAS-RHIN	BEATNIK
AUTARKY	BACULUM	BANEFUL	BASSEIN	BEAVERS
AUTHORS	BADAJOZ	BANGERS	BASSETS	BECAUSE
AUTOCUE	BAD DEBT	BANGING	BASSIST	BEDBUGS
AUTOMAT	BAD FORM	BANGKOK	BASSOON	BEDDING
AUTOPSY	BADGERS	BANGLES	BASTARD	BEDEVIL
AUTUMNS	BADNESS	BANGORS	BASTING	BEDEWED
AUXESIS	BAFFLED	BANKING	BASTION	BEDLAMS
AVAILED	BAFFLER	BANKSIA	BATCHES	BEDOUIN
AVARICE	BAFFLES	BANNERS	BATFISH	BEDPANS
AVATARS	BAGANDA	BANNING	BATHERS	BEDPOST
AVENGED	BAGASSE	BANNOCK	BATHING	BEDRAIL
AVENGER	BAGGAGE	BANQUET	BATH MAT	BEDROCK
AVENUES	BAGGIER	BANSHEE	BATHTUB	BEDROOM
AVERAGE	BAGGILY	BANTAMS	BATHYAL	BEDSIDE
AVERRED	BAGGING	BANTOID	BATISTE	BEDSORE
AVERTED	BAGHDAD	BANYANS	BATSMAN	BEDTIME
AVESTAN	BAG LADY	BAPTISM	BATSMEN	BEECHES
AVEYRON	BAGPIPE	BAPTIST	BATTENS	BEEFIER
AVIATOR	BAGWORM	BAPTIZE	BATTERS	BEEFING
AVIDITY	BAHAISM	BARBARY	BATTERY	BEEF TEA
AVIGNON	BAHAIST	BARBATE	BATTIER	BEEHIVE
AVIONIC	BAHAMAS	BARBELL	BATTING	BEELINE
AVOCADO	BAHRAIN	BARBERS	BATTLED	BEESWAX
AVOIDED	BAILEYS	BARBULE	BATTLES	BEETFLY
AVOIDER	BAILIFF	BARCHAN	BATWING	BEETLED
AVOWALS	BAILING	BAR CODE	BAUBLES	BEETLES
AVOWING	BAINITE	BARENTS	BAUHAUS	BEGGARS
AWAITED	BAITING	BARGAIN	BAULKED	BEGGARY
AWAKING	BALANCE	BARGEES	BAUTZEN	BEGGING
AWARDED	BALATON	BARGING	BAUXITE	BEGONIA
AWARDEE	BALCONY	BARILLA	BAVARIA	BEGUILE
AWARDER	BALDING	BARKERS	BAWDIER	BEHAVED

BEHINDS	BETHINK	BIOCIDE	BLEEDER	B-MOVIES
BEJEWEL	BETIDED	BIODATA	BLEEPED	BOARDED
BELATED	BETIMES	BIOHERM	BLEEPER	BOARDER
BELAYED	BETOKEN	BIOLOGY	BLEMISH	BOARISH
BELCHED	BETROTH	BIOMASS	BLENDED	BOASTED
BELCHES	BETTERS	BIONICS	BLENDER	BOASTER
BELFORT	BETTING	BIOPICS	BLESBOK	BOATERS
BELGIAN	BETWEEN	BIOPTIC	BLESSED	BOATING
BELGIUM	BETWIXT	BIOTITE	BLETHER	BOATMAN
BELIEFS	BEVELED	BIOTOPE	BLEWITS	BOATMEN
BELIEVE	BEWITCH	BIOTYPE	BLIGHTS	BOBBERY
BELLBOY	BEYOGLU	BIPLANE	BLINDED	BOBBIES
BELLEEK	BEZIQUE	BIPOLAR	BLINDLY	BOBBING
BELLIES	BIASING	BIRCHED	BLINKED	BOBBINS
BELLOWS	BIASSED	BIRCHES	BLINKER	BOBBLES
BELOVED	BIAXIAL	BIRD DOG	BLISTER	BOBSLED
BELTING	BIBCOCK	BIRDIES	BLITZED	BOBSTAY
BELTWAY	BIBELOT	BIRETTA	BLITZES	BOBTAIL
BELYING	BICYCLE	BISCUIT	BLOATED	BODICES
BEMUSED	BIDDING	BISHOPS	BLOATER	BODKINS
BENARES	BIFFING	BISMUTH	BLOCKED	BOFFINS
BENCHER	BIFILAR	BISTORT	BLONDER	BOGGIER
BENCHES	BIFOCAL	BISTROS	BLONDES	BOGGING
BENDING	BIG CATS	BITCHED	BLOODED	BOGGLED
BENEATH	BIG DEAL	BITCHES	BLOOMED	BOHEMIA
BENEFIT	BIG ENDS	BIT PART	BLOOMER	BOILERS
BENELUX	BIGENER	BITTERN	BLOOPER	BOILING
BENGALI	BIG GAME	BITTERS	BLOSSOM	BOLDEST
BENTHOS	BIGGEST	BITTIER	BLOTCHY	BOLEROS
BENZENE	BIGGIES	BITUMEN	BLOTTED	BOLETUS
BENZINE	BIGHEAD	BIVALVE	BLOTTER	BOLIVAR
BENZOIC	BIGHORN	BIVOUAC	BLOUSES	BOLIVIA
BENZOIN	BIG NAME	BIZARRE	BLOW-DRY	BOLLARD
BENZOYL	BIGNESS	BIZERTE	BLOWERS	BOLOGNA
BEQUEST	BIGOTED	BLABBED	BLOWFLY	BOLONEY
BERATED	BIGOTRY	BLABBER	BLOWIER	BOLSHIE
BEREAVE	BIG SHOT	BLACKED	BLOWING	BOLSTER
BERGAMO	BIG TIME	BLACKEN	BLOWOUT	BOLTING
BERMUDA	BIG TOPS	BLACKER	BLOW-UPS	BOLZANO
BERNESE	BIGWIGS	BLACKLY	BLUBBER	BOMBARD
BERRIES	BIJAPUR	BLADDER	BLUE GUM	BOMBAST
BERSEEM	BIKANER	BLAMING	BLUEING	BOMBERS
BERSERK	BIKINIS	BLANDER	BLUE JAY	BOMBING
BERTHED	BILBOES	BLANDLY	BLUE LAW	BONANZA
BESEECH	BILIARY	BLANKET	BLUE-SKY	BONBONS
BESIDES	BILIOUS	BLANKLY	BLUETIT	BONDAGE
BESIEGE	BILKING	BLARING	BLUFFED	BONDING
BESMEAR	BILLETS	BLARNEY	BLUFFER	BONE-DRY
BESPEAK	BILLIES	BLASTED	BLUFFLY	BONESET
BESPOKE	BILLING	BLATANT	BLUNDER	BONFIRE
BESTIAL	BILLION	BLATHER	BLUNGER	BONGOES
BESTING	BILLOWS	BLAUBOK	BLUNTED	BONIEST
BEST MAN	BILLOWY	BLAZERS	BLUNTLY	BONJOUR
BEST-OFF	BILTONG	BLAZING	BLURRED	BONKERS
BESTREW	BIMORPH	BLAZONS	BLURTED	BONNETS
BESTRID	BINDERS	BLEAKER	BLUSHED	BONNIER
BETAINE	BINDERY	BLEAKLY	BLUSHER	BONUSES
BETAKEN	BINDING	BLEATED	BLUSHES	BOOBIES
BETHELS	BINNING	BLEATER	BLUSTER	BOOBING

BOOKEND	BOWSHOT	BRINDLE	BUCKLES	BUNDLER
BOOKING	BOW TIES	BRIOCHE	BUCKRAM	BUNDLES
BOOKISH	BOXCARS	BRISKER	BUCKSAW	BUNGING
BOOKLET	BOXROOM	BRISKET	BUCOLIC	BUNGLED
BOOMING	BOXWOOD	BRISKLY	BUDDIES	BUNGLER
BOORISH	BOYCOTT	BRISTLE	BUDDING	BUNGLES
BOOSTED	BOYHOOD	BRISTLY	BUDGETS	BUNIONS
BOOSTER	BRABANT	BRITISH	BUDGING	BUNKERS
BOOTEES	BRACING	BRITONS	BUFFALO	BUNKING
BOOTING	BRACKEN	BRITTLE	BUFFERS	BUNK-UPS
BOOTLEG	BRACKET	BROADEN	BUFFETS	BUNNIES
BOOZERS	BRADAWL	BROADER	BUFFING	BUNTING
BOOZE-UP	BRAGGED	BROADLY	BUFFOON	BUOYAGE
BOOZIER	BRAGGER	BROCADE	BUGABOO	BUOYANT
BOOZILY	BRAHMAN	BROCKET	BUGANDA	BUOYING
BOOZING	BRAIDED	BROGUES	BUGBANE	BURBLED
BOPPING	BRAIDER	BROILED	BUGBEAR	BURBLER
BORACIC	BRAILLE	BROILER	BUG-EYED	BURDENS
BORAZON	BRAINED	BROKERS	BUGGERS	BURDOCK
BORDERS	BRAISED	BROMATE	BUGGERY	BUREAUX
BORDURE	BRAKING	BROMIDE	BUGGIES	BURETTE
BOREDOM	BRAMBLE	BROMINE	BUGGING	BURGEON
BORNEEL	BRAMLEY	BROMISM	BUGLERS	BURGERS
BORNITE	BRANDED	BRONCHI	BUGLOSS	BURGESS
BOROUGH	BRASHER	BRONCOS	BUILDER	BURGHAL
BORSCHT	BRASHLY	BRONZED	BUILDUP	BURGHER
BORSTAL	BRASSES	BRONZES	BUILT-IN	BURGLAR
BORZOIS	BRASSIE	BROODED	BUILT-UP	BURGLED
BOSCAGE	BRAVADO	BROODER	BUKHARA	BURIALS
BOSNIAN	BRAVAIS	BROOKED	BULBOUS	BURLIER
BOSSIER	BRAVELY	BROTHEL	BULGIER	BURMESE
BOSSILY	BRAVERY	BROTHER	BULGING	BURNERS
BOSSING	BRAVEST	BROWNED	BULIMIA	BURNING
BOTCHED	BRAVING	BROWNER	BULKIER	BURNISH
BOTCHER	BRAVURA	BROWNIE	BULKILY	BURNOUS
BOTCH-UP	BRAWLED	BROWSED	BULKING	BURNOUT
BOTTLED	BRAWLER	BROWSER	BULLACE	BURPING
BOTTLES	BRAYING	BRUCINE	BULLATE	BURRING
BOTTOMS	BRAZIER	BRUISED	BULLDOG	BURRITO
BOTTROP	BREADTH	BRUISER	BULLETS	BURROWS
BOTULIN	BREAKER	BRUISES	BULLIED	BURSARS
BOUCHEE	BREAK-IN	BRUITED	BULLIES	BURSARY
BOUDOIR	BREATHE	BRUMOUS	BULLION	BURSTER
BOULDER	BREATHY	BRUSHED	BULLISH	BURTHEN
BOUNCED	BRECCIA	BRUSHER	BULLOCK	BURTONS
BOUNCER	BREEDER	BRUSHES	BULRUSH	BURUNDI
BOUNCES	BRENNER	BRUSH-UP	BULWARK	BURWEED
BOUNDED	BREVIER	BRUSQUE	BUMBLED	BURYING
BOUNDEN	BREVITY	BRUTISH	BUMBLER	BUSBIES
BOUNDER	BREWAGE	BRYANSK	BUMBOAT	BUS BOYS
BOUQUET	BREWERY	BUBBLED	BUMMING	BUSHELS
BOURBON	BREWING	BUBBLER	BUMPERS	BUSHIER
BOURDON	BRIBERY	BUBBLES	BUMPIER	BUSHING
BOUYANT	BRICOLE	BUBONIC	BUMPILY	BUSHIRE
BOWHEAD	BRIDOON	BUCKETS	BUMPING	BUSHMAN
BOWKNOT	BRIGADE	BUCKEYE	BUMPKIN	BUSHPIG
BOWLERS	BRIGAND	BUCKING	BUNCHED	BUSHTIT
BOWLINE	BRIMFUL	BUCKLED	BUNCHES	BUSIEST
BOWLING	BRIMMER	BUCKLER	BUNDLED	BUSKERS

BUSKING	CADMIUM	CAMPERS	CARABID	CARVING
BUSSING	CAESIUM	CAMPHOR	CARACAL	CASCADE
BUS STOP	CAESURA	CAMPING	CARACAS	CASCARA
BUSTARD	CAFTANS	CAMPION	CARACUL	CASEASE
BUSTERS	CAGIEST	CAMWOOD	CARAFES	CASEATE
BUSTIER	CAGOULE	CANAPES	CARAMBA	CASEOSE
BUSTING	CAHOOTS	CANARDS	CARAMEL	CASEOUS
BUSTLED	CAIQUES	CANASTA	CARAVAN	CASERTA
BUSTLER	CAISSON	CANCANS	CARAVEL	CASHEWS
BUSTLES	CAJOLED	CANCERS	CARAWAY	CASHIER
BUST-UPS	CAJUPUT	CANDELA	CARBENE	CASHING
BUSYING	CALAMUS	CANDIED	CARBIDE	CASINGS
BUTANOL	CALCIFY	CANDIES	CARBINE	CASINOS
BUTCHER	CALCINE	CANDLER	CARBONS	CASKETS
BUTLERS	CALCITE	CANDLES	CARBOYS	CASPIAN
BUTLERY	CALCIUM	CANDOUR	CARCASS	CASQUED
BUTTERY	CALCULI	CANELLA	CARDIAC	CASQUES
BUTTIES	CALDERA	CANINES	CARDING	CASSATA
BUTTING	CALDRON	CANKERS	CARDOON	CASSAVA
BUTTOCK	CALENDS	CANNERY	CAREERS	CASSINO
BUTTONS	CALGARY	CANNIER	CAREFUL	CASSOCK
BUTYRIC	CALIBRE	CANNILY	CARFARE	CASTERS
BUTYRIN	CALICHE	CANNING	CARGOES	CASTILE
BUYOUTS	CALICOS	CANNONS	CARHOPS	CASTING
BUZZARD	CALIPEE	CANNULA	CARIBOU	CASTLED
BUZZERS	CALIPHS	CANONRY	CARIOCA	CASTLES
BUZZING	CALKING	CANOPUS	CARIOLE	CAST-OFF
BYE-BYES	CALLAIS	CANTALA	CARIOUS	CASTORS
BYELOVO	CALLANT	CANTATA	CARLINE	CASUIST
BYGONES	CALL BOX	CANTEEN	CARLING	CATALAN
BY-LINES	CALLBOY	CANTERS	CARMINE	CATALPA
BYRONIC	CALLERS	CANTHUS	CARNAGE	CATANIA
BYWORDS	CALLING	CANTING	CARNIFY	CATARRH
	CALL-INS	CANTONS	CAROLED	CATBIRD
	CALLOUS	CANTORS	CAROLUS	CATBOAT
C	CALMEST	CANVASS	CAROTID	CATCALL
CABARET	CALMING	CANYONS	CAROUSE	CATCHER
CABBAGE	CALOMEL	CANZONA	CARPALE	CATCHES
CABBALA	CALORIC	CANZONE	CAR PARK	CATECHU
CABBIES	CALORIE	CAPABLE	CARPETS	CATERED
CABEZON	CALOTTE	CAPABLY	CARPING	CATERER
CABIMAS	CALTROP	CAP-A-PIE	CAR POOL	CATFISH
CABINET	CALUMNY	CAPELIN	CARPORT	CATHEAD
CABLING	CALVARY	CAPELLA	CARRICK	CATHODE
CABOOSE	CALVING	CAPERED	CARRIED	CATKINS
CAB RANK	CALYCES	CAPITAL	CARRIER	CATLING
CACHETS	CALYCLE	CAPITOL	CARRIES	CATMINT
CACKLED	CALYPSO	CAPORAL	CARRION	CATNAPS
CACKLER	CALYXES	CAPPING	CARROTS	CAT'S-EAR
CACKLES	CAMBERS	CAPRICE	CARROTY	CAT'S EYE
CADAVER	CAMBIAL	CAPSIZE	CARRY-ON	CAT'S PAW
CADDIED	CAMBIST	CAPSTAN	CARSICK	CATSUIT
CADDIES	CAMBIUM	CAPSULE	CARTAGE	CATTALO
CADDISH	CAMBRAI	CAPTAIN	CARTELS	CATTERY
CADELLE	CAMBRIC	CAPTION	CARTERS	CATTIER
CADENCE	CAMELOT	CAPTIVE	CARTING	CATTILY
CADENCY	CAMERAL	CAPTORS	CARTONS	CATTISH
CADENZA	CAMERAS	CAPTURE	CARTOON	CATWALK
CADGERS	CAMP BED	CARABAO	CARVERS	CAUDATE

CAULINE	CHAFFED	CHASING	CHILIES	CICHLID
CAULKED	CHAFFER	CHASMAL	CHILLED	CILIARY
CAULKER	CHAFING	CHASSIS	CHILLUM	CILIATE
CAUSING	CHAGRIN	CHASTEN	CHILUNG	CIMBRIC
CAUSTIC	CHAINED	CHASTER	CHIMERA	CINDERS
CAUTERY	CHAIRED	CHATEAU	CHIMERE	CINDERY
CAUTION	CHAISES	CHATTED	CHIMING	CINEMAS
CAVALLA	CHALAZA	CHATTEL	CHIMNEY	CINERIN
CAVALRY	CHALCID	CHATTER	CHINESE	CIPHERS
CAVEATS	CHALDEA	CHAYOTE	CHINKED	CIPOLIN
CAVE-INS	CHALETS	CHEAPEN	CHINOOK	CIRCLED
CAVEMAN	CHALICE	CHEAPER	CHINTZY	CIRCLER
CAVEMEN	CHALKED	CHEAPLY	CHINWAG	CIRCLES
CAVERNS	CHALLAH	CHEATED	CHIPPED	CIRCLET
CAVETTO	CHALLIS	CHEATER	CHIPPER	CIRCUIT
CAVILED	CHALONE	CHECHEN	CHIRPED	CIRQUES
CAYENNE	CHAMBER	CHECKED	CHIRPER	CIRRATE
CEASING	CHAMFER	CHECK-IN	CHIRRUP	CIRSOID
CEDILLA	CHAMOIS	CHECKUP	CHISELS	CISSIES
CEILING	CHAMPAC	CHEDDAR	CHIVIED	CISSOID
CELADON	CHAMPED	CHEEKED	CHLORAL	CISTERN
CELEBES	CHANCED	CHEEPED	CHLORIC	CISTRON
CELESTA	CHANCEL	CHEEPER	CHOC-ICE	CITABLE
CELLARS	CHANCES	CHEERED	CHOCKED	CITADEL
CELLIST	CHANCRE	CHEERIO	CHOCTAW	CITHARA
CELLULE	CHANGED	CHEESES	CHOICER	CITIZEN
CELSIUS	CHANGER	CHEETAH	CHOICES	CITRATE
CEMBALO	CHANGES	CHELATE	CHOKERS	CITRINE
CENACLE	CHANNEL	CHEMISE	CHOKING	CITRONS
CENSORS	CHANSON	CHEMIST	CHOLERA	CIVILLY
CENSUAL	CHANTED	CHENGTU	CHOLINE	CIVVIES
CENSURE	CHANTER	CHEQUER	CHOMPED	CLACKED
CENTAUR	CHANTRY	CHEQUES	CHOOSER	CLADODE
CENTAVO	CHAOTIC	CHERISH	CHOPPED	CLAIMED
CENTERS	CHAPEAU	CHEROOT	CHOPPER	CLAIMER
CENTIME	CHAPELS	CHERUBS	CHORALE	CLAMANT
CENTNER	CHAPLET	CHERVIL	CHORDAL	CLAMBER
CENTRAL	CHAPPAL	CHESTED	CHOREAL	CLAMMED
CENTRED	CHAPPED	CHEVIOT	CHORION	CLAMOUR
CENTRES	CHAPTER	CHEVRON	CHOROID	CLAMPED
CENTRIC	CHARADE	CHEWIER	CHORTLE	CLAMPER
CENTRUM	CHARGED	CHEWING	CHORZOW	CLANGED
CENTURY	CHARGER	CHIANTI	CHOWDER	CLANGER
CEPHEUS	CHARGES	CHIAPAS	CHROMIC	CLANGOR
CERAMIC	CHARIER	CHIASMA	CHROMYL	CLANKED
CERATED	CHARILY	CHIBOUK	CHRONIC	CLAPPED
CEREALS	CHARIOT	CHICAGO	CHRONON	CLAPPER
CEREBRA	CHARITY	CHICANE	CHUCKED	CLAQUES
CERTAIN	CHARKHA	CHICANO	CHUCKLE	CLARIFY
CERTIFY	CHARLIE	CHICKEN	CHUFFED	CLARINO
CERUMEN	CHARMED	CHICORY	CHUGGED	CLARION
CERVINE	CHARMER	CHIDDEN	CHUKCHI	CLARITY
CESSION	CHARNEL	CHIDING	CHUKKER	CLARKIA
CESSPIT	CHARPOY	CHIEFLY	CHUMMED	CLASHED
CESTODE	CHARQUI	CHIFFON	CHURNED	CLASHER
CESTOID	CHARRED	CHIGGER	CHUTNEY	CLASHES
CETOOGY	CHARTED	CHIGNON	CHUVASH	CLASPED
CHABLIS	CHARTER	CHILEAN	CHYMOUS	CLASPER
CHA-CHAS	CHASERS	CHILIAD	CICADAS	CLASSED

CLASSES	CLOUDED	COFFERS	COMMODE	CONJOIN
CLASSIC	CLOUTED	COFFINS	COMMONS	CONJURE
CLASSIS	CLOWNED	COGENCY	COMMUNE	CONKERS
CLASTIC	CLOYING	COGGING	COMMUTE	CONKING
CLATTER	CLUBBED	COGNACS	COMPACT	CONNATE
CLAUSAL	CLUBMAN	COGNATE	COMPANY	CONNECT
CLAUSES	CLUCKED	COGNIZE	COMPARE	CONNING
CLAVATE	CLUMPED	COHABIT	COMPASS	CONNIVE
CLAVIER	CLUNIAC	COHERED	COMPEER	CONNOTE
CLAVIUS	CLUPEID	COHORTS	COMPERE	CONQUER
CLAWING	CLUSTER	COILING	COMPETE	CONSENT
CLAYPAN	CLUTTER	COIMBRA	COMPILE	CONSIGN
CLEANED	CLYPEAL	COINAGE	COMPLEX	CONSIST
CLEANER	CLYPEUS	COINERS	COMPLIN	CONSOLE
CLEANLY	COACHED	COINING	COMPONY	CONSOLS
CLEANSE	COACHES	COLDEST	COMPORT	CONSORT
CLEANUP	COAL GAS	COLDISH	COMPOSE	CONSULS
CLEARED	COALING	COLD WAR	COMPOST	CONSULT
CLEARER	COAL TAR	COLICKY	COMPOTE	CONSUME
CLEARLY	COAMING	COLITIC	COMPUTE	CONTACT
CLEAVED	COARSEN	COLITIS	COMRADE	CONTAIN
CLEAVER	COARSER	COLLAGE	CONATUS	CONTEMN
CLEMENT	COASTAL	COLLARD	CONCAVE	CONTEND
CLERICS	COASTED	COLLARS	CONCEAL	CONTENT
CLERKED	COASTER	COLLATE	CONCEDE	CONTEST
CLICHED	COATING	COLLECT	CONCEIT	CONTEXT
CLICHES	COAXIAL	COLLEEN	CONCEPT	CONTORT
CLICKED	COAXING	COLLEGE	CONCERN	CONTOUR
CLICKER	COBBERS	COLLIDE	CONCERT	CONTROL
CLIENTS	COBBLED	COLLIER	CONCHAL	CONTUSE
CLIMATE	COBBLER	COLLIES	CONCHES	CONVENE
CLIMBED	COBWEBS	COLLOID	CONCISE	CONVENT
CLIMBER	COCAINE	COLLUDE	CONCOCT	CONVERT
CLINGER	COCCOID	COLOBUS	CONCORD	CONVICT
CLINICS	COCCOUS	COLOGNE	CONCUSS	CONVOKE
CLINKED	COCHLEA	COLOMBO	CONDEMN	CONVOYS
CLINKER	COCKADE	COLONEL	CONDIGN	COOKERS
CLIPPED	COCKIER	COLONIC	CONDOLE	COOKERY
CLIPPER	COCKING	COLOSSI	CONDOMS	COOKIES
CLIPPIE	COCKLES	COLOURS	CONDONE	COOKING
CLIQUES	COCKNEY	COLTISH	CONDORS	COOKOUT
CLIQUEY	COCKPIT	COLUMNS	CONDUCE	COOLANT
CLOACAL	COCK-UPS	COMBATS	CONDUCT	COOLERS
CLOAKED	COCONUT	COMBERS	CONDUIT	COOLEST
CLOBBER	COCOONS	COMBINE	CONDYLE	COOLIES
CLOCHES	COCOTTE	COMBING	CONFECT	COOLING
CLOCKED	COCOYAM	COMB-OUT	CONFESS	COOLISH
CLOGGED	CODDLED	COMBUST	CONFIDE	COONTIE
CLOPPED	CODEINE	COMECON	CONFINE	COOPERS
CLOSELY	CODFISH	COMEDIC	CONFIRM	CO-OPTED
CLOSEST	CODGERS	COMFIER	CONFORM	COPAIBA
CLOSETS	CODICES	COMFITS	CONFUSE	COPEPOD
CLOSE-UP	CODICIL	COMFORT	CONFUTE	COPIERS
CLOSING	CODLING	COMFREY	CONGEAL	COPILOT
CLOSURE	COELIAC	COMICAL	CONGEST	COPINGS
CLOTHED	COEQUAL	COMINGS	CONGIUS	COPIOUS
CLOTHES	COERCED	COMMAND	CONICAL	COP-OUTS
CLOTTED	COEVALS	COMMEND	CONIFER	COPPERS
CLOTURE	COEXIST	COMMENT	CONIINE	COPPERY

COPPICE	COSTARD	COWHERD	CREOLES	CRUDEST
COPPING	CO-STARS	COWHIDE	CREOSOL	CRUDITY
COPULAR	COSTATE	COWLICK	CRESSET	CRUELLY
COPYCAT	COSTING	COWLING	CRESTED	CRUELTY
COPYING	COSTIVE	COWPATS	CRETINS	CRUISED
COPYIST	COSTUME	COWRIES	CREVICE	CRUISER
COQUINA	COTE-D'OR	COWSHED	CREW CUT	CRUISES
COQUITO	COTERIE	COWSLIP	CREWING	CRUMBLE
CORACLE	COTIDAL	COXCOMB	CRIBBED	CRUMBLY
CORBEIL	COTINGA	COYNESS	CRICKED	CRUMPET
CORBELS	COTTAGE	COYOTES	CRICKET	CRUMPLE
CORDAGE	COTTONY	COZENED	CRICOID	CRUMPLY
CORDATE	COUCHED	COZENER	CRIMEAN	CRUNCHY
CORDIAL	COUCHER	COZIEST	CRIMPED	CRUNODE
CORDING	COUCHES	CRABBED	CRIMPER	CRUPPER
CORDITE	COUGARS	CRACKED	CRIMPLE	CRUSADE
CORDOBA	COUGHED	CRACKER	CRIMSON	CRUSHED
CORDONS	COULDN'T	CRACKLE	CRINGED	CRUSHES
CORINTH	COULDST	CRACKUP	CRINGLE	CRUSTAL
CORKAGE	COULOIR	CRADLED	CRINITE	CRYBABY
CORKERS	COULOMB	CRADLES	CRINKLE	CRYOGEN
CORKING	COULTER	CRAFTED	CRINKLY	CRYPTAL
CORMOUS	COUNCIL	CRAIOVA	CRINOID	CRYPTIC
CORNCOB	COUNSEL	CRAMMED	CRIOLLO	CRYSTAL
CORNEAL	COUNTED	CRAMMER	CRIPPLE	CTENOID
CORNERS	COUNTER	CRAMPED	CRISPED	CUBBING
CORNETS	COUNTRY	CRAMPON	CRISPLY	CUBICAL
CORNICE	COUPLED	CRANIAL	CRISSAL	CUBICLE
CORNIER	COUPLER	CRANING	CRISSUM	CUBITAL
CORNISH	COUPLES	CRANIUM	CRITICS	CUCKOLD
CORNUAL	COUPLET	CRANKED	CRITTER	CUCKOOS
CORNUTE	COUPONS	CRAPPED	CROAKED	CUDBEAR
COROLLA	COURAGE	CRAPPIE	CROAKER	CUDDLED
CORONAE	COURIER	CRASHED	CROATIA	CUDGELS
CORONAL	COURSED	CRASHES	CROCEIN	CUDWEED
CORONAS	COURSER	CRASSLY	CROCHET	CUFFING
CORONER	COURSES	CRATERS	CROCKET	CUIRASS
CORONET	COURTED	CRATING	CROFTER	CUISINE
CORPORA	COURTLY	CRAVATS	CRONIES	CULICID
CORPSES	COUSINS	CRAVING	CROOKED	CULLING
CORRADE	COUTURE	CRAWLED	CROONED	CULPRIT
CORRALS	COUVADE	CRAWLER	CROONER	CULTISM
CORRECT	COVERED	CRAYONS	CROPPED	CULTIST
CORREZE	COVERER	CRAZIER	CROPPER	CULTURE
CORRIDA	COVERTS	CRAZILY	CROQUET	CULVERT
CORRODE	COVER-UP	CREAKED	CROSIER	CUMQUAT
CORRUPT	COVETED	CREAMED	CROSSED	CUMULET
CORSAGE	COVETER	CREAMER	CROSSER	CUMULUS
CORSAIR	COWARDS	CREASED	CROSSES	CUNEATE
CORSETS	COWBANE	CREASES	CROSSLY	CUNNING
CORSICA	COWBELL	CREATED	CROUTON	CUP CAKE
CORTEGE	COWBIND	CREATOR	CROWBAR	CUPOLAS
CORVINE	COWBIRD	CRECHES	CROWDED	CUPPING
COSENZA	COWBOYS	CREDENT	CROWING	CUPRITE
COSHING	COWERED	CREDITS	CROWNED	CUPROUS
COSIEST	COWFISH	CREEDAL	CROZIER	CUP TIES
COSINES	COWGIRL	CREEPER	CRUCIAL	CURABLE
COSMINE	COWHAND	CREMATE	CRUCIFY	CURABLY
COSMOID	COWHERB	CRENATE	CRUDELY	CURACAO

CURATES	CYGNETS	DAPPING	DECAPOD	DEHISCE
CURATOR	CYMBALS	DAPPLED	DECAYED	DEICIDE
CURBING	CYNICAL	DARESAY	DECEASE	DE-ICING
CURCUMA	CYPHERS	DARIOLE	DECEIVE	DEICTIC
CURDLED	CYPRESS	DARKEST	DECENCY	DEIFIED
CURE-ALL	CYPRIOT	DARKIES	DECIARE	DEIFIER
CURFEWS	CYPSELA	DARLING	DECIBEL	DEIFORM
CURIOSA	CYSTINE	DARNING	DECIDED	DEIGNED
CURIOUS	CYSTOID	DARTING	DECIDER	DEISTIC
CURLERS	CZARDAS	DASHEEN	DECIDUA	DEITIES
CURLEWS	CZARINA	DASHING	DECIMAL	DEJECTA
CURLIER		DASYURE	DECKING	DELAINE
CURLING	D	DATABLE	DECLAIM	DELAYED
CURRANT	DABBING	DATA BUS	DECLARE	DELAYER
CURRENT	DABBLED	DATIVAL	DECLASS	DELETED
CURRIED	DABBLER	DATIVES	DECLINE	DELIGHT
CURRIER	DAB HAND	DAUBERY	DECODED	DELIMIT
CURRIES	DACTYLS	DAUBING	DECORUM	DELIVER
CURRISH	DADAISM	DAUNTED	DECOYED	DELOUSE
CURSING	DADAIST	DAUNTER	DECOYER	DELPHIC
CURSIVE	DADDIES	DAUPHIN	DECREED	DELTAIC
CURSORS	DAEMONS	DAWDLED	DECREER	DELTOID
CURSORY	DAFTEST	DAWDLER	DECREES	DELUDED
CURTAIL	DAGGERS	DAWNING	DECRIAL	DELUDER
CURTAIN	DAGLOCK	DAYBOOK	DECRIED	DELUGED
CURTESY	DAHLIAS	DAYBOYS	DECRIER	DELUGES
CURVING	DAHOMAN	DAY-CARE	DECUPLE	DELVING
CUSHIER	DAHOMEY	DAYLONG	DEDUCED	DEMANDS
CUSHION	DAILIES	DAYROOM	DEEMING	DEMERIT
CUSPATE	DAIRIES	DAYTIME	DEEPEST	DEMESNE
CUSSING	DAISIES	DAZEDLY	DEEP FRY	DEMIGOD
CUSTARD	DAKOTAN	DAZZLED	DEFACED	DEMONIC
CUSTODY	DALLIED	DEACONS	DEFACER	DEMOTED
CUSTOMS	DAMAGED	DEAD END	DE FACTO	DEMOTIC
CUTAWAY	DAMAGER	DEADEYE	DEFAMED	DEMOUNT
CUTBACK	DAMAGES	DEADPAN	DEFAMER	DEMURER
CUTICLE	DAMMING	DEAF-AID	DEFAULT	DENIALS
CUTLASS	DAMNIFY	DEALATE	DEFEATS	DENIERS
CUTLERS	DAMNING	DEALERS	DEFECTS	DENIZEN
CUTLERY	DAMPERS	DEALING	DEFENCE	DENMARK
CUTLETS	DAMPEST	DEANERY	DEFIANT	DENNING
CUTOFFS	DAMPING	DEAREST	DEFICIT	DENOTED
CUTOUTS	DAMPISH	DEARIES	DEFILED	DENSELY
CUTTACK	DAMSELS	DEATHLY	DEFILER	DENSEST
CUTTERS	DAMSONS	DEBACLE	DEFILES	DENSITY
CUTTING	DANCERS	DEBASED	DEFINED	DENTATE
CUTWORK	DANCING	DEBASER	DEFINER	DENTINE
CUTWORM	DANDERS	DEBATED	DEFLATE	DENTING
CWMBRAN	DANDIER	DEBATER	DEFLECT	DENTIST
CYANATE	DANDIES	DEBATES	DEFORCE	DENTOID
CYANIDE	DANDIFY	DEBAUCH	DEFRAUD	DENTURE
CYANINE	DANDLED	DEBITED	DEFROCK	DENUDED
CYANITE	DANDLER	DEBOUCH	DEFROST	DENUDER
CYBALER	DANGERS	DEBRIEF	DEFUNCT	DENYING
CYCLING	DANGLED	DEBTORS	DEFUSED	DEONTIC
CYCLIST	DANGLER	DECADAL	DEFYING	DEPISER
CYCLOID	DANKEST	DECADES	DEGAUSS	DEPLETE
CYCLONE	DANSEUR	DECAGON	DEGRADE	DEPLORE
CYCLOPS	DAPHNIA	DECANAL	DEGREES	DEPLUME

DEPOSAL	DEVISED	DIGESTS	DISCUSS	DODGERS
DEPOSED	DEVISEE	DIGGERS	DISDAIN	DODGIER
DEPOSER	DEVISER	DIGGING	DISEASE	DODGING
DEPOSIT	DEVISOR	DIGITAL	DISEUSE	DODOISM
DEPRAVE	DEVOICE	DIGNIFY	DISGUST	DOESKIN
DEPRESS	DEVOIRS	DIGNITY	DISHFUL	DOFFING
DEPRIVE	DEVOLVE	DIGRAPH	DISHIER	DOGBANE
DEPSIDE	DEVOTED	DIGRESS	DISHING	DOGCART
DEPUTED	DEVOTEE	DILATED	DISJECT	DOG DAYS
DERANGE	DEWCLAW	DILATOR	DISJOIN	DOGFISH
DERBIES	DEWDROP	DILDOES	DISLIKE	DOGGERY
DERIDED	DEWIEST	DILEMMA	DISMAST	DOGGIES
DERIDER	DEWLAPS	DILUENT	DISMISS	DOGGING
DERIVED	DEXTRAL	DILUTED	DISOBEY	DOGGONE
DERIVER	DEXTRAN	DILUTEE	DISPLAY	DOGLEGS
DERMOID	DEXTRIN	DILUTER	DISPORT	DOG TAGS
DERRICK	DHAHRAN	DIMETER	DISPOSE	DOGTROT
DERVISH	DIABASE	DIMMERS	DISPUTE	DOGVANE
DESCALE	DIABOLO	DIMMEST	DISRATE	DOGWOOD
DESCANT	DIADEMS	DIMMING	DISROBE	DOILIES
DESCEND	DIAGRAM	DIMNESS	DISRUPT	DOLEFUL
DESCENT	DIALECT	DIMORPH	DISSECT	DOLLARS
DESERTS	DIALING	DIMPLES	DISSENT	DOLLIES
DESERVE	DIALLED	DIMWITS	DISTAFF	DOLLING
DESIGNS	DIALLER	DINERIC	DISTANT	DOLLISH
DESIRED	DIALYSE	DINETTE	DISTEND	DOLLOPS
DESIRER	DIAMINE	DINGIER	DISTICH	DOLMENS
DESIRES	DIAMOND	DINGILY	DISTORT	DOLPHIN
DESKTOP	DIANOIA	DINGLES	DISTURB	DOLTISH
DESMOID	DIAPERS	DINGOES	DISUSED	DOMAINS
DESPAIR	DIARCHY	DINKIER	DITCHED	DOMICAL
DESPISE	DIARIES	DINNERS	DITCHER	DOMINEE
DESPITE	DIARIST	DINNING	DITCHES	DONATED
DESPOIL	DIASTER	DIOCESE	DITTANY	DONATOR
DESPOND	DIAZINE	DIOPTRE	DITTIES	DONBASS
DESPOTS	DIAZOLE	DIORAMA	DIURNAL	DONEGAL
DESSERT	DIBASIC	DIORITE	DIVERGE	DONETSK
DESTINE	DIBBING	DIOXIDE	DIVERSE	DON JUAN
DESTINY	DIBBLED	DIPHASE	DIVIDED	DONKEYS
DESTROY	DIBBLER	DIPLOID	DIVIDER	DONNING
DETAILS	DIBBLES	DIPLOMA	DIVIDES	DONNISH
DETENTE	DICIEST	DIPLONT	DIVINED	DOODLED
DETERGE	DICKENS	DIPNOAN	DIVINER	DOODLER
DETINUE	DICKIER	DIPOLAR	DIVISOR	DOODLES
DETOURS	DICKIES	DIPPERS	DIVORCE	DOOMING
DETRACT	DICLINY	DIPPING	DIVULGE	DO-OR-DIE
DETRAIN	DICTATE	DIPTYCH	DIZZIER	DOORMAN
DETROIT	DICTION	DIREFUL	DIZZILY	DOORMAT
DETRUDE	DICTUMS	DIRNDLS	DNIEPER	DOORMEN
DEUTZIA	DIDDLED	DIRTIED	D-NOTICE	DOORWAY
DEVALUE	DIDICOY	DIRTIER	DOBRUJA	DOPIEST
DEVELOP	DIEBACK	DIRTILY	DOCKAGE	DORMANT
DEVIANT	DIE-CAST	DISABLE	DOCKERS	DORMERS
DEVIATE	DIEHARD	DISAVOW	DOCKETS	DORMICE
DEVICES	DIESELS	DISBAND	DOCKING	DORNICK
DEVILED	DIETARY	DISCARD	DOCTORS	DOSAGES
DEVILRY	DIETING	DISCERN	DODDERY	DOSSERS
DEVIOUS	DIFFUSE	DISCOID	DODDLES	DOSSIER
DEVISAL	DIGAMMA	DISCORD	DODGEMS	DOSSING

DOTAGES	DRESDEN	DUCHESS	DYSURIA	EDAPHIC
DOTTIER	DRESSED	DUCHIES	DYSURIC	EDDYING
DOTTING	DRESSER	DUCKIES	DZONGKA	EDGIEST
DOUBLED	DRESSES	DUCKING		EDGINGS
DOUBLER	DRIBBLE	DUCTILE	**E**	EDICTAL
DOUBLES	DRIBLET	DUDGEON	EACH WAY	EDIFICE
DOUBLET	DRIFTED	DUELING	EAGERLY	EDIFIED
DOUBTED	DRIFTER	DUELLED	EAGLETS	EDIFIER
DOUBTER	DRILLED	DUELLER	EARACHE	EDITING
DOUCHES	DRILLER	DUENNAS	EARDRUM	EDITION
DOUGHTY	DRINKER	DUFFERS	EARFLAP	EDITORS
DOUGLAS	DRIP-DRY	DUGOUTS	EARLDOM	EDUCATE
DOURINE	DRIPPED	DUKEDOM	EARLIER	EEL-LIKE
DOUSING	DRIVE-IN	DULLARD	EARLOBE	EELPOUT
DOWABLE	DRIVERS	DULLEST	EARMARK	EELWORM
DOWAGER	DRIVING	DULLING	EARMUFF	EFFACED
DOWDIER	DRIZZLE	DULOSIS	EARNERS	EFFACER
DOWDILY	DRIZZLY	DUMBEST	EARNEST	EFFECTS
DOWN-BOW	DROLLER	DUMMIES	EARNING	EFFORTS
DOWNERS	DRONING	DUMPERS	EARPLUG	EGGCUPS
DOWNIER	DRONISH	DUMPIER	EARRING	EGGHEAD
DOWNING	DROOLED	DUMPING	EARSHOT	EGG ROLL
DOWRIES	DROOPED	DUNGEON	EARTHED	EGOISTS
DOWSERS	DROPLET	DUNKING	EARTHEN	EGOTISM
DOWSING	DROPOUT	DUNKIRK	EARTHLY	EGOTIST
DOYLEYS	DROPPED	DUNNAGE	EARWIGS	EGO TRIP
DOZENTH	DROPPER	DUNNEST	EASEFUL	EIDETIC
DOZIEST	DROSHKY	DUNNING	EASIEST	EIDOLON
DRABBER	DROUGHT	DUNNITE	EAST END	EIGHTHS
DRABBLE	DROVERS	DUODENA	EASTERN	EIGHTVO
DRACHMA	DROWNED	DUOTONE	EASTERS	EINKORN
DRACHMS	DROWNER	DUPABLE	EASTING	EJECTED
DRAFTED	DROWSED	DURABLE	EATABLE	EJECTOR
DRAFTEE	DRUBBER	DURABLY	EBB TIDE	ELAMITE
DRAFTER	DRUDGED	DURANGO	EBONITE	ELAPSED
DRAGGED	DRUDGER	DURMAST	EBONIZE	ELASTIC
DRAGGLE	DRUDGES	DUSKIER	ECBOLIC	ELASTIN
DRAGNET	DRUGGED	DUSTBIN	ECCRINE	ELATION
DRAGONS	DRUGGET	DUSTERS	ECDYSIS	ELATIVE
DRAGOON	DRUIDIC	DUSTIER	ECHELON	ELBOWED
DRAINED	DRUMLIN	DUSTING	ECHIDNA	ELDERLY
DRAINER	DRUMMED	DUSTMAN	ECHINUS	ELEATIC
DRAPERS	DRUMMER	DUSTMEN	ECHOING	ELECTED
DRAPERY	DRUNKEN	DUSTPAN	ECHOISM	ELECTOR
DRAPING	DRUNKER	DUSTUPS	ECLAIRS	ELEGANT
DRASTIC	DRYABLE	DUTIFUL	ECLIPSE	ELEGIAC
DRATTED	DRYADIC	DUVETYN	ECLOGUE	ELEGIES
DRAUGHT	DRY DOCK	DVANDVA	ECOLOGY	ELEGIST
DRAWBAR	DRY-EYED	DWARFED	ECONOMY	ELEGIZE
DRAWERS	DRY LAND	DWARVES	ECORCHE	ELEMENT
DRAWING	DRYNESS	DWELLED	ECOTONE	ELEUSIS
DRAWLED	DRY-SALT	DWELLER	ECOTYPE	ELEVATE
DRAWLER	DRY-SHOD	DWINDLE	ECSTASY	ELEVENS
DREADED	DUALISM	DYARCHY	ECTHYMA	ELIDING
DREAMED	DUALIST	DYELINE	ECTOPIA	ELISION
DREAMER	DUALITY	DYEWOOD	ECTOPIC	ELITISM
DREDGED	DUBBING	DYNAMIC	ECTYPAL	ELITIST
DREDGER	DUBIETY	DYNAMOS	ECUADOR	ELIXIRS
DRENTHE	DUBIOUS	DYNASTY	EDACITY	ELLIPSE

EL MINYA	ENCODED	ENTENTE	EQUALED	ETHANOL
ELOPING	ENCODER	ENTERED	EQUALLY	ETHERIC
ELUDING	ENCOMIA	ENTERER	EQUATED	ETHICAL
ELUSION	ENCORES	ENTERIC	EQUATOR	ETHMOID
ELUSIVE	ENCRUST	ENTERON	EQUERRY	ETHYLIC
ELUVIAL	ENDARCH	ENTHRAL	EQUINOX	ETRURIA
ELUVIUM	ENDEMIC	ENTHUSE	ERASERS	EUBOEAN
ELYSIAN	END GAME	ENTICED	ERASING	EUCAINE
ELYSIUM	ENDINGS	ENTICER	ERASION	EUGENIC
ELYTRON	ENDIVES	ENTITLE	ERASURE	EUGENOL
EMANATE	ENDLESS	ENTOPIC	ERECTED	EUGLENA
EMBARGO	ENDMOST	ENTRAIN	ERECTER	EULOGIA
EMBASSY	ENDORSE	ENTRANT	ERECTLY	EUNUCHS
EMBLEMS	ENDOWED	ENTREAT	ERECTOR	EUPHONY
EMBOLIC	ENDOWER	ENTREES	EREMITE	EUPHROE
EMBOLUS	ENDUING	ENTRIES	EREPSIN	EUPLOID
EMBRACE	ENDURED	ENTROPY	ERISTIC	EUPNOEA
EMBROIL	END USER	ENTRUST	ERITREA	EURASIA
EMBRYOS	ENDWAYS	ENTWINE	ERMINES	EURATOM
EMENDED	ENEMIES	E NUMBER	ERODENT	EURIPUS
EMERALD	ENERGID	ENVELOP	ERODING	EUSTASY
EMERGED	ENFEOFF	ENVENOM	EROSION	EVACUEE
EMERSED	ENFORCE	ENVIOUS	EROSIVE	EVADING
EMETICS	ENGAGED	ENVIRON	EROTEMA	EVANGEL
EMETINE	ENGAGER	ENVYING	EROTICA	EVASION
EMIGRES	EN GARDE	ENZYMES	ERRANCY	EVASIVE
EMINENT	ENGINES	EOBIONT	ERRANDS	EVENING
EMIRATE	ENGLAND	EOSINIC	ERRATIC	EVEREST
EMITTED	ENGLISH	EPARCHY	ERRATUM	EVERTOR
EMITTER	ENGORGE	EPAULET	ERRHINE	EVICTED
EMOTION	ENGRAFT	EPEEIST	ERUDITE	EVICTOR
EMOTIVE	ENGRAIL	EPEIRIC	ERUPTED	EVIDENT
EMPALER	ENGRAIN	EPERGNE	ERZURUM	EVILEST
EMPANEL	ENGRAVE	EPIBOLY	ESBJERG	EVIL EYE
EMPATHY	ENGROSS	EPICARP	ESCAPED	EVILLER
EMPEROR	ENHANCE	EPICENE	ESCAPEE	EVINCED
EMPIRES	ENIGMAS	EPICURE	ESCAPER	EVOKING
EMPIRIC	ENJOYED	EPIDOTE	ESCAPES	EVOLUTE
EMPLACE	ENJOYER	EPIGEAL	ESCOLAR	EVOLVED
EMPORIA	ENLARGE	EPIGENE	ESCORTS	EVOLVER
EMPOWER	ENLIVEN	EPIGONE	ESERINE	EWE-NECK
EMPRESS	EN MASSE	EPIGRAM	ESKIMOS	EXACTED
EMPTIED	ENNOBLE	EPIGYNY	ESPARTO	EXACTLY
EMPTIER	ENOUNCE	EPIMERE	ESPOUSE	EXACTOR
EMPTIES	ENPLANE	EPISODE	ESPYING	EXALTED
EMPTILY	ENQUIRE	EPISOME	ESQUIRE	EXALTER
EMPYEMA	ENQUIRY	EPISTLE	ESSAYED	EXAMINE
EMULATE	ENRAGED	EPITAPH	ESSENCE	EXAMPLE
EMULOUS	ENROBER	EPITAXY	ESSONNE	EXARATE
ENABLED	EN ROUTE	EPITHET	ESTATES	EXCERPT
ENABLER	ENSIGNS	EPITOME	ESTHETE	EXCISED
ENACTED	ENSLAVE	EPIZOIC	ESTREAT	EXCITED
ENACTOR	ENSNARE	EPIZOON	ESTUARY	EXCITER
ENAMOUR	ENSUING	EPOCHAL	ETAGERE	EXCITON
ENCASED	ENSURED	EPOCHES	ETAMINE	EXCITOR
ENCHAIN	ENSURER	EPONYMY	ETCHERS	EXCLAIM
ENCHANT	ENTASIA	EPSILON	ETCHING	EXCLAVE
ENCLAVE	ENTASIS	EQUABLE	ETERNAL	EXCLUDE
ENCLOSE	ENTEBBE	EQUABLY	ETESIAN	EXCRETA

EXCRETE	EYELIDS	FANCIED	FEARFUL	FEUDING
EXCUSAL	EYESHOT	FANCIER	FEARING	FEVERED
EXCUSED	EYESORE	FANCIES	FEASTED	FEWNESS
EXCUSES	EYESPOT	FANCILY	FEASTER	FEYNESS
EXECUTE	EYEWASH	FANFARE	FEATHER	FIANCES
EXEGETE		FANNIES	FEATURE	FIASCOS
EXERGUE	F	FANNING	FEBRILE	FIBBERS
EXERTED	FABIANS	FANTAIL	FEDERAL	FIBBING
EXHALED	FABRICS	FANTAST	FEDORAS	FIBROID
EXHAUST	FACADES	FANTASY	FEEBLER	FIBROIN
EXHIBIT	FACEBAR	FANZINE	FEEDBAG	FIBROMA
EXHUMED	FACE-OFF	FARADAY	FEEDERS	FIBROUS
EXHUMER	FACIALS	FARADIC	FEEDING	FIBULAE
EXIGENT	FACINGS	FARAWAY	FEEDLOT	FIBULAR
EXILING	FACTFUL	FARCEUR	FEELERS	FIBULAS
EXISTED	FACTION	FAR EAST	FEELING	FICTILE
EXITING	FACTORS	FAR-GONE	FEIGNED	FICTION
EXODERM	FACTORY	FARMERS	FEIGNER	FIDDLED
EXOGAMY	FACTUAL	FARMING	FEINTED	FIDDLER
EXOTICA	FACULAR	FARNESS	FELINES	FIDDLES
EXPANSE	FACULTY	FARRAGO	FELLERS	FIDEISM
EX PARTE	FADABLE	FARRIER	FELLING	FIDEIST
EXPENSE	FADDISH	FARTHER	FELLOWS	FIDGETS
EXPERTS	FADDISM	FARTING	FELONRY	FIDGETY
EXPIATE	FADDIST	FARTLEK	FELSITE	FIELDED
EXPIRED	FADEOUT	FASCIAL	FELSPAR	FIELDER
EXPIRER	FAEROES	FASCIAS	FELTING	FIERCER
EXPLAIN	FAG ENDS	FASCINE	FELUCCA	FIERIER
EXPLANT	FAGGING	FASCISM	FELWORT	FIESOLE
EXPLODE	FAGGOTS	FASCIST	FEMALES	FIESTAS
EXPLOIT	FAIENCE	FASHION	FEMORAL	FIFTEEN
EXPLORE	FAILING	FASTEST	FENCERS	FIFTIES
EXPORTS	FAILURE	FASTING	FENCING	FIGHTER
EXPOSAL	FAINTED	FATALLY	FENDERS	FIG LEAF
EXPOSED	FAINTER	FATBACK	FENDING	FIGMENT
EXPOSER	FAINTLY	FAT CATS	FERMATA	FIGURAL
EXPOSES	FAIREST	FATEFUL	FERMENT	FIGURED
EXPOUND	FAIRIES	FATHEAD	FERMION	FIGURER
EXPRESS	FAIRING	FATHERS	FERMIUM	FIGURES
EXPUNGE	FAIRISH	FATHOMS	FERNERY	FIGWORT
EXSCIND	FAIR SEX	FATIGUE	FERRARA	FILARIA
EXTENTS	FAIRWAY	FATLING	FERRATE	FILBERT
EXTINCT	FALANGE	FATNESS	FERRETS	FILCHED
EXTRACT	FALBALA	FATSHAN	FERRETY	FILCHER
EXTREME	FALCATE	FATTEST	FERRIED	FILETED
EXTRUDE	FALCONS	FATTIER	FERRIES	FILIATE
EXUDING	FALLACY	FATTIES	FERRITE	FILIBEG
EXULTED	FALL GUY	FATTILY	FERROUS	FILINGS
EXURBIA	FALLING	FATTISH	FERRULE	FILLETS
EXUVIAE	FALLOUT	FATUITY	FERTILE	FILLIES
EXUVIAL	FALSELY	FATUOUS	FERVENT	FILLING
EX-WORKS	FALSEST	FAUCETS	FERVOUR	FILL-INS
EYEBALL	FALSIES	FAULTED	FESTIVE	FILLIPS
EYEBATH	FALSIFY	FAUVISM	FESTOON	FILMIER
EYEBOLT	FALSITY	FAUVIST	FETCHED	FILMILY
EYEBROW	FAMILLE	FAUX PAS	FETCHER	FILMING
EYELASH	FAMINES	FAVOURS	FETLOCK	FILMSET
EYELESS	FANATIC	FAVRILE	FETTERS	FILTERS
EYELETS	FAN BELT	FAWNING	FETUSES	FIMBRIA

FINABLE	FLAKIER	FLOCCUS	FOCUSES	FOREPAW
FINAGLE	FLAKING	FLOCKED	FOGGIER	FORERUN
FINALES	FLAMING	FLOGGED	FOGGILY	FORESAW
FINALLY	FLANEUR	FLOGGER	FOGGING	FORESEE
FINANCE	FLANGER	FLOODED	FOGHORN	FORESTS
FINBACK	FLANGES	FLOODER	FOG LAMP	FORETOP
FINCHES	FLANKED	FLOORED	FOGYISH	FOREVER
FINDING	FLANKER	FLOPPED	FOIBLES	FORFEIT
FINE ART	FLANNEL	FLORIDA	FOILING	FORGAVE
FINE-CUT	FLAPPED	FLORINS	FOISTED	FORGERS
FINESSE	FLAPPER	FLORIST	FOLACIN	FORGERY
FINFOOT	FLARE-UP	FLORUIT	FOLDERS	FORGING
FINGERS	FLARING	FLOSSED	FOLDING	FORGIVE
FINICKY	FLASHED	FLOTAGE	FOLDOUT	FORGOER
FININGS	FLASHER	FLOTSAM	FOLIAGE	FORGONE
FINLAND	FLASHES	FLOUNCE	FOLIATE	FORKFUL
FINNING	FLASKET	FLOURED	FOLIOSE	FORKING
FINNISH	FLAT-BED	FLOUTED	FOLKISH	FORLORN
FIREARM	FLATLET	FLOUTER	FOLLIES	FORMANT
FIREBOX	FLATTEN	FLOWAGE	FONDANT	FORMATE
FIREBUG	FLATTER	FLOWERS	FONDEST	FORMATS
FIREDOG	FLAUNCH	FLOWERY	FONDLED	FORMICA
FIREFLY	FLAVONE	FLOWING	FONDLER	FORMING
FIREMAN	FLAVOUR	FLUENCY	FONDUES	FORMOSA
FIREMEN	FLAWING	FLUFFED	FOOCHOW	FORMULA
FIREPAN	FLAYING	FLUIDAL	FOODIES	FORSAKE
FIRMEST	FLEABAG	FLUIDIC	FOOLERY	FORSOOK
FIRMING	FLEAPIT	FLUMMOX	FOOLING	FORTIES
FIRSTLY	FLECKED	FLUNKED	FOOLISH	FORTIFY
FIRTREE	FLEECED	FLUNKEY	FOOTAGE	FORTUNE
FISCALS	FLEECES	FLUORIC	FOOTBOY	FORWARD
FISHERY	FLEEING	FLUSHED	FOOTING	FORWENT
FISH-EYE	FLEETER	FLUSHER	FOOTMAN	FOSSILS
FISHGIG	FLEMING	FLUSHES	FOOTMEN	FOUETTE
FISHIER	FLEMISH	FLUSTER	FOOTPAD	FOULARD
FISHING	FLENSER	FLUTING	FOOTSIE	FOULEST
FISHNET	FLESHED	FLUTIST	FOOT-TON	FOULING
FISSILE	FLESHER	FLUTTER	FOOTWAY	FOUL-UPS
FISSION	FLESHES	FLUVIAL	FOOZLER	FOUNDED
FISSURE	FLESHLY	FLUXION	FOPPERY	FOUNDER
FISTULA	FLEURON	FLYABLE	FOPPISH	FOUNDRY
FITMENT	FLEXILE	FLYAWAY	FORAGED	FOURIER
FITNESS	FLEXING	FLYBACK	FORAGER	FOURTHS
FITTERS	FLEXION	FLYBLOW	FORAGES	FOUR-WAY
FITTEST	FLEXURE	FLYBOAT	FORAMEN	FOVEATE
FITTING	FLICKED	FLYBOOK	FORAYED	FOVEOLA
FIXABLE	FLICKER	FLY-FISH	FORAYER	FOWLING
FIXATED	FLIGHTS	FLY HALF	FORBADE	FOXFIRE
FIXEDLY	FLIGHTY	FLYLEAF	FORBEAR	FOXHOLE
FIXTURE	FLINGER	FLYOVER	FORBORE	FOXHUNT
FIZZIER	FLIPPED	FLYPAST	FORCEPS	FOXIEST
FIZZING	FLIPPER	FLYTRAP	FORCING	FOXLIKE
FLACCID	FLIRTED	FOALING	FORDING	FOXTAIL
FLAG DAY	FLIRTER	FOAMIER	FOREARM	FOXTROT
FLAGGED	FLITTED	FOAMING	FOREGUT	FRACTUS
FLAGGER	FLITTER	FOBBING	FOREIGN	FRAENUM
FLAGMAN	FLIVVER	FO'C'SLES	FORELEG	FRAGILE
FLAGONS	FLOATED	FOCUSED	FOREMAN	FRAILER
FLAILED	FLOATER	FOCUSER	FOREMEN	FRAILTY

FRAKTUR	FRONDED	FURNESS	GALLOWS	GATHERS
FRAME-UP	FRONTAL	FURNISH	GALUMPH	GAUCHOS
FRAMING	FRONTED	FURRIER	GAMBADO	GAUDERY
FRANKED	FROSTED	FURRING	GAMBIAN	GAUDIER
FRANKER	FROTHED	FURROWS	GAMBIER	GAUDILY
FRANKLY	FROWARD	FURROWY	GAMBITS	GAUGING
FRANTIC	FROWNED	FURTHER	GAMBLED	GAUHATI
FRAPPES	FROWNER	FURTIVE	GAMBLER	GAUZIER
FRAUGHT	FROWSTY	FUSCOUS	GAMBOGE	GAVOTTE
FRAYING	FRUITED	FUSIBLE	GAMBOLS	GAWKERS
FRAZZLE	FRUITER	FUSSIER	GAMBREL	GAWKIER
FREAKED	FRUSTUM	FUSSILY	GAMELAN	GAWKING
FRECKLE	FUCHSIA	FUSSING	GAMETAL	GAWPING
FREEBIE	FUCHSIN	FUSSPOT	GAMIEST	GAYNESS
FREEDOM	FUCK ALL	FUSTIAN	GANDERS	GAZEBOS
FREEING	FUCKERS	FUSTIER	GANGERS	GAZELLE
FREEMAN	FUCKING	FUTTOCK	GANGING	GAZETTE
FREEMEN	FUCK-UPS	FUTURES	GANGTOK	GEARBOX
FREESIA	FUDDLED	FUZZIER	GANGWAY	GEARING
FREEWAY	FUDDLES	FUZZILY	GANNETS	GECKOES
FREEZER	FUDGING	FUZZING	GANTLET	GEE-GEES
FREIGHT	FUEGIAN	FYZABAD	GAOLERS	GEELONG
FREMONT	FUELING		GAOLING	GEEZERS
FRESCOS	FUELLED	G	GAPPING	GEISHAS
FRESHEN	FUELLER	GABBING	GARAGED	GELATIN
FRESHER	FUGGIER	GABBLED	GARAGES	GELDING
FRESHET	FUKUOKA	GABBLER	GARBAGE	GELLING
FRESHLY	FULCRUM	GADDING	GARBING	GEMMATE
FRESNEL	FULGENT	GADGETS	GARBLED	GEMMING
FRETFUL	FULLEST	GADGETY	GARBLER	GEMMULE
FRETSAW	FULMARS	GADROON	GARCONS	GEMSBOK
FRETTED	FULNESS	GADWALL	GARDENS	GENAPPE
FRIABLE	FULSOME	GAFFERS	GARFISH	GENDERS
FRIBBLE	FULVOUS	GAGAUZI	GARGETY	GENERAL
FRIDAYS	FUMARIC	GAGGING	GARGLED	GENERIC
FRIDGES	FUMBLED	GAHNITE	GARGLER	GENESIS
FRIENDS	FUMBLER	GAINERS	GARGLES	GENETIC
FRIEZES	FUMBLES	GAINFUL	GARLAND	GENEVAN
FRIGATE	FUNCHAL	GAINING	GARMENT	GENIPAP
FRIGHTS	FUNDING	GAINSAY	GARNETS	GENITAL
FRILLED	FUNERAL	GAITERS	GARNISH	GENITOR
FRINGED	FUNFAIR	GALATEA	GARONNE	GENOESE
FRINGES	FUNGOID	GALEATE	GARPIKE	GENTEEL
FRISBEE	FUNGOUS	GALENIC	GARRETS	GENTIAN
FRISEUR	FUNICLE	GALICIA	GARTERS	GENTILE
FRISIAN	FUNKIER	GALILEE	GASBAGS	GENUINE
FRISKED	FUNKING	GALIPOT	GASCONY	GEODESY
FRISKER	FUNNELS	GALLANT	GASEOUS	GEOLOGY
FRISKET	FUNNIER	GALLEON	GASHING	GEORDIE
FRISSON	FUNNILY	GALLERY	GASKETS	GEORGIA
FRITTER	FUN RUNS	GALLEYS	GAS MASK	GEORGIC
FRIZZED	FURBISH	GALLFLY	GASPING	GERBILS
FRIZZER	FURCATE	GALLING	GASSIER	GERENUK
FRIZZLE	FURCULA	GALLIUM	GASSING	GERMANE
FROEBEL	FURIOSO	GALLNUT	GASTRIC	GERMANS
FROG-BIT	FURIOUS	GALLONS	GASTRIN	GERMANY
FROGMAN	FURLING	GALLOON	GATEAUX	GERUNDS
FROGMEN	FURLONG	GALLOPS	GATE-LEG	GESTALT
FROLICS	FURNACE	GALLOUS	GATEWAY	GESTAPO

GESTATE	GLASGOW	GOBBLED	GRADUAL	GREYISH
GESTURE	GLASSED	GOBBLER	GRAFTED	GREYLAG
GETABLE	GLASSES	GOBBLES	GRAFTER	GRIBBLE
GETAWAY	GLAZIER	GOBELIN	GRAINER	GRIDDLE
GETTING	GLAZING	GOBIOID	GRAMMAR	GRIEVED
GEYSERS	GLEAMED	GOBLETS	GRAMMES	GRIEVER
GHASTLY	GLEANED	GOBLINS	GRAMPUS	GRIFFIN
GHERKIN	GLEANER	GODDAMN	GRANADA	GRIFFON
GHETTOS	GLEEFUL	GODDESS	GRANARY	GRILLED
GHILLIE	GLENOID	GODHEAD	GRANDAD	GRILLER
GHOSTED	GLIADIN	GODHOOD	GRANDEE	GRILLES
GHOSTLY	GLIBBER	GODLESS	GRANDER	GRIMACE
GIBBETS	GLIDERS	GODLIER	GRANDLY	GRIMIER
GIBBING	GLIDING	GODLIKE	GRANDMA	GRIMMER
GIBBONS	GLIMMER	GODSEND	GRANDPA	GRINDER
GIBBOUS	GLIMPSE	GOGGLED	GRANGES	GRINGOS
GIBLETS	GLINTED	GOGGLES	GRANITE	GRINNED
GIDDIER	GLISTEN	GOIANIA	GRANOLA	GRINNER
GIDDILY	GLITTER	GO-KARTS	GRANTED	GRIPERS
GIGGLED	GLIWICE	GOLDEYE	GRANTEE	GRIPING
GIGGLER	GLOATED	GOLFERS	GRANTER	GRIPPED
GIGGLES	GLOATER	GOLFING	GRANTOR	GRIPPER
GIGOLOS	GLOBATE	GOLIATH	GRANULE	GRISTLE
GILBERT	GLOBOID	GONADAL	GRAPHIC	GRISTLY
GILDING	GLOBOSE	GONDOLA	GRAPNEL	GRITTED
GILLIES	GLOBULE	GOODBYE	GRAPPLE	GRIZZLE
GIMBALS	GLORIED	GOOD DAY	GRASPED	GRIZZLY
GIMLETS	GLORIES	GOODIES	GRASPER	GROANED
GIMMICK	GLORIFY	GOODISH	GRASSED	GROANER
GINGERY	GLOSSAL	GOOFIER	GRASSES	GROCERS
GINGHAM	GLOSSED	GOOFILY	GRATERS	GROCERY
GINGILI	GLOSSER	GOOFING	GRATIFY	GROGRAM
GINGIVA	GLOTTAL	GOOIEST	GRATING	GROLIER
GINSENG	GLOTTIC	GOPHERS	GRAUPEL	GROMMET
GIN TRAP	GLOTTIS	GORGING	GRAVELY	GROOMED
GIPSIES	GLOWING	GORGONS	GRAVEST	GROOMER
GIRAFFE	GLUCOSE	GORIEST	GRAVITY	GROOVED
GIRASOL	GLUEING	GORILLA	GRAVURE	GROOVES
GIRDERS	GLUMMER	GOSHAWK	GRAYEST	GROPING
GIRDING	GLUTEAL	GOSLING	GRAYING	GROSSED
GIRDLED	GLUTEUS	GO-SLOWS	GRAZIER	GROSSER
GIRDLER	GLUTTED	GOSPELS	GRAZING	GROSSES
GIRDLES	GLUTTON	GOSPLAN	GREASED	GROSSLY
GIRLISH	GLYCINE	GOSSIPS	GREASER	GROTTOS
GIRONDE	GLYPHIC	GOSSIPY	GREATER	GROUCHY
GIRONNY	GLYPTIC	GOUACHE	GREATLY	GROUNDS
GISARME	GNARLED	GOUGING	GREAVES	GROUPED
GITTERN	GNASHED	GOULASH	GRECIAN	GROUPER
GIVABLE	GNASHES	GOURAMI	GREENED	GROUPIE
GIZZARD	GNATHIC	GOURMET	GREENER	GROUSED
GLACIAL	GNAWING	GRAB BAG	GREETED	GROUSER
GLACIER	GNOCCHI	GRABBED	GREETER	GROUSES
GLADDEN	GNOMISH	GRABBER	GREISEN	GROUTER
GLADDER	GNOSTIC	GRABBLE	GREMIAL	GROWERS
GLAD EYE	GOADING	GRACILE	GREMLIN	GROWING
GLAMOUR	GO-AHEAD	GRACING	GRENADE	GROWLED
GLANCED	GOATEED	GRACKLE	GREYEST	GROWLER
GLANCES	GOATEES	GRADATE	GREYHEN	GROWN-UP
GLARING	GOBBETS	GRADING	GREYING	GROWTHS

GROYNES	GURGLED	HALAKAH	HANOVER	HATBAND
GRUBBED	GURNARD	HALAKIC	HANSARD	HATCHED
GRUBBER	GUSHERS	HALAVAH	HANSOMS	HATCHEL
GRUDGED	GUSHING	HALBERD	HANUMAN	HATCHER
GRUDGER	GUSSETS	HALCYON	HANYANG	HATCHES
GRUDGES	GUSTIER	HALDANE	HA'PENNY	HATCHET
GRUFFER	GUSTILY	HALFWAY	HAPLESS	HATEFUL
GRUFFLY	GUSTING	HALF-WIT	HAPLITE	HATLESS
GRUMBLE	GUTLESS	HALIBUT	HAPLOID	HATLIKE
GRUMOUS	GUTSIER	HALIDOM	HA'P'ORTH	HATPINS
GRUNTED	GUTTATE	HALIFAX	HAPPIER	HATTERS
GRUNTER	GUTTERS	HALLWAY	HAPPILY	HAUBERK
GRUYERE	GUTTING	HALOGEN	HAPTENE	HAUGHTY
GRYPHON	GUVNORS	HALTERE	HARAPPA	HAULAGE
G-STRING	GUZZLED	HALTERS	HARBOUR	HAULIER
GUANACO	GUZZLER	HALTING	HARDEST	HAULING
GUANASE	GWALIOR	HALVING	HARDIER	HAUNTED
GUANINE	GWYNEDD	HALYARD	HARDILY	HAUNTER
GUARANI	GWYNIAD	HAMADAN	HARDING	HAURAKI
GUARDED	GYMNAST	HAMBURG	HARD NUT	HAUTBOY
GUARDER	GYMSLIP	HAMELIN	HARD-ONS	HAUTEUR
GUAYULE	GYPPING	HAMITIC	HARDPAN	HAWKERS
GUDGEON	GYPSIES	HAMLETS	HARDTOP	HAWKING
GUESSED	GYRATED	HAMMERS	HARELIP	HAWKINS
GUESSER	GYRATOR	HAMMING	HARICOT	HAWKISH
GUESSES		HAMMOCK	HARIJAN	HAWORTH
GUESTED	H	HAMMOND	HARKING	HAWSERS
GUFFAWS	HABITAT	HAMPDEN	HARLOTS	HAYCOCK
GUIDING	HABITED	HAMPERS	HARMFUL	HAYFORK
GUILDER	HABITUE	HAMPTON	HARMING	HAYRACK
GUINEAN	HABITUS	HAMSTER	HARMONY	HAYSEED
GUINEAS	HACHURE	HAMULAR	HARNESS	HAYWARD
GUIPURE	HACKBUT	HAMULUS	HARPIES	HAYWIRE
GUITARS	HACKERS	HANAPER	HARPING	HAZARDS
GUJARAT	HACKING	HANCOCK	HARPINS	HAZIEST
GULCHES	HACKLER	HANDBAG	HARPIST	HAZLITT
GULDENS	HACKLES	HANDFUL	HARPOON	HEADERS
GULLETS	HACKNEY	HANDGUN	HARRIED	HEADIER
GULLIES	HACKSAW	HANDIER	HARRIER	HEADILY
GULLING	HADAWAY	HANDILY	HARROWS	HEADING
GULPING	HADDOCK	HANDING	HARSHER	HEADMAN
GUMBOIL	HADRIAN	HANDLED	HARSHLY	HEADMEN
GUMBOOT	HAEMOID	HANDLER	HARSLET	HEADPIN
GUMDROP	HAFNIUM	HANDLES	HARTLEY	HEADSET
GUMMIER	HAGFISH	HANDOUT	HARVARD	HEADWAY
GUMMING	HAGGARD	HANDSAW	HARVEST	HEALERS
GUMMITE	HAGGISH	HANDSEL	HARWICH	HEALING
GUMSHOE	HAGGLED	HANDSET	HARYANA	HEALTHS
GUM TREE	HAGGLER	HANDS-ON	HAS-BEEN	HEALTHY
GUNBOAT	HAGLIKE	HANDS UP	HASHING	HEAPING
GUNDOGS	HAILING	HANGARS	HASHISH	HEARING
GUNFIRE	HAIRCUT	HANGDOG	HASIDIC	HEARKEN
GUNLOCK	HAIRDOS	HANGERS	HASIDIM	HEARSAY
GUNNELS	HAIRIER	HANGING	HASSLED	HEARSES
GUNNERS	HAIRNET	HANGMAN	HASSLES	HEARTEN
GUNNERY	HAIRPIN	HANGMEN	HASSOCK	HEARTHS
GUNNING	HATTIAN	HANGOUT	HASTATE	HEATERS
GUNSHOT	HAITINK	HANG-UPS	HASTIER	HEATHEN
GUNWALE	HAKLUYT	HANKIES	HASTILY	HEATHER

HEATING	HEPATIC	HIONATE	HOLDALL	HOSIERY
HEAVENS	HEPBURN	HIPBATH	HOLDERS	HOSPICE
HEAVIER	HEPTANE	HIPBONE	HOLDING	HOSTAGE
HEAVIES	HEPTOSE	HIPLESS	HOLDUPS	HOSTELS
HEAVILY	HERALDS	HIPLIKE	HOLIBUT	HOSTESS
HEAVING	HERBAGE	HIPPEST	HOLIDAY	HOSTILE
HEBETIC	HERBALS	HIPPIES	HOLIEST	HOSTING
HEBRAIC	HERBERT	HIPSTER	HOLLAND	HOSTLER
HEBREWS	HERDING	HIRABLE	HOLLERS	HOTBEDS
HECKLED	HEREDES	HIRCINE	HOLLOWS	HOT DOGS
HECKLER	HERETIC	HIRSUTE	HOLMIUM	HOTFOOT
HECTARE	HERITOR	HIRUDIN	HOLSTER	HOTHEAD
HEDGING	HERMITS	HISSING	HOLY SEE	HOT LINE
HEDONIC	HERNIAL	HISTOID	HOMBURG	HOTNESS
HEEDFUL	HERNIAS	HISTONE	HOMERIC	HOTPOTS
HEEDING	HEROICS	HISTORY	HOME RUN	HOT RODS
HEELING	HEROINE	HITCHED	HOMIEST	HOT SEAT
HEELTAP	HEROISM	HITCHER	HOMINID	HOT SPOT
HEERLEN	HERONRY	HITCHES	HOMOLOG	HOTSPUR
HEFTIER	HERRICK	HIT LIST	HOMONYM	HOTTEST
HEFTILY	HERRING	HITTING	HONESTY	HOUDINI
HEGUMEN	HERSELF	HITTITE	HONEYED	HOUMOUS
HEIFERS	HERTZOG	HOARDED	HONIARA	HOUNDED
HEIFETZ	HESIONE	HOARDER	HONITON	HOUNDER
HEIGH-HO	HESSIAN	HOARIER	HONKIES	HOUSING
HEIGHTS	HESSITE	HOARILY	HONKING	HOUSMAN
HEINOUS	HETAERA	HOARSEN	HONOURS	HOUSTON
HEIRDOM	HETAIRA	HOARSER	HOODLUM	HOUTING
HEIRESS	HEXADIC	HOATZIN	HOODOOS	HOVERED
HEISTER	HEXAGON	HOAXERS	HOOGHLY	HOVERER
HEITIKI	HEXAPLA	HOAXING	HOOKAHS	HOWBEIT
HELICAL	HEXAPOD	HOBBEMA	HOOKERS	HOWDAHS
HELICES	HEXOSAN	HOBBIES	HOOKIES	HOWEVER
HELICON	HEYDUCK	HOBBISM	HOOKING	HOWLAND
HELLBOX	HEYSHAM	HOBBIST	HOOKUPS	HOWLERS
HELLCAT	HEYWOOD	HOBBLED	HOORAYS	HOWLING
HELLENE	HIALEAH	HOBBLER	HOOTERS	HOYDENS
HELLERY	HIBACHI	HOBLIKE	HOOTING	HOYLAKE
HELLION	HICCUPS	HOBNAIL	HOOVERS	HSIA-MEN
HELLISH	HICKORY	HOBOISM	HOPEFUL	HSINING
HELLUVA	HIDABLE	HOBOKEN	HOPHEAD	HSU-CHOU
HELMAND	HIDALGO	HOCKING	HOPKINS	HUAI-NAN
HELMETS	HIDEOUS	HOCKNEY	HOPLITE	HUBBIES
HELOISE	HIDINGS	HODEIDA	HOPPERS	HUBCAPS
HELOTRY	HIELAND	HODGKIN	HOPPING	HUDDLED
HELPFUL	HIGHBOY	HOEDOWN	HOPPLER	HUDDLER
HELPING	HIGHEST	HOELIKE	HOPSACK	HUDDLES
HEMIOLA	HIGH TEA	HOGARTH	HORDEIN	HUFFIER
HEMIPOD	HIGHWAY	HOGBACK	HORIZON	HUFFILY
HEMLINE	HIJACKS	HOGFISH	HORMONE	HUFFING
HEMLOCK	HILBERT	HOGGING	HORNETS	HUFFISH
HEMMING	HILLARY	HOGGISH	HORNIER	HUGGING
HENBANE	HILLERY	HOGLIKE	HORNILY	HUHEHOT
HENCOOP	HILLIER	HOGNOSE	HORRIFY	HULKING
HENDRIX	HILLOCK	HOGWASH	HORRORS	HULLING
HENGIST	HIMSELF	HOGWEED	HORSIER	HUMANLY
HENNERY	HINDGUT	HOISTED	HORSILY	HUMBLED
HENPECK	HINGING	HOISTER	HOSANNA	HUMBLER
HEPARIN	HINTING	HOKUSAI	HOSIERS	HUMBUGS

HUMDRUM	HYGIENE	IMMERSE	INDEXER	INNERVE
HUMERAL	HYMNALS	IMMORAL	INDEXES	INNINGS
HUMERUS	HYMNING	IMMURED	INDIANA	INQUEST
HUMIDLY	HYPED UP	IMPACTS	INDIANS	INQUIET
HUMIDOR	HYPHENS	IMPALAS	INDICAN	INQUIRE
HUMMING		IMPALED	INDICIA	INQUIRY
HUMMOCK	I	IMPALER	INDOORS	INROADS
HUMORAL	IAMBICS	IMPANEL	INDORSE	INSECTS
HUMOURS	IAPETUS	IMPASSE	INDOXYL	INSERTS
HUMPING	IBERIAN	IMPASTE	INDRAWN	INSHORE
HUNCHED	ICE AGES	IMPASTO	INDUCED	INSIDER
HUNCHES	ICEBALL	IMPEACH	INDUCER	INSIDES
HUNDRED	ICEBERG	IMPEDED	INDULGE	INSIGHT
HUNGARY	ICE CAPS	IMPEDER	INEPTLY	INSIPID
HUNGNAM	ICE-COLD	IMPERIL	INERTIA	INSOFAR
HUNKERS	ICEFALL	IMPETUS	INERTLY	INSOLES
HUNLIKE	ICELAND	IMPIETY	INEXACT	INSPECT
HUNNISH	ICE PACK	IMPINGE	INFANCY	INSPIRE
HUNTERS	ICE PICK	IMPIOUS	INFANTA	INSTALL
HUNTING	ICE RINK	IMPLANT	INFANTE	INSTANT
HURDLED	ICHNITE	IMPLEAD	INFANTS	INSTATE
HURDLER	ICICLED	IMPLIED	INFARCT	INSTEAD
HURDLES	ICICLES	IMPLODE	INFERNO	INSTEPS
HURLING	ICINESS	IMPLORE	INFIDEL	INSULAR
HURRAYS	ICTERIC	IMPORTS	INFIELD	INSULIN
HURRIED	ICTERUS	IMPOSED	INFLAME	INSULTS
HURTFUL	ID CARDS	IMPOSER	INFLATE	INSURED
HURTING	IDEALLY	IMPOUND	INFLECT	INSURER
HURTLED	IDEATUM	IMPRESA	INFLICT	INSWING
HUSBAND	IDENTIC	IMPRESS	INFLOWS	INTAKES
HUSHABY	IDIOTIC	IMPREST	INFRACT	INTEGER
HUSHING	IDOLIZE	IMPRINT	INFUSED	INTENSE
HUSKIER	IDYLLIC	IMPROVE	INFUSER	INTERIM
HUSKIES	IGNEOUS	IMPULSE	INGENUE	INTERNS
HUSKILY	IGNITED	IMPUTED	INGESTA	INTIMAL
HUSSARS	IGNITER	IMPUTER	INGOING	INTONED
HUSSEIN	IGNOBLE	INANELY	INGRAIN	INTONER
HUSSIES	IGNOBLY	INANITY	INGRATE	INTROIT
HUSSISM	IGNORED	INAPTLY	INGRESS	INTRUDE
HUSSITE	IGNORER	INBOARD	IN-GROUP	INTRUST
HUSTLED	IGUANAS	INBOUND	INGROWN	INURING
HUSTLER	IKEBANA	INBREED	INHABIT	INUTILE
HUTCHES	ILEITIS	INCENSE	INHALED	IN VACUO
HUTCHIE	ILL-BRED	INCHING	INHALER	INVADED
HUTLIKE	ILLEGAL	INCIPIT	INHERIT	INVADER
HUTMENT	ILLICIT	INCISED	INHIBIT	INVALID
HUYGENS	ILLNESS	INCISOR	IN-HOUSE	INVEIGH
HWANG HO	ILL WILL	INCITED	INHUMAN	INVERSE
HYAENAS	IMAGERY	INCITER	INHUMER	INVITED
HYAENIC	IMAGINE	INCLINE	INITIAL	INVITER
HYALINE	IMAGISM	INCLOSE	INJURED	IN VITRO
HYALITE	IMAGIST	INCLUDE	INJURER	INVOICE
HYALOID	IMAMATE	INCOMES	INKIEST	INVOKED
HYBRIDS	IMBIBED	INCROSS	INKLING	INVOKER
HYDATID	IMBIBER	INCUBUS	INKPADS	INVOLVE
HYDRANT	IMBRUTE	INCURVE	INKWELL	INWARDS
HYDRATE	IMBUING	INDENTS	INLAYER	INWEAVE
HYDRIDE	IMITATE	IN-DEPTH	INMATES	IODIZER
HYDROID	IMMENSE	INDEXED	INNARDS	IONIZED

IONIZER	JACK TAR	JIGGING	JUDAIST	KASSALA
IPOMOEA	JACOBIN	JIGGLED	JUDAIZE	KATANGA
IPSWICH	JACONET	JIGGLES	JUDASES	KATYDID
IRANIAN	JACUZZI	JIGSAWS	JUDGING	KAYAKER
IRATELY	JADEITE	JILTING	JUDOIST	KAYSERI
IRELAND	JAGGERY	JIM CROW	JUGGING	KEELING
IRENICS	JAGGING	JIMJAMS	JUGGLED	KEELSON
IRIDIUM	JAGUARS	JIMMIES	JUGGLER	KEENEST
IRKSOME	JAILERS	JINGLED	JUGULAR	KEENING
IRKUTSK	JAILING	JINGLER	JUICIER	KEEPERS
IRON AGE	JALAPIC	JINGLES	JUICILY	KEEPING
IRONIES	JALISCO	JINXING	JUICING	KEEPNET
IRONING	JAMAICA	JITTERS	JUJITSU	KEITLOA
IRONIST	JAMMIER	JITTERY	JUJUBES	KELVINS
ISAGOGE	JAMMING	JOBBERS	JUKEBOX	KENNEDY
ISCHIAL	JANGLED	JOBBERY	JUMBLED	KENNELS
ISCHIUM	JANGLER	JOBBING	JUMBLER	KENNING
ISFAHAN	JANITOR	JOBLESS	JUMBLES	KENOSIS
ISLAMIC	JANUARY	JOB LOTS	JUMPERS	KENOTIC
ISLANDS	JARGONS	JOCKEYS	JUMPIER	KENTISH
ISOBARS	JARRING	JOCULAR	JUMPILY	KERATIN
ISOBATH	JASMINE	JODHPUR	JUMPING	KERBING
ISOCHOR	JAUNTED	JOGGING	JUMP-OFF	KERNELS
ISOGAMY	JAVELIN	JOGGLED	JUNDIAI	KERNITE
ISOGENY	JAWBONE	JOGGLER	JUNGIAN	KESTREL
ISOHYET	JAYWALK	JOGGLES	JUNGLES	KESWICK
ISOLATE	JAZZIER	JOG TROT	JUNIORS	KETCHES
ISOLINE	JAZZILY	JOHN DOE	JUNIPER	KETCHUP
ISONOMY	JAZZING	JOINDER	JUNKETS	KETONIC
ISOTONE	JEALOUS	JOINERS	JUNKIES	KETOSIS
ISOTOPE	JEERING	JOINERY	JUNKING	KETTLES
ISOTOPY	JEHOVAH	JOINING	JUPITER	KEYED UP
ISOTRON	JEJUNAL	JOINTED	JURISTS	KEYHOLE
ISRAELI	JEJUNUM	JOINTER	JURY BOX	KEYNOTE
ISSUING	JELLIED	JOINTLY	JURYMAN	KEY RING
ISTHMUS	JELLIES	JOLLIED	JUSSIVE	KHADDAR
ISTRIAN	JELLIFY	JOLLIER	JUSTICE	KHAKASS
ITALIAN	JELLING	JOLLIFY	JUSTIFY	KHALIFS
ITALICS	JEMMIED	JOLLILY	JUTLAND	KHALKHA
ITCHIER	JEMMIES	JOLLITY	JUTTING	KHAMSIN
ITCHING	JENNIES	JOLTING		KHANATE
ITEMIZE	JERICHO	JONESES	**K**	KHARKOV
ITERANT	JERKIER	JONQUIL	KAFFIRS	KHERSON
ITERATE	JERKILY	JOSHING	KAFTANS	KHINGAN
ITHACAN	JERKING	JOSTLED	KAIFENG	KHOISAN
IVANOVO	JERKINS	JOSTLER	KAINITE	KIANGSI
IVORIES	JERSEYS	JOTTERS	KAISERS	KIANGSU
IZHEVSK	JESTERS	JOTTING	KALENDS	KIBBUTZ
	JESTING	JOURNAL	KALININ	KICKING
J	JESUITS	JOURNEY	KALMUCK	KICKOFF
JABBING	JETFOIL	JOURNOS	KAMPALA	KIDDERS
JACAMAR	JETPORT	JOUSTED	KANNADA	KIDDIES
JACKALS	JETTIES	JOUSTER	KANTIAN	KIDDING
JACKASS	JETTING	JOYLESS	KARACHI	KIDNEYS
JACKDAW	JEWFISH	JOYRIDE	KARAKUL	KIDSKIN
JACKETS	JEW'S-EAR	JUBILEE	KARBALA	KILDARE
JACKING	JEZEBEL	JUDAEAN	KARSTIC	KILLERS
JACKPOT	JIBBING	JUDAICA	KASHGAR	KILLICK
JACKSON	JIGGERS	JUDAISM	KASHMIR	KILLING

KILLJOY	KOFTGAR	LAMBING	LATVIAN	LEGATOR
KILOTON	KOKANEE	LAMELLA	LAUDING	LEGENDS
KILTERS	KOKOBEH	LAMENTS	LAUGHED	LEGGIER
KIMONOS	KOLKHOZ	LAMINAR	LAUGHER	LEGGING
KINDEST	KOLOMNA	LAMPERN	LAUNDER	LEGHORN
KINDLED	KONGONI	LAMPOON	LAUNDRY	LEGIBLE
KINDLER	KOOKIER	LAMPREY	LAURELS	LEGIBLY
KINDRED	KOPECKS	LANCERS	LAWLESS	LEGIONS
KINETIC	KOPEISK	LANCETS	LAWSUIT	LEGLESS
KINFOLK	KOWLOON	LANCHOW	LAWYERS	LEG-PULL
KINGCUP	KREFELD	LANCING	LAXNESS	LEGROOM
KINGDOM	KREMLIN	LANDAUS	LAYERED	LEG SIDE
KINGPIN	KRISHNA	LANDING	LAYETTE	LEGUMES
KINKIER	KRYPTON	LANDTAG	LAY-OFFS	LEGUMIN
KINKILY	KUCHING	LANGRES	LAYOUTS	LEGWORK
KINSHIP	KUMQUAT	LANGUID	LAZIEST	LE HAVRE
KINSMAN	KUNMING	LANGUOR	L-DRIVER	LEIPZIG
KINSMEN	KUNZITE	LANIARY	LEACHED	LEISTER
KIPPERS	KURDISH	LANKEST	LEACHER	LEISURE
KIPPING	KUTAISI	LANKIER	LEADERS	LEITRIM
KIRGHIZ	KUWAITI	LANKILY	LEADING	LEMMING
KIRUNDI	KWANGJU	LANOLIN	LEAD-INS	LENDERS
KISSERS	KWAZULU	LANSING	LEAFAGE	LENDING
KISSING	KWEILIN	LANTANA	LEAFIER	LENGTHS
KIT BAGS	KYANIZE	LANTERN	LEAFLET	LENGTHY
KITCHEN		LANYARD	LEAGUED	LENIENT
KITSCHY	L	LAOTIAN	LEAGUES	LENTIGO
KITTENS	LABELED	LAPDOGS	LEAKAGE	LENTILS
KITTIES	LABIALS	LAPLACE	LEAKIER	LEONINE
KITTING	LABIATE	LAPLAND	LEAKING	LEOPARD
KLAXONS	LABOURS	LAPPING	LEANEST	LEOTARD
KLEENEX	LABROID	LAPSING	LEANING	LEPORID
KNAPPER	LACIEST	LAPWING	LEAN-TOS	LEPROSE
KNAVERY	LACKEYS	LARCENY	LEAPING	LEPROSY
KNAVISH	LACKING	LARCHES	LEARNED	LEPROUS
KNEADED	LACONIC	LARDERS	LEARNER	LERWICK
KNEADER	LACQUER	LARDING	LEASHES	LESBIAN
KNEECAP	LACTASE	LARGELY	LEASING	LESIONS
KNEEING	LACTATE	LARGESS	LEATHER	LESOTHO
KNEELED	LACTEAL	LARGEST	LEAVENS	LESSEES
KNEEPAD	LACTONE	LARGISH	LEAVING	LESSONS
KNIFING	LACTOSE	LARIATS	LEBANON	LESSORS
KNIGHTS	LACUNAE	LARKING	LECHERS	LETDOWN
KNITTED	LACUNAR	LASAGNA	LECHERY	LETTERS
KNITTER	LACUNAS	LASAGNE	LECTERN	LETTING
KNOBBLY	LADDERS	LASCAUX	LECTION	LETTUCE
KNOCKED	LADDIES	LASHING	LECTURE	LEUCINE
KNOCKER	LADINGS	LASH-UPS	LEDGERS	LEUCITE
KNOCK-ON	LADLING	LASSOED	LEECHES	LEUCOMA
KNOCK-UP	LAGGARD	LASSOER	LEERIER	LEVATOR
KNOSSOS	LAGGING	LASTING	LEERING	LEVELED
KNOTTED	LAGOONS	LATCHED	LEE TIDE	LEVERED
KNOTTER	LAICISM	LATCHES	LEEWARD	LEVERET
KNOW-ALL	LAICIZE	LATCHET	LEFTIES	LEVYING
KNOW-HOW	LALLANS	LATENCY	LEFTISM	LEXICAL
KNOWING	LAMAISM	LATERAL	LEFTIST	LEXICON
KNUCKLE	LAMAIST	LATHERY	LEGALLY	LIAISED
KNUCKLY	LAMBENT	LATRINE	LEGATEE	LIAISON
KOBLENZ	LAMBERT	LATTICE	LEGATES	LIANOID

LIASSIC	LINKING	LOCKNUT	LOUSIER	LUSATIA
LIBBERS	LINKMAN	LOCKOUT	LOUSILY	LUSTFUL
LIBELED	LINKUPS	LOCKUPS	LOUSING	LUSTILY
LIBERAL	LINNETS	LOCOISM	LOUTISH	LUSTING
LIBERIA	LINOCUT	LOCULAR	LOUVAIN	LUSTRAL
LIBERTY	LINSANG	LOCUSTS	LOUVRES	LUSTRES
LIBIDOS	LINSEED	LODGERS	LOVABLE	LUTEOUS
LIBRARY	LINTELS	LODGING	LOWBORN	LYCHEES
LIBRATE	LIONESS	LOFTIER	LOWBROW	LYCHNIS
LICENCE	LIONIZE	LOFTILY	LOW-DOWN	LYCOPOD
LICENSE	LIPETSK	LOFTING	LOWERED	LYDDITE
LICKING	LIP-READ	LOGBOOK	LOWLAND	LYING-IN
LIE-DOWN	LIQUATE	LOGGERS	LOWLIER	LYNCEAN
LIFTING	LIQUEFY	LOGGIAS	LOW LIFE	LYNCHED
LIFT-OFF	LIQUEUR	LOGGING	LOWNESS	LYNCHER
LIGHTED	LIQUIDS	LOGICAL	LOW-RISE	LYRICAL
LIGHTEN	LISPING	LOGIEST	LOW TIDE	
LIGHTER	LISTING	LOGJAMS	LOYALLY	M
LIGHTLY	LITCHIS	LOGWOOD	LOYALTY	MACABRE
LIGNIFY	LITERAL	LOLLARD	LOZENGE	MACADAM
LIGNITE	LITHELY	LOLLIES	L-PLATES	MACAQUE
LIGROIN	LITHEST	LOLLING	LUBBOCK	MACEDON
LIGULAR	LITHIUM	LOMBARD	LUCERNE	MACHETE
LIGURIA	LITHOID	LONGBOW	LUCIDLY	MACHINE
LIKABLE	LITOTES	LONGEST	LUCIFER	MACRAME
LIKENED	LITTERS	LONGING	LUCKIER	MACULAR
LIKINGS	LITURGY	LONGISH	LUCKILY	MADDEST
LILTING	LIVABLE	LONG TON	LUCKNOW	MADEIRA
LIMACON	LIVENED	LOOFAHS	LUDDITE	MADISON
LIMBATE	LIVENER	LOOKERS	LUFFING	MADNESS
LIMBURG	LIVIDLY	LOOKING	LUGANDA	MADONNA
LIMEADE	LIVINGS	LOOKOUT	LUGGAGE	MADRONA
LIMIEST	LIVONIA	LOOMING	LUGGERS	MADURAI
LIMINAL	LIVORNO	LOONIER	LUGGING	MADWORT
LIMITED	LIZARDS	LOONIES	LUGHOLE	MAENADS
LIMITER	LOADING	LOOPING	LUGSAIL	MAESTRI
LIMNING	LOAFERS	LOOSELY	LUGWORM	MAESTRO
LIMOGES	LOAFING	LOOSEST	LULLABY	MAFIOSO
LIMPEST	LOANING	LOOSING	LULLING	MAGENTA
LIMPETS	LOATHED	LOOTERS	LUMBAGO	MAGGOTS
LIMPING	LOATHER	LOOTING	LUMENAL	MAGGOTY
LIMPKIN	LOATHLY	LOPPING	LUMPIER	MAGHREB
LIMPOPO	LOBBIED	LOQUATS	LUMPILY	MAGICAL
LIMULUS	LOBBIES	LORDING	LUMPING	MAGNATE
LINABLE	LOBBING	LORELEI	LUMPISH	MAGNETO
LINCTUS	LOBBYER	LORGNON	LUMP SUM	MAGNETS
LINDANE	LOBELIA	LORRIES	LUNATIC	MAGNIFY
LINDENS	LOBSTER	LOSABLE	LUNCHED	MAGNUMS
LINEAGE	LOBULAR	LOSINGS	LUNCHER	MAGPIES
LINEATE	LOCALES	LOTIONS	LUNCHES	MAHATMA
LINEMAN	LOCALLY	LOTTERY	LUNETTE	MAHICAN
LINEMEN	LOCATED	LOTTING	LUNGING	MAH-JONG
LINE-OUT	LOCATER	LOTUSES	LUPULIN	MAHONIA
LINEUPS	LOCHIAL	LOUDEST	LURCHED	MAHOUTS
LINGCOD	LOCKAGE	LOUNGED	LURCHER	MAIDENS
LINGOES	LOCKERS	LOUNGER	LURCHES	MAILBAG
LINGUAL	LOCKETS	LOUNGES	LURGIES	MAILBOX
LININGS	LOCKING	LOURDES	LURIDLY	MAILING
LINKAGE	LOCKJAW	LOURING	LURKING	MAILMAN

MAILMEN	MANNERS	MARTIAL	MEADOWS	MERMAID
MAIMING	MANNING	MARTIAN	MEALIER	MERRIER
MAINTOP	MANNISH	MARTINI	MEANDER	MERRILY
MAJESTY	MANNITE	MARTINS	MEANEST	MESARCH
MAJORCA	MANNOSE	MARTYRS	MEANING	MESHING
MAJORED	MANROPE	MARTYRY	MEASLES	MESSAGE
MAKASAR	MANSARD	MARVELS	MEASURE	MESSIAH
MAKINGS	MANSION	MARXIAN	MEATIER	MESSIER
MALABAR	MANTLED	MARXISM	MEATILY	MESSILY
MALACCA	MANTLES	MARXIST	MEDDLED	MESSINA
MALAISE	MANUALS	MASBATE	MEDDLER	MESSING
MALARIA	MANUKAU	MASCARA	MEDIACY	MESS-UPS
MALATYA	MANURED	MASCOTS	MEDIANS	MESTIZA
MALAYAN	MANURER	MASHHAD	MEDIANT	MESTIZO
MALEATE	MANX CAT	MASHING	MEDIATE	METALED
MALEFIC	MANXMAN	MASKING	MEDICAL	METAMER
MALINES	MAOISTS	MASONIC	MEDICOS	METEORS
MALINKE	MAPPING	MASONRY	MEDIUMS	METERED
MALLARD	MARABOU	MASQUES	MEDLARS	METHANE
MALLETS	MARACAS	MASSAGE	MEDLEYS	METHODS
MALLEUS	MARACAY	MASSEUR	MEDULLA	METIERS
MALLOWS	MARASCA	MASSIFS	MEEKEST	METONYM
MALMSEY	MARATHA	MASSING	MEERKAT	METOPIC
MALTASE	MARATHI	MASSIVE	MEETING	METRICS
MALTESE	MARBLED	MASTERS	MEGATON	METRIFY
MALTING	MARBLER	MASTERY	MEIOSIS	METRIST
MALTOSE	MARBLES	MASTIFF	MEIOTIC	MEXICAN
MAMILLA	MARCHED	MASTOID	MEISSEN	MIAOWED
MAMMALS	MARCHER	MASURIA	MELANGE	MIASMAL
MAMMARY	MARCHES	MATADOR	MELANIC	MIASMAS
MAMMIES	MAREMMA	MATCHED	MELANIN	MICELLE
MAMMOTH	MARGAUX	MATCHES	MELILOT	MICKEYS
MANACLE	MARGINS	MATHURA	MELISMA	MICROBE
MANAGED	MARIMBA	MATINEE	MELODIC	MICRONS
MANAGER	MARINAS	MATRONS	MELTAGE	MIDDENS
MANAGUA	MARINER	MATTERS	MELTING	MIDDLE C
MANAKIN	MARINES	MATTING	MEMBERS	MIDGETS
MANATEE	MARITAL	MATTINS	MEMENTO	MIDIRON
MANDATE	MARKERS	MATTOCK	MEMOIRS	MIDLAND
MANDREL	MARKETS	MATURED	MEMPHIS	MIDMOST
MANGERS	MARKHOR	MAUDLIN	MENACED	MIDRIFF
MANGIER	MARKING	MAULING	MENACER	MIDTERM
MANGILY	MARKUPS	MAUNDER	MENACES	MIDWEEK
MANGLED	MARLINE	MAWKISH	MENAGES	MIDWEST
MANGLER	MARLINS	MAXILLA	MENDERS	MIDWIFE
MANGLES	MARLITE	MAXIMAL	MENDING	MIDYEAR
MANGOES	MARMITE	MAXIMIN	MENDIPS	MIGHTN'T
MANHOLE	MARMOTS	MAXIMUM	MENDOZA	MIGRANT
MANHOOD	MAROONS	MAXIMUS	MENFOLK	MIGRATE
MANHOUR	MARQUEE	MAXWELL	MENIALS	MIKADOS
MANHUNT	MARQUIS	MAY DAYS	MENTHOL	MILDEST
MANIACS	MARRIED	MAYENNE	MENTION	MILDEWY
MANIKIN	MARRIER	MAYFAIR	MENTORS	MILEAGE
MANIPUR	MARRING	MAYORAL	MEOWING	MILIARY
MAN JACK	MARROWS	MAYPOLE	MERCIES	MILIEUS
MANKIND	MARSALA	MAYWEED	MERCURY	MILIEUX
MANLIER	MARSHAL	MAZURKA	MERGERS	MILITIA
MANLIKE	MARSHES	MAZZARD	MERGING	MILKERS
MAN-MADE	MARTENS	MBABANE	MERITED	MILKIER

MILKILY	MISKOLC	MOLDIER	MORONIC	MUFFINS
MILKING	MISLAID	MOLDING	MORROWS	MUFFLED
MILKMAN	MISLEAD	MOLLIFY	MORSELS	MUFFLER
MILKMEN	MISPLAY	MOLLUSC	MORTALS	MUGGERS
MILK RUN	MISREAD	MOLTING	MORTARS	MUGGIER
MILKSOP	MISRULE	MOMBASA	MORTIFY	MUGGILY
MILLDAM	MISSALS	MOMENTA	MORTISE	MUGGING
MILLERS	MISSIES	MOMENTS	MORULAR	MUGGINS
MILLINE	MISSILE	MOMMIES	MOSAICS	MUGSHOT
MILLING	MISSING	MONACAN	MOSELLE	MUGWORT
MILLION	MISSION	MONADIC	MOSEYED	MUGWUMP
MILLRUN	MISSIVE	MONARCH	MOSLEMS	MULATTO
MIMESIS	MISTAKE	MONARDA	MOSOTHO	MULCHED
MIMETIC	MISTERS	MONDAYS	MOSQUES	MULCTED
MIMICRY	MISTILY	MONEYED	MOSSIER	MULLAHS
MINABLE	MISTIME	MONGOLS	MOTHERS	MULLEIN
MINARET	MISTING	MONGREL	MOTIONS	MULLETS
MINCERS	MISTOOK	MONITOR	MOTIVES	MULLING
MINCING	MISTRAL	MONKEYS	MOTORED	MULLION
MINDERS	MISUSED	MONKISH	MOTTLED	MULLITE
MINDFUL	MISUSER	MONOCLE	MOTTOES	MUMBLED
MINDING	MISUSES	MONOMER	MOUFLON	MUMBLER
MINERAL	MITHRAS	MONSOON	MOUILLE	MUMMERS
MINGIER	MITOSIS	MONSTER	MOULDED	MUMMERY
MINGLED	MITOTIC	MONTAGE	MOULDER	MUMMIES
MINIBUS	MITTENS	MONTANA	MOULTED	MUMMIFY
MINICAB	MITZVAH	MONTANE	MOULTER	MUMMING
MINIMAL	MIXABLE	MONTHLY	MOUNTED	MUNCHED
MINIMAX	MIXED UP	MOOCHED	MOUNTER	MUNCHER
MINIMUM	MIXTURE	MOOCHER	MOUNTIE	MUNDANE
MINIMUS	MIZORAM	MOODIER	MOURNED	MUNSTER
MINIONS	MOANERS	MOODILY	MOURNER	MUNTJAC
MINIVER	MOANING	MOONEYE	MOUSERS	MURDERS
MINIVET	MOBBING	MOONILY	MOUSIER	MURKIER
MINNOWS	MOBILES	MOONING	MOUSING	MURKILY
MINORCA	MOBSTER	MOONLIT	MOUSSES	MURMURS
MINSTER	MOCKERS	MOONSET	MOUTHED	MURRAIN
MINTAGE	MOCKERY	MOORAGE	MOUTHER	MUSCLED
MINTING	MOCKING	MOORHEN	MOVABLE	MUSCLES
MINUETS	MOCK-UPS	MOORING	MOVABLY	MUSEFUL
MINUSES	MODALLY	MOORISH	MOVIOLA	MUSEUMS
MINUTED	MOD CONS	MOOTING	MUCKIER	MUSHIER
MINUTES	MODELED	MOPPETS	MUCKILY	MUSHILY
MINXISH	MODERAS	MOPPING	MUCKING	MUSICAL
MIOCENE	MODERNS	MORAINE	MUD BATH	MUSKETS
MIRACLE	MODESTY	MORALLY	MUDDIED	MUSKIER
MIRADOR	MODICUM	MORAVIA	MUDDIER	MUSKRAT
MIRAGES	MODISTE	MORCEAU	MUDDILY	MUSLIMS
MIRRORS	MODULAR	MORDANT	MUDDING	MUSSELS
MISCALL	MODULES	MORDENT	MUDDLED	MUSSING
MISCAST	MODULUS	MORDVIN	MUDDLER	MUSTANG
MISDEAL	MOFETTE	MOREISH	MUDDLES	MUSTARD
MISDEED	MOGADOR	MORELIA	MUDFISH	MUSTERS
MISERLY	MOGGIES	MORELLO	MUDFLAP	MUSTIER
MISFILE	MOGILEV	MORELOS	MUDFLAT	MUSTILY
MISFIRE	MOHICAN	MORGUES	MUDPACK	MUTABLE
MISFITS	MOIDORE	MORMONS	MUD PIES	MUTABLY
MISHAPS	MOISTEN	MORNING	MUEZZIN	MUTAGEN
MISHEAR	MOISTLY	MOROCCO	MUFFING	MUTANTS

MUTTONY	NASTILY	NERVINE	NITRIFY	NOURISH
MUZZIER	NATIONS	NERVING	NITRILE	NOVELLA
MUZZILY	NATIVES	NERVOUS	NITRITE	NOVELLE
MUZZLED	NATTIER	NERVURE	NITROSO	NOVELTY
MUZZLER	NATTILY	NEST EGG	NITROUS	NOVICES
MUZZLES	NATURAL	NESTING	NITWITS	NOWHERE
MYALGIA	NATURES	NESTLED	NIVEOUS	NOXIOUS
MYALGIC	NAUGHTY	NESTLER	NO BALLS	NOZZLES
MYCENAE	NAURUAN	NETBALL	NOBBLED	NUANCES
MYCOSIS	NAVARRE	NETSUKE	NOBBLER	NUCLEAR
MYCOTIC	NAVVIES	NETTING	NOBLEST	NUCLEIN
MYELOID	NAYARIT	NETTLED	NOCTUID	NUCLEON
MYELOMA	NEAREST	NETTLES	NOCTULE	NUCLEUS
MYIASIS	NEARING	NETWORK	NOCTURN	NUCLIDE
MYNHEER	NEATEST	NEUROMA	NODDING	NUDGING
MYOLOGY	NEBULAE	NEUTRAL	NODDLES	NUDISTS
MYOTOME	NEBULAR	NEUTRON	NODICAL	NUGGETS
MYRIADS	NEBULAS	NEWBORN	NODULAR	NUGGETY
MYRTLES	NECKING	NEW DEAL	NODULES	NULLIFY
MYSTERY	NECKLET	NEW MOON	NOGGING	NULLITY
MYSTICS	NECKTIE	NEWNESS	NOGGINS	NULL SET
MYSTIFY	NECROSE	NEW TOWN	NOISIER	NUMBERS
	NECTARY	NEW WAVE	NOISILY	NUMBING
N	NEEDFUL	NEW YEAR	NOISOME	NUMERAL
NABBING	NEEDIER	NEXUSES	NOMADIC	NUMMARY
NACELLE	NEEDING	NIAGARA	NOMBRIL	NUNATAK
NAEVOID	NEEDLED	NIBBLED	NOMINAL	NUNCIOS
NAGGERS	NEEDLES	NIBBLER	NOMINEE	NUNNERY
NAGGING	NEGATED	NIBBLES	NONAGON	NUPTIAL
NAHUATL	NEGATOR	NICKELS	NON-IRON	NURSERY
NAIADES	NEGLECT	NICKING	NONPLUS	NURSING
NAILING	NEGRESS	NICOBAR	NON-PROS	NURTURE
NAIROBI	NEGRITO	NICOSIA	NONSTOP	NUTCASE
NAIVELY	NEGROES	NIFTIER	NONSUIT	NUTGALL
NAIVETE	NEGROID	NIFTILY	NOODLES	NUTMEGS
NAIVETY	NEIGHED	NIGERIA	NOONDAY	NUTRIAS
NAKEDLY	NEITHER	NIGGARD	NO-PLACE	NUTTIER
NALCHIK	NELLIES	NIGGERS	NORFOLK	NUTTILY
NAMABLE	NELUMBO	NIGGLED	NORMANS	NUTTING
NAME DAY	NEMATIC	NIGGLER	NORWICH	NUTWOOD
NAMIBIA	NEMESES	NIGHTIE	NOSEBAG	NUZZLED
NANKEEN	NEMESIS	NIGHTLY	NOSEGAY	NYMPHAL
NANKING	NEOCENE	NIIGATA	NOSHING	NYMPHET
NANNIES	NEOGAEA	NILOTIC	NOSIEST	
NANNING	NEOGENE	NIMBLER	NOSTRIL	O
NANTUNG	NEOLITH	NINEPIN	NOSTRUM	OAKLAND
NAPHTHA	NEONATE	NINNIES	NOTABLE	OARFISH
NAPKINS	NEOTENY	NIOBITE	NOTABLY	OARLOCK
NAPPIES	NEOTYPE	NIOBIUM	NOTCHED	OARSMAN
NAPPING	NEOZOIC	NIOBOUS	NOTCHES	OARSMEN
NARKIER	NEPHEWS	NIPPERS	NOTELET	OATCAKE
NARKING	NEPHRON	NIPPIER	NOTEPAD	OATMEAL
NARRATE	NEPOTIC	NIPPILY	NOTHING	OBCONIC
NARROWS	NEPTUNE	NIPPING	NOTICED	OBELISK
NARTHEX	NEREIDS	NIPPLES	NOTICES	OBELIZE
NARWHAL	NERITIC	NIRVANA	NOTIONS	OBESITY
NASALLY	NERVATE	NITEROI	NO-TRUMP	OBEYING
NASCENT	NERVIER	NITRATE	NOUGATS	OBJECTS
NASTIER	NERVILY	NITRIDE	NOUGHTS	OBLIGED

OBLIGEE	OILRIGS	OPPOSED	OSSICLE	OUTSTAY
OBLIGER	OILSKIN	OPPOSER	OSSUARY	OUT-TAKE
OBLIGOR	OIL WELL	OPPRESS	OSTEOID	OUTTALK
OBLIQUE	OINKING	OPSONIC	OSTEOMA	OUTVOTE
OBLONGS	OKAYAMA	OPSONIN	OSTIOLE	OUTWARD
OBLOQUY	OKAYING	OPTICAL	OSTLERS	OUTWASH
OBOISTS	OKINAWA	OPTIMAL	OSTMARK	OUTWEAR
OBOVATE	OLD BOYS	OPTIMUM	OSTOSIS	OUTWORK
OBOVOID	OLD HAND	OPTIONS	OSTRAVA	OUTWORN
OBSCENE	OLD LADY	OPULENT	OSTRICH	OVARIAN
OBSCURE	OLD LAGS	OPUNTIA	OTOCYST	OVARIES
OBSERVE	OLD MAID	OQUASSA	OTOLITH	OVATION
OBTRUDE	OLD NICK	ORACLES	OTOLOGY	OVERACT
OBVERSE	OLDSTER	ORANGES	OTTOMAN	OVERAGE
OBVIATE	OLDTIME	ORATION	OUABAIN	OVERALL
OBVIOUS	OLDUVAI	ORATORS	OUGHTN'T	OVERARM
OCARINA	OLEFINE	ORATORY	OUR LADY	OVERAWE
OCCIPUT	O LEVELS	ORBITAL	OUR LORD	OVERBID
OCCLUDE	OLIVARY	ORBITED	OURSELF	OVERDID
OCEANIA	OLIVINE	ORCHARD	OUSTERS	OVERDUE
OCEANIC	OLYMPIC	ORCHIDS	OUSTING	OVERFLY
OCELLAR	OLYMPUS	ORCINOL	OUTBACK	OVERJOY
OCELLUS	OMENTUM	ORDEALS	OUTCAST	OVERLAP
OCELOTS	OMICRON	ORDERED	OUTCOME	OVERLAY
OCHROID	OMINOUS	ORDERER	OUTCROP	OVERLIE
OCREATE	OMITTED	ORDERLY	OUTDATE	OVERMAN
OCTADIC	OMITTER	ORDINAL	OUTDONE	OVERPAY
OCTAGON	OMNIBUS	ORECTIC	OUTDOOR	OVERRAN
OCTANES	ONENESS	OREGANO	OUTFACE	OVERRUN
OCTAVES	ONE-OFFS	ORGANIC	OUTFALL	OVERSAW
OCTOBER	ONEROUS	ORGANON	OUTFITS	OVERSEE
OCTOPOD	ONESELF	ORGANUM	OUTFLOW	OVERSET
OCTOPUS	ONE-STAR	ORGANZA	OUTGREW	OVERSEW
OCTUPLE	ONE-STEP	ORGASMS	OUTGROW	OVERTAX
OCULIST	ONETIME	ORIENTE	OUTHAUL	OVERTLY
ODDBALL	ON-GLIDE	ORIFICE	OUTINGS	OVERTOP
ODDMENT	ONGOING	ORIGAMI	OUTLAST	OVERUSE
ODDNESS	ONSHORE	ORIGINS	OUTLAWS	OVIDUCT
ODOROUS	ONTARIO	ORINOCO	OUTLAYS	OVIFORM
ODYSSEY	ONWARDS	ORISONS	OUTLETS	OVULATE
OEDIPAL	OOLITIC	ORKNEYS	OUTLIER	OWN GOAL
OERSTED	OOPHYTE	ORLEANS	OUTLINE	OXALATE
OESTRUS	OOSPERM	OROGENY	OUTLIVE	OXAZINE
OFFBEAT	OOSPORE	OROLOGY	OUTLOOK	OXBLOOD
OFFENCE	OOTHECA	OROTUND	OUTMOST	OXCARTS
OFFERED	OOZIEST	ORPHANS	OUTPLAY	OXHEART
OFFERER	OPACITY	ORPHREY	OUTPORT	OXIDANT
OFFHAND	OPALINE	ORTOLAN	OUTPOST	OXIDASE
OFFICER	OPEN-AIR	OSCULAR	OUTPOUR	OXIDATE
OFFICES	OPENERS	OSCULUM	OUTPUTS	OXIDIZE
OFFINGS	OPENING	OSHOGBO	OUTRAGE	OXONIAN
OFF-LOAD	OPERAND	OSMIOUS	OUTRANK	OXYACID
OFF-PEAK	OPERANT	OSMOSIS	OUTRIDE	OXYSALT
OFFSIDE	OPERATE	OSMOTIC	OUTRODE	OXYTONE
OGREISH	OPHITIC	OSMUNDA	OUTSELL	OYSTERS
OHM'S LAW	OPIATES	OSPREYS	OUTSIDE	OZONIZE
OILBIRD	OPINING	OSSEOUS	OUTSIZE	
OILCANS	OPINION	OSSETIA	OUTSOLD	**P**
OILIEST	OPOSSUM	OSSETIC	OUTSOLE	PACIFIC

PACKAGE	PANGAEA	PARRIES	PAUNCHY	PEG LEGS
PACKERS	PANICKY	PARROTS	PAUPERS	PELAGIC
PACKETS	PANICLE	PARSEES	PAUSING	PELICAN
PACK ICE	PANNIER	PARSERS	PAVANES	PELITIC
PACKING	PANNING	PARSING	PAVINGS	PELLETS
PADDIES	PANOCHA	PARSLEY	PAVIOUR	PELMETS
PADDING	PANOPLY	PARSNIP	PAWKIER	PELORIA
PADDLED	PANSIES	PARSONS	PAWKILY	PELORUS
PADDLER	PANTHER	PARTAKE	PAWNAGE	PELOTAS
PADDLES	PANTIES	PARTIAL	PAWNING	PELTATE
PADDOCK	PANTILE	PARTIED	PAWPAWS	PELTING
PADLOCK	PANTING	PARTIES	PAYABLE	PENALLY
PADRONE	PANTOUM	PARTING	PAYBEDS	PENALTY
PAGEANT	PANZERS	PARTITA	PAY DIRT	PENANCE
PAGEBOY	PAOTING	PARTITE	PAYLOAD	PENDANT
PAGINAL	PAPAYAS	PARTNER	PAYMENT	PENDENT
PAGODAS	PAPERED	PARTOOK	PAYOUTS	PENDING
PAINFUL	PAPERER	PARVENU	PAYROLL	PENGUIN
PAINING	PAPILLA	PASCHAL	PAYSLIP	PENISES
PAINTED	PAPISTS	PASSADE	PEACHES	PEN NAME
PAINTER	PAPOOSE	PASSAGE	PEACOCK	PENNANT
PAIRING	PAPPIES	PASSANT	PEAFOWL	PENNATE
PAIR-OAR	PAPPOSE	PAS SEUL	PEAHENS	PENNIES
PAISLEY	PAPRIKA	PASSING	PEAKIER	PENNING
PAJAMAS	PAPYRUS	PASSION	PEAKING	PENNONS
PALACES	PARABLE	PASSIVE	PEALING	PEN PALS
PALADIN	PARADED	PASSKEY	PEANUTS	PENSILE
PALATAL	PARADER	PASTELS	PEARLER	PENSION
PALATES	PARADES	PASTERN	PEASANT	PENSIVE
PALAVER	PARADOX	PASTE-UP	PEBBLES	PENTANE
PALE ALE	PARAGON	PASTIER	PECCANT	PENTENE
PALERMO	PARAIBA	PASTIES	PECCARY	PENTODE
PALETTE	PARAPET	PASTILY	PECCAVI	PENTOSE
PALFREY	PARASOL	PASTIME	PECKERS	PEONIES
PALINGS	PARBOIL	PASTING	PECKING	PEOPLED
PALLETS	PARCELS	PASTORS	PECKISH	PEOPLES
PALLIER	PARCHED	PASTURE	PECTASE	PEPPERS
PALLING	PARDONS	PATCHED	PECTATE	PEPPERY
PALLIUM	PAREIRA	PATCHER	PECTIZE	PEP PILL
PALMATE	PARENTS	PATCHES	PEDALED	PEPPING
PALMIER	PARESIS	PATELLA	PEDANTS	PEP TALK
PALMING	PARETIC	PATENCY	PEDDLED	PEPTIDE
PALMIRA	PARFAIT	PATENTS	PEDDLER	PEPTIZE
PALMIST	PARIAHS	PATHANS	PEDICEL	PEPTONE
PALM OIL	PARINGS	PATHWAY	PEDICLE	PERACID
PALMYRA	PARKIER	PATIALA	PEDLARS	PERCALE
PALPATE	PARKING	PATIENT	PEDOCAL	PER CENT
PALSIED	PARKWAY	PATRIAL	PEEBLES	PERCEPT
PAMPEAN	PARLEYS	PATRIOT	PEEKING	PERCHED
PANACEA	PARLOUR	PATROLS	PEELING	PERCHER
PANACHE	PARLOUS	PATRONS	PEEPERS	PERCHES
PANAMAS	PARODIC	PATTENS	PEEPING	PERCOID
PAN-ARAB	PAROLED	PATTERN	PEERAGE	PERCUSS
PANCAKE	PAROLES	PATTERS	PEERESS	PER DIEM
PANCHAX	PARONYM	PATTIES	PEERING	PEREIRA
PANDECT	PAROTIC	PATTING	PEEVING	PERFECT
PANDITS	PAROTID	PAUCITY	PEEVISH	PERFIDY
PANDORE	PARQUET	PAULINE	PEEWITS	PERFORM
PANELED	PARRIED	PAULIST	PEGGING	PERFUME

PERFUSE	PHARAOH	PIETIES	PINNULE	PLANNER
PERGOLA	PHARYNX	PIGEONS	PINTAIL	PLANTAR
PERHAPS	PHASING	PIGFISH	PINWORK	PLANTED
PERIDOT	PHASMID	PIGGERY	PINWORM	PLANTER
PERIGEE	PHELLEM	PIGGIER	PIONEER	PLANULA
PERIGON	PHILTRE	PIGGIES	PIOUSLY	PLAQUES
PERIODS	PHIZOGS	PIGGING	PIPETTE	PLASMIN
PERIQUE	PHLOXES	PIGGISH	PIPPING	PLASMON
PERIWIG	PHOBIAS	PIG IRON	PIPPINS	PLASTER
PERJURE	PHOBICS	PIGLETS	PIQUANT	PLASTIC
PERJURY	PHOCINE	PIGMENT	PIQUING	PLASTID
PERKIER	PHOENIX	PIGMIES	PIRAEUS	PLATEAU
PERKILY	PHONATE	PIGSKIN	PIRANHA	PLATINA
PERKING	PHONE-IN	PIGTAIL	PIRATED	PLATING
PERLITE	PHONEME	PIGWEED	PIRATES	PLATOON
PERMIAN	PHONEYS	PIKEMAN	PIRATIC	PLATTER
PERMING	PHONICS	PIKEMEN	PISCARY	PLAUDIT
PERMITS	PHONIER	PILEATE	PISCINA	PLAY-ACT
PERMUTE	PHONING	PILEOUS	PISCINE	PLAYBOY
PERPEND	PHRASAL	PILEUPS	PISSING	PLAYERS
PERPLEX	PHRASED	PILGRIM	PISS-UPS	PLAYFUL
PERSEID	PHRASES	PILLAGE	PISTILS	PLAYING
PERSIAN	PHRATRY	PILLARS	PISTOLS	PLAYLET
PERSIST	PHRENIC	PILLBOX	PISTONS	PLAY-OFF
PERSONA	PHYSICS	PILLION	PIT-A-PAT	PLAYPEN
PERSONS	PHYSIOS	PILLOCK	PITCHED	PLEADED
PERSPEX	PIANISM	PILLORY	PITCHER	PLEADER
PERTAIN	PIANIST	PILLOWS	PITCHES	PLEASED
PERTURB	PIANOLA	PILOTED	PITEOUS	PLEASER
PERUGIA	PIASTRE	PILSNER	PITFALL	PLEATED
PERUSAL	PIAZZAS	PILULAR	PITHEAD	PLEATER
PERUSED	PIBROCH	PIMENTO	PITHIER	PLEDGED
PERUSER	PICADOR	PIMPING	PITHILY	PLEDGER
PERVADE	PICARDY	PIMPLED	PITIFUL	PLEDGES
PERVERT	PICCOLO	PIMPLES	PIT PONY	PLEDGET
PESCARA	PICEOUS	PINBALL	PIT PROP	PLEDGOR
PESETAS	PICKAXE	PINCERS	PITTING	PLENARY
PESKIER	PICKERS	PINCHED	PITYING	PLEURAL
PESSARY	PICKETS	PINCHES	PIVOTAL	PLEURON
PESTLES	PICKIER	PINETUM	PIVOTED	PLIABLE
PETARDS	PICKING	PINFISH	PIZZAZZ	PLIANCY
PETCOCK	PICKLED	PINFOLD	PLACARD	PLICATE
PETIOLE	PICKLER	PINGING	PLACATE	PLIGHTS
PET NAME	PICKLES	PINGUID	PLACEBO	PLINTHS
PETRELS	PICK-UPS	PINHEAD	PLACING	PLODDED
PETRIFY	PICNICS	PINHOLE	PLACKET	PLODDER
PETROUS	PICOTEE	PINIEST	PLACOID	PLOESTI
PETSAMO	PICRATE	PINIONS	PLAFOND	PLONKED
PETTIER	PICRITE	PINKEST	PLAGUED	PLOPPED
PETTILY	PICTISH	PINKEYE	PLAGUER	PLOSION
PETTING	PICTURE	PINK GIN	PLAGUES	PLOSIVE
PETTISH	PIDDLED	PINKIES	PLAINER	PLOTTED
PETUNIA	PIDDOCK	PINKING	PLAINLY	PLOTTER
PFENNIG	PIDGINS	PINKISH	PLAINTS	PLOUGHS
PHAETON	PIEBALD	PINKOES	PLAITED	PLOVDIV
PHALANX	PIECING	PINNACE	PLANETS	PLOVERS
PHALLIC	PIE-EYED	PINNATE	PLANING	PLOWING
PHALLUS	PIERCED	PINNIES	PLANISH	PLUCKED
PHANTOM	PIERCER	PINNING	PLANNED	PLUCKER

PLUGGED	POMPANO	POSTING	PREDATE	PRINTER
PLUMAGE	POMPEII	POSTMAN	PREDICT	PRISING
PLUMATE	POMPOMS	POSTMEN	PREEMPT	PRISONS
PLUMBED	POMPOUS	POSTURE	PREENED	PRITHEE
PLUMBER	PONCHOS	POSTWAR	PREENER	PRIVACY
PLUMBIC	PONGIER	POTABLE	PREFABS	PRIVATE
PLUMING	PONGING	POTENCY	PREFACE	PRIVIER
PLUMMET	PONIARD	POTFULS	PREFECT	PRIVIES
PLUMPED	PONTIFF	POTHEEN	PREHEAT	PRIVILY
PLUMPER	PONTINE	POTHERB	PRELACY	PRIVITY
PLUMULE	PONTOON	POTHOLE	PRELATE	PRIZING
PLUNDER	POOCHES	POTHOOK	PRELIMS	PROBANG
PLUNGED	POODLES	POTICHE	PRELUDE	PROBATE
PLUNGER	POOFIER	POTIONS	PREMIER	PROBING
PLURALS	POOH-BAH	POTLUCK	PREMISE	PROBITY
PLUSHER	POOLING	POTOMAC	PREMISS	PROBLEM
PLUVIAL	POOPERS	POTSDAM	PREMIUM	PROCARP
PLYWOOD	POOREST	POTSHOT	PREPACK	PROCEED
POACHED	POOR LAW	POTTAGE	PREPAID	PROCESS
POACHER	POPADUM	POTTERS	PREPARE	PROCTOR
PO BOXES	POPCORN	POTTERY	PREPUCE	PROCURE
POCHARD	POPEDOM	POTTIER	PRESAGE	PRODDED
POCKETS	POP-EYED	POTTIES	PRESENT	PRODDER
PODAGRA	POPGUNS	POTTING	PRESIDE	PRODIGY
PODDING	POPLARS	POUCHED	PRESSED	PRODUCE
PODESTA	POPOVER	POUCHES	PRESSES	PRODUCT
PODGIER	POPPERS	POULARD	PRESSOR	PROFANE
PODGILY	POPPETS	POULTRY	PRESS-UP	PROFESS
PODIUMS	POPPIES	POUNCED	PRESTOS	PROFFER
PODOLSK	POPPING	POUNCES	PRESUME	PROFILE
POETESS	POPULAR	POUNDAL	PRETEND	PROFITS
POETICS	PORCHES	POUNDED	PRETEST	PRO-FORM
PO-FACED	PORCINE	POUNDER	PRETEXT	PROFUSE
POGONIA	PORKERS	POURING	PRETZEL	PROGENY
POGROMS	PORKIER	POUTING	PREVAIL	PROGRAM
POINTED	PORK PIE	POVERTY	PREVENT	PROJECT
POINTER	PORTAGE	POWDERS	PREVIEW	PROLATE
POISING	PORTALS	POWDERY	PREYING	PRO-LIFE
POISONS	PORTEND	POWERED	PREZZIE	PROLINE
POKIEST	PORTENT	POWWOWS	PRICIER	PROLONG
POLARIS	PORTERS	PRAIRIE	PRICING	PROMISE
POLEAXE	PORTICO	PRAISED	PRICKED	PROMOTE
POLECAT	PORTING	PRAISER	PRICKER	PROMPTS
POLEMIC	PORTION	PRAISES	PRICKET	PRONATE
POLICED	PORTRAY	PRALINE	PRICKLE	PRONOUN
POLITIC	POSEURS	PRANCED	PRICKLY	PROOFED
POLLACK	POSHEST	PRANCER	PRIDING	PROPANE
POLLARD	POSITED	PRATING	PRIESTS	PROPEND
POLLING	POSITIF	PRATTLE	PRIMACY	PROPENE
POLL TAX	POSSESS	PRAWNER	PRIMARY	PROPHET
POLLUTE	POSSETS	PRAYERS	PRIMATE	PROPOSE
POLTAVA	POSSUMS	PRAYING	PRIMERS	PROPPED
POLYGON	POSTAGE	PREBEND	PRIMINE	PRO RATA
POLYMER	POSTBAG	PRECAST	PRIMING	PROSAIC
POLYNYA	POSTBOX	PRECEDE	PRIMMER	PROSIER
POLYPOD	POSTERN	PRECEPT	PRIMULA	PROSILY
POLYPUS	POSTERS	PRECESS	PRINCES	PROSODY
POMMELS	POSTFIX	PRECISE	PRINKER	PROSPER
POMMIES	POSTIES	PRECOOK	PRINTED	PROTEAN

PROTECT	PULPIER	PUZZLER	QUESTER	RADICEL
PROTEGE	PULPING	PUZZLES	QUETZAL	RADICES
PROTEIN	PULPITS	PYAEMIA	QUEUING	RADICLE
PROTEST	PULSARS	PYAEMIC	QUIBBLE	RADIOED
PROTIST	PULSATE	PYGMIES	QUICHES	RADULAR
PROTIUM	PULSING	PYJAMAS	QUICKEN	RAFFISH
PROTONS	PUMPING	PYLORUS	QUICKER	RAFFLED
PROTYLE	PUMPKIN	PYRALID	QUICKIE	RAFFLER
PROUDER	PUNCHED	PYRAMID	QUICKLY	RAFFLES
PROUDLY	PUNCHER	PYRETIC	QUIETEN	RAFTERS
PROVERB	PUNCHES	PYREXIA	QUIETER	RAFTING
PROVIDE	PUNCH-UP	PYRITES	QUIETLY	RAGBAGS
PROVING	PUNDITS	PYRITIC	QUIETUS	RAGGING
PROVISO	PUNGENT	PYROGEN	QUILMES	RAGOUTS
PROVOKE	PUNIEST	PYROSIS	QUILTED	RAGTIME
PROVOST	PUNJABI	PYRRHIC	QUILTER	RAGWEED
PROWESS	PUNKAHS	PYRROLE	QUINARY	RAGWORM
PROWLED	PUNNETS	PYTHONS	QUINATE	RAGWORT
PROWLER	PUNNING		QUINCES	RAIDERS
PROXIES	PUNSTER	**Q**	QUININE	RAIDING
PROXIMA	PUNTERS	Q-FACTOR	QUINONE	RAILING
PRUDENT	PUNTING	QUACKED	QUINTAL	RAILWAY
PRUDERY	PUPPETS	QUADRAT	QUINTAN	RAIMENT
PRUDISH	PUPPIES	QUADRIC	QUINTET	RAINBOW
PRUNING	PUPPING	QUAFFER	QUINTIC	RAINIER
PRURIGO	PURGING	QUAILED	QUIPPED	RAINILY
PRUSSIA	PURISTS	QUAKERS	QUITTED	RAINING
PSALMIC	PURITAN	QUAKILY	QUITTER	RAINOUT
PSALTER	PURLIEU	QUAKING	QUITTOR	RAISERS
PSYCHED	PURLING	QUALIFY	QUIVERS	RAISING
PSYCHES	PURLOIN	QUALITY	QUIVERY	RAISINS
PSYCHIC	PURPLES	QUANGOS	QUI VIVE	RAISINY
PSYLLID	PURPORT	QUANTAL	QUIZZED	RAKE-OFF
PTERYLA	PURPOSE	QUANTIC	QUIZZER	RALEIGH
PTYALIN	PURPURA	QUANTUM	QUIZZES	RALLIED
PUBERTY	PURPURE	QUARREL	QUONDAM	RALLIER
PUBLISH	PURRING	QUARTAN	QUORATE	RALLIES
PUCCOON	PURSERS	QUARTER	QUORUMS	RALLINE
PUCKERS	PURSING	QUARTET	QUOTHED	RAMADAN
PUCKISH	PURSUED	QUARTIC	QUOTING	RAMBLED
PUDDING	PURSUER	QUARTOS		RAMBLER
PUDDLED	PURSUIT	QUASARS	**R**	RAMBLES
PUDDLER	PURVIEW	QUASHED	RABBITS	RAMEKIN
PUDDLES	PUSHERS	QUASSIA	RABBLER	RAMMING
PUDENDA	PUSHIER	QUAVERS	RABBLES	RAMMISH
PUDGIER	PUSHILY	QUAVERY	RACCOON	RAMPAGE
PUDGILY	PUSHING	QUAYAGE	RACEMIC	RAMPANT
PUERILE	PUSHROD	QUECHUA	RACHIAL	RAMPART
PUFFIER	PUSH-UPS	QUEENED	RACIEST	RAMPION
PUFFILY	PUSSIES	QUEENLY	RACISTS	RAMRODS
PUFFING	PUSTULE	QUEERED	RACKETS	RAMSONS
PUFFINS	PUTAMEN	QUEERER	RACKETY	RANCHER
PUGGING	PUT-DOWN	QUEERLY	RACKING	RANCHES
PULLETS	PUT-OFFS	QUELLED	RACOONS	RANCOUR
PULLEYS	PUTREFY	QUELLER	RACQUET	RANDIER
PULLING	PUTTERS	QUERIED	RADIALS	RANDOMS
PULL-INS	PUTTING	QUERIES	RADIANT	RANGERS
PULLMAN	PUT-UPON	QUERIST	RADIATE	RANGILY
PULLOUT	PUZZLED	QUESTED	RADICAL	RANGING

RANGOON	REACHES	RECYCLE	REGIMES	RENT BOY
RANKERS	REACTED	REDCOAT	REGINAS	RENTERS
RANKING	REACTOR	RED DEER	REGIONS	RENTIER
RANKLED	READERS	REDDEST	REGNANT	RENTING
RANSACK	READIED	REDDISH	REGOSOL	REORDER
RANSOMS	READIER	REDFISH	REGRATE	REPAIRS
RANTERS	READIES	RED FLAG	REGRESS	REPASTS
RANTING	READILY	REDHEAD	REGRETS	REPEATS
RAPHIDE	READING	RED MEAT	REGROUP	REPINED
RAPIDLY	READOUT	REDNECK	REGULAR	REPLACE
RAPIERS	REAGENT	REDNESS	REGULOS	REPLAYS
RAPISTS	REALGAR	REDOING	REGULUS	REPLETE
RAPPING	REALIGN	REDOUBT	REHOUSE	REPLEVY
RAPPORT	REALISM	REDOUND	REIFIER	REPLICA
RAPTURE	REALIST	REDPOLL	REIGNED	REPLIED
RAREBIT	REALITY	REDRAFT	REINING	REPLIER
RASBORA	REALIZE	REDRESS	REISSUE	REPLIES
RASCALS	REALTOR	REDROOT	REJECTS	REPORTS
RASHERS	REAMERS	REDSKIN	REJOICE	REPOSAL
RASHEST	REAMING	RED TAPE	RELAPSE	REPOSED
RASPING	REAPERS	REDUCED	RELATED	REPOSER
RATABLE	REAPING	REDUCER	RELATER	REPOSIT
RATABLY	REARING	REDWING	RELATOR	REPRESS
RATAFIA	REARMED	REDWOOD	RELATUM	REPRINT
RAT-A-TAT	REASONS	REEDIER	RELAXED	REPRISE
RATBAGS	REBATER	REEDING	RELAXER	REPROOF
RATCHET	REBATES	REEFERS	RELAXIN	REPROVE
RATE-CAP	REBIRTH	REEFING	RELAYED	REPTANT
RATINGS	REBOUND	REEKING	RELEASE	REPTILE
RATIONS	REBUFFS	RE-ELECT	RELIANT	REPULSE
RATLINE	REBUILD	REELING	RELIEFS	REPUTED
RAT RACE	REBUILT	RE-ENTER	RELIEVE	REQUEST
RATTIER	REBUKED	RE-ENTRY	RELINED	REQUIEM
RATTILY	REBUKER	REFACED	RELIVED	REQUIRE
RATTING	REBUKES	REFEREE	RELYING	REQUITE
RATTISH	REBUSES	REFILLS	REMAINS	REREDOS
RATTLED	RECALLS	REFINED	REMAKES	RESCIND
RATTLES	RECAPED	REFINER	REMANDS	RESCUED
RAT TRAP	RECEDED	REFLATE	REMARKS	RESCUER
RAUCOUS	RECEIPT	REFLECT	REMARRY	RESCUES
RAUNCHY	RECEIVE	REFORMS	REMATCH	RESERVE
RAVAGED	RECIPES	REFRACT	REMNANT	RESHAPE
RAVAGER	RECITAL	REFRAIN	REMODEL	RESIDED
RAVAGES	RECITED	REFRESH	REMORSE	RESIDER
RAVELED	RECITER	REFUGEE	REMOTER	RESIDUE
RAVELIN	RECKING	REFUGES	REMOULD	RESOLVE
RAVELLY	RECLAIM	REFUNDS	REMOUNT	RESORTS
RAVENER	RECLINE	REFUSAL	REMOVAL	RESOUND
RAVENNA	RECLUSE	REFUSED	REMOVED	RESPECT
RAVE-UPS	RECORDS	REFUSER	REMOVER	RESPIRE
RAVINES	RECOUNT	REFUTED	REMOVES	RESPITE
RAVINGS	RECOVER	REFUTER	RENAMED	RESPOND
RAVIOLI	RECRUIT	REGALIA	RENDING	RESTATE
RAW DEAL	RECTIFY	REGALLY	RENEGED	RESTFUL
RAWHIDE	RECTORS	REGARDS	RENEGER	RESTING
RAWNESS	RECTORY	REGATTA	RENEWAL	RESTIVE
RAZZLES	RECTRIX	REGENCY	RENEWED	RESTOCK
REACHED	RECTUMS	REGENTS	RENEWER	RESTORE
REACHER	RECURVE	REGIMEN	RENTALS	RESTYLE

RESULTS	RHAETIC	RIPPLES	ROMPERS	ROYALLY
RESUMED	RHATANY	RIPPLET	ROMPING	ROYALTY
RESUMES	RHENIUM	RIPSAWS	RONDEAU	ROZZERS
RETABLE	RHEUMIC	RIPTIDE	RONDURE	RUBBERS
RETAKEN	RHIZOID	RISIBLE	RONTGEN	RUBBERY
RETAKER	RHIZOME	RISIBLY	ROOFING	RUBBING
RETAKES	RHODIUM	RISINGS	ROOFTOP	RUBBISH
RETCHED	RHOMBIC	RISKIER	ROOKERY	RUBDOWN
RETHINK	RHOMBUS	RISKILY	ROOKIES	RUBELLA
RETICLE	RHONDDA	RISKING	ROOKING	RUBEOLA
RETINAE	RHUBARB	RISOTTO	ROOMERS	RUBICON
RETINAL	RHYMING	RISSOLE	ROOMFUL	RUBIDIC
RETINAS	RHYTHMS	RITUALS	ROOMIER	RUBIOUS
RETINOL	RIBBAND	RIVALED	ROOMILY	RUBRICS
RETINUE	RIBBING	RIVALRY	ROOMING	RUCHING
RETIRED	RIBBONS	RIVETED	ROOSTED	RUCKING
RETIRER	RIB CAGE	RIVETER	ROOSTER	RUCTION
RETORTS	RIBWORT	RIVIERA	ROOTAGE	RUDDERS
RETOUCH	RICHEST	RIVIERE	ROOTING	RUDDIER
RETRACE	RICKETS	RIVULET	ROOTLET	RUDDILY
RETRACT	RICKETY	ROACHES	ROPIEST	RUDERAL
RETREAD	RICKING	ROADBED	RORQUAL	RUFFIAN
RETREAT	RIDDING	ROAD HOG	ROSARIO	RUFFLED
RETRIAL	RIDDLED	ROADMAN	ROSEATE	RUFFLER
RETSINA	RIDDLER	ROADMEN	ROSEBUD	RUFFLES
RETURNS	RIDDLES	ROAD TAX	ROSE HIP	RUINING
REUNIFY	RIDGING	ROADWAY	ROSELLA	RUINOUS
REUNION	RIDOTTO	ROAMERS	ROSEOLA	RULABLE
REUNITE	RIFFLED	ROAMING	ROSETTE	RULINGS
REUSING	RIFFLER	ROARING	ROSIEST	RUMANIA
REVALUE	RIFLERY	ROASTED	ROSINED	RUMBLED
REVELED	RIFLING	ROASTER	ROSTERS	RUMBLER
REVELRY	RIGGING	ROBBERS	ROSTOCK	RUMBLES
REVENGE	RIGHTED	ROBBERY	ROSTRAL	RUMMAGE
REVENUE	RIGHTER	ROBBING	ROSTRUM	RUMMEST
REVERED	RIGHTLY	ROCKERS	ROTATED	RUMOURS
REVERER	RIGIDLY	ROCKERY	ROTATOR	RUMPLED
REVERIE	RIG-OUTS	ROCKETS	ROTIFER	RUNAWAY
REVERSE	RIM-FIRE	ROCKIER	ROTTERS	RUN-DOWN
REVIEWS	RIMLESS	ROCKIES	ROTTING	RUNNELS
REVILED	RIMMING	ROCKING	ROTUNDA	RUNNERS
REVILER	RIMROCK	ROCKOON	ROUBAIX	RUNNIER
REVISAL	RINGENT	RODENTS	ROUBLES	RUNNING
REVISED	RINGERS	RODLIKE	ROUGHEN	RUN-OFFS
REVISER	RINGING	ROEBUCK	ROUGHER	RUNTISH
REVIVAL	RINGLET	ROE DEER	ROUGHLY	RUNWAYS
REVIVED	RINSING	ROGUERY	ROUGING	RUPTURE
REVIVER	RIOT ACT	ROGUISH	ROULEAU	RUSHING
REVOICE	RIOTERS	ROISTER	ROUNDED	RUSSIAN
REVOKED	RIOTING	ROLL BAR	ROUNDEL	RUSTICS
REVOKER	RIOTOUS	ROLLERS	ROUNDER	RUSTIER
REVOLTS	RIPCORD	ROLLICK	ROUNDLY	RUSTILY
REVOLVE	RIPENED	ROLLING	ROUNDUP	RUSTING
REVVING	RIPENER	ROLLMOP	ROUSING	RUSTLED
REWARDS	RIP-OFFS	ROLL-ONS	ROUTINE	RUSTLER
REWIRED	RIPOSTE	ROLL-TOP	ROUTING	RUTTILY
REWRITE	RIPPING	ROLLWAY	ROWDIER	RUTTING
REWROTE	RIPPLED	ROMAGNA	ROWDILY	RUTTISH
REYNOSA	RIPPLER	ROMANCE	ROWLOCK	RYBINSK

S	SAMPANS	SATISFY	SCENTED	SCRIMPY
SABBATH	SAMPLED	SATSUMA	SCEPTIC	SCRIPTS
SACATON	SAMPLER	SATYRIC	SCEPTRE	SCROLLS
SACCATE	SAMPLES	SATYRID	SCHEMED	SCROOGE
SACCULE	SAMURAI	SAUCERS	SCHEMER	SCROTUM
SACHETS	SANCTUM	SAUCIER	SCHEMES	SCRUBBY
SACKING	SANCTUS	SAUCILY	SCHERZO	SCRUFFS
SADDEST	SANDALS	SAUCING	SCHISMS	SCRUFFY
SADDLED	SANDBAG	SAUNTER	SCHMUCK	SCRUMPY
SADDLER	SANDBAR	SAURIAN	SCHOLAR	SCRUNCH
SADDLES	SANDBOX	SAUSAGE	SCHOOLS	SCRUPLE
SADIRON	SANDERS	SAUTEED	SCIATIC	SCUDDED
SADISTS	SAND FLY	SAVABLE	SCIENCE	SCUFFED
SADNESS	SANDIER	SAVAGED	SCISSOR	SCUFFLE
SAFARIS	SANDING	SAVAGES	SCOFFED	SCULLED
SAFFIAN	SANDPIT	SAVANNA	SCOFFER	SCULLER
SAFFRON	SANGRIA	SAVANTS	SCOLDED	SCULPIN
SAFROLE	SANICLE	SAVE-ALL	SCOLDER	SCUMBLE
SAGGIER	SAN JOSE	SAVINGS	SCOLLOP	SCUMMER
SAGGING	SAN JUAN	SAVIOUR	SCONCES	SCUPPER
SAGUARO	SANTA FE	SAVOURY	SCOOPED	SCUTATE
SAHARAN	SAO LUIS	SAWBILL	SCOOPER	SCUTTLE
SAILING	SAPHENA	SAWDUST	SCOOTED	SCYTHED
SAILORS	SAPIENT	SAWFISH	SCOOTER	SCYTHES
SAINTED	SAPLESS	SAWMILL	SCOPULA	SEABIRD
SAINTLY	SAPLING	SAWN-OFF	SCORERS	SEACOCK
SALAAMS	SAPONIN	SAXHORN	SCORIFY	SEA DOGS
SALABLE	SAPPERS	SAXTUBA	SCORING	SEAFOOD
SALERNO	SAPPIER	SAYINGS	SCORNED	SEAGIRT
SALICIN	SAPPILY	SCABBLE	SCORNER	SEAGULL
SALIENT	SAPPING	SCABIES	SCORPER	SEA-LANE
SALLIED	SAPPORO	SCALARS	SCORPIO	SEALANT
SALLIER	SAPROBE	SCALDED	SCOTOMA	SEA LEGS
SALLIES	SAPSAGO	SCALENE	SCOURED	SEALERS
SALLOWS	SAPWOOD	SCALIER	SCOURER	SEALERY
SALMONS	SARACEN	SCALING	SCOURGE	SEALING
SALOONS	SARANSK	SCALLOP	SCOUSES	SEA LION
SALPINX	SARATOV	SCALPED	SCOUTED	SEAMARK
SALSIFY	SARAWAK	SCALPEL	SCOUTER	SEAMIER
SALTANT	SARCASM	SCALPER	SCOWLED	SEA MILE
SALTBOX	SARCOID	SCAMPER	SCOWLER	SEA MIST
SALTERN	SARCOMA	SCANDAL	SCRAGGY	SEANCES
SALTIER	SARCOUS	SCANDIC	SCRAPED	SEAPORT
SALTILY	SARDINE	SCANNED	SCRAPER	SEARING
SALTING	SARDIUS	SCANNER	SCRAPES	SEASICK
SALTIRE	SARKIER	SCAPOSE	SCRAPPY	SEASIDE
SALTPAN	SARNIES	SCAPULA	SCRATCH	SEASONS
SALTPOT	SARONGS	SCARABS	SCRAWLS	SEATING
SALUTED	SARONIC	SCARCER	SCRAWLY	SEATTLE
SALUTER	SASSABY	SCARIER	SCRAWNY	SEAWALL
SALUTES	SASSARI	SCARIFY	SCREAMS	SEAWARE
SALVAGE	SASSIER	SCARING	SCREECH	SEAWAYS
SALVERS	SASSING	SCARLET	SCREEDS	SEAWEED
SALVING	SATANIC	SCARPER	SCREENS	SECEDED
SALVOES	SATCHEL	SCARRED	SCREWED	SECEDER
SAMISEN	SATIATE	SCARVES	SCREWER	SECLUDE
SAMOSAS	SATIETY	SCATTED	SCRIBAL	SECONDO
SAMOVAR	SATINET	SCATTER	SCRIBER	SECONDS
SAMOYED	SATIRES	SCENERY	SCRIBES	SECRECY

SECRETE	SEQUENT	SHAFTED	SHINDIG	SHUNNER
SECRETS	SEQUINS	SHAGGED	SHINGLE	SHUNTED
SECTARY	SEQUOIA	SHAHDOM	SHINGLY	SHUNTER
SECTILE	SERAPHS	SHAKERS	SHINIER	SHUSHED
SECTION	SERBIAN	SHAKE-UP	SHINING	SHUT-EYE
SECTORS	SERFDOM	SHAKHTY	SHINNED	SHUT-OFF
SECULAR	SERGIPE	SHAKIER	SHIPPED	SHUTOUT
SECURED	SERIALS	SHAKILY	SHIPPER	SHUTTER
SECURER	SERIATE	SHAKING	SHIPWAY	SHUTTLE
SEDATED	SERICIN	SHALLOP	SHIRKED	SHYNESS
SEDILIA	SERIEMA	SHALLOT	SHIRKER	SHYSTER
SEDUCED	SERINGA	SHALLOW	SHITTED	SIALKOT
SEDUCER	SERIOUS	SHAMANS	SHIVERS	SIALOID
SEEDBED	SERMONS	SHAMBLE	SHIVERY	SIAMANG
SEEDIER	SERPENT	SHAMING	SHOCKED	SIAMESE
SEEDILY	SERPIGO	SHAMMED	SHOCKER	SIBERIA
SEEDING	SERRATE	SHAMMER	SHOEING	SIBLING
SEEKERS	SERRIED	SHAMPOO	SHOGUNS	SICKBAY
SEEKING	SERUMAL	SHANNON	SHOOING	SICKBED
SEEMING	SERVANT	SHAPELY	SHOOTER	SICKEST
SEEPAGE	SERVERS	SHAPING	SHOPPED	SICKING
SEEPING	SERVERY	SHARERS	SHOPPER	SICKLES
SEESAWS	SERVICE	SHARING	SHORING	SICK PAY
SEETHED	SERVILE	SHARPEN	SHORTED	SIDEARM
SEGMENT	SERVING	SHARPER	SHORTEN	SIDECAR
SEISMIC	SESOTHO	SHARPLY	SHORTER	SIDINGS
SEIZING	SESSILE	SHATTER	SHORTIE	SIDLING
SEIZURE	SESSION	SHAVERS	SHORTLY	SIEMENS
SEKONDI	SESTINA	SHAVING	SHOTGUN	SIERRAN
SELENIC	SETBACK	SHAWNEE	SHOT PUT	SIERRAS
SELFISH	SETLINE	SHEARED	SHOTTEN	SIESTAS
SELLERS	SETTEES	SHEARER	SHOUTED	SIEVING
SELLING	SETTERS	SHEATHE	SHOUTER	SIFTERS
SELL-OUT	SETTING	SHEATHS	SHOVELS	SIFTING
SELTZER	SETTLED	SHEAVES	SHOVING	SIGHING
SELVAGE	SETTLER	SHEBANG	SHOWERS	SIGHTED
SEMATIC	SETTLES	SHEBEEN	SHOWERY	SIGHTER
SEMINAL	SEVENTH	SHEDDER	SHOWIER	SIGHTLY
SEMINAR	SEVENTY	SHEERED	SHOWILY	SIGMATE
SEMITIC	SEVERAL	SHEERER	SHOWING	SIGMOID
SENATES	SEVERED	SHEIKHS	SHOWMAN	SIGNALS
SENATOR	SEVILLE	SHEILAS	SHOWMEN	SIGNETS
SENDERS	SEXIEST	SHEKELS	SHOW-OFF	SIGNIFY
SENDING	SEXISTS	SHELLAC	SHRIEKS	SIGNING
SEND-OFF	SEXLESS	SHELLED	SHRIFTS	SIGNORA
SEND-UPS	SEXPOTS	SHELTER	SHRIKES	SIGNORE
SENEGAL	SEXTANT	SHELVED	SHRILLY	SIGNORS
SENIORS	SEXTETS	SHELVER	SHRIMPS	SILENCE
SENORAS	SEXTILE	SHELVES	SHRINES	SILENTS
SENSATE	SEXTONS	SHERBET	SHRINKS	SILESIA
SENSING	SFUMATO	SHERIFF	SHRIVEL	SILICIC
SENSORS	SHACKED	SHERPAS	SHRIVER	SILICLE
SENSORY	SHACKLE	SHEWING	SHROUDS	SILICON
SENSUAL	SHADIER	SHIELDS	SHRUBBY	SILIQUA
SEPTATE	SHADILY	SHIFTED	SHUCKED	SILKIER
SEPTETS	SHADING	SHIFTER	SHUCKER	SILKILY
SEPTIME	SHADOOF	SHIITES	SHUDDER	SILLIER
SEQUELA	SHADOWS	SHIKOKU	SHUFFLE	SILLIES
SEQUELS	SHADOWY	SHIMMER	SHUNNED	SILTING

SILURID	SKIFFLE	SLEDGED	SMACKER	SNIFFER
SILVERS	SKI JUMP	SLEDGES	SMALL AD	SNIFFLE
SILVERY	SKILFUL	SLEEKED	SMALLER	SNIFTER
SIMIANS	SKI LIFT	SLEEKER	SMARTED	SNIGGER
SIMILAR	SKILLED	SLEEKLY	SMARTEN	SNIGGLE
SIMILES	SKILLET	SLEEPER	SMARTER	SNIPERS
SIMIOUS	SKIMMED	SLEETED	SMARTLY	SNIPING
SIMPERS	SKIMMER	SLEEVES	SMASHED	SNIPPED
SIMPLER	SKIMMIA	SLEIGHS	SMASHER	SNIPPET
SIMPLEX	SKIMPED	SLEIGHT	SMASHES	SNOGGED
SIMULAR	SKINFUL	SLENDER	SMASH-UP	SNOOKER
SINALOA	SKINNED	SLEUTHS	SMATTER	SNOOPED
SINCERE	SKINNER	SLEWING	SMEARED	SNOOPER
SINE DIE	SKI POLE	SLICING	SMEARER	SNOOZED
SINGING	SKIPPED	SLICKED	SMECTIC	SNOOZER
SINGLED	SKIPPER	SLICKER	SMELLED	SNOOZES
SINGLES	SKIPPET	SLICKLY	SMELTED	SNORERS
SINGLET	SKIRRET	SLIDING	SMELTER	SNORING
SINITIC	SKIRTED	SLIGHTS	SMIDGIN	SNORKEL
SINKERS	SKITTER	SLIMIER	SMILING	SNORTED
SINKING	SKITTLE	SLIMILY	SMIRKED	SNORTER
SINLESS	SKIVERS	SLIMMED	SMIRKER	SNOWCAP
SINNERS	SKIVING	SLIMMER	SMITING	SNOWIER
SINNING	SKULKED	SLINGER	SMITTEN	SNOWILY
SINUATE	SKULKER	SLIP-ONS	SMOKERS	SNOWING
SINUIJU	SKY-BLUE	SLIPPED	SMOKIER	SNOWMAN
SINUOUS	SKYCAPS	SLIPPER	SMOKILY	SNOWMEN
SINUSES	SKYDIVE	SLIP-UPS	SMOKING	SNUBBED
SIPHONS	SKY-HIGH	SLIPWAY	SMOLDER	SNUBBER
SIPPING	SKYJACK	SLITHER	SMOTHER	SNUFFED
SIRLOIN	SKYLARK	SLITTED	SMUDGED	SNUFFER
SIROCCO	SKYLINE	SLITTER	SMUDGES	SNUFFLE
SIRRAHS	SKYSAIL	SLIVERS	SMUGGER	SNUFFLY
SISSIER	SLACKED	SLOBBER	SMUGGLE	SNUGGLE
SISSIES	SLACKEN	SLOGANS	SMUTCHY	SOAKAGE
SISTERS	SLACKER	SLOGGED	SNACKED	SOAKING
SITCOMS	SLACKLY	SLOGGER	SNAFFLE	SO-AND-SO
SIT-DOWN	SLAGGED	SLOPING	SNAGGED	SOAPBOX
SITTERS	SLAKING	SLOPPED	SNAKILY	SOAPIER
SITTING	SLALOMS	SLOSHED	SNAKING	SOAPILY
SITUATE	SLAMMED	SLOTTED	SNAPPED	SOAPING
SIXFOLD	SLANDER	SLOTTER	SNAPPER	SOARING
SIX-PACK	SLANGED	SLOUCHY	SNARING	SOBBING
SIXTEEN	SLANTED	SLOUGHS	SNARLED	SOBERED
SIXTIES	SLAPPED	SLOUGHY	SNARLER	SOBERLY
SIZABLE	SLAPPER	SLOVENE	SNARL-UP	SOCAGER
SIZZLED	SLASHED	SLOWEST	SNATCHY	SOCIALS
SIZZLER	SLASHER	SLOWING	SNEAKED	SOCIETY
SKATING	SLASHES	SLUGGED	SNEAKER	SOCKETS
SKATOLE	SLATING	SLUICED	SNEERED	SOCKEYE
SKEPTIC	SLATTED	SLUICES	SNEERER	SOCKING
SKETCHY	SLAVERS	SLUMBER	SNEEZED	SODDING
SKEWERS	SLAVERY	SLUMMED	SNEEZER	SOD'S LAW
SKEWING	SLAVING	SLUMMER	SNEEZES	SOFTEST
SKIABLE	SLAVISH	SLUMPED	SNICKED	SOFTIES
SKIBOBS	SLAYERS	SLURPED	SNICKER	SOGGIER
SKIDDED	SLAYING	SLURRED	SNIDELY	SOGGILY
SKIDPAN	SLEDDED	SLYNESS	SNIDEST	SOILAGE
SKID ROW	SLEDDER	SMACKED	SNIFFED	SOILING

SOIREES	SOUNDER	SPICATE	SPOOKED	SQUINTY
SOJOURN	SOUNDLY	SPICERY	SPOONED	SQUIRES
SOLACED	SOUPCON	SPICIER	SPOORER	SQUIRMS
SOLACER	SOUPFIN	SPICILY	SPORRAN	SQUIRMY
SOLACES	SOURCES	SPICING	SPORTED	SQUIRTS
SOLANUM	SOUREST	SPICULE	SPORTER	SQUISHY
SOLARIA	SOURING	SPIDERS	SPORULE	STABBED
SOLDIER	SOURSOP	SPIDERY	SPOTLIT	STABBER
SOLICIT	SOUSING	SPIELER	SPOTTED	STABILE
SOLIDLY	SOUTANE	SPIGNEL	SPOTTER	STABLED
SOLIDUS	SOUTHER	SPIGOTS	SPOUSAL	STABLES
SOLOIST	SOVIETS	SPIKIER	SPOUSES	STACKED
SOLOMON	SOVKHOZ	SPIKILY	SPOUTED	STACKER
SOLUBLE	SOZZLED	SPIKING	SPOUTER	STADDLE
SOLVATE	SPACING	SPILLED	SPRAINS	STADIUM
SOLVENT	SPANCEL	SPILLER	SPRAWLS	STAFFED
SOLVERS	SPANGLE	SPINACH	SPRAWLY	STAFFER
SOLVING	SPANGLY	SPINDLE	SPRAYED	STAGGER
SOMALIA	SPANIEL	SPINDLY	SPRAYER	STAGILY
SOMATIC	SPANISH	SPIN-DRY	SPREADS	STAGING
SOMEDAY	SPANKED	SPINETS	SPRIEST	STAIDLY
SOMEHOW	SPANKER	SPINNER	SPRIGGY	STAINED
SOMEONE	SPANNED	SPINNEY	SPRINGE	STAINER
SOMEWAY	SPANNER	SPIN-OFF	SPRINGS	STAKING
SOMITAL	SPARING	SPINOSE	SPRINGY	STALEST
SONANCE	SPARKED	SPINOUS	SPRINTS	STALING
SONATAS	SPARKLE	SPINULE	SPRITES	STALKED
SONDAGE	SPARRED	SPIRAEA	SPROUTS	STALKER
SONGFUL	SPARROW	SPIRALS	SPRUCED	STALLED
SONNETS	SPARSER	SPIRANT	SPRUCES	STAMBUL
SOOCHOW	SPARTAN	SPIREME	SPUMONE	STAMENS
SOOTHED	SPASTIC	SPIRITS	SPUMOUS	STAMINA
SOOTHER	SPATHIC	SPIROID	SPURNED	STAMMEL
SOOTIER	SPATIAL	SPIRULA	SPURNER	STAMMER
SOOTILY	SPATTER	SPITING	SPURRED	STAMPED
SOPHISM	SPATULA	SPITTER	SPURTED	STAMPER
SOPHIST	SPAWNED	SPITTLE	SPUTNIK	STANCES
SOPPIER	SPAWNER	SPLASHY	SPUTTER	STANDBY
SOPPILY	SPAYING	SPLAYED	SQUABBY	STANDER
SOPPING	SPEAKER	SPLEENS	SQUACCO	STAND-IN
SOPRANO	SPEARED	SPLENIC	SQUALID	STAND-UP
SORBETS	SPEARER	SPLICED	SQUALLS	STANNIC
SORBOSE	SPECIAL	SPLICER	SQUALLY	STANZAS
SORCERY	SPECIES	SPLICES	SQUALOR	STAPLED
SORDINO	SPECIFY	SPLINTS	SQUARED	STAPLER
SORGHUM	SPECKLE	SPLODGE	SQUARER	STAPLES
SORITES	SPECTRA	SPLODGY	SQUARES	STARCHY
SOROSIS	SPECTRE	SPLURGE	SQUASHY	STARDOM
SORRIER	SPEEDED	SPOILED	SQUAWKS	STARING
SORRILY	SPEEDER	SPOILER	SQUEAKS	STARKER
SORROWS	SPELLED	SPOKANE	SQUEAKY	STARKLY
SORTIES	SPELLER	SPONDEE	SQUEALS	STARLET
SORTING	SPELTER	SPONGED	SQUEEZE	STARLIT
SORT-OUT	SPENCER	SPONGER	SQUELCH	STARRED
SOTTISH	SPENDER	SPONGES	SQUIDGY	STARTED
SOUFFLE	SPEWING	SPONGIN	SQUIFFY	STARTER
SOUGHED	SPHENIC	SPONSON	SQUILLA	STARTLE
SOULFUL	SPHERAL	SPONSOR	SQUINCH	STARVED
SOUNDED	SPHERES	SPOOFER	SQUINTS	STARVER

STASHED	STICKLE	STRANGE	STYLISH	SUICIDE
STASHES	STICK-ON	STRATAL	STYLIST	SUITING
STATANT	STICK-UP	STRATAS	STYLIZE	SUITORS
STATELY	STIFFEN	STRATUM	STYLOID	SUKHUMI
STATICS	STIFFER	STRATUS	STYLOPS	SULCATE
STATING	STIFFLY	STRAYED	STYMIED	SULKIER
STATION	STIFLED	STRAYER	STYPSIS	SULKILY
STATISM	STIFLER	STREAKS	STYPTIC	SULKING
STATIST	STIGMAS	STREAKY	STYRENE	SULLAGE
STATIVE	STILLED	STREAMS	SUAVELY	SULLIED
STATUED	STILLER	STREETS	SUAVITY	SULPHUR
STATUES	STILTED	STRETCH	SUBACID	SULTANA
STATURE	STILTON	STRETTA	SUB-AQUA	SULTANS
STATUTE	STIMULI	STRETTO	SUBARID	SUMATRA
STAUNCH	STINGER	STREWED	SUBBASE	SUMMAND
STAVING	STINKER	STREWER	SUBBASS	SUMMARY
STAYERS	STINTED	STREWTH	SUBBING	SUMMERS
STAYING	STINTER	STRIATE	SUBDUAL	SUMMERY
STEALER	STIPEND	STRIDES	SUBDUCT	SUMMING
STEALTH	STIPPLE	STRIDOR	SUBDUED	SUMMITS
STEAMED	STIPULE	STRIKER	SUBEDIT	SUMMONS
STEAMER	STIR-FRY	STRIKES	SUBERIN	SUNBEAM
STEARIC	STIRRED	STRINGS	SUBFUSC	SUNBEDS
STEARIN	STIRRER	STRINGY	SUBJECT	SUNBELT
STEELED	STIRRUP	STRIPED	SUBJOIN	SUNBIRD
STEEPED	STOCKED	STRIPER	SUBLIME	SUNBURN
STEEPEN	STOCKER	STRIPES	SUBPLOT	SUNDAES
STEEPER	STOICAL	STRIPEY	SUB ROSA	SUNDAYS
STEEPLE	STOKERS	STRIVEN	SUBSETS	SUNDIAL
STEEPLY	STOKING	STRIVER	SUBSIDE	SUNDOWN
STEERED	STOMACH	STROBIC	SUBSIDY	SUNFISH
STEERER	STOMPED	STROKED	SUBSIST	SUNGLOW
STELLAR	STOMPER	STROKES	SUBSOIL	SUN GODS
STEMMED	STONIER	STROLLS	SUBSUME	SUNLAMP
STEMMER	STONILY	STROPHE	SUBTEND	SUNLESS
STEMSON	STONING	STROPPY	SUBTLER	SUNNIER
STENCIL	STOOGES	STRUDEL	SUBTYPE	SUNNILY
STEN GUN	STOOKER	STUBBED	SUBURBS	SUNNING
STENTOR	STOOPED	STUBBLE	SUBVERT	SUNRISE
STEPPED	STOOPER	STUBBLY	SUBWAYS	SUNROOF
STEPPER	STOPGAP	STUCK-UP	SUCCEED	SUNSETS
STEPPES	STOPING	STUDDED	SUCCESS	SUNSPOT
STEPSON	STOPPED	STUDENT	SUCCOUR	SUNSTAR
STEREOS	STOPPER	STUDIED	SUCCUBI	SUNTANS
STERILE	STORAGE	STUDIES	SUCCUMB	SUNTRAP
STERLET	STOREYS	STUDIOS	SUCCUSS	SUNWISE
STERNAL	STORIED	STUFFED	SUCKERS	SUPPERS
STERNER	STORIES	STUFFER	SUCKING	SUPPING
STERNLY	STORING	STUMBLE	SUCKLED	SUPPLER
STERNUM	STORMED	STUMPED	SUCKLER	SUPPORT
STEROID	STOUTER	STUMPER	SUCRASE	SUPPOSE
STERTOR	STOUTLY	STUNNED	SUCROSE	SUPREME
STETSON	STOWAGE	STUNNER	SUCTION	SUPREMO
STEWARD	STOWING	STUNTED	SUDANIC	SURBASE
STEWING	STRAFED	STUPEFY	SUDETES	SURCOAT
STHENIC	STRAFER	STUPORS	SUFFICE	SURFACE
STIBINE	STRAINS	STUTTER	SUFFUSE	SURFEIT
STICHIC	STRAITS	STYGIAN	SUGARED	SURFERS
STICKER	STRANDS	STYLING	SUGGEST	SURFING

SURGEON	SWILLER	TACKILY	TANGLER	TAXIING
SURGERY	SWIMMER	TACKING	TANGLES	TAXIWAY
SURGING	SWINDLE	TACKLED	TANGOED	TBILIZI
SURINAM	SWINGER	TACKLER	TANGRAM	TEABAGS
SURLIER	SWINGLE	TACKLES	TANKAGE	TEACAKE
SURLILY	SWINISH	TACNODE	TANKARD	TEACHER
SURMISE	SWIPING	TACTFUL	TANKERS	TEACH-IN
SURNAME	SWIPPLE	TACTICS	TANNAGE	TEA COSY
SURPASS	SWIRLED	TACTILE	TANNATE	TEACUPS
SURPLUS	SWISHED	TACTUAL	TANNERS	TEALEAF
SURREAL	SWISHER	TADPOLE	TANNERY	TEAMING
SURREYS	SWISHES	TADZHIK	TANNING	TEAPOTS
SURVEYS	SWIVELS	TAFFETA	TANTRUM	TEARFUL
SURVIVE	SWIZZLE	TAFFIES	TAOISTS	TEAR GAS
SUSPECT	SWOLLEN	TAGGERS	TAPERED	TEARING
SUSPEND	SWOONED	TAGGING	TAPERER	TEAROOM
SUSSING	SWOOPED	TAGMEME	TAPETAL	TEASELS
SUSTAIN	SWOPPED	TAIL END	TAPETUM	TEASERS
SUTURAL	SWOTTED	TAILING	TAPHOLE	TEASHOP
SUTURED	SYCOSIS	TAILORS	TAPIOCA	TEASING
SUTURES	SYENITE	TAINTED	TAPPETS	TECHILY
SWABBED	SYLLABI	TAIYUAN	TAPPING	TECHNIC
SWABBER	SYLPHIC	TAKABLE	TAPROOM	TECTRIX
SWABIAN	SYLPHID	TAKEOFF	TAPROOT	TEDIOUS
SWADDLE	SYLVITE	TAKEOUT	TARANTO	TEEMING
SWAGGER	SYMBOLS	TAKEUPS	TARDIER	TEENAGE
SWAHILI	SYMPTOM	TAKINGS	TARDILY	TEEPEES
SWALLOW	SYNAPSE	TALCOSE	TARGETS	TEGULAR
SWAMPED	SYNCARP	TALENTS	TARIFFS	TEHERAN
SWANKED	SYNCHRO	TALIPED	TARMACS	TEKTITE
SWANNED	SYNCOPE	TALIPES	TARNISH	TELAMON
SWANSEA	SYNERGY	TALIPOT	TARRASA	TEL AVIV
SWAPPED	SYNESIS	TALKERS	TARRIED	TELEOST
SWAPPER	SYNGAMY	TALKIES	TARRING	TELERAN
SWARMED	SYNODAL	TALKING	TARSIER	TELESIS
SWARTHY	SYNODIC	TALLAGE	TARTANS	TELEXED
SWATHED	SYNONYM	TALLBOY	TARTARS	TELEXES
SWATTED	SYNOVIA	TALLEST	TASSELS	TELLERS
SWATTER	SYPHONS	TALLIED	TASTERS	TELLIES
SWAYING	SYRINGA	TALLIER	TASTIER	TELLING
SWEARER	SYRINGE	TALLIES	TASTILY	TELPHER
SWEATED	SYRPHID	TALLINN	TASTING	TELSTAR
SWEATER	SYSTEMS	TALLISH	TATOUAY	TEMPERA
SWEDISH	SYSTOLE	TALLYHO	TATTERS	TEMPERS
SWEEPER		TAMABLE	TATTIER	TEMPEST
SWEETEN	T	TAMARAU	TATTILY	TEMPING
SWEETER	TABANID	TAMARIN	TATTING	TEMPLES
SWEETIE	TABASCO	TAMBOUR	TATTLED	TEMPTED
SWEETLY	TABBIES	TAMPERE	TATTLER	TEMPTER
SWELLED	TABBING	TAMPICO	TATTOOS	TENABLE
SWELTER	TABLEAU	TAMPING	TAUNTED	TENANCY
SWERVED	TABLING	TAMPONS	TAUNTER	TENANTS
SWERVER	TABLOID	TANAGER	TAUREAN	TENCHES
SWERVES	TABORET	TANBARK	TAURINE	TENDERS
SWIFTER	TABORIN	TANDEMS	TAUTEST	TENDING
SWIFTLY	TABULAR	TANGELO	TAVERNS	TENDONS
SWIGGED	TACHYON	TANGENT	TAXABLE	TENDRIL
SWIGGER	TACITLY	TANGIER	TAX-FREE	TENFOLD
SWILLED	TACKIER	TANGLED	TAXICAB	TENNERS

TENONER	THEREON	TICKERS	TIPTOED	TOOTLER
TENPINS	THERETO	TICKETS	TIPTOES	TOOTLES
TENSELY	THERMAL	TICKING	TIRADES	TOOTSIE
TENSEST	THERMIC	TICKLED	TIREDLY	TOPARCH
TENSILE	THERMIT	TICKLER	TISSUES	TOPAZES
TENSING	THERMOS	TICKLES	TITANIA	TOPCOAT
TENSION	THEROID	TIDBITS	TITANIC	TOP DOGS
TENSIVE	THEURGY	TIDDLER	TITBITS	TOP HATS
TENTAGE	THICKEN	TIDEWAY	TITFERS	TOPIARY
TENUITY	THICKER	TIDIEST	TITHING	TOPICAL
TENUOUS	THICKET	TIDINGS	TITMICE	TOPKNOT
TEPIDLY	THICKLY	TIDYING	TITOISM	TOPLESS
TEQUILA	THIEVED	TIE-DIED	TITOIST	TOPMAST
TERBIUM	THIEVES	TIEPINS	TITRANT	TOPMOST
TERMING	THIMBLE	TIFFANY	TITRATE	TOPONYM
TERMINI	THIN AIR	TIGHTEN	TITTERS	TOPPERS
TERMITE	THINNED	TIGHTER	TITTIES	TOPPING
TERNARY	THINNER	TIGHTLY	TITULAR	TOPPLED
TERNATE	THIONIC	TIGRESS	TIZZIES	TOPSAIL
TERPENE	THIONYL	TILAPIA	TOADIED	TOPSIDE
TERRACE	THIRSTS	TILBURG	TOADIES	TOPSOIL
TERRAIN	THIRSTY	TILLAGE	TOASTED	TOPSPIN
TERRANE	THISTLE	TILLERS	TOASTER	TORCHES
TERRENE	THISTLY	TILLING	TOBACCO	TORMENT
TERRIER	THITHER	TILTING	TOBY JUG	TORNADO
TERRIFY	THORITE	TIMBALE	TOCCATA	TORONTO
TERRINE	THORIUM	TIMBERS	TOCSINS	TORPEDO
TERRORS	THOUGHT	TIMBREL	TODDIES	TORQUAY
TERSELY	THRALLS	TIMBRES	TODDLED	TORQUES
TERTIAL	THREADS	TIME LAG	TODDLER	TORREFY
TERTIAN	THREADY	TIMIDLY	TOE CAPS	TORRENT
TESSERA	THREATS	TIMPANI	TOEHOLD	TORREON
TESTACY	THREE R'S	TINAMOU	TOENAIL	TORSADE
TESTATE	THRIFTS	TINFOIL	TOFFEES	TORSION
TEST BAN	THRIFTY	TINGING	TOGGING	TORTONI
TESTERS	THRILLS	TINGLED	TOGGLES	TORTURE
TESTIER	THRIVED	TINGLER	TOHEROA	TORYISM
TESTIFY	THROATS	TIN GODS	TOILETS	TOSSING
TESTILY	THROATY	TIN HATS	TOILING	TOSS-UPS
TESTING	THRONES	TINIEST	TOLLING	TOTALED
TETANIC	THRONGS	TINKERS	TOLUATE	TOTALLY
TETANUS	THROUGH	TINKLED	TOLUENE	TOTE BAG
TETHERS	THROWER	TINKLES	TOMBOLA	TOTEMIC
TETRODE	THROW-IN	TINNIER	TOMBOLO	TOTTERY
TEXTILE	THRUSTS	TINNILY	TOMBOYS	TOTTING
TEXTUAL	THRUWAY	TINNING	TOMCATS	TOUCANS
TEXTURE	THUDDED	TINTACK	TOMFOOL	TOUCHED
THALLIC	THULIUM	TINTING	TOM-TOMS	TOUCHER
THALLUS	THUMBED	TINTYPE	TONETIC	TOUCHES
THANKED	THUMPED	TINWARE	TONGUES	TOUGHEN
THAWING	THUMPER	TINWORK	TONIGHT	TOUGHER
THEATRE	THUNDER	TIP-OFFS	TONNAGE	TOUGHLY
THEISTS	THURGAU	TIPPERS	TONNEAU	TOUPEES
THEOREM	THWACKS	TIPPING	TONSILS	TOURACO
THERAPY	THYMINE	TIPPLER	TONSURE	TOURING
THEREAT	THYROID	TIPPLES	TONTINE	TOURISM
THEREBY	THYRSUS	TIPSIER	TOOLING	TOURIST
THEREIN	THYSELF	TIPSILY	TOOTING	TOURNEY
THEREOF	TIBETAN	TIPSTER	TOOTLED	TOUSLED

TOUTING	TREHALA	TRIVETS	TUBULAR	TWEETER
TOWARDS	TREKKED	TRIVIAL	TUCKING	TWELFTH
TOWBOAT	TREKKER	TROCHAL	TUCUMAN	TWELVES
TOWELED	TRELLIS	TROCHEE	TUESDAY	TWIDDLE
TOWERED	TREMBLE	TRODDEN	TUGGING	TWIDDLY
TOWHEAD	TREMBLY	TROIKAS	TUITION	TWIGGED
TOWLINE	TREMOLO	TROJANS	TUMBLED	TWIN BED
TOWPATH	TREMORS	TROLLED	TUMBLER	TWINGES
TOWROPE	TRENTON	TROLLEY	TUMBLES	TWINING
TRACERS	TREPANG	TROLLOP	TUMBREL	TWINKLE
TRACERY	TRESSES	TROMMEL	TUMMIES	TWINNED
TRACHEA	TRESTLE	TROOPED	TUMOURS	TWIN SET
TRACING	TRIABLE	TROOPER	TUMULAR	TWIRLED
TRACKED	TRIACID	TROPHIC	TUMULTS	TWIRLER
TRACKER	TRIADIC	TROPICS	TUMULUS	TWISTED
TRACTOR	TRIBADE	TROPISM	TUNABLE	TWISTER
TRADE-IN	TRIBUNE	TROTTED	TUNEFUL	TWITTED
TRADERS	TRIBUTE	TROTTER	TUNICLE	TWITTER
TRADING	TRICEPS	TROUBLE	TUNISIA	TWOFOLD
TRADUCE	TRICKED	TROUGHS	TUNNELS	TWOSOME
TRAFFIC	TRICKER	TROUNCE	TUNNIES	TWO-STAR
TRAGEDY	TRICKLE	TROUPER	TUPPING	TWO-STEP
TRAILED	TRICKLY	TROUPES	TURBANS	TWO-TIME
TRAILER	TRICKSY	TROUSER	TURBARY	TWO-TONE
TRAINED	TRICORN	TROWELS	TURBINE	TYCHISM
TRAINEE	TRIDENT	TRUANCY	TURBOTS	TYCOONS
TRAINER	TRIDUUM	TRUANTS	TURDINE	TYLOSIS
TRAIPSE	TRIESTE	TRUCKED	TUREENS	TYMPANA
TRAITOR	TRIFLED	TRUCKER	TURFING	TYNWALD
TRAJECT	TRIFLER	TRUCKLE	TURGITE	TYPEBAR
TRAMCAR	TRIFLES	TRUDGED	TURKEYS	TYPESET
TRAMMEL	TRIGGER	TRUDGEN	TURKISH	TYPHOID
TRAMPED	TRILLED	TRUDGER	TURKMEN	TYPHOON
TRAMPER	TRILOGY	TRUDGES	TURMOIL	TYPHOUS
TRAMPLE	TRIMMED	TRUFFLE	TURNERS	TYPICAL
TRAMWAY	TRIMMER	TRUISMS	TURNERY	TYPISTS
TRANCES	TRINARY	TRUMPED	TURNING	TYRANNY
TRANSIT	TRINITY	TRUMPET	TURNIPS	TYRANTS
TRANSOM	TRINKET	TRUNDLE	TURNKEY	TYRONIC
TRAPEZE	TRIOLET	TRUSSED	TURN-OFF	TZARINA
TRAPPED	TRIPLED	TRUSSER	TURN-ONS	
TRAPPER	TRIPLET	TRUSSES	TURNOUT	U
TRASHED	TRIPLEX	TRUSTED	TURN-UPS	UDAIPUR
TRAUMAS	TRIPODS	TRUSTEE	TURPETH	UGANDAN
TRAVAIL	TRIPODY	TRUSTER	TURRETS	UGLIEST
TRAVELS	TRIPOLI	TRYPSIN	TURTLER	UKRAINE
TRAVOIS	TRIPPED	TRYPTIC	TURTLES	UKULELE
TRAWLED	TRIPPER	TRYSAIL	TUSCANY	ULAN-UDE
TRAWLER	TRIPPET	TRYSTER	TUSKERS	ULLAGED
TREACLE	TRIPURA	TSARDOM	TUSSIVE	ULULANT
TREACLY	TRIREME	TSARINA	TUSSLED	ULULATE
TREADER	TRISECT	TSARIST	TUSSLES	UMBRAGE
TREADLE	TRISMIC	T-SHIRTS	TUSSOCK	UMBRIAN
TREASON	TRISMUS	T-SQUARE	TUTORED	UMBRIEL
TREATED	TRISOME	TSUNAMI	TUXEDOS	UMLAUTS
TREATER	TRITELY	TUATARA	TWADDLE	UMPIRED
TREBLED	TRITIUM	TUBBIER	TWANGED	UMPIRES
TREBLES	TRITONE	TUBBING	TWEAKED	UMPTEEN
TREFOIL	TRIUMPH	TUBIFEX	TWEETED	UNAIDED

UNARMED	UNQUIET	UREDIAL	VALIDLY	VENTING
UNAWARE	UNQUOTE	UREDIUM	VALISES	VENTRAL
UNBONED	UNRAVEL	URETHRA	VALLEYS	VENTURE
UNBOSOM	UNREADY	URGENCY	VALONIA	VENULAR
UNBOUND	UNREEVE	URIDINE	VALUERS	VERANDA
UNBOWED	UNSCREW	URINALS	VALUING	VERBENA
UNBRACE	UNSLING	URINANT	VALVATE	VERBIFY
UNCAGED	UNSNARL	URINARY	VALVULE	VERBOSE
UNCANNY	UNSOUND	URINATE	VAMOOSE	VERDANT
UNCHAIN	UNSTICK	URINOUS	VAMPIRE	VERDICT
UNCINUS	UNSTRAP	URNLIKE	VANADIC	VERDURE
UNCIVIL	UNSTUCK	URODELE	VANDALS	VERGERS
UNCLASP	UNSWEAR	UROLITH	VANILLA	VERGING
UNCLEAN	UNTHINK	UROLOGY	VANTAGE	VERGLAS
UNCLEAR	UNTRIED	URUAPAN	VANWARD	VERISMO
UNCLOAK	UNTRUSS	URUGUAY	VAPIDLY	VERMEIL
UNCLOSE	UNTRUTH	URUMCHI	VAPOURS	VERMONT
UNCOUTH	UNTYING	USELESS	VARIANT	VERNIER
UNCOVER	UNUSUAL	USHERED	VARIATE	VERONAL
UNCROSS	UNVOICE	USUALLY	VARIETY	VERRUCA
UNCTION	UNWAGED	USURERS	VARIOLA	VERSANT
UNDERDO	UNWOUND	USURPED	VARIOLE	VERSIFY
UNDERGO	UP-AND-UP	USURPER	VARIOUS	VERSION
UNDOING	UPBRAID	UTENSIL	VARLETS	VERTIGO
UNDRESS	UPBUILD	UTERINE	VARMINT	VERVAIN
UNDYING	UPDATED	UTILITY	VARNISH	VESICAL
UNEARTH	UPDATER	UTILIZE	VARSITY	VESICLE
UNEQUAL	UPDATES	UT INFRA	VARYING	VESPERS
UNFROCK	UPDRAFT	UTOPIAN	VASSALS	VESPINE
UNGODLY	UPENDED	UTOPIAS	VASTITY	VESSELS
UNGUENT	UPFRONT	UTRECHT	VATICAN	VESTIGE
UNGULAR	UPGRADE	UTRICLE	VAUDOIS	VESTING
UNHAPPY	UPHEAVE	UT SUPRA	VAULTED	VESTRAL
UNHEARD	UPLANDS	UTTERED	VAULTER	VESTURE
UNHINGE	UPPSALA	UTTERER	VAUNTED	VETCHES
UNHORSE	UPRAISE	UTTERLY	VAUNTER	VETERAN
UNICORN	UPRIGHT	UVEITIC	VECTORS	VETIVER
UNIFIED	UPRISER	UVEITIS	VEDALIA	VETOING
UNIFIER	UPRIVER	UVULARS	VEDDOID	VETTING
UNIFORM	UPSILON	UXORIAL	VEDETTE	VEXEDLY
UNITARY	UPSTAGE		VEERING	VIADUCT
UNITIES	UPSTART	V	VEGETAL	VIBRANT
UNITING	UPSURGE	VACANCY	VEHICLE	VIBRATE
UNITIVE	UPSWEEP	VACATED	VEILING	VIBRATO
UNKEMPT	UPSWING	VACCINE	VEINING	VICENZA
UNKNOWN	UPTAKES	VACUITY	VEINLET	VICEROY
UNLATCH	UPTHROW	VACUOLE	VELAMEN	VICINAL
UNLEARN	UPTIGHT	VACUOUS	VELIGER	VICIOUS
UNLEASH	UPTURNS	VACUUMS	VELLORE	VICOMTE
UNLOOSE	UPWARDS	VAGINAL	VELOURS	VICTIMS
UNLUCKY	URAEMIA	VAGINAS	VELVETY	VICTORS
UNMAKER	URAEMIC	VAGRANT	VENALLY	VICTORY
UNMANLY	URALITE	VAGUELY	VENATIC	VICTUAL
UNMEANT	URANIAN	VAINEST	VENDACE	VICUNAS
UNMORAL	URANIDE	VALANCE	VENDING	VIDEOED
UNMOVED	URANITE	VALENCE	VENDORS	VIDICON
UNNAMED	URANIUM	VALENCY	VENEERS	VIETNAM
UNNERVE	URANOUS	VALERIC	VENISON	VIEWERS
UNPAGED	URCHINS	VALIANT	VENTAGE	VIEWING

VIKINGS	VOLAPUK	WALK-ONS	WASHTUB	WEIGHER
VILLAGE	VOLCANO	WALKOUT	WASPILY	WEIGHTS
VILLAIN	VOLLEYS	WALK-UPS	WASPISH	WEIGHTY
VILLEIN	VOLOGDA	WALLABY	WASSAIL	WEIRDER
VILLOUS	VOLTAGE	WALLAHS	WASTAGE	WEIRDIE
VILNIUS	VOLTAIC	WALLETS	WASTERS	WEIRDLY
VINASSE	VOLUBLE	WALLEYE	WASTING	WEIRDOS
VINEGAR	VOLUBLY	WALLIES	WASTREL	WELCHED
VINTAGE	VOLUMED	WALLING	WATCHED	WELCOME
VINTNER	VOLUMES	WALLOON	WATCHER	WELDERS
VIOLATE	VOLVATE	WALLOPS	WATCHES	WELDING
VIOLENT	VOMITED	WALLOWS	WATERED	WELFARE
VIOLETS	VOMITER	WALNUTS	WATERER	WELL-FED
VIOLINS	VOMITUS	WALTZED	WATTAGE	WELLIES
VIOLIST	VORLAGE	WALTZER	WATTLES	WELLING
VIRAGOS	VOTABLE	WALTZES	WAVELET	WELL-OFF
VIRELAY	VOUCHED	WANGLED	WAVEOFF	WELL-SET
VIRGATE	VOUCHER	WANGLER	WAVERED	WELSHED
VIRGINS	VOX POPS	WANGLES	WAVERER	WELSHER
VIRGOAN	VOYAGED	WANKERS	WAVIEST	WEMBLEY
VIRGULE	VOYAGER	WANKING	WAXBILL	WENCHED
VIRTUAL	VOYAGES	WANNESS	WAXIEST	WENCHER
VIRTUES	VOYEURS	WANNEST	WAXLIKE	WENCHES
VIRUSES	VULGATE	WANNING	WAXWING	WENDING
VISAGES	VULPINE	WANT ADS	WAXWORK	WENDISH
VISAING	VULTURE	WANTING	WAYBILL	WEST END
VIS-A-VIS		WAPITIS	WAYLAID	WESTERN
VISAYAN	W	WARBLED	WAYLAIN	WESTING
VISCERA	WADABLE	WARBLER	WAYSIDE	WET-LOOK
VISCOID	WADDING	WARDENS	WAYWARD	WETNESS
VISCOSE	WADDLED	WARDERS	WEAKEST	WET SUIT
VISCOUS	WADDLER	WARDING	WEALTHY	WETTEST
VISIBLE	WADDLES	WARFARE	WEANING	WETTING
VISIBLY	WAFFLED	WAR GAME	WEAPONS	WETTISH
VISIONS	WAFFLES	WARHEAD	WEARIED	WHACKED
VISITED	WAFTAGE	WARIEST	WEARIER	WHACKER
VISITOR	WAFTING	WARLIKE	WEARILY	WHALERS
VISTAED	WAGERED	WARLOCK	WEARING	WHALING
VISTULA	WAGERER	WARLORD	WEASELS	WHANGEE
VITALLY	WAGGING	WARMEST	WEATHER	WHARVES
VITAMIN	WAGGISH	WARMING	WEAVERS	WHAT FOR
VITEBSK	WAGGLED	WARM-UPS	WEAVING	WHATNOT
VITIATE	WAGGLES	WARNING	WEBBING	WHATSIT
VITORIA	WAGONER	WARPAGE	WEBFOOT	WHEATEN
VITRAIN	WAGTAIL	WARPATH	WEB-TOED	WHEEDLE
VITRIFY	WAILFUL	WARPING	WEDDING	WHEELED
VITRINE	WAILING	WARRANT	WEDGING	WHEELER
VITRIOL	WAISTED	WARRENS	WEDLOCK	WHEELIE
VITTATE	WAITERS	WARRING	WEEDIER	WHEEZED
VIVIDLY	WAITING	WARRIOR	WEEDILY	WHEEZER
VIYELLA	WAIVERS	WARSHIP	WEEDING	WHEEZES
VIZIERS	WAIVING	WARTHOG	WEEKDAY	WHEREAS
V-NECKED	WAKEFUL	WARTIME	WEEKEND	WHEREAT
VOCABLE	WAKENED	WARWICK	WEENIER	WHEREBY
VOCALIC	WAKENER	WASHDAY	WEEPING	WHEREIN
VOCALLY	WALKERS	WASHERS	WEEVILS	WHEREOF
VOICING	WALKIES	WASHERY	WEEVILY	WHEREON
VOIDING	WALKING	WASHING	WEIGELA	WHERETO
VOIOTIA	WALKMAN	WASHOUT	WEIGHED	WHERRIT

WHETHER	WILLIES	WONDERS	WRITE-IN	YORKIST
WHETTED	WILLING	WONKIER	WRITERS	YORUBAN
WHETTER	WILLOWS	WOODCUT	WRITE-UP	YOUNGER
WHICKER	WILLOWY	WOODIER	WRITHED	YOWLING
WHIFFER	WILTING	WOODMAN	WRITHER	YTTRIUM
WHIFFLE	WIMPIES	WOODSIA	WRITING	YUCATAN
WHILING	WIMPISH	WOOFERS	WRITTEN	YUCKIER
WHIMPER	WIMPLES	WOOLLEN	WROCLAW	YUKONER
WHINERS	WINCHED	WOOMERA	WRONGED	YULE LOG
WHINGED	WINCHER	WOOZIER	WRONGER	YUPPIES
WHINING	WINCHES	WOOZILY	WRONGLY	
WHIPPED	WINCING	WORDAGE	WROUGHT	Z
WHIPPER	WINDAGE	WORDIER	WRYBILL	ZAGAZIG
WHIPPET	WINDBAG	WORDILY	WRYNECK	ZAIRESE
WHIPSAW	WINDIER	WORDING	WRYNESS	ZAMBEZI
WHIRLED	WINDILY	WORKBAG	WYCH-ELM	ZAMBIAN
WHIRLER	WINDING	WORKBOX	WYOMING	ZANIEST
WHIRRED	WINDOWS	WORKDAY	WYVERNS	ZAPOTEC
WHISKED	WINDROW	WORKERS		ZAPPIER
WHISKER	WINDSOR	WORKING	X	ZAPPING
WHISKEY	WINE BAR	WORKMAN	XANTHIC	ZEALOTS
WHISPER	WINGERS	WORKMEN	XANTHIN	ZEALOUS
WHISTLE	WINGING	WORKOUT	XERARCH	ZEBRINE
WHITEST	WINGLET	WORKSHY	XEROSIS	ZEDOARY
WHITHER	WING NUT	WORKTOP	XEROTIC	ZEELAND
WHITING	WINKERS	WORLDLY	XEROXED	ZENITHS
WHITLOW	WINKING	WORMIER	XEROXES	ZEOLITE
WHITSUN	WINKLED	WORMING	XIPHOID	ZEPHYRS
WHITTLE	WINKLES	WORN-OUT	X-RAYING	ZEROING
WHIZZED	WINNERS	WORRIED		ZESTFUL
WHIZZES	WINNING	WORRIER	Y	ZHDANOV
WHOEVER	WINSOME	WORRIES	YAKKING	ZIGZAGS
WHOOPED	WINTERS	WORSHIP	YAKUTSK	ZILLION
WHOOPEE	WIRETAP	WORSTED	YANGTZE	ZINCATE
WHOOPER	WIRIEST	WOTCHER	YANKEES	ZINCITE
WHOPPED	WISE GUY	WOULD-BE	YANKING	ZIONISM
WHOPPER	WISHFUL	WOULDN'T	YAOUNDE	ZIONIST
WHORISH	WISHING	WOUNDED	YAPPING	ZIP CODE
WHORLED	WISPIER	WOUNDER	YARDAGE	ZIPPERS
WICHITA	WISPILY	WOUND-UP	YARDARM	ZIPPIER
WICKETS	WISTFUL	WRAITHS	YARNING	ZIPPING
WICKING	WITCHES	WRANGLE	YASHMAK	ZITHERS
WIDE BOY	WITHERS	WRAPPED	YAWNING	ZODIACS
WIDENED	WITHOUT	WRAPPER	YEAR DOT	ZOISITE
WIDENER	WITLESS	WREAKED	YEARNED	ZOMBIES
WIDGEON	WITNESS	WREAKER	YEARNER	ZONALLY
WIDOWED	WITTIER	WREATHE	YELLING	ZONULAR
WIDOWER	WITTILY	WREATHS	YELLOWS	ZOOLOGY
WIELDED	WIZARDS	WRECKED	YELPING	ZOOMING
WIELDER	WIZENED	WRECKER	YEREVAN	ZOOTOMY
WIGGING	WOBBLED	WRESTED	Y-FRONTS	ZORILLA
WIGGLED	WOBBLER	WRESTER	YIDDISH	ZWICKAU
WIGGLER	WOBBLES	WRESTLE	YIELDED	ZYGOSIS
WIGGLES	WOLFING	WRIGGLE	YIELDER	ZYGOTIC
WIGWAMS	WOLFISH	WRIGGLY	YINGKOW	ZYMOGEN
WILDCAT	WOLFRAM	WRINGER	YODELED	ZYMOSIS
WILDEST	WOMANLY	WRINKLE	YOGHURT	ZYMOTIC
WILDING	WOMBATS	WRINKLY	YONKERS	ZYMURGY
WILIEST				

A	ABSTRUSE	ACQUIRED	AD-LIBBER
AARDVARK	ABSURDLY	ACQUIRER	ADMIRALS
AARDWOLF	ABU DHABI	ACRE-FOOT	ADMIRERS
ABACUSES	ABUNDANT	ACRE-INCH	ADMIRING
ABAMPERE	ABUTILON	ACRIDINE	ADMITTED
ABATTOIR	ABUTMENT	ACRIDITY	ADMONISH
ABBATIAL	ABUTTALS	ACRIMONY	ADOPTING
ABBESSES	ABUTTING	ACROBATS	ADOPTION
ABDICATE	ACADEMIA	ACRODONT	ADOPTIVE
ABDOMENS	ACADEMIC	ACROLEIN	ADORABLE
ABDUCENT	ACANTHUS	ACROLITH	ADORNING
ABDUCTED	ACAPULCO	ACROMION	ADRIATIC
ABELMOSK	ACARPOUS	ACRONYMS	ADROITLY
ABEOKUTA	ACCEDING	ACROSTIC	ADULARIA
ABERDEEN	ACCENTED	ACRYLICS	ADULATOR
ABERRANT	ACCENTOR	ACTINIDE	ADULTERY
ABETTING	ACCEPTED	ACTINISM	ADUMBRAL
ABETTORS	ACCEPTOR	ACTINIUM	ADVANCED
ABEYANCE	ACCESSED	ACTINQID	ADVANCER
ABHORRED	ACCESSES	ACTIVATE	ADVANCES
ABHORRER	ACCIDENT	ACTIVELY	ADVERTED
ABIDANCE	ACCOLADE	ACTIVISM	ADVISERS
AB INITIO	ACCORDED	ACTIVIST	ADVISING
ABJECTLY	ACCORDER	ACTIVITY	ADVISORY
ABJURING	ACCOSTED	ACT OF GOD	ADVOCAAT
ABKHAZIA	ACCOUNTS	ACTUALLY	ADVOCACY
ABLATION	ACCREDIT	ACTUATED	ADVOCATE
ABLATIVE	ACCRUING	ACTUATOR	ADYNAMIA
ABLUTION	ACCURACY	ACULEATE	ADYNAMIC
ABNEGATE	ACCURATE	ACUTANCE	AEGROTAT
ABNORMAL	ACCURSED	ADAMSITE	AERATING
ABOMASUM	ACCUSERS	ADAPTERS	AERATION
ABORTING	ACCUSING	ADAPTING	AERIALLY
ABORTION	ACCUSTOM	ADAPTIVE	AEROBICS
ABORTIVE	ACCUTRON	ADDENDUM	AERODYNE
ABOUNDED	ACENTRIC	ADDICTED	AEROFOIL
ABOVE PAR	ACERBATE	ADDITION	AEROGRAM
ABRADANT	ACERBITY	ADDITIVE	AEROLITE
ABRADING	ACERVATE	ADDUCENT	AEROLOGY
ABRASION	ACESCENT	ADDUCING	AERONAUT
ABRASIVE	ACHENIAL	ADDUCTOR	AEROSOLS
ABRIDGED	ACHIEVED	ADELAIDE	AEROSTAT
ABRIDGER	ACHIEVER	ADENITIS	AESTHETE
ABROGATE	ACHILLES	ADENOIDS	AFEBRILE
ABRUPTLY	ACHROMAT	ADEQUACY	AFFECTED
ABSCISSA	ACHROMIC	ADEQUATE	AFFERENT
ABSEILED	ACICULAR	ADHERENT	AFFIANCE
ABSENCES	ACICULUM	ADHERING	AFFINITY
ABSENTED	ACID-FAST	ADHESION	AFFIRMED
ABSENTEE	ACIDNESS	ADHESIVE	AFFIRMER
ABSENTER	ACIDOSIS	ADJACENT	AFFIXING
ABSENTLY	ACIDOTIC	ADJOINED	AFFLATUS
ABSINTHE	ACID RAIN	ADJUDGED	AFFLUENT
ABSOLUTE	ACID TEST	ADJUNCTS	AFFORDED
ABSOLVED	ACIERATE	ADJURING	AFFOREST
ABSOLVER	ACOLYTES	ADJUSTED	AFFRONTS
ABSORBED	ACONITIC	ADJUTANT	AFFUSION
ABSORBER	ACOUSTIC	ADJUVANT	AFLUTTER
ABSTRACT	ACQUAINT	AD-LIBBED	AFRICANS

AGARTALA	A LA CARTE	ALLOTTED	AMMONITE
AGE GROUP	ALACRITY	ALLOTTEE	AMMONIUM
AGENCIES	ALARMING	ALLOWING	AMNESIAC
AGENESIS	ALARMISM	ALLOYING	AMNIOTIC
AGENETIC	ALARMIST	ALL RIGHT	AMOEBOID
AGENTIAL	ALBACORE	ALL-ROUND	AMORETTO
AGENTIVE	ALBANIAN	ALLSPICE	AMORTIZE
AGERATUM	ALBINISM	ALLUDING	AMOUNTED
AGGRIEVE	ALCATRAZ	ALLURING	AMPERAGE
AGIOTAGE	ALCHEMIC	ALLUSION	AMPHIPOD
AGITATED	ALCIDINE	ALLUSIVE	AMPHORAE
AGITATOR	ALCOHOLS	ALLUVIAL	AMPHORAS
AGITPROP	ALDEHYDE	ALLUVIUM	AMPOULES
AGMINATE	ALDERMAN	ALMANACS	AMPULLAR
AGNOSTIC	ALDERMEN	ALMIGHTY	AMPUTATE
AGONIZED	ALDERNEY	ALMONERS	AMPUTEES
AGRAPHIA	ALDOXIME	ALOPECIA	AMRAVATI
AGRARIAN	ALEATORY	ALPHABET	AMRITSAR
AGRESTAL	ALEHOUSE	ALPHOSIS	AMYGDALA
AGRIMONY	ALERTING	ALPINISM	AMYGDALE
AGROLOGY	ALFRESCO	ALPINIST	ANABAENA
AGRONOMY	ALGERIAN	ALSATIAN	ANABASIS
AGUEWEED	ALGERINE	ALSO-RANS	ANABATIC
AIGRETTE	ALGINATE	ALTER EGO	ANABLEPS
AIGUILLE	ALGOLOGY	ALTERING	ANABOLIC
AILERONS	ALGORISM	ALTHOUGH	ANACONDA
AILMENTS	ALHAMBRA	ALTITUDE	ANAEROBE
AIRBASES	ALICANTE	ALTRUISM	ANAGLYPH
AIRBORNE	ALIENAGE	ALTRUIST	ANAGOGIC
AIRBRAKE	ALIENATE	ALUMROOT	ANAGRAMS
AIRBRICK	ALIENISM	ALVEOLAR	ANALCITE
AIRBRUSH	ALIENIST	ALVEOLUS	ANALECTS
AIRBURST	ALIGHTED	AMALGAMS	ANALEMMA
AIRBUSES	ALIGNING	AMARANTH	ANALOGUE
AIRCRAFT	ALIQUANT	AMARELLE	ANALYSED
AIRCREWS	ALIZARIN	AMARILLO	ANALYSER
AIREDALE	ALKAHEST	AMASSING	ANALYSES
AIRFIELD	ALKALIES	AMATEURS	ANALYSIS
AIRFORCE	ALKALIFY	AMAZONAS	ANALYSTS
AIRFRAME	ALKALINE	AMBEROID	ANALYTIC
AIRINESS	ALKALIZE	AMBIENCE	ANAPAEST
AIRLANES	ALKALOID	AMBITION	ANAPHASE
AIRLIFTS	ALLANITE	AMBIVERT	ANAPHORA
AIRLINER	ALLAYING	AMBROSIA	ANARCHIC
AIRLINES	ALL CLEAR	AMBULANT	ANASARCA
AIRLOCKS	ALLEGING	AMBULATE	ANATHEMA
AIRPLANE	ALLEGORY	AMBUSHED	ANATOLIA
AIRPORTS	ALLELISM	AMBUSHES	ANCESTOR
AIR RAIDS	ALLELUIA	AMENABLE	ANCESTRY
AIRSCREW	ALLEPPEY	AMENDING	ANCHORED
AIRSHIPS	ALLERGEN	AMERICAN	ANCIENTS
AIRSPACE	ALLERGIC	AMETHYST	ANDANTES
AIRSPEED	ALLEYWAY	AMICABLE	ANDESINE
AIRSTRIP	ALLIANCE	AMICABLY	ANDESITE
AIRTIGHT	ALLOCATE	AMITOSIS	ANDIRONS
AIR-TO-AIR	ALLODIAL	AMITOTIC	ANDIZHAN
AIRWAVES	ALLODIUM	AMMETERS	ANDORRAN
AIRWOMAN	ALLOGAMY	AMMONIAC	ANDROGEN
AIRWOMEN	ALLOPATH	AMMONIFY	ANDROIDS

ANECDOTE	ANTINOMY	APPROVAL	ARMOURER
ANECHOIC	ANTIPHON	APPROVED	ARMS RACE
ANEMONES	ANTIQUES	APRES-SKI	AROMATIC
ANETHOLE	ANTITANK	APRICOTS	AROUSING
ANEURYSM	ANTONYMS	APTEROUS	ARPEGGIO
ANGELENO	ANTRORSE	APTITUDE	ARRANGED
ANGELICA	ANURESIS	APYRETIC	ARRANGER
ANGERING	ANYPLACE	AQUALUNG	ARRAYING
ANGINOSE	ANYTHING	AQUANAUT	ARRESTED
ANGLESEY	ANYWHERE	AQUARIST	ARRESTER
ANGLICAN	AORISTIC	AQUARIUM	ARRIVALS
ANGRIEST	APAGOGIC	AQUARIUS	ARRIVING
ANGSTROM	APATETIC	AQUATICS	ARROGANT
ANGULATE	APERIENT	AQUATINT	ARROGATE
ANHEDRAL	APERITIF	AQUEDUCT	ARROWING
ANIMATED	APERTURE	AQUILINE	ARSENALS
ANIMATOR	APHANITE	ARACHNID	ARSENATE
ANIMISTS	APHELIAN	ARAPAIMA	ARSENIDE
ANISETTE	APHELION	ARAWAKAN	ARSENITE
ANKERITE	APHORISM	ARBITERS	ARSONIST
ANKYLOSE	APHORIST	ARBITRAL	ARTEFACT
ANNALIST	APHORIZE	ARBOREAL	ARTERIAL
ANNEALED	APIARIAN	ARCADIAN	ARTERIES
ANNEALER	APIARIES	ARCATURE	ARTESIAN
ANNEXING	APIARIST	ARCHAEAN	ARTFULLY
ANNOTATE	APIOLOGY	ARCHAISM	ARTICLED
ANNOUNCE	APLASTIC	ARCHAIST	ARTICLES
ANNOYING	APOCRINE	ARCHAIZE	ARTIFACT
ANNUALLY	APODOSIS	ARCHDUKE	ARTIFICE
ANNULATE	APOGAMIC	ARCHIVAL	ARTINESS
ANNULLED	APOLOGIA	ARCHIVES	ARTISANS
ANNULOSE	APOLOGUE	ARCHNESS	ARTISTES
ANODYNES	APOMIXIS	ARCHWAYS	ARTISTIC
ANOINTED	APOPHYGE	ARCTURUS	ARTISTRY
ANOINTER	APOPLEXY	ARDENNES	ARYANIZE
ANOREXIA	APOSPORY	ARDENTLY	ASBESTOS
ANSERINE	APOSTASY	AREA CODE	ASCENDED
ANSWERED	APOSTATE	ARENITIC	ASCENDER
ANTABUSE	APOSTLES	AREQUIPA	ASCETICS
ANTEATER	APPALLED	ARETHUSA	ASCIDIAN
ANTECEDE	APPANAGE	ARGENTIC	ASCIDIUM
ANTEDATE	APPARENT	ARGININE	ASCOCARP
ANTELOPE	APPEALED	ARGUABLE	ASCORBIC
ANTENNAS	APPEALER	ARGUABLY	ASCRIBED
ANTERIOR	APPEARED	ARGUMENT	ASHTRAYS
ANTEROOM	APPEASED	ARIANISM	ASNIERES
ANTEVERT	APPELLEE	ARILLATE	ASPERITY
ANTHELIX	APPENDED	ARILLODE	ASPERSER
ANTHESIS	APPENDIX	ARISTATE	ASPHODEL
ANTHILLS	APPESTAT	ARKANSAS	ASPHYXIA
ANTIBODY	APPETITE	ARMAGNAC	ASPIRANT
ANTIDOTE	APPLAUSE	ARMAMENT	ASPIRATE
ANTIGENS	APPLE PIE	ARMATURE	ASPIRING
ANTIHERO	APPLIQUE	ARMBANDS	ASPIRINS
ANTI-ICER	APPLYING	ARMCHAIR	ASSAILED
ANTILLES	APPOSITE	ARMENIAN	ASSAILER
ANTIMERE	APPRAISE	ARMHOLES	ASSAMESE
ANTIMONY	APPRISED	ARMORIAL	ASSASSIN
ANTINODE	APPROACH	ARMOURED	ASSAULTS

ASSAYING	ATTEMPTS	AVERTING	BACKWARD
ASSEGAIS	ATTENDED	AVIARIES	BACKWASH
ASSEMBLE	ATTESTED	AVIATION	BACKYARD
ASSEMBLY	ATTIRING	AVIATORS	BACTERIA
ASSENTED	ATTITUDE	AVIATRIX	BACTERIN
ASSENTOR	ATTORNEY	AVIDNESS	BACTRIAN
ASSERTED	ATTUNING	AVIEMORE	BADALONA
ASSERTER	ATYPICAL	AVIFAUNA	BAD BLOOD
ASSESSED	AUBUSSON	AVIONICS	BAD DEBTS
ASSESSOR	AUCKLAND	AVOCADOS	BADGERED
ASSHOLES	AUCTIONS	AVOIDING	BADINAGE
ASSIGNAT	AUDACITY	AVOWABLE	BADLANDS
ASSIGNED	AUDIENCE	AVULSION	BADLY-OFF
ASSIGNEE	AUDITING	AWAITING	BAD-MOUTH
ASSIGNER	AUDITION	AWAKENED	BAEDEKER
ASSIGNOR	AUDITORS	AWARDING	BAFFLING
ASSISTED	AUDITORY	AWEATHER	BAGGAGES
ASSISTER	AUGSBURG	AXILLARY	BAGGIEST
ASSONANT	AUGURIES	AXIOLOGY	BAGPIPES
ASSORTED	AUGURING	AXLETREE	BAGUETTE
ASSORTER	AUGUSTLY	AYRSHIRE	BAHAMIAN
ASSUAGED	AUREOLES	AZIMUTHS	BAHRAINI
ASSUAGER	AU REVOIR	AZOTEMIA	BAILABLE
ASSUMING	AURICLES	AZOTEMIC	BAILIFFS
ASSURING	AURICULA		BAILMENT
ASSYRIAN	AUSPICES	**B**	BAILSMAN
ASTATINE	AUSTRIAN	BABBLERS	BAKELITE
ASTERISK	AUTACOID	BABBLING	BAKERIES
ASTERISM	AUTARCHY	BABIRUSA	BALANCED
ASTERNAL	AUTARKIC	BABYHOOD	BALANCER
ASTEROID	AUTHORED	BABY TALK	BALANCES
ASTHENIA	AUTISTIC	BACCARAT	BALDNESS
ASTHENIC	AUTOBAHN	BACCHIUS	BALEARIC
ASTONISH	AUTOCRAT	BACHELOR	BALINESE
ASTRAGAL	AUTOCUES	BACILLUS	BALLADES
ASTURIAS	AUTOGAMY	BACKACHE	BALLADRY
ASTUTELY	AUTOGIRO	BACKBITE	BALLARAT
ASUNCION	AUTOLYSE	BACKBONE	BALLCOCK
ATARAXIA	AUTOMATA	BACKCHAT	BALL GAME
ATHEISTS	AUTOMATE	BACKCOMB	BALLONET
ATHENIAN	AUTOMATS	BACKDATE	BALLOONS
ATHEROMA	AUTONOMY	BACK DOOR	BALLOTED
ATHLETES	AUTOSOME	BACKDROP	BALL PARK
ATHLETIC	AUTOTOMY	BACKFILL	BALLROOM
ATLANTIC	AUTOTYPE	BACKFIRE	BALLS-UPS
ATLANTIS	AUTOTYPY	BACKHAND	BALLYHOO
ATOM BOMB	AUTUMNAL	BACKINGS	BALMIEST
ATOMIZER	AUTUNITE	BACKLASH	BALMORAL
ATONABLE	AUVERGNE	BACKLESS	BALSAMIC
ATONALLY	AVADAVAT	BACKLIST	BALUSTER
ATROCITY	AVAILING	BACKLOGS	BANALITY
ATROPHIC	AVENGERS	BACKPACK	BANDAGED
ATROPINE	AVENGING	BACK SEAT	BANDAGES
ATTACHED	AVERAGED	BACKSIDE	BANDANNA
ATTACHER	AVERAGES	BACKSLID	BANDIEST
ATTACHES	AVERMENT	BACKSPIN	BANDITRY
ATTACKED	AVERRING	BACKSTAY	BANDSMAN
ATTACKER	AVERSION	BACKSTOP	BANDSMEN
ATTAINED	AVERSIVE	BACK TALK	BANDYING

BANISHED	BASIDIAL	BECKONER	BELMOPAN
BANISTER	BASIDIUM	BECOMING	BELONGED
BANKBOOK	BASILARY	BEDAUBED	BELOVEDS
BANK NOTE	BASILICA	BEDAZZLE	BELTWAYS
BANK RATE	BASILISK	BEDECKED	BEMOANED
BANKROLL	BASKETRY	BEDIMMED	BENADRYL
BANKRUPT	BASOPHIL	BED LINEN	BENEFICE
BANNOCKS	BASS CLEF	BEDOUINS	BENEFITS
BANQUETS	BASSINET	BEDPLATE	BENGHAZI
BANSHEES	BASSISTS	BEDPOSTS	BENIGNLY
BANTERED	BASSOONS	BEDROOMS	BENTWOOD
BANTERER	BASSWOOD	BEDSIDES	BENUMBED
BAPTISMS	BASTARDS	BEDSORES	BENZOATE
BAPTISTS	BASTARDY	BEDSTEAD	BEQUEATH
BAPTIZED	BASTILLE	BEDSTRAW	BEQUESTS
BARATHEA	BASTIONS	BEDTIMES	BERATING
BARBADOS	BATANGAS	BEEBREAD	BERCEUSE
BARBARIC	BATHETIC	BEECHNUT	BEREAVED
BARBECUE	BATH MATS	BEE-EATER	BERGAMET
BARBERRY	BATHROBE	BEEFCAKE	BERIBERI
BARBICAN	BATHROOM	BEEFIEST	BERTHING
BARBICEL	BATHTUBS	BEEFWOOD	BERYLINE
BAR CHART	BATHURST	BEEHIVES	BESANCON
BAR CODES	BATTENED	BEELINES	BESIEGED
BAREBACK	BATTERED	BEESWING	BESIEGER
BAREFOOT	BATTERER	BEETLING	BESMIRCH
BAREILLY	BATTIEST	BEETROOT	BESOTTED
BARENESS	BATTLING	BEFALLEN	BESOUGHT
BARGAINS	BAUHINIA	BEFITTED	BESPOKEN
BAR GRAPH	BAULKING	BEFOULER	BESTIARY
BARITONE	BAVARIAN	BEFRIEND	BESTOWAL
BARMAIDS	BAWDIEST	BEGETTER	BESTOWED
BARMIEST	BAYBERRY	BEGGARED	BESTOWER
BARNACLE	BAYONETS	BEGGARLY	BESTREWN
BARNYARD	BAZOOKAS	BEGINING	BESTRIDE
BAROGRAM	BDELLIUM	BEGINNER	BESTRODE
BARONAGE	BEACHING	BEGOTTEN	BETAKING
BARONESS	BEADIEST	BEGRUDGE	BETATRON
BARONETS	BEADINGS	BEGUILED	BETIDING
BARONIAL	BEAGLING	BEGUILER	BETRAYAL
BARONIES	BEAM-ENDS	BEHAVING	BETRAYED
BAROSTAT	BEANPOLE	BEHEADED	BETRAYER
BAROUCHE	BEARABLE	BEHOLDEN	BETTERED
BARRACKS	BEARABLY	BEHOLDER	BEVATRON
BARRAGES	BEARDING	BELABOUR	BEVELING
BARRATOR	BEAR HUGS	BELAYING	BEVELLED
BARRATRY	BEARINGS	BELCHING	BEVERAGE
BARRETTE	BEARSKIN	BELFRIES	BEWAILED
BARRIERS	BEATABLE	BELGRADE	BEWAILER
BARTERED	BEATIFIC	BELIEVED	BEWARING
BARTERER	BEATINGS	BELIEVER	BEWIGGED
BARTIZAN	BEATNIKS	BELITTLE	BEWILDER
BASEBALL	BEAUTIES	BELLBIRD	BHATPARA
BASELESS	BEAUTIFY	BELLBOYS	BIANNUAL
BASELINE	BEAUVAIS	BELLOWED	BIASSING
BASEMENT	BEAVERED	BELLOWER	BIATHLON
BASENESS	BECALMED	BELLPULL	BIBLICAL
BASE RATE	BECHAMEL	BELLWORT	BIBULOUS
BASICITY	BECKONED	BELLYFUL	BICKERED

BICKERER	BIRAMOUS	BLEACHER	BLUE BOOK
BICOLOUR	BIRCHING	BLEAKEST	BLUE CHIP
BICONVEX	BIRDBATH	BLEARIER	BLUE FILM
BICUSPID	BIRDCAGE	BLEARILY	BLUEFISH
BICYCLED	BIRD DOGS	BLEATING	BLUEGILL
BICYCLES	BIRDLIKE	BLEEDERS	BLUE GUMS
BICYCLIC	BIRDLIME	BLEEDING	BLUE JAYS
BIDDABLE	BIRDSEED	BLEEPERS	BLUE LAWS
BIENNIAL	BIRD'S-EYE	BLEEPING	BLUE MOON
BIFACIAL	BIRETTAS	BLENCHED	BLUENESS
BIFIDITY	BIRTHDAY	BLENCHER	BLUFFING
BIFOCALS	BISCUITS	BLENDERS	BLUNDERS
BIGAMIST	BISECTED	BLENDING	BLUNTING
BIGAMOUS	BISECTOR	BLENHEIM	BLURRING
BIGHEADS	BISEXUAL	BLESSING	BLURTING
BIG NAMES	BISTOURY	BLIGHTED	BLUSHERS
BIGNONIA	BITCHIER	BLIGHTER	BLUSHING
BIG SHOTS	BITCHILY	BLIMPISH	BLUSTERY
BIG STICK	BITCHING	BLINDAGE	BOARDERS
BIG-TIMER	BITINGLY	BLINDERS	BOARDING
BIG WHEEL	BIT PARTS	BLINDING	BOARFISH
BIJUGATE	BITSTOCK	BLINKERS	BOASTERS
BILABIAL	BITTERLY	BLINKING	BOASTFUL
BILBERRY	BITTERNS	BLISSFUL	BOASTING
BILINEAR	BITTIEST	BLISTERS	BOAT HOOK
BILLETED	BIVALENT	BLITHELY	BOATLOAD
BILLFISH	BIVALVES	BLITZING	BOBBINET
BILLFOLD	BIVOUACS	BLIZZARD	BOBBY PIN
BILLHOOK	BIWEEKLY	BLOATERS	BOBOLINK
BILLIARD	BIYEARLY	BLOCKADE	BOBTAILS
BILLIONS	BLABBING	BLOCKAGE	BOBWHITE
BILLOWED	BLACK ART	BLOCKING	BODILESS
BILOBATE	BLACK BOX	BLONDEST	BODLEIAN
BIMANOUS	BLACKCAP	BLOODFIN	BODY BLOW
BINAURAL	BLACKEST	BLOODILY	BODYWORK
BINDINGS	BLACK EYE	BLOODING	BOEHMITE
BINDWEED	BLACKFLY	BLOOD RED	BOGEYMAN
BIN-LINER	BLACK ICE	BLOOMERS	BOGGIEST
BINNACLE	BLACKING	BLOOMERY	BOGGLING
BINOMIAL	BLACKISH	BLOOMING	BOHEMIAN
BIO-ASSAY	BLACKLEG	BLOOPERS	BOILABLE
BIOCIDAL	BLACKOUT	BLOSSOMS	BOLDFACE
BIOCYCLE	BLACK-TIE	BLOTCHES	BOLDNESS
BIODATAS	BLACKTOP	BLOTTERS	BOLIVIAN
BIOLYSIS	BLADDERS	BLOTTING	BOLLARDS
BIOLYTIC	BLAMABLE	BLOWFISH	BOLLOCKS
BIOMETRY	BLAMEFUL	BLOWHARD	BOLLWORM
BIONOMIC	BLANCHED	BLOWHOLE	BOLSHIER
BIOPLASM	BLANDEST	BLOWIEST	BOLSTERS
BIOPSIES	BLANDISH	BLOWLAMP	BOLTHOLE
BIOSCOPE	BLANKETS	BLOWOUTS	BOLTONIA
BIOSCOPY	BLASTEMA	BLOWPIPE	BOLTROPE
BIOTITIC	BLASTING	BLOW-WAVE	BOMBSITE
BIOTYPIC	BLAST-OFF	BLOWZIER	BOMBYCID
BIPAROUS	BLASTULA	BLOWZILY	BONA FIDE
BIPHENYL	BLATANCY	BLUDGEON	BONANZAS
BIPLANES	BLAZONED	BLUE BABY	BONEFISH
BIRACIAL	BLAZONRY	BLUEBELL	BONEHEAD
BIRADIAL	BLEACHED	BLUEBIRD	BONE-IDLE

BONELESS	BOUNCILY	BREACHES	BROWNEST
BONE MEAL	BOUNCING	BREAD BIN	BROWNIES
BONFIRES	BOUNDARY	BREADNUT	BROWNING
BONHOMIE	BOUNDERS	BREADTHS	BROWNISH
BONINESS	BOUNDING	BREAKAGE	BROWSING
BONNIEST	BOUNTIES	BREAKERS	BRUISERS
BONS MOTS	BOUQUETS	BREAKING	BRUISING
BONTEBOK	BOUTIQUE	BREAK-INS	BRUITING
BOOHOOED	BOUZOUKI	BREATHER	BRUNCHES
BOOKABLE	BOWSHOTS	BREECHES	BRUNETTE
BOOKCASE	BOWSPRIT	BREEDING	BRUSHING
BOOK CLUB	BOXBERRY	BREEZILY	BRUSH-OFF
BOOKENDS	BOXBOARD	BRETHREN	BRUSH-UPS
BOOKINGS	BOXROOMS	BREVETCY	BRUSSELS
BOOKLETS	BOYCOTTS	BREVIARY	BRUTALLY
BOOKMARK	BOYISHLY	BRIBABLE	BRYOLOGY
BOOKRACK	BOY SCOUT	BRICKBAT	BRYOZOAN
BOOKSHOP	BRACELET	BRIDGING	BUBALINE
BOOKWORM	BRACHIAL	BRIEFING	BUBBLIER
BOOSTERS	BRACHIUM	BRIGHTEN	BUBBLING
BOOSTING	BRACKETS	BRIGHTON	BUCHSHEE
BOOTLACE	BRACKISH	BRIOCHES	BUCKAROO
BOOTLESS	BRACTEAL	BRISANCE	BUCKBEAN
BOOZE-UPS	BRADAWLS	BRISBANE	BUCKETED
BOOZIEST	BRAGGART	BRISKEST	BUCKHORN
BORACITE	BRAGGING	BRISLING	BUCKLERS
BORDEAUX	BRAHMANI	BRISTLED	BUCKLING
BORDELLO	BRAHMANS	BRISTLES	BUCKSHEE
BORDERED	BRAIDING	BRITCHES	BUCKSHOT
BORDERER	BRAINIER	BRITTANY	BUCKSKIN
BOREHOLE	BRAINING	BROACHED	BUDAPEST
BORINGLY	BRAINPAN	BROACHER	BUDDHISM
BOROUGHS	BRAISING	BROADEST	BUDDHIST
BORROWED	BRAMBLES	BROADWAY	BUDDLEIA
BORROWER	BRANCHED	BROCADED	BUDGETED
BORSTALS	BRANCHES	BROCCOLI	BUFFALOS
BOSPORUS	BRANCHIA	BROCHURE	BUFFERED
BOSS-EYED	BRANDIES	BROILERS	BUFFETED
BOSSIEST	BRANDING	BROILING	BUFFETER
BOTANIST	BRANDISH	BROKENLY	BUFFOONS
BOTANIZE	BRAND-NEW	BROLLIES	BUGABOOS
BOTCHERS	BRASHEST	BROMIDES	BUGBEARS
BOTCHIER	BRASILIA	BRONCHIA	BUGGERED
BOTCHILY	BRASSARD	BRONCHOS	BUILDERS
BOTCHING	BRASS HAT	BRONCHUS	BUILDING
BOTCH-UPS	BRASSICA	BRONZING	BUILDUPS
BOTHERED	BRASSIER	BROOCHES	BUKOVINI
BOTSWANA	BRASSILY	BROODERS	BULAWAYO
BOTTLING	BRATTICE	BROODIER	BULGARIA
BOTTOMRY	BRAUNITE	BROODILY	BULGIEST
BOTULISM	BRAWLERS	BROODING	BULKHEAD
BOUDOIRS	BRAWLING	BROOKING	BULKIEST
BOUFFANT	BRAWNIER	BROOKITE	BULLDOGS
BOUILLON	BRAWNILY	BROOKLYN	BULLDOZE
BOULDERS	BRAZENED	BROTHELS	BULLETIN
BOULLION	BRAZENLY	BROTHERS	BULLFROG
BOULOGNE	BRAZIERS	BROUGHAM	BULLHEAD
BOUNCERS	BRAZILIN	BROUHAHA	BULLHORN
BOUNCIER	BREACHED	BROWBEAT	BULLNECK

BULLOCKS	BYPASSES	CALFSKIN	CANNIKIN
BULLRING	BYRONISM	CALIBRED	CANNONED
BULL'S-EYE		CALIBRES	CANNONRY
BULLSHIT	C	CALIPASH	CANOEING
BULLYBOY	CABARETS	CALIPERS	CANOEIST
BULLYING	CABBAGES	CALISAYA	CANONESS
BULLY-OFF	CABIN BOY	CALLABLE	CANONIST
BULWARKS	CABINETS	CALL GIRL	CANONIZE
BUMBLING	CABLE CAR	CALLINGS	CANON LAW
BUMPIEST	CABLEWAY	CALLIOPE	CANOODLE
BUMPKINS	CABOCHON	CALLIPER	CANOPIES
BUNCHING	CABOODLE	CALLISTO	CANTATAS
BUNDLING	CABOOSES	CALLUSES	CANTEENS
BUNGALOW	CABOTAGE	CALMNESS	CANTERED
BUNGHOLE	CAB RANKS	CALOR GAS	CANTICLE
BUNGLERS	CABRILLA	CALORIES	CANTONAL
BUNGLING	CABRIOLE	CALUTRON	CANVASES
BUNTLINE	CACHALOT	CALVADOS	CANZONET
BUOYANCY	CACHEPOT	CALVARIA	CAPACITY
BURAYDAH	CACHEXIA	CALYCATE	CAPERING
BURBERRY	CACHUCHA	CALYCINE	CAPESKIN
BURBLING	CACKLERS	CALYPSOS	CAPITALS
BURDENED	CACKLING	CALYPTRA	CAPITATE
BURGHERS	CACTUSES	CAMAGUEY	CAPONIZE
BURGLARS	CADASTER	CAMBODIA	CAPRICES
BURGLARY	CADAVERS	CAMBOGIA	CAPRIFIG
BURGLING	CADDYING	CAMBRIAN	CAPRIOLE
BURGUNDY	CADENCES	CAMELEER	CAPSICUM
BURLIEST	CADENZAS	CAMELLIA	CAPSIZED
BURNOOSE	CADUCEUS	CAMEROON	CAPSTANS
BURNOUTS	CADUCITY	CAMISOLE	CAPSTONE
BURRITOS	CADUCOUS	CAMOMILE	CAPSULAR
BURROWED	CAERLEON	CAMPAGNA	CAPSULES
BURROWER	CAESURAS	CAMPAIGN	CAPTAINS
BURSITIS	CAFFEINE	CAMPANIA	CAPTIONS
BURSTING	CAGELING	CAMP BEDS	CAPTIOUS
BURTHENS	CAGINESS	CAMPECHE	CAPTIVES
BUSHBABY	CAGLIARI	CAMPFIRE	CAPTURED
BUSHBUCK	CAGOULES	CAMPHENE	CAPTURES
BUSHIEST	CAISSONS	CAMPINAS	CAPUCHIN
BUSHVELD	CAJOLERY	CAMPSITE	CAPYBARA
BUSINESS	CAJOLING	CAMPUSES	CARACARA
BUS STOPS	CAKEWALK	CAMSHAFT	CARACOLE
BUSTIEST	CALABASH	CANADIAN	CARAMELS
BUSTLING	CALABRIA	CANAIGRE	CARANGID
BUSYBODY	CALADIUM	CANAILLE	CARAPACE
BUSYNESS	CALAMINE	CANALIZE	CARAVANS
BUTANONE	CALAMINT	CANARIES	CARAWAYS
BUTCHERS	CALAMITE	CANBERRA	CARBINES
BUTCHERY	CALAMITY	CANCELED	CARBOLIC
BUTTERED	CALATHUS	CANCROID	CARBONIC
BUTTOCKS	CALCIFIC	CANDIDLY	CARBONYL
BUTTONED	CALCITIC	CANFIELD	CARBURET
BUTTRESS	CALCULUS	CANISTER	CARDAMOM
BUTYRATE	CALCUTTA	CANNABIC	CARDIGAN
BUZZARDS	CALDRONS	CANNABIN	CARDINAL
BUZZWORD	CALENDAR	CANNABIS	CARDIOID
BY-BIDDER	CALENDER	CANNIBAL	CARDITIS
BYPASSED	CALF LOVE	CANNIEST	CAREENED

CAREERED	CASUISTS	CEDILLAS	CHAINMAN
CAREFREE	CATACOMB	CEILINGS	CHAIN SAW
CARELESS	CATALASE	CELERIAC	CHAIRING
CARESSED	CATALYSE	CELERITY	CHAIRMAN
CARESSER	CATALYST	CELIBACY	CHAIRMEN
CARESSES	CATAMITE	CELIBATE	CHALAZAL
CAREWORN	CATAPULT	CELLARER	CHALDRON
CARIBOUS	CATARACT	CELLARET	CHALICES
CARILLON	CATCALLS	CELLISTS	CHALKIER
CARINATE	CATCH-ALL	CELLULAR	CHALKING
CARLISLE	CATCHFLY	CELULOID	CHAMBERS
CARNAUBA	CATCHIER	CEMENTED	CHAMBRAY
CARNIVAL	CATCHILY	CEMENTER	CHAMPING
CAROLINA	CATCHING	CEMENTUM	CHAMPION
CAROLINE	CATECHIN	CEMETERY	CHANCELS
CAROLING	CATECHOL	CENOTAPH	CHANCERY
CAROLLED	CATEGORY	CENOZOIC	CHANCIER
CAROTENE	CATENANE	CENSORED	CHANCILY
CAROUSAL	CATENARY	CENSURED	CHANCING
CAROUSED	CATENATE	CENSURES	CHANDLER
CAROUSEL	CATENOID	CENSUSES	CHANGING
CAR PARKS	CATERING	CENTAURS	CHANGSHA
CARPETED	CATHEDRA	CENTAURY	CHANGTEH
CAR POOLS	CATHETER	CENTAVOS	CHANNELS
CARPORTS	CATHEXIS	CENTERED	CHANTIES
CARRIAGE	CATHODES	CENTIARE	CHANTING
CARRIERS	CATHODIC	CENTIMES	CHANUKAH
CARRYALL	CATHOLIC	CENTRING	CHAPATTI
CARRYCOT	CATIONIC	CENTRIST	CHAPBOOK
CARRYING	CAT'S EYES	CENTROID	CHAPERON
CARRYOUT	CAT'S-FOOT	CEPHALAD	CHAPLAIN
CARTOONS	CAT'S PAWS	CEPHALIC	CHAPLETS
CARUNCLE	CATSUITS	CEPHALIN	CHAPPING
CARVINGS	CATTIEST	CERAMICS	CHAPTERS
CARYATID	CATTLEYA	CERAMIST	CHARACIN
CASANOVA	CATWALKS	CERASTES	CHARADES
CASCADED	CAUCASIA	CERATOID	CHARCOAL
CASCADES	CAUCASUS	CERCARIA	CHARENTE
CASEMATE	CAUCUSES	CEREBRAL	CHARGERS
CASEMENT	CAUDALLY	CEREBRIC	CHARGING
CASEWORK	CAULDRON	CEREBRUM	CHARIEST
CASHABLE	CAULICLE	CEREMENT	CHARIOTS
CASH-BOOK	CAULKING	CEREMONY	CHARISMA
CASH CARD	CAUSABLE	CERNUOUS	CHARLADY
CASH CROP	CAUSALLY	CEROTYPE	CHARLIES
CASH DESK	CAUSERIE	CERULEAN	CHARLOCK
CASH FLOW	CAUSEWAY	CERVELAT	CHARMERS
CASHIERS	CAUTIONS	CERVICAL	CHARMING
CASHLESS	CAUTIOUS	CERVICES	CHARQUID
CASHMERE	CAVALIER	CERVIXES	CHARRING
CASSETTE	CAVATINA	CESAREAN	CHARTERS
CASSOCKS	CAVEATOR	CESSIONS	CHARTING
CASTAWAY	CAVEFISH	CESSPITS	CHARTISM
CASTINGS	CAVICORN	CESSPOOL	CHARTIST
CAST-IRON	CAVILING	CETACEAN	CHASSEUR
CASTRATE	CAVILLED	CEVENNES	CHASTELY
CASTRATO	CAVILLER	CHACONNE	CHASTEST
CASUALLY	CAVITIES	CHAFFING	CHASTISE
CASUALTY	CAVORTED	CHAINING	CHASTITY

CHASUBLE	CHILIAST	CHRISTEN	CLAIMING
CHAT SHOW	CHILLIER	CHROMATE	CLAMBAKE
CHATTELS	CHILLIES	CHROMITE	CLAMMIER
CHATTIER	CHILLING	CHROMIUM	CLAMMILY
CHATTILY	CHILOPOD	CHROMOUS	CLAMMING
CHATTING	CHIMAERA	CHUBBIER	CLAMOURS
CHAUFFER	CHIMBOTE	CHUCKING	CLAMPING
CHEAPEST	CHIMERAS	CHUCKLED	CLANGERS
CHEATING	CHIMKENT	CHUCKLER	CLANGING
CHECKERS	CHIMNEYS	CHUCKLES	CLANKING
CHECKING	CHINAMAN	CHUGGING	CLANNISH
CHECK-INS	CHIN-CHOU	CHUKKERS	CLANSMAN
CHECKOUT	CHINDWIN	CHUMMIER	CLANSMEN
CHECKUPS	CHINKING	CHUMMILY	CLAPPERS
CHEDDITE	CHINLESS	CHUMMING	CLAPPING
CHEEKIER	CHIPMUNK	CHUNKIER	CLAPTRAP
CHEEKILY	CHIPPIES	CHURCHES	CLARINET
CHEEKING	CHIPPING	CHURLISH	CLARIONS
CHEEPING	CHIRPIER	CHURNING	CLASHING
CHEERFUL	CHIRPILY	CHUTZPAH	CLASPING
CHEERIER	CHIRPING	CHYMOSIN	CLASSICS
CHEERILY	CHIRRUPY	CIBORIUM	CLASSIER
CHEERING	CHISELED	CICATRIX	CLASSIFY
CHEETAHS	CHITCHAT	CICERONE	CLASSING
CHEKIANG	CHIVALRY	CICHLOID	CLASSISM
CHEMICAL	CHIVYING	CIMBRIAN	CLASSIST
CHEMISES	CHLORATE	CINCHONA	CLATTERS
CHEMISTS	CHLORIDE	CINCTURE	CLATTERY
CHEMURGY	CHLORINE	CINEASTE	CLAVICLE
CHENILLE	CHLORITE	CINERAMA	CLAYLIKE
CHENOPOD	CHLOROUS	CINERARY	CLAYMORE
CHEQUERS	CHOC-ICES	CINGULUM	CLEAN-CUT
CHEROKEE	CHOCKING	CINNABAR	CLEANERS
CHEROOTS	CHOICELY	CINNAMON	CLEANEST
CHERRIES	CHOICEST	CINQUAIN	CLEANING
CHERUBIC	CHOIRBOY	CIPHERED	CLEANSED
CHESSMAN	CHOISEUL	CIRCLETS	CLEANSER
CHESTIER	CHOLERIC	CIRCLING	CLEAR-CUT
CHESTILY	CHOMPING	CIRCUITS	CLEAREST
CHESTNUT	CHONGJIN	CIRCUITY	CLEARING
CHEVRONS	CHOOSIER	CIRCULAR	CLEAROUT
CHEWABLE	CHOP-CHOP	CIRCUSES	CLEARWAY
CHEWIEST	CHOPPERS	CISLUNAR	CLEAVAGE
CHEYENNE	CHOPPIER	CISTERNA	CLEAVERS
CHIASMAL	CHOPPILY	CISTERNS	CLEAVING
CHIASMIC	CHOPPING	CITADELS	CLEMATIS
CHIASMUS	CHOP SUEY	CITATION	CLEMENCY
CHIASTIC	CHORALES	CITIFIED	CLENCHED
CHICANER	CHORDATE	CITIZENS	CLENCHES
CHICANOS	CHORDING	CITREOUS	CLERICAL
CHICKENS	CHORIAMB	CITRUSES	CLERIHEW
CHICKPEA	CHORTLED	CITY HALL	CLERKDOM
CHICLAYO	CHORTLES	CIVILIAN	CLERKING
CHIGETAI	CHORUSED	CIVILITY	CLEVEITE
CHIGGERS	CHORUSES	CIVILIZE	CLEVERLY
CHIGNONS	CHOW-CHOW	CIVIL LAW	CLICKING
CHILDISH	CHOW MEIN	CIVIL WAR	CLIENTAL
CHILDREN	CHRESARD	CLACKING	CLIMATES
CHILIASM	CHRISMAL	CLAIMANT	CLIMATIC

CLIMAXED	COAHUILA	COIFFURE	COMEDOWN
CLIMAXES	COALESCE	COINAGES	COMELIER
CLIMBERS	COALFACE	COINCIDE	COMFIEST
CLIMBING	COALFISH	COINSURE	COMFORTS
CLINCHED	COALHOLE	COLANDER	COMITIES
CLINCHER	COALMINE	COLD CUTS	COMMANDO
CLINCHES	COALPORT	COLD FEET	COMMANDS
CLINGING	COARSELY	COLD FISH	COMMENCE
CLINICAL	COARSEST	COLDNESS	COMMENTS
CLINKERS	COASTERS	COLD SNAP	COMMERCE
CLINKING	COASTING	COLD SORE	COMMODES
CLIPPERS	COATINGS	COLD-WELD	COMMONER
CLIPPIES	COAT-TAIL	COLESLAW	COMMONLY
CLIPPING	COAUTHOR	COLISEUM	COMMUNAL
CLIQUISH	COBALTIC	COLLAGEN	COMMUNED
CLITORAL	COBBLERS	COLLAGES	COMMUNES
CLITORIS	COBBLING	COLLAPSE	COMMUTED
CLOAKING	COBWEBBY	COLLARED	COMMUTER
CLOCKING	COCA-COLA	COLLATED	COMPACTS
CLODDISH	COCCYGES	COLLATOR	COMPARED
CLOGGING	COCHLEAE	COLLECTS	COMPARER
CLOISTER	COCHLEAR	COLLEENS	COMPARES
CLOPPING	COCKADES	COLLEGES	COMPEERS
CLOSE-SET	COCKATOO	COLLIDED	COMPERED
CLOSETED	COCKCROW	COLLIERS	COMPERES
CLOSE-UPS	COCKEREL	COLLIERY	COMPETED
CLOSURES	COCKEYED	COLLOGUE	COMPILED
CLOTHIER	COCKIEST	COLLOQUY	COMPILER
CLOTHING	COCKNEYS	COLLUDED	COMPLAIN
CLOTTING	COCKPITS	COLOMBIA	COMPLETE
CLOUDIER	COCKSPUR	COLONELS	COMPLIED
CLOUDILY	COCKSURE	COLONIAL	COMPLIER
CLOUDING	COCKTAIL	COLONIES	COMPLINE
CLOUDLET	COCONUTS	COLONIST	COMPOSED
CLOUTING	COCOONED	COLONIZE	COMPOSER
CLOWNERY	CODDLING	COLOPHON	COMPOTES
CLOWNING	CODICILS	COLORADO	COMPOUND
CLOWNISH	CODIFIED	COLORANT	COMPRESS
CLUBBING	CODIFIER	COLOSSAL	COMPRISE
CLUBFEET	CODOMAIN	COLOSSUS	COMPUTED
CLUBFOOT	CODPIECE	COLOTOMY	COMPUTER
CLUBHAUL	COENURUS	COLOURED	COMRADES
CLUCKING	COENZYME	COLPITIS	CONATION
CLUELESS	COEQUALS	COLUBRID	CONATIVE
CLUMPING	COERCING	COLUMBIA	CONCEDED
CLUMPISH	COERCION	COLUMBIC	CONCEITS
CLUMSIER	COERCIVE	COLUMBUS	CONCEIVE
CLUMSILY	COEXTEND	COLUMNAR	CONCEPTS
CLUPEOID	COGENTLY	COLUMNED	CONCERNS
CLUSTERS	COGITATE	COMANCHE	CONCERTO
CLUSTERY	COGNATES	COMATOSE	CONCERTS
CLUTCHED	COGNOMEN	COMBATED	CONCHOID
CLUTCHES	COGWHEEL	COMBATER	CONCLAVE
COACHING	COHERENT	COMBINED	CONCLUDE
COACHMAN	COHERING	COMBINER	CONCRETE
COACHMEN	COHESION	COMBINES	CONDENSE
COACTION	COHESIVE	COMEBACK	CONDOLED
COACTIVE	COHOBATE	COMEDIAN	CONDOLER
COAGULUM	COIFFEUR	COMEDIES	CONDONED

CONDONER	CONTINUO	CORNERED	COVALENT
CONDUCED	CONTOURS	CORNETTE	COVENANT
CONDUCER	CONTRACT	CORNICES	COVENTRY
CONDUITS	CONTRAIL	CORNICHE	COVERAGE
CONDYLAR	CONTRARY	CORNIEST	COVERING
CONFEREE	CONTRAST	CORN PONE	COVERLET
CONFERVA	CONTRITE	CORONARY	COVERTLY
CONFETTI	CONTRIVE	CORONERS	COVER-UPS
CONFIDED	CONTROLS	CORONETS	COVETING
CONFIDER	CONTUSED	CORPORAL	COVETOUS
CONFINED	CONVENED	CORRIDOR	COWARDLY
CONFINES	CONVENER	CORRODED	COWBELLS
CONFLATE	CONVENTS	CORRODER	COWBERRY
CONFLICT	CONVERGE	CORSAGES	COWERING
CONFOCAL	CONVERSE	CORSAIRS	COWHANDS
CONFOUND	CONVERTS	CORSELET	COWHERDS
CONFRERE	CONVEXLY	CORSETED	COWHIDES
CONFRONT	CONVEYED	CORSETRY	COWLICKS
CONFUSED	CONVEYER	CORTEGES	COWLINGS
CONFUTED	CONVEYOR	CORTICAL	CO-WORKER
CONFUTER	CONVICTS	CORTICES	COWSHEDS
CONGENER	CONVINCE	CORUNDUM	COWSLIPS
CONGRATS	CONVOKED	CORVETTE	COXALGIA
CONGRESS	CONVOKER	CORYPHEE	COXALGIC
CONIDIAL	CONVOYED	COSECANT	COXCOMBS
CONIDIUM	CONVULSE	COSINESS	COXSWAIN
CONIFERS	COOKABLE	COSMETIC	COZENAGE
CONJOINT	COOKBOOK	COSTLIER	COZENING
CONJUGAL	COOKOUTS	COSTMARY	COZINESS
CONJUNCT	COOLABAR	COST-PLUS	CRABBIER
CONJURED	COOLANTS	COSTUMES	CRABBING
CONJURER	COOLNESS	COT DEATH	CRABWISE
CONNIVED	COONSKIN	COTENANT	CRACKERS
CONNIVER	COOPTING	COTERIES	CRACKING
CONNOTED	COOPTION	COTOPAXI	CRACKLED
CONODONT	COPILOTS	COTSWOLD	CRACKNEL
CONOIDAL	COPLANAR	COTTAGER	CRACKPOT
CONQUEST	COPPERAS	COTTAGES	CRACKUPS
CONSERVE	COPULATE	COTYLOID	CRADLING
CONSIDER	COPYBOOK	COUCHANT	CRAFTIER
CONSOLED	COPYCATS	COUCHING	CRAFTILY
CONSOLER	COPY-EDIT	COUGHING	CRAFTING
CONSOLES	COPYHOLD	COULISSE	CRAGGIER
CONSOMME	COPYISTS	COUMARIC	CRAM-FULL
CONSORTS	COQUETRY	COUMARIN	CRAMMERS
CONSPIRE	COQUETTE	COUNCILS	CRAMMING
CONSTANT	COQUILLE	COUNTERS	CRAMPING
CONSTRUE	CORACLES	COUNTESS	CRAMPONS
CONSULAR	CORACOID	COUNTIES	CRANE FLY
CONSUMED	CORDIALS	COUNTING	CRANIATE
CONSUMER	CORDLESS	COUPLETS	CRANIUMS
CONTACTS	CORDONED	COUPLING	CRANKIER
CONTANGO	CORDOVAN	COURANTE	CRANKING
CONTEMPT	CORDUROY	COURLAND	CRANKPIN
CONTENTS	CORDWOOD	COURSING	CRANNIED
CONTESTS	CORE TIME	COURTESY	CRANNIES
CONTEXTS	CORKWOOD	COURTIER	CRAPPIER
CONTINUA	CORNCOBS	COURTING	CRAPPING
CONTINUE	CORNEOUS	COUSCOUS	CRASHING

CRAVENLY	CRISTATE	CRYOLITE	CURRYING
CRAVINGS	CRITERIA	CRYONICS	CURSEDLY
CRAWFISH	CRITICAL	CRYOSTAT	CURTAINS
CRAWLERS	CRITIQUE	CRYOTRON	CURTNESS
CRAWLING	CRITTERS	CRYSTALS	CURTSIED
CRAYFISH	CROAKILY	CUBATURE	CURTSIES
CRAYONED	CROAKING	CUBE ROOT	CUSHIEST
CRAZIEST	CROCKERY	CUBICLES	CUSHIONS
CREAKIER	CROCOITE	CUBIFORM	CUSHIONY
CREAKILY	CROCUSES	CUBISIST	CUSPIDOR
CREAKING	CROFTERS	CUBISTIC	CUSSEDLY
CREAMERS	CROMLECH	CUCKOLDS	CUSTARDS
CREAMERY	CROOKING	CUCUMBER	CUSTOMER
CREAMIER	CROONERS	CUCURBIT	CUSTUMAL
CREAMING	CROONING	CUDDLIER	CUTAWAYS
CREASING	CROPPERS	CUDDLING	CUTBACKS
CREATINE	CROPPING	CUDGELED	CUTENESS
CREATING	CROSIERS	CUFF LINK	CUT GLASS
CREATION	CROSSBAR	CUL-DE-SAC	CUTICLES
CREATIVE	CROSSBOW	CULIACAN	CUTICULA
CREATORS	CROSSCUT	CULINARY	CUTINIZE
CREATURE	CROSSEST	CULOTTES	CUT-PRICE
CREDENCE	CROSS-EYE	CULOUSLY	CUTPURSE
CREDENZA	CROSSING	CULPABLE	CUTTINGS
CREDIBLE	CROSSLET	CULPABLY	CUTWATER
CREDIBLY	CROSSPLY	CULPRITS	CYANITIC
CREDITED	CROTCHES	CULTIGEN	CYANOGEN
CREDITOR	CROTCHET	CULTIVAR	CYANOSIS
CREEPERS	CROUCHED	CULTRATE	CYANOTIC
CREEPIER	CROUPIER	CULTURAL	CYCLADES
CREEPILY	CROUPOUS	CULTURED	CYCLAMEN
CREEPING	CROUTONS	CULTURES	CYCLISTS
CREMATED	CROWBARS	CULVERIN	CYCLONES
CREMATOR	CROWBOOT	CULVERTS	CYCLONIC
CREODONT	CROWDING	CUMBERED	CYCLOSIS
CREOSOTE	CROWFOOT	CUMBRIAN	CYLINDER
CRESCENT	CROWNING	CUMQUATS	CYMATIUM
CRESTING	CROZIERS	CUMULOUS	CYMOGENE
CRESYLIC	CRUCIATE	CUPBOARD	CYNICISM
CRETONNE	CRUCIBLE	CUP CAKES	CYNOSURE
CREVASSE	CRUCIFER	CUP FINAL	CYPHERED
CREVICES	CRUCIFIX	CUPIDITY	CYPRINID
CREW CUTS	CRUDITES	CUPREOUS	CYRILLIC
CREW NECK	CRUISERS	CUPULATE	CYSTEINE
CRIBBAGE	CRUISING	CURARIZE	CYSTITIS
CRIBBING	CRUMBLED	CURASSOW	CYTASTER
CRICKETS	CRUMBLES	CURATIVE	CYTIDINE
CRICKING	CRUMHORN	CURATORS	CYTOLOGY
CRIMINAL	CRUMMIER	CURCULIO	CYTOSINE
CRIMPING	CRUMPETS	CURDLING	CZARINAS
CRIMSONS	CRUMPLED	CURE-ALLS	
CRINGING	CRUNCHED	CURITIBA	D
CRINKLED	CRUSADED	CURLICUE	DABBLERS
CRINKLES	CRUSADER	CURLIEST	DABBLING
CRIPPLED	CRUSADES	CURRANTS	DABCHICK
CRIPPLES	CRUSHING	CURRENCY	DAB HANDS
CRISPATE	CRUSTIER	CURRENTS	DACTYLIC
CRISPIER	CRUSTILY	CURRICLE	DAEMONIC
CRISPING	CRUTCHES	CURRIERY	DAFFODIL

DAFTNESS	DEADENED	DECODING	DELAWARE
DAGESTAN	DEADENER	DECOLOUR	DELAYING
DAINTIER	DEADFALL	DECORATE	DELEGACY
DAINTIES	DEAD HEAT	DECOROUS	DELEGATE
DAINTILY	DEADLIER	DECOYING	DELETING
DAIQUIRI	DEADLINE	DECREASE	DELETION
DAIRYMAN	DEADLOCK	DECREPIT	DELICACY
DAIRYMEN	DEADNESS	DECRETAL	DELICATE
DALESMAN	DEAD WOOD	DECRYING	DELIGHTS
DALLYING	DEAF-AIDS	DECURVED	DELIRIUM
DALMATIA	DEAFENED	DEDICATE	DELIVERY
DALMATIC	DEAF-MUTE	DEDUCING	DELOUSED
DALTONIC	DEAFNESS	DEDUCTED	DELPHIAN
DAMAGING	DEALFISH	DEED POLL	DELUDING
DAMANHUR	DEALINGS	DEEMSTER	DELUGING
DAMASCUS	DEANSHIP	DEEPENED	DELUSION
DAMNABLE	DEARESTS	DEEPENER	DELUSIVE
DAMNABLY	DEARNESS	DEEP-LAID	DELUSORY
DAMOCLES	DEATHBED	DEEPNESS	DEMAGOGY
DAMPENED	DEATH ROW	DEERSKIN	DEMANDED
DAMPENER	DEBACLES	DEFACING	DEMANDER
DAMPNESS	DEBARKED	DEFAMING	DEMARCHE
DANDIEST	DEBARRED	DEFAULTS	DEMEANED
DANDLING	DEBASING	DEFEATED	DEMENTED
DANDRUFF	DEBATERS	DEFEATER	DEMENTIA
DANDYISH	DEBATING	DEFECATE	DEMERARA
DANDYISM	DEBILITY	DEFECTED	DEMERITS
DANEWORT	DEBITING	DEFECTOR	DEMERSAL
DANGLING	DEBONAIR	DEFENCES	DEMESNES
DANKNESS	DEBRECEN	DEFENDED	DEMIGODS
DANUBIAN	DEBUGGED	DEFENDER	DEMIJOHN
DARINGLY	DEBUNKED	DEFERENT	DEMILUNE
DARK AGES	DEBUNKER	DEFERRED	DEMISTED
DARKENED	DECADENT	DEFERRER	DEMISTER
DARKENER	DECAMPED	DEFIANCE	DEMIVOLT
DARKNESS	DECANOIC	DEFICITS	DEMOBBED
DARKROOM	DECANTED	DEFILERS	DEMOCRAT
DARLINGS	DECANTER	DEFILING	DEMOLISH
DATABASE	DECAYING	DEFINING	DEMONIAC
DATEABLE	DECEASED	DEFINITE	DEMONISM
DATELINE	DECEIVED	DEFLATED	DEMONIST
DATOLITE	DECEIVER	DEFLATOR	DEMONIZE
DAUGHTER	DECEMBER	DEFLEXED	DEMOTING
DAUNTING	DECENTLY	DEFLOWER	DEMOTION
DAUPHINE	DECIBELS	DEFOREST	DEMOTIST
DAUPHINS	DECIDING	DEFORMED	DEMPSTER
DAWDLERS	DECIDUAL	DEFORMER	DEMURELY
DAWDLING	DECIMALS	DEFRAYAL	DEMUREST
DAYBREAK	DECIMATE	DEFRAYED	DEMURRAL
DAYDREAM	DECIPHER	DEFRAYER	DEMURRED
DAYLIGHT	DECISION	DEFTNESS	DEMURRER
DAYROOMS	DECISIVE	DEFUSING	DENATURE
DAYTIMES	DECKHAND	DEGASSER	DENDRITE
DAY-TO-DAY	DECLARED	DEGRADED	DENDROID
DAZZLING	DECLARER	DEGRADER	DENIABLE
DEACONRY	DECLASSE	DEICIDAL	DENIZENS
DEAD BEAT	DECLINED	DEIFYING	DENOTING
DEAD DUCK	DECLINER	DEIGNING	DENOUNCE
DEAD ENDS	DECLINES	DEJECTED	DENTICLE

DENTINAL	DESTRUCT	DIALYTIC	DILATANT
DENTURES	DETACHED	DIAMANTE	DILATING
DENUDATE	DETACHER	DIAMETER	DILATION
DENUDING	DETAILED	DIAMONDS	DILATIVE
DEPARTED	DETAINED	DIANTHUS	DILATORY
DEPENDED	DETAINEE	DIAPASON	DILEMMAS
DEPICTED	DETAINER	DIAPAUSE	DILIGENT
DEPICTER	DETECTED	DIAPHONE	DILUTING
DEPILATE	DETECTER	DIAPHONY	DILUTION
DEPLETED	DETECTOR	DIARCHIC	DILUVIAL
DEPLORED	DETENTES	DIARISTS	DIMERISM
DEPLORER	DETERRED	DIASCOPE	DIMEROUS
DEPLOYED	DETESTED	DIASPORA	DIMETRIC
DEPONENT	DETESTER	DIASPORE	DIMINISH
DEPORTED	DETHRONE	DIASTASE	DINGDONG
DEPORTEE	DETONATE	DIASTEMA	DINGHIES
DEPOSING	DETRITAL	DIASTOLE	DINGIEST
DEPOSITS	DETRITUS	DIASTRAL	DINKIEST
DEPRAVED	DEUCEDLY	DIASTYLE	DINOSAUR
DEPRAVER	DEUTERON	DIATOMIC	DIOCESAN
DEPRIVED	DEVALUED	DIATONIC	DIOCESES
DEPRIVER	DEVIANCE	DIATRIBE	DIOPSIDE
DEPURATE	DEVIANTS	DIBBLING	DIOPTASE
DEPUTIES	DEVIATED	DICENTRA	DIOPTRAL
DEPUTING	DEVIATOR	DICHROIC	DIOPTRIC
DEPUTIZE	DEVILING	DICKERED	DIORAMIC
DERAILED	DEVILISH	DICKIEST	DIORITIC
DERANGED	DEVILLED	DICROTIC	DIOXIDES
DERELICT	DEVISING	DICTATED	DIPHENYL
DERIDING	DEVOLVED	DICTATES	DIPLEGIA
DERISION	DEVONIAN	DICTATOR	DIPLEXER
DERISIVE	DEVOTEES	DIDACTIC	DIPLOMAS
DERISORY	DEVOTING	DIDDLING	DIPLOMAT
DERIVING	DEVOTION	DIDYMIUM	DIPLOPIA
DEROGATE	DEVOURED	DIDYMOUS	DIPLOPIC
DERRICKS	DEVOURER	DIEHARDS	DIPLOPOD
DESCALED	DEVOUTER	DIELDRIN	DIPLOSIS
DESCANTS	DEVOUTLY	DIERESES	DIPSTICK
DESCENTS	DEWBERRY	DIERESIS	DIPTERAL
DESCRIBE	DEWDROPS	DIERETIC	DIPTERAN
DESCRIED	DEWINESS	DIESTOCK	DIRECTED
DESCRIER	DEWY-EYED	DIETETIC	DIRECTLY
DESERTED	DEXTROSE	DIFFERED	DIRECTOR
DESERTER	DIABASIC	DIFFRACT	DIRIMENT
DESERVED	DIABETES	DIFFUSED	DIRT BIKE
DESERVER	DIABETIC	DIFFUSER	DIRTIEST
DESIGNED	DIABOLIC	DIGAMIST	DIRT ROAD
DESIGNER	DIACIDIC	DIGAMOUS	DIRTYING
DESINENT	DIACONAL	DIGESTED	DISABLED
DESIRING	DIAGNOSE	DIGESTER	DISABUSE
DESIROUS	DIAGONAL	DIGESTIF	DISAGREE
DESISTED	DIAGRAMS	DIGGINGS	DISALLOW
DESKWORK	DIAGRAPH	DIGITATE	DISANNUL
DESOLATE	DIALECTS	DIGITIZE	DISARMED
DESPATCH	DIALLAGE	DIGITRON	DISARMER
DESPISED	DIALLING	DIGRAPHS	DISARRAY
DESPOTIC	DIALOGUE	DIHEDRAL	DISASTER
DESSERTS	DIALYSER	DIHEDRON	DISBURSE
DESTINED	DIALYSIS	DIHYBRID	DISCARDS

DISCIPLE	DISTRAIN	DOGFIGHT	DOUBLURE
DISCLAIM	DISTRAIT	DOGGEDLY	DOUBTERS
DISCLOSE	DISTRESS	DOGGEREL	DOUBTFUL
DISCORDS	DISTRICT	DOGGONED	DOUBTING
DISCOUNT	DISTRUST	DOGGY BAG	DOUGHNUT
DISCOVER	DISUNION	DOGHOUSE	DOURNESS
DISCREET	DISUNITE	DOGMATIC	DOVECOTE
DISCRETE	DISUNITY	DO-GOODER	DOVETAIL
DISCUSES	DITCHING	DOGSBODY	DOWAGERS
DISEASED	DITHEISM	DOG'S-TAIL	DOWDIEST
DISEASES	DITHEIST	DOG-TIRED	DOWNBEAT
DISENDOW	DITHERED	DOGTOOTH	DOWNCAST
DISGORGE	DITHERER	DOGTROTS	DOWNFALL
DISGRACE	DIURESIS	DOGWATCH	DOWNHAUL
DISGUISE	DIURETIC	DOGWOODS	DOWNHILL
DISHEVEL	DIVALENT	DOLDRUMS	DOWNIEST
DISHFULS	DIVE-BOMB	DOLERITE	DOWNLOAD
DISHIEST	DIVERGED	DOLOMITE	DOWNPIPE
DISINTER	DIVERTED	DOLOROSO	DOWNPLAY
DISJOINT	DIVERTER	DOLOROUS	DOWNPOUR
DISJUNCT	DIVESTED	DOLPHINS	DOWNTIME
DISKETTE	DIVIDEND	DOMELIKE	DOWNTOWN
DISLIKED	DIVIDERS	DOMESTIC	DOWNTURN
DISLIKES	DIVIDING	DOMICILE	DOWNWARD
DISLODGE	DIVI-DIVI	DOMINANT	DOWNWASH
DISLOYAL	DIVINELY	DOMINATE	DOWNWIND
DISMALLY	DIVINERS	DOMINEER	DOXASTIC
DISMAYED	DIVINING	DOMINION	DOXOLOGY
DISMOUNT	DIVINITY	DOMINIUM	DOZINESS
DISORDER	DIVINIZE	DOMINOES	DRABBEST
DISOWNED	DIVISION	DONATING	DRABNESS
DISOWNER	DIVISIVE	DONATION	DRACAENA
DISPATCH	DIVISORS	DONATIVE	DRACHMAE
DISPENSE	DIVORCED	DON JUANS	DRACHMAS
DISPERSE	DIVORCEE	DOODLING	DRACONIC
DISPIRIT	DIVORCER	DOOMSDAY	DRAFTEES
DISPLACE	DIVORCES	DOORBELL	DRAFTIER
DISPLAYS	DIVULGED	DOORJAMB	DRAFTING
DISPOSAL	DIVULGER	DOORKNOB	DRAGGIER
DISPOSED	DIZZIEST	DOORMATS	DRAGGING
DISPOSER	DJAKARTA	DOORNAIL	DRAGGLED
DISPROOF	DJIBOUTI	DOORPOST	DRAGLINE
DISPROVE	DNIESTER	DOORSILL	DRAGNETS
DISPUTED	D-NOTICES	DOORSTEP	DRAGOMAN
DISPUTER	DOCILITY	DOORSTOP	DRAGONET
DISPUTES	DOCKETED	DOORWAYS	DRAGOONS
DISQUIET	DOCKLAND	DOPINESS	DRAGROPE
DISROBED	DOCKSIDE	DORDOGNE	DRAINAGE
DISROBER	DOCKYARD	DORMANCY	DRAINING
DISSEISE	DOCTORAL	DORMOUSE	DRAMATIC
DISSENTS	DOCTORED	DORTMUND	DRAPABLE
DISSEVER	DOCTRINE	DOSSIERS	DRATTING
DISSOLVE	DOCUMENT	DOTATION	DRAUGHTS
DISSUADE	DODDERED	DOTINGLY	DRAUGHTY
DISTAFFS	DODDERER	DOTTEREL	DRAWABLE
DISTANCE	DODGIEST	DOTTIEST	DRAWBACK
DISTASTE	DOGBERRY	DOUBLETS	DRAWBORE
DISTINCT	DOGCARTS	DOUBLING	DRAWINGS
DISTRACT	DOG-EARED	DOUBLOON	DRAWLING

DRAWTUBE	DRUMHEAD	DYNAMIST	EDGEWAYS
DREADFUL	DRUMMERS	DYNAMITE	EDGINESS
DREADING	DRUMMING	DYNASTIC	EDIFICES
DREAMERS	DRUNKARD	DYNATRON	EDIFYING
DREAMILY	DRUNKEST	DYSGENIC	EDITIONS
DREAMING	DRUPELET	DYSLEXIA	EDMONTON
DREARIER	DRY-CLEAN	DYSLEXIC	EDUCABLE
DREARILY	DRY DOCKS	DYSPNOEA	EDUCATED
DREDGERS	DRY GOODS	DYTISCID	EDUCATOR
DREDGING	DRY-STONE		EDUCIBLE
DRENCHED	DUBONNET	E	EDUCTION
DRENCHER	DUCKLING	EARDROPS	EDUCTIVE
DRESSAGE	DUCKWEED	EARDRUMS	EELGRASS
DRESSERS	DUCTILES	EARLDOMS	EERINESS
DRESSIER	DUELLING	EARLIEST	EFFACING
DRESSILY	DUELLIST	EARLOBES	EFFECTED
DRESSING	DUETTIST	EARMUFFS	EFFECTER
DRIBBLED	DUISBURG	EARNINGS	EFFECTOR
DRIBBLER	DUKEDOMS	EARPHONE	EFFERENT
DRIBBLES	DULCIANA	EARPIECE	EFFICACY
DRIBLETS	DULCIMER	EARPLUGS	EFFIGIAL
DRIFTAGE	DULLARDS	EARRINGS	EFFIGIES
DRIFTERS	DULLNESS	EARSHOTS	EFFLUENT
DRIFTING	DUMBBELL	EARTHIER	EFFUSION
DRILLING	DUMB-CANE	EARTHILY	EFFUSIVE
DRINKERS	DUMBNESS	EARTHING	EGESTION
DRINKING	DUMB SHOW	EARTHNUT	EGESTIVE
DRIPPING	DUMMY RUN	EASEMENT	EGGHEADS
DRIVABLE	DUMPIEST	EASINESS	EGGPLANT
DRIVE-INS	DUMPLING	EASTERLY	EGG ROLLS
DRIVELED	DUNGAREE	EAST SIDE	EGGSHELL
DRIVEWAY	DUNGEONS	EASTWARD	EGG TIMER
DRIZZLED	DUNGHILL	EBB TIDES	EGOISTIC
DROLLERY	DUODENAL	EBBW VALE	EGOMANIA
DROLLEST	DUODENUM	ECCLESIA	EGOTISTS
DROOLING	DUOLOGUE	ECDYSIAL	EGO TRIPS
DROOPILY	DUPLEXES	ECDYSONE	EGYPTIAN
DROOPING	DURATION	ECHELONS	EIGHTEEN
DROPLETS	DURATIVE	ECHINATE	EIGHTIES
DROPOUTS	DUSHANBE	ECHINOID	EISENACH
DROPPERS	DUSKIEST	ECLECTIC	EITHER-OR
DROPPING	DUSTBINS	ECLIPSED	EJECTING
DROPSIED	DUSTBOWL	ECLIPSER	EJECTION
DROPWORT	DUSTCART	ECLIPSES	EJECTIVE
DROUGHTS	DUSTIEST	ECLIPSIS	EKISTICS
DROUGHTY	DUSTPANS	ECLIPTIC	ELAPSING
DROWNING	DUTCH CAP	ECLOGITE	ELATERID
DROWSILY	DUTCHMAN	ECLOSION	ELATERIN
DROWSING	DUTIABLE	ECONOMIC	ELBOWING
DRUBBING	DUTY-FREE	ECOTONAL	EL DORADO
DRUDGERY	DWARFING	ECOTYPIC	ELDRITCH
DRUDGING	DWARFISH	ECRASEUR	ELECTING
DRUGGETS	DWARFISM	ECSTATIC	ELECTION
DRUGGING	DWELLING	ECTODERM	ELECTIVE
DRUGGIST	DWINDLED	ECTOMERE	ELECTORS
DRUIDISM	DYARCHIC	ECTOSARC	ELECTRET
DRUMBEAT	DYESTUFF	ECUMENIC	ELECTRIC
DRUMFIRE	DYNAMICS	EDACIOUS	ELECTRON
DRUMFISH	DYNAMISM	EDENTATE	ELECTRUM

ELEGANCE	EMPHASIS	ENERGIZE	ENTENDRE
ELEMENTS	EMPHATIC	ENERVATE	ENTENTES
ELENCHUS	EMPLOYED	ENFEEBLE	ENTERING
ELENCTIC	EMPLOYEE	ENFILADE	ENTHALPY
ELEPHANT	EMPLOYER	ENFOLDED	ENTHETIC
ELEVATED	EMPORIUM	ENFOLDER	ENTHRONE
ELEVATOR	EMPTIEST	ENFORCED	ENTHUSED
ELEVENTH	EMPTYING	ENFORCER	ENTICING
EL FAIYUM	EMPYEMIC	ENGADINE	ENTIRELY
ELICITED	EMPYREAL	ENGAGING	ENTIRETY
ELICITOR	EMPYREAN	ENGENDER	ENTITIES
ELIDIBLE	EMULATED	ENGINEER	ENTITLED
ELIGIBLE	EMULATOR	ENGINERY	ENTODERM
ELISIONS	EMULSIFY	ENGRAVED	ENTOMBED
ELITISTS	EMULSION	ENGRAVER	ENTOZOIC
ELKHOUND	EMULSIVE	ENGULFED	ENTOZOON
ELLIPSES	EMULSOID	ENHANCED	ENTR'ACTE
ELLIPSIS	ENABLING	ENHANCER	ENTRAILS
ELONGATE	ENACTING	ENJOINED	ENTRANCE
ELOQUENT	ENACTIVE	ENJOINER	ENTRANTS
ELYTROID	ENACTORY	ENJOYING	ENTREATY
EMACIATE	ENAMELED	ENKINDLE	ENTRENCH
EMANATED	ENCAENIA	ENLARGED	ENTREPOT
EMANATOR	ENCAMPED	ENLARGER	ENTRESOL
EMBALMED	ENCASING	ENLISTED	ENTRYISM
EMBALMER	ENCIPHER	ENLISTER	ENTRYWAY
EMBARKED	ENCIRCLE	ENMESHED	ENTWINED
EMBATTLE	ENCLAVES	ENNEADIC	E NUMBERS
EMBEDDED	ENCLITIC	ENNEAGON	ENURESIS
EMBEZZLE	ENCLOSED	ENNOBLED	ENURETIC
EMBITTER	ENCLOSER	ENNOBLER	ENVELOPE
EMBLAZON	ENCODING	ENORMITY	ENVIABLE
EMBODIED	ENCOMIUM	ENORMOUS	ENVIABLY
EMBOLDEN	ENCROACH	ENQUIRED	ENVIRONS
EMBOLISM	ENCUMBER	ENQUIRER	ENVISAGE
EMBOSSED	ENCYCLIC	ENRAGING	ENVISION
EMBOSSER	ENDAMAGE	ENRICHED	ENWREATH
EMBRACED	ENDANGER	ENRICHER	ENZOOTIC
EMBRACER	END-BLOWN	ENROLLED	EOLITHIC
EMBRACES	ENDBRAIN	ENROLLEE	EPAULETS
EMBRYOID	ENDEARED	ENROLLER	EPHEMERA
EMENDING	ENDEMIAL	ENSCHEDE	EPIBLAST
EMERALDS	ENDEMISM	ENSCONCE	EPIBOLIC
EMERGENT	ENDERMIC	ENSEMBLE	EPICALYX
EMERGING	END GAMES	ENSHRINE	EPICOTYL
EMERITUS	ENDOCARP	ENSHROUD	EPICURES
EMERSION	ENDODERM	ENSIFORM	EPICYCLE
EMIGRANT	ENDOGAMY	ENSILAGE	EPIDEMIC
EMIGRATE	ENDOGENY	ENSLAVED	EPIDOTIC
EMINENCE	ENDORSED	ENSLAVER	EPIDURAL
EMIRATES	ENDORSEE	ENSNARED	EPIFOCAL
EMISSARY	ENDORSER	ENSNARER	EPIGRAMS
EMISSION	ENDORSOR	ENSPHERE	EPIGRAPH
EMISSIVE	ENDOSOME	ENSURING	EPILEPSY
EMITTING	ENDOWING	ENSWATHE	EPILOGUE
EMOTIONS	ENDPAPER	ENTAILED	EPINASTY
EMPATHIC	ENDPLATE	ENTAILER	EPIPHANY
EMPERORS	ENDURING	ENTANGLE	EPIPHYTE
EMPHASES	END USERS	ENTELLUS	EPISCOPE

EPISODES	ESPOUSED	EUTECTIC	EXCUSING
EPISODIC	ESPOUSER	EUXENITE	EXECRATE
EPISTLER	ESPRESSO	EVACUANT	EXECUTED
EPISTLES	ESSAYING	EVACUATE	EXECUTER
EPISTYLE	ESSAYIST	EVACUEES	EXECUTOR
EPITAPHS	ESSENCES	EVADABLE	EXEGESES
EPITASIS	ESTANCIA	EVALUATE	EXEGESIS
EPITHETS	ESTEEMED	EVANESCE	EXEGETIC
EPITOMIC	ESTERASE	EVASIONS	EXEMPLAR
EPIZOISM	ESTERIFY	EVECTION	EXEMPLUM
EPIZOITE	ESTHETES	EVENINGS	EXEMPTED
EPONYMIC	ESTIMATE	EVENNESS	EXEQUIES
EQUALING	ESTONIAN	EVENSONG	EXERCISE
EQUALITY	ESTOPPEL	EVENTFUL	EXERGUAL
EQUALIZE	ESTOVERS	EVENTIDE	EXERTING
EQUALLED	ESTRAGON	EVENTUAL	EXERTION
EQUATING	ESTRANGE	EVERMORE	EXERTIVE
EQUATION	ESURIENT	EVERSION	EX GRATIA
EQUINITY	ETCHINGS	EVERYDAY	EXHALANT
EQUIPAGE	ETERNITY	EVERYMAN	EXHALING
EQUIPPED	ETERNIZE	EVERYONE	EXHAUSTS
EQUIPPER	ETHEREAL	EVICTING	EXHIBITS
EQUITANT	ETHERIFY	EVICTION	EXHORTED
EQUITIES	ETHERIZE	EVIDENCE	EXHORTER
ERADIATE	ETHICIST	EVILDOER	EXHUMING
ERASABLE	ETHICIZE	EVILLEST	EXIGENCY
ERASURES	ETHIOPIA	EVILNESS	EXIGIBLE
ERECTILE	ETHIOPIC	EVINCING	EXIGUITY
ERECTING	ETHNARCH	EVINCIVE	EXIGUOUS
ERECTION	ETHOLOGY	EVOCABLE	EXISTENT
EREMITIC	ETHONONE	EVOCATOR	EXISTING
ERETHISM	ETHOXIDE	EVOLVING	EXITANCE
ERGOTISM	ETHYLATE	EVONYMUS	EX LIBRIS
ERIGERON	ETHYLENE	EXACTING	EXOCRINE
ERRANTRY	ETIOLATE	EXACTION	EXOERGIC
ERUMPENT	ETIOLOGY	EXALTING	EXORABLE
ERUPTING	ETRUSCAN	EXAMINED	EXORCISE
ERUPTION	EUCHARIS	EXAMINEE	EXORCISM
ERUPTIVE	EUGENICS	EXAMINER	EXORCIST
ERYTHEMA	EULACHON	EXAMPLES	EXORCIZE
ESCALADE	EULOGIES	EXARCHAL	EXORDIAL
ESCALATE	EULOGIST	EXCAVATE	EXORDIUM
ESCALOPE	EULOGIZE	EXCEEDED	EXOSPORE
ESCAPADE	EUONYMUS	EXCEEDER	EXOTERIC
ESCAPEES	EUPEPSIA	EXCELLED	EXOTOXIC
ESCAPING	EUPEPTIC	EXCEPTED	EXOTOXIN
ESCAPISM	EUPHONIC	EXCERPTS	EXPANDED
ESCAPIST	EUPHORIA	EXCESSES	EXPANDER
ESCHEWAL	EUPHORIC	EXCHANGE	EXPECTED
ESCHEWED	EUPHOTIC	EXCISING	EXPEDITE
ESCHEWER	EUPHRASY	EXCISION	EXPELLED
ESCORTED	EUPHUISM	EXCITANT	EXPELLEE
ESCULENT	EUPHUIST	EXCITING	EXPELLER
ESKIMOAN	EUPNOEIC	EXCLUDED	EXPENDED
ESKIMOID	EURASIAN	EXCLUDER	EXPENDER
ESOTERIC	EUROCRAT	EXCRETAL	EXPENSES
ESPALIER	EUROPEAN	EXCRETED	EXPERTLY
ESPECIAL	EUROPIUM	EXCRETER	EXPIABLE
ESPOUSAL	EUSTATIC	EXCURSUS	EXPIATED

EXPIATOR	FADELESS	FARMABLE	FEEDBACK
EXPIRING	FADEOUTS	FARMHAND	FEEDBAGS
EXPLICIT	FAEROESE	FARMLAND	FEELINGS
EXPLODED	FAHLBAND	FARMYARD	FEIGNING
EXPLODER	FAILINGS	FARNESOL	FEINTING
EXPLOITS	FAIL-SAFE	FAROUCHE	FELDSPAR
EXPLORED	FAILURES	FARRIERS	FELICITY
EXPLORER	FAINEANT	FARRIERY	FELINITY
EXPONENT	FAINTEST	FARROWED	FELLABLE
EXPORTED	FAINTING	FARTHEST	FELLATIO
EXPORTER	FAINTISH	FARTHING	FELONIES
EXPOSING	FAIR COPY	FASCIATE	FELSITIC
EXPOSURE	FAIR GAME	FASCICLE	FEMININE
EXPUNGED	FAIRINGS	FASCISTS	FEMINISM
EXPUNGER	FAIRLEAD	FASHIONS	FEMINIST
EXTENDED	FAIRNESS	FASTBACK	FEMINIZE
EXTENDER	FAIRWAYS	FASTENED	FENDERED
EXTENSOR	FAITHFUL	FASTENER	FENESTRA
EXTERIOR	FAIZABAD	FAST FOOD	FERETORY
EXTERNAL	FALCHION	FASTNESS	FEROCITY
EXTOLLED	FALCONER	FATALISM	FERREOUS
EXTOLLER	FALCONET	FATALIST	FERRETED
EXTORTED	FALCONRY	FATALITY	FERRETER
EXTORTER	FALDERAL	FATHEADS	FERRIAGE
EXTRACTS	FALKLAND	FATHERED	FERRITIN
EXTRADOS	FALLFISH	FATHERLY	FERRULES
EXTREMES	FALL GUYS	FATHOMED	FERRYING
EXTRORSE	FALLIBLE	FATHOMER	FERRYMAN
EXTRUDED	FALLOUTS	FATIGUED	FERRYMEN
EXULTANT	FALSETTO	FATIGUES	FERVENCY
EXULTING	FALTBOAT	FATTENED	FERVIDLY
EXUVIATE	FALTERED	FATTENER	FESTERED
EYEBALLS	FALTERER	FATTIEST	FESTIVAL
EYEBROWS	FAMILIAL	FAUBOURG	FESTOONS
EYEGLASS	FAMILIAR	FAULTIER	FETATION
EYELINER	FAMILIES	FAULTILY	FETCHING
EYEPIECE	FAMISHED	FAULTING	FETIALES
EYESHADE	FAMOUSLY	FAUSTIAN	FETICIDE
EYESIGHT	FANAGALO	FAUTEUIL	FETISHES
EYESORES	FANATICS	FAVONIAN	FETLOCKS
EYESTALK	FAN BELTS	FAVOURED	FETTERED
EYETEETH	FANCIERS	FAVOURER	FETTERER
EYETOOTH	FANCIEST	FAYALITE	FETTLING
	FANCIFUL	FEARLESS	FEVERFEW
F	FANCYING	FEARSOME	FEVERISH
FABULIST	FANCY MAN	FEASIBLE	FIASCOES
FABULOUS	FANCY MEN	FEASIBLY	FIBRILAR
FACEABLE	FANDANGO	FEASTING	FIBROSIS
FACE CARD	FANFARES	FEATHERS	FIBROTIC
FACELESS	FANLIGHT	FEATHERY	FICTIONS
FACE-LIFT	FANTASIA	FEATURED	FIDDLING
FACE PACK	FANZINES	FEATURES	FIDELITY
FACETIAE	FARADISM	FEBRIFIC	FIDGETED
FACIALLY	FARADIZE	FEBRUARY	FIDUCIAL
FACILELY	FARCEUSE	FECKLESS	FIELD DAY
FACILITY	FARCICAL	FECULENT	FIELDERS
FACTIONS	FAREWELL	FEDERATE	FIELDING
FACTIOUS	FAR-FLUNG	FEEBLEST	FIENDISH
FACTOTUM	FARINOSE	FEEDABLE	FIERCELY

FIERCEST	FIREBACK	FLANERIE	FLINGING
FIERIEST	FIREBALL	FLANKING	FLINTIER
FIFTIETH	FIREBOAT	FLANNELS	FLIP-FLOP
FIGHTERS	FIREBRAT	FLAPJACK	FLIPPANT
FIGHTING	FIREBUGS	FLAPPING	FLIPPERS
FIG LEAFS	FIRE-CURE	FLARE-UPS	FLIPPEST
FIGMENTS	FIREDAMP	FLASHERS	FLIPPING
FIGURANT	FIREDOGS	FLASHEST	FLIP SIDE
FIGURATE	FIRE-PLUG	FLASHGUN	FLIRTING
FIGURINE	FIRESIDE	FLASHIER	FLITTING
FIGURING	FIRETRAP	FLASHILY	FLOATAGE
FILAGREE	FIREWEED	FLASHING	FLOATERS
FILAMENT	FIREWOOD	FLATBOAT	FLOATING
FILARIAL	FIREWORK	FLAT FEET	FLOCCOSE
FILATURE	FIRMNESS	FLATFISH	FLOCCULE
FILCHING	FIRMWARE	FLATFOOT	FLOCKING
FILECARD	FIRST AID	FLATHEAD	FLOGGING
FILEFISH	FIRST-DAY	FLATLETS	FLOODING
FILETING	FIRTREES	FLATMATE	FLOODLIT
FILICIDE	FISCALLY	FLATNESS	FLOORAGE
FILIFORM	FISHABLE	FLAT SPIN	FLOORING
FILIGREE	FISHBOLT	FLATTERY	FLOOZIES
FILIPINO	FISHBOWL	FLATTEST	FLOPPIER
FILLETED	FISHCAKE	FLATTING	FLOPPILY
FILLINGS	FISH FARM	FLATTISH	FLOPPING
FILMIEST	FISH-HOOK	FLATWARE	FLORALLY
FILM STAR	FISHIEST	FLATWAYS	FLORENCE
FILTERED	FISHNETS	FLATWORM	FLORIDLY
FILTHIER	FISHSKIN	FLAUNTED	FLORIGEN
FILTHILY	FISHTAIL	FLAUNTER	FLORISTS
FILTRATE	FISHWIFE	FLAUTIST	FLOSSING
FIMBRIAL	FISSIPED	FLAVOURS	FLOTILLA
FINAGLER	FISSURES	FLAWLESS	FLOUNCED
FINALISM	FISTMELE	FLAXSEED	FLOUNCES
FINALIST	FITFULLY	FLEABAGS	FLOUNDER
FINALITY	FITMENTS	FLEABANE	FLOURING
FINALIZE	FITTABLE	FLEABITE	FLOURISH
FINANCED	FITTINGS	FLEAPITS	FLOUTING
FINANCES	FIVEFOLD	FLEAWORT	FLOWERED
FINDABLE	FIVEPINS	FLECKING	FLOWERER
FINDINGS	FIVE-STAR	FLECTION	FLUE-CURE
FINEABLE	FIXATION	FLEECING	FLUENTLY
FINE ARTS	FIXATIVE	FLEETEST	FLUFFIER
FINE-DRAW	FIXTURES	FLEETING	FLUFFING
FINE GAEL	FIZZIEST	FLESHIER	FLUIDICS
FINENESS	FLABBIER	FLESHING	FLUIDITY
FINESPUN	FLABBILY	FLESHPOT	FLUIDIZE
FINE-TUNE	FLAG DAYS	FLETCHER	FLUMMERY
FINGERED	FLAGGING	FLEXIBLE	FLUNKEYS
FINGERER	FLAGPOLE	FLEXIBLY	FLUNKING
FINIALED	FLAGRANT	FLEXUOUS	FLUORENE
FINISHED	FLAGSHIP	FLEXURAL	FLUORIDE
FINISHER	FLAILING	FLICKERY	FLUORINE
FINISHES	FLAKIEST	FLICKING	FLURRIED
FINITELY	FLAMBEAU	FLIMFLAM	FLURRIES
FINNMARK	FLAMENCO	FLIMSIER	FLUSHING
FINOCHIO	FLAMEOUT	FLIMSILY	FLUTISTS
FIREABLE	FLAMINGO	FLINCHED	FLUTTERS
FIREARMS	FLANDERS	FLINCHER	FLUTTERY

FLYBLOWN	FOOTSTEP	FORGINGS	FRAMABLE
FLYOVERS	FOOTWALL	FORGIVEN	FRAME-UPS
FLYPAPER	FOOTWEAR	FORGIVER	FRANCIUM
FLYPASTS	FOOTWORK	FORGOING	FRANKEST
FLYSHEET	FOOTWORN	FORJUDGE	FRANKING
FLYSPECK	FORAGING	FORK-LIFT	FRANKISH
FLYWHEEL	FORAYING	FORMABLE	FRANKLIN
FLYWHISK	FORBEARS	FORMALIN	FRAULEIN
FOAMIEST	FORBORNE	FORMALLY	FRAZZLED
FOAMLIKE	FORCE-FED	FORMERLY	FREAKING
FOB WATCH	FORCEFUL	FORMLESS	FREAKISH
FOCALIZE	FORCIBLE	FORMULAE	FRECKLED
FOCUSING	FORCIBLY	FORMULAS	FRECKLES
FOCUSSED	FORDABLE	FORMWORK	FREE-BASE
FOETUSES	FOREARMS	FORNICAL	FREEBIES
FOGBOUND	FOREBEAR	FORSAKEN	FREEBOOT
FOGGIEST	FOREBODE	FORSAKER	FREEBORN
FOGHORNS	FORECAST	FORSOOTH	FREEDMAN
FOG LAMPS	FOREDECK	FORSWEAR	FREE-FALL
FOIE GRAS	FOREDOOM	FORSWORE	FREEFONE
FOILABLE	FOREFEET	FORSWORN	FREEHAND
FOILSMAN	FOREFOOT	FORTIETH	FREEHOLD
FOISTING	FOREGOER	FORT KNOX	FREE KICK
FOLDABLE	FOREGONE	FORTRESS	FREELOAD
FOLDAWAY	FOREHAND	FORTUITY	FREE PASS
FOLDBOAT	FOREHEAD	FORTUNES	FREE PORT
FOLIATED	FOREKNOW	FORWARDS	FREEPOST
FOLKLORE	FORELAND	FORZANDO	FREE REIN
FOLK-ROCK	FORELEGS	FOSSETTE	FREESIAS
FOLKTALE	FORELIMB	FOSTERED	FREETOWN
FOLKWAYS	FORELOCK	FOSTERER	FREEWAYS
FOLLICLE	FOREMAST	FOULNESS	FREE WILL
FOLLOWED	FOREMOST	FOUL PLAY	FREEZERS
FOLLOWER	FORENAME	FOUNDERS	FREEZE-UP
FOLLOW-ON	FORENOON	FOUNDING	FREEZING
FOLLOW-UP	FORENSIC	FOUNTAIN	FREIBURG
FOMENTED	FOREPART	FOUR-BALL	FREMITUS
FOMENTER	FOREPEAK	FOUR-DEAL	FRENETIC
FONDANTS	FOREPLAY	FOUR-EYED	FRENULUM
FONDLING	FORESAIL	FOUREYES	FRENZIED
FONDNESS	FORESEEN	FOURFOLD	FREQUENT
FOOLSCAP	FORESEER	FOUR-LEAF	FRESCOES
FOOTBALL	FORESIDE	FOURSOME	FRESHEST
FOOTFALL	FORESKIN	FOUR-STAR	FRESHMAN
FOOTGEAR	FORESTAL	FOURTEEN	FRESHMEN
FOOTHILL	FORESTAY	FOVEOLAR	FRETLESS
FOOTHOLD	FORESTED	FOWLIANG	FRETSAWS
FOOTLING	FORESTER	FOWL PEST	FRETTING
FOOTMARK	FORESTRY	FOXGLOVE	FRETWORK
FOOTNOTE	FORETELL	FOXHOLES	FREUDIAN
FOOTPACE	FORETIME	FOXHOUND	FRIARIES
FOOTPADS	FORETOLD	FOXHUNTS	FRIBBLER
FOOTPATH	FOREWARN	FOXINESS	FRIBOURG
FOOTRACE	FOREWENT	FOXTROTS	FRICTION
FOOTREST	FOREWIND	FRACTION	FRIENDLY
FOOTROPE	FOREWING	FRACTURE	FRIESIAN
FOOTSIES	FOREWORD	FRAGMENT	FRIGATES
FOOTSLOG	FOREYARD	FRAGRANT	FRIGGING
FOOTSORE	FORFEITS	FRAILEST	FRIGHTEN

FRIGIDLY	FULL MOON	GAINABLE	GARMENTS
FRILLIER	FULLNESS	GAINSAID	GARNERED
FRINGING	FULL-PAGE	GALACTIC	GARRISON
FRIPPERY	FULL STOP	GALANGAL	GARROTTE
FRISBEES	FULL-TIME	GALAXIES	GASIFIER
FRISETTE	FULMINIC	GALBANUM	GASIFORM
FRISKIER	FUMAROLE	GALENISM	GASLIGHT
FRISKILY	FUMATORY	GALENIST	GAS MASKS
FRISKING	FUMBLING	GALICIAN	GASOLIER
FRISSONS	FUMELESS	GALILEAN	GASOLINE
FRITTERS	FUMIGANT	GALLANTS	GASSIEST
FRIULIAN	FUMIGATE	GALLEASS	GASTIGHT
FRIZZIER	FUMINGLY	GALLEONS	GASTRULA
FRIZZING	FUMITORY	GALLIARD	GASWORKS
FRIZZLED	FUNCTION	GALLIPOT	GATEFOLD
FRIZZLER	FUNERALS	GALLOPED	GATEPOST
FROCKING	FUNERARY	GALLOPER	GATEWAYS
FROGFISH	FUNEREAL	GALLOWAY	GATHERED
FROMENTY	FUNFAIRS	GALOSHES	GATHERER
FRONDEUR	FUNGIBLE	GALVANIC	GAUDIEST
FRONTAGE	FUNGUSES	GAMBLERS	GAULLISM
FRONTIER	FUNKIEST	GAMBLING	GAULLIST
FRONTING	FUNNELED	GAMBOLED	GAUNTLET
FRONTLET	FUNNIEST	GAMECOCK	GAUZIEST
FRONT MAN	FURBELOW	GAMENESS	GAVOTTES
FRONT MEN	FURCATED	GAMESTER	GAWKIEST
FROSTIER	FURFURAN	GAMINESS	GAZELLES
FROSTILY	FURLABLE	GAMMA RAY	GAZETTES
FROSTING	FURLONGS	GAMMONER	GAZPACHO
FROTHIER	FURLOUGH	GANDHIAN	GAZUMPED
FROTHILY	FURNACES	GANG-BANG	GAZUMPER
FROTHING	FURRIERS	GANGLAND	GELATINE
FROUFROU	FURRIERY	GANGLIAL	GELATION
FROWNING	FURRIEST	GANGLING	GELDINGS
FROWZIER	FURROWED	GANGLION	GELIDITY
FRUCTIFY	FURROWER	GANGRENE	GEMINATE
FRUCTOSE	FURTHEST	GANGSTER	GEMOLOGY
FRUGALLY	FURUNCLE	GANGWAYS	GEMSTONE
FRUITAGE	FUSELAGE	GANISTER	GENDARME
FRUIT BAT	FUSIFORM	GANTLINE	GENERALS
FRUIT FLY	FUSILIER	GANTRIES	GENERATE
FRUITFUL	FUSSIEST	GANYMEDE	GENEROUS
FRUITIER	FUSSPOTS	GAOLBIRD	GENETICS
FRUITING	FUSTIEST	GAPEWORM	GENIALLY
FRUITION	FUTILITY	GAPINGLY	GENITALS
FRUMENTY	FUTURISM	GARAGING	GENITIVE
FRUMPIER	FUTURIST	GARAMOND	GENIUSES
FRUMPISH	FUTURITY	GARBLESS	GENOCIDE
FRUSTULE	FUZZIEST	GARBLING	GENOTYPE
FUCHSIAS		GARBOARD	GENTIANS
FUCOIDAL	**G**	GARDENED	GENTILES
FUDDLING	GABBLING	GARDENER	GENTRIFY
FUELLING	GABBROIC	GARDENIA	GEODESIC
FUGACITY	GABONESE	GARGANEY	GEODETIC
FUGGIEST	GABORONE	GARGLING	GEOGNOSY
FUGITIVE	GADABOUT	GARGOYLE	GEOMANCY
FUGLEMAN	GADFLIES	GARISHLY	GEOMETER
FULCRUMS	GADGETRY	GARLANDS	GEOMETRY
FULLBACK	GAFFSAIL	GARLICKY	GEOPHAGY

GEOPHYTE	GLASSINE	GNAWABLE	GOURMAND
GEOPONIC	GLASSING	GNEISSIC	GOURMETS
GEORDIES	GLASSMAN	GNOMONIC	GOUTWEED
GEORGIAN	GLAUCOMA	GOAL LINE	GOVERNED
GEOTAXIS	GLAUCOUS	GOALPOST	GOVERNOR
GERANIAL	GLAZIERS	GOATHERD	GRAB BAGS
GERANIOL	GLAZIERY	GOATSKIN	GRABBING
GERANIUM	GLEAMING	GOAT'S-RUE	GRABBLER
GERMANIC	GLEANING	GOBBLING	GRACEFUL
GERM CELL	GLENDALE	GOD-AWFUL	GRACIOUS
GERMINAL	GLIBBEST	GODCHILD	GRADABLE
GESTALTS	GLIBNESS	GODLIEST	GRADIENT
GESTAPOS	GLIMMERS	GODSENDS	GRADUATE
GESTURAL	GLIMPSED	GODSPEED	GRAECISM
GESTURED	GLIMPSER	GODTHAAB	GRAFFITI
GESTURER	GLIMPSES	GOETHITE	GRAFFITO
GESTURES	GLINTING	GO-GETTER	GRAFTERS
GHANAIAN	GLISSADE	GOGGLING	GRAFTING
GHERKINS	GLITCHES	GOIDELIC	GRAINING
GHETTOES	GLITTERS	GOINGS-ON	GRAMPIAN
GHOSTING	GLITTERY	GOITROUS	GRANDADS
GHOULISH	GLITZIER	GOLD DUST	GRANDEES
GIANTESS	GLOAMING	GOLDFISH	GRANDEST
GIBBERED	GLOATING	GOLD LEAF	GRANDEUR
GIBBSITE	GLOBALLY	GOLDMINE	GRAND MAL
GIBINGLY	GLOBULAR	GOLD RUSH	GRANDMAS
GIDDIEST	GLOBULES	GOLF BALL	GRANDPAS
GIFT-WRAP	GLOBULIN	GOLF CLUB	GRANDSON
GIGANTIC	GLOOMFUL	GOLIATHS	GRANITIC
GIGGLING	GLOOMIER	GOLLIWOG	GRANNIES
GILTHEAD	GLOOMILY	GOLLOPER	GRANTING
GIMCRACK	GLORIOUS	GOMBROON	GRANULAR
GIMMICKS	GLORYING	GONDOLAS	GRANULES
GIMMICKY	GLOSSARY	GONIDIAL	GRAPHEME
GINGERED	GLOSSIER	GONIDIUM	GRAPHICS
GINGERLY	GLOSSILY	GONOCYTE	GRAPHITE
GINGIVAL	GLOSSING	GONOPORE	GRAPNELS
GIN RUMMY	GLOWERED	GOOD BOOK	GRAPPLED
GIN SLING	GLOW-WORM	GOODBYES	GRAPPLER
GIN TRAPS	GLOXINIA	GOODLIER	GRASPING
GIRAFFES	GLUCAGON	GOODNESS	GRASSIER
GIRDLING	GLUCINUM	GOODWILL	GRASSING
GIRLHOOD	GLUCOSIC	GOOD WORD	GRATEFUL
GIVEAWAY	GLUMMEST	GOOFIEST	GRATINGS
GIZZARDS	GLUMNESS	GOOGLIES	GRATUITY
GLABELLA	GLUTELIN	GORGEDLY	GRAVAMEN
GLABROUS	GLUTTING	GORGEOUS	GRAVELED
GLACIATE	GLUTTONS	GORGERIN	GRAVELLY
GLACIERS	GLUTTONY	GORILLAS	GRAVITAS
GLADDEST	GLYCERIC	GORINESS	GRAVITON
GLAD HAND	GLYCERIN	GORLOVKA	GRAYLING
GLADIATE	GLYCEROL	GORMLESS	GREASERS
GLADIOLI	GLYCERYL	GOSLINGS	GREASIER
GLADNESS	GLYCOGEN	GOSPODIN	GREASILY
GLAD RAGS	GLYCOLIC	GOSSAMER	GREASING
GLANCING	GLYPTICS	GOSSIPED	GREATEST
GLANDERS	GNASHING	GOSSIPER	GREEDIER
GLANDULE	GNATHION	GOTEBORG	GREEDILY
GLASSIER	GNATHITE	GOUACHES	GREENERY

GREENEST	GROWLERS	GURKHALI	HALFBACK
GREENFLY	GROWLING	GUSTIEST	HALFBEAK
GREENING	GROWN-UPS	GUTSIEST	HALF COCK
GREENISH	GRUBBIER	GUTTERED	HALF-LIFE
GREENLET	GRUBBILY	GUTTURAL	HALF-MAST
GREEN TEA	GRUBBING	GUYANESE	HALF MOON
GREETING	GRUDGING	GUZZLERS	HALF NOTE
GREMLINS	GRUESOME	GUZZLING	HALF TERM
GRENADES	GRUFFEST	GYMKHANA	HALF TIME
GRENOBLE	GRUFFISH	GYMNASTS	HALFTONE
GREY AREA	GRUMBLED	GYMSLIPS	HALF-WITS
GREYBACK	GRUMBLER	GYNANDRY	HALIBUTS
GREYNESS	GRUMBLES	GYNARCHY	HALLIARD
GRIDDLES	GRUMPIER	GYPSEOUS	HALLMARK
GRIDIRON	GRUMPILY	GYRATING	HALLOWED
GRIEVING	GRUNTING	GYRATION	HALLOWER
GRIEVOUS	GRYPHONS	GYRATORY	HALLWAYS
GRIFFINS	G-STRINGS		HALO-LIKE
GRILLAGE	GUAIACOL	H	HALYARDS
GRILLING	GUAIACUM	HABAKKUK	HAMILTON
GRIMACED	GUARANTY	HABANERA	HAMMERED
GRIMACER	GUARDANT	HABITANT	HAMMERER
GRIMACES	GUARDIAN	HABITATS	HAMMOCKS
GRIMIEST	GUARDING	HABITUAL	HAMPERED
GRIMMEST	GUERNSEY	HABITUDE	HAMPERER
GRIMNESS	GUERRERO	HABITUES	HAMSTERS
GRINDERS	GUESSING	HABSBURG	HANDBAGS
GRINDERY	GUESTING	HACIENDA	HANDBALL
GRINDING	GUFFAWED	HACKNEYS	HANDBELL
GRINNING	GUIANESE	HACKSAWS	HANDBILL
GRIPPING	GUIDABLE	HACKWORK	HANDBOOK
GRISEOUS	GUIDANCE	HADRONIC	HANDCART
GRISETTE	GUILDERS	HAEMATIC	HANDCLAP
GRISLIER	GUILEFUL	HAEMATIN	HANDCUFF
GRITTIER	GUILTIER	HAEREMAI	HANDFAST
GRITTILY	GUILTILY	HA-ERH-PIN	HANDFEED
GRITTING	GUJARATI	HAFTARAH	HANDFULS
GRIZZLED	GULFWEED	HAGGADAH	HANDGRIP
GRIZZLER	GULLIBLE	HAGGADIC	HANDGUNS
GROANING	GULLIBLY	HAGGLING	HANDHOLD
GROGGIER	GUMBOILS	HAILWOOD	HANDICAP
GROGGILY	GUMBOOTS	HAIPHONG	HANDIEST
GROMWELL	GUMBOTIL	HAIRBALL	HANDLERS
GROOMING	GUMDROPS	HAIRCUTS	HANDLESS
GROOVIER	GUMMIEST	HAIRGRIP	HANDLIKE
GROSBEAK	GUMMOSIS	HAIRIEST	HANDLING
GROSCHEN	GUMPTION	HAIRLESS	HANDLOOM
GROSSEST	GUMSHOES	HAIRLIKE	HANDMADE
GROSSING	GUM TREES	HAIRLINE	HANDOUTS
GROTTIER	GUNBOATS	HAIRNETS	HANDOVER
GROTTOES	GUNFLINT	HAIRPINS	HANDRAIL
GROUCHED	GUNMETAL	HAIRTAIL	HANDS-OFF
GROUCHES	GUNPAPER	HAIRWORM	HANDSOME
GROUNDED	GUNPOINT	HAKODATE	HANDYMAN
GROUPIES	GUNSHOTS	HALAFIAN	HANDYMEN
GROUPING	GUNSMITH	HALATION	HANGBIRD
GROUSING	GUNSTOCK	HALBERDS	HANGCHOW
GROVELED	GUNWALES	HALCYONE	HANGER-ON
GROWABLE	GURGLING	HALENESS	HANGINGS

HANGNAIL	HARRIMAN	HEADACHE	HEDONISM
HANGOUTS	HARRISON	HEADACHY	HEDONIST
HANGOVER	HARROWED	HEADBAND	HEEDLESS
HANKERED	HARROWER	HEADFAST	HEELBALL
HANKERER	HARRUMPH	HEADGEAR	HEELLESS
HANNIBAL	HARRYING	HEADHUNT	HEELPOST
HANRATTY	HARSHEST	HEADIEST	HEFTIEST
HANUKKAH	HARTFORD	HEADINGS	HEGELIAN
HAPLITIC	HARTNELL	HEADLAND	HEGEMONY
HAPLOSIS	HARUSPEX	HEADLESS	HEIGHTEN
HAPPENED	HARVESTS	HEADLIKE	HEIMDALL
HAPPIEST	HAS-BEENS	HEADLINE	HEIRLESS
HAPSBURG	HASIDISM	HEADLOCK	HEIRLOOM
HAPTERON	HASSLING	HEADLONG	HEIRSHIP
HARA-KIRI	HASSOCKS	HEADMOST	HELIACAL
HARAMBEE	HASTEFUL	HEADRACE	HELICOID
HARANGUE	HASTENED	HEADRAIL	HELIPORT
HARAPPAN	HASTENER	HEADREST	HELLADIC
HARASSED	HASTIEST	HEADROOM	HELL-BENT
HARASSER	HASTINGS	HEADSAIL	HELLCATS
HARBOURS	HATBANDS	HEADSETS	HELLENES
HARDBACK	HATCHERY	HEADSHIP	HELLENIC
HARDBAKE	HATCHETS	HEADSMAN	HELLFIRE
HARDBALL	HATCHING	HEADWARD	HELLHOLE
HARD CASH	HATCHWAY	HEADWAYS	HELMETED
HARD COPY	HATEABLE	HEADWIND	HELMINTH
HARD-CORE	HATFIELD	HEADWORD	HELMLESS
HARD DISK	HATHAWAY	HEADWORK	HELMSMAN
HARDENED	HATHORIC	HEALABLE	HELMSMEN
HARDENER	HATTERAS	HEARABLE	HELOTISM
HARDHACK	HAT TRICK	HEARINGS	HELPABLE
HARDIEST	HAULIERS	HEARTIER	HELPINGS
HARD LINE	HAUNCHED	HEARTILY	HELPLESS
HARD LUCK	HAUNCHES	HEATEDLY	HELPMANN
HARDNESS	HAUNTING	HEATHENS	HELPMATE
HARD NUTS	HAUSFRAU	HEATHERY	HELPMEET
HARD SELL	HAUTBOIS	HEATLESS	HELSINKI
HARDSHIP	HAUTBOYS	HEAT PUMP	HELVETIA
HARD TACK	HAVELOCK	HEAT RASH	HELVETIC
HARDTOPS	HAVE-NOTS	HEAT WAVE	HELVETII
HARD UPON	HAVERING	HEAVENLY	HEMIOLIC
HARDWARE	HAVILDAR	HEAVIEST	HEMIPODE
HARDWOOD	HAVOCKER	HEAVY-SET	HEMLINES
HAREBELL	HAWAIIAN	HEBDOMAD	HEMLOCKS
HARELIKE	HAWFINCH	HEBETATE	HENBANES
HARGEISA	HAWKBILL	HEBETUDE	HENCHMAN
HARICOTS	HAWK-EYED	HEBRAISM	HENCHMEN
HARIKARI	HAWKLIKE	HEBRAIST	HENEQUEN
HARINGEY	HAWKWEED	HEBRAIZE	HENG-YANG
HARKENED	HAWTHORN	HEBRIDES	HEN HOUSE
HARKENER	HAYCOCKS	HECATOMB	HEN PARTY
HARLOTRY	HAY FEVER	HECKLERS	HENRYSON
HARMLESS	HAYFORKS	HECKLING	HENSLOWE
HARMONIC	HAYMAKER	HECTARES	HEPATICA
HARPINGS	HAYSTACK	HECTORED	HEPTAGON
HARPISTS	HAZARDED	HEDGEHOG	HEPTARCH
HARPOONS	HAZELHEN	HEDGEHOP	HEPWORTH
HARRIDAN	HAZELNUT	HEDGEROW	HERACLEA
HARRIERS	HAZINESS	HEDONICS	HERACLES

HERALDED	HIGHLAND	HOLDALLS	HONEYDEW
HERALDIC	HIGH LIFE	HOLDFAST	HONG KONG
HERALDRY	HIGH MASS	HOLDINGS	HONIEDLY
HERBLIKE	HIGHNESS	HOLDOVER	HONOLULU
HERCULES	HIGH-RISE	HOLIDAYS	HONORARY
HERDSMAN	HIGH ROAD	HOLINESS	HONOURED
HERDSMEN	HIGH SEAS	HOLISTIC	HONOURER
HERDWICK	HIGH SPOT	HOLLANDS	HOODLESS
HEREDITY	HIGHTAIL	HOLLERED	HOODLIKE
HEREFORD	HIGH TECH	HOLLIDAY	HOODLUMS
HEREINTO	HIGH TIDE	HOLLOWED	HOODWINK
HERESIES	HIGH TIME	HOLLOWER	HOOFLESS
HERETICS	HIGHVELD	HOLLOWLY	HOOFLIKE
HEREUNTO	HIGHWAYS	HOLOCENE	HOOKLESS
HEREUPON	HIJACKED	HOLOGRAM	HOOKLIKE
HEREWARD	HIJACKER	HOLOTYPE	HOOKNOSE
HEREWITH	HILARITY	HOLOZOIC	HOOKWORM
HERITAGE	HILLFORT	HOLSTEIN	HOOLIGAN
HERMETIC	HILLIARD	HOLSTERS	HOOPLIKE
HERMITIC	HILLIEST	HOLYHEAD	HOOSEGOW
HERODIAS	HILLOCKS	HOLYOAKE	HOOVERED
HERPETIC	HILLSIDE	HOLYTIDE	HOPEFULS
HERRINGS	HIMATION	HOLY WEEK	HOPELESS
HERSCHEL	HINAYANA	HOLY WRIT	HOPLITIC
HERTFORD	HINCKLEY	HOMBURGS	HORATIAN
HERTZIAN	HINDERED	HOMEBODY	HORIZONS
HESIODIC	HINDERER	HOMEBRED	HORMONAL
HESITANT	HINDMOST	HOME BREW	HORMONES
HESITATE	HINDUISM	HOME HELP	HORNBEAM
HESPERIA	HIPBATHS	HOMELAND	HORNBILL
HESPERUS	HIP FLASK	HOMELESS	HORNBOOK
HESSIANS	HIPPARCH	HOMELIER	HORNFELS
HETAERIC	HIPSTERS	HOMELIKE	HORNIEST
HEXAGONS	HIRAGANA	HOMEMADE	HORNLESS
HEXAGRAM	HIRELING	HOMERIAN	HORNLIKE
HEXANOIC	HIRI MOTU	HOME RULE	HORNPIPE
HEXAPLAR	HIROHITO	HOME RUNS	HORNTAIL
HEXAPODY	HISPANIA	HOMESICK	HORNWORT
HEZEKIAH	HISPANIC	HOMESPUN	HOROLOGE
HIATUSES	HISTOGEN	HOMETOWN	HOROLOGY
HIAWATHA	HISTORIC	HOMEWARD	HOROWITZ
HIBERNAL	HITCHING	HOMEWORK	HORRIBLE
HIBERNIA	HITHERTO	HOMICIDE	HORRIBLY
HIBISCUS	HIT LISTS	HOMILIES	HORRIDLY
HICCUPED	HIVELIKE	HOMILIST	HORRIFIC
HIDDENLY	HOACTZIN	HOMINESS	HORSEBOX
HIDEAWAY	HOARDING	HOMINOID	HORSEFLY
HIDELESS	HOARIEST	HOMODONT	HORSEMAN
HIDROSIS	HOARSELY	HOMOGAMY	HORSEMEN
HIDROTIC	HOARSEST	HOMOGENY	HORSIEST
HIERARCH	HOBBLING	HOMOGONY	HOSANNAS
HIERATIC	HOBBYIST	HOMOLOGY	HOSPICES
HIGHBALL	HOBNAILS	HOMONYMS	HOSPITAL
HIGHBORN	HOCKTIDE	HONDURAN	HOSPODAR
HIGHBOYS	HOGMANAY	HONDURAS	HOSTAGES
HIGHBROW	HOGSHEAD	HONEGGER	HOSTELRY
HIGHER-UP	HOISTING	HONESTLY	HOSTLERS
HIGHJACK	HOKKAIDO	HONEWORT	HOTCHPOT
HIGH JUMP	HOLDABLE	HONEYBEE	HOTELIER

HOT FLUSH	HURDLERS	IDOLATRY	IMPLICIT
HOTHEADS	HURDLING	IDOLIZED	IMPLODED
HOTHOUSE	HURRYING	IDOLIZER	IMPLORED
HOT LINES	HURTLING	IDYLLIST	IMPLORER
HOTPLATE	HUSBANDS	IGNITING	IMPLYING
HOT SPOTS	HUSH-HUSH	IGNITION	IMPOLICY
HOT STUFF	HUSKIEST	IGNITRON	IMPOLITE
HOT WATER	HUSKLIKE	IGNOMINY	IMPORTED
HOUNDING	HUSTINGS	IGNORANT	IMPORTER
HOUNSLOW	HUSTLERS	IGNORING	IMPOSING
HOUSEBOY	HUSTLING	IGUANIAN	IMPOSTOR
HOUSEFLY	HWANG HAI	ILLATIVE	IMPOTENT
HOUSEFUL	HYACINTH	ILL-FATED	IMPRINTS
HOUSEMAN	HYDER ALI	ILLINOIS	IMPRISON
HOUSEMEN	HYDRACID	ILLIQUID	IMPROPER
HOUSETOP	HYDRANTH	ILL-TIMED	IMPROVED
HOUSINGS	HYDRANTS	ILL-TREAT	IMPROVER
HOVERERS	HYDRATED	ILLUSION	IMPUDENT
HOVERING	HYDRATES	ILLUSORY	IMPUGNED
HOWITZER	HYDRATOR	ILMENITE	IMPUGNER
HRVATSKA	HYDROGEN	IMAGINAL	IMPULSES
HSINKING	HYDROMEL	IMAGINED	IMPUNITY
HUANG HUA	HYGIENIC	IMAGINER	IMPURITY
HUCKSTER	HYMENEAL	IMBECILE	IMPUTING
HUDDLING	HYPNOSIS	IMBEDDED	INACTION
HUFFIEST	HYPNOTIC	IMBIBING	INACTIVE
HUGENESS	HYSTERIA	IMITABLE	INASMUCH
HUGGABLE	HYSTERIC	IMITATED	IN CAMERA
HUGUENOT		IMITATOR	INCENSED
HULL-LESS	I	IMMANENT	INCEPTOR
HUMANELY	IAMBUSES	IMMATURE	INCHOATE
HUMANISM	ICEBERGS	IMMERSED	INCIDENT
HUMANIST	ICEBLINK	IMMINENT	INCISING
HUMANITY	ICEBOUND	IMMOBILE	INCISION
HUMANIZE	ICEBOXES	IMMODEST	INCISIVE
HUMANOID	ICE CREAM	IMMOLATE	INCISORS
HUMBLEST	ICE LOLLY	IMMORTAL	INCISURE
HUMBLING	ICE PACKS	IMMOTILE	INCITING
HUMBOLDT	ICE PICKS	IMMUNITY	INCLINED
HUMIDIFY	ICE RINKS	IMMUNIZE	INCLINER
HUMIDITY	ICE SHEET	IMMURING	INCLINES
HUMILITY	ICE SKATE	IMPACTED	INCLOSED
HUMMOCKS	ICE WATER	IMPAIRED	INCLUDED
HUMMOCKY	ICHTHYIC	IMPAIRER	INCOMING
HUMORIST	IDEALISM	IMPALING	INCREASE
HUMOROUS	IDEALIST	IMPARITY	INCUBATE
HUMOURED	IDEALITY	IMPARTED	INCUDATE
HUMPBACK	IDEALIZE	IMPARTER	INCURRED
HUMPHREY	IDEATION	IMPASSES	INDAMINE
HUMPLIKE	IDEATIVE	IMPEDING	INDEBTED
HUNCHING	IDEE FIXE	IMPELLED	INDECENT
HUNDREDS	IDENTIFY	IMPELLER	INDENTED
HUNGERED	IDENTITY	IMPERIAL	INDENTER
HUNGRIER	IDEOGRAM	IMPERIUM	INDEXERS
HUNGRILY	IDEOLOGY	IMPETIGO	INDEXING
HUNTEDLY	IDIOCIES	IMPINGED	INDICANT
HUNTRESS	IDIOLECT	IMPINGER	INDICATE
HUNTSMAN	IDLENESS	IMPISHLY	INDICIAL
HUNTSMEN	IDOLATER	IMPLANTS	INDICTED

INDICTEE	INGATHER	INSTRUCT	INVOICED
INDIGENE	INGENUES	INSULANT	INVOICES
INDIGENT	INGESTED	INSULATE	INVOKING
INDIGOID	INGRATES	INSULTED	INVOLUTE
INDIRECT	IN-GROUPS	INSULTER	INVOLVED
INDOCILE	INGROWTH	INSURERS	INVOLVER
INDOLENT	INGUINAL	INSURING	INWARDLY
INDOLOGY	INHALANT	INTAGLIO	IODATION
INDORSED	INHALERS	INTARSIA	IODOFORM
INDUCING	INHALING	INTEGERS	IODOPSIN
INDUCTED	INHERENT	INTEGRAL	IONIZERS
INDUCTOR	INHUMANE	INTENDED	IONIZING
INDULGED	INIMICAL	INTENDER	IOTACISM
INDULGER	INIQUITY	INTENTLY	IRAKLION
INDULINE	INITIALS	INTERACT	IRISHMAN
INDUSIAL	INITIATE	INTERCOM	IRISHMEN
INDUSIUM	INJECTED	INTEREST	IRONBARK
INDUSTRY	INJECTOR	INTERIMS	IRONCLAD
INEDIBLE	INJURIES	INTERIOR	IRON-GREY
INEDIBLY	INJURING	INTERLAY	IRONWARE
INEDITED	INKBERRY	INTERMIT	IRONWOOD
INEQUITY	INKINESS	INTERMIX	IRONWORK
INERTIAL	INKSTAND	INTERNAL	IROQUOIS
INESSIVE	INKWELLS	INTERNED	IRRIGATE
INEXPERT	INLANDER	INTERNEE	IRRITANT
INFAMIES	INNATELY	INTERPOL	IRRITATE
INFAMOUS	INNER MAN	INTERRED	ISAGOGIC
INFANTAS	INNOCENT	INTERREX	ISATINIC
INFANTRY	INNOVATE	INTERSEX	ISCHEMIC
INFECTED	INNUENDO	INTERVAL	ISLANDER
INFECTOR	INOCULUM	INTIMACY	ISMAILIA
INFERIOR	INOSITOL	INTIMATE	ISOBARIC
INFERNAL	INPUTTED	INTONATE	ISOCHEIM
INFERNOS	INQUESTS	INTONING	ISOCLINE
INFERRED	INQUIRED	INTRADOS	ISOCRACY
INFERRER	INQUIRER	INTRENCH	ISOGLOSS
INFESTED	INSANELY	INTREPID	ISOGONIC
INFESTER	INSANITY	INTRIGUE	ISOLABLE
INFIDELS	INSCRIBE	INTRORSE	ISOLATED
INFINITE	INSECURE	INTRUDED	ISOLATOR
INFINITY	INSERTED	INTRUDER	ISOLOGUE
INFIXION	INSERTER	INTUBATE	ISOMERIC
INFLAMED	INSETTED	INTUITED	ISOMETRY
INFLAMER	INSETTER	INUNDANT	ISOMORPH
INFLATED	INSIDERS	INUNDATE	ISOPHONE
INFLATER	INSIGHTS	INVADERS	ISOPLETH
INFLEXED	INSIGNIA	INVADING	ISOPODAN
IN-FLIGHT	INSISTED	INVALIDS	ISOPRENE
INFLUENT	INSISTER	INVASION	ISOSTASY
INFLUXES	INSOLATE	INVASIVE	ISOTHERE
INFORMAL	INSOLENT	INVEIGLE	ISOTHERM
INFORMED	INSOMNIA	INVENTED	ISOTONIC
INFORMER	INSOMUCH	INVENTOR	ISOTOPES
INFRA DIG	INSPIRED	INVERTED	ISOTOPIC
INFRARED	INSPIRER	INVERTER	ISOTROPY
INFRINGE	INSPIRIT	INVESTED	ISRAELIS
INFUSING	INSTANCE	INVESTOR	ISSUABLE
INFUSION	INSTANTS	INVIABLE	ISSUANCE
INFUSIVE	INSTINCT	INVITING	ISTANBUL

ISTHMIAN	JEW'S HARP	JUNKYARD	KICKBACK
ISTHMOID	JEZEBELS	JURASSIC	KICKOFFS
ITALIANS	JIGGERED	JURATORY	KICKSHAW
ITCHIEST	JIGGLING	JURISTIC	KID-GLOVE
ITEMIZED	JINGLING	JUSTICES	KIDNAPED
	JINGOISM	JUSTNESS	KILKENNY
J	JINGOIST	JUVENILE	KILLDEER
JABALPUR	JIPIJAPA		KILLINGS
JABBERED	JIUJITSU	**K**	KILLJOYS
JABBERER	JOCKEYED	KAKEMONO	KILOBYTE
JACKBOOT	JOCOSELY	KALAHARI	KILOGRAM
JACKDAWS	JOCOSITY	KAMACITE	KILOVOLT
JACKFISH	JODHPURI	KAMAKURA	KILOWATT
JACKPOTS	JODHPURS	KAMIKAZE	KIMONOED
JACKSTAY	JOGGLING	KANARESE	KINABALU
JACK TARS	JOHN BULL	KANAZAWA	KINDLIER
JACOBEAN	JOHNNIES	KANDAHAR	KINDLING
JACOBIAN	JOINTING	KANGAROO	KINDNESS
JACOBITE	JOINTURE	KAOLIANG	KINDREDS
JACQUARD	JOKINGLY	KAOLINIC	KINETICS
JACUZZIS	JOLLIEST	KARELIAN	KINGBIRD
JAGGEDLY	JOLLYING	KASHMIRI	KINGBOLT
JAILBIRD	JOSTLING	KATAKANA	KINGDOMS
JALOPIES	JOTTINGS	KATMANDU	KINGFISH
JALOUSIE	JOURNALS	KATOWICE	KINGLIER
JAMAICAN	JOURNEYS	KATTEGAT	KINGPINS
JAMBOREE	JOUSTING	KAWASAKI	KINGSHIP
JAMMIEST	JOVIALLY	KAYAKERS	KING-SIZE
JAMNAGAR	JOYFULLY	KEDGEREE	KINGSTON
JANGLING	JOYOUSLY	KEENNESS	KINGWANA
JANITORS	JOYRIDER	KEEPSAKE	KINGWOOD
JAPANESE	JOYRIDES	KEESHOND	KINKAJOU
JAPANNED	JOYSTICK	KEEWATIN	KINKIEST
JAPINGLY	JUBILANT	KEIGHLEY	KINSFOLK
JAPONICA	JUBILATE	KELANTAN	KINSHASA
JAROSITE	JUBILEES	KELOIDAL	KIRIGAMI
JASMINES	JUDAIZER	KEMEROVO	KISHINEV
JAUNDICE	JUDDERED	KENNELED	KISSABLE
JAUNTIER	JUDGMENT	KENTUCKY	KITCHENS
JAUNTILY	JUDICIAL	KERATOID	KLAIPEDA
JAUNTING	JUGGLERS	KERATOSE	KLONDIKE
JAVANESE	JUGGLERY	KERCHIEF	KLYSTRON
JAVELINS	JUGGLING	KEROSENE	KNAPSACK
JAWBONES	JUGULARS	KESTEVEN	KNAPWEED
JAZZIEST	JUICIEST	KESTRELS	KNEADING
JEALOUSY	JULIENNE	KETOXIME	KNEECAPS
JEHOVIAN	JUMBLING	KEYBOARD	KNEE-DEEP
JEMMYING	JUMBO JET	KEYHOLES	KNEE-HIGH
JEOPARDY	JUMPABLE	KEY MONEY	KNEE-JERK
JEREMIAD	JUMPED-UP	KEYNOTES	KNEELING
JERKIEST	JUMPIEST	KEYPUNCH	KNICKERS
JEROBOAM	JUMPSUIT	KEY RINGS	KNIGHTED
JESUITIC	JUNCTION	KEYSTONE	KNIGHTLY
JET-BLACK	JUNCTURE	KHARTOUM	KNITTERS
JETFOILS	JUNGFRAU	KHMERIAN	KNITTING
JETLINER	JUNIPERS	KHUSKHUS	KNITWEAR
JETTISON	JUNKETER	KIAOCHOW	KNOCKERS
JEWELLED	JUNK FOOD	KIBOSHES	KNOCKING
JEWELLER	JUNK MAIL	KICKABLE	KNOCKOUT

KNOCK-UPS	LAMASERY	LATERITE	LEATHERY
KNOTHOLE	LAMBASTE	LATHERED	LEAVENED
KNOTTIER	LAMBDOID	LATINATE	LEAVINGS
KNOTTILY	LAMBENCY	LATINISM	LECITHIN
KNOTTING	LAMBSKIN	LATINIST	LECTERNS
KNOTWEED	LAME DUCK	LATINITY	LECTURED
KNOWABLE	LAMELLAR	LATINIZE	LECTURER
KNOW-ALLS	LAMENESS	LATITUDE	LECTURES
KNUCKLED	LAMENTED	LATRINES	LEEBOARD
KNUCKLES	LAMENTER	LATTERLY	LEERIEST
KOHINOOR	LAMINATE	LATTICES	LEE SHORE
KOHLRABI	LAMPOONS	LAUDABLE	LEE TIDES
KOLHAPUR	LAMPPOST	LAUDABLY	LEFT-HAND
KOLINSKY	LAMPREYS	LAUDANUM	LEFTISTS
KOMSOMOL	LANCELET	LAUGHING	LEFTOVER
KOOKIEST	LANDFALL	LAUGHTER	LEFTWARD
KOOTENAY	LANDFORM	LAUNCHED	LEFT WING
KORDOFAN	LANDINGS	LAUNCHER	LEGACIES
KOSTROMA	LANDLADY	LAUNCHES	LEGAL AID
KOWTOWED	LANDLORD	LAUREATE	LEGALESE
KOWTOWER	LANDMARK	LAUSANNE	LEGALISM
KRAKATOA	LANDMASS	LAVATION	LEGALIST
KUMAMOTO	LANDMINE	LAVATORY	LEGALITY
KUMQUATS	LANDRACE	LAVENDER	LEGALIZE
KURTOSIS	LANDSLIP	LAVISHED	LEGATEES
KUZNETSK	LANDWARD	LAVISHER	LEGATINE
KWEICHOW	LANGLAUF	LAVISHLY	LEGATION
KWEIYANG	LANGUAGE	LAWFULLY	LEGENDRY
KYPHOSIS	LANGUISH	LAWGIVER	LEGGIEST
KYPHOTIC	LANKIEST	LAWSUITS	LEGGINGS
	LANKNESS	LAXATION	LEG-PULLS
L	LANNERET	LAXATIVE	LEG SIDES
LABDANUM	LANTERNS	LAYABOUT	LEINSTER
LABELING	LANYARDS	LAYERING	LEISURED
LABELLED	LAPBOARD	LAYETTES	LEMMINGS
LABELLER	LAP-CHART	LAYSHAFT	LEMONADE
LABELLUM	LAPELLED	LAYWOMAN	LEMUROID
LABILITY	LAPIDARY	LAYWOMEN	LENGTHEN
LABOURED	LAPILLUS	LAZINESS	LENIENCY
LABOURER	LAPPETED	LAZULITE	LENINISM
LABRADOR	LAPSABLE	LAZURITE	LENINIST
LABURNUM	LAPWINGS	L-DRIVERS	LENITIVE
LACERANT	LARBOARD	LEACHING	LENTICEL
LACERATE	LARGESSE	LEADSMAN	LEOPARDS
LACEWING	LARKSOME	LEAD TIME	LEOTARDS
LACINESS	LARKSPUR	LEADWORT	LEPIDOTE
LA CORUNA	LARRIGAN	LEAFIEST	LEPORINE
LACRIMAL	LARYNGES	LEAF-LARD	LESBIANS
LACROSSE	LARYNXES	LEAFLETS	LESSENED
LACTONIC	LASHINGS	LEAGUING	LETDOWNS
LACUNOSE	LA SPEZIA	LEAKAGES	LETHALLY
LADDERED	LASSOING	LEAKIEST	LETHARGY
LADYBIRD	LAST POST	LEANINGS	LETRASET
LADYLIKE	LAST WORD	LEANNESS	LETTERED
LADYSHIP	LAS VEGAS	LEAPFROG	LETTERER
LAEVULIN	LATCHING	LEAP YEAR	LETTINGS
LAGGARDS	LATCHKEY	LEARNERS	LETTUCES
LAH-DI-DAH	LATENESS	LEARNING	LEUCITIC
LAID-BACK	LATERALS	LEASABLE	LEUKEMIA

LEVANTER	LIGHTING	LITERATE	LOLLOPED
LEVELING	LIGNEOUS	LITERATI	LOMBARDY
LEVELLED	LIGNITIC	LITHARGE	LONDONER
LEVELLER	LIGULATE	LITIGANT	LONDRINA
LEVERAGE	LIGULOID	LITIGATE	LONELIER
LEVERETS	LIGURIAN	LITTERED	LONESOME
LEVERING	LIKELIER	LITTORAL	LONE WOLF
LEVIABLE	LIKENESS	LIVELIER	LONGBOAT
LEVIGATE	LIKENING	LIVELONG	LONGBOWS
LEVITATE	LIKEWISE	LIVENING	LONGERON
LEWDNESS	LIMA BEAN	LIVERIED	LONG FACE
LEWISITE	LIMACINE	LIVERIES	LONGHAND
LEXICONS	LIMASSOL	LIVERISH	LONG-HAUL
LIAISING	LIMBLESS	LIVETRAP	LONGHORN
LIAISONS	LIMEKILN	LIVEWARE	LONGINGS
LIAONING	LIMERICK	LIVE WIRE	LONG JUMP
LIAOTUNG	LIMINESS	LIVONIAN	LONG-LIFE
LIAOYANG	LIMITARY	LIXIVIUM	LONGSHIP
LIBATION	LIMITING	LOADINGS	LONG SHOT
LIBECCIO	LIMNETIC	LOADSTAR	LONG SUIT
LIBELING	LIMONENE	LOANABLE	LONG-TERM
LIBELLED	LIMONITE	LOANWORD	LONG TONS
LIBELLEE	LIMOUSIN	LOATHING	LONGUEUR
LIBELLER	LIMPIDLY	LOBBYING	LONG WAVE
LIBERALS	LIMPNESS	LOBBYISM	LONGWAYS
LIBERATE	LINALOOL	LOBBYIST	LOOKER-ON
LIBERIAN	LINCHPIN	LOBELINE	LOOKOUTS
LIBRETTI	LINEAGES	LOBLOLLY	LOONIEST
LIBRETTO	LINEALLY	LOBOTOMY	LOONY BIN
LICENCES	LINESMAN	LOBSTERS	LOOPHOLE
LICENSED	LINESMEN	LOCALISM	LOOSEBOX
LICENSEE	LINGERED	LOCALIST	LOOSE END
LICENSER	LINGERER	LOCALITY	LOOSENED
LICHENIN	LINGERIE	LOCALIZE	LOOSENER
LICKINGS	LINGUIST	LOCATING	LOP-EARED
LICORICE	LINIMENT	LOCATION	LOP-SIDED
LIE-DOWNS	LINKABLE	LOCATIVE	LOQUITUR
LIENTERY	LINKAGES	LOCKABLE	LORDLIER
LIFE BELT	LINKWORK	LOCKOUTS	LORDOSIS
LIFEBOAT	LINOCUTS	LOCOWEED	LORDOTIC
LIFE BUOY	LINOLEUM	LOCUTION	LORDSHIP
LIFELESS	LINOTYPE	LODESTAR	LORICATE
LIFELIKE	LINSTOCK	LODGINGS	LORIKEET
LIFELINE	LIONFISH	LODGMENT	LORRAINE
LIFELONG	LIONIZED	LODICULE	LOTHARIO
LIFE PEER	LIONIZER	LOESSIAL	LOUDNESS
LIFE-SIZE	LIPOIDAL	LOFTIEST	LOUNGERS
LIFESPAN	LIPSTICK	LOGBOOKS	LOUNGING
LIFETIME	LIQUESCE	LOG CABIN	LOUSIEST
LIFE WORK	LIQUEURS	LOGICIAN	LOVEBIRD
LIFTABLE	LISSOMLY	LOGICISM	LOVELESS
LIFT-OFFS	LISTABLE	LOGISTIC	LOVELIER
LIGAMENT	LISTENED	LOGOGRAM	LOVELIES
LIGATION	LISTENER	LOGOTYPE	LOVELORN
LIGATIVE	LISTLESS	LOGOTYPY	LOVESICK
LIGATURE	LITANIES	LOITERED	LOVINGLY
LIGHT ALE	LITERACY	LOITERER	LOWBROWS
LIGHTERS	LITERALS	LOLLARDY	LOWERING
LIGHTEST	LITERARY	LOLLIPOP	LOWLANDS

LOWLIEST	LYSOZYME	MAL DE MER	MANSIONS
LOW-LYING		MALDIVES	MAN-SIZED
LOW TIDES	M	MALENESS	MANTILLA
LOW WATER	MACADMIA	MALIGNED	MANTISES
LOYALISM	MACARONI	MALIGNER	MANTISSA
LOYALIST	MACAROON	MALIGNLY	MANTLING
LOZENGES	MACERATE	MALINGER	MAN-TO-MAN
LUCIDITY	MACHETES	MALLARDS	MANUALLY
LUCKIEST	MACHINED	MALPOSED	MANURING
LUCKLESS	MACHINES	MALTREAT	MANX CATS
LUCKY DIP	MACHISMO	MALTSTER	MAPPABLE
LUDDITES	MACKEREL	MALVASIA	MAPPINGS
LUDHIANA	MACRURAL	MAMA'S BOY	MAQUETTE
LUGHOLES	MACRURAN	MAMMOTHS	MARABOUS
LUGSAILS	MADDENED	MANACLED	MARANHAO
LUGWORMS	MADHOUSE	MANACLES	MARASMIC
LUKEWARM	MADONNAS	MANAGERS	MARASMUS
LUMBERED	MADRIGAL	MANAGING	MARATHON
LUMBERER	MADURESE	MANATOID	MARAUDER
LUMINARY	MAEBASHI	MANCIPLE	MARBLING
LUMINOUS	MAENADIC	MANDALAY	MARCHERS
LUMPFISH	MAESTOSO	MANDAMUS	MARCHESA
LUMPIEST	MAESTROS	MANDARIN	MARCHESE
LUMP SUMS	MAGAZINE	MANDATED	MARCHING
LUNATICS	MAGELLAN	MANDATES	MARGARIC
LUNATION	MAGHREBI	MANDIBLE	MARGINAL
LUNCHEON	MAGIC EYE	MANDOLIN	MARIANAO
LUNCHING	MAGICIAN	MANDORLA	MARIGOLD
LUNEBURG	MAGNATES	MANDRAKE	MARIMBAS
LUNGFISH	MAGNESIA	MANDRILL	MARINADE
LUNGWORM	MAGNETIC	MAN-EATER	MARINATE
LUNGWORT	MAGNETON	MANEUVER	MARINERS
LUNULATE	MAGNETOS	MANFULLY	MARIPOSA
LURCHING	MAGNOLIA	MANGABEY	MARITIME
LURINGLY	MAHARAJA	MANGANIC	MARJORAM
LUSATIAN	MAHARANI	MANGANIN	MARKDOWN
LUSCIOUS	MAHATMAS	MANGIEST	MARKEDLY
LUSHNESS	MAHOGANY	MANGLING	MARKETED
LUSTRATE	MAIDENLY	MANGONEL	MARKETER
LUSTROUS	MAIEUTIC	MANGROVE	MARKINGS
LUTANIST	MAILABLE	MANHOLES	MARKSMAN
LUTENIST	MAILBAGS	MANHOURS	MARKSMEN
LUTEOLIN	MAILSHOT	MANHUNTS	MARMOSET
LUTETIUM	MAINLAND	MANIACAL	MAROONED
LUTHERAN	MAIN LINE	MANICURE	MAROQUIN
LUXATION	MAINMAST	MANIFEST	MARQUEES
LUXURIES	MAINSAIL	MANIFOLD	MARQUESS
LYALLPUR	MAINSTAY	MANIKINS	MARQUISE
LYCHGATE	MAINTAIN	MANITOBA	MARRIAGE
LYINGS-IN	MAJESTIC	MANLIEST	MARRIEDS
LYMPHOID	MAJOLICA	MANNERED	MARRYING
LYMPHOMA	MAJORING	MANNERLY	MARSHALS
LYNCHING	MAJORITY	MANNHEIM	MARSH GAS
LYNCH LAW	MALADIES	MANNITIC	MARTAGON
LYONNAIS	MALAGASY	MANNITOL	MARTELLO
LYREBIRD	MALAISES	MAN-OF-WAR	MARTIANS
LYRICISM	MALARIAL	MANORIAL	MARTINET
LYRICIST	MALARKEY	MANPOWER	MARTINIS
LYSOSOME	MALAYSIA	MANSARDS	MARTYRED

MARVELED	MECONIUM	MENTALLY	MIDFIELD
MARXISTS	MEDALLIC	MENTIONS	MIDLANDS
MARYLAND	MEDDLERS	MEPHITIC	MIDNIGHT
MARZIPAN	MEDDLING	MEPHITIS	MIDPOINT
MASSACRE	MEDELLIN	MERCHANT	MIDRIFFS
MASSAGED	MEDIALLY	MERCIFUL	MIDWIVES
MASSAGER	MEDIATED	MERCURIC	MIGHTIER
MASSAGES	MEDIATOR	MERGENCE	MIGHTILY
MASSEDLY	MEDICAID	MERIDIAN	MIGRAINE
MASSETER	MEDICALS	MERINGUE	MIGRANTS
MASSEURS	MEDICARE	MERISTEM	MIGRATED
MASSICOT	MEDICATE	MERISTIC	MIGRATOR
MASTERED	MEDICINE	MERITING	MILANESE
MASTERLY	MEDIEVAL	MERMAIDS	MILCH COW
MASTHEAD	MEDIOCRE	MERRIEST	MILDEWED
MASTIFFS	MEDITATE	MESCALIN	MILDNESS
MASTITIS	MEDUSOID	MESDAMES	MILEAGES
MASTODON	MEEKNESS	MESMERIC	MILEPOST
MASTOIDS	MEETINGS	MESOCARP	MILIARIA
MASURIAN	MEGALITH	MESODERM	MILITANT
MATABELE	MEGATONS	MESOGLEA	MILITARY
MATADORS	MEGAVOLT	MESOZOIC	MILITATE
MATCHBOX	MEGAWATT	MESQUITE	MILITIAS
MATCHING	MELAMINE	MESSAGES	MILKFISH
MATERIAL	MELANGES	MESSENIA	MILKIEST
MATERIEL	MELANISM	MESSIAHS	MILKMAID
MATERNAL	MELANIST	MESSIEST	MILK RUNS
MATINEES	MELANITE	MESSMATE	MILKSOPS
MATRICES	MELANOID	MESSUAGE	MILKWEED
MATRIXES	MELANOMA	MESTIZOS	MILKWORT
MATRONAL	MELANOUS	METALING	MILKY WAY
MATRONLY	MELINITE	METALLED	MILLABLE
MATTERED	MELLOWED	METALLIC	MILLIARD
MATTRESS	MELLOWER	METAMALE	MILLIARY
MATURATE	MELLOWLY	METAMERE	MILLIBAR
MATURELY	MELODEON	METAPHOR	MILLINER
MATURING	MELODIES	METAZOAN	MILLIONS
MATURITY	MELODIST	METAZOIC	MILLPOND
MAVERICK	MELODIZE	METEORIC	MILLRACE
MAXILLAR	MELTABLE	METERING	MILTONIC
MAXIMIZE	MELTDOWN	METHANOL	MIMETITE
MAXIMUMS	MEMBRANE	METHYLAL	MIMICKED
MAYORESS	MEMENTOS	METHYLIC	MIMICKER
MAYPOLES	MEMORIAL	METONYMY	MINARETS
MAZATLAN	MEMORIES	METRICAL	MINATORY
MAZURKAS	MEMORIZE	METRITIS	MINCE PIE
MEA CULPA	MEMSAHIB	MEUNIERE	MINDLESS
MEAGRELY	MENACING	MEXICALI	MIND'S EYE
MEALIEST	MENARCHE	MEZEREON	MINERALS
MEALWORM	MENDABLE	MEZEREUM	MINGIEST
MEANINGS	MENHADEN	MEZIERES	MINGLING
MEANNESS	MENIALLY	MIAOWING	MINICABS
MEANTIME	MENINGES	MICELLAR	MINIMIZE
MEASURED	MENISCUS	MICHIGAN	MINIMUMS
MEASURER	MEN-OF-WAR	MICROBES	MINISTER
MEASURES	MENOLOGY	MICRODOT	MINISTRY
MEATBALL	MEN'S ROOM	MIDBRAIN	MINORCAN
MEATIEST	MENSURAL	MIDDLE CS	MINORITY
MECHANIC	MENSWEAR	MIDDLING	MINOTAUR

MINSTERS	MOBILIZE	MONOCLES	MORIBUND
MINSTREL	MOBOCRAT	MONOCRAT	MORNINGS
MINUTELY	MOBSTERS	MONOCYTE	MOROCCAN
MINUTIAE	MOCCASIN	MONOGAMY	MORONISM
MINUTING	MOCKABLE	MONOGENY	MOROSELY
MIRACLES	MODALITY	MONOGRAM	MORPHEME
MIREPOIX	MODELING	MONOGYNY	MORPHEUS
MIRRORED	MODELLED	MONOHULL	MORPHINE
MIRTHFUL	MODELLER	MONOLITH	MORTALLY
MISAPPLY	MODERATE	MONOLOGY	MORTGAGE
MISCARRY	MODERATO	MONOMIAL	MORTISER
MISCHIEF	MODESTLY	MONOPOLY	MORTISES
MISCIBLE	MODIFIED	MONORAIL	MORTMAIN
MISCOUNT	MODIFIER	MONOSEMY	MORTUARY
MISDEEDS	MODIOLUS	MONOSOME	MOSEYING
MISERERE	MODISHLY	MONOTONE	MOSQUITO
MISERIES	MODULATE	MONOTONY	MOSSIEST
MISFIRED	MOHAMMED	MONOTYPE	MOTHBALL
MISFIRES	MOIETIES	MONOXIDE	MOTHERED
MISGUIDE	MOISTURE	MONROVIA	MOTHERLY
MISHEARD	MOLALITY	MONSIEUR	MOTILITY
MISHMASH	MOLASSES	MONSOONS	MOTIONED
MISJUDGE	MOLDAVIA	MONSTERS	MOTIONER
MISLAYER	MOLDERED	MONTAGES	MOTIVATE
MISMATCH	MOLDIEST	MONTEITH	MOTIVITY
MISNOMER	MOLDINGS	MONTREAL	MOT JUSTE
MISOGAMY	MOLECULE	MONUMENT	MOTORBUS
MISOGYNY	MOLEHILL	MOOCHING	MOTORCAR
MISOLOGY	MOLESKIN	MOODIEST	MOTORING
MISPLACE	MOLESTED	MOONBEAM	MOTORIST
MISPLEAD	MOLESTER	MOONCALF	MOTORIZE
MISPRINT	MOLLUSCS	MOONFISH	MOTORMAN
MISQUOTE	MOLYBDIC	MOONLESS	MOTORMEN
MISSHAPE	MOMENTUM	MOONRISE	MOTORWAY
MISSILES	MONACHAL	MOONSEED	MOULDIER
MISSIONS	MONADISM	MOON SHOT	MOULDING
MISSIVES	MONANDRY	MOONWORT	MOULMEIN
MISSOURI	MONARCHS	MOORCOCK	MOULTING
MISSPELL	MONARCHY	MOORHENS	MOUNTAIN
MISSPELT	MONASTIC	MOORINGS	MOUNTIES
MISSPEND	MONAURAL	MOORLAND	MOUNTING
MISSPENT	MONAZITE	MOORWORT	MOURNERS
MISSTATE	MONETARY	MOPINGLY	MOURNFUL
MISTAKEN	MONETIZE	MOQUETTE	MOURNING
MISTAKES	MONEYBOX	MORAINAL	MOUSIEST
MISTIMED	MONGOLIA	MORAINES	MOUSSAKA
MISTREAT	MONGOLIC	MORALISM	MOUTHFUL
MISTRESS	MONGOOSE	MORALIST	MOUTHING
MISTRIAL	MONGRELS	MORALITY	MOVABLES
MISTRUST	MONISTIC	MORALIZE	MOVEMENT
MISUSAGE	MONITION	MORASSES	MOVINGLY
MISUSING	MONITORS	MORATORY	MOZZETTA
MITICIDE	MONITORY	MORAVIAN	MUCHNESS
MITIGATE	MONKEYED	MORBIDLY	MUCILAGE
MITTIMUS	MONKFISH	MORBIFIC	MUCINOUS
MIXED BAG	MON-KHMER	MORBIHAN	MUCKHEAP
MIXTURES	MONKHOOD	MORDANCY	MUCKIEST
MNEMONIC	MONOACID	MOREOVER	MUCKRAKE
MOBILITY	MONOCARP	MORESQUE	MUCKWORM

MUCOSITY	MUSTERED	NARRATED	NEOGAEAN
MUD BATHS	MUSTIEST	NARRATOR	NEOMYCIN
MUDDIEST	MUTATION	NARROWED	NEONATAL
MUDDLING	MUTENESS	NARROWLY	NEOPHYTE
MUDDYING	MUTICOUS	NASALITY	NEOPLASM
MUDFLATS	MUTILATE	NASALIZE	NEOPRENE
MUDGUARD	MUTINEER	NASCENCE	NEOTERIC
MUDPACKS	MUTINIES	NASTIEST	NEPALESE
MUDSTONE	MUTINOUS	NATATION	NEPENTHE
MUENSTER	MUTINIED	NATIONAL	NEPHRITE
MUEZZINS	MUTTERED	NATIVISM	NEPOTISM
MUFFLERS	MUTTERER	NATIVIST	NEPOTIST
MUFFLING	MUTUALLY	NATIVITY	NERVIEST
MUGGIEST	MUZZIEST	NATTERED	NESCIENT
MUGGINGS	MUZZLING	NATTIEST	NEST EGGS
MUG'S GAME	MYCELIAL	NATURALS	NESTLING
MUGSHOTS	MYCELIUM	NATURISM	NETTLING
MUGWUMPS	MYCELOID	NATURIST	NETWORKS
MULATTOS	MYCETOMA	NAUPLIUS	NEURITIC
MULBERRY	MYCOLOGY	NAUSEATE	NEURITIS
MULCHING	MYELINIC	NAUSEOUS	NEURONIC
MULCTING	MYELITIS	NAUTICAL	NEUROSES
MULETEER	MYLONITE	NAUTILUS	NEUROSIS
MULHOUSE	MYOGENIC	NAVICERT	NEUROTIC
MULISHLY	MYOGRAPH	NAVIGATE	NEUTERED
MULLIONS	MYOLOGIC	NAVY BLUE	NEUTRALS
MULTIFID	MYOSOTIS	NAZARENE	NEUTRINO
MULTIPED	MYOTONIA	NAZARETH	NEUTRONS
MULTIPLE	MYOTONIC	NEAP TIDE	NEW BLOOD
MULTIPLY	MYRIAPOD	NEARCTIC	NEW BROOM
MUMBLING	MYSTICAL	NEAR EAST	NEWCOMER
MUNCHING	MYSTIQUE	NEAR MISS	NEW DEALS
MUNIMENT	MYTHICAL	NEARNESS	NEWLYWED
MUNITION		NEARSIDE	NEW MOONS
MURALIST	N	NEATNESS	NEWSCAST
MURDERED	NABOBERY	NEBRASKA	NEWSPEAK
MURDERER	NACELLES	NEBULIZE	NEWSREEL
MURICATE	NACREOUS	NEBULOUS	NEWSROOM
MURKIEST	NAGALAND	NECKBAND	NEW TOWNS
MURMANSK	NAGASAKI	NECKLACE	NEW WAVES
MURMURED	NAIL FILE	NECKLETS	NEW WORLD
MURMURER	NAILHEAD	NECKLINE	NEXT-DOOR
MURRAINS	NAINSOOK	NECKTIES	NIBBLING
MURRELET	NAISSANT	NECROSIS	NICENESS
MURRHINE	NAMANGAN	NECROTIC	NICETIES
MUSCATEL	NAME DAYS	NEEDIEST	NICHROME
MUSCLING	NAMEDROP	NEEDLESS	NICKELED
MUSCULAR	NAMELESS	NEEDLING	NICKELIC
MUSHIEST	NAMESAKE	NEGATING	NICKNACK
MUSHROOM	NAMIBIAN	NEGATION	NICKNAME
MUSICALE	NANCHANG	NEGATIVE	NICOTINE
MUSICALS	NAPHTHOL	NEGLIGEE	NIELLIST
MUSICIAN	NAPHTHYL	NEGRILLO	NIFTIEST
MUSINGLY	NAPIFORM	NEGRITIC	NIGERIAN
MUSKETRY	NARCEINE	NEGROISM	NIGGARDS
MUSKIEST	NARCISSI	NEIGHING	NIGGLERS
MUSQUASH	NARCOSIS	NEKTONIC	NIGGLING
MUSTACHE	NARCOTIC	NEMATODE	NIGHTCAP
MUSTANGS	NARKIEST	NEMBUTAL	NIGHTJAR

NIGHT OWL
NIHILISM
NIHILIST
NIHILITY
NIJMEGEN
NIMBLEST
NIMBUSES
NINEFOLD
NINEPINS
NINETEEN
NINETIES
NIPPIEST
NIRVANAS
NIRVANIC
NITRATES
NITROGEN
NITROSYL
NIVATION
NOBBLING
NOBELIUM
NOBILITY
NOBLEMAN
NOBLEMEN
NOBODIES
NOCTURNE
NODALITY
NODOSITY
NO-GO AREA
NOISIEST
NOMADISM
NOMINATE
NOMINEES
NOMISTIC
NOMOLOGY
NONESUCH
NON-EVENT
NONJUROR
NON LICET
NONMETAL
NONSENSE
NONSTICK
NONTOXIC
NONUNION
NONVOTER
NONWHITE
NOONTIME
NORMALLY
NORMANDY
NORSEMAN
NORSEMEN
NORTHERN
NORTHING
NOSEBAGS
NOSEBAND
NOSECONE
NOSEDIVE
NOSEGAYS
NOSINESS
NOSOLOGY

NOSTRILS
NOSTRUMS
NOTA BENE
NOTABLES
NOTARIAL
NOTARIES
NOTARIZE
NOTATION
NOTCHING
NOTEBOOK
NOTECASE
NOTELETS
NOTEPADS
NOTICING
NOTIFIED
NOTIFIER
NOTIONAL
NOTOGAEA
NOTORNIS
NOVATION
NOVELIST
NOVELLAS
NOVEMBER
NOVGOROD
NOWADAYS
NUBECULA
NUBILITY
NUCELLAR
NUCELLUS
NUCLEASE
NUCLEATE
NUDENESS
NUDICAUL
NUGATORY
NUISANCE
NULL SETS
NUMBERED
NUMBFISH
NUMBNESS
NUMERACY
NUMERALS
NUMERARY
NUMERATE
NUMEROUS
NUMINOUS
NUMMULAR
NUMSKULL
NUPTIALS
NURISTAN
NURSLING
NURTURED
NURTURER
NUTATION
NUT-BROWN
NUTCASES
NUTHATCH
NUTHOUSE
NUTRIENT
NUTSHELL

NUTTIEST
NUZZLING
NYMPHETS
NYSTATIN

O
OAFISHLY
OARLOCKS
OATCAKES
OBDURACY
OBDURATE
OBEDIENT
OBEISANT
OBELISKS
OBERLAND
OBITUARY
OBJECTED
OBJECTOR
OBLATION
OBLATORY
OBLIGATE
OBLIGING
OBLIQUES
OBLIVION
OBSCURED
OBSERVED
OBSERVER
OBSESSED
OBSIDIAN
OBSOLETE
OBSTACLE
OBSTRUCT
OBTAINED
OBTAINER
OBTRUDED
OBTRUDER
OBTUSELY
OBVIATED
OBVOLUTE
OCARINAS
OCCASION
OCCIDENT
OCCLUSAL
OCCUPANT
OCCUPIED
OCCUPIER
OCCURRED
OCEANIAN
OCHREOUS
OCOTILLO
OCTAGONS
OCTARCHY
OCTOBERS
OCTOROON
OCULISTS
ODDBALLS
ODDITIES
ODDMENTS
ODIOUSLY

ODOMETER
ODONTOID
ODYSSEYS
OENOLOGY
OESTRIOL
OESTRONE
OESTROUS
OFFENCES
OFFENDED
OFFENDER
OFFERING
OFF-GLIDE
OFFICERS
OFFICIAL
OFFPRINT
OFFSHOOT
OFFSHORE
OFFSTAGE
OFF-WHITE
OHMMETER
OILCLOTH
OILFIELD
OIL-FIRED
OILINESS
OIL PAINT
OILSKINS
OIL SLICK
OILSTONE
OIL WELLS
OINTMENT
OKLAHOMA
OLD FLAME
OLD GUARD
OLD HANDS
OLD MAIDS
OLDSTERS
OLD-TIMER
OLD WOMAN
OLD WOMEN
OLD WORLD
OLEANDER
OLEASTER
OLEFINIC
OLIBANUM
OLIGARCH
OLIGURIA
OLYMPIAD
OLYMPIAN
OMDURMAN
OMELETTE
OMISSION
OMITTING
OMNIVORE
OMPHALOS
ONCE-OVER
ONCOLOGY
ONCOMING
ONDOGRAM
ONE-HORSE

ONE-PIECE	ORCHITIS	OUTDOORS	OVERCOAT
ONE-SIDED	ORDAINED	OUTFACED	OVERCOME
ONE-TO-ONE	ORDAINER	OUTFALLS	OVERCOOK
ONE-TRACK	ORDERING	OUTFIELD	OVERCROP
ONLOOKER	ORDINALS	OUTFIGHT	OVERDONE
ONRUSHES	ORDINAND	OUTFLANK	OVERDOSE
ON-SCREEN	ORDINARY	OUTFLOWS	OVERDRAW
ONSTREAM	ORDINATE	OUTFOXED	OVERDREW
ONTOGENY	ORDNANCE	OUTGOING	OVERFLEW
ONTOLOGY	ORENBURG	OUT-GROUP	OVERFLOW
OOGAMOUS	ORGANDIE	OUTGROWN	OVERGROW
OOGONIAL	ORGANISM	OUT-HEROD	OVERHAND
OOGONIUM	ORGANIST	OUTHOUSE	OVERHANG
OOLOGIST	ORGANIZE	OUTLAWED	OVERHAUL
OOPHYTIC	ORGASMIC	OUTLAWRY	OVERHEAD
OOSPHERE	ORIENTAL	OUTLINED	OVERHEAR
OOSPORIC	ORIFICES	OUTLINES	OVERHEAT
OOTHECAL	ORIGINAL	OUTLIVED	OVERHUNG
OOZINESS	ORINASAL	OUTLOOKS	OVERKILL
OPALESCE	ORNAMENT	OUTLYING	OVERLAID
OPAQUELY	ORNATELY	OUTMODED	OVERLAIN
OPENCAST	ORNITHIC	OUTPOINT	OVERLAND
OPEN-EYED	OROGENIC	OUTPOSTS	OVERLAPS
OPENINGS	OROMETER	OUTRAGED	OVERLAYS
OPENNESS	ORPHANED	OUTRAGES	OVERLEAF
OPEN-PLAN	ORPIMENT	OUTREACH	OVERLOAD
OPEN SHOP	ORRERIES	OUTRIDER	OVERLONG
OPENWORK	ORTHODOX	OUTRIGHT	OVERLOOK
OPERABLE	ORTHOEPY	OUTRIVAL	OVERLORD
OPERABLY	OSCITANT	OUTSHINE	OVERMUCH
OPERATED	OSCULANT	OUTSHONE	OVERPAID
OPERATIC	OSCULATE	OUTSHOOT	OVERPASS
OPERATOR	OSNABURG	OUTSIDER	OVERPLAY
OPERETTA	OSSIFIED	OUTSIDES	OVERRATE
OPHIDIAN	OSSIFIER	OUTSMART	OVERRIDE
OPINICUS	OSTEITIC	OUTSTAND	OVERRIPE
OPINIONS	OSTEITIS	OUTSTARE	OVERRODE
OPIUMISM	OSTINATO	OUTSTRIP	OVERRULE
OPOSSUMS	OSTIOLAR	OUTSWING	OVERSEAS
OPPILATE	OSTRACOD	OUT-TAKES	OVERSEEN
OPPONENT	OTIOSITY	OUTVOTED	OVERSEER
OPPOSING	OTOSCOPE	OUTWARDS	OVERSELL
OPPOSITE	OTTOMANS	OUTWEIGH	OVERSHOE
OPPUGNER	OUTBLUFF	OUTWORKS	OVERSHOT
OPSONIZE	OUTBOARD	OVALNESS	OVERSIDE
OPTATIVE	OUTBOUND	OVARITIS	OVERSIZE
OPTICIAN	OUTBRAVE	OVATIONS	OVERSOLD
OPTIMISM	OUTBREAK	OVENBIRD	OVERSTAY
OPTIMIST	OUTBREED	OVENWARE	OVERSTEP
OPTIMIZE	OUTBURST	OVERALLS	OVERTAKE
OPTIONAL	OUTCASTE	OVERARCH	OVERTIME
OPULENCE	OUTCASTS	OVERAWED	OVERTIRE
ORACULAR	OUTCLASS	OVERBEAR	OVERTONE
ORANGERY	OUTCOMES	OVERBIDS	OVERTOOK
ORATIONS	OUTCRIES	OVERBOOK	OVERTURE
ORATORIO	OUTCROPS	OVERBORE	OVERTURN
ORBITING	OUTCROSS	OVERCALL	OVERVIEW
ORCHARDS	OUTDATED	OVERCAME	OVERWIND
ORCHITIC	OUTDOING	OVERCAST	OVERWORK

O

OVIDUCAL	PALMISTS	PARAMENT	PASSERBY
OVIPOSIT	PALMITIN	PARAMOUR	PASSIBLE
OVULATED	PALOMINO	PARANOIA	PASSIONS
OWLISHLY	PALPABLE	PARANOID	PASSKEYS
OWN GOALS	PALPABLY	PARAPETS	PASSOVER
OXBRIDGE	PALPATED	PARAQUAT	PASSPORT
OXIDASIC	PALTERER	PARASITE	PASSWORD
OXIDIZED	PALTRIER	PARASOLS	PASTERNS
OXIDIZER	PALTRILY	PARAVANE	PASTE-UPS
OXPECKER	PAMPERED	PAR AVION	PASTICHE
OXTONGUE	PAMPERER	PARAZOAN	PASTIEST
OXYGENIC	PAMPHLET	PARCELED	PASTILLE
OXYMORON	PAMPLONA	PARCENER	PASTIMES
OXYTOCIC	PANACEAN	PARCHING	PASTINGS
OXYTOCIN	PANACEAS	PARDONED	PASTORAL
OZONIZER	PANATELA	PARDONER	PASTRAMI
	PANCAKES	PARENTAL	PASTRIES
P	PANCREAS	PARHELIC	PASTURED
PACIFIED	PANDA CAR	PARIETAL	PASTURES
PACIFIER	PANDANUS	PARISHES	PATAGIUM
PACIFISM	PANDEMIC	PARISIAN	PATCHIER
PACIFIST	PANDERED	PARKIEST	PATCHILY
PACKABLE	PANDERER	PARKLAND	PATCHING
PACKAGED	PANELING	PARKWAYS	PATELLAR
PACKAGER	PANELLED	PARLANCE	PATELLAS
PACKAGES	PANGOLIN	PARLANDO	PATENTED
PADDLING	PANICKED	PARLEYED	PATENTEE
PADDOCKS	PANICLED	PARLEYER	PATENTLY
PADLOCKS	PANMIXIA	PARLOURS	PATENTOR
PAEONIES	PANNIERS	PARMESAN	PATERNAL
PAGANISM	PANNIKIN	PARODIED	PATHETIC
PAGANIST	PANOPTIC	PARODIES	PATHLESS
PAGANIZE	PANORAMA	PARODIST	PATHOGEN
PAGEANTS	PANPIPES	PAROLING	PATHWAYS
PAGINATE	PANSOPHY	PAROTOID	PATIENCE
PAGURIAN	PANTHEON	PAROXYSM	PATIENTS
PAINLESS	PANTHERS	PARROTED	PATRIALS
PAINTERS	PANTILES	PARRYING	PATRIOTS
PAINTING	PANTRIES	PARSABLE	PATRONAL
PAKISTAN	PAPACIES	PARSNIPS	PATTERED
PALADINS	PAPERBOY	PARTAKEN	PATTERNS
PALATALS	PAPERING	PARTAKER	PATULOUS
PALATIAL	PAPILLON	PARTERRE	PAUNCHES
PALATINE	PAPISTRY	PARTHIAN	PAVEMENT
PALAVERS	PAPOOSES	PARTIBLE	PAVILION
PALEFACE	PARABLES	PARTICLE	PAVONINE
PALENESS	PARABOLA	PARTINGS	PAWKIEST
PALETTES	PARADIGM	PARTISAN	PAWNSHOP
PALFREYS	PARADING	PARTNERS	PAYCHECK
PALINODE	PARADISE	PART-SONG	PAYLOADS
PALISADE	PARADROP	PART-TIME	PAYMENTS
PALLADIC	PARAFFIN	PART WORK	PAY PHONE
PALLIATE	PARAGOGE	PARTYING	PAYROLLS
PALLIDLY	PARAGONS	PAR VALUE	PAYSLIPS
PALLIEST	PARAGUAY	PARVENUS	PEACEFUL
PALL MALL	PARAKEET	PASSABLE	PEACOCKS
PALMETTE	PARALLAX	PASSABLY	PEAFOWLS
PALMETTO	PARALLEL	PASSAGES	PEA GREEN
PALMIEST	PARALYSE	PASSBOOK	PEAKIEST

PEARLIER	PENTACLE	PESHAWAR	PHYSICAL
PEARLITE	PENTAGON	PESKIEST	PHYSIQUE
PEARMAIN	PENTOMIC	PESTERED	PIACENZA
PEASANTS	PENTOSAN	PESTERER	PIACULAR
PEBBLING	PENUMBRA	PESTHOLE	PIANISTS
PECCABLE	PENZANCE	PETALINE	PIANOLAS
PECCANCY	PEOPLING	PETALODY	PIASSAVA
PECTORAL	PEPPERED	PETALOID	PIASTRES
PECULATE	PEP PILLS	PETECHIA	PICADORS
PECULIAR	PEP TALKS	PETITION	PICCOLOS
PEDAGOGY	PEPTIZER	PETIT MAL	PICKABLE
PEDALFER	PER ANNUM	PET NAMES	PICKAXES
PEDALING	PERCEIVE	PETROLIC	PICKEREL
PEDALLED	PERCHING	PETROSAL	PICKETED
PEDANTIC	PERFORCE	PETTIEST	PICKETER
PEDANTRY	PERFUMED	PETTIFOG	PICKIEST
PEDDLERS	PERFUMER	PETULANT	PICKINGS
PEDDLING	PERFUMES	PETUNIAS	PICKLING
PEDERAST	PERGOLAS	PETUNTSE	PICKLOCK
PEDESTAL	PERIANTH	PEWTERER	PICK-ME-UP
PEDICURE	PERIBLEM	PFENNIGS	PICOLINE
PEDIFORM	PERICARP	PHAETONS	PICTURED
PEDIGREE	PERIDERM	PHALANGE	PICTURES
PEDIMENT	PERIDIUM	PHANTASM	PIDDLING
PEDIPALP	PERIGEAN	PHANTASY	PIEBALDS
PEDOLOGY	PERIGEES	PHANTOMS	PIE CHART
PEDUNCLE	PERIGYNY	PHARAOHS	PIECRUST
PEEKABOO	PERILOUS	PHARISEE	PIEDMONT
PEELINGS	PERILUNE	PHARMACY	PIERCING
PEEPHOLE	PERINEUM	PHASE-OUT	PIFFLING
PEEPSHOW	PERIODIC	PHEASANT	PIGGIEST
PEERAGES	PERIOTIC	PHENETIC	PIGMENTS
PEERLESS	PERISARC	PHENOLIC	PIGSKINS
PEGBOARD	PERISHED	PHILTRES	PIGSTICK
PEIGNOIR	PERISHER	PHIMOSIS	PIGSTIES
PEKINESE	PERIWIGS	PHONE BOX	PIGSWILL
PELICANS	PERJURED	PHONE-INS	PIGTAILS
PELLAGRA	PERJURER	PHONEMES	PILASTER
PELLICLE	PERKIEST	PHONEMIC	PILCHARD
PELL-MELL	PERLITIC	PHONETIC	PILEWORT
PELLUCID	PERMEANT	PHONIEST	PILFERED
PELVISES	PERMEATE	PHOSGENE	PILFERER
PEMMICAN	PERMUTED	PHOSPHOR	PILGRIMS
PENALIZE	PERONEAL	PHOTOFIT	PILIFORM
PENANCES	PERORATE	PHOTOMAP	PILLAGED
PENCHANT	PEROXIDE	PHOTOPIA	PILLAGER
PENCILED	PERSONAL	PHOTOPIC	PILLIONS
PENDANTS	PERSONAS	PHOTOSET	PILLOCKS
PENDULUM	PERSPIRE	PHRASING	PILLOWED
PENGUINS	PERSUADE	PHRATRIC	PILOTAGE
PENITENT	PERTNESS	PHREATIC	PILOTING
PENKNIFE	PERUSALS	PHTHALIC	PIMENTOS
PEN NAMES	PERUSING	PHTHISIC	PIMIENTO
PENNANTS	PERUVIAN	PHTHISIS	PINAFORE
PENNINES	PERVADED	PHYLETIC	PINASTER
PENN'ORTH	PERVADER	PHYLLITE	PINCE-NEZ
PENOLOGY	PERVERSE	PHYLLODE	PINCHING
PENSIONS	PERVERTS	PHYLLOID	PINETREE
PENSTOCK	PERVIOUS	PHYLLOME	PINEWOOD

PING-PONG	PLANNERS	PLOUGHER	POLLUTED
PINHEADS	PLANNING	PLUCKIER	POLLUTER
PINIONED	PLANOSOL	PLUCKILY	POLO NECK
PINK GINS	PLANTAIN	PLUCKING	POLONIUM
PINKROOT	PLANTERS	PLUGGING	POLTROON
PIN MONEY	PLANTING	PLUGHOLE	POLYGALA
PINNACES	PLANULAR	PLUMBAGO	POLYGAMY
PINNACLE	PLASTERS	PLUMBERS	POLYGENE
PINNIPED	PLASTICS	PLUMBERY	POLYGLOT
PINOCHLE	PLASTRAL	PLUMBING	POLYGONS
PINPOINT	PLASTRON	PLUMBISM	POLYGYNY
PINPRICK	PLATELET	PLUMBOUS	POLYMATH
PINTABLE	PLATFORM	PLUMMIER	POLYMERS
PINT-SIZE	PLATINIC	PLUMPEST	POLYPARY
PINWHEEL	PLATINUM	PLUMPING	POLYPODY
PIONEERS	PLATONIC	PLUNGERS	POLYPOID
PIPECLAY	PLATOONS	PLUNGING	POLYPOUS
PIPEFISH	PLATTERS	PLUSHEST	POLYSEMY
PIPELINE	PLATYPUS	PLUTONIC	POLYURIA
PIPE RACK	PLAUDITS	PLUVIOUS	POLYURIC
PIPERINE	PLAUSIVE	PLYMOUTH	POLYZOAN
PIPETTES	PLAYABLE	POACEOUS	POLYZOIC
PIPEWORT	PLAYBACK	POACHERS	POMANDER
PIQUANCY	PLAYBILL	POACHING	POMOLOGY
PIRACIES	PLAYBOYS	POCKETED	PONDERED
PIRANHAS	PLAYGOER	POCKMARK	PONDERER
PIRATING	PLAYMATE	PODAGRAL	PONDWEED
PIS ALLER	PLAY-OFFS	PODGIEST	PONGIEST
PISIFORM	PLAYPENS	PODIATRY	PONIARDS
PISOLITE	PLAYROOM	PODZOLIC	PONTIFEX
PISS-TAKE	PLAYSUIT	POETICAL	PONTIFFS
PITCHERS	PLAYTIME	POIGNANT	PONTOONS
PITCHING	PLEADING	POINTERS	PONYTAIL
PITFALLS	PLEASANT	POINTING	POOFIEST
PITHEADS	PLEASING	POISONED	POOH-POOH
PITHIEST	PLEASURE	POISONER	POOR LAWS
PITIABLE	PLEATING	POKEWEED	POORLIER
PITIABLY	PLEBBIER	POKINESS	POORNESS
PITILESS	PLEBEIAN	POLARITY	POPADUMS
PIT PROPS	PLECTRUM	POLARIZE	POPINJAY
PITTANCE	PLEDGING	POLAROID	POPOVERS
PIVOTING	PLEIADES	POLEAXED	POPPADOM
PIZZERIA	PLEIN-AIR	POLECATS	POPSICLE
PLACABLE	PLEONASM	POLEMICS	POPULACE
PLACARDS	PLETHORA	POLE STAR	POPULATE
PLACATED	PLEURISY	POLICIES	PCPULISM
PLACEBOS	PLEUSTON	POLICING	POPULIST
PLACE MAT	PLIANTLY	POLISHED	POPULOUS
PLACENTA	PLIGHTED	POLISHER	PORKIEST
PLACIDLY	PLIGHTER	POLISHES	PORK PIES
PLAGUILY	PLIMSOLL	POLITELY	POROSITY
PLAGUING	PLIOCENE	POLITICO	PORPHYRY
PLAINEST	PLODDERS	POLITICS	PORPOISE
PLAITING	PLODDING	POLITIES	PORRIDGE
PLANCHET	PLONKING	POLKA DOT	PORTABLE
PLANFORM	PLOPPING	POLLARDS	PORTENTS
PLANGENT	PLOSIVES	POLLICAL	PORTHOLE
PLANKING	PLOTTING	POLLINIC	PORTICOS
PLANKTON	PLOUGHED	POLLSTER	PORTIERE

PORTIONS	PRAIRIES	PRESSMEN	PROCLAIM
PORTLIER	PRAISING	PRESS-UPS	PROCTORS
PORTRAIT	PRALINES	PRESSURE	PROCURED
PORT SAID	PRANCING	PRESTIGE	PROCURER
PORTUGAL	PRANDIAL	PRESUMED	PRODDING
POSITING	PRANKISH	PRESUMER	PRODIGAL
POSITION	PRATIQUE	PRETENCE	PRODROME
POSITIVE	PRATTLED	PRETEXTS	PRODUCED
POSITRON	PRATTLER	PRETORIA	PRODUCER
POSOLOGY	PREACHED	PRETTIER	PRODUCTS
POSSIBLE	PREACHER	PRETTIFY	PROEMIAL
POSSIBLY	PREAMBLE	PRETTILY	PROFANED
POSTBAGS	PREAXIAL	PRETZELS	PROFANER
POSTCARD	PREBENDS	PREVIEWS	PROFILED
POSTCAVA	PRECEDED	PREVIOUS	PROFILES
POSTCODE	PRECEPTS	PREZZIES	PROFITED
POSTDATE	PRECINCT	PRIAPISM	PROFITER
POST-FREE	PRECIOUS	PRICE TAG	PRO FORMA
POST HORN	PRECLUDE	PRICIEST	PROFOUND
POSTICHE	PREDATED	PRICKING	PROGRAMS
POSTINGS	PREDATOR	PRICKLED	PROGRESS
POSTLUDE	PREDELLA	PRICKLES	PROHIBIT
POSTMARK	PREENING	PRIDEFUL	PROJECTS
POST-OBIT	PREEXIST	PRIE-DIEU	PROLAPSE
POSTPAID	PREFACED	PRIESTLY	PROLIFIC
POSTPONE	PREFACER	PRIGGERY	PROLOGUE
POSTURAL	PREFACES	PRIGGISH	PROMISED
POSTURED	PREFECTS	PRIGGISM	PROMISER
POSTURER	PREFIXAL	PRIMATES	PROMISES
POSTURES	PREFIXED	PRIMEVAL	PROMISOR
POTASSIC	PREFIXES	PRIMMEST	PROMOTED
POTATION	PREGNANT	PRIMNESS	PROMOTER
POTATOES	PREJUDGE	PRIMROSE	PROMPTED
POT-AU-FEU	PRELATES	PRIMULAS	PROMPTER
POTBELLY	PRELATIC	PRIMUSES	PROMPTLY
POTBOUND	PRELUDER	PRINCELY	PRONATOR
POTENTLY	PRELUDES	PRINCESS	PRONOUNS
POTHOLER	PREMIERE	PRINTERS	PROOFING
POTHOLES	PREMIERS	PRINTING	PROPERLY
POTLUCKS	PREMISES	PRINTOUT	PROPERTY
POT PLANT	PREMIUMS	PRIORATE	PROPHAGE
POTSHERD	PREMOLAR	PRIORESS	PROPHASE
POTSHOTS	PREMORSE	PRIORIES	PROPHECY
POTSTONE	PRENATAL	PRIORITY	PROPHESY
POTTERED	PREPARED	PRISMOID	PROPHETS
POTTERER	PREPENSE	PRISONER	PROPOLIS
POTTIEST	PRESAGED	PRISSIER	PROPOSAL
POULTICE	PRESAGER	PRISSILY	PROPOSED
POUNCING	PRESAGES	PRISTINE	PROPOSER
POUNDAGE	PRESENCE	PRIVATES	PROPOUND
POUNDING	PRESENTS	PRIVIEST	PROPPING
POWDERED	PRESERVE	PRIZE DAY	PROROGUE
POWDERER	PRESIDED	PROBABLE	PROSAISM
POWERFUL	PRESIDER	PROBABLY	PROSIEST
POWERING	PRESIDIA	PROBATED	PROSODIC
PRACTICE	PRESIDIO	PROBATES	PROSPECT
PRACTISE	PRESS BOX	PROBLEMS	PROSTATE
PRAEDIAL	PRESSING	PROCAINE	PROSTYLE
PRAESEPE	PRESSMAN	PROCEEDS	PROTASIS

PROTEGEE	PULLMANS	PUSHOVER	QUEASIER
PROTEGES	PULLOUTS	PUSH-PULL	QUEASILY
PROTEINS	PULLOVER	PUSTULAR	QUECHUAN
PROTEOSE	PULMONIC	PUSTULES	QUEENDOM
PROTESTS	PULMOTOR	PUTATIVE	QUEENING
PROTOCOL	PULPIEST	PUT-DOWNS	QUEEREST
PROTOZOA	PULPWOOD	PUTSCHES	QUEERING
PROTRACT	PULSATED	PUTTERED	QUELLING
PROTRUDE	PULSATOR	PUT-UP JOB	QUENCHED
PROUDEST	PULSEJET	PUZZLERS	QUENCHER
PROVABLE	PULVINUS	PUZZLING	QUERCINE
PROVABLY	PUMMELED	PYELITIC	QUERYING
PROVENCE	PUMPKINS	PYELITIS	QUESTING
PROVENLY	PUMP ROOM	PYGIDIAL	QUESTION
PROVERBS	PUNCHEON	PYGIDIUM	QUIBBLED
PROVIDED	PUNCHIER	PYODERMA	QUIBBLER
PROVIDER	PUNCHING	PYOGENIC	QUIBBLES
PROVINCE	PUNCH-UPS	PYRAMIDS	QUIBERON
PROVISOS	PUNCTATE	PYRAZOLE	QUICKEST
PROVOKED	PUNCTUAL	PYRENEAN	QUICKIES
PROVOSTS	PUNCTURE	PYRENEES	QUICKSET
PROWL CAR	PUNGENCY	PYRENOID	QUIDDITY
PROWLERS	PUNINESS	PYREXIAL	QUIDNUNC
PROWLING	PUNISHED	PYRIDINE	QUIETEST
PROXIMAL	PUNISHER	PYRIFORM	QUIETISM
PRUDENCE	PUNITIVE	PYROSTAT	QUIETIST
PRUINOSE	PUNSTERS	PYROXENE	QUIETUDE
PRUNABLE	PUPARIAL	PYRROLIC	QUILTING
PRUNELLA	PUPARIUM	PYRRUVIC	QUINCUNX
PRUNELLE	PUPATION	PYTHONIC	QUINTETS
PRURIENT	PUPPETRY	PYXIDIUM	QUINTILE
PRURITIC	PUPPY FAT		QUIPPING
PRURITUS	PUPPYISH	Q	QUIPSTER
PRUSSIAN	PURBLIND	QUACKERY	QUIRKIER
PSALMIST	PURCHASE	QUACKING	QUIRKILY
PSALMODY	PUREBRED	QUADRANT	QUISLING
PSALTERS	PUREEING	QUADRATE	QUITTERS
PSALTERY	PURENESS	QUADROON	QUITTING
PSEPHITE	PURFLING	QUAGMIRE	QUIVERED
PSORALEA	PURIFIED	QUAILING	QUIVERER
PSYCHICS	PURIFIER	QUAINTLY	QUIXOTIC
PSYCHING	PURISTIC	QUALMISH	QUIZZING
PTEROPOD	PURITANS	QUANDARY	QUOTABLE
PTOMAINE	PURLIEUS	QUANDONG	QUOTHING
PTYALISM	PURPLISH	QUANTIFY	QUOTIENT
PUB-CRAWL	PURPOSED	QUANTITY	
PUBLICAN	PURPOSES	QUANTIZE	R
PUBLICLY	PURPURIN	QUARRELS	RABBITED
PUCKERED	PURSLANE	QUARRIED	RABBITER
PUDDINGS	PURSUANT	QUARRIER	RABBITRY
PUDDLING	PURSUERS	QUARRIES	RABIDITY
PUDENDUM	PURSUING	QUARTERN	RACCOONS
PUDGIEST	PURSUITS	QUARTERS	RACEMISM
PUFFBALL	PURULENT	QUARTETS	RACEMOSE
PUFFBIRD	PURVEYED	QUARTILE	RACIALLY
PUFFIEST	PURVEYOR	QUASHING	RACINESS
PUGILISM	PUSHBIKE	QUATRAIN	RACK-RENT
PUGILIST	PUSHCART	QUAVERED	RACQUETS
PUISSANT	PUSHIEST	QUAVERER	RADIALLY

RADIANCE	RASPINGS	REBUTTER	REDOUBLE
RADIATED	RATCHETS	RECALLED	REDOUBTS
RADIATOR	RATIFIED	RECANTED	REDSHANK
RADICALS	RATIFIER	RECANTER	REDSKINS
RADICAND	RATIONAL	RECAPPED	REDSTART
RADIOING	RATIONED	RECEDING	REDUCING
RADISHES	RATSBANE	RECEIPTS	REDUVIID
RAFFLING	RATTIEST	RECEIVED	REDWOODS
RAGGEDLY	RATTLING	RECEIVER	RE-ECHOED
RAG TRADE	RAT TRAPS	RECENTLY	REDBUCK
RAILHEAD	RAVAGING	RECEPTOR	REEDIEST
RAILINGS	RAVELING	RECESSED	REEDLING
RAILLERY	RAVELLED	RECESSES	REEF KNOT
RAILROAD	RAVELLER	RECHARGE	REELABLE
RAILWAYS	RAVENING	RECISION	REELABLY
RAINBAND	RAVENOUS	RECITALS	RE-EMPLOY
RAINBOWS	RAVISHED	RECITERS	RE-EXPORT
RAINCOAT	RAVISHER	RECITING	REFACING
RAINDROP	RAW-BONED	RECKLESS	REFEREED
RAINFALL	RAW DEALS	RECKONED	REFEREES
RAINIEST	RAWHIDES	RECKONER	REFERENT
RAINLESS	RAZOR-CUT	RECLINED	REFERRAL
RAISABLE	REACHING	RECLINER	REFERRED
RAKE-OFFS	REACTANT	RECLUSES	REFERRER
RAKISHLY	REACTING	RECOILED	REFILLED
RALLYING	REACTION	RECOILER	REFINERY
RAMAT GAN	REACTIVE	RECOMMIT	REFINING
RAMBLERS	REACTORS	RECORDED	REFINISH
RAMBLING	READABLE	RECORDER	REFITTED
RAMBUTAN	READABLY	RECOUNTS	REFLATED
RAMEKINS	READIEST	RECOUPED	REFLEXES
RAMENTUM	READINGS	RECOURSE	REFOREST
RAMIFIED	READJUST	RECOVERY	REFORMED
RAMOSITY	READOUTS	RECREANT	REFORMER
RAMPAGED	READYING	RECREATE	REFRAINS
RAMPAGER	READY-MIX	RECRUITS	REFUELED
RAMPANCY	REAFFIRM	RECTALLY	REFUGEES
RAMPARTS	REAGENTS	RECURRED	REFUGIUM
RAMULOSE	REALISTS	RECUSANT	REFUNDED
RANCHERS	REALIZED	RECYCLED	REFUNDER
RANDIEST	REALIZER	REDACTOR	REFUSALS
RANDOMLY	REALNESS	RED ALERT	REFUSING
RANKLING	REAL-TIME	REDBRICK	REFUTING
RANKNESS	REALTORS	REDCOATS	REGAINED
RANSOMED	REAPABLE	RED CROSS	REGAINER
RANSOMER	REAPPEAR	REDDENED	REGALITY
RAPACITY	REARMING	REDEEMED	REGARDED
RAPESEED	REARMOST	REDEEMER	REGATTAS
RAPIDITY	REARWARD	REDEMAND	REGELATE
RAPTNESS	REASONED	REDEPLOY	REGENTAL
RAPTURES	REASONER	REDESIGN	REGICIDE
RARA AVIS	REASSURE	RED-FACED	REGIMENS
RAREFIED	REAWAKEN	RED FLAGS	REGIMENT
RAREFIER	REBELLED	RED GIANT	REGIONAL
RARENESS	REBOUNDS	REDHEADS	REGISTER
RARITIES	REBUFFED	REDIRECT	REGISTRY
RASCALLY	REBUKING	RED LIGHT	REGRATER
RASHNESS	REBUTTAL	REDNECKS	REGROWTH
RASORIAL	REBUTTED	REDOLENT	REGULARS

REGULATE	REMEDIES	REPOUSSE	RESTATED
REGULINE	REMEMBER	REPRIEVE	REST CURE
REHASHED	REMIGIAL	REPRINTS	REST HOME
REHASHES	REMINDED	REPRISAL	RESTLESS
REHEARSE	REMINDER	REPRISES	RESTORED
REHEATER	REMITTED	REPROACH	RESTORER
REHOBOAM	REMITTER	REPROOFS	RESTRAIN
REHOUSED	REMNANTS	REPROVAL	RESTRICT
REIGNING	REMOTELY	REPROVED	REST ROOM
REIMPORT	REMOTEST	REPROVER	RESULTED
REIMPOSE	REMOULDS	REPTILES	RESUMING
REINDEER	REMOUNTS	REPUBLIC	RETAILED
REINSURE	REMOVALS	REPULSED	RETAILER
REINVEST	REMOVERS	REPULSER	RETAINED
REISSUED	REMOVING	REPULSES	RETAINER
REISSUER	RENAMING	REQUESTS	RETAKING
REISSUES	RENDERED	REQUIEMS	RETARDED
REJECTED	RENDERER	REQUIRED	RETARDER
REJECTER	RENDIBLE	REQUIRER	RETCHING
REJIGGED	RENDZINA	REQUITAL	RETICENT
REJOICED	RENEGADE	REQUITED	RETICULE
REJOICER	RENEGING	REQUITER	RETINENE
REJOINED	RENEWALS	RESCRIPT	RETINITE
REKINDLE	RENEWING	RESCUERS	RETINUED
RELAPSED	RENIFORM	RESCUING	RETINUES
RELAPSER	RENOUNCE	RESEARCH	RETIRING
RELAPSES	RENOVATE	RESEMBLE	RETORTED
RELATING	RENOWNED	RESENTED	RETORTER
RELATION	RENTABLE	RESERVED	RETRACED
RELATIVE	RENT BOYS	RESERVER	RETREADS
RELAXANT	RENT-FREE	RESERVES	RETREATS
RELAXING	RENTIERS	RESETTER	RETRENCH
RELAYING	RENT-ROLL	RESETTLE	RETRIALS
RELEASED	REOPENED	RESIDENT	RETRIEVE
RELEASER	REPAIRED	RESIDING	RETROACT
RELEASES	REPAIRER	RESIDUAL	RETROFIT
RELEGATE	REPARTEE	RESIDUES	RETRORSE
RELENTED	REPAYING	RESIDUUM	RETURNED
RELEVANT	REPEALED	RESIGNED	RETURNER
RELIABLE	REPEALER	RESIGNER	REUNIONS
RELIABLY	REPEATED	RESINATE	REUNITED
RELIANCE	REPEATER	RESINOID	REUNITER
RELIEVED	REPELLED	RESINOUS	REUSABLE
RELIEVER	REPELLER	RESISTED	REVALUED
RELIGION	REPENTED	RESISTER	REVAMPED
RELINING	REPENTER	RESISTOR	REVAMPER
RELISHED	REPEOPLE	RESOLUTE	REVEALED
RELISHES	REPETEND	RESOLVED	REVEALER
RELIVING	REPHRASE	RESOLVER	REVEILLE
RELOADED	REPINING	RESOLVES	REVELING
RELOCATE	REPLACED	RESONANT	REVELLED
REMAINED	REPLACER	RESONATE	REVELLER
REMAKING	REPLAYED	RESORTED	REVENANT
REMANDED	REPLEVIN	RESORTER	REVENGED
REMARKED	REPLICAS	RESOURCE	REVENGER
REMARKER	REPLYING	RESPECTS	REVENUED
REMARQUE	REPORTED	RESPIRED	REVEREND
REMEDIAL	REPORTER	RESPITES	REVERENT
REMEDIED	REPOSING	RESPONSE	REVERIES

REVERING	RIDDANCE	ROASTING	ROSINING
REVERSAL	RIDDLING	ROBOTICS	ROSTRUMS
REVERSED	RIDICULE	ROBOTISM	ROTARIAN
REVERSER	RIESLING	ROBUSTLY	ROTATING
REVERSES	RIFENESS	ROCAILLE	ROTATION
REVERTED	RIFFLING	ROCK CAKE	ROTATIVE
REVERTER	RIFFRAFF	ROCK DASH	ROTATORY
REVIEWAL	RIFLEMAN	ROCKETED	ROTENONE
REVIEWED	RIGADOON	ROCKETRY	ROTTENLY
REVIEWER	RIGATONI	ROCKFALL	ROTUNDAS
REVILERS	RIGHTFUL	ROCKFISH	ROUGHAGE
REVILING	RIGHTING	ROCKIEST	ROUGH-DRY
REVISERS	RIGHTISM	ROCKLING	ROUGHEST
REVISING	RIGHTIST	ROCKROSE	ROUGH-HEW
REVISION	RIGIDITY	ROCK SALT	ROUGHING
REVISORY	RIGORISM	ROCKWEED	ROULETTE
REVIVALS	RIGORIST	ROEBUCKS	ROUND-ARM
REVIVIFY	RIGOROUS	ROENTGEN	ROUNDELS
REVIVING	RIMOSITY	ROGATION	ROUNDERS
REVOKING	RINGBOLT	ROGATORY	ROUNDEST
REVOLTED	RINGBONE	ROLE PLAY	ROUNDING
REVOLTER	RINGDOVE	ROLLAWAY	ROUNDISH
REVOLUTE	RING-DYKE	ROLL BARS	ROUNDUPS
REVOLVED	RINGHALS	ROLL CALL	ROUTINES
REVOLVER	RINGLETS	ROLLMOPS	ROVE-OVER
REWARDED	RING ROAD	ROLY-POLY	ROWDIEST
REWARDER	RINGSIDE	ROMANCED	ROWDYISM
REWINDER	RINGWORM	ROMANCES	ROW HOUSE
REWIRING	RINSABLE	ROMANIES	ROWLOCKS
REWORDED	RIOT ACTS	ROMAN LAW	ROYALISM
REWORKED	RIPARIAN	ROMANSCH	ROYALIST
REWRITES	RIPCORDS	ROMANTIC	RUBBINGS
RHAETIAN	RIPENESS	RONDELET	RUBBISHY
RHAPSODY	RIPENING	RONTGENS	RUBDOWNS
RHEOBASE	RIPOSTED	ROOFLESS	RUBELITE
RHEOLOGY	RIPOSTES	ROOF RACK	RUBEOLAR
RHEOSTAT	RIPPABLE	ROOFTOPS	RUBICONS
RHETORIC	RIPPLING	ROOFTREE	RUBICUND
RH FACTOR	RIPTIDES	ROOMIEST	RUBIDIUM
RHINITIS	RISKIEST	ROOMMATE	RUBRICAL
RHIZOMES	RISOTTOS	ROOSTERS	RUCKSACK
RHIZOPOD	RISSOLES	ROOSTING	RUCKUSES
RHIZOPUS	RITENUTO	ROOT BEER	RUDDIEST
RHODESIA	RITUALLY	ROOT CROP	RUDENESS
RHODINAL	RIVALING	ROOTLESS	RUDIMENT
RHOMBOID	RIVALLED	ROOTLIKE	RUEFULLY
RHONCHAL	RIVERBED	ROPEWALK	RUFFIANS
RHONCHUS	RIVERINE	ROPINESS	RUFFLING
RHUBARBS	RIVETERS	ROSARIAN	RUGGEDLY
RHYOLITE	RIVETING	ROSARIES	RUGOSITY
RHYTHMIC	RIVIERAS	ROSEBUSH	RUINABLE
RIBALDRY	RIVULETS	ROSEFISH	RULEBOOK
RIB CAGES	ROAD HOGS	ROSE HIPS	RUMANIAN
RIBOSOME	ROADSHOW	ROSEMARY	RUMBLING
RICEBIRD	ROADSIDE	ROSEOLAR	RUMINANT
RICHNESS	ROADSTER	ROSE-ROOT	RUMINATE
RICKRACK	ROAD TEST	ROSETTES	RUMMAGED
RICKSHAW	ROADWORK	ROSEWOOD	RUMMAGER
RICOCHET	ROASTERS	ROSINESS	RUMMAGES

RUMOURED	SALESMEN	SANTIAGO	SCABIOUS
RUMPLING	SALES TAX	SANTONIN	SCABROUS
RUN-ABOUT	SALIENCE	SAO PAULO	SCAFFOLD
RUNAWAYS	SALIENTS	SAPIDITY	SCALABLE
RUNDOWNS	SALINITY	SAPIENCE	SCALABLY
RUNNER-UP	SALIVARY	SAPLINGS	SCALAWAG
RUNNIEST	SALIVATE	SAPONIFY	SCALDING
RUPTURED	SALLYING	SAPONITE	SCALENUS
RUPTURES	SALPICON	SAPPHIRE	SCALIEST
RURALISM	SALTBUSH	SAPPIEST	SCALLION
RURALIST	SALTIEST	SAPROBIC	SCALLOPS
RURALITY	SALTILLO	SAPROPEL	SCALPELS
RURALIZE	SALTLICK	SARABAND	SCALPERS
RUSH HOUR	SALTNESS	SARACENS	SCALPING
RUSTICAL	SALTPANS	SARAJEVO	SCAMMONY
RUSTIEST	SALTWORT	SARDINES	SCAMPISH
RUSTLERS	SALUTARY	SARDINIA	SCANDALS
RUSTLING	SALUTING	SARDONIC	SCANDIUM
RUTABAGA	SALVABLE	SARDONYX	SCANNERS
RUTHENIC	SALVABLY	SARGASSO	SCANNING
RUTHLESS	SALVADOR	SARKIEST	SCANSION
RYE-BROME	SALVAGED	SASHAYED	SCANTIER
RYEGRASS	SALVAGER	SASSIEST	SCANTILY
	SALZBURG	SASTRUGA	SCAPULAR
S	SAMARIUM	SATANISM	SCAPULAS
SAARLAND	SAMENESS	SATANIST	SCARCELY
SABADELL	SAMIZDAT	SATCHELS	SCARCEST
SABBATIC	SAMOVARS	SATIABLE	SCARCITY
SABOTAGE	SAMPHIRE	SATIABLY	SCARIEST
SABOTEUR	SAMPLERS	SATIATED	SCARIOUS
SABULOUS	SAMPLING	SATIRIST	SCARRING
SACKLIKE	SAMURAIS	SATIRIZE	SCATHING
SACK RACE	SANCTIFY	SATSUMAS	SCATTIER
SACREDLY	SANCTION	SATURANT	SCATTILY
SACRISTY	SANCTITY	SATURATE	SCATTING
SADDENED	SANCTUMS	SATURDAY	SCAVENGE
SADDLERS	SANDARAC	SAUCEPAN	SCENARIO
SADDLERY	SANDBAGS	SAUCIEST	SCENTING
SADDLING	SANDBANK	SAUNTERS	SCEPTICS
SADISTIC	SANDBARS	SAUROPOD	SCEPTRES
SAFENESS	SAND-CAST	SAUSAGES	SCHEDULE
SAFETIES	SAND DUNE	SAUTEING	SCHEMATA
SAGACITY	SAN DIEGO	SAVAGELY	SCHEMERS
SAGGIEST	SANDIEST	SAVAGERY	SCHEMING
SAGITTAL	SANDPITS	SAVAGING	SCHERZOS
SAILABLE	SANDSHOE	SAVANNAH	SCHILLER
SAILFISH	SANDSOAP	SAVANNAS	SCHIZOID
SAILINGS	SAND TRAP	SAVIOURS	SCHIZONT
SAILORLY	SANDWICH	SAVORIES	SCHMALTZ
SAINFOIN	SANDWORM	SAVOROUS	SCHMUCKS
SAKHALIN	SANDWORT	SAVOURED	SCHNAPPS
SALAAMED	SANENESS	SAVOYARD	SCHOLARS
SALACITY	SANGAREE	SAWBONES	SCHOLIUM
SALARIED	SANGUINE	SAWHORSE	SCHOOLED
SALARIES	SANITARY	SAWMILLS	SCHOONER
SALEABLE	SANITIZE	SAWTOOTH	SCHWERIN
SALEABLY	SANSKRIT	SCABBARD	SCIAENID
SALEROOM	SANTA ANA	SCABBIER	SCIATICA
SALESMAN	SANTAREM	SCABBILY	SCIENCES

SCILICET	SCREWIER	SEARCHES	SELFLESS
SCIMITAR	SCREWING	SEASCAPE	SELF-MADE
SCINCOID	SCREW TOP	SEASHELL	SELF-PITY
SCIRRHUS	SCRIBBLE	SEASHORE	SELF-RULE
SCISSILE	SCRIMPED	SEASONAL	SELFSAME
SCISSION	SCRIPTED	SEASONED	SELF-WILL
SCISSORS	SCROFULA	SEASONER	SELL-OUTS
SCIURINE	SCROLLED	SEAT BELT	SELVAGES
SCIUROID	SCROOGES	SEAWALLS	SEMANTIC
SCLAFFER	SCROTUMS	SEAWARDS	SEMARANG
SCLERITE	SCROUNGE	SECEDING	SEMESTER
SCLEROID	SCRUBBED	SECLUDED	SEMIARID
SCLEROMA	SCRUBBER	SECONDED	SEMIDOME
SCLEROUS	SCRUMPED	SECONDER	SEMINARS
SCOFFING	SCRUPLED	SECONDLY	SEMINARY
SCOLDING	SCRUPLES	SECRETED	SEMIOTIC
SCOLLOPS	SCRUTINY	SECRETIN	SEMITICS
SCOOPING	SCUDDING	SECRETLY	SEMITIST
SCOOTERS	SCUFFING	SECTIONS	SEMITONE
SCOOTING	SCUFFLED	SECTORAL	SEMOLINA
SCORCHED	SCUFFLES	SECURELY	SEMPLICE
SCORCHER	SCULLERS	SECUREST	SENATORS
SCORCHES	SCULLERY	SECURING	SENDABLE
SCORNFUL	SCULLING	SECURITY	SEND-OFFS
SCORNING	SCULLION	SEDATELY	SENILITY
SCORPION	SCULPSIT	SEDATING	SENORITA
SCORPIOS	SCULPTOR	SEDATION	SENSIBLE
SCORPIUS	SCUPPERS	SEDATIVE	SENSIBLY
SCOTCHED	SCURRIED	SEDIMENT	SENSUOUS
SCOT-FREE	SCURVILY	SEDITION	SENTENCE
SCOTLAND	SCUTTLED	SEDUCERS	SENTIENT
SCOTOPIA	SCUTTLES	SEDUCING	SENTINEL
SCOTOPIC	SCYTHING	SEDULITY	SENTRIES
SCOTSMAN	SEABIRDS	SEDULOUS	SEPALLED
SCOTTISH	SEABOARD	SEEDBEDS	SEPALOID
SCOURERS	SEABORNE	SEEDCASE	SEPARATE
SCOURGED	SEACOAST	SEEDCORN	SEPHARDI
SCOURGER	SEAFARER	SEEDIEST	SEPTUPLE
SCOURGES	SEAFRONT	SEEDLESS	SEQUENCE
SCOURING	SEAGIRTS	SEEDLING	SEQUINED
SCOUTING	SEAGOING	SEEDSMAN	SEQUOIAS
SCOWLING	SEAGULLS	SEEDSMEN	SERAGLIO
SCRABBLE	SEAHORSE	SEESAWED	SERAPHIC
SCRAGGED	SEALABLE	SEETHING	SERAPHIM
SCRAGGLY	SEA LEVEL	SEGMENTS	SERENADE
SCRAMBLE	SEA LIONS	SEIGNEUR	SERENATA
SCRAMMED	SEALSKIN	SEISABLE	SERENELY
SCRANTON	SEALYHAM	SEISMISM	SERENITY
SCRAPERS	SEAMIEST	SEIZABLE	SERGEANT
SCRAPING	SEA MILES	SEIZURES	SERIALLY
SCRAPPED	SEA MISTS	SELANGOR	SERIATIM
SCRATCHY	SEAMLESS	SELECTED	SERMONIC
SCRAWLED	SEAMOUNT	SELECTOR	SEROLOGY
SCRAWLER	SEAPLANE	SELENATE	SEROSITY
SCREAMED	SEAPORTS	SELENITE	SEROTINE
SCREAMER	SEA POWER	SELENIUM	SERPENTS
SCREECHY	SEAQUAKE	SELFHEAL	SERPULID
SCREENED	SEARCHED	SELF-HELP	SERRANID
SCREENER	SEARCHER	SELFHOOD	SERRATED

SERVABLE	SHANGHAI	SHIRKING	SHROUDED
SERVANTS	SHANTIES	SHIRRING	SHRUGGED
SERVICED	SHANTUNG	SHIRTIER	SHRUNKEN
SERVICES	SHAPABLE	SHIRTING	SHUCKING
SERVINGS	SHARABLE	SHITTIER	SHUDDERS
SERVITOR	SHARE-OUT	SHITTING	SHUDDERY
SESAMOID	SHARP END	SHIVERED	SHUFFLED
SESSIONS	SHARPEST	SHIVERER	SHUFFLER
SETBACKS	SHARPISH	SHIZUOKA	SHUFFLES
SETIFORM	SHARP-SET	SHOCKERS	SHUNNING
SET PIECE	SHAVABLE	SHOCKING	SHUNTERS
SETSCREW	SHAVINGS	SHODDIER	SHUNTING
SETTINGS	SHEADING	SHODDILY	SHUSHING
SETTLERS	SHEARING	SHOEBILL	SHUTDOWN
SETTLING	SHEATHED	SHOEHORN	SHUTTERS
SEVENTHS	SHEBEENS	SHOELACE	SHUTTING
SEVERELY	SHEDABLE	SHOETREE	SHUTTLED
SEVERING	SHEDDING	SHOLAPUR	SHUTTLES
SEVERITY	SHEEPDIP	SHOOTERS	SHYSTERS
SEWERAGE	SHEEPDOG	SHOOTING	SIANGTAN
SEXINESS	SHEEPISH	SHOOT-OUT	SIBERIAN
SEXOLOGY	SHEEREST	SHOPGIRL	SIBILANT
SEX ORGAN	SHEERING	SHOPLIFT	SIBILATE
SEXTANTS	SHEETING	SHOPPERS	SIBLINGS
SEXTUPLE	SHEIKDOM	SHOPPING	SICILIAN
SEXUALLY	SHELDUCK	SHOPTALK	SICKBAYS
SHABBIER	SHELLING	SHORTAGE	SICKBEDS
SHABBILY	SHELTERS	SHORT CUT	SICK CALL
SHACKING	SHELVING	SHORT-DAY	SICKENED
SHACKLED	SHENYANG	SHORTEST	SICKENER
SHACKLER	SHEPHERD	SHORTIES	SICKLIER
SHACKLES	SHERATON	SHORTING	SICKNESS
SHADDOCK	SHERBETS	SHOTGUNS	SICKROOM
SHADIEST	SHERIFFS	SHOULDER	SIDEARMS
SHADINGS	SHIELDED	SHOULDN'T	SIDEBAND
SHADOWED	SHIELDER	SHOUTING	SIDECARS
SHADOWER	SHIELING	SHOVELED	SIDE DISH
SHAFTING	SHIFTIER	SHOVELER	SIDEKICK
SHAGBARK	SHIFTILY	SHOWBOAT	SIDELINE
SHAGGIER	SHIFTING	SHOWCASE	SIDELONG
SHAGGILY	SHIFT KEY	SHOWDOWN	SIDEREAL
SHAGGING	SHILLING	SHOWERED	SIDERITE
SHAGREEN	SHIMMERY	SHOWGIRL	SIDESHOW
SHAKABLE	SHINBONE	SHOWIEST	SIDESLIP
SHAKEOUT	SHINDIGS	SHOWINGS	SIDESMAN
SHAKE-UPS	SHINGLER	SHOW-OFFS	SIDESTEP
SHAKIEST	SHINGLES	SHOWROOM	SIDEWALK
SHALLOON	SHINIEST	SHRAPNEL	SIDEWALL
SHALLOTS	SHINNIED	SHREDDED	SIDEWAYS
SHALLOWS	SHINNING	SHREDDER	SIFTINGS
SHAMABLE	SHIPABLE	SHREWDER	SIGHTING
SHAMBLED	SHIPLOAD	SHREWDLY	SIGHTSEE
SHAMBLES	SHIPMATE	SHREWISH	SIGNALED
SHAMEFUL	SHIPMENT	SHRIEKED	SIGNALLY
SHAMMIES	SHIPPERS	SHRIEKER	SIGNINGS
SHAMMING	SHIPPING	SHRIEVAL	SIGNORAS
SHAMPOOS	SHIPWORM	SHRILLER	SIGNPOST
SHAMROCK	SHIPYARD	SHRIMPER	SILASTIC
SHANDIES	SHIRKERS	SHRINKER	SILENCED

SILENCER	SIXPENCE	SLANGILY	SLOPPILY
SILENCES	SIXPENNY	SLANGING	SLOPPING
SILENTLY	SIXTEENS	SLANTING	SLOPWORK
SILICATE	SIXTIETH	SLAP-BANG	SLOSHING
SILICIDE	SIZEABLE	SLAPDASH	SLOTHFUL
SILICIFY	SIZZLERS	SLAPPING	SLOTTING
SILICONE	SIZZLING	SLASHING	SLOUCHED
SILKIEST	SKELETAL	SLATTERN	SLOUCHER
SILKWORM	SKELETON	SLAVERED	SLOUGHED
SILLABUB	SKEPTICS	SLAVERER	SLOVAKIA
SILLIEST	SKEPTISM	SLAVONIA	SLOVENIA
SILOXANE	SKETCHED	SLAVONIC	SLOVENLY
SILURIAN	SKETCHER	SLEAZIER	SLOWDOWN
SILVERED	SKETCHES	SLEAZILY	SLOWNESS
SILVERER	SKEWBACK	SLEDDING	SLOWWORM
SIMMERED	SKEWBALD	SLEDGING	SLUDGIER
SIMONIAC	SKEWERED	SLEEKEST	SLUGGARD
SIMONIST	SKIDDING	SLEEKING	SLUGGING
SIMPERED	SKIDPANS	SLEEPERS	SLUGGISH
SIMPERER	SKIJORER	SLEEPIER	SLUICING
SIMPLEST	SKI JUMPS	SLEEPILY	SLUMMING
SIMPLIFY	SKI LIFTS	SLEEPING	SLUMPING
SIMPLISM	SKILLETS	SLEETING	SLURPING
SIMULANT	SKIMMERS	SLEEVING	SLURRING
SIMULATE	SKIMMING	SLEIGHER	SLUSHIER
SINAITIC	SKIMPIER	SLICKERS	SLUTTISH
SINAPISM	SKIMPILY	SLICKEST	SMACKERS
SINCIPUT	SKIMPING	SLICKING	SMACKING
SINECURE	SKIN-DEEP	SLIDABLE	SMALL ADS
SINFONIA	SKIN-DIVE	SLIGHTED	SMALLEST
SINFULLY	SKINHEAD	SLIGHTER	SMALL FRY
SINGABLE	SKINLESS	SLIGHTLY	SMALLISH
SINGEING	SKINNIER	SLIMIEST	SMALLPOX
SINGLETS	SKINNING	SLIMMERS	SMALTITE
SINGLING	SKIPJACK	SLIMMEST	SMARMIER
SINGSONG	SKI PLANE	SLIMMING	SMARTEST
SINGULAR	SKI POLES	SLIMNESS	SMARTING
SINISTER	SKIPPERS	SLINGING	SMASHERS
SINKABLE	SKIPPING	SLINKIER	SMASHING
SINKHOLE	SKIRMISH	SLINKILY	SMASH-UPS
SINN FEIN	SKIRTING	SLINKING	SMEARING
SINOLOGY	SKITTISH	SLIPCASE	SMELLIER
SINUSOID	SKITTLES	SLIPKNOT	SMELLING
SIPHONAL	SKIVVIED	SLIPPAGE	SMELTERY
SIPHONED	SKIVVIES	SLIPPERS	SMELTING
SIRENIAN	SKULKING	SLIPPERY	SMIRCHED
SIRLOINS	SKULLCAP	SLIPPIER	SMIRCHER
SIROCCOS	SKYDIVER	SLIPPING	SMIRKING
SISSIEST	SKYLARKS	SLIP ROAD	SMITHERY
SISSYISH	SKYLIGHT	SLIPSHOD	SMITHIES
SISTERLY	SKYLINES	SLIPWAYS	SMOCKING
SISTROID	SKYWARDS	SLITHERY	SMOKABLE
SITARIST	SLACKEST	SLITTING	SMOKIEST
SIT-DOWNS	SLACKING	SLIVERER	SMOLENSK
SITOLOGY	SLAGGING	SLOBBERY	SMOOCHED
SITTINGS	SLAGHEAP	SLOE-EYED	SMOOTHED
SITUATED	SLAKABLE	SLOGGERS	SMOOTHEN
SITZMARK	SLAMMING	SLOGGING	SMOOTHER
SIX-PACKS	SLANDERS	SLOPPIER	SMOOTHIE

SMOOTHLY	SNOOZING	SOLDERER	SORROWED
SMOTHERY	SNORKELS	SOLDIERS	SORROWER
SMOULDER	SNORTERS	SOLDIERY	SORTABLE
SMUDGILY	SNORTING	SOLECISM	SOUCHONG
SMUDGING	SNOTTIER	SOLECIST	SOUFFLES
SMUGGEST	SNOTTILY	SOLEMNLY	SOUGHING
SMUGGLED	SNOWBALL	SOLENOID	SOULLESS
SMUGGLER	SNOWBIRD	SOLIDAGO	SOUNDBOX
SMUGNESS	SNOWDROP	SOLIDARY	SOUNDING
SMUTTIER	SNOWFALL	SOLIDIFY	SOURDINE
SMUTTILY	SNOWIEST	SOLIDITY	SOURNESS
SNACK BAR	SNOWLINE	SOLIHULL	SOURPUSS
SNACKING	SNOWSHED	SOLINGEN	SOUTACHE
SNAFFLED	SNOWSHOE	SOLITARY	SOUTHERN
SNAFFLES	SNUBBING	SOLITUDE	SOUTHING
SNAGGING	SNUFFBOX	SOLOISTS	SOUTHPAW
SNAPBACK	SNUFFERS	SOLONETZ	SOUVENIR
SNAPPERS	SNUFFING	SOLSTICE	SOWBREAD
SNAPPIER	SNUFFLED	SOLUTION	SOYA BEAN
SNAPPILY	SNUFFLER	SOLVABLE	SOY SAUCE
SNAPPING	SNUFFLES	SOLVENCY	SPACE-AGE
SNAPPISH	SNUGGERY	SOLVENTS	SPACE-BAR
SNAPSHOT	SNUGGLED	SOMALIAN	SPACEMAN
SNARLING	SNUGNESS	SOMBRELY	SPACEMEN
SNARL-UPS	SO-AND-SOS	SOMBRERO	SPACIOUS
SNATCHED	SOAPBARK	SOMBROUS	SPANDREL
SNATCHER	SOAPIEST	SOMEBODY	SPANGLED
SNATCHES	SOAPLESS	SOMERSET	SPANGLES
SNAZZIER	SOAPSUDS	SOMETIME	SPANIARD
SNAZZILY	SOAPWORT	SOMEWHAT	SPANIELS
SNEAKERS	SOBERING	SONANTAL	SPANKING
SNEAKIER	SOBRIETY	SONATINA	SPANNERS
SNEAKILY	SOB STORY	SONGBIRD	SPANNING
SNEAKING	SO-CALLED	SONGBOOK	SPARABLE
SNEERING	SOCIABLE	SONGSTER	SPARERIB
SNEEZING	SOCIABLY	SON-IN-LAW	SPARKING
SNICKERS	SOCIALLY	SONOBUOY	SPARKLED
SNICKING	SOCIETAL	SONORANT	SPARKLER
SNIFFING	SOCRATIC	SONORITY	SPARKLES
SNIFFLED	SODALITE	SONOROUS	SPARLING
SNIFFLER	SODAMIDE	SOOTHING	SPARRING
SNIFFLES	SODOMITE	SOOTHSAY	SPARROWS
SNIFTERS	SOFTBALL	SOOTIEST	SPARSELY
SNIGGERS	SOFT COPY	SOPHISMS	SPARSEST
SNIGGLER	SOFTENED	SOPHISTS	SPASTICS
SNIPPETS	SOFTENER	SOPPIEST	SPATTERS
SNIPPILY	SOFTNESS	SOPRANOS	SPATULAR
SNIPPING	SOFT SELL	SORBITOL	SPATULAS
SNITCHED	SOFT SOAP	SORBONNE	SPAWNING
SNITCHES	SOFT SPOT	SORCERER	SPEAKERS
SNIVELED	SOFTWARE	SORDIDLY	SPEAKING
SNIVELLY	SOFTWOOD	SOREDIUM	SPEARING
SNOBBERY	SOGGIEST	SORENESS	SPECIALS
SNOBBISH	SOJOURNS	SORICINE	SPECIFIC
SNOGGING	SOLACING	SOROCABA	SPECIMEN
SNOOPERS	SOLANDER	SORORATE	SPECIOUS
SNOOPING	SOLARIUM	SORORITY	SPECKLED
SNOOTIER	SOLARIZE	SORPTION	SPECKLES
SNOOTILY	SOLDERED	SORRIEST	SPECTATE

SPECTRAL	SPLITTER	SPUNKILY	STAGNANT
SPECTRES	SPLODGES	SPURIOUS	STAGNATE
SPECTRUM	SPLOSHED	SPURNING	STAINING
SPECULAR	SPLOSHES	SPURRING	STAIRWAY
SPECULUM	SPLURGED	SPURTING	STALKERS
SPEECHES	SPLURGES	SPUTTERS	STALKILY
SPEEDIER	SPLUTTER	SPYGLASS	STALKING
SPEEDILY	SPOILAGE	SQUABBLE	STALLING
SPEEDING	SPOILERS	SQUAD CAR	STALLION
SPEEDWAY	SPOILING	SQUADRON	STALWART
SPELAEAN	SPOLIATE	SQUALENE	STAMFORD
SPELLING	SPONDAIC	SQUALLED	STAMINAL
SPENDERS	SPONDEES	SQUALLER	STAMMERS
SPENDING	SPONGERS	SQUAMATE	STAMPEDE
SPERMARY	SPONGIER	SQUAMOUS	STAMPING
SPERMINE	SPONGILY	SQUANDER	STANCHED
SPERMOUS	SPONGING	SQUARELY	STANCHER
SPHAGNUM	SPONSION	SQUAREST	STANDARD
SPHENOID	SPONSORS	SQUARING	STANDBYS
SPHERICS	SPOOKIER	SQUARISH	STANDING
SPHEROID	SPOOKILY	SQUASHED	STAND-INS
SPHERULE	SPOOKING	SQUASHER	STANDISH
SPHINXES	SPOOKISH	SQUASHES	STANNARY
SPHYGMIC	SPOON-FED	SQUATTED	STANNITE
SPICCATO	SPOONFUL	SQUATTER	STANNOUS
SPICIEST	SPOONING	SQUAWKED	STANZAIC
SPICULUM	SPORADIC	SQUAWKER	STAPELIA
SPIKELET	SPORRANS	SQUEAKED	STAPLERS
SPIKIEST	SPORTFUL	SQUEAKER	STAPLING
SPILLAGE	SPORTIER	SQUEALED	STARCHED
SPILLING	SPORTILY	SQUEALER	STARCHER
SPILLWAY	SPORTING	SQUEEGEE	STARCHES
SPINDLES	SPORTIVE	SQUEEZED	STARDUST
SPINIFEX	SPOTLESS	SQUEEZER	STARFISH
SPINNERS	SPOTTERS	SQUEEZES	STARGAZE
SPINNEYS	SPOTTIER	SQUELCHY	STARKERS
SPINNING	SPOTTILY	SQUIGGLE	STARKEST
SPIN-OFFS	SPOTTING	SQUIGGLY	STARLESS
SPINSTER	SPOT-WELD	SQUINTED	STARLETS
SPIRACLE	SPOUTERS	SQUINTER	STARLIKE
SPIRALED	SPOUTING	SQUIRMED	STARLING
SPIRITED	SPRAINED	SQUIRMER	STARRIER
SPITEFUL	SPRAWLED	SQUIRREL	STARRILY
SPITFIRE	SPRAWLER	SQUIRTED	STARRING
SPITTING	SPRAYERS	SQUIRTER	STAR SIGN
SPITTOON	SPRAY GUN	SQUISHED	STARTERS
SPLASHED	SPRAYING	SRI LANKA	STARTING
SPLASHER	SPREADER	SRINAGAR	STARTLED
SPLATTED	SPRIGGER	STABBERS	STARTLER
SPLATTER	SPRINGER	STABBING	STARVING
SPLAYING	SPRINKLE	STABLING	STAR WARS
SPLENDID	SPRINTED	STACCATO	STARWORT
SPLENIAL	SPRINTER	STACKING	STASHING
SPLENIUS	SPROCKET	STADIUMS	STATABLE
SPLICERS	SPROUTED	STAFFING	STATICAL
SPLICING	SPRUCELY	STAFFMAN	STATIONS
SPLINTER	SPRUCING	STAGGARD	STATUARY
SPLIT END	SPRYNESS	STAGGERS	STATURES
SPLIT PEA	SPUNKIER	STAGINGS	STATUSES

STATUTES	STILLING	STRAGGLE	STUBBORN
STAYSAIL	STIMULUS	STRAGGLY	STUCCOED
STEADIED	STINGERS	STRAIGHT	STUDBOOK
STEADIER	STINGIER	STRAINED	STUDDING
STEADILY	STINGILY	STRAINER	STUDENTS
STEALING	STINGING	STRAITEN	STUDIOUS
STEALTHY	STINGRAY	STRANDED	STUDWORK
STEAMERS	STINKERS	STRANGER	STUDYING
STEAMIER	STINKING	STRANGLE	STUFFIER
STEAMILY	STINTING	STRAPPED	STUFFILY
STEAMING	STIPENDS	STRATEGY	STUFFING
STEAPSIN	STIPPLED	STRATIFY	STULTIFY
STEARATE	STIPPLER	STRAW MAN	STUMBLED
STEATITE	STIPULAR	STRAW MEN	STUMBLER
STEELIER	STIRRERS	STRAYING	STUMBLES
STEELING	STIRRING	STREAKED	STUMPIER
STEEPEST	STIRRUPS	STREAKER	STUMPING
STEEPING	STITCHED	STREAMED	STUNNERS
STEEPLES	STITCHER	STREAMER	STUNNING
STEERAGE	STITCHES	STRENGTH	STUNTING
STEERING	STOCKADE	STRESSED	STUNT MAN
STEINBOK	STOCKCAR	STRESSES	STUNT MEN
STELLATE	STOCKIER	STRETCHY	STUPIDER
STELLIFY	STOCKILY	STREUSEL	STUPIDLY
STELLITE	STOCKING	STREWING	STURDIER
STEMHEAD	STOCKIST	STRIATED	STURDILY
STEMMING	STOCKMAN	STRICKEN	STURGEON
STENCHES	STOCKMEN	STRICKLE	STUTTERS
STENCILS	STOCKPOT	STRICTER	STYLISTS
STEN GUNS	STOCKTON	STRICTLY	STYLIZED
STENOSIS	STODGIER	STRIDDEN	STYLIZER
STENOTIC	STODGILY	STRIDENT	STYLUSES
STEPPING	STOICISM	STRIGOSE	STYMYING
STEPWISE	STOLIDLY	STRIKERS	STYPTICS
STERIGMA	STOMACHS	STRIKING	SUBACUTE
STERLING	STOMACHY	STRINGER	SUBAGENT
STERNEST	STOMATAL	STRIPIER	SUBCLASS
STERNSON	STOMATIC	STRIPPED	SUBDUING
STERNUMS	STOMPING	STRIPPER	SUBERIZE
STERNWAY	STONABLE	STROBILA	SUBEROSE
STEROIDS	STONE AGE	STROKING	SUBFLOOR
STETSONS	STONEFLY	STROLLED	SUBGENUS
STEWARDS	STONIEST	STROLLER	SUBGROUP
STIBNITE	STOOPING	STRONGER	SUBHUMAN
STICKERS	STOPCOCK	STRONGLY	SUBJECTS
STICKFUL	STOPGAPS	STROPHES	SUBLEASE
STICKIER	STOPOVER	STROPHIC	SUBMERGE
STICKILY	STOPPAGE	STRUDELS	SUBORDER
STICKING	STOPPERS	STRUGGLE	SUBORNED
STICKLER	STOPPING	STRUMMED	SUBORNER
STICKPIN	STORABLE	STRUMMER	SUBOXIDE
STICK-UPS	STOREYED	STRUMPET	SUBPLOTS
STIFFEST	STORMIER	STRUNG-UP	SUBPOENA
STIFLING	STORMILY	STRUTTED	SUBSERVE
STIGMATA	STORMING	STRUTTER	SUBSHRUB
STILBENE	STOUTEST	STUBBIER	SUBSIDED
STILBITE	STOWAWAY	STUBBILY	SUBSIDER
STILETTO	STRADDLE	STUBBING	SUBSOLAR
STILLEST	STRAFING	STUBBLED	SUBSONIC

SUBSTAGE	SUNGLASS	SURVEYED	SWISHEST
SUBSUMED	SUNLAMPS	SURVEYOR	SWISHING
SUBTITLE	SUNLIGHT	SURVIVAL	SWITCHED
SUBTLEST	SUNNIEST	SURVIVED	SWITCHER
SUBTLETY	SUNRISES	SURVIVOR	SWITCHES
SUBTONIC	SUNROOFS	SUSPECTS	SWIVELED
SUBTOTAL	SUNSHADE	SUSPENSE	SWOONING
SUBTRACT	SUNSHINE	SUTURING	SWOOPING
SUBULATE	SUNSHINY	SUZERAIN	SWOPPING
SUBURBAN	SUNSPOTS	SVALBARD	SWOTTING
SUBURBIA	SUNTRAPS	SWABBING	SYBARITE
SUCCINCT	SUN VISOR	SWADDLED	SYCAMINE
SUCCINIC	SUNWARDS	SWALLOWS	SYCAMORE
SUCCUBUS	SUPERBLY	SWAMPING	SYCONIUM
SUCHLIKE	SUPEREGO	SWANKIER	SYENITIC
SUCKLING	SUPERFIX	SWANKILY	SYLLABIC
SUDANESE	SUPERIOR	SWANKING	SYLLABLE
SUDATORY	SUPERMAN	SWANNERY	SYLLABUB
SUDDENLY	SUPERMEN	SWANNING	SYLLABUS
SUFFERED	SUPERNAL	SWANSKIN	SYLVATIC
SUFFERER	SUPERSEX	SWANSONG	SYMBIONT
SUFFICED	SUPERTAX	SWAP MEET	SYMBOLIC
SUFFICER	SUPINATE	SWAPPING	SYMMETRY
SUFFIXAL	SUPINELY	SWARMING	SYMPATHY
SUFFIXES	SUPPLANT	SWASTIKA	SYMPHILE
SUFFRAGE	SUPPLEST	SWATCHES	SYMPHONY
SUFFUSED	SUPPLIED	SWATHING	SYMPOSIA
SUGARING	SUPPLIER	SWATTERS	SYMPTOMS
SUICIDAL	SUPPLIES	SWATTING	SYNAPSIS
SUICIDES	SUPPORTS	SWAYABLE	SYNAPTIC
SUITABLE	SUPPOSED	SWAY-BACK	SYNARCHY
SUITABLY	SUPPOSER	SWEARING	SYNCARPY
SUITCASE	SUPPRESS	SWEATBOX	SYNCLINE
SULKIEST	SUPREMOS	SWEATERS	SYNCOPIC
SULLENER	SURABAYA	SWEATIER	SYNDESIS
SULLENLY	SURCOATS	SWEATILY	SYNDETIC
SULLYING	SUREFIRE	SWEATING	SYNDETON
SULPHATE	SURENESS	SWEEPERS	SYNDICAL
SULPHIDE	SURETIES	SWEEPING	SYNDROME
SULPHITE	SURFABLE	SWEETEST	SYNERGIC
SULPHONE	SURFACED	SWEETIES	SYNGAMIC
SULTANAS	SURFACER	SWEET PEA	SYNONYMS
SULTANIC	SURFACES	SWEETSOP	SYNONYMY
SULTRIER	SURFBIRD	SWELLING	SYNOPSES
SULTRILY	SURFBOAT	SWERVING	SYNOPSIS
SUMATRAN	SURFLIKE	SWIFTEST	SYNOPTIC
SUMMERED	SURGEONS	SWIGGING	SYNOVIAL
SUMMITAL	SURGICAL	SWILLING	SYNTONIC
SUMMONED	SURICATE	SWIMMERS	SYPHILIS
SUM TOTAL	SURLIEST	SWIMMING	SYPHONED
SUNBAKED	SURMISED	SWIMSUIT	SYRACUSE
SUNBATHE	SURMISER	SWINDLED	SYRINGED
SUNBEAMS	SURMISES	SWINDLER	SYRINGES
SUNBELTS	SURMOUNT	SWINDLES	SYSTEMIC
SUNBURNT	SURNAMES	SWINEPOX	SYSTOLIC
SUNBURST	SURPLICE	SWINGERS	SYZYGIAL
SUNDERED	SURPRINT	SWINGING	SZCZECIN
SUNDIALS	SURPRISE	SWIRLING	SZECHWAN
SUNDRIES	SURROUND		

T	TANGENTS	TAXPAYER	TENDRILS
TABLEAUS	TANGIBLE	TEABERRY	TENEFIFE
TABLEAUX	TANGIBLY	TEA BREAK	TENEMENT
TABLEMAT	TANGIEST	TEA CADDY	TENESMIC
TABLOIDS	TANGLING	TEACAKES	TENESMUS
TABULATE	TANGOING	TEACHERS	TENORITE
TACITURN	TANGOIST	TEA CHEST	TENOTOMY
TACKIEST	TANGSHAN	TEACHING	TENSED UP
TACKLING	TANKARDS	TEACH-INS	TENSIBLE
TACONITE	TANKED UP	TEA CLOTH	TENSIONS
TACTICAL	TANTALIC	TEAHOUSE	TENTACLE
TACTLESS	TANTALUM	TEA-MAKER	TENURIAL
TADPOLES	TANTALUS	TEAM-MATE	TEOCALLI
TAFFRAIL	TANTRUMS	TEAMSTER	TEOSINTE
TAGANROG	TANZANIA	TEAMWORK	TEPHRITE
TAGMEMIC	TAP DANCE	TEA PARTY	TEPIDITY
TAHITIAN	TAPE DECK	TEARABLE	TERATISM
TAICHUNG	TAPERING	TEARAWAY	TERATOID
TAILBACK	TAPESTRY	TEARDROP	TERATOMA
TAILCOAT	TAPEWORM	TEAROOMS	TEREBENE
TAIL ENDS	TAPPABLE	TEASPOON	TERESINA
TAILGATE	TAPROOTS	TEA TOWEL	TERMINAL
TAILINGS	TARBOOSH	TECHNICS	TERMINUS
TAILLESS	TARDIEST	TECTONIC	TERMITES
TAILORED	TARGETED	TEDDY BOY	TERMITIC
TAIL PIPE	TARLATAN	TEENAGER	TERMLESS
TAILRACE	TARRAGON	TEE SHIRT	TERPENIC
TAILSKID	TARRYING	TEESSIDE	TERRACES
TAILSPIN	TARTARIC	TEETERED	TERRAINS
TAILWIND	TARTNESS	TEETHING	TERRAPIN
TAINTING	TARTRATE	TEETOTAL	TERRAZZO
TAJ MAHAL	TASHKENT	TEGMINAL	TERRIBLE
TAKEAWAY	TASKWORK	TELECAST	TERRIBLY
TAKEOFFS	TASMANIA	TELEGONY	TERRIERS
TAKEOUTS	TASSELED	TELEGRAM	TERRIFIC
TAKEOVER	TASSELLY	TELEMARK	TERTIARY
TAKORADI	TASTABLE	TELEPLAY	TERYLENE
TALAPOIN	TASTE BUD	TELETEXT	TERZETTO
TALENTED	TASTEFUL	TELETYPE	TESSERAL
TALESMAN	TASTIEST	TELEVISE	TESTABLE
TALISMAN	TATARIAN	TELEXING	TESTATOR
TALKABLE	TATTERED	TELLABLE	TEST BANS
TALK SHOW	TATTIEST	TELLTALE	TEST CARD
TALLBOYS	TATTLERS	TELLURIC	TEST CASE
TALLNESS	TATTLING	TELSONIC	TESTICLE
TALLYING	TATTOOED	TEMERITY	TESTIEST
TALLYMAN	TATTOOER	TEMPERED	TEST TUBE
TALMUDIC	TAUNTING	TEMPERER	TETANIZE
TAMANDUA	TAUTENED	TEMPESTS	TETCHIER
TAMARACK	TAUTNESS	TEMPLATE	TETCHILY
TAMARIND	TAUTOMER	TEMPORAL	TETHERED
TAMARISK	TAUTONYM	TEMPTERS	TETRACID
TAMBOURS	TAVERNER	TEMPTING	TETRAPOD
TAMEABLE	TAWDRILY	TENACITY	TETRARCH
TAMENESS	TAXATION	TENANTRY	TEUTONIC
TAMPERED	TAX HAVEN	TENDENCY	TEXTBOOK
TAMPERER	TAXINGLY	TENDERED	TEXTILES
TANDOORI	TAXI RANK	TENDERER	TEXTUARY
TANGENCY	TAXONOMY	TENDERLY	TEXTURAL

TEXTURES	THOUGHTS	TILLICUM	TOENAILS
THAILAND	THOUSAND	TIMBRELS	TOGETHER
THALAMIC	THRALDOM	TIMBUKTU	TOGOLESE
THALAMUS	THRASHED	TIME BOMB	TOILETRY
THALLIUM	THRASHER	TIMECARD	TOILETTE
THALLOID	THREADED	TIME LAGS	TOILSOME
THALLOUS	THREADER	TIMELESS	TOKENISM
THANKFUL	THREATEN	TIMELIER	TOLERANT
THANKING	THREE-PLY	TIMEWORK	TOLERATE
THANK YOU	THRENODY	TIMEWORN	TOLIDINE
THATCHED	THRESHED	TIME ZONE	TOLL-FREE
THATCHER	THRESHER	TIMIDITY	TOLLGATE
THATCHES	THRESHES	TIMOROUS	TOMAHAWK
THEARCHY	THRILLED	TINCTURE	TOMATOES
THEATRES	THRILLER	TINGLING	TOMBLIKE
THEBAINE	THRIVING	TINKERED	TOMENTUM
THEISTIC	THROBBED	TINKERER	TOMMY GUN
THEMATIC	THROMBIN	TINKLING	TOMMYROT
THEOCRAT	THROMBUS	TINNIEST	TOMORROW
THEOLOGY	THRONGED	TINNITUS	TONALITY
THEOREMS	THROTTLE	TINPLATE	TONE-DEAF
THEORIES	THROWING	TINSELLY	TONELESS
THEORIST	THROW-INS	TINSMITH	TONE POEM
THEORIZE	THRUMMED	TINTACKS	TONICITY
THEREMIN	THRUMMER	TIPPABLE	TONNAGES
THERMALS	THRUSHES	TIPPLERS	TONSURES
THERMION	THRUSTER	TIPSIEST	TOOTHIER
THERMITE	THRUWAYS	TIPSTAFF	TOOTHILY
THEROPOD	THUDDING	TIPSTERS	TOOTLING
THESPIAN	THUGGERY	TIRELESS	TOOTSIES
THESSALY	THUMBING	TIRESOME	TOPARCHY
THEURGIC	THUMBNUT	TITANATE	TOP BRASS
THIAMINE	THUMPING	TITANISM	TOPCOATS
THIAZINE	THUNDERS	TITANITE	TOP-DRESS
THIAZOLE	THUNDERY	TITANIUM	TOP-HEAVY
THICKEST	THURIBLE	TITANOUS	TOPKNOTS
THICKETS	THURIFER	TITCHIER	TOP-LEVEL
THICKSET	THURSDAY	TITHABLE	TOP-NOTCH
THIEVERY	THWACKED	TITIVATE	TOPOLOGY
THIEVING	THWACKER	TITMOUSE	TOPONYMY
THIEVISH	THWARTED	TITOGRAD	TOPOTYPE
THIMBLES	THWARTER	TITTERED	TOPPINGS
THIN-FILM	THYROIDS	TITTERER	TOPPLING
THINKING	THYRSOID	TLAXCALA	TOP-SHELL
THINNESS	TIA MARIA	TOADFISH	TORCHERE
THINNEST	TICKETED	TOADFLAX	TORCHIER
THINNING	TICKLING	TOADYING	TOREADOR
THIONINE	TICKLISH	TOADYISM	TOREUTIC
THIOUREA	TICKTACK	TO-AND-FRO	TORMENTS
THIRTEEN	TICKTOCK	TOASTERS	TORNADIC
THIRTIES	TIDDLERS	TOASTING	TORNADOS
THISTLES	TIDEMARK	TOBACCOS	TOROIDAL
THONBURI	TIDEWAYS	TOBOGGAN	TORPIDLY
THORACES	TIDINESS	TOBY JUGS	TORQUATE
THORACIC	TIE-DYING	TOCCATAS	TORRANCE
THORAXES	TIENTSIN	TOCOLOGY	TORRENTS
THORNIER	TIGHTEST	TODDLERS	TORRIDLY
THORNILY	TILEFISH	TODDLING	TORTILLA
THOROUGH	TILLABLE	TOEHOLDS	TORTIOUS

TORTOISE	TRAINERS	TRENCHES	TRIPODAL
TORTUOUS	TRAINING	TRENDIER	TRIPOSES
TORTURED	TRAIN SET	TRENDIES	TRIPPERS
TORTURER	TRAIPSED	TRENDILY	TRIPPING
TORTURES	TRAITORS	TREPHINE	TRIPTANE
TOTALING	TRAMLINE	TRESPASS	TRIPTYCH
TOTALITY	TRAMMELS	TRESSURE	TRIPWIRE
TOTALIZE	TRAMPING	TRESTLES	TRIREMES
TOTALLED	TRAMPLED	TRIADISM	TRISOMIC
TOTE BAGS	TRAMPLER	TRIAL RUN	TRISTICH
TOTEMISM	TRANNIES	TRIANGLE	TRITICUM
TOTEMIST	TRANQUIL	TRIARCHY	TRIUMPHS
TOTTERED	TRANSACT	TRIASSIC	TRIUNITY
TOTTERER	TRANSECT	TRIAXIAL	TROCHAIC
TOUCHIER	TRANSEPT	TRIAZINE	TROCHEES
TOUCHILY	TRANSFER	TRIAZOLE	TROCHLEA
TOUCHING	TRANSFIX	TRIBADIC	TROCHOID
TOUGHEST	TRANSITS	TRIBASIC	TROLLEYS
TOULOUSE	TRANSKEI	TRIBRACH	TROLLING
TOURAINE	TRANSMIT	TRIBUNAL	TROLLOPS
TOURISTS	TRANSOMS	TRIBUNES	TROMBONE
TOURISTY	TRANSUDE	TRIBUTES	TROOPERS
TOURNEYS	TRAPDOOR	TRICHINA	TROOPING
TOUSLING	TRAPEZES	TRICHITE	TROPHIES
TOWELING	TRAPEZIA	TRICHOID	TROPICAL
TOWELLED	TRAPPERS	TRICHOME	TROTLINE
TOWERING	TRAPPING	TRICKERY	TROTTERS
TOWN HALL	TRAPPIST	TRICKIER	TROTTING
TOWNSHIP	TRAPUNTO	TRICKILY	TROUBLED
TOWNSMAN	TRASHCAN	TRICKING	TROUBLER
TOWNSMEN	TRASHIER	TRICKLED	TROUBLES
TOWPATHS	TRASHILY	TRICTRAC	TROUNCED
TOWROPES	TRASHING	TRICYCLE	TROUPERS
TOXAEMIA	TRAVELED	TRIDENTS	TROUPIAL
TOXAEMIC	TRAVERSE	TRIFLING	TROUSERS
TOXICANT	TRAVESTY	TRIFOCAL	TRUCKERS
TOXICITY	TRAWLERS	TRIGGERS	TRUCKING
TRACHEAL	TRAWLING	TRIGLYPH	TRUCKLED
TRACHEAS	TREADING	TRIGONAL	TRUDGING
TRACHEID	TREADLER	TRIGRAPH	TRUE-BLUE
TRACHOMA	TREADLES	TRILBIES	TRUEBORN
TRACHYTE	TREASURE	TRILEMMA	TRUE-LIFE
TRACINGS	TREASURY	TRILLING	TRUELOVE
TRACKING	TREATIES	TRILLION	TRUENESS
TRACTATE	TREATING	TRILLIUM	TRUFFLES
TRACTILE	TREATISE	TRIMARAN	TRUISTIC
TRACTION	TREATIZE	TRIMETER	TRUJILLO
TRACTIVE	TREBLING	TRIMMERS	TRUMPERY
TRACTORS	TREE FERN	TRIMMEST	TRUMPETS
TRADABLE	TREELESS	TRIMMING	TRUMPING
TRADE GAP	TREELINE	TRIMNESS	TRUNCATE
TRADE-OFF	TREENAIL	TRIMORPH	TRUNDLED
TRAD JAZZ	TREFOILS	TRINIDAD	TRUNNION
TRADUCED	TREKKING	TRINKETS	TRUSSING
TRADUCER	TREMBLED	TRIOXIDE	TRUSTEES
TRAGOPAN	TREMBLER	TRIPLANE	TRUSTFUL
TRAILERS	TREMBLES	TRIPLETS	TRUSTIER
TRAILING	TREMOLOS	TRIPLING	TRUSTIES
TRAINEES	TRENCHER	TRIPLOID	TRUSTILY

TRUSTING	TUTELARY	TZARINAS	UNDERLIE
TRUTHFUL	TUTORAGE		UNDERPAY
TSARINAS	TUTORIAL	U	UNDERPIN
TSINGHAI	TUTORING	UBIQUITY	UNDERSEA
TSINGTAO	TV DINNER	UBI SUPRA	UNDERSET
T-SQUARES	TWADDLER	UGLIFIER	UNDERTOW
TSUSHIMA	TWANGING	UGLINESS	UNDULANT
TUBBIEST	TWEAKING	UIGURIAN	UNDULATE
TUBELESS	TWEETERS	UKULELES	UNEARNED
TUBERCLE	TWEETING	ULCERATE	UNEASIER
TUBEROSE	TWEEZERS	ULCEROUS	UNEASILY
TUBEROUS	TWELFTHS	ULTERIOR	UNENDING
TUBIFORM	TWELVEMO	ULTIMATA	UNERRING
TUBULATE	TWENTIES	ULTIMATE	UNEVENLY
TUBULOUS	TWIDDLED	ULTRAISM	UNFAIRER
TUCKERED	TWIDDLER	ULTRAIST	UNFAIRLY
TUCOTUCO	TWIDDLES	UMBONATE	UNFASTEN
TUESDAYS	TWIGGING	UMBRAGES	UNFETTER
TUG-OF-WAR	TWILIGHT	UMBRELLA	UNFILIAL
TUMBLERS	TWIN BEDS	UMPIRING	UNFOLDED
TUMBLING	TWINKLED	UNABATED	UNFOLDER
TUMBRELS	TWINKLER	UNAWARES	UNFORCED
TUMIDITY	TWINNING	UNBACKED	UNFORMED
TUMOROUS	TWIN SETS	UNBARRED	UNFREEZE
TUMULOSE	TWIRLERS	UNBEATEN	UNFURLED
TUNELESS	TWIRLING	UNBELIEF	UNGAINLY
TUNGSTEN	TWISTERS	UNBIASED	UNGUENTS
TUNGSTIC	TWISTIER	UNBIDDEN	UNGULATE
TUNGUSIC	TWISTING	UNBODIED	UNHANDED
TUNICATE	TWITCHED	UNBOLTED	UNHINGED
TUNISIAN	TWITCHER	UNBRIDLE	UNHORSED
TUNNELED	TWITCHES	UNBROKEN	UNIATISM
TUNNELER	TWITTERS	UNBUCKLE	UNIAXIAL
TUPPENCE	TWITTERY	UNBURDEN	UNICORNS
TUPPENNY	TWITTING	UNBUTTON	UNICYCLE
TURBANED	TWO-EDGED	UNCHASTE	UNIFORMS
TURBINES	TWOFACED	UNCHURCH	UNIFYING
TURBOCAR	TWOPENCE	UNCIFORM	UNIONISM
TURBOFAN	TWOPENNY	UNCINATE	UNIONIST
TURBOJET	TWO-PHASE	UNCLENCH	UNIONIZE
TURGIDLY	TWO-PIECE	UNCLE SAM	UNIPOLAR
TURKOMAN	TWO-SIDED	UNCLE TOM	UNIQUELY
TURMERIC	TWOSOMES	UNCLOTHE	UNITEDLY
TURNABLE	TWO-STEPS	UNCOINED	UNIVALVE
TURNCOAT	TWO-TIMED	UNCOMMON	UNIVERSE
TURNCOCK	TWO-TIMER	UNCORKED	UNIVOCAL
TURNINGS	TYMPANIC	UNCOUPLE	UNKENNEL
TURNKEYS	TYMPANUM	UNCTUOUS	UNKINDER
TURN-OFFS	TYNESIDE	UNDAMPED	UNKINDLY
TURNOUTS	TYPECAST	UNDERACT	UNKNOWNS
TURNOVER	TYPEFACE	UNDERAGE	UNLAWFUL
TURNPIKE	TYPE-HIGH	UNDERARM	UNLIKELY
TURNSOLE	TYPHONIC	UNDERBID	UNLIMBER
TURRETED	TYPHOONS	UNDERBUY	UNLISTED
TUSKLIKE	TYPIFIED	UNDERCUT	UNLOADED
TUSSLING	TYPIFIER	UNDERDOG	UNLOADER
TUSSOCKS	TYPOLOGY	UNDERFUR	UNLOCKED
TUSSOCKY	TYRAMINE	UNDERLAY	UNLOOSED
TUTELAGE	TYROLESE	UNDERLET	UNLOOSEN

UNLOVELY	UPDATING	UVULITIS	VARIFORM
UNMANNED	UPENDING	UXORIOUS	VARIOLAR
UNMARKED	UPGRADED		VARIORUM
UNMASKED	UPGRADER		VARISTOR
UNMASKER	UPGROWTH	V	VARITYPE
UNMUZZLE	UPHEAVAL	VACANTLY	VARMINTS
UNNERVED	UPHOLDER	VACATING	VASCULAR
UNOPENED	UPLIFTED	VACATION	VASCULUM
UNPACKED	UPLIFTER	VACCINAL	VASELINE
UNPACKER	UP-MARKET	VACCINES	VASTERAS
UNPEOPLE	UPPERCUT	VACCINIA	VASTNESS
UNPICKED	UPRAISER	VACUOLAR	VAUCLUSE
UNPLACED	UPRISING	VACUUMED	VAULTERS
UNPOLLED	UPROOTED	VAGABOND	VAULTING
UNPRICED	UPROOTER	VAGARIES	VAUNTING
UNPROVEN	UPSETTER	VAGINATE	VEGETATE
UNREASON	UPSTAGED	VAGOTOMY	VEHEMENT
UNRIDDLE	UPSTAIRS	VAGRANCY	VEHICLES
UNRIFLED	UPSTARTS	VAGRANTS	VEILEDLY
UNROLLED	UPSTREAM	VAINNESS	VELARIZE
UNSADDLE	UPSTROKE	VALANCED	VELOCITY
UNSEATED	UPSURGES	VALANCES	VENALITY
UNSEEDED	UPSWINGS	VAL-D'OISE	VENATION
UNSEEING	UPTHRUST	VALENCIA	VENDETTA
UNSEEMLY	UP-TO-DATE	VALERIAN	VENDIBLE
UNSETTLE	UPTURNED	VALIANCE	VENEERED
UNSHAPEN	URALITIC	VALIDATE	VENEERER
UNSHAVEN	URANITIC	VALIDITY	VENERATE
UNSOCIAL	URANYLIC	VALLETTA	VENEREAL
UNSPOKEN	URBANELY	VALORIZE	VENETIAN
UNSTABLE	URBANITY	VALOROUS	VENGEFUL
UNSTEADY	URBANIZE	VALUABLE	VENOMOUS
UNSTRING	URETERAL	VALUATOR	VENOSITY
UNSUITED	URETHANE	VALVULAR	VENTURED
UNSWATHE	URETHRAL	VAMBRACE	VENTURER
UNTANGLE	URETHRAS	VAMOOSED	VENTURES
UNTAPPED	URGENTLY	VAMPIRES	VENUSIAN
UNTAUGHT	URGINGLY	VAMPIRIC	VERACITY
UNTHREAD	URINATED	VANADATE	VERACRUZ
UNTIDILY	URNFIELD	VANADIUM	VERANDAS
UNTIMELY	UROCHORD	VANADOUS	VERBALLY
UNTIRING	UROLOGIC	VANGUARD	VERBATIM
UNTITLED	UROPODAL	VANILLIC	VERBIAGE
UNTOWARD	UROSCOPY	VANILLIN	VERBOTEN
UNTRUTHS	UROSTYLE	VANISHED	VERDANCY
UNUSABLE	URSULINE	VANISHER	VERDICTS
UNVALUED	URTICATE	VANQUISH	VERIFIED
UNVEILED	URUSHIOL	VAPIDITY	VERIFIER
UNVERSED	USEFULLY	VAPORIZE	VERISTIC
UNVOICED	USHERING	VAPOROUS	VERITIES
UNWASHED	USUFRUCT	VAPOURER	VERJUICE
UNWIELDY	USURIOUS	VARACTOR	VERLIGTE
UNWINDER	USURPERS	VARANASI	VERMOUTH
UNWISHED	USURPING	VARIABLE	VERONESE
UNWONTED	UTENSILS	VARIABLY	VERONICA
UNWORTHY	UTERUSES	VARIANCE	VERRUCAE
UNZIPPED	UTILIZED	VARIANTS	VERRUCAS
UP-ANCHOR	UTILIZER	VARICOSE	VERSICLE
UPCOMING	UTTERING	VARIETAL	VERSIONS

VERTEBRA	VINEYARD	VOICEFUL	WALLOPER
VERTEXES	VINNITSA	VOIDABLE	WALLOWED
VERTICAL	VINOSITY	VOIDANCE	WALLOWER
VERTICES	VINTAGER	VOLATILE	WALRUSES
VERTICIL	VINTAGES	VOLCANIC	WALTZING
VESICANT	VINTNERS	VOLCANOS	WANDERED
VESICATE	VIOLABLE	VOLITION	WANDERER
VESICLES	VIOLATED	VOLITIVE	WANDEROO
VESPERAL	VIOLATOR	VOLLEYED	WANGLING
VESPIARY	VIOLENCE	VOLLEYER	WANTONLY
VESTIGES	VIPERINE	VOLPLANE	WARANGAL
VESTMENT	VIPEROUS	VOLTAGES	WARBLERS
VESTRIES	VIRAGOES	VOLTAISM	WARBLING
VESTURAL	VIRGINAL	VOLUTION	WAR CRIES
VESUVIAN	VIRGINIA	VOLVULUS	WAR CRIME
VESUVIUS	VIRIDIAN	VOMERINE	WAR DANCE
VETERANS	VIRIDITY	VOMITING	WARDENRY
VEXATION	VIRILISM	VOMITIVE	WARDRESS
VEXILLUM	VIRILITY	VOMITORY	WARDROBE
VEXINGLY	VIROLOGY	VORACITY	WARDROOM
VIADUCTS	VIRTUOSI	VORONEZH	WARDSHIP
VIA MEDIA	VIRTUOSO	VORTEXES	WARFARIN
VIATICUM	VIRTUOUS	VORTICAL	WAR GAMES
VIBRANCY	VIRULENT	VORTICES	WARHEADS
VIBRATED	VISCACHA	VOTARESS	WARHORSE
VIBRATOR	VISCERAL	VOTARIES	WARINESS
VIBRATOS	VISCOUNT	VOTARIST	WARLOCKS
VIBRIOID	VISIONAL	VOUCHERS	WARLORDS
VIBRISSA	VISITANT	VOUCHING	WARMNESS
VIBRONIC	VISITING	VOUSSOIR	WARNINGS
VIBURNUM	VISITORS	VOWELIZE	WAR PAINT
VICARAGE	VISUALLY	VOYAGERS	WARPATHS
VICARIAL	VITALISM	VOYAGING	WARPLANE
VICELIKE	VITALIST	VULGARLY	WARRANTS
VICENARY	VITALITY	VULTURES	WARRANTY
VICEROYS	VITALIZE	VULVITIS	WARRIORS
VICINITY	VITAMINS		WARSHIPS
VICTORIA	VITELLIN	W	WARTHOGS
VICTUALS	VITIABLE	WADDLING	WASHABLE
VIDEOING	VITIATED	WAFFLING	WASHBOWL
VIENNESE	VITIATOR	WAGERING	WASHDAYS
VIETCONG	VITILIGO	WAGGLING	WASHED-UP
VIETMINH	VITREOUS	WAGON-LIT	WASHOUTS
VIEWLESS	VITULINE	WAGTAILS	WASHROOM
VIGILANT	VIVACITY	WAINSCOT	WASTABLE
VIGNETTE	VIVARIUM	WAITRESS	WASTEFUL
VIGOROSO	VIVA VOCE	WAKASHAN	WASTRELS
VIGOROUS	VIVIFIER	WAKAYAMA	WATCHDOG
VILENESS	VIVISECT	WAKELESS	WATCHFUL
VILIFIED	VIXENISH	WAKENING	WATCHING
VILIFIER	VLADIMIR	WALKABLE	WATCHMAN
VILLAGER	VOCALISE	WALKAWAY	WATCHMEN
VILLAGES	VOCALISM	WALKMANS	WATERAGE
VILLAINS	VOCALIST	WALKOUTS	WATERBED
VILLAINY	VOCALITY	WALKOVER	WATER ICE
VILLATIC	VOCALIZE	WALLAROO	WATERING
VILLEINS	VOCATION	WALLEYED	WATERLOO
VINCULUM	VOCATIVE	WALL-LIKE	WATERMAN
VINEGARY	VOICE BOX	WALLOPED	WATER RAT

WATER-SKI	WESTERLY	WHITENER	WINGLIKE
WATERWAY	WESTERNS	WHITEOUT	WING NUTS
WATT-HOUR	WESTWARD	WHITE-TIE	WINGOVER
WAVE BAND	WET DREAM	WHITINGS	WINGSPAN
WAVEFORM	WET NURSE	WHITLOWS	WINKLING
WAVELIKE	WET SUITS	WHITTLED	WINNABLE
WAVERERS	WETTABLE	WHITTLER	WINNINGS
WAVERING	WETTINGS	WHIZ-BANG	WINNIPEG
WAVINESS	WHACKING	WHIZZING	WINNOWED
WAXBERRY	WHARFAGE	WHIZZ KID	WINNOWER
WAXINESS	WHATEVER	WHODUNIT	WINTERED
WAXPLANT	WHATNOTS	WHOMEVER	WINTERER
WAXWORKS	WHATSITS	WHOOPEES	WINTRIER
WAYBILLS	WHEATEAR	WHOOPING	WINTRILY
WAYFARER	WHEEDLED	WHOOSHES	WIPED OUT
WAYLAYER	WHEEDLER	WHOPPERS	WIREDRAW
WEAKENED	WHEELIES	WHOPPING	WIRELESS
WEAKENER	WHEELING	WHOREDOM	WIRETAPS
WEAKFISH	WHEEZILY	WICKEDLY	WIRE WOOL
WEAKLING	WHEEZING	WIDE BOYS	WIREWORK
WEAKNESS	WHENEVER	WIDE-EYED	WIREWORM
WEANLING	WHEREVER	WIDENESS	WIRE-WOVE
WEAPONED	WHETTING	WIDENING	WIRINESS
WEAPONRY	WHEYFACE	WIDE-OPEN	WISEACRE
WEARABLE	WHICKERS	WIDGEONS	WISE GUYS
WEARIEST	WHIFFIER	WIDOWERS	WISENESS
WEARYING	WHIGGERY	WIELDERS	WISHBONE
WEASELED	WHIGGISH	WIELDING	WISPIEST
WEASELLY	WHIMBREL	WIGGINGS	WISTERIA
WEDDINGS	WHIMPERS	WIGGLING	WITCHERY
WEDGWOOD	WHIMSIES	WILD BOAR	WITCHING
WEEDIEST	WHINCHAT	WILDCATS	WITHDRAW
WEEKDAYS	WHINGING	WILD-EYED	WITHDREW
WEEKENDS	WHINNIED	WILDFIRE	WITHERED
WEEKLIES	WHINNIES	WILDFOWL	WITHERER
WEENIEST	WHIPCORD	WILDLIFE	WITHHELD
WEIGHING	WHIP HAND	WILDNESS	WITHHOLD
WEIGHTED	WHIPLASH	WILD OATS	WITTIEST
WEIGHTER	WHIPLIKE	WILD WEST	WIZARDRY
WEIRDEST	WHIPPETS	WILFULLY	WOBBLIER
WELCHING	WHIPPING	WILINESS	WOBBLING
WELCOMED	WHIPWORM	WILLABLE	WOEFULLY
WELCOMER	WHIRLING	WILLIWAW	WOLFFISH
WELCOMES	WHIRRING	WINCHING	WOLFLIKE
WELDABLE	WHISKERS	WINDABLE	WOMANISH
WELL-BRED	WHISKERY	WINDBAGS	WOMANIZE
WELL-DONE	WHISKIES	WINDBURN	WOMBLIKE
WELLHEAD	WHISKING	WINDFALL	WONDERED
WELL-HUNG	WHISPERS	WINDGALL	WONDERER
WELL-KNIT	WHISTLED	WINDIEST	WONDROUS
WELL-NIGH	WHISTLER	WINDLASS	WONKIEST
WELL-READ	WHISTLES	WINDMILL	WOODBINE
WELL-TO-DO	WHITE ANT	WINDPIPE	WOODCHAT
WELL-WORN	WHITECAP	WINDSAIL	WOODCOCK
WELSHERS	WHITE-EYE	WINDSOCK	WOODCUTS
WELSHING	WHITEFLY	WINDWARD	WOODENLY
WENCHING	WHITE-HOT	WINE BARS	WOODIEST
WEREWOLF	WHITE LIE	WINESKIN	WOODLAND
WESLEYAN	WHITENED	WINGLESS	WOODLARK

WOODLICE	WORSHIPS	XANTHINE	ZANINESS
WOODNOTE	WORSTING	XANTHOMA	ZANZIBAR
WOODPILE	WORST-OFF	XANTHOUS	ZAPPIEST
WOOD PULP	WORTHIER	XENOGAMY	ZARAGOZA
WOODRUFF	WORTHIES	XENOLITH	ZARATITE
WOODRUSH	WORTHILY	XEROSERE	ZEALOTRY
WOODSHED	WOUNDING	XEROXING	ZECCHINO
WOODSMAN	WRANGLED	XYLIDINE	ZENITHAL
WOODSMEN	WRANGLER	XYLOCARP	ZEOLITIC
WOODWIND	WRANGLES	XYLOTOMY	ZEPPELIN
WOODWORK	WRAPOVER		ZERO HOUR
WOODWORM	WRAPPERS	**Y**	ZHITOMIR
WOOLLENS	WRAPPING	YACHTING	ZIBELINE
WOOLLIER	WRATHFUL	YAHOOISM	ZILLIONS
WOOLLIES	WREAKING	YAMMERED	ZIMBABWE
WOOLLILY	WREATHED	YAMMERER	ZIONISTS
WOOLPACK	WRECKAGE	YARDARMS	ZIP CODES
WOOLSACK	WRECKERS	YARN-DYED	ZIPPIEST
WOOZIEST	WRECKING	YASHMAKS	ZIRCONIA
WORDBOOK	WRENCHED	YEANLING	ZIRCONIC
WORD-DEAF	WRENCHES	YEARBOOK	ZLATOUST
WORDIEST	WRESTING	YEARLING	ZODIACAL
WORDLESS	WRESTLED	YEARLONG	ZOMBIISM
WORDPLAY	WRESTLER	YEARNING	ZONATION
WORKABLE	WRETCHED	YEASTILY	ZONETIME
WORKADAY	WRETCHES	YELLOWED	ZOOCHORE
WORKBAGS	WRIGGLED	YEOMANLY	ZOOGLOEA
WORKBOOK	WRIGGLER	YEOMANRY	ZOOLATER
WORKDAYS	WRIGGLES	YIELDING	ZOOLATRY
WORKED UP	WRINGERS	YODELING	ZOOMETRY
WORKINGS	WRINGING	YODELLED	ZOOM LENS
WORKLOAD	WRINKLED	YODELLER	ZOONOSIS
WORKOUTS	WRINKLES	YOKELISH	ZOOPHILE
WORKROOM	WRISTLET	YOKOHAMA	ZOOPHYTE
WORKSHOP	WRITE-INS	YOUNGEST	ZOOSPERM
WORKTOPS	WRITE-OFF	YOUNGISH	ZOOSPORE
WORM CAST	WRITE-UPS	YOURSELF	ZOOTOMIC
WORM GEAR	WRITHING	YOUTHFUL	ZOOTOXIC
WORMHOLE	WRITINGS	YTTERBIA	ZOOTOXIN
WORMIEST	WRONGFUL	YUCKIEST	ZUCCHINI
WORMLIKE	WRONGING	YUGOSLAV	ZUGZWANG
WORMSEED	WURZBURG	YULE LOGS	ZULULAND
WORMWOOD		YULETIDE	ZWIEBACK
WORRIERS	**X**	YVELINES	ZYGOTENE
WORRYING	XANTHATE		ZYMOLOGY
WORSENED	XANTHEIN	**Z**	
WORSE-OFF	XANTHENE	ZAIBATSU	

A	ACAROLOGY	ACTIVISTS	ADULATION
ABACTINAL	ACCEDENCE	ACTRESSES	ADULATORY
ABANDONED	ACCENTING	ACTS OF GOD	ADULTERER
ABASEMENT	ACCENTUAL	ACTUALITY	ADUMBRATE
ABASHEDLY	ACCEPTANT	ACTUALIZE	AD VALOREM
ABATEMENT	ACCEPTING	ACTUARIAL	ADVANCING
ABATTOIRS	ACCESSING	ACTUARIES	ADVANTAGE
ABCOULOMB	ACCESSION	ACTUATING	ADVECTION
ABDICABLE	ACCESSORY	ACTUATION	ADVENTIVE
ABDICATED	ACCIDENCE	ACUMINATE	ADVENTURE
ABDICATOR	ACCIDENTS	ACUMINOUS	ADVERBIAL
ABDOMINAL	ACCIPITER	ACUTENESS	ADVERSARY
ABDUCTING	ACCLAIMED	ADAMANTLY	ADVERSELY
ABDUCTION	ACCLIVITY	ADAPTABLE	ADVERSITY
ABERRANCE	ACCOLADES	ADDICTION	ADVERTING
ABHORRENT	ACCOMPANY	ADDICTIVE	ADVERTISE
ABHORRING	ACCORDANT	ADDITIONS	ADVISABLE
ABIDINGLY	ACCORDING	ADDITIVES	ADVISEDLY
ABILITIES	ACCORDION	ADDRESSED	ADVOCATED
ABJECTION	ACCOSTING	ADDRESSEE	ADVOCATES
ABLUTIONS	ACCOUNTED	ADDRESSER	AEOLIPILE
ABNEGATOR	ACCRETION	ADDRESSES	AEPYORNIS
ABOLISHED	ACCRETIVE	ADDUCTION	AEROBATIC
ABOLISHER	ACCRUMENT	ADEMPTION	AERODROME
ABOLITION	ACCUMBENT	ADENOIDAL	AEROLOGIC
ABOMINATE	ACELLULAR	ADENOSINE	AEROMETER
ABORIGINE	ACESCENCE	ADHERENCE	AEROMETRY
ABORTIONS	ACETAMIDE	ADHERENTS	AEROPAUSE
ABOUNDING	ACETIFIER	ADHESIONS	AEROPHONE
ABOUT-TURN	ACETYLATE	ADHESIVES	AEROPLANE
ABRASIONS	ACETYLENE	ADIABATIC	AEROSPACE
ABRASIVES	ACETYLIDE	AD INTERIM	AESTHESIA
ABRIDGING	ACHEULIAN	ADIPOCERE	AESTHETES
ABROGATED	ACHIEVING	ADJACENCY	AESTHETIC
ABROGATOR	ACICULATE	ADJECTIVE	AESTIVATE
ABSCESSES	ACIDIFIED	ADJOINING	AETHEREAL
ABSCONDED	ACIDIFIER	ADJOURNED	AETIOLOGY
ABSCONDER	ACIDOPHIL	ADJUDGING	AFFECTING
ABSEILING	ACID TESTS	ADJUSTING	AFFECTION
ABSENTEES	ACIDULATE	ADJUTANCY	AFFECTIVE
ABSENTING	ACIDULOUS	ADJUTANTS	AFFIANCED
ABSOLVING	ACINIFORM	AD-LIBBING	AFFIDAVIT
ABSORBENT	ACOUSTICS	ADMEASURE	AFFILIATE
ABSORBING	ACQUIESCE	ADMINICLE	AFFIRMING
ABSTAINED	ACQUIRING	ADMIRABLE	AFFIXTURE
ABSTAINER	ACQUITTAL	ADMIRABLY	AFFLICTED
ABSTINENT	ACQUITTED	ADMIRALTY	AFFLUENCE
ABSTRACTS	ACQUITTER	ADMISSION	AFFORDING
ABSURDITY	ACROBATIC	ADMISSIVE	AFFRICATE
ABUNDANCE	ACRODROME	ADMITTING	AFFRONTED
ABU SIMBEL	ACROGENIC	ADMIXTURE	AFLATOXIN
ABUSIVELY	ACRONYMIC	AD NAUSEAM	AFORESAID
ABUTMENTS	ACROPETAL	ADNOMINAL	A FORTIORI
ABYSSINIA	ACROPOLIS	ADOPTIONS	AFRIKAANS
ACADEMICS	ACROSPIRE	ADORATION	AFRIKANER
ACANTHINE	ACROSTICS	ADORNMENT	AFRO-ASIAN
ACANTHOID	ACTINOPOD	ADRENALIN	AFTERBODY
ACANTHOUS	ACTIVATED	ADSORBATE	AFTERCARE
ACARIASIS	ACTIVATOR	ADSORBENT	AFTERDAMP

AFTERDECK	ALGONQUIN	ALTITUDES	AMPHIOXUS
AFTERGLOW	ALGORITHM	ALTRICIAL	AMPLIFIED
AFTERHEAT	ALICYCLIC	ALTRUISTS	AMPLIFIER
AFTERLIFE	ALIENABLE	ALUMINATE	AMPLITUDE
AFTERMATH	ALIENATED	ALUMINIUM	AMPUTATED
AFTERNOON	ALIENATOR	ALUMINIZE	AMSTERDAM
AFTERWORD	ALIGHTING	ALUMINOUS	AMUSEMENT
AGE GROUPS	ALIGNMENT	ALVEOLARS	AMUSINGLY
AGGRAVATE	ALIPHATIC	ALVEOLATE	AMYGDALIN
AGGREGATE	ALKALOSIS	AMAGASAKI	AMYLOPSIN
AGGRESSOR	ALLAHABAD	AMARYLLIS	ANABANTID
AGGRIEVED	ALLANTOIC	AMAUROSIS	ANABIOSIS
AGITATING	ALLANTOID	AMAUROTIC	ANABOLISM
AGITATION	ALLANTOIS	AMAZEMENT	ANABOLITE
AGITATORS	ALL-AROUND	AMAZINGLY	ANACLINAL
AGNOMINAL	ALLEGEDLY	AMAZONIAN	ANACLISIS
AGNOSTICS	ALLELUIAS	AMAZONITE	ANACLITIC
AGONISTIC	ALLENTOWN	AMBERGRIS	ANACONDAS
AGONIZING	ALLERGIES	AMBERJACK	ANACRUSIS
AGREEABLE	ALLERGIST	AMBIENCES	ANAEROBIC
AGREEABLY	ALLETHRIN	AMBIGUITY	ANALECTIC
AGREEMENT	ALLEVIATE	AMBIGUOUS	ANALEPTIC
AGRONOMIC	ALLEYWAYS	AMBITIONS	ANALGESIA
AHMEDABAD	ALLIANCES	AMBITIOUS	ANALGESIC
AILANTHUS	ALLIGATOR	AMBLYOPIA	ANALOGIES
AIMLESSLY	ALLOCATED	AMBLYOPIC	ANALOGIST
AIRBRAKES	ALLOGRAPH	AMBROSIAL	ANALOGIZE
AIRFIELDS	ALLOMETRY	AMBROTYPE	ANALOGOUS
AIRFORCES	ALLOMORPH	AMBULANCE	ANALOGUES
AIR-INTAKE	ALLOPATHY	AMBUSHING	ANALYSAND
AIRLETTER	ALLOPHANE	AMENDABLE	ANALYSING
AIRLIFTED	ALLOPHONE	AMENDMENT	ANALYTICS
AIRLINERS	ALLOPLASM	AMENITIES	ANAMNESIS
AIRPLANES	ALLOTMENT	AMERICANA	ANANDROUS
AIRPOCKET	ALLOTROPE	AMERICANS	ANANTHOUS
AIRSTREAM	ALLOTROPY	AMERICIUM	ANAPAESTS
AIRSTRIPS	ALLOTTING	AMERINDIC	ANAPESTIC
AIRWORTHY	ALLOWABLE	AMETHYSTS	ANAPHORAL
AITCHBONE	ALLOWABLY	AMETROPIA	ANAPLASIA
ALABAMIAN	ALLOWANCE	AMIANTHUS	ANAPLASTY
ALABASTER	ALLOWEDLY	AMIDSHIPS	ANAPTYXIS
ALARMISTS	ALLUSIONS	AMINO ACID	ANARCHISM
ALBATROSS	ALLUVIUMS	AMMOCOETE	ANARCHIST
ALBERTITE	ALMA MATER	AMMONIATE	ANARTHRIA
ALBESCENT	ALMANDINE	AMMONICAL	ANATHEMAS
ALCHEMIST	ALMS-HOUSE	AMMONITIC	ANATOLIAN
ALCHEMIZE	ALONGSIDE	AMNESIACS	ANATOMIES
ALCOHOLIC	ALOOFNESS	AMNESTIES	ANATOMIST
ALDEBARAN	ALPENGLOW	AMOEBAEAN	ANATOMIZE
ALEHOUSES	ALPHABETS	AMORALITY	ANCESTORS
ALEMANNIC	ALSATIANS	AMOROUSLY	ANCESTRAL
ALEPH-NULL	ALTERABLE	AMORPHISM	ANCHORAGE
ALERTNESS	ALTERCATE	AMORPHOUS	ANCHORESS
ALFILARIA	ALTER EGOS	AMORTIZED	ANCHORING
ALGARROBA	ALTERNATE	AMOUNTING	ANCHORITE
ALGEBRAIC	ALTIMETER	AMPERSAND	ANCHOVIES
ALGECIRAS	ALTIMETRY	AMPHIBIAN	ANCILLARY
ALGOMETER	ALTIPLANO	AMPHIBOLE	ANCIPITAL
ALGOMETRY	ALTISSIMO	AMPHIGORY	ANDALUSIA

ANDANTINO	ANTARCTIC	APODICTIC	AQUITAINE
ANDRADITE	ANTEATERS	APOENZYME	ARABESQUE
ANDROMEDA	ANTECHOIR	APOGAMOUS	ARABINOSE
ANECDOTAL	ANTEDATED	APOLOGIAS	ARACHNOID
ANECDOTES	ANTEFIXAL	APOLOGIES	ARAGONESE
ANECDOTIC	ANTELOPES	APOLOGIST	ARAGONITE
ANEMOLOGY	ANTENATAL	APOLOGIZE	ARAUCANIA
ANEUPLOID	ANTENNULE	APOPHASIS	ARAUCARIA
ANGELFISH	ANTEROOMS	APOPHYSIS	ARBITRAGE
ANGELICAL	ANTHELION	APOSTATES	ARBITRARY
ANGIOLOGY	ANTHEMION	APOSTOLIC	ARBITRATE
ANGLESITE	ANTHODIUM	APPALLING	ARBITRESS
ANGLEWORM	ANTHOLOGY	APPALOOSA	ARBOREOUS
ANGLICANS	ANTHOTAXY	APPARATUS	ARBORETUM
ANGLICISM	ANTHOZOAN	APPARITOR	ARCHAISMS
ANGLICIZE	ANTHURIUM	APPEALING	ARCHAIZER
ANGOSTURA	ANTICHLOR	APPEARING	ARCHANGEL
ANGUISHED	ANTICLINE	APPEASING	ARCHDUCAL
ANHYDRIDE	ANTIDOTES	APPELLANT	ARCHDUCHY
ANHYDRITE	ANTIGENIC	APPELLATE	ARCHDUKES
ANHYDROUS	ANTIKNOCK	APPENDAGE	ARCHENEMY
ANIMALISM	ANTIMERIC	APPENDANT	ARCHETYPE
ANIMALIST	ANTIMONIC	APPENDING	ARCHFIEND
ANIMALITY	ANTIMONYL	APPENZELL	ARCHICARP
ANIMALIZE	ANTINODAL	APPERTAIN	ARCHITECT
ANIMATING	ANTINOMIC	APPETENCE	ARCHIVIST
ANIMATION	ANTIPATHY	APPETITES	ARCHIVOLT
ANIMATISM	ANTIPHONY	APPETIZER	ARCOGRAPH
ANIMISTIC	ANTIPODAL	APPLAUDED	ARCTOGAEA
ANIMOSITY	ANTIPODES	APPLAUDER	ARCTURIAN
ANISOGAMY	ANTIQUARY	APPLE CART	ARCUATION
ANKLEBONE	ANTIQUATE	APPLEJACK	ARDUOUSLY
ANKYLOSIS	ANTIQUITY	APPLE PIES	AREA CODES
ANNALISTS	ANTISERUM	APPLIANCE	ARGENTINA
ANNAPURNA	ANTITOXIC	APPLICANT	ARGENTINE
ANNEALING	ANTITOXIN	APPOINTED	ARGENTITE
ANNELIDAN	ANTIVENIN	APPOINTEE	ARGENTOUS
ANNOTATED	ANTIWORLD	APPOINTER	ARGILLITE
ANNOTATOR	ANXIETIES	APPOINTOR	ARGUMENTS
ANNOUNCED	ANXIOUSLY	APPORTION	ARMADILLO
ANNOUNCER	APARTHEID	APPRAISAL	ARMAMENTS
ANNOYANCE	APARTMENT	APPRAISED	ARMATURES
ANNUITANT	APATHETIC	APPRAISER	ARMCHAIRS
ANNUITIES	APELDOORN	APPREHEND	ARMISTICE
ANNULLING	APENNINES	APPRESSED	ARMOURERS
ANNULMENT	APERIODIC	APPRISING	ARMOURIES
ANOESTRUS	APERITIFS	APPROBATE	ARMS RACES
ANOINTING	APERTURES	APPROVING	AROMATIZE
ANOMALIES	APETALOUS	APPULSIVE	ARPEGGIOS
ANOMALOUS	APHERESIS	APRIL FOOL	ARRAIGNED
ANONYMITY	APHIDIOUS	APRIORITY	ARRAIGNER
ANONYMOUS	APHORISMS	APTITUDES	ARRANGING
ANOPHELES	APHYLLOUS	AQUALUNGS	ARRESTING
ANORTHITE	APICULATE	AQUAPLANE	ARRIVISTE
ANOSMATIC	APISHNESS	AQUARELLE	ARROGANCE
ANOXAEMIA	APIVOROUS	AQUARIUMS	ARROGATED
ANOXAEMIC	APLANATIC	AQUATINTS	ARROGATOR
ANSWERING	APOCOPATE	AQUEDUCTS	ARROWHEAD
ANTALKALI	APOCRYPHA	AQUILEGIA	ARROWROOT

ARROWWOOD	ASSIDUOUS	ATTENTION	AUTOTOXIN
ARROWWORM	ASSIGNING	ATTENTIVE	AUTOTYPIC
ARSENICAL	ASSISTANT	ATTENUANT	AUXILIARY
ARSENIOUS	ASSISTING	ATTENUATE	AVAILABLE
ARSONISTS	ASSOCIATE	ATTESTANT	AVAILABLY
ARTEFACTS	ASSONANCE	ATTESTING	AVALANCHE
ARTEMISIA	ASSORTING	ATTITUDES	AVERAGING
ARTERIOLE	ASSUAGING	ATTORNEYS	AVERSIONS
ARTERITIS	ASSUASIVE	ATTRACTED	AVERTIBLE
ARTHRITIC	ASSUMABLE	ATTRACTOR	AVIFAUNAL
ARTHRITIS	ASSURABLE	ATTRIBUTE	AVIRULENT
ARTHROPOD	ASSURANCE	ATTRITION	AVOCATION
ARTICHOKE	ASSUREDLY	ATTRITIVE	AVOIDABLE
ARTICLING	ASSURGENT	AUBERGINE	AVOIDANCE
ARTICULAR	ASTERISKS	AUBRIETIA	AVUNCULAR
ARTIFACTS	ASTEROIDS	AU COURANT	AWAKENING
ARTIFICER	ASTHMATIC	AUCTIONED	AWARDABLE
ARTIFICES	ASTOUNDED	AUCTORIAL	AWARENESS
ARTILLERY	ASTRADDLE	AUDACIOUS	AWESTRUCK
ARTLESSLY	ASTRAKHAN	AUDIENCES	AWFULNESS
ARYTENOID	ASTROCYTE	AUDIOLOGY	AWKWARDLY
ASCENDANT	ASTRODOME	AUDIPHONE	AXIOMATIC
ASCENDING	ASTROLABE	AUDITIONS	AYAHUASCA
ASCENSION	ASTROLOGY	AUGMENTED	AYATOLLAH
ASCERTAIN	ASTRONAUT	AUGMENTOR	AYUTTHAYA
ASCOSPORE	ASTRONOMY	AU NATUREL	AZEDARACH
ASCRIBING	ASYLLABIC	AURICULAR	AZEOTROPE
ASEPALOUS	ASYMMETRY	AUSTENITE	AZIMUTHAL
ASEXUALLY	ASYMPTOTE	AUSTERELY	
ASHAMEDLY	ASYNDETIC	AUSTERITY	**B**
ASHKENAZI	ASYNDETON	AUSTRALIA	BABY TEETH
ASHKHABAD	ATARACTIC	AUTARCHIC	BABY TOOTH
ASININITY	ATAVISTIC	AUTARKIES	BACCHANAL
ASPARAGUS	ATHEISTIC	AUTHENTIC	BACCIFORM
ASPERSION	ATHENAEUM	AUTHORESS	BACHELORS
ASPERSIVE	ATHLETICS	AUTHORIAL	BACILLARY
ASPHALTED	ATLANTEAN	AUTHORITY	BACKACHES
ASPHALTIC	ATMOLYSIS	AUTHORIZE	BACKBENCH
ASPHALTUM	ATMOMETER	AUTOCLAVE	BACKBITER
ASPHYXIAL	ATMOMETRY	AUTOCRACY	BACKBOARD
ASPIRANTS	ATOM BOMBS	AUTOCRATS	BACKBONES
ASPIRATED	ATOMICITY	AUTOCROSS	BACKCLOTH
ASPIRATES	ATOMISTIC	AUTOECISM	BACKCROSS
ASPIRATOR	ATOMIZERS	AUTOGRAFT	BACKDATED
ASSAILANT	ATONALISM	AUTOGRAPH	BACK DOORS
ASSAILING	ATONALITY	AUTOICOUS	BACKDROPS
ASSASSINS	ATONEMENT	AUTOLYSIN	BACKFIRED
ASSAULTED	ATONICITY	AUTOLYSIS	BACKHANDS
ASSAULTER	ATROCIOUS	AUTOLYTIC	BACKPACKS
ASSAYABLE	ATROPHIED	AUTOMATED	BACKPEDAL
ASSEMBLED	ATTACHING	AUTOMATIC	BACK SEATS
ASSEMBLER	ATTACKERS	AUTOMATON	BACKSIDES
ASSENTING	ATTACKING	AUTONOMIC	BACKSIGHT
ASSERTING	ATTAINDER	AUTOPHYTE	BACKSLIDE
ASSERTION	ATTAINING	AUTOPSIES	BACKSPACE
ASSERTIVE	ATTEMPTED	AUTOSOMAL	BACKSTAGE
ASSESSING	ATTEMPTER	AUTOTIMER	BACKSWEPT
ASSESSORS	ATTENDANT	AUTOTOMIC	BACKTRACK
ASSIDUITY	ATTENDING	AUTOTOXIC	BACKWARDS

BACKWATER	BARBARIAN	BATTERING	BELEAGUER
BACKWOODS	BARBARISM	BATTINESS	BELEMNITE
BACKYARDS	BARBARITY	BATTLEAXE	BELGRAVIA
BACTERIAL	BARBARIZE	BATTLE CRY	BELIEVERS
BACTERIUM	BARBAROUS	BAWDINESS	BELIEVING
BACTEROID	BARBECUED	BAYONETED	BELITTLED
BADGERING	BARBECUES	BAY WINDOW	BELITTLER
BADMINTON	BARBICANS	BEACH BALL	BELLATRIX
BAGATELLE	BARBITONE	BEACHHEAD	BELLICOSE
BAGGINESS	BARCAROLE	BEACHWEAR	BELLOWING
BAG LADIES	BARCELONA	BEADINESS	BELLYACHE
BAHUVRIHI	BAR CHARTS	BEARBERRY	BELLY FLOP
BAILIWICK	BARE BONES	BEARDLESS	BELONGING
BAIN-MARIE	BAREFACED	BEARISHLY	BELVEDERE
BALACLAVA	BARGAINED	BEARNAISE	BEMOANING
BALAKLAVA	BARGAINER	BEAR'S-FOOT	BENCH MARK
BALALAIKA	BARGE POLE	BEARSKINS	BENEFICES
BALANCING	BAR GRAPHS	BEASTLIER	BENEFITED
BALCONIES	BARITONES	BEATIFIED	BENGALESE
BALEFULLY	BARNACLES	BEATITUDE	BENGALINE
BALKANIZE	BARN DANCE	BEAU MONDE	BENIGHTED
BALLASTED	BARNSTORM	BEAUTEOUS	BENIGNANT
BALLCOCKS	BARNYARDS	BEAUTIFUL	BENIGNITY
BALLERINA	BAROGRAPH	BEAUX-ARTS	BENTONITE
BALL GAMES	BAROMETER	BEAVERING	BENZIDINE
BALLISTIC	BARONETCY	BEBEERINE	BERBERINE
BALLOONED	BAROSCOPE	BECCAFICO	BEREAVING
BALLOTING	BARRACKED	BECKONING	BEREZNIKI
BALLPOINT	BARRACUDA	BECQUEREL	BERKELIUM
BALLROOMS	BARRETTES	BEDAUBING	BERYLLIUM
BALMINESS	BARRICADE	BEDECKING	BESEECHED
BALTHAZAR	BARRISTER	BEDEVILED	BESETTING
BALTIMORE	BARROW BOY	BEDFELLOW	BESIEGING
BAMBOOZLE	BARTENDER	BEDRAGGLE	BESMEARED
BANDAGING	BARTERING	BEDRIDDEN	BESPATTER
BANDANNAS	BASEBALLS	BED-SITTER	BESTIALLY
BANDEROLE	BASEBOARD	BEDSPREAD	BESTIRRED
BANDICOOT	BASELINES	BEDSTEADS	BESTOWING
BANDOLEER	BASEMENTS	BEEFEATER	BESTREWED
BANDSTAND	BASE METAL	BEEFINESS	BETE-NOIRE
BANDWAGON	BASE RATES	BEEFSTEAK	BETHLEHEM
BANDWIDTH	BASHFULLY	BEEKEEPER	BETHOUGHT
BANEBERRY	BASICALLY	BEELZEBUB	BETOKENED
BANEFULLY	BASIFIXED	BEERINESS	BETRAYALS
BANGALORE	BASILICAN	BEESTINGS	BETRAYERS
BANISHING	BASILICAS	BEETROOTS	BETRAYING
BANISTERS	BASILISKS	BEFALLING	BETROTHAL
BANKBOOKS	BASIPETAL	BEFITTING	BETROTHED
BANK DRAFT	BAS-RELIEF	BEGETTING	BETTERING
BANK NOTES	BASS CLEFS	BEGGARING	BETTER-OFF
BANKROLLS	BASSINETS	BEGINNERS	BEVELLING
BANKRUPTS	BASTINADO	BEGINNING	BEVERAGES
BANQUETED	BATH CHAIR	BEGRUDGED	BEWAILING
BANQUETTE	BATHOLITH	BEGUILING	BEWITCHED
BANTERING	BATHROBES	BEHAVIOUR	BHAGALPUR
BANTUSTAN	BATHROOMS	BEHEADING	BHARATIYA
BAPTISMAL	BATTALION	BEHOLDERS	BHAVNAGAR
BAPTIZING	BATTENING	BEHOLDING	BHUTANESE
BARBADIAN	BATTERIES	BELATEDLY	BIALYSTOK

BIBLIOTIC	BISECTION	BLETHERED	BLUNTNESS
BICIPITAL	BISECTRIX	BLIGHTERS	BLURREDLY
BICKERING	BISERRATE	BLIGHTING	BLUSTERED
BICONCAVE	BISEXUALS	BLIND DATE	BLUSTERER
BICYCLING	BISHOPRIC	BLINDFISH	BOARDROOM
BICYCLIST	BISMUTHAL	BLINDFOLD	BOARDWALK
BIDENTATE	BISMUTHIC	BLINDNESS	BOARHOUND
BIELEFELD	BISULCATE	BLIND SPOT	BOAT HOOKS
BIFARIOUS	BITCHIEST	BLINKERED	BOATHOUSE
BIFOLIATE	BITTERNUT	BLISTERED	BOATSWAIN
BIFURCATE	BITTINESS	BLIZZARDS	BOAT TRAIN
BIGAMISTS	BIVALENCY	BLOCKADED	BOBBY PINS
BIGARREAU	BIZARRELY	BLOCKADER	BOBSLEIGH
BIG DIPPER	BLABBERED	BLOCKADES	BOBTAILED
BIGENERIC	BLACKBALL	BLOCKAGES	BODY BLOWS
BIG-TIMERS	BLACK BELT	BLOCKHEAD	BODYCHECK
BIGUANIDE	BLACKBIRD	BLOCK VOTE	BODYGUARD
BIG WHEELS	BLACKBUCK	BLONDNESS	BOGGINESS
BIJECTION	BLACKCOCK	BLOOD BANK	BOHEMIANS
BIJECTIVE	BLACKDAMP	BLOODBATH	BOILINGLY
BILABIALS	BLACKENED	BLOOD FEUD	BOLDFACED
BILABIATE	BLACK EYES	BLOOD HEAT	BOLECTION
BILATERAL	BLACKFISH	BLOODLESS	BOLEGNESE
BILHARZIA	BLACKHEAD	BLOOD LUST	BOLOMETER
BILINGUAL	BLACK HOLE	BLOODROOT	BOLSHEVIK
BILIRUBIN	BLACKJACK	BLOODSHED	BOLSHIEST
BILLBOARD	BLACK LEAD	BLOODSHOT	BOLSTERED
BILLETING	BLACKLEGS	BLOOD TYPE	BOLSTERER
BILLFOLDS	BLACKLIST	BLOODWORM	BOLTHOLES
BILLHOOKS	BLACKMAIL	BLOSSOMED	BOMBARDED
BILLIARDS	BLACK MASS	BLOTCHIER	BOMBARDON
BILLIONTH	BLACKNESS	BLOTCHILY	BOMBASTIC
BILLOWING	BLACKOUTS	BLOW-DRIED	BOMBAZINE
BILLY GOAT	BLACKPOLL	BLOW-DRIES	BOMBPROOF
BILOCULAR	BLACK SPOT	BLOWFLIES	BOMBSHELL
BIMONTHLY	BLACKTAIL	BLOWHARDS	BOMBSIGHT
BIN-LINERS	BLAMELESS	BLOWHOLES	BOMBSITES
BINOCULAR	BLANCHING	BLOWLAMPS	BONA FIDES
BINOMIALS	BLANDNESS	BLOWPIPES	BONEBLACK
BINTURONG	BLANKETED	BLOWZIEST	BONE CHINA
BINUCLEAR	BLANKNESS	BLUBBERED	BONEHEADS
BIOGRAPHY	BLASPHEME	BLUDGEONS	BON VIVANT
BIOLOGIST	BLASPHEMY	BLUEBEARD	BOOBY TRAP
BIOMETRIC	BLASTEMIC	BLUEBELLS	BOOHOOING
BIONOMICS	BLASTULAR	BLUEBERRY	BOOKCASES
BIONOMIST	BLATANTLY	BLUEBIRDS	BOOK CLUBS
BIOSPHERE	BLATHERED	BLUE-BLACK	BOOKMAKER
BIOSTATIC	BLAZONING	BLUE BLOOD	BOOKMARKS
BIOSTROME	BLEACHERS	BLUE BOOKS	BOOKPLATE
BIPARTITE	BLEACHING	BLUE CHIPS	BOOKSHELF
BIPINNATE	BLEAKNESS	BLUE FILMS	BOOKSHOPS
BIRDHOUSE	BLEARIEST	BLUEGRASS	BOOKSTALL
BIRD'S-FOOT	BLEMISHED	BLUE JEANS	BOOKSTAND
BIRTHDAYS	BLEMISHER	BLUE PETER	BOOK TOKEN
BIRTHMARK	BLEMISHES	BLUEPRINT	BOOKWORMS
BIRTHRATE	BLENCHING	BLUESTONE	BOOMERANG
BIRTHROOT	BLENNIOID	BLUFFNESS	BOOMSLANG
BIRTHWORT	BLESSEDLY	BLUNDERED	BOONDOCKS
BISECTING	BLESSINGS	BLUNDERER	BOORISHLY

BOOTBLACK	BRASS BAND	BROMOFORM	BULLISHLY
BOOTLACES	BRASSERIE	BRONCHIAL	BULLRINGS
BOOTSTRAP	BRASS HATS	BRONZE AGE	BULL'S-EYES
BOOZINESS	BRASSIERE	BROODIEST	BULLY BEEF
BORDELLOS	BRASSIEST	BROOKABLE	BULLYBOYS
BORDERING	BRAVENESS	BROOKLIME	BULLY-OFFS
BOREHOLES	BRAWNIEST	BROOKWEED	BULRUSHES
BORN-AGAIN	BRAZENING	BROOMCORN	BUMBLEBEE
BORROWERS	BRAZILEIN	BROOMRAPE	BUMPINESS
BORROWING	BRAZILIAN	BROSCOPIC	BUMPTIOUS
BOSSINESS	BREACHING	BROTHERLY	BUNDESRAT
BOTANICAL	BREAD BINS	BROUGHAMS	BUNDESTAG
BOTANISTS	BREADLINE	BROWN RICE	BUNGALOWS
BOTANIZED	BREADROOT	BRUNETTES	BUNGHOLES
BOTCHIEST	BREAKABLE	BRUNSWICK	BUNKHOUSE
BOTHERING	BREAKAGES	BRUSH-OFFS	BUOYANTLY
BOTTLE-FED	BREAKAWAY	BRUSHWOOD	BUPRESTID
BOTULINUS	BREAKDOWN	BRUSHWORK	BURDENING
BOUILLONS	BREAKEVEN	BRUSQUELY	BURGEONED
BOULEVARD	BREAKFAST	BRUTALITY	BURGESSES
BOUNCIEST	BREAKNECK	BRUTALIZE	BURLESQUE
BOUNDLESS	BREATHILY	BRUTISHLY	BURLINESS
BOUNTEOUS	BREATHING	BRYOPHYTE	BURNINGLY
BOUNTIFUL	BREECHING	BRYTHONIC	BURNISHED
BOURGEOIS	BRIARROOT	BUBBLE GUM	BURNISHER
BOUTIQUES	BRIC-A-BRAC	BUBBLIEST	BURNOUSES
BOWERBIRD	BRICKWORK	BUCCANEER	BURROWING
BOW-LEGGED	BRICKYARD	BUCHAREST	BURSARIAL
BOWSPRITS	BRIEFCASE	BUCKBOARD	BURSARIES
BOWSTRING	BRIGADIER	BUCKETING	BURSIFORM
BOW WINDOW	BRILLIANT	BUCKHOUND	BURTHENED
BOX AND COX	BRIMSTONE	BUCKTEETH	BUSHELLER
BOXING DAY	BRININESS	BUCKTHORN	BUSHINESS
BOX NUMBER	BRIOLETTE	BUCKTOOTH	BUTADIENE
BOX OFFICE	BRIQUETTE	BUCKWHEAT	BUTCHERED
BOYCOTTED	BRISKNESS	BUDDHISTS	BUTTERBUR
BOYFRIEND	BRISTLING	BUDGETARY	BUTTERCUP
BOYLE'S LAW	BRITANNIA	BUDGETING	BUTTERFAT
BOY SCOUTS	BRITANNIC	BUFFALOES	BUTTERFLY
BRACELETS	BRITICISM	BUFFERING	BUTTERINE
BRACHIATE	BRITISHER	BUFFETING	BUTTERING
BRACINGLY	BROACHING	BUGGER ALL	BUTTERNUT
BRACKETED	BROAD BEAN	BUGGERING	BUTTONING
BRACTEATE	BROADBILL	BUGLEWEED	BUXOMNESS
BRACTEOLE	BROADCAST	BUHRSTONE	BUZZWORDS
BRAGGARTS	BROADENED	BUILDINGS	BYDGOSZCZ
BRAINIEST	BROAD JUMP	BUJUMBURA	BYPASSING
BRAINLESS	BROADLEAF	BULGARIAN	BY-PRODUCT
BRAINSICK	BROADLOOM	BULGINESS	BYSTANDER
BRAINWASH	BROADNESS	BULGINGLY	BYZANTINE
BRAINWAVE	BROADSIDE	BULKHEADS	BYZANTIUM
BRAKE SHOE	BROADTAIL	BULKINESS	
BRAKESMAN	BROCADING	BULLDOZED	C
BRAMBLING	BROCHETTE	BULLDOZER	CABALLERO
BRANCHIAL	BROCHURES	BULLETINS	CABIN BOYS
BRANCHING	BROKERAGE	BULLFIGHT	CABLE CARS
BRANDLING	BROMELIAD	BULLFINCH	CABLEGRAM
BRAND NAME	BROMEOSIN	BULLFROGS	CABLE-LAID
BRASHNESS	BROMINATE	BULLHORNS	CABOODLES

CABRIOLET	CANCELLER	CARBURIZE	CASEATION
CACHECTIC	CANCEROUS	CARCASSES	CASEBOUND
CACODEMON	CANDIDACY	CARCINOMA	CASE STUDY
CACOETHES	CANDIDATE	CARDBOARD	CASH CARDS
CACOETHIC	CANDLEMAS	CARDIGANS	CASH CROPS
CACOPHONY	CANDLENUT	CARDINALS	CASH DESKS
CACUMINAL	CANDYTUFT	CARD INDEX	CASHIERED
CAECILIAN	CANESCENT	CARDPUNCH	CASSAREEP
CAESAREAN	CANICULAR	CARDSHARP	CASSATION
CAFETERIA	CANISTERS	CAREENING	CASSEROLE
CAIRNGORM	CANKEROUS	CAREERING	CASSETTES
CAITHNESS	CANNELURE	CAREERISM	CASSIMERE
CALABOOSE	CANNERIES	CAREERIST	CASSOCKED
CALAMANCO	CANNIBALS	CAREFULLY	CASSOULET
CALCANEAL	CANNINESS	CARESSING	CASSOWARY
CALCANEUS	CANNONADE	CARETAKER	CASTANETS
CALCICOLE	CANNONING	CARIBBEAN	CASTAWAYS
CALCIFIED	CANNULATE	CARIBBEES	CASTIGATE
CALCIFUGE	CANOEISTS	CARILLONS	CASTILIAN
CALCIMINE	CANONICAL	CARINTHIA	CASTOR OIL
CALCULATE	CANONIZED	CARIOSITY	CASTRATED
CALCULOUS	CANOODLED	CARMELITE	CASTRATOR
CALENDARS	CAN OPENER	CARNALIST	CASUARINA
CALENDERS	CANTABILE	CARNALITY	CASUISTIC
CALENDULA	CANTALOUP	CARNATION	CASUISTRY
CALENTURE	CANTERING	CARNELIAN	CATABASIS
CALIBRATE	CANTICLES	CARNIVALS	CATABATIC
CALIPHATE	CANTONESE	CARNIVORE	CATABOLIC
CALL BOXES	CANVASSED	CARNOTITE	CATACLYSM
CALL GIRLS	CANVASSER	CAROLLING	CATACOMBS
CALLOSITY	CANVASSES	CAROTIDAL	CATALEPSY
CALLOUSLY	CAPACIOUS	CAROUSALS	CATALOGUE
CALMATIVE	CAPACITOR	CAROUSELS	CATALONIA
CALORIFIC	CAPARISON	CAROUSING	CATALYSER
CALUMNIES	CAPILLARY	CARPENTER	CATALYSIS
CALVARIES	CAPITULAR	CARPENTRY	CATALYSTS
CALVINISM	CAPITULUM	CARPETBAG	CATALYTIC
CALVINIST	CAPRICCIO	CARPETING	CATAMARAN
CALVITIES	CAPRICORN	CARPOLOGY	CATAMENIA
CAMBISTRY	CAPSAICIN	CARRAGEEN	CATAMOUNT
CAMELHAIR	CAPSICUMS	CARREFOUR	CAT-AND-DOG
CAMELLIAS	CAPSIZING	CARRIAGES	CATAPHYLL
CAMEMBERT	CAPSULATE	CARRYALLS	CATAPLASM
CAMERAMAN	CAPTAINCY	CARRYCOTS	CATAPLEXY
CAMERAMEN	CAPTAINED	CARRY-OVER	CATAPULTS
CAMISOLES	CAPTIVATE	CARTAGENA	CATARACTS
CAMPAIGNS	CAPTIVITY	CARTESIAN	CATARRHAL
CAMPANILE	CAPTURING	CARTHORSE	CATATONIA
CAMPANULA	CARAPACES	CARTILAGE	CATATONIC
CAMPFIRES	CARBAMATE	CARTOGRAM	CATCALLED
CAMPHORIC	CARBANION	CARTOUCHE	CATCH CROP
CAMPSITES	CARBAZOLE	CARTRIDGE	CATCHIEST
CAMSHAFTS	CARBINEER	CART TRACK	CATCHMENT
CANAANITE	CARBOLIZE	CARTULARY	CATCHWORD
CANAL BOAT	CARBONADO	CARTWHEEL	CATECHISM
CANALIZED	CARBONATE	CARYATIDS	CATECHIST
CANAVERAL	CARBONIZE	CARYOPSIS	CATECHIZE
CANCELING	CARBONOUS	CASANOVAS	CATERWAUL
CANCELLED	CARBUNCLE	CASCADING	CATHARSES

CATHARSIS	CENTURION	CHARWOMEN	CHILLIEST
CATHARTIC	CERACEOUS	CHASTENED	CHINATOWN
CATHEDRAL	CERATODUS	CHASTENER	CHINAWARE
CATHEPSIN	CERCARIAL	CHASTISED	CHINKIANG
CATHETERS	CEREBROID	CHASUBLES	CHINSTRAP
CATHOLICS	CEREBRUMS	CHATELAIN	CHINTZIER
CATOPTRIC	CERECLOTH	CHATOYANT	CHIPBOARD
CATTERIES	CERTAINLY	CHAT SHOWS	CHIPMUNKS
CATTINESS	CERTAINTY	CHATTERED	CHIPOLATA
CATTLEMAN	CERTIFIED	CHATTERER	CHIPPINGS
CAUCASOID	CERTITUDE	CHATTIEST	CHIROPODY
CAUDATION	CERUSSITE	CHAUFFEUR	CHIROPTER
CAULDRONS	CESAREANS	CHEAPENED	CHIRPIEST
CAUSALGIA	CESSATION	CHEAP-JACK	CHIRRUPER
CAUSALITY	CETACEANS	CHEAPNESS	CHISELING
CAUSATION	CHABAZITE	CHECKABLE	CHISELLED
CAUSATIVE	CHA-CHA-CHA	CHECKERED	CHISELLER
CAUSEWAYS	CHAETOPOD	CHECKLIST	CHITINOID
CAUTERANT	CHAFFINCH	CHECKMATE	CHITINOUS
CAUTERIZE	CHAGRINED	CHECKOUTS	CHIVALRIC
CAUTIONED	CHAIN GANG	CHECKROOM	CHLORDANE
CAVALCADE	CHAIN MAIL	CHEEKBONE	CHLORELLA
CAVALIERS	CHAIN SAWS	CHEEKIEST	CHLORIDES
CAVENDISH	CHAIR LIFT	CHEERIEST	CHLORIDIC
CAVERNOUS	CHALKIEST	CHEERLESS	CHLORITIC
CAVILLERS	CHALLENGE	CHELASHIP	CHLOROSIS
CAVILLING	CHAMELEON	CHELATION	CHLOROTIC
CAVORTING	CHAMFERER	CHELICERA	CHOCK-FULL
CEASE-FIRE	CHAMOMILE	CHELIFORM	CHOCOLATE
CEASELESS	CHAMPAGNE	CHELONIAN	CHOCOLATY
CELANDINE	CHAMPAIGN	CHEMICALS	CHOIRBOYS
CELEBRANT	CHAMPERTY	CHEMISORB	CHOKEABLE
CELEBRATE	CHAMPIONS	CHEMISTRY	CHOLEROID
CELEBRITY	CHAMPLEVE	CHEMOSTAT	CHONDRIFY
CELESTIAL	CHANCIEST	CHEMPADUK	CHONDRITE
CELESTITE	CHANCROID	CHEMURGIC	CHONDROMA
CELIBATES	CHANCROUS	CHENGCHOW	CHONDRULE
CELLARAGE	CHANDELLE	CHEONGSAM	CHOOSIEST
CELLOIDIN	CHANDLERS	CHEQUERED	CHOPHOUSE
CELLULASE	CHANDLERY	CHERBOURG	CHOPLOGIC
CELLULOID	CHANGCHOW	CHERISHED	CHOPPIEST
CELLULOSE	CHANGCHUN	CHERISHER	CHOPSTICK
CELTICIST	CHANNELED	CHERNOZEM	CHORIONIC
CEMENTING	CHANTEUSE	CHESTIEST	CHORISTER
CEMENTITE	CHAPERONS	CHESTNUTS	CHOROLOGY
CENOTAPHS	CHAPLAINS	CHEVALIER	CHORTLING
CENSORIAL	CHAPLETED	CHEVRETTE	CHORUSING
CENSORING	CHARABANC	CHICALOTE	CHRISTIAN
CENSURING	CHARACTER	CHICANERY	CHRISTMAS
CENTAURUS	CHARCOALS	CHICKADEE	CHROMATIC
CENTENARY	CHARINESS	CHICKPEAS	CHROMATID
CENTERING	CHARITIES	CHICKWEED	CHROMATIN
CENTIGRAM	CHARIVARI	CHIEFTAIN	CHROMOGEN
CENTIPEDE	CHARLATAN	CHIHUAHUA	CHRONAXIE
CENTRALLY	CHARLOTTE	CHILBLAIN	CHRONICLE
CENTRIOLE	CHARMEUSE	CHILDHOOD	CHRYSALIS
CENTRISTS	CHARTABLE	CHILDLESS	CHTHONIAN
CENTURIAL	CHARTERED	CHILDLIKE	CHUBBIEST
CENTURIES	CHARWOMAN	CHILIADAL	CHUCKLING

CHUMMIEST	CLATTERED	CLUBHOUSE	COFFEE BAR
CHUNGKING	CLAVICLES	CLUMSIEST	COFFEEPOT
CHUNKIEST	CLAVICORN	CLUSTERED	COFFERDAM
CHURCHMAN	CLAYMORES	CLUTCH BAG	COGITATED
CICATRICE	CLAYSTONE	CLUTCHING	COGITATOR
CICATRIZE	CLAYTONIA	CLUTTERED	COGNATION
CICERONES	CLEANABLE	CNIDARIAN	COGNITION
CIGARETTE	CLEANNESS	COACHWORK	COGNITIVE
CIGARILLO	CLEANSERS	COADJUTOR	COGNIZANT
CILIATION	CLEANSING	COADUNATE	COGNOMENS
CILIOLATE	CLEARANCE	COAGULANT	COGWHEELS
CIMMERIAN	CLEAR-EYED	COAGULASE	COHABITED
CINCTURES	CLEARINGS	COAGULATE	COHERENCE
CINEMATIC	CLEARNESS	COALESCED	COIFFEURS
CINERARIA	CLEARWAYS	COALFACES	COIFFURED
CINEREOUS	CLEARWING	COALFIELD	COIFFURES
CINGULATE	CLEAVAGES	COALHOLES	COINCIDED
CIPHERING	CLEMENTLY	COALHOUSE	COINTREAU
CIRALPINE	CLENCHING	COALITION	COKULORIS
CIRCADIAN	CLERGYMAN	COALMINES	COLANDERS
CIRCASSIA	CLERGYMEN	COARCTATE	COLCHICUM
CIRCINATE	CLERIHEWS	COARSENED	COLCOTHAR
CIRCUITAL	CLERKSHIP	COASTLINE	COLD CREAM
CIRCUITRY	CLIENTELE	COAT TAILS	COLD-DRAWN
CIRCULARS	CLIMACTIC	COAXINGLY	COLD FRAME
CIRCULATE	CLIMAXING	COBALTITE	COLD FRONT
CIRRHOSED	CLIMB-DOWN	COBALTOUS	COLD SNAPS
CIRRHOSIS	CLINCHERS	COCA-COLAS	COLD SORES
CIRRHOTIC	CLINCHING	COCAINISM	COLD STEEL
CIRRIPEDE	CLINGFILM	COCAINIZE	COLD SWEAT
CITATIONS	CLINGFISH	COCCOLITH	COLECTOMY
CITIZENRY	CLINICIAN	COCCYGEAL	COLICROOT
CITY HALLS	CLINOSTAT	COCHINEAL	COLICWEED
CITY-STATE	CLINQUANT	COCHLEATE	COLLAGIST
CIVICALLY	CLINTONIA	COCK-A-HOOP	COLLAPSAR
CIVILIANS	CLIPBOARD	COCKATIEL	COLLAPSED
CIVILIZED	CLIP JOINT	COCKATOOS	COLLAPSES
CIVILIZER	CLIPPINGS	COCKED HAT	COLLARING
CIVIL LIST	CLITELLUM	COCKERELS	COLLATING
CIVIL WARS	CLOAKROOM	COCKFIGHT	COLLATION
CLAIMABLE	CLOBBERED	COCKHORSE	COLLATIVE
CLAIMANTS	CLOCKWISE	COCKINESS	COLLEAGUE
CLAMBAKES	CLOCKWORK	COCKLEBUR	COLLECTED
CLAMBERED	CLOISONNE	COCKNEYFY	COLLECTOR
CLAMMIEST	CLOISTERS	COCKROACH	COLLEGIAL
CLAMOROUS	CLOISTRAL	COCKSCOMB	COLLEGIAN
CLAMOURED	CLONICITY	COCKSFOOT	COLLEGIUM
CLAMPDOWN	CLOSE CALL	COCKTAILS	COLLIDING
CLAPBOARD	CLOSEDOWN	COCOONING	COLLIGATE
CLARENDON	CLOSE-KNIT	CODIFYING	COLLIMATE
CLARIFIED	CLOSENESS	CODPIECES	COLLINEAR
CLARIFIER	CLOSETING	COELOSTAT	COLLINSIA
CLARINETS	CLOTHIERS	COENOBITE	COLLISION
CLASSICAL	CLOUDBANK	COENOCYTE	COLLOCATE
CLASSIEST	CLOUDIEST	COENOSARC	COLLODION
CLASSLESS	CLOUDLESS	COEQUALLY	COLLOIDAL
CLASSMATE	CLOUD NINE	COERCIBLE	COLLOTYPE
CLASSROOM	CLOYINGLY	COEVALITY	COLLUDING
CLATHRATE	CLUBBABLE	COEXISTED	COLLUSION

COLLUSIVE	COMMITTEE	CONCERTED	CONGRUENT
COLLUVIAL	COMMITTER	CONCERTOS	CONGRUITY
COLLUVIUM	COMMODITY	CONCIERGE	CONGRUOUS
COLLYRIUM	COMMODORE	CONCILIAR	CONHOIDAL
COLOCYNTH	COMMONAGE	CONCISELY	CONICALLY
COLOMBIAN	COMMONERS	CONCISION	CONJOINED
COLONELCY	COMMON-LAW	CONCLAVES	CONJOINER
COLONIALS	COMMOTION	CONCLUDED	CONJUGANT
COLONISTS	COMMUNING	CONCOCTED	CONJUGATE
COLONIZED	COMMUNION	CONCOCTER	CONJURERS
COLONIZER	COMMUNISM	CONCORDAT	CONJURING
COLONNADE	COMMUNIST	CONCOURSE	CONNECTED
COLORIFIC	COMMUNITY	CONCRETED	CONNECTOR
COLOR LINE	COMMUNIZE	CONCUBINE	CONNEMARA
COLOSTOMY	COMMUTATE	CONCURRED	CONNIVENT
COLOSTRAL	COMMUTERS	CONCUSSED	CONNIVING
COLOSTRUM	COMMUTING	CONDEMNED	CONNOTING
COLOUR BAR	COMPACTED	CONDEMNER	CONNUBIAL
COLOUREDS	COMPACTER	CONDENSED	CONQUERED
COLOURFUL	COMPACTLY	CONDENSER	CONQUEROR
COLOURING	COMPANDER	CONDIGNLY	CONQUESTS
COLOURIST	COMPANIES	CONDIMENT	CONSCIOUS
COLTISHLY	COMPANION	CONDITION	CONSCRIPT
COLTSFOOT	COMPARING	CONDOLING	CONSENSUS
COLUBRINE	COMPASSES	CONDONING	CONSENTED
COLUMBIAN	COMPELLED	CONDUCING	CONSENTER
COLUMBINE	COMPELLER	CONDUCIVE	CONSERVED
COLUMBITE	COMPENDIA	CONDUCTED	CONSERVER
COLUMBIUM	COMPERING	CONDUCTOR	CONSERVES
COLUMELLA	COMPETENT	CONDYLOID	CONSIGNED
COLUMNIST	COMPETING	CONDYLOMA	CONSIGNEE
COMATULID	COMPILERS	CONFERRED	CONSIGNOR
COMBATANT	COMPILERR	CONFERRER	CONSISTED
COMBATING	COMPILING	CONFERVAL	CONSOCIES
COMBATIVE	COMPLAINT	CONFESSED	CONSOLING
COMBATTED	COMPLETED	CONFESSOR	CONSOLUTE
COMBINING	COMPLETER	CONFIDANT	CONSONANT
COMBUSTOR	COMPLEXES	CONFIDENT	CONSORTED
COMEBACKS	COMPLIANT	CONFIDING	CONSORTER
COMEDIANS	COMPLYING	CONFINING	CONSORTIA
COMEDOWNS	COMPONENT	CONFIRMED	CONSPIRED
COMELIEST	COMPORTED	CONFITURE	CONSTABLE
COMFORTED	COMPOSERS	CONFLATED	CONSTANCE
COMFORTER	COMPOSING	CONFLICTS	CONSTANCY
COMICALLY	COMPOSITE	CONFLUENT	CONSTANTA
COMMANDED	COMPOSTED	CONFORMAL	CONSTANTS
COMMANDER	COMPOSURE	CONFORMED	CONSTRAIN
COMMANDOS	COMPOUNDS	CONFORMER	CONSTRICT
COMMENCED	COMPRISAL	CONFRERES	CONSTRUCT
COMMENDAM	COMPRISED	CONFUCIAN	CONSTRUED
COMMENDED	COMPUTERS	CONFUSING	CONSTRUER
COMMENSAL	COMPUTING	CONFUSION	CONSULATE
COMMENTED	COMRADELY	CONFUTING	CONSULTED
COMMENTER	CONCAVITY	CONGEALED	CONSULTER
COMMINGLE	CONCEALED	CONGENIAL	CONSUMERS
COMMINUTE	CONCEDING	CONGER EEL	CONSUMING
COMMISSAR	CONCEITED	CONGERIES	CONTACTED
COMMITTAL	CONCEIVED	CONGESTED	CONTACTOR
COMMITTED	CONCENTRE	CONGOLESE	CONTAGION

CONTAGIUM	COPYRIGHT	COSMONAUT	CRACKSMEN
CONTAINED	COQUETTES	COSMOTRON	CRAFTIEST
CONTAINER	CORALLINE	COSSETTED	CRAFTSMAN
CONTEMNER	CORALLOID	COSTA RICA	CRAFTSMEN
CONTENDED	CORALROOT	CO-STARRED	CRAGGIEST
CONTENDER	CORBICULA	COSTLIEST	CRANBERRY
CONTENTED	COR BLIMEY	COSTOTOMY	CRANKCASE
CONTESTED	CORDIALLY	COST PRICE	CRANKIEST
CONTESTER	CORDIFORM	COSTUMIER	CRAPPIEST
CONTINENT	CORDONING	COTANGENT	CRAPULOUS
CONTINUAL	COREOPSIS	COT DEATHS	CRASH-DIVE
CONTINUED	CORIANDER	COTE D'AZUR	CRASH-LAND
CONTINUER	CORKBOARD	COTENANCY	CRASSNESS
CONTINUOS	CORKSCREW	COTILLION	CRATEROUS
CONTINUUM	CORMORANT	COTTAGERS	CRAYONING
CONTORTED	CORN BREAD	COTTONADE	CRAYONIST
CONTOURED	CORNCRAKE	COTTON GIN	CRAZINESS
CONTRACTS	CORNELIAN	COTYLEDON	CREAKIEST
CONTRAILS	CORNERING	COUCHETTE	CREAMCUPS
CONTRALTO	CORNETIST	COUNSELED	CREAMIEST
CONTRASTS	CORNFIELD	COUNTABLE	CREATIONS
CONTRASTY	CORNFLOUR	COUNTDOWN	CREATURAL
CONTRIVED	CORNSTALK	COUNTERED	CREATURES
CONTUMACY	COROLLARY	COUNTLESS	CREDENDUM
CONTUMELY	CORPORALE	COUNT NOUN	CREDITING
CONTUSING	CORPORALS	COUNTRIES	CREDITORS
CONTUSION	CORPORATE	COUP D'ETAT	CREDULITY
CONTUSIVE	CORPOREAL	COUPLINGS	CREDULOUS
CONUNDRUM	CORPOSANT	COURGETTE	CREEPIEST
CONVECTOR	CORPULENT	COURT CARD	CREMATING
CONVENERS	CORPUSCLE	COURTELLE	CREMATION
CONVENING	CORRALLED	COURTEOUS	CREMATORY
CONVERGED	CORRASION	COURTESAN	CRENATION
CONVERSED	CORRASIVE	COURTIERS	CRENULATE
CONVERSER	CORRECTED	COURTLIER	CREOLIZED
CONVERTED	CORRECTLY	COURTROOM	CREOPHAGY
CONVERTER	CORRECTOR	COURTSHIP	CREOSOTED
CONVEXITY	CORRELATE	COURTYARD	CREOSOTIC
CONVEYERS	CORRIDORS	COUTURIER	CREPITANT
CONVEYING	CORRODANT	COVALENCY	CREPITATE
CONVICTED	CORRODING	COVENANTS	CRESCENDO
CONVINCED	CORROSION	COVERALLS	CRESCENTS
CONVINCER	CORROSIVE	COVERINGS	CRETINISM
CONVIVIAL	CORRUGATE	COVERLESS	CRETINOID
CONVOKING	CORRUPTED	COVERLETS	CRETINOUS
CONVOLUTE	CORRUPTER	COVER NOTE	CREVASSES
CONVOYING	CORRUPTLY	COVERTURE	CREWELIST
CONVULSED	CORSELETS	COWARDICE	CREW NECKS
COOKHOUSE	CORTICATE	CO-WORKERS	CRIBELLUM
COOPERAGE	CORTISONE	COXCOMBRY	CRICKETER
COOPERATE	CORUSCATE	COYOTILLO	CRIMINALS
COORDINAL	CORVETTES	CRAB APPLE	CRIMPLENE
COPARTNER	CORYDALIS	CRABBEDLY	CRIMSONED
COPESTONE	CORYMBOSE	CRABBIEST	CRINKLIER
COPIOUSLY	COSEISMAL	CRABSTICK	CRINKLING
COPOLYMER	COSMETICS	CRACKDOWN	CRINOLINE
COPROLITE	COSMIC RAY	CRACKLING	CRIPPLING
COPULATED	COSMOGONY	CRACKPOTS	CRISPIEST
COPYBOOKS	COSMOLOGY	CRACKSMAN	CRISPNESS

CRITERION	CRYOMETRY	CUSTOMERS	DANGEROUS
CRITICISM	CRYOPHYTE	CUSTOMIZE	DAREDEVIL
CRITICIZE	CRYOSCOPE	CUTANEOUS	DARKENING
CRITIQUES	CRYOSCOPY	CUTICULAR	DARK HORSE
CROCHETED	CRYPTOGAM	CUTLASSES	DARKROOMS
CROCHETER	CTENIDIUM	CUTPURSES	DARMSTADT
CROCODILE	CUBBYHOLE	CUTTHROAT	DARTBOARD
CROISSANT	CUBE ROOTS	CUTTINGLY	DASHBOARD
CROMLECHS	CUBISISTS	CYANAMIDE	DASHINGLY
CROOKEDLY	CUB SCOUTS	CYANOTYPE	DASTARDLY
CROP-EARED	CUCKOLDED	CYBERNATE	DATABASES
CROQUETTE	CUCULLATE	CYCLAMATE	DATA BUSES
CROSSBARS	CUCUMBERS	CYCLOIDAL	DATEDNESS
CROSSBEAM	CUDDLIEST	CYCLONITE	DATELINES
CROSSBILL	CUDGELING	CYCLOPSES	DAUGHTERS
CROSSBOWS	CUDGELLED	CYCLORAMA	DAUNTLESS
CROSSBRED	CUDGELLER	CYCLOTRON	DAVENPORT
CROSS-EYED	CUFF LINKS	CYLINDERS	DAYDREAMS
CROSSFIRE	CUIRASSES	CYMBALIST	DAYDREAMY
CROSSHEAD	CUL-DE-SACS	CYMOGRAPH	DAYFLOWER
CROSSINGS	CULLENDER	CYMOPHANE	DAYLIGHTS
CROSS-LINK	CULMINANT	CYNICALLY	DAY SCHOOL
CROSSNESS	CULMINATE	CYNOSURES	DEACONESS
CROSSOVER	CULTIVATE	CYPHERING	DEADBEATS
CROSS TALK	CULTURIST	CYPRESSES	DEAD DUCKS
CROSSTREE	CUMBERING	CYPRINOID	DEADENING
CROSSWALK	CUMBRANCE	CYRENAICA	DEAD HEATS
CROSSWIND	CUNEIFORM	CYSTEINIC	DEADLIEST
CROSSWISE	CUNNINGLY	CYSTOCARP	DEADLIGHT
CROSSWORD	CUPBEARER	CYSTOCELE	DEADLINES
CROSSWORT	CUPBOARDS	CYSTOLITH	DEADLOCKS
CROTCHETS	CUP FINALS	CYSTOTOMY	DEADLY SIN
CROTCHETY	CUPOLATED	CYTOLYSIN	DEAD MARCH
CROUCHING	CURATIVES	CYTOLYSIS	DEAFENING
CROUPIERS	CURDINESS	CYTOPLASM	DEAF-MUTES
CROWBERRY	CURETTAGE	CYTOPLAST	DEALATION
CROWNWORK	CURIOSITY		DEAMINATE
CROW'S FEET	CURIOUSLY	**D**	DEANERIES
CROW'S FOOT	CURLICUES	DACHSHUND	DEATHBEDS
CROW'S NEST	CURLINESS	DACTYLICS	DEATHBLOW
CRUCIALLY	CURLPAPER	DADAISTIC	DEATH DUTY
CRUCIBLES	CURRENTLY	DAFFODILS	DEATHLESS
CRUCIFIED	CURRICULA	DAINTIEST	DEATHLIKE
CRUCIFIER	CURRYCOMB	DAIQUIRIS	DEATH MASK
CRUCIFORM	CURSIVELY	DAIRY FARM	DEATH RATE
CRUDITIES	CURSORIAL	DAIRYMAID	DEATH TOLL
CRUELTIES	CURSORILY	DALAI LAMA	DEATH TRAP
CRUMBLIER	CURTAILED	DALLIANCE	DEATH WISH
CRUMBLING	CURTAINED	DALMATIAN	DEBARKING
CRUMMIEST	CURTILAGE	DALTONISM	DEBARMENT
CRUMPLING	CURTSYING	DAMASCENE	DEBARRING
CRUNCHIER	CURVATURE	DAMNATION	DEBATABLE
CRUNCHILY	CUSHINESS	DAMNATORY	DEBAUCHED
CRUNCHING	CUSHIONED	DAMNEDEST	DEBAUCHEE
CRUSADERS	CUSPIDATE	DAMPENING	DEBAUCHER
CRUSADING	CUSPIDORS	DAMP SQUIB	DEBAUCHES
CRUSTIEST	CUSTODIAL	DAMSELFLY	DEBENTURE
CRYBABIES	CUSTODIAN	DANDELION	DEBOUCHED
CRYOMETER	CUSTOMARY	DANDIFIED	DEBRIEFED

DEBUGGING	DEDICATEE	DELICIOUS	DEPICTIVE
DEBUNKERS	DEDICATOR	DELIGHTED	DEPICTURE
DEBUNKING	DEDUCIBLE	DELIGHTER	DEPILATOR
DEBUTANTE	DEDUCTING	DELIMITED	DEPLETING
DECADENCE	DEDUCTION	DELINEATE	DEPLETION
DECAGONAL	DEDUCTIVE	DELIRIANT	DEPLETIVE
DECALCIFY	DEED POLLS	DELIRIOUS	DEPLORING
DECALOGUE	DEEDS POLL	DELIRIUMS	DEPLOYING
DECAMPING	DEEPENING	DELIVERED	DEPORTEES
DECANTERS	DEEP FRIED	DELIVERER	DEPORTING
DECANTING	DEEP SOUTH	DELOUSING	DEPOSABLE
DECAPODAL	DEERGRASS	DELUSIONS	DEPOSITED
DECASTYLE	DEERHOUND	DEMAGOGIC	DEPOSITOR
DECATHLON	DEFALCATE	DEMAGOGUE	DEPRAVING
DECEITFUL	DEFAULTED	DEMANDANT	DEPRAVITY
DECEIVERS	DEFAULTER	DEMANDING	DEPRECATE
DECEIVING	DEFEATING	DEMANTOID	DEPRESSED
DECEMBERS	DEFEATISM	DEMARCATE	DEPRESSOR
DECENCIES	DEFEATIST	DEMEANING	DEPRIVING
DECENNIAL	DEFECATED	DEMEANOUR	DEPURATOR
DECEPTION	DEFECATOR	DEMIJOHNS	DEPUTIZED
DECEPTIVE	DEFECTING	DEMIMONDE	DERAILING
DECIDABLE	DEFECTION	DEMISABLE	DERELICTS
DECIDEDLY	DEFECTIVE	DEMISTING	DE RIGUEUR
DECIDUOUS	DEFECTORS	DEMITASSE	DERISIBLE
DECILLION	DEFENDANT	DEMOBBING	DERIVABLE
DECIMALLY	DEFENDERS	DEMOCRACY	DERMATOID
DECIMATED	DEFENDING	DEMOCRATS	DERMATOME
DECIMATOR	DEFENSIVE	DEMOTIONS	DEROGATED
DECIMETRE	DEFERENCE	DEMULCENT	DERRING-DO
DECISIONS	DEFERMENT	DEMULSIFY	DERRINGER
DECKCHAIR	DEFERRING	DEMURRAGE	DERVISHES
DECKHANDS	DEFIANTLY	DEMURRING	DESCALING
DECKHOUSE	DEFICIENT	DEMYSTIFY	DESCANTER
DECLAIMED	DEFINABLE	DENDRITIC	DESCENDED
DECLAIMER	DEFINIENS	DENIGRATE	DESCENDER
DECLARANT	DEFLATING	DENITRATE	DESCRIBED
DECLARING	DEFLATION	DENITRIFY	DESCRIBER
DECLINATE	DEFLECTED	DENOTABLE	DESCRYING
DECLINING	DEFLECTOR	DENOUNCED	DESECRATE
DECLIVITY	DEFOLIANT	DENOUNCER	DESERTERS
DECOCTION	DEFOLIATE	DENSENESS	DESERTING
DECOLLATE	DEFORMING	DENSITIES	DESERTION
DECOLLETE	DEFORMITY	DENTALIUM	DESERVING
DECOMPOSE	DEFRAUDED	DENTATION	DESICCANT
DECONTROL	DEFRAUDER	DENTIFORM	DESICCATE
DECORATED	DEFRAYING	DENTISTRY	DESIGNATE
DECORATOR	DEFROCKED	DENTITION	DESIGNERS
DECOUPAGE	DEFROSTED	DEODORANT	DESIGNING
DECREASED	DEFROSTER	DEODORIZE	DESINENCE
DECREASES	DEGRADING	DEOXIDIZE	DESIRABLE
DECREEING	DEGREE-DAY	DEPARTING	DESIRABLY
DECREMENT	DEHISCENT	DEPARTURE	DESISTING
DECRETIVE	DEHYDRATE	DEPASTURE	DESMIDIAN
DECRETORY	DEJECTION	DEPENDANT	DES MOINES
DECUMBENT	DELEGABLE	DEPENDENT	DESOLATED
DECURRENT	DELEGATED	DEPENDING	DESOLATER
DECUSSATE	DELEGATES	DEPICTING	DESPAIRED
DEDICATED	DELETIONS	DEPICTION	DESPERADO

DESPERATE	DEXEDRINE	DICROTISM	DIPTEROUS
DESPISING	DEXTERITY	DICTATING	DIRECTING
DESPOILED	DEXTEROUS	DICTATION	DIRECTION
DESPOILER	DEXTRORSE	DICTATORS	DIRECTIVE
DESPOTISM	DIABETICS	DIDACTICS	DIRECTORS
DESPUMATE	DIABLERIE	DIETETICS	DIRECTORY
DESTINIES	DIABOLISM	DIETICIAN	DIRECTRIX
DESTITUTE	DIABOLIST	DIETITIAN	DIRECT TAX
DESTROYED	DIABOLIZE	DIFFERENT	DIREFULLY
DESTROYER	DIACONATE	DIFFERING	DIRIGIBLE
DESUETUDE	DIACRITIC	DIFFICULT	DIRT BIKES
DESULTORY	DIACTINIC	DIFFIDENT	DIRT CHEAP
DETACHING	DIAERESES	DIFFUSELY	DIRTINESS
DETAILING	DIAERESIS	DIFFUSING	DIRT ROADS
DETAINEES	DIAGNOSED	DIFFUSION	DIRT TRACK
DETAINING	DIAGNOSES	DIFFUSIVE	DIRTY WORK
DETECTING	DIAGNOSIS	DIGASTRIC	DISABLING
DETECTION	DIAGONALS	DIGENESIS	DISABUSAL
DETECTIVE	DIALECTAL	DIGENETIC	DISABUSED
DETECTORS	DIALECTIC	DIGESTANT	DISACCORD
DETENTION	DIALOGISM	DIGESTING	DISAFFECT
DETERGENT	DIALOGIST	DIGESTION	DISAFFIRM
DETERMENT	DIALOGIZE	DIGESTIVE	DISAGREED
DETERMINE	DIALOGUER	DIGITALIN	DISAPPEAR
DETERRENT	DIALOGUES	DIGITALIS	DISARMING
DETERRING	DIAMAGNET	DIGITIZED	DISASTERS
DETERSIVE	DIAMETERS	DIGITIZER	DISAVOWAL
DETESTING	DIAMETRAL	DIGITOXIN	DISAVOWED
DETHRONED	DIAMETRIC	DIGLOTTIC	DISAVOWER
DETHRONER	DIANDROUS	DIGNIFIED	DISBANDED
DETONATED	DIANOETIC	DIGNITARY	DISBARRED
DETONATOR	DIAPHONIC	DIGNITIES	DISBELIEF
DETRACTED	DIAPHRAGM	DIGRAPHIC	DISBRANCH
DETRACTOR	DIAPHYSIS	DIGRESSED	DISBURDEN
DETRAINED	DIARRHOEA	DIGRESSER	DISBURSED
DETRIMENT	DIASTASIC	DILATABLE	DISBURSER
DETRITION	DIASTASIS	DILATANCY	DISCALCED
DETRUSION	DIASTATIC	DILIGENCE	DISCARDED
DEUTERIDE	DIASTOLIC	DILUTIONS	DISCARDER
DEUTERIUM	DIATHERMY	DIMENSION	DISCERNED
DEVALUATE	DIATHESIS	DIMIDIATE	DISCERNER
DEVALUING	DIATHETIC	DIMISSORY	DISCHARGE
DEVASTATE	DIATOMITE	DIM-WITTED	DISCIPLES
DEVELOPED	DIATRIBES	DINGDONGS	DISCLIMAX
DEVELOPER	DIATROPIC	DINGINESS	DISCLOSED
DEVIATING	DIAZONIUM	DINING CAR	DISCLOSER
DEVIATION	DIAZOTIZE	DINOCERAS	DISCOIDAL
DEVIATORY	DIBROMIDE	DINOSAURS	DISCOLOUR
DEVILFISH	DICHASIAL	DINOTHERE	DISCOMFIT
DEVILLING	DICHASIUM	DIOECIOUS	DISCOMMON
DEVILMENT	DICHOGAMY	DIOESTRUS	DISCOUNTS
DEVIOUSLY	DICHOTOMY	DIPHTHONG	DISCOURSE
DEVISABLE	DICHROISM	DIPLOIDIC	DISCOVERT
DEVITRIFY	DICHROITE	DIPLOMACY	DISCOVERY
DEVOLVING	DICHROMIC	DIPLOMATE	DISCREDIT
DEVOTEDLY	DICKERING	DIPLOMATS	DISCUSSED
DEVOTIONS	DICKYBIRD	DIPLOTENE	DISDAINED
DEVOURING	DICLINISM	DIPSTICKS	DISEMBARK
DEVOUTEST	DICLINOUS	DIPSWITCH	DISEMBODY

DISENABLE	DISPUTING	DIVISIONS	DORMITORY
DISENGAGE	DISREGARD	DIVORCEES	DORMOBILE
DISENTAIL	DISRELISH	DIVORCING	DORONICUM
DISESTEEM	DISREPAIR	DIVORCIVE	DOSIMETER
DISFAVOUR	DISREPUTE	DIVULGING	DOSIMETRY
DISFIGURE	DISROBING	DIVULSION	DOSSHOUSE
DISFOREST	DISRUPTED	DIVULSIVE	DOTTINESS
DISGORGED	DISRUPTER	DIXIELAND	DOUBLE BED
DISGORGER	DISSECTED	DIZZINESS	DOUBLETON
DISGRACED	DISSECTOR	DJAJAPURA	DOUBLOONS
DISGRACER	DISSEISIN	DOCKETING	DOUBTABLE
DISGUISED	DISSEISOR	DOCKYARDS	DOUBTLESS
DISGUISER	DISSEMBLE	DOCTORATE	DOUGHNUTS
DISGUISES	DISSENTED	DOCTORING	DOUGHTIER
DISGUSTED	DISSENTER	DOCTRINAL	DOVECOTES
DISHCLOTH	DISSIDENT	DOCTRINES	DOVETAILS
DISHONEST	DISSIPATE	DOCUMENTS	DOWDINESS
DISHONOUR	DISSOLUTE	DODDERERS	DOWITCHER
DISH TOWEL	DISSOLVED	DODDERING	DOWNCOMER
DISHWATER	DISSOLVER	DODECAGON	DOWNFALLS
DISINFECT	DISSONANT	DOG COLLAR	DOWNGRADE
DISINFEST	DISSUADED	DOG-EAT-DOG	DOWNPOURS
DISK DRIVE	DISSUADER	DOGFIGHTS	DOWNRANGE
DISKETTES	DISTANCED	DOGFISHES	DOWNRIGHT
DISLIKING	DISTANCES	DOGGY BAGS	DOWNSPOUT
DISLOCATE	DISTANTLY	DOGHOUSES	DOWNSTAGE
DISLODGED	DISTEMPER	DOGLEGGED	DOWNSWING
DISMANTLE	DISTENDED	DOGMATICS	DOWNTHROW
DISMASTED	DISTENDER	DOGMATISM	DOWNTURNS
DISMAYING	DISTICHAL	DOGMATIST	DOWNWARDS
DISMEMBER	DISTILLED	DOGMATIZE	DRACONIAN
DISMISSAL	DISTILLER	DO-GOODERS	DRAFTIEST
DISMISSED	DISTINGUE	DOG PADDLE	DRAFTSMAN
DISOBEYED	DISTORTED	DOLEFULLY	DRAFTSMEN
DISOBEYER	DISTORTER	DOLERITIC	DRAGGIEST
DISOBLIGE	DISTRAINT	DOLLY BIRD	DRAGHOUND
DISORDERS	DISTRICTS	DOLOMITES	DRAGOMANS
DISOWNING	DISTURBED	DOLOMITIC	DRAGONESS
DISPARAGE	DISTURBER	DOLTISHLY	DRAGONFLY
DISPARATE	DISUNITED	DOMESTICS	DRAGONISH
DISPARITY	DITHERING	DOMICILED	DRAGOONED
DISPELLED	DITHYRAMB	DOMICILES	DRAINABLE
DISPELLER	DITTANDER	DOMINANCE	DRAINPIPE
DISPENSED	DIURETICS	DOMINATED	DRAMAMINE
DISPENSER	DIURNALLY	DOMINATOR	DRAMATICS
DISPERSAL	DIVALENCY	DOMINICAL	DRAMATIST
DISPERSED	DIVERGENT	DOMINICAN	DRAMATIZE
DISPERSER	DIVERGING	DOMINIONS	DRAPERIED
DISPLACED	DIVERSELY	DONATIONS	DRAPERIES
DISPLACER	DIVERSIFY	DONNISHLY	DRAUGHTER
DISPLAYED	DIVERSION	DONORSHIP	DRAVIDIAN
DISPLAYER	DIVERSITY	DOODLEBUG	DRAWBACKS
DISPLEASE	DIVERTING	DOORBELLS	DRAWKNIFE
DISPORTED	DIVERTIVE	DOORFRAME	DRAWPLATE
DISPOSING	DIVESTING	DOORKNOBS	DREAMBOAT
DISPRAISE	DIVIDABLE	DOORNAILS	DREAMLAND
DISPROVAL	DIVIDENDS	DOORPLATE	DREAMLESS
DISPROVED	DIVINABLE	DOORSTEPS	DREAMLIKE
DISPUTANT	DIVISIBLE	DORDRECHT	DREARIEST

DRENCHING	DUSTBOWLS	EASTER EGG	EGOTISTIC
DRESSIEST	DUSTCARTS	EASTERNER	EGREGIOUS
DRESSINGS	DUSTSHEET	EASTWARDS	EGYPTIANS
DRIBBLING	DUST STORM	EASY CHAIR	EIDERDOWN
DRIFTWOOD	DUTCH BARN	EASYGOING	EIGHTFOLD
DRILLABLE	DUTCH CAPS	EASY TERMS	EIGHTIETH
DRINKABLE	DUTCH OVEN	EAVESDROP	EINDHOVEN
DRIP-DRIED	DUTIFULLY	EBULLIENT	EIRENICON
DRIPSTONE	DUTY-FREES	ECCENTRIC	EISEGESIS
DRIVELING	DWELLINGS	ECHOLALIA	EJACULATE
DRIVELLED	DWINDLING	ECHOLALIC	EKISTICAL
DRIVELLER	DYER'S-WEED	ECLAMPSIA	ELABORATE
DRIVEWAYS	DYNAMETER	ECLAMPTIC	EL ALAMEIN
DRIZZLING	DYNAMITED	ECLIPSING	ELAN VITAL
DROLLNESS	DYNAMITER	ECOLOGIST	ELASTANCE
DROMEDARY	DYNAMITIC	ECONOMICS	ELASTOMER
DROPLIGHT	DYNAMOTOR	ECONOMIES	ELATERITE
DROPPINGS	DYNASTIES	ECONOMIST	ELATERIUM
DROPSICAL	DYSENTERY	ECONOMIZE	ELBOWROOM
DROPSONDE	DYSGENICS	ECOSPHERE	ELDERSHIP
DRUBBINGS	DYSLECTIC	ECOSYSTEM	ELECTIONS
DRUGGISTS	DYSPEPSIA	ECSTASIES	ELECTORAL
DRUGSTORE	DYSPEPTIC	ECSTATICS	ELECTRICS
DRUMBEATS	DYSPHAGIA	ECTOBLAST	ELECTRIFY
DRUM MAJOR	DYSPHAGIC	ECTOMERIC	ELECTRODE
DRUMSTICK	DYSPHASIA	ECTOMORPH	ELECTRONS
DRUNKARDS	DYSPHASIC	ECTOPHYTE	ELECTUARY
DRUNKENLY	DYSPHONIA	ECTOPLASM	ELEGANTLY
DUALISTIC	DYSPHONIC	ECTOPROCT	ELEMENTAL
DUBIOUSLY	DYSPHORIA	EDDYSTONE	ELEOPTENE
DUBITABLE	DYSPHORIC	EDELWEISS	ELEPHANTS
DUBROVNIK	DYSPLASIA	EDEMATOUS	ELEVATING
DUCHESSES	DYSPNOEAL	EDIBILITY	ELEVATION
DUCKBOARD	DYSTHYMIA	EDIFICIAL	ELEVATORS
DUCKLINGS	DYSTHYMIC	EDINBURGH	ELEVENSES
DUCTILITY	DYSTROPHY	EDITORIAL	ELEVENTHS
DUDE RANCH	DZUNGARIA	EDUCATING	ELICITING
DUELLISTS		EDUCATION	ELIMINANT
DUFFEL BAG	E	EDUCATIVE	ELIMINATE
DULCIMERS	EACH OTHER	EDUCATORS	ELLESMERE
DUMBBELLS	EAGERNESS	EDUCATORY	ELLIPSOID
DUMBFOUND	EAGLE-EYED	EDWARDIAN	EL MANSURA
DUMB SHOWS	EAGLEWOOD	EFFECTING	ELOCUTION
DUMMY RUNS	EARLINESS	EFFECTIVE	ELONGATED
DUMPINESS	EARLY BIRD	EFFECTUAL	ELOPEMENT
DUMPLINGS	EARMARKED	EFFERENCE	ELOQUENCE
DUNCE'S CAP	EARNESTLY	EFFICIENT	ELSEWHERE
DUNE BUGGY	EARPHONES	EFFLUENCE	ELUCIDATE
DUNGAREES	EARPIECES	EFFLUENTS	ELUSIVELY
DUNGENESS	EARTHIEST	EFFLUVIAL	ELUTRIATE
DUODECIMO	EARTHLIER	EFFLUVIUM	EMACIATED
DUODENARY	EARTHLING	EFFORTFUL	EMANATING
DUODENUMS	EARTHRISE	EFFULGENT	EMANATION
DUOLOGUES	EARTHSTAR	EFFUSIONS	EMANATIVE
DUPLEXITY	EARTHWARD	EGGPLANTS	EMANATORY
DUPLICATE	EARTHWORK	EGGSHELLS	EMBALMERS
DUPLICITY	EARTHWORM	EGG TIMERS	EMBALMING
DURALUMIN	EASTBOUND	EGLANTINE	EMBARGOED
DUSKINESS	EAST ENDER	EGOMANIAC	EMBARGOES

EMBARKING	ENACTMENT	ENGLACIAL	ENTRAPPED
EMBARRASS	ENAMELING	ENGRAMMIC	ENTRAPPER
EMBASSIES	ENAMELLED	ENGRAVERS	ENTREATED
EMBATTLED	ENAMELLER	ENGRAVING	ENTRECHAT
EMBAYMENT	ENAMOURED	ENGROSSED	ENTRECOTE
EMBEDDING	ENCAMPING	ENGROSSER	ENTREMETS
EMBEDMENT	ENCAUSTIC	ENGULFING	ENTRE NOUS
EMBELLISH	ENCHAINED	ENHANCING	ENTRUSTED
EMBEZZLED	ENCHANTED	ENHANCIVE	ENTRYWAYS
EMBEZZLER	ENCHANTER	ENIGMATIC	ENTWINING
EMBODYING	ENCHILADA	ENJOINING	ENUCLEATE
EMBOLISMS	ENCHORIAL	ENJOYABLE	ENUMERATE
EMBOSOMED	ENCIRCLED	ENJOYABLY	ENUNCIATE
EMBOSSING	ENCLOSING	ENJOYMENT	ENVELOPED
EMBOWMENT	ENCLOSURE	ENKINDLER	ENVELOPES
EMBRACEOR	ENCOMIAST	ENLARGING	ENVIOUSLY
EMBRACERY	ENCOMIUMS	ENLIGHTEN	ENVISAGED
EMBRACING	ENCOMPASS	ENLISTING	ENVYINGLY
EMBRASURE	ENCOUNTER	ENLIVENED	ENZYMATIC
EMBROCATE	ENCOURAGE	ENLIVENER	EPARCHIAL
EMBROIDER	ENCRINITE	ENMESHING	EPHEDRINE
EMBROILED	ENCRUSTED	ENNOBLING	EPHEMERAL
EMBROILER	ENDAMOEBA	EN PASSANT	EPHEMERID
EMBRYONIC	ENDEARING	ENQUIRIES	EPHEMERIS
EMENDABLE	ENDEAVOUR	ENQUIRING	EPHEMERON
EMENDATOR	ENDLESSLY	ENRAGEDLY	EPICENISM
EMERGENCE	ENDOBLAST	EN RAPPORT	EPICENTRE
EMERGENCY	ENDOCRINE	ENRAPTURE	EPICRISIS
EMIGRANTS	ENDOERGIC	ENRICHING	EPICRITIC
EMIGRATED	ENDOLYMPH	ENROLLING	EPICUREAN
EMINENCES	ENDOMORPH	ENROLMENT	EPICURISM
EMINENTLY	ENDOPHYTE	ENSCONCED	EPICYCLIC
EMISSIONS	ENDOPLASM	ENSEMBLES	EPIDEMICS
EMMENTHAL	ENDORSING	ENSHRINED	EPIDERMAL
EMOLLIENT	ENDOSCOPE	ENSLAVING	EPIDERMIS
EMOLUMENT	ENDOSCOPY	ENSNARING	EPIDURALS
EMOTIONAL	ENDOSPERM	ENSTATITE	EPIGENOUS
EMOTIVELY	ENDOSPORE	ENSUINGLY	EPIGRAPHY
EMOTIVISM	ENDOSTEAL	ENTAILING	EPIGYNOUS
EMPANELED	ENDOSTEUM	ENTAMOEBA	EPILEPTIC
EMPATHIZE	ENDOTOXIC	ENTANGLED	EPILOGIST
EMPENNAGE	ENDOTOXIN	ENTANGLER	EPILOGUES
EMPHASIZE	ENDOWMENT	ENTELECHY	EPIMYSIUM
EMPHYSEMA	ENDURABLE	ENTENDRES	EPINASTIC
EMPIRICAL	ENDURANCE	ENTERABLE	EPIPHANIC
EMPLOYEES	ENERGETIC	ENTERALLY	EPIPHRAGM
EMPLOYERS	ENERGIZED	ENTERITIS	EPIPHYSIS
EMPLOYING	ENERGIZER	ENTERTAIN	EPIPHYTIC
EMPORIUMS	ENERGUMEN	ENTHRONED	EPIROGENY
EMPOWERED	ENERVATED	ENTHUSING	EPISCOPAL
EMPRESSES	ENERVATOR	ENTHYMEME	EPISTASIS
EMPTIABLE	EN FAMILLE	ENTITLING	EPISTATIC
EMPTINESS	ENFEEBLED	ENTOBLAST	EPISTAXIS
EMPYREUMA	ENFEEBLER	ENTOMBING	EPISTEMIC
EMULATING	ENFILADED	ENTOPHYTE	EPITAPHIC
EMULATION	ENFILADES	ENTOURAGE	EPITAXIAL
EMULATIVE	ENFOLDING	ENTRAINED	EPITHETIC
EMULSIONS	ENFORCING	ENTRANCED	EPITOMIST
EMUNCTORY	ENGINEERS	ENTRANCES	EPITOMIZE

EPIZOOTIC	ESTAMINET	EVASIVELY	EXCUSABLE
EPONYMOUS	ESTATE CAR	EVENTUATE	EXCUSABLY
EQUAL-AREA	ESTEEMING	EVERGREEN	EXECRABLE
EQUALIZED	ESTHETICS	EVERSIBLE	EXECRABLY
EQUALIZER	ESTIMABLE	EVERYBODY	EXECRATED
EQUALLING	ESTIMATED	EVICTIONS	EXECUTANT
EQUATABLE	ESTIMATES	EVIDENTLY	EXECUTING
EQUATIONS	ESTIMATOR	EVILDOERS	EXECUTION
EQUERRIES	ESTOPPAGE	EVILDOING	EXECUTIVE
EQUINOXES	ESTRANGED	EVINCIBLE	EXECUTORS
EQUIPMENT	ESTRANGER	EVOCATION	EXECUTORY
EQUIPOISE	ESTUARIAL	EVOCATIVE	EXECUTRIX
EQUIPPING	ESTUARIES	EVOLUTION	EXEGETICS
EQUISETUM	ESTUARINE	EVOLVABLE	EXEMPLARY
EQUITABLE	ESURIENCE	EXACTABLE	EXEMPLIFY
EQUITABLY	ETCETERAS	EXACTNESS	EXEMPTING
EQUIVOCAL	ETERNALLY	EXALTEDLY	EXEMPTION
EQUIVOQUE	ETHERIZER	EXAMINERS	EXEQUATUR
ERADICANT	ETHICALLY	EXAMINING	EXERCISED
ERADICATE	ETHIOPIAN	EXANIMATE	EXERCISER
ERECTABLE	ETHMOIDAL	EXANTHEMA	EXERCISES
ERECTIONS	ETHNARCHY	EXCALIBUR	EXERTIONS
ERECTNESS	ETHNOGENY	EXCAUDATE	EXFOLIATE
EREMITISM	ETHNOLOGY	EXCAVATED	EXHALABLE
ERGOGRAPH	ETHOLOGIC	EXCAVATOR	EXHAUSTED
ERGOMETER	ETHYLENIC	EXCEEDING	EXHAUSTER
ERGONOMIC	ETIOLATED	EXCELLENT	EXHIBITED
ERISTICAL	ETIQUETTE	EXCELLING	EXHIBITOR
EROGENOUS	ETRAMETER	EXCELSIOR	EXHORTING
EROSIONAL	ETYMOLOGY	EXCEPTING	EXISTENCE
EROTICISM	EUCHARIST	EXCEPTION	EXODONTIA
ERRONEOUS	EUCLIDEAN	EXCEPTIVE	EXOENZYME
ERSTWHILE	EUDEMONIA	EXCERPTER	EX OFFICIO
ERUDITELY	EUDEMONIC	EXCESSIVE	EXOGAMOUS
ERUDITION	EULOGISTS	EXCHANGED	EXOGENOUS
ERUPTIBLE	EULOGIZED	EXCHANGER	EXONERATE
ERUPTIONS	EUPHEMISM	EXCHANGES	EXORCISER
ERYTHRISM	EUPHEMIST	EXCHEQUER	EXORCISMS
ERYTHRITE	EUPHEMIZE	EXCIPIENT	EXORCISTS
ESCALADER	EUPHONIUM	EXCISABLE	EXORCIZED
ESCALATED	EUPHONIZE	EXCISEMAN	EXOSMOSIS
ESCALATOR	EUPHORBIA	EXCISIONS	EXOSMOTIC
ESCALOPES	EUPHRATES	EXCITABLE	EXOSPHERE
ESCAPABLE	EUPLASTIC	EXCITEDLY	EXOSTOSIS
ESCAPADES	EURHYTHMY	EXCLAIMED	EXOTICISM
ESCAPISTS	EUROCRATS	EXCLAIMER	EXPANDING
ESCHEWING	EUROPOORT	EXCLUDING	EXPANSILE
ESCORTING	EUTHENICS	EXCLUSION	EXPANSION
ESKISEHIR	EUTHENIST	EXCLUSIVE	EXPANSIVE
ESOPHAGUS	EUTHERIAN	EXCORIATE	EXPATIATE
ESPERANTO	EUTROPHIC	EXCREMENT	EXPECTANT
ESPIONAGE	EVACUATED	EXCRETING	EXPECTING
ESPLANADE	EVACUATOR	EXCRETION	EXPEDIENT
ESPOUSALS	EVADINGLY	EXCRETIVE	EXPEDITED
ESPOUSING	EVAGINATE	EXCRETORY	EXPEDITER
ESPRESSOS	EVALUATED	EXCULPATE	EXPELLANT
ESSAYISTS	EVALUATOR	EXCURRENT	EXPELLING
ESSENTIAL	EVAPORATE	EXCURSION	EXPENDING
ESTABLISH	EVAPORITE	EXCURSIVE	EXPENSIVE

EXPERTISE	EXTREMIST	FALCONINE	FAVOURITE
EXPIATING	EXTREMITY	FALDSTOOL	FAWNINGLY
EXPIATION	EXTRICATE	FALLACIES	FEARFULLY
EXPIATORY	EXTRINSIC	FALLALERY	FEATHERED
EXPLAINED	EXTROVERT	FALLOPIAN	FEATURING
EXPLAINER	EXTRUDING	FALSEHOOD	FEBRICITY
EXPLETIVE	EXTRUSION	FALSENESS	FEBRIFUGE
EXPLICATE	EXTRUSIVE	FALSIFIED	FEBRILITY
EXPLODING	EXUBERANT	FALSIFIER	FECULENCE
EXPLOITED	EXUBERATE	FALSITIES	FECUNDATE
EXPLOITER	EXUDATION	FALTERING	FECUNDITY
EXPLORERS	EXUDATIVE	FAMILIARS	FEDERATED
EXPLORING	EYEBALLED	FAMILY MAN	FEELINGLY
EXPLOSION	EYEBRIGHT	FAMILY MEN	FEE-PAYING
EXPLOSIVE	EYELASHES	FANATICAL	FELICIFIC
EXPONENTS	EYELETEER	FANCINESS	FELONIOUS
EXPONIBLE	EYE-OPENER	FANCY-FREE	FEMINISTS
EXPORTERS	EYEPIECES	FANCYWORK	FENESTRAL
EXPORTING	EYE SHADOW	FANDANGLE	FENUGREEK
EXPOSABLE	EYESTRAIN	FANDANGOS	FERMANAGH
EXPOSITOR		FANLIGHTS	FERMENTED
EXPOSURES	F	FAN-TAILED	FERMENTER
EXPOUNDED	FABACEOUS	FANTASIES	FEROCIOUS
EXPOUNDER	FABIANISM	FANTASIZE	FERRETING
EXPRESSED	FABRICATE	FANTASTIC	FERROCENE
EXPRESSER	FABRIKOID	FARADIZER	FERROTYPE
EXPRESSES	FACE CARDS	FARANDOLE	FERTILITY
EXPRESSLY	FACECLOTH	FAREWELLS	FERTILIZE
EXPULSION	FACE-LIFTS	FARMHANDS	FERVENTLY
EXPULSIVE	FACE PACKS	FARMHOUSE	FESTERING
EXPUNGING	FACEPLATE	FARMSTEAD	FESTIVALS
EXPURGATE	FACE-SAVER	FARMYARDS	FESTIVITY
EXQUISITE	FACETIOUS	FARRAGOES	FESTOONED
EXSECTION	FACE VALUE	FARROWING	FETICIDAL
EXSERTILE	FACSIMILE	FAR-SEEING	FETISHISM
EXSERTION	FACTIONAL	FARTHINGS	FETISHIST
EXSICCATE	FACTITIVE	FASCICLED	FETTERING
EXSTROPHY	FACTORAGE	FASCICULE	FETTUCINE
EXTEMPORE	FACTORIAL	FASCINATE	FEUDALISM
EXTENDING	FACTORIES	FASCISTIC	FEUDALIST
EXTENSION	FACTORING	FASHIONED	FEUDALITY
EXTENSITY	FACTORIZE	FASHIONER	FEUDALIZE
EXTENSIVE	FACTUALLY	FASTENERS	FEUDATORY
EXTENUATE	FACULTIES	FASTENING	FEVERWORT
EXTERIORS	FADDINESS	FATALISTS	FIBONACCI
EXTERNALS	FADDISHLY	FATEFULLY	FIBREFILL
EXTIRPATE	FADEDNESS	FATHEADED	FIBRIFORM
EXTOLLING	FAGACEOUS	FATHERING	FIBRINOUS
EXTOLMENT	FAGGOTING	FATHOMING	FICTIONAL
EXTORTING	FAINEANCE	FATIGABLE	FIDEISTIC
EXTORTION	FAINTNESS	FATIGUING	FIDGETING
EXTORTIVE	FAIRYLAND	FATTENING	FIDUCIARY
EXTRABOLD	FAIRY-LIKE	FATTINESS	FIELD DAYS
EXTRACTED	FAIRY-TALE	FATUITOUS	FIELDFARE
EXTRACTOR	FAITHFULS	FATUOUSLY	FIELDSMAN
EXTRADITE	FAITHLESS	FAULTIEST	FIELDSMEN
EXTRAVERT	FALANGISM	FAULTLESS	FIELD-TEST
EXTREMELY	FALANGIST	FAVEOLATE	FIELD TRIP
EXTREMISM	FALCONERS	FAVOURING	FIELDWORK

FIFTEENTH	FIRSTLING	FLEDGLING	FLYING FOX
FIFTIETHS	FIRST NAME	FLEETNESS	FLYLEAVES
FIGURINES	FIRST-RATE	FLESHIEST	FLYSHEETS
FILAMENTS	FISHCAKES	FLESHINGS	FLYWEIGHT
FILIATION	FISHERIES	FLESHPOTS	FLYWHEELS
FILICIDAL	FISHERMAN	FLEURETTE	FLYWHISKS
FILLETING	FISHERMEN	FLEXIONAL	FOAMINESS
FILLISTER	FISH FARMS	FLEXITIME	FOCUSABLE
FILMINESS	FISHINESS	FLICKERED	FOCUSSING
FILM STARS	FISH KNIFE	FLIGHTIER	FOETATION
FILM STOCK	FISHPLATE	FLIGHTILY	FOETICIDE
FILMSTRIP	FISH SLICE	FLIMSIEST	FOGGINESS
FILOPLUME	FISH STICK	FLINCHING	FOLIATION
FILOSELLE	FISSILITY	FLINTIEST	FOLIOLATE
FILTERING	FISTULOUS	FLINTLOCK	FOLK DANCE
FILTER TIP	FIXATIONS	FLIP-FLOPS	FOLKLORIC
FILTHIEST	FIXATIVES	FLIPPANCY	FOLKTALES
FIMBRIATE	FIXED-HEAD	FLOATABLE	FOLLICLES
FINALISTS	FIXED STAR	FLOAT-FEED	FOLLOWERS
FINALIZED	FIZZINESS	FLOCCULUS	FOLLOWING
FINANCIAL	FLABBIEST	FLOGGINGS	FOLLOW-UPS
FINANCIER	FLABELLUM	FLOODABLE	FOMENTING
FINANCING	FLACCIDLY	FLOODGATE	FOOD STAMP
FINE-GRAIN	FLAGELLAR	FLOOD TIDE	FOODSTUFF
FINE PRINT	FLAGELLUM	FLOOR SHOW	FOOLERIES
FINE-TOOTH	FLAGEOLET	FLOPHOUSE	FOOLHARDY
FINE-TUNED	FLAGPOLES	FLOPPIEST	FOOLISHLY
FINGERING	FLAGRANCE	FLORIATED	FOOLPROOF
FINGERTIP	FLAGRANCY	FLORIDITY	FOOTBALLS
FINISHING	FLAGSHIPS	FLORISTIC	FOOTBOARD
FINISTERE	FLAGSTAFF	FLOS FERRI	FOOTFALLS
FIRE ALARM	FLAGSTONE	FLOTATION	FOOT FAULT
FIREBALLS	FLAG-WAVER	FLOTILLAS	FOOTHILLS
FIREBOXES	FLAKINESS	FLOUNCING	FOOTHOLDS
FIREBRAND	FLAMELIKE	FLOUNDERS	FOOTLOOSE
FIREBREAK	FLAMINGOS	FLOURMILL	FOOTNOTES
FIREBRICK	FLAMMABLE	FLOWCHART	FOOTPATHS
FIRECREST	FLANNELED	FLOWERAGE	FOOTPLATE
FIRE DRILL	FLAPJACKS	FLOWERBED	FOOT-POUND
FIRE-EATER	FLARE PATH	FLOWERING	FOOTPRINT
FIREFLIES	FLASHBACK	FLOWERPOT	FOOTRACES
FIREGUARD	FLASHBULB	FLOWINGLY	FOOTSTALK
FIRE IRONS	FLASHCUBE	FLUCTUANT	FOOTSTALL
FIRELIGHT	FLASHGUNS	FLUCTUATE	FOOTSTEPS
FIREPLACE	FLASHIEST	FLUFFIEST	FOOTSTOOL
FIRE-PLUGS	FLASHOVER	FLUIDIZER	FORAMINAL
FIREPOWER	FLATMATES	FLUKINESS	FORBEARER
FIREPROOF	FLAT SPINS	FLUMMOXED	FORBIDDEN
FIRESIDES	FLATTENED	FLUORESCE	FORBIDDER
FIRESTONE	FLATTENER	FLUOROSIS	FORCEABLE
FIRESTORM	FLATTERED	FLUORSPAR	FORCE-FEED
FIRETHORN	FLATTERER	FLURRYING	FORCEMEAT
FIRETRAPS	FLATULENT	FLUSTERED	FORCINGLY
FIREWATER	FLAUNTING	FLUTTERED	FOREARMED
FIREWORKS	FLAUTISTS	FLUTTERER	FOREBEARS
FIRMAMENT	FLAVOROUS	FLUXIONAL	FOREBODED
FIRSTBORN	FLAVOURED	FLUXMETER	FOREBODER
FIRSTHAND	FLAVOURER	FLY-FISHER	FOREBRAIN
FIRST LADY	FLEABITES	FLY HALVES	FORECASTS

FORECLOSE	FORTIFIER	FREEZABLE	FRUSTRATE
FORECOURT	FORTITUDE	FREEZE-DRY	FRYING PAN
FOREFRONT	FORTNIGHT	FREIGHTED	FUGACIOUS
FOREGOING	FORTUNATE	FREIGHTER	FUGITIVES
FOREHANDS	FORTY-FIVE	FREMANTLE	FUKUSHIMA
FOREHEADS	FORWARDED	FRENCHIFY	FULFILLED
FOREIGNER	FORWARDER	FRENCHMAN	FULFILLER
FOREJUDGE	FORWARDLY	FRENCHMEN	FULGURITE
FORELOCKS	FOSSILIZE	FREQUENCE	FULGUROUS
FORENAMED	FOSSORIAL	FREQUENCY	FULLBACKS
FORENAMES	FOSTERAGE	FRESHENED	FULL-BLOWN
FORENSICS	FOSTERING	FRESHENER	FULL BOARD
FOREREACH	FOUNDERED	FRESHNESS	FULL DRESS
FORESHANK	FOUNDLING	FRETFULLY	FULL-FACED
FORESHEET	FOUNDRIES	FRETWORKS	FULL-GROWN
FORESHOCK	FOUNTAINS	FRIARBIRD	FULL HOUSE
FORESHORE	FOURSOMES	FRICASSEE	FULL MOONS
FORESIGHT	FOUR-WHEEL	FRICATIVE	FULL-SCALE
FORESKINS	FOVEOLATE	FRIESIANS	FULL STOPS
FORESTALL	FOXGLOVES	FRIESLAND	FULMINANT
FORESTERS	FOXHOUNDS	FRIGHTFUL	FULMINATE
FORETASTE	FOXHUNTER	FRIGIDITY	FULSOMELY
FORETOKEN	FRACTIONS	FRILLIEST	FUMAROLIC
FORETOOTH	FRACTIOUS	FRISKIEST	FUMIGATED
FOREWOMAN	FRACTURAL	FRITTERED	FUMIGATOR
FOREWOMEN	FRACTURED	FRITTERER	FUNCTIONS
FOREWORDS	FRACTURES	FRIVOLITY	FUNDAMENT
FORFEITED	FRAGILITY	FRIVOLLER	FUNGICIDE
FORFEITER	FRAGMENTS	FRIVOLOUS	FUNGIFORM
FORFICATE	FRAGRANCE	FRIZZIEST	FUNGISTAT
FORGATHER	FRAILTIES	FRIZZLING	FUNICULAR
FORGEABLE	FRAMBOISE	FROCK COAT	FUNICULUS
FORGERIES	FRAMEWORK	FROGMARCH	FUNNELING
FORGETFUL	FRANCHISE	FROGMOUTH	FUNNELLED
FORGETTER	FRANCOLIN	FROGSPAWN	FUNNINESS
FORGIVING	FRANGIBLE	FROLICKED	FUNNY BONE
FORGOTTEN	FRANGLAIS	FROLICKER	FUNNY FARM
FORLORNLY	FRANKABLE	FRONTAGES	FURBISHED
FORMALISM	FRANKNESS	FRONTALLY	FURBISHER
FORMALIST	FRATERNAL	FRONT DOOR	FURCATION
FORMALITY	FREE AGENT	FRONTIERS	FURIOUSLY
FORMALIZE	FREE-BASED	FRONT LINE	FURLOUGHS
FORMATION	FREEBOARD	FRONT-PAGE	FURNISHED
FORMATIVE	FREEHOLDS	FRONT ROOM	FURNISHER
FORMATTED	FREE HOUSE	FROSTBITE	FURNITURE
FORMICARY	FREE KICKS	FROSTIEST	FURRINESS
FORMULAIC	FREELANCE	FROSTWORK	FURROWING
FORMULARY	FREE-LIVER	FROTHIEST	FURTHERED
FORMULATE	FREEMASON	FROWSTIER	FURTHERER
FORMULISM	FREEPHONE	FROWZIEST	FURTIVELY
FORMULIST	FREE PORTS	FRUCTUOUS	FUSELAGES
FORNICATE	FREE-RANGE	FRUGALITY	FUSILLADE
FORSAKING	FREESHEET	FRUIT BATS	FUSIONISM
FORSYTHIA	FREESTONE	FRUITCAKE	FUSIONIST
FORTALEZA	FREESTYLE	FRUITIEST	FUSSINESS
FORTALICE	FREE TRADE	FRUITLESS	FUSTINESS
FORTHWITH	FREE VERSE	FRUMPIEST	FUTURISTS
FORTIETHS	FREEWHEEL		FUZZINESS
FORTIFIED	FREE WORLD		

G	GARRULOUS	GEOGRAPHY	GLADDENER
GABARDINE	GAS FITTER	GEOLOGIST	GLADIATOR
GABERDINE	GASHOLDER	GEOLOGIZE	GLADIOLUS
GABIONADE	GASLIGHTS	GEOMANCER	GLAIREOUS
GADABOUTS	GASOLINIC	GEOMANTIC	GLAMORIZE
GADOLINIC	GASOMETER	GEOMETRIC	GLAMOROUS
GADROONED	GASOMETRY	GEOMETRID	GLANDERED
GAINFULLY	GASPINGLY	GEOPHYTIC	GLANDULAR
GAINSAYER	GASSINESS	GEOPONICS	GLARINGLY
GALACTOSE	GASTRITIC	GEORGETTE	GLASSIEST
GALANTINE	GASTRITIS	GEOSTATIC	GLASSWARE
GALAPAGOS	GASTROPOD	GEOTACTIC	GLASSWORK
GALEIFORM	GASTRULAR	GEOTROPIC	GLASSWORT
GALENICAL	GATECRASH	GERANIUMS	GLEANABLE
GALINGALE	GATEHOUSE	GERIATRIC	GLEANINGS
GALLANTLY	GATEPOSTS	GERMANDER	GLEEFULLY
GALLANTRY	GATHERING	GERMANISM	GLENGARRY
GALLERIED	GAUCHERIE	GERMANITE	GLIDINGLY
GALLERIES	GAUDINESS	GERMANIUM	GLIMMERED
GALLICISM	GAUGEABLE	GERMANIZE	GLIMPSING
GALLICIZE	GAUGEABLY	GERMANOUS	GLISSADER
GALLINULE	GAULEITER	GERM CELLS	GLISSANDO
GALLIPOLI	GAUNTLETS	GERMICIDE	GLISTENED
GALLIVANT	GAUNTNESS	GERMINANT	GLITTERED
GALLONAGE	GAUZINESS	GERMINATE	GLITZIEST
GALLOPING	GAWKINESS	GERMISTON	GLOBALISM
GALLSTONE	GAZEHOUND	GERUNDIAL	GLOBALIST
GALUMPHED	GAZETTEER	GERUNDIVE	GLOBOSITY
GALVANISM	GAZIANTEP	GESTATION	GLOMERATE
GALVANIZE	GAZUMPING	GESTATORY	GLOMERULE
GALWEGIAN	GEARBOXES	GESTURING	GLOOMIEST
GAMBOGIAN	GEAR LEVER	GEYSERITE	GLORIFIED
GAMBOLING	GEARWHEEL	GHASTLIER	GLORIFIER
GAMECOCKS	GEHLENITE	GHOSTLIER	GLORY HOLE
GAMMADION	GELIGNITE	GHOST TOWN	GLOSSIEST
GAMMA RAYS	GELSEMIUM	GIBBERING	GLOSSITIC
GANDHIISM	GEMMATION	GIBBERISH	GLOSSITIS
GANG-BANGS	GEMUTLICH	GIBRALTAR	GLOTTIDES
GANGLIONS	GENDARMES	GIDDINESS	GLOTTISES
GANGPLANK	GENEALOGY	GIFT HORSE	GLOWERING
GANGSTERS	GENERABLE	GIGAHERTZ	GLOWINGLY
GAOLBIRDS	GENERALLY	GIGANTISM	GLOW-WORMS
GARDENERS	GENERATED	GILSONITE	GLUCOSIDE
GARDENIAS	GENERATOR	GILT-EDGED	GLUTAMINE
GARDENING	GENIALITY	GIMMICKRY	GLUTENOUS
GARGOYLED	GENITALIC	GINGER ALE	GLUTINOUS
GARGOYLES	GENITALLY	GINGERING	GLYCERIDE
GARIBALDI	GENITIVAL	GINGER NUT	GLYCERINE
GARLANDED	GENITIVES	GIN SLINGS	GLYCOSIDE
GARNERING	GENOCIDAL	GIPSYWORT	GOAL LINES
GARNISHED	GENOTYPIC	GIRANDOLE	GOALMOUTH
GARNISHER	GENTEELLY	GIRL GUIDE	GOALPOSTS
GARNISHES	GENTILITY	GIRLISHLY	GOATHERDS
GARNITURE	GENTLEMAN	GIRONDISM	GOATSKINS
GARRISONS	GENTLEMEN	GIRONDIST	GO-BETWEEN
GARROTTED	GENTLE SEX	GIVEAWAYS	GODFATHER
GARROTTER	GENUFLECT	GIVEN NAME	GODLESSLY
GARROTTES	GENUINELY	GLABELLAR	GODLINESS
GARRULITY	GEODESIST	GLADDENED	GODMOTHER

GODPARENT	GRANDIOSE	GRENADIER	GUARDSMAN
GO-GETTERS	GRANDIOSO	GRENADINE	GUARDSMEN
GOGGLE BOX	GRAND JURY	GREY AREAS	GUARD'S VAN
GOING-OVER	GRANDNESS	GREYBEARD	GUATEMALA
GOLDCREST	GRAND PRIX	GREYHOUND	GUAYAQUIL
GOLDEN AGE	GRAND SLAM	GREY-STATE	GUERRILLA
GOLDENEYE	GRANDSONS	GREYWACKE	GUESSABLE
GOLDENROD	GRANITITE	GRIDIRONS	GUESSWORK
GOLDFIELD	GRANIVORE	GRIEVANCE	GUESTROOM
GOLDFINCH	GRANOLITH	GRILLROOM	GUFFAWING
GOLD MEDAL	GRANTABLE	GRIMACING	GUIDELINE
GOLD-MINER	GRANULATE	GRIMALKIN	GUIDEPOST
GOLDMINES	GRANULITE	GRIMINESS	GUIDINGLY
GOLD PLATE	GRANULOMA	GRINDELIA	GUILDHALL
GOLDSMITH	GRAPESHOT	GRIPINGLY	GUILDSMAN
GOLF BALLS	GRAPEVINE	GRISAILLE	GUILELESS
GOLF CLUBS	GRAPHITIC	GRISLIEST	GUILLEMOT
GOLF LINKS	GRAPPLING	GRISTLIER	GUILLOCHE
GOLLIWOGS	GRASPABLE	GRISTMILL	GUILTIEST
GOMPHOSIS	GRASSIEST	GRITTIEST	GUILTLESS
GONDOLIER	GRASSLAND	GRIZZLING	GUINEA PIG
GONIATITE	GRASSQUIT	GROCERIES	GUITARIST
GONOPHORE	GRATICULE	GROGGIEST	GULPINGLY
GONORRHEA	GRATIFIED	GRONINGEN	GUMMATOUS
GOODLIEST	GRATIFIER	GROOMSMAN	GUMMINESS
GOOD LOOKS	GRATINGLY	GROOVIEST	GUMSHIELD
GOODNIGHT	GRATITUDE	GROPINGLY	GUN COTTON
GOOD-SIZED	GRAVELING	GROSGRAIN	GUNPOWDER
GOOD WORDS	GRAVELISH	GROSSNESS	GUNRUNNER
GOOFINESS	GRAVELLED	GROTESQUE	GUNSMITHS
GOOSANDER	GRAVENESS	GROTTIEST	GUSHINGLY
GOOSEFOOT	GRAVEYARD	GROUCHIER	GUSTATORY
GOOSENECK	GRAVIDITY	GROUCHILY	GUSTINESS
GOOSESTEP	GRAVITATE	GROUCHING	GUTTERING
GOOSINESS	GRAVY BOAT	GROUNDAGE	GYMKHANAS
GORAKHPUR	GREASE GUN	GROUNDING	GYMNASIUM
GORGEABLE	GREASIEST	GROUNDNUT	GYMNASTIC
GORGONIAN	GREAT-AUNT	GROUNDSEL	GYNAECOID
GORILLIAN	GREAT BEAR	GROUPINGS	GYNARCHIC
GORILLOID	GREATCOAT	GROVELING	GYNOECIUM
GOSPELLER	GREAT DANE	GROVELLED	GYNOPHORE
GOSSIPING	GREATNESS	GROVELLER	GYRATIONS
GOTHICISM	GREEDIEST	GRUBBIEST	GYRFALCON
GOTTINGEN	GREENBACK	GRUBSTAKE	GYROSCOPE
GOURMANDS	GREEN BEAN	GRUELLING	
GOUTINESS	GREEN BELT	GRUFFNESS	H
GOVERNESS	GREENGAGE	GRUMBLERS	HABERGEON
GOVERNING	GREENHEAD	GRUMBLING	HABITABLE
GOVERNORS	GREENHORN	GRUMPIEST	HABITABLY
GRACELESS	GREENLAND	GUANABARA	HABITUATE
GRADATION	GREENLING	GUANIDINE	HACIENDAS
GRADIENTS	GREENNESS	GUANOSINE	HACKAMORE
GRADUALLY	GREENROOM	GUARANTEE	HACKBERRY
GRADUATED	GREENSAND	GUARANTOR	HACKNEYED
GRADUATES	GREENWICH	GUARDABLE	HADROSAUR
GRADUATOR	GREENWOOD	GUARDEDLY	HAECCEITY
GRAMPUSES	GREETINGS	GUARDIANS	HAEMATEIN
GRANARIES	GREGARINE	GUARDRAIL	HAEMATITE
GRANDADDY	GREGORIAN	GUARDROOM	HAEMATOID

HAEMATOMA	HAMMERING	HARDSHIPS	HEADFIRST
HAEMOCOEL	HAMMERTOE	HARDWOODS	HEADINESS
HAEMOCYTE	HAMMURABI	HAREBELLS	HEADLANDS
HAEMOSTAT	HAMPERING	HARKENING	HEADLIGHT
HAGBUTEER	HAMPSHIRE	HARLEQUIN	HEADLINED
HAGGADIST	HAMPSTEAD	HARMATTAN	HEADLINER
HAGGARDLY	HAMSTRING	HARMFULLY	HEADLINES
HAGGISHLY	HAMSTRUNG	HARMONICA	HEADPIECE
HAGIARCHY	HANDBILLS	HARMONICS	HEADREACH
HAGIOLOGY	HANDBOOKS	HARMONIES	HEADRESTS
HAG-RIDDEN	HANDBRAKE	HARMONIST	HEADSCARF
HAIDAR ALI	HANDCARTS	HARMONIUM	HEADSHIPS
HAILSTONE	HANDCLAPS	HARMONIZE	HEADSTALL
HAILSTORM	HANDCLASP	HARMOTOME	HEADSTAND
HAIRBRUSH	HANDCRAFT	HARNESSED	HEAD START
HAIRCLOTH	HANDCUFFS	HARNESSER	HEADSTOCK
HAIRGRIPS	HANDICAPS	HARNESSES	HEADSTONE
HAIRINESS	HANDINESS	HARPOONED	HEADWARDS
HAIRLINES	HANDIWORK	HARPOONER	HEADWINDS
HAIRPIECE	HANDLEBAR	HARQUEBUS	HEADWORDS
HAIR SHIRT	HANDLOOMS	HARRIDANS	HEALINGLY
HAIR SLIDE	HANDOVERS	HARROGATE	HEALTHFUL
HAIRSTYLE	HANDRAILS	HARROVIAN	HEALTHIER
HALEAKALA	HANDSHAKE	HARROWING	HEALTHILY
HALESOWEN	HANDSPIKE	HARSHNESS	HEARKENED
HALFBACKS	HANDSTAND	HARTBEEST	HEARKENER
HALF-BAKED	HANGERS-ON	HARTSHORN	HEARTACHE
HALF BOARD	HANGNAILS	HARUSPICY	HEARTBEAT
HALF-BREED	HANGOVERS	HARVESTED	HEARTBURN
HALF-CASTE	HANKERING	HARVESTER	HEARTENED
HALF CROWN	HANSEATIC	HASDRUBAL	HEARTFELT
HALF-LIGHT	HAPHAZARD	HASHEMITE	HEARTHRUG
HALF-LIVES	HAPHTARAH	HASTENING	HEARTIEST
HALF MOONS	HAPLESSLY	HASTINESS	HEARTLAND
HALF NOTES	HAPLOLOGY	HATCHABLE	HEARTLESS
HALFPENCE	HAPPENING	HATCHBACK	HEARTSICK
HALFPENNY	HAPPINESS	HATCHMENT	HEARTSOME
HALFTONES	HAPPY HOUR	HATCHWAYS	HEARTWOOD
HALF-TRUTH	HARANGUED	HATEFULLY	HEARTWORM
HALITOSIS	HARANGUER	HAT TRICKS	HEATHERED
HALLELUJA	HARANGUES	HAUGHTIER	HEATHFOWL
HALLIARDS	HARASSING	HAUGHTILY	HEATHLIKE
HALL-JONES	HARBINGER	HAVENLESS	HEAT PUMPS
HALLMARKS	HARBOURED	HAVERSACK	HEAT WAVES
HALLOWE'EN	HARBOURER	HAVERSIAN	HEAVINESS
HALLOWING	HARDBACKS	HAVERSINE	HEAVISIDE
HALLOWMAS	HARDBOARD	HAWKSBILL	HEAVY-DUTY
HALLSTATT	HARDBOUND	HAWSEHOLE	HEBRAIZER
HALMAHERA	HARD CIDER	HAWSEPIPE	HEBRIDEAN
HALOBIONT	HARD CORES	HAWTHORNE	HECTOGRAM
HALOPHYTE	HARDCOVER	HAWTHORNS	HECTORING
HALOTHANE	HARD DISKS	HAYMAKING	HEDGEHOGS
HALTINGLY	HARD DRINK	HAYSTACKS	HEDGEROWS
HAMADRYAD	HARDENING	HAZARDING	HEDONISTS
HAMADRYAS	HARDHEADS	HAZARDOUS	HEEDFULLY
HAMAMATSU	HARDIHOOD	HEADACHES	HEELPIECE
HAMBURGER	HARDINESS	HEADBANDS	HEFTINESS
HAMERSLEY	HARD-LINER	HEADBOARD	HEGEMONIC
HAM-FISTED	HARD-NOSED	HEADDRESS	HEGUMENOS

HEIMDALLR	HESITATER	HILARIOUS	HOLE IN ONE
HEINOUSLY	HESPERIAN	HILLBILLY	HOLIDAYED
HEIRESSES	HESSONITE	HILLOCKED	HOLINSHED
HEIRLOOMS	HESYCHAST	HILLSIDES	HOLLANDER
HELGOLAND	HETAERISM	HILVERSUM	HOLLANDIA
HELICALLY	HETAERIST	HIMALAYAS	HOLLERING
HELICLINE	HETAIRISM	HIMYARITE	HOLLOWEST
HELIOSTAT	HETERODOX	HINDBRAIN	HOLLOWING
HELIOTYPE	HETERONYM	HINDERING	HOLLYHOCK
HELIOZOAN	HETEROSIS	HINDOOISM	HOLLYWOOD
HELIPORTS	HEURISTIC	HINDRANCE	HOLOCAINE
HELLDIVER	HEXACHORD	HINDSIGHT	HOLOCAUST
HELLEBORE	HEXAGONAL	HINDU KUSH	HOLOCRINE
HELLENIAN	HEXAGRAMS	HINDUSTAN	HOLOGRAMS
HELLENISM	HEXAMETER	HINGELESS	HOLOGRAPH
HELLENIST	HEXAPODIC	HINGELIKE	HOLOPHYTE
HELLENIZE	HEXASTICH	HIP FLASKS	HOLOTYPIC
HELLHOUND	HEXASTYLE	HIP POCKET	HOLSTEINS
HELLISHLY	HEXATEUCH	HIPPOCRAS	HOLSTERED
HELPFULLY	HEY PRESTO	HIPPOLYTA	HOLY GHOST
HELPMATES	HIBERNATE	HIPPOLYTE	HOLY GRAIL
HELVELLYN	HIBERNIAN	HIRELINGS	HOLYSTONE
HELVETIAN	HICCUPING	HIROSHIGE	HOME FRONT
HELVETIUS	HICKORIES	HIROSHIMA	HOMEGROWN
HEMIALGIA	HIDDENITE	HIRUNDINE	HOME GUARD
HEMICYCLE	HIDEAWAYS	HISPIDITY	HOME HELPS
HEMINGWAY	HIDEBOUND	HISTAMINE	HOMELANDS
HEMISTICH	HIDEOUSLY	HISTIDINE	HOMELIEST
HEMITROPE	HIERARCHY	HISTOGENY	HOMEMAKER
HEMSTITCH	HIERODULE	HISTOGRAM	HOME MOVIE
HENDIADYS	HIEROGRAM	HISTOLOGY	HOMEOPATH
HEN HOUSES	HIEROLOGY	HISTORIAN	HOMESTEAD
HENPECKED	HIFALUTIN	HISTORIES	HOMETOWNS
HEOMANIAC	HIGHBALLS	HIT-AND-RUN	HOME TRUTH
HEPATITIS	HIGHBROWS	HITCHCOCK	HOMEWARDS
HEPTAGONS	HIGH CHAIR	HITCHHIKE	HOMEYNESS
HEPTARCHY	HIGH-CLASS	HITLERISM	HOMICIDAL
HERACLEAN	HIGH COURT	HIT-OR-MISS	HOMICIDES
HERALDING	HIGHER-UPS	HIT PARADE	HOMILETIC
HERALDIST	HIGH-FLIER	HOARDINGS	HOMOGRAFT
HERBALIST	HIGH-FLOWN	HOARFROST	HOMOGRAPH
HERBARIAL	HIGH-GRADE	HOARHOUND	HOMOLYSIS
HERBARIUM	HIGH HORSE	HOARINESS	HOMOLYTIC
HERBICIDE	HIGH JINKS	HOATCHING	HOMONYMIC
HERBIVORE	HIGH JUMPS	HOBBESIAN	HOMOPHILE
HERCULEAN	HIGHLANDS	HOBGOBLIN	HOMOPHONE
HERCYNIAN	HIGH-LEVEL	HOBNAILED	HOMOPHONY
HEREAFTER	HIGHLIGHT	HOBNOBBED	HOMOPHYLY
HERETICAL	HIGH POINT	HO CHI MINH	HOMOPLASY
HEREUNDER	HIGH-RISES	HODOMETER	HOMOPOLAR
HERITABLE	HIGH ROADS	HODOMETRY	HOMOSPORY
HERITABLY	HIGH-SPEED	HODOSCOPE	HOMOTAXIC
HERITRESS	HIGH SPOTS	HOGGISHLY	HOMOTAXIS
HERMITAGE	HIGH TABLE	HOGSHEADS	HONEYBEES
HERMITIAN	HIGH TIDES	HOHENLOHE	HONEYCOMB
HERNIATED	HIGH-TONED	HOIDENISH	HONEYEDLY
HERODOTUS	HIGH WATER	HOI POLLOI	HONEY-LIKE
HESITANCY	HIJACKERS	HOLARCTIC	HONEYMOON
HESITATED	HIJACKING	HOLDOVERS	HONKY-TONK

HONORARIA	HOUSELEEK	HYBRIDISM	IGNITABLE
HONORIFIC	HOUSELESS	HYBRIDITY	IGNORAMUS
HONOR ROLL	HOUSELINE	HYBRIDIZE	IGNORANCE
HONOURING	HOUSEMAID	HYBRISTIC	IGNORATIO
HOODOOISM	HOUSEROOM	HYDANTOIN	IGUANODON
HOOFBOUND	HOUSETOPS	HYDATHODE	ILEOSTOMY
HOOK-NOSED	HOUSEWIFE	HYDERABAD	ILL AT EASE
HOOKWORMS	HOUSEWORK	HYDRANGEA	ILLEGALLY
HOOLIGANS	HOUSTONIA	HYDRASTIS	ILLEGIBLE
HOOTNANNY	HOVERPORT	HYDRATION	ILLEGIBLY
HOOVERING	HOWITZERS	HYDRAULIC	ILL-GOTTEN
HOPE CHEST	HOWLINGLY	HYDRAZINE	ILLIBERAL
HOPEFULLY	HOWSOEVER	HYDRAZOIC	ILLICITLY
HOPLOLOGY	HOWTOWDIE	HYDRIODIC	ILLNESSES
HOPSCOTCH	HOYDENISH	HYDROCELE	ILLOGICAL
HOREHOUND	HSUAN T'UNG	HYDROFOIL	ILL-OMENED
HORNBILLS	HUBRISTIC	HYDROLOGY	ILLUSIONS
HORNINESS	HUCKABACK	HYDROLYSE	IMAGINARY
HORNPIPES	HUCKSTERS	HYDROLYTE	IMAGINING
HORNSTONE	HUE AND CRY	HYGIENIST	IMAGISTIC
HOROLOGIC	HUFFINESS	HYPERBOLA	IMBALANCE
HOROSCOPE	HUGH CAPET	HYPERBOLE	IMBECILES
HOROSCOPY	HU-HO-HAO-T'E	HYPHENATE	IMBEDDING
HORRIFIED	HUMANISTS	HYPNOTISM	IMBRICATE
HORSEBACK	HUMANIZED	HYPNOTIST	IMBROGLIO
HORSEHAIR	HUMANIZER	HYPNOTIZE	IMIDAZOLE
HORSEHIDE	HUMANKIND	HYPOCRISY	IMITATING
HORSELESS	HUMAN-LIKE	HYPOCRITE	IMITATION
HORSELIKE	HUMANNESS	HYSTERICS	IMITATIVE
HORSEMINT	HUMANOIDS		IMITATORS
HORSEPLAY	HUMAN RACE	I	IMMANENCE
HORSESHIT	HUMBLEBEE	ICE CREAMS	IMMANENCY
HORSESHOE	HUMBUGGER	ICE HOCKEY	IMMEDIACY
HORSETAIL	HUMDINGER	ICELANDER	IMMEDIATE
HORSEWEED	HUMECTANT	ICELANDIC	IMMENSELY
HORSEWHIP	HUMERUSES	ICE SHEETS	IMMENSITY
HORSINESS	HUMIDNESS	ICE-SKATED	IMMERSING
HORTATIVE	HUMILIATE	ICE-SKATER	IMMERSION
HORTATORY	HUMORISTS	ICE SKATES	IMMIGRANT
HOSPITALS	HUMOURFUL	ICHNEUMON	IMMIGRATE
HOSPITIUM	HUMOURING	ICHNOLOGY	IMMINENCE
HOSTELLER	HUMPBACKS	ICHTHYOID	IMMINGHAM
HOSTESSES	HUMPINESS	ICONOLOGY	IMMODESTY
HOSTILELY	HUNCHBACK	IDEALISTS	IMMOLATED
HOSTILITY	HUNDREDTH	IDEALIZED	IMMOLATOR
HOTELIERS	HUNGARIAN	IDEALIZER	IMMORALLY
HOTFOOTED	HUNGERING	IDENTICAL	IMMORTALS
HOTHEADED	HUNGRIEST	IDENTIKIT	IMMOVABLE
HOTHOUSES	HUNKY-DORY	IDEOGRAMS	IMMOVABLY
HOTPLATES	HUNNISHLY	IDEOLOGUE	IMMUNIZED
HOT POTATO	HURRICANE	IDEOMOTOR	IMMUNIZER
HOTTENTOT	HURRIEDLY	IDIOBLAST	IMMUTABLE
HOT WATERS	HURTFULLY	IDIOLECTS	IMMUTABLY
HOURGLASS	HUSBANDED	IDIOMATIC	IMPACTING
HOUSEBOAT	HUSBANDER	IDIOPATHY	IMPACTION
HOUSEBOYS	HUSBANDRY	IDIOPHONE	IMPAIRING
HOUSECARL	HUSH MONEY	IDOLATERS	IMPARTIAL
HOUSECOAT	HUSKINESS	IDOLIZING	IMPARTING
HOUSEHOLD	HYACINTHS	IGNESCENT	IMPASSION

IMPASSIVE	INANITION	INDEXICAL	INFRACTOR
IMPATIENS	INAPTNESS	INDIAN INK	INFRINGED
IMPATIENT	INAUDIBLE	INDICATED	INFRINGER
IMPEACHED	INAUDIBLY	INDICATOR	INFURIATE
IMPEACHER	INAUGURAL	INDICTING	INFUSCATE
IMPEDANCE	INCAPABLE	INDIGENCE	INFUSIBLE
IMPELLENT	INCAPABLY	INDIGNANT	INFUSIONS
IMPELLING	INCARNATE	INDIGNITY	INGENIOUS
IMPENDING	INCAUTION	INDIGOTIC	INGENUITY
IMPERFECT	INCENSING	INDISPOSE	INGENUOUS
IMPERILED	INCENTIVE	INDOCHINA	INGESTING
IMPERIOUS	INCEPTION	INDOLENCE	INGESTION
IMPETRATE	INCEPTIVE	INDONESIA	INGESTIVE
IMPETUOUS	INCESSANT	INDORSING	INGLENOOK
IMPETUSES	INCIDENCE	INDRAUGHT	INGRAINED
IMPIETIES	INCIDENTS	INDUCIBLE	INGROWING
IMPINGING	INCIPIENT	INDUCTILE	INHABITED
IMPIOUSLY	INCISIONS	INDUCTING	INHALANTS
IMPLANTED	INCISURAL	INDUCTION	INHALATOR
IMPLANTER	INCLEMENT	INDUCTIVE	INHARMONY
IMPLEADER	INCLINING	INDULGENT	INHERENCE
IMPLEMENT	INCLOSING	INDULGING	INHERITED
IMPLICATE	INCLOSURE	INEBRIANT	INHERITOR
IMPLODING	INCLUDING	INEBRIATE	INHIBITED
IMPLORING	INCLUSION	INEBRIETY	INHIBITER
IMPLOSION	INCLUSIVE	INEFFABLE	INHIBITOR
IMPLOSIVE	INCOGNITO	INEFFABLY	INITIALED
IMPOLITIC	INCOME TAX	INELASTIC	INITIALER
IMPORTANT	INCOMMODE	INELEGANT	INITIALLY
IMPORTERS	INCORRECT	INEPTNESS	INITIATED
IMPORTING	INCORRUPT	INERTNESS	INITIATES
IMPORTUNE	INCREASED	INFANTILE	INITIATOR
IMPOSABLE	INCREASER	INFARCTED	INJECTING
IMPOSTORS	INCREASES	INFATUATE	INJECTION
IMPOSTURE	INCREMENT	INFECTING	INJECTIVE
IMPOTENCE	INCRETION	INFECTION	INJURABLE
IMPOUNDED	INCUBATED	INFECTIVE	INJURIOUS
IMPOUNDER	INCUBATOR	INFERABLE	INJUSTICE
IMPRECATE	INCUBUSES	INFERENCE	INKSTANDS
IMPRECISE	INCULCATE	INFERIORS	INMIGRANT
IMPRESSED	INCULPATE	INFERRING	INNER CITY
IMPRESSER	INCUMBENT	INFERTILE	INNERMOST
IMPRESSES	INCURABLE	INFESTING	INNER TUBE
IMPRINTED	INCURABLY	INFIELDER	INNERVATE
IMPRINTER	INCURIOUS	INFIGHTER	INNKEEPER
IMPROBITY	INCURRENT	INFIRMARY	INNOCENCE
IMPROMPTU	INCURRING	INFIRMITY	INNOCUOUS
IMPROVING	INCURSION	INFLAMING	INNOVATED
IMPROVISE	INCURSIVE	INFLATING	INNOVATOR
IMPRUDENT	INCURVATE	INFLATION	INNSBRUCK
IMPUDENCE	INDECENCY	INFLECTED	INNUENDOS
IMPUGNING	INDECORUM	INFLECTOR	INOCULATE
IMPULSION	INDELIBLE	INFLICTED	INORGANIC
IMPULSIVE	INDELIBLY	INFLICTER	INOTROPIC
IMPUTABLE	INDEMNIFY	INFLUENCE	IN-PATIENT
INABILITY	INDEMNITY	INFLUENZA	INPUTTING
INAMORATA	INDENTING	INFORMANT	INQUILINE
INANIMATE	INDENTION	INFORMERS	INQUIRIES
INANITIES	INDENTURE	INFORMING	INQUIRING

INQUORATE	INTERCEDE	INTUITIVE	IRRITANTS
INSCRIBED	INTERCEPT	INTUMESCE	IRRITATED
INSCRIBER	INTERCITY	INUNCTION	IRRITATOR
INSECTEAN	INTERCOMS	INUNDATED	IRRUPTION
INSELBERG	INTERCROP	INUNDATOR	IRRUPTIVE
INSENSATE	INTERDICT	INUTILITY	ISAGOGICS
INSERTING	INTERESTS	INVADABLE	ISALLOBAR
INSERTION	INTERFACE	INVALIDED	ISCHAEMIA
IN-SERVICE	INTERFERE	INVALIDLY	ISINGLASS
INSETTING	INTERFILE	INVARIANT	ISLAMABAD
INSIDE JOB	INTERFUSE	INVASIONS	ISLANDERS
INSIDIOUS	INTERIORS	INVECTIVE	ISOBARISM
INSINCERE	INTERJECT	INVEIGHED	ISOBATHIC
INSINUATE	INTERLACE	INVEIGHER	ISOCHORIC
INSIPIDLY	INTERLARD	INVEIGLED	ISOCLINAL
INSISTENT	INTERLEAF	INVEIGLER	ISOCRATIC
INSISTING	INTERLINE	INVENTING	ISOGAMETE
INSOLENCE	INTERLINK	INVENTION	ISOGAMOUS
INSOLUBLE	INTERLOCK	INVENTIVE	ISOGENOUS
INSOLVENT	INTERLOPE	INVENTORS	ISOLATING
INSOMNIAC	INTERLUDE	INVENTORY	ISOLATION
INSPECTED	INTERMENT	INVERNESS	ISOLATIVE
INSPECTOR	INTERNEES	INVERSELY	ISOLOGOUS
INSPIRING	INTERNING	INVERSION	ISOMERISM
INSTALLED	INTERNIST	INVERSIVE	ISOMERIZE
INSTALLER	INTERNODE	INVERTASE	ISOMEROUS
INSTANCED	INTERPLAY	INVERTING	ISOMETRIC
INSTANCES	INTERPOSE	INVESTING	ISONIAZID
INSTANTER	INTERPRET	INVIDIOUS	ISOOCTANE
INSTANTLY	INTERRING	INVIOLACY	ISOPROPYL
INSTIGATE	INTERRUPT	INVIOLATE	ISOSCELES
INSTILLED	INTERSECT	INVISIBLE	ISOSMOTIC
INSTILLER	INTERVALS	INVISIBLY	ISOSTATIC
INSTINCTS	INTERVENE	INVOCABLE	ISOSTERIC
INSTITUTE	INTERVIEW	INVOICING	ISOTACTIC
INSULATED	INTERWOVE	INVOLUCEL	ISOTHERAL
INSULATOR	INTESTACY	INVOLUCRE	ISOTHERMS
INSULTING	INTESTATE	INVOLVING	ISOTROPIC
INSURABLE	INTESTINE	IODOMETRY	ISRAELITE
INSURANCE	INTIMATED	IONOPAUSE	ISTHMUSES
INSURGENT	INTIMATES	IPSO FACTO	ITALICIZE
INSWINGER	INTORSION	IRASCIBLE	ITCHINESS
INTAGLIOS	INTRICACY	IRASCIBLY	ITCHY FEET
INTEGRAND	INTRICATE	IRIDOTOMY	ITCHY PALM
INTEGRANT	INTRIGUED	IRISH STEW	ITEMIZING
INTEGRATE	INTRIGUER	IRONBOUND	ITERATION
INTEGRITY	INTRIGUES	IRONSIDES	ITERATIVE
INTELLECT	INTRINSIC	IRONSTONE	ITINERANT
INTENDANT	INTRODUCE	IRONWORKS	ITINERARY
INTENDEDS	INTROITAL	IROQUOIAN	ITINERATE
INTENDING	INTROJECT	IRRADIANT	ITSY-BITSY
INTENSELY	INTROVERT	IRRADIATE	IVY LEAGUE
INTENSIFY	INTRUDERS	IRRAWADDY	
INTENSION	INTRUDING	IRREGULAR	J
INTENSITY	INTRUSION	IRRIGABLE	JABBERERS
INTENSIVE	INTRUSIVE	IRRIGATED	JABBERING
INTENTION	INTRUSTED	IRRIGATOR	JABORANDI
INTER ALIA	INTUITING	IRRITABLE	JACARANDA
INTERBRED	INTUITION	IRRITABLY	JACKASSES

JACKBOOTS	JOVIALITY	KELTICISM	KNOCKOUTS
JACK FROST	JOYLESSLY	KELTICIST	KNOTGRASS
JACKFRUIT	JOYRIDERS	KENNELING	KNOTTIEST
JACK KNIFE	JOYRIDING	KENNELLED	KNOWINGLY
JACKSHAFT	JOYSTICKS	KENTLEDGE	KNOWLEDGE
JACKSMELT	JUBILANCE	KEPT WOMAN	KNOXVILLE
JACKSNIPE	JUDDERING	KEPT WOMEN	KNUCKLING
JACOBITES	JUDGEABLE	KERATITIS	KONIOLOGY
JAILBIRDS	JUDGEMENT	KERATOSIS	KOOKINESS
JAILBREAK	JUDGESHIP	KERBSTONE	KOSCIUSKO
JAMBOREES	JUDGINGLY	KERCHIEFS	KOWTOWING
JAM-PACKED	JUDGMENTS	KERFUFFLE	KOZHIKODE
JANISSARY	JUDICABLE	KETONURIA	KRASNODAR
JANSENISM	JUDICATOR	KEYBOARDS	KRONSTADT
JANSENIST	JUDICIARY	KEYSTONES	KUIBYSHEV
JANUARIES	JUDICIOUS	KEYSTROKE	KURDISTAN
JAPANNING	JUICINESS	KIBBUTZES	KURRAJONG
JAPONICAS	JUKEBOXES	KIBBUTZIM	KWANGTUNG
JARGONIZE	JULLUNDUR	KICKBACKS	KYMOGRAPH
JAUNDICED	JUMBO JETS	KID GLOVES	
JAUNTIEST	JUMPINESS	KIDNAPING	L
JAYWALKED	JUMP-START	KIDNAPPED	LABELLING
JAYWALKER	JUMPSUITS	KIDNAPPER	LABELLOID
JEALOUSLY	JUNCTIONS	KIESERITE	LABIALISM
JEERINGLY	JUNCTURES	KILLARNEY	LABIALITY
JELLY BEAN	JUNGLE GYM	KILLIFISH	LABIALIZE
JELLYFISH	JUNKETING	KILLINGLY	LABORIOUS
JELLY ROLL	JUNOESQUE	KILOBYTES	LABOUR DAY
JEREMIADS	JURIDICAL	KILOCYCLE	LABOURERS
JERKINESS	JURY BOXES	KILOGRAMS	LABOURING
JERKINGLY	JUSTICIAR	KILOHERTZ	LABOURISM
JEROBOAMS	JUSTIFIED	KILOLITRE	LABOURIST
JERUSALEM	JUSTIFIER	KILOMETRE	LABOURITE
JESTINGLY	JUTLANDER	KILOWATTS	LABRADORS
JESUITISM	JUVENILES	KIMBERLEY	LABURNUMS
JET ENGINE	JUVENILIA	KINDLIEST	LABYRINTH
JET-SETTER	JUXTAPOSE	KINEMATIC	LACCOLITH
JET STREAM		KINGLIEST	LACERABLE
JEWELFISH	K	KINGMAKER	LACERATED
JEWELLERS	KADIYEVKA	KING'S EVIL	LACERTIAN
JEWELLERY	KAGOSHIMA	KINGSTOWN	LACHRYMAL
JEWELLING	KAISERDOM	KINKINESS	LACINIATE
JEW'S HARPS	KAMCHATKA	KINSWOMAN	LACQUERED
JIB-HEADED	KANAMYCIN	KIRKCALDY	LACQUERER
JITTERBUG	KANGAROOS	KIROVABAD	LACTATION
JOB CENTRE	KAOHSIUNG	KISANGANI	LADDERING
JOCKEYING	KAOLINITE	KITCHENER	LADIES' MAN
JOCKSTRAP	KARABINER	KITTENISH	LADIES' MEN
JOCULARLY	KARAGANDA	KITTIWAKE	LADYBIRDS
JOCUNDITY	KARAKORAM	KLEENEXES	LADYSHIPS
JOE PUBLIC	KARLSRUHE	KNACKERED	LAEVULOSE
JOINTRESS	KARYOGAMY	KNAPSACKS	LAGOMORPH
JOINTWORM	KARYOSOME	KNAVERIES	LALLATION
JOLLINESS	KARYOTYPE	KNAVISHLY	LAMAISTIC
JONKOPING	KATABATIC	KNIFE-EDGE	LAMBASTED
JORDANIAN	KATANGESE	KNIGHTING	LAMBSKINS
JOSS STICK	KATHIAWAR	KNITTABLE	LAME DUCKS
JOURNEYED	KAWAGUCHI	KNOBBLIER	LAMENTING
JOURNEYER	KEEPSAKES	KNOCKDOWN	LAMINABLE

LAMINARIA	LAUGHABLE	LENGTHILY	LIGAMENTS
LAMINATED	LAUGHABLY	LENIENTLY	LIGATURES
LAMINATES	LAUNCHING	LENINABAD	LIGHT BULB
LAMINATOR	LAUNCH PAD	LENINAKAN	LIGHTENED
LAMINITIS	LAUNDERED	LENINGRAD	LIGHT-FAST
LAMP-BLACK	LAUNDERER	LEPONTINE	LIGHTNESS
LAMPOONED	LAUNDRESS	LEPTOSOME	LIGHTNING
LAMPOONER	LAUNDRIES	LEPTOTENE	LIGHTSHIP
LAMPPOSTS	LAUREATES	LESSENING	LIGHTS-OUT
LAMPSHADE	LAVISHING	LETHALITY	LIGHT YEAR
LANCASTER	LAWGIVING	LETHARGIC	LIGNIFORM
LANCEWOOD	LAWLESSLY	LETTERBOX	LIKELIEST
LANCINATE	LAWNMOWER	LETTERING	LILY-WHITE
LAND AGENT	LAWN PARTY	LEUCOCYTE	LIMA BEANS
LANDAULET	LAXATIVES	LEUCOTOMY	LIMELIGHT
LANDFALLS	LAYABOUTS	LEUKAEMIA	LIMERICKS
LANDLORDS	LAY FIGURE	LEVANTINE	LIMESTONE
LANDMARKS	LAYPERSON	LEVELLERS	LIMEWATER
LANDMINES	LAY READER	LEVELLING	LIMITABLE
LANDOWNER	LAY SISTER	LEVIATHAN	LIMITLESS
LAND ROVER	LAZARETTO	LEVIGATOR	LIMNOLOGY
LANDSCAPE	LAZYBONES	LEVITATED	LIMOUSINE
LANDSLIDE	LEAD TIMES	LEVITATOR	LIMPIDITY
LANDSLIPS	LEAFINESS	LEXICALLY	LIMPINGLY
LANDWARDS	LEAFLETED	LIABILITY	LINCHPINS
LANGOUSTE	LEAF MOULD	LIBATIONS	LINEAMENT
LANGUAGES	LEAFSTALK	LIBELLANT	LINEARITY
LANGUEDOC	LEAKINESS	LIBELLING	LINEATION
LANGUIDLY	LEAP YEARS	LIBELLOUS	LINEOLATE
LANKINESS	LEARNABLE	LIBERALLY	LINGERERS
LANOLATED	LEARNEDLY	LIBERATED	LINGERING
LANTHANUM	LEASEBACK	LIBERATOR	LINGUISTS
LAODICEAN	LEASEHOLD	LIBERTIES	LINGULATE
LAPLANDER	LEASTWAYS	LIBERTINE	LINKOPING
LARCENIES	LEAVENING	LIBIDINAL	LINOLEATE
LARCENIST	LECHEROUS	LIBRARIAN	LINOTYPER
LARCENOUS	LECTORATE	LIBRARIES	LIONIZING
LARGENESS	LECTURERS	LIBRATION	LIPOLYSIS
LARGHETTO	LECTURING	LIBRATORY	LIPOLYTIC
LARKSPURS	LEERINGLY	LIBRETTOS	LIP-READER
LARVICIDE	LEE SHORES	LIBRIFORM	LIPSTICKS
LARYNGEAL	LEFTOVERS	LICENSEES	LIQUATION
LASHINGLY	LEFTWARDS	LICENSING	LIQUEFIED
LAS PALMAS	LEGALIZED	LICHENOID	LIQUEFIER
LASSITUDE	LEGATIONS	LICHENOUS	LIQUIDATE
LAST-DITCH	LEGENDARY	LIENTERIC	LIQUIDITY
LASTINGLY	LEGGINESS	LIFE BELTS	LIQUIDIZE
LAST STRAW	LEGGINGED	LIFEBLOOD	LIQUORICE
LATCHKEYS	LEGIONARY	LIFEBOATS	LISPINGLY
LATECOMER	LEGISLATE	LIFE BUOYS	LISTENERS
LATERALLY	LEG-WARMER	LIFE CYCLE	LISTENING
LATERITIC	LEICESTER	LIFEGUARD	LISTERISM
LATHERING	LEISURELY	LIFELINES	LIST PRICE
LATIMERIA	LEITMOTIV	LIFE PEERS	LITERALLY
LATINIZER	LEMNISCUS	LIFE-SAVER	LITERATIM
LATITUDES	LEMON CURD	LIFESPANS	LITHENESS
LATTER-DAY	LEMON SOLE	LIFE STORY	LITHIASIS
LAUDATION	LEND-LEASE	LIFESTYLE	LITHOLOGY
LAUDATORY	LENGTHIER	LIFETIMES	LITHOPONE

LITHOTOMY	LONGCLOTH	LUCKY DIPS	MADREPORE
LITHUANIA	LONGEVITY	LUCRATIVE	MADRIGALS
LITIGABLE	LONGEVOUS	LUCUBRATE	MAELSTROM
LITIGANTS	LONG FACES	LUDICROUS	MAGAZINES
LITIGATED	LONGICORN	LUFTWAFFE	MAGDEBURG
LITIGATOR	LONGINGLY	LULLABIES	MAGICALLY
LITIGIOUS	LONGITUDE	LULLINGLY	MAGIC EYES
LITTERBIN	LONG JOHNS	LUMBERING	MAGICIANS
LITTERING	LONG-LIVED	LUMBERMAN	MAGIC WAND
LITTORALS	LONG-RANGE	LUMBERMEN	MAGISTERY
LITURGICS	LONGSHIPS	LUMBRICAL	MAGISTRAL
LITURGIES	LONGSHORE	LUMINANCE	MAGMATISM
LITURGISM	LONG SHOTS	LUMINESCE	MAGNESIAN
LITURGIST	LONGUEUIL	LUMPINESS	MAGNESITE
LIVELIEST	LONGUEURS	LUNATICAL	MAGNESIUM
LIVERPOOL	LOOK-ALIKE	LUNISOLAR	MAGNETICS
LIVERWORT	LOOM-STATE	LUNITIDAL	MAGNETISM
LIVERYMAN	LOONINESS	LURIDNESS	MAGNETITE
LIVERYMEN	LOONY BINS	LURKINGLY	MAGNETIZE
LIVESTOCK	LOOPHOLES	LUSTFULLY	MAGNETRON
LIVE WIRES	LOOSE ENDS	LUSTINESS	MAGNIFICO
LIVIDNESS	LOOSE-LEAF	LUTANISTS	MAGNIFIED
LJUBLJANA	LOOSENESS	LUTHERISM	MAGNIFIER
LOADSTARS	LOOSENING	LUXURIANT	MAGNITUDE
LOADSTONE	LOQUACITY	LUXURIATE	MAGNOLIAS
LOAMINESS	LORDLIEST	LUXURIOUS	MAHARAJAH
LOANWORDS	LORDSHIPS	LYCHGATES	MAHARAJAS
LOATHSOME	LORGNETTE	LYMINGTON	MAHARANIS
LOBECTOMY	LORRY PARK	LYMPHATIC	MAILBOXES
LOCALIZED	LOST CAUSE	LYONNAISE	MAILCOACH
LOCALIZER	LOTTERIES	LYOPHILIC	MAIL ORDER
LOCAL TIME	LOUDMOUTH	LYOPHOBIC	MAILSHOTS
LOCATABLE	LOUISBURG	LYREBIRDS	MAINFRAME
LOCATIONS	LOUISIANA	LYRICALLY	MAINLINED
LOCKSMITH	LOUNGE BAR	LYRICISMS	MAIN LINES
LOCOMOTOR	LOUSEWORT	LYRICISTS	MAINMASTS
LOCUTIONS	LOUSINESS	LYSIMETER	MAINSAILS
LODESTARS	LOVEBIRDS	LYSOSOMAL	MAINSHEET
LODESTONE	LOVECHILD		MAINSTAYS
LODGEABLE	LOVELIEST	**M**	MAJESTICS
LOFTINESS	LOVING CUP	MACARONIC	MAJESTIES
LOGAOEDIC	LOW COMEDY	MACAROONS	MAJORDOMO
LOGARITHM	LOWERABLE	MACEDOINE	MAJORETTE
LOG CABINS	LOWER CASE	MACERATED	MAJOR SUIT
LOGICALLY	LOWERMOST	MACERATER	MAJUSCULE
LOGICIANS	LOWESTOFT	MACHINATE	MAKESHIFT
LOGISTICS	LOWLANDER	MACHINERY	MAKEYEVKA
LOGOGRIPH	LOWLINESS	MACHINING	MALACHITE
LOGOMACHY	LOW-MINDED	MACHINIST	MALADROIT
LOINCLOTH	LOW-NECKED	MACHMETER	MALAGUENA
LOITERERS	LOW SEASON	MACKERELS	MALANDERS
LOITERING	LOYALISTS	MACROCOSM	MALATHION
LOLLINGLY	LOYALTIES	MACROCYST	MALAYALAM
LOLLIPOPS	LUBRICANT	MACROCYTE	MALAYSIAN
LOLLOPING	LUBRICATE	MACRUROID	MALDIVIAN
LOMBARDIC	LUBRICITY	MACRUROUS	MALFORMED
LONELIEST	LUBRICOUS	MADDENING	MALGRE LUI
LONE WOLFS	LUCIFERIN	MADELEINE	MALIC ACID
LONGBOATS	LUCKINESS	MADHOUSES	MALICIOUS

MALIGNANT	MANUBRIAL	MASTICATE	MEDICATED
MALIGNING	MANUBRIUM	MASTODONS	MEDICINAL
MALIGNITY	MANY-SIDED	MATAMOROS	MEDICINES
MALLEABLE	MARACAIBO	MATCHLESS	MEDITATED
MALLEMUCK	MARATHONS	MATCHMARK	MEDITATOR
MALLEOLAR	MARAUDERS	MATCHWOOD	MEDULLARY
MALLEOLUS	MARAUDING	MATELASSE	MEGACYCLE
MALTINESS	MARCASITE	MATERIALS	MEGADEATH
MALTSTERS	MARCH-PAST	MATERNITY	MEGAHERTZ
MALVOISIE	MARDI GRAS	MATEYNESS	MEGALITHS
MAMA'S BOYS	MARE'S NEST	MATRIARCH	MEGAPHONE
MAMILLARY	MARGARINE	MATRICIDE	MEGASPORE
MAMILLATE	MARGARITA	MATRIMONY	MELANESIA
MAMMALIAN	MARGARITE	MATRONAGE	MELANOSIS
MAMMALOGY	MARGINATE	MATSUMOTO	MELATONIN
MAMMONISM	MARIGOLDS	MATSUYAMA	MELBOURNE
MAMMONIST	MARIJUANA	MATTERING	MELIORATE
MANACLING	MARINADES	MATUTINAL	MELIORISM
MAN-AT-ARMS	MARINATED	MAULSTICK	MELITOPOL
MANCHURIA	MARITALLY	MAUNDERED	MELLOWEST
MANCUNIAN	MARKDOWNS	MAUNDERER	MELLOWING
MANDARINS	MARKETEER	MAURITIAN	MELODIOUS
MANDATARY	MARKETERS	MAURITIUS	MELODIZER
MANDATING	MARKETING	MAUSOLEAN	MELODRAMA
MANDATORY	MARMALADE	MAUSOLEUM	MELTDOWNS
MANDIBLES	MARMOREAL	MAVERICKS	MELTINGLY
MANDOLINS	MARMOSETS	MAWKISHLY	MELTWATER
MANDRAKES	MAROONING	MAXILLARY	MELUNGEON
MANDRILLS	MARQUETRY	MAXIMALLY	MEMBRANES
MAN-EATERS	MARQUISES	MAXIMIZED	MEMORABLE
MAN-EATING	MARRAKECH	MAXIMIZER	MEMORABLY
MANEUVERS	MARRIAGES	MAYFLOWER	MEMORANDA
MAN FRIDAY	MARROWFAT	MAYORALTY	MEMORIALS
MANGALORE	MARSEILLE	MAYORSHIP	MEMORIZED
MANGANATE	MARSHALCY	MBUJIMAYI	MEMORIZER
MANGANESE	MARSHALED	MEANDERED	MEMSAHIBS
MANGANITE	MARSUPIAL	MEANDERER	MENADIONE
MANGANOUS	MARSUPIUM	MEANDROUS	MENAGERIE
MANGETOUT	MARTINETS	MEANS TEST	MEN-AT-ARMS
MANGINESS	MARTINMAS	MEANTIMES	MENDACITY
MANGROVES	MARTYRDOM	MEANWHILE	MENDELIAN
MANHANDLE	MARTYRING	MEASURING	MENDELISM
MANHATTAN	MARVELING	MEATBALLS	MENDICANT
MANHUNTER	MARVELLED	MEATINESS	MENISCOID
MANICURED	MARZIPANS	MECHANICS	MENOPAUSE
MANICURES	MASCULINE	MECHANISM	MEN'S ROOMS
MANIFESTO	MASOCHISM	MECHANIST	MENSTRUAL
MANIFESTS	MASOCHIST	MECHANIZE	MENSTRUUM
MANIFOLDS	MASSACRED	MEDALLION	MENTAL AGE
MANIZALES	MASSACRER	MEDALLIST	MENTALISM
MANLINESS	MASSACRES	MEDIAEVAL	MENTALITY
MANNEQUIN	MASSAGING	MEDIATING	MENTIONED
MANNERISM	MASSIVELY	MEDIATION	MENTIONER
MANNERIST	MASS MEDIA	MEDIATIVE	MENTORIAL
MANNISHLY	MASTERDOM	MEDIATIZE	MEPACRINE
MANOEUVRE	MASTERFUL	MEDIATORS	MERBROMIN
MANOMETER	MASTERING	MEDICABLE	MERCAPTAN
MANOMETRY	MASTER KEY	MEDICABLY	MERCENARY
MANTILLAS	MASTHEADS	MEDICALLY	MERCERIZE

MERCHANTS	MEZZANINE	MILLWHEEL	MISSHAPEN
MERCILESS	MEZZOTINT	MILOMETER	MISSILERY
MERCURATE	MICACEOUS	MILWAUKEE	MISSIONER
MERCURIAL	MICHOACAN	MIMICKING	MISSTATED
MERCUROUS	MICROBIAL	MINARETED	MISTAKING
MERGANSER	MICROCHIP	MINCEMEAT	MISTIMING
MERIDIANS	MICROCOPY	MINCE PIES	MISTINESS
MERINGUES	MICROCOSM	MINCINGLY	MISTLETOE
MERITEDLY	MICROCYTE	MINEFIELD	MISTRIALS
MERITLESS	MICRODONT	MINELAYER	MITICIDAL
MEROCRINE	MICROFILM	MINIATURE	MITIGABLE
MEROZOITE	MICROMESH	MINIBUSES	MITIGATED
MERRIMENT	MICROPYLE	MINIDRESS	MITIGATOR
MERRINESS	MICROSOME	MINIMALLY	MITREWORT
MERSEBURG	MICROTOME	MINIMIZED	MNEMONICS
MESCALINE	MICROTOMY	MINIMIZER	MOANINGLY
MESENTERY	MICROTONE	MINISCULE	MOBILIZED
MESICALLY	MICROWAVE	MINISKIRT	MOBOCRACY
MESMERISM	MIDDLE AGE	MINISTERS	MOCCASINS
MESMERIST	MIDDLEMAN	MINITRACK	MOCKERIES
MESMERIZE	MIDDLEMEN	MINNESOTA	MOCKINGLY
MESOMORPH	MIDDLESEX	MINOR SUIT	MODELLING
MESOPAUSE	MIDHEAVEN	MINSTRELS	MODERATED
MESOPHYLL	MIDNIGHTS	MINT JULEP	MODERATES
MESOPHYTE	MIDPOINTS	MINUSCULE	MODERATOR
MESSALINE	MIDSUMMER	MIRRORING	MODERATOS
MESSENGER	MID-WICKET	MIRTHLESS	MODERNISM
MESSIANIC	MIDWIFERY	MISADVISE	MODERNIST
MESSIEURS	MIDWINTER	MISBEHAVE	MODERNITY
MESSINESS	MIFFINESS	MISBELIEF	MODERNIZE
MESTRANOL	MIGHTIEST	MISCALLED	MODIFIERS
METABOLIC	MIGRAINES	MISCHANCE	MODIFYING
METALLINE	MIGRATING	MISCHIEFS	MODILLION
METALLING	MIGRATION	MISCOUNTS	MODULATED
METALLIST	MIGRATORY	MISCREANT	MODULATOR
METALLIZE	MILCH COWS	MISCREATE	MOISTENED
METALLOID	MILESTONE	MISDEALER	MOISTENER
METALWORK	MILITANCY	MISDIRECT	MOISTNESS
METAMERAL	MILITANTS	MISERABLE	MOLDAVIAN
METAMERIC	MILITATED	MISERABLY	MOLDAVITE
METAPHASE	MILK FLOAT	MISFIRING	MOLDERING
METAPHORS	MILKINESS	MISGIVING	MOLDINESS
METAPLASM	MILKMAIDS	MISGOVERN	MOLECULAR
METAXYLEM	MILK SHAKE	MISGUIDED	MOLECULES
METEORITE	MILK TOOTH	MISGUIDER	MOLEHILLS
METEOROID	MILLBOARD	MISHANDLE	MOLESKINS
METHADONE	MILLENARY	MISINFORM	MOLESTERS
METHODISM	MILLENNIA	MISJUDGED	MOLESTING
METHODIST	MILLEPEDE	MISJUDGER	MOLLIFIED
METHODIZE	MILLEPORE	MISLAYING	MOLLIFIER
METHOXIDE	MILLERITE	MISLEADER	MOLLUSCAN
METHYLATE	MILLIBARS	MISMANAGE	MOLYBDATE
METHYLENE	MILLIGRAM	MISNOMERS	MOLYBDOUS
METRALGIA	MILLINERS	MISONEISM	MOMENTARY
METRICIZE	MILLINERY	MISONEIST	MOMENTOUS
METRIC TON	MILLIONTH	MISPLACED	MOMENTUMS
METRIFIER	MILLIPEDE	MISPRINTS	MONACHISM
METROLOGY	MILLPONDS	MISQUOTED	MONADNOCK
METRONOME	MILLSTONE	MISREPORT	MONARCHAL

MONASTERY	MOONBEAMS	MOUSETAIL	MUSKINESS
MONATOMIC	MOON-FACED	MOUSETRAP	MUSKMELON
MONEYBAGS	MOONINESS	MOUSINESS	MUSLIMISM
MONEYLESS	MOONLIGHT	MOUSTACHE	MUSTACHES
MONEYWORT	MOONRAKER	MOUTHFULS	MUSTACHIO
MONGERING	MOONSCAPE	MOUTHPART	MUSTELINE
MONGOLIAN	MOONSHINE	MOUTHWASH	MUSTERING
MONGOLISM	MOON SHOTS	MOVEABLES	MUSTINESS
MONGOLOID	MOONSTONE	MOVEMENTS	MUTAGENIC
MONGOOSES	MOOT POINT	MOVIE STAR	MUTATIONS
MONITORED	MORACEOUS	MOVIETONE	MUTILATED
MONITRESS	MORADABAD	MOVING VAN	MUTILATOR
MONKEYING	MORALISTS	MUCIC ACID	MUTINEERS
MONKEY NUT	MORALIZED	MUCKHEAPS	MUTINYING
MONKSHOOD	MORALIZER	MUCKINESS	MUTTERERS
MONOBASIC	MORATORIA	MUCKRAKER	MUTTERING
MONOCHORD	MORBIDITY	MUCRONATE	MUTUALITY
MONOCLINE	MORDACITY	MUDDINESS	MUTUALIZE
MONOCOQUE	MORDANTLY	MUDGUARDS	MUZZINESS
MONOCRACY	MORGANITE	MUGGINESS	MYCENAEAN
MONOCULAR	MORMONISM	MUGGINSES	MYDRIASIS
MONOCYTIC	MORPHEMES	MULATTOES	MYDRIATIC
MONODRAMA	MORPHEMIC	MULETEERS	MYOGLOBIN
MONOGENIC	MORPHOSIS	MULLIONED	MYOGRAPHY
MONOGRAMS	MORSE CODE	MULTICIDE	MYOLOGIST
MONOGRAPH	MORTALITY	MULTIFOIL	MYROBALAN
MONOLATER	MORTAL SIN	MULTIFOLD	MYSTAGOGY
MONOLATRY	MORTGAGED	MULTIFORM	MYSTERIES
MONOLAYER	MORTGAGEE	MULTIHULL	MYSTICISM
MONOLITHS	MORTGAGES	MULTIPARA	MYSTIFIED
MONOLOGIC	MORTGAGOR	MULTIPLES	MYSTIFIER
MONOLOGUE	MORTICIAN	MULTIPLET	MYSTIQUES
MONOMANIA	MORTIFIED	MULTIPLEX	MYTHICIZE
MONOMERIC	MORTIFIER	MULTITUDE	MYTHOLOGY
MONOMETER	MOSAICIST	MUMMIFIED	MYXOEDEMA
MONOPHAGY	MOSCHATEL	MUNDANELY	MYXOVIRUS
MONOPHONY	MOSQUITOS	MUNICIPAL	
MONOPLANE	MOSS-GROWN	MUNIMENTS	**N**
MONOPSONY	MOSSINESS	MUNITIONS	NAHUATLAN
MONORAILS	MOTHBALLS	MURDERERS	NAILBRUSH
MONOSOMIC	MOTH-EATEN	MURDERESS	NAIL FILES
MONOSTICH	MOTHERING	MURDERING	NAIVENESS
MONOSTOME	MOTHPROOF	MURDEROUS	NAIVETIES
MONOTONIC	MOTIONING	MURKINESS	NAKEDNESS
MONOTREME	MOTIVATED	MURMURING	NAMEPLATE
MONOTYPER	MOTOCROSS	MUSACEOUS	NAMESAKES
MONOTYPIC	MOTORBIKE	MUSCADINE	NANNY GOAT
MONOXIDES	MOTORBOAT	MUSCARINE	NANOMETER
MONSIGNOR	MOTORCADE	MUSCATELS	NANTUCKET
MONSTROUS	MOTORCARS	MUSCLEMAN	NAPHTHENE
MONTAUBAN	MOTORISTS	MUSCLEMEN	NAPPINESS
MONT BLANC	MOTORIZED	MUSCOVADO	NARCISSUS
MONTERREY	MOTORWAYS	MUSCOVITE	NARCOTICS
MONTHLIES	MOULDABLE	MUSHINESS	NARCOTISM
MONTICULE	MOULDERED	MUSHROOMS	NARCOTIZE
MONTREUIL	MOULDIEST	MUSICALLY	NARRATING
MONUMENTS	MOULDINGS	MUSIC HALL	NARRATION
MONZONITE	MOUNTABLE	MUSICIANS	NARRATIVE
MOODINESS	MOUNTAINS	MUSKETEER	NARRATORS

NARROWING	NEPHOLOGY	NIGHT OWLS	NOTARIZED
NASHVILLE	NEPHRITIC	NIGHT SOIL	NOTATIONS
NASTINESS	NEPHRITIS	NIGHTTIME	NOTEBOOKS
NATIONALS	NEPHROSIS	NIGHTWEAR	NOTEPAPER
NATROLITE	NEPHROTIC	NIGROSINE	NOTIFYING
NATTERING	NEPTUNIAN	NIHILISTS	NO-TILLAGE
NATTINESS	NEPTUNIUM	NIKOLAYEV	NOTOCHORD
NATURALLY	NERVELESS	NINETEENS	NOTOGAEAN
NATURISTS	NERVINESS	NINETIETH	NOTORIETY
NAUGHTIER	NERVOUSLY	NIPPINESS	NOTORIOUS
NAUGHTILY	NESCIENCE	NIPPONESE	NOURISHED
NAUSEATED	NESTLINGS	NISI PRIUS	NOURISHER
NAUTILOID	NETWORKED	NISSEN HUT	NOVELETTE
NAVICULAR	NEUCHATEL	NITPICKER	NOVELISTS
NAVIGABLE	NEURALGIA	NITRAMINE	NOVELTIES
NAVIGABLY	NEURALGIC	NITRATION	NOVEMBERS
NAVIGATED	NEUROGLIA	NITRIDING	NOVITIATE
NAVIGATOR	NEUROLOGY	NIVERNAIS	NOVOCAINE
NEAP TIDES	NEUROPATH	NO-ACCOUNT	NOXIOUSLY
NEAR THING	NEUROTICS	NOBILIARY	NUCLEATOR
NEBULIZER	NEUROTOMY	NOBLENESS	NUCLEOLAR
NECESSARY	NEUTERING	NOCTILUCA	NUCLEOLUS
NECESSITY	NEUTRALLY	NOCTURNAL	NUCLEONIC
NECKBANDS	NEUTRETTO	NOCTURNES	NUEVO LEON
NECKCLOTH	NEVERMORE	NO-GO AREAS	NUISANCES
NECKLACES	NEW BROOMS	NOISELESS	NULLIFIED
NECKLINES	NEWCOMERS	NOISINESS	NULLIFIER
NECKPIECE	NEWLYWEDS	NOMINALLY	NULLIPARA
NECROLOGY	NEWSAGENT	NOMINATED	NULLIPORE
NECROTOMY	NEWSHOUND	NOMINATOR	NULLITIES
NECTARIAL	NEWSINESS	NOMOCRACY	NUMBERING
NECTARINE	NEWSPAPER	NOMOGRAPH	NUMBER ONE
NEEDFULLY	NEWSPRINT	NONAGONAL	NUMBER TEN
NEEDINESS	NEWSREELS	NONEDIBLE	NUMBSKULL
NEFARIOUS	NEWSROOMS	NONENTITY	NUMERABLE
NEGATIONS	NEWSSHEET	NON-EVENTS	NUMERABLY
NEGATIVED	NEWSSTAND	NON-FINITE	NUMERATOR
NEGATIVES	NEWTONIAN	NONILLION	NUMERICAL
NEGLECTED	NICARAGUA	NONPAREIL	NUMMULITE
NEGLECTER	NICCOLITE	NONPAROUS	NUMSKULLS
NEGLIGEES	NICKELING	NONSMOKER	NUNNERIES
NEGLIGENT	NICKELLED	NONVERBAL	NUREMBERG
NEGOTIANT	NICKELOUS	NONWHITES	NURSELING
NEGOTIATE	NICKNACKS	NORMALITY	NURSEMAID
NEGRITUDE	NICKNAMED	NORMALIZE	NURSERIES
NEIGHBOUR	NICKNAMES	NORMATIVE	NURSLINGS
NEMERTEAN	NICOTIANA	NORTHEAST	NURTURING
NEODYMIUM	NICOTINIC	NORTHERLY	NUTHOUSES
NEOLITHIC	NICTITATE	NORTH POLE	NUTRIENTS
NEOLOGISM	NIFTINESS	NORTHWARD	NUTRIMENT
NEOLOGIST	NIGGARDLY	NORTHWEST	NUTRITION
NEOLOGIZE	NIGHTCAPS	NORWEGIAN	NUTRITIVE
NEON LIGHT	NIGHTCLUB	NOSEBLEED	NUTSHELLS
NEOPHYTES	NIGHTFALL	NOSECONES	NUTTINESS
NEOPHYTIC	NIGHTGOWN	NOSEDIVED	NYASALAND
NEOPLASTY	NIGHTHAWK	NOSEDIVES	NYMPHALID
NEOTENOUS	NIGHTLIFE	NOSTALGIA	NYSTAGMIC
NEPHELINE	NIGHTLONG	NOSTALGIC	NYSTAGMUS
NEPHOGRAM	NIGHTMARE	NOSTOLOGY	

O	OCCUPANTS	OLIGOPOLY	ORANG-UTAN
OAST HOUSE	OCCUPIERS	OLIVE DRAB	ORATORIES
OBBLIGATO	OCCUPYING	OLIVENITE	ORATORIOS
OBCORDATE	OCCURRENT	OLYMPIADS	ORBICULAR
OBEDIENCE	OCCURRING	OLYMPIANS	ORCHESTRA
OBEISANCE	OCELLATED	OMBUDSMAN	ORDAINING
OBELISCAL	OCHLOCRAT	OMBUDSMEN	ORDERLIES
OBFUSCATE	OCTAGONAL	OMELETTES	ORDINANCE
OBJECTIFY	OCTAMETER	OMINOUSLY	ORGANELLE
OBJECTING	OCTENNIAL	OMISSIBLE	ORGANISMS
OBJECTION	OCTILLION	OMISSIONS	ORGANISTS
OBJECTIVE	OCTOPUSES	OMNIBUSES	ORGANIZED
OBJECTORS	ODALISQUE	OMNIRANGE	ORGANIZER
OBJET D'ART	ODD-JOB MAN	OMOPHAGIA	ORGANZINE
OBJURGATE	ODD MAN OUT	OMOPHAGIC	ORGIASTIC
OBLATIONS	ODD MEN OUT	ONCE-OVERS	ORIENTALS
OBLIGABLE	ODOMETERS	ONDOGRAPH	ORIENTATE
OBLIGATED	ODOURLESS	ONDOMETER	ORIGINALS
OBLIGATOR	OESTROGEN	ONEROUSLY	ORIGINATE
OBLIQUITY	OFF COLOUR	ONIONSKIN	ORNAMENTS
OBLIVIOUS	OFFENBACH	ONLOOKERS	ORNITHINE
OBNOXIOUS	OFFENDERS	ONLOOKING	OROGRAPHY
OBREPTION	OFFENDING	ONOMASTIC	OROLOGIST
OBSCENELY	OFFENSIVE	ONRUSHING	ORPHANAGE
OBSCENITY	OFFERINGS	ONSLAUGHT	ORPHANING
OBSCURANT	OFFERTORY	ONTOGENIC	ORTANIQUE
OBSCURELY	OFFHANDED	OOGENESIS	ORTHODOXY
OBSCURING	OFFICE BOY	OOGENETIC	ORTHOEPIC
OBSCURITY	OFFICIALS	OOLOGICAL	ORTHOPTER
OBSEQUENT	OFFICIANT	OPEN-ENDED	ORTHOPTIC
OBSEQUIES	OFFICIARY	OPEN-FACED	OSCILLATE
OBSERVANT	OFFICIATE	OPEN HOUSE	OSCITANCY
OBSERVERS	OFFICIOUS	OPEN SHOPS	OSMOMETER
OBSERVING	OFF-LOADED	OPERATING	OSMOMETRY
OBSESSING	OFFSHOOTS	OPERATION	OSNABRUCK
OBSESSION	OFFSPRING	OPERATIVE	OSSICULAR
OBSESSIVE	OFF-STREET	OPERATORS	OSSIFRAGE
OBSOLESCE	OGBOMOSHO	OPERCULAR	OSSIFYING
OBSTACLES	OILFIELDS	OPERCULUM	OSTENSIVE
OBSTETRIC	OIL PAINTS	OPERETTAS	OSTEOLOGY
OBSTINACY	OIL SLICKS	OPHIOLOGY	OSTEOPATH
OBSTINATE	OIL TANKER	OPPONENCY	OSTEOTOME
OBSTRUENT	OINTMENTS	OPPONENTS	OSTEOTOMY
OBTAINING	OKLAHOMAN	OPPORTUNE	OSTRACISM
OBTRUDING	OLDENBURG	OPPOSABLE	OSTRACIZE
OBTRUSION	OLD FLAMES	OPPOSABLY	OSTRICHES
OBTRUSIVE	OLD MASTER	OPPOSITES	OTHERNESS
OBVERSION	OLD SCHOOL	OPPRESSED	OTHERWISE
OBVIATING	OLD-TIMERS	OPPRESSOR	OTOCYSTIC
OBVIATION	OLEACEOUS	OPTICALLY	OTOLITHIC
OBVIOUSLY	OLEANDERS	OPTICIANS	OTOLOGIST
OCCASIONS	OLECRANAL	OPTIMISTS	OTOSCOPIC
OCCIPITAL	OLECRANON	OPTIMIZED	OUBLIETTE
OCCLUDENT	OLEOGRAPH	OPTOMETER	OUR FATHER
OCCLUSION	OLEORESIN	OPTOMETRY	OURSELVES
OCCLUSIVE	OLFACTION	OPULENTLY	OUT-AND-OUT
OCCULTISM	OLFACTORY	ORANGEADE	OUTBRAVED
OCCULTIST	OLIGARCHY	ORANGEISM	OUTBREAKS
OCCUPANCY	OLIGOCENE	ORANGEMAN	OUTBURSTS

OUTCASTES	OVERHANGS	P	PANNIKINS
OUTERMOST	OVERHAULS	PACEMAKER	PANOPLIED
OUTFACING	OVERHEADS	PACHYDERM	PANORAMAS
OUTFITTED	OVERHEARD	PACHYTENE	PANORAMIC
OUTFITTER	OVERISSUE	PACIFIERS	PANSOPHIC
OUTFOUGHT	OVERJOYED	PACIFISTS	PANTHEISM
OUTFOXING	OVERLADEN	PACIFYING	PANTHEIST
OUTGOINGS	OVERLOADS	PACKAGERS	PANTHEONS
OUTGROWTH	OVERLORDS	PACKAGING	PANTOMIME
OUTHOUSES	OVERLYING	PACKED-OUT	PANTY HOSE
OUTLASTED	OVERNIGHT	PACKHORSE	PAPARAZZI
OUTLAWING	OVERPOWER	PADLOCKED	PAPARAZZO
OUTLAYING	OVERPRINT	PAEDERAST	PAPERBACK
OUTLINING	OVERPROOF	PAEDOLOGY	PAPERBOYS
OUTLIVING	OVERRATED	PAGANIZER	PAPER CLIP
OUTNUMBER	OVERREACH	PAGEANTRY	PAPERWORK
OUT-OF-DATE	OVERREACT	PAILLASSE	PAPETERIE
OUTPLAYED	OVERRIDER	PAILLETTE	PAPILLARY
OUTRAGING	OVERRULED	PAINFULLY	PAPILLOMA
OUTRANKED	OVERSCORE	PAINTERLY	PAPILLOTE
OUTRIDDEN	OVERSEERS	PAINTINGS	PAPYRUSES
OUTRIDERS	OVERSEXED	PAINTWORK	PARABLAST
OUTRIDING	OVERSHOES	PAKISTANI	PARABOLAS
OUTRIGGER	OVERSHOOT	PALANQUIN	PARABOLIC
OUTRUNNER	OVERSIGHT	PALATABLE	PARACHUTE
OUTSIDERS	OVERSIZED	PALATABLY	PARADIGMS
OUTSKIRTS	OVERSKIRT	PALEFACES	PARADISES
OUTSPOKEN	OVERSLEEP	PALEMBANG	PARADOXES
OUTSPREAD	OVERSLEPT	PALESTINE	PARAGOGIC
OUTSTARED	OVERSPEND	PALISADES	PARAGRAPH
OUTSTAYED	OVERSPILL	PALLADIAN	PARAKEETS
OUTTALKED	OVERSTATE	PALLADIUM	PARALLELS
OUTVOTING	OVERSTOCK	PALLADOUS	PARALYSED
OUTWARDLY	OVERTAKEN	PALLIASSE	PARALYSER
OUTWITTED	OVERTAXED	PALLIATED	PARALYSES
OUTWORKER	OVERTHREW	PALLIATOR	PARALYSIS
OVATIONAL	OVERTHROW	PALMATION	PARALYTIC
OVEN-READY	OVERTONES	PALMETTOS	PARAMATTA
OVERACTED	OVERTRADE	PALMISTRY	PARAMEDIC
OVERAWING	OVERTRICK	PALMITATE	PARAMETER
OVERBLOWN	OVERTRUMP	PALOMINOS	PARAMORPH
OVERBOARD	OVERTURES	PALPATING	PARAMOUNT
OVERBORNE	OVERVIEWS	PALPATION	PARAMOURS
OVERBUILD	OVERWEIGH	PALPEBRAL	PARANOIAC
OVERCHECK	OVERWHELM	PALPITATE	PARAPLASM
OVERCLOUD	OVERWRITE	PALTRIEST	PARASITES
OVERCOATS	OVIFEROUS	PAMPERING	PARASITIC
OVERCROWD	OVIPAROUS	PAMPHLETS	PARATAXIS
OVERDOING	OVOTESTIS	PANATELAS	PARATHION
OVERDOSED	OVULATING	PANDA CARS	PARBOILED
OVERDOSES	OVULATION	PANDEMICS	PARBUCKLE
OVERDRAFT	OWNERSHIP	PANDERING	PARCELING
OVERDRAWN	OXIDATION	PANDURATE	PARCELLED
OVERDRESS	OXIDATIVE	PANEGYRIC	PARCENARY
OVERDRIVE	OXIDIZING	PANELLING	PARCHMENT
OVERFLOWN	OXYGENATE	PANELLIST	PARDONERS
OVERFLOWS	OXYGENIZE	PANHANDLE	PARDONING
OVERGLAZE	OYSTER BED	PANICKING	PAREGORIC
OVERGROWN	OZOCERITE	PANMUNJOM	PARENTAGE

PARENTING	PATCHABLE	PEDESTALS	PERCALINE
PARGETING	PATCHIEST	PEDICULAR	PER CAPITA
PARHELION	PATCHOULI	PEDICURES	PERCEIVED
PARI PASSU	PATCHWORK	PEDIGREED	PERCEIVER
PARISIANS	PATELLATE	PEDIGREES	PERCHANCE
PARLEYING	PATENTEES	PEDIMENTS	PERCHERON
PARLOR CAR	PATENTING	PEDUNCLED	PERCOLATE
PARNASSUS	PATERNITY	PEEPHOLES	PERCUSSOR
PAROCHIAL	PATHOLOGY	PEERESSES	PERDITION
PARODISTS	PATIENTLY	PEEVISHLY	PEREGRINE
PARODYING	PATRIARCH	PEGMATITE	PERENNATE
PAROICOUS	PATRICIAN	PEKINESES	PERENNIAL
PAROLABLE	PATRICIDE	PEKINGESE	PERFECTED
PARONYMIC	PATRIMONY	PELLITORY	PERFECTER
PAROTITIS	PATRIOTIC	PELMANISM	PERFECTLY
PAROXYSMS	PATRISTIC	PELTATION	PERFIDIES
PARQUETRY	PATROL CAR	PEMPHIGUS	PERFORATE
PARRICIDE	PATROLLED	PENALIZED	PERFORMED
PARROTING	PATROLLER	PENALTIES	PERFORMER
PARSIMONY	PATROLMAN	PENCHANTS	PERFUMERY
PARSONAGE	PATROLMEN	PENCILING	PERFUMING
PARTAKING	PATRONAGE	PENCILLED	PERFUSION
PARTERRES	PATRONESS	PENCILLER	PERFUSIVE
PARTHENON	PATRONIZE	PENDRAGON	PERICLASE
PARTIALLY	PATTERING	PENDULOUS	PERICLINE
PARTICLES	PATTERNED	PENDULUMS	PERICYCLE
PARTI PRIS	PAULOWNIA	PENEPLAIN	PERILYMPH
PARTISANS	PAUPERISM	PENETRANT	PERIMETER
PARTITION	PAUPERIZE	PENETRATE	PERIMETRY
PARTITIVE	PAUSINGLY	PEN FRIEND	PERIMORPH
PARTNERED	PAVEMENTS	PENINSULA	PERINATAL
PARTRIDGE	PAVILIONS	PENITENCE	PERIODATE
PART-SONGS	PAWKINESS	PENITENTS	PERIPHERY
PART WORKS	PAWNSHOPS	PENKNIVES	PERISCOPE
PARTY LINE	PAYCHECKS	PENNILESS	PERISHERS
PARTY WALL	PAYMASTER	PENNINITE	PERISHING
PAS DE DEUX	PAY PACKET	PENN'ORTHS	PERISPERM
PASO DOBLE	PAY PHONES	PENNY-WISE	PERISTOME
PASSBOOKS	PEACEABLE	PENNYWORT	PERISTYLE
PASSENGER	PEACEABLY	PEN PUSHER	PERITONEA
PASSERINE	PEACE PIPE	PENSILITY	PERITRACK
PASSERSBY	PEACETIME	PENSIONED	PERJURERS
PASSIONAL	PEARLIEST	PENSIONER	PERJURIES
PASSIVELY	PEARLITIC	PENSIVELY	PERJURING
PASSIVISM	PEARLIZED	PENTAGONS	PERKINESS
PASSIVIST	PEARMAINS	PENTAGRAM	PERMALLOY
PASSIVITY	PEASANTRY	PENTARCHY	PERMANENT
PASSOVERS	PEA SOUPER	PENTECOST	PERMEABLE
PASSPORTS	PECCARIES	PENTHOUSE	PERMEANCE
PASSWORDS	PECTINATE	PENTOXIDE	PERMEATED
PASTICHES	PECULATED	PENUMBRAL	PERMEATOR
PASTILLES	PECULATOR	PENUMBRAS	PER MENSEM
PASTINESS	PECUNIARY	PENURIOUS	PERMITTED
PASTORALE	PEDAGOGIC	PEPPERING	PERMITTER
PASTORALS	PEDAGOGUE	PEPPER POT	PERMUTING
PASTORATE	PEDALLING	PEPSINATE	PERPETUAL
PASTURAGE	PEDATIFID	PEPTIDASE	PERPIGNAN
PASTURING	PEDERASTS	PEPTONIZE	PERPLEXED
PATAGONIA	PEDERASTY	PERBORATE	PERSECUTE

PERSEVERE	PHENETOLE	PICOLINIC	PISTACHIO
PERSIMMON	PHENOCOPY	PICTORIAL	PITCH-DARK
PERSISTED	PHENOLATE	PICTURING	PITCHFORK
PERSISTER	PHENOLOGY	PIECE-DYED	PITEOUSLY
PERSONAGE	PHENOMENA	PIECEMEAL	PITHINESS
PERSONALS	PHENOTYPE	PIECEWORK	PITOT TUBE
PERSONATE	PHENOXIDE	PIE CHARTS	PIT PONIES
PERSONIFY	PHEROMONE	PIECRUSTS	PITTANCES
PERSONNEL	PHILANDER	PIERCABLE	PITUITARY
PERSPIRED	PHILATELY	PIERIDINE	PITYINGLY
PERSUADED	PHILIPPIC	PIGGERIES	PIZZICATO
PERSUADER	PHILOLOGY	PIGGISHLY	PLACARDED
PERTAINED	PHLEBITIC	PIGGYBACK	PLACATING
PERTINENT	PHLEBITIS	PIGGYBANK	PLACATION
PERTURBED	PHLYCTENA	PIGHEADED	PLACATORY
PERTUSSIS	PHNOM PENH	PIGTAILED	PLACEBOES
PERVADING	PHOENICIA	PIKEPERCH	PLACE CARD
PERVASIVE	PHOENIXES	PIKESTAFF	PLACE MATS
PERVERTED	PHONATION	PILASTERS	PLACEMENT
PERVERTER	PHONATORY	PILCHARDS	PLACENTAE
PESSARIES	PHONE BOOK	PILFERAGE	PLACENTAL
PESSIMISM	PHONEMICS	PILFERERS	PLACENTAS
PESSIMIST	PHONETICS	PILFERING	PLACIDITY
PESTERING	PHONEY WAR	PILLAGERS	PLACODERM
PESTICIDE	PHONINESS	PILLAGING	PLAIN-LAID
PESTILENT	PHONOGRAM	PILLAR BOX	PLAINNESS
PETAL-LIKE	PHONOLITE	PILLBOXES	PLAINSMAN
PETALODIC	PHONOLOGY	PILLORIED	PLAINSONG
PETECHIAL	PHONOTYPE	PILLORIES	PLAINTIFF
PETERSHAM	PHONOTYPY	PILLOWING	PLAINTIVE
PETIOLATE	PHOSPHATE	PIMPERNEL	PLANARIAN
PETIOLULE	PHOSPHENE	PINACEOUS	PLANATION
PETIT FOUR	PHOSPHIDE	PINAFORES	PLANETARY
PETITIONS	PHOSPHINE	PINCHBECK	PLANETOID
PETRIFIED	PHOSPHITE	PINCHCOCK	PLANE TREE
PETRIFIER	PHOTOCELL	PINEAPPLE	PLANGENCY
PETROLEUM	PHOTOCOPY	PINETREES	PLANISHER
PETROLOGY	PHOTOGRAM	PINEWOODS	PLANTABLE
PETTICOAT	PHOTOSTAT	PINIONING	PLANTAINS
PETTINESS	PHOTOTUBE	PINNACLES	PLASMAGEL
PETTISHLY	PHOTOTYPE	PINNATION	PLASMASOL
PETTY CASH	PHRENITIC	PINPOINTS	PLASTERED
PETULANCE	PHRENITIS	PINPRICKS	PLASTERER
PFORZHEIM	PHTHALEIN	PINSTRIPE	PLATELETS
PHAGOCYTE	PHYCOLOGY	PINTABLES	PLATE RACK
PHALANGER	PHYLLITIC	PINTADERA	PLATFORMS
PHALANGES	PHYLLOMIC	PINWHEELS	PLATINIZE
PHALANXES	PHYLOGENY	PIONEERED	PLATINOID
PHALAROPE	PHYSICALS	PIOUSNESS	PLATINOUS
PHALLUSES	PHYSICIAN	PIPE DREAM	PLATITUDE
PHANTASMS	PHYSICIST	PIPELINES	PLAUSIBLE
PHARISAIC	PHYSIQUES	PIPE RACKS	PLAUSIBLY
PHARISEES	PHYTOTRON	PIPERONAL	PLAY-ACTED
PHARYNXES	PIANISTIC	PIPESTONE	PLAYBACKS
PHASE-OUTS	PICKETING	PIPSQUEAK	PLAY DOUGH
PHEASANTS	PICKINESS	PIQUANTLY	PLAYED-OUT
PHELLOGEN	PICK-ME-UPS	PIRATICAL	PLAYFULLY
PHENACITE	PICNICKED	PIROUETTE	PLAYGOERS
PHENAZINE	PICNICKER	PISS-TAKES	PLAYGROUP

PLAYHOUSE	POINCIANA	POLYPTYCH	POSTAXIAL
PLAYMATES	POINT DUTY	POLYSOMIC	POSTCARDS
PLAYROOMS	POINTEDLY	POLYTHENE	POSTCODES
PLAYTHING	POINTLESS	POLYTONAL	POSTDATED
PLEADABLE	POINTSMAN	POLYTYPIC	POSTERIOR
PLEADINGS	POISONERS	POLYVINYL	POSTERITY
PLEASABLE	POISON GAS	POMACEOUS	POSTHASTE
PLEASANCE	POISONING	POMANDERS	POST HORNS
PLEASEDLY	POISON IVY	POMERANIA	POSTICOUS
PLEASURES	POISONOUS	POMPADOUR	POSTILION
PLEBBIEST	POKEBERRY	POMPOSITY	POSTMARKS
PLEBEIANS	POKER FACE	POMPOUSLY	POSTNATAL
PLECTRUMS	POKERWORK	PONDERING	POSTPONED
PLENARILY	POLAR BEAR	PONDEROUS	POSTPONER
PLENITUDE	POLARIZED	PONDOLAND	POSTULANT
PLENTEOUS	POLARIZER	PONTIANAK	POSTULATE
PLENTIFUL	POLAROIDS	PONYTAILS	POSTURING
PLEONASMS	POLEAXING	POORHOUSE	POTASSIUM
PLEURITIC	POLEMICAL	POORLIEST	POTATIONS
PLEXIFORM	POLE VAULT	POORLY OFF	POTBOILER
PLICATION	POLICEMAN	POOR WHITE	POTENTATE
PLIGHTING	POLICEMEN	POPE'S NOSE	POTENTIAL
PLIMSOLLS	POLISHING	POPINJAYS	POTHOLERS
PLOUGHBOY	POLITBURO	POPLITEAL	POTHOLING
PLOUGHING	POLITESSE	POPPYCOCK	POTHUNTER
PLOUGHMAN	POLITICAL	POPPYHEAD	POT PLANTS
PLOUGHMEN	POLITICOS	POPSICLES	POTPOURRI
PLUCKIEST	POLKA DOTS	POPULARLY	POTSHERDS
PLUGBOARD	POLLARDED	POPULATED	POTTERIES
PLUGHOLES	POLLINATE	POPULISTS	POTTERING
PLUMBABLE	POLLINIUM	PORBEAGLE	POTTINESS
PLUMBEOUS	POLLSTERS	PORCELAIN	POULTERER
PLUMBICON	POLL TAXES	PORCUPINE	POULTICES
PLUMB LINE	POLLUCITE	PORIFERAN	POULTRIES
PLUMMETED	POLLUTANT	PORKINESS	POUNDINGS
PLUMMIEST	POLLUTING	POROMERIC	POURBOIRE
PLUMPNESS	POLLUTION	PORPHYRIN	POUTINGLY
PLUNDERED	POLLYANNA	PORPOISES	POVERTIES
PLUNDERER	POLONAISE	PORRINGER	POWDERING
PLURALISM	POLO NECKS	PORTACRIB	POWDER KEG
PLURALIST	POLTROONS	PORTATIVE	POWER BASE
PLURALITY	POLYAMIDE	PORTENDED	POWERBOAT
PLURALIZE	POLYANDRY	PORTERAGE	POWER DIVE
PLUS FOURS	POLYBASIC	PORTFOLIO	POWERLESS
PLUSHNESS	POLYCARPY	PORTHOLES	PRACTICAL
PLUTOCRAT	POLYESTER	PORTICOES	PRACTICES
PLUTONIUM	POLYGLOTS	PORTIONED	PRACTISED
PNEUMATIC	POLYGONAL	PORTLIEST	PRAESIDIA
PNEUMONIA	POLYGONUM	PORTRAITS	PRAGMATIC
PNEUMONIC	POLYGRAPH	PORTRAYAL	PRANKSTER
POCKETFUL	POLYMATHS	PORTRAYED	PRATINGLY
POCKETING	POLYMERIC	PORTRAYER	PRATTLERS
POCKMARKS	POLYMORPH	PORTULACA	PRATTLING
PODGINESS	POLYMYXIN	POSITIONS	PRAYERFUL
POETASTER	POLYNESIA	POSITIVES	PRAYER RUG
POETESSES	POLYPHASE	POSITRONS	PREACHERS
POETICIZE	POLYPHONE	POSSESSED	PREACHIFY
POGO STICK	POLYPHONY	POSSESSOR	PREACHING
POIGNANCY	POLYPLOID	POSSIBLES	PREAMBLES

PREBENDAL	PRESCHOOL	PRINCIPAL	PROGRAMME
PRECANCEL	PRESCIENT	PRINCIPLE	PROJECTED
PRECEDENT	PRESCRIBE	PRINTABLE	PROJECTOR
PRECEDING	PRESCRIPT	PRINTINGS	PROLACTIN
PRECENTOR	PRESENCES	PRINTOUTS	PROLAMINE
PRECEPTOR	PRESENTED	PRISMATIC	PROLAPSED
PRECINCTS	PRESENTEE	PRISONERS	PROLAPSES
PRECIPICE	PRESENTER	PRISSIEST	PROLEPSIS
PRECISELY	PRESENTLY	PRIVATEER	PROLEPTIC
PRECISIAN	PRESERVED	PRIVATELY	PROLIXITY
PRECISION	PRESERVER	PRIVATION	PROLOGUES
PRECLUDED	PRESERVES	PRIVATIVE	PROLONGED
PRECOCIAL	PRESETTER	PRIVATIZE	PROLONGER
PRECOCITY	PRESHRUNK	PRIVILEGE	PROLUSION
PRECONIZE	PRESIDENT	PRIZE DAYS	PROLUSORY
PRECOOKED	PRESIDING	PROACTIVE	PROMENADE
PRECURSOR	PRESIDIUM	PROBABLES	PROMINENT
PREDATING	PRESSGANG	PROBATING	PROMISING
PREDATION	PRESSINGS	PROBATION	PROMOTERS
PREDATORS	PRESSMARK	PROBATIVE	PROMOTING
PREDATORY	PRESSROOM	PROBEABLE	PROMOTION
PREDICANT	PRESS—STUD	PROBINGLY	PROMOTIVE
PREDICATE	PRESSURED	PROBOSCIS	PROMPTING
PREDICTED	PRESSURES	PROCEDURE	PRONATION
PREDICTOR	PRESSWORK	PROCEEDED	PRONENESS
PREDIGEST	PRESTIGES	PROCEEDER	PRONGHORN
PRE—EMPTED	PRESTRESS	PROCESSED	PRONOUNCE
PRE—EMPTOR	PRESUMING	PROCESSES	PROOFREAD
PREFACING	PRETENCES	PROCESSOR	PROPAGATE
PREFATORY	PRETENDED	PROCLITIC	PROPAGULE
PREFERRED	PRETENDER	PROCONSUL	PRO PATRIA
PREFIGURE	PRETERITE	PROCREANT	PROPELLED
PREFIXING	PRETTIEST	PROCREATE	PROPELLER
PREFLIGHT	PREVAILED	PROCTORED	PROPHETIC
PREGNABLE	PREVAILER	PROCURERS	PROPONENT
PREGNANCY	PREVALENT	PROCURING	PROPOSALS
PREHEATED	PREVENTED	PRODIGALS	PROPOSERS
PREJUDGED	PREVENTER	PRODIGIES	PROPOSING
PREJUDGER	PREVIEWED	PRODROMAL	PROPRIETY
PREJUDICE	PREVISION	PRODUCERS	PROPTOSIS
PRELATISM	PRICELESS	PRODUCING	PROPYLITE
PRELATIST	PRICE TAGS	PROFANELY	PROROGUED
PRELATURE	PRICINESS	PROFANING	PROSCRIBE
PRELUDIAL	PRICKLIER	PROFANITY	PROSECTOR
PRELUSION	PRICKLING	PROFESSED	PROSECUTE
PRELUSIVE	PRIESTESS	PROFESSOR	PROSELYTE
PREMATURE	PRIMAEVAL	PROFFERED	PROSIMIAN
PREMIERED	PRIMARIES	PROFFERER	PROSINESS
PREMIERES	PRIMARILY	PROFILING	PROSODIST
PREOCCUPY	PRIMATIAL	PROFITEER	PROSPECTS
PREORDAIN	PRIME COST	PROFITING	PROSPERED
PREPACKED	PRIMENESS	PROFLUENT	PROSTATES
PREPARING	PRIME RATE	PROFUSELY	PROSTATIC
PREPAYING	PRIME TIME	PROFUSION	PROSTRATE
PREPOTENT	PRIMIPARA	PROGESTIN	PROTAMINE
PREPUTIAL	PRIMITIVE	PROGNOSES	PROTANDRY
PRERECORD	PRIMROSES	PROGNOSIS	PROTECTED
PRESAGING	PRINCEDOM	PROGRAMED	PROTECTOR
PRESBYTER	PRINCETON	PROGRAMER	PROTESTER

PROTHESIS	PUFFINESS	PUSHINESS	QUEUE-JUMP
PROTHETIC	PUGILISTS	PUSHINGLY	QUIBBLERS
PROTHORAX	PUGNACITY	PUSSYFOOT	QUIBBLING
PROTOCOLS	PUISSANCE	PUSTULANT	QUICKENED
PROTOGYNY	PULLOVERS	PUSTULATE	QUICKLIME
PROTONEMA	PULLULATE	PUTREFIED	QUICKNESS
PROTOSTAR	PULMONARY	PUTREFIER	QUICKSAND
PROTOTYPE	PULMONATE	PUTRIDITY	QUICKSTEP
PROTOXIDE	PULPINESS	PUTTERING	QUIESCENT
PROTOZOAN	PULSATILE	PUTTYROOT	QUIETENED
PROTRUDED	PULSATING	PUT-UP JOBS	QUIETISTS
PROUDNESS	PULSATION	PUY DE DOME	QUIETNESS
PROUSTITE	PULSATIVE	PYCNIDIUM	QUIETUSES
PROVENCAL	PULSATORY	PYONGYANG	QUILLWORT
PROVENDER	PULVERIZE	PYORRHOEA	QUINIDINE
PROVIDENT	PULVILLUS	PYRAMIDAL	QUINOLINE
PROVIDERS	PULVINATE	PYRETHRIN	QUINONOID
PROVIDING	PUMICEOUS	PYRETHRUM	QUINTUPLE
PROVINCES	PUMMELING	PYRIDOXAL	QUIRKIEST
PROVISION	PUMMELLED	PYROGENIC	QUISLINGS
PROVISORY	PUMP ROOMS	PYROLITIC	QUITCLAIM
PROVOKING	PUNCH BALL	PYROLYSIS	QUITTANCE
PROVOLONE	PUNCH BOWL	PYROMANCY	QUIVERFUL
PROWESSES	PUNCHIEST	PYROMANIA	QUIVERING
PROWL CARS	PUNCH LINE	PYROMETER	QUIXOTISM
PROXIMATE	PUNCTILIO	PYROMETRY	QUIZZICAL
PROXIMITY	PUNCTUATE	PYROXENIC	QUODLIBET
PRUDENTLY	PUNCTURED	PYROXYLIN	QUOTATION
PRUDISHLY	PUNCTURER		QUOTIDIAN
PRURIENCE	PUNCTURES	**Q**	QUOTIENTS
PRUSSIATE	PUNGENTLY	QUADRANTS	
PRYTANEUM	PUNISHING	QUADRATIC	**R**
PSALMISTS	PUPILLAGE	QUADRIFID	RABBINATE
PSALMODIC	PUPILLARY	QUADRILLE	RABBITING
PSEUDONYM	PUPPETEER	QUADRUPED	RABBITTED
PSORIASIS	PUPPYHOOD	QUADRUPLE	RACEHORSE
PSORIATIC	PUPPY LOVE	QUADRUPLY	RACETRACK
PSYCHICAL	PURCHASED	QUAGMIRES	RACIALISM
PSYCHOSES	PURCHASER	QUAKERISM	RACIALIST
PSYCHOSIS	PURCHASES	QUAKINESS	RACKETEER
PSYCHOTIC	PUREBREDS	QUALIFIED	RACONTEUR
PTARMIGAN	PURGATION	QUALIFIER	RADIAL-PLY
PTERYGOID	PURGATIVE	QUALITIES	RADIANCES
PTOLEMAIC	PURGATORY	QUARRELED	RADIANTLY
PUB-CRAWLS	PURIFIERS	QUARRYING	RADIATING
PUBESCENT	PURIFYING	QUARTERED	RADIATION
PUBLICANS	PURLOINED	QUARTERLY	RADIATIVE
PUBLIC BAR	PURLOINER	QUARTZITE	RADIATORS
PUBLICIST	PURPORTED	QUATRAINS	RADICALLY
PUBLICITY	PURPOSELY	QUAVERING	RADIOGRAM
PUBLICIZE	PURPOSING	QUEASIEST	RADIOLOGY
PUBLISHED	PURPOSIVE	QUEBECOIS	RAFFINOSE
PUBLISHER	PURSUANCE	QUEBRACHO	RAFFISHLY
PUCKERING	PURULENCE	QUEERNESS	RAFFLESIA
PUCKISHLY	PURVEYING	QUENCHING	RAILHEADS
PUDGINESS	PURVEYORS	QUERCETIN	RAILROADS
PUERILISM	PUSHBIKES	QUERETARO	RAIN CHECK
PUERILITY	PUSHCARTS	QUERULOUS	RAINCOATS
PUERPERAL	PUSHCHAIR	QUESTIONS	RAINDROPS

RAINFALLS	REARWARDS	RECTANGLE	REFINANCE
RAIN GAUGE	REASONING	RECTIFIED	REFITTING
RAININESS	REASSURED	RECTIFIER	REFLATING
RAINMAKER	REASSURER	RECTITUDE	REFLATION
RAINPROOF	REBATABLE	RECTOCELE	REFLECTED
RAINSTORM	REBELLING	RECTORATE	REFLECTOR
RAINWATER	REBELLION	RECTORIAL	REFLEXIVE
RAJASTHAN	REBINDING	RECTORIES	REFORMERS
RAMIFYING	REBOUNDED	RECUMBENT	REFORMING
RAMPAGING	REBUFFING	RECURRENT	REFORMISM
RAMPANTLY	REBUKABLE	RECURRING	REFORMIST
RANCIDITY	REBUTTALS	RECUSANCY	REFRACTED
RANCOROUS	REBUTTING	RECUSANTS	REFRACTOR
RANDINESS	RECALLING	RECYCLING	REFRAINED
RANDOMIZE	RECANTING	REDACTION	REFRAINER
RANGINESS	RECAPPING	RED ALERTS	REFRESHED
RANSACKED	RECAPTION	REDBREAST	REFRESHER
RANSACKER	RECAPTURE	REDBRICKS	REFUELING
RANSOMERS	RECASTING	RED CARPET	REFUELLED
RANSOMING	RECEIVERS	REDDENING	REFULGENT
RANTINGLY	RECEIVING	REDEEMERS	REFUNDING
RAPACIOUS	RECENSION	REDEEMING	REFURBISH
RAPID-FIRE	RECEPTION	REDELIVER	REFUSABLE
RAPIDNESS	RECEPTIVE	REDEVELOP	REFUTABLE
RAPTORIAL	RECESSING	RED GIANTS	REGAINING
RAPTUROUS	RECESSION	RED-HANDED	REGARDANT
RARE EARTH	RECESSIVE	RED-HEADED	REGARDFUL
RASCALITY	RECHARGED	RED INDIAN	REGARDING
RASPBERRY	RECHAUFFE	RED LIGHTS	REGENCIES
RASPINGLY	RECHERCHE	REDOLENCE	REGICIDAL
RATEPAYER	RECIPIENT	REDOUBLED	REGICIDES
RATIFYING	RECITABLE	REDOUNDED	REGIMENTS
RATIONALE	RECKONING	RED-PENCIL	REGISTERS
RATIONING	RECLAIMED	RED PEPPER	REGISTRAR
RATTINESS	RECLINATE	REDRESSED	REGRESSED
RATTLEBOX	RECLINING	REDRESSER	REGRESSOR
RAUCOUSLY	RECLUSION	REDUCIBLE	REGRETFUL
RAUNCHIER	RECLUSIVE	REDUCTASE	REGRETTED
RAUNCHILY	RECOGNIZE	REDUCTION	REGRETTER
RAUWOLFIA	RECOILING	REDUNDANT	REGROUPED
RAVELLING	RECOLLECT	RE-ECHOING	REGULABLE
RAVISHING	RECOMMEND	REEDINESS	REGULARLY
RAZORBACK	RECOMPOSE	RE-EDUCATE	REGULATED
RAZORBILL	RECONCILE	REEF KNOTS	REGULATOR
RAZOR EDGE	RECONDITE	REEKINGLY	REHASHING
REACHABLE	RECONVERT	RE-ELECTED	REHEARSAL
REACTANCE	RECORDERS	RE-ENFORCE	REHEARSED
REACTIONS	RECORDING	RE-ENTRANT	REHEARSER
READDRESS	RECOUNTAL	RE-ENTRIES	REHOUSING
READINESS	RECOUNTED	RE-EXAMINE	REIMBURSE
READY-MADE	RECOUPING	REFECTION	REINFORCE
REALIGNED	RE-COVERED	REFECTORY	REINSTALL
REALISTIC	RECOVERER	REFERABLE	REINSTATE
REALITIES	RECREANTS	REFERENCE	REINSURED
REALIZING	RECREATED	REFERENDA	REINSURER
REANIMATE	RE-CREATOR	REFERRALS	REISSUING
REAPPOINT	RECREMENT	REFERRING	REITERANT
REARGUARD	RECRUITED	REFILLING	REITERATE
REARRANGE	RECRUITER	REFINABLE	REJECTING

REJECTION	RENOVATED	REPUTABLE	REST HOMES
REJECTIVE	RENOVATOR	REPUTABLY	RESTIFORM
REJIGGING	REOPENING	REPUTEDLY	RESTIVELY
REJOICING	REPAIRING	REQUESTED	RESTOCKED
REJOINDER	REPAIRMAN	REQUESTER	RESTORERS
REJOINING	REPARABLE	REQUIRING	RESTORING
REKINDLED	REPARABLY	REQUISITE	RESTRAINT
RELAPSING	REPARTEES	REQUITING	REST ROOMS
RELATABLE	REPAYABLE	REREDOSES	RESULTANT
RELATIONS	REPAYMENT	RERUNNING	RESULTING
RELATIVES	REPEALING	RESALABLE	RESUMABLE
RELAXABLE	REPEATERS	RESCINDED	RESURFACE
RELAXEDLY	REPEATING	RESCINDER	RESURGENT
RELEASING	REPECHAGE	RESCUABLE	RESURRECT
RELEGATED	REPELLENT	RESECTION	RETAILERS
RELENTING	REPELLING	RESEMBLED	RETAILING
RELEVANCE	REPENTANT	RESEMBLER	RETAINERS
RELEVANCY	REPENTING	RESENTFUL	RETAINING
RELIEF MAP	REPERTORY	RESENTING	RETALIATE
RELIEVING	REPHRASED	RESERPINE	RETARDANT
RELIGIONS	REPLACING	RESERVING	RETARDATE
RELIGIOSE	REPLAYING	RESERVIST	RETARDING
RELIGIOUS	REPLEADER	RESERVOIR	RETELLING
RELIQUARY	REPLENISH	RESETTING	RETENTION
RELISHING	REPLETION	RESETTLED	RETENTIVE
RELIVABLE	REPLETIVE	RESHUFFLE	RETHOUGHT
RELOADING	REPLICATE	RESIDENCE	RETICENCE
RELOCATED	REPLY-PAID	RESIDENCY	RETICULES
RELUCTANT	REPORTAGE	RESIDENTS	RETICULUM
REMAINDER	REPORTERS	RESIDUARY	RETINITIS
REMAINING	REPORTING	RESIGNING	RETORSION
REMANDING	REPOSEDLY	RESILIENT	RETORTING
REMANENCE	REPOSEFUL	RESINATED	RETORTION
REMARKING	REPOSSESS	RESISTANT	RETOUCHED
REMARRIED	REPREHEND	RESISTERS	RETOUCHER
REMEDYING	REPRESENT	RESISTING	RETRACING
REMINDERS	REPRESSED	RESISTORS	RETRACTED
REMINDFUL	REPRESSER	RESITTING	RETRACTOR
REMINDING	REPRIEVED	RESNATRON	RETREADED
REMINISCE	REPRIEVER	RESOLUBLE	RETREATAL
REMISSION	REPRIEVES	RESOLVENT	RETREATED
REMISSIVE	REPRIMAND	RESOLVING	RETRIEVAL
REMITTING	REPRINTED	RESONANCE	RETRIEVED
REMODELED	REPRINTER	RESONATED	RETRIEVER
REMONTANT	REPRISALS	RESONATOR	RETROCEDE
REMONTOIR	REPROBACY	RESORBENT	RETROFIRE
REMOULDED	REPROBATE	RESORTING	RETROFLEX
REMOUNTED	REPROCESS	RESOUNDED	RETROPACK
REMOVABLE	REPRODUCE	RESOURCES	RETROUSSE
REMOVABLY	REPROVING	RESPECTED	RETURNING
REMSCHEID	REPTILIAN	RESPECTER	REUNITING
RENASCENT	REPTILOID	RESPIRING	REUTILIZE
RENDERING	REPUBLICS	RESPONDED	REVALUING
RENDITION	REPUBLISH	RESPONDER	REVAMPING
RENEGADES	REPUDIATE	RESPONSER	REVEALING
RENEWABLE	REPUGNANT	RESPONSES	REVELATOR
RENEWEDLY	REPULSING	RESTATING	REVELLING
RENOUNCED	REPULSION	REST CURES	REVELMENT
RENOUNCER	REPULSIVE	RESTFULLY	REVELROUS

REVENGING	RICKSHAWS	ROLLINGLY	RUINATION
REVERABLE	RICOCHETS	ROMANCING	RUINOUSLY
REVERENCE	RIDDANCES	ROMAN NOSE	RULEBOOKS
REVERENDS	RIDERLESS	ROMANTICS	RUMBLINGS
REVERSALS	RIDGELING	ROMPINGLY	RUMINANTS
REVERSING	RIDGEPOLE	ROOF RACKS	RUMINATED
REVERSION	RIDICULED	ROOKERIES	RUMINATOR
REVERTING	RIDICULER	ROOMINESS	RUMMAGING
REVERTIVE	RIFLEBIRD	ROOMMATES	RUN-ABOUTS
REVETMENT	RIGHTEOUS	ROOT CROPS	RUN-AROUND
REVIEWERS	RIGHT-HAND	ROOTINESS	RUNCINATE
REVIEWING	RIGHTISTS	ROOTSTOCK	RUNNERS-UP
REVISABLE	RIGHTNESS	ROQUEFORT	RUNNER-UPS
REVISIONS	RIGHTWARD	ROSACEOUS	RUNNYMEDE
REVIVABLE	RIGHT WING	ROSEWATER	RUNTINESS
REVIVABLY	RIGMAROLE	ROSINWEED	RUPTURING
REVOCABLE	RING ROADS	ROSTELLUM	RUSH HOURS
REVOCABLY	RIO GRANDE	ROTAMETER	RUSHINESS
REVOKABLE	RIOTOUSLY	ROTARIANS	RUSHINGLY
REVOKABLY	RIPOSTING	ROTATABLE	RUSHLIGHT
REVOLTING	RISKINESS	ROTATIONS	RUSSETISH
REVOLVERS	RITUALISM	ROTIFERAL	RUSTICATE
REVOLVING	RITUALIST	ROTOVATOR	RUSTICITY
REVULSION	RITUALIZE	ROTTERDAM	RUSTINESS
REVULSIVE	RIVALLING	ROTUNDITY	RUSTPROOF
REWARDING	RIVALRIES	ROUGHCAST	RUTABAGAS
REWIRABLE	RIVALROUS	ROUGHENED	RUTACEOUS
REWORDING	RIVERBEDS	ROUGH-HEWN	RUTHENIAN
REWORKING	RIVERHEAD	ROUGHNECK	RUTHENIUM
REWRITING	RIVERSIDE	ROUGHNESS	RUTILATED
REYKJAVIK	ROADBLOCK	ROUGHSHOD	RUTTINESS
RHAPSODIC	ROADHOUSE	ROUNDELAY	
RHEOMETER	ROADSHOWS	ROUNDHEAD	S
RHEOMETRY	ROADSTEAD	ROUNDNESS	SABADILLA
RHEOSTATS	ROADSTERS	ROUNDSMAN	SABOTAGED
RHEOTAXIS	ROAD TAXES	ROUNDSMEN	SABOTEURS
RHEUMATIC	ROAD TESTS	ROUND-TRIP	SACCHARIN
RH FACTORS	ROAD WORKS	ROUNDWORM	SACCULATE
RHIGOLENE	ROASTINGS	ROUTINELY	SACKCLOTH
RHINELAND	ROBBERIES	ROUTINISM	SACK RACES
RHINOLOGY	ROBOT-LIKE	ROUTINIST	SACRAMENT
RHIZOBIUM	ROCKBOUND	ROVING EYE	SACRARIUM
RHIZOIDAL	ROCK CAKES	ROWDINESS	SACRED COW
RHIZOTOMY	ROCKERIES	ROW HOUSES	SACRIFICE
RHODAMINE	ROCKETEER	ROYAL BLUE	SACRILEGE
RHODESIAN	ROCKETING	ROYALISTS	SACRISTAN
RHODOLITE	ROCKFALLS	ROYALTIES	SADDENING
RHODONITE	ROCKINESS	RUBBERIZE	SADDLEBAG
RHODOPSIN	ROCK 'N'	RUBBISHED	SADDLEBOW
RHOMBOIDS	ROLL	RUBESCENT	SAFEGUARD
RHOMBUSES	ROCK PLANT	RUBRICATE	SAFE HOUSE
RHOTACISM	ROCKSHAFT	RUBRICIAN	SAFELIGHT
RHOTACIST	ROENTGENS	RUCKSACKS	SAFETY NET
RHYMESTER	ROGUERIES	RUDACEOUS	SAFETY PIN
RHYOLITIC	ROGUISHLY	RUDBECKIA	SAFFLOWER
RHYTHMICS	ROISTERER	RUDDINESS	SAFRANINE
RIBOSOMAL	ROLE MODEL	RUDIMENTS	SAGACIOUS
RICE PADDY	ROLE PLAYS	RUFESCENT	SAGEBRUSH
RICE PAPER	ROLL CALLS	RUFFIANLY	SAGITTATE

SAILBOARD	SANTONICA	SCALLOPER	SCLEROSES
SAILCLOTH	SAPHENOUS	SCALLYWAG	SCLEROSIS
SAILPLANE	SAPIENTLY	SCAMPERED	SCLEROTIC
SAINTHOOD	SAPODILLA	SCAMPERER	SCOLDABLE
SAINTLILY	SAPPHIRES	SCANTIEST	SCOLDINGS
SAINT PAUL	SAPPINESS	SCANTLING	SCOLECITE
SAINT'S DAY	SAPRAEMIA	SCANTNESS	SCOLIOSIS
SALAAMING	SAPRAEMIC	SCAPA FLOW	SCOLIOTIC
SALACIOUS	SAPROLITE	SCAPEGOAT	SCOLLOPED
SALAD DAYS	SAPROZOIC	SCAPHOPOD	SCOMBROID
SALAMANCA	SAPSUCKER	SCAPOLITE	SCOPOLINE
SALERATUS	SARABANDS	SCARABOID	SCOPULATE
SALEROOMS	SARACENIC	SCARECROW	SCORBUTIC
SALESGIRL	SARCASTIC	SCARFSKIN	SCORCHERS
SALESROOM	SARCOCARP	SCARIFIED	SCORCHING
SALES SLIP	SARDINIAN	SCARIFIER	SCORECARD
SALES TALK	SARGASSUM	SCARINGLY	SCORIFIER
SALIMETER	SARTORIAL	SCARPERED	SCORPIOID
SALIMETRY	SARTORIUS	SCATOLOGY	SCORPIONS
SALISBURY	SASHAYING	SCATTERED	SCOTCH EGG
SALIVATED	SASKATOON	SCATTERER	SCOTCHING
SALMONOID	SASSAFRAS	SCATTIEST	SCOUNDREL
SALOON BAR	SASSENACH	SCAVENGED	SCOURGING
SALPIFORM	SATANISTS	SCAVENGER	SCOURINGS
SALTATION	SATELLITE	SCENARIOS	SCRABBLED
SALTINESS	SATIATING	SCENARIST	SCRABBLER
SALTLICKS	SATIATION	SCENTLESS	SCRAGGIER
SALTPETRE	SATINWOOD	SCEPTICAL	SCRAGGILY
SALTWATER	SATIRICAL	SCHEDULAR	SCRAGGING
SALTWORKS	SATIRIZED	SCHEDULED	SCRAMBLED
SALVAGING	SATIRIZER	SCHEDULES	SCRAMBLER
SALVATION	SATISFIED	SCHEELITE	SCRAMBLES
SAMARITAN	SATISFIER	SCHEMATIC	SCRAMMING
SAMARKAND	SATURABLE	SCHILLING	SCRAPABLE
SANATORIA	SATURATED	SCHISTOSE	SCRAPBOOK
SANCTIONS	SATURATER	SCHIZOPOD	SCRAP HEAP
SANCTUARY	SATURDAYS	SCHLEPPED	SCRAPINGS
SANDALLED	SATURNIAN	SCHLIEREN	SCRAPPIER
SANDBANKS	SATURNIID	SCHLIERIC	SCRAPPILY
SANDBLAST	SATURNINE	SCHMALTZY	SCRAPPING
SAND—BLIND	SATURNISM	SCHNAUZER	SCRATCHED
SANDBOXES	SAUCEPANS	SCHNITZEL	SCRATCHER
SAND DUNES	SAUCINESS	SCHOLARLY	SCRATCHES
SAND FLIES	SAUNTERED	SCHOLIAST	SCRAWLING
SANDINESS	SAUNTERER	SCHOOLBOY	SCRAWNIER
SANDPAPER	SAUTERNES	SCHOOLING	SCRAWNILY
SANDPIPER	SAVOURING	SCHOONERS	SCREAMING
SANDSHOES	SAXIFRAGE	SCIENTIAL	SCREECHED
SANDSTONE	SAXOPHONE	SCIENTISM	SCREECHER
SANDSTORM	SCABBARDS	SCIENTIST	SCREECHES
SAND TRAPS	SCABBIEST	SCIMITARS	SCREENING
SANFORIZE	SCABIETIC	SCINTILLA	SCREWBALL
SANGFROID	SCAFFOLDS	SCIOMANCY	SCREWIEST
SANITARIA	SCAGLIOLA	SCIRRHOID	SCREW TOPS
SANITIZED	SCALAWAGS	SCIRRHOUS	SCREWWORM
SAN MARINO	SCALDFISH	SCLERITIC	SCRIBBLED
SANS SERIF	SCALINESS	SCLERITIS	SCRIBBLER
SANTA CRUZ	SCALLIONS	SCLEROSAL	SCRIBBLES
SANTANDER	SCALLOPED	SCLEROSED	SCRIMMAGE

SCRIMPILY	SECRETIVE	SENSILLUM	SET THEORY
SCRIMPING	SECRETORY	SENSITIVE	SETTLINGS
SCRIMSHAW	SECTARIAN	SENSITIZE	SEVENFOLD
SCRIPTURE	SECTILITY	SENSORIUM	SEVENTEEN
SCROLLING	SECTIONAL	SENTENCED	SEVENTIES
SCROUNGED	SECTIONED	SENTENCES	SEVERABLE
SCROUNGER	SECTORIAL	SENTIENCE	SEVERALLY
SCRUBBERS	SECUNDINE	SENTIMENT	SEVERALTY
SCRUBBIER	SECURABLE	SENTINELS	SEVERANCE
SCRUBBING	SEDATIVES	SENTRY BOX	SEX APPEAL
SCRUBLAND	SEDENTARY	SEPARABLE	SEXENNIAL
SCRUFFIER	SEDIMENTS	SEPARABLY	SEX OBJECT
SCRUMHALF	SEDITIOUS	SEPARATED	SEX ORGANS
SCRUMMAGE	SEDUCIBLE	SEPARATES	SEXTUPLET
SCRUMPING	SEDUCTION	SEPARATOR	SEXUALITY
SCRUNCHED	SEDUCTIVE	SEPHARDIC	SFORZANDO
SCRUPLING	SEEDINESS	SEPIOLITE	SGRAFFITO
SCUFFLING	SEEDLINGS	SEPTARIAN	SHABBIEST
SCULLIONS	SEEMINGLY	SEPTARIUM	SHACKLING
SCULPTORS	SEESAWING	SEPTEMBER	SHADINESS
SCULPTURE	SEGMENTAL	SEPTENARY	SHADOW-BOX
SCUPPERED	SEGMENTED	SEPTICITY	SHADOWIER
SCURRYING	SEGREGATE	SEPTUPLET	SHADOWING
SCUTATION	SEIGNEURS	SEPULCHRE	SHAGGIEST
SCUTCHEON	SELACHIAN	SEPULTURE	SHAKEDOWN
SCUTELLAR	SELECTING	SEQUACITY	SHAKEOUTS
SCUTELLUM	SELECTION	SEQUENCER	SHAKINESS
SCUTIFORM	SELECTIVE	SEQUENCES	SHALLOWED
SCUTTLING	SELECTORS	SEQUESTER	SHALLOWER
SEABOARDS	SELENIOUS	SERAGLIOS	SHALLOWLY
SEA BREEZE	SELF-ABUSE	SERENADED	SHAMANISM
SEA CHANGE	SELF-DOUBT	SERENADER	SHAMANIST
SEAFARING	SELF-DRIVE	SERENADES	SHAMATEUR
SEAFRONTS	SELFISHLY	SERGEANCY	SHAMBLING
SEAHORSES	SELLOTAPE	SERGEANTS	SHAMBOLIC
SEAL-POINT	SEMANTICS	SERIALISM	SHAMELESS
SEALYHAMS	SEMAPHORE	SERIALIZE	SHAMPOOED
SEAMINESS	SEMBLANCE	SERICEOUS	SHAMPOOER
SEAPLANES	SEMESTERS	SERIGRAPH	SHANGRI-LA
SEA POWERS	SEMESTRAL	SERIOUSLY	SHAPELESS
SEARCHING	SEMI-BANTU	SERMONIZE	SHAPELIER
SEASCAPES	SEMIBREVE	SEROLOGIC	SHARECROP
SEASHELLS	SEMICOLON	SEROTINAL	SHARKSKIN
SEASONING	SEMIFINAL	SEROTONIN	SHARPENED
SEAT BELTS	SEMIFLUID	SERRATION	SHARPENER
SEA URCHIN	SEMILUNAR	SERRIFORM	SHARP-EYED
SEAWORTHY	SEMIOTICS	SERRULATE	SHARPNESS
SEBACEOUS	SEMIRIGID	SERVERIES	SHATTERED
SECATEURS	SEMISOLID	SERVICING	SHATTERER
SECESSION	SEMITONES	SERVIETTE	SHEARLING
SECLUDING	SEMITONIC	SERVILELY	SHEATFISH
SECLUSION	SEMIVOCAL	SERVILITY	SHEATHING
SECLUSIVE	SEMIVOWEL	SERVITORS	SHEEPDIPS
SECONDARY	SENESCENT	SERVITUDE	SHEEPDOGS
SECONDERS	SENESCHAL	SESSILITY	SHEEPFOLD
SECONDING	SENIORITY	SESSIONAL	SHEEPSKIN
SECRETARY	SENORITAS	SETACEOUS	SHEEPWALK
SECRETING	SENSATION	SET PIECES	SHEERLEGS
SECRETION	SENSELESS	SETSQUARE	SHEERNESS

SHEIKHDOM	SHOWERING	SIGNALING	SIXTEENMO
SHELDUCKS	SHOWGIRLS	SIGNALIZE	SIXTEENTH
SHELF LIFE	SHOWINESS	SIGNALLED	SIXTH FORM
SHELLFIRE	SHOWPIECE	SIGNALLER	SIXTIETHS
SHELLFISH	SHOWPLACE	SIGNALMAN	SIZARSHIP
SHELTERED	SHOWROOMS	SIGNALMEN	SKAGERRAK
SHELTERER	SHOW TRIAL	SIGNATORY	SKEDADDLE
SHEPHERDS	SHREDDERS	SIGNATURE	SKELETONS
SHIELDING	SHREDDING	SIGNBOARD	SKEPTICAL
SHIFTIEST	SHREWDEST	SIGNIFIED	SKETCHERS
SHIFT KEYS	SHRIEKING	SIGNIFIER	SKETCHIER
SHIFTLESS	SHRILLEST	SIGNORINA	SKETCHILY
SHILLINGS	SHRINKAGE	SIGNPOSTS	SKETCHING
SHIMMERED	SHRINKING	SIKKIMESE	SKETCHPAD
SHINBONES	SHRIVELED	SILENCERS	SKEWBALDS
SHININESS	SHROUDING	SILENCING	SKEWERING
SHINNYING	SHRUBBERY	SILICATES	SKEW-WHIFF
SHIPBOARD	SHRUGGING	SILICEOUS	SKIASCOPE
SHIPMATES	SHUDDERED	SILICOSIS	SKIASCOPY
SHIPMENTS	SHUFBOARD	SILIQUOSE	SKIDPROOF
SHIPOWNER	SHUFFLERS	SILKALINE	SKIJORING
SHIPSHAPE	SHUFFLING	SILKINESS	SKILFULLY
SHIPWRECK	SHUNNABLE	SILKWORMS	SKIMMINGS
SHIPYARDS	SHUTDOWNS	SILLABUBS	SKIMPIEST
SHIRTIEST	SHUTTERED	SILLINESS	SKIN-DIVED
SHIRTTAIL	SHUTTLING	SILTATION	SKIN DIVER
SHITTIEST	SIBILANCE	SILVERING	SKIN FLICK
SHIVERING	SIBILANTS	SIMAROUBA	SKINFLINT
SHOCKABLE	SIBYLLINE	SIMILARLY	SKIN GRAFT
SHODDIEST	SICCATIVE	SIMMERING	SKINHEADS
SHOEHORNS	SICKENING	SIMPATICO	SKINNIEST
SHOELACES	SICK LEAVE	SIMPERING	SKIN-TIGHT
SHOEMAKER	SICKLIEST	SIMPLETON	SKI PLANES
SHOESHINE	SICKROOMS	SIMULACRA	SKIPPERED
SHOETREES	SIC PASSIM	SIMULATED	SKITTERED
SHOOTINGS	SIDEBOARD	SIMULATOR	SKIVVYING
SHOOT-OUTS	SIDE-DRESS	SINCERELY	SKULLCAPS
SHOP FLOOR	SIDE ISSUE	SINCERITY	SKYDIVERS
SHORELESS	SIDEKICKS	SINECURES	SKYDIVING
SHORELINE	SIDELIGHT	SINGAPORE	SKYJACKED
SHORTAGES	SIDELINED	SINGINGLY	SKYJACKER
SHORTCAKE	SIDELINES	SINGLETON	SKYLARKED
SHORT CUTS	SIDE ORDER	SINGSONGS	SKYLARKER
SHORTENED	SIDERITIC	SINGULARS	SKYLIGHTS
SHORTENER	SIDEROSIS	SINGULTUS	SKYROCKET
SHORTFALL	SIDEROTIC	SINHALESE	SKYWRITER
SHORTHAND	SIDESHOWS	SINISTRAL	SLACKENED
SHORT-HAUL	SIDESLIPS	SINOLOGUE	SLACKNESS
SHORTHORN	SIDESTEPS	SINUOSITY	SLAGHEAPS
SHORT LIST	SIDESWIPE	SINUOUSLY	SLANDERED
SHORTNESS	SIDETRACK	SINUSITIS	SLANDERER
SHORT-TERM	SIDEWARDS	SIPHONAGE	SLANTWISE
SHORT TIME	SIGHTABLE	SIPHONING	SLAPHAPPY
SHORT WAVE	SIGHTINGS	SISYPHEAN	SLAPSTICK
SHOULDERS	SIGHTLESS	SITUATING	SLATINESS
SHOVELING	SIGHT-READ	SITUATION	SLATTERNS
SHOVELLED	SIGHTSEER	SITZKREIG	SLAUGHTER
SHOWCASES	SIGMATION	SIX-FOOTER	SLAVERING
SHOWDOWNS	SIGNAL BOX	SIXPENCES	SLAVISHLY

SLAVONIAN	SMOOCHING	SOAP OPERA	SOMNOLENT
SLEAZIEST	SMOOTHEST	SOAPSTONE	SONGBIRDS
SLEEKNESS	SMOOTHIES	SOAPSUDSY	SONGBOOKS
SLEEPIEST	SMOOTHING	SOARINGLY	SONGSTERS
SLEEPLESS	SMOTHERED	SOBBINGLY	SONIC BOOM
SLEEPWALK	SMUGGLERS	SOBERNESS	SONNETEER
SLICEABLE	SMUGGLING	SOBRIQUET	SON-OF-A-GUN
SLICKNESS	SMUTTIEST	SOCIALISM	SONS-IN-LAW
SLIDE RULE	SNACK BARS	SOCIALIST	SOOTINESS
SLIGHTEST	SNAFFLING	SOCIALITE	SOPHISTER
SLIGHTING	SNAKEBITE	SOCIALITY	SOPHISTIC
SLIMINESS	SNAKEROOT	SOCIALIZE	SOPHISTRY
SLINGSHOT	SNAKESKIN	SOCIETIES	SOPHOMORE
SLINKIEST	SNAKINESS	SOCIOLOGY	SOPORIFIC
SLIPCASES	SNAPPABLE	SOCIOPATH	SOPPINESS
SLIPKNOTS	SNAPPIEST	SODA WATER	SOPRANINO
SLIPNOOSE	SNAPSHOTS	SODOMITES	SORCERERS
SLIPPAGES	SNARE DRUM	SOFTENING	SORCERESS
SLIPPIEST	SNARINGLY	SOFT FRUIT	SORCEROUS
SLIP ROADS	SNATCHILY	SOFT-PEDAL	SORITICAL
SLIPSHEET	SNATCHING	SOFT SPOTS	SORRINESS
SLITHERED	SNAZZIEST	SOFT TOUCH	SORROWFUL
SLIVOVITZ	SNEAKIEST	SOFTWOODS	SORROWING
SLOBBERED	SNICKERED	SOGGINESS	SORTILEGE
SLOBBERER	SNIDENESS	SOI-DISANT	SORTITION
SLOPINGLY	SNIFFLERS	SOJOURNED	SOSNOWIEC
SLOPPIEST	SNIFFLING	SOJOURNER	SOSTENUTO
SLOUCH HAT	SNIGGERED	SOLAR CELL	SOTTO VOCE
SLOUCHILY	SNIPEFISH	SOLARIUMS	SOUBRETTE
SLOUCHING	SNITCHING	SOLAR YEAR	SOULFULLY
SLOUGHING	SNIVELING	SOLDERING	SOUL MUSIC
SLOVAKIAN	SNIVELLED	SOLDIERED	SOUNDABLE
SLOVENIAN	SNIVELLER	SOLDIERLY	SOUNDINGS
SLOWCOACH	SNOOKERED	SOLECISMS	SOUNDLESS
SLOWDOWNS	SNOOTIEST	SOLEMNIFY	SOUNDNESS
SLOWWORMS	SNOTTIEST	SOLEMNITY	SOUNDPOST
SLUDGIEST	SNOWBALLS	SOLEMNIZE	SOUP SPOON
SLUGGARDS	SNOWBERRY	SOLFATARA	SOUR CREAM
SLUMBERED	SNOW-BLIND	SOLFEGGIO	SOUTHDOWN
SLUMBERER	SNOWBLINK	SOLFERINO	SOUTHEAST
SLUSH FUND	SNOWBOUND	SOLICITED	SOUTHERLY
SLUSHIEST	SNOWDONIA	SOLICITOR	SOUTHPAWS
SMALL ARMS	SNOWDRIFT	SOLIDNESS	SOUTH POLE
SMALL BEER	SNOWDROPS	SOLILOQUY	SOUTHWARD
SMALLNESS	SNOWFALLS	SOLIPSISM	SOUTHWARK
SMALL TALK	SNOWFIELD	SOLIPSIST	SOUTHWEST
SMALL-TIME	SNOWFLAKE	SOLITAIRE	SOUVENIRS
SMARMIEST	SNOWINESS	SOLONCHAK	SOU'WESTER
SMARTENED	SNOWSHOER	SOLOTHURN	SOVEREIGN
SMARTNESS	SNOWSHOES	SOLSTICES	SOVIETISM
SMASHABLE	SNOWSTORM	SOLUTIONS	SOVIETIST
SMATTERER	SNOW-WHITE	SOLUTREAN	SOVIETIZE
SMEAR TEST	SNUB-NOSED	SOLVATION	SOYA BEANS
SMELLIEST	SNUFFLING	SOMBREROS	SPACEBAND
SMILINGLY	SNUGGLING	SOMEPLACE	SPACED OUT
SMIRCHING	SOAKINGLY	SOMETHING	SPACELESS
SMOKELESS	SOAPBERRY	SOMETIMES	SPACEPORT
SMOKINESS	SOAPBOXES	SOMEWHERE	SPACESHIP
SMOLDERED	SOAPINESS	SOMMELIER	SPACESUIT

SPACE-TIME	SPICINESS	SPOONSFUL	SQUEALING
SPACEWALK	SPICULATE	SPOROCARP	SQUEAMISH
SPADEFISH	SPIDERMAN	SPOROCYST	SQUEEGEES
SPADEWORK	SPIDERWEB	SPOROCYTE	SQUEEZERS
SPAGHETTI	SPIKENARD	SPOROGONY	SQUEEZING
SPANGLING	SPIKE-RUSH	SPOROZOAN	SQUELCHED
SPANIARDS	SPIKINESS	SPORTIEST	SQUELCHER
SPANKINGS	SPILLIKIN	SPORTS CAR	SQUIDGIER
SPARENESS	SPILLWAYS	SPORTSMAN	SQUIFFIER
SPARE PART	SPINDLIER	SPORTSMEN	SQUIGGLER
SPARERIBS	SPIN-DRIED	SPORULATE	SQUIGGLES
SPARE TYRE	SPINDRIFT	SPOT CHECK	SQUINTING
SPARINGLY	SPIN-DRYER	SPOTLIGHT	SQUIRMING
SPARKLERS	SPINELESS	SPOTTABLE	SQUIRRELS
SPARKLING	SPININESS	SPOTTIEST	SQUIRTERS
SPARK PLUG	SPINNAKER	SPRAINING	SQUIRTING
SPARTEINE	SPINNERET	SPRAWLING	SQUISHIER
SPASMODIC	SPINOSITY	SPRAY GUNS	SQUISHING
SPATIALLY	SPINSTERS	SPREADING	STABILITY
SPATTERED	SPINULOSE	SPRIGHTLY	STABILIZE
SPATULATE	SPIRALING	SPRINGBOK	STABLE BOY
SPEAKABLE	SPIRALLED	SPRINGIER	STAGE DOOR
SPEAKEASY	SPIRILLAR	SPRINGILY	STAGEHAND
SPEARHEAD	SPIRILLUM	SPRINGING	STAGE NAME
SPEARMINT	SPIRITING	SPRINKLED	STAGGERED
SPEARWORT	SPIRITOSO	SPRINKLER	STAGGERER
SPECIALLY	SPIRITUAL	SPRINKLES	STAGHOUND
SPECIALTY	SPIROGYRA	SPRINTERS	STAGINESS
SPECIFICS	SPITFIRES	SPRINTING	STAGNANCY
SPECIFIED	SPITTOONS	SPRITSAIL	STAGNATED
SPECIFIER	SPLASHIER	SPROCKETS	STAG PARTY
SPECIMENS	SPLASHILY	SPROUTING	STAIDNESS
SPECTACLE	SPLASHING	SPUNKIEST	STAINABLE
SPECTATED	SPLATTING	SPUTTERED	STAINLESS
SPECTATOR	SPLAYFOOT	SPUTTERER	STAIRCASE
SPECULATE	SPLEENFUL	SQUABBLED	STAIRHEAD
SPEECH DAY	SPLEENISH	SQUABBLER	STAIRWELL
SPEECHIFY	SPLENDOUR	SQUABBLES	STALEMATE
SPEEDBOAT	SPLENETIC	SQUAD CARS	STALENESS
SPEEDIEST	SPLENITIS	SQUADRONS	STALINISM
SPEEDSTER	SPLINTERS	SQUALIDLY	STALINIST
SPEED TRAP	SPLINTERY	SQUALLIER	STALL-FEED
SPEEDWAYS	SPLIT ENDS	SQUALLING	STALLIONS
SPEEDWELL	SPLIT PEAS	SQUAMOSAL	STALWARTS
SPELLABLE	SPLIT RING	SQUARE ONE	STAMINATE
SPELLBIND	SPLITTING	SQUARROSE	STAMINODE
SPELLINGS	SPLOSHING	SQUASHIER	STAMINODY
SPELUNKER	SPLURGING	SQUASHILY	STAMMERED
SPENDABLE	SPLUTTERS	SQUASHING	STAMMERER
SPERMATIC	SPODUMENE	SQUATNESS	STAMPEDED
SPERMATID	SPOKEN FOR	SQUATTERS	STAMPEDER
SPHAGNOUS	SPOKESMAN	SQUATTEST	STAMPEDES
SPHAGNUMS	SPONGE BAG	SQUATTING	STANCHING
SPHENODON	SPONGIEST	SQUAWKERS	STANCHION
SPHERICAL	SPONSORED	SQUAWKING	STANDARDS
SPHEROIDS	SPOOKIEST	SQUEAKERS	STANDPIPE
SPHERULAR	SPOONBILL	SQUEAKIER	STAPEDIAL
SPHINCTER	SPOON-FEED	SQUEAKING	STAR-APPLE
SPHYGMOID	SPOONFULS	SQUEALERS	STARBOARD

STARCHIER	STERILIZE	STONE-DEAD	STRICTEST
STARCHILY	STERNMOST	STONE-DEAF	STRICTURE
STARCHING	STERNNESS	STONEFISH	STRIDENCE
STARGAZER	STERNPOST	STONELESS	STRIDENCY
STARKNESS	STEVEDORE	STONE-LILY	STRIKE PAY
STARLIGHT	STICKIEST	STONEWALL	STRINGENT
STARLINGS	STICKLERS	STONEWARE	STRINGIER
STARRIEST	STICKPINS	STONEWORK	STRINGILY
STAR SIGNS	STICKSEED	STONEWORT	STRINGING
STARTLING	STICKWEED	STONINESS	STRIP CLUB
STATEHOOD	STICKY END	STOPCOCKS	STRIPIEST
STATELESS	STIFFENED	STOPLIGHT	STRIPLING
STATEMENT	STIFFENER	STOPOVERS	STRIPPERS
STATEROOM	STIFFNESS	STOPPABLE	STRIPPING
STATESIDE	STIGMATIC	STOPPAGES	STROBILUS
STATESMAN	STILETTOS	STOPPERED	STROLLERS
STATESMEN	STILLBORN	STOP PRESS	STROLLING
STATIONED	STILL LIFE	STOPWATCH	STROMATIC
STATIONER	STILLNESS	STOREROOM	STRONGARM
STATISTIC	STILTEDLY	STORMIEST	STRONGBOX
STATOCYST	STIMULANT	STORYBOOK	STRONGEST
STATOLITH	STIMULATE	STORY LINE	STRONGYLE
STATUETTE	STINGIEST	STOUTNESS	STRONTIAN
STATUS QUO	STINGRAYS	STOVEPIPE	STRONTIUM
STATUTORY	STINK-BOMB	STOWAWAYS	STROPPIER
STAUNCHED	STINKHORN	STRADDLED	STRUCTURE
STAUNCHER	STINKWEED	STRADDLER	STRUGGLED
STAUNCHLY	STINKWOOD	STRAGGLED	STRUGGLER
STAVANGER	STIPIFORM	STRAGGLER	STRUGGLES
STAVROPOL	STIPITATE	STRAIGHTS	STRUMATIC
ST BERNARD	STIPPLING	STRAINERS	STRUMMING
STEADFAST	STIPULATE	STRAINING	STRUMPETS
STEADIEST	STIR-FRIED	STRANGELY	STRUNG-OUT
STEADYING	STIRRABLE	STRANGERS	STRUTTING
STEAMBOAT	STITCHING	STRANGEST	STRYCHNIC
STEAMED-UP	STOCKADED	STRANGLED	STUBBIEST
STEAMIEST	STOCKADES	STRANGLER	STUDBOOKS
STEAM IRON	STOCKCARS	STRANGLES	STUDHORSE
STEAMSHIP	STOCK CUBE	STRANGURY	STUFFIEST
STEATITIC	STOCKFISH	STRAPLESS	STUMBLING
STEEL BAND	STOCKHOLM	STRAPPING	STUMPIEST
STEELHEAD	STOCKIEST	STRATAGEM	STUPEFIED
STEELIEST	STOCKINET	STRATEGIC	STUPEFIER
STEEL WOOL	STOCKINGS	STRAW POLL	STUPIDEST
STEELWORK	STOCKISTS	STREAKERS	STUPIDITY
STEELYARD	STOCKPILE	STREAKIER	STUPOROUS
STEEPENED	STOCKPOTS	STREAKILY	STURDIEST
STEEPNESS	STOCKROOM	STREAKING	STURGEONS
STEERABLE	STOCKYARD	STREAMERS	STUTTERED
STEERSMAN	STODGIEST	STREAMING	STUTTERER
STEERSMEN	STOICALLY	STREETCAR	STUTTGART
STELLULAR	STOKEHOLD	STRENGTHS	STYLEBOOK
STENCILED	STOKEHOLE	STRENUOUS	STYLELESS
STENOTYPE	STOLIDITY	STRESSFUL	STYLIFORM
STENOTYPY	STOMACHED	STRESSING	STYLISHLY
STEPCHILD	STOMACHIC	STRETCHED	STYLISTIC
STERADIAN	STONECHAT	STRETCHER	STYLIZING
STERILANT	STONE-COLD	STRETCHES	STYLOBATE
STERILITY	STONECROP	STRIATION	STYLOLITE

STYLOPIZE	SUBTENDED	SUNBATHED	SURROUNDS
STYPTICAL	SUBTILIZE	SUNBATHER	SURVEYING
STYROFOAM	SUBTITLED	SUNBURNED	SURVEYORS
SUABILITY	SUBTITLES	SUNDERING	SURVIVALS
SUAVENESS	SUBTOTALS	SUNDOWNER	SURVIVING
SUBALPINE	SUBVERTED	SUNFLOWER	SURVIVORS
SUBALTERN	SUBVERTER	SUN LOUNGE	SUSPECTED
SUBARCTIC	SUCCEEDED	SUNNINESS	SUSPECTER
SUBATOMIC	SUCCEEDER	SUNSHADES	SUSPENDED
SUBCLIMAX	SUCCENTOR	SUNSTROKE	SUSPENDER
SUBCORTEX	SUCCESSES	SUNTANNED	SUSPENSOR
SUBDEACON	SUCCESSOR	SUN VISORS	SUSPICION
SUBDIVIDE	SUCCINATE	SUPERABLE	SUSTAINED
SUBDUABLE	SUCCOURED	SUPERCOOL	SUSTAINER
SUBDUEDLY	SUCCOURER	SUPEREGOS	SUSURRANT
SUBEDITED	SUCCULENT	SUPERFINE	SUSURRATE
SUBEDITOR	SUCCUMBED	SUPERHEAT	SUZERAINS
SUBFAMILY	SUCCUMBER	SUPERIORS	SWADDLING
SUBJACENT	SUCKLINGS	SUPERNOVA	SWAGGERED
SUBJECTED	SUCTIONAL	SUPERPOSE	SWAGGERER
SUBJOINED	SUCTORIAL	SUPERSEDE	SWAHILIAN
SUB JUDICE	SUDORIFIC	SUPERSTAR	SWALLOWED
SUBJUGATE	SUFFERERS	SUPERVENE	SWALLOWER
SUBLEASED	SUFFERING	SUPERVISE	SWAMPLAND
SUBLEASES	SUFFICING	SUPINATOR	SWANKIEST
SUBLESSEE	SUFFIXION	SUPPERADD	SWAN'S-DOWN
SUBLESSOR	SUFFOCATE	SUPPLIANT	SWANSONGS
SUBLIMATE	SUFFRAGAN	SUPPLIERS	SWAP MEETS
SUBLIMELY	SUFFRAGES	SUPPLYING	SWARTHIER
SUBLIMITY	SUFFUSING	SUPPORTED	SWARTHILY
SUBLUNARY	SUFFUSION	SUPPORTER	SWASTIKAS
SUBMARINE	SUFFUSIVE	SUPPOSING	SWATHABLE
SUBMENTAL	SUGAR BEET	SUPPURATE	SWAYINGLY
SUBMERGED	SUGARCANE	SUPREMACY	SWAZILAND
SUBMITTAL	SUGGESTED	SUPREMELY	SWEARWORD
SUBMITTED	SUGGESTER	SUPREMITY	SWEATBAND
SUBMITTER	SUITCASES	SURAKARTA	SWEATIEST
SUBMUCOSA	SULCATION	SURCHARGE	SWEATSHOP
SUBNORMAL	SULKINESS	SURCINGLE	SWEEPBACK
SUBORNING	SULLENEST	SURCULOSE	SWEEPINGS
SUBPHYLAR	SULLIABLE	SURE THING	SWEET CORN
SUBPHYLUM	SULPHATES	SURFACING	SWEETENER
SUBPOENAS	SULPHIDES	SURFBOARD	SWEETMEAT
SUBREGION	SULPHITIC	SURFEITED	SWEETNESS
SUBROGATE	SULPHURET	SURFEITER	SWEET PEAS
SUBSCRIBE	SULPHURYL	SURFPERCH	SWEET TALK
SUBSCRIPT	SULTANATE	SURGEONCY	SWELLFISH
SUBSIDIES	SULTRIEST	SURGERIES	SWELLINGS
SUBSIDING	SUMMARIES	SURLINESS	SWELTERED
SUBSIDIZE	SUMMARILY	SURMISING	SWEPT-BACK
SUBSISTED	SUMMARIZE	SURPASSED	SWEPTWING
SUBSISTER	SUMMATION	SURPLICES	SWERVABLE
SUBSOCIAL	SUMMERING	SURPLUSES	SWIFTNESS
SUBSOILER	SUMMING-UP	SURPRISED	SWIMMABLE
SUBSTANCE	SUMMONING	SURPRISER	SWIMMERET
SUBSTRATA	SUMMONSED	SURPRISES	SWINDLERS
SUBSTRATE	SUMMONSES	SURRENDER	SWINDLING
SUBSUMING	SUMPTUARY	SURROGACY	SWINEHERD
SUBTENANT	SUMPTUOUS	SURROGATE	SWINGEING

SWING-WING	SYNONYMIC	TALMUDIST	TEARFULLY
SWINISHLY	SYNOVITIC	TAMARINDS	TEARINGLY
SWISS ROLL	SYNOVITIS	TAMIL NADU	TEASINGLY
SWITCHING	SYNTACTIC	TAMPERING	TEASPOONS
SWIVELING	SYNTHESES	TANDOORIS	TEA TOWELS
SWIVELLED	SYNTHESIS	TANGERINE	TECHINESS
SWORDBILL	SYNTHETIC	TANNERIES	TECHNICAL
SWORDFISH	SYPHERING	TANTALATE	TECHNIQUE
SWORDPLAY	SYPHILOID	TANTALITE	TECTONICS
SWORDSMAN	SYPHILOMA	TANTALIZE	TEDDY BEAR
SWORDSMEN	SYPHONING	TANTALOUS	TEDDY BOYS
SWORDTAIL	SYRINGEAL	TANZANIAN	TEDIOUSLY
SYBARITES	SYRINGING	TAP DANCER	TEENAGERS
SYBARITIC	SYSTALTIC	TAP DANCES	TEE SHIRTS
SYCAMORES		TAPE DECKS	TEETERING
SYCOPHANT	T	TAPEWORMS	TELECASTS
SYKTYVKAR	TABESCENT	TARANTISM	TELEGENIC
SYLLABARY	TABLATURE	TARANTULA	TELEGONIC
SYLLABIFY	TABLELAND	TARAXACUM	TELEGRAMS
SYLLABISM	TABLEMATS	TARDINESS	TELEGRAPH
SYLLABLES	TABLEWARE	TARGETING	TELEMETER
SYLLABUBS	TABLE WINE	TARMACKED	TELEMETRY
SYLLEPSIS	TABULABLE	TARNISHED	TELEOLOGY
SYLLEPTIC	TABULATED	TARNISHER	TELEPATHY
SYLLOGISM	TABULATOR	TARPAULIN	TELEPHONE
SYLLOGIZE	TACAMAHAC	TARTARIZE	TELEPHONY
SYLPHLIKE	TACHYLYTE	TARTAROUS	TELESCOPE
SYLVANITE	TACITNESS	TASIMETER	TELESCOPY
SYMBIOSIS	TACKINESS	TASIMETRY	TELESTICH
SYMBIOTIC	TACTFULLY	TASK FORCE	TELEVISED
SYMBOLISM	TACTICIAN	TASMANIAN	TELLINGLY
SYMBOLIST	TACTILITY	TASTE BUDS	TELLTALES
SYMBOLIZE	TAENIASIS	TASTELESS	TELLURATE
SYMBOLOGY	TAGMEMICS	TASTINESS	TELLURIAN
SYMPATHIN	TAILBACKS	TATTINESS	TELLURIDE
SYMPATRIC	TAILBOARD	TATTOOING	TELLURION
SYMPHONIC	TAILCOATS	TATTOOIST	TELLURITE
SYMPHYSIS	TAILGATED	TAUTENING	TELLURIUM
SYMPODIAL	TAILGATES	TAUTOLOGY	TELLURIZE
SYMPODIUM	TAILLIGHT	TAUTONYMY	TELLUROUS
SYMPOSIAC	TAILORING	TAXACEOUS	TELOPHASE
SYMPOSIUM	TAILPIECE	TAX HAVENS	TELPHERIC
SYNAGOGUE	TAIL PIPES	TAXIDERMY	TEMPERATE
SYNALEPHA	TAILPLANE	TAXIMETER	TEMPERING
SYNCLINAL	TAILSPINS	TAXI RANKS	TEMPLATES
SYNCOPATE	TAILSTOCK	TAXONOMIC	TEMPORARY
SYNCRETIC	TAILWINDS	TAXPAYERS	TEMPORIZE
SYNCYTIUM	TAIWANESE	TEA BREAKS	TEMPTABLE
SYNDACTYL	TAKAMATSU	TEACHABLE	TEMPTRESS
SYNDICATE	TAKEAWAYS	TEA CHESTS	TENACIOUS
SYNDROMES	TAKEOVERS	TEA CLOTHS	TENACULUM
SYNDROMIC	TALIGRADE	TEA COSIES	TENANCIES
SYNECTICS	TALISMANS	TEAGARDEN	TENDEREST
SYNERESIS	TALKATIVE	TEAHOUSES	TENDERING
SYNERGISM	TALKING-TO	TEAKETTLE	TENDERIZE
SYNERGIST	TALK SHOWS	TEALEAVES	TENDINOUS
SYNIZESIS	TALL ORDER	TEAMSTERS	TENEBRISM
SYNKARYON	TALL STORY	TEARAWAYS	TENEBRIST
SYNOEKETE	TALMUDISM	TEARDROPS	TENEBROUS

TENEMENTS	THEARCHIC	THROATILY	TITILLATE
TENNESSEE	THEATRICS	THROBBING	TITIVATED
TENSENESS	THECODONT	THRONGING	TITIVATOR
TENSILITY	THEME PARK	THROTTLED	TITLE DEED
TENSIONAL	THEME SONG	THROTTLER	TITLE PAGE
TENSORIAL	THEOCRACY	THROTTLES	TITLE ROLE
TENTACLES	THEOCRASY	THROWAWAY	TITRATION
TENTATION	THEOMANIA	THROWBACK	TITTERING
TENTATIVE	THEORISTS	THROWSTER	T-JUNCTION
TENUOUSLY	THEORIZED	THRUMMING	TOADSTONE
TEPHRITIC	THEORIZER	THRUSTERS	TOADSTOOL
TEREBINTH	THEOSOPHY	THRUSTING	TOBOGGANS
TERMAGANT	THERAPIES	THUMBNAIL	TOGLIATTI
TERMINALS	THERAPIST	THUMBTACK	TOLERABLE
TERMINATE	THERAPSID	THUNDERED	TOLERABLY
TERPINEOL	THEREFORE	THUNDERER	TOLERANCE
TERRAPINS	THEREINTO	THURINGIA	TOLERATED
TERRARIUM	THEREUPON	THURSDAYS	TOLERATOR
TERRIFIED	THEREWITH	THWACKING	TOLLBOOTH
TERRIFIER	THERMOSES	THWARTING	TOLLGATES
TERRITORY	THESAURUS	THYLACINE	TOLLHOUSE
TERRORFUL	THESPIANS	THYMIDINE	TOMAHAWKS
TERRORISM	THEURGIST	THYRATRON	TOMBOYISH
TERRORIST	THICKENED	THYRISTOR	TOMBSTONE
TERRORIZE	THICKENER	THYROXINE	TOMMY GUNS
TERSENESS	THICKHEAD	TICKETING	TOMORROWS
TERVALENT	THICKLEAF	TIDAL WAVE	TONBRIDGE
TESSERACT	THICKNESS	TIDEMARKS	TONE POEMS
TESSITURA	THIGHBONE	TIDEWATER	TONOMETER
TESTAMENT	THINKABLE	TIED HOUSE	TONOMETRY
TESTATORS	THINK TANK	TIE-DYEING	TONSILLAR
TESTATRIX	THIO-ETHER	TIGHTENED	TONSORIAL
TEST CARDS	THIOPHENE	TIGHTENER	TOOL-MAKER
TEST CASES	THIRD-RATE	TIGHTKNIT	TOOTHACHE
TESTICLES	THIRSTIER	TIGHTNESS	TOOTHCOMB
TESTIFIED	THIRSTILY	TIGHTROPE	TOOTHIEST
TESTIFIRE	THIRTIETH	TIGRESSES	TOOTHLESS
TESTIMONY	THITHERTO	TIME BOMBS	TOOTHPICK
TESTINESS	THONINESS	TIME-LAPSE	TOOTHSOME
TESTINGLY	THORNBACK	TIMELIEST	TOOTHWORT
TEST MATCH	THORNBILL	TIME LIMIT	TOP DRAWER
TEST PILOT	THORNIEST	TIMEPIECE	TOP-FLIGHT
TEST TUBES	THOUSANDS	TIMESAVER	TOPIARIAN
TETCHIEST	THRALLDOM	TIME SHEET	TOPIARIST
TETE-A-TETE	THRASHING	TIMETABLE	TOPICALLY
TETHERING	THREADFIN	TIME ZONES	TOPMINNOW
TETRAGRAM	THREADING	TIMISOARA	TOPOLOGIC
TETRALOGY	THREEFOLD	TIMOCRACY	TOPONYMIC
TETRAPODY	THREESOME	TIMPANIST	TOP-SECRET
TETRARCHY	THREE-STAR	TINCTURES	TORCHWOOD
TETROXIDE	THREONINE	TINDERBOX	TOREADORS
TEXTBOOKS	THRESHERS	TINGALING	TOREUTICS
THALASSIC	THRESHING	TINKERING	TORMENTED
THANJAVUR	THRESHOLD	TINNINESS	TORMENTIL
THANKLESS	THRIFTIER	TIN OPENER	TORMENTOR
THANKYOUS	THRIFTILY	TIPSINESS	TORNADOES
THATCHERS	THRILLERS	TIREDNESS	TORPEDOED
THATCHING	THRILLING	TITCHIEST	TORPEDOES
THEACEOUS	THROATIER	TIT FOR TAT	TORPIDITY

TORRIDITY	TRAIN SETS	TRENCHANT	TRINOMIAL
TORSIONAL	TRAIPSING	TRENCHERS	TRIOELEIN
TORTILLAS	TRAMLINES	TRENDIEST	TRIPLEXES
TORTOISES	TRAMMELER	TRENGGANU	TRIPTYCHS
TORTRICID	TRAMPLING	TREPANNED	TRIPWIRES
TORTURERS	TRANSCEND	TREPHINED	TRISECTED
TORTURING	TRANSEPTS	TREPHINES	TRISECTOR
TOTALIZER	TRANSEUNT	TREPONEMA	TRISERIAL
TOTALLING	TRANSFERS	TRIAL RUNS	TRITENESS
TOTAQUINE	TRANSFORM	TRIANGLES	TRITURATE
TOTEM POLE	TRANSFUER	TRIATOMIC	TRIUMPHAL
TOTTERING	TRANSFUSE	TRIAZOLIC	TRIUMPHED
TOUCHABLE	TRANSIENT	TRIBADISM	TRIUMPHER
TOUCHDOWN	TRANSLATE	TRIBALISM	TRIVALENT
TOUCHIEST	TRANSMUTE	TRIBALIST	TRIVIALLY
TOUCHLINE	TRANSONIC	TRIBESMAN	TRIWEEKLY
TOUCHMARK	TRANSPIRE	TRIBESMEN	TROCHLEAR
TOUCH-TYPE	TRANSPORT	TRIBOLOGY	TROMBONES
TOUCHWOOD	TRANSPOSE	TRIBUNALS	TRONDHEIM
TOUGHENED	TRANSSHIP	TRIBUNARY	TROOPSHIP
TOUGHENER	TRANSVAAL	TRIBUNATE	TROOSTITE
TOUGH LUCK	TRAPDOORS	TRIBUTARY	TROPISTIC
TOUGHNESS	TRAPEZIAL	TRICEPSES	TROPOLOGY
TOURISTIC	TRAPEZIUM	TRICHITIC	TROSSACHS
TOUT A FAIT	TRAPEZIUS	TRICHOMIC	TROUBLING
TOWELLING	TRAPEZOID	TRICHOSIS	TROUBLOUS
TOWN CLERK	TRAPPINGS	TRICHROIC	TROUNCING
TOWN CRIER	TRAPPISTS	TRICKIEST	TROUSSEAU
TOWN HALLS	TRASHCANS	TRICKLING	TROWELLER
TOWN HOUSE	TRASHIEST	TRICKSTER	TRPORIFIC
TOWNSCAPE	TRATTORIA	TRICLINIC	TRUCK FARM
TOWNSHIPS	TRAUMATIC	TRICOLOUR	TRUCKLING
TOXAPHENE	TRAVAILED	TRICOTINE	TRUCKLOAD
TOXICALLY	TRAVELING	TRICROTIC	TRUCK STOP
TOXICOSIS	TRAVELLED	TRICUSPID	TRUCULENT
TOXOPHILY	TRAVELLER	TRICYCLES	TRUELOVES
TRABEATED	TRAVERSAL	TRICYCLIC	TRUE NORTH
TRABECULA	TRAVERSED	TRIDACTYL	TRUMP CARD
TRACEABLE	TRAVERSER	TRIENNIAL	TRUMPETED
TRACHYTIC	TRAVERSES	TRIENNIUM	TRUMPETER
TRACKABLE	TREACHERY	TRIFOLIUM	TRUNCATED
TRACKLESS	TREADMILL	TRIFORIAL	TRUNCHEON
TRACKSUIT	TREASURED	TRIFORIUM	TRUNDLING
TRACTABLE	TREASURER	TRIGGERED	TRUNK CALL
TRADE GAPS	TREASURES	TRIGONOUS	TRUNKFISH
TRADEMARK	TREATABLE	TRIHEDRAL	TRUNK ROAD
TRADE NAME	TREATISES	TRIHEDRON	TRUSTABLE
TRADE-OFFS	TREATMENT	TRIHYDRIC	TRUST FUND
TRADESMAN	TREE FERNS	TRILINEAR	TRUSTIEST
TRADESMEN	TREENWARE	TRILLIONS	TSETSE FLY
TRADE WIND	TREHALOSE	TRILOBATE	TUBBINESS
TRADITION	TREILLAGE	TRILOBITE	TUBULATOR
TRADUCERS	TRELLISES	TRILOGIES	TUCKERING
TRADUCING	TREMATODE	TRIMARANS	TUG-OF-LOVE
TRAFALGAR	TREMBLING	TRIMEROUS	TUGS-OF-WAR
TRAGEDIAN	TREMOLITE	TRIMESTER	TUILERIES
TRAGEDIES	TREMOROUS	TRIMETRIC	TUITIONAL
TRAINABLE	TREMULANT	TRIMMINGS	TULIPWOOD
TRAININGS	TREMULOUS	TRINITIES	TUMBLE-DRY

TUMESCENT	TYPHLITIC	UNCREATED	UNFAILING
TUMULUSES	TYPHLITIS	UNCROWNED	UNFAIREST
TUNEFULLY	TYPHOIDAL	UNDAUNTED	UNFEELING
TUNGSTITE	TYPHOIDIN	UNDECAGON	UNFEIGNED
TUNGUSIAN	TYPICALLY	UNDECEIVE	UNFITNESS
TUNING PEG	TYPIFYING	UNDECIDED	UNFLEDGED
TUNNELERS	TYRANNIES	UNDERBODY	UNFOLDING
TUNNELING	TYRANNIZE	UNDERBRED	UNFOUNDED
TUNNELLED	TYRANNOUS	UNDERCLAY	UNFROCKED
TUNNELLER	TZETZE FLY	UNDERCOAT	UNFURLING
TUPPENCES		UNDERDOGS	UNGUARDED
TURBIDITY	U	UNDERDONE	UNGUINOUS
TURBINATE	UITLANDER	UNDERFEED	UNHANDING
TURBOJETS	UKRAINIAN	UNDERFELT	UNHAPPILY
TURBOPROP	ULAN BATOR	UNDERFOOT	UNHARNESS
TURBULENT	ULCERATED	UNDERGIRD	UNHEALTHY
TURFINESS	ULMACEOUS	UNDERGOER	UNHEARD-OF
TURGIDITY	ULOTRICHY	UNDERGONE	UNHINGING
TURKESTAN	ULTIMATUM	UNDERHAND	UNHORSING
TURNABOUT	ULULATION	UNDERHUNG	UNHURRIED
TURNCOATS	ULYANOVSK	UNDERLAIN	UNICOLOUR
TURNCOCKS	UMBELLATE	UNDERLAYS	UNIFIABLE
TURNOVERS	UMBELLULE	UNDERLIER	UNIFORMED
TURNPIKES	UMBILICAL	UNDERLINE	UNIFORMLY
TURNROUND	UMBILICUS	UNDERLING	UNIJUGATE
TURNSTILE	UMBRELLAS	UNDERMINE	UNINSURED
TURNSTONE	UMPTEENTH	UNDERMOST	UNIONISTS
TURNTABLE	UNABASHED	UNDERPAID	UNIONIZED
TURPITUDE	UNADOPTED	UNDERPASS	UNION JACK
TURQUOISE	UNADVISED	UNDERPLAY	UNIPAROUS
TUSCARORA	UNALLOYED	UNDERPLOT	UNIPLANAR
TUTIORISM	UNANIMITY	UNDERPROP	UNIRAMOUS
TUTIORIST	UNANIMOUS	UNDERRATE	UNISEXUAL
TUTORIALS	UNAPTNESS	UNDERSEAL	UNISONOUS
TUT-TUTTED	UNASHAMED	UNDERSELL	UNITARIAN
TV DINNERS	UNASSUMED	UNDERSHOT	UNIT TRUST
TWAYBLADE	UNBALANCE	UNDERSIDE	UNIVALENT
TWENTIETH	UNBARRING	UNDERSOIL	UNIVERSAL
TWICE-LAID	UNBEKNOWN	UNDERSOLD	UNIVERSES
TWICE-TOLD	UNBENDING	UNDERTAKE	UNKINDEST
TWIDDLING	UNBINDING	UNDERTINT	UNKNOWING
TWINKLING	UNBLESSED	UNDERTONE	UNLEARNED
TWISTABLE	UNBOSOMED	UNDERTOOK	UNLEASHED
TWISTEDLY	UNBOUNDED	UNDERWEAR	UNLIMITED
TWISTIEST	UNBRIDLED	UNDERWENT	UNLOADERS
TWITCHING	UNBUCKLED	UNDERWING	UNLOADING
TWITTERED	UNCANNIER	UNDESIRED	UNLOCKING
TWITTERER	UNCANNILY	UNDIVIDED	UNLOOSING
TWO-BY-FOUR	UNCEASING	UNDOUBTED	UNLUCKILY
TWO-HANDED	UNCERTAIN	UNDRESSED	UNMARRIED
TWOPENCES	UNCHARGED	UNDULANCE	UNMASKING
TWO-SEATER	UNCHARTED	UNDULATED	UNMATCHED
TWO-STROKE	UNCHECKED	UNDULATOR	UNMEANING
TWO-TIMERS	UNCONCERN	UNEARTHED	UNMINDFUL
TWO-TIMING	UNCORKING	UNEARTHLY	UNMUSICAL
TYMPANIST	UNCOUNTED	UNEASIEST	UNNATURAL
TYMPANUMS	UNCOUPLED	UNEATABLE	UNNERVING
TYPEFACES	UNCOUTHLY	UNEQUALLY	UNNOTICED
TYPEWRITE	UNCOVERED	UNETHICAL	UNOPPOSED

UNPACKING	UPHOLDING	VALIDATED	VENERATED
UNPICKING	UPHOLSTER	VALIDNESS	VENERATOR
UNPLUMBED	UPLIFTING	VALLATION	VENEZUELA
UNPOLITIC	UPPER CASE	VALLECULA	VENGEANCE
UNPOPULAR	UPPERCUTS	VALUABLES	VENIALITY
UNRAVELED	UPPER HAND	VALUATION	VENTILATE
UNREALITY	UPPERMOST	VALUELESS	VENTRICLE
UNREFINED	UPRIGHTLY	VALVELESS	VENTURERS
UNRELATED	UPRISINGS	VAMOOSING	VENTURING
UNRESERVE	UPROOTING	VAMPIRISM	VERACIOUS
UNRIDDLER	UPSETTING	VANASPATI	VERANDAED
UNROLLING	UPSTAGING	VANCOUVER	VERATRINE
UNROUNDED	URANINITE	VANDALISM	VERBALISM
UNRUFFLED	URCEOLATE	VANDALIZE	VERBALIST
UNSADDLED	URINATING	VANGUARDS	VERBALIZE
UNSAVOURY	URINATION	VANISHING	VERBOSELY
UNSCATHED	URINATIVE	VAPIDNESS	VERBOSITY
UNSCREWED	UROCHROME	VAPORETTO	VERDIGRIS
UNSEATING	UROGENOUS	VAPORIFIC	VERDUROUS
UNSECURED	UROLITHIC	VAPORIZED	VERIDICAL
UNSELFISH	UROLOGIST	VAPORIZER	VERIFYING
UNSETTLED	UROPYGIAL	VAPOURISH	VERITABLE
UNSHACKLE	UROPYGIUM	VARANGIAN	VERITABLY
UNSHEATHE	UROSCOPIC	VARIABLES	VERMICIDE
UNSIGHTED	URSA MAJOR	VARIANCES	VERMIFORM
UNSIGHTLY	URTICARIA	VARIATION	VERMIFUGE
UNSKILFUL	URUGUAYAN	VARICELLA	VERMILION
UNSKILLED	USABILITY	VARICOSIS	VERMINOUS
UNSPARING	USELESSLY	VARIEGATE	VERMONTER
UNSPOTTED	USHERETTE	VARIETIES	VERNALIZE
UNSTOPPED	USUALNESS	VARIOLATE	VERNATION
UNSTRIPED	UTILITIES	VARIOLITE	VERRUCOSE
UNSTUDIED	UTILIZING	VARIOLOID	VERSATILE
UNTANGLED	UTRICULAR	VARIOLOUS	VERSIFIER
UNTENABLE	UTTERABLE	VARIOUSLY	VERSIONAL
UNTOUCHED	UTTERANCE	VARISCITE	VERS LIBRE
UNTREATED	UTTERLESS	VARITYPER	VERTEBRAE
UNTUTORED	UVAROVITE	VARNISHED	VERTEBRAL
UNTYPICAL	UXORICIDE	VARNISHER	VERY LIGHT
UNUSUALLY		VARNISHES	VESICULAR
UNVEILING	V	VARSITIES	VESTIBULE
UNWATCHED	VACANCIES	VARYINGLY	VESTIGIAL
UNWEARIED	VACATABLE	VASECTOMY	VESTMENTS
UNWEIGHED	VACATIONS	VASOMOTOR	VESTRYMAN
UNWELCOME	VACCINATE	VASSALAGE	VETCHLING
UNWILLING	VACCINIAL	VASSALIZE	VEXATIONS
UNWINDING	VACILLANT	VECTORIAL	VEXATIOUS
UNWITTING	VACILLATE	VEERINGLY	VEXEDNESS
UNWORLDLY	VACUOLATE	VEGETABLE	VEXILLARY
UNWRITTEN	VACUOUSLY	VEGETATED	VEXILLATE
UNZIPPING	VACUUMING	VEHEMENCE	VIABILITY
UP-AND-DOWN	VAGABONDS	VEHICULAR	VIBRANTLY
UPBRAIDED	VAGINITIS	VEINSTONE	VIBRATILE
UPBRAIDER	VAGOTONIA	VELODROME	VIBRATING
UPBUILDER	VAGUENESS	VELVETEEN	VIBRATION
UP-COUNTRY	VAINGLORY	VENDETTAS	VIBRATIVE
UPGRADING	VALENCIES	VENDITION	VIBRATORS
UPHEAVALS	VALENTINE	VENEERING	VIBRISSAL
UPHOLDERS	VALIANTLY	VENERABLE	VICARAGES

VICARIATE	VITRIFIED	WAKEFULLY	WATER RATS
VICARIOUS	VITRIFORM	WAKE-ROBIN	WATERSHED
VICARSHIP	VITRIOLIC	WALBRZYCH	WATER-SICK
VICEGERAL	VIVACIOUS	WALCHEREN	WATERSIDE
VICENNIAL	VIVARIUMS	WALKABOUT	WATER VOLE
VICEREGAL	VIVA VOCES	WALKAWAYS	WATERWAYS
VICEREINE	VIVERRINE	WALKOVERS	WATERWEED
VICE VERSA	VIVIDNESS	WALLABIES	WATERWORN
VICIOUSLY	VOCALISTS	WALLBOARD	WATTMETER
VICTIMIZE	VOCALIZER	WALLCHART	WAVE BANDS
VICTORIAN	VOCATIONS	WALLOPING	WAVEGUIDE
VICTORIES	VOCATIVES	WALLOWING	WAVELLITE
VICTUALED	VOICELESS	WALLPAPER	WAVEMETER
VIDELICET	VOICE-OVER	WANDERERS	WAXWORKER
VIDEODISC	VOJVODINA	WANDERING	WAYFARERS
VIDEOTAPE	VOL-AU-VENT	WAR CLOUDS	WAYFARING
VIENTIANE	VOLCANISM	WAR CRIMES	WAYLAYING
VIEWPOINT	VOLCANIZE	WAR DANCES	WEAKENING
VIGESIMAL	VOLCANOES	WARDROBES	WEAKER SEX
VIGILANCE	VOLGOGRAD	WARDROOMS	WEAK-KNEED
VIGILANTE	VOLLEYING	WAREHOUSE	WEAKLINGS
VIGNETTES	VOLTE-FACE	WARHORSES	WEALTHIER
VILIFYING	VOLTMETER	WARMONGER	WEALTHILY
VILLAGERS	VOLUMETER	WARRANTED	WEAPONEER
VILLIFORM	VOLUMETRY	WARRANTEE	WEARINESS
VILLOSITY	VOLUNTARY	WARRANTER	WEARINGLY
VIMINEOUS	VOLUNTEER	WARRANTOR	WEARISOME
VINACEOUS	VOODOOISM	WASHBASIN	WEARPROOF
VINDICATE	VOODOOIST	WASHBOARD	WEASELING
VINEYARDS	VORACIOUS	WASHCLOTH	WEATHERED
VIOLATING	VORTICISM	WASHED-OUT	WEATHERER
VIOLATION	VORTICIST	WASHINESS	WEB-FOOTED
VIOLATIVE	VOUCHSAFE	WASHING-UP	WEB OFFSET
VIOLATORS	VOYEURISM	WASHROOMS	WEDNESDAY
VIOLENTLY	VULCANIAN	WASHSTAND	WEEDINESS
VIOLINIST	VULCANITE	WASPINESS	WEEKENDED
VIRESCENT	VULCANIZE	WASPISHLY	WEEKENDER
VIRGINALS	VULGARIAN	WASSAILER	WEEKNIGHT
VIRGINIAN	VULGARISM	WASTELAND	WEEPINESS
VIRGINITY	VULGARITY	WATCHDOGS	WEEPINGLY
VIRGULATE	VULGARIZE	WATCHWORD	WEIGHABLE
VIRTUALLY	VULNERARY	WATER BIRD	WEIGHTILY
VIRTUOSIC	VULTURINE	WATERBUCK	WEIGHTING
VIRTUOSOS	VULTUROUS	WATER BUTT	WEIRDNESS
VIRULENCE	VULVIFORM	WATER-COOL	WELCOMING
VIRULENCY		WATERFALL	WELL-ACTED
VISCIDITY	**W**	WATERFOWL	WELL-AWARE
VISCOSITY	WACKINESS	WATERHOLE	WELLBEING
VISCOUNTS	WAD MEDANI	WATER ICES	WELL-FOUND
VISIONARY	WAFER-THIN	WATER JUMP	WELL-KNOWN
VISITABLE	WAGE SLAVE	WATERLESS	WELL-LINED
VISUAL AID	WAGGISHLY	WATER LILY	WELL-MEANT
VISUALIZE	WAGONETTE	WATERLINE	WELL-OILED
VITACEOUS	WAGONLOAD	WATER MAIN	WELL-TIMED
VITALIZER	WAILINGLY	WATERMARK	WELL-TRIED
VITAMINIC	WAINSCOTS	WATERMILL	WERNERITE
VITELLINE	WAISTBAND	WATER PIPE	WESLEYANS
VITIATING	WAISTCOAT	WATER POLO	WESTBOUND
VITIATION	WAISTLINE	WATER RATE	WESTERING

WESTERNER	WHODUNITS	WITHSTAND	WORRYWART
WESTWARDS	WHOLEFOOD	WITHSTOOD	WORSENING
WET DREAMS	WHOLEMEAL	WITLESSLY	WORSHIPED
WET-NURSED	WHOLENESS	WITNESSED	WORTHIEST
WET NURSES	WHOLE NOTE	WITNESSER	WORTHLESS
WHACKINGS	WHOLESALE	WITNESSES	WOUNDABLE
WHALEBOAT	WHOLESOME	WITTICISM	WOUNDWORT
WHALEBONE	WHOSOEVER	WITTINESS	WRANGLERS
WHEAT GERM	WIDE-ANGLE	WOBBLIEST	WRANGLING
WHEATWORM	WIDE-AWAKE	WOEBEGONE	WRAPPINGS
WHEEDLING	WIDOWHOOD	WOLFHOUND	WREATHING
WHEELBASE	WIDTHWISE	WOLFSBANE	WRECKFISH
WHEELWORK	WIELDABLE	WOLVERINE	WRENCHING
WHEREFORE	WIESBADEN	WOMANHOOD	WRESTLERS
WHEREUPON	WIGWAGGER	WOMANIZED	WRESTLING
WHEREWITH	WILD BOARS	WOMANIZER	WRIGGLING
WHERRYMAN	WILDFIRES	WOMANKIND	WRINKLING
WHETSTONE	WILLEMITE	WOMAN-LIKE	WRISTBAND
WHICHEVER	WILLINGLY	WOMENFOLK	WRISTLETS
WHICKERED	WILLPOWER	WOMEN'S LIB	WRISTLOCK
WHIFFIEST	WILTSHIRE	WONDERFUL	WRITE-OFFS
WHIMPERED	WINCINGLY	WONDERING	WRONGDOER
WHIMPERER	WINDBLOWN	WOODBLOCK	WRONGNESS
WHIMSICAL	WIND-BORNE	WOODBORER	WROUGHT-UP
WHININGLY	WINDBOUND	WOODCHUCK	WULFENITE
WHINNYING	WINDBREAK	WOODCOCKS	WUPPERTAL
WHINSTONE	WINDBURNT	WOODCRAFT	WYANDOTTE
WHIPPER-IN	WINDFALLS	WOODINESS	WYCH-HAZEL
WHIPPINGS	WIND GAUGE	WOODLOUSE	
WHIP-ROUND	WINDINESS	WOODPRINT	X
WHIPSTALL	WINDINGLY	WOODSCREW	XENOCRYST
WHIPSTOCK	WINDMILLS	WOODSHEDS	XENOPHILE
WHIRLIGIG	WINDOW BOX	WOOLLIEST	XENOPHOBE
WHIRLPOOL	WINDPIPES	WOOZINESS	XERICALLY
WHIRLWIND	WINDROWER	WORCESTER	XERODERMA
WHISKERED	WINDSOCKS	WORDBREAK	XEROPHILY
WHISPERED	WINDSTORM	WORDINESS	XEROPHYTE
WHISPERER	WINDSWEPT	WORKBENCH	XYLOGRAPH
WHISTLING	WINEGLASS	WORKBOOKS	XYLOPHONE
WHITE ANTS	WINEPRESS	WORKFORCE	
WHITEBAIT	WINGSPANS	WORKHORSE	Y
WHITECAPS	WINNEBAGO	WORKHOUSE	YACHTINGS
WHITEDAMP	WINNOWING	WORKLOADS	YACHTSMAN
WHITEFISH	WINSOMELY	WORKPIECE	YACHTSMEN
WHITE FLAG	WINTERING	WORKPLACE	YAMMERING
WHITEHALL	WINTRIEST	WORKROOMS	YANKEEISM
WHITE HEAT	WIRE-GAUGE	WORKSHOPS	YARDSTICK
WHITE HOPE	WIREWORKS	WORK-STUDY	YAROSLAVL
WHITE LEAD	WIREWORMS	WORKTABLE	YAWNINGLY
WHITE LIES	WISCONSIN	WORLD BANK	YEARBOOKS
WHITE MEAT	WISECRACK	WORLDLIER	YEARLINGS
WHITENESS	WISHBONES	WORLDLING	YEARNINGS
WHITENING	WISPINESS	WORLDWIDE	YELLOWING
WHITEWALL	WISTFULLY	WORM CASTS	YELLOWISH
WHITEWASH	WITCH-HUNT	WORM-EATEN	YESTERDAY
WHITEWOOD	WITCHLIKE	WORM GEARS	YIELDABLE
WHITTLERS	WITHDRAWN	WORMHOLES	YODELLING
WHITTLING	WITHERING	WORRIEDLY	YOHIMBINE
WHIZZ KIDS	WITHERITE	WORRISOME	YOUNGSTER

YTTERBITE	ZEEBRUGGE	ZITHERIST	ZOOTOMIST
YTTERBIUM	ZEELANDER	ZOOGLOEAL	ZUCCHINIS
	ZEITGEIST	ZOOGRAPHY	ZUIDER ZEE
Z	ZEPPELINS	ZOOLOGIST	ZYGOMATIC
ZACATECAS	ZESTFULLY	ZOOMETRIC	ZYGOPHYTE
ZAMBEZIAN	ZEUGMATIC	ZOOPHILIA	ZYGOSPORE
ZAMBOANGA	ZIGZAGGED	ZOOPHILIC	ZYMOGENIC
ZANZIBARI	ZIGZAGGER	ZOOPHOBIA	ZYMOLOGIC
ZAPOTECAN	ZINKENITE	ZOOPHYTIC	ZYMOLYSIS
ZEALOUSLY	ZIONISTIC	ZOOPLASTY	ZYMOLYTIC
ZEBRA-LIKE	ZIRCALLOY	ZOOSPORIC	ZYMOMETER
ZEBRAWOOD	ZIRCONIUM	ZOOSTEROL	

A	ABYSSINIAN	ACTINOMERE	ADVENTURER
ABANDONING	ACCELERANT	ACTINOZOAN	ADVENTURES
ABBREVIATE	ACCELERATE	ACTIONABLE	ADVERBIALS
ABDICATING	ACCENTUATE	ACTIVATING	ADVERTENCE
ABDICATION	ACCEPTABLE	ACTIVATION	ADVERTISED
ABDICATIVE	ACCEPTABLY	ACTIVENESS	ADVERTISER
ABERRATION	ACCEPTANCE	ACTIVITIES	ADVOCATING
ABHORRENCE	ACCEPTEDLY	ACTOMYOSIN	ADVOCATION
ABIOGENIST	ACCESSIBLE	ADACTYLOUS	ADVOCATORY
ABIRRITANT	ACCESSIONS	ADAMANTINE	ADZUKI BEAN
ABIRRITATE	ACCESS TIME	ADAM'S APPLE	AECIOSPORE
ABJURATION	ACCIDENTAL	ADAPTATION	AERENCHYMA
ABLE-BODIED	ACCIPITRAL	ADDICTIONS	AEROBATICS
ABLE SEAMAN	ACCLAIMING	ADDIS ABABA	AEROBIOSIS
ABLE SEAMEN	ACCOMPLICE	ADDITIONAL	AEROBIOTIC
ABNEGATION	ACCOMPLISH	ADDRESSEES	AERODROMES
ABNEY LEVEL	ACCORDABLE	ADDRESSING	AERO-ENGINE
ABNORMALLY	ACCORDANCE	ADDUCEABLE	AEROGRAMME
ABOLISHING	ACCORDIONS	ADENECTOMY	AEROGRAPHY
ABOMINABLE	ACCOSTABLE	ADENOVIRUS	AEROLOGIST
ABOMINABLY	ACCOUNTANT	ADEQUATELY	AEROMETRIC
ABOMINATED	ACCOUNTING	ADIRONDACK	AERONAUTIC
ABOMINATOR	ACCREDITED	ADJECTIVAL	AEROPHAGIA
ABORIGINAL	ACCRESCENT	ADJECTIVES	AEROPHOBIA
ABORIGINES	ACCRETIONS	ADJOURNING	AEROPHOBIC
ABORTICIDE	ACCUMBENCY	ADJUDICATE	AEROPLANES
ABORTIONAL	ACCUMULATE	ADJUNCTIVE	AEROSPHERE
ABORTIVELY	ACCURATELY	ADJURATION	AEROSTATIC
ABOUT-TURNS	ACCUSATION	ADJURATORY	AESTHETICS
ABOVEBOARD	ACCUSATIVE	ADJUSTABLE	AESTIVATOR
ABRASIVELY	ACCUSINGLY	ADJUSTMENT	AFFABILITY
ABREACTION	ACCUSTOMED	ADMINISTER	AFFECTEDLY
ABRIDGABLE	ACEPHALOUS	ADMIRATION	AFFECTIONS
ABRIDGMENT	ACETABULUM	ADMIRINGLY	AFFETTUOSO
ABROGATING	ACETIC ACID	ADMISSIBLE	AFFIDAVITS
ABROGATION	ACETOMETER	ADMISSIONS	AFFILIATED
ABRUPTNESS	ACETYLENIC	ADMITTANCE	AFFILIATES
ABSCISSION	ACHIEVABLE	ADMITTEDLY	AFFINITIES
ABSCONDING	ACHONDRITE	ADMIXTURES	AFFINITIVE
ABSOLUTELY	ACHROMATIC	ADMONISHED	AFFLICTING
ABSOLUTION	ACHROMATIN	ADMONISHER	AFFLICTION
ABSOLUTISM	ACIDIFYING	ADMONITION	AFFLICTIVE
ABSOLUTORY	ACIDIMETER	ADMONITORY	AFFORDABLE
ABSOLVABLE	ACIDOMETER	ADOLESCENT	AFFORESTED
ABSORBABLE	ACIERATION	ADORNMENTS	AFFRICATES
ABSORBANCE	ACOTYLEDON	ADRENALINE	AFFRONTING
ABSORBEDLY	ACQUAINTED	ADRENERGIC	AFICIONADO
ABSORBENCY	ACQUIESCED	ADROITNESS	AFRIKANDER
ABSORBENTS	ACQUIRABLE	ADSORBABLE	AFRIKANERS
ABSORPTION	ACQUITTALS	ADSORPTION	AFTERBIRTH
ABSORPTIVE	ACQUITTING	ADULTERANT	AFTERBRAIN
ABSTAINERS	ACROBATICS	ADULTERATE	AFTERGLOWS
ABSTAINING	ACROMEGALY	ADULTERERS	AFTERIMAGE
ABSTEMIOUS	ACRONYCHAL	ADULTERESS	AFTERLIVES
ABSTENTION	ACROPHOBIA	ADULTERINE	AFTERMATHS
ABSTERGENT	ACROPHOBIC	ADULTEROUS	AFTERNOONS
ABSTINENCE	ACTABILITY	ADUMBRATED	AFTERPAINS
ABSTRACTED	ACTINIFORM	ADVANTAGES	AFTERPIECE
ABUNDANTLY	ACTINOLITE	ADVENTITIA	AFTERSHAFT

AFTERSHAVE	ALLERGENIC	AMMONIACAL	ANDROECIAL
AFTERSHOCK	ALLEVIATED	AMMUNITION	ANDROECIUM
AFTERTASTE	ALLEVIATOR	AMOEBIASIS	ANDROGENIC
AFTERWARDS	ALLIACEOUS	AMOEBOCYTE	ANECDOTAGE
AGAMICALLY	ALLIGATORS	AMORTIZING	ANECDOTIST
AGAPANTHUS	ALLITERATE	AMPELOPSIS	ANEMICALLY
AGGLUTININ	ALLOCATING	AMPERE-HOUR	ANEMOCHORE
AGGRANDIZE	ALLOCATION	AMPERE-TURN	ANEMOGRAPH
AGGRAVATED	ALLOCUTION	AMPERSANDS	ANEMOMETER
AGGREGATED	ALLOGAMOUS	AMPHEATRIC	ANEMOMETRY
AGGREGATES	ALLOMERISM	AMPHIASTER	ANEMOPHILY
AGGRESSION	ALLOMEROUS	AMPHIBIANS	ANEMOSCOPE
AGGRESSIVE	ALLOMETRIC	AMPHIBIOUS	ANESTHESIA
AGGRESSORS	ALLOPATHIC	AMPHIBOLIC	ANESTHETIC
AGITATIONS	ALLOPATRIC	AMPHIBRACH	ANEURYSMAL
AGREEMENTS	ALLOPHONIC	AMPHICTYON	ANGELOLOGY
AGRONOMICS	ALLOTMENTS	AMPHIGORIC	ANGIOSPERM
AGRONOMIST	ALLOTROPIC	AMPHIMACER	ANGLICISMS
AGRYPNOTIC	ALLOWANCES	AMPHIMIXIS	ANGLICIZED
AHMEDNAGAR	ALL-PURPOSE	AMPHOTERIC	ANGLOPHILE
AIDE-DE-CAMP	ALL-ROUNDER	AMPLIFIERS	ANGLOPHOBE
AIR-HOSTESS	ALLUREMENT	AMPLIFYING	ANGLOPHONE
AIR-LETTERS	ALLUSIVELY	AMPUTATING	ANGLO-SAXON
AIRLIFTING	ALMA MATERS	AMPUTATION	ANGULARITY
AIR-POCKETS	ALMIGHTIER	AMUSEMENTS	ANGULATION
AKTYUBINSK	ALMIGHTILY	AMYGDALATE	ANGWANTIBO
ALACRITOUS	ALMS-HOUSES	AMYGDALINE	ANIMADVERT
ALARM CLOCK	ALONGSHORE	AMYGDALOID	ANIMALCULE
ALARMINGLY	ALPENSTOCK	AMYLACEOUS	ANIMATEDLY
ALBESCENCE	ALPESTRINE	AMYLOLYSIS	ANISOTROPY
ALBUMENIZE	ALTARPIECE	ANABOLITIC	ANKYLOSAUR
ALBUMINATE	ALTAZIMUTH	ANACHORISM	ANNALISTIC
ALBUMINOID	ALTERATION	ANACOUSTIC	ANNEXATION
ALBUMINOUS	ALTERATIVE	ANACRUSTIC	ANNIHILATE
ALCHEMISTS	ALTERNATED	ANADROMOUS	ANNO DOMINI
ALCOHOLICS	ALTERNATOR	ANAGLYPHIC	ANNOTATING
ALCOHOLISM	ALTIMETERS	ANALGESICS	ANNOTATION
ALCOHOLIZE	ALTOGETHER	ANALOGICAL	ANNOTATIVE
ALDERMANIC	ALTRUISTIC	ANALYSABLE	ANNOUNCERS
ALGEBRAIST	AMALGAMATE	ANAMNESTIC	ANNOUNCING
ALGOLAGNIA	AMANUENSES	ANAMORPHIC	ANNOYANCES
ALGOLAGNIC	AMANUENSIS	ANAPAESTIC	ANNULATION
ALGONQUIAN	AMATEURISH	ANAPLASTIC	ANNULLABLE
ALGOPHOBIA	AMATEURISM	ANAPTYCTIC	ANNULMENTS
ALGORISMIC	AMBASSADOR	ANARCHISTS	ANNUNCIATE
ALGORITHMS	AMBIVALENT	ANARTHROUS	ANOINTMENT
ALIENATING	AMBOCEPTOR	ANASARCOUS	ANORTHITIC
ALIENATION	AMBULACRAL	ANASTIGMAT	ANSWERABLE
ALIGNMENTS	AMBULACRUM	ANASTOMOSE	ANSWERABLY
ALIMENTARY	AMBULANCES	ANATOMICAL	ANTAGONISM
ALKALINITY	AMBULATION	ANATOMISTS	ANTAGONIST
ALKYLATION	AMBULATORY	ANATOMIZER	ANTAGONIZE
ALLARGANDO	AMELIORANT	ANATROPOUS	ANTARCTICA
ALLEGATION	AMELIORATE	ANCESTRESS	ANTEBELLUM
ALLEGIANCE	AMENDMENTS	ANCESTRIES	ANTECEDENT
ALLEGORIES	AMERINDIAN	ANCHORAGES	ANTEDATING
ALLEGORIST	AMIABILITY	ANCHORITES	ANTE-MORTEM
ALLEGORIZE	AMIANTHINE	ANDALUSITE	ANTEPENULT
ALLEGRETTO	AMINO ACIDS	ANDERLECHT	ANTHOPHORE

ANTHRACENE	APOTHECARY	ARCHITECTS	ASSAILABLE
ANTHRACITE	APOTHECIAL	ARCHITRAVE	ASSAILANTS
ANTHRACOID	APOTHECIUM	ARCHIVISTS	ASSAILMENT
ANTHROPOID	APOTHEOSES	ARCHOPLASM	ASSAULTING
ANTIBARYON	APOTHEOSIS	ARCTOGAEAN	ASSEMBLAGE
ANTIBIOSIS	APOTROPAIC	ARC WELDING	ASSEMBLIES
ANTIBIOTIC	APPALACHIA	ARENACEOUS	ASSEMBLING
ANTIBODIES	APPARELLED	AREOGRAPHY	ASSERTIBLE
ANTICHRIST	APPARENTLY	AREOLATION	ASSERTIONS
ANTICIPANT	APPARITION	ARGENTEUIL	ASSESSABLE
ANTICIPATE	APPEALABLE	ARGILLITIC	ASSESSMENT
ANTICLIMAX	APPEARANCE	ARGUMENTUM	ASSEVERATE
ANTICLINAL	APPEASABLE	ARISTOCRAT	ASSIBILATE
ANTIDROMIC	APPENDAGES	ARITHMETIC	ASSIGNABLE
ANTIFREEZE	APPENDICES	ARMADILLOS	ASSIGNMENT
ANTIHEROES	APPENDICLE	ARMAGEDDON	ASSIMILATE
ANTILEPTON	APPENDIXES	ARMIPOTENT	ASSISTANCE
ANTILOGISM	APPERCEIVE	ARMISTICES	ASSISTANTS
ANTIMATTER	APPETIZERS	ARRAIGNING	ASSOCIABLE
ANTIMERISM	APPETIZING	ARRHYTHMIA	ASSOCIATED
ANTIMONIAL	APPLAUDING	ARROGANTLY	ASSOCIATES
ANTIMONOUS	APPLE CARTS	ARROGATING	ASSONANTAL
ANTIPHONAL	APPLIANCES	ARROGATION	ASSORTMENT
ANTIPODEAN	APPLICABLE	ARROGATIVE	ASSUMPTION
ANTIPROTON	APPLICANTS	ARROWHEADS	ASSUMPTIVE
ANTIPYRINE	APPLICATOR	ARTFULNESS	ASSURANCES
ANTIQUATED	APPOINTEES	ARTHRALGIA	ASTATICISM
ANTI-SEMITE	APPOINTING	ARTHRALGIC	ASTERIATED
ANTISEPSIS	APPOSITION	ARTHRITICS	ASTERISKED
ANTISEPTIC	APPOSITIVE	ARTHROMERE	ASTEROIDAL
ANTISOCIAL	APPRAISALS	ARTICHOKES	ASTHENOPIA
ANTISTATIC	APPRAISING	ARTICULATE	ASTHENOPIC
ANTITHESIS	APPRAISIVE	ARTIFICERS	ASTHMATICS
ANTITRADES	APPRECIATE	ARTIFICIAL	ASTIGMATIC
ANTITRAGUS	APPRENTICE	ART NOUVEAU	ASTOMATOUS
APARTMENTS	APPROACHED	ARTY-CRAFTY	ASTONISHED
APHORISTIC	APPROACHES	ASAFOETIDA	ASTOUNDING
APHRODISIA	APPROXIMAL	ASARABACCA	ASTRAGALUS
APICULTURE	APRIL FOOLS	ASBESTOSIS	ASTRINGENT
APIOLOGIST	APTERYGIAL	ASCARIASIS	ASTROLOGER
APLACENTAL	AQUAMARINE	ASCENDANCY	ASTROMETRY
APOCALYPSE	AQUAPHOBIA	ASCENDANTS	ASTRONAUTS
APOCARPOUS	AQUAPLANED	ASCETICISM	ASTRONOMER
APOCHROMAT	AQUAPLANES	ASCOGONIUM	ASTUTENESS
APOCRYPHAL	ARABESQUES	ASCOMYCETE	ASYMMETRIC
APOLITICAL	ARACHNIDAN	ASCRIBABLE	ASYMPTOTIC
APOLOGETIC	ARAUCANIAN	ASCRIPTION	ATHERMANCY
APOLOGISTS	ARBITRABLE	ASEXUALITY	ATMOSPHERE
APOLOGIZED	ARBITRATED	ASPARAGINE	ATOMICALLY
APOLOGIZER	ARBITRATOR	ASPERITIES	ATOMIC PILE
APOPHTHEGM	ARCHAISTIC	ASPERSIONS	ATROCITIES
APOPHYSATE	ARCHANGELS	ASPHALTING	ATROPHYING
APOPHYSIAL	ARCHBISHOP	ASPHALTITE	ATTACHABLE
APOPLECTIC	ARCHDEACON	ASPHYXIANT	ATTACHMENT
APOSEMATIC	ARCHERFISH	ASPHYXIATE	ATTAINABLE
APOSTASIES	ARCHESPORE	ASPIDISTRA	ATTAINMENT
APOSTATIZE	ARCHETYPAL	ASPIRATING	ATTEMPTING
APOSTOLATE	ARCHETYPES	ASPIRATION	ATTENDANCE
APOSTROPHE	ARCHIMEDES	ASPIRATORY	ATTENDANTS

ATTENTIONS	AUTUMNALLY	BALLPOINTS	BASKETWORK
ATTENUATED	AUXOCHROME	BALNEOLOGY	BAS-RELIEFS
ATTENUATOR	AVALANCHES	BALUSTRADE	BASS GUITAR
ATTESTABLE	AVANT-GARDE	BAMBOOZLED	BASSOONIST
ATTORNMENT	AVARICIOUS	BAMBOOZLER	BASTARDIZE
ATTRACTING	AVELLANEDA	BANALITIES	BASUTOLAND
ATTRACTION	AVENTURINE	BANANA SKIN	BATH CHAIRS
ATTRACTIVE	AVICULTURE	BANDERILLA	BATHOMETER
ATTRIBUTED	AVOCATIONS	BANDMASTER	BATHOMETRY
ATTRIBUTER	AVUNCULATE	BANDOLEERS	BATHYMETRY
ATTRIBUTES	AWAKENINGS	BANDSTANDS	BATHYSCAPH
ATYPICALLY	AXIOLOGIST	BANDWAGONS	BATON ROUGE
AUBERGINES	AYATOLLAHS	BANGLADESH	BATTALIONS
AUCTIONEER	AZEOTROPIC	BANISHMENT	BATTLEAXES
AUCTIONING	AZERBAIJAN	BANK DRAFTS	BATTLEDORE
AUDIBILITY	AZOBENZENE	BANKROLLED	BATTLEMENT
AUDIOGENIC		BANKRUPTCY	BATTLESHIP
AUDIOMETER	B	BANKRUPTED	BAYONETING
AUDIOMETRY	BABY-MINDER	BANNERETTE	BAY WINDOWS
AUDITIONED	BABY-SITTER	BANQUETING	BEACH BALLS
AUDITORIUM	BACCHANALS	BAPTISTERY	BEACH BUGGY
AUGMENTING	BACITRACIN	BARBARIANS	BEACHCHAIR
AUREOMYCIN	BACKBITERS	BARBARISMS	BEACHHEADS
AURICULATE	BACKBITING	BARBARIZED	BEANSPROUT
AURIFEROUS	BACKCLOTHS	BARBECUING	BEASTLIEST
AUSCULTATE	BACKCOMBED	BARBED WIRE	BEATIFYING
AUSFORMING	BACKDATING	BARBELLATE	BEATITUDES
AUSPICIOUS	BACKFIRING	BAREHEADED	BEAUJOLAIS
AUSTENITIC	BACKGAMMON	BARELEGGED	BEAUTICIAN
AUSTRALIAN	BACKGROUND	BARGAINING	BEAUTIFIED
AUSTRALOID	BACKHANDED	BARGE POLES	BEAUTY SPOT
AUSTRALORP	BACKHANDER	BARIUM MEAL	BECOMINGLY
AUTARCHIES	BACKLASHES	BARLEYCORN	BECQUERELS
AUTECOLOGY	BACK NUMBER	BARLEY WINE	BEDCLOTHES
AUTHORIZED	BACKPACKER	BAR MITZVAH	BEDEVILING
AUTHORIZER	BACKSLIDER	BARN DANCES	BEDEVILLED
AUTHORSHIP	BACKSPACES	BAROMETERS	BEDFELLOWS
AUTOCHTHON	BACKSTAIRS	BAROMETRIC	BED OF ROSES
AUTOCRATIC	BACKSTITCH	BARONESSES	BEDRAGGLED
AUTOECIOUS	BACK STREET	BARONETAGE	BED-SITTERS
AUTOGAMOUS	BACKSTROKE	BARRACKING	BEDSPREADS
AUTOGENOUS	BACKWARDLY	BARRACUDAS	BEEFEATERS
AUTOGRAPHS	BACKWATERS	BARRAMUNDA	BEFOREHAND
AUTOGRAPHY	BACULIFORM	BARRATROUS	BEFOULMENT
AUTOMATICS	BADEN-BADEN	BARRENNESS	BEFRIENDED
AUTOMATING	BAD-MOUTHED	BARRENWORT	BEGGARWEED
AUTOMATION	BAFFLEMENT	BARRICADED	BEGINNINGS
AUTOMATISM	BAGGAGE CAR	BARRICADER	BEGRUDGING
AUTOMATIST	BALACLAVAS	BARRICADES	BEHINDHAND
AUTOMATONS	BALALAIKAS	BARRISTERS	BELABOURED
AUTOMATOUS	BALDERDASH	BARROW BOYS	BELIEVABLE
AUTOMOBILE	BALDHEADED	BARTENDERS	BELIEVABLY
AUTOMOTIVE	BALIKPAPAN	BARYCENTRE	BELITTLING
AUTONOMIST	BALLASTING	BARYSPHERE	BELLADONNA
AUTONOMOUS	BALLERINAS	BASALTWARE	BELLARMINE
AUTOPHYTIC	BALLFLOWER	BASE METALS	BELLETRIST
AUTOPLASTY	BALLISTICS	BASILICATA	BELL-RINGER
AUTOSTRADA	BALLOONING	BASKETBALL	BELLWETHER
AUTOTOMIZE	BALLOONIST	BASKET-STAR	BELLYACHED

BELLYACHES	BILLY GOATS	BLACKGUARD	BLOODSTOCK
BELLY DANCE	BIMESTRIAL	BLACKHEADS	BLOODSTONE
BELLY FLOPS	BIMETALLIC	BLACKHEART	BLOOD TYPES
BELLY LAUGH	BINOCULARS	BLACK HOLES	BLOODY MARY
BELONGINGS	BINUCLEATE	BLACKJACKS	BLOOMSBURY
BENCH MARKS	BIOCELLATE	BLACKLISTS	BLOSSOMING
BENEDICITE	BIODYNAMIC	BLACK MAGIC	BLOTCHIEST
BENEFACTOR	BIOECOLOGY	BLACK MARIA	BLOW-BY-BLOW
BENEFICENT	BIOGENESIS	BLACK POWER	BLOW-DRYING
BENEFICIAL	BIOGENETIC	BLACK SHEEP	BLOWZINESS
BENEFITING	BIOGRAPHER	BLACKSHIRT	BLUBBERING
BENEVOLENT	BIOGRAPHIC	BLACKSMITH	BLUDGEONED
BENIGNANCY	BIOLOGICAL	BLACKSNAKE	BLUDGEONER
BENZOCAINE	BIOLOGISTS	BLACK SPOTS	BLUE BABIES
BENZODRINE	BIOPHYSICS	BLACKTHORN	BLUEBEARDS
BENZOFURAN	BIOPLASMIC	BLACK WIDOW	BLUEBOTTLE
BEQUEATHED	BIOPOIESIS	BLADDERNUT	BLUE CHEESE
BEQUEATHER	BIORHYTHMS	BLANCMANGE	BLUE-COLLAR
BESEECHING	BIOSTATICS	BLANKETING	BLUE MURDER
BESMEARING	BIPARIETAL	BLANK VERSE	BLUE-PENCIL
BESMIRCHED	BIPARTISAN	BLASPHEMED	BLUEPRINTS
BESPEAKING	BIPETALOUS	BLASPHEMER	BLUETHROAT
BESSARABIA	BIQUADRATE	BLASTOCOEL	BLUNDERERS
BESTIALITY	BIRD OF PREY	BLASTOCYST	BLUNDERING
BESTIALIZE	BIRKENHEAD	BLASTODERM	BLUSHINGLY
BESTIARIES	BIRTHMARKS	BLASTOMERE	BLUSTERERS
BESTIRRING	BIRTHPLACE	BLASTOPORE	BLUSTERING
BESTREWING	BIRTH RATES	BLATHERING	BOARDROOMS
BESTRIDDEN	BIRTHRIGHT	BLEACHABLE	BOARDWALKS
BESTRIDING	BIRTHSTONE	BLEARINESS	BOASTFULLY
BEST-SELLER	BISEXUALLY	BLEATINGLY	BOASTINGLY
BETELGEUSE	BISHOPBIRD	BLEMISHING	BOATHOUSES
BETHINKING	BISHOPRICS	BLETHERING	BOATSWAINS
BETOKENING	BISMUTHOUS	BLIND ALLEY	BOAT TRAINS
BETROTHALS	BISSEXTILE	BLIND DATES	BOBBY SOCKS
BETROTHING	BISULPHATE	BLIND DRUNK	BOBSLEIGHS
BETTERMENT	BISULPHIDE	BLINDFOLDS	BODYGUARDS
BEWILDERED	BISULPHITE	BLIND SPOTS	BOILER SUIT
BEWITCHING	BISYMMETRY	BLISSFULLY	BOISTEROUS
BIANNULATE	BITARTRATE	BLISTERING	BOLLOCKS-UP
BIBLIOPOLE	BITCHINESS	BLITHENESS	BOLL WEEVIL
BIBLIOTICS	BIT OF FLUFF	BLITHERING	BOLOMETRIC
BIBLIOTIST	BITTERLING	BLITHESOME	BOLSHEVIKS
BICHLORIDE	BITTERNESS	BLOCKADING	BOLSHEVISM
BICYCLISTS	BITTERWEED	BLOCKHEADS	BOLSTERING
BIENNIALLY	BITTERWOOD	BLOCKHOUSE	BOMBARDIER
BIFURCATED	BITUMINIZE	BLOCK VOTES	BOMBARDING
BIGAMOUSLY	BITUMINOUS	BLONDENESS	BOMBSHELLS
BIG BROTHER	BIVALVULAR	BLOOD BANKS	BONDHOLDER
BIG DIPPERS	BIVOUACKED	BLOODBATHS	BONEHEADED
BIJOUTERIE	BLABBERING	BLOOD COUNT	BONE MARROW
BILBERRIES	BLACKAMOOR	BLOOD FEUDS	BONESHAKER
BILINGUALS	BLACK BELTS	BLOOD GROUP	BON VIVANTS
BILIVERDIN	BLACKBERRY	BLOODHOUND	BOOBY PRIZE
BILLBOARDS	BLACKBIRDS	BLOODINESS	BOOBY TRAPS
BILLET-DOUX	BLACKBOARD	BLOOD LUSTS	BOOKBINDER
BILLIONTHS	BLACK BOXES	BLOOD MONEY	BOOKKEEPER
BILL OF FARE	BLACK DEATH	BLOOD SPORT	BOOKMAKERS
BILL OF SALE	BLACKENING	BLOODSTAIN	BOOKMOBILE

BOOKPLATES	BRATISLAVA	BUCKBOARDS	CACOGRAPHY
BOOKSELLER	BRAVISSIMO	BUCKET SEAT	CACOMISTLE
BOOKSTALLS	BRAWNINESS	BUCKET SHOP	CACOPHONIC
BOOK TOKENS	BRAZENNESS	BUDGERIGAR	CACTACEOUS
BOOMERANGS	BREADBOARD	BUFFER ZONE	CADAVERINE
BOOTBLACKS	BREADCRUMB	BUFFLEHEAD	CADAVEROUS
BOOTLEGGED	BREADFRUIT	BUFFOONERY	CADET CORPS
BOOTLEGGER	BREADLINES	BULLDOZERS	CAERPHILLY
BOOTLOADER	BREAKAWAYS	BULLDOZING	CAESAREANS
BOOTSTRAPS	BREAKDOWNS	BULLFIGHTS	CAESPITOSE
BORDERLAND	BREAKFASTS	BULLHEADED	CAFETERIAS
BORDERLINE	BREAKFRONT	BULLNECKED	CALABASHES
BORROWINGS	BREAKWATER	BUMBLEBEES	CALABOOSES
BOTANIZING	BREASTBONE	BUNCHINESS	CALAMANDER
BOTCHINESS	BREASTWORK	BUNKHOUSES	CALAMITIES
BOTHERSOME	BRECCIATED	BUNYA-BUNYA	CALAMITOUS
BOTRYOIDAL	BREEZINESS	BUON GIORNO	CALAMONDIN
BOTTLE BANK	BRICKLAYER	BURBERRIES	CALAVERITE
BOTTLE-FEED	BRIDEGROOM	BURDENSOME	CALCAREOUS
BOTTLENECK	BRIDESMAID	BUREAUCRAT	CALCEIFORM
BOTTOMLESS	BRIDGEABLE	BURGENLAND	CALCIFEROL
BOTTOM LINE	BRIDGEHEAD	BURGEONING	CALCIFUGAL
BOTTOMMOST	BRIDGEPORT	BURGLARIES	CALCIFYING
BOULEVARDS	BRIDGEWORK	BURGUNDIAN	CALCITONIN
BOUNCINESS	BRIGANTINE	BURLESQUED	CALCSINTER
BOUNDARIES	BRIGHTENER	BURLESQUER	CALCULABLE
BOWDLERISM	BRIGHTNESS	BURLESQUES	CALCULATED
BOWDLERIZE	BRIGHTWORK	BURNISHING	CALCULATOR
BOW WINDOWS	BRILLIANCE	BURTHENING	CALCULUSES
BOX NUMBERS	BRILLIANCY	BUSHBABIES	CALEDONIAN
BOX OFFICES	BRIQUETTES	BUSHHAMMER	CALIBRATED
BOYCOTTING	BRITISHERS	BUSHMASTER	CALIBRATOR
BOYFRIENDS	BROAD BEANS	BUSHRANGER	CALIFORNIA
BOYISHNESS	BROADCASTS	BUSINESSES	CALIPHATES
BRACHIOPOD	BROADCLOTH	BUS STATION	CALLOWNESS
BRACHYLOGY	BROADENING	BUSYBODIES	CALORICITY
BRACHYURAN	BROAD GAUGE	BUTCHERING	CALUMNIATE
BRACKETING	BROADSHEET	BUTTER BEAN	CALUMNIOUS
BRADYKININ	BROADSIDES	BUTTERCUPS	CALVINISTS
BRAGGINGLY	BROADSWORD	BUTTERFISH	CALYPTRATE
BRAHMANISM	BROCATELLE	BUTTERMILK	CAMEMBERTS
BRAINCHILD	BROKEN-DOWN	BUTTERWORT	CAMERLENGO
BRAIN DRAIN	BROKENNESS	BUTTON-DOWN	CAMOUFLAGE
BRAININESS	BRONCHIOLE	BUTTONHOLE	CAMPAIGNED
BRAINSTORM	BRONCHITIC	BUTTONHOOK	CAMPAIGNER
BRAINWAVES	BRONCHITIS	BUTTONWOOD	CAMPANILES
BRAKE SHOES	BRONX CHEER	BUTTRESSED	CAMPESTRAL
BRANCHIATE	BROODINESS	BUTTRESSES	CAMPGROUND
BRANDISHED	BROOMSTICK	BY-ELECTION	CAMPHORATE
BRANDISHER	BROWBEATEN	BY-PRODUCTS	CANAL BOATS
BRAND NAMES	BROWNED-OFF	BYSTANDERS	CANALIZING
BRASHINESS	BROWNSTONE		CANCELLATE
BRASS BANDS	BRUTALIZED	C	CANCELLING
BRASSBOUND	BRYOLOGIST	CABANATUAN	CANDELABRA
BRASSED OFF	BRYOPHYTIC	CABIN CLASS	CANDIDATES
BRASSERIES	BUBONOCELE	CACCIATORE	CANDLEFISH
BRASSIERES	BUCCANEERS	CACHINNATE	CANDLEPINS
BRASSINESS	BUCCINATOR	CACK-HANDED	CANDLEWICK
BRASS TACKS	BUCHENWALD	CACOGENICS	CANDLEWOOD

CANDYFLOSS	CARNASSIAL	CATCHINESS	CENTURIONS
CANKERWORM	CARNATIONS	CATCHPENNY	CEPHALOPOD
CANNELLONI	CARNELIANS	CATCHWORDS	CEREBELLAR
CANNONADES	CARNIVORES	CATECHESIS	CEREBELLUM
CANNONBALL	CAROLINIAN	CATECHISMS	CEREBRALLY
CANONICATE	CAROTENOID	CATECHISTS	CEREMONIAL
CANONICITY	CARPATHIAN	CATECHIZED	CEREMONIES
CANONIZING	CARPELLARY	CATEGORIES	CEROGRAPHY
CANOODLING	CARPELLATE	CATEGORIZE	CERTIFYING
CAN OPENERS	CARPENTERS	CATENARIAN	CERTIORARI
CANTABRIAN	CARPOPHORE	CATENATION	CERUMINOUS
CANTALOUPE	CARPOSPORE	CATENULATE	CERVICITIS
CANTALOUPS	CARRIER BAG	CATHEDRALS	CESSATIONS
CANTATRICE	CARRYING-ON	CATHOLICON	CESSIONARY
CANTILEVER	CARRY-OVERS	CATOPTRICS	CETOLOGIST
CANTILLATE	CARTHORSES	CAT'S CRADLE	CHAGRINING
CANTONMENT	CARTHUSIAN	CATTLE GRID	CHAIN GANGS
CANVASBACK	CARTILAGES	CAULESCENT	CHAINPLATE
CANVASSERS	CARTOMANCY	CAUTERIZED	CHAIN-REACT
CANVASSING	CARTOONIST	CAUTIONARY	CHAIN-SMOKE
CAOUTCHOUC	CARTRIDGES	CAUTIONING	CHAIN STORE
CAPABILITY	CART TRACKS	CAUTIOUSLY	CHAIR LIFTS
CAPACITATE	CARTWHEELS	CAVALCADES	CHAIRWOMAN
CAPACITIES	CARUNCULAR	CAVALRYMAN	CHAIRWOMEN
CAPACITIVE	CARYATIDAL	CAVALRYMEN	CHALCEDONY
CAPACITORS	CASABLANCA	CAVITATION	CHALCOCITE
CAPARISONS	CASCARILLA	CAVITY WALL	CHALKBOARD
CAPITALISM	CASE-HARDEN	CEASE-FIRES	CHALKINESS
CAPITALIST	CASEINOGEN	CEILOMETER	CHALLENGED
CAPITALIZE	CASEWORKER	CELEBRATED	CHALLENGER
CAPITATION	CASHIERING	CELEBRATOR	CHALLENGES
CAPITATIVE	CASSEROLES	CELLOBIOSE	CHALYBEATE
CAPITULATE	CASSIOPEIA	CELLOPHANE	CHAMBER POT
CAPPUCCINO	CASTIGATED	CELLULITIS	CHAMELEONS
CAPREOLATE	CASTIGATOR	CELLULOSIC	CHAMOMILES
CAPRICIOUS	CASTRATING	CEMETERIES	CHAMPIGNON
CAPRICORNS	CASTRATION	CENOTAPHIC	CHAMPIONED
CAPTAINING	CASUALNESS	CENSORABLE	CHANCELLOR
CAPTIOUSLY	CASUALTIES	CENSORIOUS	CHANCERIES
CAPTIVATED	CASUS BELLI	CENSORSHIP	CHANCINESS
CAPTIVATOR	CATABOLISM	CENSURABLE	CHANDELIER
CARAMELIZE	CATABOLITE	CENTENNIAL	CHANDIGARH
CARBOLATED	CATACLINAL	CENTESIMAL	CHANGEABLE
CARBONATED	CATACLYSMS	CENTIGRADE	CHANGEABLY
CARBON COPY	CATAFALQUE	CENTIGRAMS	CHANGELESS
CARBONIZED	CATALECTIC	CENTILITRE	CHANGELING
CARBUNCLES	CATALEPTIC	CENTILLION	CHANGEOVER
CARCINOGEN	CATALOGUED	CENTIMETRE	CHANNELLED
CARDIALGIA	CATALOGUER	CENTIPEDES	CHANNELLER
CARDIALGIC	CATALOGUES	CENTIPOISE	CHAPERONED
CARDIOGRAM	CATAMARANS	CENTRALISM	CHAPFALLEN
CARDIOLOGY	CATAMENIAL	CENTRALITY	CHAPLAINCY
CARDSHARPS	CATAPLASIA	CENTRALIZE	CHARABANCS
CAREERISTS	CATAPULTED	CENTRE-FIRE	CHARACTERS
CARELESSLY	CATARRHINE	CENTRE-FOLD	CHARGEABLE
CARETAKERS	CATASTASIS	CENTRICITY	CHARGE CARD
CARICATURE	CAT BURGLAR	CENTRIFUGE	CHARGE HAND
CARMARTHEN	CATCALLING	CENTROMERE	CHARIOTEER
CARNALLITE	CATCH CROPS	CENTROSOME	CHARITABLE

CHARITABLY	CHILLINESS	CICATRIZER	CLIENTELES
CHARLADIES	CHIMERICAL	CIGARETTES	CLINGINESS
CHARLATANS	CHIMNEYPOT	CINCHONINE	CLINGSTONE
CHARLESTON	CHIMPANZEE	CINCHONISM	CLINICALLY
CHARMINGLY	CHINABERRY	CINCHONIZE	CLINKSTONE
CHARTERING	CHINATOWNS	CINCINNATI	CLINOMETER
CHARTREUSE	CHINCHILLA	CINDERELLA	CLINOMETRY
CHASTENING	CHINQUAPIN	CINERARIUM	CLIPBOARDS
CHASTISING	CHINSTRAPS	CINNAMONIC	CLIP JOINTS
CHATELAINE	CHINTZIEST	CINQUEFOIL	CLOAKROOMS
CHATOYANCY	CHIPOLATAS	CIRCUITOUS	CLOBBERING
CHATTERBOX	CHIROMANCY	CIRCULATED	CLOCKMAKER
CHATTERERS	CHIRPINESS	CIRCULATOR	CLOCK TOWER
CHATTERING	CHISELLERS	CIRCUMCISE	CLODDISHLY
CHAUDFROID	CHISELLING	CIRCUMFLEX	CLODHOPPER
CHAUFFEURS	CHITARRONE	CIRCUMFUSE	CLOGGINESS
CHAUVINISM	CHITTAGONG	CIRCUMVENT	CLOISTERED
CHAUVINIST	CHIVALROUS	CISMONTANE	CLOSE CALLS
CHEAPENING	CHLAMYDATE	CISTACEOUS	CLOSED BOOK
CHEAPSKATE	CHLORAMINE	CISTERCIAN	CLOSEDOWNS
CHEBOKSARY	CHLORINATE	CITRIC ACID	CLOSED SHOP
CHECKLISTS	CHLOROFORM	CITRONELLA	CLOSE SHAVE
CHECKMATED	CHOANOCYTE	CITRULLINE	CLOSE THING
CHECKMATES	CHOCOLATES	CITY FATHER	CLOTHBOUND
CHECKPOINT	CHOICENESS	CITY-STATES	CLOTHES PEG
CHECKROOMS	CHOKEBERRY	CIVILITIES	CLOUDBANKS
CHEEKBONES	CHONDRITIC	CIVILIZING	CLOUDBERRY
CHEEKINESS	CHOPHOUSES	CLACTONIAN	CLOUDBURST
CHEEKPIECE	CHOPPINESS	CLADOCERAN	CLOUDINESS
CHEERFULLY	CHOPSTICKS	CLAMBERING	CLOVE HITCH
CHEERINESS	CHORIAMBIC	CLAMMINESS	CLOVERLEAF
CHEESECAKE	CHORISTERS	CLAMOURING	CLOWNISHLY
CHEESED OFF	CHRISTENED	CLAMPDOWNS	CLOYEDNESS
CHEESINESS	CHRISTENER	CLANGOROUS	CLUBFOOTED
CHELICERAL	CHRISTIANS	CLANNISHLY	CLUBHOUSES
CHEMICALLY	CHROMATICS	CLANSWOMAN	CLUMSINESS
CHEMISETTE	CHROMATIST	CLAPPED-OUT	CLUSTERING
CHEMOTAXIS	CHROMOMERE	CLARABELLA	CLUTCH BAGS
CHEQUEBOOK	CHROMONEMA	CLARIFYING	CLUTTERING
CHEQUE CARD	CHROMOSOME	CLASP KNIFE	CLYDESDALE
CHERISHING	CHRONICITY	CLASSICISM	CNIDOBLAST
CHERNOVTSY	CHRONICLED	CLASSICIST	COACERVATE
CHERUBICAL	CHRONICLER	CLASSIFIED	COACTIVITY
CHESAPEAKE	CHRONICLES	CLASSIFIER	COADJUTANT
CHESSBOARD	CHRONOGRAM	CLASSMATES	COADJUTORS
CHESTINESS	CHRONOLOGY	CLASSROOMS	COAGULABLE
CHEVALIERS	CHRYSOLITE	CLATTERING	COAGULATED
CHEVROTAIN	CHRYSOTILE	CLAVICHORD	COALBUNKER
CHEWING GUM	CHUBBINESS	CLAVICULAR	COALESCENT
CHICKEN POX	CHUCKER-OUT	CLAY PIGEON	COALESCING
CHIEFTAINS	CHUCKWALLA	CLEANSABLE	COALFIELDS
CHIFFCHAFF	CHUMMINESS	CLEAN SWEEP	COALHOUSES
CHIFFONIER	CHUNKINESS	CLEARANCES	COALITIONS
CHIHUAHUAS	CHURCHGOER	CLEFT STICK	COAPTATION
CHILBLAINS	CHURCHYARD	CLEMENTINE	COARSENESS
CHILDBIRTH	CHURLISHLY	CLERESTORY	COARSENING
CHILDISHLY	CHYLACEOUS	CLERICALLY	COASTGUARD
CHILD'S PLAY	CICATRICES	CLEVER DICK	COASTLINES
CHILIASTIC	CICATRICLE	CLEVERNESS	COAT HANGER

COAT OF ARMS	COLLISIONS	COMMONALTY	CONCEALING
COCHABAMBA	COLLOCATED	COMMONNESS	CONCEDEDLY
COCHINEALS	COLLOQUIAL	COMMON NOUN	CONCEIVING
COCKALORUM	COLLOQUIES	COMMON ROOM	CONCENTRIC
COCKCHAFER	COLLOQUIUM	COMMONWEAL	CONCEPCION
COCKED HATS	COLLOTYPIC	COMMOTIONS	CONCEPTION
COCKFIGHTS	COLONIZERS	COMMUNIONS	CONCEPTIVE
COCKHORSES	COLONIZING	COMMUNIQUE	CONCEPTUAL
COCKNEYISM	COLONNADED	COMMUNISTS	CONCERNING
COCKSCOMBS	COLONNADES	COMMUTABLE	CONCERTINA
COCONUT SHY	COLORATION	COMMUTATOR	CONCERTINO
CODSWALLOP	COLORATURA	COMPACTING	CONCESSION
COELACANTH	COLOR LINES	COMPANIONS	CONCESSIVE
COENOCYTIC	COLOSSALLY	COMPARABLE	CONCHIOLIN
COEQUALITY	COLOSSUSES	COMPARABLY	CONCHOLOGY
COERCIVELY	COLOURABLE	COMPARATOR	CONCIERGES
COERCIVITY	COLOUR BARS	COMPARISON	CONCILIATE
COEXISTENT	COLOURFAST	COMPASSION	CONCINNITY
COEXISTING	COLOURINGS	COMPATIBLE	CONCINNOUS
COFFEE BARS	COLOURLESS	COMPATIBLY	CONCLAVIST
COFFEEPOTS	COLUMBINES	COMPATRIOT	CONCLUDING
COFFEE SHOP	COLUMELLAR	COMPELLING	CONCLUSION
COFFERDAMS	COLUMNISTS	COMPENDIUM	CONCLUSIVE
COGITATING	COMANCHEAN	COMPENSATE	CONCOCTING
COGITATION	COMBATABLE	COMPETENCE	CONCOCTION
COGITATIVE	COMBATANTS	COMPETENCY	CONCOCTIVE
COGNIZABLE	COMBATTING	COMPETITOR	CONCORDANT
COGNIZANCE	COMBINABLE	COMPLACENT	CONCORDATS
COHABITANT	COMBUSTION	COMPLAINED	CONCOURSES
COHABITING	COMEDIENNE	COMPLAINER	CONCRETELY
COHERENTLY	COME-HITHER	COMPLAINTS	CONCRETING
COHESIVELY	COMELINESS	COMPLEMENT	CONCRETION
COIMBATORE	COMESTIBLE	COMPLETELY	CONCRETIVE
COINCIDENT	COMFORTERS	COMPLETING	CONCRETIZE
COINCIDING	COMFORTING	COMPLETION	CONCUBINES
COLATITUDE	COMIC OPERA	COMPLETIVE	CONCURRENT
COLCHICINE	COMIC STRIP	COMPLEXION	CONCURRING
COLD CHISEL	COMMANDANT	COMPLEXITY	CONCUSSING
COLD FISHES	COMMANDEER	COMPLIANCE	CONCUSSION
COLD FRAMES	COMMANDERS	COMPLICATE	CONCUSSIVE
COLD FRONTS	COMMANDING	COMPLICITY	CONDEMNING
COLD TURKEY	COMMEASURE	COMPLIMENT	CONDENSATE
COLEMANITE	COMMENCING	COMPONENTS	CONDENSERS
COLEOPTILE	COMMENDING	COMPORTING	CONDENSING
COLEORHIZA	COMMENTARY	COMPOSITES	CONDESCEND
COLLAGENIC	COMMENTATE	COMPOSITOR	CONDIMENTS
COLLAPSING	COMMENTING	COMPOSTING	CONDITIONS
COLLARBONE	COMMERCIAL	COMPOUNDED	CONDOLENCE
COLLAR STUD	COMMISSARS	COMPOUNDER	CONDUCIBLE
COLLATERAL	COMMISSARY	COMPREHEND	CONDUCTING
COLLATIONS	COMMISSION	COMPRESSED	CONDUCTION
COLLEAGUES	COMMISSURE	COMPRESSES	CONDUCTIVE
COLLECTING	COMMITMENT	COMPRESSOR	CONDUCTORS
COLLECTION	COMMITTALS	COMPRISING	CONEFLOWER
COLLECTIVE	COMMITTEES	COMPROMISE	CONFECTION
COLLECTORS	COMMITTING	COMPULSION	CONFERENCE
COLLEGIATE	COMMODIOUS	COMPULSIVE	CONFERMENT
COLLIERIES	COMMODORES	COMPULSORY	CONFERRING
COLLIMATOR	COMMONABLE	COMPUTABLE	CONFERVOID

CONFESSING	CONSOCIATE	CONTRARILY	COQUELICOT
CONFESSION	CONSOLABLE	CONTRASTED	COQUETRIES
CONFESSORS	CONSONANCE	CONTRAVENE	COQUETTISH
CONFIDANTS	CONSONANTS	CONTRIBUTE	COR ANGLAIS
CONFIDENCE	CONSORTIAL	CONTRITELY	CORDIALITY
CONFIRMING	CONSORTING	CONTRITION	CORDIERITE
CONFISCATE	CONSORTIUM	CONTRIVING	CORDILLERA
CONFLATING	CONSPECTUS	CONTROLLED	CORDON BLEU
CONFLATION	CONSPIRACY	CONTROLLER	CORIACEOUS
CONFLICTED	CONSPIRING	CONTROVERT	CORINTHIAN
CONFLUENCE	CONSTABLES	CONTUSIONS	CORKSCREWS
CONFORMERS	CONSTANTAN	CONUNDRUMS	CORMOPHYTE
CONFORMING	CONSTANTLY	CONVALESCE	CORMORANTS
CONFORMIST	CONSTIPATE	CONVECTION	CORNACEOUS
CONFORMITY	CONSTITUTE	CONVECTIVE	CORNCOCKLE
CONFOUNDED	CONSTRAINT	CONVECTORS	CORNCRAKES
CONFOUNDER	CONSTRUCTS	CONVENABLE	CORNED BEEF
CONFRONTED	CONSTRUING	CONVENANCE	CORNELIANS
CONFRONTER	CONSUETUDE	CONVENIENT	CORNFLAKES
CONFUSABLE	CONSULATES	CONVENTION	CORNFLOWER
CONFUSEDLY	CONSULSHIP	CONVENTUAL	CORNSTARCH
CONGEALING	CONSULTANT	CONVERGENT	CORNUCOPIA
CONGENERIC	CONSULTING	CONVERGING	CORONATION
CONGENITAL	CONSUMMATE	CONVERSANT	CORPORATOR
CONGER EELS	CONTACTING	CONVERSELY	CORPOREITY
CONGESTION	CONTACTUAL	CONVERSING	CORPULENCE
CONGESTIVE	CONTAGIONS	CONVERSION	CORPUSCLES
CONGLOBATE	CONTAGIOUS	CONVERTERS	CORRALLING
CONGREGATE	CONTAINERS	CONVERTING	CORRECTING
CONGRESSES	CONTAINING	CONVEYABLE	CORRECTION
CONGRUENCE	CONTENDERS	CONVEYANCE	CORRECTIVE
CONIFEROUS	CONTENDING	CONVICTING	CORRELATED
CONJECTURE	CONTENTING	CONVICTION	CORRELATES
CONJOINING	CONTENTION	CONVICTIVE	CORRESPOND
CONJOINTLY	CONTESTANT	CONVINCING	CORRIENTES
CONJUGABLE	CONTESTING	CONVOCATOR	CORRIGENDA
CONJUGATED	CONTEXTUAL	CONVOLUTED	CORRIGIBLE
CONJUGATOR	CONTEXTURE	CONVULSING	CORRODIBLE
CONNECTING	CONTIGUITY	CONVULSION	CORRUGATED
CONNECTION	CONTIGUOUS	CONVULSIVE	CORRUPTING
CONNECTIVE	CONTINENCE	COOKHOUSES	CORRUPTION
CONNIVANCE	CONTINENTS	COOL-HEADED	CORRUPTIVE
CONQUERING	CONTINGENT	COOPERATED	CORSETIERE
CONQUERORS	CONTINUANT	COOPERATOR	CORUSCATED
CONSCIENCE	CONTINUING	COOPTATION	COS LETTUCE
CONSCRIPTS	CONTINUITY	COOPTATIVE	COSMICALLY
CONSECRATE	CONTINUOUS	COORDINATE	COSMIC RAYS
CONSENSUAL	CONTINUUMS	COPARCENER	COSMODROME
CONSENTING	CONTORTING	COPENHAGEN	COSMOGONAL
CONSEQUENT	CONTORTION	COPPERHEAD	COSMOGONIC
CONSERVING	CONTOURING	COPROLALIA	COSMONAUTS
CONSIDERED	CONTRABAND	COPROLITIC	COSSETTING
CONSIDERER	CONTRABASS	COPROPHAGY	COSTA RICAN
CONSIGNEES	CONTRACTED	COPULATING	CO-STARRING
CONSIGNING	CONTRACTOR	COPULATION	COSTLINESS
CONSIGNORS	CONTRADICT	COPULATIVE	COST PRICES
CONSISTENT	CONTRAFLOW	COPYHOLDER	COSTUMIERS
CONSISTING	CONTRALTOS	COPYRIGHTS	COTANGENTS
CONSISTORY	CONTRARIES	COPYWRITER	COTILLIONS

COTTAGE PIE	CREAMERIES	CRUMBLIEST	CYSTOSCOPE
COTTON GINS	CREAMINESS	CRUNCHIEST	CYSTOSCOPY
COTTONSEED	CREATININE	CRUSTACEAN	CYTOCHROME
COTTONTAIL	CREATIONAL	CRUSTINESS	CYTOLOGIST
COTTONWOOD	CREATIVELY	CRYOGENICS	
COTTON WOOL	CREATIVITY	CRYOPHILIC	**D**
COUCHETTES	CREDITABLE	CRYOSCOPIC	DACHSHUNDS
COUCH GRASS	CREDITABLY	CRYPTOZOIC	DAIL EIRANN
COULOMETER	CREDIT CARD	CRYSTAL SET	DAILY BREAD
COUNCILLOR	CREDIT NOTE	CTENOPHORE	DAINTINESS
COUNCILMAN	CREEPINESS	CUBBYHOLES	DAIRY FARMS
COUNCILMEN	CREMATIONS	CUCKOLDING	DAIRYMAIDS
COUNSELLED	CREMATORIA	CUCKOOPINT	DAISY WHEEL
COUNSELLOR	CRENELLATE	CUCULIFORM	DALAI LAMAS
COUNTDOWNS	CREOSOTING	CUDDLESOME	DALMATIANS
COUNTERACT	CREPE PAPER	CUDGELLING	DAMAGEABLE
COUNTERING	CRESCENDOS	CUERNAVACA	DAMP COURSE
COUNTERSPY	CRESCENTIC	CULLENDERS	DAMP SQUIBS
COUNTESSES	CRETACEOUS	CULTIVABLE	DAMSELFISH
COUNT NOUNS	CREWELWORK	CULTIVATED	DANDELIONS
COUNTRYMAN	CRIBRIFORM	CULTIVATOR	DAPPLE-GREY
COUNTRYMEN	CRICKETERS	CULTURALLY	DAREDEVILS
COUNTY TOWN	CRIMINALLY	CUMBERSOME	DARJEELING
COUPS D'ETAT	CRIMSONING	CUMMERBUND	DARK HORSES
COURAGEOUS	CRINKLIEST	CUMULATION	DARTBOARDS
COURGETTES	CRINOLINES	CUMULATIVE	DASHBOARDS
COURT CARDS	CRISPATION	CUMULIFORM	DAUGAVPILS
COURTESANS	CRISPINESS	CUPBEARERS	DAUGHTERLY
COURTESIES	CRISSCROSS	CURABILITY	DAYDREAMED
COURTHOUSE	CRITERIONS	CURATORIAL	DAYDREAMER
COURTLIEST	CRITICALLY	CURMUDGEON	DAY-NEUTRAL
COURTSHIPS	CRITICISMS	CURRENCIES	DAY NURSERY
COURTYARDS	CRITICIZED	CURRICULAR	DAY SCHOOLS
COUTURIERS	CRITICIZER	CURRICULUM	DAY-TRIPPER
COVARIANCE	CROAKINESS	CURTAILING	DEACONSHIP
COVENANTAL	CROCHETING	CURTAINING	DEACTIVATE
COVENANTED	CROCODILES	CURVACEOUS	DEAD CENTRE
COVENANTEE	CROISSANTS	CURVATURES	DEAD LETTER
COVENANTER	CROQUETTES	CUSHIONING	DEADLINESS
COVENANTOR	CROSSBONES	CUSSEDNESS	DEADLY SINS
COVER NOTES	CROSSBREED	CUSTARD PIE	DEAD-NETTLE
COVETOUSLY	CROSSCHECK	CUSTODIANS	DEAD RINGER
COWCATCHER	CROSSHATCH	CUSTOMIZED	DEALERSHIP
CRAB APPLES	CROSS-INDEX	CUSTOM-MADE	DEATHBLOWS
CRACKBRAIN	CROSSPATCH	CUTTHROATS	DEATH MASKS
CRACKDOWNS	CROSSPIECE	CUTTLEBONE	DEATH RATES
CRAFTINESS	CROSS-REFER	CUTTLEFISH	DEATH'S-HEAD
CRANE FLIES	CROSSROADS	CYBERNETIC	DEATH SQUAD
CRANESBILL	CROSS-SLIDE	CYCLAMATES	DEATH TOLLS
CRANIOLOGY	CROSSTREES	CYCLICALLY	DEATH TRAPS
CRANIOTOMY	CROSSWALKS	CYCLOMETER	DEATHWATCH
CRANKSHAFT	CROSSWINDS	CYCLOMETRY	DEBASEMENT
CRAPULENCE	CROSSWORDS	CYCLORAMIC	DEBAUCHEES
CRAQUELURE	CROWDED OUT	CYCLOSTOME	DEBAUCHERY
CRASH-DIVED	CROWN COURT	CYCLOSTYLE	DEBAUCHING
CRASH-DIVES	CROWNPIECE	CYLINDROID	DEBENTURES
CRAVENNESS	CROW'S NESTS	CYMBALISTS	DEBILITATE
CRAYFISHES	CRUCIFIXES	CYMIFEROUS	DEBOUCHING
CREAKINESS	CRUCIFYING	CYSTECTOMY	DEBRIEFING

DEBUTANTES	DEFAULTING	DELIMITING	DEPENDABLE
DECADENTLY	DEFEASANCE	DELINEATED	DEPENDABLY
DECAHEDRAL	DEFEASIBLE	DELINEATOR	DEPENDANTS
DECAHEDRON	DEFEATISTS	DELINQUENT	DEPENDENCE
DECAMPMENT	DEFECATING	DELIQUESCE	DEPENDENCY
DECAPITATE	DEFECATION	DELIVERIES	DEPICTIONS
DECATHLONS	DEFECTIONS	DELIVERING	DEPILATION
DECEIVABLE	DEFENDABLE	DELOCALIZE	DEPILATORY
DECELERATE	DEFENDANTS	DELPHINIUM	DEPLETABLE
DECEPTIONS	DEFENSIBLE	DELTIOLOGY	DEPLORABLE
DECIMALIZE	DEFENSIBLY	DELUSIONAL	DEPLORABLY
DECIMATING	DEFENSIVES	DELUSIVELY	DEPLOYMENT
DECIMATION	DEFERMENTS	DEMAGOGUES	DEPOLARIZE
DECIPHERED	DEFERRABLE	DEMANDABLE	DEPOPULATE
DECIPHERER	DEFICIENCY	DEMARCATED	DEPORTABLE
DECISIONAL	DEFILEMENT	DEMARCATOR	DEPORTMENT
DECISIVELY	DEFINITELY	DEMEANOURS	DEPOSITARY
DECKCHAIRS	DEFINITION	DEMENTEDLY	DEPOSITING
DECLAIMING	DEFINITIVE	DEMICANTON	DEPOSITION
DECLARABLE	DEFINITUDE	DEMIVIERGE	DEPOSITORS
DECLASSIFY	DEFLAGRATE	DEMOBILIZE	DEPOSITORY
DECLENSION	DEFLECTING	DEMOCRATIC	DEPRECATED
DECLINABLE	DEFLECTION	DEMODULATE	DEPRECATOR
DECOCTIONS	DEFLECTIVE	DEMOGRAPHY	DEPRECIATE
DECOLLATOR	DEFLOWERED	DEMOISELLE	DEPRESSANT
DECOLONIZE	DEFLOWERER	DEMOLISHED	DEPRESSING
DECOLORANT	DEFOLIANTS	DEMOLISHER	DEPRESSION
DECOLORIZE	DEFOLIATED	DEMOLITION	DEPRESSIVE
DECOMPOSED	DEFOLIATOR	DEMONETIZE	DEPRIVABLE
DECOMPOSER	DEFORESTED	DEMONIACAL	DEPURATION
DECOMPOUND	DEFORESTER	DEMONOLOGY	DEPURATIVE
DECOMPRESS	DEFORMABLE	DEMORALIZE	DEPUTATION
DECORATING	DEFRAUDING	DEMOTIVATE	DEPUTIZING
DECORATION	DEFRAYABLE	DEMURENESS	DERACINATE
DECORATIVE	DEFROCKING	DEMURRABLE	DERAILLEUR
DECORATORS	DEFROSTERS	DENATURANT	DERAILMENT
DECOROUSLY	DEFROSTING	DENDRIFORM	DEREGULATE
DECOUPLING	DEFUNCTIVE	DENDROLOGY	DERISIVELY
DECREASING	DEGENERACY	DENEGATION	DERISORILY
DECREEABLE	DEGENERATE	DENIGRATED	DERIVATION
DECREE NISI	DEGRADABLE	DENIGRATOR	DERIVATIVE
DECRESCENT	DEGRESSION	DENOMINATE	DERMATITIS
DECUMBENCE	DEHISCENCE	DENOTATION	DERMATOGEN
DEDICATING	DEHUMANIZE	DENOTATIVE	DERMATOMIC
DEDICATION	DEHUMIDIFY	DENOTEMENT	DERMATOSIS
DEDICATORY	DEHYDRATED	DENOUEMENT	DEROGATING
DEDUCTIBLE	DEHYDRATOR	DENOUNCING	DEROGATION
DEDUCTIONS	DEJECTEDLY	DENSIMETER	DEROGATIVE
DEEP FREEZE	DELAMINATE	DENSIMETRY	DEROGATORY
DEEP FRYING	DELAWAREAN	DENTIFRICE	DESALINATE
DEEP-ROOTED	DELECTABLE	DENUDATION	DESCENDANT
DEEP-SEATED	DELECTABLY	DENUNCIATE	DESCENDENT
DE-ESCALATE	DELEGATING	DEODORANTS	DESCENDING
DEFACEABLE	DELEGATION	DEODORIZED	DESCRIBING
DEFACEMENT	DELIBERATE	DEODORIZER	DESECRATED
DEFALCATOR	DELICACIES	DEONTOLOGY	DESECRATOR
DEFAMATION	DELICATELY	DEOXIDIZER	DESERTIONS
DEFAMATORY	DELIGHTFUL	DEPARTMENT	DESERVEDLY
DEFAULTERS	DELIGHTING	DEPARTURES	DESHABILLE

DESICCANTS	DEVELOPERS	DIGITALISM	DISBURSING
DESICCATED	DEVELOPING	DIGITALIZE	DISCARDING
DESICCATOR	DEVIATIONS	DIGITATION	DISC BRAKES
DESIDERATA	DEVILISHLY	DIGITIFORM	DISCERNING
DESIDERATE	DEVITALIZE	DIGITIZERS	DISCHARGED
DESIGNABLE	DEVOCALIZE	DIGITIZING	DISCHARGER
DESIGNATED	DEVOLUTION	DIGNIFYING	DISCHARGES
DESIGNATOR	DEVOTEMENT	DIGRESSING	DISC HARROW
DESIGNEDLY	DEVOTIONAL	DIGRESSION	DISCIPLINE
DESISTANCE	DEVOUTNESS	DIGRESSIVE	DISC JOCKEY
DESOLATELY	DEXTRALITY	DILAPIDATE	DISCLAIMED
DESOLATING	DIABOLICAL	DILATATION	DISCLAIMER
DESOLATION	DIACAUSTIC	DILEMMATIC	DISCLOSING
DESPAIRING	DIACHRONIC	DILETTANTE	DISCLOSURE
DESPATCHED	DIACRITICS	DILETTANTI	DISCOMFORT
DESPATCHER	DIACTINISM	DILIGENTLY	DISCOMMODE
DESPATCHES	DIADROMOUS	DILLYDALLY	DISCOMPOSE
DESPERADOS	DIAGENESIS	DIMENSIONS	DISCONCERT
DESPICABLE	DIAGNOSING	DIMINISHED	DISCONNECT
DESPICABLY	DIAGNOSTIC	DIMINUENDO	DISCONTENT
DESPOILING	DIAGONALLY	DIMINUTION	DISCOPHILE
DESPONDENT	DIAKINESIS	DIMINUTIVE	DISCORDANT
DESQUAMATE	DIALECTICS	DIMORPHISM	DISCOUNTED
DESSIATINE	DIALYSABLE	DIMORPHOUS	DISCOUNTER
DESTROYERS	DIAPASONAL	DINING CARS	DISCOURAGE
DESTROYING	DIAPEDESIS	DINING ROOM	DISCOURSED
DESTRUCTOR	DIAPEDETIC	DINNER BELL	DISCOURSER
DETACHABLE	DIAPHANOUS	DIPETALOUS	DISCOURSES
DETACHMENT	DIAPHRAGMS	DIPHOSGENE	DISCOVERED
DETAINABLE	DIAPHYSIAL	DIPHTHERIA	DISCOVERER
DETAINMENT	DIARRHOEAL	DIPHTHONGS	DISCREETLY
DETECTABLE	DIASTALSIS	DIPHYLETIC	DISCREPANT
DETECTIVES	DIASTALTIC	DIPHYLLOUS	DISCRETELY
DETERGENCY	DIATHERMIC	DIPHYODONT	DISCRETION
DETERGENTS	DIATROPISM	DIPLODOCUS	DISCURSIVE
DETERMINED	DIBASICITY	DIPLOMATIC	DISCUSSANT
DETERMINER	DICHLORIDE	DIPSOMANIA	DISCUSSING
DETERRENCE	DICHROMATE	DIRECTIONS	DISCUSSION
DETERRENTS	DICKENSIAN	DIRECTIVES	DISDAINFUL
DETESTABLE	DICKYBIRDS	DIRECTNESS	DISDAINING
DETESTABLY	DICTAPHONE	DIRECTOIRE	DISEMBOGUE
DETHRONING	DICTATIONS	DIRECTRESS	DISEMBOWEL
DETONATING	DICTATRESS	DIRIGIBLES	DISEMBROIL
DETONATION	DICTIONARY	DIRT FARMER	DISENCHANT
DETONATIVE	DICTOGRAPH	DIRT TRACKS	DISENDOWER
DETONATORS	DICYNODONT	DIRTY TRICK	DISENGAGED
DETOXICANT	DIDYNAMOUS	DISABILITY	DISENTHRAL
DETOXICATE	DIE-CASTING	DISABUSING	DISENTITLE
DETRACTING	DIE-HARDISM	DISALLOWED	DISENTWINE
DETRACTION	DIELECTRIC	DISAPPOINT	DISEPALOUS
DETRACTIVE	DIETICIANS	DISAPPROVE	DISFEATURE
DETRACTORS	DIFFERENCE	DISARRANGE	DISFIGURED
DETRAINING	DIFFICULTY	DISASTROUS	DISFIGURER
DETRIMENTS	DIFFIDENCE	DISAVOWALS	DISGORGING
DETRUNCATE	DIFFRACTED	DISAVOWING	DISGRACING
DEUTOPLASM	DIFFUSIBLE	DISBANDING	DISGRUNTLE
DEUX-SEVRES	DIGESTIBLE	DISBARMENT	DISGUISING
DEVASTATED	DIGESTIONS	DISBARRING	DISGUSTING
DEVASTATOR	DIGESTIVES	DISBELIEVE	DISHABILLE

DISHARMONY	DISSATISFY	DIVERTIBLE	DOWNLOADED
DISHCLOTHS	DISSECTING	DIVESTIBLE	DOWN-MARKET
DISHEARTEN	DISSECTION	DIVESTMENT	DOWNPLAYED
DISHONESTY	DISSEMBLED	DIVINATION	DOWNSPOUTS
DISH TOWELS	DISSEMBLER	DIVINATORY	DOWNSTAIRS
DISHWASHER	DISSENSION	DIVING BELL	DOWNSTREAM
DISINCLINE	DISSENTERS	DIVINITIES	DRAGONHEAD
DISINHERIT	DISSENTING	DIVISIONAL	DRAGONROOT
DISJOINTED	DISSERVICE	DIVISIVELY	DRAGOONAGE
DISK DRIVES	DISSIDENCE	DIVULGENCE	DRAGOONING
DISLIKABLE	DISSIDENTS	DIYARBAKIR	DRAINPIPES
DISLOCATED	DISSIMILAR	DOCENTSHIP	DRAMATISTS
DISLODGING	DISSIPATED	DOCTORATES	DRAMATIZED
DISLOYALLY	DISSIPATER	DOCTRINISM	DRAMATIZER
DISLOYALTY	DISSOCIATE	DOCUMENTED	DRAMATURGE
DISMALNESS	DISSOLUBLE	DODECANESE	DRAMATURGY
DISMANTLED	DISSOLVING	DOG BISCUIT	DRAWBRIDGE
DISMANTLER	DISSONANCE	DOGCATCHER	DRAWING PIN
DISMASTING	DISSUADING	DOG COLLARS	DRAWSTRING
DISMISSALS	DISSUASION	DOGGEDNESS	DREADFULLY
DISMISSING	DISSUASIVE	DOGMATISTS	DREADLOCKS
DISMISSIVE	DISTANCING	DOGMATIZER	DREAMBOATS
DISMOUNTED	DISTENDING	DOGSBODIES	DREAMINESS
DISOBEYING	DISTENSION	DOLLARFISH	DREAMINGLY
DISOBLIGED	DISTICHOUS	DOLL'S HOUSE	DREAMLANDS
DISORDERED	DISTILLATE	DOLLY BIRDS	DREAM WORLD
DISORDERLY	DISTILLERS	DOLOROUSLY	DREARINESS
DISOWNMENT	DISTILLERY	DOMINATING	DRESSINESS
DISPARAGED	DISTILLING	DOMINATION	DRESSMAKER
DISPARAGER	DISTINCTLY	DOMINATIVE	DRILLSTOCK
DISPASSION	DISTORTING	DOMINEERED	DRIP-DRYING
DISPATCHED	DISTORTION	DOMINICANS	DRIVELLERS
DISPATCHES	DISTORTIVE	DONKEYWORK	DRIVELLING
DISPELLING	DISTRACTED	DONNYBROOK	DROLLERIES
DISPENSARY	DISTRACTER	DOORKEEPER	DROOPINESS
DISPENSERS	DISTRAINED	DOORPLATES	DROSOPHILA
DISPENSING	DISTRAINEE	DORSIGRADE	DROSSINESS
DISPERMOUS	DISTRAINOR	DOSIMETRIC	DROWSINESS
DISPERSING	DISTRAUGHT	DOSSHOUSES	DRUGSTORES
DISPERSION	DISTRESSED	DOTTED LINE	DRUM MAJORS
DISPERSIVE	DISTRIBUTE	DOUBLE BASS	DRUMSTICKS
DISPERSOID	DISTRUSTED	DOUBLE BEDS	DRUPACEOUS
DISPIRITED	DISTRUSTER	DOUBLE BIND	DRY BATTERY
DISPLACING	DISTURBING	DOUBLE CHIN	DRY-CLEANED
DISPLAYING	DISULFIRAM	DOUBLE DATE	DRY CLEANER
DISPLEASED	DISULPHATE	DOUBLE-HUNG	DUBITATION
DISPORTING	DISULPHIDE	DOUBLE-PARK	DUCKBOARDS
DISPOSABLE	DISUNITING	DOUBLE-REED	DUFFEL BAGS
DISPOSSESS	DISUTILITY	DOUBLE-STOP	DUFFEL COAT
DISPRAISER	DISYLLABIC	DOUBLE TAKE	DUMBSTRUCK
DISPROVING	DITHEISTIC	DOUBLE-TALK	DUMBWAITER
DISPUTABLE	DITHIONITE	DOUBLE TIME	DUNCE'S CAPS
DISPUTABLY	DIVARICATE	DOUBLETREE	DUNDERHEAD
DISQUALIFY	DIVE-BOMBED	DOUBTFULLY	DUODECIMAL
DISQUIETED	DIVE-BOMBER	DOUGHTIEST	DUODENITIS
DISRESPECT	DIVERGENCE	DOVETAILED	DUPABILITY
DISRUPTING	DIVERGENCY	DOWN-AND-OUT	DUPLICABLE
DISRUPTION	DIVERSIONS	DOWN-AT-HEEL	DUPLICATED
DISRUPTIVE	DIVERTEDLY	DOWNGRADED	DUPLICATES

DUPLICATOR	ECONOMIZED	ELICITABLE	EMPALEMENT
DURABILITY	ECONOMIZER	ELIMINABLE	EMPANELING
DURATIONAL	ECOSPECIES	ELIMINATED	EMPANELLED
DUSSELDORF	ECOSYSTEMS	ELIMINATOR	EMPHASIZED
DUST JACKET	ECTODERMAL	ELLIPTICAL	EMPIRICISM
DUSTSHEETS	ECTOENZYME	ELONGATING	EMPIRICIST
DUST STORMS	ECTOGENOUS	ELONGATION	EMPLOYABLE
DUTCH BARNS	ECTOMORPHY	ELONGATIVE	EMPLOYMENT
DUTCH OVENS	ECUADORIAN	ELOPEMENTS	EMPOWERING
DUTCH TREAT	ECUMENICAL	ELOQUENTLY	EMULSIFIED
DUTCH UNCLE	ECZEMATOUS	EL SALVADOR	EMULSIFIER
DYNAMISTIC	EDENTULOUS	ELUCIDATED	EMULSIONED
DYNAMITING	EDIFYINGLY	ELUCIDATOR	ENACTMENTS
DYSENTERIC	EDITORIALS	ELUTRIATOR	ENAMELLING
DYSPLASTIC	EDITORSHIP	ELUVIATION	ENAMELLIST
DYSPROSIUM	EDULCORATE	EMACIATION	ENAMELWARE
DYSTROPHIC	EDWARDIANS	EMANATIONS	ENAMELWORK
DZERZHINSK	EFFACEABLE	EMANCIPATE	ENCAMPMENT
	EFFACEMENT	EMARGINATE	ENCASEMENT
E	EFFECTIBLE	EMASCULATE	ENCASHABLE
EAGLESTONE	EFFECTUATE	EMBALMMENT	ENCASHMENT
EARLY BIRDS	EFFEMINACY	EMBANKMENT	ENCEPHALIC
EARMARKING	EFFEMINATE	EMBARGOING	ENCEPHALON
EARTHBOUND	EFFERVESCE	EMBARKMENT	ENCHAINING
EARTHINESS	EFFETENESS	EMBEZZLERS	ENCHANTERS
EARTHLIEST	EFFICIENCY	EMBEZZLING	ENCHANTING
EARTHLIGHT	EFFLORESCE	EMBITTERED	ENCHILADAS
EARTHLINGS	EFFORTLESS	EMBITTERER	ENCIPHERER
EARTHQUAKE	EFFRONTERY	EMBLAZONED	ENCIRCLING
EARTHSHINE	EFFULGENCE	EMBLAZONRY	ENCLOSABLE
EARTHWARDS	EFFUSIVELY	EMBLEMATIC	ENCLOSURES
EARTHWORKS	EGOCENTRIC	EMBLEMENTS	ENCODEMENT
EARTHWORMS	EGYPTOLOGY	EMBODIMENT	ENCOUNTERS
EAR TRUMPET	EIDERDOWNS	EMBOLDENED	ENCOURAGED
EAST ANGLIA	EIGHTEENMO	EMBOLISMIC	ENCOURAGER
EAST BERLIN	EIGHTEENTH	EMBONPOINT	ENCROACHED
EAST ENDERS	EIGHTH NOTE	EMBOSSMENT	ENCROACHER
EASTER EGGS	EIGHTIETHS	EMBOUCHURE	ENCRUSTANT
EASTERNERS	EISTEDDFOD	EMBRASURED	ENCUMBERED
EASTERTIDE	EJACULATED	EMBRASURES	ENCYCLICAL
EAST GERMAN	EJACULATOR	EMBRECTOMY	ENCYSTMENT
EAST INDIAN	ELABORATED	EMBROIDERY	ENDANGERED
EAST INDIES	ELABORATOR	EMBROILING	ENDEARMENT
EASTWARDLY	ELAEOPTENE	EMBRYOGENY	ENDEAVOURS
EASY CHAIRS	ELASTICITY	EMBRYOLOGY	ENDOCARPAL
EASY STREET	ELASTICIZE	EMENDATION	ENDOCRINAL
EASY VIRTUE	ELATEDNESS	EMENDATORY	ENDOCRINIC
EBRACTEATE	ELDERBERRY	EMETICALLY	ENDODERMAL
EBULLIENCE	ELEATICISM	EMIGRATING	ENDODERMIC
EBULLITION	ELECAMPANE	EMIGRATION	ENDODERMIS
EBURNATION	ELECTIVITY	EMIGRATIVE	ENDODONTIA
ECCENTRICS	ELECTORATE	EMISSARIES	ENDODONTIC
ECCHYMOSIS	ELECTRICAL	EMISSIVITY	ENDOENZYME
ECHINODERM	ELECTRODES	EMMENTALER	ENDOGAMOUS
ECHOPRAXIA	ELECTROJET	EMMETROPIA	ENDOGENOUS
ECOLOGICAL	ELECTRONIC	EMMETROPIC	ENDOMORPHY
ECOLOGISTS	ELEMENTARY	EMOLLIENCE	ENDOPHYTIC
ECONOMICAL	ELEVATIONS	EMOLLIENTS	ENDORSABLE
ECONOMISTS	ELEVEN-PLUS	EMOLUMENTS	ENDOSCOPIC

ENDOSMOSIS	ENTOMBMENT	EPISTERNUM	ESTATE CARS
ENDOSMOTIC	ENTOMOLOGY	EPISTOLARY	ESTHETICAL
ENDOSTOSIS	ENTOPHYTIC	EPITAPHIST	ESTIMATING
ENDOWMENTS	ENTOURAGES	EPITHELIAL	ESTIMATION
END PRODUCT	ENTRAINING	EPITHELIUM	ESTIMATIVE
ENDURINGLY	ENTRANCING	EPITOMIZED	ESTIMATORS
ENERGETICS	ENTRAPMENT	EPITOMIZER	ESTIPULATE
ENERGIZING	ENTRAPPING	EPOXY RESIN	ESTRANGING
ENERVATING	ENTREATIES	EPSOM SALTS	ETERNALITY
ENERVATION	ENTREATING	EQUABILITY	ETERNALIZE
ENERVATIVE	ENTRENCHED	EQUALIZERS	ETERNITIES
ENFACEMENT	ENTRENCHER	EQUALIZING	ETHANEDIOL
ENFEEBLING	ENTRUSTING	EQUANIMITY	ETHEREALLY
ENFILADING	ENUCLEATOR	EQUANIMOUS	ETHNICALLY
ENFLEURAGE	ENUMERATED	EQUATIONAL	ETHNOGENIC
ENFOLDMENT	ENUMERATOR	EQUATORIAL	ETHNOLOGIC
ENFORCEDLY	ENUNCIABLE	EQUESTRIAN	ETHOLOGIST
ENGAGEMENT	ENUNCIATED	EQUIPOTENT	ETHYLATION
ENGAGINGLY	ENUNCIATOR	EQUITATION	ETIOLATION
ENGENDERED	ENVELOPING	EQUIVALENT	EUBACTERIA
ENGENDERER	ENVISAGING	EQUIVOCATE	EUCALYPTOL
ENGINEERED	ENZYMOLOGY	ERADIATION	EUCALYPTUS
ENGLISHMAN	EOSINOPHIL	ERADICABLE	EUCHLORINE
ENGLISHMEN	EPEIROGENY	ERADICATED	EUDEMONICS
ENGRAVINGS	EPENTHESIS	ERADICATOR	EUDEMONISM
ENGROSSING	EPENTHETIC	ERECTILITY	EUDIOMETER
ENGULFMENT	EPEXEGESIS	ERETHISMIC	EUDIOMETRY
ENHARMONIC	EPEXEGETIC	ERGONOMICS	EUGENICIST
ENJAMBMENT	EPIBLASTIC	ERGOSTEROL	EUHEMERISM
ENJOINMENT	EPICANTHUS	ERICACEOUS	EUHEMERIST
ENJOYMENTS	EPICARDIAC	ERINACEOUS	EUHEMERIZE
ENLACEMENT	EPICARDIUM	EROGENEITY	EULOGISTIC
ENLISTMENT	EPICENTRAL	EROTEMATIC	EULOGIZING
ENLIVENING	EPICENTRES	EROTICALLY	EUPATORIUM
ENORMITIES	EPICUREANS	EROTOGENIC	EUPHAUSIID
ENORMOUSLY	EPICYCLOID	EROTOMANIA	EUPHEMISMS
ENPHYTOTIC	EPIDEICTIC	ERRATICISM	EUPHEMIZER
ENRAGEMENT	EPIDEMICAL	ERUBESCENT	EUPHONIOUS
ENRAPTURED	EPIDIDYMAL	ERUCTATION	EUPHONIUMS
ENRICHMENT	EPIDIDYMIS	ERUCTATIVE	EUPHORIANT
ENROLMENTS	EPIGASTRIC	ERUPTIONAL	EUPHUISTIC
ENSANGUINE	EPIGENESIS	ERUPTIVITY	EURE-ET-LOIR
ENSCONCING	EPIGENETIC	ERYSIPELAS	EURHYTHMIC
ENSHRINING	EPIGLOTTAL	ERYTHRITOL	EUROCHEQUE
ENSHROUDED	EPIGLOTTIS	ESCADRILLE	EUROCLYDON
ENSIGNSHIP	EPIGRAPHER	ESCALATING	EURODOLLAR
ENTAILMENT	EPIGRAPHIC	ESCALATION	EUROMARKET
ENTANGLING	EPILEPTICS	ESCALATORS	EURYPTERID
ENTEROTOMY	EPILEPTOID	ESCAPEMENT	EURYTHMICS
ENTERPRISE	EPIMORPHIC	ESCAPOLOGY	EURYTROPIC
ENTHRALLED	EPINEURIAL	ESCARPMENT	EUSTACHIAN
ENTHRALLER	EPINEURIUM	ESCHAROTIC	EUTHANASIA
ENTHRONING	EPIPHONEMA	ESCRITOIRE	EVACUATING
ENTHUSIASM	EPIPHYSEAL	ESCUTCHEON	EVACUATION
ENTHUSIAST	EPIROGENIC	ESKILSTUNA	EVACUATIVE
ENTICEMENT	EPISCOPACY	ESPADRILLE	EVALUATING
ENTICINGLY	EPISCOPATE	ESPECIALLY	EVALUATION
ENTIRENESS	EPISIOTOMY	ESPLANADES	EVALUATIVE
ENTODERMAL	EPISPASTIC	ESSENTIALS	EVANESCENT

EVANGELISM	EXECUTIVES	EXPLOITING	FACECLOTHS
EVANGELIST	EXEMPTIBLE	EXPLOSIONS	FACE-HARDEN
EVANGELIZE	EXEMPTIONS	EXPLOSIVES	FACE POWDER
EVANSVILLE	EXENTERATE	EXPORTABLE	FACE-SAVERS
EVAPORABLE	EXERCISING	EXPOSITION	FACE-SAVING
EVAPORATED	EXHALATION	EXPOSITORY	FACE-TO-FACE
EVAPORATOR	EXHAUSTING	EXPOUNDING	FACE VALUES
EVECTIONAL	EXHAUSTION	EXPRESSAGE	FACILENESS
EVEN-HANDED	EXHAUSTIVE	EXPRESSING	FACILITATE
EVENTFULLY	EXHIBITING	EXPRESSION	FACILITIES
EVENTUALLY	EXHIBITION	EXPRESSIVE	FACSIMILES
EVERGLADES	EXHIBITIVE	EXPRESSWAY	FACTITIOUS
EVERGREENS	EXHIBITORS	EXPULSIONS	FACT OF LIFE
EVERYTHING	EXHIBITORY	EXPUNCTION	FACTORABLE
EVERYWHERE	EXHILARANT	EXPURGATED	FACTORIZED
EVIDENTIAL	EXHILARATE	EXPURGATOR	FACTORSHIP
EVIL-MINDED	EXHUMATION	EXSANGUINE	FACTUALISM
EVISCERATE	EXIGENCIES	EXSICCATOR	FACTUALIST
EVOCATIONS	EXIGUOUSLY	EXTENDIBLE	FAHRENHEIT
EVOLVEMENT	EXISTENCES	EXTENSIBLE	FAINTINGLY
EXACERBATE	EXOBIOLOGY	EXTENSIONS	FAIR COPIES
EXACTINGLY	EXOCENTRIC	EXTENUATED	FAIR DINKUM
EXACTITUDE	EXODONTIST	EXTENUATOR	FAIRGROUND
EXAGGERATE	EXONERATED	EXTERNALLY	FAIR-MINDED
EXALTATION	EXONERATOR	EXTINCTION	FAIR-SPOKEN
EXAMINABLE	EXORBITANT	EXTINCTIVE	FAIRYLANDS
EXASPERATE	EXORCIZING	EXTINGUISH	FAIRY LIGHT
EX CATHEDRA	EXOSPOROUS	EXTIRPATED	FAIRY TALES
EXCAVATING	EXOTHERMIC	EXTIRPATOR	FAITHFULLY
EXCAVATION	EXOTICALLY	EXTORTIONS	FALLACIOUS
EXCAVATORS	EXOTICNESS	EXTRACTING	FALLOW DEER
EXCEEDABLE	EXPANDABLE	EXTRACTION	FALLOWNESS
EXCELLENCE	EXPANSIBLE	EXTRACTIVE	FALSE ALARM
EXCELLENCY	EXPANSIONS	EXTRACTORS	FALSEHOODS
EXCEPTABLE	EXPATIATED	EXTRADITED	FALSE START
EXCEPTIONS	EXPATIATOR	EXTRAMURAL	FALSE TEETH
EXCHANGING	EXPATRIATE	EXTRANEOUS	FALSIFYING
EXCITATION	EXPECTABLE	EXTRAVERTS	FAMILIARLY
EXCITATIVE	EXPECTANCY	EXTRICABLE	FAMILY NAME
EXCITEMENT	EXPEDIENCE	EXTRICATED	FAMILY TREE
EXCITINGLY	EXPEDIENCY	EXTROVERTS	FAMISHMENT
EXCLAIMING	EXPEDIENTS	EXTRUSIONS	FAMOUSNESS
EXCLUDABLE	EXPEDITING	EXUBERANCE	FANATICISM
EXCLUSIVES	EXPEDITION	EXULTANTLY	FANATICIZE
EXCOGITATE	EXPELLABLE	EXULTATION	FANCIFULLY
EXCORIATED	EXPENDABLE	EXULTINGLY	FANCY DRESS
EXCRESCENT	EXPERIENCE	EXUVIATION	FANCY WOMAN
EXCRETIONS	EXPERIMENT	EYEBALLING	FANCY WOMEN
EXCRUCIATE	EXPERTNESS	EYE-CATCHER	FANTASIZED
EXCULPABLE	EXPIRATION	EYEDROPPER	FANTOCCINI
EXCULPATED	EXPIRATORY	EYEGLASSES	FARCICALLY
EXCURSIONS	EXPLAINING	EYE-OPENERS	FAR EASTERN
EXCUSATORY	EXPLETIVES	EYE SHADOWS	FARFETCHED
EXECRATING	EXPLICABLE	EYEWITNESS	FARMHOUSES
EXECRATION	EXPLICABLY		FARMSTEADS
EXECRATIVE	EXPLICATED	**F**	FARSIGHTED
EXECUTABLE	EXPLICATOR	FABRICATED	FASCIATION
EXECUTANTS	EXPLICITLY	FABRICATOR	FASCICULAR
EXECUTIONS	EXPLOITERS	FABULOUSLY	FASCICULUS

FASCINATED	FEUILLETON	FIRST NAMES	FLIGHTIEST
FASHIONING	FEVERISHLY	FIRST NIGHT	FLIGHTLESS
FASTENINGS	FIANNA FAIL	FISH FINGER	FLIGHT PATH
FASTIDIOUS	FIBREBOARD	FISH KNIVES	FLIMSINESS
FASTIGIATE	FIBREGLASS	FISHMONGER	FLINTINESS
FASTNESSES	FIBRINOGEN	FISH SLICES	FLINTLOCKS
FATALISTIC	FIBROBLAST	FISH STICKS	FLIPPANTLY
FATALITIES	FIBROSITIS	FISSIPEDAL	FLIRTATION
FATHERHOOD	FICKLENESS	FISTICUFFS	FLIRTINGLY
FATHERLAND	FICTIONIST	FIVE-FINGER	FLOATATION
FATHERLESS	FICTITIOUS	FIXED-POINT	FLOCCULANT
FATHER-LIKE	FIDDLEHEAD	FIXED STARS	FLOCCULATE
FATHOMABLE	FIDDLEWOOD	FLABBINESS	FLOCCULENT
FATHOMETER	FIELD EVENT	FLABELLATE	FLOODGATES
FATHOMLESS	FIELDMOUSE	FLACCIDITY	FLOODLIGHT
FAT-SOLUBLE	FIELDSTONE	FLAGELLANT	FLOOD TIDES
FATTENABLE	FIELD-TESTS	FLAGELLATE	FLOORBOARD
FAULTINESS	FIELD TRIPS	FLAGITIOUS	FLOOR CLOTH
FAVOURABLE	FIENDISHLY	FLAGRANTLY	FLOOR SHOWS
FAVOURABLY	FIERCENESS	FLAGSTAFFS	FLOPHOUSES
FAVOURITES	FIFTEENTHS	FLAGSTONES	FLOPPINESS
FEARLESSLY	FIFTY-FIFTY	FLAG-WAVING	FLOPPY DISK
FEARNOUGHT	FIGURATION	FLAMBOYANT	FLORENTINE
FEATHER BED	FIGURATIVE	FLAMEPROOF	FLORIBUNDA
FEATHER BOA	FIGUREHEAD	FLAMINGOES	FLORISTICS
FEATHERING	FILARIASIS	FLANNELING	FLOTATIONS
FEBRIFUGAL	FILIALNESS	FLANNELLED	FLOUNDERED
FEBRUARIES	FILIBUSTER	FLARE PATHS	FLOURISHED
FECKLESSLY	FILMSETTER	FLASHBACKS	FLOURISHER
FECUNDATOR	FILMSTRIPS	FLASHBOARD	FLOURISHES
FEDERALISM	FILTERABLE	FLASHBULBS	FLOURMILLS
FEDERALIST	FILTER TIPS	FLASHCUBES	FLOUTINGLY
FEDERALIZE	FILTHINESS	FLASHINESS	FLOWCHARTS
FEDERATING	FILTRATION	FLASHLIGHT	FLOWERBEDS
FEDERATION	FINALIZING	FLASH POINT	FLOWER GIRL
FEDERATIVE	FINANCIERS	FLATFISHES	FLOWERLESS
FEEBLENESS	FINE-TUNING	FLAT-FOOTED	FLOWER-LIKE
FEET OF CLAY	FINGER BOWL	FLAT RACING	FLOWERPOTS
FEIGNINGLY	FINGERLING	FLATTENING	FLUCTUATED
FELICITATE	FINGERNAIL	FLATTERERS	FLUFFINESS
FELICITIES	FINGERTIPS	FLATTERING	FLUGELHORN
FELICITOUS	FINISTERRE	FLATULENCE	FLUID OUNCE
FELLMONGER	FINNO-UGRIC	FLAVESCENT	FLUMMOXING
FELLOWSHIP	FIRE ALARMS	FLAVOURFUL	FLUORIDATE
FELT-TIP PEN	FIREBRANDS	FLAVOURING	FLUORINATE
FEMALENESS	FIREBREAKS	FLAWLESSLY	FLUSTERING
FEMININITY	FIREBRICKS	FLEA-BITTEN	FLUTTERING
FENESTELLA	FIRE DRILLS	FLEA MARKET	FLY-BY-NIGHT
FER-DE-LANCE	FIRE-EATERS	FLECTIONAL	FLYCATCHER
FERMENTING	FIRE-EATING	FLEDGLINGS	FLY-FISHING
FEROCITIES	FIRE ENGINE	FLEECINESS	FLYING BOAT
FERRITE-ROD	FIRE ESCAPE	FLEETINGLY	FLYING FISH
FERTILIZED	FIREGUARDS	FLESHINESS	FLYSPECKED
FERTILIZER	FIREPLACES	FLESH WOUND	FLYSWATTER
FESTOONERY	FIRE-RAISER	FLETCHINGS	FLYWEIGHTS
FESTOONING	FIRESTORMS	FLEUR-DE-LIS	FOAMFLOWER
FETCHINGLY	FIRING LINE	FLICKERING	FOAM RUBBER
FETIPAROUS	FIRST-CLASS	FLICK KNIFE	FOB WATCHES
FETISHISTS	FIRST FLOOR	FLIGHT DECK	FOCAL POINT

FOLIACEOUS	FORMALISTS	FRANGIPANI	FRIZZINESS
FOLK DANCER	FORMALIZED	FRATERNITY	FROCK COATS
FOLK DANCES	FORMALIZER	FRATERNIZE	FROGHOPPER
FOLKESTONE	FORMATIONS	FRATRICIDE	FROLICKING
FOLKLORIST	FORMATTING	FRAUDULENT	FROLICSOME
FOLKSINESS	FORMIC ACID	FRAXINELLA	FRONTALITY
FOLLICULAR	FORMIDABLE	FREAKINESS	FRONTBENCH
FOLLICULIN	FORMIDABLY	FREAKISHLY	FRONT DOORS
FOLLOWABLE	FORMLESSLY	FREE AGENTS	FRONT ROOMS
FOLLOWINGS	FORMULATED	FREE-BASING	FRONTWARDS
FONDLINGLY	FORMULATOR	FREEBOARDS	FROSTBOUND
FONTANELLE	FORNICATED	FREEBOOTER	FROSTINESS
FOOD STAMPS	FORNICATOR	FREE CHURCH	FROTHINESS
FOODSTUFFS	FORSTERITE	FREEDWOMAN	FROWNINGLY
FOOTBALLER	FORSWEARER	FREE-FOR-ALL	FROWZINESS
FOOTBRIDGE	FORTE-PIANO	FREE-HANDED	FROZENNESS
FOOT-CANDLE	FORTHRIGHT	FREEHOLDER	FRUCTIFIED
FOOT FAULTS	FORTIFIERS	FREE HOUSES	FRUCTIFIER
FOOTLIGHTS	FORTIFYING	FREELANCED	FRUITCAKES
FOOTPLATES	FORTISSIMO	FREELANCER	FRUITERERS
FOOTPRINTS	FORTNIGHTS	FREELANCES	FRUIT FLIES
FOOTSTOOLS	FORTRESSES	FREE-LIVING	FRUITFULLY
FORBEARING	FORTUITISM	FREELOADED	FRUITINESS
FORBIDDING	FORTUITIST	FREELOADER	FRUIT SALAD
FORCEDNESS	FORTUITOUS	FREEMARTIN	FRUSTRATED
FORCEFULLY	FORTY-NINER	FREEMASONS	FRUSTRATER
FORE AND AFT	FORTY WINKS	FREE PARDON	FRUTESCENT
FOREARMING	FORWARDING	FREE PASSES	FRYING PANS
FOREBODING	FOSSILIZED	FREE-SPOKEN	FUDDY-DUDDY
FORECASTED	FOSTERLING	FREE-TRADER	FULFILLING
FORECASTER	FOUDROYANT	FREIGHTAGE	FULFILMENT
FORECASTLE	FOUNDATION	FREIGHTERS	FULIGINOUS
FORECLOSED	FOUNDERING	FREIGHTING	FULL-BODIED
FORECOURSE	FOUNDLINGS	FRENCH BEAN	FULL HOUSES
FORECOURTS	FOURCHETTE	FRENCH HORN	FULL-LENGTH
FOREDOOMED	FOUR-COLOUR	FRENCH KISS	FULL-RIGGED
FOREFATHER	FOUR-HANDED	FRENCH LOAF	FULL-SAILED
FOREFINGER	FOURIERISM	FRENZIEDLY	FULLY-GROWN
FOREGATHER	FOURIERIST	FREQUENTED	FULMINATED
FOREGOINGS	FOUR-IN-HAND	FREQUENTER	FULMINATOR
FOREGROUND	FOUR-POSTER	FREQUENTLY	FUMATORIUM
FOREIGN AID	FOURRAGERE	FRESHENING	FUMBLINGLY
FOREIGNERS	FOURSQUARE	FRESHWATER	FUMIGATING
FOREIGNISM	FOUR-STROKE	FRIABILITY	FUMIGATION
FOREORDAIN	FOURTEENTH	FRICANDEAU	FUNCTIONAL
FORERUNNER	FOXHUNTERS	FRICASSEES	FUNCTIONED
FORESEEING	FOXHUNTING	FRICATIVES	FUNEREALLY
FORESHADOW	FOX TERRIER	FRICTIONAL	FUNGICIDAL
FOREST-LIKE	FRACTIONAL	FRIENDLESS	FUNGICIDES
FORETELLER	FRACTURING	FRIENDLIER	FUNICULARS
FOREWARNED	FRAGMENTAL	FRIENDLIES	FUNICULATE
FOREWARNER	FRAGMENTED	FRIENDLILY	FUNNELLING
FORFEITERS	FRAGRANCES	FRIENDSHIP	FUNNY BONES
FORFEITING	FRAGRANTLY	FRIGHTENED	FUNNY FARMS
FORFEITURE	FRAMEWORKS	FRIGHTENER	FURBISHING
FORGETTING	FRANCHISED	FRILLINESS	FURNISHING
FORGIVABLE	FRANCHISES	FRISKINESS	FURTHERING
FORGIVABLY	FRANCISCAN	FRITILLARY	FURUNCULAR
FORKEDNESS	FRANCONIAN	FRITTERING	FUSIBILITY

FUSILLADES	GELATINIZE	GINGER BEER	GOATSBEARD
FUSTANELLA	GELATINOID	GINGER NUTS	GO-BETWEENS
FUTURISTIC	GELATINOUS	GINGIVITIS	GODFATHERS
FUTUROLOGY	GELDERLAND	GIPPY TUMMY	GOD-FEARING
	GEMINATION	GIRL FRIDAY	GODMOTHERS
G	GEMMACEOUS	GIRLFRIEND	GODPARENTS
GABARDINES	GEMOLOGIST	GIRL GUIDES	GOGGLE-EYED
GADOLINITE	GENERALIST	GIVEN NAMES	GOINGS-OVER
GADOLINIUM	GENERALITY	GLACIALIST	GOLD-BEATER
GAFF-RIGGED	GENERALIZE	GLACIATION	GOLD DIGGER
GAILLARDIA	GENERATING	GLACIOLOGY	GOLDEN AGES
GAINLINESS	GENERATION	GLADDENING	GOLDEN MEAN
GAINSAYING	GENERATIVE	GLADIATORS	GOLDEN RULE
GALASHIELS	GENERATORS	GLAGOLITIC	GOLDENSEAL
GALLICIZER	GENERATRIX	GLAIRINESS	GOLDFIELDS
GALLOGLASS	GENEROSITY	GLAMORIZED	GOLDILOCKS
GALLSTONES	GENEROUSLY	GLAMORIZER	GOLD MEDALS
GALLUP POLL	GENETICIST	GLANCINGLY	GOLD-MINING
GALUMPHING	GENICULATE	GLANDEROUS	GOLD-PLATED
GALVANIZED	GENIUS LOCI	GLASS FIBRE	GOLD RUSHES
GALVANIZER	GENTLEFOLK	GLASSHOUSE	GOLDSMITHS
GAMEKEEPER	GENTLENESS	GLASSINESS	GOLDTHREAD
GAMETOCYTE	GENTRIFYED	GLASS-MAKER	GOLF COURSE
GANG-BANGED	GEOCENTRIC	GLASSWORKS	GONDOLIERS
GANGLIONIC	GEOCHEMIST	GLASWEGIAN	GONIOMETER
GANGPLANKS	GEODYNAMIC	GLAUCONITE	GONIOMETRY
GANGRENOUS	GEOGNOSTIC	GLAZING-BAR	GONOCOCCAL
GARAGE SALE	GEOGRAPHER	GLEAMINGLY	GONOCOCCUS
GARBAGE CAN	GEOLOGICAL	GLIMMERING	GONOPHORIC
GARDEN CITY	GEOLOGISTS	GLIOMATOUS	GONORRHOEA
GARGANTUAN	GEOMETRIZE	GLISTENING	GOOD FRIDAY
GARISHNESS	GEOMORPHIC	GLITTERATI	GOODLINESS
GARLANDING	GEOPHAGIST	GLITTERING	GOOD LOOKER
GARNIERITE	GEOPHAGOUS	GLOATINGLY	GOODY-GOODY
GARNISHING	GEOPHYSICS	GLOBALISTS	GOOGOLPLEX
GARRISONED	GEOSCIENCE	GLOCHIDIUM	GOOSEBERRY
GARROTTING	GEOSTATICS	GLOMERULAR	GOOSEFLESH
GAS FITTERS	GEOTHERMAL	GLOMERULUS	GOOSESTEPS
GASHOLDERS	GEOTROPISM	GLOOMINESS	GORGEOUSLY
GASIFIABLE	GERATOLOGY	GLORIFYING	GORGONZOLA
GASOMETERS	GERIATRICS	GLORIOUSLY	GORMANDIZE
GASOMETRIC	GERMANIZER	GLORY HOLES	GORMLESSLY
GAS STATION	GERMICIDAL	GLOSSARIAL	GORNO-ALTAI
GASTRALGIA	GERMICIDES	GLOSSARIES	GOTHICALLY
GASTRALGIC	GERMINABLE	GLOSSARIST	GOVERNABLE
GASTROLITH	GERMINATED	GLOSSINESS	GOVERNANCE
GASTRONOME	GERMINATOR	GLOTTIDEAN	GOVERNMENT
GASTRONOMY	GERUNDIVAL	GLUCOSIDAL	GRACEFULLY
GASTROTOMY	GESTATIONS	GLUMACEOUS	GRACIOUSLY
GAS TURBINE	GESUNDHEIT	GLUTTINGLY	GRADATIONS
GATEHOUSES	GET-UP-AND-GO	GLUTTONOUS	GRADUALISM
GATEKEEPER	GHASTLIEST	GLYCOGENIC	GRADUALIST
GATHERABLE	GHOSTLIEST	GLYCOLYSIS	GRADUATING
GATHERINGS	GHOST TOWNS	GLYCOSIDIC	GRADUATION
GAUCHENESS	GHOSTWRITE	GLYCOSURIA	GRAININESS
GAULTHERIA	GIANT PANDA	GLYCOSURIC	GRAMICIDIN
GAUSSMETER	GIFTEDNESS	GNASHINGLY	GRAMINEOUS
GAZETTEERS	GIFT HORSES	GOALKEEPER	GRAMMARIAN
GEAR LEVERS	GINGER ALES	GOALMOUTHS	GRAMOPHONE

GRANADILLA	GREEN LIGHT	GUESTROOMS	HAIRSTYLES
GRANDCHILD	GREEN PAPER	GUIDELINES	HALBERDIER
GRAND OPERA	GREENSBORO	GUILDHALLS	HALF A CROWN
GRAND PIANO	GREENSHANK	GUILEFULLY	HALF-BREEDS
GRAND SLAMS	GREENSTONE	GUILLEMOTS	HALF-CASTES
GRANDS PRIX	GREEN THUMB	GUILLOTINE	HALF CROWNS
GRANDSTAND	GREGARIOUS	GUILTINESS	HALF-LENGTH
GRANGERISM	GRENADIERS	GUINEA FOWL	HALF-SISTER
GRANGERIZE	GRESSORIAL	GUINEA PIGS	HALF-TRUTHS
GRANNY KNOT	GREYHOUNDS	GUITARFISH	HALF VOLLEY
GRANOPHYRE	GREY MATTER	GUITARISTS	HALF-WITTED
GRANT-IN-AID	GRIEVANCES	GUJRANWALA	HALLELUJAH
GRANULATED	GRIEVINGLY	GULF STREAM	HALLMARKED
GRANULATOR	GRIEVOUSLY	GUNRUNNERS	HALOGENATE
GRANULITIC	GRIM REAPER	GUNRUNNING	HALOGENOID
GRAPEFRUIT	GRINDSTONE	GURGLINGLY	HALOGENOUS
GRAPEVINES	GRIPPINGLY	GYMNASIAST	HALOPHYTIC
GRAPHITIZE	GRISLINESS	GYMNASIUMS	HALTER-LIKE
GRAPHOLOGY	GRISTLIEST	GYMNASTICS	HALTERNECK
GRAPH PAPER	GRITTINESS	GYMNOSPERM	HAMBURGERS
GRAPTOLITE	GROANINGLY	GYNANDROUS	HAMMERHEAD
GRASSFINCH	GROGGINESS	GYNOPHORIC	HAMMERLESS
GRASSINESS	GROTESQUES	GYPSOPHILA	HAMMER-LIKE
GRASS ROOTS	GROTTINESS	GYROSCOPES	HAMSHACKLE
GRASS WIDOW	GROUCHIEST	GYROSCOPIC	HAMSTRINGS
GRATEFULLY	GROUND BAIT	GYROSTATIC	HANDBALLER
GRATIFYING	GROUND CREW		HANDBARROW
GRATUITIES	GROUNDLESS	H	HANDBRAKES
GRATUITOUS	GROUNDLING	HABILIMENT	HANDCUFFED
GRAUBUNDEN	GROUNDMASS	HABILITATE	HANDICRAFT
GRAVELLING	GROUNDNUTS	HABITATION	HANDLEABLE
GRAVESTONE	GROUND PLAN	HABITUALLY	HANDLEBARS
GRAVETTIAN	GROUND RENT	HABITUATED	HANDLELESS
GRAVEYARDS	GROUND RULE	HACKBUTEER	HANDMAIDEN
GRAVIMETER	GROUNDSMAN	HACKNEYISM	HAND-ME-DOWN
GRAVIMETRY	GROUNDSMEN	HADHRAMAUT	HANDPICKED
GRAVITATED	GROUNDWORK	HAECKELIAN	HANDSHAKES
GRAVITATER	GROVELLERS	HAEMAGOGUE	HANDSOMELY
GRAVY BOATS	GROVELLING	HAEMATINIC	HANDSPRING
GRAVY TRAIN	GRUBBINESS	HAEMATITIC	HANDSTANDS
GREASE GUNS	GRUBSTAKES	HAEMATOSIS	HANDSTROKE
GREASEWOOD	GRUDGINGLY	HAEMATURIA	HANKERINGS
GREASINESS	GRUESOMELY	HAEMATURIC	HANKY-PANKY
GREATCOATS	GRUMPINESS	HAEMOLYSIN	HANOVERIAN
GREAT DANES	GRUNTINGLY	HAEMOLYSIS	HAPLOLOGIC
GREAT-NIECE	GUADELOUPE	HAEMOLYTIC	HAPPENINGS
GREAT-UNCLE	GUANAJUATO	HAEMOPHILE	HAPPY EVENT
GREEDINESS	GUANTANAMO	HAGIOCRACY	HAPPY HOURS
GREEDY-GUTS	GUARANTEED	HAGIOLATER	HARANGUING
GREENBACKS	GUARANTEES	HAGIOLATRY	HARASSMENT
GREEN BEANS	GUARANTIES	HAGIOLOGIC	HARBINGERS
GREEN BELTS	GUARANTORS	HAGIOSCOPE	HARBOURAGE
GREENBRIER	GUARDHOUSE	HAILSTONES	HARBOURING
GREENFINCH	GUARDRAILS	HAILSTORMS	HARD-BITTEN
GREENFLIES	GUARDROOMS	HAIRPIECES	HARD-BOILED
GREENGAGES	GUARD'S VANS	HAIR SHIRTS	HARD CIDERS
GREENHEART	GUERRILLAS	HAIR SLIDES	HARDHEADED
GREENHORNS	GUESSINGLY	HAIRSPRING	HARD LABOUR
GREENHOUSE	GUESTHOUSE	HAIRSTREAK	HARD-LINERS

HARD LIQUOR	HEARING AID	HEMIPTERON	HEXANGULAR
HARD PALATE	HEARKENING	HEMISPHERE	HEXAVALENT
HARELIPPED	HEARTBEATS	HEMITROPIC	HIBERNACLE
HARGREAVES	HEARTBREAK	HEMOGLOBIN	HIBERNATED
HARLEQUINS	HEARTENING	HEMOPHILIA	HIBERNATOR
HARMLESSLY	HEARTHRUGS	HEMORRHAGE	HIBISCUSES
HARMONICAS	HEARTINESS	HEMORRHOID	HIDDENNESS
HARMONIOUS	HEARTSEASE	HENCEFORTH	HIERARCHAL
HARMONIUMS	HEARTTHROB	HENDECAGON	HIEROCRACY
HARMONIZED	HEATEDNESS	HENOTHEISM	HIERODULIC
HARMONIZER	HEATHBERRY	HENOTHEIST	HIEROGLYPH
HARMSWORTH	HEATHENDOM	HEN PARTIES	HIEROLOGIC
HARNESSING	HEATHENISH	HEPARINOID	HIERONYMIC
HARPOONING	HEATHENISM	HEPHAESTUS	HIERONYMUS
HARRISBURG	HEATHENIZE	HEPHAISTOS	HIEROPHANT
HARROWMENT	HEAT RASHES	HEPTAGONAL	HIGHBINDER
HARTEBEEST	HEAT SHIELD	HEPTAMETER	HIGH CHAIRS
HARTLEPOOL	HEATSTROKE	HEPTARCHIC	HIGH CHURCH
HARUSPICAL	HEAVEN-SENT	HEPTASTICH	HIGH COURTS
HARVESTERS	HEAVENWARD	HEPTATEUCH	HIGH-FLIERS
HARVESTING	HEAVY-LADEN	HERACLIDAN	HIGH-FLYING
HARVESTMAN	HEAVY WATER	HERACLITUS	HIGH-HANDED
HASH BROWNS	HEBDOMADAL	HERBACEOUS	HIGH HORSES
HASTEFULLY	HEBETATION	HERBALISTS	HIGHJACKER
HATCHBACKS	HEBETATIVE	HERBICIDAL	HIGH JUMPER
HATCHELLER	HEBRAISTIC	HERBIVORES	HIGHLANDER
HATCHERIES	HECTICALLY	HEREABOUTS	HIGHLIGHTS
HATCHET JOB	HECTOGRAPH	HEREDITARY	HIGH MASSES
HATCHET MAN	HEDONISTIC	HEREDITIST	HIGH-MINDED
HATCHET MEN	HEEDLESSLY	HERESIARCH	HIGHNESSES
HATSHEPSUT	HEIDELBERG	HERETOFORE	HIGH-OCTANE
HAUBERGEON	HEIGHTENED	HERMITAGES	HIGH POINTS
HAUGHTIEST	HEIGHTENER	HEROICALLY	HIGH PRIEST
HAUNTINGLY	HEISENBERG	HEROPHILUS	HIGH RELIEF
HAUSTELLUM	HELIANTHUS	HESITANTLY	HIGH SCHOOL
HAUSTORIAL	HELICOPTER	HESITATING	HIGH SEASON
HAUSTORIUM	HELIGOLAND	HESITATION	HIGH STREET
HAVERSACKS	HELIOGRAPH	HESITATIVE	HIGH-STRUNG
HAZARDABLE	HELIOLATER	HESPERIDES	HIGHWAYMAN
HAZARD-FREE	HELIOLATRY	HESPERIDIN	HIGHWAYMEN
HEADBOARDS	HELIOMETER	HETERODONT	HIJACKINGS
HEADCHEESE	HELIOMETRY	HETERODOXY	HILDEBRAND
HEADHUNTED	HELIOPOLIS	HETERODYNE	HILLINGDON
HEADHUNTER	HELIOTAXIS	HETEROGAMY	HIMYARITIC
HEADLIGHTS	HELIOTROPE	HETEROGONY	HINAYANIST
HEADLINING	HELIOTYPIC	HETEROLOGY	HINDENBURG
HEADMASTER	HELLBENDER	HETERONOMY	HINDERMOST
HEAD OF HAIR	HELLENIZER	HETEROTOPY	HINDRANCES
HEADPHONES	HELLESPONT	HEULANDITE	HINDUSTANI
HEADPIECES	HELMET-LIKE	HEURISTICS	HINTERLAND
HEADSPRING	HELMINTHIC	HEXADECANE	HIPHUGGERS
HEADSQUARE	HELPLESSLY	HEXAEMERIC	HIPPARCHUS
HEADSTONES	HEMELYTRAL	HEXAEMERON	HIP POCKETS
HEADSTREAM	HEMELYTRON	HEXAHEDRAL	HIPPOCRENE
HEADSTRONG	HEMICYCLIC	HEXAHEDRON	HIPPODROME
HEADWATERS	HEMIHEDRAL	HEXAMERISM	HIPPOGRIFF
HEADWORKER	HEMIPLEGIA	HEXAMEROUS	HIPPOLYTAN
HEALTH FOOD	HEMIPLEGIC	HEXAMETERS	HIPPOLYTUS
HEALTHIEST	HEMIPTERAN	HEXAMETRIC	HIPPOMENES

HISPANIOLA	HOMOGENIZE	HORSEWOMEN	HURRICANES
HISTAMINIC	HOMOGENOUS	HOSPITABLE	HURRYINGLY
HISTIOCYTE	HOMOGONOUS	HOSPITABLY	HUSBANDING
HISTOGRAMS	HOMOGRAPHS	HOSTELLERS	HUSBANDMAN
HISTOLYSIS	HOMOLOGATE	HOSTELLING	HUSBANDMEN
HISTOLYTIC	HOMOLOGIZE	HOSTELRIES	HYACINTHUS
HISTORIANS	HOMOLOGOUS	HOT-BLOODED	HYALOPLASM
HISTORICAL	HOMOLOSINE	HOTCHPOTCH	HYALURONIC
HISTRIONIC	HOMONYMITY	HOT FLUSHES	HYBRIDIZER
HITCHHIKED	HOMOOUSIAN	HOTFOOTING	HYDRANGEAS
HITCHHIKER	HOMOPHONES	HOUSEBOATS	HYDRASTINE
HITHERMOST	HOMOPHONIC	HOUSEBOUND	HYDRAULICS
HIT PARADES	HOMOPLASTY	HOUSECOATS	HYDROCORAL
HOARSENESS	HOMORGANIC	HOUSECRAFT	HYDROFOILS
HOBBYHORSE	HOMOSEXUAL	HOUSEFLIES	HYDROGRAPH
HOBGOBLINS	HOMOZYGOTE	HOUSEHOLDS	HYDROLOGIC
HOBNOBBING	HOMOZYGOUS	HOUSEMAIDS	HYDROLYSER
HOCHHEIMER	HOMUNCULAR	HOUSE OF GOD	HYDROLYSIS
HOCUS-POCUS	HOMUNCULUS	HOUSE PARTY	HYDROLYTIC
HODGEPODGE	HONESTNESS	HOUSEPLANT	HYDROMANCY
HOGARTHIAN	HONEYBUNCH	HOUSE-PROUD	HYDROPONIC
HOITY-TOITY	HONEYCOMBS	HOUSEWIVES	HYGIENISTS
HOKEY COKEY	HONEYDEWED	HOVERCRAFT	HYPERBOLAS
HOKEY-POKEY	HONEY-EATER	HOVERINGLY	HYPERBOLES
HOLDERSHIP	HONEYMOONS	HOVERTRAIN	HYPERBOLIC
HOLES IN ONE	HONORARIUM	HOW DO YOU DO	HYPHENATED
HOLIDAYING	HONORIFICS	HUA KUO-FENG	HYPNOTISTS
HOLINESSES	HONOURABLE	HUCKLEBONE	HYPNOTIZED
HOLLOWNESS	HONOURABLY	HUDDLESTON	HYPOCRITES
HOLLYHOCKS	HONOURLESS	HUGUENOTIC	HYPODERMIC
HOLOCAUSTS	HOODLUMISM	HULLABALOO	HYPOTENUSE
HOLOENZYME	HOODWINKED	HUMANENESS	HYPOTHESES
HOLOFERNES	HOODWINKER	HUMANISTIC	HYPOTHESIS
HOLOGRAPHY	HOOKEDNESS	HUMANITIES	HYSTERICAL
HOLOHEDRAL	HOOTENANNY	HUMANIZING	
HOLOPHYTIC	HOPE CHESTS	HUMBERSIDE	I
HOLUS-BOLUS	HOPELESSLY	HUMBLENESS	IAMBICALLY
HOLY SPIRIT	HORIZONTAL	HUMBLINGLY	IATROGENIC
HOMEBODIES	HORNBLENDE	HUMBUGGERY	ICEBREAKER
HOME-BREWED	HORNEDNESS	HUMDINGERS	ICE LOLLIES
HOMECOMING	HORN-RIMMED	HUMIDIFIED	ICE-SKATERS
HOME GUARDS	HOROLOGIST	HUMIDIFIER	ICE-SKATING
HOMELINESS	HOROLOGIUM	HUMIDISTAT	ICHINOMIYA
HOMEMAKERS	HOROSCOPES	HUMILIATED	ICHTHYOSIS
HOMEMAKING	HOROSCOPIC	HUMILIATOR	ICHTHYOTIC
HOME MOVIES	HORRENDOUS	HUMORESQUE	ICONOCLASM
HOME OFFICE	HORRIDNESS	HUMORISTIC	ICONOCLAST
HOMEOPATHS	HORRIFYING	HUMOROUSLY	ICONOLATER
HOMEOPATHY	HORROR FILM	HUMOURLESS	ICONOLATRY
HOMEOTYPIC	HORSEBOXES	HUMOURSOME	ICONOMATIC
HOMESTEADS	HORSEFLESH	HUMPBACKED	ICONOSCOPE
HOME TRUTHS	HORSEFLIES	HUNCHBACKS	IDEALISTIC
HOMILETICS	HORSELAUGH	HUNDREDTHS	IDEALIZING
HOMOCERCAL	HORSELEECH	HUNGRINESS	IDEATIONAL
HOMOCYCLIC	HORSE OPERA	HUNTINGDON	IDEMPOTENT
HOMOEOPATH	HORSEPOWER	HUNTRESSES	IDENTIFIED
HOMOEROTIC	HORSE SENSE	HUNTSVILLE	IDENTIFIER
HOMOGAMOUS	HORSESHOES	HURDY-GURDY	IDENTIKITS
HOMOGENATE	HORSEWOMAN	HURLY-BURLY	IDENTITIES

IDEOGRAPHY	IMMUNIZING	IMPROVISER	INCUBATING
IDEOLOGIES	IMMUNOLOGY	IMPRUDENCE	INCUBATION
IDEOLOGIST	IMPAIRMENT	IMPUDENTLY	INCUBATIVE
IDEOLOGUES	IMPALEMENT	IMPUISSANT	INCUBATORS
IDIOLECTAL	IMPALPABLE	IMPULSIONS	INCULCATED
IDIOPATHIC	IMPANATION	IMPUNITIES	INCULCATOR
IDIOPHONIC	IMPANELLED	IMPURITIES	INCULPABLE
IDOLATRIZE	IMPARTIBLE	IMPUTATION	INCULPATED
IDOLATROUS	IMPASSABLE	IMPUTATIVE	INCUMBENCY
IGNES FATUI	IMPATIENCE	IN ABSENTIA	INCUMBENTS
IGNOBILITY	IMPEACHING	INACCURACY	INCUNABULA
IGNOMINIES	IMPECCABLE	INACCURATE	INCURRABLE
IJSSELMEER	IMPECCABLY	INACTIVATE	INCURRENCE
ILL-ADVISED	IMPEDANCES	INACTIVELY	INCURSIONS
ILLEGALITY	IMPEDIMENT	INACTIVITY	INDECENTLY
ILLEGALIZE	IMPEDINGLY	INADEQUACY	INDECISION
ILLITERACY	IMPENDENCE	INADEQUATE	INDECISIVE
ILLITERATE	IMPENITENT	INAMORATAS	INDECOROUS
ILL-NATURED	IMPERATIVE	INAPPOSITE	INDEFINITE
ILLOCUTION	IMPERIALLY	INAPTITUDE	INDELICACY
ILL-STARRED	IMPERILLED	INARTISTIC	INDELICATE
ILL-TREATED	IMPERSONAL	INAUGURATE	INDENTURED
ILLUMINANT	IMPERVIOUS	INBREEDING	INDENTURES
ILLUMINATE	IMPETRATOR	INCANDESCE	INDEXATION
ILLUMINATI	IMPISHNESS	INCAPACITY	INDIAN CORN
ILLUMINISM	IMPLACABLE	INCAPARINA	INDICATING
ILLUMINIST	IMPLANTING	INCARNATED	INDICATION
ILLUSORILY	IMPLEMENTS	INCAUTIOUS	INDICATIVE
ILLUSTRATE	IMPLICATED	INCENDIARY	INDICATORS
IMAGINABLE	IMPLICITLY	INCENTIVES	INDICATORY
IMBALANCES	IMPLOSIONS	INCEPTIONS	INDICTABLE
IMBECILITY	IMPOLITELY	INCESSANCY	INDICTMENT
IMBIBITION	IMPORTANCE	INCESTUOUS	INDIGENOUS
IMBRICATED	IMPORTUNED	INCHOATION	INDIRECTLY
IMBROGLIOS	IMPORTUNER	INCHOATIVE	INDISCREET
IMITATIONS	IMPOSINGLY	INCIDENTAL	INDISCRETE
IMMACULACY	IMPOSITION	INCINERATE	INDISPOSED
IMMACULATE	IMPOSSIBLE	INCIPIENCE	INDISTINCT
IMMATERIAL	IMPOSSIBLY	INCIPIENCY	INDIVIDUAL
IMMATURELY	IMPOSTROUS	INCISIVELY	INDOCILITY
IMMATURITY	IMPOSTURES	INCITATION	INDOLENTLY
IMMEMORIAL	IMPOTENTLY	INCITEMENT	INDOLOGIST
IMMERSIBLE	IMPOUNDAGE	INCITINGLY	INDONESIAN
IMMIGRANTS	IMPOUNDING	INCIVILITY	INDOPHENOL
IMMIGRATED	IMPOVERISH	INCLEMENCY	INDUCEMENT
IMMIGRATOR	IMPREGNATE	INCLINABLE	INDUCTANCE
IMMINENTLY	IMPRESARIO	INCLOSURES	INDUCTIONS
IMMISCIBLE	IMPRESSING	INCLUDABLE	INDULGENCE
IMMOBILITY	IMPRESSION	INCLUSIONS	INDUSTRIAL
IMMOBILIZE	IMPRESSIVE	INCOHERENT	INDUSTRIES
IMMODERACY	IMPRIMATUR	INCOMMODED	INEBRIATED
IMMODERATE	IMPRINTING	INCOMPLETE	INEBRIATES
IMMODESTLY	IMPRISONED	INCONSTANT	INEDUCABLE
IMMOLATING	IMPRISONER	INCRASSATE	INEDUCABLY
IMMOLATION	IMPROBABLE	INCREASING	INEFFICACY
IMMORALIST	IMPROBABLY	INCREDIBLE	INELEGANCE
IMMORALITY	IMPROPERLY	INCREDIBLY	INELIGIBLE
IMMORTELLE	IMPROVABLE	INCREMENTS	INELOQUENT
IMMOTILITY	IMPROVISED	INCRESCENT	INEPTITUDE

INEQUALITY	INHALATION	INSENSIBLY	INTENTNESS
INEQUITIES	INHARMONIC	INSENTIENT	INTERACTED
INEVITABLE	INHERENTLY	INSERTABLE	INTER ALIOS
INEVITABLY	INHERITING	INSERTIONS	INTERBRAIN
INEXISTENT	INHIBITING	INSIDE JOBS	INTERBREED
INEXORABLE	INHIBITION	INSIGHTFUL	INTERCEDED
INEXORABLY	INHIBITIVE	INSINUATED	INTERCEDER
INEXPERTLY	INHUMANELY	INSINUATOR	INTERDICTS
INEXPIABLE	INHUMANITY	INSIPIDITY	INTERESTED
INEXPLICIT	INHUMATION	INSISTENCE	INTERFACED
IN EXTREMIS	INIMITABLE	INSOBRIETY	INTERFACES
INFALLIBLE	INIMITABLY	INSOLATION	INTERFERED
INFALLIBLY	INIQUITIES	INSOLENTLY	INTERFERER
INFARCTION	INIQUITOUS	INSOLVABLE	INTERFERON
INFATUATED	INITIALING	INSOLVENCY	INTERFLUVE
INFECTIONS	INITIALIZE	INSOLVENTS	INTERGRADE
INFECTIOUS	INITIALLED	INSOMNIACS	INTERGROUP
INFELICITY	INITIATING	INSOMNIOUS	INTERLACED
INFERENCES	INITIATION	INSOUCIANT	INTERLAKEN
INFERNALLY	INITIATIVE	INSPECTING	INTERLEAVE
INFIDELITY	INITIATORY	INSPECTION	INTERLINER
INFIELDERS	INJECTABLE	INSPECTIVE	INTERLOPER
INFIGHTING	INJECTIONS	INSPECTORS	INTERLUDES
INFILTRATE	INJUNCTION	INSPIRABLE	INTERLUNAR
INFINITELY	INJUNCTIVE	INSPIRITER	INTERMARRY
INFINITIVE	INJURY TIME	INSTALLING	INTERMENTS
INFINITUDE	INJUSTICES	INSTALMENT	INTERMEZZI
INFLATABLE	IN MEMORIAM	INSTANCING	INTERMEZZO
INFLATEDLY	INNER TUBES	INSTIGATED	INTERNALLY
INFLECTING	INNKEEPERS	INSTIGATOR	INTERNMENT
INFLECTION	INNOCENTLY	INSTILLING	INTERNODAL
INFLECTIVE	INNOMINATE	INSTILMENT	INTERNSHIP
INFLEXIBLE	INNOVATING	INSTITUTED	INTERPHASE
INFLEXIBLY	INNOVATION	INSTITUTES	INTERPHONE
INFLICTING	INNOVATIVE	INSTITUTOR	INTERPLEAD
INFLICTION	INNOVATORS	INSTRUCTED	INTERPOSAL
INFLICTIVE	INNUENDOES	INSTRUCTOR	INTERPOSED
INFLUENCED	INNUMERACY	INSTRUMENT	INTERPOSER
INFLUENCER	INNUMERATE	INSUFFLATE	INTERREGNA
INFLUENCES	INOCULABLE	INSULARISM	INTERSPACE
INFLUENZAL	INOCULATED	INSULARITY	INTERSTATE
INFORMALLY	INOCULATOR	INSULATING	INTERSTICE
INFORMANTS	INOPERABLE	INSULATION	INTERTIDAL
INFORMEDLY	INORDINACY	INSULATORS	INTERTWINE
INFRACTION	INORDINATE	INSURANCES	INTERVENED
INFRASONIC	INOSCULATE	INSURGENCE	INTERVENER
INFREQUENT	IN-PATIENTS	INSURGENCY	INTERVIEWS
INFRINGING	INQUIETUDE	INSURGENTS	INTERWEAVE
INFURIATED	INQUISITOR	INTANGIBLE	INTERWOVEN
INFUSORIAL	INSALIVATE	INTANGIBLY	INTESTINAL
INGESTIBLE	INS AND OUTS	INTEGRABLE	INTESTINES
INGLENOOKS	INSANITARY	INTEGRATED	INTIMACIES
INGLORIOUS	INSATIABLE	INTEGRATOR	INTIMATELY
INGRATIATE	INSATIABLY	INTEGUMENT	INTIMATING
INGREDIENT	INSCRIBING	INTELLECTS	INTIMATION
INGRESSION	INSECURELY	INTENDANCE	INTIMIDATE
INGRESSIVE	INSECURITY	INTENDANCY	INTINCTION
INHABITANT	INSEMINATE	INTENDMENT	INTOLERANT
INHABITING	INSENSIBLE	INTENTIONS	INTONATION

INTOXICANT	IRISHWOMAN	JAWBREAKER	KARYOPLASM
INTOXICATE	IRONICALLY	JAYWALKERS	KARYOTYPIC
INTRAMURAL	IRONMONGER	JAYWALKING	KASHMIRIAN
INTRENCHED	IRRADIANCE	JEALOUSIES	KENNELLING
INTREPIDLY	IRRADIATED	JELLY BEANS	KENTUCKIAN
INTRIGUING	IRRADIATOR	JELLY ROLLS	KERATINIZE
INTRODUCED	IRRATIONAL	JEOPARDIZE	KERCHIEFED
INTRODUCER	IRREGULARS	JERRY-BUILD	KERFUFFLES
INTROSPECT	IRRELATIVE	JERRY-BUILT	KERMANSHAH
INTROVERTS	IRRELEVANT	JESUITICAL	KERSEYMERE
INTRUSIONS	IRRELIGION	JET ENGINES	KETTLEDRUM
INTRUSTING	IRRESOLUTE	JET-SETTERS	KEYBOARDED
INTUBATION	IRREVERENT	JETTISONED	KEYBOARDER
INTUITABLE	IRRIGATING	JIGGERMAST	KEYPUNCHED
INTUITIONS	IRRIGATION	JINGOISTIC	KEYPUNCHER
INUNDATING	IRRIGATIVE	JITTERBUGS	KEYPUNCHES
INUNDATION	IRRITATING	JOB CENTRES	KHABAROVSK
INUREDNESS	IRRITATION	JOBSHARING	KIDNAPPERS
INVAGINATE	IRRITATIVE	JOCKSTRAPS	KIDNAPPING
INVALIDATE	IRRUPTIONS	JOCULARITY	KIDNEY BEAN
INVALIDING	ISENTROPIC	JOGJAKARTA	KIESELGUHR
INVALIDISM	ISOANTIGEN	JOLLY ROGER	KILMARNOCK
INVALIDITY	ISOCHEIMAL	JOSS STICKS	KILOLITRES
INVALUABLE	ISOCHRONAL	JOURNALESE	KILOMETRES
INVARIABLE	ISOCHROOUS	JOURNALISM	KILOMETRIC
INVARIABLY	ISOCYANIDE	JOURNALIST	KIMBERLITE
INVARIANCE	ISODYNAMIC	JOURNALIZE	KINCARDINE
INVEIGHING	ISOGAMETIC	JOURNEYING	KINDLINESS
INVEIGLING	ISOGLOSSAL	JOURNEYMAN	KINDNESSES
INVENTIBLE	ISOGLOTTIC	JOURNEYMEN	KINEMATICS
INVENTIONS	ISOLEUCINE	JOYFULNESS	KINGFISHER
INVERACITY	ISOMETRICS	JOYOUSNESS	KINGLINESS
INVERSIONS	ISOMORPHIC	JUBILANTLY	KINGMAKERS
INVERTIBLE	ISOPIESTIC	JUBILATION	KING-OF-ARMS
INVESTABLE	ISOSEISMAL	JUDGMENTAL	KING'S BENCH
INVESTMENT	ISOTHERMAL	JUDICATIVE	KIROVOGRAD
INVETERACY	ISOTROPOUS	JUDICATORY	KISS OF LIFE
INVETERATE	ISRAELITES	JUDICATURE	KITAKYUSHU
INVIGILATE	ITALIANATE	JUDICIALLY	KITH AND KIN
INVIGORATE	ITALICIZED	JUGGERNAUT	KITTIWAKES
INVINCIBLE	ITCHY PALMS	JUMBLE SALE	KLANGFARBE
INVINCIBLY	ITINERANCY	JUMBLINGLY	KNEECAPPED
INVIOLABLE	IVORY TOWER	JUNCACEOUS	KNEE-LENGTH
INVITATION		JUNCTIONAL	KNICK-KNACK
INVITATORY	J	JUNKETINGS	KNIFE-EDGES
INVITINGLY	JACKANAPES	JURY-RIGGED	KNIGHTHEAD
INVOCATION	JACKHAMMER	JUSTICIARY	KNIGHTHOOD
INVOCATORY	JACK-KNIFED	JUSTIFYING	KNOBBLIEST
INVOLUCRAL	JACK KNIVES	JUVENILITY	KNOCKABOUT
INVOLUTION	JACKRABBIT	JUXTAPOSED	KNOCK-KNEED
IODIZATION	JACK THE LAD		KOMMUNARSK
IODOMETRIC	JACOBITISM	K	KOOKABURRA
IONIZATION	JAGUARONDI	KABARAGOYA	KRAMATORSK
IONOSPHERE	JAILBREAKS	KANTIANISM	KREMENCHUG
IRENICALLY	JAM SESSION	KARA-KALPAK	KRIEGSPIEL
IRIDACEOUS	JAMSHEDPUR	KARYOGAMIC	KRISHNAISM
IRIDECTOMY	JANITORIAL	KARYOLYMPH	KRUGERRAND
IRIDESCENT	JARDINIERE	KARYOLYSIS	KU KLUX KLAN
IRISH STEWS	JAUNTINESS	KARYOLYTIC	KUOMINTANG

L	LARGE-SCALE	LEMON SOLES	LIGHT YEARS
LABIONASAL	LARVICIDAL	LENGTHENED	LIGNOCAINE
LABIOVELAR	LARYNGITIC	LENGTHENER	LIKELIHOOD
LABORATORY	LARYNGITIS	LENGTHIEST	LIKE-MINDED
LABOR UNION	LASCIVIOUS	LENGTHWAYS	LIKENESSES
LABOUR DAYS	LAST MINUTE	LENTAMENTE	LILIACEOUS
LABOUREDLY	LATECOMERS	LENTICULAR	LIMICOLINE
LABYRINTHS	LATENT HEAT	LENTISSIMO	LIMICOLOUS
LACERATING	LATTERMOST	LEOPARDESS	LIMITARIAN
LACERATION	LAUGHINGLY	LEPIDOLITE	LIMITATION
LACERATIVE	LAUNCH PADS	LEPRECHAUN	LIMOUSINES
LACHRYMOSE	LAUNDERING	LEPTOSOMIC	LINEAMENTS
LACKLUSTRE	LAUNDRYMAN	LESBIANISM	LINECASTER
LACQUERING	LAURACEOUS	LESSEESHIP	LINGUIFORM
LACRIMATOR	LAUREATION	LETTER BOMB	LINGUISTIC
LACTESCENT	LAURENTIAN	LETTERHEAD	LINSEED OIL
LACTIC ACID	LAVATIONAL	LEUCOCYTES	LIPOMATOUS
LACTOGENIC	LAVATORIAL	LEUCOCYTIC	LIPOPHILIC
LACTOMETER	LAVATORIES	LEUCODERMA	LIP-READING
LACTOSCOPE	LAVISHNESS	LEUCOMAINE	LIP SERVICE
LACUNOSITY	LAW-ABIDING	LEUCOPENIA	LIQUEFYING
LACUSTRINE	LAW-BREAKER	LEUCOPENIC	LIQUESCENT
LADY-KILLER	LAWFULNESS	LEUCOPLAST	LIQUIDATED
LADY'S-SMOCK	LAWNMOWERS	LEVERKUSEN	LIQUIDATOR
LAMARCKIAN	LAWN TENNIS	LEVIATHANS	LIQUIDIZED
LAMARCKISM	LAWRENCIUM	LEVIGATION	LIQUIDIZER
LAMASERIES	LAY BROTHER	LEVITATING	LIQUORICES
LAMBASTING	LAY FIGURES	LEVITATION	LISSOMNESS
LAMBDACISM	LAYPERSONS	LEXICALITY	LISTENABLE
LAMBREQUIN	LAY READERS	LEXICOLOGY	LISTLESSLY
LAMELLATED	LAY SISTERS	LIBATIONAL	LIST PRICES
LAMENTABLE	LEADERSHIP	LIBERALISM	LITERALISM
LAMENTABLY	LEAF-HOPPER	LIBERALIST	LITERALIST
LAMINATING	LEAFLETING	LIBERALITY	LITERARILY
LAMINATION	LEASEBACKS	LIBERALIZE	LITERATELY
LAMPOONERY	LEAVENINGS	LIBERATING	LITERATION
LAMPOONING	LEBENSRAUM	LIBERATION	LITERATURE
LAMPSHADES	LECTIONARY	LIBERATORS	LITHOGRAPH
LANCASHIRE	LECTORSHIP	LIBERTINES	LITHOLOGIC
LANCEOLATE	LEFT-HANDED	LIBIDINOUS	LITHOMARGE
LAND AGENTS	LEFT-HANDER	LIBRARIANS	LITHOPHYTE
LANDING NET	LEFT-WINGER	LIBRETTIST	LITHOTOMIC
LANDLADIES	LEGALISTIC	LIBREVILLE	LITHOTRITY
LANDLOCKED	LEGALIZING	LICENSABLE	LITHUANIAN
LANDLUBBER	LEGATESHIP	LICENTIATE	LITIGATING
LANDMASSES	LEGATORIAL	LICENTIOUS	LITIGATION
LAND ROVERS	LEGIBILITY	LIEUTENANT	LITTERBINS
LANDSCAPED	LEGISLATED	LIFE CYCLES	LITTERLOUT
LANDSCAPES	LEGISLATOR	LIFEGUARDS	LITURGICAL
LANDSLIDES	LEGITIMACY	LIFE JACKET	LIVABILITY
LANGLAUFER	LEGITIMATE	LIFELESSLY	LIVELIHOOD
LANGUISHED	LEGITIMISM	LIFE-SAVING	LIVELINESS
LANGUISHER	LEGITIMIST	LIFESTYLES	LIVING ROOM
LANGUOROUS	LEGITIMIZE	LIGHT BULBS	LIVING WAGE
LANIFEROUS	LEGUMINOUS	LIGHTENING	LOADSTONES
LANTHANIDE	LEG-WARMERS	LIGHTERAGE	LOBOTOMIES
LAPAROTOMY	LEISHMANIA	LIGHTHOUSE	LOBSTERPOT
LAPIDARIAN	LEITMOTIVS	LIGHTNINGS	LOBULATION
LAPIDARIES	LEMNISCATE	LIGHTSHIPS	LOCAL DERBY

LOCALISTIC	LUBRICATOR	MAGNETIZED	MANICURIST
LOCALITIES	LUBRICIOUS	MAGNETIZER	MANIFESTED
LOCALIZING	LUBUMBASHI	MAGNIFIERS	MANIFESTLY
LOCKER ROOM	LUCUBRATOR	MAGNIFYING	MANIFESTOS
LOCK KEEPER	LUGGAGE VAN	MAGNITUDES	MANIFOLDER
LOCKSMITHS	LUGUBRIOUS	MAGNUM OPUS	MANIPULATE
LOCKSTITCH	LULUABOURG	MAIDENHAIR	MANNEQUINS
LOCOMOTION	LUMBERJACK	MAIDENHEAD	MANNERISMS
LOCOMOTIVE	LUMBER-ROOM	MAIDENHOOD	MANOEUVRED
LOCULATION	LUMBERYARD	MAIDEN NAME	MANOEUVRER
LODESTONES	LUMBRICOID	MAIN CHANCE	MANOEUVRES
LOGANBERRY	LUMINARIES	MAIN CLAUSE	MAN OF STRAW
LOGARITHMS	LUMINOSITY	MAINFRAMES	MANOMETERS
LOGGERHEAD	LUMINOUSLY	MAINLINING	MANOMETRIC
LOGICALITY	LUMISTEROL	MAINSPRING	MANOR HOUSE
LOGISTICAL	LUNAR MONTH	MAINSTREAM	MANSERVANT
LOGOGRAPHY	LURCHINGLY	MAINTAINED	MANTELTREE
LOGOPAEDIC	LUSCIOUSLY	MAINTAINER	MANTICALLY
LOGORRHOEA	LUSTRATION	MAISONETTE	MANUSCRIPT
LOGROLLING	LUSTRATIVE	MAJOR-DOMOS	MANZANILLA
LOINCLOTHS	LUSTREWARE	MAJORETTES	MARASCHINO
LOIR-ET-CHER	LUSTROUSLY	MAJORITIES	MARCESCENT
LONELINESS	LUTINE BELL	MAJOR SUITS	MARCH-PASTS
LONGHAIRED	LUXEMBOURG	MAJUSCULAR	MARCONI RIG
LONG-HEADED	LUXURIANCE	MAKESHIFTS	MARE'S NESTS
LONGITUDES	LUXURIATED	MAKEWEIGHT	MARGARITAS
LONG-JUMPER	LYCOPODIUM	MALACOLOGY	MARGINALIA
LONGWINDED	LYMPHOCYTE	MALADDRESS	MARGINALLY
LOOK-ALIKES	LYOPHILIZE	MALAPROPOS	MARGUERITE
LOPHOPHORE		MALCONTENT	MARINATING
LOQUACIOUS	M	MALEFACTOR	MARINATION
LORDLINESS	MAASTRICHT	MALEFICENT	MARIONETTE
LORGNETTES	MACADAMIZE	MALEVOLENT	MARKEDNESS
LORRY PARKS	MACEBEARER	MALFEASANT	MARKETABLE
LOS ANGELES	MACEDONIAN	MALIGNANCY	MARKETABLY
LOSS LEADER	MACERATING	MALINGERED	MARKETEERS
LOST CAUSES	MACERATION	MALINGERER	MARKET TOWN
LOTUS-EATER	MACERATIVE	MALODOROUS	MARKSWOMAN
LOUDHAILER	MACHINABLE	MALPIGHIAN	MARLACIOUS
LOUDMOUTHS	MACHINATOR	MALTED MILK	MARQUISATE
LOUISVILLE	MACHINE GUN	MALTHUSIAN	MARROWBONE
LOUNGE BARS	MACHINISTS	MALTREATED	MARSHALING
LOUNGE SUIT	MACH NUMBER	MALTREATER	MARSHALLED
LOVABILITY	MACKINTOSH	MALVACEOUS	MARSHALLER
LOVE AFFAIR	MACROCOSMS	MANAGEABLE	MARSHINESS
LOVELINESS	MACROCYTIC	MANAGEABLY	MARSUPIALS
LOVEMAKING	MACROGRAPH	MANAGEMENT	MARTELLATO
LOVING CUPS	MACROPHAGE	MANAGERESS	MARTENSITE
LOWBROWISM	MACROSPORE	MANAGERIAL	MARTIAL ART
LOWER CLASS	MACULATION	MANCHINEEL	MARTIALISM
LOWER HOUSE	MADAGASCAN	MANCHURIAN	MARTIALIST
LOWERINGLY	MADAGASCAR	MANCUNIANS	MARTIAL LAW
LOWLANDERS	MADREPORAL	MANEUVERED	MARTINGALE
LOW-PITCHED	MAELSTROMS	MAN FRIDAYS	MARTINICAN
LOW PROFILE	MAGIC WANDS	MANFULNESS	MARTINIQUE
LOW-TENSION	MAGISTRACY	MANGOSTEEN	MARVELLING
LOXODROMIC	MAGISTRATE	MANHANDLED	MARVELLOUS
LUBRICANTS	MAGNA CARTA	MANIACALLY	MARVELMENT
LUBRICATED	MAGNETITIC	MANICURING	MARXIANISM

MASOCHISTS	MEDDLINGLY	MESENTERON	MICROCHIPS
MASQUERADE	MEDICAMENT	MESITYLENE	MICROCLINE
MASSACRING	MEDICATION	MESMERISTS	MICROCOSMS
MASSASAUGA	MEDICATIVE	MESMERIZED	MICROCYTIC
MASSETERIC	MEDIOCRITY	MESMERIZER	MICROFICHE
MASTECTOMY	MEDITATING	MESOCRATIC	MICROFILMS
MASTER CARD	MEDITATION	MESODERMAL	MICROGRAPH
MASTERHOOD	MEDITATIVE	MESOLITHIC	MICROMETER
MASTER KEYS	MEDIUM WAVE	MESOMORPHY	MICROMETRY
MASTERMIND	MEDULLATED	MESOPHYTIC	MICROPHONE
MASTERSHIP	MEERSCHAUM	MESOSPHERE	MICROPHYTE
MASTERWORK	MEGAGAMETE	MESOTHORAX	MICROPRINT
MASTICABLE	MEGALITHIC	MESSENGERS	MICROPYLAR
MASTICATED	MEGAPHONES	METABOLISM	MICROSCOPE
MASTICATOR	MEGAPHONIC	METABOLITE	MICROSCOPY
MASTURBATE	MEGASPORIC	METABOLIZE	MICROSEISM
MATCHBOARD	MELANCHOLY	METACARPAL	MICROSOMAL
MATCHBOXES	MELANESIAN	METACARPUS	MICROSPORE
MATCHMAKER	MELANISTIC	METACENTRE	MICROTOMIC
MATCH POINT	MELANOCYTE	METAFEMALE	MICROTONAL
MATCHSTICK	MELANOSITY	METAGALAXY	MICROWAVES
MATERIALLY	MELBURNIAN	METALLURGY	MIDDLE-AGED
MATERNALLY	MELIACEOUS	METAMERISM	MIDDLE AGES
MATO GROSSO	MELIORABLE	METAPHORIC	MIDDLEBROW
MATRIARCHS	MELIORATOR	METAPHRASE	MIDDLE EAST
MATRIARCHY	MELISMATIC	METAPHRAST	MIDDLE NAME
MATRICIDAL	MELLOPHONE	METAPHYSIC	MIDDLE WEST
MATRICIDES	MELLOWNESS	METAPLASIA	MIDLOTHIAN
MATRILOCAL	MELODRAMAS	METASTABLE	MIDSECTION
MATTERHORN	MELTING POT	METASTASIS	MIDSHIPMAN
MATTRESSES	MEMBERSHIP	METASTATIC	MIDSHIPMEN
MATURATION	MEMBRANOUS	METATARSUS	MIDWESTERN
MATURATIVE	MEMORANDUM	METATHEORY	MIGHTINESS
MAUDLINISM	MEMORIZING	METATHESIS	MIGNONETTE
MAUNDERING	MENACINGLY	METATHETIC	MIGRAINOID
MAURITANIA	MENAGERIES	METATHORAX	MIGRATIONS
MAUSOLEUMS	MENARCHEAL	METEORITES	MILEOMETER
MAXILLIPED	MENDACIOUS	METEORITIC	MILESTONES
MAXIMALIST	MENDICANCY	METHIONINE	MILITANTLY
MAXIMIZING	MENDICANTS	METHODICAL	MILITARILY
MAXISINGLE	MENINGITIC	METHODISTS	MILITARISM
MAYONNAISE	MENINGITIS	METHODIZER	MILITARIST
MAYORESSES	MEN OF STRAW	METHUSELAH	MILITARIZE
MEADOWLARK	MENOPAUSAL	METHYLATOR	MILITATING
MEAGRENESS	MENOPAUSIC	METHYLDOPA	MILITATION
MEANDERING	MENSTRUATE	METICULOUS	MILITIAMAN
MEANINGFUL	MENSTRUOUS	METOESTRUS	MILK FLOATS
MEANS TESTS	MENSURABLE	METRICALLY	MILK SHAKES
MEASLINESS	MENTAL AGES	METRICIZED	MILLENNIAL
MEASURABLE	MENTAL NOTE	METRIC TONS	MILLENNIUM
MEASURABLY	MENTIONING	METRONOMES	MILLEPEDES
MEASUREDLY	MERCANTILE	METRONOMIC	MILLESIMAL
MECHANICAL	MERCAPTIDE	METRONYMIC	MILLIGRAMS
MECHANISMS	MERCIFULLY	METROPOLIS	MILLILITRE
MECHANIZED	MERIDIONAL	METTLESOME	MILLIMETRE
MECHANIZER	MERRYMAKER	MEZZANINES	MILLIONTHS
MEDALLIONS	MERSEYSIDE	MEZZOTINTS	MILLIPEDES
MEDALLISTS	MESENCHYME	MICHAELMAS	MILLSTONES
MEDDLESOME	MESENTERIC	MICKEY FINN	MILLSTREAM

MILLWHEELS	MISPRISION	MONGRELISM	MORALIZERS
MILLWRIGHT	MISQUOTING	MONGRELIZE	MORALIZING
MILOMETERS	MISREADING	MONILIFORM	MORATORIUM
MIMEOGRAPH	MISSIONARY	MONITORIAL	MORBIDNESS
MINATORILY	MISSOURIAN	MONITORING	MORDACIOUS
MINDLESSLY	MISSPELLED	MONKEY NUTS	MORDVINIAN
MIND READER	MISSTATING	MONOCARPIC	MORGANATIC
MINEFIELDS	MISSUPPOSE	MONOCHROME	MOROSENESS
MINERALIZE	MISTAKABLE	MONOCLINAL	MORPHEUSES
MINERALOGY	MISTAKABLY	MONOCLINIC	MORPHINISM
MINERAL OIL	MISTAKENLY	MONOCRATIC	MORPHOLOGY
MINESTRONE	MISTRESSES	MONOCYCLIC	MORTAL SINS
MINIATURES	MISTRUSTED	MONOCYTOID	MORTGAGEES
MINIMALIST	MISTRUSTER	MONOECIOUS	MORTGAGING
MINIMIZING	MITIGATING	MONOGAMIST	MORTGAGORS
MINISTERED	MITIGATION	MONOGAMOUS	MORTICIANS
MINISTRANT	MITIGATIVE	MONOGENOUS	MORTIFYING
MINISTRIES	MIXABILITY	MONOGRAPHS	MORTUARIES
MINNESOTAN	MIXED GRILL	MONOGYNIST	MOSQUITOES
MINORITIES	MIXOLYDIAN	MONOGYNOUS	MOTHERHOOD
MINOR SUITS	MIZZENMAST	MONOHYBRID	MOTHERLESS
MINSTRELSY	MOBILE HOME	MONOLITHIC	MOTHER'S BOY
MINT JULEPS	MOBILIZING	MONOLOGIST	MOTHER'S DAY
MINUSCULAR	MOBOCRATIC	MONOLOGUES	MOTHER-TO-BE
MINUTENESS	MOCK-HEROIC	MONOMANIAC	MOTHERWORT
MIRACIDIAL	MODERATELY	MONOMEROUS	MOTIONLESS
MIRACIDIUM	MODERATING	MONOPHOBIA	MOTIVATING
MIRACULOUS	MODERATION	MONOPHOBIC	MOTIVATION
MIRTHFULLY	MODERATORS	MONOPHONIC	MOTIVATIVE
MISAPPLIED	MODERNISMS	MONOPLANES	MOTIVELESS
MISBEHAVED	MODERNISTS	MONOPLEGIA	MOTONEURON
MISBEHAVER	MODERNIZED	MONOPLEGIC	MOTORBIKES
MISCALLING	MODERNIZER	MONOPODIAL	MOTORBOATS
MISCARRIED	MODERNNESS	MONOPODIUM	MOTORCADES
MISCASTING	MODIFIABLE	MONOPOLIES	MOTORCYCLE
MISCELLANY	MODISHNESS	MONOPOLISM	MOTORIZING
MISCHANCES	MODULATING	MONOPOLIST	MOTOR LODGE
MISCH METAL	MODULATION	MONOPOLIZE	MOTS JUSTES
MISCONDUCT	MODULATIVE	MONOPTEROS	MOULDBOARD
MISCOUNTED	MOGADISCIO	MONOTHEISM	MOULDERING
MISCREANTS	MOHAMMEDAN	MONOTHEIST	MOULDINESS
MISERICORD	MOISTENING	MONOTONOUS	MOUNTEBANK
MISFORTUNE	MOISTURIZE	MONOVALENT	MOURNFULLY
MISGIVINGS	MOLLIFYING	MONSIGNORS	MOUSETRAPS
MISHANDLED	MOLLUSCOID	MONSTRANCE	MOUSSELINE
MISHEARING	MOLYBDENUM	MONTE CARLO	MOUSTACHES
MISJOINDER	MONADISTIC	MONTENEGRO	MOUTH ORGAN
MISJUDGING	MONADOLOGY	MONTEVIDEO	MOUTHPIECE
MISLEADING	MONANDROUS	MONTGOMERY	MOVABILITY
MISMANAGED	MONANTHOUS	MONTMARTRE	MOVIE STARS
MISMANAGER	MONARCHIES	MONUMENTAL	MOVING VANS
MISMATCHED	MONARCHISM	MONZONITIC	MOZAMBIQUE
MISMATCHES	MONARCHIST	MOONFLOWER	MOZZARELLA
MISOGAMIST	MONEGASQUE	MOONSCAPES	MUCKRAKERS
MISOGYNIST	MONETARISM	MOONSTONES	MUCKRAKING
MISOGYNOUS	MONETARIST	MOONSTRUCK	MUDDLINGLY
MISOLOGIST	MONEYBOXES	MOOT POINTS	MUDSKIPPER
MISPLACING	MONEYMAKER	MORALISTIC	MUDSLINGER
MISPRINTED	MONEY ORDER	MORALITIES	MUHAMMADAN

MULBERRIES	NAMBY-PAMBY	NEGOTIATOR	NIGHTSTICK
MULIEBRITY	NAMEPLATES	NEIGHBOURS	NIGRESCENT
MULISHNESS	NANNY GOATS	NEMATOCYST	NIHILISTIC
MULTIBIRTH	NANOSECOND	NEOLOGICAL	NIMBLENESS
MULTIMEDIA	NAPKIN RING	NEOLOGISMS	NINCOMPOOP
MULTIPLANE	NAPOLEONIC	NEON LIGHTS	NINETEENTH
MULTIPLIED	NARCISSISM	NEOPLASTIC	NINETIETHS
MULTIPLIER	NARCISSIST	NEPENTHEAN	NINETY-NINE
MULTISTAGE	NARCOLEPSY	NEPHOGRAPH	NINGSIA HUI
MULTITUDES	NARRATABLE	NEPHOSCOPE	NIPPLEWORT
MUMBLINGLY	NARRATIONS	NEPHRALGIA	NISSEN HUTS
MUMBO JUMBO	NARRATIVES	NEPHRALGIC	NITPICKERS
MUMMIFYING	NARROW BOAT	NEPHRIDIAL	NITPICKING
MUNIFICENT	NARROWNESS	NEPHRIDIUM	NITRIC ACID
MURPHY'S LAW	NASTURTIUM	NEPHROTOMY	NITROMETER
MUSCOVITES	NATATIONAL	NEPOTISTIC	NO-ACCOUNTS
MUSCULARLY	NATIONALLY	NETHERMOST	NOBEL PRIZE
MUSHROOMED	NATIONHOOD	NETTLE RASH	NOBILITIES
MUSICAL BOX	NATIONWIDE	NETTLESOME	NO-MAN'S-LAND
MUSIC HALLS	NATIVISTIC	NETWORKING	NOM DE PLUME
MUSICOLOGY	NATIVITIES	NEURECTOMY	NOMINALISM
MUSKETEERS	NATTERJACK	NEUROBLAST	NOMINALIST
MUSKETRIES	NATURAL GAS	NEUROCOELE	NOMINATING
MUSTACHIOS	NATURALISM	NEUROGENIC	NOMINATION
MUSTARD GAS	NATURALIST	NEUROLEMMA	NOMINATIVE
MUTABILITY	NATURALIZE	NEUROPATHY	NOMOGRAPHY
MUTATIONAL	NATUROPATH	NEUTRALISM	NOMOLOGIST
MUTILATING	NAUGHTIEST	NEUTRALIST	NOMOTHETIC
MUTILATION	NAUSEATING	NEUTRALITY	NONALIGNED
MUTILATIVE	NAUSEATION	NEUTRALIZE	NONCHALANT
MUTINOUSLY	NAUSEOUSLY	NEUTROPHIL	NONDRINKER
MUTUAL FUND	NAUTICALLY	NEVER-NEVER	NONESUCHES
MYASTHENIA	NAVIGATING	NEWFANGLED	NONETHICAL
MYASTHENIC	NAVIGATION	NEWS AGENCY	NONFACTUAL
MYCETOZOAN	NAVIGATORS	NEWSAGENTS	NONFERROUS
MYCOLOGIST	NEAPOLITAN	NEWSCASTER	NONFICTION
MYCORRHIZA	NEAR MISSES	NEWSHOUNDS	NONJOINDER
MYCOSTATIN	NEAR THINGS	NEWSLETTER	NONMEDICAL
MYOCARDIAL	NEBULOSITY	NEWSPAPERS	NO-NONSENSE
MYOCARDIUM	NEBULOUSLY	NEWSREADER	NONPAREILS
MYOGRAPHIC	NECROLATRY	NEWSSHEETS	NONPAYMENT
MYOPICALLY	NECROMANCY	NEWSSTANDS	NONPLUSSED
MYRIAPODAN	NECROPHOBE	NEWSVENDOR	NONSMOKERS
MYRTACEOUS	NECROPOLIS	NEWSWORTHY	NONSMOKING
MYSTAGOGIC	NEEDLEFISH	NEWTON'S LAW	NONSTARTER
MYSTAGOGUE	NEEDLESSLY	NEW ZEALAND	NONSTATIVE
MYSTERIOUS	NEEDLEWORK	NICARAGUAN	NON-STRIKER
MYSTICALLY	NE'ER-DO-WELL	NICKELLING	NONTYPICAL
MYSTIFYING	NEGATIVELY	NICKNAMING	NONVIOLENT
MYTHICIZER	NEGATIVING	NICOTINISM	NORMALIZED
MYTHOMANIA	NEGATIVISM	NIDICOLOUS	NORRKOPING
MYTHOPOEIA	NEGATIVIST	NIDIFUGOUS	NORTHBOUND
MYTHOPOEIC	NEGLECTFUL	NIGHTCLUBS	NORTHERNER
MYXOEDEMIC	NEGLECTING	NIGHTDRESS	NORTH POLES
MYXOMATOUS	NEGLIGENCE	NIGHTLIGHT	NORTHWARDS
MYXOMYCETE	NEGLIGIBLE	NIGHTMARES	NOSEBLEEDS
	NEGLIGIBLY	NIGHTSHADE	NOSEDIVING
N	NEGOTIABLE	NIGHT SHIFT	NOSOGRAPHY
NAIL-BITING	NEGOTIATED	NIGHTSHIRT	NOSOLOGIST

NOSTOLOGIC	OBLIGATING	OLDE WORLDE	ORDINARILY
NOSY PARKER	OBLIGATION	OLD MAIDISH	ORDINATION
NOTABILITY	OBLIGATIVE	OLD MASTERS	ORDONNANCE
NOTARIZING	OBLIGATORY	OLD SCHOOLS	ORDOVICIAN
NOTATIONAL	OBLIGINGLY	OLEAGINOUS	ORGANICISM
NOTEWORTHY	OBLITERATE	OLEOGRAPHY	ORGANICIST
NOTICEABLE	OBSEQUIOUS	OLIGARCHIC	ORGANISMAL
NOTICEABLY	OBSERVABLE	OLIGOCLASE	ORGANIZERS
NOTIFIABLE	OBSERVABLY	OLIGOPSONY	ORGANIZING
NOTTINGHAM	OBSERVANCE	OLIGURETIC	ORGANOLOGY
NOURISHING	OBSESSIONS	OLIVACEOUS	ORIENTATED
NOVACULITE	OBSESSIVES	OMMATIDIAL	ORIGINALLY
NOVA SCOTIA	OBSTETRICS	OMMATIDIUM	ORIGINATED
NOVELETTES	OBSTRUCTED	OMNIPOTENT	ORIGINATOR
NOVELISTIC	OBSTRUCTER	OMNISCIENT	ORNAMENTAL
NOVITIATES	OBTAINABLE	OMNIVOROUS	ORNAMENTED
NUCLEATION	OBTAINMENT	ONCOLOGIST	ORNATENESS
NUCLEONICS	OBTUSENESS	ONE ANOTHER	ORNITHOPOD
NUCLEOSIDE	OBVOLUTION	ONE-MAN BAND	ORNITHOSIS
NUCLEOTIDE	OBVOLUTIVE	ONE-SIDEDLY	OROGRAPHER
NUDIBRANCH	OCCASIONAL	ONOMASTICS	OROGRAPHIC
NULLIFYING	OCCASIONED	ONSLAUGHTS	OROLOGICAL
NUMBERLESS	OCCIDENTAL	OOPHORITIC	ORPHANAGES
NUMBSKULLS	OCCUPATION	OOPHORITIS	ORTHOCLASE
NUMERATION	OCCURRENCE	OOPS-A-DAISY	ORTHOGENIC
NUMERATIVE	OCEANARIUM	OPALESCENT	ORTHOGONAL
NUMERATORS	OCEANGOING	OPAQUENESS	OSCILLATED
NUMEROLOGY	OCEANOLOGY	OPEN-HANDED	OSCILLATOR
NUMEROUSLY	OCELLATION	OPEN LETTER	OSCULATION
NUMISMATIC	OCHLOCRACY	OPEN-MINDED	OSCULATORY
NUMMULITIC	OCTAHEDRAL	OPEN SEASON	OSMIRIDIUM
NUNCIATURE	OCTAHEDRON	OPEN SECRET	OSMOMETRIC
NURSELINGS	OCTAMEROUS	OPEN SESAME	OSSIFEROUS
NURSEMAIDS	OCTANGULAR	OPERATIONS	OSTENSIBLE
NURSERYMAN	OCTAVALENT	OPERATIVES	OSTENSIBLY
NURSERYMEN	OCTODECIMO	OPERETTIST	OSTEOBLAST
NURTURABLE	OCULOMOTOR	OPHICLEIDE	OSTEOCLAST
NUTATIONAL	ODALISQUES	OPHTHALMIA	OSTEOPATHS
NUTCRACKER	ODD-PINNATE	OPHTHALMIC	OSTEOPATHY
NUTRITIOUS	ODIOUSNESS	OPPILATION	OSTEOPHYTE
NYCTALOPIA	ODONTALGIA	OPPOSINGLY	OSTRACIZED
NYCTINASTY	ODONTALGIC	OPPOSITION	OSTRACIZER
NYMPHOLEPT	ODONTOLOGY	OPPRESSING	OSTRACODAN
	OEDEMATOUS	OPPRESSION	OTOLOGICAL
O	OENOLOGIST	OPPRESSIVE	OUANANICHE
OAFISHNESS	OESOPHAGUS	OPPRESSORS	OUBLIETTES
OAST HOUSES	OESTRADIOL	OPPROBRIUM	OUIJA BOARD
OBDURATELY	OFFENSIVES	OPTICAL ART	OUTBALANCE
OBEDIENTLY	OFFICE BOYS	OPTIMISTIC	OUTBIDDING
OBEISANCES	OFFICIALLY	OPTIMIZING	OUTBRAVING
OBELISKOID	OFFICIATED	OPTIONALLY	OUTCLASSED
OBERHAUSEN	OFFICIATOR	OPTOMETRIC	OUTFIELDER
OBFUSCATED	OFF-LICENCE	ORANGEWOOD	OUTFITTERS
OBITUARIES	OFF-LOADING	ORANGUTANG	OUTFITTING
OBITUARIST	OFF-PUTTING	ORATORICAL	OUTFLANKED
OBJECTIONS	OFFSETTING	ORCHESTRAL	OUTGENERAL
OBJECTIVES	OFF-THE-WALL	ORCHESTRAS	OUTGROWING
OBJETS D'ART	OIL-BEARING	ORDER PAPER	OUTGROWTHS
OBJURGATOR	OIL TANKERS	ORDINANCES	OUT-HERODED

OUTLANDISH	OVERSTAYED	PALM SUNDAY	PARANORMAL
OUTLASTING	OVERSTRUNG	PALPATIONS	PARAPHRASE
OUT OF DOORS	OVERTAXING	PALPEBRATE	PARAPHYSIS
OUTPATIENT	OVERTHROWN	PALPITATED	PARAPLEGIA
OUTPLAYING	OVERTHROWS	PALSY-WALSY	PARAPLEGIC
OUTPOINTED	OVERTHRUST	PALTRINESS	PARAPODIUM
OUTPOURING	OVERTOPPED	PALYNOLOGY	PARAPRAXIS
OUTRAGEOUS	OVERTURNED	PANAMANIAN	PARASELENE
OUTRANKING	OVERWEIGHT	PAN-ARABISM	PARASITISM
OUTRIGGERS	OVERWORKED	PANCAKE DAY	PARASITIZE
OUTRIVALED	OVIPOSITOR	PANCREASES	PARASTICHY
OUTRUNNING	OVULATIONS	PANCREATIC	PARATACTIC
OUTSELLING	OXIDIMETRY	PANCREATIN	PARATROOPS
OUTSHINING	OXYCEPHALY	PANEGYRICS	PARBOILING
OUTSMARTED	OXYGENATED	PANEGYRIST	PARCELLING
OUTSTARING	OXYGENIZER	PANEGYRIZE	PARCEL POST
OUTSTATION	OXYGEN MASK	PANELLISTS	PARCHMENTS
OUTSTAYING	OXYGEN TENT	PANGENESIS	PARDONABLE
OUTSTRETCH	OYSTER BEDS	PANGENETIC	PARDONABLY
OUTSWINGER	OZONOLYSIS	PANHANDLED	PARENCHYMA
OUTTALKING		PANHANDLER	PARENTERAL
OUTWEIGHED	P	PANHANDLES	PARENTHOOD
OUTWITTING	PACE BOWLER	PANICULATE	PARI-MUTUEL
OUTWORKERS	PACEMAKERS	PANJANDRUM	PARISH-PUMP
OVARIOTOMY	PACHYDERMS	PANTALOONS	PARKING LOT
OVERACTING	PACK ANIMAL	PANTHEISTS	PARK KEEPER
OVERACTIVE	PACKSADDLE	PANTOGRAPH	PARLIAMENT
OVERARCHED	PACKTHREAD	PANTOMIMES	PARLOR CARS
OVERBOOKED	PADDLEFISH	PANTOMIMIC	PARONYMOUS
OVERBURDEN	PADLOCKING	PAPAVERINE	PAROXYSMAL
OVERCHARGE	PAEDERASTS	PAPERBACKS	PARRICIDAL
OVERCOMING	PAEDERASTY	PAPERBOARD	PARRICIDES
OVERDOSAGE	PAEDIATRIC	PAPER CHASE	PARROTFISH
OVERDOSING	PAGANISTIC	PAPER CLIPS	PARSONAGES
OVERDRAFTS	PAGINATION	PAPERINESS	PARTIALITY
OVEREXPOSE	PAILLASSES	PAPER KNIFE	PARTICIPLE
OVERFLIGHT	PAINKILLER	PAPER MONEY	PARTICULAR
OVERFLOWED	PAINLESSLY	PAPER TIGER	PARTITIONS
OVERFLYING	PAINTBRUSH	PAPISTICAL	PARTITIVES
OVERHAULED	PAKISTANIS	PARABIOSIS	PARTNERING
OVERIJSSEL	PALAEOCENE	PARABIOTIC	PARTRIDGES
OVERLAPPED	PALAEOGENE	PARABOLIST	PARTURIENT
OVERLAYING	PALAEOLITH	PARABOLIZE	PARTY LINES
OVERLOADED	PALAEOZOIC	PARABOLOID	PARTY PIECE
OVERLOOKED	PALANQUINS	PARACHUTED	PARTY WALLS
OVERMANNED	PALATALIZE	PARACHUTES	PASQUINADE
OVERMASTER	PALATIALLY	PARAGRAPHS	PASSAGEWAY
OVERMATTER	PALATINATE	PARAGUAYAN	PASSENGERS
OVERPASSES	PALEACEOUS	PARALLELED	PASSIONATE
OVERPLAYED	PALIMPSEST	PARALOGISM	PASTEBOARD
OVERRATING	PALINDROME	PARALOGIST	PASTELLIST
OVERRIDDEN	PALLBEARER	PARALYSING	PASTEURISM
OVERRIDING	PALLIASSES	PARALYTICS	PASTEURIZE
OVERRULING	PALLIATING	PARAMECIUM	PAST MASTER
OVERSEEING	PALLIATION	PARAMEDICS	PASTY-FACED
OVERSHADOW	PALLIATIVE	PARAMETERS	PATCHINESS
OVERSIGHTS	PALLIDNESS	PARAMETRIC	PATCHWORKS
OVERSPILLS	PALMACEOUS	PARAMNESIA	PATENTABLE
OVERSTATED	PALMETTOES	PARANOIACS	PATERNALLY

PATHFINDER	PENETRABLE	PERFORMERS	PERSONABLE
PATHOGENIC	PENETRALIA	PERFORMING	PERSONABLY
PATISSERIE	PENETRANCE	PERICLINAL	PERSONAGES
PATRIARCHS	PENETRATED	PERICYCLIC	PERSONALLY
PATRIARCHY	PENETRATOR	PERIDERMAL	PERSONALTY
PATRICIANS	PEN FRIENDS	PERIDOTITE	PERSONATOR
PATRICIATE	PENICILLIN	PERIGYNOUS	PERSPIRING
PATRICIDAL	PENINSULAR	PERIHELION	PERSUADING
PATRICIDES	PENINSULAS	PERILOUSLY	PERSUASION
PATRILOCAL	PENITENTLY	PERIMETERS	PERSUASIVE
PATRIOTISM	PENMANSHIP	PERIMETRIC	PERTAINING
PATROL CARS	PENNYCRESS	PERIMYSIUM	PERTINENCE
PATROLLING	PENNYROYAL	PERIODICAL	PERTURBING
PATRONIZED	PENNYWORTH	PERIOSTEUM	PERVERSELY
PATRONIZER	PENOLOGIST	PERIPETEIA	PERVERSION
PATRONYMIC	PEN PUSHERS	PERIPHERAL	PERVERSITY
PATTERNING	PENSIONARY	PERIPHYTON	PERVERTING
PAWNBROKER	PENSIONERS	PERIPTERAL	PESSIMISTS
PAYMASTERS	PENSIONING	PERISARCAL	PESTICIDAL
PAY PACKETS	PENTAGONAL	PERISCOPES	PESTICIDES
PAY STATION	PENTAGRAMS	PERISCOPIC	PESTILENCE
PEACE CORPS	PENTAMETER	PERISHABLE	PETIT FOURS
PEACEFULLY	PENTAQUINE	PERISTOMAL	PETITIONED
PEACEMAKER	PENTASTICH	PERISTYLAR	PETITIONER
PEACE PIPES	PENTATEUCH	PERISTYLES	PETIT POINT
PEACHINESS	PENTATHLON	PERITONEAL	PETITS POIS
PEACH MELBA	PENTHOUSES	PERITONEUM	PETRIFYING
PEARL DIVER	PENTIMENTO	PERITRICHA	PETROGLYPH
PEARLINESS	PENTSTEMON	PERIWINKLE	PETROLATUM
PEAR-SHAPED	PEPPERCORN	PERMAFROST	PETROPOLIS
PEASHOOTER	PEPPER MILL	PERMANENCE	PETTICOATS
PEA SOUPERS	PEPPERMINT	PERMANENCY	PETULANTLY
PEBBLEDASH	PEPPER POTS	PERMANENTS	PHAGOCYTES
PECCADILLO	PEPPERWORT	PERMEATING	PHAGOCYTIC
PECTIZABLE	PEPSINOGEN	PERMEATION	PHAGOMANIA
PECULATING	PEPTIZABLE	PERMEATIVE	PHALANGEAL
PECULATION	PEPTONIZER	PERMISSION	PHALLICISM
PECULIARLY	PERACIDITY	PERMISSIVE	PHALLICIST
PEDAGOGISM	PERCEIVING	PERMITTING	PHANEROGAM
PEDAGOGUES	PERCENTAGE	PERNAMBUCO	PHANTASIES
PEDANTRIES	PERCENTILE	PERNICIOUS	PHANTASMAL
PEDERASTIC	PERCEPTION	PERNICKETY	PHARISAISM
PEDESTRIAN	PERCEPTIVE	PERORATION	PHARMACIES
PEDIATRICS	PERCEPTUAL	PEROXIDASE	PHARMACIST
PEDICULATE	PERCIPIENT	PERPETRATE	PHARYNGEAL
PEDICULOUS	PERCOLATED	PERPETUATE	PHELLODERM
PEDICURIST	PERCOLATOR	PERPETUITY	PHENACAINE
PEDIMENTAL	PERCUSSION	PERPLEXING	PHENACETIN
PEDOLOGIST	PERCUSSIVE	PERPLEXITY	PHENFORMIN
PEEPING TOM	PEREMPTORY	PERQUISITE	PHENOCRYST
PEGMATITIC	PERENNIALS	PERSECUTED	PHENOMENAL
PEJORATION	PERFECTING	PERSECUTOR	PHENOMENON
PEJORATIVE	PERFECTION	PERSEVERED	PHENOTYPIC
PELLAGROUS	PERFECTIVE	PERSIAN CAT	PHILATELIC
PELLICULAR	PERFIDIOUS	PERSIENNES	PHILIPPICS
PELLUCIDLY	PERFOLIATE	PERSIFLAGE	PHILIPPINE
PENALIZING	PERFORABLE	PERSIMMONS	PHILISTINE
PENCILLING	PERFORATED	PERSISTENT	PHILOSOPHY
PENDENTIVE	PERFORATOR	PERSISTING	PHLEBOTOMY

PHLEGMATIC	PICHICIEGO	PITYRIASIS	PLUMB LINES
PHLOGISTIC	PICKPOCKET	PLACARDING	PLUMMETING
PHLOGISTON	PICNICKERS	PLACE CARDS	PLUNDERERS
PHLOGOPITE	PICNICKING	PLACEMENTS	PLUNDERING
PHOCOMELIA	PICRIC ACID	PLAGIARISM	PLUNDEROUS
PHOENICIAN	PICROTOXIC	PLAGIARIST	PLUPERFECT
PHONE BOOKS	PICROTOXIN	PLAGIARIZE	PLURALISTS
PHONE BOXES	PICTOGRAPH	PLAINCHANT	PLURALIZER
PHONEYNESS	PIED-A-TERRE	PLAIN FLOUR	PLUTOCRACY
PHONEY WARS	PIERCINGLY	PLAINTIFFS	PLUTOCRATS
PHONICALLY	PIGEONHOLE	PLANCHETTE	PNEUMATICS
PHONOGRAPH	PIGEON-TOED	PLANETARIA	POCKETABLE
PHONOLITIC	PIGGYBACKS	PLANE TREES	POCKETBOOK
PHONOMETER	PIGGYBANKS	PLANGENTLY	POCKETFULS
PHONOSCOPE	PIGMENTARY	PLANIMETER	POCKMARKED
PHONOTYPIC	PIGSTICKER	PLANIMETRY	PODIATRIST
PHOSGENITE	PIKESTAFFS	PLANK-SHEER	POETASTERS
PHOSPHATES	PILE DRIVER	PLANKTONIC	POETICALLY
PHOSPHATIC	PILGRIMAGE	PLANOMETER	POGO STICKS
PHOSPHORIC	PILIFEROUS	PLANOMETRY	POIGNANTLY
PHOSPHORUS	PILLORYING	PLANTATION	POINSETTIA
PHOTOFLOOD	PILLOWCASE	PLASMAGENE	POINT-BLANK
PHOTOGENIC	PILLOW TALK	PLASMODIUM	POKER-FACED
PHOTOGRAPH	PILOT LIGHT	PLASMOLYSE	POLAR BEARS
PHOTOLYSIS	PIMPERNELS	PLASMOSOME	POLARITIES
PHOTOLYTIC	PIMPLINESS	PLASTERERS	POLARIZING
PHOTOMETER	PINA COLADA	PLASTERING	POLEMICIST
PHOTOMETRY	PINCERLIKE	PLASTIC ART	POLE VAULTS
PHOTOMURAL	PINCHPENNY	PLASTICINE	POLITBUROS
PHOTONASTY	PINCUSHION	PLASTICITY	POLITENESS
PHOTOPHILY	PINEAPPLES	PLASTICIZE	POLITICIAN
PHOTOPHORE	PINE MARTEN	PLAT DU JOUR	POLITICIZE
PHOTOSTATS	PINFEATHER	PLATE GLASS	POLLARDING
PHOTOTAXIS	PINGUIDITY	PLATELAYER	POLLINATED
PHOTOTONIC	PINNATIFID	PLATE RACKS	POLLINATOR
PHOTOTONUS	PINNATIPED	PLATITUDES	POLLINOSIS
PHOTOTYPIC	PINPOINTED	PLATYPUSES	POLLUTANTS
PHRASEBOOK	PINSTRIPED	PLAY-ACTING	POLONAISES
PHRENOLOGY	PINSTRIPES	PLAYFELLOW	POLYANTHUS
PHTHISICAL	PIONEERING	PLAYGROUND	POLYATOMIC
PHYLACTERY	PIPED MUSIC	PLAYGROUPS	POLYBASITE
PHYLLODIAL	PIPE DREAMS	PLAYHOUSES	POLYCARPIC
PHYLLOXERA	PIPERAZINE	PLAYSCHOOL	POLYCHAETE
PHYLOGENIC	PIPERIDINE	PLAYTHINGS	POLYCHROME
PHYSIATRIC	PIPSISSEWA	PLAYWRIGHT	POLYCHROMY
PHYSICALLY	PIPSQUEAKS	PLEASANTER	POLYCLINIC
PHYSICIANS	PIROUETTED	PLEASANTLY	POLYCYCLIC
PHYSICISTS	PIROUETTES	PLEASANTRY	POLYDACTYL
PHYSIOCRAT	PISTACHIOS	PLEASINGLY	POLYDIPSIA
PHYSIOLOGY	PISTILLATE	PLEBISCITE	POLYDIPSIC
PHYTOGENIC	PISTON RING	PLEONASTIC	POLYGAMIST
PHYTOPHAGY	PITCH-BLACK	PLESIOSAUR	POLYGAMOUS
PHYTOTOXIN	PITCHFORKS	PLEURODONT	POLYGRAPHS
PIANISSIMO	PITCHINESS	PLEUROTOMY	POLYGYNIST
PIANOFORTE	PITCHSTONE	PLEXIGLASS	POLYGYNOUS
PICARESQUE	PITH HELMET	PLIABILITY	POLYHEDRAL
PICCADILLY	PITILESSLY	PLODDINGLY	POLYHEDRON
PICCALILLI	PITOT TUBES	PLOUGHBOYS	POLYMATHIC
PICCANINNY	PITTSBURGH	PLUCKINESS	POLYMERISM

POLYMERIZE	POSTHUMOUS	PRECEDENCE	PREPACKAGE
POLYMEROUS	POSTILIONS	PRECEDENTS	PREPACKING
POLYNESIAN	POSTLIMINY	PRECENTORS	PREPAREDLY
POLYNOMIAL	POSTMARKED	PRECEPTIVE	PREPAYABLE
POLYPHAGIA	POSTMASTER	PRECESSION	PREPAYMENT
POLYPHONIC	POSTMORTEM	PRECIOSITY	PREPOSSESS
POLYPLOIDY	POST OFFICE	PRECIOUSLY	PREPOTENCY
POLYPODOUS	POSTPARTUM	PRECIPICED	PREP SCHOOL
POLYRHYTHM	POSTPONING	PRECIPICES	PRESAGEFUL
POLYSEMOUS	POSTSCRIPT	PRECIPITIN	PRESBYOPIA
POLYTHEISM	POSTULANCY	PRECISIONS	PRESBYOPIC
POLYTHEIST	POSTULANTS	PRECLUDING	PRESBYTERY
POLYVALENT	POSTULATED	PRECLUSION	PRESCHOOLS
POMERANIAN	POSTULATES	PRECLUSIVE	PRESCIENCE
POMIFEROUS	POSTULATOR	PRECOCIOUS	PRESCRIBED
POMOLOGIST	POTABILITY	PRECONCERT	PRESCRIBER
PONDERABLE	POTATO CHIP	PRECOOKING	PRESCRIPTS
POND-SKATER	POTBELLIED	PRECURSORS	PRESENT-DAY
PONTIFICAL	POTBELLIES	PRECURSORY	PRESENTERS
POOH-POOHED	POTBOILERS	PREDACIOUS	PRESENTING
POORHOUSES	POTENTATES	PREDECEASE	PRESERVERS
POOR WHITES	POTENTIATE	PREDESTINE	PRESERVING
POPE'S NOSES	POTENTILLA	PREDICABLE	PRESETTING
POPISHNESS	POTENTNESS	PREDICATED	PRESIDENCY
POPULARITY	POTHUNTERS	PREDICATES	PRESIDENTS
POPULARIZE	POTPOURRIS	PREDICTING	PRESIDIUMS
POPULATING	POULTERERS	PREDICTION	PRESIGNIFY
POPULATION	POULTRYMAN	PREDICTIVE	PRESS AGENT
PORCUPINES	POURPARLER	PREDISPOSE	PRESS BARON
PORIFEROUS	POWDER KEGS	PRE-EMINENT	PRESS BOXES
PORK BARREL	POWDER PUFF	PRE-EMPTING	PRESSGANGS
PORNOCRACY	POWDER ROOM	PRE-EMPTION	PRESSINGLY
POROUSNESS	POWER BASES	PRE-EMPTIVE	PRESS-STUDS
PORPHYROID	POWERBOATS	PRE-EMPTORY	PRESSURING
PORTAMENTO	POWER DIVES	PREEXISTED	PRESSURIZE
PORTCULLIS	POWERFULLY	PREFECTURE	PRESUMABLE
PORTENDING	POWERHOUSE	PREFERABLE	PRESUMABLY
PORTENTOUS	POWER PLANT	PREFERABLY	PRESUMEDLY
PORTFOLIOS	POWER POINT	PREFERENCE	PRESUPPOSE
PORTIONING	POZZUOLANA	PREFERMENT	PRETENDERS
PORTLINESS	PRACTICALS	PREFERRING	PRETENDING
PORT OF CALL	PRACTISING	PREFIGURED	PRETENSION
PORTRAYALS	PRAESIDIUM	PREFRONTAL	PRETTIFIED
PORTRAYING	PRAGMATICS	PREGLACIAL	PRETTINESS
PORTUGUESE	PRAGMATISM	PREGNANTLY	PREVAILING
POSITIONAL	PRAGMATIST	PREHEATING	PREVALENCE
POSITIONED	PRAIRIE DOG	PREHENSILE	PREVENIENT
POSITIVELY	PRANCINGLY	PREHENSION	PREVENTING
POSITIVISM	PRANKSTERS	PREHISTORY	PREVENTION
POSITIVIST	PRASELENIC	PREHOMINID	PREVENTIVE
POSSESSING	PRATINCOLE	PREJUDGING	PREVIEWING
POSSESSION	PRAYER RUGS	PREJUDICED	PREVIOUSLY
POSSESSIVE	PREACHMENT	PREJUDICES	PREVISIONS
POSSESSORS	PREADAMITE	PRELEXICAL	PREVOCALIC
POSSESSORY	PREAMBULAR	PREMARITAL	PRICKLIEST
POST-BELLUM	PREARRANGE	PREMAXILLA	PRIEST-HOLE
POST-CYCLIC	PREBENDARY	PREMEDICAL	PRIESTHOOD
POSTDATING	PRECARIOUS	PRENATALLY	PRIESTLIER
POSTERIORS	PRECAUTION	PRENOMINAL	PRIGGISHLY

PRIMA DONNA	PROFITEERS	PROPHECIES	PROTRACTOR
PRIMA FACIE	PROFITLESS	PROPHESIER	PROTRUDENT
PRIMAQUINE	PROFLIGACY	PROPHESIED	PROTRUDING
PRIME MOVER	PROFLIGATE	PROPHESIES	PROTRUSILE
PRIME RATES	PROFOUNDLY	PROPIONATE	PROTRUSION
PRIMITIVES	PROFUNDITY	PROPITIATE	PROTRUSIVE
PRIMORDIAL	PROGENITOR	PROPITIOUS	PROVENANCE
PRIMORDIUM	PROGLOTTIS	PROPONENTS	PROVENCALE
PRINCEDOMS	PROGNOSTIC	PROPORTION	PROVERBIAL
PRINCELING	PROGRAMERS	PROPOSABLE	PROVIDENCE
PRINCESSES	PROGRAMING	PROPOSITUS	PROVINCIAL
PRINCIPALS	PROGRAMMED	PROPOUNDED	PROVISIONS
PRINCIPIUM	PROGRAMMER	PROPOUNDER	PROVITAMIN
PRINCIPLED	PROGRAMMES	PROPRIETOR	PRUDENTIAL
PRINCIPLES	PROGRESSED	PROPULSION	PRURIENTLY
PRINTMAKER	PROGRESSES	PROPULSIVE	PSALMODIST
PRIORITIES	PROHIBITED	PROPYLAEUM	PSALTERIES
PRIORITIZE	PROHIBITER	PROROGUING	PSALTERIUM
PRISMATOID	PROJECTILE	PROSCENIUM	PSEPHOLOGY
PRISMOIDAL	PROJECTING	PROSCRIBED	PSESPHITIC
PRISON CAMP	PROJECTION	PROSECUTED	PSEUDOCARP
PRISSINESS	PROJECTIVE	PROSECUTOR	PSEUDONYMS
PRIVATEERS	PROJECTORS	PROSELYTES	PSILOCYBIN
PRIVATIONS	PROLAPSING	PROSELYTIC	PSITTACINE
PRIVATIZED	PROLOCUTOR	PROSPECTED	PSYCHIATRY
PRIVILEGED	PROLONGING	PROSPECTOR	PSYCHOLOGY
PRIVILEGES	PROMENADED	PROSPECTUS	PSYCHOPATH
PRIVY PURSE	PROMENADER	PROSPERING	PSYCHOTICS
PRIZEFIGHT	PROMENADES	PROSPERITY	PTOLEMAIST
PROCAMBIAL	PROMETHIUM	PROSPEROUS	PUB-CRAWLED
PROCAMBIUM	PROMINENCE	PROSTHESIS	PUBERULENT
PROCEDURAL	PROMISSORY	PROSTHETIC	PUBESCENCE
PROCEDURES	PROMONTORY	PROSTITUTE	PUBLIC BARS
PROCEEDING	PROMOTABLE	PROSTOMIUM	PUBLICISTS
PROCESSING	PROMOTIONS	PROSTRATED	PUBLICIZED
PROCESSION	PROMPTBOOK	PROTANOPIA	PUBLISHERS
PROCESSORS	PROMPTNESS	PROTANOPIC	PUBLISHING
PROCLAIMED	PROMULGATE	PROTECTING	PUERPERIUM
PROCLIVITY	PRONEPHRIC	PROTECTION	PUERTO RICO
PROCONSULS	PRONEPHROS	PROTECTIVE	PUGILISTIC
PROCREATED	PRONOMINAL	PROTECTORS	PUGNACIOUS
PROCREATOR	PRONOUNCED	PROTECTORY	PUISSANCES
PROCRYPTIC	PRONOUNCER	PROTEINASE	PULLULATED
PROCTOLOGY	PRONUCLEAR	PRO TEMPORE	PULSATIONS
PROCTORIAL	PRONUCLEUS	PROTESTANT	PULSIMETER
PROCUMBENT	PRO-OESTRUS	PROTESTERS	PULVERABLE
PROCURATOR	PROPAGABLE	PROTHALLIC	PULVERIZED
PRODIGALLY	PROPAGANDA	PROTHALLUS	PULVERIZER
PRODIGIOUS	PROPAGATED	PROTOHUMAN	PUMMELLING
PRODUCIBLE	PROPAGATOR	PROTONEMAL	PUNCH BALLS
PRODUCTION	PROPELLANT	PROTOPATHY	PUNCHBOARD
PRODUCTIVE	PROPELLENT	PROTOPLASM	PUNCH BOWLS
PROFESSING	PROPELLERS	PROTOPLAST	PUNCH-DRUNK
PROFESSION	PROPELLING	PROTOSTELE	PUNCHINESS
PROFESSORS	PROPENSITY	PROTOTYPAL	PUNCH LINES
PROFFERING	PROPERNESS	PROTOTYPES	PUNCTATION
PROFICIENT	PROPER NOUN	PROTOXYLEM	PUNCTILIOS
PROFITABLE	PROPERTIED	PROTOZOANS	PUNCTUALLY
PROFITABLY	PROPERTIES	PROTRACTED	PUNCTUATED

PUNCTUATOR	QUALIFIERS	RADIOPAQUE	REARRANGED
PUNCTURING	QUALIFYING	RADIOPHONY	REARRANGER
PUNISHABLE	QUANDARIES	RADIOSCOPE	REASONABLE
PUNISHMENT	QUANTIFIED	RADIOSCOPY	REASONABLY
PUNITIVELY	QUANTIFIER	RADIOSONDE	REASSEMBLE
PUPIPAROUS	QUANTITIES	RADIOTOXIC	REASSURING
PUPPETEERS	QUARANTINE	RAGAMUFFIN	REBELLIONS
PURCHASERS	QUARRELING	RAGGEDNESS	REBELLIOUS
PURCHASING	QUARRELLED	RAILROADED	REBOUNDING
PURGATIVES	QUARRELLER	RAIN CHECKS	REBUILDING
PURITANISM	QUARTERAGE	RAIN FOREST	REBUKINGLY
PURLOINING	QUARTER DAY	RAIN GAUGES	REBUTTABLE
PURPLENESS	QUARTERING	RAINMAKING	RECALLABLE
PURPORTING	QUARTERSAW	RAINSTORMS	RECAPTURED
PURPOSEFUL	QUATERNARY	RAJYA SABHA	RECEIVABLE
PURSUANCES	QUATERNION	RAKISHNESS	RECENTNESS
PURSUIVANT	QUATREFOIL	RAMPAGEOUS	RECEPTACLE
PURVEYANCE	QUEASINESS	RAMSHACKLE	RECEPTIONS
PUSH-BUTTON	QUEENSLAND	RANCH HOUSE	RECESSIONS
PUSHCHAIRS	QUENCHABLE	RANCIDNESS	RECHARGING
PUTREFYING	QUESTINGLY	RANDOMNESS	RECHRISTEN
PUTRESCENT	QUESTIONED	RANSACKING	RECIDIVISM
PUTRESCINE	QUESTIONER	RANUNCULUS	RECIDIVIST
PUZZLEMENT	QUEZON CITY	RAPPORTEUR	RECIPIENCE
PUZZLINGLY	QUICKENING	RARE EARTHS	RECIPIENTS
PYCNOMETER	QUICKSANDS	RAREFIABLE	RECIPROCAL
PYOGENESIS	QUICKSTEPS	RATABILITY	RECITATION
PYORRHOEAL	QUID PRO QUO	RATE-CAPPED	RECITATIVE
PYRACANTHA	QUIESCENCE	RATIFIABLE	RECKLESSLY
PYRIDOXINE	QUIETENING	RATIONALES	RECKONINGS
PYRIMIDINE	QUINTUPLET	RATIONALLY	RECLAIMANT
PYROGALLIC	QUIRKINESS	RATTLETRAP	RECLAIMING
PYROGALLOL	QUITTANCES	RAUNCHIEST	RECLINABLE
PYROGRAPHY	QUIZMASTER	RAVAGEMENT	RECOGNIZED
PYROLUSITE	QUONSET HUT	RAVENOUSLY	RECOGNIZEE
PYROMANCER	QUOTATIONS	RAVISHMENT	RECOGNIZER
PYROMANIAC		RAWALPINDI	RECOGNIZOR
PYROMANTIC	R	RAWINSONDE	RECOILLESS
PYROMETRIC	RABBINICAL	RAZZMATAZZ	RECOMMENCE
PYROPHORIC	RABBITFISH	REACTIONAL	RECOMPENSE
PYROSTATIC	RABBITTING	REACTIVATE	RECONCILED
PYROXENITE	RACECOURSE	REACTIVELY	RECONCILER
PYRRHOTITE	RACEHORSES	REACTIVITY	RECONSIDER
PYTHAGORAS	RACETRACKS	READERSHIP	RECORDABLE
	RACHMANISM	READJUSTED	RECORDINGS
Q	RACIALISTS	READJUSTER	RECOUNTING
QUADRANGLE	RACKETEERS	READY MONEY	RECOUPABLE
QUADRANTAL	RACK-RENTER	REAFFIRMED	RECOUPMENT
QUADRATICS	RACONTEURS	REAFFOREST	RECOVERIES
QUADRATURE	RADARSCOPE	REAL ESTATE	RE-COVERING
QUADRICEPS	RADIATIONS	REALIGNING	RECREATING
QUADRILLES	RADICALISM	REALIZABLE	RECREATION
QUADRISECT	RADIO ALARM	REALIZABLY	RECRUDESCE
QUADRIVIAL	RADIOGENIC	REALLOCATE	RECRUITING
QUADRUPEDS	RADIOGRAMS	REANIMATED	RECTANGLES
QUADRUPLED	RADIOGRAPH	REAPPEARED	RECTIFIERS
QUADRUPLET	RADIOLYSIS	REAPPRAISE	RECTIFYING
QUADRUPLEX	RADIOMETER	REARGUARDS	RECUMBENCE
QUAINTNESS	RADIOMETRY	REARMAMENT	RECUPERATE

RECURRENCE	REGELATION	REMANDMENT	REPRESSION
RED ADMIRAL	REGENERACY	REMARKABLE	REPRESSIVE
RED-BLOODED	REGENERATE	REMARKABLY	REPRIEVING
REDBREASTS	REGENSBURG	REMARRYING	REPRIMANDS
REDCURRANT	REGENTSHIP	REMEDIABLE	REPRINTING
REDECORATE	REGIMENTAL	REMEDIABLY	REPROACHED
REDEEMABLE	REGIMENTED	REMEDIALLY	REPROACHER
REDEEMABLY	REGIONALLY	REMEDILESS	REPROACHES
REDELIVERY	REGISTERED	REMEMBERED	REPROBATER
REDEMPTION	REGISTERER	REMEMBERER	REPROBATES
REDEPLOYED	REGISTRANT	REMINISCED	REPRODUCED
RED HERRING	REGISTRARS	REMISSIBLE	REPRODUCER
RED INDIANS	REGISTRIES	REMISSIONS	REPROVABLE
REDIRECTED	REGRESSING	REMISSNESS	REPTILIANS
REDISCOUNT	REGRESSION	REMITTABLE	REPUBLICAN
REDOUBLING	REGRESSIVE	REMITTANCE	REPUDIABLE
REDOUNDING	REGRETTING	REMITTENCE	REPUDIATED
RED PEPPERS	REGROUPING	REMODELING	REPUDIATOR
REDRESSING	REGULARITY	REMODELLED	REPUGNANCE
REDUCTIONS	REGULARIZE	REMODELLER	REPULSIONS
REDUNDANCY	REGULATING	REMONETIZE	REPUTATION
RE-EDUCATED	REGULATION	REMORSEFUL	REQUESTING
RE-ELECTING	REGULATIVE	REMOTENESS	REQUIESCAT
RE-ELECTION	REGULATORS	REMOULDING	REQUIRABLE
RE-ENFORCER	REGULATORY	REMOUNTING	REQUISITES
RE-ENTRANCE	REHEARSALS	REMOVAL VAN	REQUITABLE
RE-EXAMINER	REHEARSING	REMUNERATE	RESCHEDULE
RE-EXPORTER	REIMBURSED	RENDERABLE	RESCINDING
REFEREEING	REIMBURSER	RENDERINGS	RESCISSION
REFERENCER	REINFORCED	RENDEZVOUS	RESCISSORY
REFERENCES	REINSTATED	RENDITIONS	RESEARCHED
REFERENDUM	REINSTATOR	RENOUNCING	RESEARCHER
REFILLABLE	REINSURING	RENOVATING	RESEARCHES
REFINEMENT	REISSUABLE	RENOVATION	RESEMBLANT
REFINERIES	REITERATED	RENOVATIVE	RESEMBLING
REFINISHER	REJECTABLE	RENOWNEDLY	RESENTMENT
REFLECTING	REJECTIONS	RENT STRIKE	RESERVABLE
REFLECTION	REJOINDERS	REORGANIZE	RESERVEDLY
REFLECTIVE	REJUVENATE	REPAIRABLE	RESERVISTS
REFLECTORS	REKINDLING	REPARATION	RESERVOIRS
REFLEXIVES	RELATIONAL	REPARATIVE	RESETTLING
REFORESTED	RELATIVELY	REPATRIATE	RESHIPMENT
REFRACTING	RELATIVISM	REPAYMENTS	RESHUFFLED
REFRACTION	RELATIVIST	REPEALABLE	RESHUFFLES
REFRACTIVE	RELATIVITY	REPEATABLE	RESIDENCES
REFRACTORY	RELAXATION	REPEATEDLY	RESIGNEDLY
REFRAINING	RELEGATING	REPELLENCE	RESILEMENT
REFRESHFUL	RELEGATION	REPELLENTS	RESILIENCE
REFRESHING	RELENTLESS	REPENTANCE	RESILIENCY
REFRINGENT	RELEVANTLY	REPERTOIRE	RESISTANCE
REFUELLING	RELIEF MAPS	REPETITION	RESISTIBLY
REFUGEEISM	RELIEF ROAD	REPETITIVE	RESISTLESS
REFULGENCE	RELIEVABLE	REPHRASING	RESOLUTELY
REFUNDABLE	RELINQUISH	REPLICATED	RESOLUTION
REFUTATION	RELISHABLE	REPORTABLE	RESOLVABLE
REGAINABLE	RELOCATING	REPORTEDLY	RESONANCES
REGALEMENT	RELOCATION	REPOSITION	RESONANTLY
REGARDABLE	RELUCTANCE	REPOSITORY	RESONATING
REGARDLESS	REMAINDERS	REPRESSING	RESONATION

RESONATORS	REVEALABLE	RIFLE RANGE	ROUGHHOUSE
RESORCINOL	REVEALEDLY	RIFT VALLEY	ROUGHNECKS
RESORPTION	REVEALMENT	RIGHTABOUT	ROUGH PAPER
RESORPTIVE	REVEGETATE	RIGHT ANGLE	ROUGHRIDER
RESOUNDING	REVELATION	RIGHTFULLY	ROUGH STUFF
RESPECTERS	REVENGEFUL	RIGHT OF WAY	ROUNDABOUT
RESPECTFUL	REVERENCED	RIGHTWARDS	ROUNDHEADS
RESPECTING	REVERENCER	RIGMAROLES	ROUNDHOUSE
RESPECTIVE	REVERENCES	RIGORISTIC	ROUND ROBIN
RESPIRABLE	REVERENTLY	RIGOROUSLY	ROUND-TABLE
RESPIRATOR	REVERSIBLE	RINDERPEST	ROUND TRIPS
RESPONDENT	REVERTIBLE	RING BINDER	ROUSEDNESS
RESPONDING	REVETMENTS	RING FINGER	ROUSSILLON
RESPONSIVE	REVIEWABLE	RINGLEADER	ROUSTABOUT
RESPONSORY	REVILEMENT	RINGMASTER	ROUTE MARCH
RES PUBLICA	REVILINGLY	RING-NECKED	ROWING BOAT
RESTAURANT	REVISIONAL	RING-TAILED	ROYAL FLUSH
RESTHARROW	REVITALIZE	RIPPLINGLY	ROYALISTIC
RESTLESSLY	REVIVALISM	RIP-ROARING	RUB' AL KHALI
RESTOCKING	REVIVALIST	RISIBILITY	RUBBER BAND
RESTORABLE	REVIVIFIED	RISING DAMP	RUBBERNECK
RESTRAINED	REVIVINGLY	RITARDANDO	RUBBER TREE
RESTRAINER	REVOCATION	RITORNELLO	RUBBISH BIN
RESTRAINTS	REVOCATIVE	RIVER BASIN	RUBBISHING
RESTRICTED	REVOKINGLY	ROADBLOCKS	RUBBLEWORK
RESUMPTION	REVOLUTION	ROADHOUSES	RUBESCENCE
RESUMPTIVE	REVOLVABLE	ROAD ROLLER	RUBIACEOUS
RESUPINATE	REVOLVABLY	ROADRUNNER	RUBIGINOUS
RESURFACED	REWARDABLE	ROAD-TESTED	RUBRICATOR
RESURGENCE	RHAPSODIES	ROADWORTHY	RUDDERHEAD
RETAINABLE	RHAPSODIST	ROBUSTNESS	RUDDERLESS
RETAINMENT	RHAPSODIZE	ROCK BOTTOM	RUDDERPOST
RETALIATED	RHEOLOGIST	ROCK GARDEN	RUEFULNESS
RETALIATOR	RHEOMETRIC	ROCK PLANTS	RUFESCENCE
RETHINKING	RHEOSTATIC	ROCK SALMON	RUFFIANISM
RETICENTLY	RHEOTACTIC	ROISTERERS	RUGGEDNESS
RETICULATE	RHEOTROPIC	ROISTEROUS	RUMBLINGLY
RETIREMENT	RHETORICAL	ROLE MODELS	RUMINATING
RETOUCHING	RHEUMATICS	ROLE-PLAYED	RUMINATION
RETRACTILE	RHEUMATISM	ROLLED GOLD	RUMINATIVE
RETRACTING	RHEUMATOID	ROLLICKING	RUMPUS ROOM
RETRACTION	RHINESTONE	ROLLING PIN	RUNNER BEAN
RETRACTIVE	RHINOCEROS	ROLY-POLIES	RUN-OF-PAPER
RETREADING	RHINOSCOPY	ROMANESQUE	RUN-THROUGH
RETREATING	RHIZOGENIC	ROMAN NOSES	RUPTURABLE
RETRENCHED	RHIZOMORPH	ROOD SCREEN	RURITANIAN
RETRIEVERS	RHIZOPODAN	ROOF GARDEN	RUSHLIGHTS
RETRIEVING	RHOMBOIDAL	ROPE LADDER	RUSSOPHILE
RETROCHOIR	RHUMBATRON	ROSANILINE	RUSSOPHOBE
RETROGRADE	RHYMESTERS	ROSEMALING	RUSTICATED
RETROGRESS	RHYTHMICAL	ROSE WINDOW	RUSTICATOR
RETROSPECT	RIBBONFISH	ROSTELLATE	RUSTLINGLY
RETROVERSE	RIBOFLAVIN	ROTARY CLUB	RUTHENIOUS
RETURNABLE	RICKETTSIA	ROTATIONAL	RUTHERFORD
REUNIONISM	RICOCHETED	ROTISSERIE	RUTHLESSLY
REUNIONIST	RIDGEPOLES	ROTOVATORS	
REUNITABLE	RIDICULING	ROTTENNESS	S
REVANCHISM	RIDICULOUS	ROTTWEILER	SABBATICAL
REVANCHIST	RIEMANNIAN	ROUGHENING	SABOTAGING

SABULOSITY	SALMONELLA	SATINWOODS	SCHOLASTIC
SACCHARASE	SALOON BARS	SATIRIZING	SCHOOLGIRL
SACCHARATE	SALPINGIAN	SATISFYING	SCHOOLMARM
SACCHARIDE	SALTARELLO	SATURATING	SCHOOLMATE
SACCHARIFY	SALTCELLAR	SATURATION	SCHOOLWORK
SACCHARINE	SALTIGRADE	SATURNALIA	SCIENTIFIC
SACCHAROID	SALT SHAKER	SATYRIASIS	SCIENTISTS
SACCHAROSE	SALUBRIOUS	SAUERKRAUT	SCILLONIAN
SACERDOTAL	SALUTARILY	SAUNTERING	SCIOMANCER
SACRAMENTO	SALUTATION	SAUSAGE DOG	SCIOMANTIC
SACRAMENTS	SALUTATORY	SAVAGENESS	SCLEROTIUM
SACRED COWS	SALVERFORM	SAVAGERIES	SCLEROTOMY
SACREDNESS	SALZGITTER	SAXICOLOUS	SCOFFINGLY
SACRIFICED	SAMARITANS	SAXOPHONES	SCOLDINGLY
SACRIFICER	SAMARSKITE	SAXOPHONIC	SCOLLOPING
SACRIFICES	SAN ANTONIO	SCABBINESS	SCOREBOARD
SACRILEGES	SANATORIUM	SCAFFOLDER	SCORECARDS
SACRISTANS	SANCTIFIED	SCALEBOARD	SCORNFULLY
SACRISTIES	SANCTIFIER	SCALLOPING	SCORNINGLY
SACROILIAC	SANCTIMONY	SCALLYWAGS	SCORPAENID
SACROSANCT	SANCTIONED	SCALOPPINE	SCORPIONIC
SADDLEBACK	SANCTIONER	SCALPELLIC	SCOTCH EGGS
SADDLEBAGS	SANCTITUDE	SCAMPERING	SCOTCH MIST
SADDLEBILL	SANDALWOOD	SCANDALIZE	SCOTCH TAPE
SADDLERIES	SANDBAGGED	SCANDALOUS	SCOTTICISM
SADDLE-SORE	SANDBAGGER	SCANSORIAL	SCOUNDRELS
SADDLETREE	SANDCASTLE	SCANTINESS	SCOWLINGLY
SAFARI PARK	SANDERLING	SCAPEGOATS	SCRABBLING
SAFEGUARDS	SANDGROUSE	SCAPEGRACE	SCRAGGIEST
SAFE HOUSES	SANDPIPERS	SCARABAEID	SCRAMBLING
SAFETY BELT	SANDSTORMS	SCARABAEUS	SCRAPBOOKS
SAFETY LAMP	SANDWICHED	SCARCEMENT	SCRAP HEAPS
SAFETY NETS	SANDWICHES	SCARCENESS	SCRAP PAPER
SAFETY PINS	SANFORIZED	SCARCITIES	SCRAPPIEST
SAHARANPUR	SANGUINARY	SCARECROWS	SCRATCHIER
SAILBOARDS	SANGUINELY	SCAREDY CAT	SCRATCHILY
SAILOR SUIT	SANITARIAN	SCARIFYING	SCRATCHING
SAILPLANES	SANITARILY	SCARLATINA	SCRATCHPAD
SAINT LOUIS	SANITARIUM	SCARPERING	SCRAWNIEST
SAINT'S DAYS	SANITATION	SCATHINGLY	SCREECHING
SALABILITY	SANITIZING	SCATTER-GUN	SCREENABLE
SALAD CREAM	SANSKRITIC	SCATTERING	SCREENINGS
SALAMANDER	SANTA CLARA	SCATTINESS	SCREENPLAY
SALESCLERK	SANTA CLAUS	SCAVENGERS	SCREEN TEST
SALESGIRLS	SANTA MARIA	SCAVENGING	SCREWBALLS
SALES PITCH	SANTA MARTA	SCENICALLY	SCRIBBLERS
SALES SLIPS	SAPIENTIAL	SCEPTICISM	SCRIBBLING
SALES TAXES	SAPONIFIER	SCHAERBEEK	SCRIMMAGED
SALESWOMAN	SAPPANWOOD	SCHEDULING	SCRIMMAGER
SALESWOMEN	SAPPHIRINE	SCHEMATISM	SCRIMMAGES
SALICORNIA	SAPROGENIC	SCHEMATIZE	SCRIPTURAL
SALICYLATE	SAPROLITIC	SCHEMINGLY	SCROFULOUS
SALIFEROUS	SAPROPELIC	SCHERZANDO	SCROLLWORK
SALIFIABLE	SAPROPHYTE	SCHIPPERKE	SCROUNGERS
SALIMETRIC	SARCOPHAGI	SCHISMATIC	SCROUNGING
SALIVATING	SARMENTOSE	SCHIZOCARP	SCRUBBIEST
SALIVATION	SARRACENIA	SCHIZOGONY	SCRUFFIEST
SALLOWNESS	SASH WINDOW	SCHLEPPING	SCRUMMAGED
SALMANAZAR	SATELLITES	SCHNITZELS	SCRUMMAGER

SCRUMMAGES	SEE-THROUGH	SEPARATORS	SHANTYTOWN
SCRUNCHING	SEGMENTARY	SEPARATRIX	SHAPELIEST
SCRUPULOUS	SEGMENTING	SEPTENNIAL	SHARPENERS
SCRUTINEER	SEGREGABLE	SEPTICALLY	SHARPENING
SCRUTINIES	SEGREGATED	SEPTICIDAL	SHATTERING
SCRUTINIZE	SEGREGATOR	SEPTIC TANK	SHEARWATER
SCULLERIES	SEISMOLOGY	SEPTILLION	SHEATHBILL
SCULPTRESS	SELECTIONS	SEPULCHRAL	SHEATHINGS
SCULPTURAL	SELECTNESS	SEPULCHRES	SHEEPISHLY
SCULPTURED	SELENOLOGY	SEQUACIOUS	SHEEP'S EYES
SCULPTURES	SELF-ACTING	SEQUENCING	SHEEPSHANK
SCUPPERING	SELF-ACTION	SEQUENTIAL	SHEEPSHEAD
SCURRILITY	SELF-DENIAL	SEQUESTRAL	SHEEPSKINS
SCURRILOUS	SELF-ESTEEM	SEQUESTRUM	SHEET MUSIC
SCURVINESS	SELF-FEEDER	SERENADING	SHEIKHDOMS
SCUTELLATE	SELFLESSLY	SERENENESS	SHELF LIVES
SCYPHIFORM	SELF-REGARD	SERIALIZED	SHELLPROOF
SCYPHOZOAN	SELF-SEEKER	SERIGRAPHY	SHELLSHOCK
SEA ANEMONE	SELF-STYLED	SERIOCOMIC	SHELTERING
SEA BREEZES	SELF-WILLED	SERMONICAL	SHENANIGAN
SEA CAPTAIN	SELL-BY DATE	SERMONIZED	SHEPHERDED
SEA CHANGES	SELLOTAPED	SERMONIZER	SHERARDIZE
SEALED-BEAM	SEMAPHORES	SEROLOGIST	SHIBBOLETH
SEALING WAX	SEMAPHORIC	SERPENTINE	SHIFTINESS
SEAMANLIKE	SEMATOLOGY	SERVICEMAN	SHIFTINGLY
SEAMANSHIP	SEMIANNUAL	SERVICEMEN	SHIFT STICK
SEAMSTRESS	SEMIBREVES	SERVIETTES	SHILLELAGH
SEARCHABLE	SEMICIRCLE	SERVOMOTOR	SHIMMERING
SEASONABLE	SEMICOLONS	SETSQUARES	SHIPBOARDS
SEASONABLY	SEMIFINALS	SETTLEABLE	SHIPMASTER
SEASONEDLY	SEMINALITY	SETTLEMENT	SHIP-RIGGED
SEASONINGS	SEMINARIAL	SEVASTOPOL	SHIPWRECKS
SEA URCHINS	SEMINARIAN	SEVENTIETH	SHIPWRIGHT
SEBIFEROUS	SEMINARIES	SEVERANCES	SHIRE HORSE
SEBORRHOEA	SEMIQUAVER	SEVERENESS	SHIRTFRONT
SECOND BEST	SEMIVOWELS	SEVERITIES	SHIRTTAILS
SECOND-HAND	SEMIWEEKLY	SEXAGENARY	SHISH KEBAB
SECONDMENT	SENATORIAL	SEXAGESIMA	SHOALINESS
SECOND-RATE	SENEGALESE	SEXIVALENT	SHOCKINGLY
SECOND WIND	SENEGAMBIA	SEX OBJECTS	SHOCKPROOF
SECRETAIRE	SENESCENCE	SEXOLOGIST	SHODDINESS
SECRETIONS	SENSATIONS	SEXPARTITE	SHOEMAKING
SECTIONING	SENSE ORGAN	SEXTILLION	SHOESHINES
SECULARISM	SENSIBILIA	SEXTUPLETS	SHOESTRING
SECULARIST	SENSITIZED	SEYCHELLES	SHOPKEEPER
SECULARITY	SENSITIZER	SHABBINESS	SHOPLIFTED
SECULARIZE	SENSUALISM	SHADOWIEST	SHOPLIFTER
SECUNDINES	SENSUALIST	SHAGGED OUT	SHOPSOILED
SECUREMENT	SENSUALITY	SHAGGINESS	SHOPWALKER
SECURENESS	SENSUOUSLY	SHAKEDOWNS	SHOREWARDS
SECURITIES	SENTENCING	SHALLOWEST	SHORTBREAD
SEDAN CHAIR	SENTENTIAL	SHALLOWING	SHORTENING
SEDATENESS	SENTIMENTS	SHAMANISMS	SHORTFALLS
SEDUCINGLY	SEPARATELY	SHAMANISTS	SHORT LISTS
SEDUCTRESS	SEPARATING	SHAMATEURS	SHORT-LIVED
SEDULOUSLY	SEPARATION	SHAMEFACED	SHORT-RANGE
SEEMLINESS	SEPARATISM	SHAMEFULLY	SHORT STORY
SEERSUCKER	SEPARATIST	SHAMPOOING	SHOULDERED
SEETHINGLY	SEPARATIVE	SHANGHAIED	SHOVELHEAD

SHOVELLING	SIMFEROPOL	SKYJACKERS	SMOLDERING
SHOVELNOSE	SIMILARITY	SKYJACKING	SMOOTHABLE
SHOW JUMPER	SIMILITUDE	SKYLARKING	SMOOTHBORE
SHOWPIECES	SIMONIACAL	SKYROCKETS	SMOOTHNESS
SHOW TRIALS	SIMPLE LIFE	SKYSCRAPER	SMOTHERING
SHREVEPORT	SIMPLENESS	SKYWRITING	SMOULDERED
SHREWDNESS	SIMPLETONS	SLACKENING	SMUDGINESS
SHREWISHLY	SIMPLICITY	SLANDERERS	SMUTTINESS
SHREWSBURY	SIMPLIFIED	SLANDERING	SNAIL'S PACE
SHRIEVALTY	SIMPLIFIER	SLANDEROUS	SNAKEMOUTH
SHRILLNESS	SIMPLISTIC	SLANGINESS	SNAPDRAGON
SHRINKABLE	SIMULACRUM	SLANTINGLY	SNAPPINESS
SHRINK-WRAP	SIMULATING	SLASHINGLY	SNAPPINGLY
SHRIVELING	SIMULATION	SLATTERNLY	SNAPPISHLY
SHRIVELLED	SIMULATIVE	SLAVE TRADE	SNARE DRUMS
SHROUD-LAID	SIMULATORS	SLAVOPHILE	SNARLINGLY
SHROVETIDE	SINCIPITAL	SLEAZINESS	SNAZZINESS
SHUDDERING	SINECURISM	SLEEPINESS	SNEAKINESS
SHUNT-WOUND	SINECURIST	SLEEPYHEAD	SNEAKINGLY
SHUTTERING	SINE QUA NON	SLEEVELESS	SNEAK THIEF
SIALAGOGIC	SINEWINESS	SLENDERIZE	SNEERINGLY
SIALAGOGUE	SINFULNESS	SLIDE RULES	SNEEZEWORT
SIAMESE CAT	SINGHALESE	SLIGHTNESS	SNICKERING
SIBILATION	SINGLE FILE	SLINGSHOTS	SNIFFINGLY
SICKLEBILL	SINGLENESS	SLINKINESS	SNIGGERING
SICKLINESS	SINGLETONS	SLINKINGLY	SNIPPINESS
SICKNESSES	SINGULARLY	SLIPPINESS	SNIVELLERS
SICK PARADE	SINHAILIEN	SLIPPINGLY	SNIVELLING
SIDEBOARDS	SINISTROUS	SLIPSTREAM	SNOBBISHLY
SIDE DISHES	SINN FEINER	SLITHERING	SNOOKERING
SIDE EFFECT	SINOLOGIST	SLOBBERING	SNOOTINESS
SIDE ISSUES	SINUSOIDAL	SLOPPINESS	SNORKELLED
SIDELIGHTS	SISTERHOOD	SLOPWORKER	SNORTINGLY
SIDELINING	SITOSTEROL	SLOTHFULLY	SNOTTINESS
SIDE ORDERS	SITUATIONS	SLOUCH HATS	SNOWBALLED
SIDEROLITE	SIX-FOOTERS	SLOW MOTION	SNOW-CAPPED
SIDEROSTAT	SIX-SHOOTER	SLOW-WITTED	SNOWDRIFTS
SIDESADDLE	SIXTEENTHS	SLUGGISHLY	SNOWFIELDS
SIDE STREET	SIXTH FORMS	SLUICEGATE	SNOWFLAKES
SIDESTROKE	SIXTH SENSE	SLUMBERERS	SNOWMOBILE
SIDESWIPED	SKATEBOARD	SLUMBERING	SNOWPLOUGH
SIDESWIPER	SKEDADDLED	SLUMBEROUS	SNOWSTORMS
SIDESWIPES	SKETCHABLE	SLUSH FUNDS	SNUBBINGLY
SIDETRACKS	SKETCHBOOK	SLUSHINESS	SNUFFINESS
SIDEWINDER	SKETCHIEST	SMALL HOURS	SNUFFINGLY
SIGHTSEERS	SKETCHPADS	SMALL PRINT	SOAP BUBBLE
SIGNALIZED	SKIMPINESS	SMALL-SCALE	SOAP OPERAS
SIGNALLING	SKIN DIVERS	SMALL-TIMER	SOBERINGLY
SIGNATURES	SKIN DIVING	SMARAGDITE	SOBRIQUETS
SIGNIFYING	SKIN FLICKS	SMART ALECK	SOB STORIES
SIGNORINAS	SKINFLINTS	SMARTENING	SOCIALISTS
SIGNPOSTED	SKIN GRAFTS	SMARTINGLY	SOCIALITES
SILENTNESS	SKINNINESS	SMATTERING	SOCIALIZED
SILHOUETTE	SKIPPERING	SMEARINESS	SOCIALIZER
SILICULOSE	SKIRMISHED	SMEAR TESTS	SOCIALNESS
SILK SCREEN	SKIRMISHER	SMELLINESS	SOCIAL WORK
SILVERFISH	SKIRMISHES	SMIRKINGLY	SOCIOMETRY
SILVERWARE	SKITTERING	SMOKEHOUSE	SOCIOPATHY
SILVERWEED	SKITTISHLY	SMOKESTACK	SODDENNESS

SOFT-BOILED	SOUR GRAPES	SPIDERWEBS	SPRING ROLL
SOFT-FINNED	SOURPUSSES	SPIDERWORT	SPRINGTAIL
SOFT FRUITS	SOUSAPHONE	SPINAL CORD	SPRING TIDE
SOFT-HEADED	SOUTHBOUND	SPINDLIEST	SPRINGTIME
SOFT OPTION	SOUTHERNER	SPIN-DRYING	SPRINGWOOD
SOFT PALATE	SOUTHWARDS	SPINESCENT	SPRINKLERS
SOFT-SOAPED	SOU'WESTERS	SPINNAKERS	SPRINKLING
SOFT-SPOKEN	SOVEREIGNS	SPIRACULAR	SPRUCENESS
SOJOURNERS	SPACECRAFT	SPIRALLING	SPUMESCENT
SOJOURNING	SPACE PROBE	SPIRITEDLY	SPUNKINESS
SOLAR CELLS	SPACESHIPS	SPIRITLESS	SPURIOUSLY
SOLAR PANEL	SPACESUITS	SPIRITUALS	SPUTTERING
SOLAR YEARS	SPACEWOMAN	SPIRITUOUS	SPYGLASSES
SOLDERABLE	SPACIOUSLY	SPIROGRAPH	SQUABBLING
SOLDIERING	SPADICEOUS	SPIROMETER	SQUALIDITY
SOLECISTIC	SPALLATION	SPIROMETRY	SQUALLIEST
SOLEMNIZED	SPARE PARTS	SPITEFULLY	SQUAMATION
SOLEMNIZER	SPARE TYRES	SPLANCHNIC	SQUAMULOSE
SOLEMNNESS	SPARK PLUGS	SPLASHBACK	SQUANDERED
SOLENOIDAL	SPARSENESS	SPLASHDOWN	SQUANDERER
SOLFATARIC	SPARTANISM	SPLASHIEST	SQUARE KNOT
SOLICITING	SPATCHCOCK	SPLATTERED	SQUARE MEAL
SOLICITORS	SPATIALITY	SPLEENWORT	SQUARENESS
SOLICITOUS	SPATTERING	SPLENDIDLY	SQUARE ROOT
SOLICITUDE	SPEARHEADS	SPLINTERED	SQUASHIEST
SOLIDARITY	SPECIALISM	SPLIT-LEVEL	SQUEAKIEST
SOLIDIFIED	SPECIALIST	SPLIT RINGS	SQUEEZABLE
SOLIDIFIER	SPECIALITY	SPLUTTERED	SQUEEZEBOX
SOLID-STATE	SPECIALIZE	SPLUTTERER	SQUELCHIER
SOLITAIRES	SPECIATION	SPOILSPORT	SQUELCHING
SOLITARIES	SPECIFYING	SPOKESHAVE	SQUETEAGUE
SOLITARILY	SPECIOSITY	SPOLIATION	SQUIDGIEST
SOLSTITIAL	SPECIOUSLY	SPONGE BAGS	SQUIFFIEST
SOLUBILITY	SPECTACLES	SPONGE CAKE	SQUISHIEST
SOLUBILIZE	SPECTATING	SPONGINESS	STABILIZED
SOLVOLYSIS	SPECTATORS	SPONSORIAL	STABILIZER
SOMALILAND	SPECULATED	SPONSORING	STABLE BOYS
SOMATOLOGY	SPECULATOR	SPOOKINESS	STABLENESS
SOMATOTYPE	SPEECH DAYS	SPOONERISM	STAFF NURSE
SOMBRENESS	SPEECHLESS	SPORANGIAL	STAGECOACH
SOMERSAULT	SPEEDBOATS	SPORANGIUM	STAGECRAFT
SOMNOLENCE	SPEEDINESS	SPOROPHORE	STAGE DOORS
SONGSTRESS	SPEED LIMIT	SPOROPHYLL	STAGEHANDS
SONGWRITER	SPEED TRAPS	SPOROPHYTE	STAGE NAMES
SONIC BOOMS	SPELEOLOGY	SPOROZOITE	STAGGERING
SONIFEROUS	SPELLBOUND	SPORTINESS	STAGNANTLY
SONOROUSLY	SPELUNKING	SPORTINGLY	STAGNATING
SONS-OF-GUNS	SPERMACETI	SPORTIVELY	STAGNATION
SOOTHINGLY	SPERMATIUM	SPORTS CARS	STAIRCASES
SOOTHSAYER	SPERMICIDE	SPORTSWEAR	STAIRWELLS
SOPHOMORES	SPERM WHALE	SPOT CHECKS	STALACTITE
SORDIDNESS	SPERRYLITE	SPOTLESSLY	STALAGMITE
SORORICIDE	SPHALERITE	SPOTLIGHTS	STALEMATED
SORORITIES	SPHENOIDAL	SPOTTINESS	STALEMATES
SOUBRIQUET	SPHERICITY	SPREADABLE	STALKINESS
SOULLESSLY	SPHEROIDAL	SPRINGBOKS	STALWARTLY
SOUNDPROOF	SPHERULITE	SPRINGHAAS	STAMMERERS
SOUNDTRACK	SPHINCTERS	SPRINGHEAD	STAMMERING
SOUP SPOONS	SPICEBERRY	SPRINGIEST	STAMPEDING

STANCHABLE	STEPPARENT	STOMATOPOD	STRIKINGLY
STANCHIONS	STEPSISTER	STOMODAEAL	STRING BEAN
STANDPIPES	STEREOBATE	STOMODAEUM	STRINGENCY
STANDPOINT	STEREOGRAM	STONE-BLIND	STRINGENDO
STANDSTILL	STEREOPSIS	STONE FRUIT	STRINGHALT
STARCHIEST	STEREOTOMY	STONEHENGE	STRINGIEST
STARFISHES	STEREOTYPE	STONEMASON	STRIP CLUBS
STARFLOWER	STEREOTYPY	STONY BROKE	STRIPLINGS
STARGAZERS	STERICALLY	STOOPINGLY	STRIPTEASE
STARGAZING	STERILIZED	STOPPERING	STRONGHOLD
STARRINESS	STERILIZER	STOREHOUSE	STRONGNESS
STARRY-EYED	STERNWARDS	STOREROOMS	STRONG ROOM
STARVATION	STERTOROUS	STORKSBILL	STROPPIEST
STARVELING	STEVEDORES	STORMBOUND	STRUCTURAL
STATECRAFT	STEWARDESS	STORM CLOUD	STRUCTURED
STATEMENTS	STICKINESS	STORMINESS	STRUCTURES
STATEROOMS	STICK SHIFT	STORMPROOF	STRUGGLING
STATIONARY	STICKTIGHT	STORY LINES	STRUTHIOUS
STATIONERS	STICKY ENDS	STRABISMAL	STRYCHNINE
STATIONERY	STIFFENERS	STRABISMUS	STUBBINESS
STATIONING	STIFFENING	STRADDLING	STUBBORNER
STATISTICS	STIFLINGLY	STRAGGLERS	STUBBORNLY
STATOBLAST	STIGMATISM	STRAGGLIER	STUDIOUSLY
STATOSCOPE	STIGMATIST	STRAGGLING	STUFFINESS
STATUESQUE	STIGMATIZE	STRAIGHTEN	STULTIFIED
STATUETTES	STILLBIRTH	STRAIGHTER	STULTIFIER
STATUTABLE	STILL LIFES	STRAITENED	STUMPINESS
STATUTE LAW	STIMULABLE	STRAITNESS	STUNNINGLY
STAUNCHEST	STIMULANTS	STRAMONIUM	STUPEFYING
STAUNCHING	STIMULATED	STRANGLERS	STUPENDOUS
STAUROLITE	STIMULATOR	STRANGLING	STUPIDNESS
STAVESACRE	STINGINESS	STRASBOURG	STURDINESS
STAY-AT-HOME	STINGINGLY	STRATAGEMS	STUTTERERS
ST BERNARDS	STINK-BOMBS	STRATEGICS	STUTTERING
STEADINESS	STINKINGLY	STRATEGIES	STYLISTICS
STEAKHOUSE	STINKSTONE	STRATEGIST	STYLOGRAPH
STEALTHIER	STIPELLATE	STRATIFIED	STYLOLITIC
STEALTHILY	STIPULABLE	STRATIFORM	STYPTICITY
STEAMBOATS	STIPULATED	STRATOCRAT	SUBACETATE
STEAM-CHEST	STIPULATOR	STRAWBERRY	SUBACIDITY
STEAMINESS	STIR-FRYING	STRAWBOARD	SUBALTERNS
STEAM IRONS	STIRRINGLY	STRAW POLLS	SUBAQUATIC
STEAMSHIPS	STIRRUP CUP	STREAKIEST	SUBAQUEOUS
STEAMTIGHT	STITCHWORT	STREAMLINE	SUBCALIBRE
STEEL BANDS	STOCHASTIC	STREETCARS	SUBCLAVIAN
STEELINESS	STOCKADING	STREETWISE	SUBCOMPACT
STEELWORKS	STOCK CUBES	STRELITZIA	SUBCULTURE
STEEPENING	STOCKINESS	STRENGTHEN	SUBDIVIDED
STELLIFORM	STOCKPILED	STRESS MARK	SUBDIVIDER
STEM-WINDER	STOCKPILER	STRETCHERS	SUBDUCTION
STENCILING	STOCKPILES	STRETCHIER	SUBEDITING
STENCILLED	STOCKROOMS	STRETCHING	SUBEDITORS
STENCILLER	STOCK-STILL	STRIATIONS	SUBGENERIC
STENOGRAPH	STOCKYARDS	STRICTNESS	SUBGLACIAL
STENOTYPIC	STODGINESS	STRICTURES	SUBHEADING
STENTORIAN	STOKEHOLDS	STRIDENTLY	SUBJACENCY
STEPFATHER	STOMACHING	STRIDULATE	SUBJECTIFY
STEPLADDER	STOMATITIC	STRIDULOUS	SUBJECTING
STEPMOTHER	STOMATITIS	STRIGIFORM	SUBJECTION

SUBJECTIVE	SUBVERSION	SUPERFLUID	SURREALIST
SUBJOINING	SUBVERSIVE	SUPERGIANT	SURRENDERS
SUBJUGABLE	SUBVERTING	SUPERGRASS	SURROGATES
SUBJUGATED	SUCCEEDING	SUPERHUMAN	SURROUNDED
SUBJUGATOR	SUCCESSFUL	SUPERLUNAR	SURVEYABLE
SUBKINGDOM	SUCCESSION	SUPERNOVAS	SURVIVABLE
SUBLEASING	SUCCESSIVE	SUPERORDER	SUSCEPTIVE
SUBLETTING	SUCCESSORS	SUPEROXIDE	SUSPECTING
SUBLIMABLE	SUCCINCTLY	SUPERPOWER	SUSPENDERS
SUBLIMATED	SUCCOURING	SUPERSEDED	SUSPENDING
SUBLIMATES	SUCCULENCE	SUPERSEDER	SUSPENSION
SUBLIMINAL	SUCCULENTS	SUPERSONIC	SUSPENSIVE
SUBLINGUAL	SUCCUMBING	SUPERSTARS	SUSPENSOID
SUBMARINER	SUCCUSSION	SUPERTONIC	SUSPENSORY
SUBMARINES	SUCCUSSIVE	SUPERVENED	SUSPICIONS
SUBMEDIANT	SUCKERFISH	SUPERVISED	SUSPICIOUS
SUBMERGING	SUCKING PIG	SUPERVISOR	SUSTAINING
SUBMERSION	SUDDENNESS	SUPINENESS	SUSTENANCE
SUBMISSION	SUFFERABLE	SUPPLANTED	SUSTENTION
SUBMISSIVE	SUFFERANCE	SUPPLANTER	SUZERAINTY
SUBMITTING	SUFFERINGS	SUPPLEJACK	SVERDLOVSK
SUBMONTANE	SUFFICIENT	SUPPLEMENT	SWAGGERERS
SUBOCEANIC	SUFFOCATED	SUPPLENESS	SWAGGERING
SUBORBITAL	SUFFRAGISM	SUPPLETION	SWALLOWING
SUBORDINAL	SUFFRAGIST	SUPPLETIVE	SWANKINESS
SUBPOENAED	SUGAR DADDY	SUPPLETORY	SWAN-UPPING
SUBREPTION	SUGARINESS	SUPPLIABLE	SWARTHIEST
SUBROUTINE	SUGGESTING	SUPPLIANCE	SWASHINGLY
SUBSCRIBED	SUGGESTION	SUPPLIANTS	SWEARINGLY
SUBSCRIBER	SUGGESTIVE	SUPPLICANT	SWEARWORDS
SUBSECTION	SUICIDALLY	SUPPLICATE	SWEATBANDS
SUBSEQUENT	SULLENNESS	SUPPORTERS	SWEAT GLAND
SUBSIDENCE	SULPHA DRUG	SUPPORTING	SWEATINESS
SUBSIDIARY	SULPHATION	SUPPORTIVE	SWEATSHIRT
SUBSIDIZED	SULPHONATE	SUPPOSABLE	SWEATSHOPS
SUBSIDIZER	SULPHURATE	SUPPOSEDLY	SWEEPINGLY
SUBSISTENT	SULPHURIZE	SUPPRESSED	SWEEPSTAKE
SUBSISTING	SULPHUROUS	SUPPRESSOR	SWEETBREAD
SUBSPECIES	SULTANATES	SUPPURATED	SWEETBRIER
SUBSTANCES	SULTRINESS	SUPRARENAL	SWEETENERS
SUBSTATION	SUMMARIZED	SURCHARGED	SWEETENING
SUBSTITUTE	SUMMARIZER	SURCHARGER	SWEETHEART
SUBSTRATUM	SUMMATIONS	SURCHARGES	SWEETMEATS
SUBSUMABLE	SUMMERTIME	SUREFOOTED	SWEET TOOTH
SUBTANGENT	SUMMERWOOD	SURFACTANT	SWELTERING
SUBTENANCY	SUMMINGS-UP	SURFBOARDS	SWERVINGLY
SUBTENANTS	SUMMONABLE	SURFCASTER	SWIMMINGLY
SUBTENDING	SUMMONSING	SURFEITING	SWINEHERDS
SUBTERFUGE	SUNBATHERS	SURGICALLY	SWINGINGLY
SUBTILIZER	SUNBATHING	SURJECTION	SWIRLINGLY
SUBTITULAR	SUNDAY BEST	SURJECTIVE	SWISHINGLY
SUBTLENESS	SUNDOWNERS	SURMISABLE	SWISS CHARD
SUBTLETIES	SUNFLOWERS	SURMISEDLY	SWITCHABLE
SUBTRACTED	SUNGLASSES	SURMOUNTED	SWITCHBACK
SUBTRACTER	SUN LOUNGES	SURMOUNTER	SWITCHED-ON
SUBTRAHEND	SUPERBNESS	SURPASSING	SWITCHGEAR
SUBTROPICS	SUPERCARGO	SURPLUSAGE	SWIVELLING
SUBTYPICAL	SUPERCLASS	SURPRISING	SWOONINGLY
SUBVENTION	SUPERDUPER	SURREALISM	SWORDCRAFT

SWORD DANCE	TACHOMETRY	TAXIDERMAL	TENTERHOOK
SWORDSTICK	TACHYLYTIC	TAXIMETERS	TERATOLOGY
SYCOPHANTS	TACHYMETER	TAXONOMIST	TERMAGANCY
SYLLABUSES	TACHYMETRY	TAX SHELTER	TERMAGANTS
SYLLOGISMS	TACITURNLY	TEA CADDIES	TERMINABLE
SYLLOGIZER	TACTICALLY	TEAGARDENS	TERMINALLY
SYLPHIDINE	TACTICIANS	TEA PARTIES	TERMINATED
SYLVESTRAL	TACTLESSLY	TEARJERKER	TERMINATOR
SYMBIONTIC	TAENIACIDE	TEA SERVICE	TERMINUSES
SYMBOLIZED	TAENIAFUGE	TEA TROLLEY	TERRACOTTA
SYMMETRIZE	TAGLIATELE	TECHNETIUM	TERRA FIRMA
SYMPATHIES	TAILBOARDS	TECHNICIAN	TERRAMYCIN
SYMPATHIZE	TAILGATING	TECHNIQUES	TERREPLEIN
SYMPHONIES	TAILLIGHTS	TECHNOCRAT	TERRE-VERTE
SYMPHONIST	TAILORBIRD	TECHNOLOGY	TERRIFYING
SYMPHYSIAL	TAILOR-MADE	TECTRICIAL	TERRORISTS
SYMPHYSTIC	TAILPIECES	TEDDY BEARS	TERRORIZED
SYMPOSIUMS	TAKINGNESS	TEENY WEENY	TERRORIZER
SYNAGOGUES	TALCAHUANO	TELECASTER	TERRYCLOTH
SYNCARPOUS	TALEBEARER	TELEGNOSIS	TESSELLATE
SYNCHRONIC	TALISMANIC	TELEGRAPHS	TESTACEOUS
SYNCLASTIC	TALKING-TOS	TELEGRAPHY	TESTAMENTS
SYNCOPATED	TAMABILITY	TELEMETRIC	TESTICULAR
SYNCOPATOR	TAMAULIPAS	TELEPATHIC	TESTIFYING
SYNCRETISM	TAMBOURINE	TELEPHONED	TEST PILOTS
SYNCRETIST	TANANARIVE	TELEPHONER	TESTUDINAL
SYNCRETIZE	TANGANYIKA	TELEPHONES	TETCHINESS
SYNDICATED	TANGENTIAL	TELESCOPED	TETE-A-TETES
SYNDICATES	TANGERINES	TELESCOPES	TETRABASIC
SYNDICSHIP	TANGLEMENT	TELESCOPIC	TETRABRACH
SYNECDOCHE	TANTALIZED	TELESCRIPT	TETRACHORD
SYNECOLOGY	TANTALIZER	TELEVISING	TETRAGONAL
SYNERGETIC	TANTALUSES	TELEVISION	TETRAPLOID
SYNOECIOUS	TANTAMOUNT	TELEWRITER	TETRAPODIC
SYNONYMITY	TAP DANCERS	TELIOSPORE	TETRARCHIC
SYNONYMIZE	TAP DANCING	TELLING-OFF	TETRASPORE
SYNONYMOUS	TAPERINGLY	TELOPHASIC	TETRASTICH
SYNTACTICS	TAPESTRIED	TELPHERAGE	TETRATOMIC
SYNTHESIST	TAPESTRIES	TEMPERABLE	TEXTUALISM
SYNTHESIZE	TARANTELLA	TEMPERANCE	TEXTUALIST
SYNTHETISM	TARANTULAS	TEMPORIZED	TEXTURALLY
SYNTHETIST	TARDIGRADE	TEMPORIZER	THANKFULLY
SYPHILITIC	TARMACKING	TEMPTATION	THEATRICAL
SYSTEMATIC	TARNISHING	TEMPTINGLY	THEME PARKS
SYSTEMIZER	TARPAULINS	TENABILITY	THEME SONGS
	TASIMETRIC	TENDENCIES	THEMSELVES
T	TASK FORCES	TENDERABLE	THENARDITE
TABERNACLE	TASKMASTER	TENDERFEET	THEOCRATIC
TABESCENCE	TASTEFULLY	TENDERFOOT	THEODOLITE
TABLECLOTH	TATTERSALL	TENDERIZED	THEOLOGIAN
TABLE D'HOTE	TATTLINGLY	TENDERIZER	THEOLOGIES
TABLELANDS	TATTOOISTS	TENDERLOIN	THEOLOGIZE
TABLE LINEN	TAUNTINGLY	TENDERNESS	THEOPHOBIA
TABLESPOON	TAUROMACHY	TENDRILLAR	THEORETICS
TABULARIZE	TAUTOMERIC	TENEMENTAL	THEORIZING
TABULATING	TAUTONYMIC	TENNESSEAN	THEOSOPHIC
TABULATION	TAWDRINESS	TENOTOMIST	THERAPISTS
TACHOGRAPH	TAXABILITY	TENSIMETER	THEREAFTER
TACHOMETER	TAXATIONAL	TENTACULAR	THEREUNDER

THERMALIZE	THUNDEROUS	TOLERATIVE	TOXICOLOGY
THERMIONIC	THURINGIAN	TOLLBOOTHS	TRABEATION
THERMISTOR	THWARTEDLY	TOLLUIDINE	TRABECULAR
THERMOGRAM	TICKERTAPE	TOLUIC ACID	TRACHEIDAL
THERMOPILE	TICKING OFF	TOMBSTONES	TRACHEITIS
THERMOSTAT	TICKLISHLY	TOMFOOLERY	TRACHYTOID
THEROPODAN	TIDAL WAVES	TOMOGRAPHY	TRACK EVENT
THESSALIAN	TIEBREAKER	TONALITIES	TRACKLAYER
THETICALLY	TIED HOUSES	TONELESSLY	TRACKSUITS
THICKENERS	TIEMANNITE	TONGUE-TIED	TRACTILITY
THICKENING	TIGHTENING	TONIC SOL-FA	TRACTIONAL
THIEVINGLY	TIGHTROPES	TONIC WATER	TRADEMARKS
THIEVISHLY	TIGLIC ACID	TONOMETRIC	TRADE NAMES
THIMBLEFUL	TILIACEOUS	TOOL-MAKING	TRADE PRICE
THIMEROSAL	TILLANDSIA	TOOTHACHES	TRADE ROUTE
THINK TANKS	TIMBERHEAD	TOOTHBRUSH	TRADE UNION
THIOURACIL	TIMBERLINE	TOOTHCOMBS	TRADE WINDS
THIRD PARTY	TIMBERWORK	TOOTHINESS	TRADITIONS
THIRD WORLD	TIMBERYARD	TOOTHPASTE	TRADUCIBLE
THIRSTIEST	TIMEKEEPER	TOOTHPICKS	TRAFFIC JAM
THIRTEENTH	TIMELESSLY	TOPAZOLITE	TRAFFICKED
THIRTIETHS	TIME LIMITS	TOPGALLANT	TRAFFICKER
THIXOTROPY	TIMELINESS	TOP-HEAVILY	TRAGACANTH
THORIANITE	TIMEPIECES	TOPICALITY	TRAGEDIANS
THORNINESS	TIMESAVING	TOPOGRAPHY	TRAGICALLY
THOROUGHLY	TIMESERVER	TOPOLOGIST	TRAGICOMIC
THOUGHTFUL	TIME SHEETS	TOPSY-TURVY	TRAILINGLY
THOUGHT-OUT	TIME SIGNAL	TORBERNITE	TRAITOROUS
THOUSANDTH	TIME SWITCH	TORCHLIGHT	TRAJECTILE
THREADBARE	TIMETABLED	TORMENTING	TRAJECTION
THREADWORM	TIMETABLES	TORMENTORS	TRAJECTORY
THREATENED	TIMEWORKER	TORPEDOING	TRAMONTANE
THREATENER	TIMOROUSLY	TORRENTIAL	TRAMPOLINE
THREEPENCE	TIMPANISTS	TORT-FEASOR	TRANCELIKE
THREE-PHASE	TINCTORIAL	TORTUOSITY	TRANQUILLY
THREE-PIECE	TINGALINGS	TORTUOUSLY	TRANSACTED
THREESOMES	TINGLINGLY	TORTUREDLY	TRANSACTOR
THRENODIES	TIN OPENERS	TOTEMISTIC	TRANSCRIBE
THRESHOLDS	TIRELESSLY	TOTEM POLES	TRANSCRIPT
THRIFTIEST	TIRESOMELY	TOTIPOTENT	TRANSDUCER
THRIFTLESS	TITANESQUE	TOUCH-AND-GO	TRANSEPTAL
THROATIEST	TITILLATED	TOUCHDOWNS	TRANSFEREE
THROATLASH	TITIVATING	TOUCHINESS	TRANSFEROR
THROMBOGEN	TITIVATION	TOUCHINGLY	TRANSFIXED
THROMBOSES	TITLE DEEDS	TOUCHLINES	TRANSGRESS
THROMBOSIS	TITLE PAGES	TOUCHPAPER	TRANSIENCE
THROMBOTIC	TITLE ROLES	TOUCHSTONE	TRANSIENCY
THROTTLING	TITRATABLE	TOUCH-TYPED	TRANSISTOR
THROUGHOUT	TITUBATION	TOUGHENING	TRANSITION
THROUGHPUT	T-JUNCTIONS	TOURMALINE	TRANSITIVE
THROUGHWAY	TOADSTOOLS	TOURNAMENT	TRANSITORY
THROWBACKS	TOBOGGANED	TOURNIQUET	TRANSKEIAN
THUMBNAILS	TOBOGGANER	TOWER BLOCK	TRANSLATED
THUMBSCREW	TOCOPHEROL	TOWN CLERKS	TRANSLATOR
THUMBSTALL	TOILETRIES	TOWN CRIERS	TRANSLUNAR
THUMBTACKS	TOILET ROLL	TOWN HOUSES	TRANSMUTED
THUMPINGLY	TOLERANTLY	TOWNSCAPES	TRANSMUTER
THUNDERERS	TOLERATING	TOWNSWOMAN	TRANSPIRED
THUNDERING	TOLERATION	TOXALBUMIN	TRANSPLANT

TRANSPOLAR	TRIFURCATE	TROUBLEDLY	TWENTIETHS
TRANSPORTS	TRIGEMINAL	TROUSSEAUS	TWIN-BEDDED
TRANSPOSED	TRIGGERING	TROUSSEAUX	TWINFLOWER
TRANSPOSER	TRIGLYPHIC	TROY WEIGHT	TWINKLINGS
TRANSPUTER	TRIGRAPHIC	TRUCK FARMS	TWISTINGLY
TRANSUDATE	TRIHYDRATE	TRUCKLOADS	TWITTERING
TRANSVALUE	TRILATERAL	TRUCK STOPS	TYMPANITES
TRANSVERSE	TRILINGUAL	TRUCULENCE	TYMPANITIC
TRAPEZIUMS	TRILITERAL	TRUMP CARDS	TYMPANITIS
TRAPEZOIDS	TRILLIONTH	TRUMPETERS	TYPECASTER
TRASHINESS	TRILOBITES	TRUMPETING	TYPESCRIPT
TRAUMATISM	TRILOCULAR	TRUNCATING	TYPESETTER
TRAUMATIZE	TRIMESTERS	TRUNCATION	TYPEWRITER
TRAVAILING	TRIMESTRAL	TRUNCHEONS	TYPHLOLOGY
TRAVELLERS	TRIMONTHLY	TRUNK CALLS	TYPHOGENIC
TRAVELLING	TRIMORPHIC	TRUNK ROADS	TYPING POOL
TRAVELOGUE	TRINOCULAR	TRUNK ROUTE	TYPOGRAPHY
TRAVELSICK	TRIOECIOUS	TRUSTFULLY	TYPOLOGIST
TRAVERSING	TRIPARTITE	TRUST FUNDS	TYRANNICAL
TRAVERTINE	TRIPHAMMER	TRUSTINESS	TYRANNIZED
TRAVESTIES	TRIPHTHONG	TRUTHFULLY	TYRANNIZER
TREADMILLS	TRIPHYLITE	TRUTH-VALUE	TYROCIDINE
TREASURERS	TRIPINNATE	TRYINGNESS	TYROSINASE
TREASURIES	TRIPLE JUMP	TRYPTOPHAN	
TREASURING	TRIPLETAIL	TUBERCULAR	**U**
TREATMENTS	TRIPLICATE	TUBERCULIN	UBIQUITOUS
TREBLE CLEF	TRIPLICITY	TUBEROSITY	ULCERATING
TREEHOPPER	TRIPPINGLY	TUB-THUMPER	ULCERATION
TREMENDOUS	TRIPTEROUS	TUBULARITY	ULCERATIVE
TRENCHANCY	TRIRADIATE	TUBULATION	ULTIMATELY
TRENCH COAT	TRISECTING	TUFFACEOUS	ULTIMATUMS
TRENDINESS	TRISKELION	TUGS-OF-LOVE	ULTRAFICHE
TREPANNING	TRISTICHIC	TULARAEMIA	ULTRAISTIC
TREPHINING	TRITANOPIA	TULARAEMIC	ULTRASHORT
TREPPANNER	TRITANOPIC	TUMBLEDOWN	ULTRASONIC
TRESPASSED	TRITURABLE	TUMBLEWEED	ULTRASOUND
TRESPASSER	TRITURATOR	TUMESCENCE	ULTRAVIRUS
TRESPASSES	TRIUMPHANT	TUMULOSITY	UMBILICATE
TRIANGULAR	TRIUMPHING	TUMULTUOUS	UMBILIFORM
TRIBRACHIC	TRIVALENCY	TUNELESSLY	UMBRAGEOUS
TRICHIASIS	TRIVANDRUM	TUNING FORK	UMPIRESHIP
TRICHINIZE	TRIVIALITY	TUNING PEGS	UMPTEENTHS
TRICHINOUS	TRIVIALIZE	TUNNELLING	UNABRIDGED
TRICHOCYST	TROCHANTER	TURBOPROPS	UNAFFECTED
TRICHOGYNE	TROGLODYTE	TURBULENCE	UN-AMERICAN
TRICHOLOGY	TROLLEYBUS	TURGESCENT	UNASSISTED
TRICHOTOMY	TROMBONIST	TURNABOUTS	UNASSUMING
TRICHROISM	TROOPSHIPS	TURNAROUND	UNATTACHED
TRICHROMAT	TROPAEOLIN	TURNBUCKLE	UNATTENDED
TRICKINESS	TROPAEOLUM	TURNROUNDS	UNAVAILING
TRICKINGLY	TROPICALLY	TURNSTILES	UNBALANCED
TRICKSTERS	TROPICBIRD	TURNTABLES	UNBEARABLE
TRICOLOURS	TROPOLOGIC	TURPENTINE	UNBEARABLY
TRICOSTATE	TROPOPAUSE	TURQUOISES	UNBEATABLE
TRICROTISM	TROPOPHYTE	TURTLEBACK	UNBECOMING
TRIDENTATE	TROTSKYISM	TURTLEDOVE	UNBELIEVER
TRIDENTINE	TROTSKYIST	TURTLENECK	UNBENDABLE
TRIFLINGLY	TROTSKYITE	TUT-TUTTING	UNBLINKING
TRIFOLIATE	TROUBADOUR	TWELVE-TONE	UNBLUSHING

UNBOSOMING	UNDERTRUMP	UNINFORMED	UNSCREWING
UNBUCKLING	UNDERVALUE	UNINSPIRED	UNSCRIPTED
UNBURDENED	UNDERWATER	UNINTENDED	UNSEALABLE
UNCANNIEST	UNDERWORLD	UNIONISTIC	UNSEASONED
UNCARED-FOR	UNDERWRITE	UNIONIZING	UNSEEINGLY
UNCIVILITY	UNDERWROTE	UNIQUENESS	UNSETTLING
UNCOMMONLY	UNDETERRED	UNISEPTATE	UNSHAKABLE
UNCONFINED	UNDIRECTED	UNITARIANS	UNSOCIABLE
UNCOUPLING	UNDISPUTED	UNITEDNESS	UNSPECIFIC
UNCOVERING	UNDRESSING	UNIT TRUSTS	UNSTEADILY
UNCRITICAL	UNDULATING	UNIVALENCY	UNSTINTING
UNCTUOSITY	UNDULATION	UNIVERSITY	UNSTOPPING
UNCTUOUSLY	UNDULATORY	UNJUSTNESS	UNSTRAINED
UNDECEIVED	UNEARTHING	UNKINDNESS	UNSTRESSED
UNDECEIVER	UNEASINESS	UNKNOWABLE	UNSTRIATED
UNDEFEATED	UNECONOMIC	UNLAWFULLY	UNSUITABLE
UNDEFENDED	UNEDIFYING	UNLEARNING	UNSWERVING
UNDENIABLE	UNEDUCATED	UNLEASHING	UNTANGLING
UNDENIABLY	UNEMPLOYED	UNLEAVENED	UNTHANKFUL
UNDERACTED	UNENVIABLE	UNLETTERED	UNTHINKING
UNDERBELLY	UNEQUALLED	UNLICENSED	UNTIDINESS
UNDERBRUSH	UNERRINGLY	UNLOCKABLE	UNTIRINGLY
UNDERCOATS	UNEVENNESS	UNLOOSENED	UNTOWARDLY
UNDERCOVER	UNEVENTFUL	UNMANNERED	UNTRUTHFUL
UNDERCROFT	UNEXAMPLED	UNMANNERLY	UNWIELDILY
UNDERDRAIN	UNEXPECTED	UNMEASURED	UNWINDABLE
UNDERFLOOR	UNFAIRNESS	UNMERCIFUL	UNWORKABLE
UNDERGLAZE	UNFAITHFUL	UNMORALITY	UNWORTHILY
UNDERGOING	UNFAMILIAR	UNNUMBERED	UNYIELDING
UNDERGROWN	UNFATHERED	UNOCCUPIED	UP-AND-UNDER
UNDERLINED	UNFEMININE	UNOFFICIAL	UPBRAIDING
UNDERLINGS	UNFETTERED	UNORIGINAL	UPBRINGING
UNDERLYING	UNFINISHED	UNORTHODOX	UPHOLSTERY
UNDERMINED	UNFLAGGING	UNPATENTED	UPLIFTMENT
UNDERMINER	UNFORESEEN	UNPLAYABLE	UPPER CLASS
UNDERNAMED	UNFORGIVEN	UNPLEASANT	UPPER CRUST
UNDERNEATH	UNFRIENDLY	UNPREPARED	UPPER HOUSE
UNDERPANTS	UNFROCKING	UNPROMPTED	UPPER VOLTA
UNDERPRICE	UNFRUITFUL	UNPROVIDED	UPPISHNESS
UNDERPROOF	UNGENEROUS	UNPROVOKED	UPROARIOUS
UNDERQUOTE	UNGRATEFUL	UNPUNCTUAL	UPSETTABLE
UNDERRATED	UNGRUDGING	UNPUNISHED	UPSIDE DOWN
UNDERSCORE	UNGUENTARY	UNRAVELING	UPSTANDING
UNDERSEXED	UNHALLOWED	UNRAVELLED	UPWARDNESS
UNDERSHIRT	UNHAMPERED	UNRAVELLER	URAL-ALTAIC
UNDERSHOOT	UNHANDSOME	UNREADABLE	URBANENESS
UNDERSIZED	UNHERALDED	UNREADABLY	UREDOSORUS
UNDERSKIRT	UNHOLINESS	UNRELIABLE	UREDOSPORE
UNDERSLUNG	UNHOPED-FOR	UNRELIEVED	URETHRITIC
UNDERSPEND	UNHYGIENIC	UNREQUITED	URETHRITIS
UNDERSTAND	UNICAMERAL	UNRESERVED	URINALYSIS
UNDERSTATE	UNICOSTATE	UNRESOLVED	UROCHORDAL
UNDERSTOCK	UNICYCLIST	UNRIVALLED	UROGENITAL
UNDERSTOOD	UNIFOLIATE	UNRULINESS	UROSCOPIST
UNDERSTUDY	UNIFORMITY	UNSADDLING	URTICARIAL
UNDERTAKEN	UNILATERAL	UNSANITARY	URTICATION
UNDERTAKER	UNILOCULAR	UNSCHOOLED	USEFULNESS
UNDERTONES	UNIMPOSING	UNSCRAMBLE	USHERETTES
UNDERTRICK	UNIMPROVED	UNSCREENED	USQUEBAUGH

USTULATION	VELOCIPEDE	VIEWFINDER	VOL-AU-VENTS
USURPATION	VELOCITIES	VIEWPOINTS	VOLITIONAL
USURPATIVE	VELUTINOUS	VIGILANTES	VOLLEYBALL
USURPINGLY	VENATIONAL	VIGILANTLY	VOLT-AMPERE
UTILIZABLE	VENDETTIST	VIGNETTING	VOLTE-FACES
UTO-AZTECAN	VENERATING	VIGNETTIST	VOLUBILITY
UTOPIANISM	VENERATION	VIGOROUSLY	VOLUMETRIC
UTTERANCES	VENEZUELAN	VIJAYAWADA	VOLUMINOUS
UXORICIDAL	VENGEANCES	VILLAINOUS	VOLUNTEERS
UZBEKISTAN	VENGEFULLY	VILLANELLA	VOLUPTUARY
	VENOMOUSLY	VILLANELLE	VOLUPTUOUS
V	VENOUSNESS	VILLANOVAN	VORARLBERG
VACANTNESS	VENTILABLE	VINA DEL MAR	VORTICELLA
VACATIONED	VENTILATED	VINDICABLE	VOTIVENESS
VACATIONER	VENTILATOR	VINDICATED	VOUCHSAFED
VACCINATED	VENTRICLES	VINDICATOR	VULCANIZED
VACILLATED	VENTRICOSE	VINDICTIVE	VULCANIZER
VACILLATOR	VERBALIZED	VINIFEROUS	VULGARIZED
VACUUM PUMP	VERBALIZER	VINYLIDENE	VULGARIZER
VAGINISMUS	VERBAL NOUN	VIOLACEOUS	VULGARNESS
VAGOTROPIC	VERIFIABLE	VIOLATIONS	VULNERABLE
VAL-DE-MARNE	VERKRAMPTE	VIOLINISTS	VULNERABLY
VALENTINES	VERMICELLI	VIRAGINOUS	VULPECULAR
VALIDATING	VERMICIDAL	VIRESCENCE	
VALIDATION	VERMICULAR	VIROLOGIST	W
VALIDATORY	VERNACULAR	VIRTUALITY	WADDLINGLY
VALLADOLID	VERNISSAGE	VIRTUOSITY	WADING POOL
VALLECULAR	VERSAILLES	VIRTUOUSLY	WAGE SLAVES
VALPARAISO	VERTEBRATE	VIRULENTLY	WAGGA WAGGA
VALUATIONS	VERTICALLY	VISCOMETER	WAGGLINGLY
VALVULITIS	VERY LIGHTS	VISCOMETRY	WAGONS-LITS
VAMPIRE BAT	VESICATION	VISCOUNTCY	WAINWRIGHT
VANADINITE	VESICULATE	VISIBILITY	WAISTBANDS
VANDALIZED	VESPERTINE	VISITATION	WAISTCOATS
VANISHMENT	VESTIBULAR	VISITORIAL	WAISTLINES
VANQUISHED	VESTIBULES	VISUAL AIDS	WAKEY WAKEY
VANQUISHER	VESTMENTAL	VISUALIZED	WALKABOUTS
VAPORIZING	VESTMENTED	VISUALIZER	WALK OF LIFE
VAPOURABLE	VETERINARY	VITALISTIC	WALLCHARTS
VARIATIONS	VIBRACULAR	VITAL SIGNS	WALLFLOWER
VARICELLAR	VIBRACULUM	VITRESCENT	WALLPAPERS
VARICOCELE	VIBRAPHONE	VITRIFYING	WALL STREET
VARICOSITY	VIBRATIONS	VITRIOLIZE	WALL-TO-WALL
VARICOTOMY	VICEGERENT	VITUPERATE	WANDERINGS
VARIEDNESS	VICEREINES	VIVIPARITY	WANDERLUST
VARIEGATED	VICINITIES	VIVIPAROUS	WANTONNESS
VARIOLITIC	VICOMTESSE	VIVISECTOR	WAREHOUSES
VARIOMETER	VICTIMIZED	VOCABULARY	WARMING PAN
VARITYPIST	VICTIMIZER	VOCAL CORDS	WARMONGERS
VARNISHING	VICTORIANS	VOCATIONAL	WARRANTIES
VASTNESSES	VICTORIOUS	VOCIFERANT	WARRANTING
VAUDEVILLE	VICTUALING	VOCIFERATE	WASHBASINS
VAUNTINGLY	VICTUALLED	VOCIFEROUS	WASHCLOTHS
VEGETABLES	VICTUALLER	VOICE BOXES	WASHING DAY
VEGETARIAN	VIDEODISCS	VOICE-OVERS	WASHINGTON
VEGETATING	VIDEO NASTY	VOICEPRINT	WASHSTANDS
VEGETATION	VIDEOPHONE	VOLAPUKIST	WASTEFULLY
VEGETATIVE	VIDEOTAPED	VOLATILITY	WASTELANDS
VEHEMENTLY	VIETNAMESE	VOLATILIZE	WASTE PAPER

WATCHFULLY	WELLINGTON	WICKERWORK	WOODBLOCKS
WATCHMAKER	WELL-JUDGED	WICKET GATE	WOODCARVER
WATCHSTRAP	WELL-SPOKEN	WIDE-SCREEN	WOODCUTTER
WATCHTOWER	WELLSPRING	WIDESPREAD	WOODENNESS
WATCHWORDS	WELL-TURNED	WIFELINESS	WOODLANDER
WATER BIRDS	WELL-WISHER	WILDCATTED	WOODPECKER
WATERBORNE	WELL-WORDED	WILDEBEEST	WOODWORKER
WATER BUTTS	WENTLETRAP	WILDERNESS	WOOLGROWER
WATERCRAFT	WEREWOLVES	WILDFOWLER	WOOLLINESS
WATERCRESS	WESTERLIES	WILFULNESS	WORDLESSLY
WATERFALLS	WESTERNERS	WILLOWHERB	WORKAHOLIC
WATERFOWLS	WESTERNISM	WILLY-NILLY	WORKBASKET
WATERFRONT	WESTERNIZE	WINCEYETTE	WORK-HARDEN
WATERHOLES	WEST INDIAN	WINCHESTER	WORKHORSES
WATERINESS	WESTPHALIA	WINDBREAKS	WORKING DAY
WATER JUMPS	WET BLANKET	WIND-BROKEN	WORKINGMAN
WATER LEVEL	WET-NURSING	WINDEDNESS	WORKPEOPLE
WATER MAINS	WHARFINGER	WINDFLOWER	WORKPLACES
WATERMARKS	WHATSOEVER	WINDGALLED	WORK-TO-RULE
WATERMELON	WHEELBASES	WIND GAUGES	WORLD-CLASS
WATERMILLS	WHEELCHAIR	WINDJAMMER	WORLDLIEST
WATER PIPES	WHEELHOUSE	WINDLASSES	WORLD POWER
WATERPOWER	WHEEZINESS	WINDOWPANE	WORLD-WEARY
WATERPROOF	WHEEZINGLY	WINDOW-SHOP	WORRYINGLY
WATER RATES	WHENSOEVER	WINDOWSILL	WORRYWARTS
WATERSCAPE	WHEREFORES	WINDSCREEN	WORSHIPFUL
WATERSHEDS	WHETSTONES	WINDSHIELD	WORSHIPING
WATER SKIER	WHICKERING	WINDSTORMS	WORSHIPPED
WATERSPOUT	WHIMPERING	WINDSUCKER	WORSHIPPER
WATER TABLE	WHIPLASHES	WIND-SURFER	WORTHINESS
WATERTIGHT	WHIP-ROUNDS	WIND TUNNEL	WORTHWHILE
WATER VOLES	WHIPSTITCH	WINEBIBBER	WOUNDINGLY
WATERWHEEL	WHIRLABOUT	WINTERFEED	WRAITHLIKE
WATERWINGS	WHIRLIGIGS	WINTERTIME	WRATHFULLY
WATERWORKS	WHIRLINGLY	WINTRINESS	WRETCHEDLY
WATTLEBIRD	WHIRLPOOLS	WIRE-HAIRED	WRISTBANDS
WAVELENGTH	WHIRLWINDS	WIRELESSES	WRISTWATCH
WAVERINGLY	WHIRLYBIRD	WIREWORKER	WRITHINGLY
WAXED PAPER	WHISPERERS	WISECRACKS	WRONGDOERS
WEAKLINESS	WHISPERING	WISHY-WASHY	WRONGDOING
WEAK-MINDED	WHIST DRIVE	WITCHCRAFT	WRONGFULLY
WEAKNESSES	WHITEBOARD	WITCH-HAZEL	WUNDERKIND
WEAK-WILLED	WHITE DWARF	WITCH-HUNTS	
WEALTHIEST	WHITE FLAGS	WITHDRAWAL	X
WEARYINGLY	WHITE HOPES	WITHDRAWER	XANTHATION
WEATHERING	WHITE HORSE	WITHHOLDER	XENOGAMOUS
WEATHERMAN	WHITE HOUSE	WITNESS BOX	XENOLITHIC
WEATHERMEN	WHITE MAGIC	WITNESSING	XENOPHOBIA
WEAVERBIRD	WHITE METAL	WITTICISMS	XENOPHOBIC
WEDNESDAYS	WHITE PAPER	WOBBLINESS	XEROGRAPHY
WEEDKILLER	WHITE SAUCE	WOEFULNESS	XEROPHYTIC
WEEKENDERS	WHITESMITH	WOLFHOUNDS	XIPHOSURAN
WEEKENDING	WHITEWATER	WOLFRAMITE	X-RADIATION
WEEKNIGHTS	WHITTLINGS	WOLLONGONG	XYLOGRAPHY
WEIGHTLESS	WHOLEFOODS	WOMANIZERS	XYLOPHONES
WELL-ARGUED	WHOLE NOTES	WOMANIZING	XYLOPHONIC
WELL-CHOSEN	WHOLESALER	WONDERLAND	XYLOTOMIST
WELL-EARNED	WHOREHOUSE	WONDERMENT	XYLOTOMOUS
WELL-HEELED	WICKEDNESS	WONDERWORK	

Y	YESTERYEAR	Z	ZOOPHAGOUS
YARBOROUGH	YIELDINGLY	ZAPOROZHYE	ZOOPHILISM
YARDSTICKS	YLANG-YLANG	ZIGZAGGING	ZOOPHILOUS
YEASTINESS	YOSHKAR-OLA	ZINCOGRAPH	ZOOPHOBOUS
YELLOWBARK	YOUNGBERRY	ZOOGRAPHER	ZOOPLASTIC
YELLOWBIRD	YOUNGSTERS	ZOOGRAPHIC	ZWITTERION
YELLOWLEGS	YOUNGSTOWN	ZOOLATROUS	ZYGODACTYL
YELLOWTAIL	YOURSELVES	ZOOLOGICAL	ZYGOSPORIC
YELLOWWEED	YOUTHFULLY	ZOOLOGISTS	ZYMOLOGIST
YELLOWWOOD	YUGOSLAVIA	ZOOM LENSES	
YESTERDAYS		ZOOMORPHIC	

A
ABANDONEDLY
ABANDONMENT
ABBEVILLIAN
ABBREVIATED
ABBREVIATOR
ABDICATIONS
ABERRATIONS
ABIETIC ACID
ABIOGENESIS
ABIOGENETIC
ABLUTIONARY
ABNORMALITY
ABOLISHMENT
ABOMINATING
ABOMINATION
ABORIGINALS
ABORTIONIST
ABRACADABRA
ABRANCHIATE
ABRIDGMENTS
ABROGATIONS
ABSENTEEISM
ABSORBINGLY
ABSORPTANCE
ABSTENTIONS
ABSTENTIOUS
ABSTRACTING
ABSTRACTION
ABSTRACTIVE
ABSTRICTION
ABSURDITIES
ABUSIVENESS
ACADEMICALS
ACADEMICIAN
ACADEMICISM
ACARPELLOUS
ACATALECTIC
ACAULESCENT
ACCELERANDO
ACCELERATED
ACCELERATOR
ACCENTUATED
ACCEPTANCES
ACCEPTATION
ACCESSIONAL
ACCESSORIAL
ACCESSORIES
ACCESSORILY
ACCIPITRINE
ACCLAMATION
ACCLAMATORY
ACCLIMATIZE
ACCLIVITIES
ACCLIVITOUS
ACCOMMODATE
ACCOMPANIED
ACCOMPANIER
ACCOMPANIST

ACCOMPLICES
ACCORDANCES
ACCORDINGLY
ACCOUNTABLE
ACCOUNTANCY
ACCOUNTANTS
ACCULTURATE
ACCUMULABLE
ACCUMULATED
ACCUMULATOR
ACCUSATIONS
ACCUSATIVAL
ACCUSATIVES
ACCUSTOMING
ACETANILIDE
ACETYLATION
ACHIEVEMENT
ACHONDRITIC
ACHROMATISM
ACHROMATIZE
ACHROMATOUS
ACID-FORMING
ACIDIFIABLE
ACIDIMETRIC
ACIDOPHILIC
ACIDOPHILUS
ACIDULATION
ACINACIFORM
ACKNOWLEDGE
ACLINIC LINE
ACOUSTICIAN
ACQUAINTING
ACQUIESCENT
ACQUIESCING
ACQUIREMENT
ACQUISITION
ACQUISITIVE
ACQUITTANCE
ACRIFLAVINE
ACRIMONIOUS
ACROCARPOUS
ACROMEGALIC
ACTINICALLY
ACTINOMETER
ACTINOMETRY
ACTINOMYCIN
ACTUALITIES
ACUMINATION
ACUPUNCTURE
ADAM'S APPLES
ADAPTATIONS
ADIAPHORISM
ADIAPHORIST
ADIAPHOROUS
AD INFINITUM
ADIPOCEROUS
ADJOURNMENT
ADJUDICATED
ADJUDICATOR

ADJUSTMENTS
ADMIRATIONS
ADMONISHING
ADMONITIONS
ADOLESCENCE
ADOLESCENTS
ADOPTIONISM
ADOPTIONIST
ADULTERATED
ADULTERATOR
ADUMBRATING
ADUMBRATION
ADUMBRATIVE
ADVANCEMENT
ADVANCINGLY
ADVENTURERS
ADVENTURESS
ADVENTURISM
ADVENTURIST
ADVENTUROUS
ADVERBIALLY
ADVERSARIAL
ADVERSARIES
ADVERSATIVE
ADVERSITIES
ADVERTENTLY
ADVERTISERS
ADVERTISING
AEOLIAN HARP
AERODYNAMIC
AEROGRAMMES
AERONAUTICS
AEROSTATICS
AEROSTATION
AESTIVATION
AETIOLOGIST
AFFECTATION
AFFECTINGLY
AFFECTIONAL
AFFECTIVITY
AFFILIATING
AFFILIATION
AFFIRMATION
AFFIRMATIVE
AFFLICTIONS
AFFORESTING
AFFRANCHISE
AFFRICATIVE
AFGHANISTAN
AFICIONADOS
AFRO-ASIATIC
AFTERBIRTHS
AFTERBURNER
AFTEREFFECT
AFTERSHAVES
AFTERTASTES
AGELESSNESS
AGGLOMERATE
AGGLUTINANT

AGGLUTINATE	ALTARPIECES	ANAESTHETIC
AGGRADATION	ALTERATIONS	ANALEMMATIC
AGGRANDIZER	ALTERCATION	ANALYSATION
AGGRAVATING	ALTERNATELY	ANAMORPHISM
AGGRAVATION	ALTERNATING	ANAPHYLAXIS
AGGREGATING	ALTERNATION	ANARCHISTIC
AGGREGATION	ALTERNATIVE	ANASTOMOSIS
AGGRIEVEDLY	ALTERNATORS	ANASTOMOTIC
AGNOSTICISM	ALTITUDINAL	ANCIENTNESS
AGONIZINGLY	ALTOCUMULUS	ANCILLARIES
AGONY COLUMN	ALTOGETHERS	ANDROGENOUS
AGORAPHOBIA	ALTOSTRATUS	ANDROGYNOUS
AGORAPHOBIC	ALUMINOSITY	ANDROSPHINX
AGRARIANISM	ALVEOLATION	ANEMOGRAPHY
AGRICULTURE	AMALGAMATED	ANEMOMETERS
AGROBIOLOGY	AMARANTHINE	ANEMOMETRIC
AGROLOGICAL	AMBASSADORS	ANESTHETICS
AGROSTOLOGY	AMBIGUGUITY	ANESTHETIST
AIDE-MEMOIRE	AMBIGUOUSLY	ANESTHETIZE
AIDES-DE-CAMP	AMBITIOUSLY	ANFRACTUOUS
AILUROPHILE	AMBIVALENCE	ANGELICALLY
AILUROPHOBE	AMBLYGONITE	ANGIOMATOUS
AIMLESSNESS	AMELIORATED	ANGLICANISM
AIRCRAFTMAN	AMELIORATOR	ANGLICIZING
AIRCRAFTMEN	AMENABILITY	ANGLO-INDIAN
AIRLESSNESS	AMENORRHOEA	ANGLOPHILES
AIRSICKNESS	AMERICANISM	ANGLOPHILIA
AIR TERMINAL	AMERICANIZE	ANGLOPHOBES
ALARM CLOCKS	AMETHYSTINE	ANGLOPHOBIA
ALBATROSSES	AMICABILITY	ANGLO-SAXONS
ALBUMINURIA	AMINOPHENOL	ANIMALCULAR
ALBUQUERQUE	AMINOPYRINE	ANIMOSITIES
ALDOSTERONE	AMMONIATION	ANISEIKONIA
ALESSANDRIA	AMONTILLADO	ANISEIKONIC
ALGEBRAICAL	AMOROUSNESS	ANISODACTYL
ALGINIC ACID	AMOR PATRIAE	ANISOGAMOUS
ALGOLAGNIST	AMORPHOUSLY	ANISOMEROUS
ALGORITHMIC	AMORTIZABLE	ANISOMETRIC
ALKALIMETER	AMOUR-PROPRE	ANISOTROPIC
ALKALIMETRY	AMPHETAMINE	ANNABERGITE
ALKALIZABLE	AMPHIBIOTIC	ANNEXATIONS
ALL-AMERICAN	AMPHIBOLITE	ANNIHILABLE
ALLANTOIDAL	AMPHIBOLOGY	ANNIHILATED
ALLEGATIONS	AMPHICHROIC	ANNIHILATOR
ALLEGIANCES	AMPHICTYONY	ANNIVERSARY
ALLEGORICAL	AMPHISBAENA	ANNOTATIONS
ALLEVIATING	AMPHISTYLAR	ANNUNCIATOR
ALLEVIATION	AMPHITRICHA	ANOINTMENTS
ALLEVIATIVE	AMPLEXICAUL	ANOMALISTIC
ALLOCATIONS	AMPLIFIABLE	ANOMALOUSLY
ALLOGRAPHIC	AMPUTATIONS	ANONYMOUSLY
ALLOMORPHIC	AMYLOPECTIN	ANORTHOSITE
ALLOPLASMIC	ANACHRONISM	ANTAGONISMS
ALLOPURINOL	ANACOLUTHIA	ANTAGONISTS
ALL-POWERFUL	ANACOLUTHIC	ANTAGONIZED
ALL-ROUNDERS	ANACOLUTHON	ANTALKALINE
ALLUREMENTS	ANADIPLOSIS	ANTECEDENCE
ALMIGHTIEST	ANAEMICALLY	ANTECEDENTS
ALPHABETIZE	ANAESTHESIA	ANTECHAMBER

ANTEPENDIUM	APPARATUSES	ARISTOCRATS
ANTEVERSION	APPARELLING	ARMED FORCES
ANTHERIDIAL	APPARITIONS	ARMIPOTENCE
ANTHERIDIUM	APPEALINGLY	ARMOURED CAR
ANTHEROZOID	APPEARANCES	ARMOUR PLATE
ANTHOCYANIN	APPEASEMENT	AROMATICITY
ANTHOLOGIES	APPELLATION	ARONOMASTIC
ANTHOLOGIST	APPELLATIVE	ARRAIGNMENT
ANTHOLOGIZE	APPERTAINED	ARRANGEMENT
ANTHRACITIC	APPLICATION	ARRESTINGLY
ANTHRACNOSE	APPLICATIVE	ARTERIALIZE
ANTIBIOTICS	APPLICATORY	ARTHROMERIC
ANTICATHODE	APPOINTMENT	ARTHROSPORE
ANTICIPATED	APPORTIONED	ARTICULATED
ANTICIPATOR	APPORTIONER	ARTICULATOR
ANTICLASTIC	APPRECIABLE	ARTILLERIES
ANTICYCLONE	APPRECIABLY	ARTIODACTYL
ANTIFEBRILE	APPRECIATED	ARTLESSNESS
ANTIFOULING	APPREHENDED	ARYTENOIDAL
ANTIMISSILE	APPRENTICED	ASCENSIONAL
ANTINEUTRON	APPRENTICES	ASCERTAINED
ANTINUCLEAR	APPROACHING	ASCETICALLY
ANTINUCLEON	APPROBATION	ASKING PRICE
ANTIOXIDANT	APPROBATIVE	ASPERGILLUS
ANTIPATHIES	APPROPRIATE	ASPHYXIATED
ANTIPHONARY	APPROVINGLY	ASPHYXIATOR
ANTIPHRASIS	APPROXIMATE	ASPIDISTRAS
ANTIPYRESIS	APPURTENANT	ASPIRATIONS
ANTIPYRETIC	AQUACULTURE	ASSASSINATE
ANTIQUARIAN	AQUAMARINES	ASSEMBLAGES
ANTIQUITIES	AQUAPLANING	ASSEMBLYMAN
ANTIRRHINUM	AQUARELLIST	ASSEMBLYMEN
ANTI-SEMITES	AQUATICALLY	ASSENTATION
ANTI-SEMITIC	AQUICULTURE	ASSERTIVELY
ANTISEPTICS	ARALIACEOUS	ASSESSMENTS
ANTITUSSIVE	ARBITRAGEUR	ASSESSORIAL
ANTOFAGASTA	ARBITRAMENT	ASSEVERATED
ANTONOMASIA	ARBITRARILY	ASSIDUOUSLY
ANXIOUSNESS	ARBITRATING	ASSIGNATION
APHETICALLY	ARBITRATION	ASSIGNMENTS
APHRODISIAC	ARBITRATORS	ASSIMILABLE
APICULTURAL	ARBORESCENT	ASSIMILATED
APOCALYPSES	ARCHAEOLOGY	ASSOCIATING
APOCALYPTIC	ARCHAEOZOIC	ASSOCIATION
APOCOPATION	ARCHAICALLY	ASSOCIATIVE
APOCYNTHION	ARCHANGELIC	ASSORTATIVE
APOLOGETICS	ARCHBISHOPS	ASSORTMENTS
APOLOGIZING	ARCHDEACONS	ASSUAGEMENT
APOMORPHINE	ARCHDIOCESE	ASSUMPTIONS
APONEUROSIS	ARCHDUCHESS	ASSUREDNESS
APONEUROTIC	ARCHEGONIUM	ASSYRIOLOGY
APOPHYLLITE	ARCHENEMIES	ASTATICALLY
APOSIOPESIS	ARCHENTERIC	ASTERISKING
APOSIOPETIC	ARCHENTERON	ASTIGMATISM
A POSTERIORI	ARCHIPELAGO	ASTONISHING
APOSTROPHES	ARDUOUSNESS	ASTRAPHOBIA
APOTHEOSIZE	ARENICOLOUS	ASTRAPHOBIC
APPALLINGLY	ARGENTINEAN	ASTRINGENCY
APPARATCHIK	ARISTOCRACY	ASTRINGENTS

ASTROBOTANY
ASTROLOGERS
ASTROMETRIC
ASTRONAUTIC
ASTRONOMERS
ASTROSPHERE
ATELECTASIS
ATHEISTICAL
ATHERMANOUS
ATHLETICISM
ATMOSPHERES
ATMOSPHERIC
ATOMIC PILES
ATOMIZATION
ATROCIOUSLY
ATTACHE CASE
ATTACHMENTS
ATTAINMENTS
ATTEMPTABLE
ATTENDANCES
ATTENTIVELY
ATTENUATING
ATTENUATION
ATTESTATION
ATTITUDINAL
ATTRACTABLE
ATTRACTIONS
ATTRIBUTING
ATTRIBUTION
ATTRIBUTIVE
ATTRITIONAL
AUCTIONEERS
AUDACIOUSLY
AUDIOLOGIST
AUDIOMETRIC
AUDIOTYPING
AUDIOTYPIST
AUDIO-VISUAL
AUDITIONING
AUDITORIUMS
AUGMENTABLE
AURIGNACIAN
AUSCULTATOR
AUSTERENESS
AUSTERITIES
AUSTRALASIA
AUSTRALIANS
AUSTRONESIA
AUTHORITIES
AUTHORIZING
AUTOCHANGER
AUTOCRACIES
AUTOGENESIS
AUTOGENETIC
AUTOGRAPHED
AUTOGRAPHIC
AUTOKINETIC
AUTOMOBILES
AUTOPLASTIC

AUTOTROPHIC
AUXANOMETER
AUXILIARIES
AVOIRDUPOIS
AVUNCULARLY
AWESOMENESS
AWKWARDNESS
AXIOLOGICAL
AZERBAIJANI
AZOTOBACTER

B
BABY-MINDERS
BABY'S-BREATH
BABY-SITTERS
BABY-SITTING
BACCHANALIA
BACCIFEROUS
BACCIVOROUS
BACILLIFORM
BACKBENCHER
BACKBENCHES
BACKCOMBING
BACK COUNTRY
BACKGROUNDS
BACKHANDERS
BACK NUMBERS
BACKPACKERS
BACKPACKING
BACK PASSAGE
BACKPEDALED
BACKROOM BOY
BACKSLAPPER
BACKSLIDERS
BACKSLIDING
BACK STREETS
BACKSTROKES
BACKTRACKED
BACTERAEMIA
BACTERICIDE
BADDERLOCKS
BAD-MOUTHING
BAGGAGE CARS
BAGGAGE ROOM
BAHIA BLANCA
BAKER'S DOZEN
BALANCEABLE
BALEFULNESS
BALL BEARING
BALLETOMANE
BALLOONISTS
BALUCHISTAN
BALUSTRADES
BAMBOOZLING
BANANA SKINS
BANDMASTERS
BANGLADESHI
BANK ACCOUNT
BANKER'S CARD

BANK HOLIDAY
BANKROLLING
BANKRUPTING
BANTERINGLY
BARBARITIES
BARBARIZING
BARBAROUSLY
BARBITURATE
BAREFACEDLY
BARIUM MEALS
BARLEY SUGAR
BARLEY WATER
BAR MITZVAHS
BARNSTORMED
BARNSTORMER
BAROGRAPHIC
BARONETCIES
BAROTSELAND
BARQUENTINE
BARREL ORGAN
BARRICADING
BASHFULNESS
BASKERVILLE
BASS GUITARS
BASSOONISTS
BASTARDIZED
BASTINADOED
BASTINADOES
BASTNAESITE
BATHING SUIT
BATHOLITHIC
BATHOMETRIC
BATHYMETRIC
BATHYSPHERE
BATSMANSHIP
BATTLE CRIES
BATTLEFIELD
BATTLEMENTS
BATTLE ROYAL
BATTLESHIPS
BEACHCHAIRS
BEACHCOMBER
BEANSPROUTS
BEARISHNESS
BEAR'S-BREECH
BEASTLINESS
BEAUTEOUSLY
BEAUTICIANS
BEAUTIFULLY
BEAUTIFYING
BEAUTY QUEEN
BEAUTY SLEEP
BEAUTY SPOTS
BEAVERBOARD
BED AND BOARD
BEDEVILLING
BEDEVILMENT
BEFITTINGLY
BEFRIENDING

BEGUILEMENT	BIMOLECULAR	BLINDFOLDED
BEGUILINGLY	BIOCATALYST	BLINDSTOREY
BEHAVIOURAL	BIOCENOLOGY	BLOCKBUSTER
BELABOURING	BIODYNAMICS	BLOCKHOUSES
BELATEDNESS	BIOENGINEER	BLOOD COUNTS
BELEAGUERED	BIOFEEDBACK	BLOOD GROUPS
BELL-BOTTOMS	BIOGRAPHERS	BLOODHOUNDS
BELLICOSITY	BIOGRAPHIES	BLOODLESSLY
BELLIGERENT	BIOPHYSICAL	BLOOD PLASMA
BELL-RINGING	BIPARTITION	BLOOD SPORTS
BELLYACHING	BIQUADRATIC	BLOODSTAINS
BELLY BUTTON	BIQUARTERLY	BLOODSTREAM
BELLY DANCER	BIRD-BRAINED	BLOODSUCKER
BELLY DANCES	BIRDS OF PREY	BLOOD VESSEL
BELLY LAUGHS	BIRD-WATCHER	BLOTCHINESS
BENEDICTINE	BIROBIDZHAN	BLUDGEONING
BENEDICTION	BIRTHPLACES	BLUEBERRIES
BENEDICTORY	BIRTHRIGHTS	BLUE-BLOODED
BENEFACTION	BISEXUALISM	BLUEBOTTLES
BENEFACTORS	BISEXUALITY	BLUE CHEESES
BENEFICENCE	BISYMMETRIC	BLUE-EYED BOY
BENEFICIARY	BIT OF FLUFFS	BLUE MURDERS
BENEVOLENCE	BITTERSWEET	BLUNDERBUSS
BENIGHTEDLY	BIVOUACKING	BLURREDNESS
BEQUEATHING	BLACKAMOORS	BOBSLEIGHED
BEREAVEMENT	BLACKBALLED	BODHISATTVA
BERGSCHRUND	BLACKBOARDS	BODY-CENTRED
BESMIRCHING	BLACK COMEDY	BODY POLITIC
BESPATTERED	BLACKGUARDS	BOILERMAKER
BEST-SELLERS	BLACK HUMOUR	BOILERPLATE
BEST-SELLING	BLACKLEGGED	BOILER SUITS
BETES-NOIRES	BLACKLISTED	BOLLOCKS-UPS
BETULACEOUS	BLACKMAILED	BOLL WEEVILS
BEWILDERING	BLACKMAILER	BOMBARDIERS
BHUBANESWAR	BLACK MARIAS	BOMBARDMENT
BIAS BINDING	BLACK MARKET	BONDHOLDERS
BIBLIOLATRY	BLACK MASSES	BONE MARROWS
BIBLIOMANCY	BLACK MUSLIM	BONESHAKERS
BIBLIOMANIA	BLACK PEPPER	BOOBY PRIZES
BIBLIOPHILE	BLACKSHIRTS	BOOKBINDERS
BIBLIOPHISM	BLACKSMITHS	BOOKBINDERY
BIBLIOTHECA	BLACK WIDOWS	BOOKBINDING
BICARBONATE	BLADDERWORT	BOOKISHNESS
BICENTENARY	BLAMELESSLY	BOOKKEEPERS
BICEPHALOUS	BLAMEWORTHY	BOOKKEEPING
BICONCAVITY	BLANCMANGES	BOOKMOBILES
BIEDERMEIER	BLANK CHEQUE	BOOKSELLERS
BIFOLIOLATE	BLASPHEMERS	BOOMERANGED
BIFURCATING	BLASPHEMIES	BOORISHNESS
BIFURCATION	BLASPHEMING	BOOTLEGGERS
BIG BUSINESS	BLASPHEMOUS	BOOTLEGGING
BILATERALLY	BLASTOGENIC	BORDERLANDS
BILIOUSNESS	BLASTOMERIC	BORDERLINES
BILLETS-DOUX	BLASTOPORIC	BOTANICALLY
BILLIONAIRE	BLENCHINGLY	BOTHERATION
BILLOWINESS	BLEPHARITIC	BOTTLE BANKS
BILLS OF FARE	BLEPHATITIS	BOTTLE GREEN
BILLS OF SALE	BLESSEDNESS	BOTTLENECKS
BIMETALLISM	BLIND ALLEYS	BOUNDLESSLY

BOUNTEOUSLY	BRYOLOGICAL	CALIFORNIUM
BOURGEOISIE	BUCARAMANGA	CALLIGRAPHY
BOURNEMOUTH	BUCKET SEATS	CALLIPYGIAN
BOWDLERIZED	BUCKET SHOPS	CALLOUSNESS
BOYSENBERRY	BUCKLER-FERN	CALORIMETER
BRACE AND BIT	BUCOLICALLY	CALORIMETRY
BRACHIATION	BUDGERIGARS	CALUMNIATED
BRACTEOLATE	BUENOS AIRES	CALVINISTIC
BRADYCARDIA	BUFFER STATE	CALYPTROGEN
BRADYCARDIC	BUFFER STOCK	CAMARADERIE
BRAGGADOCIO	BUFFER ZONES	CAMERA-READY
BRAHMAPUTRA	BULBIFEROUS	CAMOUFLAGED
BRAIN DRAINS	BULLDOG CLIP	CAMOUFLAGES
BRAINLESSLY	BULLETPROOF	CAMPAIGNERS
BRAINSTORMS	BULLFIGHTER	CAMPAIGNING
BRAINS TRUST	BULLFINCHES	CAMPANOLOGY
BRAINTEASER	BULLISHNESS	CAMPANULATE
BRAINWASHED	BULLSHITTED	CAMPGROUNDS
BRAINWASHER	BULL TERRIER	CANALICULAR
BRANCHIOPOD	BUMPTIOUSLY	CANALICULUS
BRANDENBURG	BUNDELKHAND	CANDELABRUM
BRANDISHING	BUREAUCRACY	CANDIDACIES
BRATTISHING	BUREAUCRATS	CANDLEBERRY
BRAZZAVILLE	BURGOMASTER	CANDLELIGHT
BREADBASKET	BURLESQUING	CANDLEPOWER
BREADBOARDS	BURNISHABLE	CANDLESTICK
BREADCRUMBS	BUSHWHACKER	CANDLEWICKS
BREADFRUITS	BUSINESS END	CANINE TEETH
BREADTHWAYS	BUSINESSMAN	CANINE TOOTH
BREADWINNER	BUSINESSMEN	CANNIBALISM
BREAKFASTED	BUS STATIONS	CANNIBALIZE
BREASTPLATE	BUTCHERBIRD	CANNONBALLS
BREATHALYSE	BUTTER BEANS	CANTHARIDES
BREATHINESS	BUTTERFLIES	CANTILEVERS
BREECHBLOCK	BUTTONHOLED	CAPACIOUSLY
BREMERHAVEN	BUTTONHOLES	CAPACITANCE
BRIDGEBOARD	BUTTONMOULD	CAPILLARIES
BRISTLETAIL	BUTTRESSING	CAPILLARITY
BRITTLENESS	BUTYRACEOUS	CAPITALISTS
BRITTLE-STAR	BY-ELECTIONS	CAPITALIZED
BROADCASTER		CAPITAL LEVY
BROAD GAUGES	C	CAPITATIONS
BROADMINDED	CABINETWORK	CAPITULATED
BROADSHEETS	CABORA BASSA	CAPITULATOR
BROADSWORDS	CACOGRAPHIC	CAPRICCIOSO
BROMINATION	CACOPHONOUS	CAPRICORNUS
BRONCHIOLAR	CALCEOLARIA	CAPSULATION
BRONTOSAURI	CALCICOLOUS	CAPTIVATING
BRONX CHEERS	CALCIFEROUS	CAPTIVATION
BRONZE MEDAL	CALCIFUGOUS	CARABINIERE
BROOMSTICKS	CALCINATION	CARAVANNING
BROTHERHOOD	CALCULATING	CARBAMIDINE
BROWBEATING	CALCULATION	CARBONATION
BROWNSTONES	CALCULATORS	CARBONIZING
BRUCELLOSIS	CALEFACIENT	CARBON PAPER
BRUSQUENESS	CALEFACTION	CARBORUNDUM
BRUTALITIES	CALEFACTORY	CARBOXYLASE
BRUTALIZING	CALIBRATING	CARBOXYLATE
BRUTISHNESS	CALIBRATION	CARBUNCULAR

CARBURETTOR	CATHOLICITY	CHALLENGERS
CARBYLAMINE	CATHOLICIZE	CHALLENGING
CARCINOGENS	CATTLE GRIDS	CHAMBERLAIN
CARDINALATE	CAULIFLOWER	CHAMBERMAID
CARD INDEXES	CAUSABILITY	CHAMBER POTS
CARDIOGRAPH	CAUSATIVELY	CHAMELEONIC
CARDPUNCHES	CAUSTICALLY	CHAMPERTOUS
CARDUACEOUS	CAUSTICNESS	CHAMPIONING
CAREFULNESS	CAUTERIZING	CHANCELLERY
CARESSINGLY	CAVALIERISM	CHANCELLORS
CARICATURED	CAVERNOUSLY	CHANCROIDAL
CARICATURES	CAVITY WALLS	CHANDELIERS
CARMINATIVE	CAVO-RELIEVO	CHANGELINGS
CARNIVOROUS	CEASELESSLY	CHANGEOVERS
CAROLINGIAN	CELEBRATING	CHANNELLING
CARPOGONIAL	CELEBRATION	CHANTERELLE
CARPOGONIUM	CELEBRATIVE	CHANTICLEER
CARPOLOGIST	CELEBRITIES	CHAOTICALLY
CARRIAGEWAY	CEMENTATION	CHAPERONAGE
CARRIER BAGS	CEMENT MIXER	CHAPERONING
CARSICKNESS	CENOSPECIES	CHARGE CARDS
CARTOGRAPHY	CENTENARIAN	CHARGE HANDS
CARTOONISTS	CENTENARIES	CHARGE NURSE
CARTWHEELED	CENTENNIALS	CHARGE SHEET
CARUNCULATE	CENTIMETRES	CHARIOTEERS
CARVEL-BUILT	CENTRALIZED	CHARISMATIC
CARVING FORK	CENTREBOARD	CHASTISABLE
CASE HISTORY	CENTRE-FOLDS	CHATELAINES
CASE STUDIES	CENTREPIECE	CHATTANOOGA
CASEWORKERS	CENTRIFUGAL	CHAUFFEURED
CASSITERITE	CENTRIFUGES	CHAULMOOGRA
CASTELLATED	CENTRIPETAL	CHAUVINISTS
CASTER SUGAR	CENTROBARIC	CHEAPSKATES
CASTIGATING	CENTROMERIC	CHECKMATING
CASTIGATION	CENTROSOMIC	CHECKPOINTS
CASTING VOTE	CEPHALALGIA	CHEERLEADER
CASTOR SUGAR	CERARGYRITE	CHEERLESSLY
CATACAUSTIC	CEREBRATION	CHEESECAKES
CATACHRESIS	CEREBROSIDE	CHEESECLOTH
CATACLASTIC	CEREMONIALS	CHEF D'OEUVRE
CATACLYSMIC	CEREMONIOUS	CHELICERATE
CATADROMOUS	CEROGRAPHIC	CHELIFEROUS
CATAFALQUES	CEROPLASTIC	CHELYABINSK
CATALOGUING	CERTAINTIES	CHEMOSMOSIS
CATAPLASTIC	CERTIFIABLE	CHEMOSMOTIC
CATAPULTING	CERTIFICATE	CHEMOSPHERE
CATASTROPHE	CETOLOGICAL	CHEMOTACTIC
CAT BURGLARS	CHAETOGNATH	CHEMOTROPIC
CATCHPHRASE	CHAFFINCHES	CHEQUE CARDS
CATCHWEIGHT	CHAFING DISH	CHEREMKHOVO
CATECHISMAL	CHAIN LETTER	CHERISHABLE
CATECHISTIC	CHAIN-SMOKED	CHESHIRE CAT
CATECHIZING	CHAIN-SMOKER	CHESSBOARDS
CATEGORICAL	CHAIN STITCH	CHEVAL GLASS
CATEGORIZED	CHAIN STORES	CHIAROSCURO
CATERPILLAR	CHAIRPERSON	CHIASTOLITE
CATERWAULED	CHALCANLITE	CHICANERIES
CATHETERIZE	CHALCEDONIC	CHICHIHAERH
CATHOLICISM	CHALKBOARDS	CHICKENFEED

CHIFFONIERS	CICATRICIAL	CLOUDBURSTS
CHILDMINDER	CICATRIZANT	CLOUD-CAPPED
CHIMNEYPOTS	CINDERELLAS	CLOYINGNESS
CHIMPANZEES	CINEMASCOPE	CLUSTER BOMB
CHINCHILLAS	CIRCULARITY	COADUNATION
CHINOISERIE	CIRCULARIZE	COADUNATIVE
CHIPPENDALE	CIRCULAR SAW	COAGULATING
CHIROGRAPHY	CIRCULATING	COAGULATION
CHIROPODIST	CIRCULATION	COAGULATIVE
CHIROPTERAN	CIRCULATIVE	COALBUNKERS
CHITCHATTED	CIRCULATORY	COALESCENCE
CHLAMYDEOUS	CIRCUMCISED	COALITIONAL
CHLORINATED	CIRCUMLUNAR	COALSCUTTLE
CHLORINATOR	CIRCUMPOLAR	COARCTATION
CHLOROPHYLL	CIRCUMSPECT	COASTGUARDS
CHLOROPLAST	CIRENCESTER	COAT HANGERS
CHLOROPRENE	CITIZENSHIP	COATS OF ARMS
CHLOROQUINE	CITRONELLAL	COBBLESTONE
CHOANOCYTAL	CITY FATHERS	COCCIDIOSIS
CHOCK-A-BLOCK	CIVIL RIGHTS	COCCIFEROUS
CHOIRMASTER	CIVVY STREET	COCK-A-LEEKIE
CHOIR SCHOOL	CLAIRVOYANT	COCKCHAFERS
CHOKECHERRY	CLAMATORIAL	COCKLESHELL
CHOLESTEROL	CLANDESTINE	COCKROACHES
CHOLINERGIC	CLARINETIST	CODICILLARY
CHORDOPHONE	CLASP KNIVES	COD-LIVER OIL
CHOREODRAMA	CLASS ACTION	COEDUCATION
CHOREOGRAPH	CLASSICISTS	COEFFICIENT
CHOROGRAPHY	CLASSIFYING	COELENTERIC
CHRISMATORY	CLAVICHORDS	COELENTERON
CHRISTENDOM	CLAY PIGEONS	COERCIONARY
CHRISTENING	CLEAN-LIMBED	COERCIONIST
CHRISTMASES	CLEANLINESS	COESSENTIAL
CHRISTOLOGY	CLEAN-SHAVEN	COEXISTENCE
CHROMATINIC	CLEAN SWEEPS	COEXTENSION
CHROMINANCE	CLEAR-HEADED	COEXTENSIVE
CHROMOGENIC	CLEFT PALATE	COFFEE BREAK
CHROMONEMAL	CLEFT STICKS	COFFEE HOUSE
CHROMOPHORE	CLEISTOGAMY	COFFEE SHOPS
CHROMOPLASM	CLEVER DICKS	COFFEE TABLE
CHROMOPLAST	CLIENT STATE	COGITATIONS
CHROMOSOMAL	CLIFFHANGER	COGNITIVELY
CHROMOSOMES	CLIMACTERIC	COGNIZANCES
CHRONICALLY	CLIMATOLOGY	COGNOSCENTI
CHRONICLERS	CLINANDRIUM	COINCIDENCE
CHRONICLING	CLINOMETRIC	COINSURANCE
CHRONOGRAPH	CLOCK TOWERS	COLD-BLOODED
CHRONOMETER	CLODHOPPERS	COLD CHISELS
CHRONOMETRY	CLOISTERING	COLD COMFORT
CHRONOSCOPE	CLOSED SHOPS	COLD-HEARTED
CHRYSALISES	CLOSEFISTED	COLD STORAGE
CHRYSAROBIN	CLOSE-HAULED	COLEOPTERAN
CHRYSOBERYL	CLOSE SEASON	COLLABORATE
CHRYSOLITIC	CLOSE SHAVES	COLLAPSIBLE
CHRYSOPRASE	CLOSING TIME	COLLARBONES
CHURCHGOERS	CLOSTRIDIAL	COLLAR STUDS
CHURCHGOING	CLOSTRIDIUM	COLLECTABLE
CHURCHWOMAN	CLOTHESLINE	COLLECTANEA
CHURCHYARDS	CLOTHES PEGS	COLLECTEDLY

COLLECTIONS	COMMUNIQUES	CONCENTRATE
COLLECTIVES	COMMUNISTIC	CONCEPTACLE
COLLEMBOLAN	COMMUNITIES	CONCEPTIONS
COLLENCHYMA	COMMUTATION	CONCERNEDLY
COLLIGATION	COMMUTATIVE	CONCERTANTE
COLLIGATIVE	COMMUTATORS	CONCERTEDLY
COLLIMATION	COMPACT DISC	CONCERTGOER
COLLOCATING	COMPACTEDLY	CONCERTINAS
COLLOCATION	COMPACTNESS	CONCESSIBLE
COLOGARITHM	COMPARATIVE	CONCESSIONS
COLONIALISM	COMPARISONS	CONCILIATED
COLONIALIST	COMPARTMENT	CONCILIATOR
COLONIZABLE	COMPASSABLE	CONCLUSIONS
COLORATURAS	COMPATRIOTS	CONCOCTIONS
COLORIMETER	COMPENDIOUS	CONCOMITANT
COLOUR-BLIND	COMPENDIUMS	CONCORDANCE
COLOURISTIC	COMPENSATED	CONCUBINAGE
COLTISHNESS	COMPENSATOR	CONCURRENCE
COLUMBARIUM	COMPETENTLY	CONDEMNABLE
COMBATIVELY	COMPETITION	CONDENSABLE
COMBINATION	COMPETITIVE	CONDITIONAL
COMBINATIVE	COMPETITORS	CONDITIONED
COMBUSTIBLE	COMPILATION	CONDITIONER
COMESTIBLES	COMPLACENCE	CONDOLATORY
COME-UPPANCE	COMPLACENCY	CONDOLENCES
COMFORTABLE	COMPLAINANT	CONDOMINIUM
COMFORTABLY	COMPLAINERS	CONDONATION
COMFORTLESS	COMPLAINING	CONDUCTANCE
COMIC OPERAS	COMPLAISANT	CONDUCTIBLE
COMIC STRIPS	COMPLEMENTS	CONDUCTRESS
COMMANDANTS	COMPLEXIONS	CONFABULATE
COMMANDMENT	COMPLIANTLY	CONFECTIONS
COMME IL FAUT	COMPLICATED	CONFEDERACY
COMMEMORATE	COMPLIMENTS	CONFEDERATE
COMMENDABLE	COMPORTMENT	CONFERENCES
COMMENDABLY	COMPOSITION	CONFERMENTS
COMMENTATED	COMPOSITORS	CONFESSEDLY
COMMENTATOR	COMPOUNDING	CONFESSIONS
COMMERCIALS	COMPRESSING	CONFIDENCES
COMMINATION	COMPRESSION	CONFIDENTLY
COMMINATORY	COMPRESSIVE	CONFIDINGLY
COMMINUTION	COMPRESSORS	CONFINEMENT
COMMISERATE	COMPRISABLE	CONFISCABLE
COMMISSIONS	COMPROMISED	CONFISCATED
COMMISSURAL	COMPROMISER	CONFISCATOR
COMMITMENTS	COMPROMISES	CONFLATIONS
COMMODITIES	COMPTOMETER	CONFLICTING
COMMON NOUNS	COMPTROLLER	CONFLICTION
COMMONPLACE	COMPULSIONS	CONFLICTIVE
COMMON ROOMS	COMPUNCTION	CONFLUENCES
COMMON SENSE	COMPUTATION	CONFORMABLE
COMMOTIONAL	COMPUTERIZE	CONFORMABLY
COMMUNALISM	COMRADESHIP	CONFORMANCE
COMMUNALIST	CONCATENATE	CONFORMISTS
COMMUNALITY	CONCAVITIES	CONFOUNDING
COMMUNALIZE	CONCEALMENT	CONFRONTING
COMMUNICANT	CONCEITEDLY	CONFUSINGLY
COMMUNICATE	CONCEIVABLE	CONFUTATION
COMMUNIONAL	CONCEIVABLY	CONFUTATIVE

CONGEALMENT	CONSTERNATE	CONTROLLERS
CONGELATION	CONSTIPATED	CONTROLLING
CONGENIALLY	CONSTITUENT	CONTROVERSY
CONGESTIBLE	CONSTITUTED	CONTUMELIES
CONGREGATED	CONSTITUTER	CONTUSIONED
CONGREGATOR	CONSTRAINED	CONURBATION
CONGRESSMAN	CONSTRAINER	CONVALESCED
CONGRESSMEN	CONSTRAINTS	CONVENIENCE
CONGRUENTLY	CONSTRICTED	CONVENTICLE
CONGRUITIES	CONSTRICTOR	CONVENTIONS
CONJECTURAL	CONSTRUCTED	CONVERGENCE
CONJECTURED	CONSTRUCTOR	CONVERGENCY
CONJECTURER	CONSULSHIPS	CONVERSABLE
CONJECTURES	CONSULTANCY	CONVERSANCE
CONJOINEDLY	CONSULTANTS	CONVERSIONS
CONJUGALITY	CONSUMERISM	CONVERTIBLE
CONJUGATING	CONSUMMATED	CONVEXITIES
CONJUGATION	CONSUMMATOR	CONVEYANCER
CONJUGATIVE	CONSUMPTION	CONVEYANCES
CONJUNCTION	CONSUMPTIVE	CONVICTABLE
CONJUNCTIVA	CONTACT LENS	CONVICTIONS
CONJUNCTIVE	CONTAINMENT	CONVINCIBLE
CONJUNCTURE	CONTAMINANT	CONVIVIALLY
CONJURATION	CONTAMINATE	CONVOCATION
CONNECTIBLE	CONTEMNIBLE	CONVOCATIVE
CONNECTICUT	CONTEMPLATE	CONVOLUTION
CONNECTIONS	CONTENTEDLY	CONVOLVULUS
CONNOISSEUR	CONTENTIONS	CONVULSIONS
CONNOTATION	CONTENTIOUS	COOKERY BOOK
CONNOTATIVE	CONTENTMENT	COOPERATING
CONSCIENCES	CONTESTANTS	COOPERATION
CONSCIOUSLY	CONTEXTURAL	COOPERATIVE
CONSCRIPTED	CONTINENTAL	COOPERATORS
CONSECRATED	CONTINGENCE	COORDINATED
CONSECRATOR	CONTINGENCY	COORDINATES
CONSECUTION	CONTINGENTS	COORDINATOR
CONSECUTIVE	CONTINUALLY	COPARCENARY
CONSENSUSES	CONTINUANCE	COPLANARITY
CONSENTIENT	CONTINUATOR	COPPERPLATE
CONSEQUENCE	CONTORTIONS	COPPERSMITH
CONSERVABLE	CONTRACTILE	COPROPHILIA
CONSERVANCY	CONTRACTING	COPYWRITERS
CONSERVATOR	CONTRACTION	CORACIIFORM
CONSIDERATE	CONTRACTIVE	CORDILLERAS
CONSIDERING	CONTRACTORS	CORMOPHYTIC
CONSIGNABLE	CONTRACTUAL	CORNERSTONE
CONSIGNMENT	CONTRACTURE	CORNFLOWERS
CONSISTENCY	CONTRAFLOWS	CORNICULATE
CONSOLATION	CONTRAPTION	CORNUCOPIAS
CONSOLATORY	CONTRARIETY	COROLLARIES
CONSOLIDATE	CONTRASTING	CORONAGRAPH
CONSONANCES	CONTRASTIVE	CORONATIONS
CONSONANTAL	CONTRAVENED	CORONERSHIP
CONSORTIUMS	CONTRAVENER	CORPORALITY
CONSPECIFIC	CONTRAYERVA	CORPORATELY
CONSPICUOUS	CONTRETEMPS	CORPORATION
CONSPIRATOR	CONTRIBUTED	CORPORATIVE
CONSTANTINE	CONTRIBUTOR	CORPOREALLY
CONSTELLATE	CONTRIVANCE	CORPUSCULAR

CORRECTABLE	COURTEOUSLY	CRYPTOGAMIC
CORRECTIONS	COURTHOUSES	CRYPTOGENIC
CORRECTIVES	COURTLINESS	CRYPTOGRAPH
CORRECTNESS	COVENANTING	CRYPTOZOITE
CORRELATING	COVER CHARGE	CRYSTAL BALL
CORRELATION	COWCATCHERS	CRYSTALLINE
CORRELATIVE	CRABBEDNESS	CRYSTALLITE
CORRIGENDUM	CRACKERJACK	CRYSTALLIZE
CORROBORATE	CRANBERRIES	CRYSTALLOID
CORROSIVELY	CRANIOMETER	CRYSTAL SETS
CORRUGATION	CRANIOMETRY	CTENOPHORAN
CORRUPTIBLE	CRANKSHAFTS	CUCKOO CLOCK
CORRUPTIONS	CRASH-DIVING	CULMIFEROUS
CORRUPTNESS	CRASH HELMET	CULMINATION
CORS ANGLAIS	CRASH-LANDED	CULPABILITY
CORTICATION	CRAZY PAVING	CULTIVATING
CORUSCATING	CREAM CHEESE	CULTIVATION
CORUSCATION	CREDENTIALS	CULTIVATORS
COSIGNATORY	CREDIBILITY	CUMMERBUNDS
COS LETTUCES	CREDIT CARDS	CUNNILINGUS
COSMETICIAN	CREDIT NOTES	CUPELLATION
COSMOGONIES	CREDULOUSLY	CUPRIFEROUS
COSMOGONIST	CREMATORIUM	CUPRONICKEL
COSMOLOGIST	CRENELLATED	CURATORSHIP
COSMOPOLITE	CRENULATION	CURIOSITIES
COTERMINOUS	CREOPHAGOUS	CURIOUSNESS
COTES-DU-NORD	CREPITATION	CURMUDGEONS
COTONEASTER	CREPUSCULAR	CURRICULUMS
COTTAGE LOAF	CRESTFALLEN	CURRY POWDER
COTTON CANDY	CRIMINALITY	CURTAILMENT
COTTONTAILS	CRIMINOLOGY	CURTAIN CALL
COTYLEDONAL	CRINKLEROOT	CURVILINEAR
COUNCILLORS	CRINKLINESS	CUSPIDATION
COUNSELLING	CRITICIZING	CUSTARD PIES
COUNSELLORS	CROCIDOLITE	CUSTOMARILY
COUNTENANCE	CROCODILIAN	CUSTOM-BUILT
COUNTERFEIT	CROOKEDNESS	CUSTOMIZING
COUNTERFOIL	CROP-DUSTING	CUT-AND-DRIED
COUNTERMAND	CROSSBREEDS	CUTTING EDGE
COUNTERMINE	CROSS-GARNET	CYANIDATION
COUNTERMOVE	CROSS-LEGGED	CYANOHYDRIN
COUNTERPANE	CROSSPIECES	CYBERNATION
COUNTERPART	CROSS-STITCH	CYBERNETICS
COUNTERPLOT	CROWDEDNESS	CYCADACEOUS
COUNTERSANK	CROWN COLONY	CYCLOALKANE
COUNTERSIGN	CROWN COURTS	CYCLOHEXANE
COUNTERSINK	CROWNED HEAD	CYCLOPLEGIA
COUNTERSUNK	CROWN JEWELS	CYCLOSTYLED
COUNTERTYPE	CROWN PRINCE	CYCLOTHYMIA
COUNTERVAIL	CRUCIFEROUS	CYCLOTHYMIC
COUNTERWORD	CRUCIFIXION	CYLINDRICAL
COUNTERWORK	CRUNCHINESS	CYPERACEOUS
COUNTRIFIED	CRUSTACEANS	CYPRINODONT
COUNTRY CLUB	CRUSTACEOUS	CYPRIPEDIUM
COUNTRY SEAT	CRYOBIOLOGY	CYSTICERCUS
COUNTRYSIDE	CRYOHYDRATE	CYSTOCARPIC
COUNTY COURT	CRYOSURGERY	CYSTOSCOPIC
COUNTY TOWNS	CRYOTHERAPY	CYTOGENESIS
COUP DE GRACE	CRYPTICALLY	CYTOKINESIS

CYTOLOGICAL
CYTOLOGISTS
CYTOPLASMIC
CZESTOCHOWA

D
DACTYLOLOGY
DAGGERBOARD
DAIL EIREANN
DAIRY CATTLE
DAIRY FARMER
DAISY WHEELS
DAMNABILITY
DAMP COURSES
DANGER MONEY
DANGEROUSLY
DAPPLE-GREYS
DARDANELLES
DAREDEVILRY
DAR ES SALAAM
DATABLENESS
DAUNTLESSLY
DAYDREAMERS
DAYDREAMING
DEACTIVATOR
DEAD, LETTERS
DEAD MARCHES
DEAD RINGERS
DEAF-AND-DUMB
DEALERSHIPS
DEAMINATION
DEATH DUTIES
DEATHLESSLY
DEATHLINESS
DEATH RATTLE
DEATH'S-HEADS
DEATH SQUADS
DEBARKATION
DEBASEDNESS
DEBASEMENTS
DEBILITATED
DEBOUCHMENT
DEBRIDEMENT
DECALCIFIER
DECALESCENT
DECANEDIOIC
DECAPITATED
DECAPITATOR
DECARBONIZE
DECEITFULLY
DECELERATED
DECELERATOR
DECEPTIVELY
DECEREBRATE
DECILLIONTH
DECIMALIZED
DECIPHERING
DECKLE-EDGED
DECLAMATION

DECLAMATORY
DECLARATION
DECLARATIVE
DECLARATORY
DECLENSIONS
DECLINATION
DECLINATORY
DECLIVITIES
DECLIVITOUS
DECOLLATION
DECOLLETAGE
DECOLONIZED
DECOMPOSING
DECORATIONS
DECORTICATE
DECREPITATE
DECREPITUDE
DECRESCENCE
DECRETALIST
DECUSSATION
DEDICATEDLY
DEDICATIONS
DEDUCTIVELY
DEEP FREEZES
DEERSTALKER
DE-ESCALATED
DEFALCATION
DEFECTIVELY
DEFENCELESS
DEFENSIVELY
DEFERENTIAL
DEFICIENTLY
DEFINIENDUM
DEFINITIONS
DEFLECTIONS
DEFLORATION
DEFLOWERING
DEFOLIATING
DEFOLIATION
DEFORCEMENT
DEFORESTING
DEFORMATION
DEFORMITIES
DEFRAUDMENT
DEGENERATED
DEGENERATES
DEGLUTINATE
DEGLUTITION
DEGRADATION
DEHUMANIZED
DEHYDRATING
DEHYDRATION
DEICTICALLY
DEIFICATION
DELECTATION
DELEGATIONS
DELETERIOUS
DELIBERATED
DELIBERATOR

DELICIOUSLY
DELINEATING
DELINEATION
DELINEATIVE
DELINQUENCY
DELINQUENTS
DELIRIOUSLY
DELITESCENT
DELIVERABLE
DELIVERANCE
DELIVERYMAN
DELIVERYMEN
DELPHINIUMS
DEMAGNETIZE
DEMAGOGUERY
DEMARCATING
DEMARCATION
DEMOCRACIES
DEMOCRATIZE
DEMODULATOR
DEMOGRAPHER
DEMOGRAPHIC
DEMOLISHING
DEMOLITIONS
DEMONETIZED
DEMONICALLY
DEMONOLATER
DEMONOLATRY
DEMONSTRATE
DEMORALIZER
DEMOTIVATED
DEMOUNTABLE
DEMULSIFIER
DEMYSTIFIED
DENIGRATING
DENIGRATION
DENITRATION
DENOMINABLE
DENOMINATED
DENOMINATOR
DENOTATIONS
DENOUEMENTS
DENSIMETRIC
DENTAL FLOSS
DENTAL PLATE
DENTICULATE
DENTILABIAL
DENUMERABLE
DENUNCIATOR
DEODORIZING
DEOXYGENATE
DEOXYRIBOSE
DEPARTMENTS
DEPLORINGLY
DEPLUMATION
DEPOLARIZER
DEPOPULATED
DEPORTATION
DEPOSITIONS

DEPRAVATION	DETERMINATE	DIFFERENTLY
DEPRAVITIES	DETERMINERS	DIFFIDENTLY
DEPRECATING	DETERMINING	DIFFRACTING
DEPRECATION	DETERMINISM	DIFFRACTION
DEPRECATIVE	DETERMINIST	DIFFRACTIVE
DEPRECATORY	DETESTATION	DIFFUSENESS
DEPRECIABLE	DETONATIONS	DIFFUSIVITY
DEPRECIATED	DETRAINMENT	DIGESTIONAL
DEPRECIATOR	DETRIBALIZE	DIGITIGRADE
DEPREDATION	DETRIMENTAL	DIGNITARIES
DEPRESSIBLE	DEUTERANOPE	DIGRESSIONS
DEPRESSIONS	DEUTEROGAMY	DIHYBRIDISM
DEPRIVATION	DEUTSCHMARK	DILAPIDATED
DEPUTATIONS	DEVALUATION	DILAPIDATOR
DERAILMENTS	DEVASTATING	DILATOMETER
DERANGEMENT	DEVASTATION	DILATOMETRY
DEREGULATED	DEVASTATIVE	DILETTANTES
DERELICTION	DEVELOPABLE	DIMENSIONAL
DERIVATIONS	DEVELOPMENT	DIMERCAPROL
DERIVATIVES	DEVIOUSNESS	DIMIDIATION
DERMATOLOGY	DEVITALIZED	DIMINISHING
DESALINATED	DEVOLVEMENT	DIMINUENDOS
DESCENDABLE	DEVOTEDNESS	DIMINUTIONS
DESCENDANTS	DEVOURINGLY	DIMINUTIVES
DESCENDIBLE	DEXTEROUSLY	DINING ROOMS
DESCRIBABLE	DIACRITICAL	DINING TABLE
DESCRIPTION	DIADELPHOUS	DINNER BELLS
DESCRIPTIVE	DIAGNOSABLE	DINNER TABLE
DESECRATING	DIAGNOSTICS	DINOSAURIAN
DESECRATION	DIALECTICAL	DIOPTOMETER
DESEGREGATE	DIALOGISTIC	DIOPTOMETRY
DESENSITIZE	DIALYSATION	DIPHTHEROID
DESERVINGLY	DIAMAGNETIC	DIPHTHONGAL
DESEXUALIZE	DIAMONDBACK	DIPHYCERCAL
DESICCATING	DIAPHORESIS	DIPLOCOCCAL
DESICCATION	DIAPHORETIC	DIPLOCOCCUS
DESICCATIVE	DIAPOPHYSIS	DIPLOMATIST
DESIDERATUM	DIARTHROSIS	DIPROTODONT
DESIGNATING	DIASTROPHIC	DIPSOMANIAC
DESIGNATION	DIATESSARON	DIPSWITCHES
DESIGNATIVE	DIATOMICITY	DIRECT DEBIT
DESPATCHING	DIATONICISM	DIRECTIONAL
DESPERADOES	DICEPHALISM	DIRECTORATE
DESPERATELY	DICEPHALOUS	DIRECTORIAL
DESPERATION	DICHOGAMOUS	DIRECTORIES
DESPOILMENT	DICHOTOMIES	DIRECT TAXES
DESPONDENCY	DICHOTOMIST	DIRT FARMERS
DESPUMATION	DICHOTOMIZE	DIRTY OLD MAN
DESSERT WINE	DICHOTOMOUS	DIRTY OLD MEN
DESTABILIZE	DICHROMATIC	DIRTY TRICKS
DESTINATION	DICHROSCOPE	DISABLEMENT
DESTITUTION	DICOTYLEDON	DISACCREDIT
DESTROYABLE	DICTAPHONES	DISACCUSTOM
DESTRUCTION	DICTATIONAL	DISAFFECTED
DESTRUCTIVE	DICTATORIAL	DISAFFOREST
DESULTORILY	DIDACTICISM	DISAGREEING
DETACHMENTS	DIE-CASTINGS	DISALLOWING
DETERIORATE	DIFFERENCES	DISAPPEARED
DETERMINANT	DIFFERENTIA	DISAPPROVAL

DISAPPROVED	DISHONESTLY	DISSIPATING
DISAPPROVER	DISHONOURED	DISSIPATION
DISARMAMENT	DISHONOURER	DISSIPATIVE
DISARRANGED	DISHWASHERS	DISSOCIABLE
DISASSEMBLE	DISILLUSION	DISSOCIATED
DISASSEMBLY	DISILLUSIVE	DISSOLUTELY
DISAVOWEDLY	DISINCLINED	DISSOLUTION
DISBANDMENT	DISINFECTED	DISSOLUTIVE
DISBELIEVED	DISINFECTOR	DISSOLVABLE
DISBELIEVER	DISINTEREST	DISSONANCES
DISBURSABLE	DISINTERRED	DISSUADABLE
DISCERNIBLE	DISJOINABLE	DISSYLLABIC
DISCERNIBLY	DISJUNCTION	DISSYLLABLE
DISCERNMENT	DISJUNCTIVE	DISSYMMETRY
DISCHARGING	DISJUNCTURE	DISTASTEFUL
DISC HARROWS	DISLOCATING	DISTEMPERED
DISCIPLINAL	DISLOCATION	DISTENSIBLE
DISCIPLINED	DISLODGMENT	DISTILLABLE
DISCIPLINER	DISMANTLING	DISTINCTION
DISCIPLINES	DISMASTMENT	DISTINCTIVE
DISC JOCKEYS	DISMEMBERED	DISTINGUISH
DISCLAIMERS	DISMEMBERER	DISTORTIONS
DISCLAIMING	DISMISSIBLE	DISTRACTING
DISCLOSURES	DISMOUNTING	DISTRACTION
DISCOGRAPHY	DISOBEDIENT	DISTRACTIVE
DISCOLOURED	DISOBLIGING	DISTRAINING
DISCOMFITED	DISORDERING	DISTRESSFUL
DISCOMFITER	DISORGANIZE	DISTRESSING
DISCOMFORTS	DISPARAGING	DISTRIBUTED
DISCOMMODED	DISPARATELY	DISTRIBUTOR
DISCOMPOSED	DISPARITIES	DISTRUSTFUL
DISCONTINUE	DISPATCH BOX	DISTRUSTING
DISCORDANCE	DISPATCHING	DISTURBANCE
DISCOTHEQUE	DISPENSABLE	DISULPHURIC
DISCOUNTING	DISPIRITING	DITHYRAMBIC
DISCOURAGED	DISPLEASING	DITTOGRAPHY
DISCOURAGER	DISPLEASURE	DIVARICATOR
DISCOURSING	DISPOSITION	DIVE-BOMBERS
DISCOURTESY	DISPROVABLE	DIVE-BOMBING
DISCOVERERS	DISPUTATION	DIVERGENCES
DISCOVERIES	DISQUIETING	DIVERGENTLY
DISCOVERING	DISQUIETUDE	DIVERSIFIED
DISCREDITED	DISREGARDED	DIVERSIFIER
DISCREPANCY	DISREGARDER	DIVERSIFORM
DISCUSSIBLE	DISRELISHED	DIVERSIONAL
DISCUSSIONS	DISROBEMENT	DIVERTINGLY
DISEMBARKED	DISRUPTIONS	DIVESTITURE
DISEMBODIED	DISSECTIBLE	DIVINATIONS
DISENCUMBER	DISSECTIONS	DIVINE RIGHT
DISENGAGING	DISSEMBLERS	DIVING BELLS
DISENTANGLE	DISSEMBLING	DIVINGBOARD
DISENTHRALL	DISSEMINATE	DIVISIONISM
DISFIGURING	DISSEMINULE	DIVISIONIST
DISFORESTED	DISSENSIONS	DIVORCEABLE
DISGRACEFUL	DISSENTIENT	DIVORCEMENT
DISGRUNTLED	DISSENTIOUS	DOCTRINAIRE
DISGUISABLE	DISSEPIMENT	DOCUMENTARY
DISGUSTEDLY	DISSIMILATE	DOCUMENTING
DISHEVELLED	DISSIMULATE	DODDERINGLY

DODECAGONAL	DREADNOUGHT	ECTOPLASMIC
DODECAPHONY	DREAMLESSLY	ECTOSARCOUS
DOGBERRYISM	DREAM WORLDS	EDAPHICALLY
DOG BISCUITS	DRESS CIRCLE	EDIFICATION
DOGCATCHERS	DRESSMAKERS	EDIFICATORY
DOLABRIFORM	DRESSMAKING	EDITORIALLY
DOLEFULNESS	DRILLMASTER	EDUCABILITY
DOLL'S HOUSES	DROMEDARIES	EDUCATIONAL
DOLORIMETRY	DRUNKENNESS	EFFECTIVELY
DOMESTICATE	DRY CLEANERS	EFFECTUALLY
DOMESTICITY	DRY-CLEANING	EFFECTUATED
DOMICILIARY	DSCONTINUER	EFFERVESCED
DOMICILIATE	DUAL-PURPOSE	EFFICACIOUS
DOMINEERING	DUBIOUSNESS	EFFICIENTLY
DOORKEEPERS	DUDE RANCHES	EGALITARIAN
DOORKNOCKER	DUFFEL COATS	EGOCENTRISM
DOORSTOPPER	DUMBFOUNDED	EGOMANIACAL
DORMITORIES	DUMBFOUNDER	EGOTISTICAL
DOTTED LINES	DUMBWAITERS	EGREGIOUSLY
DOUBLE AGENT	DUNDERHEADS	EIDETICALLY
DOUBLE BINDS	DUNE BUGGIES	EIFFEL TOWER
DOUBLE-BLIND	DUPLICATING	EIGHTEENTHS
DOUBLE BLUFF	DUPLICATION	EINSTEINIAN
DOUBLE-CHECK	DUPLICATIVE	EINSTEINIUM
DOUBLE CHINS	DUPLICATORS	EISTEDDFODS
DOUBLE CREAM	DUST JACKETS	EJACULATING
DOUBLE-CROSS	DUTCH TREATS	EJACULATION
DOUBLE DATED	DUTCH UNCLES	EJACULATIVE
DOUBLE DATES	DUTIABILITY	EJACULATORY
DOUBLE-DUTCH	DUTIFULNESS	EJECTOR SEAT
DOUBLE-EDGED	DYNAMICALLY	ELABORATELY
DOUBLE-FACED	DYNAMOMETER	ELABORATING
DOUBLE FAULT	DYNAMOMETRY	ELABORATION
DOUBLE-GLAZE	DYSFUNCTION	ELABORATIVE
DOUBLE-QUICK		ELASTICALLY
DOUBLE-SPACE	**E**	ELASTIC BAND
DOUBLE TAKES	EAGER BEAVER	ELASTOMERIC
DOUBLETHINK	EARNESTNESS	ELASTOPLAST
DOUROUCOULI	EARTHENWARE	ELBOW GREASE
DOVETAILING	EARTHLINESS	ELECTIONEER
DOWN-AND-OUTS	EARTHQUAKES	ELECTORATES
DOWNGRADING	EAR TRUMPETS	ELECTORSHIP
DOWNHEARTED	EASEFULNESS	ELECTRIC EYE
DOWNLOADING	EAST ANGLIAN	ELECTRICIAN
DOWN PAYMENT	EASTERNMOST	ELECTRICITY
DOWNPLAYING	EAST GERMANY	ELECTRIFIED
DOWN-TO-EARTH	EATING APPLE	ELECTRIFIER
DOWNTRODDEN	EBULLIENTLY	ELECTROCUTE
DOXOLOGICAL	ECCLESIARCH	ELECTROFORM
DRAGONFLIES	ECCRINOLOGY	ELECTROLYSE
DRAMATIZING	ECHCHYMOSED	ELECTROLYTE
DRAMATURGIC	ECHOPRACTIC	ELECTRONICS
DRASTICALLY	ECLECTICISM	ELECTROTYPE
DRAUGHTSMAN	ECONOMETRIC	ELEGIACALLY
DRAUGHTSMEN	ECONOMIZING	ELEPHANTINE
DRAWBRIDGES	ECOSPECIFIC	ELEPHANTOID
DRAWING PINS	ECTOBLASTIC	ELICITATION
DRAWING ROOM	ECTOGENESIS	ELIGIBILITY
DRAWSTRINGS	ECTOMORPHIC	ELIMINATING

ELIMINATION	ENCEPHALOMA	ENLIGHTENED
ELIMINATIVE	ENCEPHALOUS	ENLIGHTENER
ELIZABETHAN	ENCHAINMENT	ENLISTED MAN
ELLIPSOIDAL	ENCHANTMENT	ENLISTED MEN
ELLIPTICITY	ENCHANTRESS	ENLISTMENTS
ELONGATIONS	ENCHONDROMA	ENLIVENMENT
ELUCIDATING	ENCOMIASTIC	ENNEAHEDRAL
ELUCIDATION	ENCOMPASSED	ENNEAHEDRON
ELUCIDATIVE	ENCOUNTERED	ENNISKILLEN
ELUCIDATORY	ENCOUNTERER	ENNOBLEMENT
ELUSIVENESS	ENCOURAGING	ENNOBLINGLY
ELUTRIATION	ENCROACHING	ENRAPTURING
EMANATIONAL	ENCUMBERING	ENSHROUDING
EMANCIPATED	ENCUMBRANCE	ENSLAVEMENT
EMANCIPATOR	ENCYCLICALS	ENSNAREMENT
EMASCULATED	ENDANGERING	ENTABLATURE
EMASCULATOR	ENDEARINGLY	ENTABLEMENT
EMBANKMENTS	ENDEARMENTS	ENTEROSTOMY
EMBARKATION	ENDEAVOURED	ENTEROVIRUS
EMBARRASSED	ENDEAVOURER	ENTERPRISER
EMBELLISHED	ENDEMICALLY	ENTERPRISES
EMBELLISHER	ENDLESSNESS	ENTERTAINED
EMBITTERING	ENDOBLASTIC	ENTERTAINER
EMBLAZONING	ENDOCARDIAL	ENTHRALLING
EMBLEMATIZE	ENDOCARDIUM	ENTHRALMENT
EMBOLDENING	ENDOCENTRIC	ENTHUSIASMS
EMBOLECTOMY	ENDOCRANIUM	ENTHUSIASTS
EMBRACEABLE	ENDOCRINOUS	ENTICEMENTS
EMBRACEMENT	ENDODONTICS	ENTITLEMENT
EMBROCATION	ENDODONTIST	ENTOBLASTIC
EMBROIDERED	ENDOMETRIAL	ENTOMBMENTS
EMBROIDERER	ENDOMETRIUM	ENTOMOPHILY
EMBROILMENT	ENDOMORPHIC	ENTRAINMENT
EMBRYECTOMY	ENDONEURIUM	ENTREATMENT
EMBRYOGENIC	ENDOPLASMIC	ENTRENCHING
EMENDATIONS	ENDORSEMENT	ENTRUSTMENT
EMERGENCIES	ENDOSCOPIST	ENTWINEMENT
EMIGRATIONS	ENDOSPERMIC	ENUCLEATION
EMMENAGOGIC	ENDOSPOROUS	ENUMERATING
EMMENAGOGUE	ENDOTHECIAL	ENUMERATION
EMOTIONALLY	ENDOTHECIUM	ENUMERATIVE
EMOTIONLESS	ENDOTHELIAL	ENUNCIATING
EMOTIVENESS	ENDOTHELIUM	ENUNCIATION
EMPANELLING	ENDOTHERMIC	ENUNCIATIVE
EMPANELMENT	END PRODUCTS	ENVELOPMENT
EMPERORSHIP	ENFORCEABLE	ENVIOUSNESS
EMPHASIZING	ENFORCEMENT	ENVIRONMENT
EMPIRICALLY	ENFRANCHISE	ENZYMOLYSIS
EMPLACEMENT	ENGAGEMENTS	ENZYMOLYTIC
EMPLOYMENTS	ENGENDERING	EPHEMERALLY
EMPOWERMENT	ENGINEERING	EPIDERMISES
EMPTY-HANDED	ENGLISH HORN	EPIDIASCOPE
EMPTY-HEADED	ENGORGEMENT	EPIGASTRIUM
EMULOUSNESS	ENGRAILMENT	EPIGENESIST
EMULSIFYING	ENGROSSEDLY	EPIGRAPHIST
EMULSIONING	ENGROSSMENT	EPIPHYTOTIC
ENARTHROSIS	ENHANCEMENT	EPITHALAMIC
ENCAMPMENTS	ENLARGEABLE	EPITHELIOMA
ENCAPSULATE	ENLARGEMENT	EPITOMIZING

EPOCH-MAKING	EUPHEMISTIC	EXEMPLIFIED
EQUIANGULAR	EURHYTHMICS	EXEMPLIFIER
EQUIDISTANT	EUROCHEQUES	EXERCISABLE
EQUILATERAL	EURODOLLARS	EXFOLIATION
EQUILIBRANT	EUROPEANISM	EXFOLIATIVE
EQUILIBRATE	EUROPEANIZE	EXHAUSTIBLE
EQUILIBRIST	EURYTHERMAL	EXHIBITIONS
EQUILIBRIUM	EVACUATIONS	EXHILARATED
EQUINOCTIAL	EVAGINATION	EXHILARATOR
EQUIPOLLENT	EVALUATIONS	EXHORTATION
EQUIVALENCE	EVANESCENCE	EXHORTATIVE
EQUIVALENCY	EVANGELICAL	EXHUMATIONS
EQUIVALENTS	EVANGELISTS	EXISTENTIAL
EQUIVOCALLY	EVANGELIZED	EXONERATING
EQUIVOCATED	EVANGELIZER	EXONERATION
ERADICATING	EVAPORATING	EXONERATIVE
ERADICATION	EVAPORATION	EXORABILITY
ERADICATIVE	EVAPORATIVE	EXORBITANCE
ERADICATORS	EVASIVENESS	EXOSKELETAL
ERASTIANISM	EVENING STAR	EXOSKELETON
ERGATOCRACY	EVENTUALITY	EXOTERICISM
EROSIVENESS	EVENTUATION	EXPANSIVELY
EROTOMANIAC	EVERLASTING	EXPATIATING
ERRATICALLY	EVISCERATED	EXPATIATION
ERRONEOUSLY	EVISCERATOR	EXPATRIATED
ERUBESCENCE	EXACERBATED	EXPATRIATES
ERUCTATIONS	EXAGGERATED	EXPECTANTLY
ERYSIPELOID	EXAGGERATOR	EXPECTATION
ERYTHEMATIC	EXALTEDNESS	EXPECTATIVE
ERYTHRISMAL	EXAMINATION	EXPECTORANT
ERYTHROCYTE	EXAMINATION	EXPECTORATE
ESCAPEMENTS	EXASPERATED	EXPEDIENTLY
ESCARPMENTS	EXASPERATER	EXPEDITIONS
ESCHATOLOGY	EXCAVATIONS	EXPEDITIOUS
ESCUTCHEONS	EXCEEDINGLY	EXPENDITURE
ESEMPLASTIC	EXCELLENTLY	EXPENSIVELY
ESOPHAGUSES	EXCEPTIONAL	EXPERIENCED
ESOTERICISM	EXCERPTIBLE	EXPERIENCES
ESSENTIALLY	EXCERPTTION	EXPERIMENTS
ESTABLISHED	EXCESSIVELY	EXPLAINABLE
ESTABLISHER	EXCITEDNESS	EXPLANATION
ESTATE AGENT	EXCITEMENTS	EXPLANATORY
ESTREMADURA	EXCLAMATION	EXPLICATING
ETHANEDIOIC	EXCLAMATORY	EXPLICATION
ETHEREALITY	EXCLUSIVELY	EXPLICATIVE
ETHEREALIZE	EXCOGITATOR	EXPLOITABLE
ETHICALNESS	EXCORIATING	EXPLORATION
ETHNOBOTANY	EXCORIATION	EXPLORATORY
ETHNOGENIST	EXCREMENTAL	EXPLOSIVELY
ETHNOGRAPHY	EXCRESCENCE	EXPONENTIAL
ETHNOLOGIST	EXCRESCENCY	EXPORTATION
ETIOLOGICAL	EXCULPATING	EXPOSEDNESS
ETYMOLOGIES	EXCULPATION	EXPOSITIONS
ETYMOLOGIST	EXCULPATORY	EX POST FACTO
EUCHARISTIC	EX-DIRECTORY	EXPOSTULATE
EUCHROMATIC	EXECRATIONS	EXPRESSIBLE
EUCHROMATIN	EXECUTIONER	EXPRESSIONS
EUDIOMETRIC	EXECUTORIAL	EXPRESSWAYS
EUGENICALLY	EXEMPLARILY	EXPROPRIATE

EXPURGATING	FALLIBILITY	FERRUGINOUS
EXPURGATION	FALLING STAR	FERTILIZERS
EXPURGATORY	FALSE ALARMS	FERTILIZING
EXQUISITELY	FALSE BOTTOM	FERULACEOUS
EXSICCATION	FALSE STARTS	FERVENTNESS
EXSICCATIVE	FALSIFIABLE	FESTINATION
EXSTIPULATE	FALTERINGLY	FESTSCHRIFT
EXTEMPORIZE	FAMILIARITY	FETISHISTIC
EXTENSIONAL	FAMILIARIZE	FEUDALISTIC
EXTENSIVELY	FAMILY NAMES	FIBRE OPTICS
EXTENUATING	FAMILY TREES	FIBROMATOUS
EXTENUATION	FANATICALLY	FIBROUSNESS
EXTENUATORY	FANTASIZING	FICTIONALLY
EXTERIORIZE	FARCICALITY	FIDGETINGLY
EXTERMINATE	FARINACEOUS	FIELD-EFFECT
EXTERNALISM	FARNBOROUGH	FIELD EVENTS
EXTERNALIST	FARRAGINOUS	FIELD HOCKEY
EXTERNALITY	FAR-REACHING	FIELD-HOLLER
EXTERNALIZE	FARTHERMOST	FIELD-TESTED
EXTIRPATING	FARTHINGALE	FIELDWORKER
EXTIRPATION	FASCINATING	FIFTH COLUMN
EXTIRPATIVE	FASCINATION	FIFTH-DEGREE
EXTOLLINGLY	FASCINATIVE	FIGURED BASS
EXTRACTABLE	FASHIONABLE	FIGUREHEADS
EXTRACTIONS	FAST-BREEDER	FILAMENTARY
EXTRADITING	FAST-FORWARD	FILIBUSTERS
EXTRADITION	FATEFULNESS	FILMOGRAPHY
EXTRAPOLATE	FATHER-IN-LAW	FILMSETTING
EXTRAVAGANT	FATHERLANDS	FILTHY LUCRE
EXTRAVAGATE	FATUOUSNESS	FILTRATABLE
EXTRAVASATE	FAULT-FINDER	FIMBRIATION
EXTREMENESS	FAULTLESSLY	FINANCIALLY
EXTREMITIES	FAVOURINGLY	FIN DE SIECLE
EXTRICATING	FAVOURITISM	FINE-GRAINED
EXTRICATION	FAWNINGNESS	FINES HERBES
EXTROVERTED	FEARFULNESS	FINGERBOARD
EXUBERANTLY	FEASIBILITY	FINGER BOWLS
EYE-CATCHING	FEATHER BEDS	FINGERNAILS
	FEATHER BOAS	FINGERPLATE
F	FEATHEREDGE	FINGERPRINT
FABRICATING	FEATURE FILM	FINGERSTALL
FABRICATION	FEATURELESS	FIRE BRIGADE
FABRICATIVE	FECUNDATION	FIRECRACKER
FACE-CENTRED	FECUNDATORY	FIRE ENGINES
FACETIOUSLY	FEDERALISTS	FIRE ESCAPES
FACILITATED	FEDERATIONS	FIRE FIGHTER
FACILITATOR	FELDSPATHIC	FIRE HYDRANT
FACT-FINDING	FELICITATED	FIRELIGHTER
FACTORIZING	FELICITATOR	FIREPROOFED
FACTORY FARM	FELLOWSHIPS	FIRE-RAISERS
FACTS OF LIFE	FELT-TIP PENS	FIRE-RAISING
FACTUALNESS	FEMME FATALE	FIRE STATION
FACULTATIVE	FENESTRATED	FIRING SQUAD
FAIRGROUNDS	FERMENTABLE	FIRMAMENTAL
FAIR-WEATHER	FEROCIOUSLY	FIRST COUSIN
FAIRY LIGHTS	FERRICYANIC	FIRST-DEGREE
FAITH HEALER	FERRIFEROUS	FIRST-FOOTER
FAITHLESSLY	FERRIS WHEEL	FIRST NIGHTS
FALCONIFORM	FERROCYANIC	FIRST PERSON

FIRST STRIKE	FLUOROSCOPY	FORMATIONAL
FIRST-STRING	FLYCATCHERS	FORMATIVELY
FISH-EYE LENS	FLYING BOATS	FORMICATION
FISH FARMING	FLYING FOXES	FORMULAICLY
FISH FINGERS	FLYING SQUAD	FORMULARIZE
FISHMONGERS	PLYING START	FORMULATING
FISSIONABLE	FLYSWATTERS	FORMULATION
FISSIPAROUS	FOCAL LENGTH	FORMULISTIC
FLABBERGAST	FOLK DANCERS	FORNICATING
FLAGELLANTS	FOLLICULATE	FORNICATION
FLAGELLATED	FOMENTATION	FORSWEARING
FLAMBOYANCE	FOOLISHNESS	FORTHCOMING
FLANNELETTE	FOOL'S ERRAND	FORTIFIABLE
FLANNELLING	FOOTBALLERS	FORTNIGHTLY
FLASHLIGHTS	FOOTBRIDGES	FORTUNATELY
FLASH POINTS	FOOT FAULTED	FORWARDNESS
FLAT-CHESTED	FOOT-LAMBERT	FOSSILIZING
FLATTERABLE	FOOT-POUNDAL	FOSTERINGLY
FLAUNTINGLY	FOOTSLOGGED	FOUL-MOUTHED
FLAVOURINGS	FOPPISHNESS	FOUNDATIONS
FLAVOURLESS	FORAMINIFER	FOUNTAIN PEN
FLAVOURSOME	FORASMUCH AS	FOURDRINIER
FLEA MARKETS	FORBEARANCE	FOUR-POSTERS
FLEET STREET	FORBIDDANCE	FOURTEENTHS
FLESHLINESS	FOREBODINGS	FOX TERRIERS
FLESH WOUNDS	FORECASTERS	FRACTIONARY
FLETCHERISM	FORECASTING	FRACTIONATE
FLEURS-DE-LIS	FORECLOSING	FRACTIONIZE
FLEXIBILITY	FORECLOSURE	FRACTIOUSLY
FLICK KNIVES	FOREFATHERS	FRACTURABLE
FLIGHT DECKS	FOREFINGERS	FRAGMENTARY
FLIGHTINESS	FOREGROUNDS	FRAGMENTING
FLIGHT PATHS	FOREMANSHIP	FRAME OF MIND
FLINCHINGLY	FOREQUARTER	FRANCHISING
FLIRTATIONS	FORERUNNERS	FRANCISCANS
FLIRTATIOUS	FORESEEABLE	FRANCOPHILE
FLOATATIONS	FORESHORTEN	FRANCOPHOBE
FLOCCULENCE	FORESIGHTED	FRANCOPHONE
FLOODLIGHTS	FORESTALLED	FRANKFURTER
FLOORBOARDS	FORESTALLER	FRANKLINITE
FLOOR CLOTHS	FORESTATION	FRANTICALLY
FLOORWALKER	FORETELLING	FRATERNALLY
FLOPPY DISKS	FORETHOUGHT	FRATERNIZED
FLORESCENCE	FORE-TOPMAST	FRATERNIZER
FLORILEGIUM	FORE-TOPSAIL	FRATRICIDAL
FLOUNDERING	FOREWARNING	FRATRICIDES
FLOURISHING	FORFEITABLE	FRAUDULENCE
FLOWCHARTED	FORGATHERED	FREEBOOTERS
FLOWER GIRLS	FORGETFULLY	FREE-FLOATER
FLOWERINESS	FORGET-ME-NOT	FREE-FOR-ALLS
FLUCTUATING	FORGETTABLE	FREE-HEARTED
FLUCTUATION	FORGIVENESS	FREEHOLDERS
FLUID OUNCES	FORGIVINGLY	FREELANCING
FLUORESCEIN	FORJUDGMENT	FREELOADERS
FLUORESCENT	FORLORN HOPE	FREELOADING
FLUORIDATED	FORLORNNESS	FREEMASONIC
FLUOROMETER	FORMALISTIC	FREEMASONRY
FLUOROMETRY	FORMALITIES	FREE PARDONS
FLUOROSCOPE	FORMALIZING	FREE-SWIMMER

FREETHINKER	G	GENTIANELLA
FREEWHEELED	GAFF-TOPSAIL	GENTLEMANLY
FREEZE-DRIED	GAINFULNESS	GENTLEWOMAN
FRENCH BEANS	GALLANTNESS	GENTLEWOMEN
FRENCH BREAD	GALLANTRIES	GENTRIFYING
FRENCH DOORS	GALL BLADDER	GENUFLECTED
FRENCH FRIES	GALLINACEAN	GENUFLECTOR
FRENCH HORNS	GALLIVANTED	GENUINENESS
FRENCH LEAVE	GALLUP POLLS	GEOCHEMICAL
FRENCH TOAST	GALVANIZING	GEODYNAMICS
FRENCHWOMAN	GAMEKEEPERS	GEOGRAPHERS
FREQUENCIES	GAMEKEEPING	GEOGRAPHIES
FREQUENTING	GAMETANGIAL	GEOMAGNETIC
FRETFULNESS	GAMETANGIUM	GEOPHYSICAL
FREUDIANISM	GAMETOGENIC	GEOPOLITICS
FRIENDLIEST	GAMETOPHORE	GEOSTRATEGY
FRIENDSHIPS	GAMETOPHYTE	GEOSTROPHIC
FRIGHTENING	GAMOGENESIS	GEOSYNCLINE
FRIGHTFULLY	GAMOGENETIC	GEOTECTONIC
FRINGILLINE	GANG-BANGING	GERATOLOGIC
FRIVOLITIES	GARAGE SALES	GERMANENESS
FRIVOLOUSLY	GARBAGE CANS	GERMINATING
FROGMARCHED	GARDEN PARTY	GERMINATION
FRONDESCENT	GARNISHMENT	GERM WARFARE
FRONTOLYSIS	GARRISONING	GERONTOLOGY
FRONT-RUNNER	GARRULOUSLY	GERRYMANDER
FROSTBITTEN	GASEOUSNESS	GESTATIONAL
FRUCTIFYING	GAS STATIONS	GESTICULATE
FRUGIVOROUS	GASTRECTOMY	GET-TOGETHER
FRUITLESSLY	GASTRONOMES	GHASTLINESS
FRUIT SALADS	GASTRONOMIC	GHOSTLINESS
FRUSTRATING	GASTROPODAN	GHOSTWRITER
FRUSTRATION	GASTROSCOPE	GIANT KILLER
FRUTESCENCE	GASTROSCOPY	GIANT PANDAS
FULGURATING	GASTROSTOMY	GIBBERELLIN
FULGURATION	GASTROTRICH	GIBBOUSNESS
FULL-BLOODED	GAS TURBINES	GIFT-WRAPPED
FULL-FLEDGED	GATECRASHED	GIGANTESQUE
FULL-MOUTHED	GATECRASHER	GILLYFLOWER
FULMINATING	GATEKEEPERS	GINGER BEERS
FULMINATION	GEANTICLINE	GINGERBREAD
FULMINATORY	GEGENSCHEIN	GINGER GROUP
FULSOMENESS	GELATINIZER	GIRL FRIDAYS
FUNAMBULIST	GEMMIPAROUS	GIRLFRIENDS
FUN AND GAMES	GEMMULATION	GIRLISHNESS
FUNCTIONARY	GEMOLOGICAL	GIVE-AND-TAKE
FUNCTIONING	GENDARMERIE	GLADIOLUSES
FUNDAMENTAL	GENEALOGIES	GLAMORIZING
FUNGIBILITY	GENEALOGIST	GLAMOROUSLY
FUNGISTATIC	GENERALIZED	GLARINGNESS
FURALDEHYDE	GENERALIZER	GLASSBLOWER
FURIOUSNESS	GENERALNESS	GLASSCUTTER
FURNISHINGS	GENERALSHIP	GLASSHOUSES
FURTHERANCE	GENERATIONS	GLASS-MAKING
FURTHERMORE	GENERICALLY	GLASS-WORKER
FURTHERMOST	GENETICALLY	GLAUCONITIC
FURTIVENESS	GENETIC CODE	GLEEFULNESS
	GENETICISTS	GLOBEFLOWER
	GENTEELNESS	GLOBIGERINA

GLOCHIDIATE
GLOMERATION
GLOMERULATE
GLORIFIABLE
GLOSSECTOMY
GLOSSOLALIA
GLOTTAL STOP
GLOVE PUPPET
GLOWERINGLY
GLUE-SNIFFER
GLUTATHIONE
GLYPHOGRAPH
GNATCATCHER
GOALKEEPERS
GOALKEEPING
GODCHILDREN
GODDAUGHTER
GODFORSAKEN
GODLESSNESS
GOLD-BEATING
GOLD DIGGERS
GOLD-DIGGING
GOLDEN EAGLE
GOLDEN SYRUP
GOLDFINCHES
GOLF COURSES
GONIOMETRIC
GONOCOCCOID
GONORRHOEAL
GOOD EVENING
GOOD LOOKERS
GOOD-LOOKING
GOOD MORNING
GOOD-NATURED
GOOD OFFICES
GORDIAN KNOT
GORMANDIZED
GORMANDIZER
GOSSIPINGLY
GOURMANDISE
GOURMANDISM
GOVERNESSES
GOVERNMENTS
GRACELESSLY
GRADABILITY
GRADATIONAL
GRADE SCHOOL
GRADUALNESS
GRADUATIONS
GRAECO-ROMAN
GRAMMARIANS
GRAMMATICAL
GRAMOPHONES
GRANDADDIES
GRANDFATHER
GRANDIOSITY
GRAND JURIES
GRAND MASTER
GRANDMOTHER

GRAND OPERAS
GRANDPARENT
GRAND PIANOS
GRANDSTANDS
GRANGERIZER
GRANITEWARE
GRANIVOROUS
GRANNY KNOTS
GRANOLITHIC
GRANOPHYRIC
GRANULARITY
GRANULATION
GRANULATIVE
GRANULOCYTE
GRAPEFRUITS
GRAPHICALLY
GRAPHOLOGIC
GRAPHOMOTOR
GRASSHOPPER
GRASS WIDOWS
GRAVESTONES
GRAVIMETRIC
GRAVITATING
GRAVITATION
GRAVITATIVE
GREASEPAINT
GREASY SPOON
GREAT CIRCLE
GREAT-NEPHEW
GREENBOTTLE
GREENGROCER
GREENHOUSES
GREENLANDER
GREENOCKITE
GREEN PAPERS
GREEN PEPPER
GRIDDLECAKE
GRIMACINGLY
GRINDELWALD
GRINDSTONES
GRISTLINESS
GRIZZLY BEAR
GROTESQUELY
GROTESQUERY
GROUCHINESS
GROUND CREWS
GROUND FLOOR
GROUND GLASS
GROUNDLINGS
GROUND PLANS
GROUND RENTS
GROUND RULES
GROUNDSHEET
GROUNDSPEED
GROUND STAFF
GROUNDSWELL
GRUELLINGLY
GRUMBLINGLY
GUARDEDNESS

GUARDHOUSES
GUELDER-ROSE
GUESSTIMATE
GUESTHOUSES
GUEST WORKER
GUILELESSLY
GUILLOTINED
GUILLOTINER
GUILLOTINES
GUILTLESSLY
GULLIBILITY
GUN CARRIAGE
GUNSMITHING
GURGITATION
GUTLESSNESS
GUTTA-PERCHA
GUTTER PRESS
GUTTERSNIPE
GUTTURALIZE
GYNAECOLOGY
GYPSIFEROUS
GYROCOMPASS
GYROSCOPICS
GYROSTATICS

H
HABERDASHER
HABILITATOR
HABITATIONS
HABITUATING
HABITUATION
HABITUDINAL
HADROSAURUS
HAEMACHROME
HAEMATOCELE
HAEMATOCRIT
HAEMATOLOGY
HAEMATOZOON
HAEMOCHROME
HAEMOCYANIN
HAEMOGLOBIN
HAEMOPHILIA
HAEMOPHILIC
HAEMOPTYSIS
HAEMORRHAGE
HAEMOSTASIA
HAEMOSTASIS
HAEMOSTATIC
HAGGADISTIC
HAGGARDNESS
HAGGISHNESS
HAGIOGRAPHA
HAGIOGRAPHY
HAGIOLOGIST
HAGIOSCOPIC
HAIRBREADTH
HAIRBRUSHES
HAIRDRESSER
HAIRPIN BEND

HAIR-RAISING	HARTEBEESTS	HELPFULNESS
HAIRSPRINGS	HARUM-SCARUM	HELPING HAND
HAIRSTYLIST	HARVEST HOME	HEMERALOPIA
HAIR TRIGGER	HARVESTLESS	HEMERALOPIC
HAIRWEAVING	HARVEST MOON	HEMIANOPSIA
HALCYON DAYS	HATCHET JOBS	HEMIELYTRAL
HALF-BROTHER	HATCHET-LIKE	HEMIELYTRON
HALF-HEARTED	HATEFULNESS	HEMIHYDRATE
HALF-HOLIDAY	HAUGHTINESS	HEMIMORPHIC
HALFPENNIES	HAUSTELLATE	HEMIPTEROUS
HALF-SISTERS	HAWKISHNESS	HEMISPHERES
HALF VOLLEYS	HAZARDOUSLY	HEMISPHERIC
HALLMARKING	HEADDRESSES	HEMITERPENE
HALLUCINATE	HEADHUNTERS	HEMITROPISM
HALOPHYTISM	HEADHUNTING	HEMOPHILIAC
HALTEMPRICE	HEADMASTERS	HEMORRHAGES
HALTERNECKS	HEALTH FOODS	HEMORRHOIDS
HALTINGNESS	HEALTHFULLY	HEMSTITCHER
HAMILTONIAN	HEALTHINESS	HEPPLEWHITE
HAMMERSMITH	HEARING AIDS	HEPTAHEDRAL
HAMMERSTEIN	HEART ATTACK	HEPTAHEDRON
HAMMOCK-LIKE	HEARTBROKEN	HEPTAMEROUS
HANDBREADTH	HEARTHSTONE	HEPTANGULAR
HANDCUFFING	HEARTLESSLY	HEPTAVALENT
HANDFASTING	HEARTSOMELY	HERBIVOROUS
HANDICAPPED	HEARTTHROBS	HERCULANEUM
HANDICAPPER	HEATHENNESS	HEREDITABLE
HANDICRAFTS	HEAT SHIELDS	HEREDITABLY
HAND LUGGAGE	HEAVENWARDS	HEREINAFTER
HANDMAIDENS	HEAVY-HANDED	HERETICALLY
HAND-ME-DOWNS	HEAVYWEIGHT	HERMENEUTIC
HANDWRITING	HEBDOMADARY	HERMOUPOLIS
HANDWRITTEN	HEBEPHRENIA	HERO WORSHIP
HANG GLIDING	HEBEPHRENIC	HERPETOLOGY
HAPHAZARDLY	HEBRAICALLY	HERRINGBONE
HAPLESSNESS	HECKELPHONE	HERZEGOVINA
HAPLOGRAPHY	HECTOGRAPHY	HESITATIONS
HAPPY EVENTS	HEDGEHOPPER	HESPERIDIAN
HAPPY MEDIUM	HEEDFULNESS	HESPERIDIUM
HARASSINGLY	HEGELIANISM	HESYCHASTIC
HARBOURLESS	HEIGHTENING	HETAERISTIC
HARD-AND-FAST	HEINOUSNESS	HETEROCLITE
HARDECANUTE	HELICHRYSUM	HETEROECISM
HARD-HEARTED	HELICOGRAPH	HETEROGRAFT
HARD-HITTING	HELICOPTERS	HETEROLYSIS
HARDICANUTE	HELIOCHROME	HETEROLYTIC
HARD PALATES	HELIOGRAPHS	HETEROPHONY
HARD-PRESSED	HELIOGRAPHY	HETEROPHYTE
HARDWEARING	HELIOLITHIC	HETEROPOLAR
HAREBRAINED	HELIOMETRIC	HETEROSPORY
HARMFULNESS	HELIOSTATIC	HETEROSTYLY
HARMONISTIC	HELIOTACTIC	HETEROTAXIS
HARMONIZING	HELIOTROPES	HETEROTOPIA
HARNESSLESS	HELIOTROPIC	HETEROTOPIC
HARNESS-LIKE	HELIOTROPIN	HETEROTYPIC
HARPOON-LIKE	HELLEBORINE	HEXADECIMAL
HARPSICHORD	HELLENISTIC	HEXAGONALLY
HARRIS TWEED	HELLISHNESS	HEXAHYDRATE
HARROWINGLY	HELMINTHOID	HEXASTICHIC

HEXASTICHON	HOLOCAUSTAL	HOSPITALITY
HEXATEUCHAL	HOLOGRAPHIC	HOSPITALIZE
HIBERNATING	HOLOHEDRISM	HOSPITALLER
HIBERNATION	HOLOMORPHIC	HOSTILITIES
HIBERNICISM	HOLOTHURIAN	HOT-CROSS BUN
HIDE-AND-SEEK	HOMECOMINGS	HOTHEADEDLY
HIDEOUSNESS	HOMEOPATHIC	HOT POTATOES
HIERARCHIES	HOMEOSTASIS	HOT-TEMPERED
HIERARCHISM	HOMEOSTATIC	HOURGLASSES
HIEROCRATIC	HOMERICALLY	HOUSE ARREST
HIEROGLYPHS	HOMESTEADER	HOUSEBROKEN
HIEROLOGIST	HOME STRETCH	HOUSEFATHER
HIGHFALUTIN	HOMICIDALLY	HOUSEHOLDER
HIGH JUMPERS	HOMOCENTRIC	HOUSEKEEPER
HIGHLANDERS	HOMOEOPATHS	HOUSE LIGHTS
HIGHLIGHTED	HOMOEOPATHY	HOUSEMASTER
HIGH-PITCHED	HOMOEROTISM	HOUSEMOTHER
HIGH-POWERED	HOMOGENEITY	HOUSEPARENT
HIGH PRIESTS	HOMOGENEOUS	HOUSEPLANTS
HIGH PROFILE	HOMOGENIZED	HOUSEWIFELY
HIGH-RANKING	HOMOGENIZER	HOUSEWIFERY
HIGH SCHOOLS	HOMOGRAPHIC	HOUSEWORKER
HIGH SHERIFF	HOMOIOUSIAN	HOVERCRAFTS
HIGH-TENSION	HOMOLOGICAL	HOW DO YOU DOS
HIGH TREASON	HOMOLOGIZER	HSIN-HAI-LIEN
HIGHWAY CODE	HOMOMORPHIC	HUCKLEBERRY
HIGH WYCOMBE	HOMOPHONOUS	HUCKSTERISM
HILARIOUSLY	HOMOPHYLLIC	HUDIBRASTIC
HILLBILLIES	HOMOPLASTIC	HUGUENOTISM
HINDERINGLY	HOMOPTEROUS	HULLABALOOS
HINDQUARTER	HOMO SAPIENS	HUMAN RIGHTS
HINSHELWOOD	HOMOSEXUALS	HUMDRUMNESS
HIPPEASTRUM	HOMOSPOROUS	HUMIDIFIERS
HIPPOCAMPAL	HOMOTHALLIC	HUMIDIFYING
HIPPOCAMPUS	HOMOTHERMAL	HUMILIATING
HIPPOCRATES	HOMOZYGOSIS	HUMILIATION
HIPPOCRATIC	HOMOZYGOTIC	HUMILIATIVE
HIPPOPOTAMI	HONEYCOMBED	HUMILIATORY
HIPPO REGIUS	HONEYMOONED	HUMMINGBIRD
HIRSUTENESS	HONEYMOONER	HUNCHBACKED
HISPANICISM	HONEYSUCKER	HUNGER MARCH
HISPANICIST	HONEYSUCKLE	HUNNISHNESS
HISPANICIZE	HONORARIUMS	HURRIEDNESS
HISTAMINASE	HONOURS LIST	HURTFULNESS
HISTIOCYTIC	HOODWINKING	HUSBANDLESS
HISTOLOGIST	HOOLIGANISM	HYACINTHINE
HISTORIATED	HOPEFULNESS	HYDNOCARPIC
HISTORICISM	HOPLOLOGIST	HYDRARGYRIC
HISTORICIST	HORIZONLESS	HYDRARGYRUM
HISTORICITY	HORIZONTALS	HYDROCARBON
HISTRIONICS	HORNBLENDIC	HYDROCYANIC
HITCHHIKERS	HORNET'S NEST	HYDROGENATE
HITCHHIKING	HORNSWOGGLE	HYDROGENIZE
HOBBLEDEHOY	HORROR FILMS	HYDROGENOUS
HOBBYHORSES	HORS D'OEUVRE	HYDROGRAPHY
HOGGISHNESS	HORSELAUGHS	HYDROLOGIST
HOLKAR STATE	HORSE OPERAS	HYDROLYSATE
HOLLANDAISE	HORSERADISH	HYDROMANCER
HOLOBLASTIC	HORTATORILY	HYDROMANTIC

HYDROMEDUSA	IMITATIVELY	IMPORTUNITY
HYDROMETEOR	IMMEDIATELY	IMPOSITIONS
HYDROPHOBIA	IMMEDICABLE	IMPRACTICAL
HYDROPONICS	IMMIGRATING	IMPRECATION
HYPERACTIVE	IMMIGRATION	IMPRECATORY
HYPERMARKET	IMMOBILIZED	IMPRECISION
HYPHENATING	IMMOBILIZER	IMPREGNABLE
HYPHENATION	IMMORTALITY	IMPREGNABLY
HYPNOTIZING	IMMORTALIZE	IMPREGNATED
HYPODERMICS	IMMUNOASSAY	IMPREGNATOR
HYPOTHERMIA	IMMUNOGENIC	IMPRESARIOS
	IMMUNOLOGIC	IMPRESSIBLE
I	IMPANELLING	IMPRESSIONS
ICEBREAKERS	IMPARTATION	IMPRESSMENT
ICHNOGRAPHY	IMPARTIALLY	IMPRIMATURS
ICHTHYOLOGY	IMPASSIONED	IMPRISONING
ICONOCLASTS	IMPASSIVELY	IMPROPRIATE
ICONOGRAPHY	IMPASSIVITY	IMPROPRIETY
ICONOLOGIST	IMPASTATION	IMPROVEMENT
ICOSAHEDRAL	IMPATIENTLY	IMPROVIDENT
ICOSAHEDRON	IMPEACHABLE	IMPROVINGLY
IDENTICALLY	IMPEACHMENT	IMPROVISING
IDENTIFYING	IMPECUNIOUS	IMPRUDENTLY
IDEOLOGICAL	IMPEDIMENTA	IMPUGNATION
IDIOBLASTIC	IMPEDIMENTS	IMPUISSANCE
IDIOGRAPHIC	IMPENITENCE	IMPULSIVELY
IDIOMORPHIC	IMPERATIVES	IMPUTATIONS
IDIOTICALLY	IMPERFECTLY	INADVERTENT
IDOLATRIZER	IMPERFORATE	INADVISABLE
IDOLIZATION	IMPERIALISM	INALIENABLE
IDYLLICALLY	IMPERIALIST	INALTERABLE
IGNIS FATUUS	IMPERILLING	INATTENTION
IGNOMINIOUS	IMPERIOUSLY	INATTENTIVE
IGNORAMUSES	IMPERMANENT	INAUGURATED
ILE-DE-FRANCE	IMPERMEABLE	INAUGURATOR
ILL-ASSORTED	IMPERSONATE	INCALESCENT
ILL-FAVOURED	IMPERTINENT	INCANTATION
ILLIBERALLY	IMPETRATION	INCAPSULATE
ILLIMITABLE	IMPETRATIVE	INCARCERATE
ILL-MANNERED	IMPETUOSITY	INCARDINATE
ILLOGICALLY	IMPETUOUSLY	INCARNATING
ILL-TEMPERED	IMPINGEMENT	INCARNATION
ILL-TREATING	IMPIOUSNESS	INCERTITUDE
ILLUMINANCE	IMPLAUSIBLE	INCESSANTLY
ILLUMINATED	IMPLAUSIBLY	INCIDENTALS
ILLUMINATOR	IMPLEADABLE	INCINERATED
ILLUSIONARY	IMPLEMENTAL	INCINERATOR
ILLUSIONISM	IMPLEMENTED	INCIPIENTLY
ILLUSIONIST	IMPLEMENTER	INCLINATION
ILLUSTRATED	IMPLICATING	INCLUSIVELY
ILLUSTRATOR	IMPLICATION	INCOERCIBLE
ILLUSTRIOUS	IMPLICATIVE	INCOGNIZANT
ILLUVIATION	IMPLORATION	INCOHERENCE
IMAGINARILY	IMPLORATORY	INCOME TAXES
IMAGINATION	IMPLORINGLY	INCOMMODING
IMAGINATIVE	IMPORTANTLY	INCOMPETENT
IMBRICATION	IMPORTATION	INCOMPLIANT
IMITABILITY	IMPORTUNATE	INCONGRUITY
IMITATIONAL	IMPORTUNING	INCONGRUOUS

INCONSONANT	INDULGENCES	INFREQUENCY
INCONSTANCY	INDULGENTLY	INFURIATING
INCONTINENT	INDULGINGLY	INFURIATION
INCORPORATE	INDUPLICATE	INFUSIONISM
INCORPOREAL	INDUSTRIOUS	INFUSIONIST
INCORRECTLY	INEBRIATING	INGENIOUSLY
INCREASABLE	INEBRIATION	INGENUOUSLY
INCREASEDLY	INEDIBILITY	INGRAINEDLY
INCREDULITY	INEFFECTIVE	INGRATIATED
INCREDULOUS	INEFFECTUAL	INGRATITUDE
INCREMENTAL	INEFFICIENT	INGREDIENTS
INCRIMINATE	INELEGANTLY	INGURGITATE
INCULCATING	INELOQUENCE	INHABITABLE
INCULCATION	INELUCTABLE	INHABITANCY
INCULPATING	INELUCTABLY	INHABITANTS
INCULPATION	INEQUITABLE	INHALATIONS
INCUNABULAR	INEQUITABLY	INHERITABLE
INCURIOSITY	INERTIA REEL	INHERITANCE
INCURVATION	INESCAPABLE	INHIBITABLE
INCURVATURE	INESCAPABLY	INHIBITEDLY
INDECIDUOUS	INESSENTIAL	INHIBITIONS
INDEFINABLE	INESTIMABLE	INITIALLING
INDEFINABLY	INESTIMABLY	INITIATIONS
INDEHISCENT	INEXACTNESS	INITIATIVES
INDEMNIFIED	INEXCUSABLE	INITIATRESS
INDEMNIFIER	INEXCUSABLY	INJUDICIOUS
INDEMNITIES	INEXISTENCE	INJUNCTIONS
INDENTATION	INEXPEDIENT	INJURIOUSLY
INDENTURING	INEXPENSIVE	INNER CITIES
INDEPENDENT	INFANTICIDE	INNERVATION
INDEX FINGER	INFANTILISM	INNOCUOUSLY
INDIA RUBBER	INFANTILITY	INNOVATIONS
INDICATABLE	INFANTRYMAN	INNS OF COURT
INDICATIONS	INFANTRYMEN	INNUMERABLE
INDICATIVES	INFATUATION	INNUTRITION
INDICTMENTS	INFERENTIAL	INOBSERVANT
INDIFFERENT	INFERIORITY	INOCULATING
INDIGESTION	INFERNALITY	INOCULATION
INDIGESTIVE	INFERTILITY	INOCULATIVE
INDIGNANTLY	INFESTATION	INOFFENSIVE
INDIGNATION	INFILTRATED	INOFFICIOUS
INDIGNITIES	INFILTRATOR	INOPERATIVE
INDIRECTION	INFINITIVAL	INOPPORTUNE
INDIVIDUALS	INFINITIVES	INQUILINISM
INDIVIDUATE	INFIRMARIES	INQUILINOUS
INDIVISIBLE	INFIRMITIES	INQUIRINGLY
INDIVISIBLY	INFLAMINGLY	INQUISITION
INDOCHINESE	INFLAMMABLE	INQUISITIVE
INDO-HITTITE	INFLECTIONS	INQUISITORS
INDO-IRANIAN	INFLICTIONS	IN-RESIDENCE
INDOMITABLE	INFLUENCING	INSALUBRITY
INDOMITABLY	INFLUENTIAL	INSCRIBABLE
INDO-PACIFIC	INFORMALITY	INSCRIPTION
INDUBITABLE	INFORMATION	INSCRIPTIVE
INDUBITABLY	INFORMATIVE	INSCRUTABLE
INDUCEMENTS	INFORMINGLY	INSCRUTABLY
INDUCTILITY	INFRACOSTAL	INSECTARIUM
INDUCTIONAL	INFRACTIONS	INSECTICIDE
INDUCTIVELY	INFRANGIBLE	INSECTIVORE

INSEMINATED	INTERBEDDED	INTERVIEWER
INSEMINATOR	INTERCALARY	INTERWEAVER
INSENSITIVE	INTERCALATE	INTIMATIONS
INSENTIENCE	INTERCEDING	INTIMIDATED
INSEPARABLE	INTERCEPTED	INTIMIDATOR
INSEPARABLY	INTERCEPTOR	INTOLERABLE
INSERTIONAL	INTERCESSOR	INTOLERABLY
INSESSORIAL	INTERCHANGE	INTOLERANCE
INSIDE TRACK	INTERCOSTAL	INTONATIONS
INSIDIOUSLY	INTERCOURSE	INTOXICABLE
INSINCERELY	INTERDENTAL	INTOXICANTS
INSINCERITY	INTERDICTOR	INTOXICATED
INSINUATING	INTERESTING	INTOXICATOR
INSINUATION	INTERFACING	INTRA-ATOMIC
INSINUATIVE	INTERFERING	INTRACOSTAL
INSISTENTLY	INTERFUSION	INTRACTABLE
INSOUCIANCE	INTERJECTED	INTRACTABLY
INSPECTABLE	INTERJECTOR	INTRADERMAL
INSPECTIONS	INTERLACING	INTRAVENOUS
INSPECTORAL	INTERLARDED	INTRENCHING
INSPIRATION	INTERLINEAR	INTREPIDITY
INSPIRATIVE	INTERLINGUA	INTRICACIES
INSPIRATORY	INTERLINING	INTRICATELY
INSPIRINGLY	INTERLINKED	INTRODUCING
INSTABILITY	INTERLOCKED	INTROVERTED
INSTALMENTS	INTERLOCKER	INTRUDINGLY
INSTATEMENT	INTERLOPERS	INTRUSIONAL
INSTIGATING	INTERMEZZOS	INTUITIONAL
INSTIGATION	INTERMINGLE	INTUITIVELY
INSTIGATIVE	INTERMITTOR	INTUITIVISM
INSTIGATORS	INTERNALITY	INTUITIVIST
INSTINCTIVE	INTERNALIZE	INTUMESCENT
INSTITUTING	INTERNECINE	INUNDATIONS
INSTITUTION	INTERNEURON	INVAGINABLE
INSTITUTIVE	INTERNMENTS	INVALIDATED
INSTRUCTING	INTERNSHIPS	INVALIDATOR
INSTRUCTION	INTERNUNCIO	INVENTIONAL
INSTRUCTIVE	INTERPOLATE	INVENTIVELY
INSTRUCTORS	INTERPOSING	INVENTORIAL
INSTRUMENTS	INTERPRETED	INVENTORIES
INSUFFLATOR	INTERPRETER	INVERTEBRAL
INSUPERABLE	INTERRACIAL	INVESTIGATE
INSUPERABLY	INTERRADIAL	INVESTITIVE
INTAGLIATED	INTERREGNAL	INVESTITURE
INTEGRATING	INTERREGNUM	INVESTMENTS
INTEGRATION	INTERRELATE	INVIABILITY
INTEGRATIVE	INTERROBANG	INVIDIOUSLY
INTEGUMENTS	INTERROGATE	INVIGILATED
INTELLIGENT	INTERRUPTED	INVIGILATOR
INTEMPERATE	INTERRUPTER	INVIGORATED
INTENSIFIED	INTERSECTED	INVIGORATOR
INTENSIFIER	INTERSEXUAL	INVITATIONS
INTENSIONAL	INTERSPERSE	INVOCATIONS
INTENSIVELY	INTERSTICES	INVOLUCRATE
INTENTIONAL	INTERTRIBAL	INVOLUNTARY
INTERACTING	INTERTWINED	INVOLVEMENT
INTERACTION	INTERVENING	IONOSPHERIC
INTERACTIVE	INTERVIEWED	IRIDESCENCE
INTERATOMIC	INTERVIEWEE	IRISH COFFEE

IRON CURTAIN	JOURNALIZER	LACERTILIAN
IRONMONGERS	JOYLESSNESS	LACINIATION
IRONMONGERY	JUDAIZATION	LACONICALLY
IRON RATIONS	JUDGMENT DAY	LACRIMATION
IRRADIATING	JUDICATURES	LACRIMATORY
IRRADIATION	JUDICIOUSLY	LACTALBUMIN
IRRADIATIVE	JUGGERNAUTS	LACTATIONAL
IRRECUSABLE	JUGULAR VEIN	LACTESCENCE
IRREDENTISM	JUMBLE SALES	LACTIFEROUS
IRREDENTIST	JUSTICESHIP	LADY-KILLERS
IRREDUCIBLE	JUSTICIABLE	LAEVOGYRATE
IRREDUCIBLY	JUSTIFIABLE	LAGOMORPHIC
IRREFUTABLE	JUSTIFIABLY	LAICIZATION
IRREFUTABLY	JUVENESCENT	LAMELLATION
IRREGULARLY	JUXTAPOSING	LAMELLICORN
IRRELEVANCE		LAMELLIFORM
IRRELIGIOUS	K	LAMELLOSITY
IRREMOVABLE	KALININGRAD	LAMENTATION
IRREPARABLE	KANCHIPURAM	LAMENTINGLY
IRREPARABLY	KERB CRAWLER	LAMINAR FLOW
IRRESOLUBLE	KETTLEDRUMS	LAMPROPHYRE
IRRETENTIVE	KEYBOARDERS	LANCASTRIAN
IRREVERENCE	KEYBOARDING	LANCINATION
IRREVOCABLE	KEYPUNCHERS	LANDING GEAR
IRREVOCABLY	KIDNEY BEANS	LANDING NETS
IRRITATIONS	KILIMANJARO	LANDLUBBERS
ISOCHRONIZE	KILLER WHALE	LANDSCAPING
ISODIAPHERE	KIND-HEARTED	LANDSCAPIST
ISOELECTRIC	KINDREDNESS	LANGUISHING
ISOGEOTHERM	KINETICALLY	LAPAROSCOPY
ISOLABILITY	KINETOPLAST	LAPIS LAZULI
ISOLECITHAL	KINGFISHERS	LARGE-MINDED
ISOMAGNETIC	KISS OF DEATH	LARKISHNESS
ISOMETRICAL	KITCHENETTE	LARYNGOLOGY
ISOMETROPIA	KITCHENWARE	LARYNGOTOMY
ISOMORPHISM	KITTENISHLY	LATITUDINAL
ISORHYTHMIC	KLEPTOMANIA	LAUDABILITY
ISOTONICITY	KNEECAPPING	LAUGHING GAS
ITACOLUMITE	KNICK-KNACKS	LAUNDERETTE
ITALICIZING	KNIGHTHOODS	LAURUSTINUS
ITEMIZATION	KNUCKLEBONE	LAW-BREAKERS
ITHYPHALLIC	KOOKABURRAS	LAWBREAKING
ITINERARIES	KRASNOYARSK	LAWLESSNESS
ITINERATION	KRUGERRANDS	LAWN PARTIES
IVORY TOWERS	KUALA LUMPUR	LAY BROTHERS
	KWANGCHOWAN	LEADING LADY
J	KWASHIORKOR	LEAF-CLIMBER
JACKHAMMERS	KYANIZATION	LEAPFROGGED
JACK-KNIFING	KYMOGRAPHIC	LEARNEDNESS
JACKRABBITS		LEASEHOLDER
JACTITATION	L	LEATHERBACK
JAM SESSIONS	LABIODENTAL	LEATHERETTE
JANISSARIES	LABORIOUSLY	LEATHERWOOD
JAWBREAKERS	LABOR UNIONS	LEAVE TAKING
JELLYFISHES	LABOURINGLY	LECHEROUSLY
JEOPARDIZED	LABOUR PARTY	LECITHINASE
JETTISONING	LABRADORITE	LECTURESHIP
JOIE DE VIVRE	LACCOLITHIC	LEFT-HANDERS
JOURNALISTS	LACERATIONS	LEFT-WINGERS

LEGAL TENDER	LIMNOLOGIST	LONG JUMPERS
LEGATIONARY	LIMP-WRISTED	LONGSIGHTED
LEGERDEMAIN	LINDISFARNE	LONGWEARING
LEGIONARIES	LINEAMENTAL	LOOSE CHANGE
LEGIONNAIRE	LINE DRAWING	LOOSESTRIFE
LEGISLATING	LINEN BASKET	LOPHOBRANCH
LEGISLATION	LINE OF SIGHT	LORD'S PRAYER
LEGISLATIVE	LINE PRINTER	LOSS LEADERS
LEGISLATORS	LINERTRAINS	LOTUS-EATERS
LEGISLATURE	LINGERINGLY	LOUDHAILERS
LEGITIMIZED	LINGUISTICS	LOUDMOUTHED
LEMON SQUASH	LION-HEARTED	LOUDSPEAKER
LENGTHENING	LIONIZATION	LOUNGE SUITS
LENGTHINESS	LIPOPROTEIN	LOUTISHNESS
LENTIGINOUS	LIQUEFIABLE	LOVE AFFAIRS
LEPIDOSIREN	LIQUESCENCE	LOW COMEDIES
LEPRECHAUNS	LIQUIDAMBAR	LOW-PRESSURE
LEPROSARIUM	LIQUIDATING	LOW PROFILES
LEPTORRHINE	LIQUIDATION	LOW-SPIRITED
LESE-MAJESTY	LIQUIDATORS	LOXODROMICS
LETTER BOMBS	LIQUIDIZERS	LUBRICATING
LETTERBOXES	LIQUIDIZING	LUBRICATION
LETTERHEADS	LITERALNESS	LUBRICATIVE
LETTERPRESS	LITERATURES	LUBRICATORS
LEUCOCRATIC	LITHOGRAPHS	LUCRATIVELY
LEUCODERMAL	LITHOGRAPHY	LUCUBRATION
LEUCORRHOEA	LITHOLOGIST	LUDICROUSLY
LEUCOTOMIES	LITHOMETEOR	LUGGAGE RACK
LEVEL-HEADED	LITHOPHYTIC	LUGGAGE VANS
LIABILITIES	LITHOSPHERE	LUMBERINGLY
LIBELLOUSLY	LITHOTOMIST	LUMBERJACKS
LIBERAL ARTS	LITTERATEUR	LUMBER-ROOMS
LIBERALIZED	LITTERLOUTS	LUMBERYARDS
LIBERALIZER	LITTLE WOMAN	LUMBRICALIS
LIBERALNESS	LITURGISTIC	LUMINESCENT
LIBERATRESS	LIVABLENESS	LUNAR MONTHS
LIBERTARIAN	LIVELIHOODS	LUSTFULNESS
LIBERTICIDE	LIVING ROOMS	LUTHERANISM
LIBERTINISM	LO AND BEHOLD	LUXULIANITE
LIBRATIONAL	LOATHSOMELY	LUXURIANTLY
LIBRETTISTS	LOBSTERPOTS	LUXURIATING
LICENTIATES	LOCAL COLOUR	LUXURIATION
LICKSPITTLE	LOCALIZABLE	LUXURIOUSLY
LIE DETECTOR	LOCAL OPTION	LYMPHANGIAL
LIEUTENANCY	LOCKER ROOMS	LYMPHOBLAST
LIEUTENANTS	LOCK KEEPERS	LYMPHOCYTIC
LIFE JACKETS	LOCOMOTIVES	LYTHRACEOUS
LIFE OF RILEY	LOCUM TENENS	
LIFE STORIES	LOGARITHMIC	M
LIGAMENTOUS	LOGGERHEADS	MACADAMIZER
LIGHT-FOOTED	LOGISTICIAN	MACHICOLATE
LIGHT-HEADED	LOGOGRAPHER	MACHINATION
LIGHTHOUSES	LOGOGRIPHIC	MACHINE CODE
LIGHTWEIGHT	LOGOMACHIST	MACHINEGUNS
LIKABLENESS	LOGOPAEDICS	MACHINE TOOL
LILLIPUTIAN	LOITERINGLY	MACROBIOTIC
LILY-LIVERED	LOLLIPOP MAN	MACROCOSMIC
LIMITATIONS	LOLLIPOP MEN	MACROGAMETE
LIMITLESSLY	LONDONDERRY	MACROPHAGIC

MACROSCOPIC	MANEUVERING	MASTERPIECE
MADDENINGLY	MANHANDLING	MASTERWORKS
MADEIRA CAKE	MANICHAEISM	MASTICATING
MADRIGALIAN	MANICURISTS	MASTICATION
MADRIGALIST	MANIFESTING	MASTICATORY
MAGDALENIAN	MANIFESTOES	MASTOIDITIS
MAGGOTINESS	MANIPULATED	MASTURBATED
MAGISTERIAL	MANIPULATOR	MATCHLESSLY
MAGISTRALLY	MANNERISTIC	MATCHMAKERS
MAGISTRATES	MANNISHNESS	MATCHMAKING
MAGLEMOSIAN	MANOEUVRING	MATCH POINTS
MAGNANIMITY	MANOR HOUSES	MATCHSTICKS
MAGNANIMOUS	MANSERVANTS	MATERIALISM
MAGNETIZING	MANTELPIECE	MATERIALIST
MAGNIFIABLE	MANTELSHELF	MATERIALITY
MAGNIFICENT	MANTOUX TEST	MATERIALIZE
MAHARASHTRA	MANUFACTORY	MATERNALISM
MAIDENHEADS	MANUFACTURE	MATHEMATICS
MAIDEN NAMES	MANUSCRIPTS	MATINEE IDOL
MAIDSERVANT	MARASCHINOS	MATRIARCHAL
MAILING LIST	MARCESCENCE	MATRICULANT
MAIN CLAUSES	MARCHIONESS	MATRICULATE
MAINSPRINGS	MAR DEL PLATA	MATRILINEAL
MAINTAINING	MARE CLAUSUM	MATRIMONIAL
MAINTENANCE	MARE LIBERUM	MAUDLINNESS
MAIN-TOPMAST	MARGINALITY	MAUNDY MONEY
MAINTOPSAIL	MARGINATION	MAURITANIAN
MAISONETTES	MARICULTURE	MAWKISHNESS
MAKE-BELIEVE	MARINE CORPS	MAYONNAISES
MAKHACHKALA	MARIONETTES	MEADOWSWEET
MALADJUSTED	MARKETPLACE	MEANDERINGS
MALADROITLY	MARKET PRICE	MEANINGLESS
MALAPROPIAN	MARKET TOWNS	MEASURELESS
MALAPROPISM	MARKOV CHAIN	MEASUREMENT
MALCONTENTS	MARLBOROUGH	MECHANICIAN
MALEDICTION	MARQUESSATE	MECHANISTIC
MALEDICTIVE	MARQUISETTE	MECHANIZING
MALEFACTION	MARRAM GRASS	MECKLENBURG
MALEFACTORS	MARROWBONES	MEDIASTINAL
MALEFICENCE	MARSHALLING	MEDIASTINUM
MALEVOLENCE	MARSHMALLOW	MEDICAMENTS
MALFEASANCE	MARTENSITIC	MEDICATIONS
MALFUNCTION	MARTIAL ARTS	MEDICINALLY
MALICIOUSLY	MARTINETISH	MEDICINE MAN
MALIGNANTLY	MARTINETISM	MEDICINE MEN
MALINGERERS	MARTYROLOGY	MEDIEVALISM
MALINGERING	MASCULINITY	MEDIEVALIST
MALOCCLUDED	MASKING TAPE	MEDITATIONS
MALONIC ACID	MASOCHISTIC	MEERSCHAUMS
MALPOSITION	MASONICALLY	MEGACEPHALY
MALPRACTICE	MASQUERADED	MEGALOBLAST
MALTED MILKS	MASQUERADER	MEGALOMANIA
MALTREATING	MASQUERADES	MEGALOPOLIS
MAMMALOGIST	MASSACHUSET	MEIOTICALLY
MAMMIFEROUS	MASSIVENESS	MELANCHOLIA
MAMMONISTIC	MASS-PRODUCE	MELANCHOLIC
MANAGEMENTS	MASTER CARDS	MELIORATION
MANDATORILY	MASTERFULLY	MELIORATIVE
MANDOLINIST	MASTERMINDS	MELLIFEROUS

MELLIFLUOUS	METALLOIDAL	MIND-BENDING
MELODICALLY	METALLURGIC	MIND-BLOWING
MELODIOUSLY	METALWORKER	MINDFULNESS
MELTABILITY	METAMORPHIC	MIND READERS
MELTING POTS	METANEPHROS	MIND READING
MEMBERSHIPS	METAPHYSICS	MINERALIZER
MEMORABILIA	METAPLASMIC	MINERAL OILS
MEMORANDUMS	METASTASIZE	MINESWEEPER
MEMORIALIST	METATHERIAN	MINIATURIST
MEMORIALIZE	METATHESIZE	MINIATURIZE
MEMORIZABLE	METEMPIRICS	MINIMUM WAGE
MENAQUINONE	METEOROLOGY	MINISTERIAL
MENDELEVIUM	METHODOLOGY	MINISTERING
MENDEL'S LAWS	METHYLAMINE	MINISTERIUM
MENORRHAGIA	METHYLATION	MINISTRANTS
MENORRHAGIC	METONYMICAL	MINNEAPOLIS
MENSTRUATED	METRICATION	MINOR PLANET
MENSURATION	METRICIZING	MINUTE STEAK
MENSURATIVE	METROLOGIST	MIRACLE PLAY
MENTALISTIC	MICHIGANDER	MIRROR IMAGE
MENTALITIES	MICHIGANITE	MIRTHLESSLY
MENTAL NOTES	MICKEY MOUSE	MISALLIANCE
MENTHACEOUS	MICROCOCCUS	MISANTHROPE
MENTHOLATED	MICROCOSMIC	MISANTHROPY
MENTIONABLE	MICROFICHES	MISAPPLYING
MEPROBAMATE	MICROFILMED	MISBEGOTTEN
MERCENARIES	MICROGAMETE	MISBEHAVING
MERCENARILY	MICROGRAPHY	MISCARRIAGE
MERCHANDISE	MICROGROOVE	MISCARRYING
MERCHANTMAN	MICROMETERS	MISCELLANEA
MERCHANTMEN	MICROMETRIC	MISCHIEVOUS
MERCILESSLY	MICROPHONES	MISCIBILITY
MERCURATION	MICROPHONIC	MISCONCEIVE
MERCURIALLY	MICROPHYTIC	MISCONSTRUE
MERITOCRACY	MICROREADER	MISCOUNTING
MERITORIOUS	MICROSCOPES	MISCREATION
MEROBLASTIC	MICROSCOPIC	MISDIRECTED
MERRYMAKERS	MICROSECOND	MISE-EN-SCENE
MERRYMAKING	MICROSPORIC	MISERLINESS
MESALLIANCE	MICROTOMIST	MISFEASANCE
MESENCHYMAL	MIDDLEBROWS	MISFORTUNES
MESMERIZING	MIDDLE CLASS	MISGOVERNOR
MESOBENTHOS	MIDDLE NAMES	MISGUIDANCE
MESOCEPHALY	MIDDLE-SIZED	MISGUIDEDLY
MESOGASTRIC	MIDNIGHT SUN	MISHANDLING
MESOMORPHIC	MIGRATIONAL	MISINFORMED
MESONEPHRIC	MILITARISTS	MISJUDGMENT
MESONEPHROS	MILITARIZED	MISMANAGING
MESOPHYLLIC	MILLEFLEURS	MISMATCHING
MESOPOTAMIA	MILLENARIAN	MISOGYNISTS
MESOSPHERIC	MILLILITRES	MISONEISTIC
MESOTHELIAL	MILLIMETRES	MISPRINTING
MESOTHELIUM	MILLIMICRON	MISREMEMBER
MESOTHORIUM	MILLIONAIRE	MISREPORTED
METABOLISMS	MILLISECOND	MISSING LINK
METACENTRIC	MIMEOGRAPHS	MISSISSAUGA
METAGENESIS	MIMETICALLY	MISSISSIPPI
METAGENETIC	MIMOSACEOUS	MISSPELLING
METALLOCENE	MINAS GERAIS	MISSPENDING

MISTRUSTFUL	MONOTHEISTS	MUSCULATURE
MISTRUSTING	MONOVALENCE	MUSEUM PIECE
MITHRIDATIC	MONSEIGNEUR	MUSHROOMING
MITOTICALLY	MONSTRANCES	MUSICALNESS
MIXED GRILLS	MONSTROSITY	MUSIC CENTRE
MOBILE HOMES	MONSTROUSLY	MUSKELLUNGE
MOBILIZABLE	MONS VENERIS	MUSTACHIOED
MOCKINGBIRD	MONTENEGRAN	MUTILATIONS
MODERNISTIC	MONTPELLIER	MUTTERINGLY
MODERNIZING	MOONLIGHTER	MUTTONCHOPS
MODULATIONS	MORAVIANISM	MUTUAL FUNDS
MOHAMMEDANS	MORIBUNDITY	MYCOLOGICAL
MOISTURIZED	MORNING COAT	MYCORRHIZAL
MOISTURIZER	MORNING STAR	MYELOMATOID
MOLESTATION	MORONICALLY	MYOCARDITIS
MOLLIFIABLE	MORPHOLOGIC	MYRIAPODOUS
MOLLYCODDLE	MORRIS DANCE	MYRMECOLOGY
MOLYBDENITE	MORTALITIES	MYSTERY PLAY
MOLYBDENOUS	MORTARBOARD	MYSTERY TOUR
MOMENTARILY	MORTISE LOCK	MYSTIFIEDLY
MONARCHICAL	MOSQUITO NET	MYTHOLOGIES
MONARCHISTS	MOTHER-IN-LAW	MYTHOLOGIST
MONASTERIAL	MOTHER'S BOYS	MYTHOLOGIZE
MONASTERIES	MOTHER'S RUIN	MYTHOMANIAC
MONASTICISM	MOTHERS-TO-BE	MYTHOPOEISM
MONETARISTS	MOTHPROOFED	MYTHOPOEIST
MONEYLENDER	MOTORCYCLES	MYXOMATOSIS
MONEYMAKERS	MOTOR LODGES	
MONEYMAKING	MOUNTAINEER	N
MONEY ORDERS	MOUNTAINOUS	NAILBRUSHES
MONEY SUPPLY	MOUNTAINTOP	NAIL VARNISH
MONITORSHIP	MOUNTEBANKS	NAKHICHEVAN
MONOCHASIAL	MOUTHORGANS	NAMEDROPPED
MONOCHASIUM	MOUTHPIECES	NAMEDROPPER
MONOCHROMAT	MOUTHWASHES	NAPHTHALENE
MONOCHROMIC	MUCOPROTEIN	NAPKIN RINGS
MONOCLINISM	MUCRONATION	NARAYANGANJ
MONOCLINOUS	MUDDLEDNESS	NARCISSISTS
MONOCULTURE	MUDSLINGING	NARCISSUSES
MONOGENESIS	MUHAMMADANS	NARCOLEPTIC
MONOGENETIC	MULTANGULAR	NARROW BOATS
MONOGRAMMED	MULTINOMIAL	NARROW GAUGE
MONOGRAPHER	MULTIPARITY	NASOFRONTAL
MONOGRAPHIC	MULTIPAROUS	NASOPHARYNX
MONOHYDRATE	MULTIPLEXER	NASTURTIUMS
MONOHYDROXY	MULTIPLYING	NATIONALISM
MONOLATROUS	MULTIRACIAL	NATIONALIST
MONOLINGUAL	MULTISCREEN	NATIONALITY
MONOMANIACS	MULTISTOREY	NATIONALIZE
MONOMORPHIC	MULTIVALENT	NATION STATE
MONONUCLEAR	MUNDANENESS	NATURALISTS
MONOPHAGOUS	MUNICIPALLY	NATURALIZED
MONOPHTHONG	MUNIFICENCE	NATURALNESS
MONOPOLISTS	MURDERESSES	NATUROPATHS
MONOPOLIZED	MURDEROUSLY	NATUROPATHY
MONOPOLIZER	MURMURINGLY	NAUGHTINESS
MONOSTICHIC	MUSCLE-BOUND	NEANDERTHAL
MONOSTROPHE	MUSCOVY DUCK	NEAR EASTERN
MONOSTYLOUS	MUSCULARITY	NEARSIGHTED

NECESSARIES	NIGHTMARISH	NOSOGRAPHER
NECESSARILY	NIGHT SCHOOL	NOSOGRAPHIC
NECESSITATE	NIGHTSHADES	NOSOLOGICAL
NECESSITIES	NIGHT SHIFTS	NOSY PARKERS
NECESSITOUS	NIGHTSHIRTS	NOTABLENESS
NECKERCHIEF	NIGHTSTICKS	NOTHINGNESS
NECROBIOSIS	NIGRESCENCE	NOTICE BOARD
NECROBIOTIC	NINCOMPOOPS	NOTOCHORDAL
NECROLOGIST	NINETEENTHS	NOTORIOUSLY
NECROMANCER	NINETY-NINES	NOTOTHERIUM
NECROMANTIC	NISHINOMIYA	NOURISHMENT
NECROPHILIA	NITRIFIABLE	NOVOSIBIRSK
NECROPHILIC	NITROGENIZE	NOXIOUSNESS
NECROPHOBIA	NITROGENOUS	NUCLEAR-FREE
NECROPHOBIC	NITROMETRIC	NUCLEIC ACID
NEEDFULNESS	NITROSAMINE	NUCLEOPLASM
NEEDLEPOINT	NITTY-GRITTY	NULL AND VOID
NEEDLEWOMAN	NOBEL PRIZES	NULLIFIDIAN
NEEDLEWOMEN	NOCICEPTIVE	NULLIPAROUS
NE'ER-DO-WELLS	NOCTILUCENT	NUMBERPLATE
NEFARIOUSLY	NOCTURNALLY	NUMERATIONS
NEGLIGENTLY	NOISELESSLY	NUMERICALLY
NEGOTIATING	NOISOMENESS	NUMISMATICS
NEGOTIATION	NOMADICALLY	NUMISMATIST
NEGOTIATORS	NO-MAN'S-LANDS	NUNCUPATIVE
NEIGHBOURLY	NOMENCLATOR	NURSING HOME
NEOCOLONIAL	NOMINATIONS	NUTCRACKERS
NEOLOGISTIC	NOMINATIVES	NUTRITIONAL
NEPHELINITE	NOMOGRAPHER	NYCTINASTIC
NEPHOLOGIST	NOMOGRAPHIC	NYCTITROPIC
NEPHRECTOMY	NOMOLOGICAL	NYCTOPHOBIA
NE PLUS ULTRA	NOMS DE PLUME	NYCTOPHOBIC
NERVE CENTRE	NONCHALANCE	NYMPHOLEPSY
NERVELESSLY	NONCREATIVE	NYMPHOMANIA
NERVOUSNESS	NONDESCRIPT	
NETHERLANDS	NONENTITIES	O
NEUROFIBRIL	NONETHELESS	OARSMANSHIP
NEUROLOGIST	NONEXISTENT	OBFUSCATING
NEUROMATOUS	NONFEASANCE	OBFUSCATION
NEUROPATHIC	NONHARMONIC	OBITER DICTA
NEUROPTERAN	NONILLIONTH	OBJECTIVELY
NEUROTICISM	NONIRRITANT	OBJECTIVISM
NEUROTOMIST	NONMETALLIC	OBJECTIVIST
NEUTRALIZED	NONOPERABLE	OBJECTIVITY
NEUTRALIZER	NONPARTISAN	OBJET TROUVE
NEUTRON BOMB	NONPLUSSING	OBJURGATION
NEVER-NEVERS	NONRESIDENT	OBJURGATORY
NEWSCASTERS	NONSENSICAL	OBLIGATIONS
NEWSLETTERS	NON SEQUITUR	OBLIQUITOUS
NEWSREADERS	NONSTANDARD	OBLITERATED
NEWSVENDORS	NONSTARTERS	OBLITERATOR
NEW YEAR'S DAY	NONVERBALLY	OBLIVIOUSLY
NEW YEAR'S EVE	NONVIOLENCE	OBNOXIOUSLY
NICENE CREED	NORMALIZING	OBSCENITIES
NICKELODEON	NORTHAMPTON	OBSCURATION
NICTITATION	NORTHEASTER	OBSCURITIES
NIETZSCHEAN	NORTHERNERS	OBSERVANCES
NIGHTINGALE	NORTHUMBRIA	OBSERVATION
NIGHTLIGHTS	NORTHWESTER	OBSERVATORY

OBSESSIONAL	OPEN LETTERS	OSTRACIZING
OBSOLESCENT	OPEN-MOUTHED	OSTRACODERM
OBSTINATELY	OPEN SEASONS	OSTRACODOUS
OBSTIPATION	OPEN SECRETS	OUAGADOUGOU
OBSTRUCTING	OPEN SESAMES	OUIJA BOARDS
OBSTRUCTION	OPEN VERDICT	OUTBALANCED
OBSTRUCTIVE	OPERABILITY	OUTBUILDING
OBTRUSIVELY	OPERATIONAL	OUTCLASSING
OBVIOUSNESS	OPHIOLOGIST	OUTDISTANCE
OCCASIONING	OPHTHALMIAC	OUTFIELDERS
OCCIDENTALS	OPINIONATED	OUTFIGHTING
OCCULTATION	OPINION POLL	OUTFLANKING
OCCUPATIONS	OPPORTUNELY	OUT-HERODING
OCCURRENCES	OPPORTUNISM	OUTNUMBERED
OCHLOCRATIC	OPPORTUNIST	OUT-OF-THE-WAY
OCHLOPHOBIA	OPPORTUNITY	OUTPATIENTS
OCTAHEDRITE	OPPOSITIONS	OUTPOINTING
OCTILLIONTH	OPPROBRIOUS	OUTPOURINGS
ODDS AND ENDS	OPTOMETRIST	OUTRIVALING
ODONTOBLAST	ORANGUTANGS	OUTRIVALLED
ODONTOGRAPH	ORCHESTRATE	OUTSMARTING
ODONTOPHORE	ORDERLINESS	OUTSPOKENLY
ODORIFEROUS	ORDER PAPERS	OUTSTANDING
ODOROUSNESS	ORDINATIONS	OUTSTRIPPED
OENOLOGICAL	ORGANICALLY	OUTWEIGHING
OESOPHAGEAL	ORIEL WINDOW	OVERACHIEVE
OESTROGENIC	ORIENTALISM	OVERANXIOUS
OFFENSIVELY	ORIENTALIST	OVERARCHING
OFFERTORIES	ORIENTALIZE	OVERBALANCE
OFFHANDEDLY	ORIENTATING	OVERBEARING
OFFICE BLOCK	ORIENTATION	OVERBIDDING
OFFICIALDOM	ORIGINALITY	OVERBOOKING
OFFICIALESE	ORIGINAL SIN	OVERCHARGED
OFFICIATING	ORIGINATING	OVERCHARGES
OFFICIATION	ORIGINATION	OVERCLOUDED
OFFICIOUSLY	ORIGINATORS	OVERCROPPED
OFF-LICENCES	ORNAMENTING	OVERCROWDED
OIL PAINTING	ORNITHOLOGY	OVERDEVELOP
OLD-WOMANISH	ORNITHOPTER	OVERDRAUGHT
OLEOGRAPHIC	ORTHOCENTRE	OVERDRAWING
OLIGARCHIES	ORTHODONTIC	OVERDRESSED
OLIGOCHAETE	ORTHOGRAPHY	OVEREXPOSED
OLIGOTROPHY	ORTHOPAEDIC	OVERFLOWING
OLIVE BRANCH	ORTHOPTERAN	OVERGARMENT
OMINOUSNESS	ORTHOSCOPIC	OVERHAULING
OMMATOPHORE	ORTHOSTICHY	OVERHEARING
OMNIFARIOUS	ORTHOTROPIC	OVERINDULGE
OMNIPOTENCE	OSCILLATING	OVERLAPPING
OMNIPRESENT	OSCILLATION	OVERLOADING
OMNISCIENCE	OSCILLATORS	OVERLOOKING
ONAGRACEOUS	OSCILLATORY	OVERMANNING
ONCOLOGICAL	OSCILLOGRAM	OVERPLAYING
ONE-MAN BANDS	OSMOTICALLY	OVERPOWERED
ONEROUSNESS	OSTENTATION	OVERPRODUCE
ONTOLOGICAL	OSTEOCLASIS	OVERPROTECT
OPALESCENCE	OSTEOLOGIST	OVERREACHED
OPEN-AND-SHUT	OSTEOPATHIC	OVERREACTED
OPENHEARTED	OSTEOPHYTIC	OVERRUNNING
OPENING TIME	OSTEOPLASTY	OVERSELLING

OVERSTAFFED	PANDEMONIUM	PARONOMASIA
OVERSTATING	PANDORA'S BOX	PARSON'S NOSE
OVERSTAYING	PANEGYRICAL	PARTIALNESS
OVERSTEPPED	PANHANDLERS	PARTICIPANT
OVERSTOCKED	PANHANDLING	PARTICIPATE
OVERSTUFFED	PANHELLENIC	PARTICIPIAL
OVERTOPPING	PANJANDRUMS	PARTICIPLES
OVERTURNING	PANTHEISTIC	PARTICULARS
OVERWEENING	PANTOGRAPHS	PARTICULATE
OVERWHELMED	PANTOGRAPHY	PARTING SHOT
OVERWORKING	PANTOMIMIST	PARTITIONED
OVERWROUGHT	PAPER CHASES	PARTITIONER
OVIPOSITION	PAPER-CUTTER	PARTITIVELY
OWNER-DRIVER	PAPERHANGER	PARTNERSHIP
OXIDATIONAL	PAPER KNIVES	PARTURIENCY
OXIDIMETRIC	PAPER TIGERS	PARTURITION
OXIDIZATION	PAPERWEIGHT	PARTY PIECES
OXYCEPHALIC	PAPIER-MACHE	PARTY POOPER
OXYGENATING	PAPYRACEOUS	PAS-DE-CALAIS
OXYGENATION	PARABLASTIC	PASQUINADER
OXYGEN MASKS	PARACETAMOL	PASSIBILITY
OXYGEN TENTS	PARACHUTING	PASSIONLESS
OXYHYDROGEN	PARACHUTIST	PASSION PLAY
OXYSULPHIDE	PARADOXICAL	PASSIONTIDE
OZONIFEROUS	PARAGENESIS	PASSIVENESS
OZONIZATION	PARAGENETIC	PASTEBOARDS
OZONOSPHERE	PARAGRAPHIA	PASTEURIZED
	PARAGRAPHIC	PASTEURIZER
P	PARALDEHYDE	PAST MASTERS
PACE BOWLERS	PARALEIPSIS	PAST PERFECT
PACIFICALLY	PARALLACTIC	PATCH POCKET
PACKAGE DEAL	PARALLELING	PATELLIFORM
PACKAGE TOUR	PARALLELISM	PATERNALISM
PACK ANIMALS	PARALLELIST	PATERNALIST
PACKING CASE	PARALLELLED	PATERNOSTER
PAEDIATRICS	PARAMEDICAL	PATHFINDERS
PAEDOLOGIST	PARAMORPHIC	PATHFINDING
PAINFULNESS	PARAMOUNTCY	PATHOLOGIST
PAINKILLERS	PARAPHRASED	PATISSERIES
PAINSTAKING	PARAPHRASES	PATRIARCHAL
PALAEARCTIC	PARAPLASTIC	PATRILINEAL
PALATINATES	PARAPLEGICS	PATRIMONIAL
PALEOGRAPHY	PARATHYROID	PATROL WAGON
PALEOLITHIC	PARATROOPER	PATRONIZING
PALESTINIAN	PARATYPHOID	PATRON SAINT
PALIMPSESTS	PARENTHESES	PATRONYMICS
PALINDROMES	PARENTHESIS	PAUNCHINESS
PALINDROMIC	PARENTHETIC	PAVING STONE
PALLBEARERS	PARESTHESIA	PAWNBROKERS
PALLIATIVES	PARESTHETIC	PAWNBROKING
PALPABILITY	PARI-MUTUELS	PAY ENVELOPE
PALPITATING	PARIPINNATE	PAY STATIONS
PALPITATION	PARISH CLERK	PEACH MELBAS
PAMPAS GRASS	PARISHIONER	PEACOCK BLUE
PAMPHLETEER	PARKING LOTS	PEARL DIVERS
PAN-AMERICAN	PARK KEEPERS	PEARLY GATES
PANCAKE ROLL	PARLIAMENTS	PEASHOOTERS
PANCHEN LAMA	PARLOUR GAME	PECCABILITY
PANDEMONIAC	PAROCHIALLY	PECCADILLOS

PECTINATION	PERFECTIBLE	PERSISTENCE
PECTIZATION	PERFORATING	PERSNICKETY
PECULATIONS	PERFORATION	PERSONALISM
PECULIARITY	PERFORATIVE	PERSONALIST
PECUNIARILY	PERFORMABLE	PERSONALITY
PEDESTRIANS	PERFORMANCE	PERSONALIZE
PEDICULOSIS	PERFUNCTORY	PERSONATION
PEDICURISTS	PERICARDIUM	PERSONATIVE
PEDOLOGICAL	PERICARPIAL	PERSONIFIED
PEDUNCULATE	PERICLASTIC	PERSPECTIVE
PEEPING TOMS	PERICRANIAL	PERSPICUITY
PEEVISHNESS	PERICRANIUM	PERSPICUOUS
PELARGONIUM	PERIDOTITIC	PERSUADABLE
PELLUCIDITY	PERIGORDIAN	PERSUASIONS
PELOPONNESE	PERIHELIONS	PERTINACITY
PENALTY AREA	PERIMORPHIC	PERTINENTLY
PENDULOUSLY	PERINEURIUM	PERTURBABLE
PENETRALIAN	PERIODICALS	PERTURBABLY
PENETRATING	PERIODICITY	PERVASIVELY
PENETRATION	PERIODONTAL	PERVERSIONS
PENETRATIVE	PERIODONTIC	PERVERTEDLY
PENICILLATE	PERIOD PIECE	PERVERTIBLE
PENICILLIUM	PERIOSTITIC	PESSIMISTIC
PENITENTIAL	PERIOSTITIS	PESTERINGLY
PENNYWEIGHT	PERIPATETIC	PESTIFEROUS
PENNYWORTHS	PERIPETEIAN	PESTILENCES
PENOLOGICAL	PERIPHERALS	PETITIONARY
PENSIONABLE	PERIPHERIES	PETITIONERS
PENSIVENESS	PERIPHRASES	PETITIONING
PENTADACTYL	PERIPHRASIS	PETRODOLLAR
PENTAHEDRON	PERISHABLES	PETROGRAPHY
PENTAMEROUS	PERISHINGLY	PETROLOGIST
PENTAMETERS	PERISPERMAL	PETTIFOGGER
PENTANGULAR	PERISTALSIS	PETTISHNESS
PENTATHLONS	PERISTALTIC	PHAGOMANIAC
PENTAVALENT	PERITHECIUM	PHAGOPHOBIA
PENTECOSTAL	PERITONEUMS	PHAGOPHOBIC
PENTLANDITE	PERITONITIC	PHALANSTERY
PENULTIMATE	PERITONITIS	PHANEROZOIC
PENURIOUSLY	PERIWINKLES	PHARMACISTS
PEPPERCORNS	PERLOCUTION	PHARYNGITIS
PEPPER MILLS	PERMANENTLY	PHELLOGENIC
PEPPERMINTS	PERMISSIBLE	PHENETIDINE
PEPTIC ULCER	PERMISSIBLY	PHENOLOGIST
PEPTIZATION	PERMUTATION	PHILANDERER
PERAMBULATE	PERORATIONS	PHILATELIST
PERCEIVABLE	PERPETRATED	PHILHELLENE
PERCENTAGES	PERPETRATOR	PHILIPPINES
PERCEPTIBLE	PERPETUALLY	PHILISTINES
PERCEPTIBLY	PERPETUATED	PHILOLOGIST
PERCHLORATE	PERPLEXEDLY	PHILOSOPHER
PERCHLORIDE	PERQUISITES	PHLEBOTOMIC
PERCIPIENCE	PERSECUTING	PHONETICIAN
PERCOLATING	PERSECUTION	PHONOGRAMIC
PERCOLATION	PERSECUTIVE	PHONOGRAPHS
PERCOLATIVE	PERSECUTORS	PHONOGRAPHY
PERCOLATORS	PERSEVERANT	PHONOLOGIST
PEREGRINATE	PERSEVERING	PHONOMETRIC
PERENNIALLY	PERSIAN CATS	PHONOTYPIST

PHOSPHATASE	PILOCARPINE	PLAYFULNESS
PHOSPHATIZE	PILOT LIGHTS	PLAYGROUNDS
PHOSPHORATE	PINA COLADAS	PLAYING CARD
PHOSPHORISM	PINCUSHIONS	PLAY ON WORDS
PHOSPHORITE	PINEAL GLAND	PLAYSCHOOLS
PHOSPHOROUS	PINE MARTENS	PLAYWRIGHTS
PHOTOACTIVE	PINNATISECT	PLEASANTEST
PHOTOCOPIED	PINPOINTING	PLEASURABLE
PHOTOCOPIER	PIPE CLEANER	PLEASURABLY
PHOTOCOPIES	PIPE OF PEACE	PLEASUREFUL
PHOTO FINISH	PIPERACEOUS	PLEBEIANISM
PHOTOGRAPHS	PIPISTRELLE	PLEBISCITES
PHOTOGRAPHY	PIRATICALLY	PLECTOGNATH
PHOTOMETRIC	PIROUETTING	PLEISTOCENE
PHOTONASTIC	PISCATORIAL	PLENTEOUSLY
PHOTO-OFFSET	PISCIVOROUS	PLENTIFULLY
PHOTOPERIOD	PISTON RINGS	PLEOCHROISM
PHOTOPHOBIA	PITCHBLENDE	PLEOMORPHIC
PHOTOPHOBIC	PITCHFORKED	PLICATENESS
PHOTOSETTER	PITCHOMETER	PLOUGHSHARE
PHOTOSPHERE	PITEOUSNESS	PLOUGHSTAFF
PHOTOSTATIC	PITH HELMETS	PLUM PUDDING
PHOTOTACTIC	PITIFULNESS	PLUNDERABLE
PHOTOTROPIC	PITUITARIES	PLURALISTIC
PHRASAL VERB	PLACABILITY	PLURALITIES
PHRASEBOOKS	PLAGIARISMS	PLUTOCRATIC
PHRASEOGRAM	PLAGIARISTS	PLUVIOMETER
PHRASEOLOGY	PLAGIARIZED	PLUVIOMETRY
PHTHIRIASIS	PLAGIARIZER	PNEUMECTOMY
PHYCOLOGIST	PLAGIOCLASE	PNEUMOGRAPH
PHYCOMYCETE	PLAINSPOKEN	POCKETBOOKS
PHYLLOCLADE	PLAINTIVELY	POCKETKNIFE
PHYLLOTAXIS	PLANETARIUM	POCKET MONEY
PHYLOTACTIC	PLANETOIDAL	POCOCURANTE
PHYSIATRICS	PLANIMETRIC	POCTOSCOPIC
PHYSICALISM	PLANISPHERE	PODIATRISTS
PHYSICALIST	PLANO-CONVEX	PODOPHYLLIN
PHYSIOGNOMY	PLANOGAMETE	POINSETTIAS
PHYTOGRAPHY	PLANOGRAPHY	POINTEDNESS
PICKPOCKETS	PLANOMETRIC	POINTE-NOIRE
PICKWICKIAN	PLANTAGENET	POINTILLISM
PICTORIALLY	PLANTATIONS	POINTILLIST
PICTURE BOOK	PLANTIGRADE	POINTLESSLY
PICTURE CARD	PLASMAGENIC	POINT OF VIEW
PICTURESQUE	PLASMODESMA	POISONOUSLY
PIECE OF CAKE	PLASMOLYSIS	POLARIMETER
PIECE OF WORK	PLASMOLYTIC	POLARIMETRY
PIEDMONTITE	PLASTER CAST	POLARISCOPE
PIEDS-A-TERRE	PLASTICALLY	POLARIZABLE
PIEZOMETRIC	PLASTIC ARTS	POLEMICALLY
PIGEONHOLED	PLASTICIZER	POLE VAULTED
PIGEONHOLES	PLASTOMETER	POLE VAULTER
PIGGISHNESS	PLASTOMETRY	POLICE STATE
PIGHEADEDLY	PLATELAYERS	POLICEWOMAN
PIGSTICKING	PLATINOTYPE	POLICEWOMEN
PILE DRIVERS	PLATS DU JOUR	POLITICALLY
PILGRIMAGES	PLATYRRHINE	POLITICIANS
PILLAR BOXES	PLAYER PIANO	POLITICIZED
PILLOWCASES	PLAYFELLOWS	POLITICKING

POLLEN COUNT	POSTNUPTIAL	PRE-EMINENCE
POLLINATING	POST OFFICES	PRE-EXISTENT
POLLINATION	POSTPONABLE	PRE-EXISTING
POLTERGEIST	POSTSCRIPTS	PREFATORILY
POLYANDROUS	POSTULATING	PREFECTURAL
POLYCHASIUM	POSTULATION	PREFECTURES
POLYGAMISTS	POTATO CHIPS	PREFERENCES
POLYGENESIS	POTATO CRISP	PREFIGURING
POLYGENETIC	POTENTIALLY	PREGNANCIES
POLYGLOTISM	POTTING SHED	PREHISTORIC
POLYGRAPHIC	POVERTY TRAP	PRE-IGNITION
POLYHYDROXY	POWDER PUFFS	PREJUDGMENT
POLYNUCLEAR	POWDER ROOMS	PREJUDICIAL
POLYPEPTIDE	POWER BROKER	PREJUDICING
POLYPHONOUS	POWERHOUSES	PRELIMINARY
POLYPLOIDAL	POWERLESSLY	PRELITERACY
POLYSTYRENE	POWER PLANTS	PRELITERATE
POLYTECHNIC	POWER POINTS	PREMATURELY
POLYTHEISTS	PRACTICABLE	PREMEDITATE
POLYTROPHIC	PRACTICABLY	PREMIERSHIP
POLYVALENCY	PRACTICALLY	PREMIUM BOND
POLYZOARIUM	PRAEDIALITY	PREMONITION
POMEGRANATE	PRAESIDIUMS	PREMONITORY
POMICULTURE	PRAGMATISTS	PREMUNITION
POMOLOGICAL	PRAIRIE DOGS	PREOCCUPIED
POMPOUSNESS	PRATTLINGLY	PREORDAINED
PONDEROUSLY	PRAYER WHEEL	PREPARATION
PONDICHERRY	PREARRANGED	PREPARATIVE
PONTIFICALS	PREARRANGER	PREPARATORY
PONTIFICATE	PRECAMBRIAN	PREPOSITION
POOH-POOHING	PRECAUTIONS	PREPOSITIVE
POPULARIZED	PRECAUTIOUS	PREP SCHOOLS
POPULARIZER	PRECESSIONS	PRERECORDED
POPULATIONS	PRECIPITANT	PREROGATIVE
PORK BARRELS	PRECIPITATE	PRESBYTERAL
PORNOGRAPHY	PRECIPITOUS	PRESCRIBING
PORPHYRITIC	PRECISENESS	PRESENTABLE
PORTABILITY	PRECLINICAL	PRESENTABLY
PORTERHOUSE	PRECLUDABLE	PRESENTIENT
PORTMANTEAU	PRECONCEIVE	PRESENTMENT
PORTO ALEGRE	PRECONTRACT	PRESERVABLE
PORT OF ENTRY	PRECRITICAL	PRESS AGENCY
PORTRAITIST	PREDATORILY	PRESS AGENTS
PORTRAITURE	PREDECEASED	PRESS BARONS
PORTRAYABLE	PREDECESSOR	PRESSGANGED
PORTS OF CALL	PREDESTINED	PRESSURIZED
POSITIONING	PREDICAMENT	PRESSURIZER
POSITIVISTS	PREDICATING	PRESTIGIOUS
POSITRONIUM	PREDICATION	PRESTISSIMO
POSSESSIONS	PREDICATIVE	PRESTRESSED
POSSESSIVES	PREDICATORY	PRESUMINGLY
POSSIBILITY	PREDICTABLE	PRESUMPTION
POSTAL ORDER	PREDICTABLY	PRESUMPTIVE
POSTERITIES	PREDICTIONS	PRESUPPOSED
POSTER PAINT	PREDIGESTED	PRETENDEDLY
POSTGLACIAL	PREDISPOSAL	PRETENSIONS
POSTMARKING	PREDISPOSED	PRETENTIOUS
POSTMASTERS	PREDOMINANT	PRETERITION
POSTMORTEMS	PREDOMINATE	PRETERITIVE

PRETTIFYING	PROFLIGATES	PROROGATION
PRETTY PENNY	PROFUSENESS	PROSAICALLY
PREVALENTLY	PROGENITIVE	PROSAICNESS
PREVARICATE	PROGENITORS	PROS AND CONS
PREVENTABLE	PROGNATHISM	PROSCENIUMS
PREVENTABLY	PROGNATHOUS	PROSCRIBING
PREVENTIVES	PROGRAMMERS	PROSECUTING
PRICKLINESS	PROGRAMMING	PROSECUTION
PRICKLY HEAT	PROGRESSING	PROSECUTORS
PRICKLY PEAR	PROGRESSION	PROSELYTISM
PRIESTCRAFT	PROGRESSIVE	PROSELYTIZE
PRIESTLIEST	PROHIBITING	PROSENCHYMA
PRIMA DONNAS	PROHIBITION	PROSPECTING
PRIMATOLOGY	PROHIBITIVE	PROSPECTIVE
PRIME MOVERS	PROHIBITORY	PROSPECTORS
PRIME NUMBER	PROJECTILES	PROSTATITIS
PRIMIPARITY	PROJECTIONS	PROSTHETICS
PRIMIPAROUS	PROKOPYEVSK	PROSTITUTED
PRIMITIVELY	PROLATENESS	PROSTITUTES
PRIMITIVISM	PROLEGOMENA	PROSTITUTOR
PRIMITIVIST	PROLETARIAN	PROSTRATING
PRINCIPALLY	PROLETARIAT	PROSTRATION
PRINTING INK	PROLIFERATE	PROTAGONISM
PRIORITIZED	PROLIFEROUS	PROTAGONIST
PRISON CAMPS	PROLONGMENT	PROTANDROUS
PRIVATIZING	PROMENADING	PROTECTIONS
PRIZEFIGHTS	PROMINENCES	PROTECTORAL
PROBABILISM	PROMINENTLY	PROTECTRESS
PROBABILIST	PROMISCUITY	PROTEOLYSIS
PROBABILITY	PROMISCUOUS	PROTEOLYTIC
PROBATIONAL	PROMISINGLY	PROTEROZOIC
PROBATIONER	PROMOTIONAL	PROTESTANTS
PROBLEMATIC	PROMPTITUDE	PROTHROMBIN
PROBOSCIDES	PROMULGATED	PROTOGYNOUS
PROBOSCISES	PROMULGATOR	PROTOLITHIC
PROCEEDINGS	PROMYCELIUM	PROTOPATHIC
PROCEPHALIC	PRONOUNCING	PROTOSTELIC
PROCESSIONS	PROOFREADER	PROTRACTILE
PROCHRONISM	PROOF SPIRIT	PROTRACTING
PROCLAIMING	PROPAGATING	PROTRACTION
PROCONSULAR	PROPAGATION	PROTRACTIVE
PROCREATING	PROPAGATIVE	PROTRACTORS
PROCREATION	PROPAGATORS	PROTRUDABLE
PROCRUSTEAN	PROPELLANTS	PROTRUSIONS
PROCTOSCOPE	PROPER NOUNS	PROTUBERANT
PROCTOSCOPY	PROPHESYING	PROVABILITY
PROCURATION	PROPHYLAXES	PROVIDENCES
PROCUREMENT	PROPHYLAXIS	PROVIDENTLY
PRODIGALITY	PROPINQUITY	PROVINCIALS
PRODUCTIONS	PROPITIABLE	PROVISIONAL
PROFANATION	PROPITIATED	PROVISIONED
PROFANATORY	PROPITIATOR	PROVISIONER
PROFANENESS	PROPORTIONS	PROVISORILY
PROFANITIES	PROPOSITION	PROVOCATION
PROFESSEDLY	PROPOUNDING	PROVOCATIVE
PROFESSIONS	PROPRANOLOL	PROVOKINGLY
PROFICIENCY	PROPRIETARY	PROXIMATELY
PROFITEERED	PROPRIETIES	PROXIMATION
PROFITEROLE	PROPRIETORS	PRUDENTNESS

PRUDISHNESS	PYRANOMETER	QUOTABILITY
PRUSSIC ACID	PYRARGYRITE	
PSEUDOMORPH	PYROCLASTIC	R
PSILOMELANE	PYROGALLATE	RABBIT HUTCH
PSITTACOSIS	PYROGRAPHER	RABBIT PUNCH
PSYCHEDELIA	PYROGRAPHIC	RABELAISIAN
PSYCHEDELIC	PYROMANIACS	RACECOURSES
PSYCHIATRIC	PYROTECHNIC	RACE MEETING
PSYCHICALLY	PYRRHULOXIA	RACQUETBALL
PSYCHODRAMA	PYRROLIDINE	RADIATIONAL
PSYCHOGENIC	PYTHAGOREAN	RADICALNESS
PSYCHOGRAPH		RADIOACTIVE
PSYCHOMETRY	Q	RADIO ALARMS
PSYCHOMOTOR	QUADRANGLES	RADIO BEACON
PSYCHOPATHS	QUADRENNIAL	RADIOCARBON
PSYCHOPATHY	QUADRENNIUM	RADIOGRAPHY
PTERIDOLOGY	QUADRILLION	RADIOLARIAN
PTERODACTYL	QUADRUPEDAL	RADIOLOGIST
PTOCHOCRACY	QUADRUPLETS	RADIOLUCENT
PUB-CRAWLING	QUADRUPLING	RADIOMETRIC
PUBLICATION	QUALIFIABLE	RADIOPACITY
PUBLIC HOUSE	QUALITATIVE	RADIOPHONIC
PUBLICIZING	QUANTIFIERS	RADIOSCOPIC
PUBLIC WORKS	QUANTIFYING	RADIOTHERMY
PUBLISHABLE	QUANTUM LEAP	RAFFISHNESS
PUCKISHNESS	QUARANTINED	RAGAMUFFINS
PUERTO RICAN	QUARRELLING	RAILROADING
PULCHRITUDE	QUARRELSOME	RAIN FORESTS
PULLULATING	QUARTER DAYS	RAISON D'ETRE
PULLULATION	QUARTERDECK	RALLENTANDO
PULSATILITY	QUARTER-HOUR	RAMAN EFFECT
PULVERIZING	QUARTERLIES	RAMBOUILLET
PULVERULENT	QUARTER NOTE	RANCH HOUSES
PUMPKINSEED	QUAVERINGLY	RANCOROUSLY
PUNCHED CARD	QUEENLINESS	RANGE FINDER
PUNCTILIOUS	QUEEN MOTHER	RANK AND FILE
PUNCTUALITY	QUEEN'S BENCH	RAPACIOUSLY
PUNCTUATING	QUERULOUSLY	RAPSCALLION
PUNCTUATION	QUESTIONARY	RAPTUROUSLY
PUNCTURABLE	QUESTIONERS	RAREFACTION
PUNISHINGLY	QUESTIONING	RASPBERRIES
PUNISHMENTS	QUESTION TAG	RASTAFARIAN
PURCHASABLE	QUEUE-JUMPED	RATE-CAPPING
PURCHASE TAX	QUEUE-JUMPER	RATIOCINATE
PUREBLOODED	QUIBBLINGLY	RATIONALISM
PURGATORIAL	QUICK-CHANGE	RATIONALIST
PURIFICATOR	QUICK-FREEZE	RATIONALITY
PURITANICAL	QUICKSILVER	RATIONALIZE
PURPLE HEART	QUICK-WITTED	RATTLESNAKE
PURPOSELESS	QUID PRO QUOS	RATTLETRAPS
PUSHINGNESS	QUIESCENTLY	RAUCOUSNESS
PUSSYFOOTED	QUINCUNCIAL	RAUNCHINESS
PUSSY WILLOW	QUINDECAGON	RAVEN-HAIRED
PUSTULATION	QUINTILLION	RAVISHINGLY
PUTREFIABLE	QUINTUPLETS	REACH-ME-DOWN
PUTRESCENCE	QUIVERINGLY	REACTIONARY
PYCNOMETRIC	QUIZMASTERS	REACTIONISM
PYELOGRAPHY	QUIZZICALLY	REACTIVATED
PYLORECTOMY	QUONSET HUTS	READABILITY

READDRESSED	RECUPERATOR	REIFICATION
READERSHIPS	RECURRENCES	REIMBURSING
READJUSTING	RECURRENTLY	REINCARNATE
READ-THROUGH	RECURRINGLY	REINFORCING
READY-TO-WEAR	REDACTIONAL	REINSTATING
READY-WITTED	RED ADMIRALS	REINSURANCE
REAFFIRMING	RED CRESCENT	REINTRODUCE
REALIGNMENT	REDCURRANTS	REITERATING
REALIZATION	REDECORATED	REITERATION
REALPOLITIK	REDEPLOYING	REITERATIVE
REANIMATING	REDEVELOPED	REJUVENATED
REANIMATION	REDEVELOPER	REJUVENATOR
REAPPEARING	RED HERRINGS	RELATEDNESS
REAPPORTION	REDIFFUSION	RELAXATIONS
REAPPRAISAL	REDIRECTING	RELIABILITY
REAPPRAISED	REDIRECTION	RELIEF ROADS
REAR ADMIRAL	REDOUBTABLE	RELIGIONISM
REARRANGING	REDOUBTABLY	RELIGIOSITY
REASSURANCE	REDRESSABLE	RELIGIOUSLY
REASSUREDLY	REDUCTIONAL	RELIQUARIES
REBARBATIVE	REDUNDANTLY	RELISHINGLY
RECALESCENT	REDUPLICATE	RELUCTANTLY
RECANTATION	RE-EDUCATING	RELUCTIVITY
RECAPTURING	RE-EDUCATION	REMAINDERED
RECEIVABLES	RE-ELECTIONS	REMEMBERING
RECEPTACLES	REFECTORIES	REMEMBRANCE
RECEPTIVELY	REFERENDUMS	REMINISCENT
RECEPTIVITY	REFERENTIAL	REMINISCING
RECESSIONAL	REFINEMENTS	REMITTANCES
RECIDIVISTS	REFLECTANCE	REMODELLING
RECIPROCATE	REFLECTIONS	REMONSTRANT
RECIPROCITY	REFORESTING	REMONSTRATE
RECITATIONS	REFORMATION	REMORSELESS
RECITATIVES	REFORMATIVE	REMOVAL VANS
RECLAIMABLE	REFORMATORY	REMUNERABLE
RECLAMATION	REFRACTABLE	REMUNERATED
RECLINATION	REFRAINMENT	REMUNERATOR
RECOGNITION	REFRANGIBLE	RENAISSANCE
RECOGNIZING	REFRESHMENT	RENEGOTIATE
RECOILINGLY	REFRIGERANT	RENOVATIONS
RECOLLECTED	REFRIGERATE	RENTABILITY
RECOMMENDED	REFRINGENCY	RENT STRIKES
RECOMMENDER	REFURBISHED	REORGANIZED
RECOMPENSED	REFUTATIONS	REORGANIZER
RECOMPENSER	REGENERABLE	REPARATIONS
RECONCILING	REGENERATED	REPARTITION
RECONDITION	REGIMENTALS	REPATRIATED
RECONNOITRE	REGIMENTING	REPELLINGLY
RECONSTRUCT	REGIONALISM	REPENTANTLY
RECOVERABLE	REGIONALIST	REPERTOIRES
RECREATIONS	REGISTERING	REPERTORIAL
RECREMENTAL	REGISTRABLE	REPERTORIES
RECRIMINATE	REGRETFULLY	REPETITIONS
RECRUITABLE	REGRETTABLE	REPETITIOUS
RECRUITMENT	REGRETTABLY	REPLACEABLE
RECTANGULAR	REGULARIZED	REPLACEMENT
RECTIFIABLE	REGULATIONS	REPLENISHED
RECTILINEAR	REGURGITANT	REPLENISHER
RECUPERATED	REGURGITATE	REPLETENESS

REPLEVIABLE	RESPIRATORS	REVERBERANT
REPLICATING	RESPIRATORY	REVERBERATE
REPLICATION	RESPLENDENT	REVERENCING
REPLICATIVE	RESPONDENCE	REVERENTIAL
REPOSSESSED	RESPONDENTS	REVERSIONER
REPOSSESSOR	RESPONSIBLE	REVISIONISM
REPREHENDED	RESPONSIBLY	REVISIONIST
REPREHENDER	RESPONSIONS	REVITALIZED
REPRESENTED	RESTATEMENT	REVIVALISTS
REPRESSIBLE	RESTAURANTS	REVIVIFYING
REPRESSIONS	RESTFULNESS	REVOCATIONS
REPRIEVABLE	RESTITUTION	REVOLTINGLY
REPRIMANDED	RESTITUTIVE	REVOLUTIONS
REPRIMANDER	RESTIVENESS	REVOLVINGLY
REPROACHFUL	RESTORATION	RHABDOMANCY
REPROACHING	RESTORATIVE	RHABDOMYOMA
REPROBATION	RESTRAINING	RHAMNACEOUS
REPROBATIVE	RESTRICTING	RHAPSODIZED
REPROCESSED	RESTRICTION	RHEOLOGICAL
REPRODUCERS	RESTRICTIVE	RHEOTROPISM
REPRODUCING	RESTRUCTURE	RHETORICIAN
REPROGRAPHY	RESURFACING	RHEUMATICKY
REPROVINGLY	RESURRECTED	RHINESTONES
REPUBLICANS	RESUSCITATE	RHINOLOGIST
REPUBLISHER	RETALIATING	RHINOPLASTY
REPUDIATING	RETALIATION	RHINOSCOPIC
REPUDIATION	RETALIATIVE	RHIZOMATOUS
REPUDIATIVE	RETALIATORY	RHIZOPODOUS
REPUDIATORY	RETARDATION	RHIZOSPHERE
REPULSIVELY	RETARDATIVE	RHODE ISLAND
REPUTATIONS	RETARDINGLY	RHOTACISTIC
REQUEST STOP	RETENTIVELY	RHYTHMICITY
REQUIREMENT	RETENTIVITY	RICE PADDIES
REQUISITION	RETICULATED	RICKETINESS
REQUITEMENT	RETINACULAR	RICKETTSIAL
RERADIATION	RETINACULUM	RICOCHETING
RESCHEDULED	RETINOSCOPY	RICOCHETTED
RESCINDABLE	RETIREMENTS	RIFLE RANGES
RESCINDMENT	RETOUCHABLE	RIFT VALLEYS
RESCISSIBLE	RETRACEABLE	RIGHT-ANGLED
RESEARCHERS	RETRACEMENT	RIGHT ANGLES
RESEARCHING	RETRACTABLE	RIGHTEOUSLY
RESECTIONAL	RETRACTIONS	RIGHT-HANDED
RESEMBLANCE	RETRENCHING	RIGHT-HANDER
RESENTFULLY	RETRIBUTION	RIGHT-MINDED
RESERVATION	RETRIBUTIVE	RIGHTS ISSUE
RESHUFFLING	RETRIEVABLE	RIGHTS OF WAY
RESIDENTIAL	RETRIEVABLY	RIGHT-WINGER
RESIGNATION	RETROACTION	RIGOR MORTIS
RESILIENTLY	RETROACTIVE	RING BINDERS
RESISTANCES	RETROLENTAL	RING FINGERS
RESISTENCIA	RETRO-ROCKET	RINGLEADERS
RESISTINGLY	RETROVERTED	RINGMASTERS
RESISTIVITY	REUPHOLSTER	RINSABILITY
RESOLUTIONS	REUSABILITY	RIOTOUSNESS
RESOURCEFUL	REVALUATION	RITUALISTIC
RESPECTABLE	REVEALINGLY	RIVER BASINS
RESPECTABLY	REVELATIONS	ROADHOLDING
RESPIRATION	REVENGINGLY	ROAD MANAGER

ROAD ROLLERS	RUSSOPHOBIC	SALVAGEABLE
ROAD TESTING	RUSTICATING	SALVATIONAL
ROCK-AND-ROLL	RUSTICATION	SAL VOLATILE
ROCK GARDENS	RUSTPROOFED	SAN ANTONIAN
RODENTICIDE	RUTTISHNESS	SANATORIUMS
RODOMONTADE		SANCTIFYING
ROGUISHNESS	S	SANCTIONING
ROLE PLAYING	SAARBRUCKEN	SANCTUARIES
ROLLER BLIND	SABBATARIAN	SANDBAGGING
ROLLER SKATE	SABBATICALS	SANDBLASTED
ROLLER TOWEL	SACCULATION	SANDBLASTER
ROLLICKINGS	SACRAMENTAL	SAND-CASTING
ROLLICKSOME	SACRIFICIAL	SANDCASTLES
ROLLING MILL	SACRIFICING	SANDPAPERED
ROLLING PINS	SACRILEGIST	SANDWICHING
ROLLTOP DESK	SACROILIACS	SANGUINARIA
ROMAN CANDLE	SADDENINGLY	SANGUINEOUS
ROMANTICISM	SADDLECLOTH	SANITARIUMS
ROMANTICIST	SAFARI PARKS	SAN MARINESE
ROMANTICIZE	SAFEBREAKER	SAN SALVADOR
ROOD SCREENS	SAFE-CONDUCT	SANSEVIERIA
ROOF GARDENS	SAFE-DEPOSIT	SANSKRITIST
ROOM SERVICE	SAFEGUARDED	SAPONACEOUS
ROPE LADDERS	SAFEKEEPING	SAPOTACEOUS
ROSE WINDOWS	SAFETY BELTS	SAPROPHYTIC
ROTARIANISM	SAFETY CATCH	SARCOMATOID
ROTISSERIES	SAFETY-FIRST	SARCOPHAGUS
ROTOGRAVURE	SAFETY GLASS	SARDONICISM
ROTTENSTONE	SAFETY LAMPS	SARTORIALLY
ROTUNDITIES	SAFETY MATCH	SASH WINDOWS
ROUGHCASTER	SAFETY RAZOR	SATANICALLY
ROUGH-SPOKEN	SAFETY VALVE	SATELLITIUM
ROUNDABOUTS	SAGACIOUSLY	SATIABILITY
ROUNDEDNESS	SAGITTARIAN	SATIRICALLY
ROUND ROBINS	SAGITTARIUS	SATISFIABLE
ROUSTABOUTS	SAILING BOAT	SATURNALIAS
ROWING BOATS	SAILOR SUITS	SAUDI ARABIA
RUBBER BANDS	SAINT GALLEN	SAURISCHIAN
RUBBER PLANT	SAINTLINESS	SAUROPODOUS
RUBBER STAMP	SALACIOUSLY	SAUSAGE DOGS
RUBBER TREES	SALAMANDERS	SAUSAGE ROLL
RUBBISH BINS	SALEABILITY	SAVABLENESS
RUBEFACIENT	SALESCLERKS	SAVING GRACE
RUBEFACTION	SALESPEOPLE	SAVINGS BANK
RUBICUNDITY	SALESPERSON	SAVOIR-FAIRE
RUBRICATION	SALICACEOUS	SAVOURINGLY
RUDESHEIMER	SALIENTNESS	SAXOPHONIST
RUDIMENTARY	SALINOMETER	SCAFFOLDING
RULE OF THUMB	SALINOMETRY	SCALARIFORM
RUMBUSTIOUS	SALMONBERRY	SCAMMONIATE
RUMINATIONS	SALMON TROUT	SCANDALIZED
RUMMAGE SALE	SALPINGITIC	SCANDALIZER
RUMPUS ROOMS	SALPINGITIS	SCANDINAVIA
RUNNER BEANS	SALTATORIAL	SCARABAEOID
RUNNING JUMP	SALTCELLARS	SCAREDY CATS
RUNNING MATE	SALT SHAKERS	SCAREMONGER
RUN-THROUGHS	SALUTATIONS	SCARLATINAL
RUNTISHNESS	SALVABILITY	SCATOLOGIST
RUSSOPHOBIA	SALVADORIAN	SCATTERABLE

SCENOGRAPHY	SECESSIONAL	SEMASIOLOGY
SCEPTICALLY	SECONDARILY	SEMIAQUATIC
SCHEMATIZED	SECOND-CLASS	SEMIARIDITY
SCHISMATICS	SECOND-GUESS	SEMICIRCLES
SCHISTOSITY	SECOND HANDS	SEMIDIURNAL
SCHISTOSOME	SECONDMENTS	SEMIFLUIDIC
SCHIZOPHYTE	SECOND-RATER	SEMIMONTHLY
SCHOLARSHIP	SECOND SIGHT	SEMIOTICIAN
SCHOLIASTIC	SECRET AGENT	SEMIPALMATE
SCHOOLCHILD	SECRETARIAL	SEMIQUAVERS
SCHOOLHOUSE	SECRETARIAT	SEMISKILLED
SCHOOLMARMS	SECRETARIES	SEMITONALLY
SCHOOLMATES	SECRETIVELY	SEMITRAILER
SCIENCE PARK	SECULARIZED	SEMITROPICS
SCIENTISTIC	SECULARIZER	SEMIVOCALIC
SCIENTOLOGY	SEDAN CHAIRS	SEMPITERNAL
SCINTILLATE	SEDENTARILY	SENSATIONAL
SCIRRHOSITY	SEDIMENTARY	SENSELESSLY
SCLERODERMA	SEDIMENTOUS	SENSE ORGANS
SCLEROMETER	SEDITIONARY	SENSIBILITY
SCLEROTIOID	SEDITIOUSLY	SENSITIVELY
SCOPOLAMINE	SEDUCTIVELY	SENSITIVITY
SCOREBOARDS	SEGREGATING	SENSITIZING
SCORIACEOUS	SEGREGATION	SENSUALISTS
SCORPAENOID	SEGREGATIVE	SENSUALNESS
SCOTCH BROTH	SEIGNIORAGE	SENTENTIOUS
SCOTCH MISTS	SEISMICALLY	SENTIMENTAL
SCOTCH TAPED	SEISMOGRAPH	SENTRY BOXES
SCOTOMATOUS	SEISMOLOGIC	SEPARATIONS
SCOURGINGLY	SEISMOSCOPE	SEPARATISTS
SCOUTMASTER	SELAGINELLA	SEPTAVALENT
SCRAGGINESS	SELECTIVELY	SEPTICAEMIA
SCRAPPINESS	SELECTIVITY	SEPTICAEMIC
SCRATCHIEST	SELENOGRAPH	SEPTIC TANKS
SCRATCHPADS	SELF-ASSURED	SEPTIFRAGAL
SCRAWNINESS	SELF-CENTRED	SEPTIVALENT
SCREAMINGLY	SELF-COMMAND	SEQUESTERED
SCREENPLAYS	SELF-CONCEPT	SEQUESTRANT
SCREEN TESTS	SELF-CONTROL	SEQUESTRATE
SCREWDRIVER	SELF-DEFENCE	SERENDIPITY
SCRIMMAGING	SELF-DENYING	SERIALIZING
SCRIMPINESS	SELF-EVIDENT	SERICULTURE
SCRIPTORIUM	SELF-IMPOSED	SERIES-WOUND
SCRUBBINESS	SELF-INDUCED	SERIOUSNESS
SCRUMHALVES	SELFISHNESS	SERMONIZING
SCRUMMAGING	SELF-LOADING	SERPIGINOUS
SCRUMPTIOUS	SELF-LOCKING	SERRULATION
SCRUTINEERS	SELF-PITYING	SERTULARIAN
SCRUTINIZED	SELF-RELIANT	SERVICEABLE
SCRUTINIZER	SELF-RESPECT	SERVICEABLY
SCULPTURING	SELF-SEALING	SERVICE FLAT
SCYPHISTOMA	SELF-SEEKERS	SERVICE ROAD
SEA ANEMONES	SELF-SEEKING	SERVOMOTORS
SEA CAPTAINS	SELF-SERVICE	SESQUIOXIDE
SEARCHINGLY	SELF-STARTER	SETTLEMENTS
SEARCHLIGHT	SELF-WINDING	SEVENTEENTH
SEARCH PARTY	SELL-BY DATES	SEVENTIETHS
SEASICKNESS	SELLOTAPING	SEXAGESIMAL
SEBORRHOEAL	SEMANTICIST	SEXLESSNESS

SEXOLOGISTS	SHRUBBERIES	SINOLOGICAL
SEXTODECIMO	SHRUBBINESS	SINOLOGISTS
SHADOW-BOXED	SHUTTLECOCK	SINO-TIBETAN
SHADOWGRAPH	SIAMESE CATS	SINUOSITIES
SHADOWINESS	SIAMESE TWIN	SINUOUSNESS
SHALLOWNESS	SICKENINGLY	SISTERHOODS
SHAMANISTIC	SIDE EFFECTS	SISTER-IN-LAW
SHAMELESSLY	SIDESADDLES	SITTING DUCK
SHANGHAIING	SIDESLIPPED	SITTING ROOM
SHANKS'S PONY	SIDESTEPPED	SITUATIONAL
SHANTYTOWNS	SIDESTEPPER	SIX-SHOOTERS
SHAPELESSLY	SIDE STREETS	SIXTH-FORMER
SHAPELINESS	SIDESWIPING	SIZABLENESS
SHAREHOLDER	SIDETRACKED	SKATEBOARDS
SHARP-WITTED	SIDE-WHEELER	SKEDADDLING
SHAVING FOAM	SIERRA LEONE	SKELETONIZE
SHEATH KNIFE	SIERRA MADRE	SKELETON KEY
SHEET ANCHOR	SIGHTLINESS	SKEPTICALLY
SHELLACKING	SIGHT-READER	SKETCHINESS
SHENANIGANS	SIGHTSCREEN	SKILFULNESS
SHEPHERDESS	SIGHTSEEING	SKIMMED MILK
SHEPHERDING	SIGNAL BOXES	SKIRMISHERS
SHIBBOLETHS	SIGNALIZING	SKIRMISHING
SHIFTLESSLY	SIGNATORIES	SKULDUGGERY
SHIFT STICKS	SIGNIFIABLE	SKYJACKINGS
SHIMONOSEKI	SIGNIFICANT	SKYROCKETED
SHIP BISCUIT	SIGNPOSTING	SKYSCRAPERS
SHIPBUILDER	SILHOUETTED	SLAUGHTERED
SHIPWRECKED	SILHOUETTES	SLAUGHTERER
SHIPWRIGHTS	SILICON CHIP	SLAVE DRIVER
SHIRE HORSES	SILLIMANITE	SLAVE LABOUR
SHIRTFRONTS	SILLY SEASON	SLAVISHNESS
SHIRTSLEEVE	SILVER BIRCH	SLEEPING BAG
SHISH KEBABS	SILVERINESS	SLEEPING CAR
SHIVERINGLY	SILVER MEDAL	SLEEPLESSLY
SHOCKHEADED	SILVER PAPER	SLEEPWALKED
SHOCK TROOPS	SILVER PLATE	SLEEPWALKER
SHOESTRINGS	SILVERPOINT	SLEEPYHEADS
SHOPKEEPERS	SILVERSMITH	SLENDERIZED
SHOPLIFTERS	SIMMERINGLY	SLENDERNESS
SHOPLIFTING	SIMPERINGLY	SLEUTHHOUND
SHOP STEWARD	SIMPLIFYING	SLICED BREAD
SHOPWALKERS	SIMPLON PASS	SLICE OF LIFE
SHORT-CHANGE	SIMULACRUMS	SLICKENSIDE
SHORTCOMING	SIMULATIONS	SLIDE-ACTION
SHORTHANDED	SINE QUA NONS	SLIDING DOOR
SHORT-LISTED	SINFONIETTA	SLIGHTINGLY
SHORT SHRIFT	SINGAPOREAN	SLIPPED DISC
SHORT-SPOKEN	SINGLE-BLIND	SLIPSTREAMS
SHORT-WINDED	SINGLE-CROSS	SLOOP-RIGGED
SHOULDERING	SINGLE-PHASE	SLOPINGNESS
SHOWERPROOF	SINGLE-SPACE	SLOT MACHINE
SHOW JUMPERS	SINGLE-TRACK	SLOUCHINESS
SHOW JUMPING	SINGULARITY	SLOUCHINGLY
SHOWMANSHIP	SINGULARIZE	SLOWCOACHES
SHOW OF HANDS	SINISTRORSE	SMALL CHANGE
SHOWSTOPPER	SINKING FUND	SMALLHOLDER
SHRINKINGLY	SINLESSNESS	SMALL-MINDED
SHRIVELLING	SINN FEINISM	SMALL SCREEN

SMALL-TIMERS	SOTTISHNESS	SPINY-FINNED
SMART ALECKS	SOUBRIQUETS	SPIRACULATE
SMART ALECKY	SOUGHT-AFTER	SPIRIFEROUS
SMARTY-PANTS	SOUL BROTHER	SPIRIT LEVEL
SMATTERINGS	SOULFULNESS	SPIRITUALLY
SMILINGNESS	SOUNDLESSLY	SPIRKETTING
SMITHEREENS	SOUNDTRACKS	SPIROCHAETE
SMITHSONITE	SOUP KITCHEN	SPIROMETRIC
SMOKESCREEN	SOUSAPHONES	SPITSTICKER
SMOKESTACKS	SOUTHAMPTON	SPLASHBOARD
SMOOTH-FACED	SOUTHEASTER	SPLASHDOWNS
SMORGASBORD	SOUTHERNERS	SPLASH GUARD
SMOULDERING	SOUTHWESTER	SPLASHINESS
SNAPDRAGONS	SOVEREIGNTY	SPLATTERING
SNIPERSCOPE	SOVIETISTIC	SPLAYFOOTED
SNORKELLING	SPACE HEATER	SPLENDOROUS
SNOWBALLING	SPACE PROBES	SPLENECTOMY
SNOWMOBILES	SPARINGNESS	SPLENETICAL
SNOWPLOUGHS	SPARROWHAWK	SPLINTERING
SOAP BUBBLES	SPASTICALLY	SPLIT SECOND
SOCIABILITY	SPATHACEOUS	SPLUTTERING
SOCIALISTIC	SPEAKEASIES	SPOILSPORTS
SOCIALIZING	SPEAKERSHIP	SPOKESWOMAN
SOCIOLOGIST	SPEARHEADED	SPONDYLITIS
SOCIOMETRIC	SPECIALISMS	SPONGE CAKES
SOCIOPATHIC	SPECIALISTS	SPONSORSHIP
SOFTHEARTED	SPECIALIZED	SPONTANEITY
SOFT LANDING	SPECIALNESS	SPONTANEOUS
SOFT OPTIONS	SPECIFIABLE	SPOONERISMS
SOFT PALATES	SPECIFICITY	SPOROGENOUS
SOFT-PEDALED	SPECTACULAR	SPOROGONIAL
SOFT-SOAPING	SPECTRALITY	SPOROGONIUM
SOFT TOUCHES	SPECULATING	SPOROPHYTIC
SOLANACEOUS	SPECULATION	SPORTSWOMAN
SOLARIMETER	SPECULATIVE	SPORULATION
SOLAR PANELS	SPECULATORS	SPOT CHECKED
SOLAR PLEXUS	SPEECHIFIED	SPOTTED DICK
SOLAR SYSTEM	SPEECHIFIER	SPREAD-EAGLE
SOLEMNITIES	SPEED LIMITS	SPREADSHEET
SOLEMNIZING	SPEEDOMETER	SPRINGBOARD
SOLIDIFYING	SPELLBINDER	SPRING-CLEAN
SOLILOQUIES	SPENDTHRIFT	SPRINGFIELD
SOLILOQUIST	SPERMATHECA	SPRINGINESS
SOLILOQUIZE	SPERMATOZOA	SPRING ONION
SOLIPSISTIC	SPERMICIDES	SPRING ROLLS
SOLMIZATION	SPERMOPHILE	SPRING TIDES
SOLUBLENESS	SPERM WHALES	SPRINKLINGS
SOLVABILITY	SPESSARTITE	SPUMESCENCE
SOMATICALLY	SPHEROMETER	SQUANDERERS
SOMATOLOGIC	SPHERULITIC	SQUANDERING
SOMATOPLASM	SPHINCTERAL	SQUARE DANCE
SOMERSAULTS	SPHINGOSINE	SQUARE KNOTS
SOMNOLENTLY	SPHRAGISTIC	SQUARE MEALS
SONGFULNESS	SPINA BIFIDA	SQUARE ROOTS
SON-OF-A-BITCH	SPINAL CORDS	SQUASHINESS
SOOTHSAYERS	SPINELESSLY	SQUEAMISHLY
SOPHISTRIES	SPINESCENCE	SQUELCHIEST
SORORICIDAL	SPINIFEROUS	SQUIGGLIEST
SORROWFULLY	SPINSTERISH	SQUIREARCHY

SQUIRMINGLY	STENOTYPIST	STONEWORKER
STABILIZERS	STEPBROTHER	STOOLPIGEON
STABILIZING	STEPHANOTIS	STOPWATCHES
STADIOMETER	STEPLADDERS	STOREHOUSES
STAFF NURSES	STEPPARENTS	STOREKEEPER
STAGE FRIGHT	STEPSISTERS	STORM CLOUDS
STAGE-MANAGE	STEREOGRAPH	STORYTELLER
STAGESTRUCK	STEREOMETRY	STRAGGLIEST
STAGGERBUSH	STEREOSCOPE	STRAIGHTEST
STAGING POST	STEREOSCOPY	STRAIGHT-OUT
STAG PARTIES	STEREOTAXIS	STRAIGHTWAY
STAKEHOLDER	STEREOTYPED	STRAININGLY
STALACTITES	STEREOTYPER	STRAITLACED
STALACTITIC	STEREOTYPES	STRANGENESS
STALAGMITES	STEREOTYPIC	STRANGULATE
STALAGMITIC	STERILIZERS	STRAPHANGER
STALEMATING	STERILIZING	STRATEGISTS
STALLHOLDER	STERNUTATOR	STRATHCLYDE
STANDARDIZE	STETHOSCOPE	STRATIFYING
STANDOFFISH	STETHOSCOPY	STRATOCRACY
STANDPOINTS	STEWARDSHIP	STRATOPAUSE
STARA ZAGORA	STICHICALLY	STRAWFLOWER
STAR CHAMBER	STICHOMETRY	STREAKINESS
STARCHINESS	STICK INSECT	STREAMLINED
STAR-CROSSED	STICKLEBACK	STREETLIGHT
STAR-STUDDED	STICK SHIFTS	STREET VALUE
STARTLINGLY	STIFF-NECKED	STRENUOSITY
STARVELINGS	STIGMATICAL	STRENUOUSLY
STATELINESS	STIGMATIZED	STRESS MARKS
STATELY HOME	STIGMATIZER	STRETCHABLE
STATESWOMAN	STILLBIRTHS	STRETCHIEST
STATISTICAL	STILTEDNESS	STRETCHMARK
STATOLITHIC	STIMULATING	STRIDULATED
STATUTE BOOK	STIMULATION	STRIDULATOR
STATUTORILY	STIMULATIVE	STRIKEBOUND
STAUNCHABLE	STIPENDIARY	STRING BEANS
STAUNCHNESS	STIPULATING	STRINGBOARD
STAUROLITIC	STIPULATION	STRINGENTLY
STAUROSCOPE	STIPULATORY	STRINGINESS
STAY-AT-HOMES	STIRRUP CUPS	STRINGPIECE
STEADFASTLY	STIRRUP PUMP	STRIP MINING
STEALTHIEST	STOCKBROKER	STRIPTEASES
STEAM-BOILER	STOCKHOLDER	STROBE LIGHT
STEAM-ENGINE	STOCKJOBBER	STROBOSCOPE
STEAMROLLER	STOCK MARKET	STRONGBOXES
STEAM SHOVEL	STOCKPILING	STRONGHOLDS
STEAROPTENE	STOCKTAKING	STRONG POINT
STEATOLYSIS	STOICALNESS	STRONG ROOMS
STEATOPYGIA	STOMACHACHE	STRUCTURING
STEATOPYGIC	STOMACHICAL	STRUCTURIST
STEELWORKER	STOMACH PUMP	STRUTTINGLY
STEEPLEJACK	STOMATOLOGY	STUBBORNEST
STEERAGEWAY	STONECUTTER	STUDENTSHIP
STELLARATOR	STONE FRUITS	STUDIEDNESS
STENCILLING	STONE-GROUND	STUDIO COUCH
STENOGRAPHY	STONEMASONS	STULTIFYING
STENOHALINE	STONE'S THROW	STUMBLINGLY
STENOPHAGUS	STONEWALLED	STUNTEDNESS
STENOTROPIC	STONEWALLER	STUPIDITIES

STYLISHNESS	SUBSTANTIVE	SUPERLUNARY
STYLIZATION	SUBSTATIONS	SUPERMARKET
STYLOGRAPHY	SUBSTITUENT	SUPERNATANT
STYLOPODIUM	SUBSTITUTED	SUPERNORMAL
STYLOSTIXIS	SUBSTITUTES	SUPERSCRIBE
SUBASSEMBLY	SUBSTRATIVE	SUPERSCRIPT
SUBAUDITION	SUBSUMPTION	SUPERSEDEAS
SUBAXILLARY	SUBSUMPTIVE	SUPERSEDING
SUBBASEMENT	SUBTERFUGES	SUPERSEDURE
SUBCHLORIDE	SUBTRACTING	SUPERSONICS
SUBCOMPACTS	SUBTRACTION	SUPERSTRUCT
SUBCONTRACT	SUBTRACTIVE	SUPERTANKER
SUBCONTRARY	SUBTROPICAL	SUPERVENING
SUBCORTICAL	SUBURBANITE	SUPERVISING
SUBCULTURAL	SUBVENTIONS	SUPERVISION
SUBCULTURES	SUBVERSIVES	SUPERVISORS
SUBDELIRIUM	SUCCEDANEUM	SUPERVISORY
SUBDIACONAL	SUCCEEDABLE	SUPPLANTING
SUBDIVIDING	SUCCESSIONS	SUPPLEMENTS
SUBDIVISION	SUCCESSORAL	SUPPLICANTS
SUBDOMINANT	SUCCOURABLE	SUPPLICATED
SUBDUEDNESS	SUCH AND SUCH	SUPPORTABLE
SUBHEADINGS	SUCKING PIGS	SUPPOSITION
SUBIRRIGATE	SUCTION PUMP	SUPPOSITIVE
SUBJECTABLE	SUDETENLAND	SUPPOSITORY
SUBJUGATING	SUFFERINGLY	SUPPRESSING
SUBJUGATION	SUFFICIENCY	SUPPRESSION
SUBJUNCTION	SUFFOCATING	SUPPRESSIVE
SUBJUNCTIVE	SUFFOCATION	SUPPRESSORS
SUBLIMATING	SUFFOCATIVE	SUPPURATING
SUBLIMATION	SUFFRAGETTE	SUPPURATION
SUBLITTORAL	SUFFUMIGATE	SUPPURATIVE
SUBMARGINAL	SUGGESTIBLE	SUPREMACIST
SUBMARINERS	SUGGESTIONS	SUPREMATISM
SUBMERSIBLE	SUITABILITY	SUPREMATIST
SUBMISSIONS	SULPHA DRUGS	SUPREMENESS
SUBMITTABLE	SULPHUREOUS	SURBASEMENT
SUBMULTIPLE	SUMMARINESS	SURCHARGING
SUBORDINARY	SUMMARIZING	SURFCASTING
SUBORDINATE	SUMMATIONAL	SURGEONFISH
SUBORNATION	SUMMERHOUSE	SURMOUNTING
SUBORNATIVE	SUMMERINESS	SURPASSABLE
SUBPOENAING	SUMPTUOUSLY	SURPRISEDLY
SUBREGIONAL	SUNDRENCHED	SURREALISTS
SUBROGATION	SUNLESSNESS	SURREBUTTAL
SUBROUTINES	SUNNY-SIDE UP	SURREBUTTER
SUBSCAPULAR	SUPERABOUND	SURRENDERED
SUBSCRIBERS	SUPERCHARGE	SURRENDERER
SUBSCRIBING	SUPERFAMILY	SURROGATION
SUBSECTIONS	SUPERFETATE	SURROUNDING
SUBSEQUENCE	SUPERFICIAL	SURVEILLANT
SUBSERVIENT	SUPERFLUITY	SURVIVAL KIT
SUBSIDENCES	SUPERFLUOUS	SUSCEPTANCE
SUBSIDIZERS	SUPERIMPOSE	SUSCEPTIBLE
SUBSIDIZING	SUPERINDUCE	SUSPENDIBLE
SUBSISTENCE	SUPERINTEND	SUSPENSEFUL
SUBSPECIFIC	SUPERIORITY	SUSPENSIONS
SUBSTANDARD	SUPERJACENT	SUSPICIONAL
SUBSTANTIAL	SUPERLATIVE	SUSTAINABLE

SUSTAINEDLY	SYNTHESIZED	TEETOTALISM
SUSTAINMENT	SYNTHESIZER	TEETOTALLER
SUSURRATION	SYNTHETICAL	TEGUCIGALPA
SWALLOWABLE	SYPHILITICS	TELEGNOSTIC
SWALLOW DIVE	SYPHILOLOGY	TELEGRAPHED
SWALLOWTAIL	SYSSARCOSIS	TELEGRAPHER
SWALLOWWORT	SYSSARCOTIC	TELEGRAPHIC
SWARTHINESS	SYSTEMATICS	TELEKINESIS
SWEAT GLANDS	SYSTEMATISM	TELEKINETIC
SWEATSHIRTS	SYSTEMATIST	TELEOLOGISM
SWEEPSTAKES	SYSTEMATIZE	TELEOLOGIST
SWEETBREADS		TELEPATHIST
SWEETHEARTS	T	TELEPHONING
SWEET PEPPER	TABERNACLES	TELEPHONIST
SWEET POTATO	TABLECLOTHS	TELEPRINTER
SWEET-TALKED	TABLESPOONS	TELESCOPING
SWINDLINGLY	TABLE TENNIS	TELESELLING
SWINISHNESS	TABULATIONS	TELEVISIONS
SWISS CHARDS	TACHEOMETER	TELLINGS-OFF
SWISS CHEESE	TACHOGRAPHS	TELUKBETUNG
SWITCHBACKS	TACHOMETERS	TEMERARIOUS
SWITCHBLADE	TACHOMETRIC	TEMPERAMENT
SWITCHBOARD	TACHYCARDIA	TEMPERATURE
SWITZERLAND	TACHYMETRIC	TEMPESTUOUS
SWOLLEN HEAD	TACITURNITY	TEMPORALITY
SWOLLENNESS	TACTFULNESS	TEMPORARILY
SWORD DANCER	TAGLIATELLE	TEMPORIZING
SWORD DANCES	TAKE-HOME PAY	TEMPTATIONS
SWORDFISHES	TALEBEARERS	TEMPTRESSES
SYCOPHANTIC	TALENT SCOUT	TENACIOUSLY
SYLLABOGRAM	TALKABILITY	TENDENTIOUS
SYLLOGISTIC	TALL STORIES	TENDERFOOTS
SYMBOLISTIC	TAMABLENESS	TENDERIZING
SYMBOLIZING	TAMBOURINES	TENEBROSITY
SYMBOLOGIST	TANGIBILITY	TENNIS ELBOW
SYMMETRICAL	TANTALIZING	TENORRHAPHY
SYMPATHETIC	TAPE MEASURE	TENSIBILITY
SYMPATHIZED	TARANTELLAS	TENSIOMETER
SYMPATHIZER	TARNISHABLE	TENTATIVELY
SYMPETALOUS	TARRADIDDLE	TENTERHOOKS
SYMPHONIOUS	TARTAR SAUCE	TENUOUSNESS
SYMPTOMATIC	TASKMASTERS	TEPEFACTION
SYNAGOGICAL	TASTELESSLY	TERATOGENIC
SYNCHROMESH	TAUTOLOGIES	TERATOLOGIC
SYNCHRONISM	TAUTOLOGIZE	TEREBIC ACID
SYNCHRONIZE	TAUTOMERISM	TERMINATING
SYNCHRONOUS	TAXIDERMIST	TERMINATION
SYNCHROTRON	TAX SHELTERS	TERMINATIVE
SYNCOPATING	TEARFULNESS	TERMINATORY
SYNCOPATION	TEARJERKERS	TERMINOLOGY
SYNDESMOSIS	TEA SERVICES	TERRESTRIAL
SYNDESMOTIC	TEA TROLLEYS	TERRICOLOUS
SYNDICALISM	TECHNICALLY	TERRIGENOUS
SYNDICALIST	TECHNICIANS	TERRITORIAL
SYNDICATING	TECHNICOLOR	TERRITORIES
SYNDICATION	TECHNOCRACY	TERRORISTIC
SYNECDOCHIC	TECHNOCRATS	TERRORIZING
SYNECOLOGIC	TEDIOUSNESS	TERTIUM QUID
SYNKARYONIC	TEENYBOPPER	TESSELLATED

TESTABILITY	THIN-SKINNED	TOLBUTAMIDE
TESTAMENTAL	THIOCYANATE	TOMBOYISHLY
TESTICULATE	THIRD-DEGREE	TONSILLITIS
TESTIMONIAL	THIRD PERSON	TOOTH POWDER
TESTIMONIES	THIRSTINESS	TOPDRESSING
TEST MATCHES	THIRTEENTHS	TOPOGRAPHER
TETANICALLY	THISTLEDOWN	TOPOGRAPHIC
TETRADYMITE	THIXOTROPIC	TORCHBEARER
TETRAHEDRAL	THORACOTOMY	TORMENTEDLY
TETRAHEDRON	THOROUGHPIN	TORONTONIAN
TETRAMERISM	THOUGHTLESS	TORSIBILITY
TETRAMEROUS	THOUSANDTHS	TORTICOLLAR
TETRAPLEGIA	THREADINESS	TORTICOLLIS
TETRARCHATE	THREATENING	TORTURESOME
TETRASPORIC	THREEPENCES	TORTURINGLY
TETRAVALENT	THRIFTINESS	TORTUROUSLY
THALIDOMIDE	THRILLINGLY	TOTALIZATOR
THALLOPHYTE	THROATINESS	TOTEMICALLY
THANKLESSLY	THROBBINGLY	TOTIPALMATE
THAUMATROPE	THROMBOCYTE	TOTIPOTENCY
THEATREGOER	THROUGHPUTS	TOUCHPAPERS
THEATRICALS	THROUGHWAYS	TOUCHSTONES
THENCEFORTH	THUMBSCREWS	TOUCH-TYPING
THEOBROMINE	THUNDERBIRD	TOUCH-TYPIST
THEOCENTRIC	THUNDERBOLT	TOUR DE FORCE
THEODOLITES	THUNDERCLAP	TOURMALINIC
THEODOLITIC	THYROIDITIS	TOURNAMENTS
THEOLOGIANS	THYROTROPIN	TOURNIQUETS
THEOLOGICAL	THYRSANURAN	TOUT LE MONDE
THEOLOGIZER	TICKINGS OFF	TOWER BLOCKS
THEOPHOBIAC	TICK-TACK-TOE	TOWN PLANNER
THEOREMATIC	TIDDLYWINKS	TOWNSPEOPLE
THEORETICAL	TIEBREAKERS	TOXICOGENIC
THEOSOPHISM	TIED COTTAGE	TOXOPHILITE
THEOSOPHIST	TIGHTFISTED	TOXOPLASMIC
THERAPEUTIC	TIGHT-LIPPED	TRACHEOTOMY
THEREABOUTS	TIME CAPSULE	TRACK EVENTS
THEREMINIST	TIMEKEEPERS	TRACKLAYERS
THERETOFORE	TIMESERVERS	TRACK RECORD
THERIOMORPH	TIMESERVING	TRACKSUITED
THERMIONICS	TIME-SHARING	TRADE PRICES
THERMOCLINE	TIME SIGNALS	TRADE ROUTES
THERMOGRAPH	TIMETABLING	TRADESWOMAN
THERMOLYSIS	TINDERBOXES	TRADE UNIONS
THERMOLYTIC	TIN PAN ALLEY	TRADING POST
THERMOMETER	TITANICALLY	TRADITIONAL
THERMOMETRY	TITILLATING	TRADUCEMENT
THERMOSCOPE	TITILLATION	TRADUCINGLY
THERMOSTATS	TITILLATIVE	TRAFFICATOR
THERMOTAXIC	TITLEHOLDER	TRAFFIC JAMS
THERMOTAXIS	TITTERINGLY	TRAFFICKERS
THESAURUSES	TOASTMASTER	TRAFFICKING
THICKHEADED	TOBACCONIST	TRAGEDIENNE
THICKNESSES	TOBOGGANING	TRAGICOMEDY
THICK-WITTED	TOFFEE APPLE	TRAILBLAZER
THIGMOTAXIS	TOFFEE-NOSED	TRAINBEARER
THIMBLEFULS	TOILET PAPER	TRAMPOLINER
THIMBLEWEED	TOILET ROLLS	TRAMPOLINES
THINGAMAJIG	TOILET WATER	TRANQUILITY

TRANSACTING	TREASURABLE	TROUBLINGLY
TRANSACTION	TREBLE CLEFS	TRUCULENTLY
TRANSALPINE	TRELLISWORK	TRUEHEARTED
TRANSCEIVER	TREMBLINGLY	TRUMPETWEED
TRANSCENDED	TREMULOUSLY	TRUNK ROUTES
TRANSCRIBED	TRENCHANTLY	TRUSTEESHIP
TRANSCRIBER	TRENCH COATS	TRUSTWORTHY
TRANSCRIPTS	TRENCHERMAN	TRYPANOSOME
TRANSECTION	TRENCHERMEN	TRYPSINOGEN
TRANSFERASE	TRENDSETTER	TSELINOGRAD
TRANSFERRED	TREPIDATION	TSETSE FLIES
TRANSFERRIN	TRESPASSING	TUBERCULATE
TRANSFIGURE	TRESTLETREE	TUBERCULOUS
TRANSFINITE	TRESTLEWORK	TUB-THUMPERS
TRANSFIXING	TRIABLENESS	TUB-THUMPING
TRANSFIXION	TRIANGULATE	TUMBLE-DRIED
TRANSFORMED	TRIBULATION	TUMBLE-DRYER
TRANSFORMER	TRIBUTARIES	TUMEFACIENT
TRANSFUSION	TRIBUTARILY	TUMEFACTION
TRANSFUSIVE	TRICERATOPS	TUNEFULNESS
TRANSHUMANT	TRICHINOSIS	TUNING FORKS
TRANSISTORS	TRICHLORIDE	TURBINATION
TRANSITABLE	TRICHOMONAD	TURBOCHARGE
TRANSITIONS	TRICHOTOMIC	TURBULENTLY
TRANSITIVES	TRICKLINGLY	TURGESCENCE
TRANS-JORDAN	TRICKSINESS	TURKISH BATH
TRANSLATING	TRICUSPIDAL	TURNAROUNDS
TRANSLATION	TRIGGERFISH	TURRICULATE
TRANSLATORS	TRILLIONTHS	TURTLEDOVES
TRANSLOCATE	TRIMETROGON	TURTLENECKS
TRANSLUCENT	TRIMORPHISM	TUTTI FRUTTI
TRANSMITTAL	TRINIDADIAN	TWELVEMONTH
TRANSMITTED	TRIPALMITIN	TWITCHINGLY
TRANSMITTER	TRIPLICATES	TYPECASTING
TRANSMUTING	TRIQUETROUS	TYPESCRIPTS
TRANSPADANE	TRISTICHOUS	TYPESETTERS
TRANSPARENT	TRISULPHIDE	TYPEWRITERS
TRANSPIERCE	TRITURATION	TYPEWRITING
TRANSPIRING	TRIUMVIRATE	TYPEWRITTEN
TRANSPLANTS	TRIVIALIZED	TYPICALNESS
TRANSPONDER	TROCHOPHORE	TYPING POOLS
TRANSPORTED	TROCORNERED	TYPOGRAPHER
TRANSPORTER	TROGLODYTES	TYPOGRAPHIC
TRANSPOSING	TROGLODYTIC	TYPOLOGICAL
TRANSPUTERS	TROJAN HORSE	TYRANNICIDE
TRANSURANIC	TROMBONISTS	TYRANNIZING
TRANSVAALER	TROMPE L'OEIL	TYROTHRICIN
TRANSVALUER	TROPHICALLY	TZETZE FLIES
TRANSVERSAL	TROPHOBLAST	
TRAPSHOOTER	TROPHOZOITE	U
TRAUMATIZED	TROPICALITY	ULOTRICHOUS
TRAVEL AGENT	TROPICALIZE	ULTRAFILTER
TRAVELOGUES	TROPISMATIC	ULTRAMARINE
TRAVERSABLE	TROPOPHYTIC	ULTRAMODERN
TREACHERIES	TROPOSPHERE	ULTRASONICS
TREACHEROUS	TROTSKYISTS	ULTRAVIOLET
TREACLINESS	TROUBADOURS	ULVERIZABLE
TREASONABLE	TROUBLESOME	UMBELLULATE
TREASONABLY	TROUBLE SPOT	UNACCOUNTED

UNADVISEDLY	UNDERVALUED	UNPRINTABLE
UNALTERABLE	UNDERVALUER	UNPROFESSED
UNAMBIGUOUS	UNDERWEIGHT	UNPROMISING
UNAMBITIOUS	UNDERWRITER	UNPUBLISHED
UNANIMOUSLY	UNDESIGNING	UNQUALIFIED
UNANNOUNCED	UNDESIRABLE	UNRAVELLING
UNAVAILABLE	UNDESIRABLY	UNRAVELMENT
UNAVOIDABLE	UNDEVELOPED	UNREALISTIC
UNAWARENESS	UNDISCLOSED	UNREASONING
UNBALANCING	UNDOUBTEDLY	UNREFLECTED
UNBALLASTED	UNDREAMED-OF	UNREHEARSED
UNBELIEVERS	UNDRINKABLE	UNRELENTING
UNBLEMISHED	UNDULATIONS	UNREMITTING
UNBREAKABLE	UNEQUALNESS	UNRIGHTEOUS
UNBURDENING	UNEQUIVOCAL	UNSATISFIED
UNCALLED-FOR	UNESSENTIAL	UNSATURATED
UNCERTAINLY	UNEXPLAINED	UNSAVOURILY
UNCERTAINTY	UNEXPRESSED	UNSCHEDULED
UNCHARTERED	UNFAILINGLY	UNSCRAMBLED
UNCHRISTIAN	UNFALTERING	UNSCRAMBLER
UNCIVILIZED	UNFLAPPABLE	UNSCRATCHED
UNCLEANNESS	UNFLAPPABLY	UNSHAKEABLE
UNCOMMITTED	UNFLINCHING	UNSPARINGLY
UNCONCERNED	UNFORTUNATE	UNSPEAKABLE
UNCONCLUDED	UNFULFILLED	UNSPEAKABLY
UNCONNECTED	UNGODLINESS	UNSPECIFIED
UNCONSCIOUS	UNGUICULATE	UNSTOPPABLE
UNCONTESTED	UNGULIGRADE	UNSURPASSED
UNCONVERTED	UNHAPPINESS	UNSUSPECTED
UNCONVINCED	UNHEALTHILY	UNTERWALDEN
UNCOUNTABLE	UNICELLULAR	UNTHINKABLE
UNCOUTHNESS	UNIFICATION	UNTOUCHABLE
UNCRUSHABLE	UNIFORMNESS	UNTRAVELLED
UNDECEIVING	UNINHABITED	UNUTTERABLE
UNDECIDEDLY	UNINHIBITED	UNUTTERABLY
UNDEMANDING	UNINITIATED	UNVARNISHED
UNDERACTING	UNINSPIRING	UNWARRANTED
UNDERBIDDER	UNIPERSONAL	UNWHOLESOME
UNDERCHARGE	UNIPOLARITY	UNWILLINGLY
UNDEREXPOSE	UNIVERSALLY	UNWITNESSED
UNDERGROUND	UNJUSTIFIED	UNWITTINGLY
UNDERGROWTH	UNKEMPTNESS	UP-AND-COMING
UNDERLETTER	UNKNOWINGLY	UPHOLSTERED
UNDERLINING	UNKNOWNNESS	UPHOLSTERER
UNDERMANNED	UNLOOKED-FOR	UPRIGHTNESS
UNDERMINING	UNLOOSENING	UPS AND DOWNS
UNDERPASSES	UNLUCKINESS	UPSTRETCHED
UNDERPAYING	UNMANLINESS	URANOGRAPHY
UNDERPINNED	UNMITIGATED	URINIFEROUS
UNDERPLAYED	UNNATURALLY	UROCHORDATE
UNDERRATING	UNNECESSARY	URTICACEOUS
UNDERSCORED	UNOBTRUSIVE	USELESSNESS
UNDERSELLER	UNORGANIZED	UTILITARIAN
UNDERSHIRTS	UNPALATABLE	UTILITY ROOM
UNDERSIGNED	UNPATRIOTIC	UTILIZATION
UNDERSTATED	UNPERTURBED	UTRICULITIS
UNDERTAKERS	UNPOLITICAL	
UNDERTAKING	UNPRACTICAL	V
UNDERTHRUST	UNPRACTISED	VACATIONERS

VACATIONING	VERMINATION	VOCIFERATED
VACCINATING	VERMIVOROUS	VOCIFERATOR
VACCINATION	VERNACULARS	VOLCANICITY
VACILLATING	VERRUCOSITY	VOLCANOLOGY
VACILLATION	VERSATILITY	VOLTAMMETER
VACUOLATION	VERSICOLOUR	VOLUNTARIES
VACUOUSNESS	VERTEBRATES	VOLUNTARILY
VACUUM FLASK	VERTICALITY	VOLUNTARISM
VACUUM PUMPS	VERTIGINOUS	VOLUNTARIST
VAGABONDAGE	VESTIGIALLY	VOLUNTEERED
VAGABONDISM	VETERANS DAY	VOODOOISTIC
VAGINECTOMY	VEXATIOUSLY	VOORTREKKER
VAGRANTNESS	VEXILLOLOGY	VORACIOUSLY
VALEDICTION	VIBRACULOID	VORTIGINOUS
VALEDICTORY	VIBRAPHONES	VOUCHSAFING
VALIDATIONS	VIBRATILITY	VOYEURISTIC
VALLE D'AOSTA	VIBRATINGLY	VULCANIZING
VALUATIONAL	VIBRATIONAL	VULGARITIES
VAMPIRE BATS	VICARIOUSLY	VULGARIZING
VANDALISTIC	VICEGERENCY	VULGAR LATIN
VANDALIZING	VICEROYALTY	
VANISHINGLY	VICEROYSHIP	W
VANQUISHING	VICHYSSOISE	WADING POOLS
VAPORESCENT	VICIOUSNESS	WAGGISHNESS
VAPORIMETER	VICISSITUDE	WAINSCOTING
VAPORIZABLE	VICTIMIZING	WAINSCOTTED
VAPOUR TRAIL	VICTUALLING	WAITING GAME
VARIABILITY	VIDEOPHONIC	WAITING LIST
VARIATIONAL	VIDEOTAPING	WAITING ROOM
VARICELLATE	VIEWFINDERS	WAKEFULNESS
VARICELLOID	VINAIGRETTE	WALKS OF LIFE
VARIEGATION	VINDICATING	WALLFLOWERS
VARIOLATION	VINDICATION	WALLPAPERED
VARIOUSNESS	VINDICATORY	WANDERINGLY
VASCULARITY	VINEDRESSER	WARM-BLOODED
VASECTOMIES	VINEGARROON	WARM-HEARTED
VASODILATOR	VINEYARDIST	WARMING PANS
VASOPRESSIN	VINICULTURE	WAR OF NERVES
VEGETARIANS	VINIFICATOR	WARRANTABLE
VELOCIPEDES	VIOLABILITY	WASHABILITY
VENDIBILITY	VIOLONCELLO	WASH DRAWING
VENEREOLOGY	VIRGIN BIRTH	WASHERWOMAN
VENESECTION	VIRIDESCENT	WASHERWOMEN
VENTILATING	VIROLOGICAL	WASHING DAYS
VENTILATION	VISCOMETRIC	WASPISHNESS
VENTILATIVE	VISCOUNTESS	WATCHMAKERS
VENTILATORS	VISCOUSNESS	WATCHMAKING
VENTILATORY	VISIBLENESS	WATCHSTRAPS
VENTRICULAR	VISIONARIES	WATCHTOWERS
VENTRICULUS	VISITATIONS	WATER CANNON
VENTURESOME	VISUALIZING	WATER CLOSET
VERACIOUSLY	VITICULTURE	WATERCOLOUR
VERATRIDINE	VITRESCENCE	WATERCOURSE
VERBALIZING	VITRIFIABLE	WATERED-DOWN
VERBAL NOUNS	VITUPERATOR	WATERFRONTS
VEREENIGING	VIVACIOUSLY	WATERING CAN
VERISIMILAR	VIVISECTION	WATER LEVELS
VERMICULATE	VLADIVOSTOK	WATER LILIES
VERMICULITE	VOCIFERANCE	WATERLOGGED

WATER MEADOW	WHIST DRIVES	WOLF WHISTLE
WATERMELONS	WHITEBOARDS	WOMANLINESS
WATERPROOFS	WHITE-COLLAR	WONDERFULLY
WATER SKIERS	WHITE DWARFS	WONDERINGLY
WATER SKIING	WHITE HORSES	WONDERLANDS
WATERSPOUTS	WHITE KNIGHT	WOOD ALCOHOL
WATER SUPPLY	WHITE METALS	WOODCARVING
WATER TABLES	WHITE PAPERS	WOODCUTTERS
WATER VAPOUR	WHITE PEPPER	WOODCUTTING
WATERWHEELS	WHITE-SLAVER	WOODEN SPOON
WAVELENGTHS	WHITE SPIRIT	WOODPECKERS
WAYWARDNESS	WHITETHROAT	WOODWORKING
WEALTHINESS	WHITEWASHED	WOOLGROWING
WEARABILITY	WHITEWASHER	WORD-PERFECT
WEAR AND TEAR	WHITEWASHES	WORKABILITY
WEATHERCOCK	WHITSUNTIDE	WORKAHOLICS
WEATHER SHIP	WHOLE NUMBER	WORKAHOLISM
WEATHER VANE	WHOLESALERS	WORKBASKETS
WEATHER-WISE	WHOREHOUSES	WORKBENCHES
WEDDING RING	WICKET GATES	WORKING DAYS
WEIGHBRIDGE	WILDEBEESTS	WORKING WEEK
WEIGHTINESS	WILDFOWLING	WORKMANLIKE
WELCOMENESS	WILLINGNESS	WORKMANSHIP
WELDABILITY	WINDCHEATER	WORKSTATION
WELL-ADAPTED	WINDJAMMERS	WORLD-BEATER
WELL-ADVISED	WINDOW BOXES	WORLDLINESS
WELLBEHAVED	WINDOWPANES	WORLDLY-WISE
WELL-DEFINED	WINDOW SHADE	WORLD POWERS
WELL-ENDOWED	WINDOWSILLS	WORLD SERIES
WELL-FOUNDED	WINDSCREENS	WORSHIPABLE
WELL-GROOMED	WINDSHIELDS	WORSHIPPERS
WELLINGTONS	WIND-SUCKING	WORSHIPPING
WELL-MEANING	WIND-SURFERS	WORTHLESSLY
WELL-ROUNDED	WIND-SURFING	WRIGGLINGLY
WELLSPRINGS	WIND TUNNELS	WRITING DESK
WELL-WISHERS	WIND TURBINE	WRONGDOINGS
WELL-WISHING	WINEBIBBING	WRONGHEADED
WELWITSCHIA	WINNINGNESS	WROUGHT IRON
WENSLEYDALE	WINNING POST	
WESLEYANISM	WINNIPEGGER	X
WEST COUNTRY	WINSOMENESS	XANTHOPHYLL
WESTERNIZED	WINTERGREEN	X CHROMOSOME
WESTERNMOST	WIRE NETTING	XENOGENESIS
WESTMINSTER	WIRE-TAPPING	XENOGENETIC
WESTPHALIAN	WISDOM TEETH	XENOGLOSSIA
WET BLANKETS	WISDOM TOOTH	XENOMORPHIC
WETTABILITY	WISECRACKED	XEROGRAPHER
WHEEDLINGLY	WISECRACKER	XEROGRAPHIC
WHEELBARROW	WISHFULNESS	XEROMORPHIC
WHEELCHAIRS	WISTFULNESS	XEROPHILOUS
WHEELHOUSES	WITCHDOCTOR	XEROPHYTISM
WHEELWRIGHT	WITCH-HUNTER	XYLOCARPOUS
WHEREABOUTS	WITHDRAWALS	XYLOGRAPHER
WHERESOEVER	WITHDRAWING	XYLOGRAPHIC
WHEREWITHAL	WITHHOLDING	XYLOPHAGOUS
WHIFFLETREE	WITHSTANDER	XYLOPHONIST
WHIMSICALLY	WITLESSNESS	
WHIPPING BOY	WITNESSABLE	Y
WHIRLYBIRDS	WOLFISHNESS	YACHTSWOMAN

Y CHROMOSOME	Z	ZOOMORPHISM
YELLOW FEVER	ZANTHOXYLUM	ZOOPLANKTON
YELLOW PAGES	ZEALOUSNESS	ZOOTECHNICS
YELLOWSTONE	ZESTFULNESS	ZYGOMORPHIC
YOUTH HOSTEL	ZINCIFEROUS	ZYGOTICALLY
YTTRIFEROUS	ZINCOGRAPHY	ZYMOGENESIS
YUGOSLAVIAN	ZOOCHEMICAL	ZYMOTICALLY

A	ADAPTABILITY	ALCOHOLICITY
ABBREVIATING	ADDITIONALLY	ALHAMBRESQUE
ABBREVIATION	ADHESIVENESS	ALIENABILITY
ABELIAN GROUP	ADJECTIVALLY	ALIMENTATION
ABOLITIONARY	ADJOURNMENTS	ALIMENTATIVE
ABOLITIONISM	ADJUDICATING	ALKALIMETRIC
ABOLITIONIST	ADJUDICATION	ALL-IMPORTANT
ABOMINATIONS	ADJUDICATORS	ALL-INCLUSIVE
ABORTIONISTS	ADMINISTERED	ALLITERATION
ABRACADABRAS	ADMINISTRATE	ALLITERATIVE
ABSENT-MINDED	ADSCITITIOUS	ALLOMORPHISM
ABSOLUTENESS	ADULTERATING	ALLUSIVENESS
ABSOLUTE ZERO	ADULTERATION	ALMIGHTINESS
ABSORPTIVITY	ADUMBRATIONS	ALPHABETICAL
ABSTEMIOUSLY	ADVANTAGEOUS	ALPHABETIZER
ABSTRACTEDLY	ADVENTITIOUS	ALPHANUMERIC
ABSTRACTIONS	ADVISABILITY	ALTERABILITY
ABSTRUSENESS	AERIFICATION	ALTERCATIONS
ACADEMICALLY	AERODONETICS	ALTERNATIONS
ACADEMICIANS	AERODYNAMICS	ALTERNATIVES
ACANTHACEOUS	AEROEMBOLISM	ALTIMETRICAL
ACCELERATING	AEROMECHANIC	AMALGAMATING
ACCELERATION	AERONAUTICAL	AMALGAMATION
ACCELERATIVE	AERONEUROSIS	AMATEURISHLY
ACCELERATORS	AESTHETICIAN	AMBASSADRESS
ACCENTUATING	AESTHETICISM	AMBIDEXTROUS
ACCENTUATION	AETHEREALITY	AMBITENDENCY
ACCIACCATURA	AETIOLOGICAL	AMBIVALENTLY
ACCIDENTALLY	AFFECTATIONS	AMELIORATING
ACCLAMATIONS	AFFECTEDNESS	AMELIORATION
ACCLIMATIZED	AFFECTIONATE	AMELIORATIVE
ACCLIMATIZER	AFFILIATIONS	AMERICANISMS
ACCOMMODATED	AFFIRMATIONS	AMERICANIZED
ACCOMPANISTS	AFFIRMATIVES	AMERICANIZER
ACCOMPANYING	AFORETHOUGHT	AMITOTICALLY
ACCOMPLISHED	AFRIKANERDOM	AMORTIZATION
ACCOMPLISHER	AFRO-AMERICAN	AMORTIZEMENT
ACCORDIONIST	AFTERBURNING	AMPHETAMINES
ACCOUPLEMENT	AFTEREFFECTS	AMPHIBRACHIC
ACCOUTREMENT	AFTERTHOUGHT	AMPHICOELOUS
ACCUMULATING	AGAMOGENESIS	AMPHICTYONIC
ACCUMULATION	AGAMOGENETIC	AMPHIDIPLOID
ACCUMULATIVE	AGARICACEOUS	AMPHISBAENIC
ACCUMULATORS	AGE OF CONSENT	AMPHITHEATRE
ACCUSATORIAL	AGGLOMERATED	AMPHITHECIUM
ACETALDEHYDE	AGGLUTINABLE	AMPHITROPOUS
ACHIEVEMENTS	AGGLUTINOGEN	AMPULLACEOUS
ACHILLES' HEEL	AGGRAVATIONS	AMYGDALOIDAL
ACHLAMYDEOUS	AGGREGATIONS	ANACHRONISMS
ACHLORHYDRIA	AGGRESSIVELY	ANAESTHETICS
ACKNOWLEDGED	AGONY COLUMNS	ANAESTHETIST
ACKNOWLEDGER	AGORAPHOBICS	ANAESTHETIZE
ACOUSTICALLY	AGRICULTURAL	ANAGOGICALLY
ACQUAINTANCE	AILUROPHILIA	ANAGRAMMATIC
ACQUIESCENCE	AILUROPHOBIA	ANALPHABETIC
ACQUISITIONS	AIR COMMODORE	ANALYTICALLY
ACROSTICALLY	AIR-CONDITION	ANAMORPHOSIS
ACTINOMETRIC	AIRHOSTESSES	ANAPHRODISIA
ACTINOMYCETE	AIR TERMINALS	ANAPHYLACTIC

ANARCHICALLY	APHRODISIACS	AROMATICALLY
ANASTIGMATIC	APICULTURIST	ARRAIGNMENTS
ANATHEMATIZE	APLANOSPHERE	ARRANGEMENTS
ANATOMICALLY	APOCHROMATIC	ARSENOPYRITE
ANCHORPERSON	APOCYNACEOUS	ARTESIAN WELL
ANCIEN REGIME	APOGEOTROPIC	ARTHROPODOUS
ANDROSTERONE	APOSTROPHIZE	ARTHROSPORIC
ANEMOGRAPHIC	APOTHECARIES	ARTICULATELY
ANEMOPHILOUS	APPALACHIANS	ARTICULATING
ANESTHETISTS	APPARATCHIKS	ARTICULATION
ANESTHETIZED	APPARENTNESS	ARTICULATORY
ANGLO—INDIANS	APPASSIONATO	ARTIFICIALLY
ANGLOPHILIAC	APPEASEMENTS	ARTILLERYMAN
ANGUILLIFORM	APPELLATIONS	ARTISTICALLY
ANGULARITIES	APPENDECTOMY	ASCENSION DAY
ANIMADVERTED	APPENDICITIS	ASCERTAINING
ANNEXATIONAL	APPENDICULAR	ASCOMYCETOUS
ANNIHILATING	APPERCEPTION	ASH WEDNESDAY
ANNIHILATION	APPERCEPTIVE	ASKING PRICES
ANNIHILATIVE	APPERTAINING	ASPHYXIATING
ANNOUNCEMENT	APPETIZINGLY	ASPHYXIATION
ANNUNCIATION	APPLAUDINGLY	ASSASSINATED
ANNUNCIATIVE	APPLICATIONS	ASSEMBLY LINE
ANTAGONISTIC	APPOGGIATURA	ASSEVERATING
ANTAGONIZING	APPOINTMENTS	ASSEVERATION
ANTECHAMBERS	APPORTIONING	ASSIBILATION
ANTEDILUVIAN	APPRAISINGLY	ASSIGNATIONS
ANTEMERIDIAN	APPRECIATING	ASSIMILATING
ANTE MERIDIEM	APPRECIATION	ASSIMILATION
ANTHOLOGICAL	APPRECIATIVE	ASSIMILATIVE
ANTHOLOGISTS	APPREHENDING	ASSOCIATIONS
ANTHROPOIDAL	APPREHENSION	ASTONISHMENT
ANTHROPOLOGY	APPREHENSIVE	ASTOUNDINGLY
ANTI—AIR—CRAFT	APPRENTICING	ASTRINGENTLY
ANTICATALYST	APPROACHABLE	ASTROBIOLOGY
ANTICIPATING	APPROPRIABLE	ASTROCOMPASS
ANTICIPATION	APPROPRIATED	ASTROGEOLOGY
ANTICIPATIVE	APPROXIMATED	ASTROLOGICAL
ANTICIPATORY	APPURTENANCE	ASTRONAUTICS
ANTICLERICAL	APRON STRINGS	ASTRONOMICAL
ANTICLIMAXES	AQUICULTURAL	ASTROPHYSICS
ANTICYCLONES	ARBITRAGEURS	ASYMPTOMATIC
ANTICYCLONIC	ARBORESCENCE	ASYNCHRONISM
ANTIHALATION	ARBORIZATION	ASYNCHRONOUS
ANTIMACASSAR	ARCHDEACONRY	ATHEROMATOUS
ANTIMAGNETIC	ARCHDIOCESAN	ATHLETE'S FOOT
ANTINEUTRINO	ARCHDIOCESES	ATHLETICALLY
ANTIPARALLEL	ARCHEOLOGIES	ATHWARTSHIPS
ANTIPARTICLE	ARCHESPORIAL	ATMOSPHERICS
ANTIPATHETIC	ARCHETYPICAL	ATOMIC ENERGY
ANTIPERIODIC	ARCHIPELAGIC	ATTACHE CASES
ANTIQUARIANS	ARCHIPELAGOS	ATTESTATIONS
ANTIRACHITIC	ARCHITECTURE	ATTESTED MILK
ANTI—SEMITISM	ARCHOPLASMIC	ATTITUDINIZE
ANTITHETICAL	ARCTIC CIRCLE	ATTRACTIVELY
ANTONOMASTIC	ARGILLACEOUS	ATTRIBUTABLE
AORISTICALLY	ARISTOCRATIC	AUDIOLOGICAL
APAGOGICALLY	ARMOURED CARS	AUDIOMETRIST
APERIODICITY	ARMOUR—PLATED	AUGMENTATION

AUGMENTATIVE	BARBARIANISM	BIFURCATIONS
AULD LANG SYNE	BARBARICALLY	BILHARZIASIS
AUSCULTATION	BARBITURATES	BILINGUALISM
AUSPICIOUSLY	BARLEY SUGARS	BILL OF HEALTH
AUSTRALASIAN	BARNSTORMERS	BILL OF LADING
AUSTRONESIAN	BARNSTORMING	BILL OF RIGHTS
AUTHENTICATE	BARQUISIMETO	BIOCATALYTIC
AUTHENTICITY	BARRANQUILLA	BIOCHEMISTRY
AUTISTICALLY	BARREL ORGANS	BIOECOLOGIST
AUTOANTIBODY	BASIDIOSPORE	BIOFLAVONOID
AUTOGRAPHING	BASTARDIZING	BIOGEOGRAPHY
AUTOHYPNOSIS	BASTINADOING	BIOGRAPHICAL
AUTOHYPNOTIC	BATCH PROCESS	BIOLOGICALLY
AUTOMOBILIST	BATHING SUITS	BIONOMICALLY
AUTONOMOUSLY	BATHYSPHERES	BIOPHYSICIST
AUTOROTATION	BATTERING RAM	BIOSYNTHESIS
AUTOXIDATION	BATTLEFIELDS	BIOSYNTHETIC
AVAILABILITY	BATTLE ROYALS	BIPROPELLANT
AVARICIOUSLY	BEACH BUGGIES	BIRD'S-EYE VIEW
AVICULTURIST	BEACHCOMBERS	BIRD-WATCHERS
AVITAMINOSIS	BEATIFICALLY	BIREFRINGENT
AVOGADRO'S LAW	BEAUTY QUEENS	BIRTH CONTROL
AWE-INSPIRING	BECHUANALAND	BISMUTHINITE
AZATHIOPRINE	BEDAZZLEMENT	BLABBERMOUTH
	BEGGARLINESS	BLACK AND BLUE
B	BEGRUDGINGLY	BLACKBALLING
BABY CARRIAGE	BEHAVIOURISM	BLACKBERRIES
BACCHANALIAN	BEHAVIOURIST	BLACK COUNTRY
BACKBENCHERS	BELEAGUERING	BLACKCURRANT
BACKBREAKING	BELITTLEMENT	BLACK ECONOMY
BACKHANDEDLY	BELITTLINGLY	BLACK ENGLISH
BACK OF BEYOND	BELLETRISTIC	BLACKGUARDLY
BACK PASSAGES	BELLIGERENCE	BLACK-HEARTED
BACKPEDALING	BELLIGERENCY	BLACKLEGGING
BACKPEDALLED	BELLIGERENTS	BLACKLISTING
BACKROOM BOYS	BELLY BUTTONS	BLACKMAILERS
BACKSLAPPERS	BELLY DANCERS	BLACKMAILING
BACKSLAPPING	BELLY-LANDING	BLACK MUSLIMS
BACKTRACKING	BENEDICTINES	BLACK PUDDING
BACKWARDNESS	BENEDICTIONS	BLADDERWRACK
BACKWOODSMAN	BENEFACTIONS	BLAMEFULNESS
BACKWOODSMEN	BENEFACTRESS	BLANK CHEQUES
BACTERICIDAL	BENEFICENTLY	BLAST FURNACE
BACTERIOLOGY	BENEFICIALLY	BLASTODERMIC
BAGGAGE ROOMS	BENEVOLENTLY	BLASTOSPHERE
BAKING POWDER	BENZALDEHYDE	BLINDFOLDING
BALANCED DIET	BENZOPHENONE	BLISSFULNESS
BALANCE SHEET	BENZOQUINONE	BLISTERINGLY
BALL BEARINGS	BEREAVEMENTS	BLOCKBUSTERS
BALLOTTEMENT	BESPECTACLED	BLOCK LETTERS
BALNEOLOGIST	BEWILDERMENT	BLOEMFONTEIN
BANDERILLERO	BEWITCHINGLY	BLOOD BROTHER
BANDJARMASIN	BIAURICULATE	BLOODLETTING
BANK ACCOUNTS	BIBLIOGRAPHY	BLOODSTAINED
BANKER'S CARDS	BIBLIOMANIAC	BLOODSTREAMS
BANKER'S ORDER	BIBLIOPHILES	BLOODSUCKERS
BANK HOLIDAYS	BICOLLATERAL	BLOODTHIRSTY
BANKRUPTCIES	BIELSKO-BIALA	BLOOD VESSELS
BANTAMWEIGHT	BIFLAGELLATE	BLOODY-MINDED

BLUE-EYED BOYS	BURGLAR ALARM	CARBON PAPERS
BLUESTOCKING	BURSERACEOUS	CARBURETTORS
BLUNDERINGLY	BUSINESSLIKE	CARCINOGENIC
BLUSTERINGLY	BUSINESS SUIT	CARD-CARRYING
BOARDING CARD	BUTTERSCOTCH	CARDIOGRAPHY
BOASTFULNESS	BUTTONHOLING	CARDIOLOGIST
BOBSLEIGHING	BUYER'S MARKET	CARDIOMEGALY
BODY LANGUAGE	BYELORUSSIAN	CARELESSNESS
BODY SNATCHER		CARICATURING
BODY STOCKING	C	CARICATURIST
BOILING POINT	CABIN CRUISER	CARILLONNEUR
BOISTEROUSLY	CABINET-MAKER	CARPETBAGGER
BOLSTERINGLY	CABLE RAILWAY	CARPOLOGICAL
BOMBACACEOUS	CACHINNATION	CARPOPHAGOUS
BOMBARDMENTS	CAENOGENESIS	CARRIAGEWAYS
BOOBY-TRAPPED	CAENOGENETIC	CARTE BLANCHE
BOOK-LEARNING	CALAMITOUSLY	CARTOGRAPHER
BOOMERANGING	CALCULATIONS	CARTOGRAPHIC
BOROSILICATE	CALENDAR YEAR	CARTWHEELING
BOTTOM DRAWER	CALIBRATIONS	CARVING FORKS
BOWDLERIZING	CALISTHENICS	CARVING KNIFE
BOWLING ALLEY	CALLIGRAPHER	CASH AND CARRY
BOWLING GREEN	CALLIGRAPHIC	CASH REGISTER
BRACHYLOGOUS	CALLISTHENIC	CASTELLATION
BRACKISHNESS	CALL OF NATURE	CASTING VOTES
BRAINS TRUSTS	CALORIMETRIC	CATACHRESTIC
BRAINTEASERS	CALUMNIATING	CATASTROPHES
BRAINWASHING	CALUMNIATION	CATASTROPHIC
BREADWINNERS	CAMELOPARDUS	CATCHPHRASES
BREAKFASTING	CAMI-KNICKERS	CATECHETICAL
BREASTSTROKE	CAMOUFLAGING	CATEGORIZING
BREATHALYZER	CAMP FOLLOWER	CATERPILLARS
BREATHTAKING	CANALIZATION	CATERWAULING
BREECHLOADER	CANCELLATION	CAULIFLOWERS
BRILLIANTINE	CANDELABRUMS	CAUSE CELEBRE
BRINKMANSHIP	CANDLESTICKS	CAUTIOUSNESS
BRISTLE-GRASS	CANDY-STRIPED	CAVEAT EMPTOR
BROADCASTERS	CANNIBALIZED	CELEBRATIONS
BROADCASTING	CANNON FODDER	CEMENT MIXERS
BRONCHOSCOPE	CANONIZATION	CENSORIOUSLY
BRONCHOSCOPY	CANTABRIGIAN	CENTENARIANS
BRONCOBUSTER	CANTANKEROUS	CENTRALIZING
BRONTOSAURUS	CAPABILITIES	CENTREPIECES
BRONZE MEDALS	CAPACITATION	CENTROCLINAL
BROTHERHOODS	CAPARISONNED	CENTROSPHERE
BROTHER-IN-LAW	CAPE COLOURED	CENTUPLICATE
BROWNIE POINT	CAPERCAILLIE	CEPHALOMETER
BUENAVENTURA	CAPILLACEOUS	CEPHALOMETRY
BUFFER STATES	CAPITAL GAINS	CEPHALOPODAN
BUFFER STOCKS	CAPITALIZING	CEPHALOPODIC
BULLDOG CLIPS	CAPITULATING	CEREMONIALLY
BULLET-HEADED	CAPITULATION	CEROGRAPHIST
BULLFIGHTERS	CAPRICIOUSLY	CERTIFICATED
BULLFIGHTING	CAPTIOUSNESS	CERTIFICATES
BULLHEADEDLY	CARAVANSERAI	CHAIN LETTERS
BULLSHITTING	CARBOHYDRATE	CHAIN-SMOKERS
BULL TERRIERS	CARBONACEOUS	CHAIN-SMOKING
BUNSEN BURNER	CARBON COPIES	CHAIRMANSHIP
BUREAUCRATIC	CARBON DATING	CHAIRPERSONS

CHAISE LONGUE	CHLORENCHYMA	CIVIL SERVANT
CHALCOGRAPHY	CHLORINATING	CIVIL SERVICE
CHALCOPYRITE	CHLORINATION	CLAIRVOYANCE
CHAMBERLAINS	CHLOROFORMED	CLAIRVOYANTS
CHAMBERMAIDS	CHLOROHYDRIN	CLANGOROUSLY
CHAMBER MUSIC	CHLOROPICRIN	CLANNISHNESS
CHAMPIONSHIP	CHOIRMASTERS	CLAPPERBOARD
CHANGCHIAKOW	CHOIR SCHOOLS	CLARINETTIST
CHANGELESSLY	CHOLERICALLY	CLASS ACTIONS
CHANGE OF LIFE	CHONDRIOSOME	CLASSICALITY
CHANGING ROOM	CHOREOGRAPHS	CLASSICISTIC
CHAPLAINCIES	CHOREOGRAPHY	CLASSIFIABLE
CHAPTERHOUSE	CHOROGRAPHER	CLASSIFIED AD
CHARACTERFUL	CHOROGRAPHIC	CLAUDICATION
CHARACTERIZE	CHRISTCHURCH	CLEAR-SIGHTED
CHARGE NURSES	CHRISTENINGS	CLEFT PALATES
CHARGE SHEETS	CHRISTIAN ERA	CLERESTORIED
CHARLATANISM	CHRISTIANITY	CLERESTORIES
CHARNEL HOUSE	CHRISTIANIZE	CLERK OF WORKS
CHASTISEMENT	CHRISTMAS BOX	CLIENT STATES
CHASTITY BELT	CHRISTMAS EVE	CLIFFHANGERS
CHATTERBOXES	CHRIST'S-THORN	CLIFFHANGING
CHAUFFEURING	CHROMATICISM	CLIMACTERICS
CHAUVINISTIC	CHROMATICITY	CLIMATICALLY
CHECKERBERRY	CHROMATOGRAM	CLIMATOLOGIC
CHECKERBLOOM	CHROME YELLOW	CLIMBING IRON
CHEERFULNESS	CHROMOPHORIC	CLINKER-BUILT
CHEERLEADERS	CHROMOSPHERE	CLIQUISHNESS
CHEESEBURGER	CHRONOGRAPHS	CLODDISHNESS
CHEESEPARING	CHRONOLOGIES	CLOSE-CROPPED
CHEFS D'OEUVRE	CHRONOLOGIST	CLOSED SEASON
CHEMOSPHERIC	CHRONOMETERS	CLOSE-GRAINED
CHEMOTHERAPY	CHRONOMETRIC	CLOSE SEASONS
CHEMOTROPISM	CHRONOSCOPIC	CLOSING PRICE
CHEQUERBOARD	CHURCHWARDEN	CLOSING TIMES
CHERUBICALLY	CHURLISHNESS	CLOTHESHORSE
CHESHIRE CATS	CHYMOTRYPSIN	CLOTHESLINES
CHESTERFIELD	CINCHONIDINE	CLOTHES-PRESS
CHIAROSCUROS	CINEMATHEQUE	CLOTTED CREAM
CHIEF JUSTICE	CIRCUITOUSLY	CLOVE HITCHES
CHIEF OF STAFF	CIRCULARIZED	CLOVERLEAVES
CHILDBEARING	CIRCULARIZER	CLOWNISHNESS
CHILD BENEFIT	CIRCULAR SAWS	CLUB SANDWICH
CHILDISHNESS	CIRCUMCISING	CLUSTER BOMBS
CHILDMINDERS	CIRCUMCISION	COACERVATION
CHILDMINDING	CIRCUMFLUOUS	COACHBUILDER
CHILD PRODIGY	CIRCUMFUSION	COACH STATION
CHIMNEYPIECE	CIRCUMNUTATE	COALITIONIST
CHIMNEYSTACK	CIRCUMSCRIBE	COALSCUTTLES
CHIMNEYSWEEP	CIRCUMSTANCE	COBBLESTONES
CHIROGRAPHER	CIRCUMVENTED	COCKFIGHTING
CHIROGRAPHIC	CIRCUMVENTER	COCKLESHELLS
CHIROPODISTS	CIRROCUMULUS	COCONUT SHIES
CHIROPRACTIC	CIRROSTRATUS	CODIFICATION
CHIROPRACTOR	CITIZENS' BAND	COEFFICIENTS
CHITCHATTING	CITRICULTURE	COELENTERATE
CHITTERLINGS	CIVIL DEFENCE	COENESTHESIA
CHIVALROUSLY	CIVILIZATION	COENESTHESIS
CHLORAMBUCIL	CIVIL LIBERTY	COENESTHETIC

COERCIVENESS	COMMONPLACES	CONCILIATORY
COFFEE BREAKS	COMMONWEALTH	CONCLUSIVELY
COFFEE HOUSES	COMMUNICABLE	CONCOMITANCE
COFFEE KLATCH	COMMUNICABLY	CONCOMITANTS
COFFEE TABLES	COMMUNICANTS	CONCORDANCES
COHABITATION	COMMUNICATED	CONCRESCENCE
COHESIVENESS	COMMUNICATOR	CONCUPISCENT
COINCIDENCES	COMMUNIONIST	CONCURRENCES
COINCIDENTAL	COMMUTATIONS	CONCURRENTLY
COLD SHOULDER	COMPACT DISCS	CONDEMNATION
COLEOPTEROUS	COMPANIONATE	CONDEMNATORY
COLLABORATED	COMPANIONWAY	CONDENSATION
COLLABORATOR	COMPARTMENTS	CONDESCENDED
COLLECTIVELY	COMPASS POINT	CONDITIONERS
COLLECTIVISM	COMPATRIOTIC	CONDITIONING
COLLECTIVIST	COMPELLINGLY	CONDOMINIUMS
COLLECTIVITY	COMPENSATING	CONDUCTIVITY
COLLECTIVIZE	COMPENSATION	CONDUPLICATE
COLLECTORATE	COMPENSATIVE	CONFABULATED
COLLOCATIONS	COMPENSATORY	CONFABULATOR
COLLOIDALITY	COMPETITIONS	CONFECTIONER
COLLOQUIALLY	COMPILATIONS	CONFEDERATED
COLLYWOBBLES	COMPLACENTLY	CONFEDERATES
COLONIALISTS	COMPLAINANTS	CONFERENTIAL
COLONIZATION	COMPLAISANCE	CONFESSIONAL
COLORIMETRIC	COMPLEMENTED	CONFIDENTIAL
COLOURLESSLY	COMPLETENESS	CONFINEMENTS
COLOUR SCHEME	COMPLEXITIES	CONFIRMATION
COLUMNIATION	COMPLICATING	CONFIRMATORY
COMBINATIONS	COMPLICATION	CONFISCATING
COMBUSTIBLES	COMPLIMENTED	CONFISCATION
COME-UPPANCES	COMPONENTIAL	CONFISCATORY
COMFORTINGLY	COMPOSITIONS	CONFORMATION
COMMANDEERED	COMPOS MENTIS	CONFOUNDEDLY
COMMANDMENTS	COMPREHENDED	CONFRATERNAL
COMMEMORATED	COMPRESSIBLE	CONFUCIANISM
COMMEMORATOR	COMPROMISING	CONFUCIANIST
COMMENCEMENT	COMPTROLLERS	CONFUTATIONS
COMMENDATION	COMPULSIVELY	CONGENIALITY
COMMENDATORY	COMPULSORILY	CONGENITALLY
COMMENSALISM	COMPUNCTIOUS	CONGLOBATION
COMMENSURATE	COMPUTATIONS	CONGLOMERATE
COMMENTARIAL	COMPUTERIZED	CONGLUTINANT
COMMENTARIES	CONCATENATED	CONGLUTINATE
COMMENTATING	CONCELEBRATE	CONGRATULATE
COMMENTATORS	CONCENTRATED	CONGREGATING
COMMERCIALLY	CONCENTRATES	CONGREGATION
COMMISERATED	CONCENTRATOR	CONGREGATIVE
COMMISERATOR	CONCEPTIONAL	CONIDIOPHORE
COMMISSARIAL	CONCEPTUALLY	CONJECTURING
COMMISSARIAT	CONCERTGOERS	CONJUGATIONS
COMMISSARIES	CONCERT GRAND	CONJUNCTIONS
COMMISSIONAL	CONCERTINAED	CONJUNCTIVAL
COMMISSIONED	CONCERT PITCH	CONJUNCTIVES
COMMISSIONER	CONCHIFEROUS	CONJUNCTURAL
COMMITTEEMAN	CONCHOLOGIST	CONJUNCTURES
COMMITTEEMEN	CONCILIATING	CONNECTIONAL
COMMODIOUSLY	CONCILIATION	CONNING TOWER
COMMON MARKET	CONCILIATORS	CONNOISSEURS

CONNOTATIONS	CONTEMPLATOR	COOKERY BOOKS
CONNUBIALITY	CONTEMPORARY	COOKING APPLE
CONQUISTADOR	CONTEMPORIZE	COOPERATIVES
CONSCIONABLE	CONTEMPTIBLE	COORDINATELY
CONSCRIPTING	CONTEMPTIBLY	COORDINATING
CONSCRIPTION	CONTEMPTUOUS	COORDINATION
CONSECRATING	CONTENTIONAL	COPOLYMERIZE
CONSECRATION	CONTERMINOUS	COPROPHAGOUS
CONSECRATORY	CONTESTATION	COPROPHILOUS
CONSENTIENCE	CONTEXTUALLY	COPTIC CHURCH
CONSEQUENCES	CONTIGUOUSLY	COQUETTISHLY
CONSEQUENTLY	CONTINENTALS	CORDUROY ROAD
CONSERVATION	CONTINGENTLY	CORESPONDENT
CONSERVATISM	CONTINUALITY	CORNERSTONES
CONSERVATIVE	CONTINUATION	CORN EXCHANGE
CONSERVATORY	CONTINUATIVE	CORNISH PASTY
CONSIDERABLE	CONTINUINGLY	COROLLACEOUS
CONSIDERABLY	CONTINUOUSLY	CORPORALSHIP
CONSIGNATION	CONTORTIONAL	CORPORATIONS
CONSIGNMENTS	CONTRABASSES	CORPOREALITY
CONSISTENTLY	CONTRACTIBLE	CORRECTITUDE
CONSISTORIAL	CONTRACTIONS	CORRECTIVELY
CONSOCIATION	CONTRADICTED	CORRELATIONS
CONSOLATIONS	CONTRADICTER	CORRELATIVES
CONSOLIDATED	CONTRAPTIONS	CORRESPONDED
CONSOLIDATOR	CONTRAPUNTAL	CORROBORATED
CONSPECTUSES	CONTRARINESS	CORROBORATOR
CONSPIRACIES	CONTRARIWISE	CORRUGATIONS
CONSPIRATORS	CONTRAVENING	COSMETICALLY
CONSTABULARY	CONTRIBUTING	COSMETICIANS
CONSTIPATION	CONTRIBUTION	COSMOLOGICAL
CONSTITUENCY	CONTRIBUTIVE	COSMOPOLITAN
CONSTITUENTS	CONTRIBUTORS	COSTERMONGER
CONSTITUTING	CONTRIBUTORY	COST OF LIVING
CONSTITUTION	CONTRIVANCES	COTYLEDONARY
CONSTITUTIVE	CONTROLLABLE	COTYLEDONOUS
CONSTRAINING	CONTROVERTER	COUNTENANCED
CONSTRICTING	CONTUMACIOUS	COUNTENANCES
CONSTRICTION	CONTUMELIOUS	COUNTERACTED
CONSTRICTIVE	CONURBATIONS	COUNTERBLAST
CONSTRICTORS	CONVALESCENT	COUNTERCHECK
CONSTRUCTING	CONVALESCING	COUNTERCLAIM
CONSTRUCTION	CONVECTIONAL	COUNTERFOILS
CONSTRUCTIVE	CONVENIENCES	COUNTERPANES
CONSTRUCTORS	CONVENIENTLY	COUNTERPARTS
CONSULTATION	CONVENTICLES	COUNTERPOINT
CONSULTATIVE	CONVENTIONAL	COUNTERPOISE
CONSUMMATELY	CONVERGENCES	COUNTERPROOF
CONSUMMATING	CONVERSATION	COUNTERSHAFT
CONSUMMATION	CONVERSIONAL	COUNTERSIGNS
CONSUMMATIVE	CONVERTIBLES	COUNTERTENOR
CONSUMPTIONS	CONVEYANCING	COUNTRY CLUBS
CONSUMPTIVES	CONVEYER BELT	COUNTRY DANCE
CONTAGIOUSLY	CONVINCINGLY	COUNTRY SEATS
CONTAINERIZE	CONVIVIALITY	COUNTY COURTS
CONTAMINANTS	CONVOCATIONS	COUPS DE GRACE
CONTAMINATED	CONVOLUTEDLY	COURAGEOUSLY
CONTAMINATOR	CONVOLUTIONS	COURT-MARTIAL
CONTEMPLATED	CONVULSIVELY	COVER CHARGES

COVERED WAGON	D	DEFLOCCULATE
COVETOUSNESS	DACTYLICALLY	DEFORMATIONS
COWARDLINESS	DAEMONICALLY	DEFORMEDNESS
CRACKBRAINED	DAIRY FARMERS	DEFRAUDATION
CRANIOLOGIST	DANISH PASTRY	DEGENERATING
CRANIOMETRIC	DARBY AND JOAN	DEGENERATION
CRASH BARRIER	DAY NURSERIES	DEGENERATIVE
CRASH HELMETS	DEACTIVATION	DEGRADATIONS
CRASH LANDING	DEAF-MUTENESS	DEHUMANIZING
CREEPY-CRAWLY	DEATH RATTLES	DEHUMIDIFIER
CREMATIONISM	DEATH WARRANT	DEJECTEDNESS
CREMATIONIST	DEBARKATIONS	DELAMINATION
CREMATORIUMS	DEBAUCHERIES	DELIBERATELY
CRENELLATION	DEBILITATING	DELIBERATING
CRISSCROSSED	DEBILITATION	DELIBERATION
CRISSCROSSES	DEBILITATIVE	DELIBERATIVE
CROP-SPRAYING	DEBT OF HONOUR	DELICATESSEN
CROSSBENCHER	DECALCOMANIA	DELIGHTFULLY
CROSSBENCHES	DECALESCENCE	DELIMITATION
CROSSCHECKED	DECAPITATING	DELIMITATIVE
CROSS-COUNTRY	DECAPITATION	DELIQUESCENT
CROSSCURRENT	DECARBONIZER	DELITESCENCE
CROSS-DRESSER	DECASYLLABIC	DELTIOLOGIST
CROSS-EXAMINE	DECASYLLABLE	DEMAGNETIZED
CROSS-GRAINED	DECELERATING	DEMAGNETIZER
CROSSPATCHES	DECELERATION	DEMENTEDNESS
CROSS-SECTION	DECENTRALIST	DEMILITARIZE
CROWNED HEADS	DECENTRALIZE	DEMIMONDAINE
CROWN PRINCES	DECIMALIZING	DEMOCRATIZED
CRUSH BARRIER	DECIPHERABLE	DEMODULATION
CRYOPLANKTON	DECIPHERMENT	DEMOGRAPHERS
CRYPTANALYST	DECISIVENESS	DEMOLISHMENT
CRYPTOGRAPHY	DECLAMATIONS	DEMONETIZING
CRYPTOLOGIST	DECLARATIONS	DEMONIACALLY
CRYSTAL BALLS	DECLASSIFIED	DEMONOLOGIST
CRYSTAL CLEAR	DECLENSIONAL	DEMONSTRABLE
CRYSTAL GAZER	DECLINATIONS	DEMONSTRABLY
CRYSTALLITIC	DECLINOMETER	DEMONSTRATED
CRYSTALLIZED	DECOLLETAGES	DEMONSTRATOR
CUCKOO CLOCKS	DECOLONIZING	DEMOTIVATING
CUMULATIVELY	DECOLORATION	DEMOTIVATION
CUMULONIMBUS	DECOMPOSABLE	DEMYSTIFYING
CUPBOARD LOVE	DECOMPRESSED	DENATURALIZE
CURARIZATION	DECONGESTANT	DENATURATION
CURATORSHIPS	DECONTROLLED	DENBIGHSHIRE
CURMUDGEONLY	DECORATIVELY	DENDROLOGIST
CURTAILMENTS	DECORTICATOR	DENICOTINIZE
CURTAIN CALLS	DEDUCIBILITY	DENOMINATING
CURVACEOUSLY	DEERSTALKERS	DENOMINATION
CUT AND THRUST	DE-ESCALATING	DENOMINATIVE
CUTTLEFISHES	DE-ESCALATION	DENOMINATORS
CYCLOPENTANE	DEFAMATORILY	DENOUNCEMENT
CYCLOSTOMATE	DEFICIENCIES	DENSITOMETER
CYCLOSTYLING	DEFINITENESS	DENSITOMETRY
CYSTICERCOID	DEFINITIONAL	DENTAL PLATES
CYTOCHEMICAL	DEFINITIVELY	DENTILINGUAL
CYTOGENETICS	DEFLAGRATION	DENUNCIATION
CYTOTAXONOMY	DEFLATIONARY	DENUNCIATORY
CZECHOSLOVAK	DEFLATIONIST	DEONTOLOGIST

DEPARTMENTAL	DEVALUATIONS	DIRECT DEBITS
DEPENDENCIES	DEVELOPMENTS	DIRECT OBJECT
DEPILATORIES	DEVIATIONISM	DIRECTORATES
DEPOLITICIZE	DEVIATIONIST	DIRECTORSHIP
DEPOPULATING	DEVILISHNESS	DIRECT SPEECH
DEPOPULATION	DEVIL-MAY-CARE	DIRIGIBILITY
DEPORTATIONS	DEVITALIZING	DISABILITIES
DEPOSITORIES	DEXTROGYRATE	DISABLEMENTS
DEPRAVEDNESS	DIABOLICALLY	DISACCHARIDE
DEPRECIATING	DIAGEOTROPIC	DISADVANTAGE
DEPRECIATION	DIAGRAMMATIC	DISAFFECTION
DEPRECIATORY	DIALECTICIAN	DISAFFILIATE
DEPREDATIONS	DIALECTOLOGY	DISAGREEABLE
DEPRESSINGLY	DIALLING CODE	DISAGREEABLY
DEPRIVATIONS	DIALLING TONE	DISAGREEMENT
DERACINATION	DIALYTICALLY	DISALLOWABLE
DERANGEMENTS	DIAMAGNETISM	DISALLOWANCE
DEREGULATING	DIAPOPHYSIAL	DISAMBIGUATE
DEREGULATION	DIARTHRODIAL	DISANNULMENT
DERELICTIONS	DIASTROPHISM	DISAPPEARING
DERESTRICTED	DIATHERMANCY	DISAPPOINTED
DERISIVENESS	DIATOMACEOUS	DISAPPOINTER
DERIVATIONAL	DIATONICALLY	DISAPPROVING
DERIVATIVELY	DIAZOMETHANE	DISARRANGING
DERMATOPHYTE	DIBRANCHIATE	DISASSOCIATE
DEROGATORILY	DICARBOXYLIC	DISASTROUSLY
DESALINATING	DICHROMATISM	DISBELIEVERS
DESALINATION	DICHROSCOPIC	DISBELIEVING
DESCRIPTIONS	DICTATORSHIP	DISBURSEMENT
DESEGREGATED	DICTIONARIES	DISCIPLESHIP
DESENSITIZED	DIDACTICALLY	DISCIPLINARY
DESENSITIZER	DIENCEPHALIC	DISCIPLINING
DESERVEDNESS	DIENCEPHALON	DISCLAMATION
DESIDERATION	DIESEL ENGINE	DISCOGRAPHER
DESIDERATIVE	DIETETICALLY	DISCOLOURING
DESIGNATIONS	DIFFERENTIAL	DISCOMFITING
DESIRABILITY	DIFFICULTIES	DISCOMFITURE
DESPAIRINGLY	DIGITIZATION	DISCOMMODING
DESPOLIATION	DIGRESSIONAL	DISCOMMODITY
DESPONDENTLY	DILAPIDATION	DISCOMPOSING
DESPOTICALLY	DILATABILITY	DISCOMPOSURE
DESQUAMATION	DILATATIONAL	DISCONCERTED
DESSERTSPOON	DILATOMETRIC	DISCONNECTED
DESSERT WINES	DILATORINESS	DISCONNECTER
DESTABILIZED	DILETTANTISH	DISCONSOLATE
DESTINATIONS	DILETTANTISM	DISCONTENTED
DESTRUCTIBLE	DILLYDALLIED	DISCONTINUED
DETERIORATED	DIMINISHABLE	DISCORDANTLY
DETERMINABLE	DIMINISHMENT	DISCOTHEQUES
DETERMINANTS	DINING TABLES	DISCOUNTABLE
DETHRONEMENT	DINNER JACKET	DISCOURAGING
DETOXICATION	DIOPTRICALLY	DISCOURTEOUS
DETRUNCATION	DIPHTHERITIC	DISCOVERABLE
DETUMESCENCE	DIPHTHONGIZE	DISCOVERTURE
DEUTERANOPIA	DIPLOBLASTIC	DISCREDITING
DEUTERANOPIC	DIPLOCARDIAC	DISCREETNESS
DEUTOPLASMIC	DIPLOMATISTS	DISCRETENESS
DEUTSCHE MARK	DIPROPELLANT	DISCRIMINANT
DEUTSCHMARKS	DIPSOMANIACS	DISCRIMINATE

DISCURSIVELY	DISSATISFIED	DONKEY'S YEARS
DISCUSSIONAL	DISSEMBLANCE	DOORKNOCKERS
DISDAINFULLY	DISSEMINATED	DOORSTEPPING
DISEMBARKING	DISSEMINATOR	DOORSTOPPERS
DISEMBARRASS	DISSENTIENCE	DORSIVENTRAL
DISEMBOWELED	DISSERTATION	DORSOVENTRAL
DISENCHANTED	DISSEVERANCE	DOUBLE-ACTING
DISENCHANTER	DISSIMILARLY	DOUBLE AGENTS
DISENDOWMENT	DISSIMULATED	DOUBLE BASSES
DISENTANGLED	DISSIMULATOR	DOUBLE-BEDDED
DISESTABLISH	DISSOCIATING	DOUBLE BLUFFS
DISFORESTING	DISSOCIATION	DOUBLE-DATING
DISFRANCHISE	DISSOCIATIVE	DOUBLE-DEALER
DISGORGEMENT	DISSOLUTIONS	DOUBLE-DECKER
DISGUSTINGLY	DISSYMMETRIC	DOUBLE-DOTTED
DISHEVELMENT	DISTEMPERING	DOUBLE FAULTS
DISHONOURING	DISTILLATION	DOUBLE-GLAZED
DISINCENTIVE	DISTILLATORY	DOUBLE-HEADER
DISINFECTANT	DISTILLERIES	DOUBLE-PARKED
DISINFECTING	DISTINCTIONS	DOUBLE-TALKED
DISINFECTION	DISTINCTNESS	DOUBLE-TONGUE
DISINFLATION	DISTORTIONAL	DOWN PAYMENTS
DISINGENUOUS	DISTRACTEDLY	DRACONIANISM
DISINHERITED	DISTRACTIBLE	DRACONICALLY
DISINTEGRATE	DISTRACTIONS	DRAMATICALLY
DISINTERMENT	DISTRAINABLE	DRAMATIZABLE
DISINTERRING	DISTRAINMENT	DRAUGHTBOARD
DISJOINTEDLY	DISTRIBUTARY	DRAWING BOARD
DISLOCATIONS	DISTRIBUTING	DRAWING ROOMS
DISLODGEMENT	DISTRIBUTION	DREADFULNESS
DISLOYALTIES	DISTRIBUTIVE	DREADNOUGHTS
DISMEMBERING	DISTRIBUTORS	DRESS CIRCLES
DISMOUNTABLE	DISTURBANCES	DRESSING-DOWN
DISOBEDIENCE	DITTOGRAPHIC	DRESSING GOWN
DISOPERATION	DIURETICALLY	DRESSING ROOM
DISORGANIZED	DIVARICATION	DRY BATTERIES
DISORGANIZER	DIVERSIFYING	DUCKING STOOL
DISORIENTATE	DIVERSIONARY	DUMBFOUNDING
DISPENSARIES	DIVERTICULAR	DUMORTIERITE
DISPENSATION	DIVERTICULUM	DUTCH AUCTION
DISPENSATORY	DIVERTIMENTO	DUTCH COURAGE
DISPIRITEDLY	DIVINGBOARDS	DWARFISHNESS
DISPLACEABLE	DIVINIZATION	DYNAMOMETRIC
DISPLACEMENT	DIVISIBILITY	DYSTELEOLOGY
DISPOSITIONS	DIVISIVENESS	
DISPOSSESSED	DOCTRINALITY	E
DISPOSSESSOR	DOCTRINARIAN	EAGER BEAVERS
DISPUTATIONS	DODECAHEDRAL	EARSPLITTING
DISPUTATIOUS	DODECAHEDRON	EARTHSHAKING
DISQUALIFIED	DODECAPHONIC	EAST BERLINER
DISQUALIFIER	DOGMATICALLY	EASTER-LEDGES
DISQUIETEDLY	DO-IT-YOURSELF	EAST GERMANIC
DISQUISITION	DOMESDAY BOOK	EATING APPLES
DISREGARDFUL	DOMESTICABLE	EAU DE COLOGNE
DISREGARDING	DOMESTICALLY	EAVESDROPPED
DISRELISHING	DOMESTICATED	EAVESDROPPER
DISREPUTABLE	DOMESTICATOR	EBULLIOSCOPY
DISREPUTABLY	DOMINO EFFECT	ECCENTRICITY
DISRUPTIVELY	DONKEY JACKET	ECCLESIASTIC

ECCLESIOLOGY	ELIZABETHANS	ENDOTHELIOID
ECHINOCOCCUS	ELLIPTICALLY	ENDOTHELIOMA
ECHINODERMAL	ELOCUTIONARY	ENDOTHERMISM
ECHOLOCATION	ELOCUTIONIST	ENDURABILITY
ECLECTICALLY	ELOQUENTNESS	ENERGETICIST
ECLIPTICALLY	EMANCIPATING	ENFEEBLEMENT
ECOLOGICALLY	EMANCIPATION	ENFRANCHISED
ECONOMETRICS	EMANCIPATIVE	ENFRANCHISER
ECONOMICALLY	EMANCIPATORY	ENGAGINGNESS
ECOTYPICALLY	EMARGINATION	ENGENDERMENT
ECSTATICALLY	EMASCULATING	ENGINE DRIVER
ECTOPARASITE	EMASCULATION	ENGLISH HORNS
ECUMENICALLY	EMASCULATIVE	ENGLISHWOMAN
EDACIOUSNESS	EMBARKATIONS	ENGRAFTATION
EDITORIALIST	EMBARRASSING	ENGROSSINGLY
EDITORIALIZE	EMBELLISHING	ENHANCEMENTS
EDULCORATION	EMBEZZLEMENT	ENLARGEMENTS
EFFECTUALITY	EMBITTERMENT	ENLIGHTENING
EFFECTUATING	EMBLAZONMENT	ENLIVENINGLY
EFFECTUATION	EMBRANCHMENT	ENORMOUSNESS
EFFEMINATELY	EMBROCATIONS	ENSHRINEMENT
EFFERVESCENT	EMBROIDERIES	ENSILABILITY
EFFERVESCING	EMBROIDERING	ENTANGLEMENT
EFFLORESCENT	EMBRYOLOGIST	ENTEROKINASE
EFFORTLESSLY	EMIGRATIONAL	ENTERPRISING
EFFUSIOMETER	EMOTIONALISM	ENTERTAINERS
EFFUSIVENESS	EMOTIONALIST	ENTERTAINING
EGOISTICALLY	EMOTIONALITY	ENTHRONEMENT
EGYPTOLOGIST	EMOTIONALIZE	ENTHUSIASTIC
EISTEDDFODIC	EMPATHICALLY	ENTHYMEMATIC
EJACULATIONS	EMPHATICALLY	ENTICINGNESS
EJECTOR SEATS	EMPLACEMENTS	ENTOMOLOGIST
ELABORATIONS	EMULSIFIABLE	ENTOMOLOGIZE
ELASMOBRANCH	ENANTIOMORPH	ENTRANCEMENT
ELASTICATION	ENARTHRODIAL	ENTRANCINGLY
ELASTIC BANDS	ENCEPHALITIC	ENTREATINGLY
ELECTRICALLY	ENCEPHALITIS	ENTRENCHMENT
ELECTRIC EYES	ENCHANTMENTS	ENTREPRENEUR
ELECTRICIANS	ENCIPHERMENT	ENUMERATIONS
ELECTRIFYING	ENCIRCLEMENT	ENVIABLENESS
ELECTROCUTED	ENCLITICALLY	ENVIRONMENTS
ELECTROGRAPH	ENCOMPASSING	ENVISAGEMENT
ELECTROLYSER	ENCOUNTERING	ENZOOTICALLY
ELECTROLYSIS	ENCROACHMENT	ENZYMOLOGIST
ELECTROLYTES	ENCRUSTATION	EOSINOPHILIC
ELECTROLYTIC	ENCUMBRANCER	EPENCEPHALIC
ELECTROMETER	ENCUMBRANCES	EPENCEPHALON
ELECTROMETRY	ENCYCLOPEDIA	EPHEMERALITY
ELECTRONVOLT	ENCYCLOPEDIC	EPICUREANISM
ELECTROPHONE	ENDAMAGEMENT	EPICYCLOIDAL
ELECTROPLATE	ENDANGERMENT	EPIDEMIOLOGY
ELECTROSCOPE	ENDEAVOURING	EPIGLOTTIDES
ELECTROSHOCK	ENDOCARDITIC	EPIGLOTTISES
ELECTROTONIC	ENDOCARDITIS	EPIGRAMMATIC
ELECTROTONUS	ENDOMORPHISM	EPIMORPHOSIS
ELECTROTYPER	ENDOPARASITE	EPISCOPALIAN
ELEEMOSYNARY	ENDORSEMENTS	EPISCOPALISM
ELEPHANT'S-EAR	ENDOSKELETAL	EPISODICALLY
ELEVENTH HOUR	ENDOSKELETON	EPISTEMOLOGY

EPITHALAMIUM	EXAGGERATION	EXPOSTULATED
EQUALITARIAN	EXAGGERATIVE	EXPOSTULATOR
EQUALIZATION	EXAMINATIONS	EXPRESSIONAL
EQUATABILITY	EXASPERATING	EXPRESSIVELY
EQUESTRIENNE	EXASPERATION	EXPRESSIVITY
EQUIDISTANCE	EXCELLENCIES	EXPROPRIABLE
EQUILIBRATOR	EXCHANGEABLE	EXPROPRIATED
EQUIPOLLENCE	EXCHANGE RATE	EXPROPRIATOR
EQUIVALENTLY	EXCITABILITY	EXPURGATIONS
EQUIVOCALITY	EXCLAMATIONS	EXSANGUINITY
EQUIVOCATING	EXCLUSIONARY	EX-SERVICEMAN
EQUIVOCATION	EXCOGITATION	EX-SERVICEMEN
EQUIVOCATORY	EXCOGITATIVE	EXTEMPORIZED
ERGASTOPLASM	EXCORIATIONS	EXTEMPORIZER
ERYTHROBLAST	EXCRESCENCES	EXTENDEDNESS
ERYTHROCYTIC	EXCRUCIATING	EXTENSOMETER
ERYTHROMYCIN	EXCRUCIATION	EXTERMINABLE
ESCAPOLOGIST	EXCURSIONIST	EXTERMINATED
ESCUTCHEONED	EXECUTIONERS	EXTERMINATOR
ESOTERICALLY	EXECUTORSHIP	EXTERNALIZED
ESSENTIALISM	EXEGETICALLY	EXTEROCEPTOR
ESSENTIALIST	EXEMPLIFYING	EXTINGUISHED
ESSENTIALITY	EXENTERATION	EXTINGUISHER
ESTABLISHING	EXHAUSTIVELY	EXTORTIONARY
ESTATE AGENCY	EXHIBITIONER	EXTORTIONATE
ESTATE AGENTS	EXHILARATING	EXTORTIONIST
ESTHETICALLY	EXHILARATION	EXTRADITABLE
ESTRANGEMENT	EXHILARATIVE	EXTRADITIONS
ETERNIZATION	EXHORTATIONS	EXTRAMARITAL
ETHERIZATION	EXIGUOUSNESS	EXTRAMUNDANE
ETHNOCENTRIC	EXOBIOLOGIST	EXTRANEOUSLY
ETHNOGRAPHER	EXOPEPTIDASE	EXTRANUCLEAR
ETHNOGRAPHIC	EXOPHTHALMIC	EXTRAPOLATED
ETHNOLOGICAL	EXOPHTHALMOS	EXTRAPOLATOR
ETHNOLOGISTS	EXORBITANTLY	EXTRASENSORY
ETHOXYETHANE	EXOTERICALLY	EXTRAUTERINE
ETHYL ALCOHOL	EXPANSIONARY	EXTRAVAGANCE
ETYMOLOGICAL	EXPANSIONISM	EXTRAVAGANZA
ETYMOLOGISTS	EXPANSIONIST	EXTROVERSION
EUCALYPTUSES	EXPATRIATING	EXTROVERSIVE
EUHEMERISTIC	EXPATRIATION	EYEWITNESSES
EUPHONICALLY	EXPECTATIONS	
EUPHORICALLY	EXPECTORATED	F
EUSTATICALLY	EXPECTORATOR	FABRICATIONS
EVANGELISTIC	EXPEDIENTIAL	FABULOUSNESS
EVANGELIZING	EXPERIENCING	FACELESSNESS
EVAPORIMETER	EXPERIENTIAL	FACILITATING
EVENING DRESS	EXPERIMENTAL	FACILITATION
EVEN-TEMPERED	EXPERIMENTED	FACILITATIVE
EVENTFULNESS	EXPERIMENTER	FACTIONALISM
EVISCERATING	EXPERT SYSTEM	FACTIONALIST
EVISCERATION	EXPLANATIONS	FACTIOUSNESS
EVOLUTIONARY	EXPLANTATION	FACTORY FARMS
EVOLUTIONISM	EXPLICITNESS	FACTUALISTIC
EVOLUTIONIST	EXPLOITATION	FAINT-HEARTED
EXACERBATING	EXPLOITATIVE	FAIT ACCOMPLI
EXACERBATION	EXPLORATIONS	FAITHFULNESS
EXACTINGNESS	EXPOSITIONAL	FAITH HEALERS
EXAGGERATING	EXPOSITORILY	FAITH HEALING

FALLACIOUSLY	FIGURATIVELY	FOCALIZATION
FALLING STARS	FIGURE-GROUND	FOLKLORISTIC
FALSE BOTTOMS	FIGURE SKATER	FOOL'S-PARSLEY
FAMILIARIZED	FILIBUSTERED	FOOT-AND-MOUTH
FAMILIARIZER	FILIBUSTERER	FOOT FAULTING
FAMILIARNESS	FILM PREMIERE	FOOTSLOGGING
FAMILY CIRCLE	FILTER-TIPPED	FORBEARINGLY
FAMILY DOCTOR	FINALIZATION	FORBIDDINGLY
FANCIFULNESS	FINGERBOARDS	FORCE-FEEDING
FARADIZATION	FINGERPLATES	FORCEFULNESS
FARSIGHTEDLY	FINGERPRINTS	FORCIBLENESS
FASCINATEDLY	FINGERSTALLS	FORE-AND-AFTER
FASTIDIOUSLY	FIRE BRIGADES	FORECLOSABLE
FATHER FIGURE	FIRECRACKERS	FORECLOSURES
FATHERLINESS	FIRE FIGHTERS	FOREGONENESS
FATHERS-IN-LAW	FIRE FIGHTING	FOREKNOWABLE
FATIGABILITY	FIRE HYDRANTS	FORENSICALLY
FAULT-FINDING	FIRELIGHTERS	FOREORDAINED
FAUTE DE MIEUX	FIREPROOFING	FORESHADOWED
FEARLESSNESS	FIRE STATIONS	FORESHADOWER
FEARSOMENESS	FIRING SQUADS	FORESTALLING
FEATHERBRAIN	FIRST COUSINS	FORESTALMENT
FEATURE FILMS	FIRST-FOOTING	FORESTAYSAIL
FEBRIFACIENT	FIRST-NIGHTER	FORETRIANGLE
FECKLESSNESS	FIRST REFUSAL	FORGATHERING
FEDERALISTIC	FISSIPALMATE	FORGET-ME-NOTS
FEEBLEMINDED	FISSIROSTRAL	FORMALDEHYDE
FELDSPATHOSE	FLAGELLATING	FORMLESSNESS
FELICITATING	FLAGELLATION	FORMULARIZER
FELICITATION	FLAGELLIFORM	FORMULATIONS
FELICITOUSLY	FLAMBOYANTLY	FORT-DE-FRANCE
FEMINIZATION	FLAME-THROWER	FORTUITOUSLY
FENESTRATION	FLAMMABILITY	FOSSILIZABLE
FENNELFLOWER	FLATTERINGLY	FOUNDATIONAL
FERMENTATION	FLAVOPROTEIN	FOUNTAINHEAD
FERMENTATIVE	FLEET ADMIRAL	FOUNTAIN PENS
FERRICYANIDE	FLICKERINGLY	FOURIERISTIC
FERRIS WHEELS	FLITTERMOUSE	FOURTH-DEGREE
FERROCYANIDE	FLOATABILITY	FOURTH ESTATE
FERROSILICON	FLOCCULATION	FOURTH OF JULY
FERTILIZABLE	FLOORWALKERS	FRACTIONALLY
FEVERISHNESS	FLORICULTURE	FRACTIONATOR
FIBRILLATION	FLOWCHARTING	FRAMES OF MIND
FIBRILLIFORM	FLUCTUATIONS	FRANCHE-COMTE
FIBRINOGENIC	FLUIDEXTRACT	FRANGIBILITY
FIBRINOLYSIN	FLUIDIZATION	FRANKFURTERS
FIBRINOLYSIS	FLUORESCENCE	FRANKINCENSE
FIBRINOLYTIC	FLUORIDATING	FRATERNALISM
FIBROBLASTIC	FLUORIDATION	FRATERNITIES
FICTIONALIZE	FLUORINATION	FRATERNIZING
FICTITIOUSLY	FLUOROCARBON	FRAUDULENTLY
FIDDLE-FADDLE	FLUOROMETRIC	FREAKISHNESS
FIDDLESTICKS	FLUOROSCOPIC	FREE CHURCHES
FIELD GLASSES	FLUTTERINGLY	FREE-FLOATING
FIELD MARSHAL	FLUVIOMARINE	FREESTANDING
FIELD-TESTING	FLYING DOCTOR	FREE-SWIMMING
FIELDWORKERS	FLYING PICKET	FREETHINKERS
FIENDISHNESS	FLYING SAUCER	FREETHINKING
FIFTH COLUMNS	FLYING SQUADS	FREEWHEELING

FREEZE-DRYING
FREIGHTLINER
FRENCH KISSES
FRENCH LOAVES
FRENCH POLISH
FRENETICALLY
FREQUENTABLE
FREUDIAN SLIP
FRIENDLINESS
FRIGHTENABLE
FROGMARCHING
FRONDESCENCE
FRONTBENCHER
FRONTBENCHES
FRONTIERSMAN
FRONTIERSMEN
FRONTISPIECE
FRONT-RUNNERS
FRUCTIFEROUS
FRUITFULNESS
FRUIT MACHINE
FRUMPISHNESS
FRUSTRATIONS
FUDDY-DUDDIES
FULLER'S EARTH
FULLY-FLEDGED
FULMINATIONS
FUNCTIONALLY
FUNDAMENTALS
FURFURACEOUS
FURUNCULOSIS
FUTILITARIAN
FUTUROLOGIST

G
GALACTAGOGUE
GALACTOMETER
GALACTOMETRY
GALL BLADDERS
GALLINACEOUS
GALLIVANTING
GALVANICALLY
GALVANOMETER
GALVANOMETRY
GALVANOSCOPE
GALVANOSCOPY
GAMESMANSHIP
GAMETOPHORIC
GAMETOPHYTIC
GAMOPETALOUS
GAMOPHYLLOUS
GAMOSEPALOUS
GARBAGE TRUCK
GARDEN CITIES
GASIFICATION
GASTIGHTNESS
GASTRONOMIST
GASTROPODOUS
GASTROSCOPIC

GASTRULATION
GATECRASHERS
GATECRASHING
GAVANIZATION
GEANTICLINAL
GENDER-BENDER
GENEALOGICAL
GENEALOGISTS
GENERALITIES
GENERALIZING
GENERAL STAFF
GENEROSITIES
GENEROUSNESS
GENICULATION
GENOTYPICITY
GENUFLECTING
GENUFLECTION
GEOCHEMISTRY
GEOGRAPHICAL
GEOLOGICALLY
GEOMAGNETISM
GEOMECHANICS
GEOPHYSICIST
GEOPOLITICAL
GEOSYNCLINAL
GERANIACEOUS
GERIATRICIAN
GERMANOPHILE
GERMANOPHOBE
GERONTOCRACY
GESTICULATED
GESTICULATOR
GET-TOGETHERS
GHOULISHNESS
GIANT KILLERS
GIBRALTARIAN
GIFT-WRAPPING
GIGANTICALLY
GIGANTICNESS
GINGER GROUPS
GINGERLINESS
GLABROUSNESS
GLACIOLOGIST
GLADIATORIAL
GLASSBLOWERS
GLASS-BLOWING
GLASSCUTTERS
GLAUCOMATOUS
GLIMMERINGLY
GLISTENINGLY
GLITTERINGLY
GLOBETROTTER
GLOCKENSPIEL
GLORIOUSNESS
GLOSSOGRAPHY
GLOTTAL STOPS
GLOVE PUPPETS
GLUCOGENESIS
GLUCOGENETIC

GLUE-SNIFFERS
GLUE-SNIFFING
GLUTTONOUSLY
GLYCOGENESIS
GLYCOGENETIC
GLYCOPROTEIN
GLYPHOGRAPHY
GLYPTOGRAPHY
GNOMONICALLY
GNOTOBIOTICS
GOBBLEDEGOOK
GOBBLEDYGOOK
GOLDEN EAGLES
GOLDFISH BOWL
GOLD STANDARD
GONADOTROPIN
GOOD-HUMOURED
GOODY-GOODIES
GOOSEBERRIES
GOOSE PIMPLES
GOOSESTEPPED
GORGEOUSNESS
GORMANDIZING
GOSSIPMONGER
GOVERNMENTAL
GOVERNORSHIP
GRACEFULNESS
GRACIOUSNESS
GRADE SCHOOLS
GRADUALISTIC
GRALLATORIAL
GRAMMATOLOGY
GRAM-NEGATIVE
GRAM-POSITIVE
GRANDFATHERS
GRAND MASTERS
GRANDMOTHERS
GRANDPARENTS
GRANODIORITE
GRANULOCYTIC
GRAPHOLOGIST
GRASSHOPPERS
GRATEFULNESS
GRATIFYINGLY
GRATUITOUSLY
GREASY SPOONS
GREAT CIRCLES
GREEN FINGERS
GREENGROCERS
GREENGROCERY
GREEN PEPPERS
GREGARIOUSLY
GRIEVOUSNESS
GRIZZLY BEARS
GROSSULARITE
GROUND FLOORS
GROUNDLESSLY
GROUNDSHEETS
GROUND STAFFS

GROUND STROKE
GROUNDSWELLS
GROUP CAPTAIN
GROUP THERAPY
GROVELLINGLY
GROWING PAINS
GRUESOMENESS
GUADALQUIVIR
GUARANTEEING
GUARDIANSHIP
GUERRILLAISM
GUESSTIMATES
GUEST WORKERS
GUILLOTINING
GUN CARRIAGES
GUTTERSNIPES
GUTTURALNESS
GYNAECOCRACY
GYROMAGNETIC

H
HABEAS CORPUS
HABERDASHERS
HABERDASHERY
HABILITATION
HABITABILITY
HABITATIONAL
HABITUALNESS
HACKING COUGH
HAEMATEMESIS
HAEMATOBLAST
HAEMATOCRYAL
HAEMATOGENIC
HAEMATOLOGIC
HAEMATOLYSIS
HAEMATOXYLIC
HAEMATOXYLIN
HAEMATOXYLON
HAEMOPHILIAC
HAEMOPOIESIS
HAEMOPOIETIC
HAEMORRHAGIC
HAEMORRHOIDS
HAGIOGRAPHER
HAGIOGRAPHIC
HAGIOLATROUS
HAIRDRESSERS
HAIRDRESSING
HAIRPIN BENDS
HAIR-RESTORER
HAIR'S BREADTH
HAIRSPLITTER
HAIR TRIGGERS
HALF-BROTHERS
HALF-HOLIDAYS
HALF MEASURES
HALF-TIMBERED
HALFWAY HOUSE
HALF-WITTEDLY

HALLOWEDNESS
HALLSTATTIAN
HALLUCINATED
HALLUCINATOR
HALLUCINOGEN
HALLUCINOSIS
HALOGENATION
HAMBLETONIAN
HAMMARSKJOLD
HAMMERHEADED
HAMPEREDNESS
HAMSTRINGING
HANDICAPPING
HANDKERCHIEF
HANDSOMENESS
HAPPENSTANCE
HAPPY-GO-LUCKY
HAPPY MEDIUMS
HAPTOTROPISM
HARD CURRENCY
HARD FEELINGS
HARD SHOULDER
HARE COURSING
HARLEQUINADE
HARLEY STREET
HARMLESSNESS
HARMONICALLY
HARMONIOUSLY
HARMONIZABLE
HARPSICHORDS
HARQUEBUSIER
HARTHACANUTE
HARVEST HOMES
HARVEST MOONS
HATCHET-FACED
HAUTE COUTURE
HAUTE CUISINE
HEADQUARTERS
HEADSHRINKER
HEADSTRONGLY
HEART ATTACKS
HEARTBREAKER
HEART DISEASE
HEARTENINGLY
HEART FAILURE
HEARTRENDING
HEARTSTRINGS
HEART-TO-HEART
HEARTWARMING
HEATHENISHLY
HEAVENLINESS
HEAVYHEARTED
HEAVY PETTING
HEAVYWEIGHTS
HEBDOMADALLY
HEBETUDINOUS
HEBRAIZATION
HECTOCOTYLUS
HECTOGRAPHIC

HEDGEHOPPING
HEDGE SPARROW
HEEDLESSNESS
HEILUNGKIANG
HEIR APPARENT
HELICOIDALLY
HELIOCENTRIC
HELIOCHROMIC
HELIOGABALUS
HELIOGRAPHER
HELIOGRAPHIC
HELIOGRAVURE
HELIOLATROUS
HELIOTHERAPY
HELIOTROPISM
HELLENICALLY
HELLGRAMMITE
HELPING HANDS
HELPLESSNESS
HEMICHORDATE
HEMIHYDRATED
HEMIMORPHISM
HEMIMORPHITE
HEMIPARASITE
HEMISPHEROID
HEMOPHILIACS
HENDECAGONAL
HENOTHEISTIC
HERALDICALLY
HERBACEOUSLY
HEREDITAMENT
HEREDITARILY
HEREINBEFORE
HERITABILITY
HERMANNSTADT
HERMENEUTICS
HERMENEUTIST
HERMETICALLY
HERMITICALLY
HERMOTENSILE
HEROD ANTIPAS
HEROICALNESS
HERPES ZOSTER
HERPETOLOGIC
HERRINGBONES
HERSTMONCEUX
HESITATINGLY
HETEROCERCAL
HETEROCYCLIC
HETERODACTYL
HETEROECIOUS
HETEROGAMETE
HETEROGAMOUS
HETEROGENOUS
HETEROGONOUS
HETEROGRAPHY
HETEROGYNOUS
HETEROLOGOUS
HETEROMEROUS

HETERONOMOUS
HETERONYMOUS
HETEROOUSIAN
HETEROPHYLLY
HETEROPLASTY
HETEROSEXUAL
HETEROTACTIC
HETEROZYGOTE
HETEROZYGOUS
HEXACOSANOIC
HEXAGRAMMOID
HEXAHYDRATED
HIBERNACULUM
HIBERNIANISM
HIERARCHICAL
HIERATICALLY
HIEROGLYPHIC
HIEROPHANTIC
HIGH FIDELITY
HIGH-HANDEDLY
HIGHLIGHTING
HIGHLY-STRUNG
HIGH-MINDEDLY
HIGH-PRESSURE
HIGH PROFILES
HIGH SHERIFFS
HIGH-SOUNDING
HIGH-SPIRITED
HINAYANISTIC
HINDQUARTERS
HIPPOCRENIAN
HIPPOPOTAMUS
HIRE PURCHASE
HISTOGENESIS
HISTOGENETIC
HISTOLOGICAL
HISTORICALLY
HOBBLEDEHOYS
HOBSON-JOBSON
HOHENZOLLERN
HOLIDAYMAKER
HOLISTICALLY
HOLOPHRASTIC
HOLOPLANKTON
HOLY OF HOLIES
HOME COUNTIES
HOME FROM HOME
HOMELESSNESS
HOMEOMORPHIC
HOMEOPATHIST
HOMESICKNESS
HOMOCHROMOUS
HOMOGENIZING
HOMOGONOUSLY
HOMOLOGATION
HOMOMORPHISM
HOMOPOLARITY
HOMOTAXIALLY
HOMOTHALLISM

HOMOZYGOUSLY
HONEYMOONERS
HONEYMOONING
HONEYSUCKLED
HONEYSUCKLES
HOPELESSNESS
HORIZONTALLY
HORNET'S NESTS
HORN OF PLENTY
HORRENDOUSLY
HORRIBLENESS
HORRIFICALLY
HORRIFYINGLY
HORS DE COMBAT
HORS D'OEUVRES
HORSEMANSHIP
HORSE-TRADING
HORSEWHIPPED
HORSEWHIPPER
HORTICULTURE
HORTUS SICCUS
HOSPITALIZED
HOT-CROSS BUNS
HOT-GOSPELLER
HOUSE ARRESTS
HOUSEBREAKER
HOUSEFATHERS
HOUSEHOLDERS
HOUSE HUSBAND
HOUSEKEEPERS
HOUSEKEEPING
HOUSEMASTERS
HOUSEMOTHERS
HOUSE OF CARDS
HOUSE OF LORDS
HOUSEPARENTS
HOUSE PARTIES
HOUSE SPARROW
HOUSE-TO-HOUSE
HOUSE-TRAINED
HOUSEWARMING
HOUSEY-HOUSEY
HUBBLE-BUBBLE
HUDDERSFIELD
HUGGER-MUGGER
HUMANITARIAN
HUMANIZATION
HUMILIATIONS
HUMMINGBIRDS
HUMOROUSNESS
HUMPTY DUMPTY
HUNGER STRIKE
HURDY-GURDIES
HURSTMONCEUX
HUSEIN IBN-ALI
HYALOPLASMIC
HYBRIDIZABLE
HYDNOCARPATE
HYDRASTININE

HYDROCARBONS
HYDROCEPHALY
HYDROCHLORIC
HYDRODYNAMIC
HYDROFLUORIC
HYDROGENATOR
HYDROGEN BOMB
HYDROGRAPHER
HYDROGRAPHIC
HYDROKINETIC
HYDROLYSABLE
HYDROMEDUSAN
HYDROTHERAPY
HYGIENICALLY
HYPERMARKETS
HYPNOTICALLY
HYPOCHONDRIA
HYPOCRITICAL
HYPOTHETICAL
HYSTERECTOMY
HYSTERICALLY

I
ICE-CREAM SODA
ICHNEUMON FLY
ICHNOGRAPHIC
ICHNOLOGICAL
ICHTHYOLOGIC
ICHTHYOPHAGY
ICONOCLASTIC
ICONOGRAPHER
ICONOGRAPHIC
ICONOLATROUS
ICONOLOGICAL
IDEALIZATION
IDENTIFIABLE
IDENTITY CARD
IDEOLOOGICAL
IDIOMORPHISM
IDIOSYNCRASY
IDOLATROUSLY
IGNITABILITY
ILLEGALITIES
ILLEGIBILITY
ILLEGITIMACY
ILLEGITIMATE
ILLIBERALITY
ILLITERATELY
ILLOGICALITY
ILL-TREATMENT
ILLUMINATING
ILLUMINATION
ILLUMINATIVE
ILLUSIONISTS
ILLUSORINESS
ILLUSTRATING
ILLUSTRATION
ILLUSTRATIVE
ILLUSTRATORS

IMAGINATIONS	INACCURATELY	INCORPORABLE
IMBECILITIES	INACTIVATION	INCORPORATED
IMMACULATELY	INADEQUACIES	INCORPORATOR
IMMEASURABLE	INADEQUATELY	INCORPOREITY
IMMEASURABLY	INADMISSIBLE	INCORRIGIBLE
IMMEMORIABLE	INADMISSIBLY	INCORRIGIBLY
IMMERSIONISM	INADVERTENCE	INCRASSATION
IMMERSIONIST	INAPPLICABLE	INCREASINGLY
IMMETHODICAL	INAPPLICABLY	INCRETIONARY
IMMOBILIZING	INARTICULATE	INCRIMINATED
IMMODERATELY	INAUDIBILITY	INCRIMINATOR
IMMODERATION	INAUGURATING	INCRUSTATION
IMMORALITIES	INAUGURATION	INCUBATIONAL
IMMORTALIZED	INAUSPICIOUS	INCUMBENCIES
IMMORTALIZER	INCALCULABLE	INCURABILITY
IMMOVABILITY	INCALCULABLY	INDEBTEDNESS
IMMUNE SYSTEM	INCALESCENCE	INDECISIVELY
IMMUNIZATION	INCANDESCENT	INDECLINABLE
IMMUNOLOGIST	INCANTATIONS	INDECOROUSLY
IMMUTABILITY	INCAPABILITY	INDEFEASIBLE
IMPARTIALITY	INCAPACITATE	INDEFENSIBLE
IMPEDIMENTAL	INCARCERATED	INDEFENSIBLY
IMPENETRABLE	INCARCERATOR	INDEFINITELY
IMPENITENTLY	INCARNATIONS	INDEHISCENCE
IMPERATIVELY	INCAUTIOUSLY	INDELIBILITY
IMPERCEPTION	INCENDIARISM	INDELICATELY
IMPERCEPTIVE	INCESTUOUSLY	INDEMNIFYING
IMPERFECTION	INCIDENTALLY	INDENTATIONS
IMPERFECTIVE	INCINERATING	INDEPENDENCE
IMPERIALISTS	INCINERATION	INDEPENDENCY
IMPERISHABLE	INCINERATORS	INDEPENDENTS
IMPERMANENCE	INCISIVENESS	INDEX FINGERS
IMPERSONALLY	INCIVILITIES	INDIANAPOLIS
IMPERSONATED	INCLINATIONS	INDIAN SUMMER
IMPERSONATOR	INCLINOMETER	INDICATIVELY
IMPERTINENCE	INCOGNIZANCE	INDIFFERENCE
IMPETIGINOUS	INCOHERENTLY	INDIGENOUSLY
IMPLANTATION	INCOMMODIOUS	INDIGESTIBLE
IMPLEMENTING	INCOMMUTABLE	INDIGESTIBLY
IMPLICATIONS	INCOMPARABLE	INDIRECTNESS
IMPLICITNESS	INCOMPARABLY	INDISCIPLINE
IMPOLITENESS	INCOMPATIBLE	INDISCREETLY
IMPONDERABLE	INCOMPATIBLY	INDISCRETION
IMPORTATIONS	INCOMPETENCE	INDISPUTABLE
IMPOVERISHED	INCOMPETENTS	INDISPUTABLY
IMPOVERISHER	INCOMPLETELY	INDISSOLUBLE
IMPRECATIONS	INCOMPLIANCE	INDISSOLUBLY
IMPREGNATING	INCOMPUTABLE	INDISTINCTLY
IMPREGNATION	INCONCLUSIVE	INDIVIDUALLY
IMPRESSIONAL	INCONFORMITY	INDIVIDUATOR
IMPRESSIVELY	INCONSEQUENT	INDOCTRINATE
IMPRISONMENT	INCONSISTENT	INDO-EUROPEAN
IMPROPRIATOR	INCONSOLABLE	INDOLEACETIC
IMPROVEMENTS	INCONSOLABLY	INDOMETHACIN
IMPROVIDENCE	INCONSONANCE	INDRE-ET-LOIRE
IMPUTABILITY	INCONSUMABLE	INDUSTRIALLY
INACCESSIBLE	INCONTINENCE	INEFFABILITY
INACCESSIBLY	INCONVENIENT	INEFFACEABLE
INACCURACIES	INCOORDINATE	INEFFICIENCY

INELASTICITY	INQUISITIONS	INTERLACEDLY
INEQUALITIES	INSALIVATION	INTERLAMINAR
INERADICABLE	INSALUBRIOUS	INTERLARDING
INERADICABLY	INSCRIPTIONS	INTERLINKING
INERTIA REELS	INSECTICIDAL	INTERLOCKING
INESCUTCHEON	INSECTICIDES	INTERLOCUTOR
INESSENTIALS	INSECTIVORES	INTERMARRIED
INEXACTITUDE	INSEMINATING	INTERMEDIACY
INEXPEDIENCE	INSEMINATION	INTERMEDIARY
INEXPERIENCE	INSINUATIONS	INTERMEDIATE
INEXPERTNESS	INSOLUBILITY	INTERMINABLE
INEXPLICABLE	INSPECTINGLY	INTERMINABLY
INEXPLICABLY	INSPECTIONAL	INTERMINGLED
INEXPRESSIVE	INSPECTORATE	INTERMISSION
INEXTENSIBLE	INSPIRATIONS	INTERMISSIVE
INEXTIRPABLE	INSPIRITMENT	INTERMITTENT
INEXTRICABLE	INSTALLATION	INTERMIXABLE
INEXTRICABLY	INSTILLATION	INTERMIXTURE
INFANTICIDAL	INSTITUTIONS	INTERNALIZED
INFANTICIDES	INSTRUCTIBLE	INTERNUNCIAL
INFATUATEDLY	INSTRUCTIONS	INTEROCEPTOR
INFATUATIONS	INSTRUMENTAL	INTERPELLANT
INFECTIOUSLY	INSUFFERABLE	INTERPELLATE
INFELICITOUS	INSUFFERABLY	INTERPLEADER
INFESTATIONS	INSUFFICIENT	INTERPOLATED
INFIDELITIES	INSUFFLATION	INTERPOLATER
INFILTRATING	INSURABILITY	INTERPOSABLE
INFILTRATION	INSURGENCIES	INTERPRETERS
INFILTRATIVE	INSURRECTION	INTERPRETING
INFILTRATORS	INTELLECTION	INTERPRETIVE
INFLAMMATION	INTELLECTIVE	INTERREGNUMS
INFLAMMATORY	INTELLECTUAL	INTERROGATED
INFLATIONARY	INTELLIGENCE	INTERROGATOR
INFLATIONISM	INTELLIGIBLE	INTERRUPTING
INFLATIONIST	INTELLIGIBLY	INTERRUPTION
INFLECTIONAL	INTEMPERANCE	INTERRUPTIVE
INFLORESCENT	INTENSIFIERS	INTERSECTING
INFREQUENTLY	INTENSIFYING	INTERSECTION
INFRINGEMENT	INTERACTIONS	INTERSPATIAL
INFUNDIBULAR	INTERCEPTING	INTERSPERSED
INFUNDIBULUM	INTERCEPTION	INTERSTADIAL
INFUSIBILITY	INTERCEPTIVE	INTERSTELLAR
INGLORIOUSLY	INTERCEPTORS	INTERSTITIAL
INGRATIATING	INTERCESSION	INTERTEXTURE
INGRATIATION	INTERCESSORY	INTERTWINING
INHABITATION	INTERCHANGED	INTERVENTION
INHARMONIOUS	INTERCHANGES	INTERVIEWEES
INHERITANCES	INTERCONNECT	INTERVIEWERS
INHOSPITABLE	INTERCURRENT	INTERVIEWING
INHOSPITABLY	INTERDICTION	INTERVOCALIC
INHUMANITIES	INTERDICTIVE	INTERWEAVING
INIMICALNESS	INTERESTEDLY	INTIMIDATING
INIQUITOUSLY	INTERFERENCE	INTIMIDATION
INNOVATIONAL	INTERFERTILE	INTOLERANTLY
INNUTRITIOUS	INTERFLUVIAL	INTONATIONAL
INOBSERVANCE	INTERGLACIAL	INTOXICATING
INOCULATIONS	INTERJECTING	INTOXICATION
INORDINATELY	INTERJECTION	INTOXICATIVE
INOSCULATION	INTERJECTORY	INTRACARDIAC

INTRACRANIAL	IRRESOLVABLE	KNEE BREECHES
INTRANSIGENT	IRRESPECTIVE	KNIGHT-ERRANT
INTRANSITIVE	IRRESPIRABLE	KRISTIANSAND
INTRANUCLEAR	IRRESPONSIVE	
INTRAUTERINE	IRREVERENTLY	L
INTRIGUINGLY	IRREVERSIBLE	LABORATORIES
INTRODUCIBLE	IRREVERSIBLY	LABOUR MARKET
INTRODUCTION	IRRIGATIONAL	LABOUR OF LOVE
INTRODUCTORY	IRRITABILITY	LABOURSAVING
INTROJECTION	ISOCHROMATIC	LABYRINTHINE
INTROJECTIVE	ISODIAMETRIC	LACERABILITY
INTROVERSION	ISOLATIONISM	LACHRYMOSITY
INTROVERSIVE	ISOLATIONIST	LACTOPROTEIN
INTUITIONISM	ISOTOPICALLY	LADY'S FINGERS
INTUITIONIST	ITALIANESQUE	LADY'S-SLIPPER
INTUMESCENCE		LAISSEZ-FAIRE
INTUSSUSCEPT	J	LAMENTATIONS
INVAGINATION	JACK-IN-THE-BOX	LANDING CRAFT
INVALIDATING	JACK-O'-LANTERN	LANDING FIELD
INVALIDATION	JACK ROBINSON	LANDING STAGE
INVERTEBRACY	JACKSONVILLE	LANDING STRIP
INVERTEBRATE	JE NE SAIS QUOI	LANDLUBBERLY
INVERTED SNOB	JEOPARDIZING	LANGUISHMENT
INVESTIGABLE	JET-PROPELLED	LANGUOROUSLY
INVESTIGATED	JIGSAW PUZZLE	LANTERN-JAWED
INVESTIGATOR	JOHANNESBURG	LANTERNSLIDE
INVESTITURES	JOURNALISTIC	LAPIS LAZULIS
INVIGILATING	JUDICATORIAL	LARYNGOSCOPE
INVIGILATION	JUGULAR VEINS	LARYNGOSCOPY
INVIGILATORS	JUNIOR SCHOOL	LASCIVIOUSLY
INVIGORATING	JURISCONSULT	LASER PRINTER
INVIGORATION	JURISDICTION	LAST JUDGMENT
INVIGORATIVE	JURISDICTIVE	LATEENRIGGED
INVISIBILITY	JURISPRUDENT	LATICIFEROUS
INVOCATIONAL	JUSTIFYINGLY	LATINIZATION
INVOLUCELATE	JUVENESCENCE	LAUNDERETTES
INVOLUTIONAL		LAUNDRYWOMAN
INVULNERABLE	K	LAUREATESHIP
INVULNERABLY	KALEIDOSCOPE	LEADING LIGHT
INVULTUATION	KARYOKINESIS	LEAPFROGGING
IRASCIBILITY	KARYOKINETIC	LEASEHOLDERS
IRISH COFFEES	KARYOPLASMIC	LEATHERINESS
IRONING BOARD	KERATOGENOUS	LEAVE TAKINGS
IRRADIATIONS	KERATOPLASTY	LECTURESHIPS
IRRATIONALLY	KERB CRAWLERS	LEGALIZATION
IRREDEEMABLE	KERB CRAWLING	LEGIONNAIRES
IRREDEEMABLY	KEYNESIANISM	LEGISLATRESS
IRREFRAGABLE	KEY SIGNATURE	LEGISLATURES
IRREGULARITY	KILLER WHALES	LEGITIMATELY
IRRELEVANCES	KILOWATT-HOUR	LEGITIMATION
IRRELEVANTLY	KINAESTHESIA	LEGITIMATIZE
IRRELIEVABLE	KINAESTHETIC	LEGITIMISTIC
IRREMEDIABLE	KINDERGARTEN	LEGITIMIZING
IRREMEDIABLY	KING'S COUNSEL	LENTICELLATE
IRREMISSIBLE	KING'S ENGLISH	LEOPARD'S-BANE
IRRESISTIBLE	KITCHENETTES	LEPIDOPTERAN
IRRESISTIBLY	KLEPTOMANIAC	LEPIDOPTERON
IRRESOLUTELY	KLIPSPRINGER	LETTER OPENER
IRRESOLUTION	KNACKER'S YARD	LEUCOCYTOSIS

LEUCOCYTOTIC	LONELY HEARTS	MAGNIFICENCE
LEUCOPOIESIS	LONESOMENESS	MAGNILOQUENT
LEUCOPOIETIC	LONG-DISTANCE	MAGNITOGORSK
LEUCORRHOEAL	LONG DIVISION	MAGNUM OPUSES
LEVALLOISIAN	LONG-DRAWN-OUT	MAIDENLINESS
LEXICOGRAPHY	LONGITUDINAL	MAID OF HONOUR
LEXICOLOGIST	LONGSHOREMAN	MAIDSERVANTS
LIBERALISTIC	LONGSHOREMEN	MAILING LISTS
LIBERALITIES	LONG-STANDING	MAINE-ET-LOIRE
LIBERALIZING	LONG VACATION	MAINTAINABLE
LIBERAL PARTY	LONGWINDEDLY	MAITRE D'HOTEL
LIBERTARIANS	LOOKING GLASS	MAJESTICALLY
LIBERTICIDAL	LOOSE-JOINTED	MAJOR GENERAL
LIBIDINOUSLY	LOOSE-TONGUED	MALACOLOGIST
LICENSE PLATE	LOPHOPHORATE	MALAPROPISMS
LICENTIATION	LOQUACIOUSLY	MALEDICTIONS
LICENTIOUSLY	LOSS ADJUSTER	MALEFACTRESS
LIE DETECTORS	LOST PROPERTY	MALEVOLENTLY
LIFELESSNESS	LOT-ET-GARONNE	MALFEASANCES
LIGHT-HEARTED	LOUDSPEAKERS	MALFORMATION
LIGHTWEIGHTS	LOUGHBOROUGH	MALFUNCTIONS
LIMNOLOGICAL	LOVECHILDREN	MALIGNANCIES
LINE DRAWINGS	LOWER CLASSES	MALIMPRINTED
LINE-ENGRAVER	LOW-WATER MARK	MALLEABILITY
LINEN BASKETS	LUDWIGSHAFEN	MALNOURISHED
LINE PRINTERS	LUGGAGE RACKS	MALNUTRITION
LINE PRINTING	LUGUBRIOUSLY	MALOCCLUSION
LINES OF SIGHT	LUMBERJACKET	MALPRACTICES
LINGUA FRANCA	LUMINESCENCE	MALTESE CROSS
LIQUEFACIENT	LUNCHEONETTE	MALTREATMENT
LIQUEFACTION	LUSCIOUSNESS	MAMMALOGICAL
LIQUEFACTIVE	LYMPHANGITIC	MAN-ABOUT-TOWN
LIRIODENDRON	LYMPHANGITIS	MANAGERESSES
LISTLESSNESS	LYMPHOMATOID	MANAGERIALLY
LITERALISTIC	LYSERGIC ACID	MANDARIN DUCK
LITERARINESS		MANEUVERABLE
LITERATENESS	M	MANGEL-WURZEL
LITHOGRAPHED	MACHINATIONS	MANIFESTABLE
LITHOGRAPHER	MACHINE CODES	MANIPULATING
LITHOGRAPHIC	MACHINE TOOLS	MANIPULATION
LITTERATEURS	MACKINTOSHES	MANIPULATIVE
LITTLE FINGER	MACROCLIMATE	MANIPULATORY
LITTLE PEOPLE	MACROCYTOSIS	MANNERLINESS
LITURGICALLY	MACROGRAPHIC	MANOEUVRABLE
LIVERPUDLIAN	MACRONUCLEUS	MAN OF LETTERS
LIVER SAUSAGE	MACROPHYSICS	MANSLAUGHTER
LIVERY STABLE	MACROPTEROUS	MANTELPIECES
LIVING FOSSIL	MADEMOISELLE	MANUFACTURAL
LOCAL DERBIES	MAGIC LANTERN	MANUFACTURED
LOCALIZATION	MAGISTRACIES	MANUFACTURER
LOCAL OPTIONS	MAGISTRATURE	MARCASITICAL
LOCI CLASSICI	MAGNETICALLY	MARITIME ALPS
LOCKSMITHERY	MAGNETIC HEAD	MARKET FORCES
LOCKSTITCHES	MAGNETIC POLE	MARKET GARDEN
LODGING HOUSE	MAGNETIC TAPE	MARKETPLACES
LOGANBERRIES	MAGNETIZABLE	MARKET PRICES
LOGANIACEOUS	MAGNETOGRAPH	MARKSMANSHIP
LOGISTICALLY	MAGNETOMETER	MARLINESPIKE
LOMENTACEOUS	MAGNETOMETRY	MARRIAGEABLE

MARSEILLAISE	MEN OF LETTERS	MICROBALANCE
MARSHALL PLAN	MENSTRUATING	MICROBIOLOGY
MARSHMALLOWS	MENSTRUATION	MICROCEPHALY
MARSUPIALIAN	MEPHITICALLY	MICROCIRCUIT
MARVELLOUSLY	MERCANTILISM	MICROCLIMATE
MASQUERADERS	MERCANTILIST	MICROFILMING
MASQUERADING	MERCHANDISED	MICROGRAPHER
MASSOTHERAPY	MERCHANDISER	MICROGRAPHIC
MASS-PRODUCED	MERCHANTABLE	MICROHABITAT
MASS-PRODUCER	MERCHANT BANK	MICRONUCLEUS
MASTECTOMIES	MERCHANT NAVY	MICROPHYSICS
MASTER-AT-ARMS	MERCIFULNESS	MICROSCOPIST
MASTERLINESS	MERCURIALIZE	MICROSECONDS
MASTERMINDED	MERCY KILLING	MICROSEISMIC
MASTER OF ARTS	MERETRICIOUS	MICROSTOMOUS
MASTERPIECES	MERISTEMATIC	MIDDLE COURSE
MASTERSTROKE	MEROPLANKTON	MIDDLE FINGER
MASTIGOPHORE	MERRY-GO-ROUND	MIDDLE SCHOOL
MASTURBATING	MESENTERITIS	MIDDLEWEIGHT
MASTURBATION	MESENTERONIC	MIDSUMMER DAY
MATABELELAND	MESMERICALLY	MIDWESTERNER
MATERIALISTS	MESOCEPHALIC	MILITARISTIC
MATERIALIZED	MESOGASTRIUM	MILITARIZING
MATERIALIZER	MESOGNATHISM	MILLEFEUILLE
MATHEMATICAL	MESOGNATHOUS	MILLENARIANS
MATINEE IDOLS	MESOMORPHISM	MILLIONAIRES
MATRIARCHIES	MESOMORPHOUS	MILTON KEYNES
MATRICLINOUS	MESOPOTAMIAN	MIMEOGRAPHED
MATRICULATED	MESOTHORACIC	MIND-BOGGLING
MATRICULATOR	METAGALACTIC	MINDLESSNESS
MATRONLINESS	METAGNATHISM	MINE DETECTOR
MATTER-OF-FACT	METAGNATHOUS	MINERALOGIST
MATURATIONAL	METALANGUAGE	MINERAL WATER
MAXIMIZATION	METALLICALLY	MINESWEEPERS
MEALY-MOUTHED	METALLURGIST	MINESWEEPING
MEANDERINGLY	METALWORKERS	MINIATURISTS
MEANINGFULLY	METALWORKING	MINICOMPUTER
MEASUREMENTS	METAMORPHISM	MINIFICATION
MECAMYLAMINE	METAMORPHOSE	MINIMIZATION
MECHANICALLY	METAPHORICAL	MINIMUM WAGES
MEDALLIONIST	METAPHRASTIC	MINISTRATION
MEDICAMENTAL	METAPHYSICAL	MINISTRATIVE
MEDIOCRITIES	METASOMATISM	MINOR PLANETS
MEDITATINGLY	METATHORACIC	MINUTE STEAKS
MEDITATIVELY	METEMPIRICAL	MIRACLE PLAYS
MEETINGHOUSE	METEORICALLY	MIRROR IMAGES
MEGACEPHALIC	METEOROGRAPH	MIRTHFULNESS
MEGALOCARDIA	METHACRYLATE	MISADVENTURE
MEGALOMANIAC	METHODICALLY	MISALIGNMENT
MELANCHOLIAC	METHOTREXATE	MISALLIANCES
MELANCHOLILY	METICULOUSLY	MISANTHROPES
MELODRAMATIC	METONIC CYCLE	MISANTHROPIC
MELTING POINT	METROLOGICAL	MISAPPREHEND
MEMORABILITY	METROPOLISES	MISBEHAVIOUR
MEMORIALIZER	METROPOLITAN	MISCALCULATE
MEMORIZATION	METRORRHAGIA	MISCARRIAGES
MEN-ABOUT-TOWN	MEZZO-RELIEVO	MISCEGENETIC
MENAGE A TROIS	MEZZO-SOPRANO	MISCELLANIES
MENDACIOUSLY	MICROANALYST	MISCELLANIST

MISCONCEIVED	MONOGAMOUSLY	MUCILAGINOUS
MISCONCEIVER	MONOMANIACAL	MUCOPURULENT
MISCONDUCTED	MONOMETALLIC	MUDDLE-HEADED
MISCONSTRUED	MONOMETRICAL	MULLIGATAWNY
MISDEMEANANT	MONOMORPHISM	MULTICHANNEL
MISDEMEANOUR	MONOPETALOUS	MULTIFACETED
MISDIRECTING	MONOPHTHONGS	MULTIFARIOUS
MISDIRECTION	MONOPHYLETIC	MULTIFOLIATE
MISE-EN-SCENES	MONOPHYLLOUS	MULTIFORMITY
MISINFORMANT	MONOPOLISTIC	MULTIGRAVIDA
MISINFORMING	MONOPOLIZING	MULTILAMINAR
MISINTERPRET	MONOSEPALOUS	MULTILATERAL
MISJUDGEMENT	MONOSPERMOUS	MULTILINGUAL
MISJUDGMENTS	MONOSTROPHIC	MULTINUCLEAR
MISLEADINGLY	MONOSYLLABIC	MULTIPARTITE
MISPLACEMENT	MONOSYLLABLE	MULTIPLIABLE
MISPRONOUNCE	MONOTHEISTIC	MULTIPLICAND
MISQUOTATION	MONOTONOUSLY	MULTIPLICATE
MISREPORTING	MONOTRICHOUS	MULTIPLICITY
MISREPRESENT	MONTPARNASSE	MULTIPURPOSE
MISSING LINKS	MONUMENTALLY	MULTIVALENCY
MISSIONARIES	MOONLIGHTERS	MUNICIPALITY
MISSPELLINGS	MOONLIGHTING	MUNICIPALIZE
MISSTATEMENT	MORALITY PLAY	MUNIFICENTLY
MISTREATMENT	MORALIZATION	MUSEUM PIECES
MITHRIDATISM	MORALIZINGLY	MUSICAL BOXES
MIXED-ABILITY	MORBIFICALLY	MUSIC CENTRES
MIXED DOUBLES	MORNING COATS	MUSICIANSHIP
MIXED ECONOMY	MORNING DRESS	MUSICOLOGIST
MIXED FARMING	MORNING GLORY	MYRMECOPHILE
MNEMONICALLY	MORPHALLAXIS	MYSTERIOUSLY
MOBILIZATION	MORPHOLOGIES	MYSTERY PLAYS
MOCKINGBIRDS	MORPHOLOGIST	MYSTERY TOURS
MODERATENESS	MORRIS DANCER	MYSTIFYINGLY
MODIFICATION	MORRIS DANCES	MYTHOLOGICAL
MODIFICATORY	MORTARBOARDS	MYTHOLOGISTS
MODULABILITY	MORTGAGEABLE	MYTHOLOGIZER
MODUS VIVENDI	MORTIFYINGLY	MYXOMYCETOUS
MOHAVE DESERT	MORTISE LOCKS	
MOISTURIZING	MOSQUITO NETS	N
MOLLIFYINGLY	MOTHERLINESS	NAIL SCISSORS
MOLLYCODDLED	MOTHER NATURE	NAMBY-PAMBIES
MONADELPHOUS	MOTHERS-IN-LAW	NAMEDROPPERS
MONARCHISTIC	MOTHER TONGUE	NAMEDROPPING
MONASTICALLY	MOTHPROOFING	NANOPLANKTON
MONETIZATION	MOTIONLESSLY	NANSEN BOTTLE
MONEYCHANGER	MOTIVATIONAL	NARCISSISTIC
MONEY-GRUBBER	MOTORCYCLIST	NARCOTICALLY
MONEYLENDERS	MOTORIZATION	NARROW GAUGES
MONEYLENDING	MOTOR SCOOTER	NARROW-MINDED
MONEY-SPINNER	MOULDABILITY	NARROW SQUEAK
MONISTICALLY	MOUNTAINEERS	NASALIZATION
MONKEY-PUZZLE	MOUNTAIN LION	NATIONAL DEBT
MONKEY WRENCH	MOUNTAINSIDE	NATIONALISTS
MONOCHLORIDE	MOUNTAINTOPS	NATIONALIZED
MONOCHROMIST	MOURNFULNESS	NATIONAL PARK
MONODRAMATIC	MOUTHBROODER	NATION STATES
MONOFILAMENT	MOUTH-TO-MOUTH	NATIVITY PLAY
MONOGAMISTIC	MOVABLE FEAST	NATURALISTIC

NATURALIZING	NITROBENZENE	NYCTITROPISM
NATUROPATHIC	NITROMETHANE	NYMPHOLEPTIC
NAUSEATINGLY	NO-CLAIM BONUS	NYMPHOMANIAC
NAUSEOUSNESS	NOCTAMBULISM	
NAUTICAL MILE	NOCTAMBULIST	O
NAVIGABILITY	NOCTILUCENCE	OBERAMMERGAU
NAVIGATIONAL	NOCTURNALITY	OBITER DICTUM
NEANDERTHALS	NOLENS VOLENS	OBJECT LESSON
NEBULIZATION	NOMENCLATURE	OBLANCEOLATE
NEBULOUSNESS	NOMINALISTIC	OBLATE SPHERE
NECESSITATED	NONAGENARIAN	OBLIGATIONAL
NECKERCHIEFS	NONALIGNMENT	OBLIGATORILY
NECROLOGICAL	NONCHALANTLY	OBLITERATING
NECROMANCERS	NONCOMBATANT	OBLITERATION
NECROPHILIAC	NONCOMMITTAL	OBLITERATIVE
NECROPHILISM	NONCONDUCTOR	OBSCURANTISM
NECROPOLISES	NONCORRODING	OBSCURANTIST
NEEDLESSNESS	NONESSENTIAL	OBSEQUIOUSLY
NEGATIVENESS	NONEXISTENCE	OBSERVATIONS
NEGATIVE POLE	NONEXPLOSIVE	OBSOLESCENCE
NEGATIVISTIC	NONFICTIONAL	OBSOLETENESS
NEGLECTFULLY	NONFLAMMABLE	OBSTETRICIAN
NEGOTIATIONS	NONIDENTICAL	OBSTREPEROUS
NEIGHBOURING	NONIDIOMATIC	OBSTRUCTIONS
NEMATOCYSTIC	NONMALIGNANT	OCCASIONALLY
NEOANTHROPIC	NONOPERATIVE	OCCUPATIONAL
NEOCLASSICAL	NONPOISONOUS	OCEANOGRAPHY
NEOLOGICALLY	NONPOLITICAL	OCTOGENARIAN
NEOTERICALLY	NONRESIDENCE	OCTOSYLLABIC
NEPHELOMETER	NONRESIDENTS	OCTOSYLLABLE
NEPHOLOGICAL	NONRESISTANT	ODONTOGRAPHY
NERVE CENTRES	NONSCHEDULED	ODONTOLOGIST
NERVE-RACKING	NONSECTARIAN	ODONTOPHORAL
NETHERLANDER	NON SEQUITURS	OESOPHAGUSES
NETTLE RASHES	NONSTRATEGIC	OFFICE BLOCKS
NEURASTHENIA	NONTECHNICAL	OFFICEHOLDER
NEURASTHENIC	NONVIOLENTLY	OFF-THE-RECORD
NEUROLOGICAL	NORTHEASTERN	OIL PAINTINGS
NEUROLOGISTS	NORTHEASTERS	OLD-FASHIONED
NEUROPTEROUS	NORTHERNMOST	OLD SCHOOL TIE
NEUROSURGEON	NORTHUMBRIAN	OLD TESTAMENT
NEUROSURGERY	NORTHWESTERN	OLD WIVES' TALE
NEUROTICALLY	NOTEWORTHILY	OLEORESINOUS
NEUROTOMICAL	NOTICE BOARDS	OLIGOTROPHIC
NEUTRALIZING	NOTIFICATION	OLYMPIC GAMES
NEUTRON BOMBS	NOURISHINGLY	OMNIPRESENCE
NEVERTHELESS	NOUVEAU RICHE	ONEIROCRITIC
NEW BRUNSWICK	NOVOKUZNETSK	ONE-SIDEDNESS
NEWFOUNDLAND	NUBIAN DESERT	ONE-TRACK MIND
NEWS AGENCIES	NUCLEOPHILIC	ONE-UPMANSHIP
NEWSPAPERMAN	NUMBERPLATES	ONOMASIOLOGY
NEW TESTAMENT	NUMEROUSNESS	ONOMATOPOEIA
NEW ZEALANDER	NUMINOUSNESS	ONOMATOPOEIC
NICOTINAMIDE	NUMISMATISTS	ONYCHOPHORAN
NIDIFICATION	NURSERY RHYME	OOPHORECTOMY
NIETZSCHEISM	NURSING HOMES	OPEN-HANDEDLY
NIGHTDRESSES	NUTRITIONIST	OPENING TIMES
NIGHTINGALES	NUTRITIOUSLY	OPEN-MINDEDLY
NIMBOSTRATUS	NUTS AND BOLTS	OPEN SANDWICH

OPEN VERDICTS	OUTBUILDINGS	PALEOGRAPHER
OPERA GLASSES	OUTDISTANCED	PALEONTOLOGY
OPERATICALLY	OUTGENERALED	PALETTE KNIFE
OPHIOLOGICAL	OUTLANDISHLY	PALINGENESIS
OPHTHALMITIS	OUTMANOEUVRE	PALINGENETIC
OPINION POLLS	OUTNUMBERING	PALPITATIONS
OPPORTUNISTS	OUTRAGEOUSLY	PALYNOLOGIST
OPPOSABILITY	OUTRIVALLING	PAMPHLETEERS
OPPOSITENESS	OUTSTRETCHED	PANCAKE ROLLS
OPPOSITIONAL	OUTSTRIPPING	PANCHROMATIC
OPPRESSINGLY	OVERBALANCED	PANDANACEOUS
OPPRESSIVELY	OVERBURDENED	PANDEMONIUMS
OPSONIZATION	OVERCAPACITY	PANHELLENISM
OPTIMIZATION	OVERCAUTIOUS	PANHELLENIST
ORATORICALLY	OVERCHARGING	PANOPTICALLY
ORBICULARITY	OVERCLOUDING	PANTECHNICON
ORCHESTRA PIT	OVERCRITICAL	PANTISOCRACY
ORCHESTRATED	OVERCROPPING	PANTOGRAPHER
ORCHIDACEOUS	OVERCROWDING	PANTOGRAPHIC
ORDINARINESS	OVERDRESSING	PAPERHANGERS
ORGAN GRINDER	OVEREMPHATIC	PAPERHANGING
ORGANICISTIC	OVERESTIMATE	PAPERWEIGHTS
ORGANIZATION	OVEREXPOSING	PAPULIFEROUS
ORGANOGRAPHY	OVERGENEROUS	PARABOLOIDAL
ORGANOLEPTIC	OVERINDULGED	PARACHRONISM
ORGANOLOGIST	OVERMASTERED	PARACHUTISTS
ORIEL WINDOWS	OVERPOPULATE	PARADE GROUND
ORIENTALISTS	OVERPOWERING	PARADIGMATIC
ORIENTATIONS	OVERREACHING	PARADISIACAL
ORIENTEERING	OVERREACTING	PARAESTHESIA
ORNAMENTALLY	OVERREACTION	PARAESTHETIC
OROGENICALLY	OVERSHADOWED	PARAHYDROGEN
OROLOGICALLY	OVERSHOOTING	PARALANGUAGE
ORTHOCEPHALY	OVERSIMPLIFY	PARALLEL BARS
ORTHODONTICS	OVERSLEEPING	PARALLELISMS
ORTHOGENESIS	OVERSTEPPING	PARALLELLING
ORTHOGENETIC	OVERSTOCKING	PARALOGISTIC
ORTHOGRAPHER	OVERTHROWING	PARALYSATION
ORTHOGRAPHIC	OVERWHELMING	PARAMAGNETIC
ORTHOMORPHIC	OWNER-DRIVERS	PARAMILITARY
ORTHOPAEDICS	OXYACETYLENE	PARAMORPHISM
ORTHOPAEDIST	OXYGENIZABLE	PARAPHRASING
ORTHOPTEROUS		PARAPHRASTIC
ORTHORHOMBIC	P	PARASITICIDE
ORTHOTROPISM	PACIFICATION	PARASITOLOGY
ORTHOTROPOUS	PACKAGE DEALS	PARATHYROIDS
OSCILLATIONS	PACKAGE TOURS	PARATROOPERS
OSCILLOGRAPH	PACKING CASES	PARENTHESIZE
OSCILLOSCOPE	PADDLING POOL	PARISH CLERKS
OSSIFICATION	PAEDOGENESIS	PARISHIONERS
OSTENTATIOUS	PAEDOGENETIC	PARISYLLABIC
OSTEOBLASTIC	PAEDOLOGICAL	PARKING LIGHT
OSTEOCLASTIC	PAGANIZATION	PARKING METER
OSTEOLOGICAL	PAINTBRUSHES	PARLOUR GAMES
OSTEOMALACIA	PALAEOBOTANY	PAROCHIALISM
OSTEOPLASTIC	PALAEOGRAPHY	PARSIMONIOUS
OSTRACIZABLE	PALAEOLITHIC	PARSON'S NOSES
OTHERWORLDLY	PALATABILITY	PART EXCHANGE
OUTBALANCING	PALATIALNESS	PARTIALITIES

PARTICIPANTS	PERFIDIOUSLY	PETROGRAPHIC
PARTICIPATED	PERFOLIATION	PETROLOGICAL
PARTICIPATOR	PERFORATIONS	PETROLOGISTS
PARTICULARLY	PERFORMANCES	PETROZAVODSK
PARTING SHOTS	PERFORMATIVE	PETTIFOGGING
PARTISANSHIP	PERICARDITIC	PETTY LARCENY
PARTITIONING	PERICARDITIS	PETTY OFFICER
PARTNERSHIPS	PERICYNTHION	PHAGOCYTOSIS
PART OF SPEECH	PERILOUSNESS	PHANEROGAMIC
PARTY POOPERS	PERIMORPHISM	PHANEROPHYTE
PASQUEFLOWER	PERINEPHRIUM	PHARMACOLOGY
PASSE-PARTOUT	PERINEURITIC	PHARYNGOLOGY
PASSIONATELY	PERINEURITIS	PHARYNGOTOMY
PASSION PLAYS	PERIODICALLY	PHELLODERMAL
PASTEURIZING	PERIODONTICS	PHENANTHRENE
PAST PERFECTS	PERIOD PIECES	PHENOLOGICAL
PATCH POCKETS	PERIONYCHIUM	PHENOMENALLY
PATERNALISTS	PERIPHERALLY	PHI BETA KAPPA
PATERNOSTERS	PERIPHRASTIC	PHILADELPHIA
PATHETICALLY	PERITRICHOUS	PHILADELPHUS
PATHOGENESIS	PERMANENT WAY	PHILANDERERS
PATHOGENETIC	PERMANGANATE	PHILANDERING
PATHOLOGICAL	PERMEABILITY	PHILANTHROPY
PATHOLOGISTS	PERMISSIVELY	PHILATELISTS
PATRIARCHATE	PERMITTIVITY	PHILHARMONIC
PATRIARCHIES	PERMUTATIONS	PHILISTINISM
PATRICLINOUS	PERNICIOUSLY	PHILODENDRON
PATROL WAGONS	PERPETRATING	PHILOLOGICAL
PATRON SAINTS	PERPETRATION	PHILOLOGISTS
PAVING STONES	PERPETRATORS	PHILOSOPHERS
PAY ENVELOPES	PERPETUATING	PHILOSOPHIES
PEACEFULNESS	PERPETUATION	PHILOSOPHIZE
PEANUT BUTTER	PERPETUITIES	PHLEBOTOMIST
PEASE PUDDING	PERPLEXITIES	PHONEMICALLY
PECCADILLOES	PERSECUTIONS	PHONE-TAPPING
PECKING ORDER	PERSEVERANCE	PHONETICALLY
PEDANTICALLY	PERSISTENTLY	PHONETICIANS
PEDIATRICIAN	PERSONA GRATA	PHONOGRAPHER
PEJORATIVELY	PERSONALIZED	PHONOLOGICAL
PENALIZATION	PERSONIFYING	PHONOLOGISTS
PENALTY AREAS	PERSPECTIVES	PHONOTACTICS
PENDENTE LITE	PERSPICACITY	PHOSPHATURIA
PENITENTIARY	PERSPIRATION	PHOSPHATURIC
PENNSYLVANIA	PERSPIRATORY	PHOSPHOLIPID
PENNULTIMATE	PERSPIRINGLY	PHOSPHORESCE
PENNY PINCHER	PERSUASIVELY	PHOSPHORITIC
PENNY WHISTLE	PERTINACIOUS	PHOTOACTINIC
PENTARCHICAL	PERTURBATION	PHOTOCATHODE
PEPTIC ULCERS	PERTURBINGLY	PHOTOCHEMIST
PERADVENTURE	PERVERSENESS	PHOTOCOMPOSE
PERAMBULATED	PERVERSITIES	PHOTOCOPIERS
PERAMBULATOR	PERVIOUSNESS	PHOTOCOPYING
PERCEPTIONAL	PESTILENTIAL	PHOTOCURRENT
PERCEPTIVELY	PETALIFEROUS	PHOTODYNAMIC
PERCEPTIVITY	PETERBOROUGH	PHOTOENGRAVE
PERCOLATIONS	PETIT LARCENY	PHOTOGEOLOGY
PERCUTANEOUS	PETRIFACTION	PHOTOGRAPHED
PEREGRINATOR	PETRODOLLARS	PHOTOGRAPHER
PEREMPTORILY	PETROGRAPHER	PHOTOGRAPHIC

PHOTOGRAVURE
PHOTOKINESIS
PHOTOKINETIC
PHOTOMETRIST
PHOTOMONTAGE
PHOTONEUTRON
PHOTONUCLEAR
PHOTOPHILOUS
PHOTOPOLYMER
PHOTOSPHERIC
PHOTOSTATTED
PHOTOTHERAPY
PHOTOTHERMIC
PHOTOTROPISM
PHRASAL VERBS
PHRASEOGRAPH
PHRENOLOGIST
PHYCOLOGICAL
PHYLETICALLY
PHYSICALNESS
PHYSIOCRATIC
PHYSIOGNOMIC
PHYSIOGRAPHY
PHYSIOLOGIES
PHYSIOLOGIST
PHYSOSTOMOUS
PHYTOGENESIS
PHYTOGENETIC
PHYTOHORMONE
PHYTOPHAGOUS
PICCANINNIES
PICKERELWEED
PICTURE BOOKS
PICTURE CARDS
PIECE OF EIGHT
PIECES OF WORK
PIGEONHOLING
PIGMENTATION
PILOT OFFICER
PINEAL GLANDS
PINK ELEPHANT
PIPE CLEANERS
PIPES OF PEACE
PISCICULTURE
PITCHFORKING
PITIABLENESS
PITILESSNESS
PITTER-PATTER
PLACENTATION
PLACE SETTING
PLAGIARISTIC
PLAGIARIZING
PLAGIOCLIMAX
PLAIN-CLOTHES
PLAIN SAILING
PLANETARIUMS
PLANETESIMAL
PLANISPHERIC
PLANO-CONCAVE

PLANOGRAPHIC
PLASTERBOARD
PLASTER CASTS
PLASTOMETRIC
PLATONICALLY
PLAUSIBILITY
PLAYER PIANOS
PLAYING CARDS
PLAYING FIELD
PLAYS ON WORDS
PLEASANTNESS
PLEASANTRIES
PLEASINGNESS
PLEIOTROPISM
PLEOMORPHISM
PLIMSOLL LINE
PLODDINGNESS
PLOUGHSHARES
PLUMBIFEROUS
PLUM PUDDINGS
PLUTOCRACIES
PLUVIOMETRIC
PNEUMOCOCCUS
PNEUMOTHORAX
POET LAUREATE
POINTILLISTS
POINT OF ORDER
POINTS OF VIEW
POINT-TO-POINT
POLARIMETRIC
POLARIZATION
POLAROGRAPHY
POLE POSITION
POLE VAULTERS
POLE VAULTING
POLICE STATES
POLICYHOLDER
POLITICIZING
POLLEN COUNTS
POLLING BOOTH
POLTERGEISTS
POLYANTHUSES
POLYCENTRISM
POLYCHAETOUS
POLYCYTHEMIA
POLYEMBRYONY
POLYETHYLENE
POLYISOPRENE
POLYMORPHISM
POLYMORPHOUS
POLYPETALOUS
POLYPHYLETIC
POLYPHYODONT
POLYRHYTHMIC
POLYSEPALOUS
POLYSULPHIDE
POLYSYLLABIC
POLYSYLLABLE
POLYSYNDETON

POLYTECHNICS
POLYTHEISTIC
POLYTONALIST
POLYTONALITY
POLYURETHANE
POMEGRANATES
PONS ASINORUM
PONTIFICATED
PONTIFICATES
PONY-TREKKING
POOR RELATION
POOR-SPIRITED
POPOCATEPETL
POPULARIZING
POPULOUSNESS
PORNOGRAPHER
PORNOGRAPHIC
PORPHYROPSIN
PORT-AU-PRINCE
PORTCULLISES
PORTE-COCHERE
PORTENTOUSLY
PORTERHOUSES
PORT HARCOURT
PORTMANTEAUS
PORTMANTEAUX
PORTS OF ENTRY
POSITIVENESS
POSITIVE POLE
POSITIVISTIC
POSSESSIVELY
POSTAGE STAMP
POSTAL ORDERS
POSTDILUVIAL
POSTDILUVIAN
POSTDOCTORAL
POSTER COLOUR
POSTER PAINTS
POSTGRADUATE
POSTHUMOUSLY
POSTMERIDIAN
POST MERIDIEM
POSTPONEMENT
POSTPOSITION
POSTPOSITIVE
POSTPRANDIAL
POTATO BEETLE
POTATO CRISPS
POTENTIALITY
POTTER'S WHEEL
POTTING SHEDS
POTTY-TRAINED
POVERTY TRAPS
POWER BROKERS
POWERFULNESS
POWER STATION
PRACTICALITY
PRACTITIONER
PRAGMATISTIC

PRAISEWORTHY	PREOCCUPYING	PROBATIONARY
PRASEODYMIUM	PREORDAINING	PROBATIONERS
PRAYER WHEELS	PREPARATIONS	PROBOSCIDEAN
PREAMPLIFIER	PREPAREDNESS	PROCATHEDRAL
PREARRANGING	PREPONDERANT	PROCESSIONAL
PREBENDARIES	PREPONDERATE	PROCLAMATION
PRECARIOUSLY	PREPOSITIONS	PROCLIVITIES
PRECEDENTIAL	PREPOSSESSED	PROCONSULATE
PRECENTORIAL	PREPOSTEROUS	PROCTOLOGIST
PRECEPTORATE	PRERECORDING	PRODIGIOUSLY
PRECEPTORIAL	PREREQUISITE	PRODUCTIONAL
PRECESSIONAL	PREROGATIVES	PRODUCTIVELY
PRECIOUSNESS	PRESBYTERATE	PRODUCTIVITY
PRECIPITANCE	PRESBYTERIAL	PROFANATIONS
PRECIPITATED	PRESBYTERIAN	PROFESSIONAL
PRECIPITATES	PRESBYTERIES	PROFESSORIAL
PRECIPITATOR	PRESCRIPTION	PROFICIENTLY
PRECISIANISM	PRESCRIPTIVE	PROFITEERING
PRECISIONISM	PRESENTATION	PROFITLESSLY
PRECISIONIST	PRESENTATIVE	PROFIT MARGIN
PRECOCIOUSLY	PRESENTIMENT	PROFOUNDNESS
PRECOGNITION	PRESERVATION	PROFUNDITIES
PRECOGNITIVE	PRESERVATIVE	PROGESTERONE
PRECONCEIVED	PRESIDENCIES	PROGRAMMABLE
PRECONDITION	PRESIDENTIAL	PROGRAMMATIC
PRECONSCIOUS	PRESS CUTTING	PROGRESSIONS
PREDECEASING	PRESS GALLERY	PROGRESSIVES
PREDECESSORS	PRESSGANGING	PROHIBITIONS
PREDESTINATE	PRESSINGNESS	PROJECTIONAL
PREDESTINING	PRESS RELEASE	PROLEGOMENAL
PREDETERMINE	PRESSURIZING	PROLEGOMENON
PREDICAMENTS	PRESUMPTIONS	PROLETARIANS
PREDICTIVELY	PRESUMPTUOUS	PROLIFERATED
PREDIGESTING	PRESUPPOSING	PROLIFICALLY
PREDIGESTION	PRETTY-PRETTY	PROLIFICNESS
PREDILECTION	PREVAILINGLY	PROLONGATION
PREDISPOSING	PREVARICATED	PROMISED LAND
PREDOMINANCE	PREVARICATOR	PROMONTORIES
PREDOMINATED	PREVENTIVELY	PROMULGATING
PREDOMINATOR	PREVIOUSNESS	PROMULGATION
PRE-ECLAMPSIA	PRICKLY PEARS	PROMULGATORS
PRE-EMINENTLY	PRIDE OF PLACE	PRONOMINALLY
PRE-EMPTIVELY	PRIESTLINESS	PRONOUNCEDLY
PRE-EXISTENCE	PRIEST-RIDDEN	PROOFREADERS
PREFABRICATE	PRIGGISHNESS	PROOFREADING
PREFECTORIAL	PRIME NUMBERS	PROPAEDEUTIC
PREFERENTIAL	PRIMOGENITOR	PROPAGANDISM
PREFORMATION	PRIMORDIALLY	PROPAGANDIST
PREGNABILITY	PRIMULACEOUS	PROPAGANDIZE
PREJUDGEMENT	PRIMUM MOBILE	PROPENSITIES
PREJUDGMENTS	PRINCELINESS	PROPHESIABLE
PREMARITALLY	PRINCIPAL BOY	PROPHYLACTIC
PREMAXILLARY	PRINCIPALITY	PROPITIATING
PREMEDITATED	PRINTABILITY	PROPITIATION
PREMEDITATOR	PRIORITIZING	PROPITIATIVE
PREMENSTRUAL	PRISMATOIDAL	PROPITIATORY
PREMIERSHIPS	PRIVATE PARTS	PROPITIOUSLY
PREMIUM BONDS	PRIVY COUNCIL	PROPORTIONAL
PREMONITIONS	PRIZEFIGHTER	PROPORTIONED

PROPOSITIONS
PROROGATIONS
PROSCRIPTION
PROSCRIPTIVE
PROSECUTABLE
PROSECUTIONS
PROSELYTIZED
PROSELYTIZER
PROSOPOPOEIA
PROSPECTUSES
PROSPEROUSLY
PROSTITUTING
PROSTITUTION
PROSTRATIONS
PROTACTINIUM
PROTAGONISTS
PROTECTIVELY
PROTECTORATE
PROTESTATION
PROTESTINGLY
PROTHALAMION
PROTHONOTARY
PROTOHISTORY
PROTOMORPHIC
PROTOPLASMIC
PROTOPLASTIC
PROTOSEMITIC
PROTOTHERIAN
PROTOTROPHIC
PROTOZOOLOGY
PROTRACTEDLY
PROTUBERANCE
PROVERBIALLY
PROVIDENTIAL
PROVINCIALLY
PROVISIONING
PROVOCATIONS
PRUDENTIALLY
PRUSSIAN BLUE
PSEPHOLOGIST
PSEUDONYMITY
PSEUDONYMOUS
PSEUDOPODIUM
PSYCHIATRIST
PSYCHOACTIVE
PSYCHOBABBLE
PSYCHOGNOSIS
PSYCHOGRAPHY
PSYCHOLOGIES
PSYCHOLOGISM
PSYCHOLOGIST
PSYCHOLOGIZE
PSYCHOMETRIC
PSYCHOPATHIC
PSYCHOSEXUAL
PSYCHOSOCIAL
PSYCHROMETER
PTERIDOPHYTE
PTERIDOSPERM

PTERODACTYLS
PUBLICATIONS
PUBLIC HOUSES
PUBLIC SCHOOL
PUBLIC SECTOR
PUBLIC SPIRIT
PUGNACIOUSLY
PULVERULENCE
PUMPERNICKEL
PUNCHED CARDS
PUNITIVENESS
PURIFICATION
PURIFICATORY
PURISTICALLY
PURPLE HEARTS
PURPOSE-BUILT
PURPOSEFULLY
PURSE STRINGS
PUSSYFOOTING
PUSSY WILLOWS
PUTREFACTION
PUTREFACTIVE
PYELOGRAPHIC
PYRIDOXAMINE
PYROCATECHOL
PYROCHEMICAL
PYROELECTRIC
PYROGNOSTICS
PYROLIGNEOUS
PYROMANIACAL
PYROMORPHITE
PYROPHYLLITE
PYROSULPHATE
PYROTECHNICS

Q
QUADRAGESIMA
QUADRANGULAR
QUADRAPHONIC
QUADRILLIONS
QUADRINOMIAL
QUADRIPLEGIA
QUADRIPLEGIC
QUADRIVALENT
QUADRUMANOUS
QUALIFYINGLY
QUANTIFIABLE
QUANTITATIVE
QᵁANTIZATION
QUANTUM LEAPS
QUAQUAVERSAL
QUARANTINING
QUARTER-BOUND
QUARTERFINAL
QUARTERLIGHT
QUARTER NOTES
QUARTERSTAFF
QUEEN CONSORT
QUEEN MOTHERS

QUELQUE CHOSE
QUESTIONABLE
QUESTIONABLY
QUESTION MARK
QUESTION TAGS
QUESTION TIME
QUEUE-JUMPERS
QUEUE-JUMPING
QUINDECAPLET
QUINQUENNIAL
QUINQUENNIUM
QUINTESSENCE
QUIXOTICALLY
QUIZZICALITY

R
RABBIT WARREN
RABBLE-ROUSER
RACE MEETINGS
RACEMIZATION
RADICALISTIC
RADIO BEACONS
RADIOBIOLOGY
RADIOCHEMIST
RADIOELEMENT
RADIOGRAPHER
RADIOGRAPHIC
RADIOISOTOPE
RADIOLOGICAL
RADIOLOGISTS
RADIONUCLIDE
RADIOTHERAPY
RAISON D'ETRES
RALLENTANDOS
RAMBUNCTIOUS
RAMENTACEOUS
RAMIFICATION
RANGE FINDERS
RANKINE SCALE
RAPHAELESQUE
RAPSCALLIONS
RASTAFARIANS
RATIFICATION
RATIOCINATOR
RATIONALISTS
RATIONALIZED
RATIONALIZER
RATTLESNAKES
RAVENOUSNESS
RAYLEIGH DISC
RAZZLE-DAZZLE
REACH-ME-DOWNS
REACTIVATING
REACTIVATION
REACTIVENESS
READDRESSING
READJUSTABLE
READJUSTMENT
REAFFIRMANCE

REAFFORESTED	REDUCIBILITY	REPARABILITY
REALIGNMENTS	REDUNDANCIES	REPATRIATING
REALIZATIONS	REDUPLICATED	REPATRIATION
REALLOCATION	REEFER JACKET	REPERCUSSION
REAL PROPERTY	RE-EMPLOYMENT	REPERCUSSIVE
REAPPEARANCE	RE-EXAMINABLE	REPLACEMENTS
REAPPRAISALS	REFLATIONARY	REPLENISHING
REAPPRAISING	REFLECTINGLY	REPLICATIONS
REAR ADMIRALS	REFLECTIONAL	REPOSITORIES
REASSURANCES	REFORMATIONS	REPOSSESSING
REASSURINGLY	REFRACTIONAL	REPOSSESSION
REAUMUR SCALE	REFRACTORILY	REPREHENDING
REBELLIOUSLY	REFRESHINGLY	REPREHENSION
RECALCITRANT	REFRESHMENTS	REPREHENSIVE
RECALESCENCE	REFRIGERANTS	REPREHENSORY
RECANTATIONS	REFRIGERATED	REPRESENTING
RECAPITALIZE	REFRIGERATOR	REPRESSIVELY
RECAPITULATE	REFURBISHING	REPRIMANDING
RECEIVERSHIP	REFUTABILITY	REPROACHABLE
RECEPTIONIST	REGENERATING	REPROACHABLY
RECESSIONALS	REGENERATION	REPROCESSING
RECIDIVISTIC	REGENERATIVE	REPRODUCIBLE
RECIPROCALLY	REGISTRATION	REPRODUCTION
RECIPROCATED	REGULARIZING	REPRODUCTIVE
RECIPROCATOR	REGURGITATED	REPROGRAPHIC
RECKLESSNESS	REHABILITATE	REPUTABILITY
RECOGNITIONS	REIMBURSABLE	REQUEST STOPS
RECOGNIZABLE	REIMPOSITION	REQUIREMENTS
RECOGNIZABLY	REIMPRESSION	REQUISITIONS
RECOGNIZANCE	REINCARNATED	RESCHEDULING
RECOLLECTING	REINVESTMENT	RESEARCHABLE
RECOLLECTION	REITERATIONS	RESEMBLANCES
RECOLLECTIVE	REJUVENATING	RESERVATIONS
RECOMMENDING	REJUVENATION	RESERVEDNESS
RECOMMITMENT	RELATIONSHIP	RESETTLEMENT
RECOMPENSING	RELATIVISTIC	RESIDENTIARY
RECONCILABLE	RELENTLESSLY	RESIDENTSHIP
RECONCILABLY	RELINQUISHED	RESIGNATIONS
RECONNOITRED	RELINQUISHER	RESIGNEDNESS
RECONNOITRER	REMAINDERING	RESINIFEROUS
RECONSIDERED	REMAINDERMAN	RESINOUSNESS
RECONSTITUTE	REMEMBRANCER	RESOLUBILITY
RECONVERSION	REMEMBRANCES	RESOLUTENESS
RECORD PLAYER	REMINISCENCE	RESOLUTIONER
RECREATIONAL	REMONSTRANCE	RESOLVEDNESS
RECRIMINATED	REMONSTRATED	RESOUNDINGLY
RECRIMINATOR	REMONSTRATOR	RESOURCELESS
RECUPERATING	REMORSEFULLY	RESPECTFULLY
RECUPERATION	REMOVABILITY	RESPECTIVELY
RECUPERATIVE	REMUNERATING	RESPLENDENCE
RED BLOOD CELL	REMUNERATION	RESPONSIVELY
REDECORATING	REMUNERATIVE	RESTATEMENTS
REDEMANDABLE	RENAISSANCES	RESTAURATEUR
REDEMPTIONAL	RENEGOTIABLE	RESTLESSNESS
REDEPLOYMENT	RENEWABILITY	RESTORATIONS
REDEVELOPING	RENOUNCEMENT	RESTORATIVES
REDINTEGRATE	RENUNCIATION	RESTRAINABLE
REDISTRIBUTE	RENUNCIATIVE	RESTRAINEDLY
RED-LETTER DAY	REORGANIZING	RESTRICTEDLY

RESTRICTIONS	RIGHT-HAND MEN	SAILING BOATS
RESTRUCTURED	RIGHTS ISSUES	SAINT-ETIENNE
RESUPINATION	RIGHT-WINGERS	SALAMANDRINE
RESURRECTING	RIGOROUSNESS	SALESMANSHIP
RESURRECTION	RING-STREAKED	SALES PITCHES
RESUSCITABLE	RIO DE JANEIRO	SALIFICATION
RESUSCITATED	ROAD MANAGERS	SALINOMETRIC
RESUSCITATOR	ROCKING CHAIR	SALMON TROUTS
RETICULATION	ROCKING HORSE	SALPIGLOSSIS
RETINOSCOPIC	ROLLER BLINDS	SALUTARINESS
RETRACTILITY	ROLLER SKATED	SALUTATORILY
RETRENCHABLE	ROLLER-SKATER	SALVATIONISM
RETRENCHMENT	ROLLER SKATES	SALVATIONIST
RETROCESSION	ROLLER TOWELS	SAMARITANISM
RETROCESSIVE	ROLLICKINGLY	SANCTIFIABLE
RETROFLEXION	ROLLING MILLS	SANCTIONABLE
RETROGRESSED	ROLLING STOCK	SANDBLASTING
RETRO-ROCKETS	ROLLING STONE	SANDPAPERING
RETROVERSION	ROLL OF HONOUR	SAN FRANCISCO
REUNIONISTIC	ROLLTOP DESKS	SANGUINARILY
REVALUATIONS	ROMAN CANDLES	SANGUINENESS
REVEGETATION	ROMAN NUMERAL	SANGUINOLENT
REVELATIONAL	ROMANTICALLY	SANITARINESS
REVERBERATED	ROMANTICISTS	SAN SEBASTIAN
REVERBERATOR	ROMANTICIZED	SANTALACEOUS
REVERENDSHIP	ROOMING HOUSE	SANTO DOMINGO
REVERENTNESS	ROOTLESSNESS	SAONE-ET-LOIRE
REVERSIONARY	ROSE-COLOURED	SAPINDACEOUS
REVISABILITY	ROTARY TILLER	SAPONIFIABLE
REVISIONISTS	ROUGH DIAMOND	SAPROPHAGOUS
REVITALIZING	ROUND BRACKET	SARCOMATOSIS
REVIVABILITY	ROUTE MARCHES	SARDONICALLY
REVIVALISTIC	ROYAL FLUSHES	SARSAPARILLA
REVOCABILITY	RUBBER DINGHY	SASKATCHEWAN
REVOKABILITY	RUBBERNECKED	SATIRIZATION
REVULSIONARY	RUBBER PLANTS	SATISFACTION
RHAPSODISTIC	RUBBER STAMPS	SATISFACTORY
RHAPSODIZING	RULES OF THUMB	SATISFYINGLY
RHESUS FACTOR	RUMINATINGLY	SATURABILITY
RHETORICALLY	RUMINATIVELY	SAUDI ARABIAN
RHETORICIANS	RUMMAGE SALES	SAUSAGE ROLLS
RHINOCEROSES	RUMOURMONGER	SAVING GRACES
RHINOCEROTIC	RUNNING JUMPS	SAVINGS BANKS
RHINOLOGICAL	RUNNING MATES	SAXOPHONISTS
RHINOPLASTIC	RUN-OF-THE-MILL	SCALABLENESS
RHIZOCARPOUS	RURALIZATION	SCANDALIZING
RHODODENDRON	RUSTPROOFING	SCANDALOUSLY
RHOMBOHEDRAL	RUTHLESSNESS	SCANDINAVIAN
RHOMBOHEDRON		SCAREMONGERS
RHYMING SLANG	S	SCARIFICATOR
RHYTHMICALLY	SABBATARIANS	SCARLET FEVER
RHYTHM METHOD	SACCHARINITY	SCARLET WOMAN
RIBONUCLEASE	SACRILEGIOUS	SCARLET WOMEN
RICHTER SCALE	SADISTICALLY	SCATOLOGICAL
RICOCHETTING	SAFEBREAKERS	SCATTERBRAIN
RIDICULOUSLY	SAFEGUARDING	SCENESHIFTER
RIGHTFULNESS	SAFETY ISLAND	SCENOGRAPHER
RIGHT-HANDERS	SAFETY RAZORS	SCENOGRAPHIC
RIGHT-HAND MAN	SAFETY VALVES	SCHAFFHAUSEN

SCHEMATIZING	SEISMOGRAPHS	SEVERANCE PAY
SCHIZOMYCETE	SEISMOGRAPHY	SEXAGENARIAN
SCHIZOPHYTIC	SEISMOLOGIST	SEXCENTENARY
SCHIZOTHYMIA	SEISMOSCOPIC	SEXTILLIONTH
SCHIZOTHYMIC	SELENOGRAPHY	SEXTUPLICATE
SCHOLARSHIPS	SELENOLOGIST	SHADOW-BOXING
SCHOLASTICAL	SELF-ABSORBED	SHAHJAHANPUR
SCHOOLFELLOW	SELF-ANALYSIS	SHAMATEURISM
SCHOOLHOUSES	SELF-ASSEMBLY	SHAMEFACEDLY
SCHOOL-LEAVER	SELF-CATERING	SHAMEFULNESS
SCHOOLMASTER	SELF-COLOURED	SHARECROPPER
SCHORLACEOUS	SELF-DESTRUCT	SHAREHOLDERS
SCIENCE PARKS	SELF-EDUCATED	SHARPSHOOTER
SCINTILLATED	SELF-EFFACING	SHARP-SIGHTED
SCINTILLATOR	SELF-EMPLOYED	SHARP-TONGUED
SCLERENCHYMA	SELF-INTEREST	SHATTERINGLY
SCLEROMETRIC	SELFLESSNESS	SHATTERPROOF
SCOLOPENDRID	SELF-PORTRAIT	SHAVING CREAM
SCORNFULNESS	SELF-RELIANCE	SHEATH KNIVES
SCOTCH TAPING	SELF-REPROACH	SHEEPISHNESS
SCOTCH WHISKY	SELF-STARTERS	SHEEPSHEARER
SCOTLAND YARD	SELLING POINT	SHEET ANCHORS
SCOUTMASTERS	SEMANTICALLY	SHELLACKINGS
SCRATCHINESS	SEMICIRCULAR	SHELLSHOCKED
SCRATCH PAPER	SEMIDETACHED	SHEPHERD'S PIE
SCREWDRIVERS	SEMIDIAMETER	SHETLAND PONY
SCRIPTWRITER	SEMIFINALIST	SHIFTINGNESS
SCROBICULATE	SEMIFLUIDITY	SHILLY-SHALLY
SCRUPULOUSLY	SEMINIFEROUS	SHIMMERINGLY
SCRUTINIZING	SEMIOTICIANS	SHIPBUILDERS
SCURRILOUSLY	SEMIPRECIOUS	SHIPBUILDING
SCUTELLATION	SEMITROPICAL	SHIPWRECKING
SEAMSTRESSES	SEMIVITREOUS	SHIRTSLEEVES
SEARCHLIGHTS	SEMPITERNITY	SHIRTWAISTER
SEASONALNESS	SENARMONTITE	SHOCKABILITY
SEASON TICKET	SENSIBLENESS	SHOCKINGNESS
SECESSIONISM	SENSITOMETER	SHOCKING PINK
SECESSIONIST	SENSITOMETRY	SHOOTING STAR
SECLUDEDNESS	SENSORIMOTOR	SHOP STEWARDS
SECOND COMING	SENSUOUSNESS	SHORT-CHANGED
SECOND COUSIN	SEPARABILITY	SHORT-CHANGER
SECOND-DEGREE	SEPARATENESS	SHORT CIRCUIT
SECOND NATURE	SEPARATISTIC	SHORTCOMINGS
SECOND PERSON	SEPTILATERAL	SHORT-LISTING
SECOND-STRING	SEPTILLIONTH	SHORTSIGHTED
SECRET AGENTS	SEPTUAGESIMA	SHORT STORIES
SECRETARIATS	SEPTUPLICATE	SHORT-WAISTED
SECRETIONARY	SEQUENTIALLY	SHOW BUSINESS
SECRET POLICE	SEQUESTRABLE	SHOWSTOPPERS
SECTARIANISM	SEQUESTRATED	SHOWSTOPPING
SECTIONALISM	SEQUESTRATOR	SHREWISHNESS
SECTIONALIST	SERIAL NUMBER	SHUDDERINGLY
SECTIONALIZE	SERICULTURAL	SHUFFLEBOARD
SECULARISTIC	SERVICEBERRY	SHUTTLECOCKS
SECULARIZING	SERVICE FLATS	SIAMESE TWINS
SECURITY RISK	SERVICE ROADS	SICK HEADACHE
SEDULOUSNESS	SESQUIALTERA	SIDEROSTATIC
SEGMENTATION	SEVENTEENTHS	SIDESLIPPING
SEINE-ET-MARNE	SEVENTY-EIGHT	SIDESTEPPING

SIDETRACKING	SLOVENLINESS	SOUND EFFECTS
SIDE-WHEELERS	SLUGGARDNESS	SOUNDPROOFED
SIDI-BEL-ABBES	SLUGGISHNESS	SOUP KITCHENS
SIERRA NEVADA	SLUMBERINGLY	SOUSAPHONIST
SIGHT-READERS	SLUTTISHNESS	SOUTHEASTERN
SIGHT-READING	SMALL FORTUNE	SOUTHERNMOST
SIGNIFICANCE	SMALLHOLDERS	SOUTHERNWOOD
SIGN LANGUAGE	SMALLHOLDING	SOUTHWESTERN
SILHOUETTING	SMASH-AND-GRAB	SPACE HEATERS
SILICIFEROUS	SMILACACEOUS	SPACE SHUTTLE
SILICON CHIPS	SMOKESCREENS	SPACE STATION
SILIQUACEOUS	SMOOTH-SPOKEN	SPACIOUSNESS
SILVERFISHES	SMORGASBORDS	SPEAKING TUBE
SILVER MEDALS	SNAGGLETOOTH	SPEARHEADING
SILVERSMITHS	SNAKE CHARMER	SPECIALISTIC
SILVICULTURE	SNAP FASTENER	SPECIALITIES
SIMILARITIES	SNAPPISHNESS	SPECIALIZING
SIMPLE-MINDED	SNEAKINGNESS	SPECIFICALLY
SIMULTANEITY	SNEAK PREVIEW	SPECIOUSNESS
SIMULTANEOUS	SNEAK THIEVES	SPECTACULARS
SINANTHROPUS	SNICKERINGLY	SPECTROGRAPH
SINGLE-ACTING	SNIGGERINGLY	SPECTROMETER
SINGLE-ACTION	SNOBBISHNESS	SPECTROMETRY
SINGLE-DECKER	SNOOPERSCOPE	SPECTROSCOPE
SINGLE-HANDED	SOCIALIZABLE	SPECTROSCOPY
SINGLE-MINDED	SOCIAL WORKER	SPECULATIONS
SINGULARNESS	SOCIOLOGICAL	SPEECHIFYING
SINISTERNESS	SOCIOLOGISTS	SPEECHLESSLY
SINISTRORSAL	SOCIOMETRIST	SPEEDOMETERS
SINKING FUNDS	SODA FOUNTAIN	SPEEDWRITING
SIPHONOPHORE	SOFT LANDINGS	SPELEOLOGIST
SIPHONOSTELE	SOFT-PEDALING	SPELLBINDERS
SISTERLINESS	SOFT-PEDALLED	SPELLBINDING
SISTERS-IN-LAW	SOLARIZATION	SPENDTHRIFTS
SITTING DUCKS	SOLAR SYSTEMS	SPERMATHECAL
SITTING ROOMS	SOLICITATION	SPERMATOCYTE
SKELETON KEYS	SOLICITOUSLY	SPERMATOZOAL
SKIPPING-ROPE	SOLIDIFIABLE	SPERMATOZOID
SKITTISHNESS	SOLIFLUCTION	SPERMATOZOON
SKYROCKETING	SOLILOQUIZED	SPERMOGONIUM
SLANDEROUSLY	SOLITARINESS	SPHRAGISTICS
SLAUGHTERING	SOLITUDINOUS	SPHYGMOGRAPH
SLAUGHTEROUS	SOLVENT ABUSE	SPICK-AND-SPAN
SLAVE DRIVERS	SOMATOLOGIST	SPIEGELEISEN
SLAVONICALLY	SOMATOPLEURE	SPINSTERHOOD
SLEDGEHAMMER	SOMERSAULTED	SPIRITEDNESS
SLEEPING BAGS	SOMNAMBULANT	SPIRIT LEVELS
SLEEPING CARS	SOMNAMBULATE	SPIRITUALISM
SLEEPING PILL	SOMNAMBULISM	SPIRITUALIST
SLEEPWALKERS	SOMNAMBULIST	SPIRITUALITY
SLEEPWALKING	SON ET LUMIERE	SPIRITUALIZE
SLENDERIZING	SONG AND DANCE	SPIRITUOSITY
SLIDING DOORS	SONOROUSNESS	SPIROGRAPHIC
SLIDING SCALE	SOOTHINGNESS	SPITEFULNESS
SLIPPERINESS	SOPHISTICATE	SPLASH GUARDS
SLIPPINGNESS	SOPORIFEROUS	SPLENDIDNESS
SLIPSTREAMED	SOUL BROTHERS	SPLENOMEGALY
SLOTHFULNESS	SOULLESSNESS	SPLIT SECONDS
SLOT MACHINES	SOUND BARRIER	SPOKESPEOPLE

SPOKESPERSON	STEAM SHOVELS	STOREKEEPING
SPONGIOBLAST	STEATOPYGOUS	STORM TROOPER
SPOON-FEEDING	STEATORRHOEA	STORMY PETREL
SPORADICALLY	STEEPLECHASE	STORYTELLERS
SPOROGENESIS	STEEPLEJACKS	STORYTELLING
SPORTFULNESS	STELLIFEROUS	STOUTHEARTED
SPORTIVENESS	STENOGRAPHER	STOVEPIPE HAT
SPOT-CHECKING	STENOGRAPHIC	STRADIVARIUS
SPOTLESSNESS	STENOTHERMAL	STRAGGLINGLY
SPOTLIGHTING	STEPBROTHERS	STRAIGHTAWAY
SPOTTED DICKS	STEPCHILDREN	STRAIGHTEDGE
SPREAD-EAGLED	STEPDAUGHTER	STRAIGHTENED
SPREADSHEETS	STEREOCHROME	STRAIGHTENER
SPRINGBOARDS	STEREOCHROMY	STRAIGHTNESS
SPRING ONIONS	STEREOGRAPHY	STRAINEDNESS
SPURIOUSNESS	STEREOISOMER	STRAITJACKET
SQUAMOUSNESS	STEREOMETRIC	STRANGLEHOLD
SQUARE DANCES	STEREOPHONIC	STRANGULATED
SQUARE-RIGGED	STEREOPTICON	STRAPHANGERS
SQUARE-RIGGER	STEREOSCOPIC	STRAPHANGING
SQUEEZEBOXES	STEREOTACTIC	STRATICULATE
SQUELCHINGLY	STEREOTROPIC	STRATIGRAPHY
SQUIRRELFISH	STEREOTYPING	STRATOCRATIC
STADDLESTONE	STEREOVISION	STRATOSPHERE
STAFF OFFICER	STERILIZABLE	STRAWBERRIES
STAGECOACHES	STERNUTATION	STREAMLINING
STAGE-MANAGED	STERNUTATIVE	STREET VALUES
STAGE MANAGER	STERNUTATORY	STREETWALKER
STAGE WHISPER	STERTOROUSLY	STRENGTHENED
STAGGERINGLY	STETHOSCOPES	STRENGTHENER
STAGING POSTS	STETHOSCOPIC	STREPTOCOCCI
STAINABILITY	STICHOMETRIC	STREPTOMYCIN
STAINED GLASS	STICK INSECTS	STRETCHINESS
STAKEHOLDERS	STICKLEBACKS	STRETCHMARKS
STALACTIFORM	STICKY WICKET	STRIDULATING
STALLHOLDERS	STIGMASTEROL	STRIDULATION
STALWARTNESS	STIGMATIZING	STRIDULATORY
STAMMERINGLY	STILBOESTROL	STRIKINGNESS
STANDARDIZED	STILETTO HEEL	STRIP CARTOON
STANDARDIZER	STINKINGNESS	STRIP MININGS
STANDARD LAMP	STIPULATIONS	STROBE LIGHTS
STANDARD TIME	STIRRUP PUMPS	STROBILATION
STANDING ROOM	STOCKBREEDER	STROBOSCOPES
STANDOFF HALF	STOCKBROKERS	STROBOSCOPIC
STANNIFEROUS	STOCKHOLDERS	STROMATOLITE
STAR CHAMBERS	STOCK-IN-TRADE	STRONG-MINDED
STAR-SPANGLED	STOCKJOBBERS	STRONG POINTS
STARTING GATE	STOCKJOBBERY	STRONG-WILLED
STATELY HOMES	STOCK MARKETS	STRONTIANITE
STATEN ISLAND	STOICHIOLOGY	STROPHANTHIN
STATIONARILY	STOMACHACHES	STROPHANTHUS
STATION BREAK	STOMACH PUMPS	STRUCTURALLY
STATION HOUSE	STONECUTTING	STRUGGLINGLY
STATION WAGON	STONEMASONRY	STRYCHNINISM
STATISTICIAN	STONEWALLERS	STUBBORNNESS
STAYING POWER	STONEWALLING	STUDDINGSAIL
STEAK TARTARE	STONY-HEARTED	STUDIOUSNESS
STEALTHINESS	STOOLPIGEONS	STUFFED SHIRT
STEAMROLLERS	STOREKEEPERS	STUPEFACIENT

STUPEFACTION	SUCTION PUMPS	SURRENDERING
STUPEFYINGLY	SUDORIFEROUS	SURROUNDEDLY
STUPENDOUSLY	SUFFRAGETTES	SURROUNDINGS
STUTTERINGLY	SUFFRUTICOSE	SURVEILLANCE
STYLOGRAPHIC	SUGAR DADDIES	SURVEYORSHIP
STYRACACEOUS	SUGGESTINGLY	SURVIVAL KITS
SUBALTERNATE	SUGGESTIVELY	SUSCEPTIVITY
SUBANTARCTIC	SUITABLENESS	SUSPICIOUSLY
SUBAURICULAR	SULPHONAMIDE	SUSTAININGLY
SUBCELESTIAL	SULPHURATION	SWAGGERINGLY
SUBCLIMACTIC	SUMMARIZABLE	SWALLOW DIVES
SUBCOMMITTEE	SUMMERHOUSES	SWASHBUCKLER
SUBCONSCIOUS	SUMMER SCHOOL	SWEEPINGNESS
SUBCONTINENT	SUNDAY SCHOOL	SWEET-AND-SOUR
SUBCUTANEOUS	SUPERABILITY	SWEET PEPPERS
SUBDEACONATE	SUPERANNUATE	SWEET-TALKING
SUBDIACONATE	SUPERCHARGED	SWEET WILLIAM
SUBDIVISIONS	SUPERCHARGER	SWELTERINGLY
SUBERIZATION	SUPERCILIARY	SWIMMING BATH
SUBINFEUDATE	SUPERCILIOUS	SWIMMING POOL
SUBJECTIVELY	SUPEREMINENT	SWITCHBLADES
SUBJECTIVISM	SUPERFICIARY	SWITCHBOARDS
SUBJECTIVIST	SUPERGLACIAL	SWIZZLE STICK
SUBJECTIVITY	SUPERGRASSES	SWORD DANCERS
SUBJUNCTIVES	SUPERIMPOSED	SYLLABICALLY
SUBMAXILLARY	SUPERLATIVES	SYMBOLICALLY
SUBMERSIBLES	SUPERMARKETS	SYMBOLOGICAL
SUBMISSIVELY	SUPERNATURAL	SYMMETALLISM
SUBMITTINGLY	SUPERPOSABLE	SYMPATHIZERS
SUBNORMALITY	SUPERSEDABLE	SYMPATHIZING
SUBORDINATED	SUPERSESSION	SYNAESTHESIA
SUBORDINATES	SUPERSTITION	SYNAESTHETIC
SUBPRINCIPAL	SUPERSTRATUM	SYNAPTICALLY
SUBSCRIPTION	SUPERTANKERS	SYNARTHROSIS
SUBSCRIPTIVE	SUPERVENIENT	SYNCHROFLASH
SUBSEQUENTLY	SUPPLEMENTAL	SYNCHRONIZED
SUBSERVIENCE	SUPPLEMENTED	SYNCHRONIZER
SUBSIDIARIES	SUPPLEMENTER	SYNCHROSCOPE
SUBSIDIARILY	SUPPLETORILY	SYNCLINORIUM
SUBSIDIZABLE	SUPPLICATING	SYNDACTYLISM
SUBSISTINGLY	SUPPLICATION	SYNDETICALLY
SUBSTANTIATE	SUPPLICATORY	SYNDICALISTS
SUBSTANTIVAL	SUPPOSITIONS	SYNDIOTACTIC
SUBSTANTIVES	SUPPOSITIOUS	SYNONYMOUSLY
SUBSTITUTING	SUPPRESSIBLE	SYNOPTICALLY
SUBSTITUTION	SUPRAGLOTTAL	SYNTHESIZERS
SUBSTITUTIVE	SUPRALIMINAL	SYNTHESIZING
SUBSTRUCTURE	SUPRAORBITAL	SYNTONICALLY
SUBTEMPERATE	SUPRAPROTEST	SYSTEMATIZED
SUBTERRANEAN	SUPREMACISTS	SYSTEMATIZER
SUBTRACTIONS	SUPREME BEING	SYSTEMICALLY
SUBURBANITES	SUPREME COURT	
SUBVERSIVELY	SUREFOOTEDLY	T
SUCCEDANEOUS	SURFACE-TO-AIR	TABERNACULAR
SUCCEEDINGLY	SURMOUNTABLE	TABLE MANNERS
SUCCESSFULLY	SURPASSINGLY	TABLE-TURNING
SUCCESSIONAL	SURPRISINGLY	TACHEOMETRIC
SUCCESSIVELY	SURREALISTIC	TACHYCARDIAC
SUCCINCTNESS	SURREJOINDER	TACTLESSNESS

TADZHIKISTAN	TETRACYCLINE	TIED COTTAGES
TALCUM POWDER	TETRAHEDRITE	TIME CAPSULES
TALENT SCOUTS	TETRAPTEROUS	TIME EXPOSURE
TALKING POINT	TETRASTICHIC	TIME-HONOURED
TAMBOURINIST	TETRAVALENCY	TIMELESSNESS
TANGENTIALLY	TEUTONICALLY	TIME SWITCHES
TAPE MEASURES	THALAMICALLY	TIMOROUSNESS
TAPE RECORDER	THALLOPHYTIC	TIRELESSNESS
TARAMASALATA	THANKFULNESS	TIRESOMENESS
TARDENOISIAN	THANKSGIVING	TITANIFEROUS
TARTARIC ACID	THAUMATOLOGY	TITLEHOLDERS
TASTEFULNESS	THEANTHROPIC	TITTLE-TATTLE
TAUROMACHIAN	THEATREGOERS	TOASTING FORK
TAUTOLOGICAL	THEATRICALLY	TOASTMASTERS
TAXIDERMISTS	THEISTICALLY	TOBACCONISTS
TECHNICALITY	THEMATICALLY	TOFFEE APPLES
TECHNOGRAPHY	THEOCENTRISM	TOGETHERNESS
TECHNOLOGIES	THEOPHYLLINE	TOMFOOLERIES
TECHNOLOGIST	THEORETICIAN	TONE LANGUAGE
TECTONICALLY	THEORIZATION	TONELESSNESS
TEENYBOPPERS	THERAPEUTICS	TONSILLOTOMY
TEETER-TOTTER	THEREINAFTER	TOOTHBRUSHES
TEETOTALLERS	THERMOCOUPLE	TOPDRESSINGS
TELAESTHESIA	THERMOGENOUS	TOP-HEAVINESS
TELAESTHETIC	THERMOGRAPHY	TOPOGRAPHERS
TELAUTOGRAPH	THERMOLABILE	TORMENTINGLY
TELEGRAPHERS	THERMOMETERS	TORREFACTION
TELEGRAPHESE	THERMOMETRIC	TORTUOUSNESS
TELEGRAPHING	THERMOSCOPIC	TOTALITARIAN
TELEOLOGICAL	THERMOS FLASK	TOTALIZATORS
TELEOLOGISTS	THERMOSIPHON	TOURIST CLASS
TELEPHONE BOX	THERMOSPHERE	TOUT ENSEMBLE
TELEPHONISTS	THERMOSTABLE	TOWN PLANNERS
TELEPRINTERS	THERMOSTATIC	TOWN PLANNING
TELEPROMPTER	THERMOTROPIC	TOXICOLOGIST
TELEUTOSPORE	THEURGICALLY	TOXOPHILITIC
TELEVISIONAL	THICK-SKINNED	TRACEABILITY
TELGENICALLY	THIEVISHNESS	TRACE ELEMENT
TELLUROMETER	THIGMOTACTIC	TRACHEOPHYTE
TEMPERAMENTS	THIGMOTROPIC	TRACHEOSTOMY
TEMPERATURES	THINGAMAJIGS	TRACHOMATOUS
TENANT FARMER	THIOSINAMINE	TRACING PAPER
TEN-GALLON HAT	THIOSULPHATE	TRACK RECORDS
TERATOLOGIST	THIRD PARTIES	TRACTABILITY
TERCENTENARY	THOROUGHBRED	TRACUCIANIST
TEREBINTHINE	THOROUGHFARE	TRADESCANTIA
TERGIVERSATE	THOROUGHNESS	TRADESPEOPLE
TERMINATIONS	THOUGHTFULLY	TRADING POSTS
TERRIBLENESS	THREE-QUARTER	TRADING STAMP
TERRIFICALLY	THREE-WHEELER	TRADITIONIST
TERRIFYINGLY	THROMBOCYTIC	TRADUCIANISM
TERRITORIALS	THUNDERBOLTS	TRAFFICATORS
TESSELLATION	THUNDERCLAPS	TRAFFIC LIGHT
TESTAMENTARY	THUNDERCLOUD	TRAGEDIENNES
TESTIMONIALS	THUNDERINGLY	TRAILBLAZING
TESTOSTERONE	THUNDEROUSLY	TRAILER HOUSE
TEST-TUBE BABY	THUNDERSTONE	TRAINBEARERS
TETANIZATION	THUNDERSTORM	TRAITOROUSLY
TETRACHORDAL	TICKLISHNESS	TRAJECTORIES

TRAMPISHNESS	TREMENDOUSLY	TWO-WAY MIRROR
TRANQUILLITY	TRENDSETTERS	TYPIFICATION
TRANQUILLIZE	TRENDSETTING	TYPOGRAPHERS
TRANSACTIONS	TREPHINATION	TYRANNICALLY
TRANSCENDENT	TRIBULATIONS	TYRANNICIDAL
TRANSCENDING	TRICHINIASIS	
TRANSCRIBING	TRICHOCYSTIC	U
TRANSCURRENT	TRICHOGYNIAL	UBIQUITOUSLY
TRANSDUCTION	TRICHOLOGIST	UGLIFICATION
TRANSFERABLE	TRICHOPTERAN	UGLY DUCKLING
TRANSFERENCE	TRICHROMATIC	ULTRAMONTANE
TRANSFERRING	TRICK OR TREAT	ULTRAMUNDANE
TRANSFIGURED	TRIFURCATION	UMBILICATION
TRANSFORMERS	TRIGGER-HAPPY	UNACCEPTABLE
TRANSFORMING	TRIGLYCERIDE	UNACCUSTOMED
TRANSFORMISM	TRIGONOMETRY	UNACQUAINTED
TRANSFORMIST	TRILINGUALLY	UNAFFECTEDLY
TRANSFUSIBLE	TRIMOLECULAR	UNANSWERABLE
TRANSFUSIONS	TRIPARTITION	UNAPPEALABLE
TRANSGRESSED	TRIPHTHONGAL	UNASSAILABLE
TRANSGRESSOR	TRIPLE-TONGUE	UNASSUMINGLY
TRANSHUMANCE	TRIPLICATION	UNATTAINABLE
TRANSITIONAL	TRIPOLITANIA	UNATTRACTIVE
TRANSITORILY	TRIUMPHANTLY	UNBELIEVABLE
TRANSLATABLE	TRIUMVIRATES	UNBELIEVABLY
TRANSLATIONS	TRIVIALITIES	UNBIASEDNESS
TRANSLUCENCE	TRIVIALIZING	UNCHALLENGED
TRANSLUCENCY	TROCHAICALLY	UNCHARITABLE
TRANSMIGRANT	TROCHOIDALLY	UNCHARITABLY
TRANSMIGRATE	TROJAN HORSES	UNCHASTENESS
TRANSMISSION	TROLLEYBUSES	UNCINARIASIS
TRANSMISSIVE	TROMBIDIASIS	UNCLASSIFIED
TRANSMITTERS	TROOP CARRIER	UNCOMMERCIAL
TRANSMITTING	TROPHALLAXIS	UNCOMMONNESS
TRANSMOGRIFY	TROPOPHILOUS	UNCONFORMITY
TRANSMUNDANE	TROUBLEMAKER	UNCONSENTING
TRANSMUTABLE	TROUBLE SPOTS	UNCONSIDERED
TRANSOCEANIC	TROUSER PRESS	UNCONVINCING
TRANSPARENCY	TRUSTABILITY	UNCOVENANTED
TRANSPIRABLE	TRUSTEESHIPS	UNCRITICALLY
TRANSPLANTED	TRUSTFULNESS	UNCTUOUSNESS
TRANSPLANTER	TRUTHFULNESS	UNDECEIVABLE
TRANSPONDERS	TRYPANOSOMAL	UNDEMOCRATIC
TRANSPORTERS	TRYPARSAMIDE	UNDERACHIEVE
TRANSPORTING	TUBERCULOSIS	UNDERBELLIES
TRANSPORTIVE	TUMBLE-DRYERS	UNDERCHARGED
TRANSPOSABLE	TUMBLE-DRYING	UNDERCLOTHES
TRANSUDATORY	TUMULTUOUSLY	UNDERCURRENT
TRANSVAALIAN	TUNELESSNESS	UNDERCUTTING
TRANSVERSELY	TUNNEL VISION	UNDERDEVELOP
TRANSVESTISM	TURBELLARIAN	UNDERDRESSED
TRANSVESTITE	TURBIDIMETER	UNDEREXPOSED
TRANSYLVANIA	TURBOCHARGED	UNDERGARMENT
TRAPSHOOTING	TURBOCHARGER	UNDERGROUNDS
TRAUMATIZING	TURKISH BATHS	UNDERNOURISH
TRAVEL AGENCY	TURNING POINT	UNDERPAYMENT
TRAVEL AGENTS	TU-WHIT TU-WHOO	UNDERPINNING
TREBLE CHANCE	TWISTABILITY	UNDERPLAYING
TREELESSNESS	TWO-FACEDNESS	UNDERSCORING

UNDERSELLING	UNOFFICIALLY	USURIOUSNESS
UNDERSHERIFF	UNPARALLELED	UTILITY ROOMS
UNDERSTAFFED	UNPERFORATED	UTTAR PRADESH
UNDERSTATING	UNPLEASANTLY	UXORIOUSNESS
UNDERSTUDIED	UNPOPULARITY	
UNDERSTUDIES	UNPREJUDICED	V
UNDERSURFACE	UNPRINCIPLED	VACCINATIONS
UNDERTAKINGS	UNPRODUCTIVE	VACILLATIONS
UNDERVALUING	UNPROFITABLE	VACUUM FLASKS
UNDERWRITERS	UNQUESTIONED	VACUUM-PACKED
UNDERWRITING	UNREASONABLE	VAINGLORIOUS
UNDERWRITTEN	UNREASONABLY	VALEDICTIONS
UNDESIRABLES	UNRECKONABLE	VALENCIENNES
UNDETERMINED	UNRECOGNIZED	VALORIZATION
UNDISCHARGED	UNREFLECTIVE	VALUABLENESS
UNECONOMICAL	UNREGENERACY	VANQUISHABLE
UNEMPLOYABLE	UNREGENERATE	VANQUISHMENT
UNEMPLOYMENT	UNRESERVEDLY	VANTAGEPOINT
UNEVENTFULLY	UNRESPONSIVE	VAPORESCENCE
UNEXPRESSIVE	UNRESTRAINED	VAPORIZATION
UNEXPURGATED	UNRESTRICTED	VAPOROUSNESS
UNFAITHFULLY	UNSANCTIONED	VAPOUR TRAILS
UNFATHOMABLE	UNSATURATION	VARICOLOURED
UNFATHOMABLY	UNSCIENTIFIC	VASODILATION
UNFAVOURABLE	UNSCRAMBLING	VAUDEVILLIAN
UNFAVOURABLY	UNSCRUPULOUS	VAUDEVILLIST
UNFLAGGINGLY	UNSEARCHABLE	VEGETATIONAL
UNFLATTERING	UNSEASONABLE	VELARIZATION
UNFORGIVABLE	UNSEASONABLY	VENERABILITY
UNFORTUNATES	UNSEEMLINESS	VENERATIONAL
UNFREQUENTED	UNSEGREGATED	VENGEFULNESS
UNGAINLINESS	UNSETTLEMENT	VENIPUNCTURE
UNGOVERNABLE	UNSTEADINESS	VENTRICOSITY
UNGRATEFULLY	UNSTRATIFIED	VERBENACEOUS
UNHESITATING	UNSTRUCTURED	VERIDICALITY
UNHYPHENATED	UNSUCCESSFUL	VERIFICATION
UNIDENTIFIED	UNSUSPECTING	VERIFICATIVE
UNIFOLIOLATE	UNTENABILITY	VERTEBRATION
UNILATERALLY	UNTHINKINGLY	VERTICILLATE
UNIMAGINABLE	UNTIMELINESS	VESICULATION
UNIMPRESSIVE	UNTOUCHABLES	VESTAL VIRGIN
UNINFLUENCED	UNTOWARDNESS	VIBRAPHONIST
UNINTERESTED	UNTRAMMELLED	VICE-CHAIRMAN
UNIONIZATION	UNWIELDINESS	VICISSITUDES
UNISEXUALITY	UNWORTHINESS	VICTORIANISM
UNITARIANISM	UNWRITTEN LAW	VICTORIA PLUM
UNIVERSALISM	UPHOLSTERERS	VICTORIOUSLY
UNIVERSALIST	UPHOLSTERING	VIDEO NASTIES
UNIVERSALITY	UPRIGHT PIANO	VIGOROUSNESS
UNIVERSALIZE	UPROARIOUSLY	VILIFICATION
UNIVERSITIES	UP-TO-DATENESS	VILLAHERMOSA
UNKINDLINESS	URANOGRAPHER	VILLEURBANNE
UNLAWFULNESS	URANOGRAPHIC	VINDICTIVELY
UNLIKELIHOOD	URBANIZATION	VINICULTURAL
UNLIKELINESS	URETHROSCOPE	VIN ORDINAIRE
UNMANAGEABLE	URETHROSCOPY	VIOLONCELLOS
UNMEASURABLE	URINOGENITAL	VIRGIN'S-BOWER
UNMISTAKABLE	USER-FRIENDLY	VIRIDESCENCE
UNMISTAKABLY	USUFRUCTUARY	VIRTUOUSNESS

VISCEROMOTOR	WATER MEADOWS	WINDING SHEET
VISCOUNTCIES	WATERPROOFED	WINDOW SHADES
VISITATIONAL	WAYS AND MEANS	WIND TURBINES
VISITATORIAL	WEATHERBOARD	WINEGLASSFUL
VISITING CARD	WEATHER-BOUND	WINGLESSNESS
VISITORS' BOOK	WEATHERCOCKS	WINSTON-SALEM
VITALIZATION	WEATHERGLASS	WINTERBOURNE
VITICULTURAL	WEATHERPROOF	WINTER SPORTS
VITICULTURER	WEATHER SHIPS	WISCONSINITE
VITREOUSNESS	WEATHER VANES	WISECRACKING
VITUPERATION	WEDDING RINGS	WITCHDOCTORS
VITUPERATIVE	WEIGHBRIDGES	WITCH-HUNTING
VIVIFICATION	WEIGHTLESSLY	WITCHING HOUR
VIVISECTIONS	WEIGHT LIFTER	WITHDRAWABLE
VIXENISHNESS	WELFARE STATE	WITHEREDNESS
VOCABULARIES	WELL-ADJUSTED	WITHSTANDING
VOCALIZATION	WELL-ASSORTED	WITNESS BOXES
VOCIFERATING	WELL-ATTENDED	WOLF WHISTLES
VOCIFERATION	WELL-BALANCED	WOLLASTONITE
VOCIFEROUSLY	WELL-DESERVED	WOMANISHNESS
VOIDABLENESS	WELL-DISPOSED	WONDER-WORKER
VOLCANICALLY	WELL-EDUCATED	WONDROUSNESS
VOLTA REDONDA	WELL-EQUIPPED	WOODENHEADED
VOLUMINOSITY	WELL-FAVOURED	WOOLGATHERER
VOLUMINOUSLY	WELL-GROUNDED	WOOLLY-HEADED
VOLUNTARYISM	WELL-INFORMED	WORDLESSNESS
VOLUNTARYIST	WELL-MANNERED	WORKER-PRIEST
VOLUNTEERING	WELL-PROVIDED	WORKING CLASS
VOLUPTUARIES	WELL-RECEIVED	WORKING ORDER
VOLUPTUOUSLY	WELL-SITUATED	WORKING PARTY
VOMITURITION	WELL-TEMPERED	WORKING WEEKS
VOTE OF THANKS	WELSH RAREBIT	WORKINGWOMAN
VOWELIZATION	WELTERWEIGHT	WORKSTATIONS
VULCANIZABLE	WENSLEYDALES	WORLD-BEATERS
	WESTERLINESS	WORLD-BEATING
W	WESTERNIZING	WORLDSHAKING
WAITING LISTS	WETTING AGENT	WRATHFULNESS
WAITING ROOMS	WHEELBARROWS	WRETCHEDNESS
WALKIE-TALKIE	WHEELWRIGHTS	WRISTWATCHES
WALKING STICK	WHENCESOEVER	WRITER'S CRAMP
WALL PAINTING	WHEREWITHALS	WRITING DESKS
WALLPAPERING	WHIGGISHNESS	WRITING PAPER
WANKEL ENGINE	WHIMPERINGLY	WRONGFULNESS
WAREHOUSEMAN	WHIMSICALITY	
WARMONGERING	WHIPPING BOYS	X
WARS OF NERVES	WHIPPOORWILL	X CHROMOSOMES
WASH DRAWINGS	WHITE KNIGHTS	XERODERMATIC
WASTEFULNESS	WHITE-LIVERED	XIPHISTERNUM
WASTE PRODUCT	WHITE SLAVERY	
WATCHFULNESS	WHITEWASHING	Y
WATER BISCUIT	WHITE WEDDING	Y CHROMOSOMES
WATER BUFFALO	WHOLE-HEARTED	YELLOWHAMMER
WATER CANNONS	WHOLE NUMBERS	YIELDINGNESS
WATER CLOSETS	WHORTLEBERRY	YOUTHFULNESS
WATERCOLOURS	WICKET KEEPER	YOUTH HOSTELS
WATERCOURSES	WIFE SWAPPING	
WATERING CANS	WILDERNESSES	Z
WATERING HOLE	WILL-O'-THE-WISP	ZINCOGRAPHER
WATERMANSHIP	WINDCHEATERS	ZINCOGRAPHIC

ZOOCHEMISTRY	ZOOTOMICALLY	ZYGAPOPHYSIS
ZOOGEOGRAPHY	ZWITTERIONIC	ZYGOMORPHISM
ZOOSPERMATIC		

A	AFTERTHOUGHTS	ANIMADVERSION
ABBREVIATIONS	AGGIORNAMENTO	ANIMADVERTING
ABNORMALITIES	AGGLOMERATING	ANIMALIZATION
ABOLITIONISTS	AGGLOMERATION	ANISOMETROPIA
ABORTIFACIENT	AGGLOMERATIVE	ANNEXATIONISM
ABSORBABILITY	AGGLUTINATION	ANNEXATIONIST
ACCELEROMETER	AGGLUTINATIVE	ANNIVERSARIES
ACCENTUATIONS	AGGRAVATINGLY	ANNOUNCEMENTS
ACCEPTABILITY	AGREEABLENESS	ANSWERABILITY
ACCESSIBILITY	AGRICULTURIST	ANTAGONIZABLE
ACCESSORINESS	AGROBIOLOGIST	ANTHRAQUINONE
ACCIDENT-PRONE	AIR COMMODORES	ANTHROPOMETRY
ACCLIMATIZING	AIRCRAFTWOMAN	ANTHROPOPATHY
ACCOMMODATING	AIRWORTHINESS	ANTHROPOPHAGI
ACCOMMODATION	AIX-EN-PROVENCE	ANTHROPOSOPHY
ACCOMMODATIVE	ALCOHOLICALLY	ANTICLIMACTIC
ACCOMPANIMENT	ALCOHOLOMETER	ANTICLINORIUM
ACCOMPLISHING	ALGEBRAICALLY	ANTICLOCKWISE
ACCOUTREMENTS	ALLEGORICALLY	ANTIGENICALLY
ACCREDITATION	ALLOCHTHONOUS	ANTIHISTAMINE
ACCULTURATION	ALPHA AND OMEGA	ANTILOGARITHM
ACCUMULATIONS	ALTERNATIVELY	ANTIMACASSARS
ACETIFICATION	ALUMINIFEROUS	ANTIMONARCHIC
ACETYLCHOLINE	ALUMINOTHERMY	ANTINOMICALLY
ACHILLES' HEELS	AMALGAMATIONS	ANTIPERSONNEL
ACIDIFICATION	AMBASSADORIAL	ANTIPRAGMATIC
ACKNOWLEDGING	AMBIDEXTERITY	ANTISPASMODIC
ACOTYLEDONOUS	AMBIGUGUITIES	ANTISUBMARINE
ACQUAINTANCES	AMBIGUOUSNESS	APATHETICALLY
ACQUIESCENTLY	AMBITIOUSNESS	APERIODICALLY
ACQUIRED TASTE	AMERICANIZING	APHELIOTROPIC
ACQUISITIVELY	AMNIOCENTESIS	APLANATICALLY
ACRIMONIOUSLY	AMORPHOUSNESS	APOCHROMATISM
ACROBATICALLY	AMPHIBLASTULA	APODICTICALLY
ACRYLONITRILE	AMPHIPROSTYLE	APOGEOTROPISM
ACTINOMORPHIC	AMPHITHEATRES	APOSTROPHIZED
ACTINOMYCOSIS	AMPHITRICHOUS	APPLICABILITY
ACTINOMYCOTIC	AMPLIFICATION	APPORTIONABLE
ACTINOTHERAPY	AMUSEMENT PARK	APPORTIONMENT
ACTINOURANIUM	ANACHRONISTIC	APPRECIATIONS
ACTUALIZATION	ANAEROBICALLY	APPREHENSIBLE
ADDRESSOGRAPH	ANAESTHETISTS	APPREHENSIONS
ADENOIDECTOMY	ANAESTHETIZED	APPROPRIATELY
ADIAPHORISTIC	ANAGRAMMATISM	APPROPRIATING
ADMEASUREMENT	ANAGRAMMATIST	APPROPRIATION
ADMINISTERING	ANAGRAMMATIZE	APPROXIMATELY
ADMINISTRATOR	ANAPHORICALLY	APPROXIMATING
ADMISSIBILITY	ANAPHRODISIAC	APPROXIMATION
ADMONISHINGLY	ANATHEMATIZED	APPURTENANCES
ADSORBABILITY	ANATOMIZATION	AQUICULTURIST
ADVANCED LEVEL	ANCHORPERSONS	ARABIC NUMERAL
ADVENTURESSES	ANDHRA PRADESH	ARBITRARINESS
ADVENTUROUSLY	ANEMOMETRICAL	ARBORICULTURE
ADVERTISEMENT	ANESTHETIZING	ARCHAEOLOGIST
AEROMECHANICS	ANFRACTUOSITY	ARCHBISHOPRIC
AESTHETICALLY	ANGIOSPERMOUS	ARCHIDIACONAL
AFFENPINSCHER	ANGLICIZATION	ARCHIMANDRITE
AFFIRMATIVELY	ANGLO-AMERICAN	ARCHIPELAGOES
AFFORESTATION	ANGLO-CATHOLIC	ARCHITECTONIC

ARCHITECTURAL
ARGENTIFEROUS
ARGILLIFEROUS
ARGUMENTATION
ARGUMENTATIVE
ARISTOCRACIES
ARITHMETICIAN
AROMATIZATION
ARRIERE-PENSEE
ARTERIOVENOUS
ARTESIAN WELLS
ARTICULATIONS
ARTIFICIALITY
ARTS AND CRAFTS
ARUNDINACEOUS
ASCERTAINABLE
ASCERTAINMENT
ASPERGILLOSIS
ASSASSINATING
ASSASSINATION
ASSAULT COURSE
ASSEMBLY LINES
ASSERTIVENESS
ASSET-STRIPPER
ASSEVERATIONS
ASSIDUOUSNESS
ASSIGNABILITY
ASSYRIOLOGIST
ASTHENOSPHERE
ASTHMATICALLY
ASTIGMATISTIC
ASTONISHINGLY
ASTRODYNAMICS
ASTROPHYSICAL
ASYNDETICALLY
ATAVISTICALLY
ATHEISTICALLY
ATOMISTICALLY
ATROCIOUSNESS
ATTAINABILITY
ATTENTIVENESS
ATTITUDINIZER
ATTRIBUTIVELY
AUBERVILLIERS
AUDACIOUSNESS
AUGMENTATIONS
AUSTRALASIANS
AUSTRO-ASIATIC
AUTECOLOGICAL
AUTHENTICALLY
AUTHENTICATED
AUTHENTICATOR
AUTHORITARIAN
AUTHORITATIVE
AUTHORIZATION
AUTOBIOGRAPHY
AUTOCATALYSIS
AUTOCHTHONISM
AUTOCHTHONOUS

AUTOMATICALLY
AUTONOMICALLY
AUTOSTABILITY
AUXILIARY VERB
AXIOMATICALLY

B
BABY CARRIAGES
BACCALAUREATE
BACK FORMATION
BACKPEDALLING
BACKWARDATION
BACTERIOLYSIS
BACTERIOLYTIC
BACTERIOPHAGE
BALANCED DIETS
BALANCE SHEETS
BALKANIZATION
BALLISTICALLY
BALNEOLOGICAL
BALSAMIFEROUS
BAMBOOZLEMENT
BANDSPREADING
BANKER'S ORDERS
BANTAMWEIGHTS
BARBAROUSNESS
BAREFACEDNESS
BASIDIOMYCETE
BATTERING RAMS
BATTLE CRUISER
BATTLE-SCARRED
BEAST OF BURDEN
BEATIFICATION
BEAUTY PARLOUR
BEHAVIOURALLY
BEHAVIOURISTS
BELISHA BEACON
BELLES-LETTRES
BELLY-LANDINGS
BELO HORIZONTE
BENEFICIARIES
BERCHTESGADEN
BEWILDERINGLY
BIBLIOGRAPHER
BIBLIOGRAPHIC
BICENTENARIES
BIG BANG THEORY
BIGHEADEDNESS
BIGNONIACEOUS
BILLS OF HEALTH
BILLS OF LADING
BILLS OF RIGHTS
BIODEGRADABLE
BIOECOLOGICAL
BIOENERGETICS
BIOMETRICALLY
BIOSTATICALLY
BIOTECHNOLOGY
BIRD OF PASSAGE

BIRD'S-EYE VIEWS
BIREFRINGENCE
BLABBERMOUTHS
BLACK AND WHITE
BLACKBERRYING
BLACK COMEDIES
BLACKCURRANTS
BLACKGUARDISM
BLACK PUDDINGS
BLAMELESSNESS
BLANDISHMENTS
BLANTYRE-LIMBE
BLASPHEMOUSLY
BLAST FURNACES
BLASTOGENESIS
BLIND MAN'S BUFF
BLOOD BROTHERS
BLOODCURDLING
BLOODLESSNESS
BLOOD PRESSURE
BLOOD RELATION
BLOTTING PAPER
BLUE-PENCILLED
BLUESTOCKINGS
BLUNDERBUSSES
BOARDING CARDS
BOARDINGHOUSE
BODY SNATCHERS
BODY STOCKINGS
BOILING POINTS
BOMBASTICALLY
BOOBY TRAPPING
BOON COMPANION
BORAGINACEOUS
BOTTLE-FEEDING
BOTTOM DRAWERS
BOUGAINVILLEA
BOUILLABAISSE
BOUNDLESSNESS
BOUNTEOUSNESS
BOUNTIFULNESS
BOUSTROPHEDON
BOWLING ALLEYS
BOWLING GREENS
BRACHYCEPHALY
BRACHYPTEROUS
BRAINLESSNESS
BRAINSTORMING
BRASSICACEOUS
BRASS KNUCKLES
BROADMINDEDLY
BROKEN-HEARTED
BROMELIACEOUS
BRONCHIAL TUBE
BRONCHOSCOPIC
BROTHERLINESS
BROTHERS-IN-LAW
BROWNIE GUIDES
BROWNIE POINTS

BRUTALIZATION
BUBONIC PLAGUE
BUILDING BLOCK
BULLETIN BOARD
BUMPTIOUSNESS
BUNSEN BURNERS
BURDEN OF PROOF
BUREAUCRACIES
BUREAUCRATISM
BURGLAR ALARMS
BURNT OFFERING
BUSH TELEGRAPH
BUSINESS CLASS
BUSINESS SUITS
BUSINESSWOMAN
BUTCHER'S-BROOM
BUTTERFINGERS
BUTYRALDEHYDE

C
CABIN CRUISERS
CABINET-MAKERS
CABLE RAILWAYS
CALCARIFEROUS
CALCIFICATION
CALCULABILITY
CALENDAR MONTH
CALENDAR YEARS
CALLIGRAPHIST
CALLISTHENICS
CALORIFICALLY
CAMPANOLOGIST
CAMP FOLLOWERS
CANCELLATIONS
CANNIBALISTIC
CANNIBALIZING
CANONIZATIONS
CAPACIOUSNESS
CAPARISONNING
CAPE COLOUREDS
CAPITAL LEVIES
CAPITULATIONS
CAPRIFICATION
CARAVANSERAIS
CARBOHYDRATES
CARBON DIOXIDE
CARBONIFEROUS
CARBONIZATION
CARBURIZATION
CARCINOMATOID
CARDINAL POINT
CARDIOGRAPHER
CARDIOGRAPHIC
CARDIOLOGICAL
CARICATURISTS
CARNIFICATION
CARPETBAGGERS
CARPET SWEEPER
CARRIER PIGEON

CARTILAGINOUS
CARTOGRAPHERS
CARVING KNIVES
CASE HISTORIES
CASH DISPENSER
CASH REGISTERS
CASSEGRAINIAN
CASUISTICALLY
CATASTROPHISM
CATASTROPHIST
CATCHMENT AREA
CATECHIZATION
CATECHOLAMINE
CATEGORICALLY
CATHARTICALLY
CAT-O'-NINE-TAILS
CAUTERIZATION
CAYENNE PEPPER
CENTRE FORWARD
CEPHALIZATION
CEPHALOMETRIC
CEPHALOTHORAX
CEREBROSPINAL
CEREMONIALISM
CEREMONIALIST
CEREMONIOUSLY
CERTIFICATION
CERTIFICATORY
CERTIFIED MAIL
CERTIFIED MILK
CHAFING DISHES
CHAIN REACTION
CHAIN STITCHES
CHAIRMANSHIPS
CHAISE LONGUES
CHALCOGRAPHER
CHALCOGRAPHIC
CHALLENGEABLE
CHAMPIONSHIPS
CHANCELLERIES
CHANGEABILITY
CHANGE RINGING
CHANGING ROOMS
CHANTRY CHAPEL
CHARACTERIZED
CHARACTERLESS
CHARGEABILITY
CHARGE ACCOUNT
CHARNEL HOUSES
CHARTER MEMBER
CHASTISEMENTS
CHASTITY BELTS
CHATEAUBRIAND
CHEERLESSNESS
CHEMISORPTION
CHEMORECEPTOR
CHESTERFIELDS
CHEVAL GLASSES
CHIAROSCURISM

CHIAROSCURIST
CHIEF JUSTICES
CHIEFS OF STAFF
CHIEFTAINSHIP
CHILDLESSNESS
CHIMNEYBREAST
CHIMNEY CORNER
CHIMNEYPIECES
CHIMNEYSTACKS
CHIMNEYSWEEPS
CHIROPRACTORS
CHLAMYDOSPORE
CHLOROBENZENE
CHLOROFORMING
CHLOROMYCETIN
CHLOROPLASTIC
CHONDRIOSOMAL
CHONDROMATOUS
CHOREOGRAPHED
CHOREOGRAPHER
CHOREOGRAPHIC
CHRISTIANIZER
CHRISTIAN NAME
CHRISTMAS CAKE
CHRISTMAS CARD
CHRISTMASTIDE
CHRISTMASTIME
CHRISTMAS TREE
CHRISTOLOGIST
CHROMATICALLY
CHROMATICNESS
CHROMATOLYSIS
CHROMATOPHORE
CHROMOPLASMIC
CHROMOPROTEIN
CHROMOSPHERIC
CHRONOBIOLOGY
CHRONOGRAPHER
CHRONOGRAPHIC
CHRONOLOGICAL
CHRYSANTHEMUM
CHURCHWARDENS
CICATRIZATION
CINEMATICALLY
CINEMATOGRAPH
CIRCULARIZING
CIRCUMAMBIENT
CIRCUMCISIONS
CIRCUMFERENCE
CIRCUMFLEXION
CIRCUMSCRIBED
CIRCUMSPECTLY
CIRCUMSTANCES
CIRCUMVALLATE
CIRCUMVENTING
CIRCUMVENTION
CIVIL ENGINEER
CIVILIZATIONS
CIVIL SERVANTS

CLAIRAUDIENCE	COMMISERATION	CONCRETIONARY
CLANDESTINELY	COMMISERATIVE	CONCUPISCENCE
CLAPPERBOARDS	COMMISSARIATS	CONDEMNATIONS
CLARIFICATION	COMMISSIONERS	CONDEMNED CELL
CLARINETTISTS	COMMISSIONING	CONDENSED MILK
CLASSIFIED ADS	COMMUNALISTIC	CONDESCENDING
CLASSLESSNESS	COMMUNICATING	CONDESCENSION
CLASS STRUGGLE	COMMUNICATION	CONDITIONALLY
CLAUSTROPHOBE	COMMUNICATIVE	CONDUCIVENESS
CLAVICHORDIST	COMMUNICATORY	CONDUCTOR RAIL
CLEARANCE SALE	COMMUNITARIAN	CONDYLOMATOUS
CLEAR-HEADEDLY	COMMUNITY HOME	CONFABULATING
CLEARINGHOUSE	COMMUNIZATION	CONFABULATION
CLEISTOGAMOUS	COMPANIONABLE	CONFABULATORY
CLERKS OF WORKS	COMPANIONABLY	CONFECTIONARY
CLIMACTERICAL	COMPANIONSHIP	CONFECTIONERS
CLIMATOLOGIST	COMPANIONWAYS	CONFECTIONERY
CLIMBING FRAME	COMPARABILITY	CONFEDERACIES
CLIMBING IRONS	COMPARATIVELY	CONFEDERATING
CLOSED-CIRCUIT	COMPARTMENTAL	CONFEDERATION
CLOSED SEASONS	COMPASSIONATE	CONFESSIONALS
CLOSING PRICES	COMPASS POINTS	CONFESSIONARY
CLOTHES HANGER	COMPATIBILITY	CONFIGURATION
CLOTHESHORSES	COMPATRIOTISM	CONFIRMATIONS
CLUSTER-BOMBED	COMPENDIOUSLY	CONFISCATIONS
COACHBUILDERS	COMPETITIVELY	CONFLAGRATION
COACH STATIONS	COMPLAININGLY	CONFLAGRATIVE
COBELLIGERENT	COMPLAISANTLY	CONFORMATIONS
COCAINIZATION	COMPLEMENTARY	CONFRATERNITY
COCKER SPANIEL	COMPLEMENTING	CONFRONTATION
COCKTAIL STICK	COMPLICATEDLY	CONGLOMERATES
CODECLINATION	COMPLICATIONS	CONGLOMERATIC
CODIFICATIONS	COMPLIMENTARY	CONGRATULATED
COEDUCATIONAL	COMPLIMENTING	CONGRATULATOR
COLD-BLOODEDLY	COMPOSITIONAL	CONGREGATIONS
COLD-HEARTEDLY	COMPREHENDING	CONGRESSIONAL
COLLABORATING	COMPREHENSION	CONGRESSWOMAN
COLLABORATION	COMPREHENSIVE	CONJUGATIONAL
COLLABORATIVE	COMPRESSIONAL	CONJUNCTIONAL
COLLABORATORS	COMPUTABILITY	CONNECTING ROD
COLLETIVISTIC	COMPUTATIONAL	CONNING TOWERS
COLLOQUIALISM	COMPUTERIZING	CONNOTATATIVE
COLOUR SCHEMES	CONCATENATING	CONQUISTADORS
COMBAT FATIGUE	CONCATENATION	CONSANGUINITY
COMBINING FORM	CONCAVO-CONVEX	CONSCIENTIOUS
COMMANDEERING	CONCENTRATING	CONSCIOUSNESS
COMMANDERSHIP	CONCENTRATION	CONSECUTIVELY
COMMAND MODULE	CONCENTRATIVE	CONSEQUENTIAL
COMMEMORATING	CONCENTRICITY	CONSERVANCIES
COMMEMORATION	CONCEPTUALISM	CONSERVATIVES
COMMEMORATIVE	CONCEPTUALIST	CONSERVATOIRE
COMMENCEMENTS	CONCEPTUALIZE	CONSIDERATELY
COMMENDATIONS	CONCERT GRANDS	CONSIDERATION
COMMENSURABLE	CONCERTINAING	CONSISTENCIES
COMMERCIALISM	CONCESSIONARY	CONSOLIDATING
COMMERCIALIST	CONCHOLOGICAL	CONSOLIDATION
COMMERCIALITY	CONCHOLOGISTS	CONSPICUOUSLY
COMMERCIALIZE	CONCOMITANTLY	CONSPIRATRESS
COMMISERATING	CONCRETE MIXER	CONSTELLATION

CONSTELLATORY
CONSTERNATION
CONSTITUTIONS
CONSTRAINEDLY
CONSTRICTIONS
CONSTRUCTIBLE
CONSTRUCTIONS
CONSULTANCIES
CONSULTATIONS
CONSUMMATIONS
CONTACT LENSES
CONTAINERIZED
CONTAMINATING
CONTAMINATION
CONTAMINATORS
CONTEMPLATING
CONTEMPLATION
CONTEMPLATIVE
CONTENTIOUSLY
CONTEXTUALIZE
CONTINGENCIES
CONTINUATIONS
CONTORTIONIST
CONTRABANDIST
CONTRABASSIST
CONTRABASSOON
CONTRACEPTION
CONTRACEPTIVE
CONTRACTILITY
CONTRACTIONAL
CONTRACTUALLY
CONTRADICTING
CONTRADICTION
CONTRADICTIVE
CONTRADICTORY
CONTRAPUNTIST
CONTRAVENTION
CONTRIBUTIONS
CONTROVERSIAL
CONTROVERSIES
CONVALESCENCE
CONVALESCENTS
CONVERSATIONS
CONVERSAZIONE
CONVERTIPLANE
CONVEXO-CONVEX
CONVEYER BELTS
CONVOCATIONAL
CONVOLVULUSES
COOKING APPLES
COOPERATIVELY
CORDUROY ROADS
CORELIGIONIST
CO-RESPONDENCY
CO-RESPONDENTS
CORN EXCHANGES
CORPS DE BALLET
CORRESPONDENT
CORRESPONDING

CORRIGIBILITY
CORROBORATING
CORROBORATION
CORROBORATIVE
CORROBORATORS
CORRODIBILITY
CORROSIVENESS
CORRUPTIONIST
COSIGNATORIES
COSMOPOLITANS
COSMOPOLITISM
COST-EFFECTIVE
COSTERMONGERS
COTERMINOUSLY
COTTAGE CHEESE
COTTAGE LOAVES
COTTON-PICKING
COUNTENANCING
COUNTERACTING
COUNTERACTION
COUNTERACTIVE
COUNTERATTACK
COUNTERBLASTS
COUNTERCHARGE
COUNTERCLAIMS
COUNTERFEITED
COUNTERFEITER
COUNTERMANDED
COUNTERPOINTS
COUNTERPOISED
COUNTERPOISES
COUNTERSIGNED
COUNTERTENORS
COUNTERWEIGHT
COUNTINGHOUSE
COUNTRY COUSIN
COUNTRY DANCES
COUNTY COUNCIL
COURTEOUSNESS
COURT MARTIALS
COURTS-MARTIAL
COVERED WAGONS
CRAFTSMANSHIP
CRANIOLOGICAL
CRASH BARRIERS
CRASH LANDINGS
CRASSULACEOUS
CREAM OF TARTAR
CREDIT ACCOUNT
CREDIT SQUEEZE
CREME DE MENTHE
CRIMINOLOGIST
CRISSCROSSING
CROSSBENCHERS
CROSSBREEDING
CROSSCHECKING
CROSSCURRENTS
CROSS-DRESSERS
CROSS-DRESSING

CROSS-EXAMINED
CROSS-EXAMINER
CROSS-HATCHING
CROSS-PURPOSES
CROSS-QUESTION
CROSS-REFERRED
CROSS-SECTIONS
CROSS-STITCHES
CROWN COLONIES
CROWN PRINCESS
CRUISE MISSILE
CRUISERWEIGHT
CRUSH BARRIERS
CRYOBIOLOGIST
CRYPTANALYSIS
CRYPTANALYTIC
CRYPTOCLASTIC
CRYPTOGRAPHER
CRYPTOGRAPHIC
CRYSTAL GAZERS
CRYSTAL GAZING
CRYSTALLINITY
CRYSTALLIZING
CUMULOSTRATUS
CURTAIN RAISER
CUSTODIANSHIP
CYBERNETICIST
CYLINDRICALLY
CYTOCHEMISTRY
CYTOTAXONOMIC

D
DADAISTICALLY
DADDY LONGLEGS
DAGUERREOTYPE
DAGUERREOTYPY
DAMAGEABILITY
DAMNIFICATION
DANDIFICATION
DARK CONTINENT
DASTARDLINESS
DAUGHTER-IN-LAW
DEAD RECKONING
DEATH WARRANTS
DEBTS OF HONOUR
DECAPITATIONS
DECEITFULNESS
DECENTRALIZED
DECEPTIVENESS
DECEREBRATION
DECLAMATORILY
DECLARATORILY
DECLASSIFYING
DECOMPOSITION
DECOMPRESSING
DECOMPRESSION
DECOMPRESSIVE
DECONGESTANTS
DECONTAMINANT

DECONTAMINATE	DESPICABILITY	DISAPPEARANCE
DECONTROLLING	DESSERTSPOONS	DISAPPOINTING
DECORTICATION	DESTABILIZING	DISARTICULATE
DECREPITATION	DESTRUCTIVELY	DISASSOCIATED
DEDUCTIBILITY	DESULTORINESS	DISBURDENMENT
DEFECTIVENESS	DETACHABILITY	DISBURSEMENTS
DEFENSIBILITY	DETERIORATING	DISCHARGEABLE
DEFENSIVENESS	DETERIORATION	DISCIPLINABLE
DEFERENTIALLY	DETERIORATIVE	DISCOLORATION
DEFIBRILLATOR	DETERMINATION	DISCOMMODIOUS
DEFORESTATION	DETERMINATIVE	DISCOMPOSEDLY
DEGLUTINATION	DETERMINISTIC	DISCONCERTING
DEHYDROGENASE	DETESTABILITY	DISCONCERTION
DEHYDROGENATE	DETRIMENTALLY	DISCONFORMITY
DEHYDROGENIZE	DEUTEROGAMIST	DISCONNECTING
DELETERIOUSLY	DEVASTATINGLY	DISCONNECTION
DELIBERATIONS	DEVELOPMENTAL	DISCONNECTIVE
DELICATESSENS	DEVIATIONISTS	DISCONTENTING
DELICIOUSNESS	DEVOLUTIONARY	DISCONTINUING
DELINQUENCIES	DEVOTIONALITY	DISCONTINUITY
DELIQUESCENCE	DEXTEROUSNESS	DISCONTINUOUS
DELIRIOUSNESS	DEXTROGLUCOSE	DISCOUNT STORE
DEMAGNETIZING	DIAGEOTROPISM	DISCOURTESIES
DEMAGOGICALLY	DIAGNOSTICIAN	DISCREDITABLE
DEMERARA SUGAR	DIALECTICIANS	DISCREDITABLY
DEMERITORIOUS	DIALLING CODES	DISCREPANCIES
DEMILITARIZED	DIALLING TONES	DISCRETIONARY
DEMOCRATIZING	DIALYSABILITY	DISCRIMINATED
DEMOLITIONIST	DIAMETRICALLY	DISCRIMINATOR
DEMONOLOGICAL	DIAPHRAGMATIC	DISEMBODIMENT
DEMONSTRATING	DIATHERMANOUS	DISEMBOWELING
DEMONSTRATION	DIATONIC SCALE	DISEMBOWELLED
DEMONSTRATIVE	DIAZOTIZATION	DISENABLEMENT
DEMONSTRATORS	DICHLAMIDEOUS	DISENGAGEMENT
DENATIONALIZE	DICTATORIALLY	DISENTAILMENT
DENDRITICALLY	DICTATORSHIPS	DISENTANGLING
DENDROLOGICAL	DIESEL ENGINES	DISFIGUREMENT
DENOMINATIONS	DIFFERENTIALS	DISFRANCHISED
DENSITOMETRIC	DIFFERENTIATE	DISGRACEFULLY
DENTAL SURGEON	DIFFUSIBILITY	DISHARMONIOUS
DENTICULATION	DIGESTIBILITY	DISHONOURABLE
DENUNCIATIONS	DILAPIDATIONS	DISHONOURABLY
DEODORIZATION	DILLYDALLYING	DISILLUSIONED
DEONTOLOGICAL	DIMENSIONLESS	DISINCENTIVES
DEOXIDIZATION	DIM-WITTEDNESS	DISINFECTANTS
DEOXYGENATION	DINNER JACKETS	DISINHERITING
DEPENDABILITY	DINNER SERVICE	DISINTEGRABLE
DEPERSONALIZE	DIPHENYLAMINE	DISINTEGRATED
DEPRECATINGLY	DIPSOMANIACAL	DISINTEGRATOR
DEPRECATORILY	DIRECT CURRENT	DISINTERESTED
DEPRESSOMOTOR	DIRECT OBJECTS	DISINTERMENTS
DERMATOLOGIST	DIRECTORSHIPS	DISINVESTMENT
DERMATOPHYTIC	DISADVANTAGED	DISMANTLEMENT
DERMATOPLASTY	DISADVANTAGES	DISMEMBERMENT
DESCRIPTIVELY	DISAFFECTEDLY	DISOBEDIENTLY
DESCRIPTIVISM	DISAFFILIATED	DISOBLIGINGLY
DESEGREGATING	DISAFFIRMANCE	DISORIENTATED
DESEGREGATION	DISAFFORESTED	DISPARAGEMENT
DESENSITIZING	DISAGREEMENTS	DISPARAGINGLY

DISPASSIONATE	DOUBLE-CROSSES	ELECTROCUTING
DISPATCH BOXES	DOUBLE-DEALERS	ELECTROCUTION
DISPENSATIONS	DOUBLE-DEALING	ELECTROGRAPHY
DISPLACEMENTS	DOUBLE-DECKERS	ELECTROMAGNET
DISPOSABILITY	DOUBLE FEATURE	ELECTROMERISM
DISPOSITIONAL	DOUBLE FIGURES	ELECTROMETRIC
DISPOSSESSING	DOUBLE-GLAZING	ELECTROMOTIVE
DISPOSSESSION	DOUBLE-JOINTED	ELECTROPHILIC
DISPOSSESSORY	DOUBLE-PARKING	ELECTROPHONIC
DISPROPORTION	DOUBLE-TALKING	ELECTROPHORUS
DISPUTABILITY	DOWNHEARTEDLY	ELECTROPLATER
DISQUALIFYING	DOWNING STREET	ELECTROSCOPIC
DISQUISITIONS	DOWN'S SYNDROME	ELECTROSTATIC
DISRESPECTFUL	DRAINING BOARD	ELECTROVALENT
DISSATISFYING	DRAMATIC IRONY	ELEPHANTIASIC
DISSEMINATING	DRAMATIZATION	ELEPHANTIASIS
DISSEMINATION	DRAWING BOARDS	ELEPHANT'S-FOOT
DISSEMINATIVE	DRESSING GOWNS	EMBARRASSMENT
DISSEPIMENTAL	DRESSING ROOMS	EMBELLISHMENT
DISSERTATIONS	DRESSING TABLE	EMBRYOLOGICAL
DISSIMILARITY	DRINKING WATER	EMBRYONICALLY
DISSIMILATION	DRUM MAJORETTE	EMILIA-ROMAGNA
DISSIMILATIVE	DRYOPITHECINE	EMINENCE GRISE
DISSIMILATORY	DUALISTICALLY	EMOTIONLESSLY
DISSIMILITUDE	DUCKING STOOLS	EMPHYSEMATOUS
DISSIMULATING	DUCTLESS GLAND	EMPIRICALNESS
DISSIMULATION	DUPLICABILITY	EMPLOYABILITY
DISSIMULATIVE	DUTCH AUCTIONS	EMULSION PAINT
DISSOLUBILITY	DWELLING HOUSE	ENCAPSULATION
DISSOLUTENESS	DYED-IN-THE-WOOL	ENCAUSTICALLY
DISTASTEFULLY	DYSMENORRHOEA	ENCEPHALOGRAM
DISTILLATIONS		ENCHANTRESSES
DISTINCTIVELY	E	ENCOMPASSMENT
DISTINGUISHED	EAST-NORTHEAST	ENCOURAGEMENT
DISTINGUISHER	EAST-SOUTHEAST	ENCOURAGINGLY
DISTRESSINGLY	EAVESDROPPERS	ENCROACHINGLY
DISTRIBUTABLE	EAVESDROPPING	ENCROACHMENTS
DISTRIBUTIONS	ECCENTRICALLY	ENCULTURATION
DISTRUSTFULLY	ECCLESIASTICS	ENCULTURATIVE
DITRANSITIVES	ECCLESIOLATER	ENCUMBERINGLY
DIVERSIFIABLE	ECCLESIOLATRY	ENCYCLOPEDIAS
DIVISION LOBBY	ECONOMIZATION	ENCYCLOPEDISM
DOCTRINAIRISM	ECTOPARASITIC	ENCYCLOPEDIST
DOCUMENTARIES	ECUMENICALISM	ENDOCRINOLOGY
DOCUMENTARILY	EDITORIALIZER	ENDODONTOLOGY
DOCUMENTATION	EDUCATED GUESS	ENDOLYMPHATIC
DODECAPHONISM	EFFECTIVENESS	ENDOMETRIOSIS
DODECAPHONIST	EFFERVESCENCE	ENDOPARASITIC
DOGMATIZATION	EFFERVESCIBLE	ENDOPEPTIDASE
DOG'S BREAKFAST	EFFICACIOUSLY	ENERGETICALLY
DOMESTICATING	EFFLORESCENCE	ENFRANCHISING
DOMESTICATION	EGOCENTRICITY	ENGINE DRIVERS
DOMESTICATIVE	EGOTISTICALLY	ENIGMATICALLY
DOMESTICITIES	EGREGIOUSNESS	ENLIGHTENMENT
DONKEY JACKETS	EGYPTOLOGICAL	ENROLLED NURSE
DOSIMETRICIAN	ELABORATENESS	ENTANGLEMENTS
DOUBLE-CHECKED	ELECTIONEERER	ENTERTAINMENT
DOUBLE-CROSSED	ELECTRIC CHAIR	ENTHRALLINGLY
DOUBLE-CROSSER	ELECTRIFIABLE	ENTHRONEMENTS

ENTOMOLOGICAL
ENTOMOLOGISTS
ENTOMOPHAGOUS
ENTOMOPHILOUS
ENTOMOSTRACAN
ENTREPRENEURS
ENUNCIABILITY
ENVIRONMENTAL
ENZYMOLOGICAL
EPIGRAMMATISM
EPIGRAMMATIST
EPIGRAMMATIZE
EPILEPTICALLY
EPIPHENOMENAL
EPIPHENOMENON
EPIPHYTICALLY
EPISCOPALIANS
EPITOMIZATION
EPIZOOTICALLY
EQUESTRIANISM
EQUILIBRATION
EQUILIBRISTIC
EQUIMOLECULAR
EQUIPONDERANT
EQUIPONDERATE
EQUIPOTENTIAL
EQUITABLENESS
EQUIVOCATIONS
ERGONOMICALLY
ERRONEOUSNESS
ERYSIPELATOUS
ESCAPOLOGISTS
ESCHATOLOGIST
ESPIRITO SANTO
ESPRIT DE CORPS
ESTABLISHMENT
ESTIMABLENESS
ESTRANGEMENTS
ETHNOCENTRISM
ETHNOGRAPHERS
ETHOLOGICALLY
ETIOLOGICALLY
EUSPORANGIATE
EVAPORABILITY
EVENTUALITIES
EVERLASTINGLY
EVERY WHICH WAY
EVOCATIVENESS
EXAGGERATEDLY
EXAGGERATIONS
EXAMINATIONAL
EXANTHEMATOUS
EXASPERATEDLY
EXCEPTIONABLE
EXCEPTIONALLY
EXCESSIVENESS
EXCHANGE RATES
EXCLAMATIONAL
EXCLAMATORILY

EXCLUDABILITY
EXCLUSIVENESS
EXCOMMUNICATE
EXCURSIVENESS
EXCUSABLENESS
EXECRABLENESS
EXEMPLARINESS
EXEMPLIFIABLE
EXEMPLI GRATIA
EXHIBITIONISM
EXHIBITIONIST
EXPANSIBILITY
EXPANSIONISTS
EXPANSIVENESS
EXPECTORATING
EXPECTORATION
EXPEDITIONARY
EXPEDITIOUSLY
EXPENDABILITY
EXPENSIVENESS
EXPERIMENTING
EXPERT SYSTEMS
EXPLANATORIES
EXPLANATORILY
EXPLOSIVENESS
EXPONENTIALLY
EXPORTABILITY
EXPOSTULATING
EXPOSTULATION
EXPOSTULATORY
EXPRESSIONISM
EXPRESSIONIST
EXPROPRIATING
EXPROPRIATION
EXPROPRIATORS
EXQUISITENESS
EXTEMPORARILY
EXTEMPORIZING
EXTENDIBILITY
EXTENSIBILITY
EXTENSIVENESS
EXTENUATINGLY
EXTERMINATING
EXTERMINATION
EXTERMINATIVE
EXTERMINATORS
EXTERNALIZING
EXTEROCEPTIVE
EXTERRITORIAL
EXTINGUISHANT
EXTINGUISHERS
EXTINGUISHING
EXTORTIONABLE
EXTORTIONISTS
EXTRACELLULAR
EXTRAGALACTIC
EXTRAJUDICIAL
EXTRAORDINARY
EXTRAPOLATING

EXTRAPOLATION
EXTRAPOLATIVE
EXTRAPOSITION
EXTRAVAGANCES
EXTRAVAGANTLY
EXTRAVAGANZAS
EXTRAVAGATION
EXTRAVASATION
EXTRAVASCULAR
EXTRINSICALLY
EYEBROW PENCIL
EYE-CATCHINGLY

F
FACETIOUSNESS
FACTORABILITY
FACTORIZATION
FAITHLESSNESS
FALLOPIAN TUBE
FALSIFICATION
FAMILIARITIES
FAMILIARIZING
FAMILY DOCTORS
FANTASTICALLY
FASCICULATION
FASCINATINGLY
FASCISTICALLY
FATHEADEDNESS
FATHER FIGURES
FAULTLESSNESS
FEATHERBEDDED
FEATHERSTITCH
FEATHER-VEINED
FEATHERWEIGHT
FEATURE-LENGTH
FEEDING BOTTLE
FELICITATIONS
FELLOW FEELING
FELONIOUSNESS
FEMMES FATALES
FEROCIOUSNESS
FERRIMAGNETIC
FERROCHROMIUM
FERROCONCRETE
FERROELECTRIC
FERROMAGNETIC
FERTILIZATION
FEUDALIZATION
FEUILLETONISM
FEUILLETONIST
FIBROVASCULAR
FICTIONALIZED
FIELD MARSHALS
FIELD OF VISION
FIGHTER-BOMBER
FIGURED BASSES
FIGURE OF EIGHT
FIGURE SKATERS
FIGURE-SKATING

FILIBUSTERING	FRACTIONATION	GEOSTATIONARY
FILING CABINET	FRACTIOUSNESS	GEOTACTICALLY
FILM PREMIERES	FRACTOCUMULUS	GEOTROPICALLY
FILTERABILITY	FRACTOSTRATUS	GERIATRICIANS
FINANCIAL YEAR	FRAGMENTATION	GERMANIZATION
FINE-TOOTH COMB	FRANCHISEMENT	GERMAN MEASLES
FINGERPRINTED	FREDERIKSBERG	GERMANOPHILIA
FIRST OFFENDER	FREEZING POINT	GERMANOPHOBIA
FISH-EYE LENSES	FREIGHTLINERS	GERONTOCRATIC
FISSION-FUSION	FRENCH WINDOWS	GERONTOLOGIST
FLABBERGASTED	FREQUENTATION	GERRYMANDERED
FLAGELLANTISM	FREQUENTATIVE	GESTICULATING
FLAME-THROWERS	FREUDIAN SLIPS	GESTICULATION
FLAVOPURPURIN	FRIDGE-FREEZER	GESTICULATIVE
FLEET ADMIRALS	FRIGHTENINGLY	GHETTO BLASTER
FLESH AND BLOOD	FRIGHTFULNESS	GLACIOLOGICAL
FLIRTATIOUSLY	FRINGE BENEFIT	GLAMORIZATION
FLOATING-POINT	FRIVOLOUSNESS	GLAMOROUSNESS
FLOATING VOTER	FRONTBENCHERS	GLOBETROTTERS
FLOODLIGHTING	FRONTISPIECES	GLOBETROTTING
FLORIANOPOLIS	FRONTOGENESIS	GLOBULIFEROUS
FLORICULTURAL	FRUITLESSNESS	GLOCKENSPIELS
FLORISTICALLY	FRUIT MACHINES	GLORIFICATION
FLOURISHINGLY	FRUMENTACEOUS	GLOSSOGRAPHER
FLYING COLOURS	FULL-FASHIONED	GLUTINOUSNESS
FLYING DOCTORS	FUNCTIONALISM	GLYPHOGRAPHER
FLYING OFFICER	FUNCTIONALIST	GLYPHOGRAPHIC
FLYING PICKETS	FUNCTIONARIES	GLYPTOGRAPHER
FLYING SAUCERS	FUNDAMENTALLY	GLYPTOGRAPHIC
FOLLOW-THROUGH	FUNNY BUSINESS	GOLDEN JUBILEE
FONTAINEBLEAU	FUTURE PERFECT	GOLDEN WEDDING
FOOD POISONING		GOLDFISH BOWLS
FOOD PROCESSOR	G	GOOD AFTERNOON
FOOLHARDINESS	GALLICIZATION	GOOD-NATUREDLY
FOOL'S PARADISE	GALLOWS HUMOUR	GOOD SAMARITAN
FOOTBALL POOLS	GALVANOMETRIC	GOOSESTEPPING
FORAMINIFERAL	GALVANOSCOPIC	GOVERNABILITY
FOREIGN OFFICE	GALVANOTROPIC	GRACELESSNESS
FOREJUDGEMENT	GAMBREL-ROOFED	GRADE CROSSING
FOREKNOWINGLY	GAMETOGENESIS	GRAMINIVOROUS
FOREKNOWLEDGE	GAMMA GLOBULIN	GRAMMAR SCHOOL
FORENSICALITY	GARBAGE TRUCKS	GRAMMATICALLY
FOREORDAINING	GARDEN PARTIES	GRAM-MOLECULAR
FORESHADOWING	GARRULOUSNESS	GRANDCHILDREN
FORESHORTENED	GASTROSCOPIST	GRANDDAUGHTER
FOREWARNINGLY	GEIGER COUNTER	GRANDILOQUENT
FORGETFULNESS	GELANDESPRUNG	GRANULOMATOUS
FORGIVINGNESS	GELSENKIRCHEN	GRAPHEMICALLY
FORKLIFT TRUCK	GENDER-BENDERS	GRAPHICALNESS
FORMALIZATION	GENERALISSIMO	GRAPHIC DESIGN
FORMATIVENESS	GENERAL STRIKE	GRAPHOLOGISTS
FORMIDABILITY	GENERATION GAP	GRAPPLING IRON
FORTIFICATION	GENTIANACEOUS	GRATIFICATION
FORTITUDINOUS	GENUFLECTIONS	GRAVITATIONAL
FORTUNE HUNTER	GEOCHRONOLOGY	GREEN-FINGERED
FORTUNE-TELLER	GEODYNAMICIST	GROTESQUENESS
FOSSILIFEROUS	GEOMETRICALLY	GROUND STROKES
FOSSILIZATION	GEOMORPHOLOGY	GROUP CAPTAINS
FOUNDATIONARY	GEOPOLITICIAN	GROUP PRACTICE

GUARDIAN ANGEL
GUBERNATORIAL
GUIDED MISSILE
GUILELESSNESS
GUILTLESSNESS
GYMNOSPERMISM
GYMNOSPERMOUS
GYNAECOCRATIC
GYNAECOLOGIST
GYNANDROMORPH

H
HACKING COUGHS
HAEMATOGENOUS
HAEMATOLOGIST
HAEMODIALYSIS
HAEMOPHILIOID
HAEMORRHOIDAL
HAGIOGRAPHIES
HAILE SELASSIE
HAIR-RESTORERS
HAIR-SPLITTING
HALF-HEARTEDLY
HALFWAY HOUSES
HALICARNASSUS
HALLUCINATING
HALLUCINATION
HALLUCINATORY
HAMILCAR BARCA
HANDKERCHIEFS
HAPHAZARDNESS
HARD-HEARTEDLY
HARD-LUCK STORY
HARD OF HEARING
HARD SHOULDERS
HARMONIZATION
HARUN AL-RASHID
HAZARDOUSNESS
HEADSHRINKERS
HEALTHFULNESS
HEARTBREAKING
HEARTBROKENLY
HEART DISEASES
HEARTLESSNESS
HEARTSICKNESS
HEARTSOMENESS
HEART-TO-HEARTS
HEATH ROBINSON
HEAVY HYDROGEN
HEAVY INDUSTRY
HEDGE SPARROWS
HEEBIE-JEEBIES
HEIRS APPARENT
HELLENIZATION
HELMINTHIASIS
HELMINTHOLOGY
HELTER-SKELTER
HEMICELLULOSE
HENDECAHEDRON

HEPTADECANOIC
HEPTAMETRICAL
HERBIVOROUSLY
HEREDITAMENTS
HEREFORDSHIRE
HERMAPHRODITE
HERNIORRHAPHY
HEROIC COUPLET
HERPES SIMPLEX
HERPETOLOGIST
HERTFORDSHIRE
HETEROGENEITY
HETEROGENEOUS
HETEROGENESIS
HETEROGENETIC
HETEROGRAPHIC
HETEROMORPHIC
HETEROPLASTIC
HETEROPTEROUS
HETEROSEXUALS
HETEROSPOROUS
HETEROSTYLOUS
HETEROTHALLIC
HETEROTROPHIC
HETEROZYGOSIS
HEURISTICALLY
HIERACOSPHINX
HIEROGLYPHICS
HIEROGLYPHIST
HIGH-AND-MIGHTY
HIGH CHURCHMAN
HIGH EXPLOSIVE
HIGHLAND FLING
HIGH-PRESSURED
HIGH-WATER MARK
HILARIOUSNESS
HILDEBRANDIAN
HILDEBRANDINE
HISTOCHEMICAL
HOBSON'S CHOICE
HOIDENISHNESS
HOLE-AND-CORNER
HOLIDAYMAKERS
HOLIDAYMAKING
HOLY COMMUNION
HOME ECONOMICS
HOMEOMORPHISM
HOMILETICALLY
HOMOCHROMATIC
HOMOEROTICISM
HOMOGENEOUSLY
HOMOIOTHERMIC
HOMOLOGICALLY
HOMOLOGRAPHIC
HOMOOUSIANISM
HOMOSEXUALITY
HONEYDEW MELON
HONORIFICALLY
HORNS OF PLENTY

HORRIFICATION
HORRIPILATION
HORSE CHESTNUT
HORSEWHIPPING
HORTICULTURAL
HOSPITALIZING
HOT-GOSPELLERS
HOT-GOSPELLING
HOT-HEADEDNESS
HOUSEBREAKERS
HOUSEBREAKING
HOUSEHOLD NAME
HOUSE HUSBANDS
HOUSEMISTRESS
HOUSES OF CARDS
HOUSE SPARROWS
HOUSEWARMINGS
HOYDENISHNESS
HUCKLEBERRIES
HUMANITARIANS
HUMILIATINGLY
HUNDREDWEIGHT
HUNGER MARCHER
HUNGER MARCHES
HUNGER STRIKER
HUNGER STRIKES
HUNTING GROUND
HURRICANE LAMP
HYALURONIDASE
HYBRIDIZATION
HYDRAULICALLY
HYDROCEPHALIC
HYDROCEPHALUS
HYDROCHLORIDE
HYDRODYNAMICS
HYDROELECTRIC
HYDROGENATION
HYDROGEN BOMBS
HYDROKINETICS
HYDROLYSATION
HYPERCRITICAL
HYPOCHONDRIAC

I
IATROGENICITY
ICE-CREAM SODAS
ICHTHYOLOGIST
ICONOMATICISM
IDEALIZATIONS
IDENTICAL TWIN
IDENTITY CARDS
IDEOLOGICALLY
IDIOMATICALLY
IDIOSYNCRATIC
IGNOMINIOUSLY
ILL-CONSIDERED
ILLE-ET-VILAINE
ILLOCUTIONARY
ILLUMINATIONS

ILLUSIONISTIC	INATTENTIVELY	INDISPOSITION
ILLUSTRATIONS	INAUGURATIONS	INDISTINCTIVE
ILLUSTRIOUSLY	INCANDESCENCE	INDIVIDUALISM
IMAGINATIVELY	INCANTATIONAL	INDIVIDUALIST
IMAGISTICALLY	INCAPACITATED	INDIVIDUALITY
IMITATIVENESS	INCAPSULATION	INDIVIDUALIZE
IMMATERIALISM	INCARCERATING	INDIVIDUATION
IMMATERIALIST	INCARCERATION	INDOCTRINATED
IMMATERIALITY	INCARDINATION	INDOCTRINATOR
IMMATERIALIZE	INCLINATIONAL	INDOLEBUTYRIC
IMMIGRATIONAL	INCOMBUSTIBLE	INDUPLICATION
IMMISCIBILITY	INCOMMUNICADO	INDUSTRIALISM
IMMORTALIZING	INCOMPETENTLY	INDUSTRIALIST
IMMUNIZATIONS	INCONCEIVABLE	INDUSTRIALIZE
IMMUNOGENETIC	INCONCEIVABLY	INDUSTRIOUSLY
IMMUNOTHERAPY	INCONDENSABLE	INEDUCABILITY
IMPALPABILITY	INCONGRUITIES	INEFFECTIVELY
IMPARIPINNATE	INCONGRUOUSLY	INEFFECTUALLY
IMPARTIBILITY	INCONSEQUENCE	INEFFICACIOUS
IMPASSABILITY	INCONSIDERATE	INEFFICIENTLY
IMPASSIONEDLY	INCONSISTENCY	INELIGIBILITY
IMPASSIVENESS	INCONSPICUOUS	INEVITABILITY
IMPECCABILITY	INCONSTANCIES	INEXHAUSTIBLE
IMPECUNIOUSLY	INCONTESTABLE	INEXHAUSTIBLY
IMPERCEPTIBLE	INCONTESTABLY	INEXORABILITY
IMPERCEPTIBLY	INCONVENIENCE	INEXPENSIVELY
IMPERFECTIONS	INCONVERTIBLE	INEXPERIENCED
IMPERFORATION	INCONVINCIBLE	INEXPRESSIBLE
IMPERIALISTIC	INCORPORATING	INEXPRESSIBLY
IMPERIOUSNESS	INCORPORATION	INFALLIBILITY
IMPERMISSIBLE	INCORPORATIVE	INFANT PRODIGY
IMPERSONALITY	INCORPOREALLY	INFECTIVENESS
IMPERSONALIZE	INCORRECTNESS	INFERENTIALLY
IMPERSONATING	INCORRUPTIBLE	INFILTRATIONS
IMPERSONATION	INCORRUPTIBLY	INFINITESIMAL
IMPERSONATORS	INCREDIBILITY	INFLAMMATIONS
IMPERTINENTLY	INCREDULOUSLY	INFLECTEDNESS
IMPERTURBABLE	INCREMENTALLY	INFLEXIBILITY
IMPERTURBABLY	INCRIMINATING	INFLORESCENCE
IMPETUOUSNESS	INCRIMINATION	INFLUENCEABLE
IMPLACABILITY	INCRIMINATORY	INFLUENTIALLY
IMPONDERABLES	INCRUSTATIONS	INFORMATIONAL
IMPORTUNATELY	INCULPABILITY	INFORMATIVELY
IMPOSSIBILITY	INDEFATIGABLE	INFRINGEMENTS
IMPOVERISHING	INDEFATIGABLY	INFURIATINGLY
IMPRACTICABLE	INDENTURESHIP	INGENUOUSNESS
IMPRACTICABLY	INDEPENDENTLY	INGRAINEDNESS
IMPRACTICALLY	INDESCRIBABLE	INGURGITATION
IMPRESSIONISM	INDESCRIBABLY	INHOSPITALITY
IMPRESSIONIST	INDETERMINACY	INIMITABILITY
IMPROBABILITY	INDETERMINATE	INJUDICIOUSLY
IMPROPRIATION	INDETERMINISM	INLAND REVENUE
IMPROPRIETIES	INDETERMINIST	INNOCUOUSNESS
IMPROVABILITY	INDIAN SUMMERS	INNOVATIONIST
IMPROVIDENTLY	INDIFFERENTLY	INOCULABILITY
IMPROVISATION	INDISCERNIBLE	INOFFENSIVELY
IMPULSIVENESS	INDISCRETIONS	INOPERABILITY
INADVERTENTLY	INDISPENSABLE	INOPPORTUNELY
INAPPROPRIATE	INDISPENSABLY	INORGANICALLY

INQUISITIONAL	INTERLAMINATE	INVESTIGATION
INQUISITIVELY	INTERLOCUTION	INVESTIGATIVE
INQUISITORIAL	INTERLOCUTORS	INVESTIGATORS
INSATIABILITY	INTERLOCUTORY	INVIDIOUSNESS
INSCRIPTIONAL	INTERLUNATION	INVINCIBILITY
INSECTIVOROUS	INTERMARRIAGE	INVIOLABILITY
INSENSIBILITY	INTERMARRYING	INVOLUNTARILY
INSENSITIVELY	INTERMEDIATOR	IRONING BOARDS
INSENSITIVITY	INTERMINGLING	IRRATIONALITY
INSIDIOUSNESS	INTERMISSIONS	IRRECLAIMABLE
INSIGNIFICANT	INTERMITTENCE	IRRECOVERABLE
INSOLVABILITY	INTERNALIZING	IRRECOVERABLY
INSPECTORATES	INTERNATIONAL	IRREFRANGIBLE
INSPECTORSHIP	INTEROCEPTIVE	IRRELIGIONIST
INSPIRATIONAL	INTEROSCULATE	IRREPLACEABLE
INSPIRITINGLY	INTERPELLATOR	IRREPLEVIABLE
INSTABILITIES	INTERPERSONAL	IRREPRESSIBLE
INSTALLATIONS	INTERPOLATING	IRREPRESSIBLY
INSTANTANEOUS	INTERPOLATION	IRRESPONSIBLE
INSTIGATINGLY	INTERPOLATIVE	IRRESPONSIBLY
INSTINCTIVELY	INTERPOSINGLY	IRRETRIEVABLE
INSTITUTIONAL	INTERPOSITION	IRRETRIEVABLY
INSTRUCTIONAL	INTERPRETABLE	ISOAGGLUTININ
INSTRUCTIVELY	INTERRACIALLY	ISODIMORPHISM
INSUBORDINATE	INTERRELATION	ISODIMORPHOUS
INSUBSTANTIAL	INTERROGATING	ISOELECTRONIC
INSUFFICIENCY	INTERROGATION	ISOGEOTHERMAL
INSUPPORTABLE	INTERROGATIVE	ISOLATIONISTS
INSURRECTIONS	INTERROGATORS	ISOMERIZATION
INSUSCEPTIBLE	INTERROGATORY	ISOSPONDYLOUS
INTANGIBILITY	INTERRUPTIBLE	ITALICIZATION
INTEGRABILITY	INTERRUPTIONS	
INTEGUMENTARY	INTERSECTIONS	**J**
INTELLECTUALS	INTERSPERSING	JACK-O'-LANTERNS
INTELLIGENTLY	INTERSPERSION	JARGONIZATION
INTEMPERATELY	INTERSTRATIFY	JELLIFICATION
INTENTIONALLY	INTERTROPICAL	JET PROPULSION
INTERACTIONAL	INTERVENTIONS	JIGGERY-POKERY
INTERACTIVELY	INTRACELLULAR	JIGSAW PUZZLES
INTERACTIVITY	INTRAMUSCULAR	JOB'S COMFORTER
INTERBREEDING	INTRANSIGENCE	JOLLIFICATION
INTERCALARILY	INTRAPERSONAL	JUDICIOUSNESS
INTERCALATION	INTRATELLURIC	JUGLANDACEOUS
INTERCALATIVE	INTRAVASATION	JUNIOR SCHOOLS
INTERCELLULAR	INTRAVENOUSLY	JURISPRUDENCE
INTERCEPTIONS	INTRINSICALLY	JUSTICIARSHIP
INTERCESSIONS	INTRODUCTIONS	JUSTIFICATION
INTERCHANGING	INTROGRESSION	JUSTIFICATORY
INTERCLAVICLE	INTROSPECTION	JUXTAPOSITION
INTERCOLUMNAR	INTROSPECTIVE	
INTERCURRENCE	INTUITIVENESS	**K**
INTEREST GROUP	INVARIABILITY	KALEIDOSCOPES
INTERESTINGLY	INVENTIVENESS	KALEIDOSCOPIC
INTERFACIALLY	INVENTORIABLE	KANGAROO COURT
INTERFERINGLY	INVERTEBRATES	KANGCHENJUNGA
INTERGALACTIC	INVERTED COMMA	KARL-MARX-STADT
INTERGRADIENT	INVERTED SNOBS	KERATOPLASTIC
INTERJECTIONS	INVERTIBILITY	KETTLEDRUMMER
INTERLACEMENT	INVESTIGATING	KEY SIGNATURES

KIDDERMINSTER	LEXICOGRAPHER	MAGNETIC FIELD
KIDNEY MACHINE	LEXICOGRAPHIC	MAGNETIC HEADS
KINDERGARTENS	LEXICOLOGICAL	MAGNETIC NORTH
KIND-HEARTEDLY	LIBRARIANSHIP	MAGNETIC POLES
KINEMATICALLY	LICENSE PLATES	MAGNETIC TAPES
KINETIC ENERGY	LICENSING LAWS	MAGNETIZATION
KINETONUCLEUS	LIEBFRAUMILCH	MAGNETOMETRIC
KING'S COUNSELS	LIECHTENSTEIN	MAGNETOMOTIVE
KING'S EVIDENCE	LIFE PRESERVER	MAGNETOSPHERE
KIRKCUDBRIGHT	LIGHT AIRCRAFT	MAGNIFICATION
KITCHEN GARDEN	LIGHT-FINGERED	MAGNIFICENTLY
KLEPTOMANIACS	LIGHT-HEADEDLY	MAGNILOQUENCE
KNIGHTS-ERRANT	LIGNIFICATION	MAGNITUDINOUS
KNOWLEDGEABLE	LIMITLESSNESS	MAGNOLIACEOUS
KNOWLEDGEABLY	LINE-ENGRAVING	MAIDS OF HONOUR
KNUCKLE-DUSTER	LINGUA FRANCAS	MAJOR GENERALS
KWANGSI-CHUANG	LITHOGRAPHING	MALACOLOGICAL
	LITIGIOUSNESS	MALACOSTRACAN
L	LITTLE FINGERS	MALADJUSTMENT
LABIALIZATION	LIVERY COMPANY	MALADMINISTER
LABORIOUSNESS	LIVERY STABLES	MALADROITNESS
LABOURS OF LOVE	LIVING FOSSILS	MALFORMATIONS
LACKADAISICAL	LOATHSOMENESS	MALFUNCTIONED
LACTOBACILLUS	LODGING HOUSES	MALICIOUSNESS
LADY-IN-WAITING	LOGOGRAMMATIC	MALIMPRINTING
LAEVOROTATION	LONGSUFFERING	MALTHUSIANISM
LAEVOROTATORY	LONG VACATIONS	MANAGEABILITY
LAMELLIBRANCH	LOSS ADJUSTERS	MANDARIN DUCKS
LANCE CORPORAL	LOWER EAST SIDE	MANGEL-WURZELS
LANDING FIELDS	LOW-PASS FILTER	MANIFESTATION
LANDING STAGES	LOW-WATER MARKS	MANIPULATABLE
LANDING STRIPS	LUBRICATIONAL	MANIPULATIONS
LANDOWNERSHIP	LUDICROUSNESS	MANTELSHELVES
LANTERNSLIDES	LUNATIC FRINGE	MANUFACTURERS
LAPAROSCOPIES	LUNCHEONETTES	MANUFACTURING
LARYNGOLOGIST	LYMPHADENITIS	MANY-SIDEDNESS
LARYNGOSCOPIC	LYMPHATICALLY	MARAGING STEEL
LASER PRINTERS	LYMPHOBLASTIC	MARCHIONESSES
LATCHKEY CHILD	LYMPHOCYTOSIS	MARKETABILITY
LATEROVERSION	LYMPHOCYTOTIC	MARKET GARDENS
LATIN AMERICAN	LYMPHOPOIESIS	MARRIAGE LINES
LAUGHINGSTOCK	LYMPHOPOIETIC	MARRONS GLACES
LAUNDRY BASKET		MARTYRIZATION
LEADING LADIES	M	MARTYROLOGIST
LEADING LIGHTS	MACARONICALLY	MASSACHUSETTS
LEATHERJACKET	MACHIAVELLIAN	MASSIF CENTRAL
LECHEROUSNESS	MACHICOLATION	MASS-PRODUCING
LEGISLATORIAL	MACHINABILITY	MASTERFULNESS
LEISHMANIASIS	MACHINEGUNNED	MASTERMINDING
LEISURELINESS	MACRENCEPHALY	MASTERS-AT-ARMS
LEPIDOPTERIST	MACROCLIMATIC	MASTERS OF ARTS
LEPIDOPTEROUS	MACROECONOMIC	MASTERSTROKES
LEPTOCEPHALUS	MACROMOLECULE	MASTIGOPHORAN
LEPTOPHYLLOUS	MACRONUTRIENT	MASTOIDECTOMY
LETHARGICALLY	MADE-TO-MEASURE	MATCHLESSNESS
LETTER OPENERS	MADRIGALESQUE	MATERFAMILIAS
LETTER-PERFECT	MAGIC LANTERNS	MATERIALISTIC
LETTERPRESSES	MAGISTERIALLY	MATERIALIZING
LEVEL CROSSING	MAGNANIMOUSLY	MATERNALISTIC

MATHEMATICIAN	METHODIZATION	MISTRUSTINGLY
MATRICULATING	METHODOLOGIES	MISUNDERSTAND
MATRICULATION	METHODOLOGIST	MISUNDERSTOOD
MATRILOCALITY	METHYL ALCOHOL	MITOCHONDRIAL
MATURE STUDENT	METRONIDAZOLE	MITOCHONDRION
MAXILLIPEDARY	METROPOLITANS	MIXED BLESSING
MEANINGLESSLY	MEZZO-SOPRANOS	MIXED METAPHOR
MEASURABILITY	MICROANALYSIS	MOBILE LIBRARY
MECHANIZATION	MICROANALYTIC	MOBILIZATIONS
MEDIATIZATION	MICROCEPHALIC	MODERNIZATION
MEDIATORIALLY	MICROCHEMICAL	MODIFIABILITY
MEDIEVALISTIC	MICROCLIMATIC	MODIFICATIONS
MEDITERRANEAN	MICROCOMPUTER	MODUS OPERANDI
MEETINGHOUSES	MICRODETECTOR	MOHAMMEDANISM
MEGACEPHALOUS	MICRONUTRIENT	MOLLIFICATION
MEGALOBLASTIC	MICROORGANISM	MOLLYCODDLING
MEGALOMANIACS	MICROPARASITE	MOMENT OF TRUTH
MEGALOPOLITAN	MICROPHYSICAL	MONEYCHANGERS
MELODIOUSNESS	MICROTONALITY	MONEY-GRUBBERS
MELODRAMATIST	MIDDLEBROWISM	MONEY-GRUBBING
MELTING POINTS	MIDDLE EASTERN	MONEY-SPINNERS
MENSTRUATIONS	MIDDLE FINGERS	MONKEY-PUZZLES
MENSURATIONAL	MIDDLESBROUGH	MONOCHROMATIC
MERCENARINESS	MIDDLE SCHOOLS	MONOCOTYLEDON
MERCERIZATION	MIDDLEWEIGHTS	MONOGRAMMATIC
MERCHANDISING	MIDDLE WESTERN	MONOMETALLISM
MERCHANT BANKS	MID-LIFE CRISES	MONOMETALLIST
MERCILESSNESS	MID-LIFE CRISIS	MONOMOLECULAR
MERCURIALNESS	MILK CHOCOLATE	MONONUCLEOSIS
MERCUROCHROME	MILLENNIALIST	MONOPHTHONGAL
MERCY KILLINGS	MILLIONAIRESS	MONOPSONISTIC
MERITOCRACIES	MIMEOGRAPHING	MONOSYLLABISM
MERITORIOUSLY	MINE DETECTORS	MONOSYLLABLES
MERRY-GO-ROUNDS	MINERALOGICAL	MONOTREMATOUS
MERTHYR TYDFIL	MINERALOGISTS	MONSTROSITIES
MESENCEPHALIC	MINERAL WATERS	MONS VENERISES
MESENCEPHALON	MINICOMPUTERS	MONUMENTALITY
MESMERIZATION	MINISTERIALLY	MOONLIGHT FLIT
MESSIANICALLY	MIRABILE DICTU	MORALITY PLAYS
METABOLICALLY	MIRTHLESSNESS	MORAL MAJORITY
METABOLIZABLE	MISADVENTURES	MORNING PRAYER
METACHROMATIC	MISCALCULATED	MORPHEMICALLY
METALANGUAGES	MISCEGENATION	MORPHOGENESIS
METALLIFEROUS	MISCELLANEOUS	MORPHOGENETIC
METALLIZATION	MISCHIEVOUSLY	MORPHOLOGICAL
METALLOGRAPHY	MISCONCEIVING	MORPHOPHONEME
METALLURGICAL	MISCONCEPTION	MORRISDANCERS
METALLURGISTS	MISCONDUCTING	MORTIFICATION
METAMERICALLY	MISCONSTRUING	MOTHER COUNTRY
METAMORPHOSED	MISDEMEANOURS	MOTHER-OF-PEARL
METAMORPHOSES	MISERABLENESS	MOTHER TONGUES
METAMORPHOSIS	MISGOVERNMENT	MOTION PICTURE
METAPHOSPHATE	MISJUDGEMENTS	MOTORCYCLISTS
METAPHYSICIAN	MISMANAGEMENT	MOTOR SCOOTERS
METASTABILITY	MISPROPORTION	MOUNTAIN LIONS
METEMPIRICIST	MISQUOTATIONS	MOUNTAINSIDES
METENCEPHALIC	MISSISSIPPIAN	MOUNTEBANKERY
METENCEPHALON	MISSTATEMENTS	MOUTH-WATERING
METEOROLOGIST	MISTRUSTFULLY	MOVABLE FEASTS

MOVING PICTURE
MUHAMMADANISM
MULTICELLULAR
MULTICOLOURED
MULTINATIONAL
MULTIPLE STORE
MULTITUDINOUS
MULTIVIBRATOR
MUMMIFICATION
MURDEROUSNESS
MUSICAL CHAIRS
MUSICOLOGICAL
MYCOBACTERIUM
MYRMECOLOGIST
MYSTIFICATION
MYTHICIZATION

N
NARCOANALYSIS
NARCOTIZATION
NARROW SQUEAKS
NATIONAL DEBTS
NATIONALISTIC
NATIONALITIES
NATIONALIZING
NATIONAL PARKS
NATIONAL TRUST
NATIVITY PLAYS
NAUTICAL MILES
NEARSIGHTEDLY
NECESSARY EVIL
NECESSITARIAN
NECESSITATING
NECESSITATION
NECESSITATIVE
NECESSITOUSLY
NECKERCHIEVES
NECROPHILIACS
NEFARIOUSNESS
NEGATIVE POLES
NEGLIGIBILITY
NEGOTIABILITY
NEGRI SEMBILAN
NEIGHBOURHOOD
NEMATHELMINTH
NEOCLASSICISM
NEOCLASSICIST
NEOPLASTICISM
NERVELESSNESS
NERVOUS SYSTEM
NEUROFIBRILAR
NEUROMUSCULAR
NEUROSURGICAL
NEUROVASCULAR
NEW TECHNOLOGY
NICKELIFEROUS
NIGGARDLINESS
NIGHTCLUBBING
NIGHTMARISHLY

NIGHT WATCHMAN
NITRIFICATION
NITROBACTERIA
NITROGLYCERIN
NITROPARAFFIN
NOISELESSNESS
NOLI-ME-TANGERE
NOLLE PROSEQUI
NOMENCLATURES
NOMOGRAPHICAL
NOMOLOGICALLY
NONAGENARIANS
NONAGGRESSION
NONAPPEARANCE
NONATTENDANCE
NONCOMBATANTS
NONCOMPLIANCE
NONCONCURRENT
NONCONDUCTORS
NONCONFORMISM
NONCONFORMIST
NONCONFORMITY
NONCONTAGIOUS
NONCOOPERATOR
NONINDUSTRIAL
NONINFECTIOUS
NONPRODUCTIVE
NONRETURNABLE
NONSENSICALLY
NORADRENALINE
NORFOLK JACKET
NORMALIZATION
NORTHEASTERLY
NORTHEASTWARD
NORTH OSSETIAN
NORTHWESTERLY
NORTHWESTWARD
NOSOLOGICALLY
NOSTALGICALLY
NOTICEABILITY
NOTIFICATIONS
NOTORIOUSNESS
NUCLEAR ENERGY
NUCLEAR FAMILY
NUCLEAR WINTER
NUCLEONICALLY
NUCLEOPLASMIC
NUCLEOPROTEIN
NUISANCE VALUE
NULLIFICATION
NUMEROLOGICAL
NUMISMATOLOGY
NURSERY RHYMES
NURSERY SCHOOL
NYMPHAEACEOUS
NYMPHOMANIACS

O
OBJECTIONABLE

OBJECTIONABLY
OBJECTIVENESS
OBJECTIVISTIC
OBJECT LESSONS
OBLATE SPHERES
OBLIVIOUSNESS
OBNOXIOUSNESS
OBSERVATIONAL
OBSERVATORIES
OBSESSIVENESS
OBSTETRICALLY
OBSTETRICIANS
OBSTRUCTIONAL
OBSTRUCTIVELY
OBTAINABILITY
OBTRUSIVENESS
OCCASIONALISM
OCCIDENTALISM
OCCIDENTALIST
OCCIDENTALIZE
OCCLUSIVENESS
OCEANOGRAPHER
OCEANOGRAPHIC
OCTOGENARIANS
ODONTOBLASTIC
ODONTOGLOSSUM
ODONTOGRAPHIC
ODONTOLOGICAL
OFFENSIVENESS
OFFHANDEDNESS
OFFICEHOLDERS
OFFICIOUSNESS
OLD AGE PENSION
OLD-BOY NETWORK
OLD SCHOOL TIES
OLD WIVES' TALES
OLIGOPOLISTIC
OLIVE BRANCHES
OMMATOPHOROUS
ONE-NIGHT STAND
ONE-TRACK MINDS
ONTOGENICALLY
ONTOLOGICALLY
OPENHEARTEDLY
OPERATIONALLY
OPERATIVENESS
OPHTHALMOLOGY
OPISTHOBRANCH
OPPORTUNENESS
OPPORTUNISTIC
OPPORTUNITIES
OPPOSITIONIST
OPPROBRIOUSLY
ORCHESTRA PITS
ORCHESTRATING
ORCHESTRATION
ORDINARY LEVEL
ORDZHONIKIDZE
ORGAN GRINDERS

ORGANIZATIONS	PAINSTAKINGLY	PATRONIZINGLY
ORGANOGENESIS	PALAEOGRAPHIC	PEACEABLENESS
ORGANOGENETIC	PALAEONTOLOGY	PEACE OFFERING
ORGANOGRAPHIC	PALAEOZOOLOGY	PECKING ORDERS
ORGANOLOGICAL	PALEOGRAPHERS	PECTORAL CROSS
ORGANOTHERAPY	PALETTE KNIVES	PECULIARITIES
ORIENTALISTIC	PALYNOLOGICAL	PEDAGOGICALLY
ORIENTATIONAL	PANCHROMATISM	PEDESTRIANIZE
ORNAMENTATION	PANDORA'S BOXES	PEDIATRICIANS
ORNITHISCHIAN	PANIC STATIONS	PEDUNCULATION
ORNITHOLOGIST	PANIC-STRICKEN	PELOPONNESIAN
ORTHOCEPHALIC	PANORAMICALLY	PELTIER EFFECT
ORTHOEPICALLY	PANSOPHICALLY	PENEPLANATION
ORTHOGNATHISM	PANTECHNICONS	PENETRABILITY
ORTHOGNATHOUS	PAPAVERACEOUS	PENETRATINGLY
ORTHOHYDROGEN	PAPILLOMATOUS	PENETRATIVELY
ORTHOSTICHOUS	PARABOLICALLY	PENICILLATION
OSCILLOGRAPHY	PARADE GROUNDS	PENITENTIALLY
OSTENSIBILITY	PARADOXICALLY	PENNILESSNESS
OSTEOMALACIAL	PARAGOGICALLY	PENNSYLVANIAN
OSTEOMYELITIS	PARALLELOGRAM	PENNY-DREADFUL
OTHER-DIRECTED	PARALYTICALLY	PENNY-FARTHING
OUTBOARD MOTOR	PARAMAGNETISM	PENNY-PINCHERS
OUTDISTANCING	PARANOIACALLY	PENNY-PINCHING
OUTGENERALING	PARAPHERNALIA	PENNY WHISTLES
OUTGENERALLED	PARASITICALLY	PENTANOIC ACID
OUTMANOEUVRED	PARASITICIDAL	PEPPER-AND-SALT
OUTSPOKENNESS	PARASYNTHESIS	PEPTONIZATION
OUTSTANDINGLY	PARASYNTHETON	PERAMBULATING
OVERABUNDANCE	PARENT COMPANY	PERAMBULATION
OVERAMBITIOUS	PARENTHETICAL	PERAMBULATORS
OVERBALANCING	PAR EXCELLENCE	PERAMBULATORY
OVERBEARINGLY	PARKING GARAGE	PERCUSSION CAP
OVERBURDENING	PARKING LIGHTS	PERCUSSIONIST
OVERCONFIDENT	PARKING METERS	PEREGRINATION
OVERCRITICIZE	PARKINSON'S LAW	PERFECTIONISM
OVERCULTIVATE	PARLIAMENTARY	PERFECTIONIST
OVERDEVELOPED	PARROT-FASHION	PERFUNCTORILY
OVERELABORATE	PART EXCHANGES	PERICARPOIDAL
OVEREMPHASIZE	PARTHENOCARPY	PERICHONDRIUM
OVERESTIMATED	PARTICIPATING	PERIODIC TABLE
OVERESTIMATES	PARTICIPATION	PERISHABILITY
OVERINDULGING	PARTICIPIALLY	PERISSODACTYL
OVERMASTERING	PARTI-COLOURED	PERMANENT WAVE
OVERPOPULATED	PARTICULARISM	PERMANENT WAYS
OVERREACTIONS	PARTICULARIST	PERMUTATIONAL
OVERSHADOWING	PARTICULARITY	PERPENDICULAR
OVERSTATEMENT	PARTICULARIZE	PERSEVERATION
OVERSUBSCRIBE	PARTS OF SPEECH	PERSONALISTIC
OVERWEENINGLY	PASSEMENTERIE	PERSONALITIES
OVOVIVIPAROUS	PASSIONFLOWER	PERSONALIZING
OWNER-OCCUPIED	PASSIONLESSLY	PERSONIFIABLE
OWNER-OCCUPIER	PASSIVIZATION	PERSPECTIVISM
OYSTERCATCHER	PATENT LEATHER	PERSPICACIOUS
	PATERFAMILIAS	PERVASIVENESS
P	PATERNALISTIC	PERVERTEDNESS
PADDLE STEAMER	PATHOGNOMONIC	PETROCHEMICAL
PADDLING POOLS	PATRIOTICALLY	PETROL STATION
PAEDIATRICIAN	PATRISTICALLY	PETROPAVLOVSK

PETTY OFFICERS	PINKING SHEARS	POSSIBILITIES
PHARMACEUTICS	PISCICULTURAL	POSTAGE STAMPS
PHARMACOGNOSY	PITCHED BATTLE	POSTER COLOURS
PHARMACOPOEIA	PLACE SETTINGS	POSTE RESTANTE
PHARYNGOSCOPE	PLAGIOTROPISM	POSTGRADUATES
PHARYNGOSCOPY	PLAINTIVENESS	POSTMAN'S KNOCK
PHELLOGENETIC	PLASTIC BULLET	POST OFFICE BOX
PHENOMENALISM	PLATINIFEROUS	POSTOPERATIVE
PHENOMENALIST	PLATINIRIDIUM	POSTPONEMENTS
PHENOMENOLOGY	PLATINIZATION	POTATO BEETLES
PHENOTHIAZINE	PLATINUM-BLOND	POTENTIOMETER
PHENYLALANINE	PLATITUDINIZE	POTTER'S WHEELS
PHI BETA KAPPAS	PLATITUDINOUS	POTTY-TRAINING
PHILANTHROPIC	PLATYHELMINTH	POWERLESSNESS
PHILHELLENISM	PLAYING FIELDS	POWER POLITICS
PHILOSOPHICAL	PLENTEOUSNESS	POWER STATIONS
PHILOSOPHIZED	PLENTIFULNESS	POWER STEERING
PHILOSOPHIZER	PLIMSOLL LINES	PRACTICAL JOKE
PHI-PHENOMENON	PLOUGHMANSHIP	PRACTITIONERS
PHOSPHORYLASE	PLURALIZATION	PRAGMATICALLY
PHOTOCHEMICAL	PNEUMATICALLY	PRAYER MEETING
PHOTOCOMPOSER	PNEUMATOLYSIS	PRAYING MANTIS
PHOTODYNAMICS	PNEUMATOMETER	PREADAPTATION
PHOTOELECTRIC	PNEUMATOMETRY	PREADOLESCENT
PHOTOELECTRON	PNEUMATOPHORE	PRECAUTIONARY
PHOTOEMISSION	PNEUMOGASTRIC	PRECEPTORSHIP
PHOTOEMISSIVE	PNEUMONECTOMY	PRECIOUS METAL
PHOTOENGRAVER	POETIC JUSTICE	PRECIOUS STONE
PHOTO FINISHES	POETIC LICENCE	PRECIPITATELY
PHOTOGRAPHERS	POETS LAUREATE	PRECIPITATING
PHOTOGRAPHING	POINTLESSNESS	PRECIPITATION
PHOTOPERIODIC	POINTS OF ORDER	PRECIPITATIVE
PHOTORECEPTOR	POINT-TO-POINTS	PRECIPITOUSLY
PHOTOSTATTING	POISONOUSNESS	PRECONCEPTION
PHRASEOGRAPHY	POLE POSITIONS	PRECONDITIONS
PHRASEOLOGIST	POLICE OFFICER	PRECONIZATION
PHRENOLOGICAL	POLICE STATION	PREDATORINESS
PHYCOMYCETOUS	POLIOMYELITIS	PREDETERMINED
PHYLLOQUINONE	POLLING BOOTHS	PREDETERMINER
PHYSICALISTIC	POLLINIFEROUS	PREDICABILITY
PHYSICAL JERKS	POLYADELPHOUS	PREDICATIVELY
PHYSIOGNOMIES	POLYCHROMATIC	PREDILECTIONS
PHYSIOGNOMIST	POLYCOTYLEDON	PREDOMINANTLY
PHYSIOGRAPHER	POLYDACTYLOUS	PREDOMINATING
PHYSIOGRAPHIC	POLYEMBRYONIC	PREDOMINATION
PHYSIOLOGICAL	POLYGALACEOUS	PREFABRICATED
PHYSIOLOGISTS	POLYGONACEOUS	PREFABRICATOR
PHYSIOTHERAPY	POLYPROPYLENE	PREFERABILITY
PHYSOCLISTOUS	POLYPROTODONT	PREFIGURATION
PHYSOSTIGMINE	POLYSYLLABLES	PREFIGURATIVE
PHYTOPLANKTON	POLYSYLLOGISM	PREFIGUREMENT
PICTURESQUELY	POLYSYNTHESIS	PREJUDGEMENTS
PICTURE WINDOW	PONDERABILITY	PRELIMINARIES
PIECES OF EIGHT	PONDEROUSNESS	PRELIMINARILY
PIEZOELECTRIC	PONTIFICATING	PREMATURENESS
PIGEON-CHESTED	POOR RELATIONS	PREMEDICATION
PIGHEADEDNESS	PORCELLANEOUS	PREMEDITATION
PILOT OFFICERS	PORNOGRAPHERS	PREMEDITATIVE
PINK ELEPHANTS	POSITIVE POLES	PREOCCUPATION

PREORDINATION	PROFIT MARGINS	PROVING GROUND
PREPARATORILY	PROFIT SHARING	PROVISIONALLY
PREPONDERANCE	PROGNOSTICATE	PROVOCATIVELY
PREPONDERATED	PROGRESSIONAL	PROXIMATENESS
PREPOSITIONAL	PROGRESSIVELY	PSEPHOLOGICAL
PREPOSSESSING	PROGRESSIVISM	PSEPHOLOGISTS
PREPOSSESSION	PROGRESSIVIST	PSEUDOMORPHIC
PRE-RAPHAELITE	PROHIBITIVELY	PSYCHIATRISTS
PREREQUISITES	PROJECTIONIST	PSYCHOANALYSE
PRESBYTERIANS	PROLEPTICALLY	PSYCHOANALYST
PRESCRIPTIBLE	PROLIFERATING	PSYCHOANALYZE
PRESCRIPTIONS	PROLIFERATION	PSYCHOBIOLOGY
PRESENTATIONS	PROLIFERATIVE	PSYCHODYNAMIC
PRESENTIMENTS	PROLONGATIONS	PSYCHOGENESIS
PRESERVATIVES	PROMENADE DECK	PSYCHOGENETIC
PRESS AGENCIES	PROMINENTNESS	PSYCHOGNOSTIC
PRESS CUTTINGS	PROMISCUOUSLY	PSYCHOGRAPHIC
PRESS RELEASES	PROMISED LANDS	PSYCHOHISTORY
PRESSURE GROUP	PROMISINGNESS	PSYCHOKINESIS
PRESSURE POINT	PROMOTIVENESS	PSYCHOKINETIC
PRESUMPTIVELY	PRONOMINALIZE	PSYCHOLOGICAL
PRETENTIOUSLY	PRONOUNCEABLE	PSYCHOLOGISTS
PRETERNATURAL	PRONOUNCEMENT	PSYCHOMETRICS
PREVARICATING	PRONUNCIATION	PSYCHOPHYSICS
PREVARICATION	PROPAGABILITY	PSYCHOSOMATIC
PREVARICATORS	PROPAGANDISTS	PSYCHOSURGERY
PRICELESSNESS	PROPAGANDIZED	PSYCHOTHERAPY
PRIMARY COLOUR	PROPAGATIONAL	PSYCHOTICALLY
PRIMARY SCHOOL	PROPAROXYTONE	PSYCHROPHILIC
PRIMARY STRESS	PROPHETICALLY	PTERIDOLOGIST
PRIME MERIDIAN	PROPHYLACTICS	PTERIDOPHYTIC
PRIME MINISTER	PROPITIATIOUS	PUBLIC COMPANY
PRIMITIVENESS	PROPORTIONATE	PUBLIC SCHOOLS
PRIMITIVISTIC	PROPORTIONING	PULVERIZATION
PRIMOGENITURE	PROPOSITIONAL	PUNCTILIOUSLY
PRINCE CONSORT	PROPOSITIONED	PUNISHABILITY
PRINCIPAL BOYS	PROPRIETARILY	PURITANICALLY
PRINTED MATTER	PROPRIETORIAL	PURPLE PASSAGE
PRINTING PRESS	PROPRIOCEPTOR	PURPOSELESSLY
PRISONER OF WAR	PROSCRIPTIONS	PURPOSIVENESS
PRISON VISITOR	PROSELYTIZERS	PUSILLANIMITY
PRIVATE MEMBER	PROSELYTIZING	PUSILLANIMOUS
PRIVATE SCHOOL	PROSOPOPOEIAL	PYRHELIOMETER
PRIVATE SECTOR	PROSTAGLANDIN	PYROPHOSPHATE
PRIVATIZATION	PROSTATECTOMY	
PRIZEFIGHTERS	PROTECTIONISM	Q
PRIZEFIGHTING	PROTECTIONIST	QUADRICIPITAL
PROBABILISTIC	PROTECTORATES	QUADRILATERAL
PROBABILITIES	PROTEINACEOUS	QUADRILLIONTH
PROCESS-SERVER	PROTESTANTISM	QUADRIPARTITE
PROCLAMATIONS	PROTESTATIONS	QUADRISECTION
PROCONSULATES	PROTHETICALLY	QUADRIVALENCY
PROCRASTINATE	PROTOCHORDATE	QUADRUPLICATE
PROCTOLOGICAL	PROTOHISTORIC	QUADRUPLICITY
PRODUCIBILITY	PROTOLANGUAGE	QUALIFICATION
PROFESSIONALS	PROTUBERANCES	QUALIFICATORY
PROFESSORIATE	PROTUBERANTLY	QUALITATIVELY
PROFESSORSHIP	PROVINCIALISM	QUANTUM THEORY
PROFITABILITY	PROVINCIALITY	QUARTERFINALS

QUARTERMASTER
QUARTERSTAFFS
QUARTERSTAVES
QUARTZIFEROUS
QUEENS CONSORT
QUEEN'S COUNSEL
QUEEN'S ENGLISH
QUERULOUSNESS
QUESTIONINGLY
QUESTION MARKS
QUESTIONNAIRE
QUICK-TEMPERED
QUINDECENNIAL
QUINQUAGESIMA
QUINQUEVALENT
QUINTILLIONTH
QUINTUPLICATE
QUODLIBETICAL
QUOTATION MARK

R
RABBIT HUTCHES
RABBIT PUNCHES
RABBIT WARRENS
RABBLE-ROUSING
RACK-AND-PINION
RADIOACTIVATE
RADIOACTIVITY
RADIOCHEMICAL
RADIOGRAPHERS
RADIOISOTOPIC
RADIOTELEGRAM
RADIOTELETYPE
RAG-AND-BONE MAN
RAMIFICATIONS
RANCOROUSNESS
RANDOMIZATION
RAPPROCHEMENT
RAPTUROUSNESS
RAREFACTIONAL
RATEABLE VALUE
RATIOCINATION
RATIONALISTIC
RATIONALIZING
REACTIONARIES
READJUSTMENTS
READ-WRITE HEAD
REAFFIRMATION
REAFFORESTING
REALISTICALLY
REAPPOINTMENT
REARRANGEMENT
RECALCITRANCE
RECAPITULATED
RECEPTIONISTS
RECEPTION ROOM
RECESSIVENESS
RECIPROCALITY
RECIPROCATING

RECIPROCATION
RECIPROCATIVE
RECOGNITIONAL
RECOLLECTIONS
RECOMBINATION
RECOMMENDABLE
RECOMPENSABLE
RECOMPOSITION
RECONCILEMENT
RECONCILINGLY
RECONDITENESS
RECONDITIONED
RECONDITIONER
RECONNOITRING
RECONSIDERING
RECONSTITUENT
RECONSTITUTED
RECONSTRUCTED
RECONSTRUCTOR
RECORD-CHANGER
RECORD LIBRARY
RECORD PLAYERS
RECRIMINATING
RECRIMINATION
RECRIMINATIVE
RECRIMINATORY
RECRUDESCENCE
RECRYSTALLIZE
RECTIFICATION
RED BLOOD CELLS
REDEEMABILITY
REDEVELOPMENT
REDISTRIBUTED
RED-LETTER DAYS
REDUPLICATING
REDUPLICATION
REDUPLICATIVE
REEFER JACKETS
RE-ENFORCEMENT
RE-EXAMINATION
RE-EXPORTATION
REFERENCE BOOK
REFLEXIVENESS
REFORESTATION
REFORMATIONAL
REFORMATORIES
REFRACTOMETER
REFRACTOMETRY
REFRIGERATING
REFRIGERATION
REFRIGERATIVE
REFRIGERATORS
REFURBISHMENT
REGARDFULNESS
REGIMENTATION
REGISTRARSHIP
REGISTRATIONS
REGRETFULNESS
REGURGITATING

REGURGITATION
REHABILITATED
REIGN OF TERROR
REIMBURSEMENT
REIMPORTATION
REINCARNATING
REINCARNATION
REINFORCEMENT
REINSTATEMENT
REJUVENESCENT
RELATIONSHIPS
RELIGIOUSNESS
RELINQUISHING
REMINISCENCES
REMISSIBILITY
REMONSTRANCES
REMONSTRATING
REMONSTRATION
REMONSTRATIVE
REMORSELESSLY
REMOTE CONTROL
RENEGOTIATION
RENSSELAERITE
RENUNCIATIONS
REPEATABILITY
REPELLINGNESS
REPERCUSSIONS
REPLENISHMENT
REPOSEFULNESS
REPREHENDABLE
REPREHENSIBLE
REPREHENSIBLY
REPRESENTABLE
REPROACHFULLY
REPROACHINGLY
REPRODUCTIONS
REPUBLICANISM
REPUBLICANIZE
REPUBLICATION
REPUBLISHABLE
REPULSIVENESS
REQUISITIONED
REQUISITIONER
RESENTFULNESS
RESISTIBILITY
RESISTIVENESS
RESOLVABILITY
RESOURCEFULLY
RESPIRABILITY
RESPIRATIONAL
RESPLENDENTLY
RESTAURANT CAR
RESTAURATEURS
RESTRAININGLY
RESTRICTIVELY
RESTRUCTURING
RESURRECTIONS
RESUSCITATING
RESUSCITATION

RESUSCITATIVE	RUMOURMONGERS	SCIENTOLOGIST
RETAINABILITY		SCILLY ISLANDS
RETENTIVENESS	S	SCINTILLATING
RETICULATIONS	SABRE-RATTLING	SCINTILLATION
RETINOSCOPIST	SACCHARIMETER	SCLEROPROTEIN
RETROACTIVELY	SACCHAROMETER	SCOLOPENDRINE
RETROACTIVITY	SACRIFICEABLE	SCORCHED EARTH
RETROGRESSING	SACRIFICIALLY	SCORIFICATION
RETROGRESSION	SACRIFICINGLY	SCRIPTWRITERS
RETROGRESSIVE	SACROSANCTITY	SCRIPTWRITING
RETROSPECTION	SADOMASOCHISM	SCULPTURESQUE
RETROSPECTIVE	SADOMASOCHIST	SEANAD EIREANN
RETURNABILITY	SAFETY CATCHES	SEARCH PARTIES
REUNIFICATION	SAFETY CURTAIN	SEARCH WARRANT
REUTILIZATION	SAFETY ISLANDS	SEASON TICKETS
REVEALABILITY	SAFETY MATCHES	SEAWORTHINESS
REVELATIONIST	SAGACIOUSNESS	SECESSIONISTS
REVERBERATING	SAINT LAWRENCE	SECLUSIVENESS
REVERBERATION	SALACIOUSNESS	SECONDARINESS
REVERBERATIVE	SALAD DRESSING	SECOND COUSINS
REVERBERATORY	SALPINGECTOMY	SECOND-GUESSED
REVERENTIALLY	SALVATION ARMY	SECOND THOUGHT
REVERSIBILITY	SALVATIONISTS	SECRETARYSHIP
REVOLUTIONARY	SAN BERNARDINO	SECRETIVENESS
REVOLUTIONIST	SANCTIMONIOUS	SECRET SERVICE
REVOLUTIONIZE	SAND-BLINDNESS	SECURITY RISKS
RHABDOMANTIST	SANDWICH BOARD	SEDENTARINESS
RHAPSODICALLY	SAN FRANCISCAN	SEDIMENTARILY
RHIZOCEPHALAN	SANGUINOLENCY	SEDIMENTATION
RHIZOMORPHOUS	SANITARY TOWEL	SEDIMENTOLOGY
RHODOCHROSITE	SAN LUIS POTOSI	SEDITIOUSNESS
RHODODENDRONS	SANTA CATARINA	SEDUCTIVENESS
RIBEIRAO PRETO	SAPROGENICITY	SEGREGATIONAL
RIGHTEOUSNESS	SARCASTICALLY	SEINE-MARITIME
RIGHT TRIANGLE	SARCOPHAGUSES	SEISMOGRAPHER
ROCK-AND-ROLLER	SATANICALNESS	SEISMOGRAPHIC
ROCKING CHAIRS	SATIRICALNESS	SEISMOLOGISTS
ROCKING HORSES	SATISFACTIONS	SELECTIVENESS
ROGUES' GALLERY	SATURNINENESS	SELENOGRAPHER
ROLLER COASTER	SCANDALMONGER	SELENOGRAPHIC
ROLLER-SKATERS	SCARIFICATION	SELF-ABASEMENT
ROLLER SKATING	SCATTERBRAINS	SELF-ADDRESSED
ROLLING STONES	SCENESHIFTERS	SELF-ANNEALING
ROLL OF HONOURS	SCEPTICALNESS	SELF-APPOINTED
ROLL-ON ROLL-OFF	SCHEMATICALLY	SELF-ASSERTION
ROMAN CATHOLIC	SCHIZOCARPOUS	SELF-ASSERTIVE
ROMAN NUMERALS	SCHIZOGENESIS	SELF-ASSURANCE
ROMANTICIZING	SCHIZOGENETIC	SELF-CONFESSED
ROOMING HOUSES	SCHIZOMYCETIC	SELF-CONFIDENT
RORSCHACH TEST	SCHIZOPHRENIA	SELF-CONSCIOUS
ROTARY TILLERS	SCHIZOPHRENIC	SELF-CONTAINED
ROTTEN BOROUGH	SCHOLARLINESS	SELF-DECEPTION
ROUGH-AND-READY	SCHOLASTICATE	SELF-DECEPTIVE
ROUGH DIAMONDS	SCHOLASTICISM	SELF-DEFEATING
ROUND BRACKETS	SCHOOLFELLOWS	SELF-EVIDENTLY
ROUND-THE-CLOCK	SCHOOL-LEAVERS	SELF-IMPORTANT
ROYAL HIGHNESS	SCHOOLMARMISH	SELF-INDUCTION
RUBBERNECKING	SCHOOLMASTERS	SELF-INDUCTIVE
RUBBER-STAMPED	SCHOOLTEACHER	SELF-INDULGENT

SELF-INFLICTED	SHOOTING STICK	SOLICITATIONS
SELF-KNOWLEDGE	SHOP ASSISTANT	SOLICITORSHIP
SELF-PITYINGLY	SHORT-CHANGING	SOLILOQUIZING
SELF-POSSESSED	SHORT CIRCUITS	SOLVAY PROCESS
SELF-PROPELLED	SHORT-TEMPERED	SOMATOPLASTIC
SELF-RESTRAINT	SHOULDER BLADE	SOMATOPLEURAL
SELF-RIGHTEOUS	SHOULDER STRAP	SOMERSAULTING
SELF-SACRIFICE	SHROVE TUESDAY	SOMNAMBULANCE
SELF-SATISFIED	SICK HEADACHES	SOMNAMBULATOR
SELLER'S MARKET	SIDESPLITTING	SOMNAMBULISTS
SELLING-PLATER	SIERRA LEONEAN	SONS-OF-BITCHES
SELLING POINTS	SIGHTLESSNESS	SOPHISTICALLY
SEMASIOLOGIST	SIGMOIDOSCOPE	SOPHISTICATED
SEMIAUTOMATIC	SIGMOIDOSCOPY	SOPHISTICATES
SEMICONDUCTOR	SIGNATURE TUNE	SOPHISTICATOR
SEMICONSCIOUS	SIGNIFICANTLY	SOPORIFICALLY
SEMIDETACHEDS	SIGNIFICATION	SORROWFULNESS
SEMIFINALISTS	SIGNIFICATIVE	SOUL-SEARCHING
SEMIPALATINSK	SILENT PARTNER	SOUNDING BOARD
SEMIPARASITIC	SILVER BIRCHES	SOUNDLESSNESS
SEMIPERMEABLE	SILVER JUBILEE	SOUNDPROOFING
SEMIPORCELAIN	SILVER-TONGUED	SOUTHEASTERLY
SEMPER FIDELIS	SILVER WEDDING	SOUTHEASTWARD
SEMPER PARATUS	SILVICULTURAL	SOUTHERLINESS
SENIOR CITIZEN	SIMPLE MACHINE	SOUTHWESTERLY
SENSATIONALLY	SINGLE-DECKERS	SOUTHWESTWARD
SENSELESSNESS	SINGULARITIES	SOVIETIZATION
SENSITIVENESS	SIPHONOSTELIC	SPACE SHUTTLES
SENSITIZATION	SITTING TARGET	SPACE STATIONS
SENTENTIOUSLY	SIXTEENTH NOTE	SPASMODICALLY
SENTIMENTALLY	SKEET SHOOTING	SPEAKING TUBES
SEQUENTIALITY	SKIRTING BOARD	SPECIAL BRANCH
SEQUESTRATING	SLAP AND TICKLE	SPECIAL SCHOOL
SEQUESTRATION	SLEDGEHAMMERS	SPECIFICATION
SERBO-CROATIAN	SLEEPING PILLS	SPECIFICATIVE
SERGEANT MAJOR	SLEEPLESSNESS	SPECTACULARLY
SERIALIZATION	SLEIGHT OF HAND	SPECTROGRAPHY
SERIAL NUMBERS	SLIDING SCALES	SPECTROMETRIC
SERICULTURIST	SLIPSTREAMING	SPECTROSCOPES
SERJEANT AT LAW	SMALL FORTUNES	SPECTROSCOPIC
SERVICE CHARGE	SMALLHOLDINGS	SPECULATIVELY
SEVENTH HEAVEN	SMELLING SALTS	SPEECH THERAPY
SEVEN-YEAR ITCH	SMOOTH-TONGUED	SPELEOLOGICAL
SEWING MACHINE	SNAKE CHARMERS	SPELEOLOGISTS
SEXAGENARIANS	SNAP FASTENERS	SPENDING MONEY
SEXPLOITATION	SNEAK PREVIEWS	SPERMATICALLY
SHAKESPEAREAN	SNOW BLINDNESS	SPERMATOPHORE
SHAMELESSNESS	SOCIAL CLIMBER	SPERMATOPHYTE
SHAPELESSNESS	SOCIALIZATION	SPHERICALNESS
SHARP PRACTICE	SOCIAL SCIENCE	SPHEROIDICITY
SHARPSHOOTERS	SOCIAL SERVICE	SPHINGOMYELIN
SHEEPSHEARING	SOCIAL WORKERS	SPHYGMOGRAPHY
SHEPHERDESSES	SOCIOECONOMIC	SPINE-CHILLING
SHIFTLESSNESS	SOCIOLINGUIST	SPINELESSNESS
SHIP'S CHANDLER	SODA FOUNTAINS	SPINNING JENNY
SHIRTWAISTERS	SOFT-PEDALLING	SPINNING WHEEL
SHOCK ABSORBER	SOLDERING IRON	SPIRITUALISTS
SHOOTING MATCH	SOLDIERLINESS	SPIRITUALIZER
SHOOTING STARS	SOLEMNIZATION	SPIT AND POLISH

SPITTING IMAGE	STIFF UPPER LIP	SUBSCRIPTIONS
SPLAYFOOTEDLY	STILETTO HEELS	SUBSERVIENTLY
SPLENDIFEROUS	STIMULATINGLY	SUBSIDIZATION
SPLINTER GROUP	STIPENDIARIES	SUBSTANTIALLY
SPONTANEOUSLY	STOCKBREEDERS	SUBSTANTIATED
SPORTSMANLIKE	STOCKBREEDING	SUBSTANTIATOR
SPORTSMANSHIP	STOCK EXCHANGE	SUBSTANTIVELY
SPREAD-EAGLING	STOICHIOMETRY	SUBSTANTIVIZE
SPRIGHTLINESS	STOLONIFEROUS	SUBSTITUTABLE
SPRING CHICKEN	STOMATOPLASTY	SUBSTITUTIONS
SPRING-CLEANED	STORM TROOPERS	SUBSTRUCTURAL
SQUANDERINGLY	STORMY PETRELS	SUBSTRUCTURES
SQUARE-BASHING	STOVEPIPE HATS	SUBTILIZATION
SQUARE BRACKET	STRAIGHTEDGES	SUBVENTIONARY
SQUEAMISHNESS	STRAIGHTENING	SUFFICIENCIES
SQUIREARCHIES	STRAIGHT-FACED	SUFFOCATINGLY
STABILIZATION	STRAIGHT FIGHT	SUFFRAGANSHIP
STAFF OFFICERS	STRAITJACKETS	SUFFRAGETTISM
STAFF SERGEANT	STRANGLEHOLDS	SUFFUMIGATION
STAGE MANAGERS	STRANGULATING	SULPHADIAZINE
STAGE-MANAGING	STRANGULATION	SULPHURIC ACID
STAGE WHISPERS	STRATEGICALLY	SUMMARIZATION
STAMINIFEROUS	STRATIGRAPHER	SUMMER SCHOOLS
STANDARDIZING	STRATIGRAPHIC	SUMPTUOUSNESS
STANDARD LAMPS	STRATOCUMULUS	SUNDAY SCHOOLS
STANDING ORDER	STRATOSPHERIC	SUPERABUNDANT
STANDOFFISHLY	STRAW-COLOURED	SUPERADDITION
STAPHYLOCOCCI	STREETWALKERS	SUPERANNUATED
STARCH-REDUCED	STRENGTHENING	SUPERCALENDER
STARTING BLOCK	STRENUOUSNESS	SUPERCHARGERS
STARTING GATES	STREPTOCOCCAL	SUPERCHARGING
STARTING PRICE	STREPTOCOCCUS	SUPERCOLUMNAR
STATELESSNESS	STREPTOKINASE	SUPEREMINENCE
STATE-OF-THE-ART	STRIKEBREAKER	SUPERFETATION
STATESMANLIKE	STRIP CARTOONS	SUPERFICIALLY
STATESMANSHIP	STRIP LIGHTING	SUPERFLUIDITY
STATION BREAKS	STROBILACEOUS	SUPERFLUOUSLY
STATION HOUSES	STROMATOLITIC	SUPERHUMANITY
STATIONMASTER	STRUCTURALISM	SUPERIMPOSING
STATION WAGONS	STRUCTURALIST	SUPERINTENDED
STATISTICALLY	STUDENTS' UNION	SUPERLATIVELY
STATISTICIANS	STUDIO COUCHES	SUPERNATATION
STEADFASTNESS	STUFFED SHIRTS	SUPERNUMERARY
STEAMROLLERED	STYLISTICALLY	SUPERORDINATE
STEEPLECHASER	SUBCOMMITTEES	SUPERPHYSICAL
STEEPLECHASES	SUBCONTINENTS	SUPERPOSITION
STEERING WHEEL	SUBCONTRACTED	SUPERSENSIBLE
STENOGRAPHERS	SUBCONTRACTOR	SUPERSTITIONS
STENOPETALOUS	SUBDIVISIONAL	SUPERSTITIOUS
STENOPHYLLOUS	SUBEQUATORIAL	SUPERVENIENCE
STEPPING-STONE	SUBIRRIGATION	SUPPLANTATION
STERCORACEOUS	SUBJECT MATTER	SUPPLEMENTARY
STEREOGRAPHIC	SUBLIEUTENANT	SUPPLEMENTING
STEREOSCOPIST	SUBMACHINE GUN	SUPPLICATIONS
STEREOTROPISM	SUBORDINATING	SUPPLY TEACHER
STEREOTYPICAL	SUBORDINATION	SUPPOSITIONAL
STERILIZATION	SUBORDINATIVE	SUPPOSITORIES
STICKING POINT	SUBPOPULATION	SUPRANATIONAL
STICK-IN-THE-MUD	SUBREPTITIOUS	SURFACE-ACTIVE

SURREPTITIOUS	TELEPHOTO LENS	THORACOPLASTY
SURROGATESHIP	TELEPROMPTERS	THOROUGHBREDS
SURVIVABILITY	TELEUTOSPORIC	THOROUGHFARES
SUSTENTACULAR	TELEVISIONARY	THOROUGHGOING
SWASHBUCKLING	TEMPERABILITY	THOROUGHPACED
SWEET NOTHINGS	TEMPERAMENTAL	THOUGHTLESSLY
SWIMMING BATHS	TEMPERATENESS	THREATENINGLY
SWIMMING POOLS	TEMPESTUOUSLY	THREE-CORNERED
SWIZZLE STICKS	TEMPORARINESS	THREE-DAY EVENT
SWOLLEN HEADED	TEMPORIZATION	THREE-LINE WHIP
SWORDSMANSHIP	TEMPORIZINGLY	THREMMATOLOGY
SYBARITICALLY	TENACIOUSNESS	THUNDERCLOUDS
SYLLABOGRAPHY	TENANT FARMERS	THUNDERSHOWER
SYLLEPTICALLY	TENDENTIOUSLY	THUNDERSTORMS
SYLLOGISTICAL	TENDERHEARTED	THUNDERSTRUCK
SYLLOGIZATION	TENDERIZATION	THYROIDECTOMY
SYMBOLIZATION	TEN-GALLON HATS	TIME-AND-MOTION
SYMMETRICALLY	TENPIN BOWLING	TIME-CONSUMING
SYMPATHECTOMY	TENTATIVENESS	TIME EXPOSURES
SYMPATHOLYTIC	TERGIVERSATOR	TIME SIGNATURE
SYMPATRICALLY	TERMINABILITY	TINTINNABULAR
SYMPHONICALLY	TERMINATIONAL	TINTINNABULUM
SYMPHYSICALLY	TERMINOLOGIES	TITILLATINGLY
SYNARTHRODIAL	TERMINOLOGIST	TITTLE-TATTLED
SYNCHRONISTIC	TERPSICHOREAN	TITTLE-TATTLER
SYNCHRONIZING	TERRACED HOUSE	TOAD-IN-THE-HOLE
SYNDICALISTIC	TERRESTRIALLY	TOASTING FORKS
SYNTACTICALLY	TERRORIZATION	TOILET-TRAINED
SYNTHETICALLY	TESTIFICATION	TOLERABLENESS
SYPHILOLOGIST	TETARTOHEDRAL	TOLERATIONISM
SYRINGOMYELIA	TETRABASICITY	TOLERATIONIST
SYRINGOMYELIC	TETRACHLORIDE	TONE LANGUAGES
SYSTEMATIZING	TETRADYNAMOUS	TONGUE TWISTER
SYSTEMATOLOGY	TETRASTICHOUS	TONSILLECTOMY
SYSTEMIZATION	TETRASYLLABIC	TOOTHSOMENESS
SYZYGETICALLY	TETRASYLLABLE	TOPOGRAPHICAL
	THALASSOCRACY	TOPOLOGICALLY
T	THANKLESSNESS	TORTOISESHELL
TACHISTOSCOPE	THANKSGIVINGS	TOTIPALMATION
TACHYPHYLAXIS	THEANTHROPISM	TOXICOLOGICAL
TALKATIVENESS	THEANTHROPIST	TOXICOLOGISTS
TALKING POINTS	THEATRICALITY	TOXOPLASMOSIS
TANGENTIALITY	THENCEFORWARD	TRACE ELEMENTS
TANTALIZATION	THEOLOGICALLY	TRACHEOTOMIST
TANTALIZINGLY	THEORETICALLY	TRADE UNIONISM
TAPE RECORDERS	THERIOMORPHIC	TRADE UNIONIST
TARN-ET-GARONNE	THERMOCHEMIST	TRADING ESTATE
TARTARIZATION	THERMODYNAMIC	TRADING STAMPS
TASTELESSNESS	THERMOGENESIS	TRADITIONALLY
TAX-DEDUCTIBLE	THERMOGRAPHER	TRAFFIC CIRCLE
TAXONOMICALLY	THERMOGRAPHIC	TRAFFIC ISLAND
TECHNOLOGICAL	THERMONUCLEAR	TRAFFIC LIGHTS
TECHNOLOGISTS	THERMOPLASTIC	TRAFFIC WARDEN
TEETER-TOTTERS	THERMOSETTING	TRAGICOMEDIES
TELAUTOGRAPHY	THERMOS FLASKS	TRAILER HOUSES
TELEGRAPH POLE	THERMOSTATICS	TRANQUILLIZED
TELEMARKETING	THERMOTHERAPY	TRANQUILLIZER
TELENCEPHALIC	THERMOTROPISM	TRANSACTINIDE
TELENCEPHALON	THIGMOTROPISM	TRANSACTIONAL

TRANSATLANTIC	TROPHOBLASTIC	UNDERCHARGING
TRANSCAUCASIA	TROUBLEMAKERS	UNDERCURRENTS
TRANSCENDENCE	TRUCIAL STATES	UNDERDRAINAGE
TRANSCENDENCY	TRUSTWORTHILY	UNDEREMPLOYED
TRANSCRIBABLE	TRUTH-FUNCTION	UNDERESTIMATE
TRANSCRIPTION	TUBERCULATION	UNDEREXPOSING
TRANSFIGURING	TUBULIFLOROUS	UNDEREXPOSURE
TRANSFORMABLE	TURBOCHARGERS	UNDERGARMENTS
TRANSGRESSING	TURBOCHARGING	UNDERGRADUATE
TRANSGRESSION	TURBO-ELECTRIC	UNDERHANDEDLY
TRANSGRESSIVE	TURING MACHINE	UNDERMININGLY
TRANSGRESSORS	TURNING CIRCLE	UNDERPAINTING
TRANSISTORIZE	TURNING POINTS	UNDERPINNINGS
TRANSLATIONAL	TWO-WAY MIRRORS	UNDERSTANDING
TRANSLATORIAL	TYPOGRAPHICAL	UNDERSTUDYING
TRANSLITERATE	TYRANNIZINGLY	UNDISCIPLINED
TRANSLOCATION	TYRANNOSAURUS	UNDISTRIBUTED
TRANSMIGRATOR	TYRANNOUSNESS	UNEARTHLINESS
TRANSMISSIBLE		UNENLIGHTENED
TRANSMISSIONS	**U**	UNEQUIVOCALLY
TRANSMITTANCE	UGLY DUCKLINGS	UNEXCEPTIONAL
TRANSMITTANCY	ULTRANATIONAL	UNEXPERIENCED
TRANSMUTATION	UMBELLIFEROUS	UNFALTERINGLY
TRANSPARENTLY	UMBILICAL CORD	UNFAMILIARITY
TRANSPIRATION	UNACCOMPANIED	UNFASHIONABLE
TRANSPIRATORY	UNACCOUNTABLE	UNFEELINGNESS
TRANSPLANTING	UNACCOUNTABLY	UNFLINCHINGLY
TRANSPORTABLE	UNADULTERATED	UNFORESEEABLE
TRANSPORT CAFE	UNADVENTUROUS	UNFORGETTABLE
TRANSPORTEDLY	UNADVISEDNESS	UNFORGETTABLY
TRANSPOSITION	UNASHAMEDNESS	UNFORTUNATELY
TRANSSHIPMENT	UNBELIEVINGLY	UNFOUNDEDNESS
TRANSVESTITES	UNBENDINGNESS	UNGUARDEDNESS
TRANSYLVANIAN	UNBLESSEDNESS	UNHEALTHINESS
TRAPEZOHEDRAL	UNCEASINGNESS	UNICAMERALISM
TRAPEZOHEDRON	UNCEREMONIOUS	UNICAMERALIST
TRAUMATICALLY	UNCERTAINNESS	UNILATERALISM
TREACHEROUSLY	UNCIRCUMCISED	UNILLUSTRATED
TREASURERSHIP	UNCLEANLINESS	UNIMPEACHABLE
TREASURE TROVE	UNCOMFORTABLE	UNIMPEACHABLY
TREMULOUSNESS	UNCOMFORTABLY	UNINHABITABLE
TREPONEMATOUS	UNCOMPENSATED	UNINHIBITEDLY
TRIANGULARITY	UNCOMPETITIVE	UNINTELLIGENT
TRIANGULATION	UNCOMPLAINING	UNINTENTIONAL
TRIATOMICALLY	UNCOMPLICATED	UNINTERRUPTED
TRIBOELECTRIC	UNCONCERNEDLY	UNITED NATIONS
TRICENTENNIAL	UNCONDITIONAL	UNIVERSALNESS
TRICHOLOGISTS	UNCONDITIONED	UNMENTIONABLE
TRICHOMONADAL	UNCONFORMABLE	UNMUSICALNESS
TRICHROMATISM	UNCONSCIOUSLY	UNNATURALNESS
TRIGONOMETRIC	UNCONSTRAINED	UNNECESSARILY
TRILATERATION	UNCONSUMMATED	UNOBTRUSIVELY
TRILINGUALISM	UNCOORDINATED	UNPRECEDENTED
TRIMETHADIONE	UNCROWNED KING	UNPREDICTABLE
TRIPLOBLASTIC	UNDECIDEDNESS	UNPRETENTIOUS
TRIPOLITANIAN	UNDERACHIEVED	UNQUALIFIABLE
TRISACCHARIDE	UNDERACHIEVER	UNQUESTIONING
TROOP CARRIERS	UNDERBREEDING	UNREADABILITY
TROPHALLACTIC	UNDERCARRIAGE	UNRELENTINGLY

UNRELIABILITY
UNREMITTINGLY
UNREPRESENTED
UNRUFFLEDNESS
UNSAVOURINESS
UNSELFISHNESS
UNSERVICEABLE
UNSIGHTLINESS
UNSOCIABILITY
UNSUBSTANTIAL
UNSUITABILITY
UNWARRANTABLE
UNWILLINGNESS
UNWRITTEN LAWS
UPRIGHT PIANOS
UP-TO-THE-MINUTE
URETHROSCOPIC
UTI POSSIDETIS
UTTERABLENESS

V
VACILLATINGLY
VACUUM CLEANER
VALUE-ADDED TAX
VALUE JUDGMENT
VALUELESSNESS
VANTAGE POINTS
VAPOURABILITY
VAPOURISHNESS
VARICOSE VEINS
VARIOLIZATION
VASOINHIBITOR
VAULTING HORSE
VEGETARIANISM
VENEREOLOGIST
VENETIAN BLIND
VENTRILOQUIAL
VENTRILOQUISM
VENTRILOQUIST
VENTRILOQUIZE
VERACIOUSNESS
VERBALIZATION
VERBIFICATION
VERITABLENESS
VERMICULATION
VERMINOUSNESS
VERNACULARISM
VERNALIZATION
VERSIFICATION
VESTAL VIRGINS
VEXATIOUSNESS
VEXED QUESTION
VEXILLOLOGIST
VICARIOUSNESS
VICE PRESIDENT
VICIOUS CIRCLE
VICTIMIZATION
VICTORIA CROSS
VICTORIA PLUMS

VILIFICATIONS
VINDICABILITY
VINICULTURIST
VIOLONCELLIST
VISCOUNTESSES
VISIONARINESS
VISITING CARDS
VISITORS' BOOKS
VISUALIZATION
VITRIFICATION
VITRIOLICALLY
VIVACIOUSNESS
VIVISECTIONAL
VOCIFERATIONS
VOICELESSNESS
VOLATILIZABLE
VOLCANIZATION
VOLCANOLOGIST
VOLUNTARINESS
VOLUNTARISTIC
VOTE OF CENSURE
VOTES OF THANKS
VOUCHSAFEMENT
VRAISEMBLANCE
VULCANIZATION
VULGARIZATION
VULNERABILITY

W
WALKIE-TALKIES
WALKING PAPERS
WALKING STICKS
WALL PAINTINGS
WARM-HEARTEDLY
WASHINGTONIAN
WASTE PRODUCTS
WATER BISCUITS
WATER BUFFALOS
WATERING HOLES
WATERING PLACE
WATERPROOFING
WATER SOFTENER
WATER SUPPLIES
WATTLE AND DAUB
WEARISOMENESS
WEATHER-BEATEN
WEATHERBOARDS
WEIGHT LIFTERS
WEIGHT LIFTING
WELFARE STATES
WELL-APPOINTED
WELL-CONNECTED
WELL-DEVELOPED
WELL-PRESERVED
WELL-QUALIFIED
WELL-SUPPORTED
WELL-THOUGHT-OF
WELSH RAREBITS
WELTERWEIGHTS

WEST-NORTHWEST
WEST-SOUTHWEST
WETTING AGENTS
WHEELER-DEALER
WHIMSICALNESS
WHIPPOORWILLS
WHITE ELEPHANT
WHITE WEDDINGS
WHOLESOMENESS
WHOOPING COUGH
WICKET KEEPERS
WIDE-AWAKENESS
WILDCAT STRIKE
WILHELMSHAVEN
WILL-O'-THE-WISPS
WILLOW PATTERN
WINDING SHEETS
WINDOW-DRESSER
WINDOW-SHOPPED
WINDOW-SHOPPER
WING COMMANDER
WITHDRAWNNESS
WITHERINGNESS
WITWATERSRAND
WOLVERHAMPTON
WOMEN'S STUDIES
WONDERFULNESS
WONDER-WORKING
WOODCRAFTSMAN
WOOLGATHERING
WORD BLINDNESS
WORD PROCESSOR
WORK-HARDENING
WORSHIPPINGLY
WORTHLESSNESS
WRONGHEADEDLY

X
XANTHOCHROISM
XEROPHTHALMIA
XEROPHTHALMIC

Y
YACHTSMANSHIP
YEOMAN SERVICE
YOUNG MARRIEDS

Z
ZEBRA CROSSING
ZEUGMATICALLY
ZIGZAGGEDNESS
ZINJANTHROPUS
ZOOGEOGRAPHER
ZOOGEOGRAPHIC
ZOOSPORANGIAL
ZOOSPORANGIUM
ZYGAPOPHYSEAL
ZYGODACTYLISM
ZYGODACTYLOUS

A
ABOVE-MENTIONED
ABSENT-MINDEDLY
ABSORBEFACIENT
ABSTEMIOUSNESS
ABSTRACTEDNESS
ABSTRACTIONISM
ACCLIMATIZABLE
ACCOMMODATIONS
ACCOMPANIMENTS
ACCOMPLISHABLE
ACCOMPLISHMENT
ACCOUNTABILITY
ACCUMULATIVELY
ACHONDROPLASIA
ACHROMATICALLY
ACKNOWLEDGMENT
ACQUIRED TASTES
ACROSS-THE-BOARD
ACTION STATIONS
ADENOCARCINOMA
ADMINISTRATION
ADMINISTRATIVE
ADMINISTRATORS
ADMINISTRATRIX
ADULT EDUCATION
ADVANCED LEVELS
ADVANTAGEOUSLY
AEROBALLISTICS
AEROMECHANICAL
AFFECTIONATELY
AFOREMENTIONED
AGGLOMERATIONS
AGGRANDIZEMENT
AGGRESSIVENESS
AGRICULTURISTS
AGROBIOLOGICAL
AGUASCALIENTES
AIR-CONDITIONED
AIR VICE-MARSHAL
ALCOHOLIZATION
ALLEGORIZATION
ALL-IN WRESTLING
ALLITERATIVELY
ALLOPATHICALLY
ALLOPATRICALLY
ALLOTROPICALLY
ALPES MARITIMES
ALPHABETICALLY
ALSACE-LORRAINE
ALTRUISTICALLY
AMARANTHACEOUS
AMATEURISHNESS
AMBASSADORSHIP
AMBASSADRESSES
AMBIDEXTROUSLY
AMERICAN INDIAN
AMMONIFICATION
AMPHIARTHROSIS

AMPHIBOLOGICAL
AMPHIPROSTYLAR
AMUSEMENT PARKS
ANACARDIACEOUS
ANAESTHETIZING
ANAMNESTICALLY
ANAMORPHOSCOPE
ANATHEMATIZING
ANDORRA LA VELLA
ANGINA PECTORIS
ANGLO-AMERICANS
ANGLO-CATHOLICS
ANIMADVERSIONS
ANISODACTYLOUS
ANTAGONIZATION
ANTHROPOLOGIST
ANTHROPOMETRIC
ANTHROPOPATHIC
ANTHROPOSOPHIC
ANTICHLORISTIC
ANTICIPATORILY
ANTIDEPRESSANT
ANTIHISTAMINES
ANTILOGARITHMS
ANTIMONARCHIST
ANTIPERSPIRANT
ANTIPHLOGISTIC
ANTIPRAGMATISM
ANTIQUATEDNESS
ANTIREPUBLICAN
ANTISEPTICALLY
ANTITHETICALLY
APARTMENT HOUSE
APOLOGETICALLY
APOPLECTICALLY
APOSTROPHIZING
APPENDECTOMIES
APPENDICECTOMY
APPORTIONMENTS
APPRECIATIVELY
APPREHENSIVELY
APPRENTICESHIP
APPROPRIATIONS
APPROVED SCHOOL
APPROXIMATIONS
ARABIC NUMERALS
ARCHAEOLOGICAL
ARCHAEOLOGISTS
ARCHBISHOPRICS
ARCHETYPICALLY
ARCHIDIACONATE
ARCHIEPISCOPAL
ARCHIMANDRITES
ARCHITECTONICS
ARITHMETICALLY
ARITHMETICIANS
ARRONDISSEMENT
ARTICULATENESS
ARTIODACTYLOUS

ASSASSINATIONS
ASSAULT COURSES
ASSET-STRIPPING
ASSOCIATIONISM
ASTIGMATICALLY
ASTROLOGICALLY
ASTRONAVIGATOR
ASTRONOMICALLY
ASTROPHYSICIST
ASYMMETRICALLY
ASYMPTOTICALLY
ATTRACTIVENESS
AUF WIEDERSEHEN
AUSPICIOUSNESS
AUTHENTICATING
AUTHENTICATION
AUTHENTICITIES
AUTHORITARIANS
AUTHORIZATIONS
AUTOBIOGRAPHER
AUTOBIOGRAPHIC
AUTOCRATICALLY
AUTOIONIZATION
AUTOMATIC PILOT
AUTOPHYTICALLY
AUTORADIOGRAPH
AUTOSUGGESTION
AUTOSUGGESTIVE
AUXILIARY VERBS
AWE-INSPIRINGLY

B
BACCALAUREATES
BACK FORMATIONS
BACKHANDEDNESS
BACK-SEAT DRIVER
BACTERIOLOGIST
BACTERIOPHAGIC
BACTERIOSTASIS
BACTERIOSTATIC
BALANCE OF POWER
BALANCE OF TRADE
BALSAMINACEOUS
BANANA REPUBLIC
BANNER HEADLINE
BAROMETRICALLY
BASIDIOSPOROUS
BASTARDIZATION
BATCH PROCESSED
BATHING MACHINE
BATTLE CRUISERS
BE-ALL AND END-ALL
BEASTS OF BURDEN
BEATIFICATIONS
BEAUTIFICATION
BEAUTY PARLOURS
BELISHA BEACONS
BERBERIDACEOUS
BIBLIOGRAPHERS

BIBLIOGRAPHIES
BIOCLIMATOLOGY
BIODEGRADABLES
BIOENGINEERING
BIOGENETICALLY
BIOGRAPHICALLY
BIOLUMINESCENT
BIPARTISANSHIP
BIRD OF PARADISE
BIRDS OF PASSAGE
BITUMINIZATION
BLACK MARKETEER
BLANK CARTRIDGE
BLOCK AND TACKLE
BLOOD POISONING
BLOOD PRESSURES
BLOOD RELATIONS
BLOODTHIRSTILY
BLUE-PENCILLING
BOARDINGHOUSES
BOARDING SCHOOL
BOIS DE BOULOGNE
BOISTEROUSNESS
BOLOMETRICALLY
BOON COMPANIONS
BOUCHES-DU-RHONE
BOUGAINVILLEAS
BOUILLABAISSES
BOULEVERSEMENT
BOWDLERIZATION
BRACHYCEPHALIC
BRACHYDACTYLIA
BRACHYDACTYLIC
BREAD-AND-BUTTER
BREATHLESSNESS
BREMSSTRAHLUNG
BRONCHIAL TUBES
BRONCHIECTASIS
BRONCHOSCOPIST
BRUSSELS SPROUT
BUILDING BLOCKS
BULLETIN BOARDS
BULLHEADEDNESS
BUREAU DE CHANGE
BURNT OFFERINGS
BUSMAN'S HOLIDAY

C
CADAVEROUSNESS
CALAMINE LOTION
CALENDAR MONTHS
CALLIGRAPHISTS
CAMPANOLOGISTS
CAMPANULACEOUS
CANTANKEROUSLY
CAPITALIZATION
CAPPARIDACEOUS
CAPRICIOUSNESS
CARBON MONOXIDE

CARCINOMATOSIS
CARDINAL POINTS
CARDIOVASCULAR
CARPET SWEEPERS
CARRIER PIGEONS
CARRYING CHARGE
CARTOGRAPHICAL
CARTRIDGE PAPER
CASEMENT WINDOW
CASH AND CARRIES
CASH DISPENSERS
CATCHMENT AREAS
CATECHETICALLY
CATEGORIZATION
CATHERINE WHEEL
CATHODE RAY TUBE
CAUSES CELEBRES
CENSORIOUSNESS
CENTRAL HEATING
CENTRALIZATION
CENTRE FORWARDS
CENTRIFUGATION
CERCOPITHECOID
CHAIN REACTIONS
CHAISES LONGUES
CHANGEABLENESS
CHANTRY CHAPELS
CHARACTERISTIC
CHARACTERIZING
CHARGE ACCOUNTS
CHARITABLENESS
CHARLATANISTIC
CHARTER MEMBERS
CHECHENO-INGUSH
CHEMOSYNTHESIS
CHEMOSYNTHETIC
CHEMOTHERAPIST
CHEST OF DRAWERS
CHICKENHEARTED
CHIEF CONSTABLE
CHIEF EXECUTIVE
CHIEF INSPECTOR
CHIEFTAINSHIPS
CHILD PRODIGIES
CHIMNEYBREASTS
CHIMNEY CORNERS
CHINCHERINCHEE
CHINESE LANTERN
CHINLESS WONDER
CHLOROPHYLLOID
CHLOROPHYLLOUS
CHLOROTHIAZIDE
CHLORPROMAZINE
CHLORPROPAMIDE
CHOLINESTERASE
CHOREOGRAPHERS
CHOREOGRAPHING
CHRISTIAN NAMES
CHRISTMAS BOXES

CHRISTMAS CAKES
CHRISTMAS CARDS
CHRISTMAS TREES
CHRISTOLOGICAL
CHROMATOGRAPHY
CHROMATOPHORIC
CHRYSANTHEMUMS
CIGARETTE PAPER
CINCHONIZATION
CINEMATOGRAPHY
CIRCUIT BREAKER
CIRCUMAMBIENCE
CIRCUMAMBULATE
CIRCUMFERENCES
CIRCUMLOCUTION
CIRCUMLOCUTORY
CIRCUMNAVIGATE
CIRCUMNUTATION
CIRCUMSCISSILE
CIRCUMSCRIBING
CIRCUMSPECTION
CIRCUMSTANTIAL
CIRCUMVOLUTION
CIRCUMVOLUTORY
CIVIL ENGINEERS
CLARIFICATIONS
CLASS-CONSCIOUS
CLASSIFICATION
CLASSIFICATORY
CLAUSTROPHOBIA
CLAUSTROPHOBIC
CLEARANCE SALES
CLEARINGHOUSES
CLEAR-SIGHTEDLY
CLIMBING FRAMES
CLOAK-AND-DAGGER
CLOTHES HANGERS
CLUB SANDWICHES
CLUSTER BOMBING
COCK-A-DOODLE-DOO
COCKER SPANIELS
COCKTAIL LOUNGE
COCKTAIL STICKS
COESSENTIALITY
COFFEE KLATCHES
COINCIDENTALLY
COLD SHOULDERED
COLLAPSIBILITY
COLLECTIVE FARM
COLLECTIVE NOUN
COLLECTOR'S ITEM
COLLOQUIALISMS
COLORADO BEETLE
COLOURFASTNESS
COLOURLESSNESS
COMBINING FORMS
COMBUSTIBILITY
COMFORTABLY OFF
COMFORT STATION

COMMAND MODULES
COMMENSURATION
COMMERCIALIZED
COMMISERATIONS
COMMISSIONAIRE
COMMITTEE STAGE
COMMON FRACTION
COMMON-OR-GARDEN
COMMUNICATIONS
COMMUNITY CHEST
COMMUNITY HOMES
COMPLEMENTIZER
COMPREHENSIBLE
COMPREHENSIBLY
COMPREHENSIONS
COMPREHENSIVES
COMPULSIVENESS
CONCATENATIONS
CONCAVO-CONCAVE
CONCELEBRATION
CONCENTRATIONS
CONCEPTUALIZED
CONCESSIONAIRE
CONCRETE JUNGLE
CONCRETE MIXERS
CONCRETIZATION
CONDEMNED CELLS
CONDENSABILITY
CONDITIONALITY
CONDUCTOR RAILS
CONDUPLICATION
CONFABULATIONS
CONFEDERATIONS
CONFIDENTIALLY
CONFIGURATIONS
CONFLAGRATIONS
CONFORMABILITY
CONFRONTATIONS
CONGLOMERATION
CONGLUTINATIVE
CONGRATULATING
CONGRATULATION
CONGRATULATORY
CONGREGATIONAL
CONJUNCTIVITIS
CONNECTING RODS
CONQUISTADORES
CONSANGUINEOUS
CONSCRIPTIONAL
CONSERVATIONAL
CONSERVATIVELY
CONSERVATOIRES
CONSERVATORIES
CONSIDERATIONS
CONSOLIDATIONS
CONSPIRATORIAL
CONSTABULARIES
CONSTANTINOPLE
CONSTELLATIONS

CONSTITUENCIES
CONSTITUTIONAL
CONSTRUCTIONAL
CONSTRUCTIVELY
CONSTRUCTIVISM
CONSTRUCTIVIST
CONSUETUDINARY
CONTAGIOUSNESS
CONTAINERIZING
CONTEMPORARIES
CONTEMPORARILY
CONTEMPTUOUSLY
CONTINENTALISM
CONTINENTALIST
CONTINENTALITY
CONTORTIONISTS
CONTRACEPTIVES
CONTRACT BRIDGE
CONTRADICTIONS
CONTRAINDICANT
CONTRAINDICATE
CONTRAPOSITION
CONTRAPUNTALLY
CONTRAVENTIONS
CONTRIBUTORIAL
CONTROVERTIBLE
CONTUMACIOUSLY
CONTUMELIOUSLY
CONVENTIONALLY
CONVERSATIONAL
CONVERSAZIOONI
CONVERTIBILITY
CONVEXO-CONCAVE
COPPER-BOTTOMED
CORELIGIONISTS
CORNISH PASTIES
CORPORATION TAX
CORRESPONDENCE
CORRESPONDENTS
CORRUPTIBILITY
CORTICOSTEROID
CORTICOSTERONE
CORTICOTROPHIN
COUNTERACTIONS
COUNTERATTACKS
COUNTERBALANCE
COUNTERFEITERS
COUNTERFEITING
COUNTERMANDING
COUNTERMEASURE
COUNTERMENSURE
COUNTERPOISING
COUNTERSHADING
COUNTERSIGNING
COUNTERSINKING
COUNTERVAILING
COUNTINGHOUSES
COUNTRY COUSINS
COUNTY COUNCILS

COURAGEOUSNESS
COURT-MARTIALED
COURT OF INQUIRY
COVERING LETTER
CREDIBILITY GAP
CREDITABLENESS
CREDIT ACCOUNTS
CREDIT SQUEEZES
CREEPY-CRAWLIES
CRIMINOLOGICAL
CRIMINOLOGISTS
CROCODILE TEARS
CROSS-COUNTRIES
CROSS-EXAMINERS
CROSS-EXAMINING
CROSS-FERTILIZE
CROSS-POLLINATE
CROSS-REFERENCE
CROSS-REFERRING
CROSS-SECTIONAL
CRUISE MISSILES
CRYPTAESTHESIA
CRYPTOGRAPHERS
CSECHOSLOVAKIA
CUCURBITACEOUS
CURRENT ACCOUNT
CURRICULA VITAE
CURTAIN RAISERS
CURVILINEARITY
CYANOCOBALAMIN
CYBERNETICALLY
CYTOTAXONOMIST

D

DAGUERREOTYPER
DAGUERREOTYPES
DANISH PASTRIES
DATA PROCESSING
DAUGHTERLINESS
DAUGHTERS-IN-LAW
DAY OF RECKONING
DECEIVABLENESS
DECENTRALIZING
DECIMALIZATION
DECLASSIFIABLE
DECLENSIONALLY
DECOLONIZATION
DECOLORIZATION
DECONTAMINATED
DECONTAMINATOR
DEFENESTRATION
DEFLOCCULATION
DEGENERATENESS
DEHUMANIZATION
DELECTABLENESS
DELIBERATENESS
DELIGHTFULNESS
DELOCALIZATION
DEMILITARIZING

DEMISEMIQUAVER	DISBELIEVINGLY	DISSUASIVENESS
DEMOBILIZATION	DISCIPLINARIAN	DISTENSIBILITY
DEMOCRATICALLY	DISCOLORATIONS	DISTINGUISHING
DEMONETIZATION	DISCOMPOSINGLY	DISTRIBUTIONAL
DEMONSTRATIONS	DISCONNECTEDLY	DISTRIBUTIVELY
DEMORALIZATION	DISCONNECTIONS	DIURETICALNESS
DENATIONALIZED	DISCONSOLATELY	DIVERTICULITIS
DENOMINATIONAL	DISCONSOLATION	DIVERTICULOSIS
DENTAL SURGEONS	DISCONTENTEDLY	DIVERTISSEMENT
DEPLORABLENESS	DISCONTENTMENT	DNEPROPETROVSK
DEPOLARIZATION	DISCONTINUANCE	DO-IT-YOURSELFER
DEPOSIT ACCOUNT	DISCOUNTENANCE	DOMESTIC ANIMAL
DERMATOLOGICAL	DISCOUNT STORES	DOUBLE-BREASTED
DERMATOLOGISTS	DISCOURAGEMENT	DOUBLE-CHECKING
DERMATOPLASTIC	DISCOURAGINGLY	DOUBLE-CROSSERS
DEROGATORINESS	DISCOURTEOUSLY	DOUBLE-CROSSING
DESTRUCTIONIST	DISCRIMINATING	DOUBLE ENTENDRE
DETERMINEDNESS	DISCRIMINATION	DOUBLE FEATURES
DEVIL'S ADVOCATE	DISCRIMINATORY	DOUBTING THOMAS
DEVITALIZATION	DISCURSIVENESS	DRAINING BOARDS
DEXTROROTATION	DISEMBARKATION	DRAMATIZATIONS
DEXTROROTATORY	DISEMBOGUEMENT	DRESSING TABLES
DIABOLICALNESS	DISEMBOWELLING	DRESS REHEARSAL
DIAGNOSTICALLY	DISEMBOWELMENT	DRIVING LICENCE
DIALECTOLOGIST	DISENCHANTMENT	DRUM MAJORETTES
DIAMOND JUBILEE	DISENFRANCHISE	DUCKS AND DRAKES
DIAMOND WEDDING	DISENTHRALMENT	DUCTLESS GLANDS
DIAPHANOUSNESS	DISEQUILIBRIUM	DWELLING HOUSES
DIAPHOTOTROPIC	DISESTABLISHED	DYER'S-GREENWEED
DICHROMATICISM	DISFEATUREMENT	DYNAMOELECTRIC
DICOTYLEDONOUS	DISFIGUREMENTS	DYSMENORRHOEAL
DIELECTRICALLY	DISFORESTATION	
DIESEL-ELECTRIC	DISFRANCHISING	E
DIFFERENTIABLE	DISGRUNTLEMENT	ECCENTRICITIES
DIFFERENTIATED	DISHEARTENMENT	ECCLESIASTICAL
DIFFERENTIATOR	DISILLUSIONING	ECCLESIOLOGIST
DIFFRACTOMETER	DISINCLINATION	ECONOMETRICIAN
DIGITALIZATION	DISINFESTATION	EDITIO PRINCEPS
DIMENHYDRINATE	DISINGENUOUSLY	EDUCATIONALIST
DIMENSIONALITY	DISINHERITANCE	EFFERVESCENTLY
DINITROBENZENE	DISINTEGRATING	EFFERVESCINGLY
DINNER SERVICES	DISINTEGRATION	EFFORTLESSNESS
DINOFLAGELLATE	DISINTEGRATIVE	EGALITARIANISM
DIPLOMATICALLY	DISJOINTEDNESS	EGOCENTRICALLY
DIPLOSTEMONOUS	DISORDERLINESS	ELDER STATESMAN
DIRECTIONALITY	DISORIENTATING	ELDER STATESMEN
DIRECT TAXATION	DISORIENTATION	ELECTIONEERING
DISAFFILIATING	DISPARAGEMENTS	ELECTRA COMPLEX
DISAFFILIATION	DISPENSABILITY	ELECTROCHEMIST
DISAFFORESTING	DISPENSATIONAL	ELECTROCUTIONS
DISAPPEARANCES	DISPUTATIOUSLY	ELECTRODEPOSIT
DISAPPOINTEDLY	DISQUALIFIABLE	ELECTRODYNAMIC
DISAPPOINTMENT	DISQUIETEDNESS	ELECTROGRAPHIC
DISAPPROBATION	DISRESPECTABLE	ELECTROKINETIC
DISAPPROVINGLY	DISSERTATIONAL	ELECTRONICALLY
DISARRANGEMENT	DISSERVICEABLE	ELECTROSTATICS
DISARTICULATOR	DISSIMULATIONS	ELECTROSURGERY
DISASSOCIATING	DISSOCIABILITY	ELECTROTHERMAL
DISASSOCIATION	DISSOLVABILITY	ELECTROVALENCY

ELEMENTARINESS	EVEN-HANDEDNESS	FEDERALIZATION
ELLIPTICALNESS	EVENING DRESSES	FEEDING BOTTLES
EMBARRASSINGLY	EVIL-MINDEDNESS	FELICITOUSNESS
EMBARRASSMENTS	EVOLUTIONISTIC	FEMME DE CHAMBRE
EMBELLISHMENTS	EXACERBATINGLY	FERMENTABILITY
EMBLEMATICALLY	EXAGGERATINGLY	FERRIMAGNETISM
EMOTIONALISTIC	EXASPERATINGLY	FERROMAGNESIAN
EMPHATICALNESS	EXCEPTIONALITY	FERROMAGNETISM
EMULSIFICATION	EXCLAUSTRATION	FERROMANGANESE
EMULSION PAINTS	EXCOMMUNICABLE	FICTIONALIZING
ENANTIOMORPHIC	EXCOMMUNICATED	FICTITIOUSNESS
ENCAPSULATIONS	EXCOMMUNICATOR	FIDEICOMMISSUM
ENCEPHALOGRAPH	EXCRUCIATINGLY	FIELDS OF VISION
ENCOURAGEMENTS	EXHAUSTIBILITY	FIFTH COLUMNIST
ENDOCRINE GLAND	EXHAUSTIVENESS	FIGHTING CHANCE
ENDOCRINOLOGIC	EXHIBITIONISTS	FIGURATIVENESS
ENDOPHYTICALLY	EXHILARATINGLY	FIGURE OF SPEECH
ENDOSMOTICALLY	EXISTENTIALISM	FIGURES OF EIGHT
ENFANT TERRIBLE	EXISTENTIALIST	FILING CABINETS
ENFORCEABILITY	EXOTHERMICALLY	FILLING STATION
ENGAGEMENT RING	EXPANSIONISTIC	FINANCIAL YEARS
ENHARMONICALLY	EXPENSE ACCOUNT	FINE-TOOTH COMBS
ENLIGHTENINGLY	EXPERIMENTALLY	FINGERPRINTING
ENROLLED NURSES	EXPOSTULATIONS	FINSTERAARHORN
ENTEROGASTRONE	EXPRESSIONISTS	FIRST OFFENDERS
ENTERPRISINGLY	EXPRESSIONLESS	FISSIONABILITY
ENTERTAININGLY	EXPRESSIVENESS	FLABBERGASTING
ENTERTAINMENTS	EXPROPRIATIONS	FLIGHT SERGEANT
ENTOMOSTRACOUS	EXTEMPORANEOUS	FLOATING VOTERS
EPEXEGETICALLY	EXTENDED FAMILY	FLORICULTURIST
EPICONTINENTAL	EXTENSIONALITY	FLOWER-OF-AN-HOUR
EPIDEMIOLOGIST	EXTINGUISHABLE	FLYING BUTTRESS
EPIGENETICALLY	EXTINGUISHMENT	FLYING OFFICERS
EPIGRAPHICALLY	EXTORTIONATELY	FOLLOW-MY-LEADER
EPISTEMOLOGIST	EXTRACANONICAL	FOLLOW-THROUGHS
EQUIPONDERANCE	EXTRACTABILITY	FOOD PROCESSORS
EQUIVOCATINGLY	EXTRANEOUSNESS	FORBIDDEN FRUIT
ERYTHROBLASTIC	EXTRAVEHICULAR	FORBIDDINGNESS
ERYTHROPOIESIS	EYEBROW PENCILS	FOREIGN AFFAIRS
ERYTHROPOIETIC		FOREORDAINMENT
ESCAPE VELOCITY	F	FORESHORTENING
ESCHATOLOGICAL	FACTITIOUSNESS	FORETHOUGHTFUL
ESTABLISHMENTS	FACTORY FARMING	FORE-TOPGALLANT
ESTATE AGENCIES	FAINT-HEARTEDLY	FORKLIFT TRUCKS
ESTERIFICATION	FAIR-MINDEDNESS	FORTHRIGHTNESS
ETERNALIZATION	FAIRY GODMOTHER	FORTIFICATIONS
ETHERIFICATION	FAITS ACCOMPLIS	FORTUITOUSNESS
ETHNOCENTRISMS	FALLACIOUSNESS	FORTUNE HUNTERS
ETHNOLOGICALLY	FALLOPIAN TUBES	FORTUNE-TELLERS
ETYMOLOGICALLY	FALSE PRETENCES	FORWARD-LOOKING
EULOGISTICALLY	FALSIFICATIONS	FOUNDING FATHER
EUPHONICALNESS	FAMILY PLANNING	FOUR-LETTER WORD
EUPHORBIACEOUS	FARSIGHTEDNESS	FRATERNIZATION
EUPHUISTICALLY	FASTIDIOUSNESS	FREE ENTERPRISE
EUSTACHIAN TUBE	FATALISTICALLY	FREEZING POINTS
EUTROPHICATION	FAVOURABLENESS	FRENCH DRESSING
EVANGELICALISM	FEATHERBEDDING	FRENCH POLISHED
EVANGELIZATION	FEATHERBRAINED	FRIDGE-FREEZERS
EVAPORATED MILK	FEATHERWEIGHTS	FRIENDLESSNESS

FRINGE BENEFITS
FRUCTIFICATION
FULLY-FASHIONED
FUNCTIONALISTS
FUNDAMENTALISM
FUNDAMENTALIST
FUNDAMENTALITY
FUNERAL PARLOUR
FURFURALDEHYDE
FUTURISTICALLY

G
GALACTOPOIESIS
GALACTOPOIETIC
GALVANOTROPISM
GASTROVASCULAR
GEIGER COUNTERS
GELATINIZATION
GENEALOGICALLY
GENERALISSIMOS
GENERALIZATION
GENERAL STRIKES
GENTRIFICATION
GEOCENTRICALLY
GEOGRAPHICALLY
GERMAN SHEPHERD
GERONTOLOGICAL
GERRYMANDERING
GESTICULATIONS
GHETTO BLASTERS
GLANDULAR FEVER
GLOBE ARTICHOKE
GLOBETROTTINGS
GLORIFICATIONS
GLORY-OF-THE-SNOW
GLOSSY MAGAZINE
GLUCOCORTICORD
GOLDEN JUBILEES
GOLDEN WEDDINGS
GOLD-OF-PLEASURE
GOOD-FOR-NOTHING
GOOD-HUMOUREDLY
GOOD SAMARITANS
GRACE-AND-FAVOUR
GRADE CROSSINGS
GRAMMAR SCHOOLS
GRAMMATICALITY
GRAMMATOLOGIST
GRANDDAUGHTERS
GRANDILOQUENCE
GRANGERIZATION
GRAPHITIZATION
GRAPPLING IRONS
GRATIFICATIONS
GRATUITOUSNESS
GREGARIOUSNESS
GREGORIAN CHANT
GROUNDLESSNESS
GROUP PRACTICES

GUARDIAN ANGELS
GUIDED MISSILES
GUY FAWKES NIGHT
GYNAECOLOGICAL
GYNAECOLOGISTS
GYROSTABILIZER

H
HABERDASHERIES
HAEMACYTOMETER
HAEMAGGLUTININ
HAEMATOBLASTIC
HAEMATOGENESIS
HAEMATOPOIESIS
HAEMATOPOIETIC
HAEMATOTHERMAL
HAEMOCYTOMETER
HALFPENNYWORTH
HALFWITTEDNESS
HALICARNASSIAN
HALLUCINATIONS
HALLUCINOGENIC
HANDICRAFTSMAN
HAPAX LEGOMENON
HARD CURRENCIES
HARD-HEADEDNESS
HARMONIOUSNESS
HARPSICHORDIST
HEADMASTERSHIP
HEADSTRONGNESS
HEARTRENDINGLY
HEARTWARMINGLY
HEATHENISHNESS
HEBRAISTICALLY
HEGIRA CALENDAR
HELTER-SKELTERS
HEMEL HEMPSTEAD
HEMISPHEROIDAL
HENRIETTA MARIA
HEREDITABILITY
HEREDITARINESS
HERMAPHRODITES
HERMAPHRODITIC
HERMAPHRODITUS
HEROIC COUPLETS
HERO WORSHIPPED
HERPES LABIALIS
HETEROCHROMOUS
HETEROGONOUSLY
HETEROLECITHAL
HETEROMORPHISM
HETERONOMOUSLY
HETERONYMOUSLY
HETEROPHYLLOUS
HETEROPOLARITY
HETEROSEXUALLY
HIERARCHICALLY
HIGH COMMISSION
HIGH EXPLOSIVES

HIGH-HANDEDNESS
HIGHLAND FLINGS
HIGH-MINDEDNESS
HIGH-PRESSURING
HIGH-PRINCIPLED
HIGH TECHNOLOGY
HIGH WATER MARKS
HIPPOPOTAMUSES
HISTOCHEMISTRY
HISTOLOGICALLY
HISTOLYTICALLY
HISTOPATHOLOGY
HISTOPLASMOSIS
HISTORICALNESS
HISTORIOGRAPHY
HISTRIONICALLY
HOEK VAN HOLLAND
HOLDING COMPANY
HOLIER-THAN-THOU
HOMOCHROMATISM
HOMOGENIZATION
HOMOIOUSIANISM
HOMOPHONICALLY
HONEYDEW MELONS
HONOURABLENESS
HORATIUS COCLES
HORIZONTALNESS
HORRENDOUSNESS
HORROR-STRICKEN
HORSE CHESTNUTS
HORTICULTURIST
HOSPITABLENESS
HOT-WATER BOTTLE
HOUSEHOLD NAMES
HOUSEMAID'S KNEE
HOUSE OF COMMONS
HOUSING PROJECT
HUMIDIFICATION
HUMOURLESSNESS
HUNGER MARCHERS
HUNGER STRIKERS
HUNTING GROUNDS
HURRICANE LAMPS
HYDROCELLULOSE
HYDROCORTISONE
HYDROGENOLYSIS
HYDROLOGICALLY
HYDROMAGNETICS
HYDROMECHANICS
HYPERBOLICALLY
HYPERSENSITIVE
HYPOCHONDRIACS
HYPOCRITICALLY
HYPODERMICALLY
HYPOTHETICALLY
HYSTERECTOMIES

I
ICEBERG LETTUCE

ICHNEUMON FLIES	INCOORDINATION	INTELLECTUALLY
ICHTHYOPHAGOUS	INDECIPHERABLE	INTELLIGENTSIA
IDEALISTICALLY	INDECIPHERABLY	INTENTIONALITY
IDENTICAL TWINS	INDECOROUSNESS	INTERCESSIONAL
IDENTIFICATION	INDEFINITENESS	INTERCOMMUNION
IDEOLOOGICALLY	INDESTRUCTIBLE	INTERDEPENDENT
IDIOSYNCRASIES	INDESTRUCTIBLY	INTEREST GROUPS
ILLEGALIZATION	INDETERMINABLE	INTERFERENTIAL
ILLEGITIMATELY	INDETERMINABLY	INTERFEROMETER
ILLIMITABILITY	INDIFFERENTISM	INTERFEROMETRY
ILLUSTRATIONAL	INDIFFERENTIST	INTERFERTILITY
ILLUSTRATIVELY	INDIGENOUSNESS	INTERGRADATION
IMMETHODICALLY	INDIRECT OBJECT	INTERJECTIONAL
IMMOBILIZATION	INDIRECT SPEECH	INTERLOCUTRESS
IMMUNOGENETICS	INDISCRIMINATE	INTERMEDIARIES
IMMUNOGLOBULIN	INDISPOSITIONS	INTERMIGRATION
IMMUNOREACTION	INDISTINCTNESS	INTERMITTENTLY
IMPARISYLLABIC	INDIVIDUALISTS	INTERMITTINGLY
IMPEACHABILITY	INDIVIDUALIZED	INTERMOLECULAR
IMPERCEPTIVITY	INDIVIDUALIZER	INTERNATIONALE
IMPERMEABILITY	INDIVISIBILITY	INTERNATIONALS
IMPERSONATIONS	INDOCTRINATING	INTERPELLATION
IMPERTURBATION	INDOCTRINATION	INTERPENETRANT
IMPLAUSIBILITY	INDOMITABILITY	INTERPENETRATE
IMPLEMENTATION	INDUBITABILITY	INTERPLANETARY
IMPOLITENESSES	INDUSTRIALISTS	INTERPOLATIONS
IMPRACTICALITY	INDUSTRIALIZED	INTERPOSITIONS
IMPREGNABILITY	INEFFECTUALITY	INTERPRETATION
IMPRESSIONABLE	INELUCTABILITY	INTERPRETATIVE
IMPRESSIONABLY	INERTIA SELLING	INTERRELATIONS
IMPRESSIONALLY	INESSENTIALITY	INTERROGATIONS
IMPRESSIONISTS	INESTIMABILITY	INTERROGATIVES
IMPRESSIVENESS	INEXCUSABILITY	INTERSECTIONAL
IMPROVISATIONS	INFECTIOUSNESS	INTERSEXUALITY
INADVISABILITY	INFLAMMABILITY	INTERSPERSEDLY
INALIENABILITY	INFLAMMATORILY	INTERTWININGLY
INALTERABILITY	INFRALAPSARIAN	INTERVENTIONAL
INAPPRECIATIVE	INFRANGIBILITY	INTOLERABILITY
INAPPREHENSIVE	INFRASTRUCTURE	INTOXICATINGLY
INAPPROACHABLE	INGRATIATINGLY	INTRACTABILITY
INARTICULATELY	INHABITABILITY	INTRACUTANEOUS
INARTISTICALLY	INHARMONIOUSLY	INTRAMOLECULAR
INAUSPICIOUSLY	INHERITABILITY	INTRANSIGENTLY
INCANDESCENTLY	INITIALIZATION	INTRANSITIVELY
INCAPACITATING	IN LOCO PARENTIS	INTRODUCTORILY
INCAPACITATION	INNUMERABILITY	INVERTED COMMAS
INCAUTIOUSNESS	INQUISITIONIST	INVESTIGATIONS
INCESTUOUSNESS	INSANITARINESS	INVIGORATINGLY
INCOMMENSURATE	INSCRUTABILITY	IODOMETRICALLY
INCOMMODIOUSLY	INSEPARABILITY	IRRECONCILABLE
INCOMMUNICABLE	INSIGNIFICANCE	IRRECONCILABLY
INCOMPLETENESS	INSTITUTIONARY	IRREDUCIBILITY
INCOMPRESSIBLE	INSTRUCTORSHIP	IRREFUTABILITY
INCONCLUSIVELY	INSUFFICIENTLY	IRREGULARITIES
INCONSIDERABLE	INSUPERABILITY	IRREMOVABILITY
INCONSISTENTLY	INSUPPRESSIBLE	IRREPARABILITY
INCONVENIENCED	INSURMOUNTABLE	IRREPROACHABLE
INCONVENIENCES	INSURRECTIONAL	IRREPROACHABLY
INCONVENIENTLY	INTEGRATIONIST	IRRESOLUBILITY

IRREVOCABILITY	LITHOLOGICALLY	MESDEMOISELLES
ISOPIESTICALLY	LOCAL AUTHORITY	METACHROMATISM
	LOCUS CLASSICUS	METALLOGRAPHER
J	LONGITUDINALLY	METALLOGRAPHIC
JACK-IN-THE-BOXES	LONG-SUFFERANCE	METAMORPHOSING
JOB'S COMFORTERS	LONGWINDEDNESS	METAPHORICALLY
JOLLIFICATIONS	LOOKING GLASSES	METAPHYSICALLY
JOURNALIZATION	LOVING KINDNESS	METAPSYCHOLOGY
JURISDICTIONAL	LOXODROMICALLY	METASTATICALLY
JUSTICIABILITY	LUGUBRIOUSNESS	METEMPSYCHOSIS
JUSTIFIABILITY		METEOROGRAPHIC
	M	METEOROLOGICAL
K	MACADAMIZATION	METEOROLOGISTS
KAISERSLAUTERN	MACHINEGUNNING	METHAEMOGLOBIN
KAMENSK-URALSKI	MACROECONOMICS	METHODICALNESS
KANGAROO COURTS	MACROEVOLUTION	METHODOLOGICAL
KERATINIZATION	MACROMOLECULAR	METICULOUSNESS
KIDNEY MACHINES	MAGNETIC FIELDS	MICROBAROGRAPH
KINDERGARTENER	MAGNIFICATIONS	MICROBIOLOGIST
KITCHEN GARDENS	MAHALLA EL KUBRA	MICROCEPHALOUS
KNICKERBOCKERS	MALACOPHYLLOUS	MICROCHEMISTRY
KNIGHT-ERRANTRY	MALACOSTRACOUS	MICROCIRCUITRY
KNUCKLE-DUSTERS	MALE CHAUVINIST	MICROCOMPUTERS
KOSOVO-METOHIJA	MALFUNCTIONING	MICROECONOMICS
	MALPIGHIACEOUS	MICROMETEORITE
L	MALTESE CROSSES	MICROORGANISMS
LABOUR EXCHANGE	MANIFESTATIONS	MICROPARASITIC
LAMELLIROSTRAL	MANIPULABILITY	MICROPROCESSOR
LANCE CORPORALS	MANNERLESSNESS	MICROPYROMETER
LARGE INTESTINE	MANOMETRICALLY	MICROSTOMATOUS
LARYNGOLOGICAL	MANUFACTURABLE	MICROSTRUCTURE
LARYNGOSCOPIST	MARCHING ORDERS	MIDDLE-DISTANCE
LASCIVIOUSNESS	MARKET GARDENER	MIGHT-HAVE-BEENS
LATITUDINARIAN	MARKET RESEARCH	MILITARIZATION
LAUGHINGSTOCKS	MARTYROLOGICAL	MILITARY POLICE
LAUNDRY BASKETS	MASON-DIXON LINE	MILLENARIANISM
LAW OF THE JUNGLE	MASSAGE PARLOUR	MINERALIZATION
LEADING ARTICLE	MASSOTHERAPIST	MISAPPLICATION
LEAVE OF ABSENCE	MASS PRODUCTION	MISAPPREHENDED
LEFT-HANDEDNESS	MATHEMATICALLY	MISAPPROPRIATE
LEGALISTICALLY	MATHEMATICIANS	MISCALCULATING
LEGERDEMAINIST	MATTER-OF-FACTLY	MISCALCULATION
LEGITIMIZATION	MATURE STUDENTS	MISCONCEPTIONS
LENDING LIBRARY	MAUNDY THURSDAY	MISINFORMATION
LETTER OF CREDIT	MEANINGFULNESS	MISINTERPRETED
LEVEL CROSSINGS	MECHANOTHERAPY	MISINTERPRETER
LEXICOGRAPHERS	MEDDLESOMENESS	MISREPRESENTED
LIBERALIZATION	MEDITATIVENESS	MISREPRESENTER
LIBERAL STUDIES	MEGALOCEPHALIC	MIXED ECONOMIES
LIBERTARIANISM	MEGALOMANIACAL	MIXED METAPHORS
LIBIDINOUSNESS	MEGAPHONICALLY	MOCK-HEROICALLY
LICENTIATESHIP	MEGASPOROPHYLL	MOCK TURTLE SOUP
LICENTIOUSNESS	MELANCHOLINESS	MODERNIZATIONS
LIFE EXPECTANCY	MENDACIOUSNESS	MOMENTS OF TRUTH
LIFE PRESERVERS	MENTAL HOSPITAL	MONGRELIZATION
LIGHT AIRCRAFTS	MEPHISTOPHELES	MONKEY BUSINESS
LIGNOCELLULOSE	MERCAPTOPURINE	MONKEY WRENCHES
LIKE-MINDEDNESS	MERCHANT NAVIES	MONOCARPELLARY
LINGUISTICALLY	MERETRICIOUSLY	MONOCHROMATISM

MONOLITHICALLY
MONOPOLIZATION
MONOPROPELLANT
MONOSACCHARIDE
MOONLIGHT FLITS
MORALISTICALLY
MORGANATICALLY
MORNING GLORIES
MORPHOPHONEMIC
MOTHER SUPERIOR
MOTIONLESSNESS
MOTION PICTURES
MOTIVELESSNESS
MOUNTAINEERING
MOVING PICTURES
MUCOMEMBRANOUS
MUCOUS MEMBRANE
MULTIFACTORIAL
MULTIFARIOUSLY
MULTILATERALLY
MULTINATIONALS
MULTIPLE STORES
MULTIPLICATION
MULTIPLICATIVE
MUNICIPALITIES
MUSTARD PLASTER
MYELENCEPHALIC
MYELENCEPHALON
MYOCARDIOGRAPH
MYOGRAPHICALLY
MYRMECOLOGICAL
MYRMECOPHAGOUS
MYRMECOPHILOUS
MYSTAGOGICALLY
MYSTERIOUSNESS

N
NANSEN PASSPORT
NARCOSYNTHESIS
NASOPHARYNGEAL
NATIONAL ANTHEM
NATURAL HISTORY
NATURALIZATION
NATURAL SCIENCE
NEANDERTHAL MAN
NEBUCHADNEZZAR
NEGLECTFULNESS
NEIGHBOURHOODS
NEOCOLONIALISM
NEOCOLONIALIST
NERVOUS SYSTEMS
NEUROPATHOLOGY
NEUTRALIZATION
NEWFOUNDLANDER
NEWS CONFERENCE
NEWSWORTHINESS
NIGHT BLINDNESS
NIGHT WATCHMANS
NIL DESPERANDUM

NINE DAYS' WONDER
NITROCELLULOSE
NITROGLYCERINE
NOBLESSE OBLIGE
NO-CLAIM BONUSES
NOLO CONTENDERE
NONATTRIBUTIVE
NONCOMMITTALLY
NONCONFORMISTS
NONCOOPERATION
NONCOOPERATIVE
NONDISJUNCTION
NONEQUIVALENCE
NONINFLAMMABLE
NONPROGRESSIVE
NON PROSEQUITUR
NONRESIDENTIAL
NONRESTRICTIVE
NONSTIMULATING
NORFOLK JACKETS
NORTHERN LIGHTS
NORTH-NORTHEAST
NORTH-NORTHWEST
NORTHUMBERLAND
NOTEWORTHINESS
NOUVEAUX RICHES
NO-WIN SITUATION
NUCLEAR REACTOR
NUCLEAR WINTERS
NURSERY SCHOOLS
NUTRITIOUSNESS
NYCTAGINACEOUS
NYMPHOMANIACAL

O
OBSEQUIOUSNESS
OBSERVABLENESS
OBSTREPEROUSLY
OBSTRUCTIONISM
OBSTRUCTIONIST
OCCUPATIONALLY
OCEANOGRAPHERS
OEDIPUS COMPLEX
OLD PEOPLE'S HOME
OLIGARCHICALLY
OLIGOPSONISTIC
ONE-ARMED BANDIT
ONEIROCRITICAL
ONE-NIGHT STANDS
OPEN-HANDEDNESS
OPEN-MINDEDNESS
OPEN SANDWICHES
OPEN UNIVERSITY
OPERATIONALISM
OPHTHALMOSCOPE
OPHTHALMOSCOPY
OPPOSITE NUMBER
OPPRESSIVENESS
OPTIMISTICALLY

ORCHESTRATIONS
ORDINARY LEVELS
ORDINARY SEAMAN
ORDNANCE SURVEY
ORGANIZATIONAL
ORGANIZED CRIME
ORGANOGRAPHIST
ORGANOMETALLIC
ORNITHOLOGICAL
ORNITHOLOGISTS
OROBANCHACEOUS
OROGRAPHICALLY
ORTHOCHROMATIC
ORTHODOX CHURCH
ORTHOGENICALLY
ORTHOGRAPHICAL
ORTHOPHOSPHATE
OSCILLOGRAPHIC
OSMOMETRICALLY
OSTENTATIOUSLY
OSTEOARTHRITIC
OSTEOARTHRITIS
OSTEOLOGICALLY
OTOLARYNGOLOGY
OUTBOARD MOTORS
OUTGENERALLING
OUTLANDISHNESS
OUTMANOEUVRING
OUTRAGEOUSNESS
OVERCAPITALIZE
OVERCOMPENSATE
OVERDEVELOPING
OVERENTHUSIASM
OVERESTIMATING
OVERESTIMATION
OVERINDULGENCE
OVERPOPULATION
OVERPOWERINGLY
OVERPRODUCTION
OVERPROTECTION
OVERSIMPLIFIED
OVERSTATEMENTS
OVERSUBSCRIBED
OVER-THE-COUNTER
OVERWHELMINGLY
OWNER-OCCUPIERS
OXYHAEMOGLOBIN
OYSTERCATCHERS

P
PACHYDERMATOUS
PADDLE STEAMERS
PAEDIATRICIANS
PAEDOMORPHOSIS
PAGANISTICALLY
PALAEANTHROPIC
PALAEETHNOLOGY
PALAEOBOTANIST
PALATALIZATION

PALEONTOLOGIST	PERSON-TO-PERSON	PLANCK CONSTANT
PAN-AMERICANISM	PERSUADABILITY	PLASTER OF PARIS
PANCAKE LANDING	PERSUASIVENESS	PLASTIC BULLETS
PANGENETICALLY	PERTINACIOUSLY	PLASTICIZATION
PANHELLENISTIC	PETIT BOURGEOIS	PLASTIC SURGEON
PAPILLOMATOSIS	PETIT LARCENIST	PLASTIC SURGERY
PARABOLIZATION	PETROCHEMICALS	PLATINOCYANIDE
PARALLELEPIPED	PETROCHEMISTRY	PLATINUM BLONDE
PARALLELOGRAMS	PETROLEUM JELLY	PLATITUDINIZER
PARAPHERNALIAS	PETROL STATIONS	PLEA BARGAINING
PARAPSYCHOLOGY	PETTY BOURGEOIS	PLEONASTICALLY
PARASITOLOGIST	PETTY LARCENIES	PLETHYSMOGRAPH
PARATACTICALLY	PHANTASMAGORIA	PLUMBER'S FRIEND
PARENCHYMATOUS	PHANTASMAGORIC	PNEUMATIC DRILL
PARKING GARAGES	PHARMACEUTICAL	PNEUMOBACILLUS
PARSIMONIOUSLY	PHARMACOLOGIST	PNEUMOCONIOSIS
PARTHENOCARPIC	PHARMACOPOEIAL	PNEUMODYNAMICS
PARTICULARIZED	PHARMACOPOEIAS	POIKILOTHERMAL
PARTICULARIZER	PHARMACOPOEIST	POLEMONIACEOUS
PARTURIFACIENT	PHARYNGOLOGIST	POLICE OFFICERS
PASSIONATENESS	PHARYNGOSCOPIC	POLICE STATIONS
PASSIONFLOWERS	PHENOBARBITONE	POLITICIZATION
PASSIVE SMOKING	PHENOTYPICALLY	POLLING STATION
PASTEURIZATION	PHILANTHROPIST	POLYCARPELLARY
PAST PARTICIPLE	PHILATELICALLY	POLYCHROMATISM
PATE DE FOIE GRAS	PHILOLOGICALLY	POLYMERIZATION
PATENT MEDICINE	PHILOSOPHIZING	POLYNUCLEOTIDE
PATHOLOGICALLY	PHLEGMATICALLY	POLYPHONICALLY
PAVEMENT ARTIST	PHONOLOGICALLY	POLYSACCHARIDE
PEACE OFFERINGS	PHOSPHOPROTEIN	POLYSYNTHESISM
PENITENTIARIES	PHOSPHORESCENT	POOR-SPIRITEDLY
PENNY DREADFULS	PHOSPHOROSCOPE	POPULARIZATION
PENNY-FARTHINGS	PHOTOCHEMISTRY	PORPHYROGENITE
PENNY-HALFPENNY	PHOTOCONDUCTOR	PORTENTOUSNESS
PEPPERCORN RENT	PHOTOENGRAVING	PORTULACACEOUS
PERAMBULATIONS	PHOTOGENICALLY	POSSESSIVENESS
PERCEIVABILITY	PHOTOGRAMMETRY	POSTMILLENNIAL
PERCEPTIBILITY	PHOTOPERIODISM	POSTPOSITIONAL
PERCUSSION CAPS	PHOTOSENSITIVE	POTENTIALITIES
PERCUSSIONISTS	PHOTOSENSITIZE	PRACTICABILITY
PEREGRINATIONS	PHOTOSYNTHESIS	PRACTICALITIES
PEREMPTORINESS	PHOTOSYNTHETIC	PRACTICAL JOKES
PERFECTIBILITY	PHOTOTYPICALLY	PRAISEWORTHILY
PERFECTIONISTS	PHRASEOGRAPHIC	PRAYER MEETINGS
PERFIDIOUSNESS	PHRASEOLOGICAL	PREADOLESCENCE
PERIMETRICALLY	PHTHALOCYANINE	PREARRANGEMENT
PERISCOPICALLY	PHYTOGEOGRAPHY	PRECARIOUSNESS
PERLOCUTIONARY	PHYTOPATHOLOGY	PRECIOUS METALS
PERMANENT WAVES	PHYTOSOCIOLOGY	PRECIOUS STONES
PERMISSIBILITY	PICTURE WINDOWS	PRECIPITATIONS
PERMISSIVENESS	PIEZOCHEMISTRY	PRECOCIOUSNESS
PERNICIOUSNESS	PILGRIM FATHERS	PRECONCEPTIONS
PERNICKETINESS	PINCER MOVEMENT	PREDACIOUSNESS
PEROXIDE BLONDE	PINNATIPARTITE	PREDESTINARIAN
PERPENDICULARS	PINS AND NEEDLES	PREDESTINATION
PERSONABLENESS	PISCICULTURIST	PREDETERMINATE
PERSONAL COLUMN	PITCH-BLACKNESS	PREDETERMINERS
PERSONAL ESTATE	PITCHED BATTLES	PREDETERMINING
PERSONAL STEREO	PLAIN CHOCOLATE	PREDICTABILITY

PREDISPOSITION	PROHIBITIONARY	PURSE STRINGSES
PREFABRICATING	PROHIBITIONISM	PYELONEPHRITIS
PREFABRICATION	PROHIBITIONIST	PYRAMID SELLING
PREFERENTIALLY	PROJECTIONISTS	PYRHELIOMETRIC
PREFIGURATIONS	PROLETARIANISM	PYROMETALLURGY
PREMEDITATEDLY	PROLIFERATIONS	PYROMETRICALLY
PREOCCUPATIONS	PROMENADE DECKS	PYROPHOTOMETER
PREORDINATIONS	PRONOUNCEMENTS	PYROPHOTOMETRY
PREPONDERANTLY	PRONUNCIATIONS	PYROTECHNICSES
PREPONDERATING	PROPAEDEUTICAL	PYRRHIC VICTORY
PREPONDERATION	PROPAGANDIZING	
PREPOSSESSIONS	PROPER FRACTION	Q
PREPOSTEROUSLY	PROPITIOUSNESS	QUADRAGENARIAN
PRE-RAPHAELITES	PROPORTIONALLY	QUADRILATERALS
PRESCRIPTIVELY	PROPORTIONMENT	QUALIFICATIONS
PRESCRIPTIVISM	PROPOSITIONING	QUANTIFICATION
PRESCRIPTIVIST	PROPRIETORALLY	QUANTITATIVELY
PRESENCE OF MIND	PROPRIOCEPTIVE	QUARTERMASTERS
PRESENTATIONAL	PROSENCEPHALON	QUEEN'S COUNSELS
PRESENT PERFECT	PROSPEROUSNESS	QUEEN'S EVIDENCE
PRESERVABILITY	PROSTHETICALLY	QUESTION MASTER
PRESIDENT-ELECT	PROSTHODONTICS	QUESTIONNAIRES
PRESS GALLERIES	PROSTHODONTIST	QUINQUEFOLIATE
PRESSURE COOKER	PROTECTIONISTS	QUINQUEPARTITE
PRESSURE GROUPS	PROTECTIVENESS	QUINQUEVALENCY
PRESSURE POINTS	PROTHONOTARIAL	QUINTESSENTIAL
PRESSURIZATION	PROTOZOOLOGIST	QUOTATION MARKS
PRESUMPTUOUSLY	PROTRACTEDNESS	
PRESUPPOSITION	PROTRUSIVENESS	R
PREVARICATIONS	PROVENTRICULAR	RADIOBIOLOGIST
PREVENTIVENESS	PROVENTRICULUS	RADIOCHEMISTRY
PRIMA BALLERINA	PROVIDENTIALLY	RADIO FREQUENCY
PRIMARY COLOURS	PROVINCIALISMS	RADIOSENSITIVE
PRIMARY SCHOOLS	PROVING GROUNDS	RADIOTELEGRAPH
PRIME MINISTERS	PSEUDOMORPHISM	RADIOTELEMETRY
PRINCE CHARMING	PSYCHOANALYSED	RADIOTELEPHONE
PRINCES CONSORT	PSYCHOANALYSIS	RADIOTELEPHONY
PRINCIPALITIES	PSYCHOANALYSTS	RADIO TELESCOPE
PRINCIPAL PARTS	PSYCHOANALYTIC	RADIOTHERAPIST
PRINTED CIRCUIT	PSYCHOANALYZER	RAILWAY STATION
PRISONERS OF WAR	PSYCHOCHEMICAL	RAMBUNCTIOUSLY
PRISON VISITORS	PSYCHODRAMATIC	RAMPAGEOUSNESS
PRIVATE MEMBERS	PSYCHODYNAMICS	RANUNCULACEOUS
PRIVATE SCHOOLS	PSYCHOLINGUIST	RAPPROCHEMENTS
PRIVATE SOLDIER	PSYCHOLOGISTIC	RASTAFARIANISM
PRO BONO PUBLICO	PSYCHONEUROSIS	RATEABLE VALUES
PROCRASTINATED	PSYCHONEUROTIC	RATE OF EXCHANGE
PROCRASTINATOR	PSYCHOPHYSICAL	REAFFIRMATIONS
PROCRYPTICALLY	PSYCHOSOMATICS	REAL-TIME SYSTEM
PRODIGIOUSNESS	PSYCHOSURGICAL	REARRANGEMENTS
PRODUCTION LINE	PSYCHOTECHNICS	REASONABLENESS
PRODUCTIVENESS	PTERIDOLOGICAL	REBELLIOUSNESS
PROFESSIONALLY	PUBLIC NUISANCE	RECAPITULATING
PROFESSORIALLY	PUBLIC-SPIRITED	RECAPITULATION
PROFESSORSHIPS	PUGILISTICALLY	RECAPITULATIVE
PROGESTATIONAL	PUGNACIOUSNESS	RECEPTION ROOMS
PROGNOSTICATED	PURCHASABILITY	RECKLINGHAUSEN
PROGNOSTICATOR	PURPLE PASSAGES	RECOMMENCEMENT
PROGRAMME MUSIC	PURPOSEFULNESS	RECOMMENDATION

RECOMMENDATORY
RECONCILIATION
RECONCILIATORY
RECONDITIONING
RECONNAISSANCE
RECONSTITUTING
RECONSTITUTION
RECONSTRUCTING
RECONSTRUCTION
RECONSTRUCTIVE
RECORD-BREAKING
RECOVERABILITY
RECREATION ROOM
RECRIMINATIONS
RECRUDESCENCES
RECTANGULARITY
RECTIFICATIONS
REDEVELOPMENTS
REDINTEGRATION
REDINTEGRATIVE
REDISTRIBUTING
REDISTRIBUTION
REFERENCE BOOKS
REFLECTIVENESS
REFRACTIVENESS
REFRACTOMETRIC
REFRACTORINESS
REFRANGIBILITY
REGARDLESSNESS
REGISTERED POST
REGISTER OFFICE
REGISTRATIONAL
REGISTRY OFFICE
REGRESSIVENESS
REGULARIZATION
REHABILITATING
REHABILITATION
REHABILITATIVE
REIGNS OF TERROR
REIMBURSEMENTS
REINCARNATIONS
REINFORCEMENTS
REINSTALLATION
REINSTATEMENTS
REINTRODUCTION
REJUVENESCENCE
RELATIVE CLAUSE
RELENTLESSNESS
RELINQUISHMENT
REMARKABLENESS
REMEMBRANCE DAY
REMONETIZATION
REMORSEFULNESS
REMUNERABILITY
REMUNERATIVELY
REORGANIZATION
REPETITIVENESS
REPLACEABILITY
REPORTED SPEECH

REPRESENTATION
REPRESENTATIVE
REPRESSIVENESS
REPRIMANDINGLY
REQUISITIONARY
REQUISITIONING
RESPECTABILITY
RESPECTFULNESS
RESPONSIBILITY
RESPONSIVENESS
RESTAURANT CARS
RESTRICTEDNESS
RESTRICTIONIST
RESURRECTIONAL
RETRACTABILITY
RETRIEVABILITY
RETROGRADATION
RETROGRADATORY
RETRO-OPERATIVE
RETROSPECTIVES
REVERBERATIONS
REVEREND MOTHER
REVISED VERSION
REVITALIZATION
REVIVIFICATION
REVOLUTIONIZED
REVOLUTIONIZER
RHEUMATIC FEVER
RHINENCEPHALIC
RHINENCEPHALON
RHIZOCEPHALOUS
RHYTHM AND BLUES
RICINOLEIC ACID
RIDICULOUSNESS
RIGHT TRIANGLES
RIO GRANDE DO SUL
ROADWORTHINESS
ROARING FORTIES
ROCKET-LAUNCHER
ROCKY MOUNTAINS
ROENTGENOPAQUE
ROLLER COASTERS
ROMAINE LETTUCE
ROMAN CATHOLICS
RORSCHACH TESTS
ROTTEN BOROUGHS
ROUGH-AND-TUMBLE
RUBBER DINGHIES
RUBBER-STAMPING
RUBBING ALCOHOL
RUDIMENTARILLY

S
SACRAMENTALISM
SACRAMENTALIST
SACRAMENTALITY
SACRAMENTARIAN
SACRILEGIOUSLY
SADOMASOCHISTS

SAFE-DEPOSIT BOX
SAFETY CURTAINS
SALAD DRESSINGS
SALUBRIOUSNESS
SANCTIFICATION
SANDWICH BOARDS
SANDWICH COURSE
SANGUINARINESS
SANITARY TOWELS
SANTIAGO DE CUBA
SAPONIFICATION
SATISFACTIONAL
SATISFACTORILY
SAVINGS ACCOUNT
SAWN-OFF SHOTGUN
SAXIFRAGACEOUS
SCANDALIZATION
SCANDALMONGERS
SCANDALOUSNESS
SCATTERBRAINED
SCHEMATIZATION
SCHISMATICALLY
SCHIZOMYCETOUS
SCHIZOPHRENICS
SCHIZOPHYCEOUS
SCHOOLCHILDREN
SCHOOLMISTRESS
SCHOOLTEACHERS
SCIENCE FICTION
SCIENTIFICALLY
SCINTILLOMETER
SCOTCH WHISKIES
SCREEN PRINTING
SCRUBBING BRUSH
SCRUPULOUSNESS
SCRUTINIZINGLY
SCURRILOUSNESS
SEARCH WARRANTS
SEASONABLENESS
SECOND-GUESSING
SECOND THOUGHTS
SECULARIZATION
SEGREGATIONIST
SELF-ABNEGATION
SELF-ABSORPTION
SELF-ANALYTICAL
SELF-CONFIDENCE
SELF-CONTROLLED
SELF-DESTRUCTED
SELF-DISCIPLINE
SELF-EFFACEMENT
SELF-EMPLOYMENT
SELF-GOVERNMENT
SELF-IMPORTANCE
SELF-INDUCTANCE
SELF-INDULGENCE
SELF-INFLICTION
SELF-INTERESTED
SELF-JUSTIFYING

SELF-POSSESSION	SILICIFICATION	SPERMATOPHYTIC
SELF-PROTECTION	SILVER JUBILEES	SPERMATORRHOEA
SELF-RESPECTFUL	SILVER WEDDINGS	SPERMIOGENESIS
SELF-RESPECTING	SILVICULTURIST	SPERMIOGENETIC
SELF-SUFFICIENT	SIMAROUBACEOUS	SPHEROIDICALLY
SELF-SUPPORTING	SIMPLE FRACTURE	SPHYGMOGRAPHIC
SEMAPHORICALLY	SIMPLE INTEREST	SPINNING WHEELS
SEMASIOLOGICAL	SIMPLE MACHINES	SPINTHARISCOPE
SEMICENTENNIAL	SIMPLIFICATION	SPIRITLESSNESS
SEMICONDUCTION	SIMPLIFICATIVE	SPIRITUALISTIC
SEMICONDUCTORS	SIMPLISTICALLY	SPIROCHAETOSIS
SEMIELLIPTICAL	SIMULTANEOUSLY	SPIRONOLACTONE
SEMIPARASITISM	SINGLE-BREASTED	SPITTING IMAGES
SENIOR CITIZENS	SINGLE-MINDEDLY	SPLINTER GROUPS
SENSATIONALISM	SINKIANG-UIGHUR	SPONGIOBLASTIC
SENSATIONALIST	SINKING FEELING	SPORADICALNESS
SENTIMENTALISM	SIPHONOPHOROUS	SPRECHSTIMMUNG
SENTIMENTALIST	SITTING TARGETS	SPRING CHICKENS
SENTIMENTALITY	SIXTEENTH NOTES	SPRING-CLEANING
SENTIMENTALIZE	SKIRTING BOARDS	SQUADRON LEADER
SEPARATIVENESS	SLANDEROUSNESS	SQUARE BRACKETS
SEPTUAGENARIAN	SLATTERNLINESS	STAFF SERGEANTS
SEQUESTRATIONS	SLAUGHTERHOUSE	STAGE DIRECTION
SERGEANT-AT-ARMS	SLIPSHODDINESS	STAMPING GROUND
SERGEANT MAJORS	SLOTTED SPATULA	STANDARD-BEARER
SERIALIZATIONS	SLUGGARDLINESS	STANDING ORDERS
SERIOCOMICALLY	SLUMBEROUSNESS	STANDOFF HALVES
SERJEANT-AT-ARMS	SMALL INTESTINE	STAPHYLOCOCCAL
SERVICEABILITY	SOCIAL CLIMBERS	STAPHYLOCOCCUS
SERVICE CHARGES	SOCIAL SCIENCES	STAPHYLOPLASTY
SERVICE STATION	SOCIAL SECURITY	STARTING BLOCKS
SERVOMECHANISM	SOCIAL SERVICES	STARTING PRICES
SESQUIPEDALIAN	SOCIOLOGICALLY	STATE'S EVIDENCE
SEWING MACHINES	SOCIOPOLITICAL	STATIONARINESS
SHAGGY-DOG STORY	SODIUM CHLORIDE	STATIONMASTERS
SHAMEFACEDNESS	SOLDERING IRONS	STATUESQUENESS
SHEET LIGHTNING	SOLICITOUSNESS	STEAMROLLERING
SHEPHERD'S-PURSE	SOLIDIFICATION	STEAMTIGHTNESS
SHERARDIZATION	SOMNAMBULATION	STEERING WHEELS
SHETLAND PONIES	SOMNAMBULISTIC	STEPPING-STONES
SHIHCHIACHUANG	SOPHISTICATION	STERCORICOLOUS
SHILLY-SHALLIED	SOUL-DESTROYING	STERCULIACEOUS
SHILLYSHALLIER	SOUNDING BOARDS	STEREOMETRICAL
SHIP'S CHANDLERS	SOUTHEASTWARDS	STEREOSPECIFIC
SHOCK ABSORBERS	SOUTHERN LIGHTS	STERTOROUSNESS
SHOCK TREATMENT	SOUTH-SOUTHEAST	STICKING POINTS
SHOOTING STICKS	SOUTH-SOUTHWEST	STIGMATIZATION
SHOP ASSISTANTS	SOUTHWESTWARDS	STINGING NETTLE
SHOPPING CENTRE	SPATIOTEMPORAL	STOCHASTICALLY
SHORT-CIRCUITED	SPECIALIZATION	STOCKBROKERAGE
SHORTSIGHTEDLY	SPECIAL LICENCE	STOCK EXCHANGES
SHOTGUN WEDDING	SPECIAL SCHOOLS	STOCKING-FILLER
SHOULDER BLADES	SPECIFICATIONS	STOICHIOMETRIC
SHOULDER STRAPS	SPECTROGRAPHIC	STORE DETECTIVE
SIDEWALK ARTIST	SPECTROSCOPIST	STRAIGHT FIGHTS
SIGMOIDOSCOPIC	SPEECHLESSNESS	STRAIGHTJACKET
SIGNATURE TUNES	SPERMATOGONIAL	STRATICULATION
SIGNIFICATIONS	SPERMATOGONIUM	STRATIFICATION
SILENT PARTNERS	SPERMATOPHORAL	STRAWBERRY MARK

STREET-CREDIBLE
STREPTOTHRICIN
STRETCHABILITY
STRETCHER PARTY
STRIDULOUSNESS
STRIKEBREAKERS
STRIKEBREAKING
STRONG LANGUAGE
STRONG-MINDEDLY
STUDENTS' UNIONS
STULTIFICATION
STUMBLING BLOCK
STUPENDOUSNESS
SUBALTERNATION
SUBCONSCIOUSLY
SUBCONTINENTAL
SUBCONTRACTING
SUBCONTRACTORS
SUBCUTANEOUSLY
SUBINFEUDATION
SUBINFEUDATORY
SUBJECTABILITY
SUBJECTIVISTIC
SUBJECT-RAISING
SUBLIEUTENANCY
SUBLIEUTENANTS
SUBMACHINE GUNS
SUBMERSIBILITY
SUBMICROSCOPIC
SUBMISSIVENESS
SUBSIDIARINESS
SUBSTANTIALISM
SUBSTANTIALIST
SUBSTANTIALITY
SUBSTANTIATING
SUBSTANTIATION
SUBSTANTIATIVE
SUBTERRESTRIAL
SUBVERSIVENESS
SUCCESSFULNESS
SUCCESSIVENESS
SUGGESTIBILITY
SUGGESTIVENESS
SULPHANILAMIDE
SULPHATHIAZOLE
SULPHISOXAZOLE
SULPHONMETHANE
SULPHURIZATION
SULPHUROUSNESS
SUPERABUNDANCE
SUPERANNUATION
SUPERCILIOUSLY
SUPERCONDUCTOR
SUPERELEVATION
SUPERFICIALITY
SUPERINCUMBENT
SUPERINDUCTION
SUPERINTENDENT
SUPERINTENDING

SUPERNATURALLY
SUPERNORMALITY
SUPERPHOSPHATE
SUPERSATURATED
SUPERSCRIPTION
SUPERSONICALLY
SUPERSTRUCTURE
SUPPLY TEACHERS
SUPPORTABILITY
SUPPORTING PART
SUPRAMOLECULAR
SUPRASEGMENTAL
SUREFOOTEDNESS
SURGICAL SPIRIT
SURPASSINGNESS
SURPRISINGNESS
SUSCEPTIBILITY
SUSPENDIBILITY
SUSPENSIVENESS
SUSPICIOUSNESS
SWIMMING TRUNKS
SYMBIONTICALLY
SYMBOLICALNESS
SYMMETRIZATION
SYMPATHIZINGLY
SYMPTOMATOLOGY
SYNCHRONICALLY
SYNCRETIZATION
SYNERGETICALLY
SYNONYMOUSNESS
SYNTHESIZATION
SYNTHETIZATION
SYPHILITICALLY
SYSTEMATICALLY
SYSTEMS ANALYST

T
TACHISTOSCOPIC
TAUTOLOGICALLY
TECHNICALITIES
TELANGIECTASIS
TELANGIECTATIC
TELAUTOGRAPHIC
TELEGRAPH POLES
TELEMETRICALLY
TELEOLOGICALLY
TELEPATHICALLY
TELEPHONE BOXES
TELESCOPICALLY
TELETYPESETTER
TERCENTENARIES
TERGIVERSATION
TERGIVERSATORY
TERMINOLOGICAL
TERRACED HOUSES
TERRITORIALISM
TERRITORIALIST
TERRITORIALITY
TERRITORIALIZE

TERROR-STRICKEN
TEST-TUBE BABIES
TETRAETHYL LEAD
THAUMATROPICAL
THEOCENTRICITY
THEOCRATICALLY
THEOLOGIZATION
THEOSOPHICALLY
THERIANTHROPIC
THERMAESTHESIA
THERMOCHEMICAL
THERMODYNAMICS
THERMOELECTRIC
THERMOELECTRON
THERMOJUNCTION
THERMOMAGNETIC
THERMOPLASTICS
THIOCYANIC ACID
THOUGHTFULNESS
THREE-DAY EVENTS
THREE-HALFPENCE
THREE-LINE WHIPS
THREE-POINT TURN
THRIFTLESSNESS
THROMBOPLASTIC
THROMBOPLASTIN
THYMELAEACEOUS
THYROTOXICOSIS
TIERRA DEL FUEGO
TIME IMMEMORIAL
TIME SIGNATURES
TITTLE-TATTLING
TOILET TRAINING
TO-ING AND FRO-ING
TONGUE TWISTERS
TORTOISESHELLS
TRACTION ENGINE
TRADE UNIONISTS
TRADING ESTATES
TRADITIONALISM
TRADITIONALIST
TRADUCIANISTIC
TRAFFIC CIRCLES
TRAFFIC ISLANDS
TRAFFIC WARDENS
TRAGICOMICALLY
TRAITOROUSNESS
TRANQUILLIZERS
TRANQUILLIZING
TRANSCAUCASIAN
TRANSCENDENTAL
TRANSCENDENTLY
TRANSCENDINGLY
TRANSCRIPTIONS
TRANSFERENTIAL
TRANSFORMATION
TRANSFORMATIVE
TRANSGRESSIBLE
TRANSGRESSIONS

TRANSISTORIZED	UNACCOUNTED-FOR	UNQUESTIONABLY
TRANSITIONALLY	UNAPPRECIATIVE	UNRECOGNIZABLE
TRANSITIVENESS	UNAPPROACHABLE	UNRESERVEDNESS
TRANSITORINESS	UNAPPROPRIATED	UNRESTRAINEDLY
TRANS-JORDANIAN	UNAVOIDABILITY	UNSATISFACTORY
TRANSLITERATED	UNBEARABLENESS	UNSCRUPULOUSLY
TRANSLITERATOR	UNBECOMINGNESS	UNTHANKFULNESS
TRANSMIGRATION	UNCOMPROMISING	UNTHINKABILITY
TRANSMIGRATIVE	UNCONSCIONABLE	UNTOUCHABILITY
TRANSMIGRATORY	UNCONSCIONABLY	UPSIDE-DOWNNESS
TRANSMISSIVITY	UNCONTAMINATED	UPSTANDINGNESS
TRANSMOGRIFIED	UNCONTROLLABLE	UPWARDLY-MOBILE
TRANSMUTATIONS	UNCONVENTIONAL	UST-KAMENOGORSK
TRANSPARENCIES	UNCONVINCINGLY	UTILITARIANISM
TRANSPLANTABLE	UNCORROBORATED	
TRANSPORTATION	UNDERACHIEVERS	**V**
TRANSPORT CAFES	UNDERACHIEVING	VACUUM CLEANERS
TRANSPOSITIONS	UNDERCARRIAGES	VALERIANACEOUS
TRANSVALUATION	UNDERESTIMATED	VALETUDINARIAN
TRANSVERSENESS	UNDERESTIMATES	VALUE JUDGMENTS
TRAUMATIZATION	UNDERGRADUATES	VASOINHIBITORY
TRAVEL AGENCIES	UNDERMENTIONED	VAULTING HORSES
TRAVELSICKNESS	UNDERNOURISHED	VEGETABLE KNIFE
TREASURE TROVES	UNDERSECRETARY	VEGETATIVENESS
TREMENDOUSNESS	UNDERSTANDABLE	VENDING MACHINE
TRICHINIZATION	UNDERSTANDABLY	VENETIAN BLINDS
TRICHOMONIASIS	UNDERSTANDINGS	VENTRILOQUISTS
TRICHOTOMOUSLY	UNDERSTATEMENT	VENTURE CAPITAL
TRICK OR TREATED	UNDERVALUATION	VERISIMILITUDE
TRIDIMENSIONAL	UNDESIRABILITY	VERTICILLASTER
TRINITROCRESOL	UNECONOMICALLY	VERTICILLATION
TRINITROPHENOL	UNENTHUSIASTIC	VESPERTILIONID
TRISOCTAHEDRAL	UNEVENTFULNESS	VESTED INTEREST
TRISOCTAHEDRON	UNEXPECTEDNESS	VEXED QUESTIONS
TRISTAN DA CUNHA	UNFAITHFULNESS	VICE-CHANCELLOR
TRIVIALIZATION	UNFLAPPABILITY	VICE-PRESIDENCY
TROUBLESHOOTER	UNFRIENDLINESS	VICIOUS CIRCLES
TROUSER PRESSES	UNFRUITFULNESS	VICTORIOUSNESS
TUMULTUOUSNESS	UNGRATEFULNESS	VILLAINOUSNESS
TUNBRIDGE WELLS	UNHANDSOMENESS	VINDICTIVENESS
TURBOGENERATOR	UNHOLY ALLIANCE	VISHAKHAPATNAM
TURF ACCOUNTANT	UNICELLULARITY	VITRIFIABILITY
TURKISH DELIGHT	UNIDENTIFIABLE	VITRIOLIZATION
TURNING CIRCLES	UNIDIRECTIONAL	VITUPERATIVELY
TWO-DIMENSIONAL	UNIFORMITARIAN	VIVISECTIONIST
TYRANNICALNESS	UNINCORPORATED	VOCIFEROUSNESS
	UNINTELLIGENCE	VOLATILIZATION
U	UNINTELLIGIBLE	VOLCANOLOGICAL
UBIQUITOUSNESS	UNIPERSONALITY	VOLUMETRICALLY
ULTIMOGENITURE	UNIVERSALISTIC	VOLUMINOUSNESS
ULTRAMODERNISM	UNIVERSAL JOINT	VOLUPTUOUSNESS
ULTRAMODERNIST	UNKNOWABLENESS	VOROSHILOVGRAD
ULTRAMONTANISM	UNMENTIONABLES	VOTES OF CENSURE
ULTRAMONTANIST	UNPLEASANTNESS	VULGAR FRACTION
ULTRASONICALLY	UNPRACTICALITY	VULGARIZATIONS
ULTRASTRUCTURE	UNPREMEDITATED	VULVOVAGINITIS
UMBILICAL CORDS	UNPREPAREDNESS	
UNACCOMMODATED	UNPROFESSIONAL	**W**
UNACCOMPLISHED	UNQUESTIONABLE	WARRANTABILITY

WARRANT OFFICER
WASHING MACHINE
WATERCOLOURIST
WATERING PLACES
WATERPROOFNESS
WATER-REPELLENT
WATER-RESISTANT
WATER SOFTENERS
WATERTIGHTNESS
WEAK-MINDEDNESS
WEATHERABILITY
WEATHERPROOFED
WEATHER STATION
WEIGHTLESSNESS
WELL-ACCUSTOMED
WELL-ACQUAINTED
WELL-DOCUMENTED
WESTERNIZATION

WHEELER-DEALERS
WHEELER-DEALING
WHIMSICALITIES
WHIPPERSNAPPER
WHITE BLOOD CELL
WHITE ELEPHANTS
WHOLE-HEARTEDLY
WHORTLEBERRIES
WILDCAT STRIKES
WILD-GOOSE CHASE
WIND INSTRUMENT
WINDOW DRESSING
WINDOW-SHOPPERS
WINDOW-SHOPPING
WIND-POLLINATED
WING COMMANDERS
WOMEN'S MOVEMENT
WORCESTER SAUCE

WORD PROCESSING
WORD PROCESSORS
WORKING PARTIES
WORLD-WEARINESS
WORSHIPFULNESS
WORTHWHILENESS

X
XANTHOPHYLLOUS
XEROPHYTICALLY

Y
YOUTH HOSTELLER

Z
ZEBRA CROSSINGS
ZINGIBERACEOUS

A
ACANTHOCEPHALAN
ACCLIMATIZATION
ACCOMMODATINGLY
ACCOMPLISHMENTS
ACHONDROPLASTIC
ACHROMATIZATION
ACIDIMETRICALLY
ACKNOWLEDGEABLE
ACKNOWLEDGMENTS
ACOUSTIC COUPLER
ACQUISITIVENESS
ADMINISTRATIONS
AERODYNAMICALLY
AFFRANCHISEMENT
AGGLUTINABILITY
AGRANULOCYTOSIS
AIR CHIEF MARSHAL
AIR-CONDITIONING
AIRCRAFT CARRIER
AIR VICE-MARSHALS
ALGORITHMICALLY
ALIMENTARY CANAL
ALPHABETIZATION
AMARYLLIDACEOUS
AMBASSADORSHIPS
AMERICAN INDIANS
AMERICANIZATION
AMUSEMENT ARCADE
ANABOLIC STEROID
ANARCHISTICALLY
ANCYLOSTOMIASIS
ANIMAL HUSBANDRY
ANIMATED CARTOON
ANOMALISTICALLY
ANTARCTIC CIRCLE
ANTEPENULTIMATE
ANTHROPOCENTRIC
ANTHROPOGENESIS
ANTHROPOGENETIC
ANTHROPOLOGICAL
ANTHROPOLOGISTS
ANTHROPOMETRIST
ANTHROPOMORPHIC
ANTICHOLINERGIC
ANTICLERICALISM
ANTI-IMPERIALISM
ANTI-IMPERIALIST
ANTILOGARITHMIC
ANTINATIONALIST
ANTIPERISTALSIS
ANTIPERSPIRANTS
APARTMENT HOUSES
APOCALYPTICALLY
APPRENTICESHIPS
APPROACHABILITY
APPROPRIATENESS
APPROVED SCHOOLS
ARCHIEPISCOPATE

ARCHITECTURALLY
ARGUMENTATIVELY
ARTERIALIZATION
ASCLEPIADACEOUS
ASSOCIATE DEGREE
ASTRONAUTICALLY
ASTRONAVIGATION
ASTROPHYSICISTS
ATHEROSCLEROSIS
ATHEROSCLEROTIC
ATMOSPHERICALLY
ATTORNEY GENERAL
AUDIOMETRICALLY
AUTHORITATIVELY
AUTOBIOGRAPHIES
AUTOCORRELATION
AUTOGRAPHICALLY
AUTOMATIC PILOTS
AUTORADIOGRAPHY
AUTOTRANSFORMER
AVERSION THERAPY

B
BACHELOR'S
   DEGREE
BACK-SEAT DRIVERS
BACTERIOLOGICAL
BACTERIOLOGISTS
BACTERIOPHAGOUS
BALLROOM DANCING
BANANA REPUBLICS
BANNER HEADLINES
BASIDIOMYCETOUS
BATCH PROCESSING
BATHING MACHINES
BATHOMETRICALLY
BATHYMETRICALLY
BED AND BREAKFAST
BENEFIT OF
   CLERGY
BIBLIOGRAPHICAL
BIBLIOPHILISTIC
BINOCULAR VISION
BIOASTRONAUTICS
BIOGEOGRAPHICAL
BIOLUMINESCENCE
BIOTECHNOLOGIST
BIRDS OF PARADISE
BISYMMETRICALLY
BLACK MARKETEERS
BLACKWATER FEVER
BLAMEWORTHINESS
BLANK CARTRIDGES
BLOCK AND TACKLES
BLOOD-AND-THUNDER
BOARDING SCHOOLS
BONDED WAREHOUSE
BROADMINDEDNESS
BROKEN-HEARTEDLY

BRUSSELS SPROUTS
BUBBLE AND
   SQUEAK
BUILDING SOCIETY
BUREAU DE
   CHANGES
BUSMAN'S
   HOLIDAYS

C
CABLE TELEVISION
CANNIBALIZATION
CAPRIFOLIACEOUS
CARPOMETACARPUS
CARRYING CHARGES
CASEMENT WINDOWS
CATEGORIZATIONS
CATHERINE WHEELS
CATHETERIZATION
CATHODE RAY
   TUBES
CATHOLICIZATION
CENTRE OF
   GRAVITY
CEPHALOCHORDATE
CEPHALOTHORACIC
CEREBROVASCULAR
CEREMONIOUSNESS
CHAPTER AND
   VERSE
CHARACTERISTICS
CHARENT-MARITIME
CHARGE D'AFFAIRES
CHECKING ACCOUNT
CHEMICAL WARFARE
CHEMOTACTICALLY
CHEMOTROPICALLY
CHENOPODIACEOUS
CHESTS OF DRAWERS
CHIEF CONSTABLES
CHIEF INSPECTORS
CHINESE CHEQUERS
CHINESE LANTERNS
CHINLESS WONDERS
CHLORAMPHENICOL
CHOLECALCIFEROL
CHOLECYSTECTOMY
CHONDRIFICATION
CHROMATOGRAPHER
CHROMATOGRAPHIC
CHROMATOPHOROUS
CHRONOGRAMMATIC
CHRONOLOGICALLY
CHUCK-WILL'S-WIDOW
CHURCH OF ENGLAND
CIGARETTE HOLDER
CIGARETTE PAPERS
CINEMATOGRAPHER
CINEMATOGRAPHIC

CIRCUIT BREAKERS
CIRCULARIZATION
CIRCUMAMBULATOR
CIRCUMFERENTIAL
CIRCUMLOCUTIONS
CIRCUMNAVIGABLE
CIRCUMNAVIGATED
CIRCUMNAVIGATOR
CIRCUMSCRIPTION
CIRCUMSTANTIATE
CIRCUMVALLATION
CLANDESTINENESS
CLASSIFICATIONS
CLAUSTROPHOBICS
CLEAR-HEADEDNESS
CLERMONT-FERRAND
CLOUD-CUCKOO-LAND
COCK-A-DOODLE-
  DOOS
COCKNEYFICATION
COCKTAIL LOUNGES
COFFEE-TABLE
  BOOK
COLD-BLOODEDNESS
COLD-HEARTEDNESS
COLD-SHOULDERING
COLLECTIVE FARMS
COLLECTIVE NOUNS
COLLECTOR'S
  ITEMS
COLLISION COURSE
COLORADO BEETLES
COLOUR BLINDNESS
COMBINATION LOCK
COMEDY OF
  MANNERS
COMFORT STATIONS
COMITY OF NATIONS
COMMERCIALISTIC
COMMERCIALIZING
COMMISSIONAIRES
COMMITTEE STAGES
COMMON FRACTIONS
COMMUNALIZATION
COMMUNICABILITY
COMMUNITY CENTRE
COMMUNITY CHESTS
COMPASSIONATELY
COMPETITIVENESS
COMPLICATEDNESS
COMPREHENSIVELY
COMPRESSIBILITY
COMPUTERIZATION
CONCEPTUALISTIC
CONCEPTUALIZING
CONCESSIONAIRES
CONCRETE JUNGLES
CONFECTIONERIES
CONFIDENCE TRICK

CONFIDENTIALITY
CONFIGURATIONAL
CONFRATERNITIES
CONGLOMERATIONS
CONGRATULATIONS
CONSCIENCE MONEY
CONSCIENTIOUSLY
CONSCRIPTIONIST
CONSENTING ADULT
CONSERVATIONISM
CONSERVATIONIST
CONSIDERATENESS
CONSPICUOUSNESS
CONSTITUTIONALS
CONSUMER DURABLE
CONTEMPORANEITY
CONTEMPORANEOUS
CONTEMPTIBILITY
CONTENTIOUSNESS
CONTORTIONISTIC
CONTRACTIBILITY
CONTRAINDICATED
CONTROVERSIALLY
CONVENIENCE FOOD
CONVENTIONALISM
CONVENTIONALIST
CONVENTIONALITY
CONVENTIONALIZE
CONVOLVULACEOUS
CORRELATIVENESS
CORRESPONDINGLY
COSMOPOLITANISM
COST-EFFECTIVELY
COTTAGE HOSPITAL
COTTAGE INDUSTRY
COUNTERATTACKED
COUNTERATTACKER
COUNTERBALANCED
COUNTERBALANCES
COUNTERCLAIMANT
COUNTERIRRITANT
COUNTERMEASURES
COUNTERPROPOSAL
COURT-MARTIALING
COURT-MARTIALLED
COURTS OF INQUIRY
COVERING LETTERS
CREDIBILITY GAPS
CROSS-FERTILIZED
CROSSOPTERYGION
CROSS-QUESTIONED
CROSS-QUESTIONER
CROSS-REFERENCES
CROWN PRINCESSES
CRYSTALLIZATION
CRYSTALLOGRAPHY
CURRENT ACCOUNTS
CURRICULUM VITAE

D
DAYLIGHT ROBBERY
DAYS OF RECKONING
DECALCIFICATION
DECARBONIZATION
DECARBOXYLATION
DECIPHERABILITY
DECOMPOSABILITY
DECONTAMINATING
DECONTAMINATION
DECONTAMINATIVE
DEFINITE ARTICLE
DEHYDROGENATION
DELIRIUM TREMENS
DEMAGNETIZATION
DEMOCRATIZATION
DEMONSTRABILITY
DEMONSTRATIONAL
DEMONSTRATIVELY
DEMULSIFICATION
DEMYSTIFICATION
DENATIONALIZING
DENITRIFICATION
DEPARTMENTALISM
DEPARTMENTALIZE
DEPARTMENT STORE
DEPENDENT CLAUSE
DEPOSIT ACCOUNTS
DERMATOGLYPHICS
DERMATOPHYTOSIS
DESCRIPTIVENESS
DESENSITIZATION
DESEXUALIZATION
DESTABILIZATION
DESTRUCTIBILITY
DESTRUCTIVENESS
DETRIBALIZATION
DEVELOPMENT AREA
DEVIL'S ADVOCATES
DEVITRIFICATION
DIALECTOLOGICAL
DIAMAGNETICALLY
DIAMOND JUBILEES
DIAMOND WEDDINGS
DIAPHOTOTROPISM
DICHOTOMIZATION
DIESEL-HYDRAULIC
DIFFERENTIATING
DIFFERENTIATION
DIGITAL COMPUTER
DIRECTION FINDER
DISADVANTAGEOUS
DISAPPOINTINGLY
DISAPPOINTMENTS
DISARTICULATION
DISCIPLINARIANS
DISCONCERTINGLY
DISCONTINUATION
DISCONTINUITIES

DISCONTINUOUSLY
DISCOUNTENANCED
DISCOURAGEMENTS
DISCRETIONARILY
DISENCUMBERMENT
DISENTANGLEMENT
DISESTABLISHING
DISHEARTENINGLY
DISHEARTENMENTS
DISILLUSIONMENT
DISINCLINATIONS
DISINFLATIONARY
DISINTERESTEDLY
DISORDERLY HOUSE
DISORGANIZATION
DISPASSIONATELY
DISREPUTABILITY
DISRESPECTFULLY
DISSATISFACTION
DISSATISFACTORY
DISSERTATIONIST
DISSIMILARITIES
DISTASTEFULNESS
DISTINCTIVENESS
DISTINGUISHABLE
DISTRACTIBILITY
DISTRUSTFULNESS
DITHYRAMBICALLY
DIVERSIFICATION
DIVISION LOBBIES
DO-IT-YOURSELFERS
DOLICHOCEPHALIC
DOMESTIC ANIMALS
DOMESTIC SCIENCE
DOMESTIC SERVICE
DORSIVENTRALITY
DOUBLE-BARRELLED
DOUBLE ENTENDRES
DRAUGHTSMANSHIP
DRESS REHEARSALS
DRIVING LICENCES
DUAL CARRIAGEWAY
DUAL CITIZENSHIP
DUTCH ELM DISEASE

E
EARTHSHATTERING
ECCLESIASTICISM
ECCLESIOLOGICAL
EDUCATED GUESSES
EDUCATIONALISTS
ELECTRIC BLANKET
ELECTRIFICATION
ELECTROACOUSTIC
ELECTROANALYSIS
ELECTROANALYTIC
ELECTROCHEMICAL
ELECTRODIALYSIS
ELECTRODYNAMICS

ELECTROKINETICS
ELECTROLYSATION
ELECTROMAGNETIC
ELECTRONEGATIVE
ELECTROPHORESIS
ELECTROPHORETIC
ELECTROPOSITIVE
ELECTROSURGICAL
ELEVATED RAILWAY
EMANCIPATIONIST
EMINENCES GRISES
ENANTIOMORPHISM
ENCEPHALOGRAPHY
ENCHONDROMATOUS
ENCOMIASTICALLY
ENDOCRINE GLANDS
ENDOCRINOLOGIST
ENDOTHERMICALLY
ENDOWMENT POLICY
ENFRANCHISEMENT
ENGAGEMENT RINGS
ENTENTE CORDIALE
ENTREPRENEURIAL
ENVIRONMENTALLY
EPIDEMIOLOGICAL
EPISCOPALIANISM
EPISTEMOLOGICAL
EPITHELIOMATOUS
EQUALITARIANISM
ETERNAL TRIANGLE
ETHEREALIZATION
ETHNOCENTRICITY
EUCHARISTICALLY
EUDIOMETRICALLY
EUPHEMISTICALLY
EUROPEANIZATION
EUSTACHIAN TUBES
EVERLASTINGNESS
EXCEPTIONALNESS
EXCHANGEABILITY
EXCLAMATION MARK
EXCOMMUNICATING
EXCOMMUNICATION
EXCOMMUNICATIVE
EXEMPLIFICATION
EXEMPLIFICATIVE
EXHIBITIONISTIC
EXPEDITIOUSNESS
EXPENSE ACCOUNTS
EXPERIMENTALISM
EXPERIMENTALIST
EXPERIMENTATION
EXPOSTULATINGLY
EXPRESSIONISTIC
EXTEMPORARINESS
EXTEMPORIZATION
EXTERIORIZATION
EXTERNALIZATION
EXTRACURRICULAR

EXTRAORDINARILY

F
FAIRY GODMOTHERS
FAMILIARIZATION
FAMILY ALLOWANCE
FASHIONABLENESS
FATHER CHRISTMAS
FEATURELESSNESS
FELLOW TRAVELLER
FEUILLETONISTIC
FIDEICOMMISSARY
FIFTH COLUMNISTS
FIGURES OF SPEECH
FILLING STATIONS
FINISHING SCHOOL
FIRST LIEUTENANT
FLIBBERTIGIBBET
FLIGHT SERGEANTS
FLIRTATIOUSNESS
FOOT-POUND-SECOND
FOREIGN EXCHANGE
FORESIGHTEDNESS
FORKED LIGHTNING
FORMULARIZATION
FOUNDATION STONE
FOUNDING FATHERS
FOUR-DIMENSIONAL
FOUR-LETTER WORDS
FOURTH DIMENSION
FRACTIONIZATION
FRAGMENTARINESS
FRANKFURT AM
  MAIN
FREE ASSOCIATION
FRENCH POLISHING
FRIENDLY SOCIETY
FULL-BLOODEDNESS
FUNDAMENTALISTS
FUNERAL DIRECTOR
FUNERAL PARLOURS
FUTILITARIANISM

G
GASTROENTERITIC
GASTROENTERITIS
GASTRONOMICALLY
GENERAL DELIVERY
GENERAL ELECTION
GENERALIZATIONS
GENTLEMAN-AT-
  ARMS
GENTLEMAN FARMER
GENTLEMANLINESS
GENTLEMEN-AT-
  ARMS
GERMAN SHEPHERDS
GLOBE ARTICHOKES
GLOSSY MAGAZINES

GLOUCESTERSHIRE
GLUCONEOGENESIS
GNOTOBIOTICALLY
GOLDEN HANDSHAKE
GOOD-FOR-NOTHINGS
GOOD-NATUREDNESS
GORNO-BADAKHSHAN
GOVERNOR-GENERAL
GRAPHIC DESIGNER
GREGORIAN CHANTS
GUTTURALIZATION
GYNANDROMORPHIC

H
HACKNEY CARRIAGE
HAEMAGGLUTINATE
HAEMOFLAGELLATE
HAEMOGLOBINURIA
HALF-HEARTEDNESS
HALL OF RESIDENCE
HALLUCINATIONAL
HAMAMELIDACEOUS
HAMMER AND
  SICKLE
HARD-HEARTEDNESS
HARD LUCK STORIES
HARMONISTICALLY
HARVEST FESTIVAL
HEARTBREAKINGLY
HEARTBROKENNESS
HEAVY-HANDEDNESS
HEIR PRESUMPTIVE
HELIOCENTRICITY
HELIOMETRICALLY
HELIOTROPICALLY
HELLENISTICALLY
HELMINTHOLOGIST
HENDECASYLLABIC
HENDECASYLLABLE
HERBIVOROUSNESS
HEREDITARIANISM
HERMAPHRODITISM
HERMENEUTICALLY
HERO-WORSHIPPING
HETEROCHROMATIC
HETEROCHROMATIN
HETEROGENEOUSLY
HETEROSEXUALITY
HEXACHLOROPHENE
HEXYLRESORCINOL
HIGH COMMISSIONS
HIGHER EDUCATION
HIMACHAL PRADESH
HIPPOCRATIC OATH
HISPANICIZATION
HISTORIC PRESENT
HISTORIOGRAPHER
HISTORIOGRAPHIC
HOLOBLASTICALLY

HOLOGRAPHICALLY
HOLY ROMAN EMPIRE
HOMEOPATHICALLY
HOMOCENTRICALLY
HOMOGENEOUSNESS
HOMOPLASTICALLY
HORTICULTURALLY
HOSPITALIZATION
HOT-WATER BOTTLES
HOUSEHOLDERSHIP
HOUSEWIFELINESS
HOUSING PROJECTS
HUMANITARIANISM
HUMANITARIANIST
HUNTINGDONSHIRE
HYDROBROMIC ACID
HYDROGENIZATION
HYDROMECHANICAL
HYDROMETALLURGY
HYPERCRITICALLY

I
ICEBERG LETTUCES
IDIOMORPHICALLY
IMMEASURABILITY
IMMERSION HEATER
IMMORTALIZATION
IMMUNOCHEMISTRY
IMMUNOGENICALLY
IMMUNOLOGICALLY
IMPECUNIOUSNESS
IMPENETRABILITY
IMPERISHABILITY
IMPONDERABILITY
IMPRESCRIPTIBLE
IMPRESSIONISTIC
IMPROBABILITIES
IMPROVISATIONAL
INACCESSIBILITY
INADMISSIBILITY
INAPPLICABILITY
INAPPROPRIATELY
INATTENTIVENESS
INCALCULABILITY
INCIDENTAL MUSIC
INCOMMENSURABLE
INCOMMUNICATIVE
INCOMMUTABILITY
INCOMPARABILITY
INCOMPATIBILITY
INCOMPREHENSION
INCOMPREHENSIVE
INCOMPUTABILITY
INCONGRUOUSNESS
INCONSEQUENTIAL
INCONSIDERATELY
INCONSIDERATION
INCONSISTENCIES
INCONSOLABILITY

INCONSPICUOUSLY
INCONVENIENCING
INCORRIGIBILITY
INCREDULOUSNESS
INDECENT ASSAULT
INDEFEASIBILITY
INDEFENSIBILITY
INDEMNIFICATION
INDETERMINISTIC
INDIGESTIBILITY
INDIRECT OBJECTS
INDISCRETIONARY
INDISPUTABILITY
INDISSOLUBILITY
INDIVIDUALISTIC
INDIVIDUALIZING
INDUSTRIALIZING
INDUSTRIOUSNESS
INEFFACEABILITY
INEFFECTIVENESS
INEXPENSIVENESS
INEXPLICABILITY
INEXTENSIBILITY
INEXTRICABILITY
INFANT PRODIGIES
INFINITESIMALLY
INFRASTRUCTURES
INFUNDIBULIFORM
INJUDICIOUSNESS
INOFFENSIVENESS
INOPPORTUNENESS
INQUISITIVENESS
INQUISITORIALLY
INSENSIBILITIES
INSIGNIFICANTLY
INSTALLMENT PLAN
INSTANTANEOUSLY
INSTRUMENTALISM
INSTRUMENTALIST
INSTRUMENTALITY
INSTRUMENTATION
INSUBORDINATELY
INSUBORDINATION
INSURANCE POLICY
INSURRECTIONARY
INSURRECTIONISM
INSURRECTIONIST
INTELLECTUALISE
INTELLECTUALISM
INTELLECTUALIST
INTELLECTUALITY
INTELLECTUALIZE
INTELLIGIBILITY
INTENSIFICATION
INTERCHANGEABLE
INTERCHANGEABLY
INTERCLAVICULAR
INTERCOLLEGIATE
INTERCONNECTION

INTERDEPENDENCE
INTERFEROMETRIC
INTERLAMINATION
INTERLOCUTORILY
INTERNALIZATION
INTERNAL REVENUE
INTERNATIONALES
INTERNATIONALLY
INTEROSCULATION
INTERPENETRABLE
INTERPRETATIONS
INTERROGATINGLY
INTERROGATIONAL
INTERROGATIVELY
INTERROGATORIES
INTERROGATORILY
INTERSCHOLASTIC
INTERVENTIONISM
INTERVENTIONIST
INTRANSIGENTIST
INTROSPECTIONAL
INTROSPECTIVELY
INTUSSUSCEPTION
INTUSSUSCEPTIVE
INVESTIGATIONAL
INVOLUNTARINESS
INVOLUNTATARILY
INVULNERABILITY
IRREDEEMABILITY
IRREFRAGABILITY
IRREMISSIBILITY
IRRESISTIBILITY
IRRESOLVABILITY
IRREVERSIBILITY

J
JACK-OF-ALL-
   TRADES
JAPANESE LANTERN
JEHOVAH'S WITNESS
JUMPING-OFF
   PLACE
JURISPRUDENTIAL
JUXTAPOSITIONAL

K
KABARDINO-BALKAR
KIND-HEARTEDNESS

L
LABOUR EXCHANGES
LABOUR-INTENSIVE
LABYRINTHICALLY
LACKADAISICALLY
LADIES-IN-
   WAITING
LAISSEZ-FAIREISM
LARGE INTESTINES
LATERAL THINKING

LAUGHING JACKASS
LEADING ARTICLES
LEADING QUESTION
LETTERS OF CREDIT
LEVEL-HEADEDNESS
LIGHT-HEADEDNESS
LIGHTNING STRIKE
LILY OF THE
   VALLEY
LIVERY COMPANIES
LOGARITHMICALLY
LOIRE-ATLANTIQUE
LOPHOBRANCHIATE
LOURENCO MARQUES

M
MACHINE-READABLE
MACROCOSMICALLY
MACROSCOPICALLY
MACROSPORANGIUM
MAGNANIMOUSNESS
MAGNETOCHEMICAL
MAGNETOELECTRIC
MAGNIFYING GLASS
MALACOPTERYGIAN
MALASSIMILATION
MALE CHAUVINISTS
MALPRACTITIONER
MANIC-DEPRESSIVE
MANIFESTATIONAL
MANNERISTICALLY
MANOEUVRABILITY
MARKET GARDENERS
MARKET GARDENING
MARRIAGEABILITY
MARSHALLING YARD
MARXISM-LENINISM
MARXIST-LENINIST
MASSAGE PARLOURS
MASTER OF SCIENCE
MATERIALIZATION
MEANINGLESSNESS
MECHANISTICALLY
MEGALOCEPHALOUS
MELANCHOLICALLY
MELLIFLUOUSNESS
MEMORIALIZATION
MENISPERMACEOUS
MENSTRUAL PERIOD
MENTAL DEFECTIVE
MENTAL HOSPITALS
MENTALISTICALLY
MEPHISTOPHELEAN
MEROBLASTICALLY
METACINNABARITE
METAGENETICALLY
METALLURGICALLY
METAMATHEMATICS
METHODISTICALLY

METROPOLITANISM
MICROBIOLOGICAL
MICROBIOLOGISTS
MICROELECTRONIC
MICROPHOTOGRAPH
MICROPROCESSORS
MICROSCOPICALLY
MICROSPORANGIUM
MICROSPOROPHYLL
MIDDLE OF
   NOWHERE
MIDDLE-OF-THE-
   ROAD
MINIATURIZATION
MISAPPLICATIONS
MISAPPREHENDING
MISAPPREHENSION
MISAPPREHENSIVE
MISAPPROPRIATED
MISCALCULATIONS
MISCELLANEOUSLY
MISCHIEVOUSNESS
MISCONSTRUCTION
MISINTERPRETING
MISREPRESENTING
MISTRUSTFULNESS
MOBILE LIBRARIES
MODERNISTICALLY
MOLOTOV COCKTAIL
MONCHEN-GLADBACH
MONOGRAPHICALLY
MOOG SYNTHESIZER
MORNING SICKNESS
MORPHOLOGICALLY
MORPHOPHONEMICS
MOTHER COUNTRIES
MOTHER SUPERIORS
MOVING STAIRCASE
MULTITUDINOUSLY
MUSTARD PLASTERS
MUTATIS MUTANDIS
MYTHOLOGIZATION

N
NAGORNO-KARABAKH
NATIONAL ANTHEMS
NATIONALIZATION
NATIONAL SERVICE
NATURAL SCIENCES
NEARSIGHTEDNESS
NEGATIVE-RAISING
NEIGHBOURLINESS
NEOARSPHENAMINE
NEOLOGISTICALLY
NEUROHYPOPHYSIS
NEUROPATHICALLY
NEUROPHYSIOLOGY
NEUROPSYCHIATRY
NEUROSURGICALLY

NEWS CONFERENCES
NIGHTMARISHNESS
NINE DAYS'
   WONDERS
NITROCHLOROFORM
NITROGENIZATION
NOMOGRAPHICALLY
NON COMPOS MENTIS
NONCONTRIBUTING
NONCONTRIBUTORY
NONINTERVENTION
NONINTOXICATING
NONPRODUCTIVITY
NON-PROFIT-MAKING
NONSENSICALNESS
NONSTANDARDIZED
NOTWITHSTANDING
NOUVELLE CUISINE
NO-WIN SITUATIONS
NUCLEAR FAMILIES
NUCLEAR REACTORS
NUMBER-CRUNCHING

O
OBJECTIFICATION
OBSERVATION POST
OBSTRUCTIONISTS
OBSTRUCTIVENESS
OESTROGENICALLY
OLD AGE PENSIONER
OLD PEOPLE'S
   HOMES
OLIGOSACCHARIDE
OMNIDIRECTIONAL
ONE-ARMED BANDITS
OPENHEARTEDNESS
OPERATING SYSTEM
OPHTHALMOLOGIST
OPHTHALMOSCOPIC
OPINIONATEDNESS
OPISTHOGNATHISM
OPISTHOGNATHOUS
OPPOSITE NUMBERS
ORIENTALIZATION
ORNITHORHYNCHUS
ORTHOCHROMATISM
ORTHOPSYCHIATRY
OSTEOPATHICALLY
OVERCAPITALIZED
OVERCOMPENSATED
OVERDEVELOPMENT
OVERSIMPLIFYING
OXYTETRACYCLINE

P
PAINSTAKINGNESS
PALAEOBOTANICAL
PALAEOGRAPHICAL
PALAEONTOGRAPHY

PALAEONTOLOGIST
PALAEOZOOLOGIST
PALEONTOLOGISTS
PANCAKE LANDINGS
PANTHEISTICALLY
PARAGENETICALLY
PARAGRAPHICALLY
PARALLACTICALLY
PARASITOLOGICAL
PARASYMPATHETIC
PARENT COMPANIES
PARENTHETICALLY
PARLIAMENTARIAN
PARTHENOGENESIS
PARTHENOGENETIC
PARTICULARISTIC
PARTICULARITIES
PARTICULARIZING
PASSIFLORACEOUS
PASSIONLESSNESS
PAST PARTICIPLES
PATENT MEDICINES
PATHETIC FALLACY
PAVEMENT ARTISTS
PELICAN CROSSING
PENTATONIC SCALE
PENTOTHAL SODIUM
PEPPERCORN RENTS
PEREGRINE FALCON
PERFUNCTORINESS
PERIODONTICALLY
PERIPATETICALLY
PERISTALTICALLY
PEROXIDE BLONDES
PERPENDICULARLY
PERSONAL COLUMNS
PERSONALITY CULT
PERSONALIZATION
PERSONAL PRONOUN
PERSONAL STEREOS
PERSONA NON GRATA
PERSONIFICATION
PERSPICACIOUSLY
PERSPICUOUSNESS
PESSIMISTICALLY
PHANTASMAGORIAS
PHARMACODYNAMIC
PHARMACOGNOSIST
PHARMACOGNOSTIC
PHARMACOLOGICAL
PHARMACOLOGISTS
PHARYNGOLOGICAL
PHENOLPHTHALEIN
PHENYLKETONURIA
PHILANTHROPISTS
PHILOSOPHICALLY
PHLEBOSCLEROSIS
PHOSPHATIZATION
PHOSPHOCREATINE

PHOSPHORESCENCE
PHOTOCONDUCTION
PHOTOELASTICITY
PHOTOGRAMMETRIC
PHOTOJOURNALISM
PHOTOJOURNALIST
PHOTOLITHOGRAPH
PHOTOMECHANICAL
PHOTOMETRICALLY
PHOTOMICROGRAPH
PHOTOMULTIPLIER
PHOTOSENSITIZED
PHOTOTELEGRAPHY
PHOTOTOPOGRAPHY
PHOTOTRANSISTOR
PHOTOTYPOGRAPHY
PHOTOZINCOGRAPH
PHYSICOCHEMICAL
PHYSIOTHERAPIST
PHYTOGEOGRAPHER
PHYTOPLANKTONIC
PICTURE-POSTCARD
PICTURESQUENESS
PIEZOMETRICALLY
PINCER MOVEMENTS
PITHECANTHROPUS
PLASMOLYTICALLY
PLASTIC SURGEONS
PLATINUM BLONDES
PLATYHELMINTHIC
PLEASURABLENESS
PLENIPOTENTIARY
PLEUROPNEUMONIA
PLOUGHMAN'S LUNCH
PLUMBAGINACEOUS
PLUMBER'S FRIENDS
PLUTOCRATICALLY
PNEUMATIC DRILLS
POIKILOTHERMISM
POISON-PEN LETTER
POLICE CONSTABLE
POLITICAL ASYLUM
POLLING STATIONS
POLYGENETICALLY
POLYGRAPHICALLY
POLYUNSATURATED
PORTMANTEAU WORD
POST OFFICE BOXES
POVERTY-STRICKEN
POWER OF ATTORNEY
PRAYING MANTISES
PREACHIFICATION
PRECANCELLATION
PRECIPITOUSNESS
PREDISPOSITIONS
PREFERENTIALITY
PREHISTORICALLY
PREPOSITIONALLY
PRESBYTERIANISM

PRESCRIPTIVISTS
PRESENTABLENESS
PRESENTATIONISM
PRESENTATIONIST
PRESS CONFERENCE
PRESSURE COOKERS
PRESTIDIGITATOR
PRESTIGIOUSNESS
PRESUMPTIVENESS
PRESUPPOSITIONS
PRETENTIOUSNESS
PRETERNATURALLY
PRIMA BALLERINAS
PRIMARY STRESSES
PRINCE CHARMINGS
PRINTED CIRCUITS
PRINTING PRESSES
PRIVATE SOLDIERS
PRIVY COUNCILLOR
PROBLEMATICALLY
PROCRASTINATING
PROCRASTINATION
PRODUCTION LINES
PROFESSIONALISM
PROFESSIONALIST
PROGENITIVENESS
PROGNOSTICATING
PROGNOSTICATION
PROGNOSTICATIVE
PROGNOSTICATORS
PROGRESSIVENESS
PROHIBITIONISTS
PROHIBITIVENESS
PROLETARIANNESS
PROMISCUOUSNESS
PROPER FRACTIONS
PROPORTIONALITY
PROPORTIONATELY
PROPYLENE GLYCOL
PROSELYTIZATION
PROSENCHYMATOUS
PROTOZOOLOGICAL
PROVOCATIVENESS
PSEPHOLOGICALLY
PSEUDOMUTUALITY
PSYCHEDELICALLY
PSYCHIATRICALLY
PSYCHOACOUSTICS
PSYCHOANALYSING
PSYCHOBIOLOGIST
PSYCHOGENICALLY
PSYCHOLOGICALLY
PSYCHOMETRICIAN
PSYCHOPATHOLOGY
PSYCHOSEXUALITY
PSYCHOTECHNICAL
PSYCHOTHERAPIST
PSYCHOTOMIMETIC
PTOLEMAIC SYSTEM

PUBLIC COMPANIES
PUBLIC NUISANCES
PUBLIC OWNERSHIP
PUBLIC RELATIONS
PULCHRITUDINOUS
PUNCTILIOUSNESS
PUNCTUATION MARK
PURITANICALNESS
PURPOSELESSNESS
PUSILLANIMOUSLY
PYROELECTRICITY

Q
QUADRUPLICATION
QUARRELSOMENESS
QUARTER SESSIONS
QUATERCENTENARY
QUEEN'S EVIDENCES
QUESTION MASTERS
QUICK-WITTEDNESS
QUINQUAGENARIAN
QUINTUPLICATION
QUODLIBETICALLY

R
RADIOACTIVATION
RADIOBIOLOGICAL
RADIOLOCATIONAL
RADIOMICROMETER
RADIOPHONICALLY
RADIOSCOPICALLY
RADIOTELEGRAPHY
RADIOTELEPHONIC
RADIO TELESCOPES
RADIOTHERAPISTS
RAILWAY STATIONS
RASTAFARIANISMS
RATE OF EXCHANGES
RATIONALIZATION
REAFFORESTATION
REAL-ESTATE AGENT
REARGUARD ACTION
RECAPITULATIONS
RECOGNIZABILITY
RECOMMENDATIONS
RECONCILABILITY
RECONNAISSANCES
RECONSIDERATION
RECONSTRUCTIBLE
RECONSTRUCTIONS
RECORD LIBRARIES
RECREATION ROOMS
REDOUBTABLENESS
REFRESHER COURSE
REGISTERED NURSE
REGISTER OFFICES
REGISTRY OFFICES
REGIUS PROFESSOR
RELATIVE CLAUSES

RELATIVE PRONOUN
REMORSELESSNESS
REPETITIOUSNESS
REPRESENTATIONS
REPRESENTATIVES
REPROACHFULNESS
REPRODUCIBILITY
RESOURCEFULNESS
RESPECTABLENESS
RESPONSIBLENESS
RESTRICTIVENESS
RESURRECTIONARY
RESURRECTIONISM
RESURRECTIONIST
RETROGRESSIVELY
RETROSPECTIVELY
REVEREND MOTHERS
REVOLUTIONARIES
REVOLUTIONARILY
REVOLUTIONIZING
RHOMBENCEPHALON
RIBONUCLEIC ACID
RIGHT-HANDEDNESS
RIGHT-MINDEDNESS
RITUALISTICALLY
ROGUES' GALLERIES
ROMANTICIZATION
ROUGH-AND-TUMBLES
ROUND-SHOULDERED
ROYAL HIGHNESSES
RUMBUSTIOUSNESS
RUSSIAN ROULETTE

S
SADOMASOCHISTIC
SALES RESISTANCE
SANCTIMONIOUSLY
SANDWICH COURSES
SAPROPHYTICALLY
SARRACENIACEOUS
SATURATION POINT
SAVINGS ACCOUNTS
SAWN-OFF SHOTGUNS
SCHISTOSOMIASIS
SCHOOL OF THOUGHT
SCINTILLATINGLY
SCLERODERMATOUS
SCRUMPTIOUSNESS
SEA ISLAND COTTON
SECONDARY MODERN
SECONDARY STRESS
SECOND CHILDHOOD
SECOND-IN-
    COMMAND
SECURITY COUNCIL
SEINE-SAINT-DENIS
SELECT COMMITTEE
SELF-CENTREDNESS
SELF-CONFIDENTLY

SELF-CONSCIOUSLY SPANISH-AMERICAN SUPERINTENDENTS
SELF-DESTRUCTING SPECIALIZATIONS SUPERLATIVENESS
SELF-DESTRUCTION SPECIAL LICENCES SUPERNATURALISM
SELF-DISCIPLINED SPECIAL PLEADING SUPERNATURALIST
SELF-EXAMINATION SPECIFIC GRAVITY SUPERNUMERARIES
SELF-EXPLANATORY SPECULATIVENESS SUPERSTITIOUSLY
SELF-IMPORTANTLY SPEECHIFICATION SUPERSTRUCTURAL
SELF-IMPROVEMENT SPEECH THERAPIST SUPERSTRUCTURES
SELF-INDULGENTLY SPERMATOGENESIS SUPPLEMENTARILY
SELF-LIQUIDATING SPERMATOGENETIC SUPPLEMENTATION
SELF-POLLINATION SPINNING JENNIES SUPPLY AND DEMAND
SELF-POSSESSEDLY SPLIT INFINITIVE SUPPORTING PARTS
SELF-REPROACHFUL SPONTANEOUSNESS SURREPTITIOUSLY
SELF-RIGHTEOUSLY SPUR-OF-THE- SUSCEPTIBLENESS
SELF-SACRIFICING   MOMENT SWIMMING COSTUME
SELF-SUFFICIENCY SQUADRON LEADERS SWORD OF DAMOCLES
SENSATIONALISTS STAGE DIRECTIONS SYCOPHANTICALLY
SENSE OF OCCASION STAMPING GROUNDS SYLLABIFICATION
SENTENTIOUSNESS STANDARD-BEARERS SYMBOL-FORMATION
SENTIMENTALISTS STANDARDIZATION SYMBOLISTICALLY
SENTIMENTALIZED STANDOFFISHNESS SYMMETRICALNESS
SEPTUAGENARIANS STAPHYLOPLASTIC SYMPATHETICALLY
SERGEANTS-AT- STAPHYLORRHAPHY SYMPATHOMIMETIC
  ARMS STAR-OF-BETHLEHEM SYMPTOMATICALLY
SERVICE STATIONS STARS AND STRIPES SYNCHRONIZATION
SERVOMECHANICAL STARVATION WAGES SYNCHRONOUSNESS
SERVOMECHANISMS STATE DEPARTMENT SYNECDOCHICALLY
SESQUICARBONATE STEREOCHEMISTRY SYNECOLOGICALLY
SHARP-WITTEDNESS STEREOISOMERISM SYNOPTIC GOSPELS
SHILLY-SHALLYING STEREOISOMETRIC SYSTEMATIZATION
SHOOTING GALLERY STICKING PLASTER SYSTEMS ANALYSTS
SHOOTING MATCHES STINGING NETTLES
SHOPPING CENTRES STOCKBROKER BELT T
SHORT-CIRCUITING STOCKING-FILLERS TACHOMETRICALLY
SHORT-HANDEDNESS STOICHIOLOGICAL TACHYMETRICALLY
SHORTHAND TYPIST STORE DETECTIVES TARSOMETATARSAL
SHOTGUN WEDDINGS STRAIGHTFORWARD TARSOMETATARSUS
SHRINKING VIOLET STRAIGHTJACKETS TECHNOLOGICALLY
SICKNESS BENEFIT STRATIFICATIONS TECHNOSTRUCTURE
SIDEWALK ARTISTS STRAWBERRY MARKS TELEGRAPHICALLY
SIESMOLOGICALLY STRETCHER-BEARER TELEPHOTOGRAPHY
SIMPLE FRACTURES STUMBLING BLOCKS TELEPHOTO LENSES
SIMPLICIDENTATE SUBORDINATENESS TELESTEREOSCOPE
SIMPLIFICATIONS SUBSISTENCE CROP TELETYPESETTING
SINGULARIZATION SUBSPECIFICALLY TEMPERAMENTALLY
SINISTRODEXTRAL SUBSTANTIVENESS TEMPESTUOUSNESS
SITUATION COMEDY SUGGESTIBLENESS TENDENTIOUSNESS
SLAUGHTERHOUSES SULPHUREOUSNESS TENDERHEARTEDLY
SLEEPING PARTNER SUNRISE INDUSTRY TERMINOLOOGICAL
SLOTTED SPATULAS SUPERADDITIONAL TERRITORIAL ARMY
SLOUGH OF DESPOND SUPERCONDUCTION TETRABRANCHIATE
SMALL INTESTINES SUPERCONDUCTIVE THEOREMATICALLY
SMALL-MINDEDNESS SUPERCONDUCTORS THERAPEUTICALLY
SOCIAL DEMOCRATS SUPERFLUOUSNESS THERIANTHROPISM
SOCIALISTICALLY SUPERIMPOSITION THERMIONIC VALVE
SOCIOLINGUISTIC SUPERINCUMBENCE THERMOBAROGRAPH
SOFT FURNISHINGS SUPERINDUCEMENT THERMOCHEMISTRY
SOFTHEARTEDNESS SUPERINTENDENCE THERMOSTABILITY
SOLEMNIFICATION SUPERINTENDENCY THICKHEADEDNESS

THICK-WITTEDNESS
THOUGHTLESSNESS
THREE-LEGGED RACE
THREE-POINT TURNS
THROMBOEMBOLISM
THYROCALCITONIN
TIGHTFISTEDNESS
TIGHTROPE WALKER
TIMES IMMEMORIAL
TOPOGRAPHICALLY
TOTALITARIANISM
TOWER OF STRENGTH
TRACTION ENGINES
TRADITIONALISTS
TRAINING COLLEGE
TRANSCRIPTIONAL
TRANSFERABILITY
TRANSFIGURATION
TRANSFIGUREMENT
TRANSFORMATIONS
TRANSGRESSINGLY
TRANSILLUMINATE
TRANSISTORIZING
TRANSLATABILITY
TRANSLITERATING
TRANSLITERATION
TRANSMOGRIFYING
TRANSMUTATIONAL
TRANSPARENTNESS
TRANSPLANTATION
TRANSPOSABILITY
TRANSPOSITIONAL
TRANSUBSTANTIAL
TREACHEROUSNESS
TREASONABLENESS
TRIBROMOETHANOL
TRICK OR TREATING
TRINITROBENZENE
TRINITROTOLUENE
TROPICALIZATION
TROUBLESHOOTERS
TROUBLESOMENESS
TRUSTWORTHINESS
TRYPANOSOMIASIS
TURF ACCOUNTANTS
TYPOGRAPHICALLY
TYRANNOSAURUSES

U
ULTRACENTRIFUGE
ULTRAFILTRATION

ULTRAMICROMETER
ULTRAMICROSCOPE
ULTRAMICROSCOPY
ULTRASTRUCTURAL
UNBELIEVABILITY
UNCEREMONIOUSLY
UNCHALLENGEABLE
UNCOMMUNICATIVE
UNCOMPLIMENTARY
UNCONCERNEDNESS
UNCONDITIONALLY
UNCONNECTEDNESS
UNCONSCIOUSNESS
UNDEMONSTRATIVE
UNDERCAPITALIZE
UNDEREMPLOYMENT
UNDERESTIMATING
UNDERESTIMATION
UNDERHANDEDNESS
UNDERPRIVILEGED
UNDERPRODUCTION
UNDERSTATEMENTS
UNDER-THE-COUNTER
UNDISTINGUISHED
UNEMPLOYABILITY
UNEQUIVOCALNESS
UNEXCEPTIONABLE
UNEXCEPTIONABLY
UNFLINCHINGNESS
UNFORTUNATENESS
UNHOLY ALLIANCES
UNINTERRUPTEDLY
UNIVERSAL JOINTS
UNKNOWN QUANTITY
UNOBTRUSIVENESS
UNPARLIAMENTARY
UNPRECEDENTEDLY
UNPREMEDITATION
UNPRETENTIOUSLY
UNPROFITABILITY
UNPRONOUNCEABLE
UNSOPHISTICATED
UNWHOLESOMENESS

V
VALETUDINARIANS
VALUE-ADDED TAXES
VASCULARIZATION
VASOCONSTRICTOR
VEGETABLE KNIVES
VEGETABLE MARROW

VENDING MACHINES
VENEREAL DISEASE
VENTRILOQUISTIC
VENTURESOMENESS
VERTIGINOUSNESS
VESPERTILIONINE
VESTED INTERESTS
VICE-CHANCELLORS
VICISSITUDINARY
VICTORIA CROSSES
VIRGINIA CREEPER
VITAL STATISTICS
VIVISECTIONISTS
VOYEURISTICALLY
VULGAR FRACTIONS

W
WALRUS MOUSTACHE
WARM-BLOODEDNESS
WARM-HEARTEDNESS
WARRANT OFFICERS
WASHING MACHINES
WEATHERBOARDING
WEATHER FORECAST
WEATHERPROOFING
WEATHER STATIONS
WELL-CONSTRUCTED
WELL-ESTABLISHED
WELL-INTENTIONED
WHIPPERSNAPPERS
WHISTLE-STOP
  TOUR
WHITE BLOOD CELLS
WHITED SEPULCHRE
WILD-GOOSE CHASES
WIND INSTRUMENTS
WIND-POLLINATION
WINDSCREEN WIPER
WISHFUL THINKING
WRONGHEADEDNESS

X
XENOMORPHICALLY
XEROGRAPHICALLY

Y
YOUTH HOSTELLERS
YOUTH HOSTELLING

Z
ZYGOPHYLLACEOUS

COUNTRIES OF THE WORLD

COUNTRY	CAPITAL	CURRENCY
AFGHANISTAN	KABUL	AFGHANI (PUL)
ALBANIA	TIRANA	LEK (QINDAR)
ALGERIA	ALGIERS	DINAR (CENTIME)
ARGENTINA	BUENOS AIRES	AUSTRAL (CENTAVO)
AUSTRALIA	CANBERRA	DOLLAR (CENT)
AUSTRIA	VIENNA	SCHILLING (GROSCHEN)
BANGLADESH	DHAKA	TAKA (POISHA)
BELGIUM	BRUSSELS	FRANC (CENTIME)
BOLIVIA	LA PAZ	PESO (CENTAVO)
BOTSWANA	GABORONE	PULA (THEBE)
BRAZIL	BRASILIA	CRUZADO (CENTAVO)
BULGARIA	SOFIA	LEV (STOTINKA)
BURMA	RANGOON	KYAT (PYA)
CAMBODIA	PHNOM PENH	RIEL (SEN)
CANADA	OTTAWA	DOLLAR (CENT)
CHILE	SANTIAGO	ESCUDO (CENTAVO)
CHINA	PEKING	YUAN (FEN)
COLOMBIA	BOGOTA	PESO (CENTAVO)
COSTA RICA	SAN JOSE	COLON (CENTIMO)
CUBA	HAVANA	PESO (CENTAVO)
CYPRUS	NICOSIA	POUND (CENT)
CZECHOSLOVAKIA	PRAGUE	KORUNA (HELLER)
DENMARK	COPENHAGEN	KRONE (ORE)
DOMINICAN REPUBLIC	SANTO DOMINGO	PESO (CENTAVO)
ECUADOR	QUITO	SUCRE (CENTAVO)
EGYPT	CAIRO	POUND (PIASTRE)
EL SALVADOR	SAN SALVADOR	COLON (CENTAVO)
ETHIOPIA	ADDIS ABABA	BIRR (CENT)
FINLAND	HELSINKI	MARKKA (PENNI)
FRANCE	PARIS	FRANC (CENTIME)
THE GAMBIA	BANJUL	DALASI (BUTUT)
GERMANY (DEMOCRATIC REPUBLIC OF)	EAST BERLIN	MARK (PFENNIG)
GERMANY (FEDERAL REPUBLIC OF)	BONN	DEUTSCHE MARK (PFENNIG)
GHANA	ACCRA	CEDI (PESEWA)
GREECE	ATHENS	DRACHMA (LEPTON)
GUATEMALA	GUATEMALA CITY	QUETZAL (CENTAVO)
HAITI	PORT-AU-PRINCE	GOURDE (CENTIME)
HONDURAS	TEGUCIGALPA	LEMPIRA (CENTAVO)
HONG KONG	VICTORIA	DOLLAR (CENT)
HUNGARY	BUDAPEST	FORINT (FILLER)
ICELAND	REYKJAVIK	KRONA (EYRIR)
INDIA	NEW DELHI	RUPEE (PAISA)
INDONESIA	JAKARTA	RUPIAH (SEN)
IRAN	TEHRAN	RIAL (DINAR)
IRAQ	BAGHDAD	DINAR (FILS)
IRELAND	DUBLIN	POUND (PENCE)
ISRAEL	JERUSALEM	SHEKEL (AGORA)
ITALY	ROME	LIRA (CENTESIMO)
JAMAICA	KINGSTON	DOLLAR (CENT)
JAPAN	TOKYO	YEN
JORDAN	AMMAN	DINAR (FILS)
KENYA	NAIROBI	SHILLING (CENT)
KOREA (DEMOCRATIC PEOPLE'S REPUBLIC OF)	P'YONGYANG	WON (CHON)

COUNTRIES OF THE WORLD

COUNTRY	CAPITAL	CURRENCY
KOREA (REPUBLIC OF)	SEOUL	WON (JEON)
KUWAIT	KUWAIT	DINAR (FILS)
LAOS	VIENTIANE	KIP (AT)
LEBANON	BEIRUT	POUND (PIASTRE)
LIBERIA	MONROVIA	DOLLAR (CENT)
LIBYA	TRIPOLI	DINAR (DIRHAM)
LUXEMBOURG	LUXEMBOURG	FRANC
MADAGASCAR	ANTANANAIVO	FRANC MALGACHE
MALAWI	LILONGWE	KWACHA (TAMBALA)
MALAYSIA	KUALA LUMPUR	DOLLAR (CENT)
MALTA	VALLETTA	LIRA (CENT)
MAURITIUS	PORT LOUIS	RUPEE (CENT)
MEXICO	MEXICO CITY	PESO (CENTAVO)
MONGOLIA	ULAN BATOR	TUGRIK (MONGO)
MOROCCO	RABAT	DIRHAM (CENTIME)
NEPAL	KATHMANDU	RUPEE (PAISA)
NETHERLANDS	AMSTERDAM	FLORIN (CENT)
NEW ZEALAND	WELLINGTON	DOLLAR (CENT)
NICARAGUA	MANAGUA	CORDOBA (CENTAVO)
NIGERIA	ABUJA	NAIRA (KOBO)
NORWAY	OSLO	KRONE (ORE)
PAKISTAN	ISLAMABAD	RUPEE (PAISA)
PANAMA	PANAMA CITY	BALBOA (CENT)
PARAGUAY	ASUNCION	GUARANI (CENTIMO)
PERU	LIMA	INTI (CENTIMO)
PHILIPPINES	MANILA	PESO (CENTAVO)
POLAND	WARSAW	ZLOTY (GROSZ)
PORTUGAL	LISBON	ESCUDO (CENTAVO)
ROMANIA	BUCHAREST	LEU (BAN)
SAUDI ARABIA	RIYADH	RIYAL (HALALAS)
SEYCHELLES	VICTORIA	RUPEE (CENT)
SIERRA LEONE	FREETOWN	LEONE (CENT)
SINGAPORE	SINGAPORE CITY	DOLLAR (CENT)
SOUTH AFRICA	PRETORIA	RAND (CENT)
SPAIN	MADRID	PESETA (CENTIMO)
SRI LANKA	COLOMBO	RUPEE (CENT)
SUDAN	KHARTOUM	POUND (PIASTRE)
SWEDEN	STOCKHOLM	KRONA (ORE)
SWITZERLAND	BERN	FRANC (CENTIME)
SYRIA	DAMASCUS	POUND (PIASTRE)
TAIWAN	TAIBEI	DOLLAR (CENT)
TANZANIA	DODOMA	SHILLING (CENT)
THAILAND	BANGKOK	BAHT (STANGS)
TUNISIA	TUNIS	DINAR (MILLIEME)
TURKEY	ANKARA	LIRA (KURUS)
UGANDA	KAMPALA	SHILLING (CENT)
UNITED KINGDOM	LONDON	POUND (PENCE)
UNITED STATES OF AMERICA	WASHINGTON, DC	DOLLAR (CENT)
URUGUAY	MONTEVIDEO	PESO (CENTESIMO)
USSR (SOVIET UNION)	MOSCOW	ROUBLE (COPECK)
VENEZUELA	CARACAS	BOLIVAR
VIETNAM	HANOI	DONG (XU)
YUGOSLAVIA	BELGRADE	DINAR (PARA)
ZAIRE	KINSHASA	ZAIRE (LIKUTA)
ZAMBIA	LUSAKA	KWACHA (NGWEE)
ZIMBABWE	HARARE	DOLLAR (CENT)

ENGLISH COUNTIES

COUNTY	ADMINISTRATIVE CENTRE	COUNTY	ADMINISTRATIVE CENTRE
AVON	BRISTOL	NORFOLK	NORWICH
BEDFORDSHIRE	BEDFORD	NORTHAMPTONSHIRE	NORTHAMPTON
BERKSHIRE	READING	NORTHUMBERLAND	MORPETH
BUCKINGHAMSHIRE	AYLESBURY	NOTTINGHAMSHIRE	NOTTINGHAM
CAMBRIDGESHIRE	CAMBRIDGE	OXFORDSHIRE	OXFORD
CHESHIRE	CHESTER	*RUTLAND	OAKHAM
CLEVELAND	MIDDLESBOROUGH	SALOP (name for	
CORNWALL	TRURO	Shropshire	
*CUMBERLAND	CARLISLE	between 1974	
CUMBRIA	CARLISLE	and 1980)	
DERBYSHIRE	MATLOCK	SHROPSHIRE	SHREWSBURY
DEVON	EXETER	SOMERSET	TAUNTON
DORSET	DORCHESTER	STAFFORDSHIRE	STAFFORD
DURHAM	DURHAM	SUFFOLK	IPSWICH
ESSEX	CHELMSFORD	SURREY	KINGSTON UPON
GLOUCESTERSHIRE	GLOUCESTER		THAMES
†GREATER	MANCHESTER	SUSSEX, EAST	LEWES
MANCHESTER		SUSSEX, WEST	CHICHESTER
HAMPSHIRE	WINCHESTER	†S. YORKSHIRE	BARNSLEY
HEREFORD AND	WORCESTER	†TYNE AND WEAR	NEWCASTLE-UPON-
WORCESTER			TYNE
*HEREFORDSHIRE	HEREFORD	WARWICKSHIRE	WARWICK
HERTFORDSHIRE	HERTFORD	*WESTMORLAND	KENDAL
HUMBERSIDE	BEVERLEY	WIGHT, ISLE OF	NEWPORT, IOW
*HUNTINGDONSHIRE	HUNTINGDON	WILTSHIRE	TROWBRIDGE
KENT	MAIDSTONE	†W. MIDLANDS	BIRMINGHAM
LANCASHIRE	PRESTON	†W. YORKSHIRE	WAKEFIELD
LEICESTERSHIRE	LEICESTER	YORKSHIRE,	NORTHALLERTON
LINCOLNSHIRE	LINCOLN	NORTH	
†MERSEYSIDE	LIVERPOOL		

*indicates a former county
| metropolitan county

WELSH COUNTIES

COUNTY	ADMINISTRATIVE CENTRE	COUNTY	ADMINISTRATIVE CENTRE
*ANGLESEY	LLANGEFNI	*MERIONETH	DOLGELLAU
*BRECONSHIRE	BRECON	MID GLAMORGAN	CARDIFF
*CAERNARVONSHIRE	CAERNARVON	*MONMOUTHSHIRE	NEWPORT
*CARDIGANSHIRE	ABERYSTWYTH	*MONTGOMERYSHIRE	WELSHPOOL
*CARMARTHENSHIRE	CARMARTHEN	*PEMBROKESHIRE	HAVERFORDWEST
CLWYD	MOLD	POWYS	LLANDRINDOD
*DENBIGHSHIRE	RUTHIN		WELLS
DYFED	CARMARTHEN	*RADNORSHIRE	LLANDRINDOD
*FLINTSHIRE	MOLD		WELLS
*GLAMORGAN	CARDIFF	S. GLAMORGAN	CARDIFF
GWENT	CWMBRAN	W. GLAMORGAN	SWANSEA
GWYNEDD	CAERNARFON		

* indicates a former county

SCOTTISH REGIONS AND COUNTIES

REGION OR COUNTY	ADMINISTRATIVE CENTRE	REGION OR COUNTY	ADMINISTRATIVE CENTRE
*ABERDEEN	ABERDEEN	*LANARK	HAMILTON
*ANGUS	FORFAR	LOTHIAN	EDINBURGH
*ARGYLL	LOCHGILPHEAD	*MIDLOTHIAN	EDINBURGH
*AYR	AYR	*MORAY	ELGIN
*BANFF	BANFF	*NAIRN	NAIRN
*BERWICK	DUNS	ORKNEY	KIRKWALL
BORDERS	NEWTON ST. BOSWELLS	*ORKNEY	KIRKWALL
		*PEEBLES	PEEBLES
*BUTE	ROTHESAY	*PERTH	PERTH
*CAITHNESS	WICK	*RENFREW	PAISLEY
CENTRAL	STIRLING	*ROSS AND CROMARTY	DINGWALL
*CLACKMANNAN	ALLOA	*ROXBURGH	NEWTOWN ST. BOSWELLS
*DUMBARTON	DUMBARTON		
*DUMFRIES	DUMFRIES		
DUMFRIES AND GALLOWAY	DUMFRIES	*SELKIRK	SELKIRK
		SHETLAND	LERWICK
*EAST LOTHIAN	HADDINGTON	*STIRLING	STIRLING
FIFE	FIFE	STRATHCLYDE	GLASGOW
*FIFE	CUPAR	*SUTHERLAND	GOLSPIE
GRAMPIAN	ABERDEEN	TAYSIDE	DUNDEE
HIGHLAND	INVERNESS	WESTERN ISLES	LEWIS
*INVERNESS	INVERNESS	*WEST LOTHIAN	LINLITHGOW
*KINCARDINE	STONEHAVEN	*WIGTOWN	STRANRAER
*KINROSS	KINROSS	*ZETLAND	LERWICK
*KIRKCUDBRIGHT	KIRKCUDBRIGHT		

* indicates former Scottish county

COUNTIES OF NORTHERN IRELAND

COUNTY	COUNTY TOWN	COUNTY	COUNTY TOWN
ANTRIM	BELFAST	LONDONDERRY	LONDONDERRY
ARMAGH	ARMAGH	TYRONE	OMAGH
DOWN	DOWNPATRICK		
FERMANAGH	ENNISKILLEN		

AMERICAN STATES

STATE	NICKNAME	CAPITAL
ALABAMA (ALA.)		MONTGOMERY
ALASKA		JUNEAU
ARIZONA (ARIZ.)	OCOTILLO	PHOENIX
ARKANSAS (ARK.)		LITTLE ROCK
CALIFORNIA (CAL.)	GOLDEN	SACRAMENTO
COLORADO (COLO.)	CENTENNIAL	DENVER
CONNECTICUT (CONN.)	NUTMEG	HARTFORD
DELAWARE (DEL.)	DIAMOND	DOVER
FLORIDA (FLA.)	SUNSHINE	TALLAHASSEE
GEORGIA (GA.)	PEACH	ATLANTA
HAWAII	ALOHA	HONOLULU
IDAHO	GEM	BOISE
ILLINOIS (ILL.)	PRAIRIE	SPRINGFIELD
INDIANA (IND.)		INDIANAPOLIS
IOWA	HAWKEYE	DES MOINES
KANSAS (KAN.)	SUNFLOWER	TOPEKA
KENTUCKY (KY.)		FRANKFORT
LOUISIANA (LA.)	PELICAN	BATON ROUGE
MAINE (ME.)	PINETREE	AUGUSTA
MARYLAND (MD.)	OLDLINE	ANNAPOLIS
MASSACHUSETTS (MASS.)	BAY	BOSTON
MICHIGAN (MICH.)	WOLVERINE	LANSING
MINNESOTA (MINN.)	NORTHSTAR	ST. PAUL
MISSISSIPPI (MISS.)	MAGNOLIA	JACKSON
MISSOURI (MO.)	SHOWME	JEFFERSON CITY
MONTANA (MONT.)	TREASURE	HELENA
NEBRASKA (NEBR.)	CORNHUSKER	LINCOLN
NEVADA (NEV.)	SILVER	CARSON CITY
NEW HAMPSHIRE (N.H.)		CONCORD
NEW JERSEY (N.J.)	GARDEN	TRENTON
NEW MEXICO (N. MEX.)		SANTA FE
NEW YORK (N.Y.)	EMPIRE	ALBANY
NORTH CAROLINA (N.C.)	TARHEEL	RALEIGH
NORTH DAKOTA (N. DAK.)	SIOUX	BISMARCK
OHIO	BUCKEYE	COLUMBUS
OKLAHOMA (OKLA.)		OKLAHOMA CITY
OREGON (OREG.)	BEAVER	SALEM
PENNSYLVANIA (PA.)	KEYSTONE	HARRISBURG
RHODE ISLAND (R.I.)		PROVIDENCE
SOUTH CAROLINA (S.C.)		COLUMBIA
SOUTH DAKOTA (S. DAK.)	COYOTE	PIERRE
TENNESSEE (TENN.)	VOLUNTEER	NASHVILLE
TEXAS (TEX.)	LONESTAR	AUSTIN
UTAH	MORMAN	SALT LAKE CITY
VERMONT (VT.)		MONTPELIER
VIRGINIA (VA.)		RICHMOND
WASHINGTON (WASH.)	EVERGREEN	OLYMPIA
WEST VIRGINIA (W.VA.)	MOUNTAIN	CHARLESTON
WISCONSIN (WIS.)	BADGER	MADISON
WYOMING (WYO.)	EQUALITY	CHEYENNE

THE CHEMICAL ELEMENTS

NAME	SYMBOL	NAME	SYMBOL	NAME	SYMBOL
ACTINIUM	AC	GOLD	AU	PRASEODYMIUM	PR
ALUMINUM	AL	HAFNIUM	HF	RADIUM	RA
AMERICIUM	AM	HELIUM	HE	RADON	RN
ANTIMONY	SB	HOLMIUM	HO	RHENIUM	RE
ARGON	AR	HYDROGEN	H	RHODIUM	RH
ARSENIC	AS	INDIUM	IN	RUBIDIUM	RB
ASTATINE	AT	IODINE	I	RUTHENIUM	RU
BARIUM	BA	IRIDIUM	IR	SAMARIUM	SM
BERKELIUM	BK	IRON	FE	SCANDIUM	SC
BERYLLIUM	BE	KRYPTON	KR	SELENIUM	SE
BISMUTH	BI	LANTHANUM	LA	SILICON	SI
BORON	B	LAWRENCIUM	LR	SILVER	AG
BROMINE	BR	LEAD	PB	SODIUM	NA
CADMIUM	CD	LITHIUM	LI	STRONTIUM	SR
CAESIUM	CS	LUTETIUM	LU	SULPHUR	S
CALCIUM	CA	MAGNESIUM	MG	TANTALUM	TA
CALIFORNIUM	CF	MANGANESE	MN	TECHETIUM	TC
CARBON	C	MENDELEVIUM	MD	TELLURIUM	TE
CERIUM	CE	MERCURY	HG	TERBIUM	TB
CHLORINE	CL	MOLYBDENUM	MO	THALLIUM	TL
CHROMIUM	CR	NEODYMIUM	ND	THORIUM	TH
COBALT	CO	NEON	NE	THULIUM	TM
COLUMBIUM	CB	NEPTUNIUM	NP	TIN	SN
COPPER	CU	NICKEL	NI	TITANIUM	TI
CURIUM	CM	NIOBIUM	NB	TUNGSTEN	W
DYSPROSIUM	DY	NITROGEN	N	URANIUM	U
EINSTEINIUM	ES	NOBELIUM	NO	VANADIUM	V
ERBIUM	ER	OSMIUM	OS	WOLFRAM	W
EUROPIUM	EU	OXYGEN	O	XENON	XE
FERMIUM	FM	PALLADIUM	PD	YTTERBIUM	YB
FLUORINE	F	PHOSPHORUS	P	YTTRIUM	Y
FRANCIUM	FR	PLATINUM	PT	ZINC	ZN
GADOLINIUM	GD	PLUTONIUM	PU	ZIRCONIUM	ZR
GALLIUM	GA	POLONIUM	PO		
GERMANIUM	GE	POTASSIUM	K		

THE PLANETS AND THEIR NAMED SATELLITES

EARTH	MOON
MARS	PHOBOS, DEIMOS
MERCURY	
VENUS	
JUPITER	METIS, ADRASTEA, AMALTHEA, THEBE, IO, EUROPA, GANYMEDE, CALLISTO, LEDA, MILALIA, LYSITHEA, ELARA, ANANKE, CARME, PASIPHAE, SINOPE.
NEPTUNE	TRITON, NEREID
PLUTO	CHARON
SATURN	MIMAS, ENCELADUS, TETHYS, DIONE, RHEA, TITAN, HYPERION, IAPETUS, PHOEBE, JANUS
URANUS	MIRANDA, ARIEL, UMBRIEL, TITANIA, OBERON

MINOR PLANETS

ACHILLES	ATEN	EUPHROSYNE	ICARUS
ADONIS	CERES	HEBE	IRIS
AMOR	CHIRON	HERMES	JUNO
APOLLO	EROS	HIDALGO	PALLAS
ASTRAEA	EUNOMIA	HYGIEA	VESTA

THE CONSTELLATIONS

3
ARA
LEO

4
APUS
CRUX
GRUS
LYNX
LYRA
PAVO
VELA

5
ARIES
CETUS
DRACO
HYDRA
INDUS
LEPUS
LIBRA
LUPUS
MENSA
MUSCA
NORMA
ORION
PYXIS
VIRGO

6
ANTLIA
AQUILA
AURIGA
BOOTES
CAELUM
CANCER

CARINA
CORVUS
CRATER
CYGNUS
DORADO
FORNAX
GEMINI
HYDRUS
OCTANS
PICTOR
PISCES
PUPPIS
SCUTUM
TAURUS
TUCANA
VOLANS

7
CEPHEUS
COLUMBA
LACERTA
PEGASUS
PERSEUS
PHOENIX
SAGITTA
SERPENS
SEXTANS

8
AQUARIUS
CIRCINUS
EQUULEUS
ERIDANUS
HERCULES
LEO MINOR
SCORPIUS

SCULPTOR

9
ANDROMEDA
CENTAURUS
CHAMELEON
DELPHINUS
MONOCEROS
OPHIUCHUS
RETICULUM
URSA MAJOR
URSA MINOR
VULPECULA

10
CANIS MAJOR
CANIS MINOR
CASSIOPEIA
HOROLOGIUM
TRIANGULUM

11
CAPRICORNUS
SAGITTARIUS
TELESCOPIUM

12 & OVER
CAMELOPARDALIS
CANES VENATICI
COMA BERENICES
CORONA AUSTRALIS
CORONA BOREALIS
MICROSCOPIUM
PISCIS AUSTRINUS
TRIANGULUM AUSTRALE

NAMED NEAREST AND BRIGHTEST STARS

ROSS
VEGA
WOLF
CYGNI
DENEB
RIGEL
SIRUS
SPICA
ADHARA
ALTAIR
CASTOR
CRUCIS
KRUGER

LUYTEN
POLLUX
SHAULA
SIRIUS
ANTARES
CANOPUS
CAPELLA
LALANDE
PROCYON
PROCYON
REGULUS
TAU CETI
ACHERNAR

ARCTURUS
BARNARD'S
CENTAURI
KAPTEYN'S
ALDEBARAN
BELLATRIX
FOMALHAUT
BETELGEUSE
EPSILON INDI
ALPHA CENTAURI
EPSILON ERIDANI
PROXIMA CENTAURI

CLOUDS

CIRRUS
CUMULUS
STRATUS
ALTOCUMULUS

ALTOSTRATUS
CIRROCUMULUS
CIRROSTRATUS
CUMULONIMBUS

NIMBOSTRATUS
STRATOCUMULUS

GREEK AND ROMAN MYTHOLOGY

AJAX _ Greek warrior
ATLAS _ bore heaven on his shoulders
HADES _ the Underworld
JASON _ led Argonauts in search of the Golden Fleece
MIDAS _ his touch turned everything to gold
ADONIS _ renowned for his beauty
CHARON _ boatman who rowed dead across river Styx
OEDIPUS _ king of Thebes; married his mother
OLYMPUS _ a mountain; the home of the gods
ORPHEUS _ skilled musician
PANDORA _ the first woman; opened box which
  released all varieties of evil
ROMULUS _ founder of Rome
ULYSSES _ Roman name for **ODYSSEUS**
ACHILLES _ Greek hero; invulnerable except
  for heel
CERBERUS _ three-headed dog, guarded Hades
HERACLES _ famed for his courage and
  strength; performed the twelve labours
HERCULES _ Roman name for **HERACLES**
ODYSSEUS _ Greek hero of Trojan war
AGAMEMNON _ king of Mycenae
NARCISSUS _ beautiful youth who fell in love
  with his own reflection
HELEN OF TROY _ famed for her beauty; cause of Trojan war

GREEK GODS	ROMAN EQUIVALENT
EOS _ goddess of dawn	AURORA
PAN _ god of woods and fields	FAUNUS
ARES _ god of war	MARS
EROS _ god of love	CUPID
HEBE _ goddess of youth	JUVENTAS
HERA _ queen of heaven, goddess of women and marriage	JUNO
RHEA _ goddess of nature	CYBELE
ZEUS _ supreme god; god of sky and weather	JUPITER
FATES _ 3 goddesses who determine man's destiny, Clotho, Lachesis and Atropos	
PLUTO _ god of the underworld	PLUTO
APOLLO _ god of poetry, music and prophecy	APOLLO
ATHENE _ goddess of wisdom	MINERVA
CRONOS _ god of agriculture	SATURN
HECATE _ goddess of witchcraft	HECATE
HELIOS _ god of the sun	SOL
HERMES _ messenger of gods	MERCURY
HESTIA _ goddess of the hearth	VESTA
HYPNOS _ god of sleep	SOMNUS
PLUTUS _ god of wealth	
SELENE _ goddess of the moon	LUNA
ARTEMIS _ goddess of the moon	DIANA
DEMETER _ goddess of agriculture	CERES
CHARITES _ 3 daughters of Zeus, Euphrosyne, Aglaia and Thalia; personified grace, beauty and charm	GRACES
DIONYSUS _ god of wine and fertility	BACCHUS
POSEIDON _ god of the sea	NEPTUNE
THANATOS _ god of death	MORS
APHRODITE _ goddess of beauty and love	VENUS
ASCLEPIUS _ god of medical art	AESCULAPIUS
HEPHAESTUS _ god of destructive fire	VULCAN
PERSEPHONE _ goddess of the Underworld	PROSERPINE

ROMAN GODS	GREEK EQUIVALE
SOL	HELIOS
JUNO	HERA
LUNA	SELENE
MARS	ARES
MORS	THANATOS
CERES	DEMETER
CUPID	EROS
DIANA	ARTEMIS
PLUTO	PLUTO
VENUS	APHRODITE
VESTA	HESTIA
APOLLO	APOLLO
AURORA	EOS
CYBELE	RHEA
FAUNUS	PAN
GRACES	CHARITES
HECATE	HECATE
SATURN	CRONOS
SOMNUS	HYPNOS
VULCAN	HEPHAESTUS
BACCHUS	DIONYSUS
JUPITER	ZEUS
MERCURY	HERMES
MINERVA	ATHENE
NEPTUNE	POSEIDON
JUVENTAS	HEBE
PROSPERINE	PERSEPHONE
AESCULAPIUS	ASCLEPIUS

THE NINE MUSES

CALLIOPE	EPIC POETRY
CLIO	HISTORY
ERATO	LOVE POETRY
EUTERPE	LYRIC POETRY
MELPOMENE	TRAGEDY
POLYHYMNIA	SACRED SONG
TERPSICHORE	DANCING
THALIA	COMEDY
URANIA	ASTRONOMY

SEVEN DEADLY SINS

PRIDE	LUST	GLUTTONY	SLOTH
COVETOUSNESS	ENVY	ANGER	

SEVEN WONDERS OF THE WORLD

THE PYRAMIDS OF EGYPT
THE COLOSSUS OF RHODES
THE HANGING GARDENS OF BABYLON
THE MAUSOLEUM OF HALICARNASSUS
THE STATUE OF ZEUS AT OLYMPIA
THE TEMPLE OF ARTEMIS AT EPHESUS
THE PHAROS OF ALEXANDRIA

SEVEN VIRTUES

FAITH	JUSTICE	TEMPERANCE
FORTITUDE	LOVE (CHARITY)	
HOPE	PRUDENCE	

NORSE MYTHOLOGY

oddess of the dead
god of fertility and crops
god of evil
supreme god; god of wisdom
god of thunder
_ god of poetry
_ goddess of love and night
_ god of night
D _ the home of the gods

BALDER _ god of the summer sun
FRIGGA _ goddess of married love
HEIMDAL _ guardian of Asgard
VALHALLA _ hall in Asgard where
Odin welcomed the souls of he-
roes killed in battle
VALKYRIES _ nine handmaidens of
Odin

EGYPTIAN MYTHOLOGY

the sun go.ᵌ
_ god of evil
S _ goddess of fertility
US _ hawk-headed god of light
TH _ god of wisdom
N-RA _ supreme god

ANUBIS _ jackel-headed son of
Osiris
HATHOR _ cow-headed goddess of
love
OSIRIS _ ruler of the afterlife

BOOKS OF THE BIBLE

E BOOKS OF THE OLD TESTAMENT

ENESIS
XODUS
EVITICUS
NUMBERS
DEUTERONOMY
JOSHUA
JUDGES
RUTH
1 SAMUEL
2 SAMUEL
1 KINGS
2 KINGS
1 CHRONICLES
2 CHRONICLES
EZRA
NEHEMIAH
ESTHER
JOB
PSALMS
PROVERBS
ECCLESIASTES
SONG OF SOLOMON

ISAIAH
JEREMIAH
LAMENTATIONS
EZEKIEL
DANIEL
HOSEA
JOEL
AMOS
OBADIAH
JONAH
MICAH
NAHUM
HABAKKUK
ZEPHANIAH
HAGGAI
ZECHARIAH
MALACHI

THE BOOKS OF THE NEW TESTAMENT

MATTHEW
MARK
LUKE
JOHN

THE ACTS
ROMANS
1 CORINTHIANS
2 CORINTHIANS
GALATIANS
EPHESIANS
PHILIPPIANS
COLOSSIANS
1 THESSALONIANS
2 THESSALONIANS
1 TIMOTHY
2 TIMOTHY
TITUS
PHILEMON
HEBREWS
JAMES
1 PETER
2 PETER
1 JOHN
2 JOHN
3 JOHN
JUDE
REVELATIONS

ANDREW _ fisherman and brother of Peter; one of 12 Apostles.

BARABBAS _ robber and murderer; in prison with Jesus and released instead of him.

BARNABAS _ Cypriot missionary, introduced Paul to the Church.

BARTHOLOMEW _ possibly same person as Nathaniel, one of the 12 Apostles.

CAIAPHAS _ high priest of the Jews; Jesus brought to him after arrest.

GABRIEL _ angel who announced birth of Jesus to Mary; and of John the Baptist to Zechariah.

HEROD _ 1. the Great, ruled when Jesus was born. 2. Antipas, son of Herod the Great ruled when John the Baptist was murdered. 3. Agrippa, killed James (brother of John). 4. Agrippa II, before whom Paul was tried.

JAMES _ 1. the Greater, one of 12 Apostles, brother of John. 2. the Less, one of 12 Apostles. 3. leader of the Church in Jerusalem and author of the new testament epistle.

JESUS _ founder of Christianity.

JOHN _ youngest of 12 Apostles.

JOHN THE BAPTIST _ announced coming of Jesus, and baptized him.

JOSEPH _ 1. husband of Mary the mother of Jesus. 2. of Arimathaea, a secret disciple of Jesus.

JUDAS ISCARIOT _ the disciple who betrayed Jesus.

LAZARUS _ brother of Mary and Martha, raised from the dead by Jesus.

LUKE _ companion of Paul, author of Luke and Acts.

MARK _ author of the Gospel; companion of Paul, Barnabas, and Peter.

MARTHA _ sister of Mary and Lazarus, friend of Jesus.

MARY _ 1. mother of Jesus. 2. sister of Martha and Lazarus. 3. Magdalene, cured by Jesus and the first to see him after the resurrection.

MATTHEW _ one of 12 Apostles, author of the gospel.

MATTHIAS _ chosen to replace the apostle Judas.

MICHAEL _ a chief archangel.

NATHANIEL _ see Bartholomew.

NICODEMUS _ a Pharisee who had a secret meeting with Jesus.

PAUL _ formerly Saul of Tarsus, persecutor of Christians; renamed after his conversion. Apostle to the Gentiles and author of Epistles.

PETER _ Simon, one of 12 Apostles; denied Jesus before the crucifixion but later became leader of the Church.

PHILIP _ one of 12 Apostles.

PILATE _ Roman procurator of Judea; allowed Jesus to be crucified.

SALOME _ 1. wife of Zebedee, mother of James and John. 2. daughter of Herodias; danced before Herod for the head of John the Baptist.

SAUL _ see Paul.

SIMON _ 1. Simon Peter see Peter. 2. the Canaanite, one of 12 Apostles. 3. one of Jesus' four brothers. 4. the leper, in whose house Jesus was anointed. 5. of Cyrene, carried the cross of Jesus. 6. the tanner, in whose house Peter had his vision.

STEPHEN _ Christian martyr, stoned to death.

THOMAS _ one of 12 Apostles, named "Doubting" because he doubted the resurrection.

TIMOTHY _ Paul's fellow missionary; two of Paul's Epistles are to him.

TITUS _ convert and companion of Paul who wrote him one Epistle.

AARON _ elder brother of Moses; 1st high priest of Hebrews.

ABEL _ second son of Adam and Eve; murdered by brother Cain.

ABRAHAM _ father of Hebrew nation.

ABSALOM _ David's spoilt third son; killed after plotting against his father.

ADAM _ the first man created; husband of Eve.

BAAL _ fertility god of Canaanites and Phoenicians.

BATHSHEBA _ mother of Solomon.

BELSHAZZAR _ last king of Babylon, son of Nebuchadnezzar; Daniel interpreted his vision of writing on the wall as foretelling the downfall of his kingdom.

BENJAMIN _ youngest son of Jacob and Rachel. His descendants formed one of the 12 tribes of Israel.

CAIN _ first son of Adam and Eve; murdered his brother Abel.

DANIEL _ prophet at the court of Nebuchadnezzar with a gift for interpreting dreams.

DAVID _ slayed the giant Goliath.

DELILAH _ a Philistine seducer and betrayer of Samson.

ELIJAH _ Hebrew prophet, taken into heaven in a fiery chariot.

ELISHA _ prophet and disciple of Elijah.

ENOCH _ father of Methuselah.

EPHRAIM _ son of Joseph; founded one of the 12 tribes of Israel.

ESAU _ elder of Isaac's twin sons; tricked out of his birthright by his younger brother Jacob.

ESTHER _ beautiful Israelite woman; heroically protected her people.

EVE _ first woman; created as companion for Adam in Garden of Eden.

EZEKIEL _ prophet of Israel captured by Babylonians.

GIDEON _ Israelite hero and judge.

GOLIATH _ Philistine giant killed by David.

HEZEKIAH _ king of Judah (C 715_686 BC).

ISAAC _ son of Abraham and Sarah, conceived in their old age; father of Jacob and Esau.

ISAIAH _ the greatest old testament prophet.

ISHMAEL _ Abraham's son by Hagar, hand-maiden to his wife, Sarah, rival of Isaac.

ISRAEL _ new name given to Jacob after reconciliation with Esau.

JACOB _ second son of Isaac and Rebekah, younger twin of Esau whom he tricked out of his inheritance. The 12 tribes of Israel were named after his 12 sons.

JEREMIAH _ one of the great prophets; foretold destruction of Jerusalem.

JEZEBEL _ cruel and lustful wife of Ahab, king of Israel.

JOB _ long-suffering and pious inhabitant of Uz.

JONAH _ after ignoring God's commands he was swallowed by a whale.

JONATHAN _ eldest son of Saul and close friend of David.

JOSEPH _ favourite son of Jacob and Rachel with his "coat of many colours"; sold into slavery by his jealous brothers.

JOSHUA _ succeeded Moses and led Israelites against Canaan. He defeated Jericho where the walls fell down.

JUDAH _ son of Jacob and Leah.

LOT _ nephew of Abraham.

METHUSELAH _ son of Enoch, the oldest person ever (969 years).

MIRIAM _ sister of Aaron and Moses whom she looked after as a baby; prophetess and leader of Israelites.

MOSES _ Israel's great leader and lawgiver, he led the Israelites out of captivity in Egypt to the promised land of Canaan. Received ten commandments from Jehovah on Mt. Sinai.

NATHAN _ Hebrew prophet at courts of David and Solomon.

NEBUCHADNEZZAR _ king of Babylon.

NOAH _ grandson of Methusaleh, father of Shem, Ham and Japheth; built ark to save his family and all animal species from the flood.

REBEKAH _ wife of Isaac, mother of Jacob and Esau.

RUTH _ Moabite who accompanied her mother-in-law Naomi to Bethlehem. Remembered for her loyalty.

SAMSON _ Israelite judge of great physical strength; seduced and betrayed by Delilah.

SAMUEL _ prophet and judge of Israel.

SARAH _ wife of Abraham, mother of Isaac.

SAUL _ first king of Israel.

SOLOMON _ son of David and Bathsheba; remembered for his great wisdom and wealth.

ABJECTLY	BLACKCAP	CHECKY	CROCKERY	EXHIBITS
ACQUAINT	BLACKISH	CHEEKILY	CROZIERS	EXHORTED
ACQUIRED	BLAZONED	CHEMURGY	CRUCIFIX	EXHUMED
ACQUIRER	BLITZING	CHEQUE	CUMQUAT	EXHUMER
ADEQUACY	BLOWZIER	CHEQUER	CUMQUATS	EXHUMING
ADJUDGED	BLOWZY	CHEQUERS	CYPHERED	EXIGENCY
ADJUVANT	BODYWORK	CHEQUES	CZARINAS	EXOGAMY
ADVOCACY	BOMBYCID	CHICKENS	DABCHICK	EXORCISM
AFFIXED	BONANZAS	CHICKPEA	DAZEDLY	EXORCIZE
AFFIXES	BOOKSHOP	CHINTZ	DECKHAND	EXPANDED
AFFIXING	BOOKWORM	CHINTZY	DEFLEXED	EXPECTED
AGONIZED	BOOZIEST	CHIPMUNK	DEJECTED	EXPENDED
AMORTIZE	BOOZILY	CHIVALRY	DEMIJOHN	EXPERTLY
APOPHYGE	BOTANIZE	CHIVYING	DEPUTIZE	EXPIABLE
APOPLEXY	BOUQUETS	CHOCKING	DIGITIZE	EXPLICIT
APPENDIX	BOUTIQUE	CHOPPILY	DOCKYARD	EXPLODED
AQUARIUM	BOUZOUKI	CHUCKING	DOORJAMB	EXPUNGED
AQUATICS	BOXBOARD	CHUCKLED	DOZENTH	FANZINE
AQUEDUCT	BOXROOMS	CHUCKLER	DRAWBACK	FANZINES
ARCHWAYS	BOXWOOD	CHUCKLES	DUCKWEED	FASTBACK
ASPHYXIA	BOYISHLY	CHUMMILY	DYSLEXIA	FEEDBACK
ATOMIZER	BRACKISH	CHUTZPAH	DYSLEXIC	FERVENCY
AXIOLOGY	BRAZENED	CINQUAIN	DZONGKA	FEVERFEW
AZIMUTH	BRAZENLY	CITIZENS	EFFICACY	FINALIZE
AZIMUTHS	BRAZIERS	CIVILIZE	EJECTIVE	FINICKY
AZOTEMIA	BREEZILY	CLIMAXED	EMBLAZON	FIREBACK
AZOTEMIC	BRONZED	CLIMAXES	EMPYEMIC	FISHBOWL
AZYGOUS	BRONZING	CLIQUISH	ENJOYING	FISHCAKE
BABYHOOD	BRONZY	COCKEYED	ENQUIRY	FIXABLE
BACKACHE	BRYOZOAN	COCKNEYS	ENTOZOIC	FIXATIVE
BACKCHAT	BUCKHORN	COENZYME	ENZOOTIC	FIXEDLY
BACKCOMB	BUCKSHEE	COEQUALS	ENZYME	FIZGIG
BACKDROP	BUCKSHOT	COLLOQUY	ENZYMES	FLAPJACK
BACKFILL	BULLDOZE	COLONIZE	EPIZOIC	FLAXSEED
BACKFIRE	BUSYBODY	COMEBACK	EPIZOISM	FLEXIBLE
BACKHAND	CADENZA	COMPLEX	EPIZOITE	FLEXIBLY
BACKLASH	CADENZAS	CONJUNCT	EQUABLY	FLICKERY
BACKSTAY	CALYXES	CONQUEST	EQUALITY	FLOOZIES
BACKWARD	CANALIZE	CONVEXLY	EQUALIZE	FLOOZY
BACKWASH	CANONIZE	COPYBOOK	EQUERRY	FLUMMOX
BACKYARD	CANZONET	COPYHOLD	EQUINITY	FLYAWAY
BANDBOX	CAPSIZE	COQUETRY	EQUINOX	FLYBACK
BANQUETS	CAPSIZED	COQUETTE	EQUIPAGE	FLYBLOWN
BAPTIZE	CASQUED	COQUILLE	EQUIPPED	FLYBOOK
BAPTIZED	CERVIXES	CORYZA	EQUIPPER	FLYSPECK
BARTIZAN	CHAFFED	COWLICKS	ETHOXIDE	FLYWHEEL
BAZOOKA	CHAFFING	COWPOX	EXACTLY	FLYWHISK
BAZOOKAS	CHAFFY	COXALGIC	EXAMPLES	FOLKWAYS
BEEFCAKE	CHALAZAL	COXCOMB	EXARCHAL	FOOZLER
BEESWAX	CHAMBRAY	COXCOMBS	EXCAVATE	FORMWORK
BENZOATE	CHAPBOOK	COXSWAIN	EXCEEDED	FORZANDO
BENZOIC	CHARLOCK	COZENAGE	EXCEPTED	FOXFIRE
BENZOYL	CHARQUI	COZENED	EXCERPTS	FOXGLOVE
BENZYL	CHARQUID	COZENING	EXCHANGE	FOXHOLE
BEQUEATH	CHAUFFER	COZILY	EXCLAVE	FOXHOLES
BEQUESTS	CHECKED	COZINESS	EXCLUDED	FOXHOUND
BETWIXT	CHECKERS	CRAYFISH	EXEMPLAR	FOXHUNT
BEZIQUE	CHECKING	CRAZIEST	EXEMPTED	FOXHUNTS
BIBCOCK	CHECKOUT	CRAZILY	EXEQUIES	FOXLIKE
BICONVEX	CHECKUP	CREDENZA	EXHALING	FREEZER
BIWEEKLY	CHECKUPS	CRITIQUE	EXHIBIT	FREEZERS

FREEZING	HEBRAIZE	ITEMIZED	JUICILY	MISJUDGE
FRENZIED	HEIFETZ	JABBERED	JUKEBOX	MISQUOTE
FRENZY	HEMLOCKS	JABBERER	JUMBLING	MOBILIZE
FREQUENT	HENEQUEN	JABBING	JUMPABLE	MONAZITE
FRIEZES	HEPWORTH	JACKAL	JUMPIEST	MONEYBOX
FROWZIER	HERTZIAN	JACKASS	JUMPILY	MOQUETTE
FROWZY	HEXADIC	JACKBOOT	JUMPING	MORALIZE
FRUCTIFY	HEXAGONS	JACKDAW	JUMPSUIT	MOSQUITO
FULLBACK	HEXAGRAM	JACKDAWS	JUNKING	MOTORIZE
FURZY	HEXANOIC	JACKED	JUNKYARD	MUCKHEAP
GAMECOCK	HEXAPLAR	JACKETS	JUSTIFY	MUCKWORM
GAZEBOS	HEXAPOD	JACKING	KERCHIEF	MUDPACKS
GAZPACHO	HEXAPODY	JACKPOT	KETOXIME	MUSQUASH
GAZUMPED	HEYDUCK	JACKPOTS	KEYPUNCH	MUZAK
GAZUMPER	HICKORY	JACKSTAY	KIBBUTZ	MYCOLOGY
GIMCRACK	HIGHBOY	JAGGEDLY	KILLJOY	MYOGRAPH
GIMMICKS	HIGHBOYS	JAMBOREE	KILLJOYS	MYSTIQUE
GIMMICKY	HIGHBROW	JAMMIEST	KITSCHY	NAPHTHYL
GLAZIERY	HIGHJACK	JAMMING	KNIGHTLY	NIGHTJAR
GREYBACK	HIGHVELD	JAPINGLY	KOWTOWED	OBJECTED
GUFFAWED	HIGHWAY	JAPONICA	KUMQUAT	OBJECTOR
GYMKHANA	HIGHWAYS	JAWBONE	KUMQUATS	OBLIQUES
HACKNEY	HIJACK	JAWBONES	KUNZITE	OBLOQUY
HACKNEYS	HIJACKED	JAYWALK	KYPHOSIS	OPAQUELY
HACKSAW	HIJACKER	JEMMIED	KYPHOTIC	OPTIMIZE
HACKSAWS	HIJACKS	JEMMYING	LATCHKEY	ORTHODOX
HAFIZ	HINCKLEY	JEOPARDY	LIQUEFY	OUTFOXED
HALFBACK	HIPPARCH	JERKIEST	LIQUESCE	OVERJOY
HALFBEAK	HOACTZIN	JERKILY	LOCALIZE	OVERSIZE
HALFWAY	HOATZIN	JERKING	LOCKJAW	OXAZINE
HAMMOCK	HOCKNEY	JEROBOAM	LYMPHOID	OXBRIDGE
HAMMOCKS	HOGBACK	JEWELLED	LYSOZYME	OXIDIZE
HANDCUFF	HOLOZOIC	JEZEBEL	MACAQUE	OXIDIZED
HARDBACK	HOMEBODY	JEZEBELS	MAGAZINE	OXPECKER
HARDHACK	HOMESICK	JIBBING	MAHARAJA	OXYACID
HARUSPEX	HOMEWORK	JIFFY	MAJESTIC	OXYTOCIC
HATCHERY	HOMOGAMY	JINXED	MAJESTY	OXYTOCIN
HATCHWAY	HOODWINK	JINXES	MAJORITY	PANCHAX
HAVELOCK	HOOKWORM	JINXING	MAQUETTE	PARAQUAT
HAVOCKER	HORIZON	JOBBERY	MARJORAM	PARKWAYS
HAWFINCH	HORIZONS	JOBBING	MAROQUIN	PAROXYSM
HAWKBILL	HOROWITZ	JOCKEY	MARQUEES	PATHWAYS
HAWKISH	HORSEBOX	JOCKEYED	MARQUESS	PAYCHECK
HAWKWEED	HOWITZER	JOCKEYS	MARQUISE	PENALIZE
HAYBOX	HUFFILY	JOCOSELY	MARZIPAN	PERJURY
HAYCOCK	HUMANIZE	JOCOSITY	MATCHBOX	PHALANX
HAYCOCKS	HUMIDIFY	JODHPURI	MAVERICK	PHARMACY
HAYFORK	HUMMOCK	JODHPURS	MAWKISH	PHARYNX
HAYFORKS	HUMMOCKS	JOHNNY	MAXIMIZE	PHIZOG
HAYMAKER	HUMMOCKY	JOKINGLY	MAZILY	PHIZOGS
HAYRACK	HUMPBACK	JOLLYING	MAZURKA	PHOENIX
HAYSTACK	HUMPLIKE	JONQUIL	MAZURKAS	PHYSIQUE
HAZARDED	HYACINTH	JOVIALLY	MEMORIZE	PICKAXE
HAZARDS	ICEBOXES	JOYFUL	MESOZOIC	PICKAXES
HAZELHEN	ICHTHYIC	JOYFULLY	MESTIZOS	PIQUANCY
HAZELNUT	IDOLIZED	JOYOUSLY	METAZOAN	PIQUING
HAZIEST	IMMUNIZE	JOYRIDER	METAZOIC	PLAYBACK
HAZILY	INEQUITY	JOYRIDES	MEZEREON	PLUCKILY
HAZINESS	INFLEXED	JOYSTICK	MIMICKED	POLARIZE
HEADACHY	INIQUITY	JUDGMENT	MINIMIZE	POLYGAMY
HEADWORK	INQUIRY	JUGGLERY	MINXISH	POLYZOAN

SPECIAL-WORD LIST

POLYZOIC	QUERYING	SITZMARK	SYMPHONY	WHINCHAT
POPINJAY	QUIBBLE	SIXPENCE	TAXINGLY	WHIPCORD
POPQUIZ	QUIBBLED	SIXPENNY	TAXIWAY	WHIPLASH
POSTFIX	QUIBBLER	SIZEABLE	TAXONOMY	WHIPLIKE
PRATIQUE	QUIBBLES	SKETCHY	TAXPAYER	WHIPPING
PREFIXAL	QUICHE	SKIJORER	TEXTBOOK	WHIPWORM
PREFIXED	QUICHES	SKIMPILY	THEORIZE	WHISKERY
PREFIXES	QUICK	SKIVVIED	THIAZINE	WHISKEY
PREJUDGE	QUICKEN	SKYDIVER	THWACKED	WHISKING
PRETZELS	QUICKER	SKYLIGHT	THWACKER	WHOMEVER
PRIZING	QUICKEST	SLEAZILY	THWACKS	WHOPPING
PROJECTS	QUICKIE	SMALLPOX	TOADFLAX	WICKEDLY
PROPHECY	QUICKIES	SNUFFBOX	TOMAHAWK	WIZARD
PROTOZOA	QUICKLY	SPHINXES	TOXAEMIC	WIZARDRY
PROXIMAL	QUICKSET	SPHYGMIC	TOXICITY	WIZARDS
PSYCHIC	QUIDNUNC	SPINIFEX	TRAPEZES	WIZENED
PSYCHICS	QUIETISM	SQUABBLE	TRAPEZIA	WOMANIZE
PSYCHING	QUIFF	SQUALLY	TWEEZERS	WOMBLIKE
PUFFBIRD	QUIFFS	SQUAMATE	UNIQUELY	WOODCOCK
PUSHBIKE	QUINCUNX	SQUARELY	UNZIPPED	WOODWORK
PYJAMAS	QUIPPED	SQUARISH	VANQUISH	WOOLPACK
PYRAZOLE	QUIPPING	SQUASHED	VAPORIZE	WOOZIER
PYREXIA	QUIPSTER	SQUASHER	VERJUICE	WOOZIEST
PYROXENE	QUIRKIER	SQUASHES	VEXEDLY	WOOZILY
QUACK	QUIRKILY	SQUASHY	VEXINGLY	WOOZY
QUACKED	QUIRKY	SQUAWK	VIXENISH	WORKADAY
QUACKERY	QUIVERED	SQUAWKED	VIZIERS	WORKBOX
QUACKING	QUIVERER	SQUAWKER	WALKAWAY	WORKDAYS
QUACKS	QUIVERY	SQUAWKS	WALTZED	WORKSHOP
QUADRIC	QUIXOTIC	SQUEAKED	WALTZER	WORKSHY
QUAFF	QUIZ	SQUEAKER	WALTZES	WRYNECK
QUAFFER	QUONDAM	SQUEAKS	WALTZING	XANTHIC
QUAGMIRE	QUOTABLE	SQUEAKY	WASHBOWL	XANTHOMA
QUAINTLY	QUOTHED	SQUEEZE	WATCHFUL	XENOGAMY
QUAKED	QWERTY	SQUEEZED	WAVEFORM	XERARCH
QUAKES	RACQUETS	SQUEEZER	WAVEOFF	XIPHOID
QUAKILY	REQUIEMS	SQUEEZES	WAXBILL	XYLIDINE
QUAKING	REVIVIFY	SQUEEZY	WAXLIKE	XYLOCARP
QUALIFY	RHIZOID	SQUELCH	WAXPLANT	XYLOTOMY
QUALITY	RHIZOME	SQUELCHY	WAXWING	YASHMAK
QUALMISH	RHIZOMES	SQUIDGY	WAXWORK	YASHMAKS
QUANDARY	RHIZOPOD	SQUIFFY	WAXWORKS	ZAFFER
QUANTIFY	RHIZOPUS	SQUIGGLE	WEEKDAYS	ZAIBATSU
QUANTITY	RHYTHMIC	SQUIGGLY	WHACKED	ZAPPED
QUARTZ	RICKSHAW	SQUINCH	WHACKER	ZAPPIER
QUARTZY	SAMIZDAT	SQUINTY	WHACKING	ZAPPIEST
QUASHED	SARDONYX	SQUIRMED	WHEEZE	ZAPPING
QUASHING	SCHERZO	SQUIRMER	WHEEZED	ZAPPY
QUAVERED	SCHERZOS	SQUIRMY	WHEEZER	ZEALOTRY
QUAVERER	SCHIZOID	SQUISHED	WHEEZES	ZEDOARY
QUAVERS	SCHIZONT	SQUISHY	WHEEZILY	ZENITHAL
QUAVERY	SCHMALTZ	STANZAIC	WHEEZING	ZENITHS
QUAYAGE	SCHMUCK	STYLIZE	WHEEZY	ZEOLITIC
QUEASILY	SCHMUCKS	STYLIZED	WHEYFACE	ZEPHYR
QUEENDOM	SEAQUAKE	SUBJECTS	WHICKER	ZEPHYRS
QUEENLY	SEIZABLE	SUFFIXAL	WHICKERS	ZEPPELIN
QUEERLY	SEQUENCE	SUFFIXES	WHIFFER	ZESTFUL
QUENCH	SEXOLOGY	SUPERFIX	WHIFFIER	ZIBELINE
QUENCHED	SHADDOCK	SWEATBOX	WHIFFLE	ZIPPED
QUENCHER	SHAMROCK	SWINEPOX	WHIFFY	ZIPPER
QUERCINE	SICKBAYS	SYMPATHY	WHIGGISH	ZIPPERS

SPECIAL-WORD LIST

ZIPPIER	ZODIACS	ZOOLATRY	ZOOTOMY	ZYGOTENE
ZIPPIEST	ZOMBIE	ZOOLOGY	ZOOTOXIC	ZYGOTIC
ZIPPING	ZOMBIES	ZOOMETRY	ZOOTOXIN	ZYMASE
ZIPPY	ZOMBIISM	ZOOMING	ZUCCHINI	ZYMOGEN
ZIRCONIA	ZONALLY	ZOOPHILE	ZWIEBACK	ZYMOLOGY
ZIRCONIC	ZONETIME	ZOOPHYTE	ZYGOSE	ZYMOTIC
ZITHERS	ZONKED	ZOOSPERM	ZYGOSIS	ZYMURGY
ZODIACAL	ZOOCHORE	ZOOSPORE	ZYGOTE	ZYXOMMA

NOTES

NOTES

NOTES

NOTES